P9-DES-921

Would Marketing be easier to learn if you could...

...use your textbook in a way that best suits your learning style?

...find out exactly what you don't know BEFORE you read the chapter?

...link directly to multimedia for the concepts you need to explore further?

PEARSON **mymarketinglab**™

created for you, with your success in mind.

www.mypearsonmarketinglab.com

MARKETING

An Introduction, 9e

Gary Armstrong

University of North Carolina

Philip Kotler

Northwestern University

PEARSON

Prentice
Hall

Upper Saddle River, NJ 07458

Library of Congress Cataloging-in-Publication Data
Armstrong, Gary (Gary M.)
    Marketing: an introduction / Gary Armstrong and Philip Kotler.—9th ed.
       p.   cm.
    Includes bibliographical references and index.
    ISBN-13: 978-0-13-602113-1
1. Marketing.   I. Kotler, Philip. II.   Title.
    HF5415.K625 2009
658.8—dc22

                                            2007050465

NOTICE:
This work is protected by U.S. copyright laws and is provided solely for the use of college instructors in reviewing course materials for classroom use. Dissemination or sale of this work, or any part (including on the World Wide Web) is not permitted.

AVP/Executive Editor: Melissa Sabella
AVP/EIC: David Parker
Product Development Manager: Ashley Santora
Editorial Project Manager: Melissa Pellerano
Marketing Manager: Anne K. Fahlgren
Marketing Assistant: Susan Osterlitz
Associate Director, Production Editorial: Judy Leale
Production Project Manager: Kerri Tomasso
Permissions Coordinator: Charles Morris
Senior Operations Supervisor: Arnold Vila
Operations Specialist: Michelle Klein
Creative Director: Leslie Osher
Interior Design: Tamara Newnam
Senior Art Director: Janet Slowik
Art Director: Heather Scott
Cover Design: Tamara Newnam
Cover Photo: Carpix
Image Manager: Keri Jean Miksza
Director, Image Resource Center: Melinda Patelli
Manager, Rights and Permissions: Zina Arabia
Manager, Visual Research: Beth Brenzel
Manager, Cover Visual Research & Permissions: Karen Sanatar
Image Permission Coordinator: Richard Rodrigues
Composition/Full-Service Project Management: Lynn Steines, S4Carlisle Publishing Services
Printer/Binder: Quebecor World Color/Versailles
Typeface: 10/12 Times

Credits and acknowledgements borrowed from other sources and reproduced, with permission, in this textbook appear on the appropriate page within text; photo credits appear on page C1.

Note: Every effort has been made to provide accurate and current Internet information in this book. However, the Internet and information posted on it are constantly changing, so it is inevitable that some of the Internet addresses listed in this textbook will change.

Copyright © 2009, 2007, 2005, 2003, 2000 by Pearson Education, Inc., Upper Saddle River, New Jersey 07458. Pearson Prentice Hall. All rights reserved. Printed in the United States of America. This publication is protected by Copyright and permission should be obtained from the publisher prior to any prohibited reproduction, storage in a retrieval system, or transmission in any form or by an means, electronic, mechanical, photocopying, recording, or likewise. For information regarding permission(s), write to: Rights and Permissions Department.

Pearson Prentice Hall™ is a trademark of Pearson Education, Inc.
Pearson® is a registered trademark of Pearson plc
Prentice Hall® is a registered trademark of Pearson Education, Inc.

Pearson Education Ltd., London
Pearson Education Singapore, Pte, Ltd.
Pearson Education Canada, Ltd.
Pearson Education—Japan

Pearson Education Australia PTY, Limited
Pearson Education North Asia Ltd.
Pearson Educatión de Mexico, S.A. de C.V.
Pearson Education Malaysia, Pte. Ltd.

10 9 8 7 6 5 4 3 2 1
ISBN-13: 978-0-13-602113-1
ISBN-10: 0-13-602113-1

To Kathy, Betty, Mandy, Matt, KC, Keri,
Delaney, Molly, Macy, and Ben; Nancy, Amy, Melissa, and Jessica

About the Authors

As a team, Gary Armstrong and Philip Kotler provide a blend of skills uniquely suited to writing an introductory marketing text. Professor Armstrong is an award-winning teacher of undergraduate business students. Professor Kotler is one of the world's leading authorities on marketing. Together they make the complex world of marketing practical, approachable, and enjoyable.

Gary Armstrong is Crist W. Blackwell Distinguished Professor of Undergraduate Education in the Kenan-Flagler Business School at the University of North Carolina at Chapel Hill. He holds undergraduate and masters degrees in business from Wayne State University in Detroit, and he received his Ph.D. in marketing from Northwestern University. Dr. Armstrong has contributed numerous articles to leading business journals. As a consultant and researcher, he has worked with many companies on marketing research, sales management, and marketing strategy.

But Professor Armstrong's first love has always been teaching. His Blackwell Distinguished Professorship is the only permanent endowed professorship for distinguished undergraduate teaching at the University of North Carolina at Chapel Hill. He has been very active in the teaching and administration of Kenan-Flagler's undergraduate program. His administrative posts have included Chair of Marketing, Associate Director of the Undergraduate Business Program, Director of the Business Honors Program, and many others. He works closely with business student groups and has received several campus-wide and Business School teaching awards. He is the only repeat recipient of school's highly regarded Award for Excellence in Undergraduate Teaching, which he has received three times. Professor Armstrong recently received the UNC Board of Governors Award for Excellence in Teaching, the highest teaching honor bestowed by the sixteen-campus University of North Carolina system.

Philip Kotler is S. C. Johnson & Son Distinguished Professor of International Marketing at the Kellogg School of Management, Northwestern University. He received his master's degree at the University of Chicago and his Ph.D. at M.I.T., both in economics. Dr. Kotler is author of *Marketing Management* (Prentice-Hall), now in its thirteenth edition and the world's most widely used marketing text book in graduate schools of business worldwide. He has authored dozens of other successful books and has written more than 100 articles in leading journals. He is the only three-time winner of the coveted Alpha Kappa Psi award for the best annual article in the *Journal of Marketing*.

Professor Kotler was named the first recipient of two major awards: the *Distinguished Marketing Educator of the Year Award* given by the American Marketing Association and the *Philip Kotler Award for Excellence in Health Care Marketing* presented by the Academy for Health Care Services Marketing. His numerous other major honors include the Sales and Marketing Executives International *Marketing Educator of the Year Award;* The European Association of Marketing Consultants and Trainers *Marketing Excellence Award;* the *Charles Coolidge Parlin Marketing Research Award;* and the *Paul D. Converse Award,* given by the American Marketing Association to honor "outstanding contributions to science in marketing. In a recent *Financial Times* poll of 1,000 senior executives across the world, Professor Kotler was ranked as the fourth "most influential business writer/guru" of the twenty-first century.

Dr. Kotler has served as chairman of the College on Marketing of the Institute of Management Sciences, a director of the American Marketing Association, and a trustee of the Marketing Science Institute. He has consulted with many major U.S. and international companies in the areas of marketing strategy and planning, marketing organization, and international marketing. He has traveled extensively throughout Europe, Asia, and South America, advising companies and governments about global marketing practices and opportunities.

Brief Contents

Contents

PART 2   UNDERSTANDING THE MARKETPLACE AND CONSUMERS   62

Welcome to the Ninth Edition!

Top marketers all share a common goal: ***putting the consumer at the heart of marketing.*** Today's marketing is all about creating customer value and building profitable customer relationships. It starts with understanding customer needs and wants, deciding which target markets the organization can best serve, and developing value propositions by which the organization can attract, keep, and grow targeted consumers. If the organization does these things well, it will reap the rewards in terms of market share, profits, and customer equity. More than any other marketing text, the ninth edition of *Marketing: An Introduction* presents and develops this integrative customer-value/customer-relationship framework from beginning to end.

This ninth edition of *Marketing: An Introduction* makes learning and teaching marketing more effective, easier, and more enjoyable than ever. Students learning marketing want a broad, complete picture of basic marketing principles and practices without drowning in a sea of details. With its streamlined approach, *Marketing: An Introduction* strikes a careful balance between depth of coverage and ease of learning. Unlike more abbreviated texts, it provides a complete overview of marketing. Unlike longer, more complex texts, its moderate length makes it easy to digest in a given semester or quarter. This text is a valuable resource for students, both in this course and in their careers. And with the exciting addition of mymarketinglab, both students and professors can be assured that students will come to class prepared.

Marketing: An Introduction presents all the latest marketing thinking and practice. It casts marketing in an innovative framework, one that positions marketing simply as the art and science of creating value for customers in order to capture value from the customers in return. As Jim Stengel, Procter & Gamble's Global Marketing Chief puts it, *"It's not about telling and selling. . . . It's about bringing a [customer] relationship mindset to everything we do."*

In *Marketing: An Introduction,* you'll see how *customer value*—creating it and capturing it—drives every marketing strategy. Fasten your seatbelt. . . .

Gary Armstrong

Philip Kotler

Gary Armstrong
University of North Carolina
at Chapel Hill

Philip Kotler
Northwestern University

Preface

Five Major Value Themes

The ninth edition of *Marketing: An Introduction* builds on five major value themes:

1. *Creating value for customers in order to capture value from customers in return.* Today's outstanding marketing companies understand the marketplace and customer needs, design value-creating marketing strategies, development integrated marketing programs that deliver value and satisfaction, and build strong customer relationships. In return, they capture value from customers in the form of sales, profits, and customer equity.

    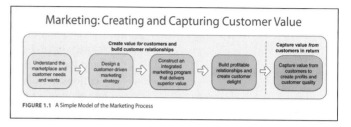

    Marketing: Creating and Capturing Customer Value

    FIGURE 1.1 A Simple Model of the Marketing Process

    This innovative customer value *framework* is introduced at the start of Chapter 1 in a five-step marketing process model, which details how marketing *creates* customer value and *captures* value in return. The framework is carefully explained in the first two chapters, providing students with a solid foundation. The framework is then integrated throughout the remainder of the text.

2. *Building and managing strong brands to create brand equity.* Well-positioned brands with strong brand equity provide the basis upon which to build profitable customer relationships. Today's marketers must position their brands powerfully and manage them well. The ninth edition provides a deep focus on brands, anchored by a Chapter 7 section on Branding Strategy: Building Strong Brands.

3. *Measuring and managing return on marketing.* Marketing managers must ensure that their marketing dollars are being well spent. In the past, many marketers spent freely on big, expensive marketing programs, often without thinking carefully about the financial returns on their spending. But all that has changed—measuring and managing return on marketing investments has become an important part of strategic marketing decision making. The ninth edition specifically addresses return on marketing investment in Chapter 2 and revisits this important topic in sections throughout the text.

4. *Harnessing new marketing technologies.* New digital and other high-tech marketing developments are dramatically changing consumers and marketers and the ways in which they relate to one another. The ninth edition thoroughly explores the new technologies impacting marketing, from "Web 2.0" in Chapter 1 to new-age digital marketing and online technologies in Chapters 12 and 14 to the exploding use of social networks and customer-generated marketing in Chapters 1, 5, 12, 14, and elsewhere.

5. *Marketing in a socially responsible way around the globe.* As technological developments make the world an increasingly smaller place, marketers must be good at marketing their brands globally and in socially responsible ways. The ninth edition integrates global marketing and social responsibility topics throughout the text. It then provides focused coverage on each topic in Chapters 15 and and 16, respectively.

What's New in the Ninth Edition?

We've thoroughly revised the ninth edition of *Marketing: An Introduction* to reflect the major trends and forces that are impacting marketing in this age of customer value and relationships. Here are just some of the changes you'll find in this edition.

- This ninth edition continues to build on and extend the innovative **customer-value framework** from previous editions. The customer value model presented in the first chapter is now more fully integrated throughout the remainder of the book. No other marketing text presents such a clear and comprehensive customer-value approach.
- Throughout the ninth edition, we address the rapidly **changing nature of today's customer relationships**—the new emphasis on creating two-way dialogs and making brands

a part of consumers' live and conversations. For just a few examples, see Chapter 1 (the section on the Changing Nature of Customer Relationships, which includes a Marketing at Work highlight on customer-generated marketing); Chapter 4 (qualitative approaches to gaining deeper customer insights); Chapter 5 (a new section on marketing through social networks); Chapter 8 (a new section on customer-driven new product development); Chapter 12 (the shift toward more personalized, interactive one-to-one communications); and Chapter 14 (online social networks, customer communities, and the new interactive digital media).

- The **integrated marketing communications** chapters have been completely restructured to reflect sweeping shifts in how today's marketers communicate value to customers.

  - A newly revised Chapter 12—Integrated Marketing Communications: Advertising and Public Relations—addresses today's **shifting integrated marketing communications model**. It tells how marketers are adding a host of new-age media—everything from interactive TV and the Internet to iPods and cell phones—to reach more carefully targeted customers with more personalized messages.
  - Advertising and public relations are now combined in Chapter 12, which includes expanded discussions on "Madison & Vine" (the merging of advertising and entertainment to break through the clutter), return on advertising, and other important topics. A restructured Chapter 13 now combines personal selling and sales promotion.
  - A **new Chapter 14—Direct and Online Marketing**—provides focused new coverage of direct marketing and its fastest-growing arm, marketing on the Internet. The new chapter includes a section on new digital direct marketing technologies, such as mobile phone marketing, podcasts and vodcasts, and interactive TV. It also includes an innovative new section on online social networks and customer communities.

- Chapter 9 contains a new section on managing new-product development, covering new **customer-driven, team-based, holistic new-product development** approaches.
- Several chapters contain new and expanded discussions of the burgeoning use of **social networks**—how marketers are tapping digital online networks such as YouTube, MySpace, and others and even creating their own social networks to build stronger, closer relationships between their brands and customers. We've also integrated discussions and examples of the growing use of customer-generated marketing to enhance, capture, and communicate the customer-brand experience.
- A **new Appendix 1—Company Cases**—provides 16 new company cases by which students can apply what they learn to actual company situations. The ninth edition also features many new video cases, with brief end-of-chapter summaries and discussion questions.
- In line with the text's emphasis on **measuring and managing return on marketing,** we've added a **new Appendix 3: Marketing by the Numbers**. This comprehensive new appendix introduces students to the marketing financial analysis that helps to guide, assess, and support marketing decisions in this age of marketing accountability. The Return on Marketing section in Chapter 2 has also been revised, as have the return on advertising and return on selling discussions in later chapters.

A Learning Approach

Features

- *Chapter-opening vignette and Marketing at Work exhibits* highlight the stories that reveal the drama of modern marketing. Just a few examples:

  - Staples held back its now-familiar "Staples: That was easy" repositioning campaign for more than a year. First, it had to *live* the slogan.
  - Ryanair—Europe's original, largest, and most profitable low-fares airline—appears to have found a radical new pricing solution: Fly free!
  - Almost unimaginably big Wal-Mart knows that its low price value proposition will never give it an "edgy" image. Its brand is about saving people money so that they can live better.

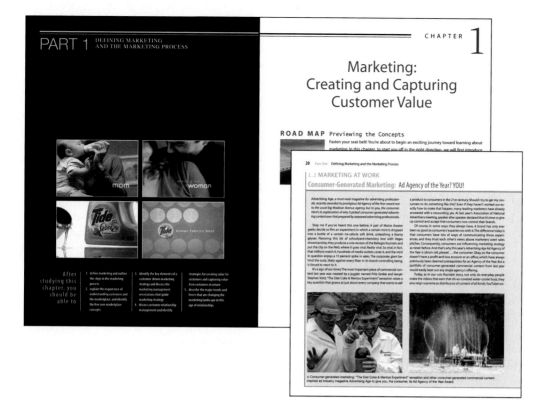

- Procter & Gamble is learning fast about the hot new world of online social networking, experimenting with all kinds of online communities for its many megabrands—from MySpace, Facebook, and YouTube to its own community Web sites.

- *Road Map: Previewing the Concepts.* Briefly previews chapter concepts, links them with previous chapter concepts, outlines chapter learning objectives, and introduces the chapter-opening vignette.
- *Linking the Concepts.* "Concept checks" inserted at key points in each chapter serve as "speed bumps" to slow students down to be certain they are grasping and applying key concepts and linkages.
- *Rest Stop: Reviewing the Concepts.* Summary of key concepts at the end of each chapter reviews chapter concepts and summarizes for each chapter objective.
- *Travel Log.* Discussing the Issues and Applications Questions help students to keep track of and apply what they've studied in the chapter.
- *Under the Hood: Focus on Technology.* Application exercises and questions focus attention and discussion on important marketing technologies in this digital age.

> **Under the Hood:** Focus on Technology
>
> Could you and a fellow student develop a business that would employ more that 10,000 people and be valued at over $120 billion in just over a decade? That's exactly what two Stanford University graduate students, Larry Page and Sergey Brin, did. They founded Google, the world's largest Internet search engine. Google is used in more than 100 countries and generates revenues from its online search services and highly targeted advertising. At Google's headquarters in Mountain View, California, known as "Googleplex," employees ("Googlers") are encouraged to be innovative. As a result, in addition to its original search engine capabilities, Google has launched a host of new products.
> **1.** Identify five products Google has introduced in addition to its search engine service. Are they successful? How many of
>
> these were you aware of before this exercise? Visit Google Labs (labs.google.com) to learn about new products that are still in the testing stage—"a few of our favorite ideas that still aren't quite ready for primetime." Briefly discuss what you found. (AACSB: Communication; Use of IT)
> **2.** Read the article about Google's new-product development process at www.businessweek.com/technology/content/jun2006/tc20060629_411177.htm. What is Google's philosophy regarding new products? Do you think it is appropriate? (AACSB: Communication; Reflective Thinking; Use of IT)

- *Focus on Ethics.* Situation descriptions and questions highlight important issues in marketing ethics.

> **Focus on Ethics**
>
> "Green marketing" has been around for a long time and has experienced renewed growth in the past decade. In response, several companies are developing eco-friendly products and touting their environmental conscientiousness. Greenpeace, an environmental activist group, is pushing legislation that would ban the production of incandescent light bulbs. Greenpeace called Philips Electronics a "climate criminal" because it produces these types of light bulbs. However, not all of the new products developed in response to consumers' desires for more environmentally friendly products live up to their promises.
> **1.** Find examples of new products developed in response to growing environmental concern. Have marketers been successful with these new products? (AACSB: Communication; Reflective Thinking)
> **2.** Not all "green" products live up to their claims. Is it ethical for marketers to continue to offer these products? (AACSB: Communication; Ethical Reasoning)

- *Marketing Plan.* Appendix 2 provides a sample marketing plan that helps students to apply and understand important marketing planning concepts.

• *Marketing by the Numbers.* A new Appendix 3 introduces students to the marketing financial analysis that helps to guide, assess, and support marketing decisions.

• *Video cases.* Every chapter is supplemented with a video case that brings the material to life, accompanied by a brief written exercise and questions to get the discussion going.

• *Company cases.* Appendix 1 supplies 16 full company cases, all new to the ninth edition, by which students can apply marketing concepts to actual company situations.

AACSB Support

This book supports Association to Advance Collegiate Schools of Business (AACSB) International accreditation. Each chapter ends with a collection of exercises: Travel Log, Under the Hood: Focus on Technology, and Focus on Ethics. In every chapter, next to each exercise, we provide a specific AACSB tagging logo to help instructors identify those exercises that support AACSB learning goals. We also provide AACSB tagging for many of the questions in the Test Item File that accompanies the textbook and mymarketinglab.

A Total Teaching and Learning Package

A successful marketing course requires more than a well-written book. Today's classroom requires a dedicated teacher and a fully-integrated teaching system. A total package of teaching and learning supplements extends this edition's emphasis on effective teaching and learning. The following aids support *Marketing: An Introduction.*

Supplements for Instructors

How often does this happen to you? You walk in to teach your Principles of Marketing class excited to help students connect the concepts in their reading assignment with the real world of marketing, only to find that very few of the students actually read the assignment so:

• You have to spend your class time explaining the concepts the students should have learned the night before.
• You have no time to talk about the fun stuff.

What if everyday your students came to class prepared? How would this change the dynamic in your classroom, and how much more fun would you and your students have every day? Think that this possibility is only a dream? mymarketinglab can help make that dream a reality everyday with:

- Self-Assessment
- Customized Study Plans
- Robust Aggregate Reporting
- Organized and adapted for YOUR course
- Defensible assessment

Find out more at mypearsonmarketinglab.com

The following supplements are available to adopting instructors.

Instructor's Manual with Video Guide (ISBN: 0-13-602114-X)

The instructor's handbook for this text provides suggestions for using features and elements of the text. This *Instructor's Manual* includes a chapter overview, objectives, a detailed lecture outline (incorporating key terms, text art, chapter objectives, and references to various pedagogical elements), and support for end-of-chapter material. Also included is a "Great Ideas" section that offers barriers to effective learning, student projects/assignments, classroom management strategies, and more, to provide a springboard for innovative learning experiences in the classroom. The Instructor's Manual also features the following elements:

- Support for end-of-chapter material along with additional student projects and "Outside Examples" assignments, offering instructors additional lecture material. The examples may be a further development of a concept or company briefly mentioned in the chapter, or perhaps new material that helps to further develop a concept in the text.
- "Professors on the Go!" serves to bring key material upfront in the manual, where an instructor who is short on time can take a quick look and find key points and assignments to incorporate into the lecture, without having to page through all the material provided for each chapter.
- Annotated Instructor's Notes, which serve as a quick reference for the entire supplements package. Suggestions for using materials from the Instructor's Manual, PowerPoint slides, Test Item File, Video Library, and online material are offered for each section within every chapter. (This content is found on the IRC online only.)

Test Item File (ISBN: 0-13-602125-5)

Featuring more than 2,000 questions, 100+ questions per chapter, this *Test Item File* has been written specifically for the ninth edition. Questions range from multiple-choice and true/false to essay and application. All questions offer level of difficulty and page references.

For each question that tests a standard from the Association to Advance Collegiate Schools of Business (AACSB), we use one of the following annotations:

- Communication
- Ethical Reasoning
- Analytical Skills
- Use of Information Technology
- Multicultural and Diversity
- Reflective Thinking

Instructor's Resource Center

Register. Redeem. Login.

At www.prenhall.com/irc instructors can access a variety of print, media, and presentation resources available with this text in downloadable, digital format. For most texts, resources are also available for course management platforms such as Blackboard, WebCT, and Course Compass.

Once you register, you will not have additional forms to fill out, or multiple usernames and passwords to remember to access new titles and/or editions. As a registered faculty member, you can log in directly to download resource files, and receive immediate access and instructions for installing Course Management content to your campus server.

Need help? Our dedicated technical support team is ready to assist instructors with questions about the media supplements that accompany this text. Visit: http://247.prenhall.com/ for answers to frequently asked questions and toll-free user support phone numbers.

Available via a password-protected site at www.prenhall.com/kotler or on CD-ROM (0-13-602126-3). Resources include:

- *Instructor's Manual:* View chapter-by-chapter or download the entire manual as a .zip file.
- *Test Item File:* View chapter-by-chapter or download the entire test item file as a .zip file.
- *TestGen (online only):* Download this easy-to-use software; it's preloaded with the ninth edition test questions and a user's manual.
- *Image bank (on CD only):* Access many of the images, ads, and illustrations featured in the text. Ideal for PowerPoint customization.
- *PowerPoints:* When it comes to PowerPoints, Prentice Hall knows one size does not fit all. That's why we offer instructors more than one option.

    PowerPoint BASIC: This simple presentation includes only basic outlines and key points from each chapter. No animation or forms of rich media are integrated, which makes the total file size manageable and easier to share online or via e-mail. BASIC was also designed for instructors who prefer to customize PowerPoints and want to be spared from having to strip out animation, embedded files, or other media rich features.

    PowerPoint MEDIA RICH (on CD only): This media-rich alternative includes basic outlines and key points from each chapter, plus advertisements and art from the text, images not included in the text, discussion questions, Web links, and embedded video snippets from the accompanying video library. This is the best option for a complete presentation solution. Instructors can further customize this presentation using the image library featured on the Instructor's Resource Center on CD-ROM.

    PowerPoints for Classroom Response Systems (CRS): These Q&A style slides are designed for classrooms using "clickers" or classroom response systems. Instructors who are interested in making CRS a part of their course should contact their Prentice Hall representative for details and a demonstration. CRS is a fun and easy way to make your classroom more interactive.
- *Online Courses:* See OneKey below. Compatible with BlackBoard and WebCT.

TestGen Test Generating Software

Prentice Hall's test-generating software is available from the *IRC Online* (www.prenhall.com/kotler).

- PC/Mac compatible; preloaded with all of the Test Item File questions.
- Manually or randomly view test bank questions and drag-and-drop to create a test.
- Add or modify test bank questions using the built-in Question Editor.
- Print up to 25 variations of a single test and deliver the test on a local area network using the built-in QuizMaster feature.
- Free customer support is available at media.support@pearsoned.com or call 1-800-6-PROFESSOR between 8:00 A.M. and 5:00 P.M. CST.

Custom Videos

The video library features 16 exciting segments for this edition. All segments are available online (www.prenhall.com/armstrongvideo) and on DVD (ISBN: 0-13-602117-4). Here are just a few of the videos offered:

- Meredith and its ability to create relationships with customers through target marketing
- Ziba and its unique approach to designing new products
- Progressive's innovation in direct and Internet marketing
- Crispin Porter + Bogusky successfully integrating marketing communications
- Google and the manner in which it has revolutionized Internet advertising and consumers' online experience

Transparencies (ISBN: 0-13-602115-8)

Features 15 to 20 color acetates per chapter selected from the Media-rich set of PowerPoints, which includes images from the text.

Supplements for Students

OneKey

Available through Course Compass, Blackboard, and WebCT, classroom resources for students are available in one spot. Resources include:

- Quizzing for review
- Case Pilot to aid in analyzing cases
- Marketing Toolkit: Interactive Modules to aid in review of understanding key concepts
- Marketing Updates: Bringing current articles to the classroom
- Much more

OneKey requires an access code, which professors can ask to be shrink-wrapped with new copies of this text. Please contact your local sales representative for the correct ISBN. Codes may also be purchased separately at www.prenhall.com/marketing.

Study Guide (ISBN: 0-13-602121-2)

The 9th edition study guide with flashcards provides students on the go with a valuable resource. It consists of detailed chapter outlines, student exercises, plus exercises correlated to award-winning print advertisements. The study guide is delivered in one compact binder and can be packaged at a low cost with new copies of this text. The study guide can also be purchased separately at www.prenhall.com/marketing.

Companion Website

Found at www.prenhall.com/armstrong, the Companion Website offers two student quizzes per chapter. The Concept Check Quiz is to be administered prior to reviewing the chapter, in order to assess the student's initial understanding. The Concept Challenge Quiz is to be administered after reviewing the chapter.

More Stand-Out Resources

CourseSmart is an exciting new *choice* for students looking to save money. As an alternative to purchasing the print textbook, students can purchase an electronic version of the same content and save up to 50 percent off the suggested list price of the print text. With a CourseSmart eTextbook, students can search the text, make notes online, print out reading assignments that incorporate lecture notes, and bookmark important passages for later review. For more information, or to purchase access to the CourseSmart eTextbook, visit www.coursesmart.com.

Classroom Response Systems (CRS)

This exciting new wireless polling technology makes classrooms, no matter how large or small, even more interactive because it enables instructors to pose questions to their students, record results, and display those results instantly. Students answer questions using compact remote control style transmitters. Prentice Hall has partnerships with leading classroom response systems providers and can show you everything you need to know about setting up and using a CRS system. We'll provide the classroom hardware, software, and support and show you how your students can save.

- Enhance interactivity
- Capture attention
- Get instant feedback
- Access comprehension

Learn more at www.prenhall.com/crs.

Coming Fall 2008

Study on the go with VangoNotes—chapter reviews from your text in downloadable mp3 format. Now wherever you are—whatever you're doing—you can study by listening to the following for each chapter of your textbook:

- *Big Ideas:* Your "need to know" for each chapter
- *Key Terms:* Audio "flashcards" to help you review key concepts and terms
- *Rapid Review:* A quick drill session—use it right before your test

VangoNotes are **flexible**; download all the material directly to your player, or only the chapters you need. And they're **efficient**. Use them in your car, at the gym, walking to class, or wherever. So get yours today. And get studying.

VangoNotes.com.

Acknowledgments

No book is the work only of its authors. We greatly appreciate the valuable contributions of several people who helped make this new edition possible. We owe very special thanks to Keri Miksza for her deep and valuable involvement and advice throughout *every* phase of the project. We thank Andy Norman of Drake University for his skillful development of company cases and video cases and for his assistance in preparing selected marketing stories. Thanks also go to Laurie Babin of the University of Louisiana at Monroe for her dedicated efforts in preparing the new Marketing by the Numbers appendix and end-of-chapter materials, plus Classroom Response System (CRS) PowerPoints; Marian Wood for her help in creating the Marketing Plan appendix; Tony L. Henthorne for his work on the Instructor's Manual; Karen E. James for development of the Basic and Media Rich PowerPoints; Bonnie Flaherty for her work on the Test Item File.

Many reviewers at other colleges and universities provided valuable comments and suggestions for this and previous editions. We are indebted to the following colleagues for their thoughtful inputs:

Ninth Edition Reviewers

Chris Adalikwu, Concordia College

Doug Albertson, University of Portland

Christie Amato, University of North Carolina, Charlotte

Corinne Asher, Henry Ford Community College

Bruce Bailey, Otterbein College

Turina Bakken, Madison Area Technical College

David Bambridge, Warner Southern College

Donald Barnes, Mississippi State University

Susan Baxter, Bethune-Cookman College

David Beck, Delaware Valley College

Colleen Bee, University of San Diego

Kenn Bennett, Irvine Valley College

Carl Bergemann, Arapahoe Community College

Donna Bergenstock, Muhlenberg College

Charles Besio, Southern Methodist University

John Bierer, University of Southern Maine

James Black, University of Maine

Alan Blake, New Hampshire Technical Institute

David Bland, Cape Fear Community College

Ross Blankenship, State Fair Community College

Earl Boatwright, Bowling Green State University

Kimberly Boyer, Washington University

Kevin Bradord, Somerset Community College, Laurel North

Donald Brady, Millersville University

Jenell Bramlage, University of Northwestern Ohio

Frederic Brunel, Boston University

Jeff Bruns, Bacone College

Kendrick Brunson, Liberty University

Derrell Bulls, Texas Woman's University

Gary Bumgarner, Mountain Empire Community College

Dale Cake, Pennsylvania State University

Jacqueline Callery, Robert Morris College

Guadalupe Campos, Borough of Manhattan Community College

Frank Carothers, Somerset Community College

Ray Carpenter, Indian River Community College

Erin Cavusgil, Michigan State University

Larry Chase, Tompkins Cortland Community College

Yun Chu, Frostburg State University

Janet Ciccarelli, Herkimer County Community College

Patricia Clarke, Boston College

Joyce Claterbos, University of Kansas

Gloria Cockerell, Collin County Community College

D. M. Coleman, Miami University of Oxford

Kathleen Conklin, St. John Fisher College

Craig Conrad, Western Illinois University

Scott Cragin, Missouri Southern State University

Martha Cranford, Stanly Community College

Carter Crockett, Westmont College

John Cronin, Western Connecticut State University

Julia Cronin Gilmore, Bellevue University

Stanley Dabrowski, Hudson County Community College

Richard M. Daiely, University of Texas at Arlington

Cynthia Davies, Rosemont College

David Davis, South Dakota State University

Helen Davis, Jefferson Community College

Tamara Dawson, Redlands Community College

Beth Deinert, Southeast Community College

Lola Dial, Robeson Community College

Susan Dik, University of Hawaii

Claudiu Dimofte, Georgetown University

Dennis Dowds, Hudson Valley Community College

John Drea, Western Illinois University

Robert Drevs, University of Notre Dame

Jose Duran, Riverside Community College

Robert Eames, Calvin College

C. R. Echard, Glenville State College

Robert Erffmeyer, University of Wisconsin, Eau Claire

Scott Erickson, Ithaca College

Denis Fiorentino, Fitchburg State College

Harry Fisher, Eureka College

Judy Foxman, Southern Methodist University

Jodi Frank, Harrisburg Area Community College

Douglas Friedman, Pennsylvania State University, Harrisburg

Karen Fritz, Bridgewater College

David Furman, Clayton State University

Jeff Gauer, Gallaudet University

John Gauld, University of Georgia

Paul Gentine, Bethany College

Katie Ghahramani, Johnson County Community College

Gaetan Giannini, Cedar Crest College

John (Jack) Gifford, Miami University of Ohio

Bill Godair, Landmark College

Dennis Goecks, Chemeketa Community College

James Gould, Pace University

Bryan Greenberg, Elizabethtown College

Bob Gregory, Bellevue University

J. D. Griffith, Brigham Young University, Idaho

Alice Griswold, Clarke College

Perry Haan, Tiffin University

Dorothy Harpool, Wichita State University

Tim Hartman, Ohio University

Joseph Hartnett, St. Charles Community College

Tim Heinze, Waynesburg College

James Hess, Ivy Tech Community College

Stacey Hills, Utah State University

Tanawat Hirunyawipada, University of North Texas

David Houghton, Northwest Nazarene University

George Hozier, Fort Lewis College

Doug Hurd, Fort Scott Community College

Mick Jackowski, Metropolitan State College of Denver

Donald Jackson, Ferris State University

Frank Jacobson, Vanguard University of Southern California

Charles Jaeger, Southern Oregon University

James Jarrard, University of Wisconsin, Platteville

Carol Johanek, Washington University

Luke Kachersky, Baruch College

Marlene Kahla, Stephen F. Austin State University

Karl Kampschroeder, St. Mary's University

Faye Kao, University of Wisconsin, Eau Claire

Janice Karlen, LaGuardia Community College

Eric Karson, Villanova University

Erdener Kaynak, Pennsylvania State University

Eileen Kearney, Montgomery County Community College

Philip Kearney, Niagara Community College

Jennifer Keeling Bond, Colorado State University

Wayne Keene, Stephens College

Jeremy Kees, Villanova University

William J. Kehoe, University of Virginia

Dale Kehr, University of Memphis

DeAnna Kempf, Middle Tennessee State University

David Kimball, Elms College

Greg Kitzmiller, Indiana University

Gary Kritz, Seton Hall University

Claudia Kubowicz Malhotra, University of North Carolina, Chapel Hill

Jean Kujawa, Lourdes College

Chris Lachapelle, Mercyhurst College

Curt Laird, University of Charleston

Roger Lall, DePaul University

Jodi Landgaard, Minnesota West Community & Technical College

Felix Lao, Baker College

Robert Lauterborn, University of North Carolina at Chapel Hill

James Lawson, Mississippi State University, Meridian Campus

David Levy, Des Moines Area Community College - West

Frank Lilja, Pine Technical School

Ingrid Lin, Saint Xavier University

Ann Little, High Point University

Karen Loveland, Texas A&M University, Corpus Christi

Marvin Lovett, University of Texas at Brownsville

Dolly Loyd, University of Southern Mississippi

Leslie Lukasik, Skagit Valley College, Whidbey Island

Kerri Lum, Kapiolani Community College

Larry Maes, Davenport University

Igor Makienko, Loyola University of New Orleans

Jennifer Malarski, Lake Superior College

Manuel Mares, Florida National College

Craig Martin, Western Kentucky University

Deanna Martin, Southwest Mississippi Community College

Nora Martin, University of South Carolina

Wendy Martin, Trinity International University

James Mason, Oklahoma State University

Brenda McAleer, University of Maine at Augusta

Chip Miller, Drake University

Jakki Mohr, University of Montana

Ed Mosher, Laramie County Community College

Jay Mulki, Northeastern University

Lewis Myers, St. Edward's University

Elaine Notarantonio, Bryant University

Gail Olmsted, Springfield Technical Community College

Lois Olson, San Diego State University

John O'Malley, New York University

Carol Osborne, University of Southern Florida

Joseph Ouellette, Bryant University

Karen Palumbo, University of St. Francis

Glenn Perser, Houston Community College

Karen Petersen, Augustana College

Joanna Phillips, Western Kentucky University

Ray Polchow, Zane State University

Sandra Rahman, Framingham State College

Bobby Reynolds, Troy University eCampus

Eric Rios, Eastern University

Chin Robinson, Oral Roberts University

Heidi Rottier, Bradley University

June Roux, Delaware Technical & Community College

Patricia A. Ryan, College of the Canyons

Doreen Sams, Georgia College & State University

Nanette Sanders-Cobb, Craven Communtiy College

William Sannwald, San Diego State University

Anshu Saran, University of Texas of the Permian Basin

Diana Scales, Tennessee State University

Fritz Scherz, Morrisville State College

Jeff Schmidt, University of Oklahoma

Kirk Schueler, University of Michigan

Joe Schwartz, Georgia College and State University

Stephen Schwarz, Saint John's University

Biagio Sciacca, Pennsylvania State University

Del Shepard, Simpson College

Scott Sherwood, Metropolitan State College of Denver

Bill Shockley, Bluefield College

Jonathan Silver, Alvernia College

Rob Simon, University of Nebraska, Lincoln

Ruth Smith, St. Anselm's College

Latanya Smith, Edinboro University of Pennsylvania

Gene Steidinger, Loras College

Alex Stein, Goucher College

Peter Stone, Spartanburg Community College

Chad Storlie, Creighton University

J. P. Stratton, Furman University

Karolina Sudwoj-Nogalska, University of Cincinnati

G. Knude Swensen, Dickinson State University

Albert J. Taylor, Coastal Carolina University

Michael Taylor, Marietta College

Surinder Tikoo, State University of New York, New Paltz

Donna Tillman, California State University, Pomona

Lisa Toms, Southern Arkansas University

Patrick Tormey, Iona College

Jessica Town-Gunderson, St. Cloud Technical College
Carrie Trimble, Illinois Wesleyan University
Carolyn Tripp, Western Illinois University
Leo Trudel, University of Maine
Gary Tucker, Oklahoma City Community College
Joseph Turner, College of The Ablemarle
David Urban, Virginia Commonwealth University
Chandu Valluri, St. Mary's University of Minnesota
Brian Vander Schee, University of Pittsburgh–Bradford
Alexia Vanides, University of California, Berkeley
Richard Vaughan, University of St. Francis

Candace Vogelsong, Cecil Community College
Simon Walls, Fort Lewis College
D.J. Wasmer, Saint Mary-of-the-Woods College
Joyce Whitehorn, University of Alaska, Fairbanks
Bob Willis, Rogers State University
Doug Wilson, University of Oregon
Kelly Wolfe, Webber International University
David Wright, Abilene Christian University
Donna Yancey, University of North Alabama
Joan Zielinski, Northwestern University
Gail Zwart, Riverside Community College, Norco Campus

Former Reviewers

Abi Almeer, Nova University
Ajay Manrai, University of Delaware
Alan Brokaw, Michigan Technological University
Alejandro Camacho, University of Georgia
Alison Pittman, Brevard Community College
Andre San Augustine, University of Arizona
Andrea Weeks, Fashion Institute of Design and Merchandising
Ann Kuzma, Minnesota State University–Mankato
Andrew T. Norman, Drake University
Arnold Bornfriend, Worcester State College
Arvid Anderson, University of North Carolina–Wilmington
Bill Worley, Allan Hancock College
Carol Gwin, Baylor University
Charles Goeldner, University of Colorado–Boulder
Dave Olsen, North Hennepin Community College
David Forlani, University of North Florida
Debbora Meflin, Bullock–California State Polytechnic University
Deborah Owens, University of Akron
Dee Smith, Lansing Community College
Diana Grewel, University of Miami
Donald Boyer, Jefferson College
Donald McBane, Clemson University
Donald Self, Auburn University–Montgomery

Donna Tillman, California State Polytechnic University
Dorothy Maas, Delaware County Community College
Dwight Scherban, Central Connecticut College
Eberhard Scheuing, St. John's University
Ed Laube, Macomb Community College
Eileen Keller, Kent State University
Eric Kulp, Middlesex Community College
Eric Pratt, New Mexico State University
Esther Headley, Wichita State University
Eugene Gilbert, California State University–Sacramento
Gemmy Allen, Mountain View College
George Paltz, Erie Community College
Gerald Cavallo, Fairfield University
Gordon Snider, California Polytechnic School of San Luis Obispo
Gregory Lincoln, Westchester Community College
Herbert Miller, University of Texas–Austin
Herbert Sherman, Long-Island University–Southhampton
Ira Teich, Long Island University
Jack Forrest, Middle Tennessee State University
Jack Sheeks, Broward Community College
James Jeck, North Carolina State University
James Kennedy, Navarro College
James McAlexander, Oregon State University

Jeff Schmidt, University of Illinois-Champaign–Urbana

Jeffrey B. Schmidt, University of Oklahoma

Jerry L. Thomas, San Jose State University

Jim Muney, Valdosta State

Jim Spiers, Arizona State University

Joan Mizis, St. Louis Community College

Joel Porrish, Springfield College

John de Young, Cumberland County College

John Gauthier, Gateway Technical Institute

John Lloyd, Monroe Community College

June Cotte, University of Connecticut

Karen Stone, Southern New Hampshire University

Kathy Illing, Greenville Technical College

Lalita Manrai, University of Delaware

Lana Podolak, Community College of Beaver County

Lee Dickson, Florida International University

Lee Nueman, Bucks County Community College

Linda Moroble, Dallas County Community College

Lucette Comer, Florida International University

Mark Mitchell, University of South Carolina–Spartanburg

Martha Leham, Diablo Valley College

Mee-Shew Cheung, University of Tennessee

Melissa Moore, Mississippi State University

Melissa Moore, University of Connecticut

Memoush Banton, University of Miami

Mery Yeagle, University of Maryland

Michael Conard, Teikyo Post University

Mike Dotson, Appalachian State University

P. Renee Foster, Delta State University

Patrick J. Demerath, Troy University–Montgomery Campus

Paul Dowling, University of Utah

Paul R. Redig, Milwaukee Area Tech College–Mequon Campus

Pamela Schindler, Wittenburg University

Peter T. Doukas, Westchester Community College

Peter Stone, Spartanburg Technical College

Raj Sethuraman, University of Iowa

Rajshri Agarwal, Iowa State University

Randall Mertz, Mesa Community College

Raymond Schwartz, Montclair State University

Rebecca Ratner, University of North Carolina at Chapel Hill

Renee Florsheim, Loyola Marymount University

Reshima H. Shah, University of Pittsburgh

Richard Hansen, Ferris State University

Richard (Rich) Brown, Freed–Hardeman University

Rick Polio, University of Bridgeport

Robert C. Reese, Illinois Valley Community College

Robert Jones, California State University–Fullerton

Robert L. Powell, Gloucester County College

Robert Moore, University of Connecticut

Robert Ross, Wichita State University

Roberta Schultz, Western Michigan University

Rodger Singley, Illinois State University

Ron Cooley, South Suburban College

Ron Lennon, Barry University

Ron Young, Kalamazoo Valley Community College

Ronald Cutter, Southwest Missouri State University

S. Allen Broyles, University of Tennessee

Sana Akili, Iowa State University

Sandra Heusinkveld, Normandale Community College

Sandra Moulton, Technical College of Alamance

Steve Hoeffler, University of North Carolina at Chapel Hill

Steve Taylor, Illinois State University

Steve Vitucci, Tarleton State University–Central Texas

Summer White, Massachusetts Bay Community College

Tammy Pappas, Eastern Michigan University

Thomas Drake, University of Miami

Thomas Paczkowski, Cayuga Community College

Turina R. Bakken, Madison Area Tech College

Veronica Miller, Mount Saint Mary's College

William Carner, University of Texas–Austin

William Morgenroth, University of South Carolina-Columbia

William Rodgers, St. Cloud State University

We also owe a great deal to the people at Prentice Hall who helped develop this book. Project Manager Melissa Pellerano provided invaluable support and assistance and ably managed many facets of this complex revision project. We would also like to thank Kerri Tomasso, Judy Leale, Wendy Craven, David Parker, Melissa Sabella, Kate Moore, and Heather Scott. We are proud to be associated with the fine professionals at Prentice Hall.

Finally, we owe many thanks to our families for all of their support and encouragement—Kathy, Betty, Mandy, Matt, KC, Keri, Delaney, Molly, Macy, and Ben from the Armstrong family and Nancy, Amy, Melissa, and Jessica from the Kotler family. To them, we dedicate this book.

Gary Armstrong
Philip Kotler

smelling
like a
mom

smelling like
a **woman**

Tide
febreze
freshness

Tide
febreze
knows fabrics best

**After
ng this
ter, you
ould be
able to**

1. define marketing and outline the steps in the marketing process
2. explain the importance of understanding customers and the marketplace, and identify the five core marketplace

3. identify the key elements of a customer-driven marketing strategy and discuss the marketing management orientations that guide marketing strategy
4. discuss customer relationship

strategies for creating valu customers and capturing va *from* customers in return
5. describe the major trends a forces that are changing the marketing landscape in this age of relationships

Marketing: Creating and Capturing Customer Value

ROAD MAP Previewing the Concepts

Fasten your seat belt! You're about to begin an exciting journey toward learning about marketing. In this chapter, to start you off in the right direction, we will first introduce you to the basic concepts. What *is* marketing? Simply put, marketing is managing profitable customer relationships. The aim of marketing is to create value for customers and to capture value in return. Chapter 1 is organized around five steps in the marketing process—from understanding customer needs, to designing customer-driven marketing strategies and programs, to building customer relationships and capturing value for the firm. Understanding these basic concepts, and forming your own ideas about what they really mean to you, will give you a solid foundation for all that follows.

Our first stop: Procter & Gamble, one of the world's largest and most respected marketing companies. P&G makes and markets a who's who list of consumer megabrands, including the likes of Tide, Crest, Bounty, Charmin, Puffs, Pampers, Pringles, Gillette, Dawn, Ivory, Febreze, Swiffer, Olay, Cover Girl, Pantene, Scope, NyQuil, Duracell, and a hundred more. It's also the world's largest advertiser, spending an eye-popping $8.2 billion each year on advertising worldwide, "telling and selling" consumers on the benefits of using its products. But look deeper and you'll see that this premier marketer does far more than just "tell and sell." P&G's stated purpose is to provide products that "improve the lives of the world's consumers." The company's products really do create value for consumers by solving their problems. In return, customers reward P&G with their brand loyalty and buying dollars. You'll see this creating-customer-value-to-capture-value-in-return theme repeated throughout the first chapter and throughout the text. But for now, let's get things rolling with a good P&G story.

Creating customer value. Building meaningful customer relationships. All this sounds pretty lofty, especially for a company like P&G, which sells seemingly mundane, low-involvement consumer products such as detergents and shampoos, toothpastes and fabric softeners, and toilet paper and disposable diapers. Can you really develop a meaningful relationship with a laundry detergent? For P&G, the resounding answer is *yes*.

For example, take P&G's Tide. More than 60 years ago, Tide revolutionized the industry as the first detergent to use synthetic compounds rather than soap chemicals for cleaning clothes. Tide really does get clothes clean. For decades, Tide's marketers have positioned the brand on superior functional performance, with hard-hitting ads showing before-and-after cleaning comparisons. But as it turns out, to consumers, Tide means a lot more than just getting grass stains out of that old pair of jeans.

For several years, P&G has been on a mission to unearth and cultivate the deep connections that customers have with its products. Two years ago, P&G global marketing chief James Stengel mandated that the company's brands must "speak to consumers eye to eye" rather than relentlessly driving product benefits. "We need to think beyond consuming . . . and to really directly understand the role and the meaning the brand has in [consumers'] lives," says Stengel. Behind this strategy lies the realization that competitors can quickly copy product benefits, such as cleaning power. However, they can't easily copy how consumers *feel* about a brand. Consequently, P&G's true strength lies in the relationships that it builds between its brands and customers.

Under this mandate, the Tide marketing team decided that it needed a new message for the brand. Tide's brand share, although large, had been stagnant for several years. Also, as a result of its hard-hitting functional advertising, consumers saw the Tide brand as arrogant, self-absorbed, and very male. The brand needed to recapture the hearts and minds of its core female consumers.

So the team set out to gain a deeper understanding of the emotional connections that women have with their laundry. Rather than conducting the usual focus groups and research surveys, however, marketing executives and strategists from P&G and its longtime ad agency, Saatchi & Saatchi, went into a two-week consumer immersion. They tagged along with women in Kansas City, Missouri, and Charlotte, North Carolina, as they worked, shopped, and ran errands, and they sat in on discussions to hear women talk about what's important to them. "We got to an incredibly deep and personal level," says a Tide marketing executive. "We wanted to understand the role of laundry in their life." But "one of the great things," adds a Saatchi strategist, "is we didn't talk [to consumers] about their laundry habits [and practices]. We talked about their lives, what their needs were, how they felt as women. And we got a lot of rich stuff that we hadn't tapped into before."

For members of the Tide team who couldn't join the two-week consumer odyssey, including Saatchi creative people, the agency videotaped the immersions, prepared scripts, and hired actresses to portray consumers in an hour-long play titled "Pieces of Her." "They were actually very good actresses who brought to life many dimensions of women," says the Saatchi executive. "It's difficult to inspire creatives sometimes. And [their reaction to the play] was incredible. There was crying and laughing. And you can see it in the [later] work. It's just very connected to women."

From the customer immersions, the marketers learned that, although Tide and laundry aren't the most important things in customers' lives, women are very emotional about their clothing. For example, "there was the joy a plus-size, divorced woman described when she got a whistle from her boyfriend while wearing her "foolproof" (sexiest) outfit." According to one P&G account: "Day-to-day fabrics in women's lives hold meaning and touch them in many ways. Women like taking care of their clothes and fabrics because they are filled with emotions, stories, feelings, and memories. The fabrics in their lives (anything from jeans to sheets) allow them to express their personalities, their multidimensions as women, their attitudes." Such insights impacted everything the brand did moving forward. Tide, the marketers decided, can do more than solve women's laundry problems. It can make a difference in something they truly care about—the fabrics that touch their lives.

Based on these insights, P&G and Saatchi develop an award-winning advertising campaign, built around the theme "Tide knows fabrics best." Rather than the mostly heartless demonstrations and side-by-side comparisons of past Tide advertising, the new campaign employs rich visual imagery and meaningful emotional connections. The "Tide knows fabrics best" slogan says little about cleaning. Instead, the message is that Tide lets women focus on life's important things. "One of our rallying cries was to get out of the laundry basket and into [your] life," says a Tide marketer.

The "Tide knows fabrics best" ads have just the right mix of emotional connections and soft sell. In one TV commercial, a pregnant woman dribbles ice cream on the one last shirt that still fits. It's Tide with Bleach to the rescue, so that "your clothes can outlast your cravings." Another ad shows touching scenes of a woman first holding a baby and then cuddling romantically with her husband, all to the tune of "Be My Baby." Tide with Febreze, says the ad, can mean "the difference between smelling like a mom and smelling like a woman." In a third ad, a woman plays with her daughter at a park, still in her white slacks from the office, thanks to her confidence in Tide with Bleach. "Your work clothes. Your play clothes. Yup, they're the same clothes," the ad concludes. "Tide with bleach: For looking great, it's child's play." In all, the "Tide knows fabrics best" campaign shows women that Tide really does make a difference in fabrics that touch their lives.

So . . . back to that original question: *Can* you develop a relationship with a laundry detergent brand? Some critics wonder if P&G is taking this relationship thing too seriously. "Everybody wants to elevate their brand to this kind of more rarefied level," says one brand consultant, "but at the end of the day detergent is detergent." But it's hard to argue with success, and no brand is more successful than Tide. P&G's flagship brand captures an incredible 43 percent share of the cluttered and competitive laundry detergent market. That's right, 43 percent and growing—including a seven percent increase in the year following the start of the "Tide knows fabrics best" campaign.

If you ask P&G global marketing chief Stengel, he'd say that kind of success comes from deeply understanding consumers and connecting the company's brands to their lives. Stengel wants P&G to be more than a one-way communicator with customers. He wants it to be "a starter of conversations and a solver of consumers' problems." "It's not about telling and selling," he says. "It's about bringing a [customer] relationship mindset to everything we do."[1]

Today's successful companies have one thing in common: Like Procter & Gamble, they are strongly customer focused and heavily committed to marketing. These companies share a passion for understanding and satisfying customer needs in well-defined target markets. They motivate everyone in the organization to help build lasting customer relationships based on creating value. P&G's chief global marketer, Jim Stengel, puts it this way: "If we're going to make one big bet on our future—right here, right now—I'd say that the smart money is on building [customer] relationships."[2]

What Is Marketing?

Marketing, more than any other business function, deals with customers. Although we will soon explore more-detailed definitions of marketing, perhaps the simplest definition is this one: *Marketing is managing profitable customer relationships.* The twofold goal of marketing is to attract new customers by promising superior value and to keep and grow current customers by delivering satisfaction.

Wal-Mart has become the world's largest retailer—the world's largest *company*—by delivering on its promise, "Save money. Live Better." At Disney theme parks, "imagineers" work wonders in their quest to "make a dream come true today." Apple fulfills its motto to "Think Different" with dazzling, customer-driven innovation that captures customer imaginations and loyalty. Its wildly successful iPod grabs more than 70 percent of the music player market; its iTunes music store captures nearly 90 percent of the song download business.[3]

Sound marketing is critical to the success of every organization. Large for-profit firms such as Procter & Gamble, Toyota, Target, Apple, and Marriott use marketing. But so do not-for-profit organizations such as colleges, hospitals, museums, symphony orchestras, and even churches.

You already know a lot about marketing—it's all around you. You see the results of marketing in the abundance of products in your nearby shopping mall. You see marketing in the advertisements that fill your TV screen, spice up your magazines, stuff your mailbox, or enliven your Web pages. At home, at school, where you work, and where you play, you see marketing in almost everything you do. Yet, there is much more to marketing than meets the consumer's casual eye. Behind it all is a massive network of people and activities competing for your attention and purchases.

This book will give you a complete introduction to the basic concepts and practices of today's marketing. In this chapter, we begin by defining marketing and the marketing process.

Marketing Defined

What *is* marketing? Many people think of marketing only as selling and advertising. And no wonder—every day we are bombarded with television commercials, direct-mail offers, sales calls, and Internet pitches. However, selling and advertising are only the tip of the marketing iceberg.

Today, marketing must be understood not in the old sense of making a sale—"telling and selling"—but in the new sense of *satisfying customer needs*. If the marketer understands consumer needs; develops products and services that provide superior customer value; and prices, distributes, and promotes them effectively, these products will sell easily. In fact, according to management guru Peter Drucker, "The aim of marketing is to make selling unnecessary."[4] Selling and advertising are only part of a larger "marketing mix"—a set of marketing tools that work together to satisfy customer needs and build customer relationships.

Broadly defined, marketing is a social and managerial process by which individuals and organizations obtain what they need and want through creating and exchanging value with others. In a narrower business context, marketing involves building profitable, value-laden exchange relationships with customers. Hence, we define **marketing** as the process by which companies create value for customers and build strong customer relationships in order to capture value from customers in return.[5]

Marketing

Marketing is the activity, set of institutions, and processes for creating, communicating, delivering, and exchanging offerings that have value for customers, clients, partners, and society at-large.

The Marketing Process

Figure 1.1 presents a simple five-step model of the marketing process. In the first four steps, companies work to understand consumers, create customer value, and build strong customer relationships. In the final step, companies reap the rewards of creating superior customer value. By creating value *for* consumers, they in turn capture value *from* consumers in the form of sales, profits, and long-term customer equity.

In this and the next chapter, we will examine the steps of this simple model of marketing. In this chapter, we will review each step but focus more on the customer relationship steps—understanding customers, building customer relationships, and capturing value from customers. In Chapter 2, we'll look more deeply into the second and third steps—designing marketing strategies and constructing marketing programs.

Understanding the Marketplace and Customer Needs

As a first step, marketers need to understand customer needs and wants and the marketplace within which they operate. We now examine five core customer and marketplace concepts: (1) *needs, wants, and demands*; (2) *marketing offers (products, services, and experiences)*; (3) *value and satisfaction*; (4) *exchanges and relationships*; and (5) *markets*.

Customer Needs, Wants, and Demands

Needs

States of felt deprivation.

The most basic concept underlying marketing is that of human needs. Human **needs** are states of felt deprivation. They include basic *physical* needs for food, clothing, warmth, and safety; *social* needs for belonging and affection; and *individual* needs for knowledge and self-expression. These needs were not created by marketers; they are a basic part of the human makeup.

Wants

The form human needs take as shaped by culture and individual personality.

Wants are the form human needs take as they are shaped by culture and individual personality. An American *needs* food but *wants* a Big Mac, french fries, and a soft drink. A per-

FIGURE 1.1

A Simple Model of the Marketing Process

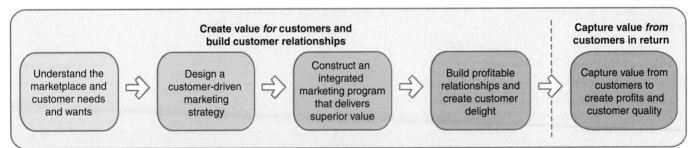

son in Papua New Guinea *needs* food but *wants* taro, rice, yams, and pork. Wants are shaped by one's society and are described in terms of objects that will satisfy needs. When backed by buying power, wants become **demands**. Given their wants and resources, people demand products with benefits that add up to the most value and satisfaction.

Outstanding marketing companies go to great lengths to learn about and understand their customers' needs, wants, and demands. They conduct consumer research and analyze mountains of customer data. Their people at all levels—including top management—stay close to customers. For example, at Southwest Airlines, all senior executives handle bags, check in passengers, and serve as flight attendants once every quarter. Harley-Davidson's chairman regularly mounts his Harley and rides with customers to get feedback and ideas. And at Build-A-Bear Workshop, one of the country's fastest-growing retailers, founder and chief executive Maxine Clark regularly visits her stores around the world, meeting customers, chatting with employees, and just getting to know the young people who buy her products. "I'm on a lot of online buddy lists," she says.[6]

Demands
Human wants that are backed by buying power.

Market Offerings—Products, Services, and Experiences

Consumers' needs and wants are fulfilled through **market offerings**—some combination of products, services, information, or experiences offered to a market to satisfy a need or want. Market offerings are not limited to physical *products*. They also include *services*—activities or benefits offered for sale that are essentially intangible and do not result in the ownership of anything. Examples include banking, airline, hotel, tax preparation, and home repair services. More broadly, market offerings also include other entities, such as *persons, places, organizations, information,* and *ideas.* For example, beyond promoting its banking services, LaSalle Bank runs ads asking people to donate used or old winter clothing to the Salvation Army. In this case, the "market offering" is helping to keep those who are less fortunate warm.

Market offering
Some combination of products, services, information, or experiences offered to a market to satisfy a need or want.

Marketing myopia
The mistake of paying more attention to the specific products a company offers than to the benefits and experiences produced by these products.

Many sellers make the mistake of paying more attention to the specific products they offer than to the benefits and experiences produced by these products. These sellers suffer from **marketing myopia**. They are so taken with their products that they focus only on existing wants and lose sight of underlying customer needs.[7] They forget that a product is only a tool to solve a consumer problem. A manufacturer of quarter-inch drill bits may think that the customer needs a drill bit. But what the customer *really* needs is a quarter-inch hole. These sellers will have trouble if a new product comes along that serves the customer's need better or less expensively. The customer will have the same *need* but will *want* the new product.

Smart marketers look beyond the attributes of the products and services they sell. By orchestrating several services and products, they create *brand experiences* for consumers. For example, Walt Disney World is an experience; so is a ride on a Harley-Davidson motorcycle or a visit to your local Starbucks. "We're not in the business of filling bellies," says Starbucks founder Howard Schultz, "we're in the business of filling souls."[8] Similarly, Hewlett-Packard recognizes that a personal computer is much more than just a collection of wires and electrical components. It's an intensely personal user experience: "There is hardly anything that you own that is *more* personal. Your personal computer is your backup brain. It's your life. . . . It's your astonishing strategy, staggering proposal, dazzling calculation. It's your autobiography, written in a thousand daily words."[9]

■ Market offerings are not limited to physical products. For example, LaSalle Bank runs ads asking people to donate used or old winter clothing to the Salvation Army. In this case, the "marketing offer" is helping to keep those who are less fortunate warm.

Customer Value and Satisfaction

Consumers usually face a broad array of products and services that might satisfy a given need. How do they choose among these many market offerings? Customers form expectations about the value and satisfaction that various market offerings will deliver and buy accordingly. Satisfied customers buy again and tell others about their good experiences. Dissatisfied customers often switch to competitors and disparage the product to others.

Marketers must be careful to set the right level of expectations. If they set expectations too low, they may satisfy those who buy but fail to attract enough buyers. If they raise expectations too high, buyers will be disappointed. Customer value and customer satisfaction are key building blocks for developing and managing customer relationships. We will revisit these core concepts later in the chapter.

Exchanges and Relationships

Exchange
The act of obtaining a desired object from someone by offering something in return.

Marketing occurs when people decide to satisfy needs and wants through exchange relationships. **Exchange** is the act of obtaining a desired object from someone by offering something in return. In the broadest sense, the marketer tries to bring about a response to some market offering. The response may be more than simply buying or trading products and services. A political candidate, for instance, wants votes, a church wants membership, an orchestra wants an audience, and a social action group wants idea acceptance.

Marketing consists of actions taken to build and maintain desirable exchange *relationships* with target audiences involving a product, service, idea, or other object. Beyond simply attracting new customers and creating transactions, the goal is to retain customers and grow their business with the company. Marketers want to build strong relationships by consistently delivering superior customer value. We will expand on the important concept of managing customer relationships later in the chapter.

Markets

Market
The set of all actual and potential buyers of a product or service.

The concepts of exchange and relationships lead to the concept of a market. A **market** is the set of actual and potential buyers of a product. These buyers share a particular need or want that can be satisfied through exchange relationships.

Marketing means managing markets to bring about profitable customer relationships. However, creating these relationships takes work. Sellers must search for buyers, identify their needs, design good market offerings, set prices for them, promote them, and store and deliver them. Activities such as consumer research, product development, communication, distribution, pricing, and service are core marketing activities.

Although we normally think of marketing as being carried on by sellers, buyers also carry on marketing. Consumers do marketing when they search for the goods they need at prices they can afford. Company purchasing agents do marketing when they track down sellers and bargain for good terms.

Figure 1.2 shows the main elements in a modern marketing system. In the usual situation, marketing involves serving a market of final consumers in the face of competitors. The company and competitors research the market and interact with consumers to under-

FIGURE 1.2

Elements of a Modern Marketing System

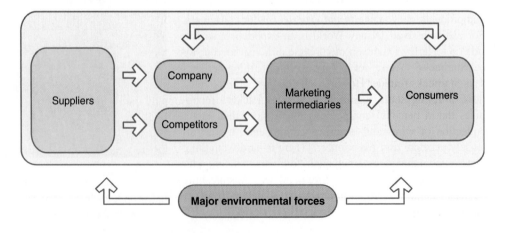

stand their needs and obtain their inputs. Then they assemble and send their respective market offerings and messages to consumers, either directly or through marketing intermediaries. All of the actors in the system are affected by major environmental forces (demographic, economic, physical, technological, political/legal, and social/cultural).

Each party in the system adds value for the next level. All of the arrows represent relationships that must be developed and managed. Thus, a company's success at building profitable relationships depends not only on its own actions but also on how well the entire system serves the needs of final consumers. Wal-Mart cannot fulfill its promise of low prices unless its suppliers provide merchandise at low costs. And Ford cannot deliver high quality to car buyers unless its dealers provide outstanding sales and service.

Designing a Customer-Driven Marketing Strategy

Once it fully understands consumers and the marketplace, marketing management can design a customer-driven marketing strategy. We define **marketing management** as the art and science of choosing target markets and building profitable relationships with them. The marketing manager's aim is to find, attract, keep, and grow target customers by creating, delivering, and communicating superior customer value.

Marketing management
The art and science of choosing target markets and building profitable relationships with them.

To design a winning marketing strategy, the marketing manager must answer two important questions: *What customers will we serve (what's our target market)?* and *How can we serve these customers best (what's our value proposition)?* We will discuss these marketing strategy concepts briefly here, and then look at them in more detail in the next chapter.

Selecting Customers to Serve

The company must first decide *who* it will serve. It does this by dividing the market into segments of customers (*market segmentation*) and selecting which segments it will go after (*target marketing*). Some people think of marketing management as finding as many customers as possible and increasing demand. But marketing managers know that they cannot serve all customers in every way. By trying to serve all customers, they may not serve any customers well. Instead, the company wants to select only customers that it can serve well and profitably. For example, Nordstrom stores profitably target affluent professionals; Family Dollar stores profitably target families with more modest means.

Some marketers may even seek *fewer* customers and reduced demand. For example, Yosemite National Park is badly overcrowded in the summer and many power companies have trouble meeting demand during peak usage periods. In these and other cases of excess demand, companies may practice *demarketing* to reduce the number of customers or to shift their demand temporarily or permanently. For instance, many power companies now sponsor programs that help customers reduce their power usage through peak-load control devices, better energy use monitoring, and heating system tune-up incentives. Progress Energy even offers an Energy Manager on Loan program that provides school systems and other public customers with a cost-free on-site energy expert to help them find energy-savings opportunities.

Ultimately, marketing managers must decide which customers they want to target and on the level, timing, and nature of their demand. Simply put, marketing management is *customer management* and *demand management*.

Choosing a Value Proposition

The company must also decide how it will serve targeted customers—how it will *differentiate and position* itself in the marketplace. A company's *value proposition* is the set of benefits or values it promises to deliver to consumers to satisfy their needs. Keebler cookies are "baked by little elves in a hollow tree" but Nabisco's Oreos are "Milk's favorite cookie." With cell phones, Nokia is "Connecting People—anyone, anywhere," whereas

■ Value propositions: Land Rover lets you "Go Beyond"—to "get a taste of adventure, whatever your tastes."

with Apple's iPhone, "Touching is believing." And BMW promises "the ultimate driving machine," whereas Land Rover lets you "Go Beyond"—to "get a taste of adventure, whatever your tastes."

Such value propositions differentiate one brand from another. They answer the customer's question "Why should I buy your brand rather than a competitor's?" Companies must design strong value propositions that give them the greatest advantage in their target markets.

Marketing Management Orientations

Marketing management wants to design strategies that will build profitable relationships with target consumers. But what *philosophy* should guide these marketing strategies? What weight should be given to the interests of customers, the organization, and society? Very often, these interests conflict.

There are five alternative concepts under which organizations design and carry out their marketing strategies: the *production, product, selling, marketing,* and *societal marketing concepts.*

Production concept
The idea that consumers will favor products that are available and highly affordable and that the organization should therefore focus on improving production and distribution efficiency.

The Production Concept The **production concept** holds that consumers will favor products that are available and highly affordable. Therefore, management should focus on improving production and distribution efficiency. This concept is one of the oldest orientations that guides sellers.

The production concept is still a useful philosophy in some situations. For example, computer maker Lenovo dominates the highly competitive, price-sensitive Chinese PC market through low labor costs, high production efficiency, and mass distribution. However, although useful in some situations, the production concept can lead to marketing myopia. Companies adopting this orientation run a major risk of focusing too narrowly on their own operations and losing sight of the real objective—satisfying customer needs and building customer relationships.

Product concept
The idea that consumers will favor products that offer the most quality, performance, and features and that the organization should therefore devote its energy to making continuous product improvements.

The Product Concept The **product concept** holds that consumers will favor products that offer the most in quality, performance, and innovative features. Under this concept, marketing strategy focuses on making continuous product improvements.

Product quality and improvement are important parts of most marketing strategies. However, focusing *only* on the company's products can also lead to marketing myopia. For example, some manufacturers believe that if they can "build a better mousetrap, the world will beat a path to their door." But they are often rudely shocked. Buyers may well be looking for a better solution to a mouse problem but not necessarily for a better mousetrap. The better solution might be a chemical spray, an exterminating service, or something else that works even better than a mousetrap. Furthermore, a better mousetrap will not sell unless the manufacturer designs, packages, and prices it attractively; places it in convenient distribution channels; brings it to the attention of people who need it; and convinces buyers that it is a better product.

Selling concept
The idea that consumers will not buy enough of the firm's products unless it undertakes a large-scale selling and promotion effort.

The Selling Concept Many companies follow the **selling concept**, which holds that consumers will not buy enough of the firm's products unless it undertakes a large-scale selling and promotion effort. The concept is typically practiced with unsought goods—those that buyers do not normally think of buying, such as insurance or blood donations. These industries must be good at tracking down prospects and selling them on product benefits.

Such aggressive selling, however, carries high risks. It focuses on creating sales transactions rather than on building long-term, profitable customer relationships. The aim often is to sell what the company makes rather than making what the market wants. It assumes

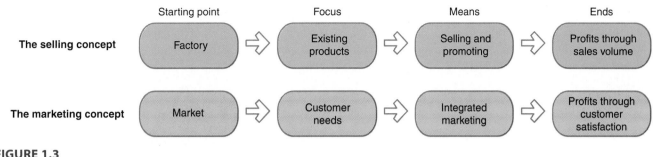

	Starting point	Focus	Means	Ends
The selling concept	Factory	Existing products	Selling and promoting	Profits through sales volume
The marketing concept	Market	Customer needs	Integrated marketing	Profits through customer satisfaction

FIGURE 1.3

The Selling and Marketing Concepts Contrasted

that customers who are coaxed into buying the product will like it. Or, if they don't like it, they will possibly forget their disappointment and buy it again later. These are usually poor assumptions.

The Marketing Concept The **marketing concept** holds that achieving organizational goals depends on knowing the needs and wants of target markets and delivering the desired satisfactions better than competitors do. Under the marketing concept, customer focus and value are the *paths* to sales and profits. Instead of a product-centered "make and sell" philosophy, the marketing concept is a customer-centered "sense and respond" philosophy. It views marketing not as "hunting," but as "gardening." The job is not to find the right customers for your product but to find the right products for your customers.

Figure 1.3 contrasts the selling concept and the marketing concept. The selling concept takes an *inside-out* perspective. It starts with the factory, focuses on the company's existing products, and calls for heavy selling and promotion to obtain profitable sales. It focuses primarily on customer conquest—getting short-term sales with little concern about who buys or why.

In contrast, the marketing concept takes an *outside-in* perspective. As Herb Kelleher, Southwest Airlines' colorful CEO, puts it, "We don't have a marketing department; we have a customer department." The marketing concept starts with a well-defined market, focuses on customer needs, and integrates all the marketing activities that affect customers. In turn, it yields profits by creating lasting relationships with the right customers based on customer value and satisfaction.

Implementing the marketing concept often means more than simply responding to customers' stated desires and obvious needs. *Customer-driven* companies research current customers deeply to learn about their desires, gather new product and service ideas, and test proposed product improvements. Such customer-driven marketing usually works well when a clear need exists and when customers know what they want.

In many cases, however, customers *don't* know what they want or even what is possible. For example, even 20 years ago, how many consumers would have thought to ask for now-commonplace products such as cell phones, notebook computers, iPods, digital cameras, 24-hour online buying, and satellite navigation systems in their cars? Such situations call for *customer-driving* marketing—understanding customer needs even better than customers themselves do and creating products and services that meet existing and latent needs, now and in the future. As an executive at 3M puts it: "Our goal is to lead customers where they want to go before *they* know where they want to go."

Marketing concept
The marketing management philosophy that holds that achieving organizational goals depends on knowing the needs and wants of target markets and delivering the desired satisfactions better than competitors do.

■ Customer-driving marketing: Even 20 years ago, how many consumers would have thought to ask for now-commonplace products such as cell phones, personal digital assistants, notebook computers, iPods, and digital cameras? Marketers must often understand customer needs even better than the customers themselves do.

FIGURE 1.4

Three Considerations Underlying
the Societal Marketing Concept

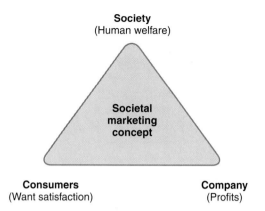

Society
(Human welfare)

**Societal
marketing
concept**

Consumers
(Want satisfaction)

Company
(Profits)

Societal marketing concept

The idea that a company's marketing decisions should consider consumers' wants, the company's requirements, consumers' long-run interests, and society's long-run interests.

The Societal Marketing Concept The **societal marketing concept** questions whether the pure marketing concept overlooks possible conflicts between consumer *short-run wants* and consumer *long-run welfare*. Is a firm that satisfies the immediate needs and wants of target markets always doing what's best for consumers in the long run? The societal marketing concept holds that marketing strategy should deliver value to customers in a way that maintains or improves both the consumer's *and the society's* well-being.

Consider the fast-food industry. You may view today's giant fast-food chains as offering tasty and convenient food at reasonable prices. Yet many consumer nutritionists and environmental groups have voiced strong concerns. They point to fast feeders such as Hardee's, who are promoting monster meals such as the Monster Thickburger—two 1/3-pound slabs of Angus beef, four strips of bacon, three slices of American cheese, and mayonnaise on a buttered bun, delivering 1,420 calories and 102 grams of fat. Such unhealthy fare, the critics claim, is leading consumers to eat too much of the wrong foods, contributing to a national obesity epidemic. What's more, the products are wrapped in convenient packaging but this leads to waste and pollution. Thus, in satisfying short-term consumer wants, the highly successful fast-food chains may be harming consumer health and causing environmental problems in the long run.[10]

As Figure 1.4 shows, companies should balance three considerations in setting their marketing strategies: company profits, consumer wants, *and* society's interests. Johnson & Johnson does this well. Its concern for societal interests is summarized in a company document called "Our Credo," which stresses honesty, integrity, and putting people before profits. Under this credo, Johnson & Johnson would rather take a big loss than ship a bad batch of one of its products.

Consider the tragic tampering case in which eight people died in 1982 from swallowing cyanide-laced capsules of Tylenol, a Johnson & Johnson brand. Although Johnson & Johnson believed that the pills had been altered in only a few stores, not in the factory, it quickly recalled all of its product and launched an information campaign to instruct and reassure consumers. The recall cost the company $100 million in earnings. In the long run, however, the company's swift recall of Tylenol strengthened consumer confidence and loyalty, and today Tylenol remains one of the nation's leading brands of pain reliever.

Johnson & Johnson management has learned that doing what's right benefits both consumers and the company. Says former CEO Ralph Larsen, "The Credo should not be

Our Credo

We believe our first responsibility is to the doctors, nurses and patients, to mothers and fathers and all others who use our products and services. In meeting their needs everything we do must be of high quality. We must constantly strive to reduce our costs in order to maintain reasonable prices. Customers' orders must be serviced promptly and accurately. Our suppliers and distributors must have an opportunity to make a fair profit.

We are responsible to our employees, the men and women who work with us throughout the world. Everyone must be considered as an individual. We must respect their dignity and recognize their merit. They must have a sense of security in their jobs. Compensation must be fair and adequate, and working conditions clean, orderly and safe. We must be mindful of ways to help our employees fulfill their family responsibilities. Employees must feel free to make suggestions and complaints. There must be equal opportunity for employment, development and advancement for those qualified. We must provide competent management, and their actions must be just and ethical.

We are responsible to the communities in which we live and work and to the world community as well. We must be good citizens — support good works and charities and bear our fair share of taxes. We must encourage civic improvements and better health and education. We must maintain in good order the property we are privileged to use, protecting the environment and natural resources.

Our final responsibility is to our stockholders. Business must make a sound profit. We must experiment with new ideas. Research must be carried on, innovative programs developed and mistakes paid for. New equipment must be purchased, new facilities provided and new products launched. Reserves must be created to provide for adverse times. When we operate according to these principles, the stockholders should realize a fair return.

Johnson & Johnson

■ The societal marketing concept: Johnson & Johnson's Credo stresses putting people before profits.

viewed as some kind of social welfare program . . . it's just plain good business. If we keep trying to do what's right, at the end of the day we believe the marketplace will reward us." Thus, over the years, Johnson & Johnson's dedication to consumers and community service has made it one of America's most-admired companies *and* one of the most profitable.[11]

Preparing an Integrated Marketing Plan and Program

The company's marketing strategy outlines which customers the company will serve and how it will create value for these customers. Next, the marketer develops an integrated marketing program that will actually deliver the intended value to target customers. The marketing program builds customer relationships by transforming the marketing strategy into action. It consists of the firm's *marketing mix,* the set of marketing tools the firm uses to implement its marketing strategy.

The major marketing mix tools are classified into four broad groups, called the *four Ps* of marketing: product, price, place, and promotion. To deliver on its value proposition, the firm must first create a need-satisfying market offering (product). It must decide how much it will charge for the offering (price) and how it will make the offering available to target consumers (place). Finally, it must communicate with target customers about the offering and persuade them of its merits (promotion). The firm must blend all of these marketing mix tools into a comprehensive *integrated marketing program* that communicates and delivers the intended value to chosen customers. We will explore marketing programs and the marketing mix in much more detail in later chapters.

Linking the Concepts

Stop here for a moment and stretch your legs. What have you learned so far about marketing? For the moment, set aside the more formal definitions we've examined and try to develop your own understanding of marketing.

- In *your own words*, what *is* marketing? Write down *your* definition. Does your definition include such key concepts as customer value and relationships?
- What does marketing *mean* to you? How does it affect your life on a daily basis?
- What brand of athletic shoes did you purchase last? Describe your relationship with Nike, New Balance, Reebok, Adidas, or whatever company made the shoes you purchased.

Building Customer Relationships

The first three steps in the marketing process—understanding the marketplace and customer needs, designing a customer-driven marketing strategy, and constructing marketing programs—all lead up to the fourth and most important step: building profitable customer relationships.

Customer Relationship Management

Customer relationship management is perhaps the most important concept of modern marketing. Some marketers define customer relationship management narrowly as a customer data management activity (a practice called *CRM*). By this definition, it involves managing detailed information about individual customers and carefully managing customer "touch points" in order to maximize customer loyalty. We will discuss this narrower CRM activity in Chapter 4 dealing with marketing information.

Most marketers, however, give the concept of customer relationship management a broader meaning. In this broader sense, **customer relationship management** is the overall process of building and maintaining profitable customer relationships by delivering

Customer relationship management
The overall process of building and maintaining profitable customer relationships by delivering superior customer value and satisfaction.

superior customer value and satisfaction. It deals with all aspects of acquiring, keeping, and growing customers.

Relationship Building Blocks: Customer Value and Satisfaction The key to building lasting customer relationships is to create superior customer value and satisfaction. Satisfied customers are more likely to be loyal customers and to give the company a larger share of their business.

Customer-perceived value

The customer's evaluation of the difference between all the benefits and all the costs of a marketing offer relative to those of competing offers.

Customer Value Attracting and retaining customers can be a difficult task. Customers often face a bewildering array of products and services from which to choose. A customer buys from the firm that offers the highest **customer-perceived value**—the customer's evaluation of the difference between all the benefits and all the costs of a market offering relative to those of competing offers.

For example, consider the "premium denim" trend that has recently sent jeans prices skyrocketing. A pair of Paige Premium Denim jeans, for instance, starts at $169. A woman who buys a pair of Paige jeans gains a number of benefits. First, owner and designer Paige Adams-Gellar, a former model for premium denim brands, uses the knowledge she learned from the field to design jeans from the female perspective. Says Paige, "Most of us weren't blessed with perfect genes but we're bringing you the next best thing: perfect jeans." Her denim "will lift the derriere, lengthen your legs, and slenderize your hips and thighs—all with an uncompromising commitment to feminine detail and quality." In all, says Paige, her jeans are a real value—they will fit you better and last longer. When deciding whether to purchase a pair, customers will weigh these and other perceived values of owning Paige jeans against the money and psychic costs of acquiring them.

Customers often do not judge values and costs "accurately" or "objectively." They act on *perceived* value. For example, as compared to a pair of less expensive jeans that you'd pull off the shelf at Gap, do Paige jeans really provide superior quality and that perfect fit and look? If so, are they worth the much higher price? It's all a matter of personal value perceptions, but for many women the answer is yes. One woman notes that, for her, premium jeans always seem to fit just right, making the price irrelevant. "I work, so I have the money to buy them," she says. "I think they're worth it."[12]

Customer satisfaction

The extent to which a product's perceived performance matches a buyer's expectations.

Customer Satisfaction **Customer satisfaction** depends on the product's perceived performance relative to a buyer's expectations. If the product's performance falls short of expectations, the customer is dissatisfied. If performance matches expectations, the customer is satisfied. If performance exceeds expectations, the customer is highly satisfied or delighted.

Outstanding marketing companies go out of their way to keep important customers satisfied. Most studies show that higher levels of customer satisfaction lead to greater customer loyalty, which in turn results in better company performance. Smart companies aim to *delight* customers by promising only what they can deliver, then delivering *more* than they promise. Delighted customers not only make repeat purchases, they become "customer evangelists" who tell others about their good experiences with the product (see Marketing at Work 1.1).[13]

For companies interested in delighting customers, exceptional value and service are more than a set of policies or actions—they are a companywide attitude, an important part of the overall company culture. For example, year after year, Lexus ranks at or near the top of the auto industry in terms of customer satisfaction. Its passion for satisfying customers is summed up in The Lexus Covenant, a founding philosophy in which the company pledges that "Lexus will treat each customer as we would a guest in our home." Lexus promises to create "the most satisfying automobile ownership experience" and "to always exceed expectations." Here's an example:[14]

A man bought his first new Lexus—a $45,000 piece of machinery. He could afford a Mercedes, a BMW, or a Cadillac, but he bought the Lexus. He took delivery of his new honey and started to drive it home, luxuriating in the smell of the leather interior and the glorious handling. On a whim, he turned on the radio. His favorite classical music station came on in splendid quadraphonic sound that ricocheted

1.1 MARKETING AT WORK

Bike Friday: Creating Customer Evangelists

Margaret Day loves to talk about her bicycle—almost as much as she loves to ride it. And that's a good thing for custom-cycle maker Bike Friday: Day, a 70-something Australian, has made about 100 customer referrals worth more than $300,000 in sales since she purchased her first bike 10 years ago "I simply cannot stop telling people about the Bike Friday," she says. Her most recent referral, in March, garnered almost $5,000 worth of bicycle sales for the company.

You can't buy that kind of loyalty but you can cultivate it—and that's precisely what Green Gear Cycling (known as Bike Friday after its signature product) has done. Through bike clubs, newsletters, Web forums, and a referral rewards program, it has built a community of delighted customer evangelists whose word-of-mouth testimony has proven more effective for the company than mounting an expensive advertising campaign. "We get key customers who are excited to be involved," says Bike Friday's Lynette Chiang. "They attract others and this creates community."

Chiang is Bike Friday's chief Customer Evangelist, the company's official World Traveler and marketing chief. Her job is to create customer delight and build customer relationships. "The role of the evangelist is to make a connection with a human being. In selling loyalty and a brand, you need to understand that brands need to be built for the long haul." Bike Friday is a small company with an even smaller marketing budget. So its customer evangelism strategy has been crucial to the company's success.

■ Delighting customers: Bike Friday has built a core of delighted "customer evangelists" who can't wait to tell others about their Bike Friday experiences.

It doesn't hurt that the unusual styling of the custom-fit, high-end travel bikes catches plenty of eyes—and prospects. Bike Friday bikes fold in seconds, pack into a standard airline suitcase, and ride like a full-size performance bike. The curiosity factor has proven a powerful way to reach new customers, particularly in the company's early years when marketing money was tight. "The nature of anything custom is you will have or generate an interest group, community group, or cult," says Chiang. "We call it a community." Creating relationships and community makes sense given the nature of the company's target market. "Bike Friday's customers are not fickle teens," says one observer, "but 40-something, well-heeled professionals who travel extensively and cherish personalized service." The Bike Friday Web site, newsletter, and catalog are filled with pictures of happy owners biking all over the world.

Bike Friday has cultivated this community in a number of ways, most notably through its 30 Bike Friday Clubs of America (and Beyond). Chiang describes these groups as self-perpetuating loyalty centers in the field, whose activities provide a social outlet for riders and help to generate referrals. The clubs are free to anyone, regardless of what brand of bike they ride. However, it usually doesn't take long for the Bike Friday enthusiasts in the clubs to convert the nonbelievers.

The "Community" page on the Bike Friday Web site welcomes new owners into the fold: "Come get to know the rest of the community," it suggests. "Buying your Bike Friday travel bike was just the beginning. Now you are automatically a member of a family of Bike Friday enthusiasts crisscrossing the globe on their little wheels." The site also invites the faithful to send photos and share travel stories. "We want to see you using your new bike," it says. To create interaction, Bike Friday also op-

erates Yak!, an e-mail discussion list that lets owners swap tips, tricks, and travel ideas relating to Bike Friday. Besides creating chat, the discussion list provides great feedback. Chiang reads the forum daily, looking for ways to create even more customer delight.

Bike Friday enthusiasts usually can't wait to tell others about their Bike Friday experiences. So the company formalizes the process through a referral awards program. Customers receive a set of 12 prepaid postage cards with their name and that of the Bike Friday expert who sold them their bike. Whenever customers meet someone whose interest is piqued by their bike, they fill out a card and drop it in the mail. Bike Friday then mails information to the contact. It also captures this interaction in its database so that riders who make a referral receive a bonus if their prospect purchases a bike. Customers can choose either a $50 check or $75 credit toward future products. Evangelist Margaret Day accumulated enough referral credits to recently purchase a $2,000 bike.

All of this customer delight has paid off handsomely for Bike Friday, creating what is essentially a voluntary customer sales force. Delighted customers can be far more persuasive than ads and other formal marketing communications. "These people have battle-tested your product or service," says a marketing communications expert. "They're so passionate about it, and they tell things in their own words to others." So far, Bike Friday's referral program has accounted for more than a third of its 10,000 customers. Last year alone, 29 percent of the company's sales came from referrals. "We did a lot more press releases and advertisements early on," explains Hanna Scholz, Bike Friday's marketing manager. "But we realized our customers were our best advertisers—if we made them happy."

Sources: Portions adapted from "The Power of One," *CMO*, October 2005, accessed at www.cmomagazine.com/read/100105/power_one.html. Other quotes and information from Ben McConnell and Jackie Huba, "The Evangelist with the Folding Bicycle," October 2002, accessed at www.creatingcustomerevangelists.com/resources/evangelists/lynette_chiang.asp; www.galfromdownunder.com, accessed March 2007; and www.bikefriday.com, accessed October 2007.

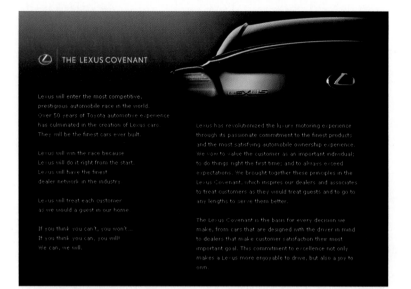

■ Customer satisfaction: Exceptional customer value and service are more than a set of policies or actions—they are an important part of the overall company culture. The Lexus Covenant pledges that "Lexus will treat each customer as we would a guest in our home."

around the interior. He pushed the second button; it was his favorite news station. The third button brought his favorite talk station that kept him awake on long trips. The fourth button was set to his daughter's favorite rock station. In fact, every button was set to his specific tastes. The customer knew the car was smart, but was it psychic? No. The mechanic at Lexus had noted the radio settings on his trade-in and duplicated them on the new Lexus. The customer was delighted. This was his car now—through and through! No one told the mechanic to do it. It's just part of the Lexus philosophy: Delight a customer and continue to delight that customer, and you will have a customer for life. What the mechanic did cost Lexus nothing. Yet it solidified the relationship that could be worth high six figures to Lexus in customer lifetime value. Such relationship-building passions in dealerships around the country have made Lexus the nation's top-selling luxury vehicle.

However, although the customer-centered firm seeks to deliver high customer satisfaction relative to competitors, it does not attempt to *maximize* customer satisfaction. A company can always increase customer satisfaction by lowering its price or increasing its services. But this may result in lower profits. Thus, the purpose of marketing is to generate customer value profitably. This requires a very delicate balance: The marketer must continue to generate more customer value and satisfaction but not "give away the house."

Customer Relationship Levels and Tools Companies can build customer relationships at many levels, depending on the nature of the target market. At one extreme, a company with many low-margin customers may seek to develop *basic relationships* with them. For example, Procter & Gamble does not phone or call on all of its Tide consumers to get to know them personally. Instead, P&G creates relationships through brand-building advertising, sales promotions, and its Tide FabricCare Network Web site (www.Tide.com). At the other extreme, in markets with few customers and high margins, sellers want to create *full partnerships* with key customers. For example, P&G customer teams work closely with Wal-Mart, Safeway, and other large retailers. In between these two extreme situations, other levels of customer relationships are appropriate.

Today, most leading companies are developing customer loyalty and retention programs. Beyond offering consistently high value and satisfaction, marketers can use specific marketing tools to develop stronger bonds with consumers. For example, many companies now offer *frequency marketing programs* that reward customers who buy frequently or in large amounts. Airlines offer frequent-flyer programs, hotels give room upgrades to their frequent guests, and supermarkets give patronage discounts to "very important customers." Some of these programs can be spectacular. To cater to its very best customers, Neiman Marcus created its InCircle Rewards program:

> InCircle members, who must spend at least $5,000 a year using their Neiman Marcus credit cards to be eligible, earn points with each purchase—one point for each dollar charged. They then cash in points for anything from a New York lunch experience for two at one of the "Big Apple's hottest beaneries" (5,000 points) or a Sony home theater system (25,000 points) to a three-day personalized bullfighting course, including travel to a ranch in Northern Baja for some practical training (50,000 points). For 500,000 points, InCircle members can get a six-night Caribbean cruise, and for 1.5 million points, a Yamaha grand piano. Among the top prizes (for 5 million points!) are a J. Mendal custom-made sable coat valued at $200,000 and a private concert in the InCircler's home by jazz instrumentalist Chris Botti.[15]

Other companies sponsor *club marketing programs* that offer members special benefits and create member communities. For example, Harley-Davidson sponsors the Harley Owners Group (H.O.G.), which gives Harley riders "an organized way to share their passion and show their pride." H.O.G membership benefits include two magazines (*Hog Tales* and *Enthusiast*), a *H.O.G. Touring Handbook,* a roadside assistance program, a specially designed insurance program, theft reward service, a travel center, and a "Fly & Ride" program enabling members to rent Harleys while on vacation. The worldwide club now numbers more than 1,500 local chapters and over 1 million members.[16]

To build customer relationships, companies can add structural ties as well as financial and social benefits. A business marketer might supply customers with special equipment or online linkages that help them manage their orders, payroll, or inventory. For example, McKesson Corporation, a leading pharmaceutical wholesaler, has set up a Supply Management Online system that helps retail pharmacy customers manage their inventories, order entry, and shelf space. The system also helps McKesson's medical-surgical supply and equipment customers optimize their supply purchasing and materials management operations.

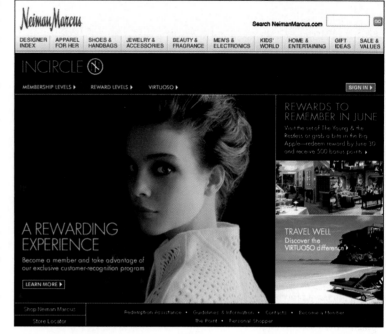

■ Relationship building tools: Neiman Marcus created its InCircle Rewards program to cater to its very best customers.

The Changing Nature of Customer Relationships

Significant changes are occurring in the ways in which companies are relating to their customers. Yesterday's big companies focused on mass marketing to all customers at arm's length. Today's companies are building deeper, more direct, and more lasting relationships with more carefully selected customers. Here are some important trends in the way companies and customers are relating to one another.

Relating with More Carefully Selected Customers Few firms today still practice true mass marketing—selling in a standardized way to any customer who comes along. Today, most marketers realize that they don't want relationships with every customer. Instead, they now are targeting fewer, more profitable customers. Called *selective relationship management,* many companies now use customer profitability analysis to weed out losing customers and to target winning ones for pampering. Once they identify profitable customers, firms can create attractive offers and special handling to capture these customers and earn their loyalty.

But what should the company do with unprofitable customers? If it can't turn them into profitable ones, it may even want to "fire" customers that are too unreasonable or that cost more to serve than they are worth. For example, consumer electronics retailer Best Buy recently rolled out a new "Customer-Centricity" strategy that distinguishes between its best customers (called *angels*) and less profitable ones (called *demons*). The aim is to embrace the angels while ditching the demons.[17]

The *angels* include the 20 percent of Best Buy customers who produce the bulk of its profits. They snap up high-definition televisions, portable electronics, and newly released DVDs without waiting for markdowns or rebates. In contrast, the *demons* form an "underground of bargain-hungry shoppers intent on wringing every nickel of savings out of the big retailer. They load up on loss leaders . . . then flip the goods at a profit on eBay. They slap down rock-bottom price quotes from Web sites and demand that Best Buy make good on its lowest-price pledge."

To attract the angels, Best Buy's Customer-Centricity stores now stock more merchandise and offer better service to these good customers. For example, the stores set up digital photo centers and a "Geek Squad," which offers one-on-one

■ Best Buy's "Customer-Centricity" strategy serves its best customers (angels) and exorcizes less profitable ones (demons). Clerks steer high-income "Barrys" into the store's Magnolia Home Theater Center, a comfy store within a store that mimics the media rooms popular with home-theater fans.

in-store or at-home computer assistance to high-value buyers. Best Buy also set up a Reward Zone loyalty program, in which regular customers can earn points toward discounts on future purchases. To discourage the demons, Best Buy removed them from its marketing lists, reduced the promotions and other sales tactics that tended to attract them, and installed a 15 percent restocking fee.

However, Best Buy didn't stop there. Customer analysis revealed that its best customers fell into five groups: "Barrys," high-income men; "Jills," suburban moms; "Buzzes," male technology enthusiasts; "Rays," young family men on a budget; and small business owners. Each Customer-Centricity store now aligns its product and service mix to reflect the make-up of these customers in its market area. Best Buy then trains store clerks in the art of serving the angels and exorcising the demons. At stores targeting Barrys, for example, blue-shirted sales clerks steer promising candidates to the store's Magnolia Home Theater Center, a comfy store within a store that mimics the media rooms popular with home-theater fans. The centers feature premium home-theater systems and knowledgeable, no-pressure home-theater consultants. So far, Customer Centricity stores have "clobbered" the traditional Best Buy stores, with many posting sales gains more than triple those of stores with conventional formats. As one store manager puts it: "The biggest thing now is to build better relationships with [our best] customers."

Relating More Deeply and Interactively Beyond choosing customers more selectively, companies are now relating with chosen customers in deeper, more meaningful ways. Rather than relying only on one-way, mass-media messages, today's marketers are incorporating new, more interactive approaches that help build targeted, two-way customer relationships.

The deeper nature of today's customer relationships results in part from the rapidly changing communications environment. New technologies have profoundly changed the ways in which people relate to one another. For example, thanks to explosive advances in Internet and computer technology, people can now interact in direct and surprisingly personal ways with large groups of others, whether nearby or scattered around the world. New tools for relating include everything from e-mail, blogs, Web sites, and video sharing to online communities and social networks such as MySpace, Facebook, YouTube, and Second Life.

This changing communications environment also affects how consumers relate to companies and products. Increasingly, marketers are using the new communications approaches in building closer customer relationships. The aim is to create deeper consumer involvement and a sense of community surrounding a brand—to make the brand a meaningful part of consumers' conversations and lives. "Becoming part of the conversation between consumers is infinitely more powerful than handing down information via traditional advertising," says one marketing expert. "It [makes] consumers . . . a part of the process, rather than being dumb recipients of the message from on high—and that is of huge potential value to brands."[18]

However, at the same time that the new communications tools create relationship-building opportunities for marketers, they also create challenges. They give consumers greater power and control. Today's consumers have more information about brands than ever before, and they have a wealth of platforms for airing and sharing their brand views with other consumers. And more than ever before, consumers can choose the brand conversations and exchanges in which they will participate. According to Mark Parker, chief executive of Nike, the new power of the consumer is "the most compelling change we've seen over the past four or five years. They are dictating what the dialogue is, how we're conducting it, and it's definitely a two-way conversation."[19]

Chapter 1   Marketing: Creating and Capturing Customer Value   **19**

Greater consumer control means that, in building customer relationships, companies can no longer rely on marketing by *intrusion*. They must practice marketing by *attraction*—creating market offerings and messages that involve consumers rather than interrupt them. Hence, most marketers now augment their mass-media marketing efforts with a rich mix of direct marketing approaches that promote brand-consumer interaction. For example, many are participating in the exploding world of *online social networks* or creating online communities of their own. Toyota, the world's fourth-largest advertiser, spends $2.8 billion a year on media advertising. But it also sells Scions at Second Life and maintains a Scion presence in MySpace, Gaia Online, and other cyber hangouts. And the company's Toyota.com/hybrids site creates a community in which more than 15,500 Prius, Camry, and Highlander hybrid "believers" meet to share videos and messages on their experiences with and reasons for buying hybrid vehicles.

Similarly, Nike spends close to $300 million a year on media advertising. But it also employs a host of other marketing activities designed to build brand community and deeper customer relationships.[20]

■ Creating community with consumers: Toyota's Scion maintains a presence on MySpace, where it has more than 12,000 friends.

Twice a week, 30 or more people gather at the Nike store in Portland, Oregon, and go for an evening run. Afterward the members of the Niketown running club chat in the store over refreshments. Nike's staff keeps track of their performances and hails members who have logged more than 100 miles. The event is a classic example of up-close-and-personal relationship building with core customers. Nike augments such events with an online social network aimed at striking up meaningful long-term interactions with even more runners. Its Nike Plus running Web site lets customers with iPod-linked Nike shoes upload, track, and compare their performances. More than 200,000 runners are now using the Nike Plus site and more than half visit the site at least four times a week. The goal is to have 15 percent of the world's 100 million runners using the system.

Another Nike social networking site—joga.com—targets the world's soccer fans. During the eight weeks surrounding the 2006 World Cup, the joga.com site was used by more than 1 million people to establish personalized World Cup pages. A related video of Ronaldinho, the Brazilian star, was downloaded 32 million times. According to Charlie Denson, president of the Nike brand, the huge success of such sites has persuaded the company to divide its Nike brand operations into six categories—running, basketball, soccer, men's fitness, women's fitness, and sports culture—with brand teams that will develop closer relationships with each specific consumer community.

As a part of the new customer control and dialog, consumers themselves are now creating brand conversations and messages on their own. And increasingly, companies are even *inviting* consumers to play a more active role in shaping brand messages and ads. For example, Doritos and the NFL ran consumer-developed ads on last year's Super Bowl. Other companies, including marketing heavyweights such as Coca-Cola, McDonald's, and BMW, have snagged brand-related consumer videos from YouTube and other popular video-sharing sites and turned them into commercial messages. **Consumer-generated marketing**, whether invited by marketers or uninvited, has become a significant marketing force. In fact, last

Consumer-generated marketing
Marketing messages, ads, and other brand exchanges created by consumers themselves—both invited and uninvited.

1.2 MARKETING AT WORK

Consumer-Generated Marketing: Ad Agency of the Year? YOU!

Advertising Age, a must-read magazine for advertising professionals, recently awarded its prestigious Ad Agency of the Year award not to the usual big Madison Avenue agency, but to you, the consumer. Here's its explanation of why it picked consumer-generated advertising content over that prepared by seasoned advertising professionals.

Stop me if you've heard this one before. A pair of Maine theater geeks decide to film an experiment in which a certain mint is dropped into a bottle of a certain no-calorie soft drink, unleashing a foamy geyser. Flavoring this bit of schoolyard-chemistry lore with Vegas showmanship, they produce a cola version of the Bellagio fountain and put the clip on the Web, where it goes viral. Really viral. So viral, in fact, that millions watch it, hundreds of media outlets cover it, and the mint in question enjoys a 15 percent spike in sales. The corporate giant behind the soda, likely against every fiber in its brand-controlling being, is forced to react to it.

It's a sign of our times: The most important piece of commercial content last year was created by a juggler named Fritz Grobe and lawyer Stephen Voltz. "The Diet Coke & Mentos Experiment" sensation raises a key question that gnaws at just about every company that wants to sell a product to consumers in the 21st century: Should I try to get my consumers to do something like this? Even if they haven't worked out exactly how to make that happen, many leading marketers have already answered with a resounding yes. At last year's Association of National Advertisers meeting, speaker after speaker declared that it's time to give up control and accept that consumers now control their brands.

Of course, in some ways, they always have. A brand has only ever been as good as consumers' experiences with it. The difference today is that consumers have lots of ways of communicating those experiences, and they trust each other's views above marketers' overt sales pitches. Consequently, consumers are influencing marketing strategy as never before. And that's why this year's *Advertising Age* Ad Agency of the Year is (drum roll, please) … the consumer. Okay, so the consumer doesn't have a profit-and-loss account or an office, which have always previously been deemed prerequisites for an Agency of the Year. But a portfolio of consumer-generated commercial content from last year would easily beat out any single agency's offering.

Today, as in our cola fountain story, not only do everyday people make the videos that earn that oh-so-coveted water-cooler buzz, they also reign supreme as distributors of content of all kinds. YouTube's ex-

■ Consumer-generated marketing: "The Diet Coke & Mentos Experiment" sensation and other consumer-generated commercial content inspired ad industry magazine *Advertising Age* to give you, the consumer, its Ad Agency of the Year Award.

year, *Advertising Age* magazine awarded its coveted Ad Agency of the Year designation to—you guessed it—the consumer. "The explosion of video, blogs, Web sites, [and consumer-generated ads] confirmed what we knew all along," says the magazine. When it comes to creative messages, "the consumer is king."[21] (See Marketing at Work 1.2.)

Partner Relationship Management

Partner relationship management
Working closely with partners in other company departments and outside the company to jointly bring greater value to customers.

When it comes to creating customer value and building strong customer relationships, today's marketers know that they can't go it alone. They must work closely with a variety of marketing partners. In addition to being good at *customer relationship management*, marketers must also be good at **partner relationship management**. Major changes are occur-

plosion glopped a big new pile of distractions into an already cluttered communications world, which means that if you want anybody to see your ad, you'd better hope people are frenetically e-mailing links to it.

Here are just a few examples of last year's consumer-generated marketing content. Two moonlighting comedians threw together video of themselves amateurishly rapping about Chicken McNuggets and slapped it on the Internet—McDonald's used the video in a popular New York-area commercial. BMW found a 1998 video of a pair of exultant children unwrapping a Nintendo on Christmas morning and then paid to use it in a new spot. MasterCard invited customers to help create a new "Priceless" commercial, received 100,000 submissions, and showed the winning ad on regular TV. The credit card giant's priceless.com site is now loaded with good consumer video.

And then there's the Super Bowl. Long a showcase for ad agencies' finest productions, last year's ad spectacular was invaded by the unwashed masses. Frito-Lay's Doritos solicited 30-second ads from consumers and ran the best two during the game. One of the ads, which showed a supermarket checkout girl getting frisky with a shopper, was judged in one poll as 67 percent more effective than the average Super Bowl ad in improving viewer opinion of the advertised product. The other Doritos ad, showing a young driver flirting with a pretty girl, cost only $12.79 to produce (the cost of four bags of chips) but was judged 45 percent more effective. The ads were extremely popular with viewers, both during and after the big game. The checkout girl ad received 850,000 views on YouTube the next day alone. "What this means is: You've got some kid with a video camera and he's playing on the same field as everyone else," says one ad agency veteran.

For years, countless big marketing thinkers have repeatedly made the case that the consumer is in control. A more interactive media environment gives consumers the tools to be better informed and less susceptible to the one-way communication model favored by most large ad agencies. When asked about this changing environment, your average big-shot agency talks about making "compelling content," the kind of stuff that people actively seek out in contrast to the spots hurled at them during breaks on *CSI: Miami*.

That phrase "compelling content" represents a lot of things, including sticky Web sites that are fun to tool around on; informative, no-BS blogs that inform consumers rather than snow them; and plain old funny or moving video snippets that people are eager to pass on to their friends. The problem is that last year the most compelling content wasn't made by highly paid ad-agency teams and aired on TV. Nobody

did it better than amateurs working with digital video cameras and Macs, and uploading onto YouTube—proving that you don't need a big medium or production budget to create catchy work.

Does the new wave of consumer-generated marketing mean the end of the big ad agency as we know it? Not likely. But the fact that an amateur could turn out a winning Doritos ad for $12.79, versus the $1 million or more that many large agencies spent crafting more spectacular but less effective ads, suggests that there are some lessons to be learned. As one ad agency creative executive suggests, "It's gonna keep professional idea makers on their toes." Marketers now "perk up when you talk about this stuff," he says.

The next big question will be whether marketers and agencies can find ways to effectively harness consumer-generated creativity—so unpolished and unaccountable—and deploy it in the service of their brands. That's still a pretty open-ended question, given how short some early attempts have fallen. For every Diet Coke & Mentos clip that's grown into a viral craze, there are several marketer-led disasters. For example, General Motors' Chevy Tahoe off-roaded into the consumer-content arena and, to its shock, found that some people aren't so crazy about the gas-guzzling SUV. At Chevy's invitation, consumers create some very creative ads, but many of the ads centered on the big vehicle's poor gas mileage and negative environmental impact. You can be sure there will be more gimmicky, awkward attempts to cash in on consumer-generated content.

Still, big marketers are starting to think in the right direction. Even Coca-Cola, after it initially sulked about the Diet Coke & Mentos experiment, decided to incorporate the videos and other user-generated footage into its Web site. And then there's Procter & Gamble. At the Association of National Advertisers meeting, P&G's CEO, A. G. Lafley, urged companies to invite more customer interaction and to "let go" of their brands. Coming from the normally tightly controlling P&G, such a provocative statement deeply impacted the advertiser audience.

The same could be said of Lafley showing an animated Pringles commercial made by a U.K. teen to the audience full of advertisers. And you know what? The clip was pretty good.

Sources: Adapted from Matthew Creamer, "John Doe Edges Out Jeff Goodby," *Advertising Age*, January 8, 2007, pp. S4–S5; with information from Frank Ahrens, "$2 Million Airtime, $13 Ad: In the YouTube Era, Even Super Bowl Advertisers Are Turning to Amateurs," *Washington Post*, January 31, 2007, accessed at www.washingtonpost.com; Elinor Mills, "Frito-Lay Turns to Netizens for Ad Creation," *CNET News*, March 21, 2007, accessed at www.cnetnews.com; Laura Petrecca, "Amateurs' Ad Ideas Come Up with Winners," *USA Today*, February 13, 2007.

ring in how marketers partner with others inside and outside the company to jointly bring more value to customers.

Partners Inside the Company   Traditionally, marketers have been charged with understanding customers and representing customer needs to different company departments. The old thinking was that marketing is done only by marketing, sales, and customer-support people. However, in today's more connected world, marketing no longer has sole ownership of customer interactions. Every functional area can interact with customers, especially electronically. The new thinking is that every employee must be customer focused. David Packard, late cofounder of Hewlett-Packard, wisely said, "Marketing is far too important to be left only to the marketing department."[22]

Today, rather than letting each department go its own way, firms are linking all departments in the cause of creating customer value. Rather than assigning only sales and marketing people to customers, they are forming cross-functional customer teams. For example, Procter & Gamble assigns "customer development teams" to each of its major retailer accounts. These teams—consisting of sales and marketing people, operations specialists, market and financial analysts, and others—coordinate the efforts of many P&G departments toward helping the retailer be more successful.

Marketing Partners Outside the Firm Changes are also occurring in how marketers connect with their suppliers, channel partners, and even competitors. Most companies today are networked companies, relying heavily on partnerships with other firms.

Marketing channels consist of distributors, retailers, and others who connect the company to its buyers. The *supply chain* describes a longer channel, stretching from raw materials to components to final products that are carried to final buyers. For example, the supply chain for personal computers consists of suppliers of computer chips and other components, the computer manufacturer, and the distributors, retailers, and others who sell the computers.

Through *supply chain management,* many companies today are strengthening their connections with partners all along the supply chain. They know that their fortunes rest not just on how well they perform. Success at building customer relationships also rests on how well their entire supply chain performs against competitors' supply chains. These companies don't just treat suppliers as vendors and distributors as customers. They treat both as partners in delivering customer value. On the one hand, for example, Lexus works closely with carefully selected suppliers to improve quality and operations efficiency. On the other hand, it works with its franchise dealers to provide top-grade sales and service support that will bring customers in the door and keep them coming back.

Capturing Value from Customers

The first four steps in the marketing process outlined in Figure 1.1 involve building customer relationships by creating and delivering superior customer value. The final step involves capturing value in return, in the form of current and future sales, market share, and profits. By creating superior customer value, the firm creates highly satisfied customers who stay loyal and buy more. This, in turn, means greater long-run returns for the firm. Here, we discuss the outcomes of creating customer value: customer loyalty and retention, share of market and share of customer, and customer equity.

Creating Customer Loyalty and Retention

Good customer relationship management creates customer delight. In turn, delighted customers remain loyal and talk favorably to others about the company and its products. Studies show big differences in the loyalty of customers who are less satisfied, somewhat satisfied, and completely satisfied. Even a slight drop from complete satisfaction can create an enormous drop in loyalty. Thus, the aim of customer relationship management is to create not just customer satisfaction, but customer delight.[23]

Companies are realizing that losing a customer means losing more than a single sale. It means losing the entire stream of purchases that the customer would make over a lifetime of patronage. For example, here is a dramatic illustration of **customer lifetime value**:

Customer lifetime value
The value of the entire stream of purchases that the customer would make over a lifetime of patronage.

> Stew Leonard, who operates a highly profitable four-store supermarket in Connecticut and New York, says that he sees $50,000 flying out of his store every time he sees a sulking customer. Why? Because his average customer spends about $100 a week, shops 50 weeks a year, and remains in the area for about 10 years. If this customer has an unhappy experience and switches to another supermarket, Stew Leonard's has lost $50,000 in revenue. The loss can be much greater if the disappointed customer shares the bad experience with other customers and causes them to defect. To keep customers coming back, Stew Leonard's has created what the

New York Times has dubbed the "Disneyland of Dairy Stores," complete with costumed characters, scheduled entertainment, a petting zoo, and animatronics throughout the store. From its humble beginnings as a small dairy store in 1969, Stew Leonard's has grown at an amazing pace. It's built 29 additions onto the original store, which now serves more than 300,000 customers each week. This legion of loyal shoppers is largely a result of the store's passionate approach to customer service. Rule #1 at Stew Leonard's—The customer is always right. Rule #2—If the customer is ever wrong, reread rule #1![24]

■ Customer lifetime value: To keep customers coming back, Stew Leonard's has created the "Disneyland of dairy stores." Rule #1—The customer is always right. Rule #2—If the customer is ever wrong, reread rule #1!

Stew Leonard is not alone in assessing customer lifetime value. Lexus estimates that a single satisfied and loyal customer is worth more than $600,000 in lifetime sales. The customer lifetime value of a Taco Bell customer exceeds $12,000.[25] Thus, working to retain and grow customers makes good economic sense. In fact, a company can lose money on a specific transaction but still benefit greatly from a long-term relationship.

This means that companies must aim high in building customer relationships. Customer delight creates an emotional relationship with a product or service, not just a rational preference. L.L.Bean, long known for its outstanding customer service and high customer loyalty, preaches the following "golden rule": Sell good merchandise, treat your customers like human beings, and they'll always come back for more." A customer relationships expert agrees: "If you want your customers to be more loyal, you must prove that you have their best interests at heart. Your concern for the customer's welfare must be so strong that it even occasionally trumps (gasp!) your own concern for immediate profits."[26]

Growing Share of Customer

Beyond simply retaining good customers to capture customer lifetime value, good customer relationship management can help marketers to increase their **share of customer**—the share they get of the customer's purchasing in their product categories. Thus, banks want to increase "share of wallet." Supermarkets and restaurants want to get more "share of stomach." Car companies want to increase "share of garage" and airlines want greater "share of travel."

Share of customer
The portion of the customer's purchasing that a company gets in its product categories.

To increase share of customer, firms can offer greater variety to current customers. Or they can train employees to cross-sell and up-sell in order to market more products and services to existing customers. For example, Amazon.com is highly skilled at leveraging relationships with its 50 million customers to increase its share of each customer's purchases. Originally an online bookseller, Amazon.com now offers customers music, videos, gifts, toys, consumer electronics, office products, home improvement items, lawn and garden products, apparel and accessories, jewelry, and an online auction. In addition, based on each customer's purchase history, the company recommends related products that might be of interest. In this way, Amazon.com captures a greater share of each customer's spending budget.

Building Customer Equity

We can now see the importance of not just acquiring customers, but of keeping and growing them as well. One marketing consultant puts it this way: "The only value your company will ever create is the value that comes from customers—the ones you have now and the ones you will have in the future. Without customers, you don't have a business."[27] Customer relationship management takes a long-term view. Companies want not only to create profitable customers, but to "own" them for life, capture their customer lifetime value, and earn a greater share of their purchases.

Customer equity

The total combined customer lifetime values of all of the company's customers.

What Is Customer Equity? The ultimate aim of customer relationship management is to produce high *customer equity*.[28] **Customer equity** is the total combined customer lifetime values of all of the company's current and potential customers. Clearly, the more loyal the firm's profitable customers, the higher the firm's customer equity. Customer equity may be a better measure of a firm's performance than current sales or market share. Whereas sales and market share reflect the past, customer equity suggests the future. Consider Cadillac:

In the 1970s and 1980s, Cadillac had some of the most loyal customers in the industry. To an entire generation of car buyers, the name "Cadillac" defined American luxury. Cadillac's share of the luxury car market reached a whopping 51 percent in 1976. Based on market share and sales, the brand's future looked rosy. However, measures of customer equity would have painted a bleaker picture. Cadillac customers were getting older (average age 60) and average customer lifetime value was falling. Many Cadillac buyers were on their last car. Thus, although Cadillac's market share was good, its customer equity was not. Compare this with BMW. Its more youthful and vigorous image didn't win BMW the early market share war. However, it did win BMW younger customers with higher customer lifetime values. The result: In the years that followed, BMW's market share and profits soared while Cadillac's fortunes eroded badly. Thus, market share is not the answer. We should care not just about current sales but also about future sales. Customer lifetime value and customer equity are the name of the game. Recognizing this, Cadillac is now making the Caddy cool again by targeting a younger generation of consumers with new high-performance models and its highly successful Break Through advertising campaign. Sales are up 35 percent over the past five years. More important, the future looks promising.[29]

■ To increase customer lifetime value and customer equity, Cadillac is cool again. It's highly successful Break Through ad campaign targets a younger generation of consumer.

Building the Right Relationships with the Right Customers Companies should manage customer equity carefully. They should view customers as assets that need to be managed and maximized. But not all customers, not even all loyal customers, are good investments. Surprisingly, some loyal customers can be unprofitable, and some disloyal customers can be profitable. Which customers should the company acquire and retain? "Up to a point, the choice is obvious: Keep the consistent big spenders and lose the erratic small spenders," says one expert. "But what about the erratic big spenders and the consistent small spenders? It's often unclear whether they should be acquired or retained, and at what cost."[30]

The company can classify customers according to their potential profitability and manage its relationships with them accordingly. Figure 1.5 classifies customers into one of four relationship groups, according to their profitability and projected loyalty.[31] Each group requires a different relationship management strategy. "Strangers" show low potential profitability and little projected loyalty. There is little fit between the company's offerings and their needs. The relationship management strategy for these customers is simple: Don't invest anything in them.

"Butterflies" are potentially profitable but not loyal. There is a good fit between the company's offerings and their needs. However, like real butterflies, we can enjoy them for only a short while and then they're gone. An example is stock market investors who trade shares often and in large amounts, but who enjoy hunting out the best deals without build-

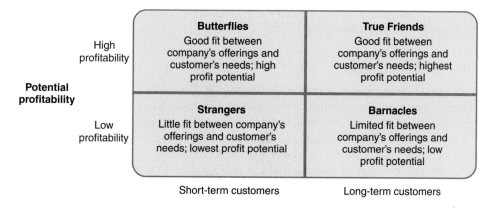

FIGURE 1.5

Customer Relationship Groups

Source: Reprinted by permission of *Harvard Business Review.* Adapted from "Mismanagement of Customer Loyalty" by Werner Renartz and V. Kumar, July 2002, p. 93. Copyright © by the president and fellows of Harvard College; all rights reserved.

ing a regular relationship with any single brokerage company. Efforts to convert butterflies into loyal customers are rarely successful. Instead, the company should enjoy the butterflies for the moment. It should use promotional blitzes to attract them, create satisfying and profitable transactions with them, and then cease investing in them until the next time around.

"True friends" are both profitable and loyal. There is a strong fit between their needs and the company's offerings. The firm wants to make continuous relationship investments to delight these customers and nurture, retain, and grow them. It wants to turn true friends into "true believers," who come back regularly and tell others about their good experiences with the company.

"Barnacles" are highly loyal but not very profitable. There is a limited fit between their needs and the company's offerings. An example is smaller bank customers who bank regularly but do not generate enough returns to cover the costs of maintaining their accounts. Like barnacles on the hull of a ship, they create drag. Barnacles are perhaps the most problematic customers. The company might be able to improve their profitability by selling them more, raising their fees, or reducing service to them. However, if they cannot be made profitable, they should be "fired."

The point here is an important one: Different types of customers require different relationship management strategies. The goal is to build the *right relationships* with the *right customers.*

Linking the Concepts

We've covered a lot of territory. Again, slow down for a moment and develop *your own* thoughts about marketing.

- In *your own words*, what *is* marketing and what does it seek to accomplish?
- How well does Lexus manage its relationships with customers? What customer relationship management strategy does it use? What relationship management strategy does Wal-Mart use?
- Think of a company for which you are a "true friend." What strategy does this company use to manage its relationship with you?

The Changing Marketing Landscape

Every day, dramatic changes are occurring in the marketplace. Richard Love of Hewlett-Packard observes, "The pace of change is so rapid that the ability to change has now become a competitive advantage." Yogi Berra, the legendary New York Yankees catcher and manager, summed it up more simply when he said, "The future ain't what it used to be." As the marketplace changes, so must those who serve it.

In this section, we examine the major trends and forces that are changing the marketing landscape and challenging marketing strategy. We look at four major developments: the digital age, rapid globalization, the call for more ethics and social responsibility, and the growth of not-for-profit marketing.

The Digital Age

The recent technology boom has created a digital age. The explosive growth in computer, telecommunications, information, transportation, and other technologies has had a major impact on the ways companies bring value to their customers.

Now, more than ever before, we are all connected to each other and to things near and far in the world around us. Where it once took weeks or months to travel across the United States, we can now travel around the globe in only hours or days. Where it once took days or weeks to receive news about important world events, we now see them as they are occurring through live satellite broadcasts. Where it once took weeks to correspond with others in distant places, they are now only moments away by phone or the Internet.

The technology boom has provided exciting new ways to learn about and track customers, and to create products and services tailored to individual customer needs. Technology is also helping companies to distribute products more efficiently and effectively. And it's helping them to communicate with customers in large groups or one-to-one.

Through videoconferencing, marketing researchers at a company's headquarters in New York can look in on focus groups in Chicago or Paris without ever stepping onto a plane. With only a few clicks of a mouse button, a direct marketer can tap into online data services to learn anything from what car you drive to what you read to what flavor of ice cream you prefer. Or, using today's powerful computers, marketers can create their own detailed customer databases and use them to target individual customers with offers designed to meet their specific needs.

Technology has also brought a new wave of communication and advertising tools—ranging from cell phones, iPods, DVRs, Web sites, and interactive TV to video kiosks at airports and shopping malls. Marketers can use these tools to zero in on selected customers with carefully targeted messages. Through the Internet, customers can learn about, design, order, and pay for products and services, without ever leaving home. Then, through the marvels of express delivery, they can receive their purchases in less than 24 hours. From virtual reality displays that test new products to online virtual stores that sell them, the technology boom is affecting every aspect of marketing.

Internet

A vast public web of computer networks, which connects users of all types all around the world to each other and to an amazingly large information repository.

Perhaps the most dramatic new technology is the **Internet**. Today, the Internet links individuals and businesses of all types to each other and to information all around the world. It allows anytime, anywhere connections to information, entertainment, and communication. Companies are using the Internet to build closer relationships with customers and marketing partners. Beyond competing in traditional market*places,* they now have access to exciting new market*spaces.*

The Internet has now become a truly a global phenomenon. The number of Internet users worldwide now stands at almost 1.2 billion and will reach an estimated 1.8 billion by 2010.[32] This growing and diverse Internet population means that all kinds of people are now going to the Web for information and to buy products and services.

Internet usage surged in the 1990s with the development of the user-friendly World Wide Web. During the overheated Web frenzy of the late 1990s, dot-coms popped up everywhere, selling everything from books, toys, and CDs to furniture, home mortgages, and 100-pound bags of dog food via the Internet. The frenzy cooled during the "dot-com meltdown" of 2000, when many poorly conceived e-tailers and other Web start-ups went out of business. Today, a new version of the Internet has emerged—a

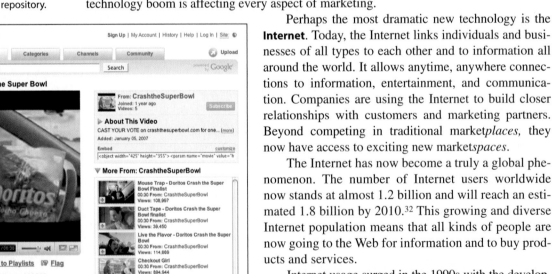

■ Web 2.0—a "second coming" of the Internet—offers a fast-growing set of new Web technologies for connecting with customers. Here, Doritos posts its Crash the Super Bowl finalists on YouTube.

"second coming" of the Web often referred to as *Web 2.0*. Web 2.0 involves a more reasoned and balanced approach to marketing online. It also offers a fast-growing set of new Web technologies for connecting with customers, such as Weblogs (blogs) and vlogs (video-based blogs), social networking sites, and video-sharing sites. The interactive, community-building nature of these new technologies makes them ideal for relating with consumers.[33]

Online marketing is now the fastest-growing form of marketing. These days, it's hard to find a company that doesn't use the Web in a significant way. In addition to the "click-only" dot-coms, most traditional "brick-and-mortar" companies have now become "click-and-mortar" companies. They have ventured online to attract new customers and build stronger relationships with existing ones. Today, some 65 percent of American online users now use the Internet to shop.[34] Business-to-business e-commerce is also booming. It seems that almost every business has set up shop on the Web.

Thus, the technology boom is providing exciting new opportunities for marketers. We will explore the impact of the new marketing technologies in future chapters, especially Chapter 14.

Rapid Globalization

As they are redefining their relationships with customers and partners, marketers are also taking a fresh look at the ways in which they relate with the broader world around them. In an increasingly smaller world, many marketers are now connected *globally* with their customers and marketing partners.

Today, almost every company, large or small, is touched in some way by global competition. A neighborhood florist buys its flowers from Mexican nurseries, and a large U.S. electronics manufacturer competes in its home markets with giant Korean rivals. A fledgling Internet retailer finds itself receiving orders from all over the world at the same time that an American consumer-goods producer introduces new products into emerging markets abroad.

American firms have been challenged at home by the skillful marketing of European and Asian multinationals. Companies such as Toyota, Nokia, Nestlé, Sony, and Samsung have often outperformed their U.S. competitors in American markets. Similarly, U.S. companies in a wide range of industries have developed truly global operations, making and selling their products worldwide. Quintessentially American McDonald's now serves 52 million customers daily in 31,600 restaurants worldwide—some 65 percent of its revenues come from outside the United States. Similarly, Nike markets in more than 160 countries, with non-U.S. sales accounting for 53 percent of its worldwide sales. Even MTV Networks has joined the elite of global brands—its 137 channels worldwide deliver localized versions of its pulse-thumping fare to teens in 419 million homes in 164 countries around the globe.[35]

Today, companies are not only trying to sell more of their locally produced goods in international markets, they also are buying more supplies and components abroad. For example, Isaac Mizrahi, one of America's top fashion designers, may choose cloth woven from Australian wool with designs printed in Italy. He will design a dress and e-mail the drawing to a Hong Kong agent, who will place the order with a Chinese factory. Finished dresses will be air-freighted to New York, where they will be redistributed to department and specialty stores around the country.

Thus, managers in countries around the world are increasingly taking a global, not just local, view of the company's industry, competitors, and opportunities. They are asking: What is global marketing? How does it differ from domestic marketing? How do global competitors and forces affect our business? To what extent should we "go global"? We will discuss the global marketplace in more detail in Chapter 15.

■ U.S. companies in a wide range of industries have developed truly global operations. Quintessentially American McDonald's captures 65 percent of its revenues from outside of the United States.

The Call for More Ethics and Social Responsibility

Marketers are reexamining their relationships with social values and responsibilities and with the very Earth that sustains us. As the worldwide consumerism and environmentalism movements mature, today's marketers are being called upon to take greater responsibility for the social and environmental impact of their actions. Corporate ethics and social responsibility have become hot topics for almost every business. And few companies can ignore the renewed and very demanding environmental movement.

The social-responsibility and environmental movements will place even stricter demands on companies in the future. Some companies resist these movements, budging only when forced by legislation or organized consumer outcries. More forward-looking companies, however, readily accept their responsibilities to the world around them. They view socially responsible actions as an opportunity to do well by doing good. They seek ways to profit by serving the best long-run interests of their customers and communities.

Some companies—such as Patagonia, Ben & Jerry's, Honest Tea, and others—are practicing "caring capitalism," setting themselves apart by being civic-minded and responsible. They are building social responsibility and action into their company value and mission statements. For example, when it comes to environmental responsibility, outdoor gear marketer Patagonia is "committed to the core." "Those of us who work here share a strong commitment to protecting undomesticated lands and waters," says the company's Web site. "We believe in using business to inspire solutions to the environmental crisis." Patagonia backs these words with actions. Each year it pledges at least 1 percent of its sales or 10 percent of its profits, whichever is greater, to the protection of the natural environment.[36] We will revisit the topic of marketing and social responsibility in greater detail in Chapter 16.

The Growth of Not-for-Profit Marketing

In the past, marketing has been most widely applied in the for-profit business sector. In recent years, however, marketing also has become a major part of the strategies of many not-for-profit organizations, such as colleges, hospitals, museums, zoos, symphony orchestras, and even churches. The nation's nonprofits face stiff competition for support and membership. Sound marketing can help them to attract membership and support. Consider the marketing efforts of the San Francisco Zoo:

The San Francisco Zoological Society aggressively markets the zoo's attractions to what might be its most important customer segment—children of all ages. It starts with a well-designed "product." The expanded Children's Zoo is specially designed to encourage parent-child interaction and discussions about living together with animals. The zoo provides close-up encounters with critters ranging from companion animals and livestock to the wildlife in our backyards and beyond. Children can groom livestock or collect eggs at the Family Farm, peer through microscopes in the Insect Zoo, crawl through a child-sized burrow at the Meerkats and Prairie Dogs exhibit, and lots more. To get the story out, attract visitors, and raise funds, the zoo sponsors innovative advertising, an informative Web site, and exciting family events. The most popular event is the annual ZooFest for Kids. "Bring your children, parents, grandparents, and friends to participate in the San Francisco Zoo's most popular annual family fundraiser—ZooFest for Kids!" the zoo in-

■ Not-for-profit marketing: The San Francisco Zoological Society aggressively markets the zoo's attractions to what might be its most important customer segment—children of all ages.

vites. "Get your face painted, enjoy up-close encounters with animals, eat yummy treats, and much, much more." ZooFest planners market the event to local businesses, which supply food and entertainment. The event usually nets about $50,000, money that goes to support the Zoo's conservation and education programs. "With music in the air and tables heaped high with food," notes one observer, "ZooFest for Kids [has] a magic about it befitting the beginning of summer"—magic created by good marketing.[37]

Similarly, private colleges, facing declining enrollments and rising costs, are using marketing to compete for students and funds. Many performing arts groups—even those with seasonal sellouts—face huge operating deficits that they must cover by more aggressive donor marketing. Finally, many long-standing not-for-profit organizations—the YMCA, the Salvation Army, the Girl Scouts—have lost members and are now modernizing their missions and "products" to attract more members and donors.[38]

Government agencies have also shown an increased interest in marketing. For example, the U.S. military has a marketing plan to attract recruits to its different services, and various government agencies are now designing *social marketing campaigns* to encourage energy conservation and concern for the environment or to discourage smoking, excessive drinking, and drug use. Even the once-stodgy U.S. Postal Service has developed innovative marketing to sell commemorative stamps, promote its priority mail services against those of its competitors, and lift its image. In all, the U.S. government is the nation's 29th-largest advertiser, with an annual advertising budget of more than $1.2 billion.[39]

So, What Is Marketing? Pulling It All Together

At the start of this chapter, Figure 1.1 presented a simple model of the marketing process. Now that we've discussed all of the steps in the process, Figure 1.6 presents an expanded model that will help you pull it all together. What is marketing? Simply put, marketing is the process of building profitable customer relationships by creating value for customers and capturing value in return.

The first four steps of the marketing process focus on creating value for customers. The company first gains a full understanding of the marketplace by researching customer needs and managing marketing information. It then designs a customer-driven marketing strategy based on the answers to two simple questions. The first question is "What consumers will we serve?" (market segmentation and targeting). Good marketing companies know that they cannot serve all customers in every way. Instead, they need to focus their resources on the customers they can serve best and most profitably. The second marketing strategy question is "How can we best serve targeted customers?" (differentiation and positioning). Here, the marketer outlines a value proposition that spells out what values the company will deliver in order to win target customers.

With its marketing strategy decided, the company now constructs an integrated marketing program—consisting of a blend of the four marketing mix elements, or the four Ps—that transforms the marketing strategy into real value for customers. The company develops product offers and creates strong brand identities for them. It prices these offers to create real customer value and distributes the offers to make them available to target consumers. Finally, the company designs promotion programs that communicate the value proposition to target consumers and persuade them to act on the market offering.

Perhaps the most important step in the marketing process involves building value-laden, profitable relationships with target customers. Throughout the process, marketers practice customer relationship management to create customer satisfaction and delight. In creating customer value and relationships, however, the company cannot go it alone. It must work closely with marketing partners both inside the company and throughout the

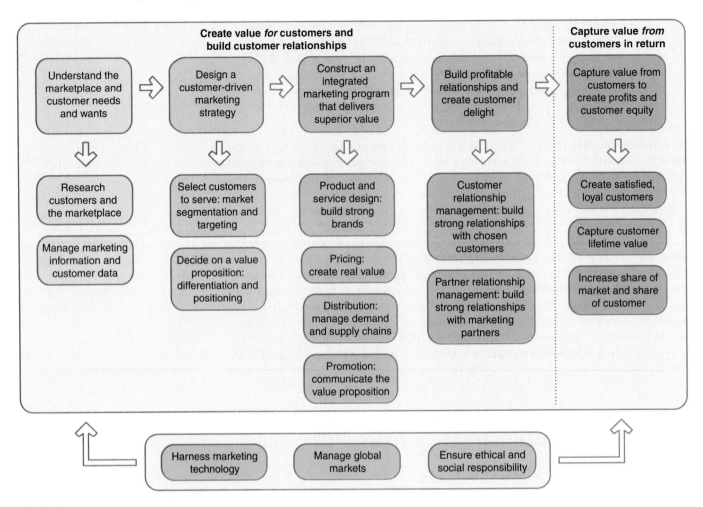

FIGURE 1.6

An Expanded Model of the Marketing Process

marketing system. Thus, beyond practicing good customer relationship management, firms must also practice good partner relationship management.

The first four steps in the marketing process create value *for* customers. In the final step, the company reaps the rewards of its strong customer relationships by capturing value *from* customers. Delivering superior customer value creates highly satisfied customers who will buy more and will buy again. This helps the company to capture customer lifetime value and greater share of customer. The result is increased long-term customer equity for the firm.

Finally, in the face of today's changing marketing landscape, companies must take into account three additional factors. In building customer and partner relationships, they must harness marketing technology, take advantage of global opportunities, and ensure that they act in an ethical and socially responsible way.

Figure 1.6 provides a good roadmap to future chapters of the text. Chapters 1 and 2 introduce the marketing process, with a focus on building customer relationships and capturing value from customers. Chapters 3, 4, and 5 address the first step of the marketing process—understanding the marketing environment, managing marketing information, and understanding consumer and business buyer behavior. In Chapter 6, we look more deeply into the two major marketing strategy decisions: selecting which customers to serve (segmentation and targeting) and deciding on a value proposition (differentiation and positioning). Chapters 8 through 14 discuss the marketing mix variables, one by one. Then, the final two chapters examine special marketing considerations: global marketing and marketing ethics and social responsibility.

REST STOP ⤤ REVIEWING THE CONCEPTS

Today's successful companies—whether large or small, for profit or not for profit, domestic or global—share a strong customer focus and a heavy commitment to marketing. The goal of marketing is to build and manage profitable customer relationships. Marketing seeks to attract new customers by promising superior value and to keep and grow current customers by delivering satisfaction. To be successful, companies will need to be strongly market focused.

1. Define marketing and outline the steps in the marketing process.

Marketing is the process by which companies create value for customers and build strong customer relationships in order to capture value from customers in return.

The marketing process involves five steps. The first four steps create value for customers. First, marketers need to understand the marketplace and customer needs and wants. Next, marketers design a customer-driven marketing strategy with the goal of getting, keeping, and growing target customers. In the third step, marketers construct a marketing program that actually delivers superior value. All of these steps form the basis for the fourth step, building profitable customer relationships and creating customer delight. In the final step, the company reaps the rewards of strong customer relationships by capturing value from customers.

2. Explain the importance of understanding customers and the marketplace, and identify the five core marketplace concepts.

Outstanding marketing companies go to great lengths to learn about and understand their customers' needs, wants, and demands. This understanding helps them to design want-satisfying market offerings and build value-laden customer relationships by which they can capture customer lifetime value and greater share of customer. The result is increased long-term customer equity for the firm.

The core marketplace concepts are needs, wants, and demands; market offerings (products, services, and experiences); value and satisfaction; exchange and relationships; and markets. Wants are the form taken by human needs when shaped by culture and individual personality. When backed by buying power, wants become demands. Companies address needs by putting forth a value proposition, a set of benefits that they promise to consumers to satisfy their needs. The value proposition is fulfilled through a market offering, which delivers customer value and satisfaction, resulting in long-term exchange relationships with customers.

3. Identify the key elements of a customer-driven marketing strategy and discuss the marketing management orientations that guide marketing strategy.

To design a winning marketing strategy, the company must first decide *who* it will serve. It does this by dividing the market into segments of customers (*market segmentation*) and selecting which segments it will cultivate (*target marketing*). Next, the company must decide *how* it will serve targeted customers (how it will *differentiate and position* itself in the marketplace).

Marketing management can adopt one of five competing market orientations. The *production concept* holds that management's task is to improve production efficiency and bring down prices. The *product concept* holds that consumers favor products that offer the most in quality, performance, and innovative features; thus, little promotional effort is required. The *selling concept* holds that consumers will not buy enough of the organization's products unless it undertakes a large-scale selling and promotion effort. The *marketing concept* holds that achieving organizational goals depends on determining the needs and wants of target markets and delivering the desired satisfactions more effectively and efficiently than competitors do. The *societal marketing concept* holds that generating customer satisfaction *and* long-run societal well-being are the keys to both achieving the company's goals and fulfilling its responsibilities.

4. Discuss customer relationship management and identify strategies for creating value *for* customers and capturing value *from* customers in return.

Broadly defined, *customer relationship management* is the process of building and maintaining profitable customer relationships by delivering superior customer value and satisfaction. The aim of customer relationship management is to produce high *customer equity,* the total combined customer lifetime values of all of the company's customers. The key to building lasting relationships is the creation of superior *customer value* and *satisfaction.*

Companies want not only to acquire profitable customers, but to build relationships that will keep them and grow "share of customer." Different types of customers require different customer relationship management strategies. The marketer's aim is to build the *right relationships* with the *right customers.* In return for creating value *for* targeted customers, the company captures value *from* customers in the form of profits and customer equity.

In building customer relationships, good marketers realize that they cannot go it alone. They must work closely with marketing partners inside and outside the company. In addition to being good at customer relationship management, they must also be good at *partner relationship management.*

5. Describe the major trends and forces that are changing the marketing landscape in this age of relationships.

Dramatic changes are occurring in the marketing arena. The boom in computer, telecommunications, information, transportation, and other technologies has created exciting new ways to learn about and track customers, and to create products and services tailored to individual customer needs. It has also allowed new approaches by which marketers can target consumers more selectively and build closer, two-way customer relationships.

In an increasingly smaller world, many marketers are now connected *globally* with their customers and marketing partners. Today, almost every company, large or small, is touched in some way by global competition. Today's marketers are also reexamining their ethical and societal responsibilities. Marketers are being called upon to take greater responsibility for the social and environmental impact of their actions. Finally, in the past, marketing has been most widely applied in the for-profit business sector. In recent years, however, marketing also has become a major part of the strategies of many not-for-profit organizations, such as colleges, hospitals, museums, zoos, symphony orchestras, and even churches.

Pulling it all together, as discussed throughout the chapter, the major new developments in marketing can be summed up in a single word: *relationships*. Today, marketers of all kinds are taking advantage of new opportunities for building relationships with their customers, their marketing partners, and the world around them.

Navigating the Key Terms

Customer equity (24)
Customer-generated marketing (19)
Customer lifetime value (22)
Customer-perceived value (14)
Customer relationship management (13)
Customer satisfaction (14)
Demands (7)
Exchange (8)

Internet (26)
Market (8)
Marketing (6)
Marketing concept (11)
Marketing management (9)
Marketing myopia (7)
Market offering (7)
Needs (6)

Partner relationship management (20)
Product concept (10)
Production concept (10)
Selling concept (10)
Share of customer (23)
Societal marketing concept (12)
Wants (6)

Travel Log

Discussing the Issues

1. Explain the goal of marketing and how companies achieve it. (AACSB: Communication)

2. Compare and contrast customer needs, wants, and demands. (AACSB: Communication)

3. Why is target market selection important for a customer-driven marketing strategy? How might target market selection impact customer satisfaction? (AACSB: Communication)

4. Name and describe the five different marketing management orientations. Which orientation do you believe your school follows when marketing its undergraduate program? (AACSB: Communication; Reflective Thinking)

5. Explain the difference between *share of customer* and *customer equity*. How does an understanding of share of customer help marketers attain higher customer equity? (AACSB: Communication; Reflective Thinking)

6. Discuss how the Internet impacts marketing. (AACSB: Communication)

Application Questions

1. Estimate how much you might be worth to an automobile manufacturer if you purchased a model offered by that manufacturer for every automobile purchase you make for the rest of your life. What factors should you consider when deriving an estimate of your lifetime value to that manufacturer? (AACSB: Communication; Reflective Thinking)

2. In a small group, develop an after-school child care service targeted toward working mothers. How will you enable them to get the best value? Define what you mean by value and develop the value proposition of your offering for this target market. (AACSB: Communication; Reflective Thinking)

3. Ask five consumers to describe an instance when they were dissatisfied with a marketing exchange, one in which they were satisfied, and one in which they were delighted. Ask them why they were or weren't satisfied and why they were delighted instead of merely satisfied. Also ask about the impact of these experiences on their long-term relationships with a company and loyalty to the brand. Report on what you learned. (AACSB: Communication; Reflective Thinking)

Under the Hood: Focus on Technology

Cutting-edge technology is now being used to improve customer service in the food service industry. The person taking your order at a fast-food drive-thru may not be in the restaurant—in fact, he or she may not even be in the state and could possibly be in another country. Several McDonald's restaurants in Colorado, Minnesota, and Missouri process orders through a centralized fa-

cility in Colorado, and other fast-feeders such as Hardee's and Carl's Jr. are joining in. High-speed data connections and voice-over-Internet protocol technology, or VoIP, enable businesses to outsource this task so that workers can concentrate on preparing the food and filling orders accurately. Some systems take temporary digital images of customers or cars placing orders so that workers can avoid mix-ups and speed up service. Domino's Pizza uses Internet technology for order placements and is launching a text-message ordering system for registered customers. Sit-down restaurants are also experimenting with table-side phone ordering and are placing credit/debit swipes at customers' fingertips. In Asia, customers routinely use their smart phones or palm computers to place an order from anywhere, and we will see this technology in the United States in the near future. Customers must be careful, however, because professional order takers are better at up-selling (that is, getting customers to order more-expensive options) and increasing the average order size.

1. What are the advantages and disadvantages of such technologies for marketers? How does this technology add value for customers? (AACSB: Communication; Reflective Thinking)

2. Although such technology is being used in restaurant service applications, discuss other areas where it can add value for customers. (AACSB: Communication; Reflective Thinking)

Focus on Ethics

Marketing to children has always been controversial. Indeed, in the 1970s, the Federal Trade Commission considered prohibiting all advertising to children, and in some other countries it is illegal to advertise to children. Now, with the child obesity rate in the United States greater than 18 percent and predicted to exceed 20 percent in just a few years, there is pressure on marketers, in general, and food marketers, in particular, to curb their marketing practices to children. Studies report that children view more than 20 food ads each day with over 90 percent of them promoting high-fat, high-sugar products. The marketing concept focuses on satisfying customers' needs and wants, but are marketers crossing the line when they cater to younger consumers' wants for products that may counter parental wishes or that may be unhealthy?

1. What ethical responsibilities do companies that market products having potentially adverse health effects have to consumers? (AACSB: Communication; Ethical Reasoning)

2. What actions are marketers taking to market their products to children more ethically? Discuss industry initiatives that help marketers market to children more responsibly. (AACSB: Communication; Ethical Reasoning)

Video Case

Harley-Davidson

Few brands engender such intense loyalty as that found in the hearts of Harley-Davidson owners. Why? Because the company's marketers spend a great deal of time thinking about customers. They want to know who customers are, how they think and feel, and why they buy a Harley. That attention to detail has helped build Harley-Davidson into a $5 billion company with more than 900,000 Harley Owners Group (HOG) members, the largest company-sponsored owner's group in the world.

Harley sells much more than motorcycles. The company sells a feeling of independence, individualism, and freedom. These strong emotional connections have made Harley-Davidson ownership much more of a lifestyle than only a product consumption experience. To support that lifestyle, Harley-Davidson recognizes that its most important marketing tool is the network of individuals that ride Harleys. For this reason, Harley-Davidson engages its customer base through company-sponsored travel adventures, events, and other things such as clothes and accessories both for riders and for those who simply like to associate with the brand.

After viewing the video featuring Harley-Davidson, answer the following questions about managing profitable customer relationships.

1. How does Harley-Davidson build long-term customer relationships?

2. What is Harley-Davidson's value proposition?

3. Relate the concept of customer equity to Harley-Davidson. How does Harley-Davidson's strategy focus on the right relationships with the right customers?

After dying this apter, you should be able to

1. explain companywide strategic planning and its four steps
2. discuss how to design business portfolios and develop growth strategies
3. explain marketing's role in marketing works with its partners to create and deliver customer value
4. describe the elements of a customer-driven marketing strategy and mix and the forces
5. list the marketing management functions, including the elements of a marketing plan, and discuss the importance of measuring and managing return on marketing

CHAPTER 2

Company and Marketing Strategy: Partnering to Build Customer Relationships

ROAD MAP

Previewing the Concepts

In the first chapter, we explored the marketing process by which companies create value for consumers in order to capture value in return. On this leg of our journey, we dig deeper into steps two and three of the marketing process—designing customer-driven marketing strategies and constructing marketing programs. To begin, we look at the organization's overall strategic planning. Next, we discuss how marketers, guided by the strategic plan, partner closely with others inside and outside the firm to serve customers. We then examine marketing strategy and planning—how marketers choose target markets, position their market offerings, develop a marketing mix, and manage their marketing programs. Finally, we look at the important step of measuring and managing return on marketing investment.

But first, let's look under NASCAR's hood. In only a few years, NASCAR has grown swiftly from a pastime for beer-guzzling Bubbas into a national marketing phenomenon. How? Through customer-driven marketing strategy. NASCAR creates high-octane experiences that result in strong relationships with its tens of millions of fans. In return, NASCAR captures value from these fans, both for itself and for its many sponsors. Read on and see how NASCAR does it.

Whardown race tracks? Think again! These days, NASCAR (the National Association for Stock Car Auto Racing) is much, much more. In fact, it's one great marketing organization. And for fans, NASCAR is a lot more than stock car races. It's a high-octane, totally involving experience.

As for the stereotypes, throw them away. NASCAR is now the second-highest rated regular season sport on TV—only the NFL draws more viewers—and races are seen in 150 countries in 23 languages. NASCAR fans are young, affluent, and decidedly family oriented—40 percent are women. What's more, they are 75 million strong and passionate about NASCAR. A hardcore NASCAR fan spends nearly $700 a year on NASCAR-related clothing, collectibles, and other items.

What's NASCAR's secret? Perhaps no organization is more customer driven—NASCAR focuses single-mindedly on creating customer relationships. For fans, the NASCAR relationship develops through a careful blend of live racing events, abundant media coverage, and compelling Web sites.

Each year, fans experience the adrenalin-charged, heart-stopping excitement of NASCAR racing firsthand by attending national tours to some two dozen tracks around the country. NASCAR is America's number-one live spectator sport, holding 17 of the 20 top-attended sporting events last year. More than 200,000 people attended the recent Daytona 500, compared to the 70,000 that attended the last Super Bowl.

At these events, fans hold tailgate parties, camp and cook out, watch the cars roar around the track, meet the drivers, and swap stories with other NASCAR enthusiasts. Track facilities even include RV parks next to and right inside the racing oval. What other sport lets you drive your beat-up RV or camper into the stadium and sit on it to watch the event? NASCAR really cares about its customers and goes out of its way to show them a good time. For example, rather than fleecing fans with overpriced food and beer, NASCAR tracks encourage fans to bring their own. Such actions mean that NASCAR might lose a sale today, but it will keep the customer tomorrow.

To further the customer relationship, NASCAR makes the sport a wholesome family affair. The environment is safe for kids—uniformed security guards patrol the track to keep things in line. The family atmosphere extends to the drivers, too. Unlike the aloof and often distant athletes in other sports, NASCAR drivers seem like regular guys. They are friendly and readily available to mingle with fans and sign autographs. Fans view drivers as good role models, and the long NASCAR tradition of family involvement creates the next generation of loyal fans.

Can't make it to the track? No problem. An average NASCAR event reaches 18 million TV viewers. Last year alone, NASCAR events captured more than 300 million viewers. Well-orchestrated coverage and in-car cameras put fans in the middle of the action, giving them vicarious thrills that keep them glued to the screen. "When the network gets it right, my surround-sound bothers my neighbors but makes my ears happy," says Angela Kotula, a 35-year-old human resources professional.

NASCAR also delivers the NASCAR experience through its engaging Web sites. NASCAR.com serves up a glut of information and entertainment—in-depth news, stats, standings, driver bios, background information, online games, community discussions, and merchandise. More than 300,000 die-hard fans subscribe to TrackPass to get up-to-the-minute standings, race video, streaming audio from the cars, and access to a host of archived audio and video highlights. TrackPass with PitCommand even delivers a real-time data feed, complete with the GPS locations of cars and data from drivers' dashboards.

But a big part of the NASCAR experience is the feeling that the sport, itself, is personally accessible. Anyone who knows how to drive feels that he or she, too, could be a champion NASCAR driver. As 48-year-old police officer Ed Sweat puts it: "Genetics did not bless me with the height of a basketball player, nor was I born to have the bulk of a lineman in the NFL. But . . . on any given Sunday, with a rich sponsor, the right car, and some practice, I could be draftin' and passin', zooming to the finish line, trading paint with Tony Stewart. . . . Yup, despite my advancing age and waistline, taking Zocor, and driving by a gym . . . I could be Dale Jarrett!"

Ultimately, such fan enthusiasm translates into financial success for NASCAR—and for its sponsors. Television networks pay on average $555 million per year for the rights to broadcast NASCAR events. With everything from NASCAR-branded bacon to its own series of Harlequin romance novels, the sport is third in licensed merchandise sales, behind only the NFL and the NCAA. NASCAR itself sells $2 billion in merchandise a year.

And marketing studies show that NASCAR's fans are three times more loyal to the sport's sponsors than fans of any other sport. Seventy-two percent of NASCAR fans consciously purchase sponsors' products because of the NASCAR connection. Just ask dental hygienist Jenny German, an ardent fan of driver Jeff Gordon. According to one account: "She actively seeks out any product he endorses. She drinks Pepsi instead of Coke, eats Edy's ice cream for desert, and owns a pair of Ray-Ban sunglasses." "'If they sold underwear with the number 24 on it, I'd have it on,' German says."

Because of such loyal fan relationships, NASCAR has attracted more than 250 big-name sponsors, from Wal-Mart, Home Depot, and Target to Procter & Gamble, UPS, Coca-Cola, and the U.S. Army. In all, corporations spend more than $1 billion a year for NASCAR sponsorships and promotions. Sprint Nextel is shelling out $750 million over a span of 10 years to be a NASCAR sponsor and to put its name on the Nextel Cup Series (or the Sprint Cup Series as of 2008). "I could pay you $1 million to try and not run into our name at a NASCAR race and you would lose," says a Sprint Nextel spokesperson.

Other sponsors eagerly pay on average $18 million to $20 million per year to sponsor a top car and to get their corporate colors and logos emblazoned on team uniforms and on the hoods or side panels of team cars. Or they pay $3 million to $5 million a year to become the "official" (fill-in-the-blank) of NASCAR racing. Is it worth the price? Office Depot certainly thinks so. It began sponsoring a car when its surveys showed that 44 percent of rival Staples' customers would switch office supply retailers if Office Depot hooked up with NASCAR.

So if you're still thinking of NASCAR as rednecks and moonshine, you'd better think again. NASCAR is a premier customer-driven marketing organization that knows how to create customer value that translates into deep and lasting customer relationships. "Better than any other sport," says a leading sports marketing executive, "NASCAR listens to its fans and gives them what they want." In turn, fans reward NASCAR and its sponsors with deep loyalty and the promise of lasting profits.[1]

Like NASCAR, outstanding marketing organizations employ strongly customer-driven marketing strategies and programs that create customer value and relationships. These marketing strategies and programs, however, are guided by broader companywide strategic plans, which must also be customer focused. Thus, to understand the role of marketing, we must first understand the organization's overall strategic planning process. For the sake of their long-term success, companies must look ahead and develop strategies that meet the future needs of customers and the changing conditions in their industries.

Companywide Strategic Planning: Defining Marketing's Role

Each company must find the game plan for long-run survival and growth that makes the most sense given its specific situation, opportunities, objectives, and resources. This is the focus of **strategic planning**—the process of developing and maintaining a strategic fit between the organization's goals and capabilities and its changing marketing opportunities.

Strategic planning sets the stage for the rest of the planning in the firm. Companies usually prepare annual plans, long-range plans, and strategic plans. The annual and long-range plans deal with the company's current businesses and how to keep them going. In contrast, the strategic plan involves adapting the firm to take advantage of opportunities in its constantly changing environment.

At the corporate level, the company starts the strategic planning process by defining its overall purpose and mission (see Figure 2.1). This mission then is turned into detailed supporting objectives that guide the whole company. Next, headquarters decides what portfolio of businesses and products is best for the company and how much support to give each one. In turn, each business and product develops detailed marketing and other departmental plans that support the companywide plan. Thus, marketing planning occurs at the business-unit, product, and market levels. It supports company strategic planning with more detailed plans for specific marketing opportunities.

> **Strategic planning**
> The process of developing and maintaining a strategic fit between the organization's goals and capabilities and its changing marketing opportunities.

Defining a Market-Oriented Mission

An organization exists to accomplish something. At first, it has a clear purpose or mission, but over time its mission may become unclear as the organization grows, adds new products and markets, or faces new conditions in the environment. When management senses that the organization is drifting, it must renew its search for purpose. It is time to ask: What is our business? Who is the customer? What do consumers value? What *should* our business be? These simple-sounding questions are among the most difficult the company will ever have to answer. Successful companies continuously raise these questions and answer them carefully and completely.

Many organizations develop formal mission statements that answer these questions. A **mission statement** is a statement of the organization's purpose—what it wants to accomplish in the larger environment. A clear mission statement acts as an "invisible hand" that guides people in the organization. Studies have shown that firms with well-crafted mission statements have better organizational and financial performance.[2]

> **Mission statement**
> A statement of the organization's purpose—what it wants to accomplish in the larger environment.

FIGURE 2.1

Steps in Strategic Planning

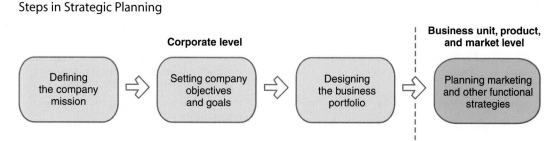

search.ebay.com/hula skirts
/portable video games
/mystery novels
/baseball tickets
/all-terrain tires
/dome tents
/stain removers

/ranch land
/hedge trimmers
/golf shoes
/video cellphones
/flip-flops
/digital sports watches
/horseshoe sets

/laptops
/swimming trunks
/digital cameras
/sprinklers
/sun hats
/lawnmowers
/artificial turf

you can get **it** on eb¥

■ Mission statements: eBay's mission is "to provide a global trading platform where practically anyone can trade practically anything—you can get it on eBay."

Some companies define their missions myopically in product or technology terms ("We make and sell furniture" or "We are a chemical-processing firm"). But mission statements should be *market oriented* and defined in terms of customer needs. Products and technologies eventually become outdated, but basic market needs may last forever.

A market-oriented mission statement defines the business in terms of satisfying basic customer needs. For example, Nike isn't just a shoe and apparel manufacturer—it wants "to bring inspiration and innovation to every athlete* in the world. (*If you have a body, you are an athlete.)" Likewise, eBay's mission isn't simply to hold online auctions and trading. Its mission is "to provide a global trading platform where practically anyone can trade practically anything—you can get *it* on eBay." It wants to be a unique Web community in which people can safely shop around, have fun, and get to know each other, for example, by chatting at the eBay Café. Table 2.1 provides several other examples of product-oriented versus market-oriented business definitions.[3]

Management should avoid making its mission too narrow or too broad. A pencil manufacturer that says it is in the communication equipment business is stating its mission too broadly. Missions should be *realistic*. Singapore Airlines would be deluding itself if it adopted the mission to become the world's largest airline. Missions should also be *specific*. Many mission statements are written for public relations purposes and lack specific, workable guidelines. Too often, they "are platitudes incorporating quality and customer satisfaction, often with an 'employees are our most important assets' kicker," say one analyst. "They're too long to remember, too vague to be meaningful, and too dull to inspire."[4] Such generic statements sound good but provide little real guidance or inspiration.

TABLE 2.1 **Market-Oriented Business Definitions**	Company	**Product-Oriented Definition**	**Market-Oriented Definition**
	Amazon.com	We sell books, videos, CDs, toys, consumer electronics, and other products online.	We make the Internet buying experience fast, easy, and enjoyable—we're the place where you can discover anything you want to buy online.
	America Online	We provide online services.	We create customer connectivity, anytime, anywhere.
	Disney	We run theme parks.	We create fantasies— a place where America still works the way it's supposed to.
	eBay	We hold online auctions.	We provide a global marketplace where practically anyone can trade practically anything—a Web community where people can shop around, have fun, and get to know each other.
	Home Depot	We sell tools and home repair and improvement items.	We empower consumers to achieve the homes of their dreams.
	Charles Schwab	We are a brokerage firm.	We are the guardian of our customers' financial dreams.
	Revlon	We make cosmetics.	We sell lifestyle and self-expression; success and status; memories, hopes, and dreams.
	Ritz-Carlton Hotels	We rent rooms.	We create the Ritz-Carlton experience—one that enlivens the senses, instills well-being, and fulfills even the unexpressed needs of our guests.
	Wal-Mart	We run discount stores.	We deliver low prices every day and help people to save money so they can live better.

Missions should fit the *market environment*. The Girl Scouts of America would not recruit successfully in today's environment with its former mission: "to prepare young girls for motherhood and wifely duties." Today, its mission is to build girls of courage, confidence, and character, who make the world a better place. The organization should also base its mission on its *distinctive competencies*. Finally, mission statements should be *motivating*. A company's mission should not be stated as making more sales or profits—profits are only a reward for undertaking a useful activity. A company's employees need to feel that their work is significant and that it contributes to people's lives. For example, Microsoft's aim is to help people to "realize their potential"—"your potential, our passion" says the company. Target's mission is to "Expect more. Pay less."

Setting Company Objectives and Goals

The company needs to turn its mission into detailed supporting objectives for each level of management. Each manager should have objectives and be responsible for reaching

48 miles per kernel.

How much ethanol can a company extract from corn? Today, BASF helps increase both the quality and quantity of corn that farmers can grow. So it is now possible to improve corn supplies for ethanol production without reducing the crops intended for the kitchen table. And with more BASF agricultural innovations on the way, there's no telling how much mileage our efforts may yield down the road. Learn more at basf.com/stories

Helping Make Products Better™

□ · BASF The Chemical Company

them. For example, giant chemical company BASF makes and markets a diverse product mix includes everything from chemicals, plastics, and agricultural products to crude oil and natural gas. But BASF does more than just make chemicals. Its mission is to work with commercial customers in numerous industries to help them employ these chemicals to find innovative solutions and better products for their consumers.

This broad mission leads to a hierarchy of objectives, including business objectives and marketing objectives. BASF's overall objective is to build profitable customer relationships by developing better products. It does this by investing in research—nearly 10 percent of BASF's employees work in research and development. R&D is expensive and requires improved profits to plow back into research programs. So improving profits becomes another major BASF objective. Profits can be improved by increasing sales or reducing costs. Sales can be increased by improving the company's share of domestic and international markets. These goals then become the company's current marketing objectives.[5]

Marketing strategies and programs must be developed to support these marketing objectives. To increase its market share, BASF might increase its products' availability and promotion in existing markets. To enter new global markets, the company can create new local partnerships within targeted countries. For example, BASF's Agricultural Products division has begun targeting China's farmers with a line of insecticides. To bring the right crop protection solutions to these farmers, BASF has formed working relationships with several Chinese agricultural research organizations, such as Nanjing Agricultural University.[6]

These are BASF's broad marketing strategies. Each broad marketing strategy must then be defined in greater detail. For example, increasing the product's promotion may require more salespeople, advertising, and public relations efforts; if so, both requirements will need to be spelled out. In this way, the firm's mission is translated into a set of objectives for the current period.

■ BASF's overall marketing objective is to work with commercial customer/partners to "help make products better." For example, it works with agricultural firms to "increase both the quality and quantity of corn that farmers can grow . . . to improve supplies for ethanol production without reducing crops intended for the kitchen table."

Designing the Business Portfolio

Guided by the company's mission statement and objectives, management now must plan its **business portfolio**—the collection of businesses and products that make up the company. The best business portfolio is the one that best fits the company's strengths and weaknesses

Business portfolio
The collection of businesses and products that make up the company.

to opportunities in the environment. Business portfolio planning involves two steps. First, the company must analyze its *current* business portfolio and decide which businesses should receive more, less, or no investment. Second, it must shape the *future* portfolio by developing strategies for growth and downsizing.

Analyzing the Current Business Portfolio The major activity in strategic planning is business **portfolio analysis**, whereby management evaluates the products and businesses making up the company. The company will want to put strong resources into its more profitable businesses and phase down or drop its weaker ones.

Management's first step is to identify the key businesses making up the company. These can be called the strategic business units. A *strategic business unit* (SBU) is a unit of the company that has a separate mission and objectives and that can be planned independently from other company businesses. An SBU can be a company division, a product line within a division, or sometimes a single product or brand.

The next step in business portfolio analysis calls for management to assess the attractiveness of its various SBUs and decide how much support each deserves. Most companies are well advised to "stick to their knitting" when designing their business portfolios. It's usually a good idea to focus on adding products and businesses that fit closely with the firm's core philosophy and competencies.

The purpose of strategic planning is to find ways in which the company can best use its strengths to take advantage of attractive opportunities in the environment. So most standard portfolio analysis methods evaluate SBUs on two important dimensions—the attractiveness of the SBU's market or industry and the strength of the SBU's position in that market or industry. The best-known portfolio-planning method was developed by the Boston Consulting Group, a leading management consulting firm.[7]

The Boston Consulting Group Approach Using the Boston Consulting Group (BCG) approach, a company classifies all its SBUs according to the **growth-share matrix** shown in Figure 2.2. On the vertical axis, *market growth rate* provides a measure of market attractiveness. On the horizontal axis, *relative market share* serves as a measure of company strength in the market. The growth-share matrix defines four types of SBUs:

> *Stars.* Stars are high-growth, high-share businesses or products. They often need heavy investment to finance their rapid growth. Eventually their growth will slow down, and they will turn into cash cows.
>
> *Cash cows.* Cash cows are low-growth, high-share businesses or products. These established and successful SBUs need less investment to hold their market share. Thus, they produce a lot of cash that the company uses to pay its bills and to support other SBUs that need investment.
>
> *Question marks.* Question marks are low-share business units in high-growth markets. They require a lot of cash to hold their share, let alone increase it. Management must think hard about which question marks it should try to build into stars and which should be phased out.

Portfolio analysis
The process by which management evaluates the products and businesses making up the company.

Growth-share matrix
A portfolio-planning method that evaluates a company's strategic business units in terms of their market growth rate and relative market share. SBUs are classified as stars, cash cows, question marks, or dogs.

FIGURE 2.2
The BCG Growth-Share Matrix

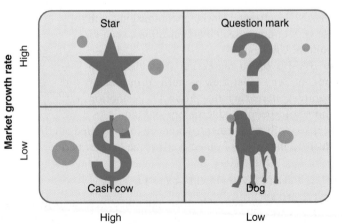

Dogs. Dogs are low-growth, low-share businesses and products. They may generate enough cash to maintain themselves but do not promise to be large sources of cash.

The 10 circles in the growth-share matrix represent a company's 10 current SBUs. The company has two stars, two cash cows, three question marks, and three dogs. The areas of the circles are proportional to the SBU's dollar sales. This company is in fair shape, although not in good shape. It wants to invest in the more promising question marks to make them stars and to maintain the stars so that they will become cash cows as their markets mature. Fortunately, it has two good-sized cash cows. Income from these cash cows will help finance the company's question marks, stars, and dogs. The company should take some decisive action concerning its dogs and its question marks. The picture would be worse if the company had no stars, if it had too many dogs, or if it had only one weak cash cow.

Once it has classified its SBUs, the company must determine what role each will play in the future. One of four strategies can be pursued for each SBU. The company can invest more in the business unit in order to *build* its share. Or it can invest just enough to *hold* the SBU's share at the current level. It can *harvest* the SBU, milking its short-term cash flow regardless of the long-term effect. Finally, the company can *divest* the SBU by selling it or phasing it out and using the resources elsewhere.

As time passes, SBUs change their positions in the growth-share matrix. Each SBU has a life cycle. Many SBUs start out as question marks and move into the star category if they succeed. They later become cash cows as market growth falls, then finally die off or turn into dogs toward the end of their life cycle. The company needs to add new products and units continuously so that some of them will become stars and, eventually, cash cows that will help finance other SBUs.

Problems with Matrix Approaches   The BCG and other formal methods revolutionized strategic planning. However, such centralized approaches have limitations. They can be difficult, time consuming, and costly to implement. Management may find it difficult to define SBUs and measure market share and growth. In addition, these approaches focus on classifying *current* businesses but provide little advice for *future* planning.

Because of such problems, many companies have dropped formal matrix methods in favor of more customized approaches that are better suited to their specific situations. Moreover, unlike former strategic-planning efforts, which rested mostly in the hands of senior managers at company headquarters, today's strategic planning has been decentralized. Increasingly, companies are placing responsibility for strategic planning in the hands of cross-functional teams of divisional managers who are close to their markets.

For example, consider The Walt Disney Company. Most people think of Disney as theme parks and wholesome family entertainment. But in the mid-1980s, Disney set up a powerful, centralized strategic planning group to guide the company's direction and growth. Over the next two decades, the strategic planning group turned The Walt Disney Company into a huge but diverse collection of media and entertainment businesses. The sprawling Disney grew to include everything from theme resorts and film studios (Walt Disney Pictures, Touchstone Pictures, Hollywood Pictures, and others) to media networks (ABC plus Disney Channel, ESPN, A&E, History Channel, and a half dozen others) to consumer products and a cruise line. The newly transformed company proved hard to manage and performed unevenly. Recently, Disney's new chief executive disbanded the centralized strategic planning unit, decentralizing its functions to Disney division managers.

■ Managing the business portfolio: Most people think of Disney as theme parks and wholesome family entertainment but over the past two decades, it's become a sprawling collection of media and entertainment businesses that requires big doses of the famed "Disney Magic" to manage.

2.1 MARKETING AT WORK
Starbucks Coffee: Where Growth Is Really Perking

More than 25 years ago, Howard Schultz hit on the idea of bringing a European-style coffeehouse to America. He believed that people needed to slow down, to "smell the coffee" and enjoy life a little more. The result is Starbucks. This coffeehouse doesn't sell just coffee, it sells *The Starbucks Experience*—the comfy velvety chairs, the hissing steam, the rich aromas. Its coffee shops "provide an uplifting experience that enriches people's lives one moment, one human being, one extraordinary cup of coffee at a time." Starbucks gives customers what it calls a "third place"—away from home and away from work.

Starbucks is now a powerhouse premium brand in a category in which only cheaper commodity products once existed. Some 40 million customers a week flock to its nearly 13,500 shops in 40 countries. Growth is the engine that keeps Starbucks perking, and over the past two decades, the company's sales and profits have risen like steam off a mug of hot java. Starbucks targets (and regularly achieves) amazing revenue growth exceeding 20 percent each year. In fact, Schultz recently announced that he wants to triple sales in the next 5 years. During the past 10 years, Starbucks has delivered a nearly 26 percent average annual return to investors.

■ Strategies for growth: To maintain its phenomenal growth in an increasingly overcaffeinated marketplace, Starbucks has brewed up an ambitious multipronged growth strategy.

Starbucks's success, however, has drawn a full litter of copycats, ranging from direct competitors such as Caribou Coffee to fast-food merchants (such as McDonald's McCafé) and even discounters (Kicks Coffee Café at a Wal-Mart). These days it seems that everyone is peddling their own brand of premium coffee. In the early 1990s, there were only 200 coffeehouses in the United States. Today there are more than 21,400. To maintain its phenomenal growth in an increasingly overcaffeinated marketplace, Starbucks has brewed up an ambitious, multipronged growth strategy. Let's examine the key elements of this strategy:

More store growth: Some 85 percent of Starbucks's sales comes from its own stores. So, not surprisingly, Starbucks is opening new stores at a breakneck pace. Eleven years ago, Starbucks had just 1,015 stores, total—that's about 1,400 fewer than it plans to build in the coming year alone. Starbucks's strategy is to put stores *everywhere*. In Seattle, there's a Starbucks for every 9,400 people; in Manhattan, there's one for every 12,000. One three-block

stretch in Chicago contains six of the trendy coffee bars. In New York City, there are two Starbucks in one Macy's store. In fact, cramming so many stores close together caused one satirical publication to run this headline: "A New Starbucks Opens in the Restroom of Existing Starbucks." The company's ultimate goal is 40,000 stores worldwide.

Enhanced Starbucks Experience: Beyond opening new shops, Starbucks is adding in-store products and features that get customers to stop in more often, stay longer, and buy more. Its beefed-up menu now includes hot breakfast sandwiches plus lunch and dinner items, increasing the average customer purchase. The chain has tested everything from Krispy Kreme doughnuts and Fresh Fields gourmet sandwiches to Greek pasta salads and assorted chips. And it recently began adding a line of nonfat items, so that Starbucks now "offers a little of everything to match your mood and lifestyle."

Developing Strategies for Growth and Downsizing   Beyond evaluating current businesses, designing the business portfolio involves finding businesses and products the company should consider in the future. Companies need growth if they are to compete more effectively, satisfy their stakeholders, and attract top talent. "Growth is pure oxygen," states one executive. "It creates a vital, enthusiastic corporation where people see genuine opportunity." At the same time, a firm must be careful not to make growth itself an objective. The company's objective must be "profitable growth."

Marketing has the main responsibility for achieving profitable growth for the company. Marketing must identify, evaluate, and select market opportunities and lay down strategies for capturing them. One useful device for identifying growth opportunities is the **product/market expansion grid**, shown in Figure 2.3.[8] We apply it here to Starbucks (see Marketing at Work 2.1).

First, Starbucks management might consider whether the company can achieve deeper **market penetration**—making more sales to current customers without changing its prod-

Product/market expansion grid
A portfolio-planning tool for identifying company growth opportunities through market penetration, market development, product development, or diversification.

Market penetration
A strategy for company growth by increasing sales of current products to current market segments without changing the product.

To get customers to hang around longer, Starbucks offers wireless Internet access in most of its stores. The chain also offers in-store music downloads, letting customers burn their own CDs while sipping their lattes. Out of cash? No problem—just swipe your prepaid Starbucks card on the way out ("a Starbucks store in your wallet"). Or use your Starbucks Card Duetto Visa (a credit card that also serves as a gift, stored-value, and rewards card).

New retail channels: The vast majority of coffee in America is bought in retail stores and brewed at home. To capture this demand, Starbucks has also pushed into America's supermarket aisles. It has a co-branding deal with Kraft, under which Starbucks roasts and packages its coffee and Kraft markets and distributes it. Beyond supermarkets, Starbucks has forged an impressive set of new ways to bring its brand to market. Some examples: Host Marriott operates Starbucks kiosks in America's airports, and several airlines serve Starbucks coffee to their passengers. Starbucks has installed coffee shops in most Borders Books and Target stores. Starbucks also sells gourmet coffee, tea, gifts, and related goods through business and consumer catalogs. And its Web site, StarbucksStore.com, has become a kind of "lifestyle portal" on which it sells coffee, tea, coffee-making equipment, compact discs, gifts, and collectibles.

New products and store concepts: Starbucks has partnered over the years with several firms to extend its brand into new categories. For example, it joined with PepsiCo to stamp the Starbucks brand on bottled Frappuccino drinks and its DoubleShot espresso drink. Starbucks ice cream, marketed in a joint venture with Dreyer's, is now the leading brand of coffee ice cream. Starbucks has also diversified into the entertainment business. Starbucks Entertainment "selects the best in music, books, and film to offer Starbucks customers the opportunity to discover quality entertainment in a fun and convenient way as a part of their daily coffee experience." The entertainment initiative includes Hear Music (the Sound of Starbucks), which selects and sells music in Starbucks shops and also produces music CDs under its own label. Hear Music now runs its own XM Satellite Radio station, and Starbucks is opening new Starbucks Hear Music Coffeehouses in a number of major U.S. cities. The company has also teamed with Apple to create a Starbucks Entertainment area on the Apple iTunes store.

International growth: Finally, Starbucks has taken its American-brewed concept global. In 1996, the company had only 11 coffeehouses outside North America. By 2004, the number had grown to more than 3,500 stores in 39 international markets, from Paris to Osaka to Oman and Beijing. Starbucks continues to open new international stores at a rate of close to 400 per year.

Although Starbucks's growth strategy so far has met with amazing success, many analysts are now expressing strong concerns. What's wrong with Starbucks's rapid expansion? Critics worry that the company may be overextending the Starbucks brand name and diluting the Starbucks experience. People pay $4.50 for a caffe latte, say the critics, because of the brand's coffee-brewing expertise, cozy ambiance, and exclusivity. When you see the Starbucks name plastered on everything from airport coffee cups to supermarket packages, you wonder.

Even Schultz worries that operational streamlining that has accompanied rapid growth may have led to "the watering down of the Starbucks experience" and the "commoditization of our brand." Other critics fear that, by pursuing such a broad-based growth strategy, Starbucks will stretch its resources too thin or lose its focus. According to one strategist, Starbucks should "pull back . . . and make coffee the core again."

Still others, however, remain true believers. Some even see similarities between Starbucks and a young McDonald's, which rode the humble hamburger to such incredible success. In fact, Starbucks has more stores, greater revenues, and better stock returns than McDonald's did at the same point in its growth. And Starbucks still has a lot of growing to do before it gets as large as McDonald's is today.

Only time will tell whether Starbucks turns out to be the next McDonald's—it all depends on how well the company manages growth. Says Schultz, "We are in the second inning of a nine-inning game. We are just beginning to tap into all sorts of new markets, new customers, and new products." For now, things are really perking. But Starbucks has to be careful that it doesn't boil over.

Sources: Quotes and other information from "U.S. Coffee Shops Still Simply Too Hot to Handle," accessed at www.marketresearchworld.net, August 8, 2007; "Company Profile," May 2007, accessed at www.starbucks.com/aboutus/Company_Profile.pdf; Burt Helm, "Saving Starbucks' Soul," *BusinessWeek,* April 9, 2007, pp. 56–62; Curt Woodward, "Weak Coffee: Some Question If Starbucks Expansion May Dilute the Brand," *Marketing News,* May 15, 2007, p. 11; and Starbucks annual reports and other information accessed at www.starbucks.com, November 2007.

ucts. It might add new stores in current market areas to make it easier for more customers to visit. In fact, Starbucks is adding an average of 46 stores a week internationally, 52 weeks a year—its ultimate goal is 40,000 stores worldwide. Improvements in advertising, prices, service, menu selection, or store design might encourage customers to stop by more often, stay longer, or to buy more during each visit. For example, Starbucks has

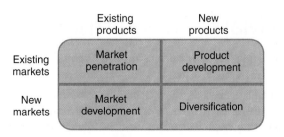

FIGURE 2.3

The Product/Market Expansion Grid

Market development
A strategy for company growth by identifying and developing new market segments for current company products.

Product development
A strategy for company growth by offering modified or new products to current market segments.

Diversification
A strategy for company growth through starting up or acquiring businesses outside the company's current products and markets.

Downsizing
Reducing the business portfolio by eliminating products of business units that are not profitable or that no longer fit the company's overall strategy.

added drive-through windows to many of its stores. A Starbucks Card lets customers pre-pay for coffee and snacks or give the gift of Starbucks to family and friends. And to get customers to hang around longer, Starbucks offers wireless Internet access in most of its stores.

Second, Starbucks management might consider possibilities for **market development**—identifying and developing new markets for its current products. For instance, managers could review new *demographic markets*. Perhaps new groups—such as seniors or ethnic groups—could be encouraged to visit Starbucks coffee shops for the first time or to buy more on each visit. Managers also could review new *geographical markets*. Starbucks is now expanding swiftly into new U.S. markets, especially smaller cities. And it's expanding rapidly in new global markets. In 1996, Starbucks had only 11 coffeehouses outside North America. It now has nearly 4,000, with plenty of room to grow. "We're just scratching the surface in China," says Starbucks' CEO. "We have [250] stores and the potential for more than 2,000 there."

Third, management could consider **product development**—offering modified or new products to current markets. For example, Starbucks recently added fruit juice Frappuchino beverages to its menu to draw in more non-coffee drinkers and breakfast sandwiches to bolster its morning business. To capture consumers who brew their coffee at home, Starbucks has also pushed into America's supermarket aisles. It has a co-branding deal with Kraft, under which Starbucks roasts and packages its coffee and Kraft markets and distributes it. And the company is forging ahead into new consumer categories. For example, it has brought out a line of Starbucks coffee liqueurs.

Fourth, Starbucks might consider **diversification**—starting up or buying businesses outside of its current products and markets. For example, Starbucks' 1999 purchase of Hear Music was so successful that it spurred the creation of a new Starbucks Entertainment division. Beginning with just selling and playing compilation CDs, Starbucks' Hear Music now has its own XM Satellite Radio station. It is also installing kiosks (called Media Bars) in select Starbucks stores that let customers download music and burn their own CDs while sipping their lattes. The newly formed Hear Music label has recently signed inaugural CDs by such legendary artists as Paul McCartney and Joni Mitchell.

In a more extreme diversification, Starbucks has partnered with Lion's Gate to coproduce movies and then market them in Starbucks coffeehouses. Starbucks supported the partnership's first film, *Akeelah and the Bee,* by sprinkling flashcards around the stores, stamping the movie's logo on its coffee cups, and placing spelling-bee-caliber words on the store chalkboards. Such new ventures have left some analysts asking whether Starbucks is diversifying too broadly, at the risk of diluting its market focus. They are asking, "What do movies have to do with Starbucks coffee and the Starbucks experience?"

Companies must not only develop strategies for *growing* their business portfolios but also strategies for **downsizing** them. There are many reasons that a firm might want to abandon products or markets. The market environment might change, making some of the company's products or markets less profitable. The firm may have grown too fast or entered areas where it lacks experience. This can occur when a firm enters too many foreign markets without the proper research or when a company introduces new products that do not offer superior customer value. Finally, some products or business units simply age and die.

When a firm finds brands or businesses that are unprofitable or that no longer fit its overall strategy, it must carefully prune, harvest, or divest them. Weak businesses usually require a disproportionate amount of management attention. Managers should focus on promising growth opportunities, not fritter away energy trying to salvage fading ones.

Planning Marketing: Partnering to Build Customer Relationships

The company's strategic plan establishes what kinds of businesses the company will operate in and its objectives for each. Then, within each business unit, more detailed planning takes place. The major functional departments in each unit—marketing, finance, accounting, purchasing, operations, information systems, human resources, and others—must work together to accomplish strategic objectives.

Marketing plays a key role in the company's strategic planning in several ways. First, marketing provides a guiding *philosophy*—the marketing concept—that suggests that company strategy should revolve around building profitable relationships with important consumer groups. Second, marketing provides *inputs* to strategic planners by helping to identify attractive market opportunities and by assessing the firm's potential to take advantage of them. Finally, within individual business units, marketing designs *strategies* for reaching the unit's objectives. Once the unit's objectives are set, marketing's task is to help carry them out profitably.

Customer value is the key ingredient in the marketer's formula for success. However, as we noted in Chapter 1, marketers alone cannot produce superior value for customers. Although marketing plays a leading role, it can be only a partner in attracting, keeping, and growing customers. In addition to *customer relationship management,* marketers must also practice *partner relationship management.* They must work closely with partners in other company departments to form an effective *value chain* that serves the customer. Moreover, they must partner effectively with other companies in the marketing system to form a competitively superior *value delivery network.* We now take a closer look at the concepts of a company value chain and value delivery network.

Partnering with Other Company Departments

Each company department can be thought of as a link in the company's **value chain**.[9] That is, each department carries out value-creating activities to design, produce, market, deliver, and support the firm's products. The firm's success depends not only on how well each department performs its work but also on how well the various departments coordinate their activities.

Value chain
The series of departments that carry out value-creating activities to design, produce, market, deliver, and support a firm's products.

For example, Wal-Mart's goal is to create customer value and satisfaction by providing shoppers with the products they want at the lowest possible prices. Marketers at Wal-Mart play an important role. They learn what customers need and stock the stores' shelves with the desired products at unbeatable low prices. They prepare advertising and merchandising programs and assist shoppers with customer service. Through these and other activities, Wal-Mart's marketers help deliver value to customers.

However, the marketing department needs help from the company's other departments. Wal-Mart's ability to offer the right products at low prices depends on the purchasing department's skill in developing the needed suppliers and buying from them at low cost. Wal-Mart's information technology department must provide fast and accurate information about which products are selling in each store. And its operations people must provide effective, low-cost merchandise handling.

A company's value chain is only as strong as its weakest link. Success depends on how well each department performs its work of adding customer value and on how well the activities of various departments are coordinated. At Wal-Mart, if purchasing can't obtain the lowest prices from suppliers, or if operations can't distribute merchandise at the lowest costs, then marketing can't deliver on its promise of lowest prices.

Ideally, then, a company's different functions should work in harmony to produce value for consumers. But, in practice, departmental relations are full of conflicts and misunderstandings. The marketing department takes the consumer's point of view. But when marketing tries to develop customer satisfaction, it can cause other departments to do a poorer job *in their terms.* Marketing department actions can increase purchasing costs, disrupt production schedules, increase inventories, and create budget headaches. Thus, the other departments may resist the marketing department's efforts.

■ The value chain: Wal-Mart's ability to offer the right products at low prices depends on the contributions of people in all of the company's departments— marketing, purchasing, information systems, finance, and operations.

Yet marketers must find ways to get all departments to "think consumer" and to develop a smoothly functioning value chain. Marketing managers need to work closely with managers of other functions to develop a system of functional plans under which the different departments can work together to accomplish the company's overall strategic objectives. The idea is to "maximize the customer experience across the organization and its various customer touch points," say a marketing consultant. Jack Welch, the highly regarded former GE CEO, told his employees: "Companies can't give job security. Only customers can!" He emphasized that all GE people, regardless of their department, have an impact on customer satisfaction and retention. His message: "If you are not thinking customer, you are not thinking."[10]

Partnering with Others in the Marketing System

In its quest to create customer value, the firm needs to look beyond its own value chain and into the value chains of its suppliers, distributors, and, ultimately, customers. Consider McDonald's. McDonald's nearly 32,000 restaurants worldwide serve more than 52 million customers daily, capturing more than 40 percent of the burger market.[11] People do not swarm to McDonald's only because they love the chain's hamburgers. In fact, consumers typically rank McDonald's behind Burger King and Wendy's in taste. Consumers flock to the McDonald's *system*, not just to its food products. Throughout the world, McDonald's finely tuned system delivers a high standard of what the company calls QSCV—quality, service, cleanliness, and value. McDonald's is effective only to the extent that it successfully partners with its franchisees, suppliers, and others to jointly deliver exceptionally high customer value.

More companies today are partnering with the other members of the supply chain to improve the performance of the customer **value delivery network**. For example, Toyota knows the importance of building close relationships with its suppliers. In fact, it even includes the phrase "achieve supplier satisfaction" in its mission statement.

Achieving satisfying supplier relationships has been a cornerstone of Toyota's stunning success. In one recent survey of parts makers—which measured items such as degree of trust, open and honest communication, amount of help given to reduce costs, and the opportunity to make a profit—Toyota scored far higher than competitors. On a scale of 1 to 500, with an industry mean of 270, Toyota rated 415, whereas GM rated 174 and Ford rated just 162. U.S. competitors often alienate their suppliers through self-serving, heavy-handed dealings. "The [U.S. automakers] set annual cost-reduction targets [for the parts they buy]," says one

Value delivery network
The network made up of the company, suppliers, distributors, and ultimately customers who "partner" with each other to improve the performance of the entire system.

■ Toyota partners with its suppliers and helps them meet its very high expectations. Creating satisfied suppliers helps Toyota produce lower-cost, higher-quality cars, which in turn results in more satisfied customers.

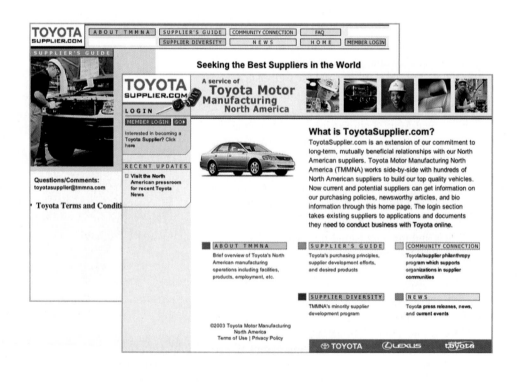

supplier. "To realize those targets, they'll do anything. [They've unleashed] a reign of terror, and it gets worse every year." Says another, "[Ford] seems to send its people to "hate school" so that they learn how to hate suppliers."

By contrast, rather than bullying suppliers, Toyota partners with them and helps them to meet its very high expectations. Toyota learns about their businesses, conducts joint improvement activities, helps train supplier employees, gives daily performance feedback, and actively seeks out supplier concerns. The high supplier satisfaction means that Toyota can rely on suppliers to help it improve its own quality, reduce costs, and develop new products quickly. For example, when Toyota recently launched a program to reduce prices by 30 percent on 170 parts that it would buy for its next generation of cars, suppliers didn't complain. Instead, they pitched in, trusting that Toyota would help them achieve the targeted reductions, in turn making them more competitive and profitable in the future. In all, creating satisfied suppliers helps Toyota to produce lower-cost, higher-quality cars, which in turn results in more satisfied customers.[12]

Increasingly in today's marketplace, competition no longer takes place between individual competitors. Rather, it takes place between the entire value delivery networks created by these competitors. Thus, Toyota's performance against Ford depends on the quality of Toyota's overall value delivery network versus Ford's. Even if Toyota makes the best cars, it might lose in the marketplace if Ford's dealer network provides more customer-satisfying sales and service.

◇ Linking the Concepts

Here's a good place to pause for a moment to think about and apply what you've read in the first part of this chapter.

- Why are we talking about companywide strategic planning in a marketing text? What *does* strategic planning have to do with marketing?
- What are Starbucks' mission and strategy? What role does marketing play in helping Starbucks to accomplish its mission and strategy?
- What roles do other Starbucks departments play, and how can Starbucks' marketers partner with these departments to maximize overall customer value?

Marketing Strategy and the Marketing Mix

The strategic plan defines the company's overall mission and objectives. Marketing's role and activities are shown in Figure 2.4, which summarizes the major activities involved in managing a customer-driven marketing strategy and the marketing mix.

Consumers stand in the center. The goal is to create value for customers and build profitable customer relationships. Next comes **marketing strategy**—the marketing logic by which the company hopes to create this customer value and achieve these profitable relationships. The company decides which customers it will serve (segmentation and targeting) and how (differentiation and positioning). It identifies the total market, then divides it into smaller segments, selects the most promising segments, and focuses on serving and satisfying customers in these segments.

Guided by marketing strategy, the company designs an integrated *marketing mix* made up of factors under its control—product, price, place, and promotion (the four Ps). To find the best marketing strategy and mix, the company engages in marketing analysis, planning, implementation, and control. Through these activities, the company watches and adapts to the actors and forces in the marketing environment. We will now look briefly at each activity. Then, in later chapters, we will discuss each one in more depth.

Marketing strategy
The marketing logic by which the business unit hopes to create customer value and achieve profitable customer relationships.

FIGURE 2.4

Managing Marketing Strategy
and the Marketing Mix

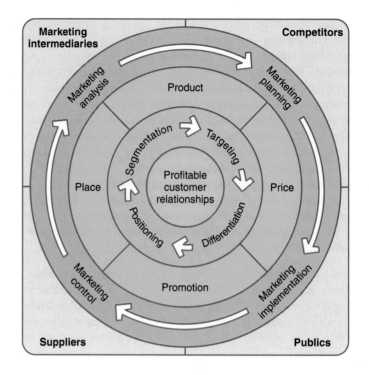

Customer-Driven Marketing Strategy

As we emphasized throughout Chapter 1, to succeed in today's competitive marketplace, companies need to be customer centered. They must win customers from competitors, then keep and grow them by delivering greater value. But before it can satisfy consumers, a company must first understand their needs and wants. Thus, sound marketing requires a careful customer analysis.

Companies know that they cannot profitably serve all consumers in a given market—at least not all consumers in the same way. There are too many different kinds of consumers with too many different kinds of needs. And most companies are in a position to serve some segments better than others. Thus, each company must divide up the total market, choose the best segments, and design strategies for profitably serving chosen segments. This process involves *market segmentation, market targeting, differentiation,* and *positioning.*

Market segmentation

Dividing a market into distinct groups of buyers who have distinct needs, characteristics, or behavior and who might require separate products or marketing programs.

Market Segmentation The market consists of many types of customers, products, and needs. The marketer must determine which segments offer the best opportunities. Consumers can be grouped and served in various ways based on geographic, demographic, psychographic, and behavioral factors. The process of dividing a market into distinct groups of buyers who have different needs, characteristics, or behavior who might require separate products or marketing programs is called **market segmentation**.

Market segment

A group of consumers who respond in a similar way to a given set of marketing efforts.

Every market has segments, but not all ways of segmenting a market are equally useful. For example, Tylenol would gain little by distinguishing between low-income and high-income pain reliever users if both respond the same way to marketing efforts. A **market segment** consists of consumers who respond in a similar way to a given set of marketing efforts. In the car market, for example, consumers who want the biggest, most comfortable car regardless of price make up one market segment. Consumers who care mainly about price and operating economy make up another segment. It would be difficult to make one car model that was the first choice of consumers in both segments. Companies are wise to focus their efforts on meeting the distinct needs of individual market segments.

Market targeting

The process of evaluating each market segment's attractiveness and selecting one or more segments to enter.

Market Targeting After a company has defined market segments, it can enter one or many of these segments. **Market targeting** involves evaluating each market segment's attractiveness and selecting one or more segments to enter. A company should target segments in which it can profitably generate the greatest customer value and sustain it over time.

A company with limited resources might decide to serve only one or a few special segments or "market niches." Such "nichers" specialize in serving customer segments that major competitors overlook or ignore. For example, Ferrari sells only 1,500 of its very high-performance cars in the United States each year, but at very high prices—from an eye-opening $190,000 for its Ferrari F430 model to an absolutely astonishing $2 million for its FXX super sports car, which can be driven only on race tracks (it sold 10 in the United States last year). Most nichers aren't quite so exotic. White Wave, maker of Silk Soymilk, has found its niche as the nation's largest soymilk producer. And Veterinary Pet Insurance is tiny compared with the insurance industry giants, but it captures a profitable 60 percent share of all health insurance policies for our furry—or feathery—friends (see Marketing at Work 2.2).

Alternatively, a company might choose to serve several related segments—perhaps those with different kinds of customers but with the same basic wants. Abercrombie & Fitch, for example, targets college students, teens, and kids with the same upscale, casual clothes and accessories in different outlets: the original Abercrombie & Fitch, Hollister, and Abercrombie. Or a large company might decide to offer a complete range of products to serve all market segments.

Most companies enter a new market by serving a single segment, and if this proves successful, they add segments. Large companies eventually seek full market coverage. They want to be the General Motors of their industry. GM says that it makes a car for every "person, purse, and personality." The leading company normally has different products designed to meet the special needs of each segment.

Market Differentiation and Positioning After a company has decided which market segments to enter, it must decide how it will differentiate its market offering for each targeted segment and what positions it wants to occupy in those segments. A product's *position* is the place the product occupies, relative to competitors' products, in consumers' minds. Marketers want to develop unique market positions for their products. If a product is perceived to be exactly like others on the market, consumers would have no reason to buy it.

Positioning is arranging for a product to occupy a clear, distinctive, and desirable place relative to competing products in the minds of target consumers. As one positioning expert puts it, positioning is "why a shopper will pay a little more for your brand."[13] Thus, marketers plan positions that distinguish their products from competing brands and give them the greatest advantage in their target markets.

Thus, Wal-Mart promises "save money, live better"; Target says "expect more, pay less." MasterCard gives you "priceless experiences"; and whether it's an everyday moment or the moment of a lifetime, "life takes Visa." And wireless provider Helio tells you "Don't call us a phone company. Don't call it a phone." Instead, Helio offers "advanced mobile services and exclusive, high-end, beautiful devices for consumers who have mobile at the

Positioning
Arranging for a product to occupy a clear, distinctive, and desirable place relative to competing products in the minds of target consumers.

■ Positioning: Wireless provider Helio proclaims "Don't call us a phone company. Don't call it a phone."

2.2 MARKETING AT WORK

Niching: Health Insurance for Our Furry—or Feathery—Friends

Health insurance for pets? MetLife, Prudential, Northwestern Mutual, and most other large insurance companies haven't paid much attention to it. But that leaves plenty of room for more-focused nichers, for whom pet health insurance has become a lucrative business. The largest of the small competitors is Veterinary Pet Insurance (VPI). VPI's mission is to "be the trusted choice of America's pet lovers."

VPI was founded in 1980 by a veterinarian with a heart. The veterinarian never intended to leave his practice, but his life took a dramatic turn when he visited a local grocery store and was identified by a client's daughter as "the man who killed Buffy." He had euthanized the family dog two weeks earlier. He immediately began researching the possibility of creating pet medical insurance. "There is nothing more frustrating for a veterinarian than knowing that you can heal a sick patient but the owner lacks the financial resources and instructs you to put the pet down," says the vet. "I wanted to change that."

Pet insurance is a still-small but fast-growing segment of the insurance business. Insiders think the industry offers huge potential. Currently, 63 percent of all U.S. households own at least one pet. Collectively, Americans own some 75 million dogs, 88 million cats, 142 million freshwater fish, 10 million saltwater fish, 16 million birds, 24 million small animals, 13 million reptiles, and 14 million horses. A recent survey showed that 94 percent of pet owners attribute human personality traits to their pets. More than two-thirds have included their pets in holiday celebrations and one-third characterize their pet as a child. Some 42 percent of dogs now sleep in the same bed as their owners. Americans spend a whopping $41 billion a year on their pets, more than the gross domestic product of all but 64 countries in the world. They spend $9.8 billion of that on pet health care.

Unlike in Britain and Sweden, where almost half of all pet owners carry pet health insurance, relatively few pet owners in the United States now carry such coverage. However, a recent study of pet owners found that nearly 75 percent are willing to go into debt to pay for veterinary care for their furry—or feathery—companions. And for many pet medical procedures, they'd have to! If not diagnosed quickly, even a mundane ear infection in a dog can result in $1,000 worth of medical treatment. Ten days of dialysis treatment can reach $12,000 and cancer treatment as much as $40,000. All of this adds up to a lot of potential growth for pet health insurers.

VPI's plans cover a multitude of pet medical problems and conditions. The insurance helps pay for office calls, prescriptions, treatments, lab fees, x-rays, surgery, and hospitalization. Like its handful of competitors, VPI issues health insurance policies for dogs and cats. Unlike its competitors, VPI covers a menagerie of exotic pets as well. Among other critters, the Avian and Exotic Pet Plan covers birds, rabbits, ferrets, rats, guinea pigs, snakes and other reptiles, iguanas, turtles, hedgehogs, and potbellied pigs. "There's such a vast array of pets," says a VPI executive. "And people love them. We have to respect that."

How's VPI doing in its niche? It's growing like a newborn puppy. VPI is by far the largest of the handful of companies that offer pet insurance, providing more than 60 percent of all U.S. pet insurance policies. Since its inception, VPI has issued more than 1 million policies, and it now serves more than 450,000 policyholders. Sales have grown rapidly, exceeding $110 million in policy premiums last year. That might not amount to much for the likes of MetLife, Prudential, or Northwestern

FAMILY *Redefined*.

Enroll Today at PETINSURANCE.COM or 800-944-1649

He's not just a dog. He's your baby and deserves the best medical care. VPI Pet Insurance helps pay for your pet's lab fees, medications, surgeries, X-rays, and more. We even offer coverage for routine care, including vaccinations and prescription flea control. Plus, you're free to use any veterinarian. That's the kind of protection you need for all your family members. Call today for a free quote.

All applications are subject to underwriting approval. / Read your policy for complete coverage details. / Underwritten by Veterinary Pet Insurance Company (CA). Brea, CA. / National Casualty Company (NatC), Madison, WI, an A+15 rated company / ©2006 Veterinary Pet Insurance Company

■ Nichers: Market nicher VPI is growing faster than a newborn puppy. Its mission is to "be the trusted choice of America's pet lovers."

Mutual, which rack up tens of billions of dollars in yearly revenues. But it's profitable business for nichers like VPI. And there's room to grow. Only about 3 percent of pet owners currently buy pet insurance.

"Pet health insurance is no longer deemed so outlandish in a world where acupuncture for cats, hospice of dogs, and Prozac for ferrets are part of a veterinarian's routine," says one analyst. Such insurance is a real godsend for VPI's policyholders. Just ask Joe and Paula Sena, whose cocker spaniel, Elvis, is receiving radiation treatments for cancer. "He is not like our kids—he is our kid," says Ms. Sena. "He is a kid in a dog's body." VPI is making Elvis's treatments possible by picking up a lion's share of the costs. As more people adopt the Sena's view towards their pets, its hard to think the pet industry isn't just beginning to stretch its paws.

Sources: See Diane Brady and Christopher Palmeri, "The Pet Economy," *BusinessWeek*, August 6, 2007, pp. 45–54; Yilu Zhao, "Break a Leg, Fluffy, If You Have Insurance," *New York Times*, June 30, 2002; Damon Darlin, "Vet Bills and the Priceless Pet: What's a Practical Owner to Do?" *New York Times*, May 13, 2006; "New National Pet Owners Survey Details Two Decades of Evolving American Pet Ownership," American Pet Products Manufacturers Association, June 18, 2007, accessed at www.appma.com; "Multiple Pet Owners with VPI Pet Insurance Represent 17% of All Policyholders," p. 1; and information accessed at www.petinsurance.com, November 2007.

center of their lives." Such deceptively simple statements form the backbone of a product's marketing strategy.

In positioning its product, the company first identifies possible customer value differences that provide competitive advantages upon which to build the position. The company can offer greater customer value either by charging lower prices than competitors do or by offering more benefits to justify higher prices. But if the company *promises* greater value, it must then *deliver* that greater value. Thus, effective positioning begins with **differentiation**—actually *differentiating* the company's market offering so that it gives consumers more value. Once the company has chosen a desired position, it must take strong steps to deliver and communicate that position to target consumers. The company's entire marketing program should support the chosen positioning strategy.

Differentiation
Actually differentiating the market offering to create superior customer value.

Developing an Integrated Marketing Mix

After deciding on its overall marketing strategy, the company is ready to begin planning the details of the marketing mix, one of the major concepts in modern marketing. The **marketing mix** is the set of controllable, tactical marketing tools that the firm blends to produce the response it wants in the target market. The marketing mix consists of everything the firm can do to influence the demand for its product. The many possibilities can be collected into four groups of variables known as the "four *Ps*": *product, price, place,* and *promotion*. Figure 2.5 shows the marketing tools under each *P*.

Product means the goods-and-services combination the company offers to the target market. Thus, a Ford Escape consists of nuts and bolts, spark plugs, pistons, headlights, and thousands of other parts. Ford offers several Escape models and dozens of optional features. The car comes fully serviced and with a comprehensive warranty that is as much a part of the product as the tailpipe.

Price is the amount of money customers must pay to obtain the product. Ford calculates suggested retail prices that its dealers might charge for each Escape. But Ford dealers rarely charge the full sticker price. Instead, they negotiate the price with each customer, offering discounts, trade-in allowances, and credit terms. These actions adjust prices for the current competitive situation and bring them into line with the buyer's perception of the car's value.

Place includes company activities that make the product available to target consumers. Ford partners with a large body of independently owned dealerships that sell the company's many different models. Ford selects its dealers carefully and supports them strongly. The

Marketing mix
The set of controllable tactical marketing tools—product, price, place, and promotion—that the firm blends to produce the response it wants in the target market.

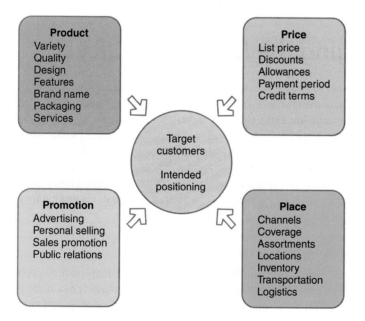

FIGURE 2.5
The Four *Ps* of the Marketing Mix

dealers keep an inventory of Ford automobiles, demonstrate them to potential buyers, negotiate prices, close sales, and service the cars after the sale.

Promotion means activities that communicate the merits of the product and persuade target customers to buy it. Ford Motor Company spends more than $2.5 billion each year on U.S. advertising, more than $800 per vehicle, to tell consumers about the company and its many products.[14] Dealership salespeople assist potential buyers and persuade them that Ford is the best car for them. Ford and its dealers offer special promotions—sales, cash rebates, low financing rates—as added purchase incentives.

An effective marketing program blends all of the marketing mix elements into an integrated marketing program designed to achieve the company's marketing objectives by delivering value to consumers. The marketing mix constitutes the company's tactical tool kit for establishing strong positioning in target markets.

Some critics think that the four Ps may omit or underemphasize certain important activities. For example, they ask, "Where are services?" Just because they don't start with a *P* doesn't justify omitting them. The answer is that services, such as banking, airline, and retailing services, are products too. We might call them *service products*. "Where is packaging?" the critics might ask. Marketers would answer that they include packaging as just one of many product decisions. All said, as Figure 2.5 suggests, many marketing activities that might appear to be left out of the marketing mix are subsumed under one of the four Ps. The issue is not whether there should be 4, 6, or 10 Ps so much as what framework is most helpful in designing integrated marketing programs.

There is another concern, however, that is valid. It holds that the four Ps concept takes the seller's view of the market, not the buyer's view. From the buyer's viewpoint, in this age of customer value and relationships, the four Ps might be better described as the four Cs:[15]

4Ps	4Cs
Product	Customer solution
Price	Customer cost
Place	Convenience
Promotion	Communication

Thus, whereas marketers see themselves as selling products, customers see themselves as buying value or solutions to their problems. And customers are interested in more than just the price; they are interested in the total costs of obtaining, using, and disposing of a product. Customers want the product and service to be as conveniently available as possible. Finally, they want two-way communication. Marketers would do well to think through the four Cs first and then build the four Ps on that platform.

Managing the Marketing Effort

In addition to being good at the *marketing* in marketing management, companies also need to pay attention to the *management*. Managing the marketing process requires the four marketing management functions shown in Figure 2.6—*analysis, planning, implementation,* and *control*. The company first develops companywide strategic plans and then translates them into marketing and other plans for each division, product, and brand. Through implementation, the company turns the plans into actions. Control consists of measuring and evaluating the results of marketing activities and taking corrective action where needed. Finally, marketing analysis provides information and evaluations needed for all of the other marketing activities.

Marketing Analysis

Managing the marketing function begins with a complete analysis of the company's situation. The marketer should conduct a **SWOT analysis**, by which it evaluates the company's overall strengths (S), weaknesses (W), opportunities (O), and threats (T) (see Figure 2.7). Strengths include internal capabilities, resources, and positive situational factors that may help the company to serve its customers and achieve its objectives. Weaknesses include in-

SWOT analysis
An overall evaluation of the company's strengths (S), weaknesses (W), opportunities (O), and threats (T).

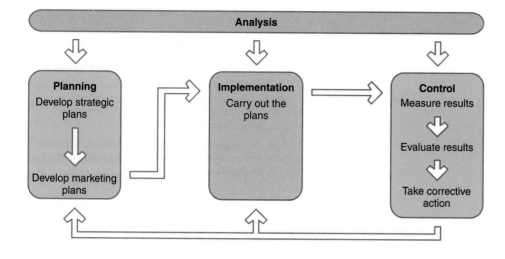

FIGURE 2.6

Marketing Analysis, Planning, Implementation, and Control

ternal limitations and negative situational factors that may interfere with the company's performance. Opportunities are favorable factors or trends in the external environment that the company may be able to exploit to its advantage. And threats are unfavorable external factors or trends that may present challenges to performance.

The company should analyze its markets and marketing environment to find attractive opportunities and identify environmental threats. It should analyze company strengths and weaknesses as well as current and possible marketing actions to determine which opportunities it can best pursue. The goal is to match the company's strengths to attractive opportunities in the environment, while eliminating or overcoming the weaknesses and minimizing the threats. Marketing analysis provides inputs to each of the other marketing management functions. We discuss marketing analysis more fully in Chapter 3.

Marketing Planning

Through strategic planning, the company decides what it wants to do with each business unit. Marketing planning involves deciding on marketing strategies that will help the company attain its overall strategic objectives. A detailed marketing plan is needed for each business, product, or brand. What does a marketing plan look like? Our discussion focuses on product or brand marketing plans.

Table 2.2 outlines the major sections of a typical product or brand marketing plan. (See Appendix 2 for a sample marketing plan.) The plan begins with an executive summary, which quickly overviews major assessments, goals, and recommendations. The main section of the plan presents a detailed SWOT analysis of the current marketing situation as well as potential threats and opportunities. The plan next states major objectives for the brand and outlines the specifics of a marketing strategy for achieving them.

A *marketing strategy* consists of specific strategies for target markets, positioning, the marketing mix, and marketing expenditure levels. It outlines how the company intends to create value for target customers in order to capture value in return. In this section, the planner explains how each strategy responds to the threats, opportunities, and critical issues spelled out earlier in the plan. Additional sections of the marketing plan lay out an action

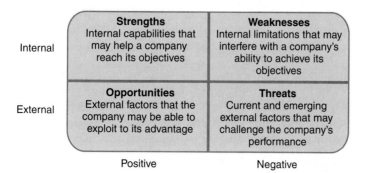

FIGURE 2.7

SWOT Analysis

	Section	Purpose
TABLE 2.2 Contents of a Marketing Plan	Executive summary	Presents a brief summary of the main goals and recommendations of the plan for management review, helping top management to find the plan's major points quickly. A table of contents should follow the executive summary.
	Current marketing situation	Describes the target market and company's position in it, including information about the market, product performance, competition, and distribution. This section includes: • A *market description,* which defines the market and major segments then reviews customer needs and factors in the marketing environment that may affect customer purchasing. • A *product review,* which shows sales, prices, and gross margins of the major products in the product line. • A review of *competition,* which identifies major competitors and assesses their market positions and strategies for product quality, pricing, distribution, and promotion. • A review of *distribution,* which evaluates recent sales trends and other developments in major distribution channels.
	Threats and opportunities analysis	Assesses major threats and opportunities that the product might face, helping management to anticipate important positive or negative developments that might have an impact on the firm and its strategies.
	Objectives and issues	States the marketing objectives that the company would like to attain during the plan's term and discusses key issues that will affect their attainment. For example, if the goal is to achieve a 15 percent market share, this section looks at how this goal might be achieved.
	Marketing strategy	Outlines the broad marketing logic by which the business unit hopes to create customer value and relationships and the specifics of target markets, positioning, and marketing expenditure levels. How will the company create value for customers in order to capture value from customers in return? This section also outlines specific strategies for each marketing mix element and explains how each responds to the threats, opportunities, and critical issues spelled out earlier in the plan.
	Action programs	Spells out how marketing strategies will be turned into specific action programs that answer the following questions: *What* will be done? *When* will it be done? *Who* will do it? *How* much will it cost?
	Budgets	Details a supporting marketing budget that is essentially a projected profit-and-loss statement. It shows expected revenues (forecasted number of units sold and the average net price) and expected costs (of production, distribution, and marketing). The difference is the projected profit. Once approved by higher management, the budget becomes the basis for materials buying, production scheduling, personnel planning, and marketing operations.
	Controls	Outlines the control that will be used to monitor progress and allow higher management to review implementation results and spot products that are not meeting their goals. It includes measures of return on marketing investment.

program for implementing the marketing strategy along with the details of a supporting *marketing budget.* The last section outlines the controls that will be used to monitor progress, measure return on marketing investment, and take corrective action.

Marketing Implementation

Planning good strategies is only a start toward successful marketing. A brilliant marketing strategy counts for little if the company fails to implement it properly. **Marketing implementation** is the process that turns marketing *plans* into marketing *actions* in order to accomplish strategic marketing objectives. Whereas marketing planning addresses the *what* and *why* of marketing activities, implementation addresses the *who, where, when,* and *how.*

Marketing implementation
The process that turns marketing strategies and plans into marketing actions in order to accomplish strategic marketing objectives.

Many managers think that "doing things right" (implementation) is as important as, or even more important than, "doing the right things" (strategy). The fact is that both are critical to success, and companies can gain competitive advantages through effective implementation. One firm can have essentially the same strategy as another, yet win in the marketplace through faster or better execution. Still, implementation is difficult—it is often easier to think up good marketing strategies than it is to carry them out.

In an increasingly connected world, people at all levels of the marketing system must work together to implement marketing strategies and plans. At Black & Decker, for example, marketing implementation for the company's power tools, outdoor equipment, and other products requires day-to-day decisions and actions by thousands of people both inside and outside the organization. Marketing managers make decisions about target segments, branding, packaging, pricing, promoting, and

■ Marketers must continually plan their analysis, implementation, and control activities.

distributing. They talk with engineering about product design, with manufacturing about production and inventory levels, and with finance about funding and cash flows. They also connect with outside people, such as advertising agencies to plan ad campaigns and the news media to obtain publicity support. The sales force urges Home Depot, Lowe's, Wal-Mart, and other retailers to advertise Black & Decker products, provide ample shelf space, and use company displays.

Successful marketing implementation depends on how well the company blends its people, organizational structure, decision and reward systems, and company culture into a cohesive action program that supports its strategies. At all levels, the company must be staffed by people who have the needed skills, motivation, and personal characteristics. The company's formal organization structure plays an important role in implementing marketing strategy; so do its decision and reward systems. For example, if a company's compensation system rewards managers for short-run profit results, they will have little incentive to work toward long-run market-building objectives.

Finally, to be successfully implemented, the firm's marketing strategies must fit with its company culture, the system of values and beliefs shared by people in the organization. Studies show that the most successful companies have almost cultlike cultures built around strong, market-oriented missions. At companies such as Dell, Nordstrom, Toyota, P&G, and Four Seasons Hotels, employees share a strong vision and know in their hearts what's right for their company and its customers.

Marketing Department Organization

The company must design a marketing organization that can carry out marketing strategies and plans. If the company is very small, one person might do all of the research, selling, advertising, customer service, and other marketing work. As the company expands, a marketing department emerges to plan and carry out marketing activities. In large companies, this department contains many specialists. Thus, General Electric and Microsoft have product and market managers, sales managers and salespeople, market researchers, advertising experts, and many other specialists. To head up such large marketing organizations, many companies have now created a *chief marketing officer* (or CMO) position.

Modern marketing departments can be arranged in several ways. The most common form of marketing organization is the *functional organization.* Under this organization, different marketing activities are headed by a functional specialist—a sales manager, advertising manager, marketing research manager, customer-service manager, or new-product manager. A company that sells across the country or internationally often uses a *geographic organization.* Its sales and marketing people are assigned to specific countries, regions, and districts. Geographic organization allows salespeople to settle into a territory, get to know their customers, and work with a minimum of travel time and cost.

Companies with many very different products or brands often create a *product management organization*. Using this approach, a product manager develops and implements a complete strategy and marketing program for a specific product or brand. Product management first appeared at Procter & Gamble in 1929. A new company soap, Camay, was not doing well, and a young P&G executive was assigned to give his exclusive attention to developing and promoting this product. He was successful, and the company soon added other product managers.[16] Since then, many firms, especially consumer-products companies, have set up product management organizations.

For companies that sell one product line to many different types of markets and customers that have different needs and preferences, a *market* or *customer management organization* might be best. A market management organization is similar to the product management organization. Market managers are responsible for developing marketing strategies and plans for their specific markets or customers. This system's main advantage is that the company is organized around the needs of specific customer segments.

Large companies that produce many different products flowing into many different geographic and customer markets usually employ some *combination* of the functional, geographic, product, and market organization forms. This ensures that each function, product, and market receives its share of management attention. However, it can also add costly layers of management and reduce organizational flexibility. Still, the benefits of organizational specialization usually outweigh the drawbacks.

Marketing organization has become an increasingly important issue in recent years. As we discussed in Chapter 1, many companies are finding that today's marketing environment calls for less focus on products, brands, and territories and more focus on customers and customer relationships. More and more companies are shifting their brand management focus toward *customer management*—moving away from managing just product or brand profitability and toward managing customer profitability and customer equity. And many companies now organize their marketing operations around major customers. They think of themselves not as managing portfolios of brands but as managing portfolios of customers. For example, companies such as Procter & Gamble and Black & Decker have large teams, or even whole divisions, set up to serve large customers such as Wal-Mart, Target, Safeway, or Home Depot.

Marketing Control

Marketing control
The process of measuring and evaluating the results of marketing strategies and plans and taking corrective action to ensure that objectives are achieved.

Because many surprises occur during the implementation of marketing plans, the marketing department must practice constant marketing control. **Marketing control** involves evaluating the results of marketing strategies and plans and taking corrective action to ensure that objectives are attained. Marketing control involves four steps. Management first sets specific marketing goals. It then measures its performance in the marketplace and evaluates the causes of any differences between expected and actual performance. Finally, management takes corrective action to close the gaps between its goals and its performance. This may require changing the action programs or even changing the goals.

Operating control involves checking ongoing performance against the annual plan and taking corrective action when necessary. Its purpose is to ensure that the company achieves the sales, profits, and other goals set out in its annual plan. It also involves determining the profitability of different products, territories, markets, and channels.

Strategic control involves looking at whether the company's basic strategies are well matched to its opportunities. Marketing strategies and programs can quickly become outdated, and each company should periodically reassess its overall approach to the marketplace. A major tool for such strategic control is a **marketing audit**. The marketing audit is a comprehensive, systematic, independent, and periodic examination of a company's environment, objectives, strategies, and activities to determine problem areas and opportunities. The audit provides good input for a plan of action to improve the company's marketing performance.[17]

Marketing audit
A comprehensive, systematic, independent, and periodic examination of a company's environment, objectives, strategies, and activities to determine problem areas and opportunities and to recommend a plan of action to improve the company's marketing performance.

The marketing audit covers *all* major marketing areas of a business, not just a few trouble spots. It assesses the marketing environment, marketing strategy, marketing organization, marketing systems, marketing mix, and marketing productivity and profitability. The audit is normally conducted by an objective and experienced outside party. The findings may come as a surprise—and sometimes as a shock—to management. Management then decides which actions make sense and how and when to implement them.

Measuring and Managing Return on Marketing Investment

Marketing managers must ensure that their marketing dollars are being well spent. In the past, many marketers spent freely on big, expensive marketing programs, often without thinking carefully about the financial returns on their spending. They believed that marketing produces intangible outcomes, which do not lend themselves readily to measures of productivity or return. But all that is changing:

> For years, corporate marketers have walked into budget meetings like neighborhood junkies. They couldn't always justify how well they spent past handouts or what difference it all made. They just wanted more money—for flashy TV ads, for big-ticket events, for, you know, getting out the message and building up the brand. But those heady days of blind budget increases are fast being replaced with a new mantra: measurement and accountability. Armed with reams of data, increasingly sophisticated tools, and growing evidence that the old tricks simply don't work, there's hardly a marketing executive today who isn't demanding a more scientific approach to help defend marketing strategies in front of the chief financial officer. Marketers want to know the actual return on investment (ROI) of each dollar. They want to know it often, not just annually. . . . Companies in every segment of American business have become obsessed with honing the science of measuring marketing performance. "Marketers have been pretty unaccountable for many years," notes one expert. "Now they are under big pressure to estimate their impact."[18]

In response, marketers are developing better measures of *return on marketing investment.* **Return on marketing investment** (or *marketing ROI*) is the net return from a marketing investment divided by the costs of the marketing investment. It measures the profits generated by investments in marketing activities.

It's true that marketing returns can be difficult to measure. In measuring financial ROI, both the *R* and the *I* are uniformly measured in dollars. But there is as yet no consistent definition of marketing ROI. "It's tough to measure, more so than for other business expenses," says one analyst. "You can imagine buying a piece of equipment . . . and then measuring the productivity gains that result from the purchase," he says. "But in marketing, benefits like advertising impact aren't easily put into dollar returns. It takes a leap of faith to come up with a number."[19] A recent survey of top marketing executives found that although 58 percent of the companies surveyed have formal accountability programs, only 28 percent are satisfied with their ability to use marketing ROI measures to take action.[20]

A company can assess return on marketing in terms of standard marketing performance measures, such as brand awareness, sales, or market share. Campbell Soup uses sales and share data to evaluate specific advertising campaigns. For example, analysis revealed that its recent Soup at Hand advertising campaign, which depicted real-life scenarios of consumers using the portable soup, nearly doubled both the product's trial rate and repeat use rate after the first year. The Soup at Hand campaign received a Gold Effie, an advertising industry award based on marketing effectiveness.[21]

Many companies are assembling such measures into *marketing dashboards*—meaningful sets of marketing performance measures in a single display used to monitor strategic marketing performance. Just as automobile dashboards

Return on marketing investment (or *marketing ROI*)
The net return from a marketing investment divided by the costs of the marketing investment.

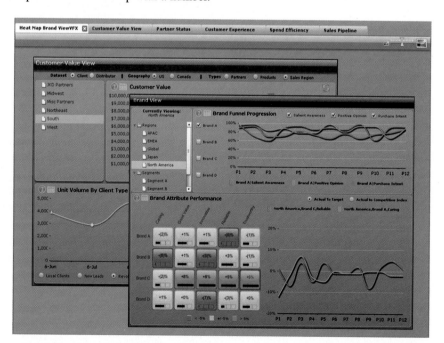

■ Many companies are assembling marketing dashboards—meaningful sets of marketing performance measures in a single display used set and adjust their marketing strategies.

FIGURE 2.8

Return on Marketing

Source: Adapted from Roland T. Rust, Katherine N. Lemon, and Valerie A. Zeithamal, "Return on Marketing: Using Consumer Equity to Focus Marketing Strategy," *Journal of Marketing,* January 2004, p. 112.

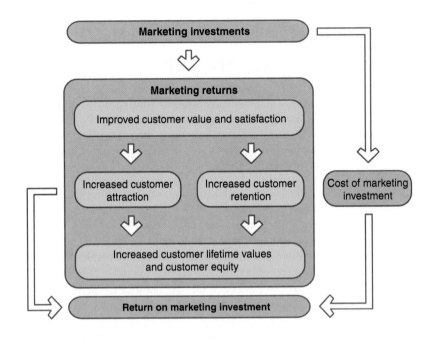

present drivers with details on how their cars are performing, the marketing dashboard gives marketers the detailed measures they need to assess and adjust their marketing strategies.[22]

Increasingly, however, beyond standard performance measures, marketers are using customer-centered measures of marketing impact, such as customer acquisition, customer retention, and customer lifetime value. Figure 2.8 views marketing expenditures as investments that produce returns in the form of more profitable customer relationships.[23] Marketing investments result in improved customer value and satisfaction, which in turn increases customer attraction and retention. This increases individual customer lifetime values and the firm's overall customer equity. Increased customer equity, in relation to the cost of the marketing investments, determines return on marketing investment.

Regardless of how it's defined or measured, the return on marketing investment concept is here to stay. "Marketing ROI is at the heart of every business," says an AT&T marketing executive. "[We've added another P to the marketing mix]—for *profit and loss* or *performance.* We absolutely have to . . . quantify the impact of marketing on the business. You can't improve what you can't measure."[24]

REST STOP REVIEWING THE CONCEPTS

In Chapter 1, we defined *marketing* and outlined the steps in the marketing process. In this chapter, we examined companywide strategic planning and marketing's role in the organization. Then, we looked more deeply into marketing strategy and the marketing mix and reviewed the major marketing management functions. So you've now had a pretty good overview of the fundamentals of modern marketing. In future chapters, we'll expand on these fundamentals.

1. Explain companywide strategic planning and its four steps.

Strategic planning sets the stage for the rest of the company's planning. Marketing contributes to strategic planning, and the overall plan defines marketing's role in the company. Although formal planning offers a variety of benefits to companies, not all companies use it or use it well.

Strategic planning involves developing a strategy for long-run survival and growth. It consists of four steps: defining the company's mission, setting objectives and goals, designing a business portfolio, and developing functional plans. *Defining a clear company mission* begins with drafting a formal mission statement, which should be market oriented, realistic, specific, motivating, and consistent with the market environment. The mission is then transformed into detailed *supporting goals and objectives* to guide the entire company. Based on those goals and objectives, headquarters designs a *business portfolio,* deciding which businesses and products should receive more or fewer resources. In turn, each business and product unit must develop *detailed marketing plans* in line with the companywide plan.

2. Discuss how to design business portfolios and develop growth strategies.

Guided by the company's mission statement and objectives, management plans its *business portfolio,* or the collection of businesses and products that make up the company. The firm wants to produce a business portfolio that best fits its strengths and weaknesses to opportunities in the environment. To do this, it must analyze and adjust its *current* business portfolio and develop growth and downsizing strategies for adjusting the *future* portfolio. The company might use a formal portfolio-planning method. But many companies are now designing more-customized portfolio-planning approaches that better suit their unique situations. The *product/market expansion grid* suggests four possible growth paths: market penetration, market development, product development, and diversification.

3. Explain marketing's role in strategic planning and how marketing works with its partners to create and deliver customer value.

Under the strategic plan, the major functional departments—marketing, finance, accounting, purchasing, operations, information systems, human resources, and others—must work together to accomplish strategic objectives. Marketing plays a key role in the company's strategic planning by providing a *marketing concept philosophy* and *inputs* regarding attractive market opportunities. Within individual business units, marketing designs *strategies* for reaching the unit's objectives and helps to carry them out profitably.

Marketers alone cannot produce superior value for customers. A company's success depends on how well each department performs its customer value-adding activities and how well the departments work together to serve the customer. Thus, marketers must practice *partner relationship management.* They must work closely with partners in other company departments to form an effective *value chain* that serves the customer.

And they must partner effectively with other companies in the marketing system to form a competitively superior *value delivery network.*

4. Describe the elements of a customer-driven marketing strategy and mix and the forces that influence it.

Consumer value and relationships are at the center of marketing strategy and programs. Through market segmentation, targeting, differentiation, and positioning, the company divides the total market into smaller segments, selects segments it can best serve, and decides how it wants to bring value to target consumers. It then designs an *integrated marketing mix* to produce the response it wants in the target market. The marketing mix consists of product, price, place, and promotion decisions.

5. List the marketing management functions, including the elements of a marketing plan, and discuss the importance of measuring and managing return on marketing investment.

To find the best strategy and mix and to put them into action, the company engages in marketing analysis, planning, implementation, and control. The main components of a *marketing plan* are the executive summary, current marketing situation, threats and opportunities, objectives and issues, marketing strategies, action programs, budgets, and controls. To plan good strategies is often easier than to carry them out. To be successful, companies must also be effective at *implementation*—turning marketing strategies into marketing actions.

Much of the responsibility for implementation goes to the company's marketing department. Marketing departments can be organized in one or a combination of ways: *functional marketing organization, geographic organization, product management organization,* or *market management organization.* In this age of customer relationships, more and more companies are now changing their organizational focus from product or territory management to customer relationship management. Marketing organizations carry out *marketing control,* both operating control and strategic control. They use *marketing audits* to determine marketing opportunities and problems and to recommend short-run and long-run actions to improve overall marketing performance.

Marketing managers must ensure that their marketing dollars are being well spent. Today's marketers face growing pressures to show that they are adding value in line with their costs. In response, marketers are developing better measures of *return on marketing investment.* Increasingly, they are using customer-centered measures of marketing impact as a key input into their strategic decision making.

Navigating the Key Terms

Business portfolio (39)
Differentiation (51)
Diversification (44)
Downsizing (44)
Growth-share matrix (40)
Market development (44)
Market penetration (42)
Market segment (48)
Market segmentation (48)

Market targeting (48)
Marketing audit (56)
Marketing control (56)
Marketing implementation (54)
Marketing mix (51)
Marketing strategy (47)
Mission statement (37)
Portfolio analysis (40)
Positioning (49)

Product development (44)
Product/market expansion grid (42)
Return on marketing investment (57)
Strategic planning (37)
SWOT analysis (52)
Value chain (45)
Value delivery network (46)

Travel Log

Discussing the Issues

1. Define strategic planning. List and briefly describe the four steps that lead managers and the firm through the strategic planning process. What role does marketing play in strategic planning? (AACSB: Communication)

2. Describe the Boston Consulting Group's approach to portfolio analysis and identify the problems associated with it. (AACSB: Communication)

3. Compare and contrast the four product/market expansion grid strategies and provide an example of each. (AACSB: Communication)

4. Discuss the differences between market segmentation, targeting, differentiation, and positioning. (AACSB: Communication)

5. Define each of the four Ps. What insights might a firm gain by considering the four Cs rather than the four Ps? (AACSB: Communication; Reflective Thinking)

6. What is return on marketing investment? Why is it difficult to measure? (AACSB: Communication; Reflective Thinking)

Application Questions

1. Explain what a SWOT analysis involves. Develop a SWOT analysis for a bank in your community. (AACSB: Communication; Reflective Thinking)

2. In a small group, visit Web sites of familiar companies (such as Nike, Kraft, or Caterpillar) until you find a company with a good mission statement. Evaluate this statement using the five attributes of a good mission statement outlined in the chapter. (AACSB: Communication; Reflective Thinking; Use of IT)

3. Unlike other advertising awards, Effie awards are not granted solely for creative execution. They are given for "Ideas that Work." Visit www.effie.org to learn about these awards and to read published case studies about winners. Present one case study to the class. (AACSB: Communication; Use of IT)

Under the Hood: Focus on Technology

Visit the Web sites of several car manufacturers and you will see the technological innovations offered with today's vehicles. From GPS navigation systems to audio and DVD entertainment systems, advanced technologies are enhancing today's car-owning experience. Microsoft, known mostly for its computer operating systems, has been working with Fiat to develop a new "infotainment" system known as Blue&Me. Currently offered only in limited Fiat models, the system integrates mobile phones, MP3 players, and an Internet connection through controls mounted on the steering wheel. The new technology will also contain a navigation system, weather and traffic forecasts, and antitheft devices.

1. According to the product/market expansion grid, which strategy best describes Microsoft's expansion into automobile applications? (AACSB: Communication; Use of IT; Reflective Thinking)

2. How is Fiat an important member of Microsoft's value delivery network? (AACSB: Communication; Reflective Thinking)

Focus on Ethics

You've learned that a customer-driven marketing strategy incorporates market segmentation, targeting, differentiation, and positioning. Procter & Gamble excels at developing offerings based on customer-driven marketing. It markets more than 100 different brands in more than 20 consumer-product categories. For example, P&G offers seven brands of body wash and soaps, six brands of laundry detergent, and three brands of dish soap. Each brand is targeted to satisfy the needs of a specific market segment. But are consumers' needs really that different when it comes to cleaning our bodies, clothes, or dishes? Or is the company simply creating meaningless product differences to hype in its advertising to consumers?

1. Go to www.pg.com to learn about the brands offered by P&G. Select one product category in which P&G offers multiple brands. What is P&G's positioning for each brand in that product category? Then, visit a store and record the prices of each brand, using a common basis such as price per ounce. Write a brief report on what you learn. Are there meaningful positioning differences between the brands? Are any price differences you find justified? (AACSB: Communication; Reflective Thinking)

2. Some marketing critics argue that many such products are simply commodities and no one brand is better than another. Are their real differences in the actual formulations of the P&G brands you investigated? Is it right for P&G to position brands in a way that consumers perceive them to be different and then price them accordingly? (AACSB: Communication; Ethical Reasoning)

Video Case

Mayo Clinic

The Mayo Clinic has a long history of providing health care. But more important, the Mayo Clinic has demonstrated innovation. It has pioneered or perfected many medical procedures, focused on accumulating and creating medical knowledge, and revolutionized health care organization by developing the group practice concept. The Mayo clinic perfected the human side of medicine to deepen the relationship with customers. It now treats more than 600,000 patients every year. Because of its focus on the customer, patients are quick to extol the virtues of the clinic and the medical miracles performed therein.

Although the Mayo Clinic thrived for decades without a formal marketing effort, in 1999 it formed an Office of Brand Management to help build its brand and foster positive perceptions. This has led the clinic to partner with numerous third-party companies in order to take the organization and the brand in new directions, serving the customer base in ever-expanding ways.

After viewing the video featuring the Mayo Clinic, answer the following questions about its marketing strategy.

1. What is the Mayo Clinic's mission? Who are its target customers and what is its relationship with these customers?

2. What is the Mayo Clinic's marketing mix? Discuss how the organization manages its marketing mix within its marketing strategy.

3. How are the Mayo Clinic's partnering activities helping it to achieve its mission and strategy?

BE OPEN TO NEW POSSIBILITIES.

NEW ASIAN SALAD   i'm lovin' it®

After studying this chapter, you should be able to

1. describe the environmental forces that affect the company's ability to serve its customers
2. explain how changes in the demographic and economic environments affect marketing decisions
3. identify the major trends in the firm's natural and technological environments
4. explain the key changes in the political and cultural environments
5. discuss how companies can react to the marketing environment

CHAPTER 3

Analyzing the Marketing Environment

ROAD MAP Previewing the Concepts

In Part 1 (Chapters 1 and 2), you learned about the basic concepts of marketing and the steps in the marketing process for building profitable relationships with targeted consumers. In Part 2, we'll look deeper into the first step of the marketing process—understanding the marketplace and customer needs and wants. In this chapter, you'll discover that marketing does not operate in a vacuum but rather in a complex and changing environment. Other *actors* in this environment—suppliers, intermediaries, customers, competitors, publics, and others—may work with or against the company. Major environmental *forces*—demographic, economic, natural, technological, political, and cultural—shape marketing opportunities, pose threats, and affect the company's ability to serve customers and develop lasting relationships with them. To understand marketing, and to develop effective marketing strategies, you must first understand the environment in which marketing operates.

First, we'll look at an American icon, McDonald's. More than half a century ago, Ray Kroc spotted an important shift in U.S. consumer lifestyles and bought a small chain of restaurants. He built that chain into the vast McDonald's fast-food empire. But although the shifting marketing environment brought opportunities for McDonald's, it has also created challenges.

I n 1955, Ray Kroc, a 52-year-old salesman of milk-shake-mixing machines, discovered a string of seven restaurants owned by Richard and Maurice McDonald. Kroc saw the McDonald brothers' fast-food concept as a perfect fit for America's increasingly on-the-go, time-squeezed, family-oriented lifestyles. Kroc bought the small chain for $2.7 million and the rest is history.

McDonald's grew quickly to become the world's largest fast-feeder. Its more than 31,000 restaurants worldwide now serve 52 million customers each day, racking up systemwide sales of almost $60 billion annually. The Golden Arches are one of the world's most familiar symbols, and other than Santa Claus, no character in the world is more recognizable than Ronald McDonald. "By making fast food respectable for middle-class families," says one industry analyst, "the Golden Arches did for greasy spoons what Holiday Inn did for roadside motels in the 1950s and what Sam Walton later did for the discount retail store." Says another, "McDonald's is much more than an ordinary fast-food chain. It is a cultural mirror [that] reflects the evolution of American eating habits."

But just as the changing marketplace has provided opportunities for McDonald's, it has also presented challenges. In fact, by early in this decade, the once-shiny Golden Arches had lost some of their luster, as the company struggled to address shifting consumer lifestyles. While McDonald's remained the nation's most visited fast-food chain, its sales growth slumped, and its market share fell by more than 3 percent between 1997 and 2003. In 2002, the company posted its first-ever quarterly loss.

What happened? In this age of obesity lawsuits and $5 lattes, McDonald's seemed a bit out of step with the times. Consumers were looking for fresher, better-tasting food and more upscale atmospheres. As a result, McDonald's was losing share to what the industry calls "fast-casual" restaurants. New competitors such as Panera Bread, Baja Fresh, Pret a Manger, and Cosi were offering more-imaginative meals in more-fashionable surroundings. And for busy consumers who'd rather "eat-out-in," even the local supermarket offered a full selection of preprepared, ready-to-serve gourmet meals to go.

Americans were also seeking healthier eating options. Fast-food patrons complained about too few healthy menu choices. Worried about their health, many customers were eating less at fast-food restaurants. As the market leader, McDonald's bore the brunt of much of this criticism. In one lawsuit, the parents of two teenage girls even charged that McDonald's was responsible for their children's obesity and related health problems, including diabetes.

Reacting to these challenges, in early 2003, McDonald's announced a turnaround plan—the "Plan to Win"—to better align the company with the new marketplace realities. The plan included the following initiatives:

Back to Basics—McDonald's began refocusing on what made it successful: consistent products and reliable service. It began pouring money back into existing stores, speeding up service, training employees, and monitoring restaurants to make sure they stay bright and clean. It's also "re-imaging" its restaurants, with clean, simple, more-modern interiors and amenities such as live plants, wireless Internet access, and flat-screen TVs showing cable news. McDonald's now promises to be a "forever young" brand.

If You Can't Lick 'Em, Join 'Em—To find new ways to compete better with the new breed of fast-casual competitors, and to expand its customer base, McDonald's has experimented with new restaurant concepts. For example, it has opened more than 1,000 attached *McCafé* coffee shops in 34 countries, which offer leather seating, a knowledgeable staff, and espresso in porcelain cups, along with made-to-order drinks, muffins, pastries, and gourmet sandwiches. Kids can still get their Happy Meals but parents can feast on more sophisticated fare.

*"It's what i **eat** and what i **do** . . . i'm lovin' it"*—McDonald's has unveiled a major multifaceted education campaign to help consumers better understand the keys to living balanced, active lifestyles. The "it's what i **eat** and what i **do** . . . i'm lovin' it" theme underscores the important interplay between eating right and staying active. The company assembled a Global Advisory Council of outside experts in the areas of nutrition, wellness, and activity to provide input on its menu choice and variety, education outreach, and promoting physical fitness. A trimmer, fitter Ronald McDonald has expanded his role as Chief Happiness Officer to be global ambassador of fun, fitness, and children's well-being, inspiring and encouraging kids and families around the world to eat well and stay active. McDonald's has also refreshed its Web site to offer tips on how to lead a balanced active lifestyle, and last year McDonald's became the first restaurant chain to place nutritional information on its packaging. Even the harshest McDonald's critics, although still skeptical, applaud these actions.

Improving the Fare—McDonald's has worked to provide more choice and variety on its menu. For example, it introduced a "Go Active! Happy Meal" for adults, featuring a Premium Salad, a bottle of Dasani water, and a "Stepometer," which measures physical activity by tracking daily steps. It now offers Chicken McNuggets made with white meat, Chicken Selects whole-breast strips, low-fat "milk jugs," and a line of salads, such as its Fruit & Walnut Salad, consisting of apple slices with a side of low-fat vanilla yogurt and candied walnuts. Within only a year of introducing its salads, McDonald's became the world's largest salad seller—it has sold more than 516 million salads to date.

McDonald's efforts to realign itself with the changing marketing environment have paid off handsomely. By almost any measure, the fast-food giant is now back in shape. The company is posting steady, even startling, sales and profit increases. Since announcing its Plan to Win, McDonald's has increased its sales by 42 percent and profits have almost quadrupled. The fast-food giant now commands nearly half of the U.S. burger market, three times more than either Burger King or Wendy's. It looks like customers and stockholders alike are humming the chain's catchy jingle, "I'm lovin' it."

McDonald's knows that as the marketing environment changes, the company must change with it. "We've learned. We've evolved. We think we've cracked the code," says McDonald's CEO James Skinner. "We're always evolving to meet the changing needs of our customers."[1]

Marketers need to be good at building relationships with customers, others in the company, and external partners. To do this effectively, however, they must understand the major environmental forces that surround all of these relationships. A company's **marketing environment** consists of the actors and forces outside marketing that affect marketing management's ability to build and maintain successful relationships with target customers. Like McDonald's, successful companies know the vital importance of constantly watching and adapting to the changing environment.

More than any other group in the company, marketers must be the environmental trend trackers and opportunity seekers. Although every manager in an organization needs to observe the outside environment, marketers have two special aptitudes. They have disciplined methods—marketing research and marketing intelligence—for collecting information about the marketing environment. They also spend more time in the customer and competitor environments. By carefully studying the environment, marketers can adapt their strategies to meet new marketplace challenges and opportunities.

The marketing environment is made up of a *microenvironment* and a *macroenvironment*. The **microenvironment** consists of the actors close to the company that affect its ability to serve its customers—the company, suppliers, marketing intermediaries, customer markets, competitors, and publics. The **macroenvironment** consists of the larger societal forces that affect the microenvironment—demographic, economic, natural, technological, political, and cultural forces. We look first at the company's microenvironment.

Marketing environment
The actors and forces outside marketing that affect marketing management's ability to build and maintain successful relationships with target customers.

Microenvironment
The actors close to the company that affect its ability to serve its customers—the company, suppliers, marketing intermediaries, customer markets, competitors, and publics.

Macroenvironment
The larger societal forces that affect the microenvironment—demographic, economic, natural, technological, political, and cultural forces.

The Company's Microenvironment

Marketing management's job is to build relationships with customers by creating customer value and satisfaction. However, marketing managers cannot do this alone. Figure 3.1 shows the major actors in the marketer's microenvironment. Marketing success will require building relationships with other company departments, suppliers, marketing intermediaries, customers, competitors, and various publics, which combine to make up the company's value delivery network.

The Company

In designing marketing plans, marketing management takes other company groups into account—groups such as top management, finance, research and development (R&D), purchasing, operations, and accounting. All these interrelated groups form the internal environment. Top management sets the company's mission, objectives, broad strategies, and policies. Marketing managers make decisions within the strategies and plans made by top management. As we discussed in Chapter 2, marketing managers must work closely with other company departments. Other departments have an impact on the marketing department's plans and actions. And under the marketing concept, all of these functions must "think consumer." They should work in harmony to provide superior customer value and relationships.

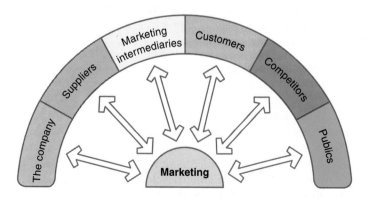

FIGURE 3.1
Actors in the Microenvironment

Suppliers

Suppliers form an important link in the company's overall customer value delivery system. They provide the resources needed by the company to produce its goods and services. Supplier problems can seriously affect marketing. Marketing managers must watch supply availability—supply shortages or delays, labor strikes, and other events can cost sales in the short run and damage customer satisfaction in the long run. Marketing managers also monitor the price trends of their key inputs. Rising supply costs may force price increases that can harm the company's sales volume.

Most marketers today treat their suppliers as partners in creating and delivering customer value. Wal-Mart goes to great lengths to work with its suppliers. For example, it helps them to test new products in its stores. And its Supplier Development Department publishes a *Supplier Proposal Guide* and maintains a supplier Web site, both of which help suppliers to navigate the complex Wal-Mart buying process. "Wal-Mart talks tough and remains a demanding customer," says one supplier executive, but "it also helps you get there."[2] It knows that good partner relationship management results in success for Wal-Mart, suppliers, and, ultimately, its customers.

Marketing Intermediaries

Marketing intermediaries

Firms that help the company to promote, sell, and distribute its goods to final buyers.

Marketing intermediaries help the company to promote, sell, and distribute its products to final buyers. They include resellers, physical distribution firms, marketing services agencies, and financial intermediaries. *Resellers* are distribution channel firms that help the company find customers or make sales to them. These include wholesalers and retailers who buy and resell merchandise. Selecting and partnering with resellers is not easy. No longer do manufacturers have many small, independent resellers from which to choose. They now face large and growing reseller organizations such as Wal-Mart, Target, Home Depot, Costco, and Best Buy. These organizations frequently have enough power to dictate terms or even shut smaller manufacturers out of large markets.

Physical distribution firms help the company to stock and move goods from their points of origin to their destinations. Working with warehouse and transportation firms, a company must determine the best ways to store and ship goods, balancing factors such as cost, delivery, speed, and safety. *Marketing services agencies* are the marketing research firms, advertising agencies, media firms, and marketing consulting firms that help the company target and promote its products to the right markets. *Financial intermediaries* include banks, credit companies, insurance companies, and other businesses that help finance transactions or insure against the risks associated with the buying and selling of goods.

Like suppliers, marketing intermediaries form an important component of the company's overall value delivery system. In its quest to create satisfying customer relationships, the company must do more than just optimize its own performance. It must partner effectively with marketing intermediaries to optimize the performance of the entire system.

Thus, today's marketers recognize the importance of working with their intermediaries as partners rather than simply as channels through which they sell their products. For example, when Coca-Cola signs on as the exclusive beverage provider for a fast-food chain, such as McDonald's, Wendy's, or Subway, it provides much more than just soft drinks. It also pledges powerful marketing support.

> Coke assigns cross-functional teams dedicated to understanding the finer points of each retail partner's business. It conducts a staggering amount of research on beverage consumers and shares these insights with its partners. It analyzes the demographics of U.S. zip code areas and helps partners to determine which Coke brands are preferred in their areas. Coca-Cola has even studied the design of drive-through menu boards to better understand which layouts, fonts, letter sizes, colors, and visuals induce consumers to order more food and drink. Based on such insights, the Coca-Cola FoodService group develops marketing programs and merchandising tools that help its retail partners to improve their beverage sales and

profits. For example, it recently created its Ponle Mas Sabor Con Coca-Cola program designed to help retail partners take full advantage of opportunities in the fast-growing Hispanic market. Coca-Cola FoodService's Web site, www.CokeSolutions.com, provides retailers with a wealth of information, business solutions, and merchandising tips. Such intense partnering efforts have made Coca-Cola a runaway leader in the U.S. fountain soft-drink market.[3]

■ Partnering with intermediaries: Coca-Cola pledges powerful marketing support to its retail partners. The CokeSolutions.com Web site provides retailers with a wealth of information, business solutions, and merchandising tips

Customers

The company needs to study five types of customer markets closely. *Consumer markets* consist of individuals and households that buy goods and services for personal consumption. *Business markets* buy goods and services for further processing or for use in their production process, whereas *reseller markets* buy goods and services to resell at a profit. *Government markets* are made up of government agencies that buy goods and services to produce public services or transfer the goods and services to others who need them. Finally, *international markets* consist of those buyers in other countries, including consumers, producers, resellers, and governments. Each market type has special characteristics that call for careful study by the seller.

Competitors

The marketing concept states that to be successful, a company must provide greater customer value and satisfaction than its competitors do. Thus, marketers must do more than simply adapt to the needs of target consumers. They also must gain strategic advantage by positioning their offerings strongly against competitors' offerings in the minds of consumers.

No single competitive marketing strategy is best for all companies. Each firm should consider its own size and industry position compared to those of its competitors. Large firms with dominant positions in an industry can use certain strategies that smaller firms cannot afford. But being large is not enough. There are winning strategies for large firms, but there are also losing ones. And small firms can develop strategies that give them better rates of return than large firms enjoy.

Publics

The company's marketing environment also includes various publics. A **public** is any group that has an actual or potential interest in or impact on an organization's ability to achieve its objectives. We can identify seven types of publics.

Public

Any group that has an actual or potential interest in or impact on an organization's ability to achieve its objectives.

- *Financial publics* influence the company's ability to obtain funds. Banks, investment houses, and stockholders are the major financial publics.
- *Media publics* carry news, features, and editorial opinion. They include newspapers, magazines, and radio and television stations.
- *Government publics*. Management must take government developments into account. Marketers must often consult the company's lawyers on issues of product safety, truth in advertising, and other matters.
- *Citizen-action publics*. A company's marketing decisions may be questioned by consumer organizations, environmental groups, minority groups, and others. Its public relations department can help it stay in touch with consumer and citizen groups.
- *Local publics* include neighborhood residents and community organizations. Large companies usually appoint a community relations officer to deal with the community, attend meetings, answer questions, and contribute to worthwhile causes.

"Nothing is impossible"

is the motto that drives Carol Olney. Her spirited approach is why her peers have chosen her to be Wal-Mart's 2004 National Teacher of the Year. This honor has earned her school a $25,000 donation from Wal-Mart to recognize the education and inspiration she provides her special-needs students.

Caring about education means supporting it. More than $4 million was awarded to 3,600 schools of Local and State Teachers of the Year by their neighborhood Wal-Mart stores and SAM'S CLUBs in 2004. This year Wal-Mart will give back more than $150 million overall to the communities we serve.

Visit us on the Web at www.walmartfoundation.org.

■ Publics: Wal-Mart's Good WORKS efforts, such as the Wal-Mart Teacher of the Year program, recognize the importance of community publics.

Demography
The study of human populations in terms of size, density, location, age, gender, race, occupation, and other statistics.

- *General public.* A company needs to be concerned about the general public's attitude toward its products and activities. The public's image of the company affects its buying.
- *Internal publics* include workers, managers, volunteers, and the board of directors. Large companies use newsletters and other means to inform and motivate their internal publics. When employees feel good about their company, this positive attitude spills over to external publics.

A company can prepare marketing plans for these major publics as well as for its customer markets. Suppose the company wants a specific response from a particular public, such as goodwill, favorable word of mouth, or donations of time or money. The company would need to design an offer to this public that is attractive enough to produce the desired response.

The Company's Macroenvironment

The company and all of the other actors operate in a larger macroenvironment of forces that shape opportunities and pose threats to the company. Figure 3.2 shows the six major forces in the company's macroenvironment. In the remaining sections of this chapter, we examine these forces and show how they affect marketing plans.

Demographic Environment

Demography is the study of human populations in terms of size, density, location, age, gender, race, occupation, and other statistics. The demographic environment is of major interest to marketers because it involves people, and people make up markets. The world population is growing at an explosive rate. It now exceeds 6.6 billion people and will grow to 8.1 billion by the year 2030.[4] The world's large and highly diverse population poses both opportunities and challenges.

Changes in the world demographic environment have major implications for business. For example, consider China. More than a quarter century ago, to curb its skyrocketing population, the Chinese government passed regulations limiting families to one child each. As a result, Chinese children—known as "little emperors and empresses"—have been showered with attention and luxuries under what's known as the "six-pocket syndrome."

FIGURE 3.2

Major Forces in the Company's Macroenvironment

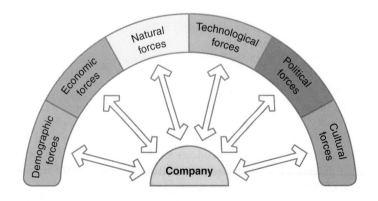

As many as six adults—two parents and four doting grandparents—may be indulging the whims of each only child.

The little emperors, now ranging in age from newborns to mid-twenties, are affecting markets for everything from children's products to financial services, restaurants, and luxury goods. Parents with only children at home now spend about 40 percent of their income on their cherished child, creating huge market opportunities for children's educational products. For example, Time Warner targeted the lucrative Chinese coddled-kiddies market with an interactive language course called English Time, a 200-lesson, 40-CD set that takes as long as four years for a child to complete. The course sells for $3,300, more than a year's salary for many Chinese parents.[5]

At the other end of the spectrum, Starbucks is targeting China's older little emperors, positioning itself as a new kind of informal but indulgent meeting place.[6]

> China's one-child rule created a generation who have been pampered by parents and grandparents and have the means to make indulgent purchases. Instead of believing in traditional Chinese collective goals, these young people embrace individuality. "Their view of this world is very different," says the president of Starbucks Greater China. "They have never gone through the hardships of our generation." Starbucks is in sync with that, he says, given its customized drinks, personalized service, and original music compilations.

■ Demographics and business: China's one-child rule has created a generation that has been pampered by parents and grandparents and that has the means to make indulgent purchases, creating opportunities for marketers.

Interestingly, the one-child policy is creating another major Chinese demographic development—a rapidly aging population. In what some deem a potential "demographic earthquake," by 2024 an estimated 58 percent of the Chinese population will be over age 40. And because of the one-child policy, close to 75 percent of all Chinese households will be childless, either because they chose to have no children or because their only child has left the nest. The result is an aging society that will need to be more self-reliant, which in turn will cause a large growth in service markets such as senior education, leisure clubs, and nursing homes.[7]

Thus, marketers keep close track of demographic trends and developments in their markets, both at home and abroad. They track changing age and family structures, geographic population shifts, educational characteristics, and population diversity. Here, we discuss the most important demographic trends in the United States.

Changing Age Structure of the Population The U.S. population stood at over 302 million in 2007 and may reach almost 364 million by the year 2030.[8] The single most important demographic trend in the United States is the changing age structure of the population. The U.S. population contains several generational groups. Here, we discuss the three largest groups—the baby boomers, Generation X, and the Millennials—and their impact on today's marketing strategies.

The Baby Boomers The post-World War II baby boom produced 78 million **baby boomers**, born between 1946 and 1964. Over the years, the baby boomers have been one of the most powerful forces shaping the marketing environment. Today's baby boomers account for nearly 30 percent of the population, spend about $2.3 trillion annually, and hold three-quarters of the nation's financial assets.[9]

The youngest boomers are now in their early-to-mid forties; the oldest are entering their sixties. The maturing boomers are rethinking the purpose and value of their work, responsibilities, and relationships. As they reach their peak earning and spending years, the

Baby boomers
The 78 million people born during the baby boom following World War II and lasting until 1964.

boomers constitute a lucrative market for financial services, new housing and home re-modeling, travel and entertainment, eating out, health and fitness products, and just about everything else.

It would be a mistake to think of the boomers as aging and slowing down. In fact, the boomers are spending $30 billion a year on *anti* aging products and services. And unlike previous generations, boomers are likely to retire later and work more after final retirement. Rather than viewing themselves as phasing out, they see themselves as entering new life phases. According to one observer:[10]

> The boomers thrive on change and reinvention. They did not grow up with the Internet, but they readily go online to plot out vacations and seek bargains. They grew up with television, but they have embraced TiVO and VCRs and other technologies that let them scoot past commercials. They may not like rap music, but they'll listen to their own music on the same types of iPods that their children use. The older boomers get, the younger they seem to feel. . . . They see retirement not as an end but as just another stage in life.

Toyota recognizes these changing boomer life phases. Ads for its Toyota Highlander show empty-nest boomers and declare "For your newfound freedom." Similarly, Curves fitness centers targets older women, but not grandmas in rocking chairs. Curves' older regulars "want to be strong and fit," says the expert. "They just don't want to go into Gold's Gym and be surrounded by spandex-clad Barbie dolls."[11] Similarly, cosmetics brands such as Dove, L'Oreal, Cover Girl, and Olay use 50- or 60-something spokesmodels such as Diane Keaton and Christie Brinkley to appeal to boomer women. And they use sensible, aspirational appeals aimed at confident older consumers who aren't trying to fight the aging process. "Boomers are saying, 'I'm aging, but I'm going to do it in a way that's graceful and still about who I am,'" says a marketer for Unilever's Dove Pro-Age brand.[12]

Perhaps no one is targeting the baby boomers more fervently than the financial services industry. In coming years, the aging boomers will transfer some $30 trillion in retirement nest eggs and other savings into new investments. They'll also be inheriting $8 trillion as their parents pass away. Thus, the boomers will be needing lots of money management help. An Ameriprise Financial marketer explains, "It's not just about the rational numbers. It's about how you are going to reinvent yourself for what could be 30 or 40 years of retirement." An Ameriprise ad promises retiring boomers that the company will "help you envision what exactly you want to do in the next phase of your life."[13] (See Marketing at Work 3.1.)

Generation X   The baby boom was followed by a "birth dearth," creating another generation of 49 million people born between 1965 and 1976. Author Douglas Coupland calls them **Generation X** because they lie in the shadow of the boomers and lack obvious distinguishing characteristics. Others call them the "baby busters" or the "generation caught in the middle" (between the larger baby boomers and later Millennials).

The Generation Xers are defined as much by their shared experiences as by their age. Increasing parental divorce rates and higher employment for their mothers made them the first generation of latchkey kids. Having grown up during times of recession and corporate downsizing, they developed a more cautious economic outlook. They care about the environment and respond favorably to socially responsible companies. Although they seek success, they are less materialistic; they prize experience, not acquisition. They are cautious romantics who want a better quality of life and are more interested in job satisfaction than in sacrificing personal happiness and growth for promotion. For many of the 30 million Gen Xers that are parents, family comes first, career second.[14]

The Gen Xers are a more skeptical bunch. "Marketing to Gen Xers is difficult," says one marketer, "and it's all about word of mouth. You can't tell them you're good, and they have zero interest in a slick brochure that says so. . . . They have a lot of 'filters' in place." Another marketer agrees: "Sixty-three percent of this group will research products before they consider a purchase. [They are also] creating extensive communities to exchange information. Even though nary a handshake occurs, the information swap is trusted and thus is more powerful than any marketing pitch ever could be.[15]

Generation X
The 45 million people born between 1965 and 1976 in the "birth dearth" following the baby boom.

3.1 MARKETING AT WORK
Ameriprise Financial: Still a Boomer Market

As the largest demographic bulge in America's history, the baby boomers have always been a hot market to companies across a wide range of industries. These days, as the boomers reach their peak earning years and look ahead toward retirement, they've become downright irresistible to the financial services industry. In fact, Ameriprise Financial, a long-standing firm (formerly American Express Financial Advisors) with a new brand name and a fresh new start, is pretty much staking its future on cultivating the baby boomers. Its entire positioning rests on a bedrock of helping the aging boomers to realize their preretirement and retirement experiences through its Dream > Plan > Track approach to financial planning.

The baby boomers make up a huge and growing financial services market. Ameriprise Financial estimates that America's 41 million affluent and mass-affluent households hold more than $19 trillion in investable assets. More than half of these affluent households are headed by baby boomers. What's more, the first boomers, now in their 60s, will initiate a retirement gold rush that will continue for more than two decades. By the time that the last boomer turns 65 in 2029, the boomers will control more than 40 percent of the nation's disposable income. During that time and beyond, the boomers will need a heap of financial planning help.

Consequently, whereas the eyes of marketers in some industries are now wandering toward the younger and fresher Millennials generation, the aging boomers comprise the bulk of revenues for Ameriprise Financial and other financial services firms. According to one expert, "If you are in the financial services industry, *this* is the baby-boomer decade."

But Ameriprise Financial knows that the boomers are very different from previous generations of preretirees and that connecting with them will require a deep understanding of what makes them tick. The image of the doddering old fool in mismatched flannel, pouring lemonade for the grandkids simply doesn't resonate with today's boomer consumer. The boomers don't think of themselves as getting old. And they don't think of themselves as retiring—it's more like shifting gears and striking out in new directions. The boomers won't need help just managing their money, they'll need help planning for and realizing life's next phases. For Ameriprise Financial, says the company's CEO, "it all begins with understanding our client's dreams." And "Dreams don't retire."

To better understand just what those retirement dreams entail, Ameriprise Financial linked up with baby-boomer experts to conduct a large-scale New Retirement Mindscape study. It learned that retirement is characterized by five distinct stages, such as Imagination (the 6 to 15 years preceding retirement when people envision the retirement they want) and Liberation (the year following retirement when people begin reconnecting with their families, pursuing hobbies, traveling, and starting new businesses). Another key finding was that people want a financial advisor who understands them—this was rated just as important as return on their investments.

■ Targeting the baby boomers: The positioning of Ameriprise Financial rests on a bedrock of helping the boomers to discover and realize their retirement dreams. And "Dreams don't retire."

Based on these findings, Ameriprise Financial developed a *Dream Book* guide that helps boomers to explore their retirement dreams and create a life strategy for retirement. It's "the best book on retirement—the one you'll write—that will help you get to a retirement defined by your dreams." The *Dream Book* guide becomes one of the first steps in the *Dream > Plan > Track* approach to financial planning through which more than 12,500 personal advisors from Ameriprise Financial form long-term relationships with clients. So far, the company has distributed more than a million of the popular planning guides.

Ameriprise Financial also used the New Retirement Mindscape study results to shape an innovative "Dreams don't retire" advertising campaign. The new campaign shuns the typical industry "Are *you* ready for retirement?" message of fear. Instead, it focuses on the positive, aspirational aspects of retirement—on what's next. The first phase of the ad campaign features 1960s icon Dennis Hopper, star of boomer-era counterculture classics such as *Easy Rider*. At 70 years old, Hopper himself is not a boomer. But boomers see him as an older brother type, one who has lived true to himself and done things his own way.

In the ads, Hopper talks plainly about what retirement means before the action shifts to boomers tackling ambitious retirement tasks, such as building a boat or designing an eco-friendly new home. One commercial, set in a field of yellow daisies, hits the old flower-power boomers right where they live. Speaking and looking directly into the lens, an impassioned Hopper says, "Some people say that dreams are like delicate little flowers. Wrong! Dreams are powerful. Dreams are what make you say 'When I'm 64, I'm going to start a new business. I want to make my own movie.' Flower power was then—your dreams are now."

(continues)

In another commercial, Hopper stands on an expansive white-sand ocean beach reading from a dictionary. "To withdraw, to go away, to disappear—that's how the dictionary defines retirement," he intones. Tossing the dictionary aside, he continues, "Time to redefine! Your generation is definitely not headed for bingo night. In fact, you can write a book about how you're going to turn retirement upside-down. I just don't see you playing shuffleboard—'ya know what I mean? The thing about dreams is—they don't retire." All of the ads employ a 1960s-style red chair as a visual icon. The chair symbolizes the launching pad for boomers' retirement dreams—it is an "anti-rocking chair."

The boomer-focused campaign has hit the right target with the right message. Although they scored low with the general audience, the ads hit it big with boomers. Half of the target group liked the ads a lot or somewhat, and 79 percent rated the ads as very effective or somewhat effective (both very good numbers, given that they're, well, ads). Perhaps more important, thanks to the campaign, the newly minted Ameriprise Financial brand achieved over 40 percent awareness in just eight months. And the company experienced double-digit sales and profits growth in the year following the start of the campaign. "We know that these ads are striking a chord," says the chief marketing officer for Ameriprise Financial.

According to an industry analyst, "Ameriprise Financial looks well on the way to securing a perch among the largest financial service providers serving baby boomers headed for retirement—it's a sleeping giant." But when it comes to catering to baby boomers, this giant isn't napping. It's working face to face with more than two million clients, "Putting millions of dreams on track. One dream at a time." As one ad promises: "What do you dream of doing in retirement? Maybe you want to go back to school. Start a second career. Visit the Spanish Steps. Work on that short game. Or maybe you're not even sure.... Ameriprise Financial [will help you] envision what exactly you want to do in the next phase of your life ... and develop a plan to help get you there."

Sources: Quotes and other information from Laura Petrecca, "More Marketers Target Boomers' Eyes, Wallets," *USA Today*, February 26, 2007; "New Evolution of Ameriprise Financial Advertising Emphasizes That 'Dreams Don't Retire,'" September 7, 2006, accessed at www.ameriprise.com; Jack Willoughby, "Ameriprise Comes Alive," *Wall Street Journal*, August 27, 2006; Claudia H. Deutsch, "Not Getting Older, Just More Scrutinized," *New York Times*, October 11, 2006, accessed at www.nyt.com; Lisa Shidler, "Baby Boomers Are Tough Customers," *Investment News*, March 12, 2007, p. 28; and annual reports and various pages at www.ameriprise.com, accessed September 2007.

Once labeled as "the MTV generation" and viewed as body-piercing slackers who whined about "McJobs," the Gen Xers have grown up and are now taking over. The Gen Xers are displacing the lifestyles, culture, and materialistic values of the baby boomers. They represent close to $1.4 trillion in annual purchasing power. With so much potential, many companies are focusing on Gen Xers as an important target segment. For example, Hyatt will soon open an international hotel chain named Andaz targeting Gen X business travelers.[16]

Hyatt is positioning Andaz as an unpretentious upscale hotel catering to customers looking for fresh, uncomplicated luxury that is timeless and gimmick-free. Andaz is squarely aimed at the maturing Generation X market. Gen Xers are now evolving from their grungy 20th-century adolescence and rapidly becoming the major market segment for business travel. Like all great demographic segments, they demand alternative brands to those patronized by their parents—the baby boomers. Xers are notoriously uncomfortable with generic global brands and prefer to seek out local specialties and experiences instead. Whereas their parents might prefer hotels with identical bathrooms from Amsterdam to Zurich, Xers like to celebrate local differences. Andaz will attempt to cater to this by allowing each of its hotels to celebrate their local autonomy through different designs and offerings. In fact, the word Andaz means personal style. Andaz will also cater to the Xer market by offering organic food and environmentally sound operating principles. The first U.S. Andaz hotel will be located on New York City's Wall Street. Hyatt pitches the new hotel as a "luxury lifestyle brand" that "expresses individual style and personal independence in an environment of casual elegance. It offers local personality, innovative design, and a relaxed atmosphere, plus unpretentious, responsive, personalized service."

Millennials (or Generation Y)
The 83 million children of the baby boomers, born between 1977 and 2000.

Millennials Both the baby boomers and Gen Xers will one day be passing the reins to the **Millennials** (also called Generation Y or the echo boomers). Born between 1977 and 2000, these children of the baby boomers number 83 million, dwarfing the Gen Xers and larger even than the baby boomer segment. This groups includes several age cohorts: *tweens* (aged 8–12), *teens* (13–18); and *young adults* (the twenty-somethings). The younger Millennials are just beginning to wield their buying power. The older ones have now graduated from college and are moving up in their careers, significantly expanding both their earning and their spending. The Millennials are a diverse bunch. Whereas the baby boomers were 80 percent white, 45 percent of Millennials describe their race as something other than white.[17]

One thing that all of the Millennials have in common is their utter fluency and comfort with computer, digital, and Internet technology. "Whereas Gen X spent a lot of time in front of the TV," says one expert, the Millennials "are always 'on.' They're consumers of every imaginable means of communication: TV, radio, cell phone, Internet, video games—often simultaneously."[18] Here's a typical Millennial profile:[19]

A. J. Hunter can't start the day without first pulling out his laptop. Each morning, the 21-year-old Ball State University junior downloads his schedule onto his Mac Powerbook, which—along with his iPod and cell phone—is always close at hand. Hunter is a typical tech-savvy college student. He can access the social networking site Facebook from his cell phone. He uses e-mail and instant messaging anywhere on the wireless campus. He downloads music to his laptop and his iPod, and he uses a 2-gigabyte flash drive provided by the university to transfer files and songs and to access his digital portfolio. Technology is so second nature, "I can't even think of when I use it and when I don't. It's such a part of life," he says. Hunter isn't a techno-geek. He's just a "digital native"—a term that has been used to describe Millennials, the first generation who grew up in a world filled with computers, cell phones, cable TV, and online social networks.

■ The Millennials are always "on." They're consumers of every imaginable means of communication: TV, radio, cellphone, PC, Internet, video games—often simultaneously.

Each Millennial segment constitutes a huge and attractive market. However, reaching these message-saturated segments effectively requires creative marketing approaches. For example, the automobile industry is aggressively targeting this new generation of car buyers. By 2010, the Millennials will buy one of every four new cars sold in the United States. Toyota even created a completely new brand—the Scion—targeted to Millennials, along with a new approach for marketing it.[20]

Scion's success depended on understanding the new Millennial generation, one that demands authenticity, respect for their time, and products built just for them. So Toyota positioned the Scion on *personalization*. It appealed to the new youth-culture club of "tuners," young fans of tricked-out vehicles (such as BMW's wildly successful Mini Cooper) who wanted to customize their cars from bumper to bumper. The Scion offers a host of options that allow lots of room for self-expression. According to a Scion marketer, the spunky little car is a "blank canvas on which the consumer can make the car what they would like it to be."

To speak to the Millennials, Toyota shunned traditional marketing approaches and instead focused on creating buzz. Scion's young marketing team held "ride-and-drive" events to generate spontaneous test drives. It put brochures in alternative publications such as *Urb* and *Tokion*, and it sponsored events at venues ranging from hip-hop nightclubs and urban pubs to library lawns. And, of course, Scion maintains a heavy presence on all of the Millennials' favorite digital haunts, from videos on YouTube and cell phone text messages to social networking sites such as MySpace, Gaia Online, and Whyville. "We want to [reach out to these younger buyers] without shouting 'buy this car,'" says the Scion marketer. Thanks to such innovative targeting and marketing, Toyota now sells some 170,000 Scions a year, almost three times its initial annual target. Most importantly, the Scion is bringing a new generation of buyers into the Toyota family.

Generational Marketing Do marketers need to create separate products and marketing programs for each generation? Some experts warn that marketers need to be careful about turning off one generation each time they craft a product or message that appeals effectively to another. Others caution that each generation spans decades of time and many socioeconomic levels. For example, marketers often split the baby boomers into three smaller groups—leading boomers, core boomers, and trailing boomers—each with its own beliefs and behaviors. Similarly, they split the Millennials into tweens, teens, and young adults.

Thus, marketers need to form more precise age-specific segments within each group. More important, defining people by their birth date may be less effective than segmenting them by their lifestyle, life stage, or the common values they seek in the products they buy. We will discuss many other ways to segment markets in Chapter 6.

The Changing American Family

The "traditional household" consists of a husband, wife, and children (and sometimes grandparents). Yet, the once American ideal of the two-child, two-car suburban family has lately been losing some of its luster.

In the United States today, married couples with children make up only 23 percent of the nation's 114 million households; married couples without children make up 29 percent; and single parents comprise another 16 percent. A full 32 percent are nonfamily households—single live-alones or adult live-togethers of one or both sexes.[21]

More people are divorcing or separating, choosing not to marry, marrying later, or marrying without intending to have children. Marketers must increasingly consider the special needs of nontraditional households, because they are now growing more rapidly than traditional households. Each group has distinctive needs and buying habits.

The number of working women has also increased greatly, growing from under 40 percent of the U.S. workforce in late 1950s to 59 percent today. Both husband and wife work in 57 percent of all married-couple families. Meanwhile, more men are staying home with their children, managing the household while their wives go to work. According to the census, the number of stay-at-home dads has risen 18 percent since 1994.[22]

The significant number of women in the workforce has spawned the child day care business and increased consumption of career-oriented women's clothing, financial services, and convenience foods and services. An example is Peapod, the nation's leading Internet grocer. Using Peapod, instead of trekking to the grocery store, battling traffic, and waiting in line, busy working moms and dads can simply buy their groceries online. Peapod offers a virtual selection of more than 10,000 grocery store products and delivers customers' orders to their doorsteps. We "bring a world of food to your door," says Peapod—it's "the solution to today's busy lifestyles." Peapod fulfilled its 10 millionth order this year. More important, it figures that it has saved its busy customers about 10 million hours in trips to the grocery store.[23]

Geographic Shifts in Population

This is a period of great migratory movements between and within countries. Americans, for example, are a mobile people, with about 14 percent of all U.S. residents moving each year. Over the past two decades, the U.S. population has shifted toward the Sunbelt states. The West and South have grown, whereas the Midwest and Northeast states have lost population.[24] Such population shifts interest marketers because people in different regions buy differently. For example, research shows that people in Seattle buy more toothbrushes per capita than people in any other U.S. city; people in Salt Lake City eat more candy bars; and people in Miami drink more prune juice.

Also, for more than a century, Americans have been moving from rural to metropolitan areas. In the 1950s, they made a massive exit from the cities to the suburbs. Today, the migration to the suburbs continues. And more and more Americans are moving to "micropolitan areas," small cities located beyond congested metropolitan areas. Drawing refugees from rural and suburban America, these smaller micros offer many of the advantages of metro areas—jobs, restaurants, diversions, community organizations—but without the population crush, traffic jams, high crime rates, and high property taxes often associated with heavily urbanized areas.[25]

The shift in where people live has also caused a shift in where they work. For example, the migration toward micropolitan and suburban areas has resulted in a rapid increase in the number of people who "telecommute"—work at home or in a remote office and conduct their business by phone, fax, modem, or the Internet. This trend, in turn, has created a booming SOHO (small office/home office) market. An estimated 10 percent of today's workforce works from home with the help of electronic conveniences such as PCs, cell phones, fax machines, PDA devices, and fast Internet access. And a recent study estimates that 2 million American businesses support some kind of telecommuting program.[26]

Many marketers are actively courting the home office segment of this lucrative SOHO market. For example, Visa runs ads targeting people who run small businesses out of their homes. And FedEx Kinko's is much more than just a self-service copy shop. Targeting small office/home office customers, it services as a well-appointed office outside the home. People can come to a FedEx Kinko's store to do all their office jobs: They can copy, send and receive faxes, use various programs on the computer, go on the Internet, order stationery and other printed supplies, ship packages, and even rent a conference room or conduct a teleconference. FedEx Kinko's ads tell small business and home office customers, "Your total solution for all your business needs is closer than you think."

A Better-Educated, More White-Collar, More Professional Population The U.S. population is becoming better educated. For example, in 2004, 86 percent of the U.S. population over age 25 had completed high school and 28 percent had completed college, compared with 69 percent and 17 percent in 1980. Moreover, nearly two-thirds of high school graduates now enroll in college within 12 months of graduating.[27]

■ Visa targets the burgeoning small office/home office market. "Your business is your life," notes this ad. And "Life takes Visa."

The rising number of educated people will increase the demand for quality products, books, magazines, travel, personal computers, and Internet services.

The workforce also is becoming more white-collar. Between 1950 and 1985, the proportion of white-collar workers rose from 41 percent to 54 percent, that of blue-collar workers declined from 47 percent to 33 percent, and that of service workers increased from 12 percent to 14 percent. Between 1983 and 1999, the proportion of managers and professionals in the work force increased from 23 percent to more than 30 percent. Job growth is now strongest for professional workers and weakest for manufacturers. Between 2004 and 2014, the number of professional workers is expected to increase 21 percent and manufacturing is expected to decline 5 percent.[28]

Increasing Diversity Countries vary in their ethnic and racial makeup. At one extreme is Japan, where almost everyone is Japanese. At the other extreme is the United States, with people from virtually all nations. The United States has often been called a melting pot—diverse groups from many nations and cultures have melted into a single, more homogenous whole. Instead, the United States seems to have become more of a "salad bowl" in which various groups have mixed together but have maintained their diversity by retaining and valuing important ethnic and cultural differences.

Marketers are facing increasingly diverse markets, both at home and abroad as their operations become more international in scope. The U.S. population is about 66 percent white, with Hispanics at 15 percent and African Americans at a little more than 13 percent. The U.S. Asian American population now totals about 5 percent of the population, with the remaining 1 percent made up of American Indian, Eskimo, and Aleut. Moreover, more than

34 million people living in the United States—more than 12 percent of the population—were born in another country. The nation's ethnic populations are expected to explode in coming decades. By 2050, Hispanics will comprise an estimated 24 percent of the U.S. population, with Asians at 9 percent.[29]

Most large companies, from Procter & Gamble, Sears, Wal-Mart, Allstate, and Bank of America to Levi Strauss and General Mills, now target specially designed products, ads, and promotions to one or more of these groups. For example, Allstate worked with Kang & Lee Advertising, a leading multicultural marketing agency, to create an award-winning marketing campaign aimed at the single largest Asian group in the country—Chinese Americans. Creating culturally significant messages for this market was no easy matter. Perhaps the most daunting task was translating Allstate's iconic "You're In Good Hands With Allstate®" slogan into Chinese.[30]

■ Multicultural marketing: Allstate created an award-winning marketing campaign aimed at the single largest Asian group in the country—Chinese Americans. The most daunting task: translating Allstate's iconic "You're In Good Hands With Allstate®" slogan into Chinese.

There's nary a U.S.-born citizen who doesn't know that, when it comes to insurance, you are in good hands with Allstate. But to Chinese Americans, Allstate was not the first insurance company that came to mind. So Allstate asked Kang & Lee Advertising to help it translate the "good hands" concept into the Chinese market. The trick was to somehow make the company's longtime brand identity relevant to this group. Problem was, the English slogan just doesn't make sense in any Chinese dialect. After months of qualitative consumer research and discussion with Chinese American Allstate agents, Kang & Lee came up with a Chinese-language version of the tag line, which, roughly translated, says "turn to our hands, relax your heart, and be free of worry." The campaign started in Seattle and New York and has since expanded to California. Studies in the first two cities show that awareness of Allstate in the Chinese American community had doubled within six months of the start of the campaign.

Diversity goes beyond ethnic heritage. For example, many major companies have recently begun to explicitly target gay and lesbian consumers. A Simmons Research study of readers of the National Gay Newspaper Guild's 12 publications found that, compared to the average American, respondents are 12 times more likely to be in professional jobs, almost twice as likely to own a vacation home, 8 times more likely to own a notebook computer, and twice as likely to own individual stocks. More than two-thirds have graduated from college and 21 percent hold a master's degree. They are twice as likely as the general population to have a household income over $250,000. In all, the gay and lesbian market spent more than $690 billion on goods and services last year.[31]

With hit TV shows such as *Queer Eye for the Straight Guy* and *The Ellen DeGeneres Show,* and Oscar-winning movies such as *Brokeback Mountain* and *Capote,* the lesbian, gay, bisexual, and transgender (LGBT) community has increasingly emerged into the public eye. A number of media now provide companies with access to this market. For example, PlanetOut Inc., a leading global media company, exclusively serves the LGBT community with several successful magazines (*Out, The Advocate, Out Traveler*) and Web sites (Gay.com, PlanetOut.com, Out&About.com). In 2005, media giant Viacom's MTV Networks introduced LOGO, a cable television network aimed at gays and lesbians and their friends and family. LOGO is now available in 27 million U.S. households. More than 60 mainstream marketers have advertised on LOGO, including Ameriprise Financial, Anheuser-Busch, Continental Airlines, Dell, Levi-Strauss, eBay, Johnson & Johnson, Orbitz, Sears, Sony, and Subaru.

Companies in a wide range of industries are now targeting the LGBT community with gay-specific marketing efforts. For example, IBM fields a paid, full-time sales force dedicated to bringing LGBT decision makers in contact with the company. IBM also targets the gay small-business community with ads in *The Advocate, Out,* and 30 other gay-themed publications. American Airlines has a dedicated LGBT sales team, sponsors gay community events, and offers a special gay-oriented Web site (www.aa.com/rainbow) that features travel deals, an e-newsletter, podcasts, and a gay events calendar. The airline's focus on gay consumers has earned it double-digit revenue growth from the LGBT community each year for more than a decade. Levi's recently ran the same ad with different endings for gay and straight audiences:[32]

> A spot from the jeans maker features a young, attractive male in his second-floor apartment slipping on his Levi's. The motion of yanking up his pants inexplicably causes the street below his apartment to get pulled up as well, crashing through his floor and bringing with it an equally attractive female in a telephone booth. In the end, the guy gets the girl. But if you watch the ad on gay cable network LOGO, the same guy with the magic jeans is greeted by a fetching blond gentleman, and the two of them run off together in the same manner as their heterosexual counterparts.

Another attractive diversity segment is the nearly 54 million adults with disabilities in the United States—a market larger than African Americans or Hispanics—representing more than $200 billion in annual spending power. This market is expected to grow as the baby boomers age. People with disabilities appreciate products that work for them. Explains Jim Tobias, president of Inclusive Technologies, a consultancy specializing in accessible products, "those with disabilities tend to be brand evangelists for products they love. Whereas consumers may typically tell 10 friends about a favorite product, people with disabilities might spread the word to 10 times that [many]."[33]

How are companies trying to reach these consumers? Many marketers now recognize that the worlds of people with disabilities and those without disabilities are one in the same. Says one marketer, "The 'us and them' paradigm is obsolete." Consider the following Avis example:[34]

> A common theme in much of the recent crop of mainstream ads, in fact, is that the disability is virtually an afterthought. A recent New York Marathon-themed print ad for car rental company Avis features an image of a marathoner in a wheelchair, but the copy—"We honor participants of the New York Marathon for spirit, courage, and unrelenting drive"—addresses the racers at large. Since 2003, Avis has offered a suite of products and services that make vehicles more accessible to renters with disabilities, helping to make travel easier and less stressful for everyone. Most recently, Avis has become the official sponsor of the Achilles Track Club, an international organization that supports individuals with disabilities who want to participate in mainstream athletics. Says an Avis marketing executive, "The Achilles athletes themselves truly exemplify the character we strive for at Avis, with their 'we try harder' spirit. Some are amputees back from Iraq; others are visually impaired. But now all of them are setting their sights on what they can achieve."

As the population in the United States grows more diverse, successful marketers will continue to diversify their marketing programs to take advantage of opportunities in fast-growing segments.

■ Avis targets people with disabilities by offering a suite of products and services that make vehicles more accessible. It also sponsors the Achilles Track Club, which supports individuals with disabilities who want to participate in mainstream athletics.

Linking the Concepts

Pull over here for a moment and think about how deeply these demographic factors impact all of us and, as a result, marketers' strategies.

- Apply these demographic developments to your own life. Think of some specific examples of how the changing demographic factors affect you and your buying behavior.
- Identify a specific company that has done a good job of reacting to the shifting demographic environment—generational segments (baby boomers, Gen Xers, or Millennials), the changing American family, and increased diversity. Compare this company to one that's done a poor job.

Economic Environment

Economic environment
Factors that affect consumer buying power and spending patterns.

Markets require buying power as well as people. The **economic environment** consists of factors that affect consumer purchasing power and spending patterns. Nations vary greatly in their levels and distribution of income. Some countries have *subsistence economies*— they consume most of their own agricultural and industrial output. These countries offer few market opportunities. At the other extreme are *industrial economies,* which constitute rich markets for many different kinds of goods. Marketers must pay close attention to major trends and consumer spending patterns both across and within their world markets. Following are some of the major economic trends in the United States.

Changes in Income Throughout the 1990s, American consumers fell into a consumption frenzy, fueled by income growth, a boom in the stock market, rapid increases in housing values, and other economic good fortune. They bought and bought, seemingly without caution, amassing record levels of debt. However, the free spending and high expectations of those days were dashed by the recession of the early 2000s. In fact, we are now facing the age of the "squeezed consumer." Along with rising incomes in some segments have come increased financial burdens. Consumers now face repaying debts acquired during earlier spending splurges, increased household and family expenses, and saving ahead for children's college tuition payments and retirement.

These financially squeezed consumers have adjusted to their changing financial situations and are spending more carefully. *Value marketing* has become the watchword for many marketers. Rather than offering high quality at a high price, or lesser quality at very low prices, marketers are looking for ways to offer today's more financially cautious buyers greater value—just the right combination of product quality and good service at a fair price.

Marketers should pay attention to *income distribution* as well as average income. Income distribution in the United States is still very skewed. At the top are *upper-class* consumers, whose spending patterns are not affected by current economic events and who are a major market for luxury goods. There is a comfortable *middle class* that is somewhat careful about its spending but can still afford the good life some of the time. The *working class* must stick close to the basics of food, clothing, and shelter and must try hard to save. Finally, the *underclass* (persons on welfare and many retirees) must count their pennies when making even the most basic purchases.

Over the past three decades, the rich have grown richer, the middle class has shrunk, and the poor have remained poor. The top 1 percent of American families now control 33.4 percent of the nation's net worth, up 3.3 points from 1989. By contrast, the bottom 90 percent of families now control only 30.4 percent of the net worth, down 3.5 points.[35]

This distribution of income has created a tiered market. Many companies—such as Nordstrom and Neiman-Marcus department stores—aggressively target the affluent. Others—such as Dollar General and Family Dollar stores—target those with more modest means. In fact, such dollar stores are now the fastest-growing retailers in the nation. Still other companies tailor their marketing offers across a range of markets, from the affluent to the less affluent. For example, many high-end fashion designers whose designs sell at sky-high prices to those who can afford it now also sell merchandise at prices that the masses can manage.[36]

Isaac Mizrahi, a high-end fashion designer, pioneered the "fashion for the masses" trend by offering a line of clothing and accessories at Target. Now, other designers such as Nicole Miller and Stella McCartney are offering less expensive lines at JC Penney and H&M, respectively. And Vera Wang, known for her $10,000 wedding gowns found in boutiques and high-end retailers such as Bergdorf Goodman, will be offering a line called "Simply Vera—Vera Wang" at Kohl's starting Fall 2007. In the fall collection, a Vera Wang gold brocade skirt that is nearly identical to a skirt that fetches $890 at high-end department stores will sell for $68 at Kohl's.

Changes in Consumer Spending Patterns Food, housing, and transportation use up the most household income. However, consumers at different income levels have different spending patterns. Some of these differences were noted over a century ago by Ernst Engel, who studied how people shifted their spending as their income rose. He found that as family income rises, the percentage spent on food declines, the percentage spent on housing remains about constant (except for such utilities as gas, electricity, and public services, which decrease), and both the percentage spent on most other categories and that devoted to savings increase. **Engel's laws** generally have been supported by later studies.

Changes in major economic variables such as income, cost of living, interest rates, and savings and borrowing patterns have a large impact on the marketplace. Companies watch these variables by using economic forecasting. Businesses do not have to be wiped out by an economic downturn or caught short in a boom. With adequate warning, they can take advantage of changes in the economic environment.

Engel's laws
Differences noted over a century ago by Ernst Engel in how people shift their spending across food, housing, transportation, health care, and other goods and services categories as family income rises.

Natural Environment

The **natural environment** involves the natural resources that are needed as inputs by marketers or that are affected by marketing activities. Environmental concerns have grown steadily during the past three decades. In many cities around the world, air and water pollution have reached dangerous levels. World concern continues to mount about the possibilities of global warming, and many environmentalists fear that we soon will be buried in our own trash.

Marketers should be aware of several trends in the natural environment. The first involves growing *shortages of raw materials*. Air and water may seem to be infinite resources, but some groups see long-run dangers. Air pollution chokes many of the world's large cities, and water shortages are already a big problem in some parts of the United States and the world. By 2030, more than one in three of the world's human beings will not have enough water to drink.[37] Renewable resources, such as forests and food, also must be used wisely. Nonrenewable resources, such as oil, coal, and various minerals, pose a serious problem. Firms making products that require these scarce resources face large cost increases, even if the materials do remain available.

A second environmental trend is *increased pollution*. Industry will almost always damage the quality of the natural environment. Consider the disposal of chemical and nuclear wastes; the dangerous mercury levels in the ocean; the quantity of chemical pollutants in the soil and food supply; and the littering of the environment with nonbiodegradable bottles, plastics, and other packaging materials.

A third trend is *increased government intervention* in natural resource management. The governments of different countries vary in their concern and efforts to promote a clean environment. Some, such as the German government, vigorously pursue environmental quality. Others, especially many poorer nations, do little about pollution, largely because they lack the needed funds or political will. Even the richer nations lack the vast funds and political accord needed to mount a worldwide environmental effort. The general hope is that companies around the world will accept more social responsibility, and that less expensive devices can be found to control and reduce pollution.

In the United States, the Environmental Protection Agency (EPA) was created in 1970 to set and enforce pollution standards and to conduct pollution research. In the future, companies doing business in the United States can expect continued strong controls from government and pressure groups. Instead of opposing regulation, marketers should help develop solutions to the material and energy problems facing the world.

Natural environment
Natural resources that are needed as inputs by marketers or that are affected by marketing activities.

■ Responding to the consumer demands for more environmentally responsible products, GE is using "ecomagination" to create products for a better world.

Concern for the natural environment has spawned the so-called green movement. Today, enlightened companies go beyond what government regulations dictate. They are developing *environmentally sustainable* strategies and practices in an effort to create a world economy that the planet can support indefinitely. They are responding to consumer demands with more environmentally responsible products. For example, General Electric is using its "ecomagination" to create products for a better world—cleaner aircraft engines, cleaner locomotives, cleaner fuel technologies.

Other companies are developing recyclable or biodegradable packaging, recycled materials and components, better pollution controls, and more energy-efficient operations. For example, HP is pushing legislation to force recycling of old TVs, computers, and other electronic gear:[38]

> HP wants your old PCs back. A few years ago, when environmentalists in Washington State began agitating to banish high-tech junk from landfills and scrub the nation's air and water of lead, chromium, mercury, and other toxins prevalent in digital debris, they found an unexpected ally: Hewlett-Packard. Teaming up with greens and retailers, HP took on IBM, Apple, and several major TV manufacturers, which were resisting recycling programs because of the costs. Aided by HP's energetic lobbying, the greens persuaded state lawmakers to adopt a landmark program that forces electronics companies to foot the bill for recycling their old equipment. With HP's help, the movement to recycle electronic refuse, or "e-waste," is now spreading across the nation.
>
> HP's efforts have made it the darling of environmentalists, but its agenda isn't entirely altruistic. Take-back laws play to the company's strategic strengths. For decades the computer maker has invested in recycling systems, giving it a head start against competitors. Last year, HP recovered 187 million pounds of electronics globally—equivalent to 600 jumbo jets. It's goal is to reduce energy consumption 20 percent by 2010. No other electronics maker has a recycling and resale program on this scale. "We see legislation coming," says HP's vice-president for corporate, social, and environmental responsibility. "A lot of companies haven't stepped up to the plate. . . . If we do this right, it becomes an advantage to us."

Thus, companies today are looking to do more than just good deeds. More and more, they are recognizing the link between a healthy ecology and a healthy economy. They are learning that environmentally responsible actions can also be good business.

Technological Environment

The **technological environment** is perhaps the most dramatic force now shaping our destiny. Technology has released such wonders as antibiotics, robotic surgery, miniaturized electronics, laptop computers, and the Internet. It also has released such horrors as nuclear missiles, chemical weapons, and assault rifles. It has released such mixed blessings as the automobile, television, and credit cards.

Our attitude toward technology depends on whether we are more impressed with its wonders or its blunders. For example, what would you think about having tiny little transmitters implanted in all of the products you buy that would allow tracking products from their point of production though use and disposal? On the one hand, it would provide many advantages to both buyers and sellers. On the other hand, it could be a bit scary. Either way, it's already happening:[39]

> Envision a world in which every product contains a tiny transmitter, loaded with information. As you stroll through the supermarket aisles, shelf sensors detect your selections and beam ads to your shopping cart screen, offering special deals on related products. As your cart fills, scanners detect that you might be buying for a dinner party; the screen suggests a wine to go with the meal you've planned. When you leave the store, exit scanners total up your purchases and automatically charge them to your credit card. At home, readers track what goes into and out of your pantry, updating your shopping list when stocks run low. For Sunday dinner, you pop a Butterball turkey into your "smart oven," which follows instructions from an embedded chip and cooks the bird to perfection.
>
> Seem far-fetched? Not really. In fact, it might soon become a reality, thanks to tiny radio-frequency identification (RFID) transmitters—or "smart chips"—that can be embedded in the products you buy. Beyond benefits to consumers, the RFID chips also give producers and retailers an amazing new way to track their products electronically—anywhere in the world, anytime, automatically—from factories, to warehouses, to retail shelves, to recycling centers. RFID technology is already in use. Every time consumers flash an ExxonMobil Speed-Pass card to purchase gas at the pump or an E-Z Pass card to breeze through an automated toll booth, they're using an RFID chip. Many large firms are adding fuel to the RFID fire. Procter & Gamble plans to have the chips on products in broad distribution as soon as 2008. And at the request of megaretailers such as Wal-Mart, Best Buy, and Albertson's, suppliers have now begun placing RFID tags on selected products.

The technological environment changes rapidly. Think of all of today's common products that were not available 100 years ago, or even 30 years ago. Abraham Lincoln did not know about automobiles, airplanes, radios, or the electric light. Woodrow Wilson did not know about television, aerosol cans, automatic dishwashers, air conditioners, antibiotics, or computers. Franklin Delano Roosevelt did not know about xerography, synthetic detergents, tape recorders, birth control pills, jet engines, or earth satellites. John F. Kennedy did not know about personal computers, cell phones, iPods, or the Internet.

New technologies create new markets and opportunities. However, every new technology replaces an older technology. Transistors hurt the vacuum-tube industry, xerography hurt the carbon-paper business, CDs hurt phonograph records, and digital photography hurt the film business. When old industries fought or ignored new technologies, their businesses declined. Thus, marketers should watch the technological environment closely.

Technological environment
Forces that create new technologies, creating new product and market opportunities.

■ Technological environment: Technology is perhaps the most dramatic force shaping the marketing environment.

Companies that do not keep up will soon find their products outdated. And they will miss new product and market opportunities.

The United States leads the world in research and development spending. Total U.S. R&D spending reached an estimated $338 billion last year. The federal government was the largest R&D spender at about $98 billion.[40] Scientists today are researching a wide range of promising new products and services, ranging from practical solar energy, electric cars, and organ transplants to mind-controlled computers and genetically engineered food crops.

Today's research usually is carried out by research teams rather than by lone inventors such as Thomas Edison, Samuel Morse, or Alexander Graham Bell. Many companies are adding marketing people to R&D teams to try to obtain a stronger marketing orientation. Scientists also speculate on fantasy products, such as flying cars, three-dimensional televisions, and space colonies. The challenge in each case is not only technical but also commercial—to make *practical, affordable* versions of these products.

As products and technology become more complex, the public needs to know that these are safe. Thus, government agencies investigate and ban potentially unsafe products. In the United States, the Food and Drug Administration (FDA) has set up complex regulations for testing new drugs. The Consumer Product Safety Commission sets safety standards for consumer products and penalizes companies that fail to meet them. Such regulations have resulted in much higher research costs and in longer times between new-product ideas and their introduction. Marketers should be aware of these regulations when applying new technologies and developing new products.

Political Environment

Marketing decisions are strongly affected by developments in the political environment. The **political environment** consists of laws, government agencies, and pressure groups that influence or limit various organizations and individuals in a given society.

Legislation Regulating Business Even the most liberal advocates of free-market economies agree that the system works best with at least some regulation. Well-conceived regulation can encourage competition and ensure fair markets for goods and services. Thus, governments develop *public policy* to guide commerce—sets of laws and regulations that limit business for the good of society as a whole. Almost every marketing activity is subject to a wide range of laws and regulations.

Increasing Legislation Legislation affecting business around the world has increased steadily over the years. The United States has many laws covering issues such as competition, fair trade practices, environmental protection, product safety, truth in advertising, consumer privacy, packaging and labeling, pricing, and other important areas (see Table 3.1). The European Commission has been active in establishing a new framework of laws covering competitive behavior, product standards, product liability, and commercial transactions for the nations of the European Union.

Several countries have gone further than the United States in passing strong consumerism legislation. For example, Norway bans several forms of sales promotion—trading stamps, contests, premiums—as being inappropriate or unfair ways of promoting products. Thailand requires food processors selling national brands to also market low-price brands, so that low-income consumers can find economy brands on the shelves. In India, food companies must obtain special approval to launch brands that duplicate those already existing on the market, such as additional cola drinks or new brands of rice.

Understanding the public policy implications of a particular marketing activity is not a simple matter. For example, in the United States, there are many laws created at the national, state, and local levels, and these regulations often overlap. Aspirins sold in Dallas are governed both by federal labeling laws and by Texas state advertising laws. Moreover, regulations are constantly changing—what was allowed last year may now be prohibited, and what was prohibited may now be allowed. Marketers must work hard to keep up with changes in regulations and their interpretations.

Business legislation has been enacted for a number of reasons. The first is to *protect companies* from each other. Although business executives may praise competition, they sometimes try to neutralize it when it threatens them. So laws are passed to define and pre-

Political environment
Laws, government agencies, and pressure groups that influence and limit various organizations and individuals in a given society.

TABLE 3.1 Major U.S. Legislation Affecting Marketing

Legislation	Purpose
Sherman Antitrust Act (1890)	Prohibits monopolies and activities (price fixing, predatory pricing) that restrain trade or competition in interstate commerce.
Federal Food and Drug Act (1906)	Forbids the manufacture or sale of adulterated or fraudulently labeled foods and drugs. Created the Food and Drug Administration.
Clayton Act (1914)	Supplements the Sherman Act by prohibiting certain types of price discrimination, exclusive dealing, and tying clauses (which require a dealer to take additional products in a seller's line).
Federal Trade Commission Act (1914)	Establishes a commission to monitor and remedy unfair trade methods.
Robinson-Patman Act (1936)	Amends Clayton Act to define price discrimination as unlawful. Empowers FTC to establish limits on quantity discounts, forbid some brokerage allowances, and prohibit promotional allowances except when made available on proportionately equal terms.
Wheeler-Lea Act (1938)	Makes deceptive, misleading, and unfair practices illegal regardless of injury to competition. Places advertising of food and drugs under FTC jurisdiction.
Lanham Trademark Act (1946)	Protects and regulates distinctive brand names and trademarks.
National Traffic and Safety Act (1958)	Provides for the creation of compulsory safety standards for automobiles and tires.
Fair Packaging and Labeling Act (1966)	Provides for the regulation of packaging and labeling of consumer goods. Requires that manufacturers state what the package contains, who made it, and how much it contains.
Child Protection Act (1966)	Bans sale of hazardous toys and articles. Sets standards for child-resistant packaging.
Federal Cigarette Labeling and Advertising Act (1967)	Requires that cigarette packages contain the following statement: "Warning: The Surgeon General Has Determined That Cigarette Smoking Is Dangerous to Your Health."
National Environmental Policy Act (1969)	Establishes a national policy on the environment. The 1970 Reorganization Plan established the Environmental Protection Agency.
Consumer Product Safety Act (1972)	Establishes the Consumer Product Safety Commission and authorizes it to set safety standards for consumer products as well as exact penalties for failure to uphold those standards.
Magnuson-Moss Warranty Act (1975)	Authorizes the FTC to determine rules and regulations for consumer warranties and provides consumer access to redress, such as the class action suit.
Children's Television Act (1990)	Limits number of commercials aired during children's programs.
Nutrition Labeling and Education Act (1990)	Requires that food product labels provide detailed nutritional information.
Telephone Consumer Protection Act (1991)	Establishes procedures to avoid unwanted telephone solicitations. Limits marketers' use of automatic telephone-dialing systems and artificial or prerecorded voices.
Americans with Disabilities Act (1991)	Makes discrimination against people with disabilities illegal in public accommodations, transportation, and telecommunications.
Children's Online Privacy Protection Act (2000)	Prohibits Web sites or online services operators from collecting personal information from children without obtaining consent from a parent and allowing parents to review information collected from their children.
Do-Not-Call Implementation Act (2003)	Authorized the FTC to collect fees from sellers and telemarketers for the implementation and enforcement of a National Do-Not-Call Registry.

vent unfair competition. In the United States, such laws are enforced by the Federal Trade Commission and the Antitrust Division of the Attorney General's office.

The second purpose of government regulation is to *protect consumers* from unfair business practices. Some firms, if left alone, would make shoddy products, invade consumer privacy, tell lies in their advertising, and deceive consumers through their packaging and pricing. Unfair business practices have been defined and are enforced by various agencies.

The third purpose of government regulation is to *protect the interests of society* against unrestrained business behavior. Profitable business activity does not always create a better quality of life. Regulation arises to ensure that firms take responsibility for the social costs of their production or products.

Changing Government Agency Enforcement International marketers will encounter dozens, or even hundreds, of agencies set up to enforce trade policies and regulations. In the United States, Congress has established federal regulatory agencies, such as the Federal Trade Commission, the Food and Drug Administration, the Federal Communications Commission, the Federal Energy Regulatory Commission, the Federal Aviation Administration, the Consumer Product Safety Commission, and the Environmental Protection Agency.

Because such government agencies have some discretion in enforcing the laws, they can have a major impact on a company's marketing performance. At times, the staffs of these agencies have appeared to be overly eager and unpredictable. Some of the agencies sometimes have been dominated by lawyers and economists who lacked a practical sense of how business and marketing work. In recent years, the Federal Trade Commission has added staff marketing experts, who can better understand complex business issues.

New laws and their enforcement will continue to increase. Business executives must watch these developments when planning their products and marketing programs. Marketers need to know about the major laws protecting competition, consumers, and society. They need to understand these laws at the local, state, national, and international levels.

Increased Emphasis on Ethics and Socially Responsible Actions Written regulations cannot possibly cover all potential marketing abuses, and existing laws are often difficult to enforce. However, beyond written laws and regulations, business is also governed by social codes and rules of professional ethics.

Socially Responsible Behavior Enlightened companies encourage their managers to look beyond what the regulatory system allows and simply "do the right thing." These socially responsible firms actively seek out ways to protect the long-run interests of their consumers and the environment.

The recent rash of business scandals and increased concerns about the environment have created fresh interest in the issues of ethics and social responsibility. Almost every aspect of marketing involves such issues. Unfortunately, because these issues usually involve conflicting interests, well-meaning people can honestly disagree about the right course of action in a given situation. Thus, many industrial and professional trade associations have suggested codes of ethics. And more companies are now developing policies, guidelines, and other responses to complex social responsibility issues.

The boom in Internet marketing has created a new set of social and ethical issues. Critics worry most about online privacy issues. There has been an explosion in the amount of personal digital data available. Users, themselves, supply some of it. They voluntarily place highly private information on social networking sites such as MySpace or on genealogy sites, which are easily searched by anyone with a PC.

However, much of the information is systematically developed by businesses seeking to learn more about their customers, often without consumers realizing that they are under the microscope. Legitimate businesses plant cookies on consumers' PCs and collect, analyze, and share digital data from every mouse click consumers make at their Web sites. Critics are concerned that companies may now know *too* much, and that some companies might use digital data to take unfair advantage of consumers. Although most companies fully disclose their Internet privacy policies, and most work to use data to benefit their customers, abuses do occur. As a result, consumer advocates and policymakers are taking action to protect consumer privacy.

Throughout the text, we present Marketing at Work exhibits that summarize the main public policy and social responsibility issues surrounding major marketing decisions. These exhibits discuss the legal issues that marketers should understand and the common ethical and societal concerns that marketers face. In Chapter 16, we discuss a broad range of societal marketing issues in greater depth.

Cause-Related Marketing To exercise their social responsibility and build more positive images, many companies are now linking themselves to worthwhile causes. These days, every product seems to be tied to some cause. Buy a pink mixer from KitchenAid and support breast cancer research. Purchase Ethos water from Starbucks and help bring clean water to children around the world. For every Staples Easy Button you buy, the office supplies retailer will donate about $5 to Boys and Girls Clubs of America. Order the City Harvest Tasting Menu at Le Bernardin in New York City, and the restaurant donates $5 to City Harvest, which feeds the hungry by rescuing millions of pounds of edible food thrown away each year by the city's food businesses. Pay for these purchases with the right charge card and you can support a local cultural arts group or help fight heart disease.

Cause-related marketing has become a primary form of corporate giving. It lets companies "do well by doing good" by linking purchases of the company's products or services with fund-raising for worthwhile causes or charitable organizations. Companies now sponsor dozens of cause-related marketing campaigns each year. Many are backed by large budgets and a full complement of marketing activities.

Consider the cause-marketing activities of Home Depot. Last year, the home improvement retailer received the Golden Halo Award, given each year by the Cause Marketing Forum to one business for its leadership and outstanding efforts in the field of cause marketing. Here's just one example of Home Depot's many cause-marketing initiatives:

Home Depot is a founding sponsor of KaBoom!, a nonprofit organization that envisions a great place to play within walking distance of every child in America through the construction of community playgrounds around the nation. Home Depot provides financial support, materials, and volunteers in an ongoing effort to help KaBoom! accomplish this mission. For example, last year, Home Depot announced that it would work with KaBoom! to create and refurbish 1,000 playspaces in 1,000 days, a commitment of $25 million and 1 million volunteer hours. Home Depot also works with its suppliers to develop cause-marketing initiatives that support KaBoom!. It recently partnered with Swing-N-Slide, a do-it-yourself backyard play system producer, to raise money by contributing $30 to KaBoom! for each Brookview No-Cut backyard playground kit sold at Home Depot. Swing-N-Slide also released a special edition of its Racing Roadster toddler swing in Home Depot orange. Home Depot donates 5 percent of the retail price of each Racing Roadster swing to KaBoom!. Such efforts "will help KaBoom! and Home Depot bring the gift of play to countless communities nationwide," says KaBoom!'s CEO. They will also help Home Depot to build closer relationships with consumers in the communities that its stores serve.[41]

■ Cause-related marketing: Home Depot links with KaBoom! to "create a great place to play within walking distance of every child in America." Supporting KaBoom! helps Home Depot to build stronger relationships with customers by giving back to the communities its stores serve.

Cause-related marketing has stirred some controversy. Critics worry that cause-related marketing is more a strategy for selling than a strategy for giving—that "cause-related" marketing is really "cause-exploitative" marketing. Thus, companies using cause-related marketing might find themselves walking a fine line between increased sales and an improved image, and facing charges of exploitation.

However, if handled well, cause-related marketing can greatly benefit both the company and the cause. The company gains an effective marketing tool while building a more positive public image. The charitable organization or cause gains greater visibility and important new sources of funding. Spending on cause-related marketing has skyrocketed from only $120 million in 1990 to more than $1.44 billion in 2007.[42]

Cultural Environment

The **cultural environment** is made up of institutions and other forces that affect a society's basic values, perceptions, preferences, and behaviors. People grow up in a particular society that shapes their basic beliefs and values. They absorb a worldview that defines their relationships with others. The following cultural characteristics can affect marketing decision making.

Persistence of Cultural Values People in a given society hold many beliefs and values. Their core beliefs and values have a high degree of persistence. For example, most Americans believe in working, getting married, giving to charity, and being honest. These beliefs shape more

Cultural environment
Institutions and other forces that affect society's basic values, perceptions, preferences, and behaviors.

specific attitudes and behaviors found in everyday life. *Core* beliefs and values are passed on from parents to children and are reinforced by schools, churches, business, and government.

Secondary beliefs and values are more open to change. Believing in marriage is a core belief; believing that people should get married early in life is a secondary belief. Marketers have some chance of changing secondary values but little chance of changing core values. For example, family-planning marketers could argue more effectively that people should get married later than that they should not get married at all.

Shifts in Secondary Cultural Values   Although core values are fairly persistent, cultural swings do take place. Consider the impact of popular music groups, movie personalities, and other celebrities on young people's hairstyling and clothing norms. Marketers want to predict cultural shifts in order to spot new opportunities or threats. Several firms offer "futures" forecasts in this connection. For example, the Yankelovich Monitor has tracked consumer value trends for years. Its annual State of the Consumer analyzes and interprets the forces that shape consumers' lifestyles and their marketplace interactions. The major cultural values of a society are expressed in people's views of themselves and others, as well as in their views of organizations, society, nature, and the universe.

People's Views of Themselves   People vary in their emphasis on serving themselves versus serving others. Some people seek personal pleasure, wanting fun, change, and escape. Others seek self-realization through religion, recreation, or the avid pursuit of careers or other life goals. People use products, brands, and services as a means of self-expression, and they buy products and services that match their views of themselves.

The Yankelovich Monitor identifies several consumer segments whose purchases are motivated by self-views. Here are two examples:[43]

■ People's self-views: With its "priceless" campaign, MasterCard targets "Adventurers" who imagine themselves doing things others wouldn't dare do. MasterCard can help them quickly set up the experience of a lifetime.

Do-It-Yourselfers—Recent Movers. Embodying the whole do-it-yourself attitude, these active consumers not only tackle home improvement projects on their own, but they also view the experience as a form of self-expression. They view their homes as their havens, especially when it's time to kick back and relax. Undertaking decorating, remodeling, and auto maintenance projects to save money and have fun, Do-It-Yourselfers view their projects as personal victories over the high-priced marketplace. Mostly GenX families with children at home, these consumers also enjoy playing board and card games and renting movies. As recent movers, they're actively spending to turn their new home into a castle.

Adventurers. These adventuresome individuals rarely follow a single path or do the same thing twice. These folks view the experience as far more exciting than the entertainment value. Although they may be appreciative of the arts (including movies, museums, photography, and music), they are more likely to engage in activities most think are too dangerous, and they like to view themselves as doing things others wouldn't dare to do.

Marketers can target their products and services based on such self-views. For example, MasterCard targets Adventurers who might want to use their credits cards to quickly set up the experience of a lifetime. It tells these consumers, "There are some things in life that money can't buy. For everything else, there's MasterCard."

People's Views of Others   In past decades, observers have noted several shifts in people's attitudes toward others. Recently, for example, many trend trackers have seen a new wave of "cocooning," in which people are going out less with others and are staying home more to enjoy the creature comforts of home and hearth—from the networked home office to home entertainment centers.

> Nearly half of major league baseball's 30 clubs are luring smaller crowds this year. Empty seats aren't just a baseball phenomenon. Rock concert attendance was off 12 percent. Entertainment promoters blame everything from unseasonable weather to high gas prices for the lousy attendance numbers. . . . But industry watchers also believe shifting consumer behavior is at work: Call it Cocooning in the Digital Age. With DVD players in most homes, broadband connections proliferating, scores of new video game titles being released each year, and nearly 400 cable channels, consumers can be endlessly entertained right in their own living room—or home theater. Add in the high costs and bother of going out, and more and more people are trading the bleachers for the couch.[44]

This trend suggests a greater demand for home improvement, home office, and home entertainment products. "As the . . . 'nesting' or 'cocooning' trend continues, with people choosing to stay home and entertain more often, the trend of upgrading outdoor living spaces has [grown rapidly]," says a home industry analyst. People are adding bigger decks with fancy gas-ready barbeques, outdoor Jacuzzis, and other amenities that make the old house "home, sweet home" for family and friends.[45]

People's Views of Organizations   People vary in their attitudes toward corporations, government agencies, trade unions, universities, and other organizations. By and large, people are willing to work for major organizations and expect them, in turn, to carry out society's work.

The late 1980s saw a sharp decrease in confidence in and loyalty toward America's business and political organizations and institutions. In the workplace, there has been an overall decline in organizational loyalty. During the 1990s, waves of company downsizings bred cynicism and distrust. And in this decade, corporate scandals at Enron, WorldCom, and Tyco; record-breaking profits for big oil companies during a time of all-time high prices at the pump; and other questionable activities have resulted in a further loss of confidence in big business. Many people today see work not as a source of satisfaction but as a required chore to earn money to enjoy their nonwork hours. This trend suggests that organizations need to find new ways to win consumer and employee confidence.

People's Views of Society   People vary in their attitudes toward their society; patriots defend it, reformers want to change it, malcontents want to leave it. People's orientation to their society influences their consumption patterns and attitudes toward the marketplace. American patriotism has been increasing gradually for the past two decades. It surged, however, following the September 11 terrorist attacks and the Iraq war. For example, the summer following the start of the Iraq war saw a surge of pumped-up Americans visiting U.S. historic sites, ranging from the Washington, D.C., monuments, Mount Rushmore, the Gettysburg battlefield, and the *USS Constitution* ("Old Ironsides") to Pearl Harbor and the Alamo. Following these peak periods, patriotism in the United States still remains high. A recent global survey on "national pride" found that Americans ranked number one among the 34 democracies polled.[46]

Marketers respond with patriotic products and promotions, offering everything from floral bouquets to clothing with patriotic themes. Although most of these marketing efforts are tasteful and well received, waving the red, white, and blue can prove tricky. Except in cases where companies tie product sales to charitable contributions, such flag-waving promotions can be viewed as attempts to cash in on triumph or tragedy. Marketers must take care when responding to such strong national emotions.

People's Views of Nature   People vary in their attitudes toward the natural world. Some feel ruled by it, others feel in harmony with it, and still others seek to master it. A long-term trend has been people's growing mastery over nature through technology and the belief that nature is bountiful. More recently, however, people have recognized that nature is finite and fragile, that it can be destroyed or spoiled by human activities.

This renewed love of things natural has created a 63-million-person "lifestyles of health and sustainability" (LOHAS) market, consumers who seek out everything from natural, organic, and nutritional products to fuel-efficient cars and alternative medicine. This segment spends nearly $300 billion annually on such products. In the words of one such consumer:[47]

> I am not an early adopter, a fast follower, or a mass-market stampeder. But I am a gas-conscious driver. So that's why I was standing in a Toyota dealership . . . this week, the latest person to check out a hybrid car. Who needs $40 fill-ups? After tooling around in three different hybrid car brands—Toyota, Honda, and a Ford—I thought: How cool could this be? Saving gas money and doing well by the environment. Turns out there's a whole trend-watchers' classification for people who think like that: LOHAS. Lifestyles of Health and Sustainability. Buy a hybrid. Shop at places like Whole Foods. Pick up the Seventh Generation paper towels at Albertsons. No skin off our noses. Conscientious shopping, with no sacrifice or hippie stigma.

Many marketers are now tracking and responding to such cultural trends. For example, Wal-Mart recently developed a Live Better Index by which in tracks the attitudes of its 180 million annual shoppers. The first Live Better Index tracked consumers' decisions regarding eco-friendly products such as compact fluorescent light bulbs, organic milk, and concentrated liquid laundry detergents in reduced packaging. The index shows that 11 percent of Americans now consider themselves to be converts to more sustainable living and that 43 percent say they will be "extremely green" within the next five years. Not to be outdone, Home Depot unveiled a new Eco Options product classification that will make it easier for customers to choose all-natural and biodegradable products.[48]

Food producers have also found fast-growing markets for natural and organic products. Consider Earthbound Farm, a company that grows and sells organic produce. It started in 1984 as a 2.5-acre raspberry farm in California's Carmel Valley. Founders Drew and Myra Goodman wanted to do the right thing by farming the land organically and producing food they'd feel good about serving to their family, friends, and neighbors. Today, Earthbound Farm has grown to become the world's largest producer of organic vegetables, with 30,000 acres under plow, annual sales of $278 million, and products available in 80 percent of America's supermarkets.

In total, the U.S. organic-food market generated $15.9 billion in sales last year, a 325 percent increase since 1997. Niche marketers, such as Whole Foods Markets, have sprung up to serve this market, and traditional food chains such as Kroger and Safeway have added separate natural and organic food sections. Even pet owners are joining the movement as they become more aware of what goes into Fido's food. Almost every major pet food brand now offers several types of natural foods.[49]

People's Views of the Universe   Finally, people vary in their beliefs about the origin of the universe and their place in it. Although most Americans practice religion, religious conviction and practice have been dropping off gradually through the years. Some futurists, however, have noted a renewed interest in spirituality, perhaps as

ORGANIC FOOD
IS MORE THAN OUR BUSINESS. IT'S OUR
PASSION.

More than 20 years ago, Earthbound Farm started as a backyard garden where we grew food we felt good about feeding our friends and family. And that meant farming organically. Today, Earthbound Farm's commitment to the health of those who enjoy our harvest is stronger than ever. We're proud that our work helps make the world a healthier place and makes it easier for you to choose delicious organic salads, fruits and vegetables every day.

Earthbound Farm • *Food to live by*® • www.ebfarm.com

Food to Live By: The Earthbound Farm Organic Cookbook is now available wherever books are sold. More than 250 delicious recipes from the farm that brings organic produce to millions of people every week.

■ Riding the trend towards all things natural, Earthbound Farm has grown to become the world's largest producer of organic salads, fruits, and vegetables, with product in 80 percent of America's supermarkets.

a part of a broader search for a new inner purpose. People have been moving away from materialism and dog-eat-dog ambition to seek more permanent values—family, community, earth, faith—and a more certain grasp of right and wrong.

"Americans are on a spiritual journey, increasingly concerned with the meaning of life and issues of the soul and spirit," observes one expert. People "say they are increasingly looking to religion—Christianity, Judaism, Hinduism, Islam, and others—as a source of comfort in a chaotic world." This new spiritualism affects consumers in everything from the television shows they watch and the books they read to the products and services they buy. "Since consumers don't park their beliefs and values on the bench outside the marketplace," adds the expert, "they are bringing this awareness to the brands they buy. Tapping into this heightened sensitivity presents a unique marketing opportunity for brands."[50]

Linking the Concepts

Slow down and cool your engine. You've now read about a large number of environmental forces. How are all of these environments *linked* with each other? With company marketing strategy?

- How are major demographic forces linked with economic changes? With major cultural trends? How are the natural and technological environments linked? Think of an example of a company that has recognized one of these links and turned it into a marketing opportunity.
- Is the marketing environment uncontrollable—something that the company can only prepare for and react to? Or can companies be proactive in changing environmental factors? Think of a good example that makes your point, then read on.

Responding to the Marketing Environment

Someone once observed, "There are three kinds of companies: those who make things happen, those who watch things happen, and those who wonder what's happened."[51] Many companies view the marketing environment as an uncontrollable element to which they must react and adapt. They passively accept the marketing environment and do not try to change it. They analyze the environmental forces and design strategies that will help the company avoid the threats and take advantage of the opportunities the environment provides.

Other companies take a *proactive* stance toward the marketing environment. Rather than simply watching and reacting, these firms take aggressive actions to affect the publics and forces in their marketing environment. Such companies hire lobbyists to influence legislation affecting their industries and stage media events to gain favorable press coverage. They run advertorials (ads expressing editorial points of view) to shape public opinion. They press lawsuits and file complaints with regulators to keep competitors in line, and they form contractual agreements to better control their distribution channels.

By taking action, companies can often overcome seemingly uncontrollable environmental events. For example, whereas some companies view the seemingly ceaseless online rumor mill as something over which they have no control, others work proactively to prevent or counter negative word of mouth:[52]

One e-mail recently circulating in Washington said that a former government lawyer knew a guy whose dog had to be put to sleep because he walked on a floor cleaned with Procter & Gamble's Swiffer WetJet, licked his paws and developed liver disease. Although the claim was proved false by toxicologists, it has been neither quick nor easy for P&G to squelch the story. But P&G learned long ago that it was best to face a false rumor head-on. Years before, P&G endured a nasty rumor that the stars-and-moon trademark the company then displayed on its

3.2 MARKETING AT WORK
YourCompanySucks.com

The Internet has been hailed by marketers as the great new relational medium. Companies use the Web to engage customers, gain insights into their needs, and create customer community. In turn, Web-empowered consumers share their brand experiences with companies and with each other. All of this back-and-forth helps both the company and its customers. But sometimes, the dialog can get nasty. Consider these examples:

A tattooed, 210-pound Richard Hatch—one of the few people in this world with a passion for both Harley-Davidson motorcycles and collecting cute little toys—gets into a shouting match with an employee in his local Wal-Mart store. He claims that the store's employees are snapping up the best Hot Wheels and NASCAR collectible toy cars before they hit the shelves. Wal-Mart bans him from the store and the angry Hatch retaliates by creating the WalMartSucks.com Web site. The Web site sprouts beyond Hatch's wildest dreams of revenge. Customers by the thousands write to attack rude Wal-Mart store managers, complain about alleged insects in the aisles, and even offer shoplifting tips.

■ Today, armed with only a PC and a broadband connection, the little guy can take it public against corporate America. By listening and proactively responding to such seemingly uncontrollable environmental events, companies can prevent the negatives from spiraling out of control or even turn them into positives.

Blogger Jeff Jarvis posts a series of irate messages to his BuzzMachine blog about the many failings of his Dell computer and his struggles with Dell's customer support. The post quickly draws national attention, and an open letter posted by Jarvis to Dell founder Michael Dell becomes the third most linked-to post on the blogosphere the day after it appears. Jarvis's headline—Dell Hell—becomes shorthand for the ability of a lone blogger to deliver a body blow to an unsuspecting business.

MSN Money columnist Scott Burns accuses Home Depot of being a "consistent abuser" of customers' time. Within hours, MSN's servers are caving under the weight of 14,000 blistering e-mails and

posts from angry Home Depot customers who storm the MSN comment room, taking the company to task for pretty much everything. It is the biggest response in MSN Money's history.

Extreme events? Not anymore. "Web 2.0" has turned the traditional power relationship between businesses and consumers upside-down. In the good old days, disgruntled consumers could do little more than bellow at a company service rep or shout out their complaints from a street corner. Now, armed with only a PC and a broadband connection, they can take it public, airing their gripes to millions on blogs, chats, or hate sites devoted exclusively to their least favorite corporations.

packaging was linked with Satanism. The rumor was disseminated through fliers and, much later, e-mails. At one point, fliers even claimed that P&G officials had appeared on TV talk shows confirming the rumor. Rather than letting the rumor lie, P&G reacted strongly by soliciting support from a range of religious leaders as well as from its employees, who worked to convince members of their own churches that the rumors were false. It publicized letters from the TV networks saying that no P&G executives had appeared on the TV shows. And once P&G identified people it said had spread the rumor—some of whom it says worked for competitors—it pressed charges to get them to confess and stop distributing the information. Some of them did confess, and litigation is still pending against others.

Marketing management cannot always control environmental forces. In many cases, it must settle for simply watching and reacting to the environment. For example, a company would have little success trying to influence geographic population shifts, the economic environment, or major cultural values. But whenever possible, smart marketing managers will take a *proactive* rather than *reactive* approach to the marketing environment (see Marketing at Work 3.2).

"I hate" and "sucks" sites are becoming almost commonplace. These sites target some highly respected companies with some highly *dis*respectful labels: PayPalSucks.com (aka NoPayPal); WalMart-blows.com; Microsucks.com; NorthWorstAir.org (Northwest Airlines); AllStateInsurancesucks.com; BestBuysux.org; DeltaREALLYsucks.com; and UnitedPackageSmashers.com (UPS), to name only a few.

Some of these sites and other Web attacks air legitimate complaints that should be addressed. Others, however, are little more than anonymous, vindictive slurs that unfairly ransack brands and corporate reputations. Some of the attacks are only a passing nuisance; others can draw serious attention and create real headaches.

How should companies react to Web attacks? The real quandary for targeted companies is figuring out how far they can go to protect their images without fueling the already raging fire. One point upon which all experts seem to agree: Don't try to retaliate in kind. "It's rarely a good idea to lob bombs at the fire starters," says one analyst. "Preemption, engagement, and diplomacy are saner tools."

Some companies have tried to silence the critics through lawsuits but few have succeeded. For example, Wal-Mart's attorneys threatened Richard Hatch with legal action unless he shut down his Wal-Mart sucks Web site. However, Hatch stood up to the $350 billion retailer and Wal-Mart eventually backed down. As it turns out, a company has legal recourse only when the unauthorized use of its trademarks, brand names, or other intellectual property is apt to be confusing to the public. And no reasonable person is likely to be confused that Wal-Mart maintains and supports a site tagged Walmartsucks.com. Beyond the finer legal points, Wal-Mart also feared that a lawsuit would only draw more attention to the consumer hate site.

Given the difficulties of trying to sue consumer online criticisms out of existence, some companies have tried other strategies. For example, most big companies now routinely buy up Web addresses for their firm names preceded by the words "Ihate" or followed by "sucks.com." For example, Procter & Gamble has registered ihateprocterandgamble.com and, interestingly, febrezekillspets.com. But this approach is easily thwarted, as Wal-Mart learned when it registered ihatewalmart.com, only to find that someone else then registered ireallyhatewalmart.com.

In general, attempts to block, counterattack, or shut down consumer attacks may be shortsighted. Such criticisms are often based on real consumer concerns and unresolved anger. Hence, the best strategy might be to proactively monitor these sites and respond to the concerns they express. "The most obvious thing to do is talk to the customer and try to deal with the problem, instead of putting your fingers in your ears," advises one consultant. For example, Home Depot CEO Francis Blake drew praise when he heeded the criticisms expressed in the MSN Money onslaught and responded positively. Blake posted a heartfelt letter in which he thanked critic Scott Burns, apologized to angry customers, and promised to make things better. He also created a new company site to deal specifically with Home Depot service problems.

Many companies have now set up teams of specialists that monitor Web conversations and engage disgruntled consumers. Others hire firms such as BuzzLogic, which creates "conversation maps" tracking not just who's talking about a company's product but also which opinions matter most. BuzzLogic recently helped computer maker Lenovo head off its own Dell Hell moment. When tech-oriented blogger Rick Klau posted his frustrations over his Lenovo ThinkPad's faulty hard drive, BuzzLogic quickly picked up the post and alerted Lenovo. Within only a few hours, Klau received a phone call from David Churbuck, Lenovo's VP of global Web marketing. Churbuck offered to fix the problem, turning Klau's rants into raves. The *good* news was picked up by other bloggers before the *bad* news could catch fire.

Thus, by listening and proactively responding to seemingly uncontrollable events in the environment, companies can prevent the negatives from spiraling out of control or even turn them into positives. Who knows? With the right responses, WalMart-blows.com might even become WalMart-rules.com. Then again, probably not.

Sources: Quotes, excerpts, and other information from Michelle Conlin, "Web Attack," *BusinessWeek,* April 16, 2007, pp. 54–56; Oliver Ryan, "The Buzz Around Buzz," *Fortune,* March 19, 2007, p. 46; Charles Wolrich, "Top Corporate Hate Sites," *Forbes,* March 8, 2005, accessed at www.forbes.com/2005/03/07/cx_cw_0308hate.html; Gemma Charles, "Complaints Are There to Be Heard," *Marketing,* January 10, 2007, p. 15; "Top 10 Service Complaint Sites," *Time Out New York,* March 8, 2007, accessed at www.timeout.com; and "Master Class: Cyber-Bullying (of Business), *Management Today,* June 2007, p. 24.

REST STOP ➜ REVIEWING THE CONCEPTS

In this chapter and the next two chapters, you'll examine the environments of marketing and how companies analyze these environments to better understand the marketplace and consumers. Companies must constantly watch and manage the *marketing environment* in order to seek opportunities and ward off threats. The marketing environment consists of all the actors and forces influencing the company's ability to transact business effectively with its target market.

1. Describe the environmental forces that affect the company's ability to serve its customers.

The company's *microenvironment* consists of other actors close to the company that combine to form the company's value de-livery network or that affect its ability to serve its customers. It includes the company's *internal environment* —its several departments and management levels—as it influences marketing decision making. *Marketing channel firms* —suppliers and marketing intermediaries, including resellers, physical distribution firms, marketing services agencies, and financial intermediaries—cooperate to create customer value. Five types of customer *markets* include consumer, business, reseller, government, and international markets. *Competitors* vie with the company in an effort to serve customers better. Finally, various *publics* have an actual or potential interest in or impact on the company's ability to meet its objectives.

The *macroenvironment* consists of larger societal forces that affect the entire microenvironment. The six forces making up the company's macroenvironment include demographic, economic, natural, technological, political, and cultural forces. These forces shape opportunities and pose threats to the company.

2. Explain how changes in the demographic and economic environments affect marketing decisions.

Demography is the study of the characteristics of human populations. Today's *demographic environment* shows a changing age structure, shifting family profiles, geographic population shifts, a better-educated and more white-collar population, and increasing diversity. The *economic environment* consists of factors that affect buying power and patterns. The economic environment is characterized by more consumer concern for value and shifting consumer spending patterns. Today's squeezed consumers are seeking greater value—just the right combination of good quality and service at a fair price. The distribution of income also is shifting. The rich have grown richer, the middle class has shrunk, and the poor have remained poor, leading to a two-tiered market. Many companies now tailor their marketing offers to two different markets—the affluent and the less affluent.

3. Identify the major trends in the firm's natural and technological environments.

The *natural environment* shows three major trends: shortages of certain raw materials, higher pollution levels, and more government intervention in natural resource management.

Environmental concerns create marketing opportunities for alert companies. The *technological environment* creates both opportunities and challenges. Companies that fail to keep up with technological change will miss out on new product and marketing opportunities.

4. Explain the key changes in the political and cultural environments.

The *political environment* consists of laws, agencies, and groups that influence or limit marketing actions. The political environment has undergone three changes that affect marketing worldwide: increasing legislation regulating business, strong government agency enforcement, and greater emphasis on ethics and socially responsible actions. The *cultural environment* is made up of institutions and forces that affect a society's values, perceptions, preferences, and behaviors. The environment shows trends toward digital "cocooning," a lessening trust of institutions, increasing patriotism, greater appreciation for nature, a new spiritualism, and the search for more meaningful and enduring values.

5. Discuss how companies can react to the marketing environment.

Companies can passively accept the marketing environment as an uncontrollable element to which they must adapt, avoiding threats and taking advantage of opportunities as they arise. Or they can take a *proactive* stance, working to change the environment rather than simply reacting to it. Whenever possible, companies should try to be proactive rather than reactive.

Reviewing the Key Terms

Baby boomers (69)
Cultural environment (85)
Demography (68)
Economic environment (78)
Engel's laws (79)

Generation X (70)
Macroenvironment (65)
Marketing environment (65)
Marketing intermediaries (66)
Microenvironment (65)

Millennials (Generation Y) (72)
Natural environment (79)
Political environment (82)
Public (67)
Technological environment (81)

Travel Log

Discussing the Issues

1. Name and describe the elements of a company's microenvironment and give an example showing why each is important. (AASCB: Communication)

2. What is *demography* and why are marketers interested in it? List some of the demographic trends of interest to marketers. (AACSB: Communication)

3. Discuss the trends in the natural environment that marketers must be aware of and provide examples of companies' responses to them. (AACSB: Communication)

4. Discuss reasons why business legislation is enacted. What role do businesses and industry groups play in shaping such legislation? (AACSB: Communication; Reflective Thinking)

5. Compare and contrast core beliefs/values and secondary beliefs/values. Provide an example of each and discuss the potential impact marketers have on each. (AACSB: Communication; Reflective Thinking)

6. How should marketers respond to the changing environment? (AACSB: Communication)

Application Questions

1. China and India are emerging markets that will have a significant impact on the world in coming years. The term "Chindia" has been used to describe the growing power of these two countries. Discuss two trends related to Chindia's power and its impact on marketers in the United States. (AACSB: Communication; Reflective Thinking)

2. The Federal Trade Commission (FTC) has regulatory authority over marketing practices. Visit www.ftc.gov to learn about this agency and how it regulates business activities in general and marketing activities in particular. Describe the process the FTC uses if a complaint is made and discuss one FTC case related to marketing. (AACSB: Communication; Use of IT)

3. Cause-related marketing has grown considerably over the past 10 years. Visit www.causemarketingforum.com and learn about companies that have won Halo Awards for outstanding cause-related marketing programs. Present two award-winning case studies to your class. (AACSB: Communication; Use of IT)

Under the Hood: Focus on Technology

First there was the television, then the computer, and now there's the "third screen"—mobile phones. The first and second screens—TV and the computer—are heavily commercialized, and so too will be the third screen. Mobile marketing involves any type of marketing message—voice, text, image, or video—delivered to a handheld portable device such as a cell phone, iPhone, or BlackBerry. Though still in its infancy in the United States, mobile marketing has grown rapidly in other countries. It has spawned an industry group—the Mobile Marketing Association (MMA)—and an academic journal entitled the *International Journal of Mobile Marketing*. Marketers in the United States are treading carefully but some are having suc-

cess, such as Coca-Cola's Sprite campaign targeted to teens and Meijer's (a Midwestern discount retail chain) "gas alerts" informing consumers of price changes three hours before they take effect.

1. Learn more about mobile marketing and discuss its applications. Develop a mobile marketing campaign for a brand of your choice. (AACSB: Communication; Reflective Thinking)

2. Which demographic group or groups will more likely accept mobile marketing? Explain your answer. (AACSB: Communication; Reflective Thinking)

Focus on Ethics

You've probably heard of a monopoly, in which one powerful seller controls a market of many buyers. But have you ever heard of a *monopsony?* A monopsony involves one powerful buyer and many sellers. The buyer is so powerful that it can drive prices down. An example is Wal-Mart, the world's largest retailer. Wal-Mart's power allows it to get the lowest possible prices from its suppliers. Similarly, wine-making giant Ernest & Gallo has so much power buying grapes that growers have to concede to the wine maker's demands for lower prices.

1. Is it fair that a buyer can exert so much power over a supplier? Are there any benefits to consumers? (AACSB: Communication; Ethical Reasoning)

2. Do you think the government should step in and set minimum price levels? Discuss the consequences of your answer. (AACSB: Communication; Reflective Thinking)

Video Case

American Express

Understanding consumers and their needs can be a challenge. As the American population diversifies, and as consumers redefine their values and preferences, marketers work to provide relevant products and services that meet consumers' changing needs and wants. For American Express, keeping up with environmental shifts translates into creating new marketing offers. American Express issued its first charge card in 1958. Within five years, it had more than 1 million cards in use. The company now offers more than 20 consumer cards, 14 small business cards, and customizable corporate cards. Some cards target very specific consumers. For example, the IN:CHICAGO, IN:NYC, and IN:LA cards offer cardholders special perks for local shopping, dining, and entertainment. By targeting such specific consumers, American Express builds strong relationships with the right customers.

After viewing the video featuring American Express, answer the following questions about the marketing environment.

1. Visit the American Express Web site (www.americanexpress.com) to learn more about the different cards that American Express offers. Select three of the macroenvironmental forces discussed in the chapter. How does American Express adjust its marketing mix in response to trends within each of these forces?

2. How does American Express deal with the various publics in its microenvironment?

3. Is American Express taking a proactive approach to managing its marketing environment? How?

Sirius and ZIBA.
Reinventing the satellite radio experience.

SIRIUS
SATELLITE RADIO
THE BEST RADIO ON RADIO™

After studying this chapter, you should be able to

1. explain the importance of information in gaining insights about the marketplace and customers

2. define the marketing information system and discuss its parts

3. outline the steps in the marketing research process

4. explain how companies analyze and use marketing information

5. discuss the special issues some marketing researchers face, including public policy and ethics issues

Managing Marketing Information to Gain Customer Insights

ROAD MAP Previewing the Concepts

In the previous chapter, you learned about the complex and changing marketing environment. In this chapter, we'll continue our exploration of how marketers gain insights into consumers and the marketplace. We'll look at how companies develop and manage information about important marketplace elements—customers, competitors, products, and marketing programs. We'll examine marketing information systems designed to assess the firm's marketing information needs, develop the needed information, and help managers to use the information to gain actionable customer and market insights. To succeed in today's marketplace, companies must know how to turn mountains of marketing information into fresh customer insights that will help them deliver greater value to customers.

We'll start this chapter of our journey with a story about ZIBA, a product design consultancy that helps its clients to create new products that connect strongly with customers. ZIBA's designs don't start in a research lab. ZIBA's first step is to research consumers and get to know them—*really* get to know them. Then, based on the deep insights garnered from consumer research, ZIBA designs products that turn consumers' heads and open their wallets.

Z IBA is a new-product design consultancy. In its own words, it "helps companies to create meaningful ideas, designs, and experiences that consumers crave." ZIBA knows that good product design begins with good marketing research. But it does much, much more than just gather facts about market demographics and consumer buying patterns. It digs in and *really* gets to know consumers. More than just gathering facts and figures, it develops deep customer and market insights. Driven by a self-described "almost unnatural obsession for understanding consumers," ZIBA innovates with soul.

The company's long odyssey into the hearts and hungers of consumers began in 1989 with—of all things—a squeegee. An entrepreneur hired the consultancy to craft a hip-looking tool for cleaning gunky shower stalls. Rather than pouring through market data or conducting the usual consumer surveys, ZIBA dispatched a small team of designers to plumb the mysteries of the American bathroom. It spent 10 days shadowing people as they bent to their noxious task, photographing the ballet-like movements of window washers, and even studying silk screeners to glean the ergonomics of handling a squeegee-like device.

Such surveillance eventually led to a sculptured, cylindrical handle, about the size of a shampoo bottle, which held two removable, wave-shaped plastic blades. Dubbed the Clerét, the freestanding cleaning tool looked like no other squeegee that had come before. Elegantly simple in its design and effective in its performance, it landed in the Smithsonian's permanent design collection. It also claimed the Industrial Designers Society of America's best-designed new consumer product award (check it out at www.cleret.com/aboutus.html). Best of all, since the Clerét's launch, the start-up has sold $40 million worth of the thing. From that point on, every ZIBA design would grow out of its unique research approach of first decoding the consumer's mind in order to forge key customer insights.

At the heart of ZIBA's success is its Consumer Insights and Trends Group, an interesting mix of social anthropologists, cultural ethnographers, user-experience wizards, trend trackers, brand translators, and cool hunters, headed by creative director Steve McCallion. McCallion argues that it's not enough to study the average user and ask them what they want. "We're going for something deeper—to understand *why* people want what they want," he says. "Our ability to invent is solely dependent on our ability to capture that dynamic relationship between the brand and the culture that finds it relevant."

So when Sirius Satellite Radio enlisted ZIBA to fashion a handheld receiver (what would later become the Sirius S50 and the new Stiletto), McCallion and his customer insights squad went in for a deep dive, spreading out across Portland, Boston, and Nashville to spend some quality time with 44 Sirius subscribers. They toured people's CD collections, hung out with them at Saturday afternoon tailgating parties, studied how they accessorized their cars, and got them to rift on why music matters to them.

Then, back at ZIBA's studios, the team spent weeks harvesting raw data, photographs, and field notes, seeking deeper customer insights. McCallion edited the material down to a de-

sign target—the "iPod fatigued"—and assembled more-focused profiles of Sirius users, such as the "intelligent fan" (dials into a wide range of sports; listens to the radio while attending Red Sox games) and the "business charismatic" (drives a BMW 5 Series; holds a platinum frequent-flier card).

Working from the profiles, McCallion and the insights team crafted a perceptive positioning statement—"discovery, portability, personalization"—that drove the entire design process as ZIBA tested and refined scores of prototypes. They knew the business charismatic was looking for a device that wouldn't detract from a car's interior, so they urged designers to give the S50 and the Stiletto a simple, accessible interface. The intelligent fan was keen on portability, and by storyboarding scenarios for the S50, the team discovered that many people wanted to use it to record programming and play it back later. They also pushed for a prominent media dial and a lustrous black finish, based on the conviction that both were powerfully reminiscent of "radio."

"We all have memories of listening to the radio when we were kids," says McCallion. "We wanted to tap into those memories; they help you emotionally connect with the product." Apparently, McCallion and ZIBA scored a hit—the S50 became one of the holiday season's top sellers and took yet another gold medal from the Industrial Designers Society of America.

ZIBA has come a long way from contemplating shower stalls. Thanks to its innovative research approach, ZIBA is now one of the nation's hottest design consultancies. Today, its clients include a who's who list of Fortune 100 heavyweights such as P&G, Microsoft, FedEx, and Whirlpool, as well as an assortment of small technology start-ups and service organizations. ZIBA's doing something right: It walked off with four Industrial Design Excellence Awards this year, the most of any single consultancy.

ZIBA teaches its clients that successful new products don't begin in their R&D labs. They begin with a deep understanding of customers and their emotional connections to the products they buy and use. Whether it's a squeegee or a high-tech consumer communications device, innovative new products start with innovative consumer research that provides fresh customer and market insights.[1]

As the ZIBA story highlights, good products and marketing programs begin with good customer information. Companies also need an abundance of information on competitors, resellers, and other actors and marketplace forces. But more than just gathering information, marketers must *use* the information to gain powerful *customer and market insights*.

Marketing Information and Customer Insights

To create value for customers and to build meaningful relationships with them, marketers must first gain fresh, deep insights into what customers need and want. Companies use such customer insights to develop competitive advantage. "In today's hypercompetitive world," states a marketing expert, "the race for competitive advantage is really a race for customer and market insights." Such insights come from the good marketing information.[2]

Consider Apple's phenomenally successful iPod. The iPod wasn't the first digital music player but Apple was the first to get it right. Apple's research uncovered a key insight about how people want to consume digital music—they want to take all their music with them but they want personal music players to be unobtrusive. This insight led to two key design goals—make it as small as a deck of cards and build it to hold 1,000 songs. Add a dash of Apple's design and usability magic to this insight, and you have a recipe for a blockbuster. Apple's expanded iPod line now captures more than a 75 percent market share.

But although customer and market insights are important for building customer value and relationships, these insights can be very difficult to obtain. Customer needs and buying motives are often anything but obvious—consumers themselves usually can't tell you exactly what they need and why they buy. To gain good customer insights, marketers must effectively manage marketing information from a wide range of sources.

Today's marketers have ready access to plenty of marketing information. With the recent explosion of information technologies, companies can now generate information in great quantities. In fact, most marketing managers are overloaded with data and often overwhelmed by it. For example, Wal-Mart refreshes sales data from checkout scanners hourly, adding a billion rows of data a day, equivalent to about 96,000 DVD movies. That's a *lot* of data to analyze.[3] Still, despite this data glut, marketers frequently complain that they lack enough information of the right kind. They don't need *more* information, they need *better* information. And they need to make better *use* of the information they already have. Says another marketing information expert, "transforming today's vast, ever-increasing volume of consumer information into actionable marketing insights . . . is the number-one challenge for digital-age marketers."[4]

Thus, a company's marketing research and information system must do more than simply generate lots of information. The real value of marketing research and marketing information lies in how it is used—in the **customer insights** that it provides. "The value of the market research department is not determined by the number of studies that it does," says the marketing expert, "but by the business value of the *insights* that it produces and the decisions that it influences.[5]

Based on such thinking, many companies are now restructuring and renaming their marketing research and information functions. They are creating "customer insights teams," headed by a vice president of customer insights and made up of representatives from all of the firm's functional areas. For example, the head of marketing research at Kraft Foods is called the director of consumer insights and strategy.

Customer insight groups collect customer and market information from a wide variety of sources—ranging from traditional marketing research studies to mingling with and observing consumers to monitoring consumer online conversations about the company and its products. Then, they *use* the marketing information to develop important customer insights from which the company can create more value for its customers. For example, Unilever's customer insights group states its mission simply as "getting better at understanding our consumers and meeting their needs."

Thus, companies must design effective marketing information systems that give managers the right information, in the right form, at the right time and help them to use this information to create customer value and stronger customer relationships. A **marketing information system (MIS)** consists of people and procedures for assessing information needs, developing the needed

Customer insights
Fresh understandings of customers and the marketplace derived from marketing information that become the basis for creating customer value and relationships.

Marketing information system (MIS)
People and procedures for assessing information needs, developing the needed information, and helping decision makers to use the information to generate and validate actionable customer and market insights.

■ The marketing information glut: Transforming today's vast, ever-increasing volume of consumer information into actionable marketing insights is the number-one challenge for digital-age marketers.

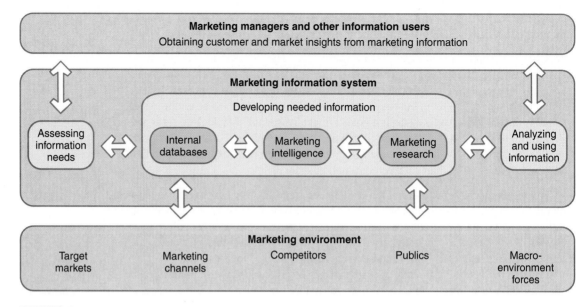

FIGURE 4.1
The Marketing Information System

information, and helping decision makers to use the information to generate and validate actionable customer and market insights.

Figure 4.1 shows that the MIS begins and ends with information users—marketing managers, internal and external partners, and others who need marketing information. First, it interacts with these information users to *assess information needs*. Next, it interacts with the marketing environment to *develop needed information* through internal company databases, marketing intelligence activities, and marketing research. Finally, the MIS helps users to analyze and use the information to develop customer insights, make marketing decisions, and manage customer relationships.

Assessing Marketing Information Needs

The marketing information system primarily serves the company's marketing and other managers. However, it may also provide information to external partners, such as suppliers, resellers, or marketing services agencies. For example, Wal-Mart's RetailLink system gives key suppliers access to information on customer buying patterns and inventory levels. And Dell creates tailored Premium Pages for large customers, giving them access to product design, order status, and product support and service information. In designing an information system, the company must consider the needs of all of these users.

A good marketing information system balances the information users would *like* to have against what they really *need* and what is *feasible* to offer. The company begins by interviewing managers to find out what information they would like. Some managers will ask for whatever information they can get without thinking carefully about what they really need. Too much information can be as harmful as too little.

Other managers may omit things they ought to know, or they may not know to ask for some types of information they should have. For example, managers might need to know about surges in favorable or unfavorable consumer "word-of-Web" discussions about their brands on blogs or online social networks. Because they do not know about these discussions, they do not think to ask about them. The MIS must monitor the marketing environment in order to provide decision makers with information they should have in order to better understand customers and make key marketing decisions.

Sometimes the company cannot provide the needed information, either because it is not available or because of MIS limitations. For example, a brand manager might want to know how competitors will change their advertising budgets next year and how these changes will affect industry market shares. The information on planned budgets probably is not available. Even if it is, the company's MIS may not be advanced enough to forecast resulting changes in market shares.

Finally, the costs of obtaining, analyzing, storing, and delivering information can mount quickly. The company must decide whether the value of insights gained from additional information is worth the costs of providing it, and both value and cost are often hard to assess. By itself, information has no worth; its value comes from its *use*. In many cases, additional information will do little to change or improve a manager's decision, or the costs of the information may exceed the returns from improved customer insights and decision making. Marketers should not assume that additional information will always be worth obtaining. Rather, they should weigh carefully the costs of getting more information against the benefits resulting from it.[6]

Developing Marketing Information

Marketers can obtain the needed information from *internal data, marketing intelligence,* and *marketing research.*

Internal Data

Many companies build extensive **internal databases**, electronic collections of consumer and market information obtained from data sources within the company network. Marketing managers can readily access and work with information in the database to identify marketing opportunities and problems, plan programs, and evaluate performance.

Information in the database can come from many sources. The marketing department furnishes information on customer transactions, demographics, psychographics, and buying behavior. The customer service department keeps records of customer satisfaction or service problems. The accounting department prepares financial statements and keeps detailed records of sales, costs, and cash flows. Operations reports on production schedules, shipments, and inventories. The sales force reports on reseller reactions and competitor activities, and marketing channel partners provide data on point-of-sale transactions. Harnessing such information can provide powerful customer insights and competitive advantage.

Here is an example of how one company uses its internal database to make better marketing decisions:

> Pizza Hut's database contains detailed customer data on 40 million U.S. households, gleaned from phone orders, online orders, and point-of-sale transactions at its more than 6,600 restaurants around the nation. The company can slice and dice the data by favorite toppings, what you ordered last, and whether you buy a salad with your cheese and pepperoni pizza. It then uses all this data to enhance customer relationships. For example, based on extensive analysis of several years of purchase transactions, Pizza Hut designed a VIP (Very Into Pizza) program to retain its best customers. It invites these customers to join the VIP program for $14.95 and receive a free large pizza. Then, for every two pizzas ordered each month, VIP customers automatically earn a coupon for another free large pizza. Pizza Hut tracks VIP purchases and targets members with additional e-mail offers. In all, the campaign not only retained Pizza Hut's top customers but attracted new customers as well. The program also generated a lot on online buzz.

Internal databases
Electronic collections of consumer and market information obtained from data sources within the company network.

■ Internal databases: Pizza Hut can slice and dice its extensive customer database by favorite toppings, what you ordered last, and whether you buy a salad with your cheese and pepperoni pizza, targeting coupon offers to specific households based on past buying behaviors and preferences.

Says one blogger, "So who is always on my mind when I feel like pizza? Who is sending me coupons and free things that make me want to get pizza rather than make dinner? You got it, Pizza Hut. They had me buy in and now they'll have my loyalty. They make it so easy that I wouldn't want to bother getting it anywhere else."[7]

Internal databases usually can be accessed more quickly and cheaply than other information sources, but they also present some problems. Because internal information was often collected for other purposes, it may be incomplete or in the wrong form for making marketing decisions. For example, sales and cost data used by the accounting department for preparing financial statements must be adapted for use in evaluating the value of specific customer segment, sales force, or channel performance. Data also ages quickly; keeping the database current requires a major effort. In addition, a large company produces mountains of information, which must be well integrated and readily accessible so that managers can find it easily and use it effectively. Managing that much data requires highly sophisticated equipment and techniques.

Marketing Intelligence

Marketing intelligence

The systematic collection and analysis of publicly available information about consumers, competitors, and developments in the marketing environment.

Marketing intelligence is the systematic collection and analysis of publicly available information about consumers, competitors, and developments in the marketplace. The goal of marketing intelligence is to improve strategic decision making by understanding the consumer environment, assessing and tracking competitors' actions, and providing early warnings of opportunities and threats.

Marketing intelligence gathering has grown dramatically as more and more companies are now busily eavesdropping on the marketplace and snooping on their competitors. Techniques range from monitoring Internet buzz or observing consumers firsthand to quizzing the company's own employees, benchmarking competitors' products, researching the Internet, lurking around industry trade shows, and even rooting through rivals' trash bins.

Good marketing intelligence can help marketers to gain insights into how consumers talk about and connect with their brands. Many companies send out teams of trained observers to mix and mingle with customers as they use and talk about the company's products. Other companies routinely monitor consumers' online chatter. For example, Ford employs marketing intelligence firm BrandIntel to monitor blogs and other Internet sites.[8] Ford wants to know what people are saying about its products, their performance, and their looks. It also wants to know about any important issues—positive or negative—that might have consumers buzzing online about specific Ford models. For example, if BrandIntel discovers unanswered product questions or service complaints, it forwards them to Ford's customer-service staff. When appropriate, the service staff can respond online, identifying themselves and asking if they can join the online discussions.

Companies also need to actively monitor competitors' activities. Firms use competitive intelligence to gain early warnings of competitor moves and strategies, new-product launches, new or changing markets, and potential competitive strengths and weaknesses. A recent analysis by consulting firm PriceWaterhouseCoopers found that companies employing competitive intelligence as a critical element in their strategic thinking grow 20 percent faster than those that do not.[9]

Much competitor intelligence can be collected from people inside the company—executives, engineers and scientists, purchasing agents, and the sales force. The company can also obtain important intelligence information from suppliers, resellers, and key customers. Or it can get good information by observing competitors and monitoring their published information. It can buy and analyze competitors' products, monitor their sales, check for new patents, and examine various types of physical evidence. For example, one company regularly checks out competitors' parking lots—full lots might indicate plenty of work and prosperity; half-full lots might suggest hard times.

Some companies have even rifled their competitors' garbage, which is legally considered abandoned property once it leaves the premises. In one elaborate garbage-snatching incident, AirCanada was recently caught rifling through rival WestJet's dumpsters in efforts to find evidence that WestJet was illegally tapping into Air Canada's computers.[10] In another case, Procter & Gamble admitted to "dumpster diving" at rival Unilever's headquarters. Unilever's dumpsters yielded a wealth of information about strategies for Unilever's hair care brands. However, when news of the questionable tactics reached top P&G managers, they were shocked and immediately stopped the project. Although P&G claims it broke no laws, it noted that dumpster raids violated its business policies.

Competitors often reveal intelligence information through their annual reports, business publications, trade show exhibits, press releases, advertisements, and Web pages. The Web has become an invaluable source of competitive intelligence. Using Internet search engines, marketers can search specific competitor names, events, or trends and see what turns up. Moreover, most companies now place volumes of information on their Web sites, providing details to attract customers, partners, suppliers, investors, or franchisees. This can provide a wealth of useful information about competitors' strategies, markets, new products, facilities, and other happenings.

Intelligence seekers can also pore through any of thousands of online databases. Some are free. For example, the U.S. Security and Exchange Commission's database provides a huge stockpile of financial information on public competitors, and the U.S. Patent Office and Trademark database reveals patents competitors have filed. And for a fee, companies can subscribe to any of the more than 3,000 online databases and information search services such as Dialog, Hoover's, DataStar, LexisNexis, Dow Jones News Retrieval, ProQuest, and Dun & Bradstreet's Online Access. Notes

■ Marketing intelligence: Procter & Gamble admitted to "dumpster diving" at rival Unilever's Helene Curtis headquarters. When P&G's top management learned of the questionable practice, it stopped the project, voluntarily informed Unilever, and set up talks to right whatever competitive wrongs had been done.

a marketing intelligence consul-tant, companies "are often surprised that there's so much out there to know. They're busy with their day-to-day operations and they don't realize how much information can be obtained with a few strategic keystrokes."[11]

The intelligence game goes both ways. Facing determined marketing intelligence efforts by competitors, most companies are now taking steps to protect their own information. For example, Unilever conducts widespread competitive intelligence training. Employees are taught not just how to collect intelligence information but also how to protect company information from competitors. According to a former Unilever staffer, "We were even warned that spies from competitors could be posing as drivers at the minicab company we used." Unilever even performs random checks on internal security. Says the former staffer, "At one [internal marketing] conference, we were set up when an actor was employed to infiltrate the group. The idea was to see who spoke to him, how much they told him, and how long it took to realize that no one knew him. He ended up being there for a long time."[12]

The growing use of marketing intelligence raises a number of ethical issues. Although most of the preceding techniques are legal, and some are considered to be shrewdly competitive, some may involve questionable ethics. Clearly, companies should take advantage of publicly available information. However, they should not stoop to snoop. With all the legitimate intelligence sources now available, a company does not need to break the law or accepted codes of ethics to get good intelligence.

Marketing Research

In addition to marketing intelligence information about general consumer, competitor, and marketplace happenings, marketers often need formal studies that provide customer and market insights for specific marketing situations and decisions. For example, Budweiser wants to know what appeals will be most effective in its Super Bowl advertising. Google wants to know how Web searchers will react to a proposed redesign of its site. Or Samsung

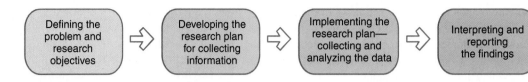

FIGURE 4.2
The Marketing Research Process

wants to know how many and what kinds of people will buy its next-generation plasma televisions. In such situations, marketing intelligence will not provide the detailed information needed. Managers will need marketing research.

Marketing research is the systematic design, collection, analysis, and reporting of data relevant to a specific marketing situation facing an organization. Companies use marketing research in a wide variety of situations. For example, marketing research gives marketers insights into customer motivations, purchase behavior, and satisfaction. It can help them to assess market potential and market share or to measure the effectiveness of pricing, product, distribution, and promotion activities.

Marketing research

The systematic design, collection, analysis, and reporting of data relevant to a specific marketing situation facing an organization.

Some large companies have their own research departments that work with marketing managers on marketing research projects. This is how Procter & Gamble, GE, and many other corporate giants handle marketing research. In addition, these companies—like their smaller counterparts—frequently hire outside research specialists to consult with management on specific marketing problems and conduct marketing research studies. Sometimes firms simply purchase data collected by outside firms to aid in their decision making.

The marketing research process has four steps (see Figure 4.2): defining the problem and research objectives, developing the research plan, implementing the research plan, and interpreting and reporting the findings.

Defining the Problem and Research Objectives

Marketing managers and researchers must work closely together to define the problem and agree on research objectives. The manager best understands the decision for which information is needed; the researcher best understands marketing research and how to obtain the information. Defining the problem and research objectives is often the hardest step in the research process. The manager may know that something is wrong, without knowing the specific causes.

Exploratory research

Marketing research to gather preliminary information that will help define problems and suggest hypotheses.

Descriptive research

Marketing research to better describe marketing problems, situations, or markets, such as the market potential for a product or the demographics and attitudes of consumers.

Causal research

Marketing research to test hypotheses about cause-and-effect relationships.

After the problem has been defined carefully, the manager and researcher must set the research objectives. A marketing research project might have one of three types of objectives. The objective of **exploratory research** is to gather preliminary information that will help define the problem and suggest hypotheses. The objective of **descriptive research** is to describe things, such as the market potential for a product or the demographics and attitudes of consumers who buy the product. The objective of **causal research** is to test hypotheses about cause-and-effect relationships. For example, would a 10 percent decrease in tuition at a private college result in an enrollment increase sufficient to offset the reduced tuition? Managers often start with exploratory research and later follow with descriptive or causal research.

The statement of the problem and research objectives guides the entire research process. The manager and researcher should put the statement in writing to be certain that they agree on the purpose and expected results of the research.

Developing the Research Plan

Once the research problems and objectives have been defined, researchers must determine the exact information needed, develop a plan for gathering it efficiently, and present the plan to management. The research plan outlines sources of existing data and spells out the specific research approaches, contact methods, sampling plans, and instruments that researchers will use to gather new data.

Research objectives must be translated into specific information needs. For example, suppose Unilever decides to conduct research on how consumers would react to a proposed new premium cologne line sold under its Axe brand. The Axe line of body sprays, shower gels, and deodorant has grown rapidly in recent years to become the world's top male grooming brand. Axe targets 18- to 24-year-old males with a coolly seductive, adventurous, and unconventional positioning that promises to give them "an edge in the dating game."[13]

However, as these young consumers age, research suggests that many see themselves as outgrowing the inexpensive body sprays and switching to cologne.[14] Creating a line of cologne fragrances for the Axe brand would be expensive but might help to keep current customers as they mature. The proposed research might call for the following specific information:

- The demographic, economic, and lifestyle characteristics of current Axe users. (Maturing teen and young adult users might move readily to Axe cologne if it's priced right, carries a more mature scent, and is positioned to meet their changing life styles.)
- Characteristics and usage patterns of young male cologne users: What do they need and expect from their fragrances, where do they buy them, when and how do they use them, and what existing cologne brands and price points are most popular? (The new Axe cologne will need strong, relevant positioning in the crowded men's fragrance market.)
- Retailer reactions to the proposed new product line: Would they stock it? Where would they display it? (Failure to get retailer support would hurt sales of the premium cologne.)
- Forecasts of sales of both the new and current Axe products. (Will the new cologne line create new sales or simply take sales from the current Axe products? Will the cologne increase Unilever's overall profits?)

Axe brand managers will need these and many other types of information to decide whether and how to introduce the new cologne product.

The research plan should be presented in a *written proposal*. A written proposal is especially important when the research project is large and complex or when an outside firm carries it out. The proposal should cover the management problems addressed and the research objectives, the information to be obtained, and the way the results will help management decision making. The proposal also should include research costs.

To meet the manager's information needs, the research plan can call for gathering secondary data, primary data, or both. **Secondary data** consist of information that already exists somewhere, having been collected for another purpose. **Primary data** consist of information collected for the specific purpose at hand.

Secondary data
Information that already exists somewhere, having been collected for another purpose.

Primary data
Information collected for the specific purpose at hand.

Gathering Secondary Data

Researchers usually start by gathering secondary data. The company's internal database provides a good starting point. However, the company can also tap a wide assortment of external information sources, including commercial data services and government sources (see Table 4.1).

Companies can buy secondary data reports from outside suppliers. For example, ACNielsen sells buyer data from a panel of more than 265,000 households in 27 countries worldwide, with measures of trial and repeat purchasing, brand loyalty, and buyer demographics. Simmons sells information on more than 8,000 brands in 460 product categories, including detailed consumer profiles that assess everything from the products consumers buy and the brands they prefer to their lifestyles, attitudes, and media preferences. The *Monitor* service by Yankelovich sells information on important social and lifestyle trends. These and other firms supply high-quality data to suit a wide variety of marketing information needs.[15]

Using **commercial online databases**, marketing researchers can conduct their own searches of secondary data sources. General database services such as Dialog, ProQuest, and LexisNexis put an incredible wealth of information at the keyboards of marketing decision makers. Beyond commercial Web sites offering information for a fee, almost every industry association, government agency, business publication, and news medium offers free information to those tenacious enough to find their Web sites. There are so many Web sites offering data that finding the right ones can become an almost overwhelming task.

Commercial online databases
Computerized collections of information available from online commercial sources or via the Internet.

Web search engines can also be a big help in locating relevant secondary information sources. However, they can also be very frustrating and inefficient. For example, an Axe

TABLE 4.1 Selected External Information Sources

For business data:

ACNielsen Corporation (www.acnielsen.com) provides point-of-sale scanner data on sales, market share, and retail prices; data on household purchasing; and data on television audiences (a unit of VNU NV).

Simmons Market Research Bureau (www.smrb.com) provides detailed analysis of consumer patterns in 400 product categories in selected markets.

Information Resources Inc. (www.infores.com) provides supermarket scanner data for tracking grocery product movement and new-product purchasing data.

IMS Health (www.imshealth.com) tracks drug sales, monitors performance of pharmaceutical sales representatives, and offers pharmaceutical market forecasts.

Arbitron (www.arbitron.com) provides local-market and Internet radio audience and advertising expenditure information, among other media and ad spending data.

J.D. Power and Associates (www.jdpower.com) provides information from independent consumer surveys of product and service quality, customer satisfaction, and buyer behavior.

Dun & Bradstreet (www.dnb.com) maintains a database containing information on more than 50 million individual companies around the globe.

comScore Networks (www.comscore.com) provides consumer behavior information and geodemographic analysis of Internet and digital media users around the world.

Thomson Dialog (www.dialog.com) offers access to more than 900 databases containing publications, reports, newsletters, and directories covering dozens of industries.

LexisNexis (www.lexisnexis.com) features articles from business, consumer, and marketing publications plus tracking of firms, industries, trends, and promotion techniques.

Factiva (www.factiva.com) specializes in in-depth financial, historical, and operational information on public and private companies.

Hoover's Inc. (www.hoovers.com) provides business descriptions, financial overviews, and news about major companies around the world.

CNN (www.cnn.com) reports U.S. and global news and covers the markets and news-making companies in detail.

American Demographics (www.demographics.com) reports on demographic trends and their significance for businesses.

For government data:

Securities and Exchange Commission Edgar database (www.sec.gov) provides financial data on U.S. public corporations.

Small Business Administration (www.sba.gov) features information and links for small business owners.

Federal Trade Commission (www.ftc.gov) shows regulations and decisions related to consumer protection and antitrust laws.

Stat-USA (www.stat-usa.gov), a Department of commerce site, highlights statistics on U.S. business and international trade.

U.S. Census (www.census.gov) provides detailed statistics and trends about the U.S. population.

U.S. Patent and Trademark Office (www.uspto.gov) allows searches to determine who has filed for trademarks and patents.

For Internet data:

ClickZ (www.clickz.com) brings together a wealth of information about the Internet and its users, from consumers to e-commerce.

Interactive Advertising Bureau (www.iab.net) covers statistics about advertising on the Internet.

Jupiter Research (www.jupiterresearch.com) monitors Web traffic and ranks the most popular sites.

marketer Googling "men's cologne" would come up with some 430,000 hits! Still, well-structured, well-designed Web searches can be a good starting point to any marketing research project. For example, the fourth hit in the "men's cologne" Google search list takes you to www.epinions.com/Fragrances-Cologne, where you can read consumer reviews and price comparisons of more than 100 men's cologne brands.

Secondary data can usually be obtained more quickly and at a lower cost than primary data. Also, secondary sources can sometimes provide data an individual company cannot collect on its own—information that either is not directly available or would be too expensive to collect. For example, it would be too expensive for Axe marketers to conduct a continuing retail store audit to find out about the market shares, prices, and displays of competitors' brands. But it can buy the InfoScan service from Information Resources Inc., which provides this information based on scanner and other data from 34,000 supermarkets in markets around the nation.[16]

Secondary data can also present problems. The needed information may not exist—researchers can rarely obtain all the data they need from secondary sources. For example, Unilever will not find existing information about consumer reactions to a new cologne line that it has not yet placed on the market. Even when data can be found, they might not be very usable. The researcher must evaluate secondary information carefully to make certain it is *relevant* (fits research project needs), *accurate* (reliably collected and reported), *current* (up-to-date enough for current decisions), and *impartial* (objectively collected and reported).

Primary Data Collection

Secondary data provide a good starting point for research and often help to define research problems and objectives. In most cases, however, the company must also collect primary data. Just as researchers must carefully evaluate the quality of secondary information, they also must take great care when collecting primary data. They need to make sure that it will be relevant, accurate, current, and unbiased. Table 4.2 shows that designing a plan for primary data collection calls for a number of decisions on *research approaches, contact methods, sampling plan,* and *research instruments.*

Research Approaches Research approaches for gathering primary data include observation, surveys, and experiments. Here, we discuss each one in turn.

Observational Research **Observational research** involves gathering primary data by observing relevant people, actions, and situations. For example, a bank might evaluate possible new branch locations by checking traffic patterns, neighborhood conditions, and the location of competing branches.

Researchers often observe consumer behavior to glean customer insights they can't obtain by simply asking customers questions. For instance, Fisher-Price has set up an observation lab in which it can observe the reactions of little tots to new toys. The Fisher-Price Play Lab is a sunny, toy-strewn space where lucky kids get to test Fisher-Price prototypes, under the watchful eyes of designers who hope to learn what will get kids worked up into a new-toy frenzy. And Kimberly-Clark invented a new way to observe behavior through the eyes of consumers:[17]

A few years back, Kimberly-Clark saw sales of its Huggies baby wipes slip just as the company was preparing to launch a line of Huggies baby lotions and bath products. When traditional research didn't yield any compelling customer insights, K-C's marketers decided they could get more useful feedback just from watching customers' daily lives. They came up with camera-equipped "glasses" to be worn by consumers at home, so that researchers could see what they saw. It didn't take long to spot the problems—and the opportunities. Although women in focus groups talked about changing babies at a diaper table, the truth was they changed them on beds, floors, and on top of washing machines in awkward positions. The researchers could see they were struggling with wipe containers and lotions requiring two hands. So the company redesigned the wipe package with

America's leading provider of consumer product purchase, shopping and media usage behavior, including detailed demographic, psychographic, lifestyle and attudinal descriptions

For Over 50 Years, the Voice of the American Consumer **Simmons** An Experian Company

Surveying over 30,000 people annually gathering information on almost 8,000 brands in more than 460 data categories.

Newly Expanded
National Consumer Study (NCS)
Unifying the Simmons National Consumer Study and Simmons National Hispanic Consumer Study
■ The first syndicated research study that fully integrates the consumer behavior of Hispanic Americans with the total U.S. population

Teens Study/Kids Study
■ National survey of teens ages 12-17
■ National survey of kids ages 6-11

Simmons BehaviorGraphics™
■ Powerful segmentation system linking Simmons NCS and National TV ratings

Simmons Integrated Marketing Solutions
■ Custom Media Studies
■ Data Integrations

SimmonsLOCAL
■ Localized projections of NCS in all 207 continental U.S. DMAs

Simmons & Microsoft MapPoint
■ Mapping capabilities for Simmons' 8,000 brands down to zip code level

■ Create a report online in real time

■ Map results instantaneously in MapPoint

29 Broadway, 2nd Floor, New York, NY 10006 | (212) 863.4500 | www.smrb.com

■ Gathering secondary data: Commercial database services such as Simmons sell an incredible wealth of information on everything from the products consumers buy and the brands they prefer to their lifestyles, attitudes, and media preferences. Simmons is "the voice of the American consumer."

Observational research
Gathering primary data by observing relevant people, actions, and situations.

Research Approaches	Contact Methods	Sampling Plan	Research Instruments	
Observation	Mail	Sampling unit	Questionnaire	**TABLE 4.2 Planning Primary Data Collection**
Survey	Telephone	Sample size	Mechanical instruments	
Experiment	Personal	Sampling procedure		
	Online			

a push-button one-handed dispenser and designed lotion and shampoo bottles that can be grabbed and dispensed easily with one hand.

Observational research can obtain information that people are unwilling or unable to provide. In some cases, observation may be the only way to obtain the needed information. In contrast, some things simply cannot be observed, such as feelings, attitudes and motives, or private behavior. Long-term or infrequent behavior is also difficult to observe. Finally, observations can be very difficult to interpret. Because of these limitations, researchers often use observation along with other data collection methods.

A wide range of companies now use **ethnographic research**. Ethnographic research involves sending trained observers to watch and interact with consumers in their "natural habitat." Consider this example:[18]

Ethnographic research
A form of observational research that involves sending trained observers to watch and interact with consumers in their "natural habitat."

Marriott hired design firm IDEO to help it take a fresh look at business travel and to rethink the hotel experience for an increasingly important customer: the young, tech-savvy road warrior. Rather than doing the usual customer surveys or focus group research, IDEO dispatched a team of consultants, including a designer, anthropologist, writer, and architect, on a six-week trip to mingle with customers and get an up-close and personal view of them.

By "living with the natives" (hanging out in hotel lobbies), they learned that hotels are not generally good at serving small groups of business travelers. Hotel lobbies tend to be dark and better suited to killing time than conducting casual business. One IDEO consultant recalls watching a female business traveler drinking wine in the lobby while trying not to spill it on papers spread out on a desk. "There are very few hotel services that address [such] problems," he says. The result: Marriott is reinventing the lobbies of its Marriott and Renaissance Hotels, creating a "social zone," with small tables, brighter lights, and wireless Web access, that is better suited to meetings. Another area will allow solo travelers to work or unwind in larger, quiet, semi-private spaces where they won't have to worry about spilling coffee on their laptops or papers.

■ Ethnographic research: After "living with the natives" (hanging out in hotel lobbies and observing business travelers), Marriott is reinventing the lobbies of its Marriott and Renaissance Hotels, creating a "social zone" with small tables, brighter lights, and wireless Web access where travelers can work or unwind.

Ethnographic research often yields the kinds of details that just don't emerge from traditional research questionnaires or focus groups. Whereas traditional quantitative research approaches seek to test known hypotheses and obtain answers to well-defined product or strategy questions, observational research can generate fresh customer and market insights. "The beauty of ethnography," says a research expert, "is that it provides a richer understanding of consumers than does traditional research. Yes, companies are still using focus groups, surveys, and demographic data to glean insights into the consumer's mind. But closely observing people where they live and work . . . allows companies to zero in on their customers' unarticulated desires."[19]

Survey research
Gathering primary data by asking people questions about their knowledge, attitudes, preferences, and buying behavior.

Survey Research **Survey research**, the most widely used method for primary data collection, is the approach best suited for gathering *descriptive* information. A company that wants to know about people's knowledge, attitudes, preferences, or buying behavior can often find out by asking them directly.

The major advantage of survey research is its flexibility—it can be used to obtain many different kinds of information in many different situations. Surveys addressing almost any marketing question or decision can be conducted by phone or mail, in person, or on the Web. However, survey research also presents some problems. Sometimes people are unable to answer survey questions because they cannot remember or have never thought about what they do and why. People may be unwilling to respond to unknown interviewers or about things they consider private. Respondents may answer survey questions even when they do not know the answer in order to appear smarter or more informed. Or they may try to help the interviewer by giving pleasing answers. Finally, busy people may not take the time, or they might resent the intrusion into their privacy.

Experimental Research   Whereas observation is best suited for exploratory research and surveys for descriptive research, **experimental research** is best suited for gathering *causal* information. Experiments involve selecting matched groups of subjects, giving them different treatments, controlling unrelated factors, and checking for differences in group responses. Thus, experimental research tries to explain cause-and-effect relationships.

For example, before adding a new sandwich to its menu, McDonald's might use experiments to test the effects on sales of two different prices it might charge. It could introduce the new sandwich at one price in one city and at another price in another city. If the cities are similar, and if all other marketing efforts for the sandwich are the same, then differences in sales in the two cities could be related to the price charged.

Experimental research
Gathering primary data by selecting matched groups of subjects, giving them different treatments, controlling related factors, and checking for differences in group responses.

Contact Methods Information can be collected by mail, telephone, personal interview, or online. Table 4.3 shows the strengths and weaknesses of each of these contact methods.

Mail, Telephone, and Personal Interviewing   *Mail questionnaires* can be used to collect large amounts of information at a low cost per respondent. Respondents may give more honest answers to more personal questions on a mail questionnaire than to an unknown interviewer in person or over the phone. Also, no interviewer is involved to bias the respondent's answers.

However, mail questionnaires are not very flexible—all respondents answer the same questions in a fixed order. Mail surveys usually take longer to complete, and the response rate—the number of people returning completed questionnaires—is often very low. Finally, the researcher often has little control over the mail questionnaire sample. Even with a good mailing list, it is hard to control *who* at the mailing address fills out the questionnaire.

Telephone interviewing is one of the best methods for gathering information quickly, and it provides greater flexibility than mail questionnaires. Interviewers can explain difficult questions and, depending on the answers they receive, skip some questions or probe on others. Response rates tend to be higher than with mail questionnaires, and interviewers can ask to speak to respondents with the desired characteristics or even by name.

However, with telephone interviewing, the cost per respondent is higher than with mail questionnaires. Also, people may not want to discuss personal questions with an interviewer. The method introduces interviewer bias—the way interviewers talk, how they ask questions, and other differences may affect respondents' answers. Different interviewers may interpret and record responses differently, and under time pressures some interviewers might even cheat by recording answers without asking questions. Finally, in this age of do-not-call lists and promotion-harassed consumers, potential survey respondents are increasingly hanging up on telephone interviewers rather than talking with them.

	Mail	Telephone	Personal	Online
Flexibility	Poor	Good	Excellent	Good
Quantity of data that can be collected	Good	Fair	Excellent	Good
Control of interviewer effects	Excellent	Fair	Poor	Fair
Control of sample	Fair	Excellent	Good	Excellent
Speed of data collection	Poor	Excellent	Good	Excellent
Response rate	Poor	Poor	Good	Good
Cost	Good	Fair	Poor	Excellent

TABLE 4.3 Strengths and Weaknesses of Contact Methods

Source: Adapted with permission of the authors. From *Marketing Research: Measurement and Method,* 7th ed., by Donald S. Tull and Del I. Hawkins. Copyright 1993 by Macmillan Publishing Company.

Personal interviewing takes two forms—individual and group interviewing. *Individual interviewing* involves talking with people in their homes or offices, on the street, or in shopping malls. Such interviewing is flexible. Trained interviewers can guide interviews, explain difficult questions, and explore issues as the situation requires. They can show subjects actual products, advertisements, or packages and observe reactions and behavior. However, individual personal interviews may cost three to four times as much as telephone interviews.

Group interviewing consists of inviting six to ten people to meet with a trained moderator to talk about a product, service, or organization. Participants normally are paid a small sum for attending. The moderator encourages free and easy discussion, hoping that group interactions will bring out actual feelings and thoughts. At the same time, the moderator "focuses" the discussion—hence the name **focus group interviewing**.

Focus group interviewing
Personal interviewing that involves inviting six to ten people to gather for a few hours with a trained interviewer to talk about a product, service, or organization. The interviewer "focuses" the group discussion on important issues.

Researchers and marketers watch the focus group discussions from behind one-way glass, and comments are recorded in writing or on video for later study. Today, focus group researchers can even use videoconferencing and Internet technology to connect marketers in distant locations with live focus group action. Using cameras and two-way sound systems, marketing executives in a far-off boardroom can look in and listen, using remote controls to zoom in on faces and pan the focus group at will.

Along with observational research, focus group interviewing has become one of the major qualitative marketing research tools for gaining fresh insights into consumer thoughts and feelings. However, focus group studies present some challenges. They usually employ small samples to keep time and costs down, and it may be hard to generalize from the results. Moreover, consumers in focus groups are not always open and honest about their real feelings, behavior, and intentions in front of other people.

Thus, although focus groups are still widely used, many researchers are tinkering with focus group design. For example, Cammie Dunaway, chief marketing officer at Yahoo!, prefers "immersion groups"—four or five people with whom Yahoo!'s product designers talk informally, without a focus group moderator present. That way, rather than just seeing videos of consumers reacting to a moderator, Yahoo! staffers can work directly with select customers to design new products and programs. "The outcome is richer if [consumers] feel included in our process, not just observed," says Dunaway.[20]

Still other researchers are changing the environments in which they conduct focus groups. To help consumers relax and to elicit more authentic responses, they use settings that are more comfortable and more relevant to the products being researched. For example, to get a better understanding of how women shave their legs, Schick Canada created the "Slow Sip" sessions designed to be like a simple get-together with girlfriends.

■ New focus group environments: To create a more congenial setting in which women could open up and share personal shaving and moisturizing stories, Schick sponsored "Slow Sip" sessions in local cafes.

In these Slow Sip sessions, participants gathered round at a local café to sip coffee or tea and munch on snacks together. The structure was loose, and the congenial setting helped the women to open up and share personal shaving and moisturizing stories on a subject that might have been sensitive in a more formal setting. The Slow Sip sessions produced a number of new customer insights. For example, researchers discovered that the message for their Schick Quattro for Women razor—that Quattro has four-blade technology—was too technical. Women don't care about the engineering behind a razor, they care about shaving results. As a result, Schick Canada repositioned the Quattro as offering a smooth, long-lasting shave. As a side benefit, participants enjoyed the sessions so much that they wanted to stick around for more. They became a kind of ongoing advisory board for Schick's marketers and "brand ambassadors" for Schick's products.[21]

Online Marketing Research   The growth of the Internet has had a dramatic impact on the conduct of marketing research. Increasingly, researchers are collecting primary data through **online marketing research**—*Internet surveys, online panels, experiments,* and even *online focus groups.* Online research spending by U.S. companies has soared to $1.35 billion, up from just $253 million in 2000. Web-based research now accounts for 17 percent of all U.S. marketing research spending.[22]

Online research can take many forms. A company can use the Web as a survey medium. It can include a questionnaire on its Web site and offer incentives for completing it. It can use e-mail, Web links, or Web pop-ups to invite people to answer questions and possibly win a prize. It can create online panels that provide regular feedback or conduct live discussions or online focus groups. Beyond surveys, researchers can conduct experiments on the Web. They can experiment with different prices, use different headlines, or offer different product features on different Web sites or at different times to learn the relative effectiveness of their offers. Or they can set up virtual shopping environments and use them to test new products and marketing programs. Finally, a company can learn about the behavior of online customers by following their click streams as they visit the Web site and move to other sites.

The Internet is especially well suited to *quantitative* research—conducting marketing surveys and collecting data. Two-thirds of all Americans now have access to the Web, making it a fertile channel for reaching a broad cross section of consumers. As response rates for traditional survey approaches decline and costs increase, the Web is quickly replacing mail and the telephone as the dominant data collection methodology. One industry analyst estimates that consumer packaged-goods firms may now invest as much as two-thirds of their total quantitative survey budgets online. And Internet surveys now command nearly 80 percent of all online research spending.[23]

Web-based survey research offers some real advantages over traditional phone and mail approaches. The most obvious advantages are speed and low costs. "Faster. Cheaper. It boils down to that," concludes a marketing research executive.[24] By going online, researchers can quickly and easily distribute Internet surveys to thousands of respondents simultaneously via e-mail or by posting them on selected Web sites. Responses can be almost instantaneous, and because respondents themselves enter the information, researchers can tabulate, review, and share research data as they arrive.

Online research usually costs much less than research conducted through mail, phone, or personal interviews. Using the Internet eliminates most of the postage, phone, interviewer, and data-handling costs associated with the other approaches. As a result, Internet surveys typically cost 15 to 20 percent less than mail surveys and 30 percent less than phone surveys. Moreover, sample size has little impact on costs. Once the questionnaire is set up, there's little difference in cost between 10 and 10,000 respondents on the Web.

Beyond their speed and cost advantages, Web-based surveys also tend to be more interactive and engaging, easier to complete, and less intrusive than traditional phone or mail surveys. As a result, they usually garner higher response rates. The Internet is an excellent medium for reaching the hard-to-reach—the often-elusive teen, single, affluent, and well-educated audiences. It's also good for reaching working mothers and other people who lead busy lives. Such people are well represented online, and they can respond in their own space and at their own convenience.

Whereas marketing researchers have rushed to use the Internet for quantitative surveys and data collection, they have been slower to adopt *qualitative* Web-based research approaches—such as online focus groups or depth interviews. However, although most online research spending goes to quantitative applications, many marketers have learned that the Internet can provide a fast, low-cost way to gain qualitative customer insights as well.[25]

Looking for better methods of predicting consumer acceptance to potential new products, Pepsi recently turned to Invoke Solutions, an online consumer research

Online marketing research
Collecting primary data online through Internet surveys, online focus groups, Web-based experiments, or tracking consumers online behavior.

company, which maintained several instant-message-style online panels of 80 to 100 people. Using the panels, Pepsi delved into attitudes among Gen Xers toward drinking mineral water. In just a few hours, the beverage marketer was able to gather and process detailed feedback from hundreds of consumers. At first, Pepsi marketers were jazzed that the group liked the idea of high levels of mineral content in water. But after further exchanges with the online panel, Pepsi beverage scientists on the scene squelched higher mineral levels; that would require adding sugar, which consumers didn't want, to make the taste acceptable. Using the online panels, "conclusions that could take three to four months to sort out through regular focus groups . . . got settled in a few hours," says an Invoke executive.

Online focus groups

Gathering a small group of people online with a trained moderator to chat about a product, service, or organization and gain qualitative insights about consumer attitudes and behavior.

The primary qualitative Web-based research approach is **online focus groups**. Such focus groups offer many advantages over traditional focus groups. Participants can log in from anywhere—all they need is a laptop and a Web connection. Thus, the Internet works well for bringing together people from different parts of the country or world, especially those in higher-income groups who can't spare the time to travel to a central site. Also, researchers can conduct and monitor online focus groups from just about anywhere, eliminating travel, lodging, and facility costs. Finally, although online focus groups require some advance scheduling, results are almost immediate.

Online focus groups can take any of several formats. Most occur in real time, in the form of online chat room discussions in which participants and a moderator sit around a virtual table exchanging comments. Alternatively, researchers might set up an online message board on which respondents interact over the course of several days or a few weeks. Participants log in daily and comment on focus group topics. The focus group moderator monitors the online interactions and redirects the discussion as required to keep the group on track. This ongoing message board format gives participants a chance to reflect on their responses, talk to others, and check out products in the real world as the group progresses. It also gives researchers the opportunity to make ongoing adjustments as the discussion unfolds. As a result, this online approach can produce much more data and deeper insights than single-session, in-person focus groups.

Although low in cost and easy to administer, online focus groups can lack the real-world dynamics of more personal approaches. The online world is devoid of the eye contact, body language, and direct personal interactions found in traditional focus group research. And the Internet format—running, typed commentary and online "emoticons" (punctuation marks that express emotion, such as :-) to signify happiness)—greatly restricts respondent expressiveness. The impersonal nature of the Internet can prevent people from interacting with each other in a normal way and getting excited about a concept.

To overcome these shortcomings, some researchers are now adding real-time audio and video to their online focus groups. For example, online research firm Channel M2 "puts the human touch back into online research" by assembling focus group participants in people-friendly "virtual interview rooms."

Participants are recruited using traditional methods and then sent a Web camera so that both their verbal and nonverbal reactions can be recorded. Participants are then provided instructions via e-mail, including a link to the Channel M2 online interviewing room and a toll-free teleconference number to call. At the appointed

■ Some researchers have now added real-time audio and video to their online focus groups. For example, Channel M2 "puts the human touch back into online research" by assembling focus group participants in people-friendly "virtual interview rooms."

time, when they click on the link and phone in, participants sign on and see the Channel M2 interview room, complete with live video of the other participants, text chat, screen or slide sharing, and a whiteboard. Once the focus group is underway, questions and answers occur in "real time" in a remarkably lively setting. Participants comment spontaneously—verbally, via text messaging, or both. Researchers can "sit in" on the focus group from anywhere, seeing and hearing every respondent. Or they can review a recorded version at a later date.

Although the use of online marketing research is growing rapidly, both quantitative and qualitative Web-based research does have drawbacks. For one, restricted Internet access can make it difficult to get a broad cross section of respondents—a third of all U.S. adults still lack Web access. However, with Internet penetration growing, this is less of a problem.[26] Another major problem is controlling who's in the online sample. Without seeing respondents, it's difficult to know who they really are. Finally, online surveys can be dry and lacking in dynamics compared with other, more-personal approaches.

To overcome such sample and context problems, many online research firms use opt-in communities and respondent panels. For example, online research firm Greenfield Online provides access to 12 million opt-in panel members in more than 40 countries. Advances in technology—such as the integration of animation, streaming audio and video, and virtual environments—also help to overcome online research dynamics limitations.

Perhaps the most explosive issue facing online researchers concerns consumer privacy. Some fear that unethical researchers will use the e-mail addresses and confidential responses gathered through surveys to sell products after the research is completed. They are concerned about the use of technologies that collect personal information online without the respondents' consent. Failure to address such privacy issues could result in angry, less-cooperative consumers and increased government intervention. Despite these concerns, most industry insiders predict healthy growth for online marketing research.[27]

Sampling Plan   Marketing researchers usually draw conclusions about large groups of consumers by studying a small sample of the total consumer population. A **sample** is a segment of the population selected for marketing research to represent the population as a whole. Ideally, the sample should be representative so that the researcher can make accurate estimates of the thoughts and behaviors of the larger population.

Designing the sample requires three decisions. First, *who* is to be surveyed (what *sampling unit*)? The answer to this question is not always obvious. For example, to study the decision-making process for a family automobile purchase, should the researcher interview the husband, wife, other family members, dealership salespeople, or all of these? The researcher must determine what information is needed and who is most likely to have it.

Second, *how many* people should be surveyed (what *sample size*)? Large samples give more reliable results than small samples. However, larger samples usually cost more, and it is not necessary to sample the entire target market or even a large portion to get reliable results. If well chosen, samples of less than 1 percent of a population can often give good reliability.

Third, *how* should the people in the sample be *chosen* (what *sampling procedure*)? Table 4.4 describes different kinds of samples. Using *probability samples*, each population member has a known chance of being included in the sample, and researchers can calculate confidence limits for sampling error. But when probability sampling costs too much or takes too much time, marketing researchers often take *nonprobability samples*, even though their sampling error cannot be measured. These varied ways of drawing samples have different costs and time limitations as well as different accuracy and statistical properties. Which method is best depends on the needs of the research project.

Research Instruments   In collecting primary data, marketing researchers have a choice of two main research instruments—the *questionnaire* and *mechanical devices*. The *questionnaire* is by far the most common instrument, whether administered in person, by phone, or online.

Questionnaires are very flexible—there are many ways to ask questions. *Closed-end questions* include all the possible answers, and subjects make choices among them. Examples include multiple-choice questions and scale questions. *Open-end questions* allow

Sample
A segment of the population selected for marketing research to represent the population as a whole.

TABLE 4.4 Types of Samples	**Probability Sample**	
	Simple random sample	Every member of the population has a known and equal chance of selection.
	Stratified random sample	The population is divided into mutually exclusive groups (such as age groups), and random samples are drawn from each group.
	Cluster (area) sample	The population is divided into mutually exclusive groups (such as blocks), and the researcher draws a sample of the groups to interview.
	Nonprobability Sample	
	Convenience sample	The researcher selects the easiest population members from which to obtain information.
	Judgment sample	The researcher uses his or her judgment to select population members who are good prospects for accurate information.
	Quota sample	The researcher finds and interviews a prescribed number of people in each of several categories.

respondents to answer in their own words. In a survey of airline users, Southwest might simply ask, "What is your opinion of Southwest Airlines?" Or it might ask people to complete a sentence: "When I choose an airline, the most important consideration is. . . ." These and other kinds of open-end questions often reveal more than closed-end questions because respondents are not limited in their answers. Open-end questions are especially useful in exploratory research, when the researcher is trying to find out *what* people think but not measuring *how many* people think in a certain way. Closed-end questions, on the other hand, provide answers that are easier to interpret and tabulate.

Researchers should also use care in the *wording* and *ordering* of questions. They should use simple, direct, unbiased wording. Questions should be arranged in a logical order. The first question should create interest if possible, and difficult or personal questions should be asked last so that respondents do not become defensive. A carelessly prepared questionnaire usually contains many errors (see Table 4.5).

Although questionnaires are the most common research instrument, researchers also use *mechanical instruments* to monitor consumer behavior. Nielsen Media Research attaches *people meters* to television sets in selected homes to record who watches which programs. Retailers use *checkout scanners* to record shoppers' purchases.

Other mechanical devices measure subjects' physical responses. For example, advertisers use eye cameras to study viewers' eye movements while watching ads—at what points their eyes focus first and how long they linger on any given ad component. IBM's BlueEyes technology interprets human facial reactions by tracking pupil, eyebrow, and mouth movements. BlueEyes offers a host of potential marketing uses, perhaps through

TABLE 4.5 A "Questionable Questionnaire"	Suppose that a summer camp director has prepared the following questionnaire to use in interviewing the parents of prospective campers. How would you assess each question?
	1. What is your income to the nearest hundred dollars? *People don't usually know their income to the nearest hundred dollars, nor do they want to reveal their income that closely. Moreover, a researcher should never open a questionnaire with such a personal question.*
	2. Are you a strong or weak supporter of overnight summer camping for your children? *What do "strong" and "weak" mean?*
	3. Do your children behave themselves well at a summer camp? Yes ( ) No ( ) *"Behave" is a relative term. Furthermore, are yes and no the best response options for this question? Besides, will people answer this honestly and objectively? Why ask the question in the first place?*
	4. How many camps mailed or e-mailed information to you last year? This year? *Who can remember this?*
	5. What are the most salient and determinant attributes in your evaluation of summer camps? *What are salient and determinant attributes? Don't use big words on me!*
	6. Do you think it is right to deprive your child of the opportunity to grow into a mature person through the experience of summer camping? *A loaded question. Given the bias, how can any parent answer yes?*

marketing machines that "know how you feel" and react accordingly. An elderly man squints at a bank's ATM screen and the font size doubles almost instantly. A woman at a shopping center kiosk smiles at a travel ad, prompting the device to print out a travel discount coupon.

Still other researchers are applying "neuromarketing," measuring brain activity to learn how consumers feel and respond. Marketing scientists using MRI scans have learned that "strong brands trigger activity in parts of the brain associated with self-identification, positive emotions, and rewards." According to one observer, it "turns out the Nike's swoosh is more than just a feel-good brand logo. It actually lights up your brain."[28] Here's another example of neuromarketing at work:[29]

Thirty-four bathroom-cleanser users recently went to a research lab to watch "Prison Visitor," the much-awarded TV spot for Unilever's Vim line of home cleaners, positioned as a product that "deals with the toughest dirt." The ad shows a young girl visiting her distraught mother, who appears to be behind a prison glass but is revealed to be scrubbing a grimy shower. Researchers wanted a "clean read" on the ad, so they tested consumers in the places where the ad never aired and where the product wasn't yet available. Participants reacted strongly to a "hands on glass" sequence, particularly during a dramatic "I love you, Momma!" "I love you

■ Mechanical measures of consumer response: Some marketers apply neuromarketing—peering into consumers' mind by measuring brain activity to discover how they respond to brands and marketing.

too, baby!" exchange. However, the scenes showing the product demonstration and brand message evoked a much weaker response. In all, the ad stirred up very strong, mostly negative emotions. Follow-up interviews showed that consumers actually hated the ad. How did researchers measure viewers' response to such emotionally charged advertising? Easy. Each participant in the study was asked how they felt about the ad. Oh, and even more telling, there were six electrodes attached to each person's head. Welcome to the world of neuromarketing, which peers into consumers' mind by measuring brain activity to discover how consumers respond to brands and marketing.

Implementing the Research Plan

The researcher next puts the marketing research plan into action. This involves collecting, processing, and analyzing the information. Data collection can be carried out by the company's marketing research staff or by outside firms. The data collection phase of the marketing research process is generally the most expensive and the most subject to error. Researchers should watch closely to make sure that the plan is implemented correctly. They must guard against problems with contacting respondents, with respondents who refuse to cooperate or who give biased answers, and with interviewers who make mistakes or take shortcuts.

Researchers must also process and analyze the collected data to isolate important information and findings. They need to check data for accuracy and completeness and code it for analysis. The researchers then tabulate the results and compute statistical measures.

Interpreting and Reporting the Findings

The market researcher must now interpret the findings, draw conclusions, and report them to management. The researcher should not try to overwhelm managers with numbers and fancy statistical techniques. Rather, the researcher should present important findings and insights that are useful in the major decisions faced by management.

However, interpretation should not be left only to the researchers. They are often experts in research design and statistics, but the marketing manager knows more about the problem and the decisions that must be made. The best research means little if the manager blindly accepts faulty interpretations from the researcher. Similarly, managers may be biased—they might tend to accept research results that show what they expected and to reject those that they did not expect or hope for. In many cases, findings can be interpreted in different ways, and discussions between researchers and managers will help point to the best interpretations. Thus, managers and researchers must work together closely when interpreting research results, and both must share responsibility for the research process and resulting decisions.

Linking the Concepts

Whew! We've covered a lot of territory. Hold up a minute, take a breather, and see if you can apply the marketing research process you've just studied.

- What specific kinds of research can Unilever's Axe brand manager use to learn more about its customers' preferences and buying behaviors? Sketch out a brief research plan for assessing potential reactions to a new Axe cologne line.

- Could you use the marketing research process to analyze your career opportunities and job possibilities? (Think of yourself as a "product" and employers as potential "customers.") What would your research plan look like?

Analyzing and Using Marketing Information

Information gathered in internal databases and through marketing intelligence and marketing research usually requires more analysis. And managers may need help applying the information to gain customer and market insights that will improve their marketing decisions. This help may include advanced statistical analysis to learn more about the relationships within a set of data. Information analysis might also involve the application of analytical models that will help marketers make better decisions.

Once the information has been processed and analyzed, it must be made available to the right decision makers at the right time. In the following sections, we look deeper into analyzing and using marketing information.

Customer Relationship Management (CRM)

The question of how best to analyze and use individual customer data presents special problems. Most companies are awash in information about their customers. In fact, smart companies capture information at every possible customer *touch point*. These touch points include customer purchases, sales force contacts, service and support calls, Web site visits, satisfaction surveys, credit and payment interactions, market research studies—every contact between the customer and the company.

The trouble is that this information is usually scattered widely across the organization. It is buried deep in the separate databases and records of different company departments. To overcome such problems, many companies are now turning to **customer relationship management (CRM)** to manage detailed information about individual customers and carefully manage customer touch points in order to maximize customer loyalty.

CRM first burst onto the scene in the early 2000s. Many companies rushed in, implementing overly ambitious CRM programs that produced disappointing results and many failures. More recently, however, companies are moving ahead more cautiously and implementing CRM systems that really work. By 2010, U.S. companies will spend an estimated $18 billion on CRM systems from companies such as Oracle, Microsoft, Salesforce.com, and SAS.[30]

Customer relationship management (CRM)
Managing detailed information about individual customers and carefully managing customer "touch points" in order to maximize customer loyalty.

CRM consists of sophisticated software and analytical tools that integrate customer information from all sources, analyze it in depth, and apply the results to build stronger customer relationships. CRM integrates everything that a company's sales, service, and marketing teams know about individual customers to provide a 360-degree view of the customer relationship.

CRM analysts develop *data warehouses* and use sophisticated *data mining* techniques to unearth the riches hidden in customer data. A data warehouse is a companywide electronic database of finely detailed customer information that needs to be sifted through for gems. The purpose of a data warehouse is not just to gather information, but to pull it together into a central, accessible location. Then, once the data warehouse brings the data together, the company uses high-powered data mining techniques to sift through the mounds of data and dig out interesting findings about customers.

These findings often lead to marketing opportunities. For example, Wal-Mart's huge database provides deep insights for marketing decisions. A few years ago, as Hurricane Ivan roared toward the Florida coast, reports one observer, the giant retailer "knew exactly what to rush onto the shelves of stores in the hurricane's path—strawberry Pop Tarts. By mining years of sales data from just prior to other hurricanes, [Wal-Mart] figured out that shoppers would stock up on Pop Tarts—which don't require refrigeration or cooking."[31]

■ CRM: Sophisticated software and analytical tools from companies like Saleforce.com help marketers to integrate everything that a company's sales, service, and marketing teams know about individual customers to provide a 360-degree view of the customer relationship.

By using CRM to understand customers better, companies can provide higher levels of customer service and develop deeper customer relationships. They can use CRM to pinpoint high-value customers, target them more effectively, cross-sell the company's products, and create offers tailored to specific customer requirements. For example, Harrah's Entertainment, the world's largest casino operator, maintains a vast customer database and uses its CRM system to manage day-to-day relationships with important customers at its 40 casinos around the world (see Marketing at Work 4.1).

CRM benefits don't come without cost or risk, either in collecting the original customer data or in maintaining and mining it. The most common CRM mistake is to view CRM only as a technology and software solution. But technology alone cannot build profitable customer relationships. "CRM is not a technology solution—you can't achieve . . . improved customer relationships by simply slapping in some software," says a CRM expert. Instead, CRM is just one part of an effective overall *customer relationship management strategy*. "Focus on the *R*," advises the expert. "Remember, a relationship is what CRM is all about."[32]

When it works, the benefits of CRM can far outweigh the costs and risks. Based on a study by SAP, customers using its mySAP CRM software reported an average 10 percent increase in customer retention and a 30 percent increase in sales leads. Overall, 90 percent of the companies surveyed increased in value from use of the software and reported an attractive return on investment. The study's conclusion: "CRM pays off." "No question that companies are getting tremendous value out of this," says a CRM consultant. "Companies [are] looking for ways to bring disparate sources of customer information together, then get it to all the customer touch points." The powerful new CRM techniques can unearth "a wealth of information to target that customer, to hit their hot button."[33]

Distributing and Using Marketing Information

Marketing information has no value until it is used to gain customer insights and make better marketing decisions. Thus, the marketing information system must make the information

4.1 MARKETING AT WORK
Harrah's Hits the CRM Jackpot

Companies everywhere covet the title "The world's greatest." Giant casino operator Harrah's Entertainment rightly claims that title in the gaming industry. Following its recent acquisition of Caesars Entertainment, Harrah's now captures a huge $9.6 billion in revenues from its properties around the nation and world. The Harrah's portfolio includes such star-studded casino and gaming brands as Harrah's, Caesars, Horseshoe, Bally's, Flamingo, Showboat, and The World Series of Poker.

The recent Caesars acquisition only adds to the luster of what was an already very successful company. In the four years prior to the acquisition, Harrah's annual sales grew 37 percent and profits soared 76 percent. Harrah's stock is worth nearly two and a half times its value five years ago, suggesting that Wall Street is betting on a bright future for the gaming giant.

Why has Harrah's been so successful? Everyone at Harrah's will quickly tell you that it's all about managing customer relationships. When you get right down to it, in physical terms, all casinos are pretty much alike. Most customers can't distinguish one company's slot machines, game tables, restaurants, and hotel rooms from another's. What sets Harrah's apart is the way it relates to its customers and creates customer loyalty. During the past decade, Harrah's has become *the* model for good CRM and customer-loyalty management.

At the heart of the Harrah's CRM strategy is its pioneering card-based Total Rewards program, the gaming industry's first and by far most successful loyalty program. Total Rewards members receive points based on the amount they spend at Harrah's facilities. They can then redeem the points for a variety of perks, such as cash, food, merchandise, rooms, and hotel show tickets. Total Rewards forms the basis for a two-part CRM process. First, the company uses Total Rewards to collect a mother lode of information about customers. Then, it mines this information to identify important customers and finely tune its market offerings to their specific needs.

Harrah's maintains a vast customer database. More than 80 percent of Harrah's customers worldwide—40 million customers in all—use a Total Rewards card. That's roughly one out of six adults in the United States alone. Information from every swipe of every card at

■ Customer relationship management: Harrah's CRM system helps the company to focus its branding, marketing, and service development strategies on the needs of its most important customers. "We're trying to figure out which products sell, and we're trying to increase our customer loyalty."

each of Harrah's 40 casinos zips off to a central computer in Memphis, Tennessee. That's a lot of information. Harrah's current data warehouse can store up to 30 terabytes (30 trillion bytes) of data, roughly

readily available to the managers and others who make marketing decisions or deal with customers. In some cases, this means providing managers with regular performance reports, intelligence updates, and reports on the results of research studies.

But marketing managers may also need nonroutine information for special situations and on-the-spot decisions. For example, a sales manager having trouble with a large customer may want a summary of the account's sales and profitability over the past year. Or a retail store manager who has run out of a best-selling product may want to know the current inventory levels in the chain's other stores. Increasingly, therefore, information distribution involves entering information into databases and making it available in a timely, user-friendly way.

Many firms use a company *intranet* to facilitate this process. The intranet provides ready access to research information, stored reports, shared work documents, contact information for employees and other stakeholders, and more. For example, iGo, a catalog and Web retailer, integrates incoming customer service calls with up-to-date database information about

three times the volume of data contained in the U.S. Library of Congress.

Analyzing all this information gives Harrah's detailed insights into casino operations. For example, "visualization software" can generate a dynamic "heat map" of a casino floor, with machines glowing red when at peak activity, then turning blue and then white as the action moves elsewhere. More importantly, the information provides insights into the characteristics and behavior of individual customers—who they are, how often they visit, how long they stay, and how and how much they gamble and entertain.

From its Total Rewards data, Harrah's has learned that 26 percent of its customers produce 82 percent of revenues. And these best customers aren't the "high rollers" that have long been the focus of the industry. Rather, they are ordinary folks from all walks of life—middle-aged and retired teachers, bankers, and doctors who have discretionary income and time. More often than not, these customers visit casinos for an evening, rather than staying overnight at the hotel, and they are more likely to play at the slots than at tables. What motivates them? It's mostly the intense anticipation and excitement of gambling itself.

Using such insights, Harrah's focuses its marketing and service development strategies on the needs of its best customers. For example, the company's advertising reflects the feeling of exuberance that target customers seek. The data insights also help Harrah's do a better job of managing day-to-day customer relationships. After a day's gaming, by the next morning, it knows which customers should be rewarded with free show tickets, dinner vouchers, or room upgrades.

In fact, Harrah's is now starting to process customer information in real time, from the moment customers swipe their rewards cards, creating the ideal link between data and the customer experience. Harrah's chief information office calls this "operational CRM." Based on up-to-the-minute customer information, he explains, "the hotel clerk can see your history and determine whether you should get a room upgrade, based on booking levels in the hotel at that time and on your past level of play. A person might walk up to you while you're playing and offer you $5 to play more slots, or a free meal, or maybe just wish you a happy birthday."

Harrah's CRM and customer-loyalty efforts are paying off like a royal flush. The company has found that happy customers are much more loyal—whereas customer spending decreases by 10 percent based on an unhappy casino experience, it increases by 24 percent with a happy experience. And Harrah's Total Rewards customers appear to be a happier bunch. Compared with nonmembers, member customers visit the company's casinos more frequently, stay longer, and spend more of their gambling and entertainment dollars in Harrah's rather than in rival casinos. Since setting up Total Rewards, Harrah's has seen its share of customers' average annual gambling budgets rise 20 percent, and revenue from customers' gambling at Harrah's rather than their "home casino" has risen 18 percent.

Harrah's CEO Gary Loveman calls Total Rewards "the vertebrae of our business" and says, "it touches, in some form or fashion, 85 percent of our revenue." He says that Harrah's "customer-loyalty strategy [and] relationship marketing . . . are constantly bringing us closer to our customers so we better understand their preferences, and from that understanding we are able to improve the entertainment experiences we offer." Another Harrah's executive puts it even more simply: "It's no different from what a good retailer or grocery store does. We're trying to figure out which products sell, and we're trying to increase our customer loyalty." Ka-ching! Through smart CRM investments, Harrah's has hit the customer-loyalty jackpot.

Sources: Quotes and other information from Suzette Parmley, "Wooing with Loyalty," *Philadelphia Inquirer*, February 28, 2007; Phil Bligh and Doug Turk, "Cashing In on Customer Loyalty," *Customer Relationship Management*, June 1, 2004, p. 48; Thomas Hoffman, "Harrah's Bets on Loyalty Program in Caesars Deal," *Computerworld*, June 27, 2005, p. 10; Daniel Lyons, "Too Much Information," *Forbes*, December 13, 2004, p. 110; Suzette Parmley "When Its Customers Return, a Casino Always Wins," *Philadelphia Inquirer*, April 15, 2005; Kai Ryssdal and Andrew Park, "Harrah's Database of Gamblers," transcript from *Marketplace*, August 4, 2005; Neal A. Martin, "A Tempting Wager," *Barron's*, April 10, 2006, pp. 28–30; John S. Webster, "Harrah's CTO Tim Stanley Plays 'Operational CRM,'" June 7, 2006, accessed at www.computerworld.com; Harrah's, *Hoover's Company Records*, www.hoovers.com, accessed, November 2007; and Harrah's annual reports and other information accessed at http://investor.harrahs.com/phoenix.zhtml?c=84772&p=irol-reportsAnnual, August 2007.

customers' Web purchases and e-mail inquiries. By accessing this information on the intranet while speaking with the customer, iGo's service representatives can get a well-rounded picture of each customer's purchasing history and previous contacts with the company.

In addition, companies are increasingly allowing key customers and value-network members to access account, product, and other data on demand through *extranets*. Suppliers, customers, resellers, and select other network members may access a company's extranet to update their accounts, arrange purchases, and check orders against inventories to improve customer service. For example, Wal-Mart's RetailLink extranet system provides suppliers with a two-year history of every product's daily sales in every Wal-Mart store worldwide, letting them track when and where their products are selling and current inventory levels. And Target's PartnersOnline extranet lets its supplier/partners review current sales, inventory, delivery, and forecasting data. Such information sharing helps Target, its suppliers, and its customers by elevating the performance of the supply chain.[34]

Thanks to modern technology, today's marketing managers can gain direct access to the information system at any time and from virtually any location. They can tap into the system while working at a home office, from a hotel room, or from the local Starbuck's through a wireless network—anyplace where they can turn on a laptop and link up. Such systems allow managers to get the information they need directly and quickly and to tailor it to their own needs. From just about anywhere, they can obtain information from company or outside databases, analyze it using statistical software, prepare reports and presentations, and communicate directly with others in the network.

Linking the Concepts

Let's stop here for a bit, think back, and be certain that you've got the "big picture" concerning marketing information systems.

- What's the overall goal of an MIS? How are the individual components linked and what does each contribute? Take another look at Figure 4.1—it provides a good organizing framework for the entire chapter.
- Apply the MIS framework to Converse (a Nike company). How might Converse go about assessing marketing managers' information needs, developing the needed information, and helping managers to analyze and use the information to gain actionable customer and market insights?

Other Marketing Information Considerations

This section discusses marketing information in two special contexts: marketing research in small businesses and nonprofit organizations and international marketing research. Finally, we look at public policy and ethics issues in marketing research.

Marketing Research in Small Businesses and Nonprofit Organizations

Just like larger firms, small organizations need market information and the customer and market insights that it can provide. Start-up businesses need information about their potential customers, industries, competitors, unfilled needs, and reactions to new market offers. Existing small businesses must track changes in customer needs and wants, reactions to new products, and changes in the competitive environment.

Managers of small businesses and nonprofit organizations often think that marketing research can be done only by experts in large companies with big research budgets. True, large-scale research studies are beyond the budgets of most small businesses. However, many of the marketing research techniques discussed in this chapter also can be used by smaller organizations in a less formal manner and at little or no expense. Consider how one small-business owner conducted market research on a shoestring before even opening his doors:[35]

After a string of bad experiences with his local dry cleaner, Robert Byerley decided to open his own dry-cleaning business. But before jumping in, he conducted plenty of market research. He needed a key customer insight: How would he make his cleaners stand out? To start, Byerley spent an entire week in the library and online, researching the dry-cleaning industry. To get input from potential customers, using a marketing firm, Byerley held focus groups on the store's name, look, and brochure. He also took clothes to the 15 best competing cleaners in town and had focus group members critique their work. Based on his research, he made a list of features for his new business. First on his list: quality. His business would stand behind everything it did. Not on the list: cheap prices. Creating the perfect dry-cleaning establishment simply didn't fit with a discount operation.

■ Small businesses need market research, too. Before opening his own dry cleaning business, Bibbentuckers owner Robert Byerley conducted plenty of low budget market research, including talking with prospective customers. "You have to think like Procter & Gamble."

His research complete, Byerley opened Bibbentuckers, a high-end dry cleaner positioned on high-quality service and convenience. It featured a bank-like drive-through area with curbside delivery. A computerized bar code system read customer cleaning preferences and tracked clothes all the way through the cleaning process. Byerley added other differentiators, such as decorative awnings, refreshments, and TV screens. "I wanted a place . . . that paired five-star service and quality with an establishment that didn't look like a dry cleaner," he says. The market research yielded results. Today, Bibbentuckers is a thriving three-store operation.

"Too [few] small-business owners have a . . . marketing mind-set," says a small-business consultant. "You have to think like Procter & Gamble. What would they do before launching a new product? They would find out who their customer is and who their competition is."[36]

Managers of small businesses and nonprofit organizations can obtain good marketing insights simply by *observing* things around them. For example, retailers can evaluate new locations by observing vehicle and pedestrian traffic. They can monitor competitor advertising by collecting ads from local media. They can evaluate their customer mix by recording how many and what kinds of customers shop in the store at different times. In addition, many small-business managers routinely visit their rivals and socialize with competitors to gain insights.

Managers can conduct informal *surveys* using small convenience samples. The director of an art museum can learn what patrons think about new exhibits by conducting informal focus groups—inviting small groups to lunch and having discussions on topics of interest. Retail salespeople can talk with customers visiting the store; hospital officials can interview patients. Restaurant managers might make random phone calls during slack hours to interview consumers about where they eat out and what they think of various restaurants in the area.

Managers also can conduct their own simple *experiments*. For example, by changing the themes in regular fund-raising mailings or e-mails and watching the results, a nonprofit manager can find out much about which marketing strategies work best. By varying newspaper advertisements, a store manager can learn the effects of things such as ad size and position, price coupons, and media used.

Small organizations can obtain most of the secondary data available to large businesses. In addition, many associations, local media, chambers of commerce, and government agencies provide special help to small organizations. The U.S. Small Business Administration offers dozens of free publications and a Web site (www.sbaonline.sba.gov) that give advice on topics ranging from starting, financing, and expanding a small business to ordering business cards. Other excellent Web resources for small businesses include the U.S. Census Bureau (www.census.gov) and the Bureau of Economic Analysis (www.bea.gov).

The business sections at local libraries can also be a good source of information. Local newspapers often provide information on local shoppers and their buying patterns. Finally, small businesses can collect a considerable amount of information at very little cost on the

Internet. They can scour competitor and customer Web sites and use Internet search engines to research specific companies and issues.

In summary, secondary data collection, observation, surveys, and experiments can all be used effectively by small organizations with small budgets. However, although these informal research methods are less complex and less costly, they still must be conducted with care. Managers must think carefully about the objectives of the research, formulate questions in advance, recognize the biases introduced by smaller samples and less skilled researchers, and conduct the research systematically.[37]

International Marketing Research

International marketing research has grown tremendously over the past decade. In 1995, the top 25 global marketing research organizations had total combined revenues of $5.7 billion, with 45 percent of these revenues coming from outside companies' home countries. By 2005, total revenues for these organizations had grown to $14.4 billion, and the out-of-home-country share had grown to more than 67 percent.[38]

International marketing researchers follow the same steps as domestic researchers, from defining the research problem and developing a research plan to interpreting and reporting the results. However, these researchers often face more and different problems. Whereas domestic researchers deal with fairly homogenous markets within a single country, international researchers deal with diverse markets in many different countries. These markets often vary greatly in their levels of economic development, cultures and customs, and buying patterns.

In many foreign markets, the international researcher may have a difficult time finding good secondary data. Whereas U.S. marketing researchers can obtain reliable secondary data from dozens of domestic research services, many countries have almost no research services at all. Some of the largest international research services do operate in many countries. For example, ACNielsen Corporation (owned by VNU NV, the world's largest marketing research company) has offices in more than 100 countries, from Schaumburg, Illinois to Hong Kong to Nicosia, Cyprus.[39] However, most research firms operate in only a relative handful of countries. Thus, even when secondary information is available, it usually must be obtained from many different sources on a country-by-country basis, making the information difficult to combine or compare.

Because of the scarcity of good secondary data, international researchers often must collect their own primary data. For example, they may find it difficult simply to develop

■ Some of the largest research services firms have large international organizations. ACNielsen has offices in more than 100 countries, here Germany and Japan.

good samples. U.S. researchers can use current telephone directories, e-mail lists, census tract data, and any of several sources of socioeconomic data to construct samples. However, such information is largely lacking in many countries.

Once the sample is drawn, the U.S. researcher usually can reach most respondents easily by telephone, by mail, on the Internet, or in person. Reaching respondents is often not so easy in other parts of the world. Researchers in Mexico cannot rely on telephone, Internet, and mail data collection—most data collection is door to door and concentrated in three or four of the largest cities. In some countries, few people have phones or personal computers. For example, whereas there are 900 main telephone lines, 651 cell phones, and 544 PCs per thousand people in the United States; there are only 168 phone lines, 358 cell phones, and 54 PCs per thousand in Mexico. In Kenya, the numbers drop to 9 phone lines, 73 cell phones, and 4 PCs per thousand people. In some countries, the postal system is notoriously unreliable. In Brazil, for instance, an estimated 30 percent of the mail is never delivered. In many developing countries, poor roads and transportation systems make certain areas hard to reach, making personal interviews difficult and expensive.[40]

Cultural differences from country to country cause additional problems for international researchers. Language is the most obvious obstacle. For example, questionnaires must be prepared in one language and then translated into the languages of each country researched. Responses then must be translated back into the original language for analysis and interpretation. This adds to research costs and increases the risks of error.

Translating a questionnaire from one language to another is anything but easy. Many idioms, phrases, and statements mean different things in different cultures. For example, a Danish executive noted, "Check this out by having a different translator put back into English what you've translated from English. You'll get the shock of your life. I remember [an example in which] 'out of sight, out of mind' had become 'invisible things are insane.'"[41]

Consumers in different countries also vary in their attitudes toward marketing research. People in one country may be very willing to respond; in other countries, nonresponse can be a major problem. Customs in some countries may prohibit people from talking with strangers. In certain cultures, research questions often are considered too personal. For example, in many Latin American countries, people may feel embarrassed to talk with researchers about their choices of shampoo, deodorant, or other personal care products. Similarly, in most Muslim countries, mixed-gender focus groups are taboo, as is videotaping female-only focus groups.

Even when respondents are *willing* to respond, they may not be *able* to because of high functional illiteracy rates. And middle-class people in developing countries often make false claims in order to appear well-off. For example, in a study of tea consumption in India, over 70 percent of middle-income respondents claimed that they used one of several national brands. However, the researchers had good reason to doubt these results—more than 60 percent of the tea sold in India is unbranded generic tea.

Despite these problems, as global marketing grows, global companies have little choice but to conduct such international marketing research. Although the costs and problems associated with international research may be high, the costs of not doing it—in terms of missed opportunities and mistakes—might be even higher. Once recognized, many of the problems associated with international marketing research can be overcome or avoided.

Public Policy and Ethics in Marketing Research

Most marketing research benefits both the sponsoring company and its consumers. Through marketing research, companies learn more about consumers' needs, resulting in more satisfying products and services and stronger customer relationships. However, the misuse of marketing research can also harm or annoy consumers. Two major public policy and ethics issues in marketing research are intrusions on consumer privacy and the misuse of research findings.

Intrusions on Consumer Privacy Many consumers feel positive about marketing research and believe that it serves a useful purpose. Some actually enjoy being interviewed and giving their opinions. However, others strongly resent or even mistrust marketing research. They worry that marketers are building huge databases full of personal information about

4.2 MARKETING AT WORK

Tracking Consumers on the Web: Smart Targeting or a Little Creepy?

On the Internet today, everybody knows who you are. In fact, legions of Internet companies also know your gender, your age, the neighborhood you live in, that you like pickup trucks, and that you spent, say, three hours and 43 seconds on a Web site for pet lovers on a rainy day in January. All that data streams through myriad computer networks, where it's sorted, catalogued, analyzed, and then used to deliver ads aimed squarely at you, potentially anywhere you travel on the Web. It's called *behavioral targeting*—tracking consumers' online browsing behavior and using it to target ads to them.

Targeting ads on the Web is nothing new. Sites such as Google and Yahoo! routinely place ads related to keyword searches alongside the search results. Most of Google's more than $10 billion in revenues come from search-related advertising. But consider this revealing fact: Internet users spend a mere 5 percent of their time actually searching. The rest of the time, they're trolling the vast expanse of Internet space. To fill that space more effectively, online advertisers are now deploying a new breed of supersmart, supertargeted display ads geared to individual Web-browsing behavior.

What you do when you aren't searching—the other 95 percent of the time you spend online—is pure gold to advertisers. And companies such as Yahoo!, Microsoft's MSN, and AOL are busy mining that gold, helping advertisers to target ads based on just about everything you do on the Internet. Yahoo!, the Web's most visited destination, has an estimated 131 million monthly unique visitors to its sites. By dropping "cookies" onto every Web browser that calls up one of its sites, Yahoo! has amassed a staggering amount of data about its users.

Yahoo!'s head of research and data, Usama Fayyad, rides herd on the 12 terabytes of user information that flow into Yahoo!'s servers every day, more than the entire inventory of the Library of Congress. Fittingly, Fayyad is a former rocket scientist whose resume includes a seven-year stint at NASA's Jet Propulsion Lab. He's an intense numbers guy who

■ Behavioral targeting: Wherever you go on the Internet, marketers are looking over your shoulder, then targeting you with ads based on your Web browsing behavior. Is it smart marketing or just "a little bit creepy"?

went on to found two data-mining companies, one of which he sold to Yahoo!. Fayyad and his group crunch all that online user data, blend it with information about what people do on Yahoo!'s search engine, and feed it into models that predict consumer behavior. This has led Fayyad to an important conclusion: What you do on the Web reveals far more about you than what you type into a search box.

Armed with this mass of data, Yahoo! often sells ad space based not on a site's content but on an individual consumer's online behavior. Say you

customers. Or they fear that researchers might use sophisticated techniques to probe our deepest feelings, peek over our shoulders as we shop, or eavesdrop on our conversations and then use this knowledge to manipulate our buying.

There are no easy answers when it comes to marketing research and privacy. For example, is it a good or bad thing that marketers track and analyze consumers' Web clicks and target ads to individuals based on their browsing behavior? (See Marketing at Work 4.2.) Should we applaud or resent the fact that ConAgra, the giant food company known for its Butterball turkeys and Healthy Choice meals, listens in on consumer Web discussions to learn all it can about diet trends and reactions to its brands?

On the one hand, most online chatter is public information, and listening in helps ConAgra to improve its products and bring more value to customers. On the other hand, although it tracks only public forums, the company does not inform consumers or obtain participants' formal consent. Many consumers would find it disconcerting to learn that ConAgra and other companies are tuning in on their online conversations. Interestingly, however, many consumers don't seem to mind. Occasionally, the monitoring of discussion groups itself becomes a topic of online conversation. In one online car forum, a discussion of BuzzMetrics (a Nielsen company that spe-

spent time at Yahoo! Autos sizing up cars based on fuel efficiency, then clicked over to Yahoo's Green Center to read about alternative fuels, then looked at cars on eBay (which has a partnership with Yahoo!). Fayyad can probably predict your next move. In fact, he says he can tell with 75 percent certainty which of the 300,000 monthly visitors to Yahoo! Autos will actually purchase a car within the next three months. And the next time you visit Yahoo! Sports or Finance, you'll likely see ads for hybrid cars.

Also moving quickly into online display advertising are a special breed of behavioral targeting advertising agencies, such as Tacoda (www.tacoda.com) and Revenue Science (www.revenuescience.com). To get an even broader view of what consumers are thinking and doing online, such agencies track consumer behavior across multiple Web sites. This lets them merge audience data from one group of sites with ad placements on another. So if you surf home lawn and garden sites, don't be surprised to see ads for Scotts lawn products the next time you visit Weather.com. Or if you seek car-buying advice at sites such as Edmunds.com or nadaguides.com, expect to see some ads for the very types of cars you researched the next time you visit your favorite ESPN site to catch up on the latest sports scores.

Noticeably absent from the behavioral targeting fray is Google. As the leading search engine, it could certainly track its users' behavior to develop supertargeting capabilities for online display ads. But the company says it won't do this. In fact, it says it's not going to employ the sort of behavioral targeting used by Yahoo! because it doesn't want to snoop on its users. "People are most often not aware that cookies are collecting data on their surfing behavior," says a Google executive. "It's murky in terms of privacy."

Privacy! Yup. As you've no doubt already considered, that's the downside and the biggest danger to the rapidly expanding world of behavioral targeting. As the practice becomes more common, it faces a growing potential for consumer backlash. One analyst calls it "the dark art of behavioral ad targeting"—eavesdropping on consumers without their knowledge or consent. Critics envision a world in which unscrupulous marketers stalk consumers on the Web and invade their privacy with unwanted ads and manipulative marketing schemes.

Proponents, however, claim that behavioral targeting benefits more than abuses consumers. "What we have here is person-centric marketing," says the CEO of Tacoda, one of the first and largest behavioral targeting advertising agencies. "That's been the holy grail of brand advertisers for a long, long time." Behavioral ad targeting takes information from users Web browsing behavior and feeds back ads that are more relevant to their needs and interests.

Although the practice may seem sinister to some consumers, advertisers like what they see so far. According to one survey, more than half of marketers already use behavioral targeting and another third plan to start this year. Spending on behavioral targeting grew to an estimated $1.5 billion in 2007 and is expected to reach $2.1 billion in 2008.

So far, companies have respected user privacy and have guarded the personally identifiable consumer information they collect. To lessen consumer fears of big-brother-type spying, some behavioral targeting networks are even offering opt-out measures to consumers. For example, Tacoda announced a Consumer Choice initiative, under which it will inform every targeted consumer of their exposure to the network at least every six months. "We're aware of our responsibility to maintain trust with consumers and believe the benefits of preserving consumer choice far outweigh the risks," says a Tacoda executive.

But as more and more companies enter the behavioral targeting ad space, the chances of the tactic getting a bad name grow. "We have something new and powerful," says Tacoda's CEO, "and there are likely to be people who abuse it." Abusive or beneficial, it'll be a hard sell to consumers. As one analyst observes, following consumers online and stalking them with ads just "feels a little creepy."

Sources: Portions adapted from Paul Sloan, "The Quest for the Perfect Online Ad," *Business 2.0,* March 2007, pp. 88–92. Other quotes and information from Brian Morissey, "Limits of Search Lead Some to Web Behavior," *Adweek,* March 27, 2006, p. 11; Sam Matthews and Will Cooper, "Behavioral Targeting Networks Let Consumers Choose to Opt Out," *New Media Age,* November 16, 2006, p. 10; Sam Matthews, "Behavioral Targeting Still Not Appreciated," *New Age Media,* December 14, 2006, p. 2; and Steve Smith, "Behavioral Targeting Could Change the Game," *EContent,* January–February 2007, p. 22.

cializes in tracking consumer-generated media, including online exchanges) and its research for General Motors produced no objections—just disbelief that the carmaker could listen to their conversations and still produce such unappealing products. Consumers often moan that companies do not listen to them. Perhaps the monitoring of discussion groups can provide an answer to that problem.[42]

Consumers may also have been taken in by previous "research surveys" that actually turned out to be attempts to sell them something. Still other consumers confuse legitimate marketing research studies with promotional efforts and say "no" before the interviewer can even begin. Most, however, simply resent the intrusion. They dislike mail, telephone, or Web surveys that are too long or too personal or that interrupt them at inconvenient times.

Increasing consumer resentment has become a major problem for the marketing research industry, leading to lower survey response rates in recent years. One study found that 59 percent of consumers had refused to give information to a company because they thought it was not really needed or too personal, up from 42 percent five years earlier. And 71 percent of consumers believe that protecting information is more of a concern now than it was a few years ago. "Some shoppers are unnerved by the idea of giving up any information at all," says an analyst. When asked for something as seemingly harmless as a zip code, "one woman told me she always gives the zip code for Guam, and another said she never surrenders any information, not even a zip code, because 'I don't get paid to help them with market research.'"[43]

The research industry is considering several options for responding to this problem. One example is the Council for Marketing and Opinion Research's "Your Opinion Counts" and "Respondent Bill of Rights" initiatives to educate consumers about the benefits of marketing research and to distinguish it from telephone selling and database building. The industry also has considered adopting broad standards, perhaps based on The International Chamber of Commerce's International Code of Marketing and Social Research Practice. This code outlines researchers' responsibilities to respondents and to the general public. For example, it says that researchers should make their names and addresses available to participants. It also bans companies from representing activities such as database compilation or sales and promotional pitches as research.[44]

Most major companies—including IBM, CitiGroup, American Express, Bank of America, and Microsoft—have now appointed a "chief privacy officer (CPO)," whose job is to safeguard the privacy of consumers who do business with the company. IBM's CPO claims that her job requires "multidisciplinary thinking and attitude." She needs to get all company departments, from technology, legal, and accounting to marketing and communications, working together to safeguard customer privacy.[45]

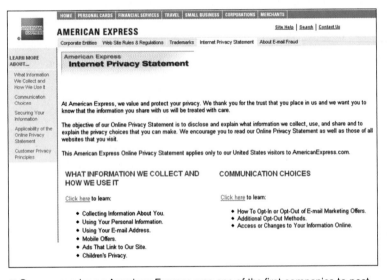

■ Consumer privacy: American Express was one of the first companies to post its privacy policies on the Web. "American Express respects your privacy and is committed to protecting it at all times."

American Express, which deals with a considerable volume of consumer information, has long taken privacy issues seriously. The company developed a set of formal privacy principles in 1991, and in 1998 it became one of the first companies to post privacy policies on its Web site. Its online Internet privacy statement tells customers in clear terms what information American Express collects and how it uses it, how it safeguards the information, and how it uses the information to market to its customers (with instructions on how to opt out).[46]

In the end, if researchers provide value in exchange for information, customers will gladly provide it. For example, Amazon.com's customers do not mind if the firm builds a database of products they buy in order to provide future product recommendations. This saves time and provides value. Similarly, Bizrate users gladly complete surveys rating online seller sites because they can view the overall ratings of others when making purchase decisions. The best approach is for researchers to ask only for the information they need, to use it responsibly to provide customer value, and to avoid sharing information without the customer's permission.

Misuse of Research Findings Research studies can be powerful persuasion tools; companies often use study results as claims in their advertising and promotion. Today, however, many research studies appear to be little more than vehicles for pitching the sponsor's products. In fact, in some cases, the research surveys appear to have been designed just to produce the intended effect. Few advertisers openly rig their research designs or blatantly misrepresent the findings; most abuses tend to be subtle "stretches."

For example, the choice or wording in a survey can greatly affect the conclusions reached. One Black Flag survey asked: "A roach disk . . . poisons a roach slowly. The dying roach returns to the nest and after it dies is eaten by other roaches. In turn these roaches become poisoned and die. How effective do you think this type of product would be in killing roaches?" Not surprisingly, 79 percent said effective.[47]

Recognizing that surveys can be abused, several associations—including the American Marketing Association, Marketing Research Association, and the Council of American Survey Research Organizations (CASRO)—have developed codes of research ethics and standards of conduct. For example, the CASRO Code of Standards and Ethics for Survey Research outlines researcher responsibilities to respondents, including confidentiality, privacy, and avoidance of harassment. It also outlines major responsibilities in reporting results to clients and the public.[48] In the end, however, unethical or inappropriate actions cannot simply be regulated away. Each company must accept responsibility for policing the conduct and reporting of its own marketing research to protect consumers' best interests and its own.

REST STOP ➦ REVIEWING THE CONCEPTS

To create value for customers and to build meaningful relationships with them, marketers must first gain fresh, deep insights into what customers need and want. Such insights come from good marketing information. As a result of the recent explosion of marketing, companies can now obtain great quantities of information, sometimes even too much. The challenge is to transform today's vast volume of consumer information into actionable customer and market insights. A company's marketing research and information system must do more than simply generate lots of information. The real value of marketing research and marketing information lies in how it is used—in the customer insights that it provides.

1. Explain the importance of information in gaining insights about the marketplace and customers.

The marketing process starts with a complete understanding of the marketplace and consumer needs and wants. Thus, the company needs sound information in order to produce superior value and satisfaction for customers. The company also requires information on competitors, resellers, and other actors and forces in the marketplace. Increasingly, marketers are viewing information not only as an input for making better decisions but also as an important strategic asset and marketing tool.

2. Define the marketing information system and discuss its parts.

The *marketing information system (MIS)* consists of people and procedures for assessing information needs, developing the needed information, and helping decision makers to use the information to generate and validate actionable customer and market insights. A well-designed information system begins and ends with users.

The MIS first *assesses information needs.* The marketing information system primarily serves the company's marketing and other managers, but it may also provide information to external partners. Then, the MIS *develops information* from internal databases, marketing intelligence activities, and marketing research. *Internal databases* provide information on the company's own operations and departments. Such data can be obtained quickly and cheaply but often needs to be adapted for marketing decisions. *Marketing intelligence* activities supply everyday information about developments in the external marketing environment. *Market research* consists of collecting information relevant to a specific marketing problem faced by the company. Lastly, the MIS helps users to analyze and use the information to develop customer insights, make marketing decisions, and manage customer relationships.

3. Outline the steps in the marketing research process.

The first step in the marketing research process involves *defining the problem and setting the research objectives,* which may be exploratory, descriptive, or causal research. The second step consists of *developing a research plan* for collecting data from primary and secondary sources. The third step calls for *implementing the marketing research plan* by gathering, processing, and analyzing the information. The fourth step consists of *interpreting and reporting the findings.* Additional information analysis helps marketing managers apply the information and provides them with sophisticated statistical procedures and models from which to develop more rigorous findings.

Both *internal* and *external* secondary data sources often provide information more quickly and at a lower cost than primary data sources, and they can sometimes yield information that a company cannot collect by itself. However, needed information might not exist in secondary sources. Researchers must also evaluate secondary information to ensure that it is *relevant, accurate, current,* and *impartial.* Primary research must also be evaluated for these features. Each primary data collection method—*observational, survey,* and *experimental*—has its own advantages and disadvantages. Similarly, each of the various research contact methods—mail, telephone, personal interview, and online—also has its own advantages and drawbacks.

4. Explain how companies analyze and use marketing information.

Information gathered in internal databases and through marketing intelligence and marketing research usually requires more analysis. This may include advanced statistical analysis or the application of analytical models that will help marketers make better decisions. To analyze individual customer data, many companies have now acquired or developed special software and analysis techniques—called *customer relationship management (CRM)*—that integrate, analyze, and apply the mountains of individual customer data contained in their databases.

Marketing information has no value until it is used to make better marketing decisions. Thus, the marketing information system must make the information available to the managers and others who make marketing decisions or deal with customers. In some cases, this means providing regular reports and updates; in other cases it means making nonroutine information available for special situations and on-the-spot decisions. Many firms use company intranets and extranets to facilitate this process. Thanks to modern technology, today's marketing managers can gain direct access to the information system at any time and from virtually any location.

5. Discuss the special issues some marketing researchers face, including public policy and ethics issues.

Some marketers face special marketing research situations, such as those conducting research in small business, nonprofit, or international situations. Marketing research can be conducted effectively by small businesses and nonprofit organizations with limited budgets. International marketing researchers follow the same steps as domestic researchers but often face more and different problems. All organizations need to react responsibly to major public policy and ethical issues surrounding marketing research, including issues of intrusions on consumer privacy and misuse of research findings.

Navigating the Key Terms

Causal research (102)
Commercial online databases (103)
Customer insights (97)
Customer relationship management (CRM) (114)
Descriptive research (102)
Ethnographic research (106)

Experimental research (107)
Exploratory research (102)
Focus group interviewing (108)
Internal databases (99)
Marketing information system (MIS) (97)
Marketing intelligence (100)
Marketing research (102)

Observational research (105)
Online focus groups (110)
Online marketing research (109)
Primary data (103)
Sample (111)
Secondary data (103)
Survey research (106)

Travel Log

Discussing the Issues

1. Describe a marketing information system (MIS) and discuss the real value of marketing research and marketing information. (AACSB: Communication)

2. Compare and contrast internal databases, marketing intelligence, and marketing research as means for developing marketing information. (AACSB: Communication)

3. Name and describe the three research approaches for gathering primary data. Explain when each approach is appropriate. (AACSB: Communication)

4. Discuss the pros and cons of using questionnaires versus mechanical devices to collect primary data. (AACSB: Communication)

5. Explain customer relationship management (CRM) and how it helps companies develop customer insights. (AACSB: Communication)

6. Discuss the challenges U.S. researchers might encounter when conducting research in other countries. (AACSB; Communication)

Application Questions

1. Describe the research process for a small business or nonprofit organization in your community. How does it differ compared to that for a larger business or organization? (AACSB: Communication; Reflective Thinking)

2. Assume you work for Outback Steakhouse, and your work group is tasked to assess customer satisfaction. Assign a different contact method used in marketing research to each member of your group to discuss the strengths and weaknesses of each. Write a brief report explaining which method your work group agreed would be appropriate for this task and support your recommendation. (AACSB: Communication; Reflective Thinking)

3. One source of competitive marketing intelligence is a company's Web site. Visit Gateway's Web site (www.gateway.com) and identify information that might be useful to competitors. Write a brief report of what you found. (AACSB: Communication; Use of IT)

Under the Hood: Focus on Technology

Zoomerang is an online research tool used by many businesses and other organizations. It provides services such as online surveys, focus groups, sample selection from a national panel, and survey design. Conducting a survey can be as simple as adapting a current questionnaire to an online format and sampling current customers, or surveys can be developed by Zoomerang and a sample selected from the millions of respondents in their online panel. Zoomerang can even conduct a survey in several languages. Visit Zoomerang's Web site (http://info.zoomerang.com) and answer the following questions:

1. Discuss the benefits of using this service. (AACSB: Communication; Use of IT)

2. How might a university use this service to assess whether students are receiving a valuable education? (AACSB: Communication; Reflective Thinking)

Focus on Ethics

Marketing information is necessary for marketers to develop customer and market insights to better meet the needs of customers. Research respondents often are asked personal information that they might not want shared with others. Advances in technology enable the collection of large amounts of personal and behavioral information on consumers. However, gathering such information concerns individual consumers, consumer protection groups, and government agencies. Legitimate marketing researchers follow codes of ethics to use consumer information responsibly, and there are laws in place to protect consumers' privacy.

1. The Council of American Survey Research Organizations (CASRO) is a trade group representing survey researchers and provides a code of ethics for its members. Visit www.casro.org and write a brief summary of the code of ethics for survey researchers. (AACSB: Communication; Use of IT)

2. Do consumers have a "right" to privacy? Discuss some federal laws in place to protect consumers' privacy. (AACSB: Communication)

Video Case

Burke

For more than 75 years, Burke has been helping marketers to understand the marketplace and build stronger relationships with customers. As a full-service, custom marketing research firm, the company helps its clients better understand everything from how consumers make purchase decisions to what drives customer loyalty. Burke was founded in 1931, when researchers went door to door to gather information. Today, the company uses a rich variety of methods to reach consumers, including telephone and Web interviewing, direct mail, and online surveys.

Burke helps marketers discover information about customers, competitors, products, and marketing programs. But more than just gathering information, Burke's services help clients use the information to gain customer insights. With sophisticated computer analysis, Burke offers the right information, in the right form, at the right time to help them make better marketing decisions.

After viewing the video featuring Burke, answer the following questions about marketing research.

1. What process does Burke use to define the research question?

2. How does Burke's process for marketing research compare to the steps outlined in the chapter?

3. How does marketing research, the Burke way, help clients build strong relationships with customers?

After studying this chapter, you should be able to

1. describe the consumer market and the major factors that influence consumer buyer behavior
2. identify and discuss the stages in the buyer decision process
3. describe the adoption and diffusion process for new products
4. define the business market and identify the major factors that influence business buyer behavior
5. list and define the steps in the business buying decision process

CHAPTER 5

Understanding Consumer and Business Buyer Behavior

ROAD MAP **Previewing the Concepts**

In the previous chapter, you studied how marketers obtain, analyze, and use marketing information to gain customer and market insights as a basis for creating customer value and relationships. In this chapter, you'll continue your marketing journey with a closer look at the most important element of the marketplace—customers. The aim of marketing is to affect how customers think about and behave toward the organization and its market offerings. But to affect the *whats, whens,* and *hows* of buying behavior, marketers must first understand the *whys.* We look first at *final consumer* buying influences and processes and then at the buying behavior of *business customers.* You'll see that understanding buying behavior is an essential but very difficult task.

Our first point of interest: Harley-Davidson, maker of the nation's top-selling heavyweight motorcycles. Who rides these big Harley "Hogs"? What moves them to tattoo their bodies with the Harley-Davidson emblem, abandon home and hearth for the open road, and flock to Harley rallies by the hundreds of thousands? *You* might be surprised, but Harley-Davidson knows *very* well.

Few brands engender such intense loyalty as that found in the hearts of Harley-Davidson owners. Harley buyers are granitelike in their devotion to the brand. "You don't see people tattooing Yamaha on their bodies," observes the publisher of *American Iron,* an industry publication. And according to another industry insider, "For a lot of people, it's not that they want a motorcycle; it's that they want a Harley—the brand is that strong."

Each year, in early March, more than 350,000 Harley bikers rumble through the streets of Daytona Beach, Florida, to attend the Daytona Bike Week celebration. Bikers from across the nation lounge on their low-slung Harleys, swap biker tales, and sport T-shirts proclaiming things like, "I'd rather push a Harley than drive a Honda."

Riding such intense emotions, Harley-Davidson has rumbled its way to the top of the heavyweight motorcycle market. Harley's "Hogs" capture 26 percent of all U.S. bike sales and almost 50 percent of the heavyweight segment. For several years running, sales have outstripped supply, with customer waiting lists of up to two years for popular models and street prices running well above suggested list prices. During the past ten years, annual revenues and earnings have grown at better than 14 percent and 23 percent, respectively. By 2007, Harley-Davidson had experienced

21 straight years of record sales and income, and its stock was at a record high.

Harley-Davidson's marketers spend a great deal of time thinking about customers and their buying behavior. They want to know who their customers are, what they think and how they feel, and why they buy a Harley Fat Boy Softail rather than a Yamaha or a Kawasaki or a big Honda American Classic. What is it that makes Harley buyers so fiercely loyal? These are difficult questions; even Harley owners themselves don't know exactly what motivates their buying. But Harley management puts top priority on understanding customers and what makes them tick.

Who rides a Harley? You might be surprised. Motorcycles are attracting a new breed of riders—older, more affluent, and better educated. "While the outlaw bad-boy biker image is what we might typically associate with Harley riders," says an analyst, "they're just as likely to be CEOs and investment bankers." "You take off the leathers and the helmet and you'll never know who you'll find," says one hard-core Harley enthusiast, himself a former New York City producer. "We're a varied lot. . . . America, at it's very best . . . a melting pot." The average Harley customer is a 47-year-old male with a median household income of $82,000. Today, women make more than 12 percent of Harley purchases. Harley-Davidson makes good bikes, and to keep up with its shifting market, the company has upgraded its showrooms and sales approaches. But Harley customers are buying a lot more than just a quality bike and a smooth sales pitch. To gain a better understanding of customers' deeper motivations, Harley-Davidson conducted focus groups in which it invited bikers to make cut-and-paste collages of pictures that expressed their feelings about Harley-Davidson motorcycles. (Can't you just see a bunch of hard-core bikers doing this?) It then mailed out 16,000 surveys containing a typical battery of psychological, sociological, and demographic questions as well as subjective questions such as "Is Harley more typified by a brown bear or a lion?"

The research revealed seven core customer types: adventure-loving traditionalists, sensitive pragmatists, stylish status seekers, laid-back campers, classy capitalists, cool-headed loners, and cocky misfits. However, all owners appreciated their Harleys for the same basic reasons. "It didn't matter if you were the guy who swept the floors of the factory or if you were the CEO at that factory, the attraction to Harley was very similar," says a Harley-Davidson executive. "Independence, freedom, and power were the universal Harley appeals."

"It's much more than a machine," says the analyst. "It is part of their own self-expression and lifestyle." Another analyst suggests that owning a Harley makes you "the toughest, baddest guy on the block. Never mind that [you're] a dentist or an accountant. You [feel] wicked astride all that power." Your Harley renews your spirits and announces your independence. As the Harley-Davidson Web site's homepage announces, "Thumbing the starter of a Harley-Davidson does a lot more than fire the engine. It fires the imagination." Adds a Harley-Davidson dealer: "We sell a dream here." The classic look, the throaty sound, the very idea of a Harley—all contribute to its mystique. Owning this "American legend" makes you a part of something bigger, a member of the Harley-Davidson family.

Such strong emotions and motivations are captured in a classic Harley-Davidson advertisement. The ad shows a close-up of an arm, the bicep adorned with a Harley-Davidson tattoo. The headline asks, "When was the last time you felt this strongly about anything?" The ad copy outlines the problem and suggests a solution: "Wake up in the morning and life picks up where it left off. . . . What once seemed exciting has now become part of the numbing routine. It all begins to feel the same. Except when you've got a Harley-Davidson. Something strikes a nerve. The heartfelt thunder rises up, refusing to become part of the background. Suddenly things are different. Clearer. More real. As they should have been all along. Riding a Harley changes you from within. The effect is permanent. Maybe it's time you started feeling this strongly. Things are different on a Harley."[1]

The Harley-Davidson example shows that many different factors affect consumer buying behavior. Buying behavior is never simple, yet understanding it is the essential task of marketing management. First we explore the dynamics of the consumer market and consumer buyer behavior. We then examine business markets and the business buying process.

Consumer buyer behavior
The buying behavior of final consumers—individuals and households who buy goods and services for personal consumption.

Consumer market
All the individuals and households who buy or acquire goods and services for personal consumption.

Consumer Markets and Consumer Buyer Behavior

Consumer buyer behavior refers to the buying behavior of final consumers—individuals and households who buy goods and services for personal consumption. All of these final consumers combine to make up the **consumer market**. The American consumer market consists of more than 300 million people who consume more than $12 trillion worth of goods and services each year, making it one of the most attractive consumer markets in the world. The world consumer market consists of more than 6.6 *billion* people who annually consume an estimated $65 trillion worth of goods and services.[2]

Consumers around the world vary tremendously in age, income, education level, and tastes. They also buy an incredible variety of goods and services. How these diverse consumers relate with each other and with other elements of the world around them impacts their choices among various products, services, and companies. Here we examine the fascinating array of factors that affect consumer behavior.

Model of Consumer Behavior

Consumers make many buying decisions every day. Most large companies research consumer buying decisions in great detail to answer questions about what consumers buy, where they buy, how and how much they buy, when they buy, and why they buy. Marketers can study actual consumer purchases to find out what they buy, where, and how much. But learning about the *whys* of consumer buying behavior is not so easy—the answers are often locked deep within the consumer's mind.

"For companies with billions of dollars on the line, the buying decision is the most crucial part of their enterprise," states one consumer behavior analyst. "Yet no one really knows how the human brain makes that choice." Often, consumers themselves don't know exactly what influences their purchases. "Buying decisions are made at an unconscious level," says the analyst, "and . . . consumers don't generally give very reliable answers if you simply ask them, 'Why did you buy this?' "[3]

The central question for marketers is: How do consumers respond to various marketing efforts the company might use? The starting point is the stimulus-response model of buyer behavior shown in Figure 5.1. This figure shows that marketing and other stimuli enter the consumer's "black box" and produce certain responses. Marketers must figure out what is in the buyer's black box.

Marketing stimuli consist of the Four Ps: product, price, place, and promotion. Other stimuli include major forces and events in the buyer's environment: economic, technological, political, and cultural. All these inputs enter the buyer's black box, where they are turned into a set of observable buyer responses: the buyer's brand and company relationship behavior and what he or she buys, when, where, and how often.

The marketer wants to understand how the stimuli are changed into responses inside the consumer's black box, which has two parts. First, the buyer's characteristics influence how he or she perceives and reacts to the stimuli. Second, the buyer's decision process itself affects the buyer's behavior. We look first at buyer characteristics as they affect buyer behavior and then discuss the buyer decision process.

Characteristics Affecting Consumer Behavior

Consumer purchases are influenced strongly by cultural, social, personal, and psychological characteristics, shown in Figure 5.2. For the most part, marketers cannot control such factors, but they must take them into account.

Cultural Factors Cultural factors exert a broad and deep influence on consumer behavior. The marketer needs to understand the role played by the buyer's *culture, subculture,* and *social class.*

FIGURE 5.1

Model of Buyer Behavior

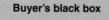

Marketing and other stimuli	**Buyer's black box**	**Buyer responses**
Marketing — Product, Price, Place, Promotion **Other** — Economic, Technological, Social, Cultural	Buyer's characteristics Buyer decision process	Buying attitudes and preferences Purchase behavior: what the buyer buys, when, where, and how much Brand and company relationship behavior

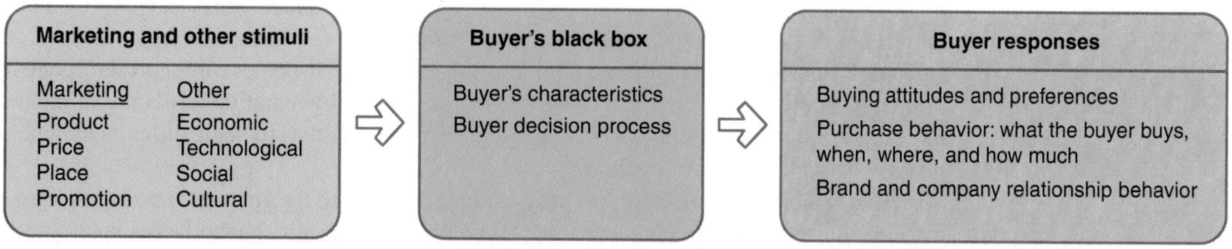

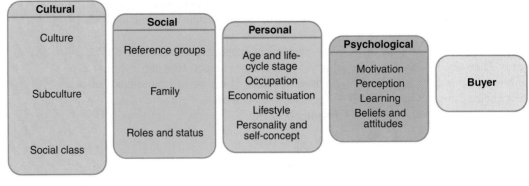

FIGURE 5.2
Factors Influencing Consumer Behavior

Culture
The set of basic values, perceptions, wants, and behaviors learned by a member of society from family and other important institutions.

Culture   **Culture** is the most basic cause of a person's wants and behavior. Human behavior is largely learned. Growing up in a society, a child learns basic values, perceptions, wants, and behaviors from the family and other important institutions. A child in the United States normally learns or is exposed to the following values: achievement and success, activity and involvement, efficiency and practicality, progress, hard work, material comfort, individualism, freedom, humanitarianism, youthfulness, and fitness and health. Every group or society has a culture, and cultural influences on buying behavior may vary greatly from country to country. Failure to adjust to these differences can result in ineffective marketing or embarrassing mistakes.

Marketers are always trying to spot *cultural shifts* in order to discover new products that might be wanted. For example, the cultural shift toward greater concern about health and fitness has created a huge industry for health-and-fitness services, exercise equipment and clothing, organic foods, and a variety of diets. The shift toward informality has resulted in more demand for casual clothing and simpler home furnishings.

Subculture
A group of people with shared value systems based on common life experiences and situations.

Subculture   Each culture contains smaller **subcultures**, or groups of people with shared value systems based on common life experiences and situations. Subcultures include nationalities, religions, racial groups, and geographic regions. Many subcultures make up important market segments, and marketers often design products and marketing programs tailored to their needs. Examples of four such important subculture groups include Hispanic, African American, Asian American, and mature consumers.

The U.S. *Hispanic market*—Americans of Cuban, Mexican, Central American, South American, and Puerto Rican descent—consists of some 45 million consumers. The U.S. Hispanic population has grown fivefold since 1966, making it the fastest growing U.S. subsegment. By 2020, this group will make up about 20 percent of the U.S. population. Hispanic purchasing power now exceeds $800 billion and is expected to top $1.2 trillion by 2012, an 86 percent increase over 2003 levels.[4]

Although Hispanic consumers share many characteristics and behaviors with the mainstream buying public, there are also distinct differences. Hispanic consumers tend to buy more branded, higher-quality products—generics don't sell well to this group. They tend to make shopping a family affair, and children have a big say in what brands they buy. Perhaps more important, Hispanics are very brand loyal, and they favor companies who show special interest in them.[5]

Even within the Hispanic market, there exist many distinct subsegments based on nationality, age, and other factors. For example, a company's product or message may be more relevant to one nationality over another, such as Mexicans, Costa Ricans, Argentineans, or Cubans. Language is another issue. Older, first-generation Hispanics might prefer Spanish as their primary or only language. Younger, second- or third-generation Hispanics might be more comfortable with English. Companies must be sensitive to such differences when marketing to the Hispanic segment.[6]

Most major marketers now produce products tailored to the Hispanic market and promote them using Spanish-language ads and media. For example, Home Depot spent more than $48 million on Hispanic advertising last year, making it the nation's fifth-most advertised brand in that market.[7] Home depot has also developed products designed specifically for Hispanics. Hispanic spending on home improvement projects has increased more than 75 percent over the past seven years, triple the rate of non-Hispanic households. So, after learning that painting is one of the most popular Hispanic home improvement projects, Home Depot created a new line of paint colors with Spanish names and special cultural associations.[8]

> Mention the color Hunter Green to Martha Kruse, senior multicultural marketing manager at Home Depot, and the Peruvian can't relate. But tell her Verde Amazonas and there is an immediate visual association. To reach out to Hispanic consumers through color and culture, Home Depot launched Colores Orígenes (which in Spanish means "the origin of one's roots"), a line of more than 70 paint colors. At first glance, the colors don't look much different. But closer inspection reveals a distinct and vibrant color palate that evokes images of food and icons popular in Hispanic culture. "Each has a little story," says Kruse. Mango Jugoso is a juicy mango, and *elote* is the Mexican word for buttery yellow corn. Horchata is a Mexican rice drink. Cafe Expreso suggests sociability to Cubans who love very strong coffee. "These are copies of the colors that we know Hispanics love," Krause affirms. Home Depot initially debuted Colores Orígenes in only its 400 most heavily Hispanic stores. But the line proved so popular, the retailer has now rolled out the line to all of its stores.

With annual buying power of $799 billion, estimated to reach $981 billion by 2010, the nation's 38.7 million *African American* consumers also attract much marketing attention. The U.S. black population is growing in affluence and sophistication. Although more price conscious than other segments, blacks are also strongly motivated by quality and selection. Brands are important. So is shopping—black consumers seem to enjoy shopping more than other groups, even for something as mundane as groceries. Black consumers are also the most fashion conscious of the ethnic groups.[9]

In recent years, many companies have developed special products, appeals, and marketing programs for African American consumers. For example, P&G's roots run deep in this market. Procter & Gamble currently spends six times more on media targeting black consumers than it did just five years ago. It has a long history of using black spokespeople in its ads, beginning in 1969 with entertainer Bill Cosby endorsing Crest. Today, you'll see Angela Bassett promoting the benefits of Olay body lotion for black skin, Tiger Woods discussing the virtues of Gillette razors, and Queen Latifah in commercials promoting a Cover Girl line for black women. "The new Queen Collection was inspired by me to celebrate the beauty of women of color," says Latifah, "and it gives women the confidence they are looking for by accentuating our natural features."[10]

P&G has also tailored a number of its products to the special preferences of African American consumers. For example, when market research showed that blacks prefer more scents and flavors, P&G added new scents to Gain detergent and flavors to Crest Whitening Expressions toothpaste. And the consumer products giant has created a line of Pantene Relaxed and Natural shampoos specially formulated for women of color. Such moves have made P&G an acknowledged leader in serving African American consumers. Says one industry watcher, "Without question, P&G has to be seen as one of the companies that other companies pattern their behavior after."[11]

■ Procter & Gamble's roots run deep in targeting African American consumers. For example, its Cover Girl Queen Latifah line is specially formulated "to celebrate the beauty of women of color."

快人一步，確保財運滾滾到！

Keep one step ahead to ensure your wealth
of fortune will arrive again and again!   ● PNC BANK

LEADING THE WAY.

■ Targeting Asian Americans: Because of the segment's affluence
and rapidly growing buying power, financial institutions like PNC
Bank cater directly to this segment with specially developed ads
and marketing programs.

Asian Americans are the most affluent U.S. demographic segment. They now number more than 14.4 million and wield more than $400 billion in annual spending power, expected to reach $579 billion in 2010. They are the second-fastest-growing population subsegment after Hispanics. Chinese Americans constitute the largest group, followed by Filipinos, Japanese Americans, Asian Indians, and Korean Americans. The U.S. Asian American population is expected to more than double by 2050, when it will make up more than 9 percent of the U.S. population.[12]

Asian consumers may be the most tech-savvy segment—more than 85 percent of English-speaking Asian Americans go online regularly and are most comfortable with Internet technologies such as online banking and instant messaging. As a group, Asian consumers shop frequently and are the most brand conscious of all the ethnic groups. They can be fiercely brand loyal.[13]

Because of the segment's rapidly growing buying power, many firms are now targeting the Asian American market. For example, PNC Bank continues to build its relationship with Asian Americans through a series of advertising and public relations campaigns that focus on family values and savings, both central to the Asian American culture. Starting with its Lunar New Year campaign last year, celebrating the most important holiday in many Asian cultures, PNC Bank promotes specific services such as account openings and small business banking tailored specifically to Korean and Chinese customers. The bank sponsors events such as the PNC Merry Wind Summer Festival, complete with ethnic food, family entertainment, and free financial consultations. It also provides in-language financial consultants at many branch locations.[14]

As the U.S. population ages, *mature consumers* are becoming a very attractive market. Now 68 million strong, the population of U.S. seniors will more than double in the next 25 years. The 65-and-over crowd alone numbers close to 37 million, more than 12 percent of the population. Mature consumers are better off financially than are younger consumer groups. Because mature consumers have more time and money, they are an ideal market for exotic travel, restaurants, high-tech home entertainment products, leisure goods and services, designer furniture and fashions, financial services, and health care services.[15]

Their desire to look as young as they feel also makes more-mature consumers good candidates for cosmetics and personal care products, health foods, fitness products, and other items that combat the effects of aging. The best strategy is to appeal to their active, multidimensional lives. For example, many beauty and style brands now contain product lines geared towards battling effects of aging. Dove's ProAge hair and skin care product line claims that "Beauty has no age limit." ProAge ads feature active and attractive, real women who seem to be benefiting from the product's promise. Says one ad, "Embrace the best years of your life with Dove ProAge, a new line of products for skin and hair created to let women in their best years realize the beautiful potential that lies within. This isn't anti-age, it's pro-age."

Social class

Relatively permanent and ordered divisions in a society whose members share similar values, interests, and behaviors.

Social Class   Almost every society has some form of social class structure. **Social classes** are society's relatively permanent and ordered divisions whose members share similar values, interests, and behaviors. Social scientists have identified the seven American social classes shown in Figure 5.3.

Social class is not determined by a single factor, such as income, but is measured as a combination of occupation, income, education, wealth, and other variables. In some social systems, members of different classes are reared for certain roles and cannot change their social positions. In the United States, however, the lines between social classes are not fixed and rigid; people can move to a higher social class or drop into a lower one.

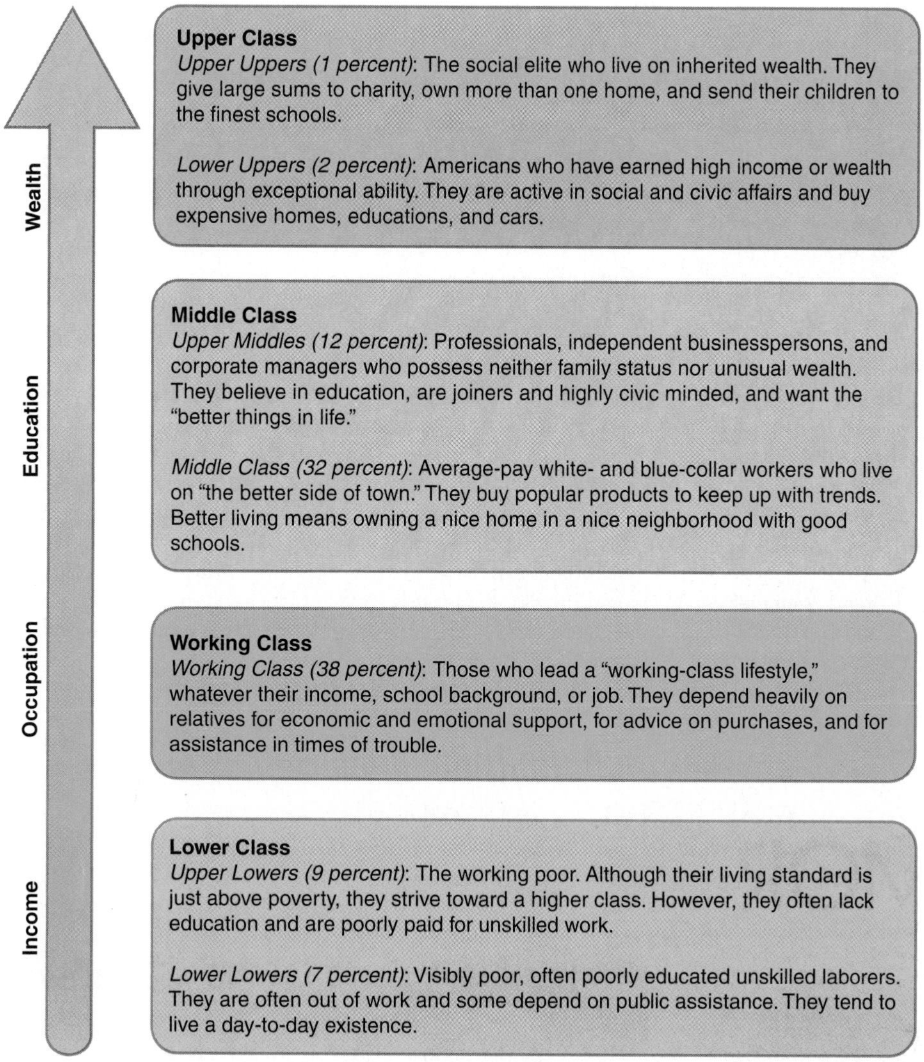

Wealth → **Education** → **Occupation** → **Income**

Upper Class
Upper Uppers (1 percent): The social elite who live on inherited wealth. They give large sums to charity, own more than one home, and send their children to the finest schools.

Lower Uppers (2 percent): Americans who have earned high income or wealth through exceptional ability. They are active in social and civic affairs and buy expensive homes, educations, and cars.

Middle Class
Upper Middles (12 percent): Professionals, independent businesspersons, and corporate managers who possess neither family status nor unusual wealth. They believe in education, are joiners and highly civic minded, and want the "better things in life."

Middle Class (32 percent): Average-pay white- and blue-collar workers who live on "the better side of town." They buy popular products to keep up with trends. Better living means owning a nice home in a nice neighborhood with good schools.

Working Class
Working Class (38 percent): Those who lead a "working-class lifestyle," whatever their income, school background, or job. They depend heavily on relatives for economic and emotional support, for advice on purchases, and for assistance in times of trouble.

Lower Class
Upper Lowers (9 percent): The working poor. Although their living standard is just above poverty, they strive toward a higher class. However, they often lack education and are poorly paid for unskilled work.

Lower Lowers (7 percent): Visibly poor, often poorly educated unskilled laborers. They are often out of work and some depend on public assistance. They tend to live a day-to-day existence.

FIGURE 5.3
The Major American Social Classes

Marketers are interested in social class because people within a given social class tend to exhibit similar buying behavior. Social classes show distinct product and brand preferences in areas such as clothing, home furnishings, leisure activity, and automobiles.

Social Factors A consumer's behavior also is influenced by social factors, such as the consumer's *small groups, family,* and *social roles* and *status.*

Groups and Social Networks Many small **groups** influence a person's behavior. Groups that have a direct influence and to which a person belongs are called membership groups. In contrast, reference groups serve as direct (face-to-face) or indirect points of comparison or reference in forming a person's attitudes or behavior. People often are influenced by reference groups to which they do not belong. For example, an aspirational group is one to which the individual wishes to belong, as when a young basketball player hopes to someday emulate basketball star Lebron James and play in the NBA.

Marketers try to identify the reference groups of their target markets. Reference groups expose a person to new behaviors and lifestyles, influence the person's attitudes and self-concept, and create pressures to conform that may affect the person's product and brand choices. The importance of group influence varies across products and brands. It tends to be strongest when the product is visible to others whom the buyer respects.

Marketers of brands subjected to strong group influence must figure out how to reach **opinion leaders**—people within a reference group who, because of special skills,

Group
Two or more people who interact to accomplish individual or mutual goals.

Opinion leader
Person within a reference group who, because of special skills, knowledge, personality, or other characteristics, exerts influence on others.

5.1 MARKETING AT WORK

Tremor and Vocalpoint: What's the Latest Buzz?

Gina Lavagna is the ideal pitch gal. After receiving information about Sony's latest compact digital music player and six $10-off coupons, she rushed four of her teen chums to a mall near her home to show them the cool new device, which sells for $99 and up. "I've probably told 20 people about it," she says, adding, "At least 10 are extremely interested in getting one." Her parents got her one for Christmas.

Procter & Gamble couldn't ask for a better salesperson than Donna Wetherell. The gregarious Columbus, Ohio, mom works at a customer service call center unaffiliated with P&G, where she knows some 300 co-workers by name. Lately, Wetherell has spent so much time at work talking about P&G products and handing out discount coupons that her colleagues have given her a nickname. "I am called the coupon lady," Wetherell says.

Multiply Gina Lavagna by 230,000 teens, and Donna Wetherell by 450,000 moms, and you'll get a notion of the size and impact of P&G's huge and carefully cultivated stealth marketing force. Gina and Donna aren't just any consumers. They're members of P&G's Tremor and Vocalpoint word-of-mouth marketing arms—natural-born buzzers on a mission to spread the word about P&G and other companies' brands among their peers.

It all started six years ago when P&G created Tremor, a word-of-mouth network to reach teens. Teens are maddeningly difficult to reach through traditional channels—more than other consumer groups, they tend to ignore mass-media messages or even to resent them. Tremor taps the power of peer-to-peer personal endorsements that cut through the advertising clutter. Tremorites deliver the word in school cafeterias, at sleepovers, by cell phone, and by e-mail.

Initially focused only on P&G brands, Tremor's forces were soon being tapped to talk up other companies' brands. More than 80 percent of Tremor's campaigns are now for non-P&G brands, such as Coca-Cola, Toyota, Kraft, and shoe company Vans. Tremor has been so successful that P&G has built a massive new network—Vocalpoint—focusing on moms. The moms market is a much bigger and more affluent target than teens, and a market that's more relevant to most P&G products. Initially, Vocalpoint has focused on moms with school-age kids, women who interact more with other moms.

■ Tremor and Vocalpoint, separate marketing arms of Procter & Gamble, have enlisted armies of buzzers to create word-of-mouth for brands. "We know that the most powerful form of marketing is a message from a trusted friend."

knowledge, personality, or other characteristics, exert social influence on others. Some experts call this 10 percent of Americans *the influentials* or *leading adopters*. One recent study found that these influencers are "four times more likely than average consumers to belong to five or more organizations, four times more likely to be considered experts, and twice as likely to recommend a product they like, in which case they are four times more likely to tell 11 people or more."[16]

Marketers often try to identify opinion leaders for their products and direct marketing efforts toward them. They use *buzz marketing* by enlisting or even creating opinion leaders to spread the word about their brands. For example, Tremor and Vocalpoint, separate mar-

To fill their enormous ranks, Tremor and Vocalpoint recruit online for what they call "connectors"—people with vast networks of friends and a gift for gab. For example, whereas average teens have only about 25 names on their instant messaging buddy lists, Tremorites average 150. And whereas the average mom talks to 5 people daily, Vocalpoint moms talk to 20 to 25. These connectors are carefully screened—only about 10 percent of those who apply are accepted. In addition to connectedness, the company is looking for natural talkers with large doses of inquisitiveness and persuasiveness.

Except for educating Tremorites and Vocalpointers about products and supplying them with samples and coupons, the company doesn't coach the teens and moms. The connectors themselves choose whether or not to pitch the product to friends and what to say. For example, when Gina Lavagna learned from Tremor about Clairol Herbal Essences Fruit Fusions Shampoo and Noxzema face wash, it was her own idea to invite her pals over so they could try it.

Tremorites and Vocalpointers also do the work without pay. What's in it for them? For one thing, they receive a steady flow of coupons and samples. But more than that, says CEO Knox, the company promises two things. First, it "provides you with cool new ideas before your friends have them," with the thrill of being an insider. Second, it gives them a voice. "They're filled with great ideas, and they don't think anybody listens to them," says Knox. "It's an empowering proposition [just to be heard]."

Buzz marketing is one of today's hottest new marketing practices. Still, jumping onto the buzz bandwagon carries some risks. For example, because Tremor and Vocalpoint connectors aren't coached or controlled, word of mouth can quickly backfire. If the teens and moms like what they see, they'll be quick to share the good news. If not, they might be even quicker to share the bad. Says one word-of-mouth expert, it's "like playing with fire: It can be a positive force when harnessed for the good, but fires are very destructive when they are out of control. If word of mouth goes against you, you're sunk."

Moreover, some advocacy groups and others question the ethics, even the legality, of recruiting people to promote products by word-of-mouth without disclosing that fact. One such group, Commercial Alert, has filed a complaint with the FTC against Tremor and several small buzz marketing agencies. But Tremor insiders ardently defend their own campaigns and buzz marketing in general. "We encourage [connectors] to talk freely, whether positively or negatively. We do not give them a script," says a company spokeswoman. Knox agrees. "The connectors need to be free to say whatever it is they want to say. It's [really just] natural human behavior. . . . People like talking to people about things they think help them."

Despite the risks and criticisms, Tremor and Vocalpoint are producing striking results. According to one analyst, most companies see a 10 to 30 percent boost in sales after employing the word-of-mouth networks. Consider these examples:

Shamrock Farms of Phoenix launched a new chocolate-malt-flavored milk in Phoenix and Tucson. The launch tactics were identical in both cities, with one exception: 2,100 Phoenix Tremorites received product information, coupons, and stickers. Shamrock reports that after 23 weeks, sales of the new milk flavor were 18 percent higher in Phoenix than in Tucson. Coupon redemption in Phoenix was 21 percent higher than the dairy had ever achieved. To Shamrock's pleasant surprise, overall milk sales in Phoenix rose by 4 percent as well.

In traditional ads introducing new Dawn Direct Foam, P&G stressed its potent grease-cutting power. But in packets mailed to Vocalpoint moms, it showed the detergent and a smiling girl on the outside with these words in big letters: "Mom, can I help?" A pamphlet inside explained that the soap is so fun to use that kids would want to help out with the dishes. To reinforce the point, the packet included a little sponge in the shape of a child's foot, plus a dozen $1.50 coupons. "We have to enable a conversation to take place," CEO Knox says. "Kids not doing enough chores is a conversation taking place among moms." Donna Wetherell, the Vocalpoint connector in Columbus, says she talked about Dawn Direct Foam with about 100 female co-workers at her call center. "There are a lot of women there who have kids," says Wetherell, 51, who has a daughter, 17. "We were all interested." Adds Lavonda Harrington, 28, another Columbus connector: "My daughter loves the foot-shaped sponge." That kind of buzz may explain the explosive sales results in the three test markets. Dawn unit sales in those locations were double those of markets without a Vocalpoint effort.

Thus, business is buzzing at P&G—and the Tremor and Vocalpoint grapevines are growing faster than Jack's beanstalk. Says CEO Knox, "We know that the most powerful form of marketing is [a] message from a trusted friend."

Sources: Extracts adapted from Robert Berner, "I Sold It through the Grapevine," *BusinessWeek,* May 29, 2006, pp. 32–34; and Melanie Wells, "Kid Nabbing," *Forbes,* February 2, 2004, p. 84. Quotes and other information from Samar Farah, "Making Waves," *CMO Magazine,* July 2005; Jeff Gelles, "Tremor: Shaky Stuff," *The Seattle Times,* December 4, 2005; Bruce Horovitz, "P&G 'Buzz Marketing' Unit Hit with Complaint," *USA Today,* October 19, 2005; Todd Wasserman, "Q+A: P&G Buzz Program Tremor Moving on to Mothers," *Brandweek,* September 26, 2006, p. 15; Jack Neff, "P&G Provides Product Launchpad, A Buzz Network of Moms," *Advertising Age,* March 20, 2006, p. 1; Barbara Correa, "Pssssst! Have You Tasted This? Mothers Sound Off in Word-of-Mouth Campaigns," *Knight Ridder Tribune Business News,* October 14, 2006, p.1; and http://business.tremor.com and http://business.vocalpoint.com, accessed October 2007.

keting arms of Procter & Gamble, have enlisted armies of buzzers to create word of mouth, not just for P&G products but for those of other client companies as well (see Marketing at Work 5.1).

Over the past few years, a new type of social interaction has exploded onto the scene—online social networking. **Online social networks** are online communities where people socialize or exchange information and opinions. Social networking media range from blogs to social networking Web sites, such as MySpace.com and YouTube, to entire virtual worlds, such as Second Life. This new form of high-tech buzz has big implications for marketers.

Online social networks
Online social communities—blogs, social networking Web sites, or even virtual worlds—where people socialize or exchange information and opinions.

Personal connections—forged through words, pictures, video, and audio posted just for the [heck] of it—are the life of the new Web, bringing together the estimated 60 million bloggers, more than 100 million MySpace.com users (230,000 more sign up every day), and millions more on single-use social networks where people share one category of stuff, like Flickr (photos), Del.icio.us (links), Digg (news stories), Wikipedia (encyclopedia articles), and YouTube (video). . . . It's hard to overstate the coming impact of these new network technologies on business: They hatch trends and build immense waves of interest in specific products. They serve up giant, targeted audiences to advertisers. They edge out old media with the loving labor of amateurs. They effortlessly provide hyperdetailed data to marketers. The new social networking technologies provide an authentic, peer-to-peer channel of communication that is far more credible than any corporate flackery.[17]

Marketers are working to harness the power of these new social networks to promote their products and build closer customer relationships. Instead of throwing more one-way commercial messages at ad-weary consumers, they hope to use social networks to *interact* with consumers and become a part of their conversations and lives. For example, brands ranging from The Honda Element and Wendy's to Victoria's Secret have set up MySpace pages and marketing campaigns. Victoria Secret's page (www.myspace.com/vspink) offers downloadable games and stationery along with a chance to get your "pink panty profile." The site has more than 200,000 "friends." And Burger King set up an ultrapopular MySpace profile of the King. Now, people on MySpace can become friends with brand mascots, movies, cell phone companies, and even deodorants.[18]

■ Online social networks: A rush of marketers—like Adidas—are now setting up their brands and even selling digital goods in Second Life, the Internet-based digital world that is "imagined, created, and owned" by its more than nearly 6 million residents.

A rush of marketers—from Dell and Sears to BMW and Adidas—are now setting up their brands and even selling digital goods in Second Life, the Internet-based digital world that is "imagined, created, and owned" by its more than nearly 6 million residents. Adidas has sold 21,000 pairs of virtual shoes in Second Life and the average avatar (your Second Life character) spends 20 minutes in its store.[19]

Other companies regularly post ads or custom videos on video-sharing sites such as YouTube.

When Adidas reintroduced its adicolor shoe, a customizable white-on-white sneaker with a set of seven color markers, it signed on seven top creative directors to develop innovative videos designed especially for downloading to iPods and other handhelds. The directors were given complete creative control to interpret their assigned color as they saw fit. "The directors that we chose we feel have a good deal of underground street cred," says an Adidas marketing executive. The project was not tied specifically to the product. Rather, the directors were asked to "celebrate color, customization, and personal expression." The diverse set of short films was then released, one film a week, via e-mail and sites such as YouTube. The films drew more than 2.1 million viewers within three weeks, 20 million within the first two months, and the numbers were growing exponentially with each new release.[20]

Companies can even create their own social networks. For example, Turner Broadcasting's Super Deluxe.com offers original comedy shorts along with community features that help comedy fans to connect with one another. Procter & Gamble set up Capessa (capessa.yahoo.com), "a gathering place for women looking to change their lives—from getting fit to finding love, changing careers to dealing with illness—and to share the wisdom they have learned along the way." The site gives women a place to express themselves and P&G an opportunity to observe and learn more about their needs and feelings.[21]

But marketers must be careful when tapping into online social networks. Results are difficult to measure and control. Ultimately, the users control the content, so online network marketing attempts can easily backfire. For example, when Chevrolet launched a Web contest inviting folks to create their own ads for its Chevy Tahoe, it quickly lost control. Says one observer, "the entries that got passed around, blogged about, and eventually covered in the mainstream media were all about the SUV's abysmal gas mileage and melting polar ice caps." One user-generated ad proclaimed, "Like this snowy wilderness? Better get your fill of it now. Then say hello to global warming." Another concluded, "$70 to fill up the tank, which will last less than 400 miles. Chevy Tahoe."[22] We will dig deeper into online social network as a marketing tool in Chapter 14.

Family   Family members can strongly influence buyer behavior. The family is the most important consumer buying organization in society, and it has been researched extensively. Marketers are interested in the roles and influence of the husband, wife, and children on the purchase of different products and services.

Husband-wife involvement varies widely by product category and by stage in the buying process. Buying roles change with evolving consumer lifestyles. In the United States, the wife traditionally has been the main purchasing agent for the family in the areas of food, household products, and clothing. But with 70 percent of women holding jobs outside the home and the willingness of husbands to do more of the family's purchasing, all this is changing. Men now account for about 40 percent of all food-shopping dollars. Women influence 85 percent of all car-buying decisions and account for 60 percent of all new car purchases outright. In all, women now make almost 85 percent of all purchases, spending two-thirds of the nation's GDP.[23]

Such changes suggest that marketers in industries that have sold their products to only men or only women are now courting the opposite sex. For example, after realizing that women today account for 50 percent of all technology purchases, Dell has stepped up its efforts to woo women buyers.[24]

> Managers from Dell's marketing and public relations staff met earlier this year with editors and sales reps at a dozen publications. Their mission wasn't too surprising: Get editors to print more about Dell's computers, televisions, and pocketPCs. It was the choice of magazines that was unusual, including Oprah Winfrey's *O at Home, Ladies' Home Journal,* and *CosmoGIRL*—not exactly publications on the company's regular radar screen. In barely six months, though, Dell's laser printer, plasma TV, and notebook computer were featured as must-haves in gift guides in shelter magazines *Real Simple* and *O at Home.* Besides the women's magazines, Dell is running ads on women-centric cable-TV channels such as Oxygen and Lifetime Television. Until recently, says Dell's director of customer experience, "you wouldn't have seen any Dell ads on these women's channels."

Children may also have a strong influence on family buying decisions. The nation's 36 million kids age 3 to 11 wield an estimated $18 billion in disposable income. They also influence an additional $115 billion that their families spend on them in

■ Children may have a strong influence on family buying decisions for everything from cell phones to restaurants to cars. To capture such family buying influences, Chevrolet runs ads like this one for its Uplander sports van in kid-focused *Nickelodeon Magazine,* featuring a family Big Wish Sweepstakes.

areas such as food, clothing, entertainment, and personal care items. For example, one recent study found that kids significantly influence family decisions about where they take vacations and what cars and cell phones they buy. As a result, marketers of cars, full-service restaurants, cell phones, and travel destinations are now placing ads on networks such as Cartoon Network and Toon Disney. Nickelodeon recently signed multimillion-dollar advertising deals with Chevrolet and Kia. Chevrolet runs TV ads on Nickelodeon television and print ads in *Nickelodeon Magazine* for its Uplander sports van.[25]

Roles and Status   A person belongs to many groups—family, clubs, organizations. The person's position in each group can be defined in terms of both role and status. A role consists of the activities people are expected to perform according to the persons around them. Each role carries a status reflecting the general esteem given to it by society.

People usually choose products appropriate to their roles and status. Consider the various roles a working mother plays. In her company, she plays the role of a brand manager; in her family, she plays the role of wife and mother; at her favorite sporting events, she plays the role of avid fan. As a brand manager, she will buy the kind of clothing that reflects her role and status in her company.

Personal Factors   A buyer's decisions also are influenced by personal characteristics such as the buyer's *age and life-cycle stage, occupation, economic situation, lifestyle,* and *personality and self-concept.*

Age and Life-Cycle Stage   People change the goods and services they buy over their lifetimes. Tastes in food, clothes, furniture, and recreation are often age related. Buying is also shaped by the stage of the family life cycle—the stages through which families might pass as they mature over time. Marketers often define their target markets in terms of life-cycle stage and develop appropriate products and marketing plans for each stage.

Traditional family life-cycle stages include young singles and married couples with children. Today, however, marketers are increasingly catering to a growing number of alternative, nontraditional stages such as unmarried couples, singles marrying later in life, childless couples, same-sex couples, single parents, extended parents (those with young adult children returning home), and others.

RBC Royal Bank has identified five life-stage segments. The *Youth* segment includes customers younger than 18. *Getting Started* consists of customers aged 18 to 35 who are going through first experiences, such as graduation, first credit card, first car, first loan, marriage, and first child. *Builders,* customers aged 35 to 50, are in their peak earning years. As they build careers and family, they tend to borrow more than they invest. *Accumulators,* aged 50 to 60, worry about saving for retirement and investing wisely. Finally, *Preservers,* customers over 60, want to maximize their retirement income to maintain a desired lifestyle. RBC markets different services to the different segments. For example, with Builders, who face many expenses, it emphasizes loans and debt-load management services.[26]

Occupation   A person's occupation affects the goods and services bought. Blue-collar workers tend to buy more rugged work clothes, whereas executives buy more business suits. Marketers try to identify the occupational groups that have an above-average interest in their products and services. A company can even specialize in making products needed by a given occupational group.

For example, Carhartt makes rugged, durable, no-nonsense work clothes—what it calls "original equipment for the American worker. From coats to jackets, bibs to overalls . . . if the apparel carries the name Carhartt, the performance will be legendary." Its Web site carries real-life testimonials of hard-working Carhartt customers. One electrician, battling the cold in Canada's arctic region, reports wearing Carhartt's lined Arctic bib overalls, Arctic jacket, and other clothing for more than two years without a single "popped button, ripped pocket seam, or stuck zipper." And an animal trainer in California says of his favorite pair of Carhartt jeans: "Not only did they keep me warm but they stood up to one playful lion and her very sharp claws."[27]

Economic Situation   A person's economic situation will affect product choice. Marketers of income-sensitive goods watch trends in personal income, savings, and interest rates. If economic indicators point to a recession, marketers can take steps to redesign, reposition, and reprice their products closely. Some marketers target consumers who have lots of money and resources, charging prices to match. For example, Rolex positions its luxury watches as "a tribute to elegance, an object of passion, a symbol for all time." Other marketers target consumers with more modest means. Timex makes more affordable watches that "take a licking and keep on ticking."

Lifestyle   People coming from the same subculture, social class, and occupation may have quite different lifestyles. **Lifestyle** is a person's pattern of living as expressed in his or her psychographics. It involves measuring consumers' major AIO dimensions—activities (work, hobbies, shopping, sports, social events), interests (food, fashion, family, recreation), and opinions (about themselves, social issues, business, products). Lifestyle captures something more than the person's social class or personality. It profiles a person's whole pattern of acting and interacting in the world.

Lifestyle
A person's pattern of living as expressed in his or her activities, interests, and opinions.

When used carefully, the lifestyle concept can help marketers understand changing consumer values and how they affect buying behavior. Consumers don't just buy products, they buy the values and lifestyles those products represent. "People's product choices are becoming more and more like value choices," says one marketer. "It's not, 'I like this water, the way it tastes.' It's 'I feel like this car, or this show, is more reflective of who I am.'"

For example, Pottery Barn, with its different store formats, sells more than just home furnishings. It sells a lifestyle to which its customers aspire. Pottery Barn Kids offers idyllic scenes of the perfect childhood, whereas PB Teens offer trendy fashion-forward self-expression. The flagship Pottery Barn stores serve an upscale yet casual, family- and friend-focused lifestyle—affluent but sensibly so.[28]

■ Lifestyle: Consumers don't just buy products, they buy the values and lifestyles those products represent. Georgia Boot proudly targets "guys who are comfortable with who they are."

Shortly after Hadley MacLean got married, she and her husband, Doug, agreed that their old bed had to go. It was a mattress and box spring on a cheap metal frame, a relic of Doug's Harvard days. But Hadley never anticipated how tough it would be to find a new bed. "We couldn't find anything we liked, even though we were willing to spend the money," says Hadley, a 31-year-old marketing director. It turned out to be much more than just finding a piece of furniture at the right price. It was a matter of emotion: They needed a bed that meshed with their lifestyle—with who they are and where they are going. The couple finally ended up at the Pottery Barn on Boston's upscale Newbury Street, where Doug fell in love with a mahogany sleigh bed that Hadley had spotted in the store's catalog. The couple was so pleased with how great it looked in their Dutch Colonial home that they hurried back to the store for a set of end tables. And then they bought a quilt. And a mirror for the living room. And some stools for the dining room. "We got kind of addicted," Hadley confesses.

Personality and Self-Concept   Each person's distinct personality influences his or her buying behavior. **Personality** refers to the unique psychological characteristics that lead to relatively consistent and lasting responses to one's own environment. Personality is usually described in terms of traits such as self-confidence, dominance, sociability, autonomy, defensiveness, adaptability, and aggressiveness. Personality can be useful in analyzing consumer behavior for certain product or brand choices.

Personality
The unique psychological characteristics that lead to relatively consistent and lasting responses to one's environment.

The idea is that brands also have personalities, and that consumers are likely to choose brands with personalities that match their own. A *brand personality* is the specific mix of human traits that may be attributed to a particular brand. One researcher identified five brand personality traits:[29]

1. Sincerity (down-to-earth, honest, wholesome, and cheerful)
2. Excitement (daring, spirited, imaginative, and up-to-date)
3. Competence (reliable, intelligent, and successful)
4. Sophistication (upper class and charming)
5. Ruggedness (outdoorsy and tough)

Most well-known brands are strongly associated with one particular trait: Jeep with "ruggedness," Apple with "excitement," CNN with "competence," and Dove with "sincerity." Hence, these brands will attract persons who are high on the same personality traits.

Many marketers use a concept related to personality—a person's *self-concept* (also called *self-image*). The basic self-concept premise is that people's possessions contribute to and reflect their identities; that is, "we are what we have." Thus, in order to understand consumer behavior, the marketer must first understand the relationship between consumer self-concept and possessions.

Apple applies these concepts in a recent series of ads that characterize two people as computers—one guy plays the part of an Apple Mac and the other plays a PC. The two have very different personalities and self-concepts. "Hello, I'm a Mac," says the guy on the right, who's younger and dressed in jeans. "And I'm a PC," says the one on the left, who's wearing dweeby glasses and a jacket and tie. The two men discuss the relative advantages of Macs versus PCs, with the Mac coming out on top. The ads present the Mac brand personality as young, laid back, and hip. The PC is portrayed as buttoned down, corporate, and a bit dorky. The message? If you see yourself as young and with it, you need a Mac.[30]

Motive (drive)
A need that is sufficiently pressing to direct the person to seek satisfaction of the need.

Psychological Factors A person's buying choices are further influenced by four major psychological factors: *motivation*, *perception*, *learning*, and *beliefs* and *attitudes*.

Motivation A person has many needs at any given time. Some are biological, arising from states of tension such as hunger, thirst, or discomfort. Others are psychological, arising from the need for recognition, esteem, or belonging. A need becomes a motive when it is aroused to a sufficient level of intensity. A **motive** (or drive) is a need that is sufficiently pressing to direct the person to seek satisfaction. Psychologists have developed theories of human motivation. Two of the most popular—the theories of Sigmund Freud and Abraham Maslow—have quite different meanings for consumer analysis and marketing.

Sigmund Freud assumed that people are largely unconscious about the real psychological forces shaping their behavior. He saw the person as growing up and repressing many urges. These urges are never eliminated or under perfect control; they emerge in dreams, in slips of the tongue, in neurotic and obsessive behavior, or ultimately in psychoses.

Freud's theory suggests that a person's buying decisions are affected by subconscious motives that even the buyer may not fully understand. Thus, an aging baby boomer who buys a sporty BMW 330Ci convertible might explain that he simply likes the feel of the wind in his thinning hair. At a deeper level, he may be trying to impress others with his success. At a still deeper level, he may be buying the car to feel young and independent again.

The term *motivation research* refers to qualitative research designed to probe consumers' hidden, subconscious motivations. Consumers often don't know or can't describe just why they act as

■ Motivation: An aging baby boomer who buys a sporty convertible might explain that he simply likes the feel of the wind in his thinning hair. At a deeper level, he may be buying the car to feel young and independent again.

they do. Thus, motivation researchers use a variety of probing techniques to uncover underlying emotions and attitudes toward brands and buying situations.

Many companies employ teams of psychologists, anthropologists, and other social scientists to carry out motivation research. One ad agency routinely conducts one-on-one, therapy-like interviews to delve into the inner workings of consumers. Another company asks consumers to describe their favorite brands as animals or cars (say, Cadillacs versus Chevrolets) in order to assess the prestige associated with various brands. Still others rely on hypnosis, dream therapy, or soft lights and mood music to plumb the murky depths of consumer psyches.

Such projective techniques seem pretty goofy, and some marketers dismiss such motivation research as mumbo jumbo. But many marketers use such touchy-feely approaches, now sometimes called *interpretive consumer research,* to dig deeply into consumer psyches and develop better marketing strategies.[31]

Abraham Maslow sought to explain why people are driven by particular needs at particular times. Why does one person spend much time and energy on personal safety and another on gaining the esteem of others? Maslow's answer is that human needs are arranged in a hierarchy, as shown in Figure 5.4, from the most pressing at the bottom to the least pressing at the top.[32] They include *physiological* needs, *safety* needs, *social* needs, *esteem* needs, and *self-actualization* needs.

A person tries to satisfy the most important need first. When that need is satisfied, it will stop being a motivator and the person will then try to satisfy the next most important need. For example, starving people (physiological need) will not take an interest in the latest happenings in the art world (self-actualization needs), nor in how they are seen or esteemed by others (social or esteem needs), nor even in whether they are breathing clean air (safety needs). But as each important need is satisfied, the next most important need will come into play.

Perception   A motivated person is ready to act. How the person acts is influenced by his or her own perception of the situation. All of us learn by the flow of information through our five senses: sight, hearing, smell, touch, and taste. However, each of us receives, organizes, and interprets this sensory information in an individual way. **Perception** is the process by which people select, organize, and interpret information to form a meaningful picture of the world.

Perception
The process by which people select, organize, and interpret information to form a meaningful picture of the world.

People can form different perceptions of the same stimulus because of three perceptual processes: selective attention, selective distortion, and selective retention. People are exposed to a great amount of stimuli every day. For example, people are exposed to an estimated 3,000 to 5,000 ad messages every day.[33] It is impossible for a person to pay attention to all these stimuli. *Selective attention*—the tendency for people to screen out most of the information to which they are exposed—means that marketers must work especially hard to attract the consumer's attention.

Even noticed stimuli do not always come across in the intended way. Each person fits incoming information into an existing mind-set. *Selective distortion* describes the tendency of

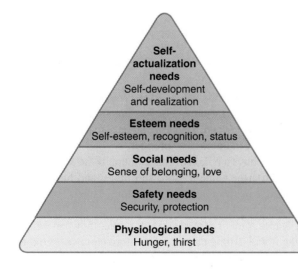

FIGURE 5.4
Maslow's Hierarchy of Needs

■ Selective perception: It's impossible for people to pay attention to the thousands of ads they're exposed to every day, so they screen most of them out.

people to interpret information in a way that will support what they already believe. For example, if you distrust a company, you might perceive even honest ads from the company as questionable. Selective distortion means that marketers must try to understand the mind-sets of consumers and how these will affect interpretations of advertising and sales information.

People also will forget much of what they learn. They tend to retain information that supports their attitudes and beliefs. Because of *selective retention,* consumers are likely to remember good points made about a brand they favor and to forget good points made about competing brands. Because of selective attention, distortion, and retention, marketers must work hard to get their messages through. This fact explains why marketers use so much drama and repetition in sending messages to their market.

Interestingly, although most marketers worry about whether their offers will be perceived at all, some consumers worry that they will be affected by marketing messages without even knowing it—through *subliminal advertising.* In 1957, a researcher announced that he had flashed the phrases "Eat popcorn" and "Drink Coca-Cola" on a screen in a New Jersey movie theater every five seconds for 1/300th of a second. He reported that although viewers did not consciously recognize these messages, they absorbed them subconsciously and bought 58 percent more popcorn and 18 percent more Coke. Suddenly advertisers and consumer-protection groups became intensely interested in subliminal perception. People voiced fears of being brainwashed, and California and Canada declared the practice illegal. Although the researcher later admitted to making up the data, the issue has not died. Some consumers still fear that they are being manipulated by subliminal messages.

Numerous studies by psychologists and consumer researchers have found little or no link between subliminal messages and consumer behavior. Recent brain wave studies have found that in certain circumstances, our brains may register subliminal messages. However, it appears that subliminal advertising simply doesn't have the power attributed to it by its critics. Most advertisers scoff at the notion of an industry conspiracy to manipulate consumers through "invisible" messages. Says one industry insider: "[Some consumers believe we are] wizards who can manipulate them at will. Ha! Snort! Oh my sides! As we know, just between us, most of [us] have difficulty getting a 2 percent increase in sales with the help of $50 million in media and extremely *liminal* images of sex, money, power, and other [motivators] of human emotion. The very idea of [us] as puppeteers, cruelly pulling the strings of consumer marionettes, is almost too much to bear."[34]

Learning

Changes in an individual's behavior arising from experience.

Learning When people act, they learn. **Learning** describes changes in an individual's behavior arising from experience. Learning theorists say that most human behavior is learned. Learning occurs through the interplay of drives, stimuli, cues, responses, and reinforcement.

A *drive* is a strong internal stimulus that calls for action. A drive becomes a motive when it is directed toward a particular *stimulus object.* For example, a person's drive for self-actualization might motivate him or her to look into buying a digital camera. The consumer's response to the idea of buying a camera is conditioned by the surrounding cues. *Cues* are minor stimuli that determine when, where, and how the person responds. For example, the person might spot several camera brands in a shop window, hear of a special sale price, or discuss cameras with a friend. These are all cues that might influence a consumer's *response* to his or her interest in buying the product.

Suppose the consumer buys a Nikon digital camera. If the experience is rewarding, the consumer will probably use the camera more and more, and his or her response will be *reinforced.* Then, the next time the consumer shops for a camera, or for binoculars or some similar product, the probability is greater that he or she will buy a Nikon product. The practical significance of learning theory for marketers is that they can build up demand for a product by associating it with strong drives, using motivating cues, and providing positive reinforcement.

Beliefs and Attitudes   Through doing and learning, people acquire beliefs and attitudes. These, in turn, influence their buying behavior. A **belief** is a descriptive thought that a person holds about something. Beliefs may be based on real knowledge, opinion, or faith and may or may not carry an emotional charge. Marketers are interested in the beliefs that people formulate about specific products and services, because these beliefs make up product and brand images that affect buying behavior. If some of the beliefs are wrong and prevent purchase, the marketer will want to launch a campaign to correct them.

People have attitudes regarding religion, politics, clothes, music, food, and almost everything else. **Attitude** describes a person's relatively consistent evaluations, feelings, and tendencies toward an object or idea. Attitudes put people into a frame of mind of liking or disliking things, of moving toward or away from them. Our digital camera buyer may hold attitudes such as "Buy the best," "The Japanese make the best electronics products in the world," and "Creativity and self-expression are among the most important things in life." If so, the Nikon camera would fit well into the consumer's existing attitudes.

Attitudes are difficult to change. A person's attitudes fit into a pattern, and to change one attitude may require difficult adjustments in many others. Thus, a company should usually try to fit its products into existing attitudes rather than attempt to change attitudes. Of course, there are exceptions in which the cost of trying to change attitudes may pay off handsomely:

> By 1994, milk consumption had been in decline for 20 years. The general perception was that milk was unhealthy, outdated, just for kids, or good only with cookies and cake. To counter these notions, the National Fluid Milk Processors Education Program (MilkPEP) began an ad campaign featuring milk be-mustached celebrities and the tag line Got Milk? The campaign has not only been wildly popular, it has been successful as well—not only did it stop the decline, milk consumption actually increased. The campaign is still running.
>
> Although initially targeted at women in their twenties, the campaign has been expanded to other target markets and has gained cult status with teens, much to their parents' delight. Starting with basic print ads featuring a musician (Kelly Clarkson), actor (Sara Ramirez), or sports idol (Marvin Harrison), the campaign has naturally spread to the Internet. At the industry's Web site (www.bodybymilk.com), young folks can bid on gear using saved milk UPCs, go behind the scenes of the latest Got Milk? photo shoot, or get facts about "everything you ever need to know about milk." There are milk moustache My-Space pages of celebrities such as David Beckham. The milk marketers even created the world's first branded emoticon—the milk moustache :-{).[35]

We can now appreciate the many forces acting on consumer behavior. The consumer's choice results from the complex interplay of cultural, social, personal, and psychological factors.

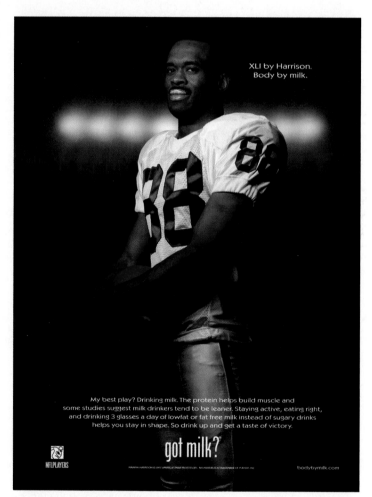

Belief

A descriptive thought that a person holds about something.

Attitude

A person's consistently favorable or unfavorable evaluations, feelings, and tendencies toward an object or idea.

■ Attitudes are difficult to change, but the National Fluid Milk Processor's wildly popular milk moustache campaign succeeded in changing attitudes toward milk.

The Buyer Decision Process

Now that we have looked at the influences that affect buyers, we are ready to look at how consumers make buying decisions. Figure 5.5 shows that the buyer decision process consists of five stages: *need recognition, information search, evaluation of alternatives, purchase decision,* and *postpurchase behavior.* Clearly, the buying process starts long before the actual purchase and continues long after. Marketers need to focus on the entire buying process rather than on just the purchase decision.

The figure suggests that consumers pass through all five stages with every purchase. But in more routine purchases, consumers often skip or reverse some of these stages. A woman buying her regular brand of toothpaste would recognize the need and go right to the purchase decision, skipping information search and evaluation. However, we use the model in Figure 5.5 because it shows all the considerations that arise when a consumer faces a new and complex purchase situation.

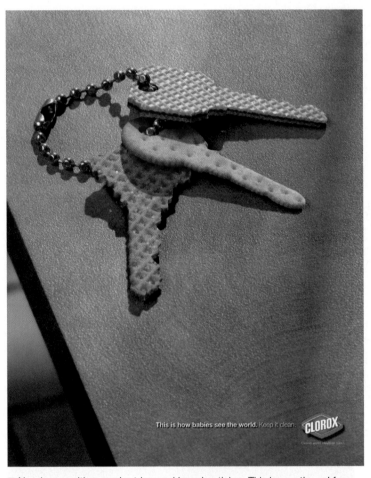

■ Need recognition can be triggered by advertising. This innovative ad from Clorox urges parents: "This is how babies see the world. Keep it clean."

Need Recognition The buying process starts with *need recognition*—the buyer recognizes a problem or need. The need can be triggered by *internal stimuli* when one of the person's normal needs—hunger, thirst, sex—rises to a level high enough to become a drive. A need can also be triggered by *external stimuli.* For example, an advertisement or a discussion with a friend might get you thinking about buying a new car. At this stage, the marketer should research consumers to find out what kinds of needs or problems arise, what brought them about, and how they led the consumer to this particular product.

Information Search An interested consumer may or may not search for more information. If the consumer's drive is strong and a satisfying product is near at hand, the consumer is likely to buy it then. If not, the consumer may store the need in memory or undertake an *information search* related to the need. For example, once you've decided you need a new car, at the least, you will probably pay more attention to car ads, cars owned by friends, and car conversations. Or you may actively search the Web, phone friends, and gather information in other ways. The amount of searching you do will depend on the strength of your drive, the amount of information you start with, the ease of obtaining more information, the value you place on additional information, and the satisfaction you get from searching.

Consumers can obtain information from any of several sources. These include *personal sources* (family, friends, neighbors, acquaintances), *commercial sources* (advertising, salespeople, Web sites, dealers, packaging, displays), *public sources* (mass media, consumer rating organizations, Internet searches), and *experiential sources* (handling, examining, using the product). The relative influence of these information sources varies with the product and the buyer. Generally, the consumer receives the most information about a product from commercial sources—those controlled by the marketer. The most effective sources, however, tend to be personal. Commercial sources normally *inform* the buyer, but personal sources *legitimize* or *evaluate* products for the buyer. As one marketer states, "It's rare that an advertising campaign can be as effective as a neighbor leaning over the fence and saying, 'This is a wonderful product.'"[36]

As more information is obtained, the consumer's awareness and knowledge of the available brands and features increase. In your car information search, you may learn about

FIGURE 5.5

Buyer Decision Process

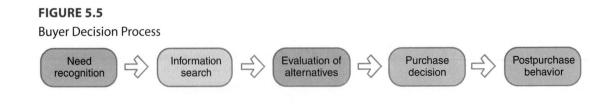

the several brands available. The information might also help you to drop certain brands from consideration. A company must design its marketing mix to make prospects aware of and knowledgeable about its brand. It should carefully identify consumers' sources of information and the importance of each source.

Evaluation of Alternatives   We have seen how the consumer uses information to arrive at a set of final brand choices. How does the consumer choose among the alternative brands? The marketer needs to know about *alternative evaluation*—that is, how the consumer processes information to arrive at brand choices. Unfortunately, consumers do not use a simple and single evaluation process in all buying situations. Instead, several evaluation processes are at work.

The consumer arrives at attitudes toward different brands through some evaluation procedure. How consumers go about evaluating purchase alternatives depends on the individual consumer and the specific buying situation. In some cases, consumers use careful calculations and logical thinking. At other times, the same consumers do little or no evaluating; instead they buy on impulse and rely on intuition. Sometimes consumers make buying decisions on their own; sometimes they turn to friends, consumer guides, or salespeople for buying advice.

Suppose you've narrowed your car choices to three brands. And suppose that you are primarily interested in four attributes—styling, operating economy, warranty, and price. By this time, you've probably formed beliefs about how each brand rates on each attribute. Clearly, if one car rated best on all the attributes, we could predict that you would choose it. However, the brands will no doubt vary in appeal. You might base your buying decision on only one attribute, and your choice would be easy to predict. If you wanted styling above everything else, you would buy the car that you think has the best styling. But most buyers consider several attributes, each with different importance. If we knew the importance that you assigned to each of the four attributes, we could predict your car choice more reliably.

Marketers should study buyers to find out how they actually evaluate brand alternatives. If they know what evaluative processes go on, marketers can take steps to influence the buyer's decision.

Purchase Decision   In the evaluation stage, the consumer ranks brands and forms purchase intentions. Generally, the consumer's *purchase decision* will be to buy the most preferred brand, but two factors can come between the purchase *intention* and the purchase *decision*. The first factor is the *attitudes of others*. If someone important to you thinks that you should buy the lowest-priced car, then the chances of your buying a more expensive car are reduced.

The second factor is *unexpected situational factors*. The consumer may form a purchase intention based on factors such as expected income, expected price, and expected product benefits. However, unexpected events may change the purchase intention. For example, the economy might take a turn for the worse, a close competitor might drop its price, or a friend might report being disappointed in your preferred car. Thus, preferences and even purchase intentions do not always result in actual purchase choice.

Postpurchase Behavior   The marketer's job does not end when the product is bought. After purchasing the product, the consumer will be satisfied or dissatisfied and will engage in *postpurchase behavior* of interest to the marketer. What determines whether the buyer is satisfied or dissatisfied with a purchase? The answer lies in the relationship between the *consumer's expectations* and the product's *perceived performance*. If the product falls short of expectations, the consumer is disappointed; if it meets expectations, the consumer is satisfied; if it exceeds expectations, the consumer is delighted. The larger the gap between expectations and performance, the greater the consumer's dissatisfaction. This suggests that sellers should promise only what their brands can deliver so that buyers are satisfied.

Almost all major purchases, however, result in **cognitive dissonance**, or discomfort caused by postpurchase conflict. After the purchase, consumers are satisfied with the benefits of the chosen brand and are glad to avoid the drawbacks of the brands not bought. However, every purchase involves compromise. So consumers feel uneasy about acquiring the drawbacks of the chosen brand and about losing the benefits of the brands not purchased. Thus, consumers feel at least some postpurchase dissonance for every purchase.[37]

Cognitive dissonance
Buyer discomfort caused by postpurchase conflict.

Why is it so important to satisfy the customer? Customer satisfaction is a key to building profitable relationships with consumers—to keeping and growing consumers and reaping their customer lifetime value. Satisfied customers buy a product again, talk favorably to others about the product, pay less attention to competing brands and advertising, and buy other products from the company. Many marketers go beyond merely *meeting* the expectations of customers—they aim to *delight* the customer.

A dissatisfied consumer responds differently. Bad word of mouth often travels farther and faster than good word of mouth. It can quickly damage consumer attitudes about a company and its products. But companies cannot simply rely on dissatisfied customers to volunteer their complaints when they are dissatisfied. Most unhappy customers never tell the company about their problem. Therefore, a company should measure customer satisfaction regularly. It should set up systems that *encourage* customers to complain. In this way, the company can learn how well it is doing and how it can improve.

By studying the overall buyer decision, marketers may be able to find ways to help consumers move through it. For example, if consumers are not buying a new product because they do not perceive a need for it, marketing might launch advertising messages that trigger the need and show how the product solves customers' problems. If customers know about the product but are not buying because they hold unfavorable attitudes toward it, the marketer must find ways either to change the product or change consumer perceptions.

New product
A good, service, or idea that is perceived by some potential customers as new.

Adoption process
The mental process through which an individual passes from first hearing about an innovation to final adoption.

The Buyer Decision Process for New Products

We have looked at the stages buyers go through in trying to satisfy a need. Buyers may pass quickly or slowly through these stages, and some of the stages may even be reversed. Much depends on the nature of the buyer, the product, and the buying situation.

We now look at how buyers approach the purchase of new products. A **new product** is a good, service, or idea that is perceived by some potential customers as new. It may have been around for a while, but our interest is in how consumers learn about products for the first time and make decisions on whether to adopt them. We define the **adoption process** as "the mental process through which an individual passes from first learning about an innovation to final adoption," and *adoption* as the decision by an individual to become a regular user of the product.[38]

Stages in the Adoption Process Consumers go through five stages in the process of adopting a new product:

- *Awareness:* The consumer becomes aware of the new product, but lacks information about it.
- *Interest:* The consumer seeks information about the new product.
- *Evaluation:* The consumer considers whether trying the new product makes sense.
- *Trial:* The consumer tries the new product on a small scale to improve his or her estimate of its value.
- *Adoption:* The consumer decides to make full and regular use of the new product.

■ The adoption process: This Gillette Fusion ad encourages trial by offering coupons.

This model suggests that the new-product marketer should think about how to help consumers move through these stages. For example, to encourage consumers to try its new Gillette Fusion razor, P&G featured coupons offering substantial savings. Similarly, a luxury car producer might find that many potential customers know about and are interested in its new model but aren't buying because of uncertainty about the model's benefits and the high price. The producer could launch a "take one home for the weekend" promotion to high-value prospects to move them into the trial process and lead them to purchase.

Individual Differences in Innovativeness   People differ greatly in their readiness to try new products. In each product area, there are "consumption pioneers" and early adopters. Other individuals adopt new products much later. People can be classified into the adopter categories shown in Figure 5.6. After a slow start, an increasing number of people adopt the new product. The number of adopters reaches a peak and then drops off as fewer nonadopters remain. Innovators are defined as the first 2.5 percent of the buyers to adopt a new idea (those beyond two standard deviations from mean adoption time); the early adopters are the next 13.5 percent (between one and two standard deviations); and so forth.

The five adopter groups have differing values. *Innovators* are venturesome—they try new ideas at some risk. *Early adopters* are guided by respect—they are opinion leaders in their communities and adopt new ideas early but carefully. The *early majority* are deliberate—although they rarely are leaders, they adopt new ideas before the average person. The *late majority* are skeptical—they adopt an innovation only after a majority of people have tried it. Finally, *laggards* are tradition bound—they are suspicious of changes and adopt the innovation only when it has become something of a tradition itself.

This adopter classification suggests that an innovating firm should research the characteristics of innovators and early adopters and should direct marketing efforts toward them. In general, innovators tend to be relatively younger, better educated, and higher in income than later adopters and nonadopters. They are more receptive to unfamiliar things, rely more on their own values and judgment, and are more willing to take risks. They are less brand loyal and more likely to take advantage of special promotions such as discounts, coupons, and samples.

Influence of Product Characteristics on Rate of Adoption   The characteristics of the new product affect its rate of adoption. Some products catch on almost overnight (iPod), whereas others take a long time to gain acceptance (HDTV). Five characteristics are especially important in influencing an innovation's rate of adoption. For example, consider the characteristics of HDTV in relation to the rate of adoption:

- *Relative advantage:* the degree to which the innovation appears superior to existing products. The greater the perceived relative advantage of using HDTV—say, in picture quality and ease of viewing—the sooner HDTVs will be adopted.
- *Compatibility:* the degree to which the innovation fits the values and experiences of potential consumers. HDTV, for example, is highly compatible with the lifestyles of the TV-watching public. However, it is not yet completely compatible with the programming and broadcasting systems currently available to consumers.
- *Complexity:* the degree to which the innovation is difficult to understand or use. HDTVs are not very complex and, therefore, once more programming is available and prices come down, will take less time to penetrate U.S. homes than more complex innovations.
- *Divisibility:* the degree to which the innovation may be tried on a limited basis. HDTVs are still relatively expensive. This will slow the rate of adoption.
- *Communicability:* the degree to which the results of using the innovation can be observed or described to others. Because HDTV lends itself to demonstration and description, its use will spread faster among consumers.

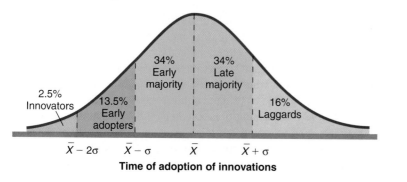

FIGURE 5.6

Adopter Categorization on the Basis of Relative Time of Adoption of Innovations

Source: Reprinted with the permission of The Free Press, a Division of Simon & Schuster, from *Diffusion of Innovations,* Fifth Edition, by Everett M. Rogers. Copyright © 2003 by the Free Press.

Other characteristics influence the rate of adoption, such as initial and ongoing costs, risk and uncertainty, and social approval. The new-product marketer must research all these factors when developing the new product and its marketing program.

Linking the Concepts

Here's a good place to pull over and apply the concepts you've examined in the first part of this chapter.

- Think about a specific major purchase you've made recently. What buying process did you follow? What major factors influenced your decision?
- Pick a company or brand that we've discussed in a previous chapter—Nike, NASCAR, Harrah's Entertainment, P&G's Tide, ESPN, Burton, or another. How does the company you chose use its understanding of customers and their buying behavior to build better customer relationships?
- Think about a company such as Intel, which sells its products to computer makers and other businesses rather than to final consumers. How would Intel's marketing to business customers differ from Starbucks's marketing to final consumers? The second part of the chapter deals with this issue.

Business Markets and Business Buyer Behavior

In one way or another, most large companies sell to other organizations. Companies such as DuPont, Boeing, IBM, Caterpillar, and countless other firms sell *most* of their products to other businesses. Even large consumer-products companies, which make products used by final consumers, must first sell their products to other businesses. For example, General Mills makes many familiar consumer brands—Big G cereals (Cheerios, Wheaties, Total, Golden Grahams); baking products (Pillsbury, Betty Crocker, Gold Medal flour); snacks (Nature Valley, Chex Mix, Pop Secret); Yoplait Yogurt; Haagen-Das ice cream; and others. But to sell these products to consumers, General Mills must first sell them to its wholesaler and retailer customers, who in turn serve the consumer market.

Business buyer behavior

The buying behavior of the organizations that buy goods and services for use in the production of other products and services or for the purpose of reselling or renting them to others at a profit.

Business buyer behavior refers to the buying behavior of the organizations that buy goods and services for use in the production of other products and services that are sold, rented, or supplied to others. It also includes the behavior of retailing and wholesaling firms that acquire goods to resell or rent them to others at a profit. In the *business buying process,* business buyers determine which products and services their organizations need to purchase and then find, evaluate, and choose among alternative suppliers and brands. *Business-to-business (B-to-B) marketers* must do their best to understand business markets and business buyer behavior. Then, like businesses that sell to final buyers, they must build profitable relationships with business customers by creating superior customer value.

Business Markets

The business market is *huge.* In fact, business markets involve far more dollars and items than do consumer markets. For example, think about the large number of business transactions involved in the production and sale of a single set of Goodyear tires. Various suppliers sell Goodyear the rubber, steel, equipment, and other goods that it needs to produce the tires. Goodyear then sells the finished tires to retailers, who in turn sell them to consumers. Thus, many sets of *business* purchases were made for only one set of *consumer* purchases. In addition, Goodyear sells tires as original equipment to manufacturers who install them on new vehicles, and as replacement tires to companies that maintain their own fleets of company cars, trucks, buses, or other vehicles.

In some ways, business markets are similar to consumer markets. Both involve people who assume buying roles and make purchase decisions to satisfy needs. However, business markets differ in many ways from consumer markets. The main differences are in *market structure and demand,* the *nature of the buying unit,* and the *types of decisions and the decision process* involved.

Market Structure and Demand The business marketer normally deals with *far fewer but far larger buyers* than the consumer marketer does. Even in large business markets, a few buyers often account for most of the purchasing. For example, when Goodyear sells replacement tires to final consumers, its potential market includes the owners of the millions of cars currently in use in the United States and around the world. But Goodyear's fate in the business market depends on getting orders from one of only a handful of large automakers. Similarly, Black & Decker sells its power tools and outdoor equipment to tens of millions of consumers worldwide. However, it must sell these products through three huge retail customers—Home Depot, Lowe's, and Wal-Mart—which, combined, account for more than half its sales.

Further, business demand is **derived demand**—it ultimately derives from the demand for consumer goods. Hewlett-Packard and Dell buy Intel microprocessor chips because consumers buy personal computers. If consumer demand for PCs drops, so will the demand for computer chips. Therefore, B-to-B marketers sometimes promote their products directly to final consumers to increase business demand. For example, Intel advertises heavily to personal computer buyers through selling them on the virtues of Intel microprocessors. In ads, it tells consumers that "great computing starts with Intel inside." The increased demand for Intel chips boosts demand for the PCs containing them, and both Intel and its business partners win.

Derived demand
Business demand that ultimately comes from (derives from) the demand for consumer goods.

Many business markets have *inelastic demand;* that is, total demand for many business products is not affected much by price changes, especially in the short run. A drop in the price of leather will not cause shoe manufacturers to buy much more leather unless it results in lower shoe prices that, in turn, will increase consumer demand for shoes.

Finally, business markets have more *fluctuating demand.* The demand for many business goods and services tends to change more—and more quickly—than the demand for consumer goods and services does. A small percentage increase in consumer demand can cause large increases in business demand. Sometimes a rise of only 10 percent in consumer demand can cause as much as a 200 percent rise in business demand during the next period.

Nature of the Buying Unit Compared with consumer purchases, a business purchase usually involves *more decision participants* and a *more professional purchasing effort.* Often, business buying is done by trained purchasing agents who spend their working lives learning how to buy better. The more complex the purchase, the more likely it is that several people will participate in the decision-making process. Buying committees made up of technical experts and top management are common in the buying of major goods. Beyond this, B-to-B marketers now face a new breed of higher-level, better-trained supply managers. Therefore, companies must have well-trained marketers and salespeople to deal with these well-trained buyers.

■ Derived demand: Intel advertises heavily to personal computer buyers, selling them on the virtues of Intel microprocessors—both Intel and its business partners benefit.

Types of Decisions and the Decision Process Business buyers usually face *more complex* buying decisions than do consumer buyers. Purchases often involve large sums of money, complex technical and economic considerations, and interactions among many people at many

5.2 MARKETING AT WORK

Ikea: Working with Suppliers to Keep Customers Clamoring for More

IKEA, the world's largest furniture retailer, is the quintessential global cult brand. Last year, more than 410 million shoppers flocked to the Scandinavian retailer's more than 250 huge stores in 34 countries, generating more than $22 billion in sales. Most of the shoppers are loyal IKEA customers—many are avid apostles. From Beijing to Moscow to Middletown, Ohio, all are drawn to the IKEA lifestyle, one built around trendy but simple and practical furniture at affordable prices. According to *BusinessWeek:*

> Perhaps more than any other company in the world, IKEA has become a curator of people's lifestyles, if not their lives. At a time when consumers face so many choices for everything they buy, IKEA provides a one-stop sanctuary for coolness. IKEA is far more than a furniture merchant. It sells a lifestyle that customers around the world embrace as a signal that they've arrived, that they have good taste and recognize value. "If it wasn't for IKEA," writes British design magazine *Icon*, "most people would have no access to affordable contemporary design."

■ Giant Swedish furniture retailer IKEA doesn't just buy from its suppliers, it involves them deeply in the process of delivering a stylish and affordable lifestyle to IKEA's customers worldwide—here in Saudi Arabia.

As the world's Ambassador of Kul (Swedish for fun), IKEA is growing at a healthy clip. Sales have leapt over 22 percent since last year. IKEA plans to open 22 new megastores this year, including outlets in Western China, Japan, and Portugal. In the United States, it plans to expand from its current 34 stores to more than 50 stores by 2013. In fact, the biggest obstacle to growth isn't opening new stores and attracting customers. Rather, it's finding enough of the right kinds of *suppliers* to help design and produce the billions of dollars of goods that those customers will carry out of its stores. IKEA currently relies on about 1,800 suppliers in more than 50 countries to stock its shelves. If the giant retailer continues at its current rate of growth, it will need to double its supply network by 2010.

It turns out that creating beautiful, durable furniture at low prices is no easy proposition. It calls for a resolute focus on design and an obsession for low costs. IKEA knows that it can't go it alone. Instead, it must develop close partnerships with suppliers around the globe who can help it develop simple new designs and keep costs down. Here's how the company describes its approach, and the importance of suppliers:

> To manufacture beautiful, durable furniture at low prices is not so easy.... We can't do it alone.... First we do our part. Our designers work with manufacturers to find smart ways to make furniture using existing production processes. Then our buyers look all over the world for good suppliers with the most suitable raw materials. Next, we buy in bulk—on a global scale—so that we can get the best deals, and you can get the lowest price. Then you do your part. Using the IKEA catalog and visiting the store, you choose the furniture yourself and pick it up at the self-serve warehouse. Because most items are packed flat, you can get them home easily and assemble them yourself. This means we don't charge you

levels of the buyer's organization. Because the purchases are more complex, business buyers may take longer to make their decisions. The business buying process also tends to be *more formalized* than the consumer buying process. Large business purchases usually call for detailed product specifications, written purchase orders, careful supplier searches, and formal approval.

Finally, in the business buying process, the buyer and seller are often much *more dependent* on each other. B-to-B marketers may roll up their sleeves and work closely with their customers during all stages of the buying process—from helping customers define problems, to finding solutions, to supporting after-sale operation. They often customize their offerings to individual customer needs. In the short run, sales go to suppliers who meet buyers' immediate product and service needs. In the long run, however, business-to-business marketers keep a customer's sales and create customer value by meeting current needs *and* by partnering with customers to help them solve their problems.

In recent years, relationships between customers and suppliers have been changing from downright adversarial to close and chummy. In fact, many customer companies are now practicing *supplier development*, systematically developing networks of supplier-partners to

for things you can easily do on your own. So together we save money . . . for a better everyday life.

At IKEA, design is important. But no matter how good the design, a product won't find its way to the showroom unless it's also affordable. IKEA goes to the ends of the earth to find supply partners who can help it to create just the right product at just the right price. According to the *BusinessWeek* writer, IKEA "once contracted with ski makers—experts in bent wood—to manufacture its Poang armchairs, and it has tapped makers of supermarket carts to turn out durable sofas."

The design process for a new IKEA product can take up to three years. IKEA's designers start with a basic customer value proposition. Then, they work closely with key suppliers to bring that proposition to market. Consider IKEA's Olle chair, developed in the late 1990s. Based on customer feedback, designer Evamaria Ronnegard set out to create a sturdy, durable kitchen chair that would fit into any décor, priced at $52. Once her initial design was completed and approved, IKEA's 45 trading offices searched the world and matched the Olle with a Chinese supplier, based on both design and cost efficiencies.

Together, Ronnegard and the Chinese supplier refined the design to improve the chair's function and reduce its costs. For example, the supplier modified the back leg angle to prevent the chair from tipping easily. This also reduced the thickness of the seat without compromising the chair's strength, reducing both costs and shipping weight. However, when she learned that the supplier planned to use traditional wood joinery methods to attach the chair back to the seat, Ronnegard intervened. That would require that the chair be shipped in a costly L-shape, which by itself would inflate the chair's retail price to $58. Ronnegard convinced the supplier to go with metal bolts instead. The back-and-forth design process worked well. IKEA introduced its still-popular Olle chair at the $52 target price. (Through continued design and manufacturing refinements, IKEA and its supplier have now reduced the price to just $29.)

Throughout the design and manufacturing process, the depth of the supplier partnership impressed Ronnegard. "My job really hit home when I got a call from the supplier in China, who had a question about some aspect of the chair," she recalls. "There he was, halfway around the world, and he was calling me about my chair." Now,

Ronnegard is often on-site in China or India or Vietnam, working face to face with suppliers as they help to refine her designs.

Another benefit of close collaboration with suppliers is that they can often help IKEA to customize its designs to make them sell better in local markets. In China, for example, at the suggestion of a local supplier, IKEA stocked 250,000 plastic placemats commemorating the year of the rooster. The placemats sold out in only three weeks.

Thus, before IKEA can sell the billions of dollars worth of products its customer covet, it must first find suppliers who can help it design and make all those products. IKEA doesn't just rely on spot suppliers who might be available when needed. Instead, it has systematically developed a robust network of supplier-partners that reliably provide the more than 10,000 items it stocks. And more than just buying from suppliers, IKEA involves them deeply in the process of designing and making stylish but affordable products to keep IKEA's customers coming back. Working together, IKEA and its suppliers have kept fans like Jen Segrest clamoring for more:

At least once a year, Jen Segrest, a 36-year-old freelance Web designer, and her husband travel 10 hours round-trip from their home in Middletown, Ohio, to the IKEA in Schaumburg, Illinois, near Chicago. "Every piece of furniture in my living room is IKEA—except for an end table, which I hate. And next time I go to IKEA I'll replace it," says Segrest. To lure the retailer to Ohio, Segrest has even started a blog called OH! IKEA. The banner on the home page reads "IKEA in Ohio—Because man cannot live on Target alone."

Turns out, IKEA has answered Segrest's request and is planning to open an IKEA outside of Cincinnati in 2008. How Swede is that?

Sources: Extracts, quotes, and other information from Kerry Capell, "How the Swedish Retailer Became a Global Cult Brand," *BusinessWeek*, November 14, 2005, p. 103; Shari Kulha, "Behind the Scenes at IKEA," *The Guardian*, September 29, 2005, p. 8; Greta Guest, "Inside IKEA's Formula for Global Success," *Detroit Free Press*, June 3, 2006; IKEA, *Hoover's Company Records*, March 2007, accessed at www.hoovers.com; "IKEA Group Stores," accessed at www.ikea-group.ikea.com/corporate/about_ikea/ ikea_group_stores.html, November 2007; and "Our Vision: A Better Everyday Life," accessed at www.ikea.com, November 2007.

ensure an appropriate and dependable supply of products and materials that they will use in making their own products or resell to others. For example, Caterpillar no longer calls its buyers "purchasing agents"—they are managers of "purchasing and supplier development." Wal-Mart doesn't have a "Purchasing Department," it has a "Supplier Development Department." And giant Swedish furniture retailer IKEA doesn't just buy from its suppliers, it involves them deeply in the process of delivering a stylish and affordable lifestyle to IKEA's customers (see Marketing at Work 5.2).

Business Buyer Behavior

At the most basic level, marketers want to know how business buyers will respond to various marketing stimuli. Figure 5.7 shows a model of business buyer behavior. In this model, marketing and other stimuli affect the buying organization and produce certain buyer responses. These stimuli enter the organization and are turned into buyer responses. In order to design good marketing strategies, the marketer must understand what happens within the organization to turn stimuli into purchase responses.

FIGURE 5.7

A Model of Business Buyer Behavior

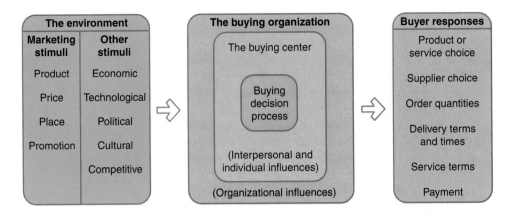

Within the organization, buying activity consists of two major parts: the buying center, made up of all the people involved in the buying decision, and the buying decision process. The model shows that the buying center and the buying decision process are influenced by internal organizational, interpersonal, and individual factors as well as by external environmental factors.

The model in Figure 5.7 suggests four questions about business buyer behavior: What buying decisions do business buyers make? Who participates in the buying process? What are the major influences on buyers? How do business buyers make their buying decisions?

Major Types of Buying Situations   There are three major types of buying situations.[39] At one extreme is the *straight rebuy*, which is a fairly routine decision. At the other extreme is the *new task*, which may call for thorough research. In the middle is the *modified rebuy,* which requires some research.

In a **straight rebuy**, the buyer reorders something without any modifications. It is usually handled on a routine basis by the purchasing department. Based on past buying satisfaction, the buyer simply chooses from the various suppliers on its list. "In" suppliers try to maintain product and service quality. They often propose automatic reordering systems so that the purchasing agent will save reordering time. "Out" suppliers try to find new ways to add value or exploit dissatisfaction so that the buyer will consider them.

In a **modified rebuy**, the buyer wants to modify product specifications, prices, terms, or suppliers. The modified rebuy usually involves more decision participants than does the straight rebuy. The in suppliers may become nervous and feel pressured to put their best foot forward to protect an account. Out suppliers may see the modified rebuy situation as an opportunity to make a better offer and gain new business.

A company buying a product or service for the first time faces a **new-task** situation. In such cases, the greater the cost or risk, the larger the number of decision participants and the greater their efforts to collect information will be. The new-task situation is the marketer's greatest opportunity and challenge. The marketer not only tries to reach as many key buying influences as possible but also provides help and information.

The buyer makes the fewest decisions in the straight rebuy and the most in the new-task decision. In the new-task situation, the buyer must decide on product specifications, suppliers, price limits, payment terms, order quantities, delivery times, and service terms. The order of these decisions varies with each situation, and different decision participants influence each choice.

Many business buyers prefer to buy a complete solution to a problem from a single seller instead of buying separate products and services from several suppliers and putting them together. The sale often goes to the firm that provides the most complete *system* for meeting the customer's needs and solving its problems. Such **systems selling** (or **solutions selling**) is often a key business marketing strategy for winning and holding accounts.

Thus, transportation and logistics giant UPS does more than just ship packages for its business customers. It develops entire solutions to customers' transportation and logistics problems. For example, UPS bundles a complete spectrum of services that support Nikon's consumer products supply chain—including logistics, transportation, freight, and customs brokerage services—into one smooth-running system.[40]

Straight rebuy
A business buying situation in which the buyer routinely reorders something without any modifications.

Modified rebuy
A business buying situation in which the buyer wants to modify product specifications, prices, terms, or suppliers.

New task
A business buying situation in which the buyer purchases a product or service for the first time.

Systems selling (or solutions selling)
Selling a complete solution to a problem, helping buyers to avoid all the separate decisions involved in a complex buying situation.

When Nikon entered the digital camera market, it decided that it needed an entirely new distribution strategy as well. But rather than handling distribution in-house, it asked transportation and logistics giant UPS to design a complete system for moving its entire electronics product line from its Asian factories to retail stores throughout the United States, Latin America, and the Caribbean. Now, products leave Nikon's Asian manufacturing centers and arrive on American retailers' shelve in as few as two days, with UPS handling everything in between. UPS first manages air and ocean freight and related customs brokerage to bring Nikon products from Korea, Japan, and Indonesia to its Louisville, Kentucky operations center. There, UPS can either "kit" the Nikon merchandise with accessories such as batteries and chargers or repackage it for in-store display. Finally, UPS distributes the products to thousands of retailers across the United States or exports them to Latin American or Caribbean retail outlets and distributors. Along the way, UPS tracks the goods and provides Nikon with a "snap shot" of the entire supply chain, letting Nikon keep retailers informed of delivery times and adjust them as needed.

Participants in the Business Buying Process Who does the buying of the trillions of dollars' worth of goods and services needed by business organizations? The decision-making unit of a buying organization is called its **buying center**: all the individuals and units that play a role in the business purchase decision-making process. This group includes the actual users of the product or service, those who make the buying decision, those who influence the buying decision, those who do the actual buying, and those who control buying information.

The buying center is not a fixed and formally identified unit within the buying organization. It is a set of buying roles assumed by different people for different purchases. Within the organization, the size and makeup of the buying center will vary for different products and for different buying situations. For some routine purchases, one person—say a purchasing agent—may assume all the buying center roles and serve as the only person involved in the buying decision. For more complex purchases, the buying center may include 20 or 30 people from different levels and departments in the organization.

The buying center concept presents a major marketing challenge. The business marketer must learn who participates in the decision, each participant's relative influence, and what evaluation criteria each decision participant uses. This can be difficult. "In the good old days, the decision maker was easy to find," notes one sales manager. "Now it's tougher. There are consensus decisions, committee decisions, decision teams, subcommittees, influencers . . . it's a regular jungle out there."[41]

For example, the medical products and services group of Cardinal Health sells disposable surgical gowns to hospitals. It identifies the hospital personnel involved in this buying decision as the vice president of purchasing, the operating room administrator, and the surgeons. Each participant plays a different role. The vice president of purchasing analyzes whether the hospital should buy disposable gowns or reusable gowns. If analysis favors disposable gowns, then the operating room administrator compares competing products and prices and makes a choice. This administrator considers the gown's absorbency, antiseptic quality, design, and cost and normally buys the brand that meets requirements at the lowest cost. Finally, surgeons affect the decision later by reporting their satisfaction or dissatisfaction with the brand.

The buying center usually includes some obvious participants who are involved formally in the buying decision. For example, the decision to buy a corporate jet will probably involve the company's CEO, chief pilot, a purchasing agent, some legal staff, a member of top management, and others formally charged with the buying decision. It may also involve less obvious, informal participants, some of whom may actually make or strongly affect the buying decision. Sometimes, even the people in the buying center are not aware of all the

> **Buying center**
> All the individuals and units that participate in the business buying-decision process.

■ Buying Center: Cardinal Health deals with a wide range of buying influences, from purchasing executives and hospital administrators to the surgeons who actually use its products.

buying participants. For example, the decision about which corporate jet to buy may actually be made by a corporate board member who has an interest in flying and who knows a lot about airplanes. This board member may work behind the scenes to sway the decision. Many business buying decisions result from the complex interactions of ever-changing buying center participants.

Major Influences on Business Buyers   Business buyers are subject to many influences when they make their buying decisions. Some marketers assume that the major influences are economic. They think buyers will favor the supplier who offers the lowest price or the best product or the most service. They concentrate on offering strong economic benefits to buyers. However, business buyers actually respond to both economic and personal factors. Far from being cold, calculating, and impersonal, business buyers are human and social as well. They react to both reason and emotion.

Today, most B-to-B marketers recognize that emotion plays an important role in business buying decisions. For example, you might expect that an advertisement promoting large trucks to corporate fleet buyers would stress objective technical, performance, and economic factors. However, one ad for Volvo heavy-duty trucks shows two drivers arm-wrestling and claims, "It solves all your fleet problems. Except who gets to drive." It turns out that, in the face of an industry-wide driver shortage, the type of truck a fleet provides can help it to attract qualified drivers. The Volvo ad stresses the raw beauty of the truck and its comfort and roominess, features that make it more appealing to drivers. The ad concludes that Volvo trucks are "built to make fleets more profitable and drivers a lot more possessive."[42]

When suppliers' offers are very similar, business buyers have little basis for strictly rational choice. Because they can meet organizational goals with any supplier, buyers can allow personal factors to play a larger role in their decisions. However, when competing products differ greatly, business buyers are more accountable for their choice and tend to pay more attention to economic factors. Figure 5.8 lists various groups of influences on business buyers—environmental, organizational, interpersonal, and individual.

Environmental Factors   Business buyers are heavily influenced by factors in the current and expected *economic environment,* such as the level of primary demand, the economic outlook, and the cost of money. Another environmental factor is *shortages* in key materials. Many companies now are more willing to buy and hold larger inventories of scarce materials to ensure adequate supply. Business buyers also are affected by technological, political, and competitive developments in the environment. Finally, *culture and customs* can strongly influence business buyer reactions to the marketer's behavior and strategies, especially in the international marketing environment. The business buyer must watch

■ Emotions play an important role in business buying: This Volvo truck ad mentions objective factors, such as efficiency and ease of maintenance. But it stresses more emotional factors such as the raw beauty of the truck and its comfort and roominess, features that make "drivers a lot more possessive."

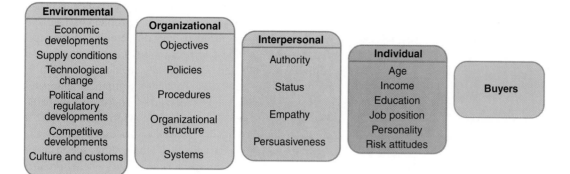

FIGURE 5.8

Major Influences on Business Buyer Behavior

these factors, determine how they will affect the buyer, and try to turn these challenges into opportunities.

Organizational Factors   Each buying organization has its own objectives, policies, procedures, structure, and systems, and the business marketer must understand these factors well. Questions such as these arise: How many people are involved in the buying decision? Who are they? What are their evaluative criteria? What are the company's policies and limits on its buyers?

Interpersonal Factors   The buying center usually includes many participants who influence each other, so *interpersonal factors* also influence the business buying process. However, it is often difficult to assess such interpersonal factors and group dynamics. Buying center participants do not wear tags that label them as "key decision maker" or "not influential." Nor do buying center participants with the highest rank always have the most influence. Participants may influence the buying decision because they control rewards and punishments, are well liked, have special expertise, or have a special relationship with other important participants. Interpersonal factors are often very subtle. Whenever possible, business marketers must try to understand these factors and design strategies that take them into account.

Individual Factors   Each participant in the business buying decision process brings in personal motives, perceptions, and preferences. These individual factors are affected by personal characteristics such as age, income, education, professional identification, personality, and attitudes toward risk. Also, buyers have different buying styles. Some may be technical types who make in-depth analyses of competitive proposals before choosing a supplier. Other buyers may be intuitive negotiators who are adept at pitting the sellers against one another for the best deal.

The Business Buying Process Figure 5.9 lists the eight stages of the business buying process.[43] Buyers who face a new-task buying situation usually go through all stages of the buying process. Buyers making modified or straight rebuys may skip some of the stages. We will examine these steps for the typical new-task buying situation.

FIGURE 5.9

Stages of the Business Buying Process

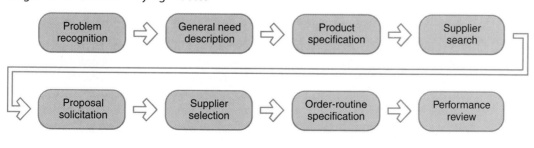

■ Problem recognition: Sharp uses ads like this one to alert customers to potential problems and then provide solutions.

Problem Recognition   The buying process begins when someone in the company recognizes a problem or need that can be met by acquiring a specific product or service. *Problem recognition* can result from internal or external stimuli. Internally, the company may decide to launch a new product that requires new production equipment and materials. Or a machine may break down and need new parts. Perhaps a purchasing manager is unhappy with a current supplier's product quality, service, or prices. Externally, the buyer may get some new ideas at a trade show, see an ad, or receive a call from a salesperson who offers a better product or a lower price.

In fact, in their advertising, business marketers often alert customers to potential problems and then show how their products provide solutions. For example, a Sharp ad notes that a multifunction printer can present data security problems and asks "Is your MFP a portal for identity theft?" The solution? Sharp's data security kits "help prevent sensitive information from falling into the wrong hands."

General Need Description   Having recognized a need, the buyer next prepares a *general need description* that describes the characteristics and quantity of the needed item. For standard items, this process presents few problems. For complex items, however, the buyer may need to work with others—engineers, users, consultants—to define the item. The team may want to rank the importance of reliability, durability, price, and other attributes desired in the item. In this phase, the alert business marketer can help the buyers define their needs and provide information about the value of different product characteristics.

Value analysis

An approach to cost reduction in which components are studied carefully to determine if they can be redesigned, standardized, or made by less costly methods of production.

Product Specification   The buying organization next develops the item's technical *product specifications,* often with the help of a value analysis engineering team. **Value analysis** is an approach to cost reduction in which components are studied carefully to determine if they can be redesigned, standardized, or made by less costly methods of production. The team decides on the best product characteristics and specifies them accordingly. Sellers, too, can use value analysis as a tool to help secure a new account. By showing buyers a better way to make an object, outside sellers can turn straight rebuy situations into new-task situations that give them a chance to obtain new business.

Supplier Search   The buyer now conducts a *supplier search* to find the best vendors. The buyer can compile a small list of qualified suppliers by reviewing trade directories, doing computer searches, or phoning other companies for recommendations. Today, more and more companies are turning to the Internet to find suppliers. For marketers, this has leveled the playing field—the Internet gives smaller suppliers many of the same advantages as larger competitors.

The newer the buying task, and the more complex and costly the item, the greater the amount of time the buyer will spend searching for suppliers. The supplier's task is to get listed in major directories and build a good reputation in the marketplace. Salespeople should watch for companies in the process of searching for suppliers and make certain that their firm is considered.

Proposal Solicitation   In the *proposal solicitation* stage of the business buying process, the buyer invites qualified suppliers to submit proposals. In response, some suppliers will send only a catalog or a salesperson. However, when the item is complex or expensive, the buyer will usually require detailed written proposals or formal presentations from each potential supplier.

Business marketers must be skilled in researching, writing, and presenting proposals in response to buyer proposal solicitations. Proposals should be marketing documents, not just technical documents. Presentations should inspire confidence and should make the marketer's company stand out from the competition.

Supplier Selection   The members of the buying center now review the proposals and select a supplier or suppliers. During *supplier selection,* the buying center often will draw up a list of the desired supplier attributes and their relative importance. Such attributes include product and service quality, reputation, on-time delivery, ethical corporate behavior, honest communication, and competitive prices. The members of the buying center will rate suppliers against these attributes and identify the best suppliers.

Buyers may attempt to negotiate with preferred suppliers for better prices and terms before making the final selections. In the end, they may select a single supplier or a few suppliers. Many buyers prefer multiple sources of supplies to avoid being totally dependent on one supplier and to allow comparisons of prices and performance of several suppliers over time. Today's supplier development managers want to develop a full network of supplier-partners that can help the company bring more value to its customers.

Order-Routine Specification   The buyer now prepares an *order-routine specification.* It includes the final order with the chosen supplier or suppliers and lists items such as technical specifications, quantity needed, expected time of delivery, return policies, and warranties. In the case of maintenance, repair, and operating items, buyers may use blanket contracts rather than periodic purchase orders. A blanket contract creates a long-term relationship in which the supplier promises to resupply the buyer as needed at agreed prices for a set time period.

Many large buyers now practice *vendor-managed inventory,* in which they turn over ordering and inventory responsibilities to their suppliers. Under such systems, buyers share sales and inventory information directly with key suppliers. The suppliers then monitor inventories and replenish stock automatically as needed.

Performance Review   In this stage, the buyer reviews supplier performance. The buyer may contact users and ask them to rate their satisfaction. The *performance review* may lead the buyer to continue, modify, or drop the arrangement. The seller's job is to monitor the same factors used by the buyer to make sure that the seller is giving the expected satisfaction.

The eight-stage buying-process model provides a simple view of the business buying as it might occur in a new-task buying situation. The actual process is usually much more complex. In the modified rebuy or straight rebuy situation, some of these stages would be compressed or bypassed. Each organization buys in its own way, and each buying situation has unique requirements.

Different buying center participants may be involved at different stages of the process. Although certain buying-process steps usually do occur, buyers do not always follow them in the same order, and they may add other steps. Often, buyers will repeat certain stages of the process. Finally, a customer relationship might involve many different types of purchases ongoing at a given time, all in different stages of the buying process. The seller must manage the total customer relationship, not just individual purchases.

E-Procurement: Buying on the Internet
Advances in information technology have changed the face of the B-to-B marketing process. Online purchasing, often called *e-procurement,* has grown rapidly in recent years.

Companies can do e-procurement in any of several ways. They can conduct *reverse auctions,* in which they put their purchasing requests online and invite suppliers to bid for the business. Or they can use online *trading exchanges,* through which companies work collectively to facilitate the trading process. For example, Exostar is an online trading exchange that connects buyers and sellers in the aerospace and defense industry. Its goal is to improve trading efficiency and reduce costs among industry trading partners. Initially a collaboration between five leading aerospace and defense companies—Boeing, Lockheed Martin, Raytheon, BAE Systems, and Rolls-Royce—Exostar has now connected more than 300 procurement systems and 34,000 trading partners in 20 countries around the world.

Companies can conduct e-procurement by setting up their own *company buying sites.* For example, General Electric operates a company trading site on which it posts its buying needs and invites bids, negotiates terms, and places orders. Or the company can create *extranet links* with key suppliers. For instance, they can create direct procurement accounts with suppliers

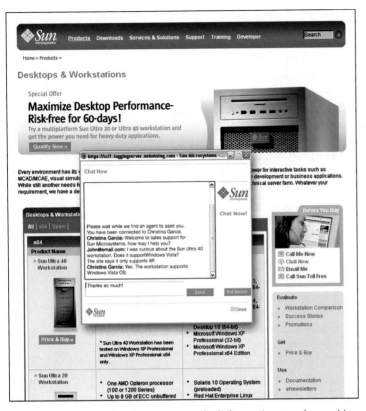

■ Online buying: This Sun Microsystems site helps customers who want to purchase online by providing deep information on its thousands of complex products and services. Users who still need help can take advantage of the sites interactive features to request an immediate phone call, e-mail, or live online chat with a Sun rep.

such as Dell or Office Depot, through which company buyers can purchase equipment, materials, and supplies.

B-to-B marketers can help customers who wish to purchase online by creating well designed, easy-to-use Web sites. For example, *BtoB* magazine recently rated the site of Sun Microsystems—a market leader in network computing hardware, software, and services—as one of its "10 great B-to-B Web sites":

A few years ago, Sun Microsystems completely redesigned its Web site. Most important, it wanted to find a better way to present deep information on its thousands of complex server, storage, and software products and services while also giving the site a more humanistic view. Sun came up with a tab-driven menu design that puts an enormous amount of information within only a few clicks of customer's computers. Action-oriented menu labels—such as Evaluate, Get, Use, and Maintain—leave nothing to the imagination and make navigation a snap. Beyond product pictures and specifications, the site provides video walkthroughs of products, along with "success stories" of how other customers have benefited from doing business with Sun. Customers can even create personalized MySun portals. "We provide you with a customized experience," says Sun's VP-Sun Web experience. "Maybe you've downloaded software. Based on that download, you'll see a filtered blog, training classes that are available, and a link to unreleased code you can try out. It's integrated support tailored to the type of Sun products you use." Users who still need help can take advantage of the site's interactive features to request an immediate phone call, an e-mail, or a live online chat in English, French, German, or Spanish with a Sun rep.[44]

E-procurement gives buyers access to new suppliers, lowers purchasing costs, and hastens order processing and delivery. In turn, business marketers can connect with customers online to share marketing information, sell products and services, provide customer support services, and maintain ongoing customer relationships.

So far, most of the products bought online are MRO materials—maintenance, repair, and operations. For instance, Hewlett-Packard spends 95 percent of its $13 billion MRO budget via e-procurement. And last year Delta Air Lines purchased $6.2 billion worth of fuel online. National Semiconductor has automated almost all of the company's 3,500 monthly requisitions to buy materials ranging from the sterile booties worn in its fabrication plants to state-of-the-art software. Even the Baltimore Aquarium uses e-procurement to buy everything from exotic fish to feeding supplies. It recently spent $6 billion online for architectural services and supplies to help construct the new exhibit "Animal Planet Australia: Wild Extremes."[45]

The actual dollar amount spent on these types of MRO materials pales in comparison to the amount spent for items such as airplane parts, computer systems, and steel tubing. Yet, MRO materials make up 80 percent of all business orders, and the transaction costs for order processing are high. Thus, companies have much to gain by streamlining the MRO buying process on the Web.

Business-to-business e-procurement yields many benefits. First, it shaves transaction costs and results in more efficient purchasing for both buyers and suppliers. A Web-powered purchasing program eliminates the paperwork associated with traditional requisition and ordering procedures. One study found that e-procurement cuts down requisition-to-order costs by an average of 58 percent.[46]

E-procurement reduces the time between order and delivery. Time savings are particularly dramatic for companies with many overseas suppliers. Adaptec, a leading supplier of computer storage, used an extranet to tie all of its Taiwanese chip suppliers together in a kind of virtual family. Now messages from Adaptec flow in seconds from its headquarters to its Asian partners, and Adaptec has reduced the time between the order and delivery of its chips from as long as 16 weeks to just 55 days—the same turnaround time for companies that build their own chips.

Finally, beyond the cost and time savings, e-procurement frees purchasing people to focus on more-strategic issues. For many purchasing professionals, going online means reducing drudgery and paperwork and spending more time managing inventory and working creatively with suppliers. "That is the key," says the HP executive. "You can now focus people on value-added activities. Procurement professionals can now find different sources and work with suppliers to reduce costs and to develop new products."[47]

The rapidly expanding use of e-purchasing, however, also presents some problems. For example, at the same time that the Web makes it possible for suppliers and customers to share business data and even collaborate on product design, it can also erode decades-old customer-supplier relationships. Many firms are using the Web to search for better suppliers.

E-purchasing can also create potential security disasters. Although e-mail and home banking transactions can be protected through basic encryption, the secure environment that businesses need to carry out confidential interactions is often still lacking. Companies are spending millions for research on defensive strategies to keep hackers at bay. Cisco Systems, for example, specifies the types of routers, firewalls, and security procedures that its partners must use to safeguard extranet connections. In fact, the company goes even further—it sends its own security engineers to examine a partner's defenses and holds the partner liable for any security breach that originates from its computer.

REST STOP ⟩⟩ REVIEWING THE CONCEPTS

This chapter is the last of three chapters that address understanding the marketplace and consumers. Here, we've looked closely at *consumer* and *business buyer behavior.* The American consumer market consists of more than 300 million people who consume many trillions of dollars' worth of goods and services each year. The business market involves even more dollars and items than the consumer market. Understanding buyer behavior is one of the biggest challenges marketers face.

1. Describe the consumer market and the major factors that influence consumer buyer behavior.

The *consumer market* consists of all the individuals and households who buy or acquire goods and services for personal consumption. A simple model of consumer behavior suggests that marketing stimuli and other major forces enter the consumer's "black box." This black box has two parts: buyer characteristics and the buyer's decision process. Once in the black box, the inputs result in buyer responses, such as buying attitudes and preferences and purchase behavior.

Consumer buyer behavior is influenced by four key sets of buyer characteristics: cultural, social, personal, and psychological. Understanding these factors can help marketers to identify interested buyers and to shape products and appeals to serve consumer needs better. *Culture* is the most basic determinant of a person's wants and behavior. People in different cultural, subcultural, and social class groups have different product and brand preferences. *Social factors*—such as small group, social network, and family influences—strongly affect product and brand choices, as do *personal characteristics,* such as age, life-cycle stage, occupation, economic circumstances, lifestyle, and personality. Finally, consumer buying behavior is influenced by four major sets of *psychological factors*—motivation, perception, learning, and be-

liefs and attitudes. Each of these factors provides a different perspective for understanding the workings of the buyer's black box.

2. Identify and discuss the stages in the buyer decision process.

When making a purchase, the buyer goes through a decision process consisting of need recognition, information search, evaluation of alternatives, purchase decision, and postpurchase behavior. During *need recognition,* the consumer recognizes a problem or need that could be satisfied by a product or service. Once the need is recognized, the consumer moves into the *information search* stage. With information in hand, the consumer proceeds to *alternative evaluation* and assesses brands in the choice set. From there, the consumer makes a *purchase decision* and actually buys the product. In the final stage of the buyer decision process, *postpurchase behavior,* the consumer takes action based on satisfaction or dissatisfaction. The marketer's job is to understand the buyer's behavior at each stage and the influences that are operating.

3. Describe the adoption and diffusion process for new products.

The product *adoption process* is made up of five stages: awareness, interest, evaluation, trial, and adoption. New-product marketers must think about how to help consumers move through these stages. With regard to the *diffusion process* for new products, consumers respond at different rates, depending on consumer and product characteristics. Consumers may be innovators, early adopters, early majority, late majority, or laggards. Each group may require different marketing approaches. Marketers often try to bring their new products to the attention of potential early adopters, especially those who are opinion leaders.

4. Define the business market and identify the major factors that influence business buyer behavior.

The *business market* consists of all organizations that buy goods and services for use in the production of other products and services or for the purpose of reselling or renting them to others at a profit. As compared to consumer markets, business markets usually have fewer, larger buyers who are more geographically concentrated. Business demand is derived demand, and the business buying decision usually involves more, and more professional, buyers.

Business buyers make decisions that vary with the three types of *buying situations*: straight rebuys, modified rebuys, and new tasks. The decision-making unit of a buying organization—the *buying center*—can consist of many different persons playing many different roles. The business marketer needs to know the following: Who are the major buying center participants? In what decisions do they exercise influence and to what degree? What evaluation criteria does each decision participant use? The business marketer also needs to understand the major environmental, organizational, interpersonal, and individual influences on the buying process.

5. List and define the steps in the business buying decision process.

The *business buying decision process* itself can be quite involved, with eight basic stages: problem recognition, general need description, product specification, supplier search, proposal solicitation, supplier selection, order-routine specification, and performance review. Buyers who face a new-task buying situation usually go through all stages of the buying process. Buyers making modified or straight rebuys may skip some of the stages. Companies must manage the overall customer relationship, which often includes many different buying decisions in various stages of the buying decision process.

Recent advances in information technology have given birth to online purchasing or "e-procurement." Such online purchasing gives buyers access to new suppliers, lowers purchasing costs, and hastens order processing and delivery. However, it can also erode customer-supplier relationships and create potential security problems. Still, business marketers are increasingly connecting with B-to-B customers online to share marketing information, sell products and services, provide customer support services, and maintain ongoing customer relationships.

Navigating the Key Terms

Adoption process (148)
Attitude (145)
Belief (145)
Business buyer behavior (150)
Buying center (155)
Cognitive dissonance (147)
Consumer buying behavior (130)
Consumer market (130)
Culture (132)

Derived demand (151)
E-procurement (159)
Group (135)
Learning (144)
Lifestyle (141)
Modified rebuy (154)
Motive (or drive) (142)
New product (148)
New task (154)

Online social networks (137)
Opinion leaders (135)
Perception (143)
Personality (141)
Social class (134)
Straight rebuy (154)
Subculture (132)
Systems selling (154)
Value analysis (158)

Travel Log

Discussing the Issues

1. Explain why marketers study buyer behavior and discuss characteristics affecting consumer behavior. Which characteristic(s) would have the greatest impact on your decision to purchase a computer and why? (AACSB: Communication; Reflective Thinking)

2. Discuss the stages of the consumer buyer decision process and describe how you or your family used this process to make a purchase. (AACSB: Communication; Reflective Thinking)

3. How might a marketer influence a consumer's information search through each of the four information sources discussed in the chapter? Which source do you think marketers should focus on to build long-term relationships with customers? (AACSB: Communication; Reflective Thinking)

4. Explain why a new product doesn't necessarily need to be "new," and discuss the adoption process individuals go through when deciding whether to adopt a new product. (AACSB: Communication)

5. Discuss how business markets are similar to and different from consumer markets. What does this mean for a

company attempting to sell goods to other organizations? (AACSB: Communication)

6. Name and describe the major types of buying situations for business buyers. (AACSB: Communication)

Application Questions

1. Interview a college student and an older adult (middle-aged or older) regarding the purchase of their automobiles. Based on what you learned in this chapter, ask them which, if any, cultural, social, personal, and psychological factors influenced their decision process and choice. Ask them to describe the process they went through in making their decision and explain it in terms of the consumer buying process discussed in the chapter. Ask them if they are satisfied or dissatisfied with their purchase and if they took any action based on that. Write a report about your interviews. (AACSB: Communication)

2. Talk to five people about purchasing a high-definition television (regardless of whether they have purchased one or not). Try to talk to individuals of different ages, genders, income levels, and occupations. Based on your understanding of the adopter categories discussed in the

chapter, categorize each individual and explain why you have identified him or her in that category. (AACSB: Communication; Reflective Thinking)

3. Interview a business person to learn how purchases are made in his or her organization. Ask this person to describe a straight rebuy, a modified rebuy, and a new-task buying situation that took place recently or that he or she is aware of (define them if necessary). Did the buying process differ based on the type of product or purchase situation? Ask the business person to explain the role he or she played in a recent purchase and to discuss the factors that influenced the decision. Write a brief report of your interview by applying the concepts you learned in this chapter regarding business buyer behavior. (AACSB: Communication; Reflective Thinking)

Under the Hood: Focus on Technology

There are several sources for buyers to research when making complex decisions such as purchasing an automobile. Kelly Blue Book is one such source (www.kbb.com). This Web site helps consumers find a car based on criteria such as price range, manufacturer, type of automobile, gas mileage, number of passengers, and others. Once the consumer selects what he or she desires, this site provides alternatives for consideration. Consumers can then compare different alternatives that they might be considering. This source also provides reviews and ratings from other sources (such as J.D. Power Quality Ratings, Safety Ratings).

1. Describe the types of information sources from which consumers can obtain information, and explain the type of information source Kelly Blue Book represents. Click on the "About Us" link at the bottom of the homepage to learn more about Kelly Blue Book. Do you think this source is very effective in influencing consumers? Explain why or why not. (AACSB: Communication; Use of IT; Reflective Thinking)

2. Click on the "Perfect Car Finder" under the "Compare and Explore" link on the left side of the homepage and select the features you would like in your next automobile. Once you have a set of alternatives, compare at least two of them using the "Compare Cars" link under the "Compare and Explore" link. Do you think this resource would help you when making an actual purchase decision? Explain the stage(s) of the consumer buyer decision process that this exercise represents. (AACSB: Communication; Use of IT; Reflective Thinking)

Focus on Ethics

One factor that influences consumers' purchase decisions is culture, and one important element of a society's culture is social class. In the United States, the lines between social classes are not fixed and rigid, as people can move to a higher or lower class. However, in other countries, such as India, this is not the case. India has a complex caste system in which members are born into one caste and expected to remain at that level, which influences their lifestyles and consumption behavior. India's complex caste system is rooted in Hinduism and includes thousands of castes and subcastes that are traditionally related to occupations. With India's high-tech boom, though, American companies are increasingly coming into India and hiring workers regardless of social caste. Although some higher-caste citizens and the government are supportive of advancing lower-caste workers, others are criticizing these companies for disregarding the long-standing social caste system.

1. Learn more about India's caste system and describe how economic growth is changing the culture in that country. What impact does this have on consumer behavior? (AACSB: Communication; Reflective Thinking)

2. Is it ethical for U.S. companies operating in India to ignore the country's caste system? Alternatively, is it ethical by U.S. standards to reinforce such a system when operating in India? (AACSB: Communication; Multicultural and Diversity; Ethical Reasoning)

Video Case

Wild Planet

Chances are that when you hear the term *socially responsible business,* a handful of companies leap to mind, such as Ben & Jerry's and The Body Shop. Although these companies and their founders led the revolution for socially responsible business, a new generation of entrepreneurs has now taken up the reigns. Today, socially responsible companies recognize that beyond "doing good" they must also bring value to consumers.

For example, Wild Planet markets high-quality, nonviolent toys that encourage kids to be imaginative and creative and to explore the world around them. But Wild Planet sells more than just toys. It sells positive play experiences. To better understand those experiences, the company conducts a tremendous amount of consumer research through state-of-the-art methods to better understand consumer buyer behavior. Wild Planet even created a Toy Opinion Panel to evaluate current products and develop new-product ideas.

After viewing the video featuring Wild Planet, answer the following questions about consumer buyer behavior.

1. Explain how each of the four sets of factors affecting consumer behavior affects the consumer purchase process as it relates to toys from Wild Planet.

2. What demographic segment of consumers is Wild Planet targeting?

3. Visit the Wild Planet Web site at www.wildplanet.com to learn more about the company. How does the Web site help consumers through the buyer decision process?

After studying this chapter, you

1. define the major steps in designing a customer-driven marketing strategy: market segmentation, targeting

2. list and discuss the major bases for segmenting consumer and business markets

3. explain how companies

4. discuss how companies differentiate and position their products for maximum competitive advantage

6

Customer-Driven Marketing Strategy: Creating Value for Target Customers

ROAD MAP Previewing the Concepts

So far, you've learned what marketing is and about the importance of understanding consumers and the marketplace environment. With that as background, you're now ready to delve deeper into marketing strategy and tactics. This chapter looks further into key customer-driven marketing strategy decisions—how to divide up markets into meaningful customer groups (*segmentation*), choose which customer groups to serve (*targeting*), create market offerings that best serve targeted customers (*differentiation*), and position the offerings in the minds of consumers (*positioning*). Then, the chapters that follow explore the tactical marketing tools—the Four Ps—by which marketers bring these strategies to life.

As an opening example of segmentation, targeting, differentiation, and positioning at work, let's look at Dunkin' Donuts. Dunkin', a largely Eastern U.S. coffee chain, has ambitious plans to expand into a national powerhouse, on a par with Starbucks. But Dunkin' is no Starbucks. In fact, it doesn't want to be. It targets a very different kind of customer with a very different value proposition. Grab yourself some coffee and read on.

Dunkin' Donuts recently paid dozens of faithful customers in Phoenix, Chicago, and Charlotte, North Carolina, $100 a week to buy coffee at Starbucks instead. At the same time, the no-frills coffee chain paid Starbucks' customers to make the opposite switch. When it later debriefed the two groups, Dunkin' says it found them so polarized that company researchers dubbed them "tribes"—each of whom loathed the very things that made the other tribe loyal to their coffee shop. Dunkin' fans viewed Starbucks as pretentious and trendy, whereas Starbucks loyalists saw Dunkin' as plain and unoriginal. "I don't get it," one Dunkin' regular told researchers after visiting Starbucks. "If I want to sit on a couch, I stay at home."

William Rosenberg opened the first Dunkin' Donuts in Quincy, Massachusetts, in 1950. Residents flocked to his store each morning for the coffee and fresh doughnuts. Rosenberg started franchising the Dunkin' Donuts name and the chain grew rapidly throughout the Midwest and Southeast. By the early 1990s, however, Dunkin' was losing breakfast sales to morning sandwiches at McDonald's and Burger King. Starbucks and other high-end cafés began sprouting up, bringing more competition. Sales slid as the company clung to its strategy of selling sugary doughnuts by the dozen.

In the mid-1990s, however, Dunkin' shifted its focus from doughnuts to coffee in the hope that promoting a more frequently consumed item would drive store traffic. The coffee push worked. Coffee now makes up 64 percent of sales—doughnuts make up a mere 17 percent of sales. Dunkin' sells 2.7 million cups of coffee a day, nearly one billion cups a year. And Dunkin's sales have surged more than 40 percent during the past four years. Based on this recent success, Dunkin' now has ambitious plans to expand into a national coffee powerhouse, on a par with Starbucks, the nation's largest coffee chain. The chain currently has more than 5,400 U.S. restaurants in 34 states and plans to open another 10,000 stores nationwide by 2020.

But Dunkin' is not Starbucks. In fact, it doesn't want to be. To succeed, it must have its own clear vision of just which customers it wants to serve (what *segments* and *targeting*) and how (what *positioning* or *value proposition*). Dunkin' and Starbucks target very different customers, who want very different things from their favorite coffee shops. Starbucks is strongly positioned as a sort of high-brow "third place"—outside the home and office—featuring couches, eclectic music, wireless Internet access, and art-splashed walls. Dunkin' has a decidedly more low-brow, "everyman" kind of positioning.

With its makeover, Dunkin' plans to move upscale—a bit but not too far—to rebrand itself as a quick but appealing alternative to specialty coffee shops and fast-food chains. A prototype Dunkin' store in Euclid, Ohio, outside Cleveland, features rounded granite-style coffee bars, where workers make espresso drinks face-to-face with customers. Open-air pastry cases brim with yogurt parfaits and fresh fruit, while a carefully orchestrated pop-music soundtrack is piped throughout.

Yet Dunkin' built itself on serving simple fare to working-class customers. Inching upscale without alienating that base will prove tricky. There will be no couches in the new stores. And Dunkin' renamed a new hot sandwich a "stuffed melt" after customers complained that calling it a "panini" was too fancy. "We're walking that [fine] line," says Regina Lewis, the chain's vice president of consumer insights. "The thing about the Dunkin' tribe is, they see through the hype."

Dunkin's research showed that although loyal Dunkin' customers want nicer stores, they were bewildered and turned off by the atmosphere at Starbucks. They groused that crowds of laptop users made it difficult to find a seat. They didn't like Starbucks' "tall," "grande," and "venti" lingo for small, medium, and large coffees. And they couldn't understand why anyone would pay as much as $4 for a cup of coffee. "It was almost as though they were a group of Martians talking about a group of Earthlings," says an executive from Dunkin's ad agency. One customer told researchers that lingering in a Starbucks felt like "celebrating Christmas with people you don't know." The Starbucks customers that Dunkin' paid to switch were equally uneasy in Dunkin' shops. "The Starbucks people couldn't bear that they weren't special anymore," says the ad executive.

Such opposing opinions aren't surprising, given the differences in the two stores' customers. About 45 percent of Dunkin' Donuts' customers have an annual household income between $45,000 and $100,000 a year, with 30 percent earning less than that and 25 percent earning more. Dunkin's customers include blue- and white-collar workers across all age, race, and income demographics. By contrast, Starbucks targets a higher-income, more professional group.

But Dunkin' researchers concluded that it wasn't income that set the two tribes apart, as much as an ideal: Dunkin' tribe members want to be part of a crowd, whereas members of the Starbucks tribe want to stand out as individuals. "The Starbucks tribe, they seek out things to make them feel more important," says Dunkin' VP Lewis. Members of the Dunkin' Donuts tribe "don't need to be any more important than they are."

Based on such findings, Dunkin' executives have made dozens of store-redesign decisions, big and small, ranging from where to put the espresso machines to how much of its signature pink and orange color scheme to retain to where to display its fresh baked goods. Out went the square laminate tables, to be replaced by round imitation-granite tabletops and sleek chairs. Dunkin' covered store walls in espresso brown and dialed down the pink and orange tones. Executives considered but held off on installing wireless Internet access because customers "just don't feel it's Dunkin' Donuts." Executives continue to discuss dropping the word "donut" from its signs to convey that its menu is now broader.

To grab a bigger share of customer, Dunkin' is expanding its menu beyond breakfast with hearty sweet and savory snacks that can substitute for meals, such as smoothies and personal pizzas. The new Euclid store is doing three times the sales of other stores in its area, partly because more customers are coming after 11 a.m. for new gourmet cookies and flatbread sandwiches. Focus groups liked the hot flatbreads and smoothies but balked at tiny pinwheels of dough stuffed with various fillings. Customers said "they felt like something at a fancy cocktail hour," says Lewis, and they weren't substantial enough.

Stacey Stevens, a 34-year-old Euclid resident who recently visited the new Dunkin' prototype store, said she noticed it felt different than other Dunkin' locations. "I don't remember there being lots of music," she said, while picking up a dozen doughnuts. "I like it in here." She said it felt "more upbeat" than Starbucks. One Euclid store manager even persuaded Richard Wandersleben to upgrade from a regular coffee to a $2.39 latte during a recent visit. The 73-year-old retired tool-and-die maker, who drinks about three cups of coffee a day, says the Dunkin' Donuts latte suited him fine. "It's a little creamier" than regular coffee, he said.

Dunkin' knows that it'll take some time to refresh its image. And whatever else happens, it plans to stay true to the needs and preferences of the Dunkin' tribe. Dunkin's "not going after the Starbucks coffee snob," says one analyst, it's "going after the average Joe." Dunkin's positioning and value proposition are well personified by the chain's new spokesperson, TV food personality Rachael Ray, who's been described by some as an everyday person's Martha Stewart. Says Dunkin' Donuts brand president Robert Rodriguez, "Rachael's philosophy of creating quality meals quickly and without pretense for busy people leading busy lives is the same driving force behind the Dunkin' Donuts brand."[1]

Companies today recognize that they cannot appeal to all buyers in the marketplace, or at least not to all buyers in the same way. Buyers are too numerous, too widely scattered, and too varied in their needs and buying practices. Moreover, the companies themselves vary widely in their abilities to serve different segments of the market. Instead, like Dunkin' Donuts, a company must identify the parts of the market that it can serve best and most profitably. It must design customer-driven marketing strategies that build the *right* relationships with the *right* customers.

Thus, most companies have moved away from mass marketing and toward *target marketing*—identifying market segments, selecting one or more of them, and developing products and marketing programs tailored to each. Instead of scattering their marketing efforts (the "shotgun" approach), firms are focusing on the buyers who have greater interest in the values they create best (the "rifle" approach).

Figure 6.1 shows the four major steps in designing a customer-driven marketing strategy. In the first two steps, the company selects the customers that it will serve. **Market segmentation** involves dividing a market into smaller groups of buyers with distinct needs, characteristics, or behaviors that might require separate marketing strategies or mixes. The company identifies different ways to segment the market and develops profiles of the resulting market segments. **Market targeting** (or **targeting**) consists of evaluating each market segment's attractiveness and selecting one or more market segments to enter.

In the final two steps, the company decides on a value proposition—on how it will create value for target customers. **Differentiation** involves actually differentiating the firm's market offering to create superior customer value. **Positioning** consists of arranging for a market offering to occupy a clear, distinctive, and desirable place relative to competing products in the minds of target consumers. We discuss each of these steps in turn.

Market segmentation
Dividing a market into smaller groups with distinct needs, characteristics, or behaviors that might require separate marketing strategies or mixes.

Market targeting (targeting)
The process of evaluating each market segment's attractiveness and selecting one or more segments to enter.

Differentiation
Actually differentiating the market offering to create superior customer value.

Positioning
Arranging for a market offering to occupy a clear, distinctive, and desirable place relative to competing products in the minds of target consumers.

Market Segmentation

Markets consist of buyers, and buyers differ in one or more ways. They may differ in their wants, resources, locations, buying attitudes, and buying practices. Through market segmentation, companies divide large, heterogeneous markets into smaller segments that can be reached more efficiently and effectively with products and services that match their unique needs. In this section, we discuss four important segmentation topics: segmenting consumer markets, segmenting business markets, segmenting international markets, and requirements for effective segmentation.

FIGURE 6.1   Designing a Customer-Driven Marketing Strategy

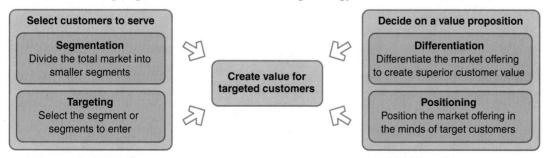

Segmenting Consumer Markets

There is no single way to segment a market. A marketer must try different segmentation variables, alone and in combination, to find the best way to view the market structure. Table 6.1 outlines the major variables that might be used in segmenting consumer markets. Here we look at the major *geographic, demographic, psychographic,* and *behavioral* variables.

Geographic segmentation

Dividing a market into different geographical units such as nations, states, regions, counties, cities, or neighborhoods.

Geographic Segmentation **Geographic segmentation** calls for dividing the market into different geographical units such as nations, regions, states, counties, cities, or even neighbor-

TABLE 6.1 Major Segmentation Variables for Consumer Markets		
Geographic		
World region or country	North America, Western Europe, Middle East, Pacific Rim, China, India, Canada, Mexico	
Country region	Pacific, Mountain, West North Central, West South Central, East, North Central, East South Central, South Atlantic, Middle Atlantic, New England	
City or metro size	Under 5,000; 5,000–20,000; 20,000–50,000; 50,000–100,000; 100,000–250,000; 250,000–500,000; 500,000–1,000,000; 1,000,000–4,000,000; over 4,000,000	
Density	Urban, suburban, ex-urban, rural	
Climate	Northern, southern	
Demographic		
Age	under 6, 6–11, 12–19, 20–34, 35–49, 50–64, 65+	
Gender	Male, female	
Family size	1–2, 3–4, 5+	
Family life cycle	Young, single; married, no children; married with children; single parents, unmarried couples; older, married, no children under 18; older, single; other	
Income	Under $20,000; $20,000–$30,000; $30,000–$50,000; $50,000–$100,000; $100,000–$250,000; $250,000 and over	
Occupation	Professional and technical; manager, officials, and proprietors; clerical; sales, craftspeople; supervisors; farmers; retired; students; homemakers; unemployed	
Education	Grade school or less; some high school; high school graduate; some college; college graduate	
Religion	Catholic, Protestant, Jewish, Muslim, Hindu, other	
Race	Asian, Hispanic, Black, White	
Generation	Baby boomer, Generation X, Millennials	
Nationality	North American, South American, British, French, German, Italian, Japanese	
Psychographics		
Social class	Lower lowers, upper lowers, working class, middle class, upper middles, lower uppers, upper uppers	
Lifestyle	Achievers, strivers, survivors	
Personality	Compulsive, gregarious, authoritarian, ambitious	
Behavioral		
Occasions	Regular occasion; special occasion; holiday; seasonal	
Benefits	Quality, service, economy, convenience, speed	
User status	Nonuser, ex-user, potential user, first-time user, regular user	
User rates	Light user, medium user, heavy user	
Loyalty status	None, medium, strong, absolute	
Readiness stage	Unaware, aware, informed, interested, desirous, intending to buy	
Attitude toward product	Enthusiastic, positive, indifferent, negative, hostile	

hoods. A company may decide to operate in one or a few geographical areas, or to operate in all areas but pay attention to geographical differences in needs and wants.

Many companies today are localizing their products, advertising, promotion, and sales efforts to fit the needs of individual regions, cities, and even neighborhoods. For example, one consumer-products company ships additional cases of its low-calorie snack foods to stores in neighborhoods near Weight Watchers clinics. Kraft developed Post's Fiesta Fruity Pebbles cereal for areas high in Hispanics. Coca-Cola developed four ready-to-drink canned coffees for the Japanese market, each targeted to a specific geographic region. Procter & Gamble introduced Curry Pringles in England and Funky Soy Sauce Pringles in Asia.[2]

Other companies are seeking to cultivate as-yet-untapped geographic territory. For example, many large companies are fleeing the fiercely competitive major cities and suburbs to set up shop in small-town America. Consider Home Depot:[3]

> Home Depot is getting ready to unveil a junior version of its stores, roughly half the size of a regular store. These stores, geared toward small markets and vacation areas that can't support a full-size store, are designed to offer a more intimate neighborhood hardware store setting. For example, Georgia will get its first small-scale Home Depot this year, near Lake Hartwell. Another store is on tap for Milledgeville next year. "We think there's a tremendous opportunity in smaller markets where it's harder to find land for a full-size store, and where they don't need a full-size store," says a Home Depot executive.

In contrast, other retailers are developing new store concepts that will give them access to higher-density urban areas. For example, Wal-Mart has been complementing its supercenters by opening small, supermarket-style Neighborhood Market grocery stores in markets where full-size stores are impractical.[4]

Demographic Segmentation **Demographic segmentation** divides the market into groups based on variables such as age, gender, family size, family life cycle, income, occupation, education, religion, race, generation, and nationality. Demographic factors are the most popular bases for segmenting customer groups. One reason is that consumer needs, wants, and usage rates often vary closely with demographic variables. Another is that demographic variables are easier to measure than most other types of variables. Even when marketers first define segments using other bases, such as benefits sought or behavior, they must know segment demographic characteristics in order to assess the size of the target market and to reach it efficiently.

Demographic segmentation
Dividing the market into groups based on variables such as age, gender, family size, family life cycle, income, occupation, education, religion, race, generation, and nationality.

Age and life-cycle segmentation
Dividing a market into different age and life-cycle groups.

Age and Life-Cycle Stage Consumer needs and wants change with age. Some companies use **age and life-cycle segmentation**, offering different products or using different marketing approaches for different age and life-cycle groups. For example, for kids, Abbott Laboratories sells NutriPals "balanced nutrition" drinks and snacks featuring cartoon characters on the product labels. For adults, it sells Ensure, promising "nutrition to help stay healthy, active, and energetic." And Nintendo, long known for its youth-oriented video games, now offers older generations a game called *Brain Age,* designed to "exercise the noggin" and keep the mind young. Nintendo's aim is to attract older nongamers who might find skill-building games more appealing than, say, *Grand Theft Auto* or *World of Warcraft.*"[5]

Marketers must be careful to guard against stereotypes when using age and life-cycle segmentation. Although some 80-year-olds require wheelchairs, others play tennis. Similarly, whereas some 40-year-old couples are sending their children off to college, others are just beginning new families. Thus, age is often a poor predictor of a person's life cycle, health, work, family

■ Age and life-cycle segmentation: Known mostly for its youth-oriented video games, Nintendo now offers older generations a game called *Brain Age,* designed "exercise the noggin" and keep the mind young.

status, needs, and buying power. Companies marketing to mature consumers usually employ positive images and appeals. For example, take the RV industry, which heavily targets older baby boomers. The older boomers, now empty-nesters, use an RV to visit their grandchildren or to see America at their own pace. They are rediscovering the excitement of life and have the means to play it out. To appeal to these consumers, the RV industry uses ads showing active and engaged boomers discovering new horizons, urging them to "Go RVing."

Gender segmentation
Dividing a market into different groups based on gender.

Gender **Gender segmentation** has long been used in clothing, cosmetics, toiletries, and magazines. For example, Procter & Gamble was among the first with Secret, a brand specially formulated for a woman's chemistry, packaged and advertised to reinforce the female image. More recently, many mostly women's cosmetics makers have begun marketing men's lines. For instance, Nivea markets Nivea for Men, "an advanced line of enriching skincare and soothing aftershave products specially designed for the active, healthy men's lifestyle," and offers a four-step guide to perfect men's care.

A neglected gender segment can offer new opportunities, in markets ranging from motorcycles to guitars. For example, 10 years ago, 96 percent of guitars were purchased by and for men. Daisy Rock Guitars, The Girl Guitar Company, is changing that statistic one guitar at a time. Starting with a daisy-shaped guitar with a leafy headstock, Daisy Rock now offers a complete line of smaller, lighter, professional-quality guitars with fun shapes and glossy finishes geared toward women. Guitars range from girly butterfly, heart, and daisy shapes for younger girls to glossy red, black, purple, and pink guitars for women. Daisy Rock's sales have doubled each year since the company was founded in 2000, last year reaching $2.4 million.[6]

Income segmentation
Dividing a market into different income groups.

Income The marketers of products and services such as automobiles, clothing, cosmetics, financial services, and travel have long used **income segmentation**. Many companies target affluent consumers with luxury goods and convenience services. Stores such as Neiman Marcus pitch everything from expensive jewelry and fine fashions to glazed Australian apricots priced at $20 a pound. And credit-card companies offer superpremium credit cards dripping with perks, such as VISA's Signature card, MasterCard's World card, and American Express's superelite Centurion card. The much-coveted black Centurion card is issued by invitation only, to customers who spend more than $150,000 a year on other AmEx cards and meet other not-so-clear requirements. Then, the select few who do receive the card pay a $2,500 annual fee just for the privilege of carrying it.

However, not all companies that use income segmentation target the affluent. For example, many retailers—such as the Dollar General, Family Dollar, and Dollar Tree store

■ Psychographic segmentation: The American Express "My life. My card" campaign provides glimpses into the lifestyles of famous people with whom consumers might identify, here Ellen DeGeneres.

chains—successfully target low- and middle-income groups. The core market for such stores is families with incomes under $30,000. When Family Dollar real-estate experts scout locations for new stores, they look for lower-middle-class neighborhoods where people wear less-expensive shoes and drive old cars that drip a lot of oil.

With their low-income strategies, the dollar stores are now the fastest-growing retailers in the nation. They have been so successful that giant discounters are taking notice. For example, Target has installed a dollar aisle—the "1 Spot"—in its stores. And supermarkets such as Kroger and A&P are launching "10 for $10" promotions. And some experts predict that, to meet the dollar store threat, Wal-Mart will eventually buy one of these chains or start one of its own.[7]

Psychographic Segmentation **Psychographic segmentation** divides buyers into different groups based on social class, lifestyle, or personality characteristics. People in the same demographic group can have very different psychographic makeups.

In Chapter 5, we discussed how the products people buy reflect their *lifestyles.* As a result, marketers often segment their markets by consumer lifestyles and base their marketing strategies on lifestyle appeals. For example, American Express promises "a card that fits your life." Its "My life. My card." campaign provides glimpses into the lifestyles of famous people with whom consumers might want to identify, from pro surfer Laird Hamilton and television personality Ellen DeGeneres to screen stars Robert DeNiro and Kate Winslet.

Marketers also use *personality* variables to segment markets. For example, cruise lines target adventure seekers. Royal Caribbean appeals to high-energy couples and families with hundreds of activities such as rock walls and ice-skating. Its commercials, set to the Iggy Pop's "Lust for Life," tells them that "this is more than a cruise" and orders them to "get out there." By contrast, the Regent Seven Seas Cruise Line targets more serene and cerebral adventurers, mature couples seeking a more elegant ambiance and exotic destinations, such as the Orient. Regent invites them to come along as "luxury goes exploring."[8]

Behavioral Segmentation **Behavioral segmentation** divides buyers into groups based on their knowledge, attitudes, uses, or responses to a product. Many marketers believe that behavior variables are the best starting point for building market segments.

Occasions Buyers can be grouped according to occasions when they get the idea to buy, actually make their purchase, or use the purchased item. **Occasion segmentation** can help firms build up product usage. For example, most consumers drink orange juice in the morning, but orange growers have promoted drinking orange juice as a cool, healthful refresher at other times of the day. By contrast, Coca-Cola's "Good Morning" campaign attempts to increase Coke consumption by promoting the soft drink as an early morning pick-me-up.

Some holidays, such as Mother's Day and Father's Day, were originally promoted partly to increase the sale of candy, flowers, cards, and other gifts. And many marketers prepare special offers and ads for holiday occasions. For example, Peeps creates different shaped sugar-and-fluffy-marshmallow treats for Easter, Valentine's Day, Halloween, and Christmas when it captures most of its sales but advertises that Peeps are "Always in Season" to increase the demand for nonholiday occasions.

Benefits Sought A powerful form of segmentation is to group buyers according to the different *benefits* that they seek from the product. **Benefit segmentation** requires finding the major benefits people look for in the product class, the kinds of people who look for each benefit, and the major brands that deliver each benefit.

Psychographic segmentation
Dividing a market into different groups based on social class, lifestyle, or personality characteristics.

Behavioral segmentation
Dividing a market into groups based on consumer knowledge, attitudes, uses, or responses to a product.

Occasion segmentation
Dividing the market into groups according to occasions when buyers get the idea to buy, actually make their purchase, or use the purchased item.

Benefit segmentation
Dividing the market into groups according to the different benefits that consumers seek from the product.

GOOD MORNING

■ Occasion segmentation: Coca-Cola's "Good Morning" campaign attempts to increase Coke consumption by promoting the soft drink as an early morning pick-me-up.

Champion athletic wear segments its markets according to benefits that different consumers seek from their activewear. For example, "Fit and Polish" consumers seek a balance between function and style—they exercise for results but want to look good doing it. "Serious Sports Competitors" exercise heavily and live in and love their activewear—they seek performance and function. By contrast, "Value-Seeking Moms" have low sports interest and low activewear involvement—they buy for the family and seek durability and value. Thus, each segment seeks a different mix of benefits. Champion must target the benefit segment or segments that it can serve best and most profitably using appeals that match each segment's benefit preferences.

User Status   Markets can be segmented into nonusers, ex-users, potential users, first-time users, and regular users of a product. Marketers want to reinforce and retain regular users, attract targeted nonusers, and reinvigorate relationships with ex-users.

Included in the potential user group are consumers facing life-stage changes—such as newlyweds and new parents—who can be turned into heavy users. For example, upscale kitchen and cookware retailer Williams-Sonoma actively targets newly engaged couples. Eight-page ad inserts in bridal magazines show a young couple strolling through a park or talking intimately in the kitchen over a glass of wine. The bride-to-be asks, "Now that I've found love, what else do I need?" Pictures of Williams-Sonoma knife sets, toasters, glassware, and pots and pans provide some strong clues. The retailer also offers a bridal registry, of course. But it plans to take its registry a step further next year. Through a program called "The Store Is Yours," it will open its stores early, by appointment, for couples to visit and make their wish lists. This segment is very important to Williams-Sonoma. About half the people who register are new to the brand—and they'll be buying a lot of kitchen and cookware in the future.[9]

Usage Rate   Markets can also be segmented into light, medium, and heavy product users. Heavy users are often a small percentage of the market but account for a high percentage of total consumption. For example, fast-feeder Burger King targets what it calls "Super Fans," young (age 18 to 34), Whopper-wolfing males who make up 18 percent of the chain's customers but account for almost half of all customer visits. They eat at Burger King an average of 16 times a month.[10] Burger King targets these Super Fans openly with ads that exalt monster burgers containing meat, cheese, and more meat and cheese that can turn "innies into outies."

Despite claims by some consumers that the fast-food chains are damaging their health, these heavy users are extremely loyal. "They insist they don't need saving," says one analyst, "protesting that they are far from the clueless fatties anti-fast-food activists make them out to be." Even the heaviest users "would have to be stupid not to know that you can't eat only burgers and fries and not exercise," he says.[11]

Loyalty Status   A market can also be segmented by consumer loyalty. Consumers can be loyal to brands (Tide), stores (Nordstrom), and companies (Toyota). Buyers can be divided into groups according to their degree of loyalty. Some consumers are completely loyal—they buy one brand all the time. For example, Apple has an almost cultlike following of loyal users:[12]

It's the "Cult of the Mac," and it's populated by "macolytes." Urbandictionary.com defines a *macolyte* as "One who is fanatically devoted to Apple products." (Sample usage: "He's a macolyte; don't even *think* of mentioning Microsoft within earshot.") How about Anna Zisa, a graphic designer from Milan who doesn't really like tattoos but stenciled an Apple tat on her behind. "It just felt like the most me thing to have," says Zisa. "I like computers. The apple looks good and sexy. All the comments I have heard have been positive, even from

■ Consumer loyalty: "Macolytes"—fanatically loyal Apple users—helped keep Apple afloat during the lean years, and they are now at the forefront of Apple's burgeoning iPod, iTunes, and iPhone empire.

Linux and Windows users." And then there's Taylor Barcroft, who has spent the past 11 years traveling the country in an RV on a mission to be the Mac cult's ultimate "multimedia historical videographer." He goes to every Macworld Expo, huge trade shows centered on the Mac, as well as all kinds of other tech shows—and videotapes anything and everything Apple. He's accumulated more than 3,000 hours of footage. And he's never been paid a dime to do any of this, living off an inheritance. Barcroft owns 17 Macs. Such fanatically loyal users helped keep Apple afloat during the lean years, and they are now at the forefront of Apple's burgeoning iPod, iTunes, and iPhone empire.

Others consumers are somewhat loyal—they are loyal to two or three brands of a given product or favor one brand while sometimes buying others. Still other buyers show no loyalty to any brand. They either want something different each time they buy or they buy whatever's on sale.

A company can learn a lot by analyzing loyalty patterns in its market. It should start by studying its own loyal customers. For example, by studying "macolytes," Apple can better pinpoint its target market and develop marketing appeals. By studying its less-loyal buyers, the company can detect which brands are most competitive with its own. By looking at customers who are shifting away from its brand, the company can learn about its marketing weaknesses.

Using Multiple Segmentation Bases Marketers rarely limit their segmentation analysis to only one or a few variables. Rather, they often use multiple segmentation bases in an effort to identify smaller, better-defined target groups. Thus, a bank may not only identify a group of wealthy retired adults but also, within that group, distinguish several segments based on their current income, assets, savings and risk preferences, housing, and lifestyles.

Several business information services—such as Claritas, Experian, Acxiom, and MapInfo—provide multivariable segmentation systems that merge geographic, demographic, lifestyle, and behavioral data to help companies segment their markets down to zip codes, neighborhoods, and even households. One of the leading segmentation systems is PRIZM NE (New Evolution) system by Claritas. PRIZM NE classifies every American household based on a host of demographic factors—such as age, educational level, income, occupation, family composition, ethnicity, and housing—and behavioral and lifestyle factors—such as purchases, free-time activities, and media preferences.

PRIZM NE classifies U.S. households into 66 demographically and behaviorally distinct segments, organized into 14 different social groups. PRIZM NE segments carry such exotic names as "Kids & Cul-de-Sacs," "Gray Power," "Blue Blood Estates," "Mayberry-ville," "Shotguns & Pickups," "Old Glories," "Multi-Culti Mosaic," "Big City Blues," and "Bright Lites L'il City." The colorful names help to bring the clusters to life.[13]

PRIZM NE and other such systems can help marketers to segment people and locations into marketable groups of like-minded consumers. Each cluster has its own pattern of likes, dislikes, lifestyles, and purchase behaviors. For example, "Blue Blood Estates" neighborhoods, part of the Elite Suburbs social group, are suburban areas populated by elite, super-rich families. People in this segment are more likely to own an Audi A8, take a ski vacation, shop at Talbots, and read *Architectural Digest.* In contrast, the "Shotguns & Pickups" segment, part of the Middle America social group, is populated by rural blue-collar workers

■ Using Claritas' PRIZM NE system, marketers can paint a surprisingly precise picture of who you are and what you might buy. PRIZM NE segments carry such exotic names as "Kids & Cul-de-Sacs," "Gray Power," "Blue Blood Estates," "Shotguns & Pickups," and "Bright Lites L'il City."

and families. People in this segment are more likely to go hunting, buy hard rock music, drive a Dodge Ram, watch the Daytona 500 on TV, and read *North American Hunter*.

Such segmentation provides a powerful tool for marketers of all kinds. It can help companies to identify and better understand key customer segments, target them more efficiently, and tailor market offerings and messages to their specific needs.

Segmenting Business Markets

Consumer and business marketers use many of the same variables to segment their markets. Business buyers can be segmented geographically, demographically (industry, company size), or by benefits sought, user status, usage rate, and loyalty status. Yet, business marketers also use some additional variables, such as customer *operating characteristics, purchasing approaches, situational factors,* and *personal characteristics*. By going after segments instead of the whole market, companies can deliver just the right value proposition to each segment served and capture more value in return.

Almost every company serves at least some business markets. For example, we've discussed American Express as the "My life. My card." company that offers credit cards to end consumers. But American Express also targets businesses in three segments—merchants, corporations, and small businesses. It has developed distinct marketing programs for each segment.

In the merchants segment, American Express focuses on convincing new merchants to accept the card and on managing relationships with those that already do. For larger corporate customers, the company offers a corporate card program, which includes extensive employee expense and travel management services. It also offers this segment a wide range of asset management, retirement planning, and financial education services.

Finally, for small business customers, American Express has created OPEN: For Business, a system of small business cards and financial services. It includes credit cards and lines of credit, special usage rewards, financial monitoring and spending report features, and 24/7 customized financial support services. "OPEN is how we serve small business," says American Express.[14]

Many companies set up separate systems for dealing with larger or multiple-location customers. For example, Steelcase, a major producer of office furniture, first segments customers into 10 industries, including banking, insurance, and electronics. Next, company salespeople work with independent Steelcase dealers to handle smaller, local, or regional Steelcase customers in each segment. But many national, multiple-location customers, such as Exxon/Mobile or IBM, have special needs that may reach beyond the scope of individual dealers. So Steelcase uses national accounts managers to help its dealer networks handle its national accounts.

Within a given target industry and customer size, the company can segment by purchase approaches and criteria. As in consumer segmentation, many marketers believe that *buying behavior* and *benefits* provide the best basis for segmenting business markets.

Segmenting International Markets

Few companies have either the resources or the will to operate in all, or even most, of the countries that dot the globe. Although some large companies, such as Coca-Cola or Sony, sell products in more than 200 countries, most international firms focus on a smaller set. Operating in many countries presents new challenges. Different countries, even those that are close together, can vary greatly in their economic, cultural, and political makeup. Thus, just as they do within their domestic markets, international firms need to group their world markets into segments with distinct buying needs and behaviors.

Companies can segment international markets using one or a combination of several variables. They can segment by *geographic location,* grouping countries by regions such as Western Europe, the Pacific Rim, the Middle East, or Africa. Geographic segmentation assumes that nations close to one another will have many common traits and behaviors. Although this is often the case, there are many exceptions. For example, although the United States and Canada have much in common, both differ culturally and economically from neighboring Mexico. Even within a region, consumers can differ widely. For example, some U.S. marketers lump all Central and South American countries together. However, the

Dominican Republic is no more like Brazil than Italy is like Sweden. Many Central and South Americans don't even speak Spanish, including 188 million Portuguese-speaking Brazilians and the millions in other countries who speak a variety of Indian dialects.

World markets can also be segmented on the basis of *economic factors*. For example, countries might be grouped by population income levels or by their overall level of economic development. A country's economic structure shapes its population's product and service needs and, therefore, the marketing opportunities it offers. Countries can be segmented by *political and legal factors* such as the type and stability of government, receptivity to foreign firms, monetary regulations, and the amount of bureaucracy. *Cultural factors* can also be used, grouping markets according to common languages, religions, values and attitudes, customs, and behavioral patterns.

Segmenting international markets based on geographic, economic, political, cultural, and other factors assumes that segments should consist of clusters of countries. However, as new communications technologies, such as satellite TV and the Internet, connect consumers around the world, marketers can define and reach segments of like-minded consumers no matter where in the world they are. Using **intermarket segmentation**, they form segments of consumers who have similar needs and buying behavior even though they are located in different countries. For example, Lexus targets the world's well-to-do, regardless of their country. Swedish furniture giant IKEA targets the aspiring global middle class—it sells good-quality furniture that ordinary people worldwide can afford. And Coca-Cola creates special programs to target teens, core consumers of its soft drinks the world over.[15]

Intermarket segmentation
Forming segments of consumers who have similar needs and buying behavior even though they are located in different countries.

Coca-Cola wants to relate to the world's teens. But to do that in this digital era takes more than big-budget ads in the mass media. You have to reach teens where they live. And increasingly, everywhere in the world, that's on the Web. So click to the http://www.coke.com/ Web site, here or in any of dozens of countries around the globe, and check out the growing collection of youth-oriented video clips and musical podcasts available via links on the front page. This is "The Coke Show," the online centerpiece of the soft-drink giant's newest global teen marketing campaign, driven by the slogan, "Welcome to the Coke side of life." The video files include glimpses of a dancing superhero, an awkward social encounter, and a guy so distracted by a pretty girl that he drives his bike into a pond. They are by turns hip, slick, and playful, the better to reinforce a branding message aimed at equating Coke with youthful good times. And almost all these video clips and podcasts are consumer generated. "This is not a promotional thing. This is a part of a commitment on a global basis to connect with teens and other consumers," says the Coca-Cola's group manager of global interactive marketing. Over time, the "Welcome to the Coke side of life" campaign will reach all 200 countries in which Coca-Cola does business, with Coke.com intended to be a primary destination for teens. "We have to stay constantly connected," says the Coca-Cola executive. "Whatever environments attract teens on a global basis—the Web, mobile phones, gaming—we need to be there."

■ Intermarket segmentation: Coke targets the world's teens where they live—online. Click on coke.com anywhere in the world—here Chile, Luxembourg, and the United States—and you see "The Coke Show," the centerpiece of Coke's global teen campaign.

Requirements for Effective Segmentation

Clearly, there are many ways to segment a market, but not all segmentations are effective. For example, buyers of table salt could be divided into blond and brunette customers. But hair color obviously does not affect the purchase of salt. Furthermore, if all salt buyers bought the same amount of salt each month, believed that all salt is the same, and wanted to pay the same price, the company would not benefit from segmenting this market.

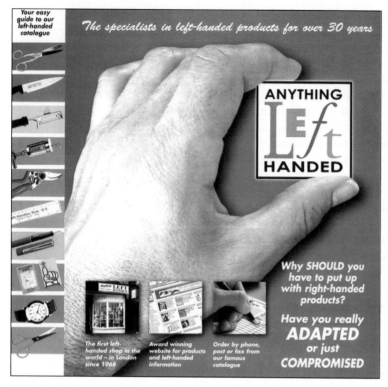

The "Leftie" segment can be hard to identify and measure. As a result, few companies tailor their offers to left-handers. However, some nichers such as Anything Left-Handed in the United Kingdom target this segment.

To be useful, market segments must be

- *Measurable:* The size, purchasing power, and profiles of the segments can be measured. Certain segmentation variables are difficult to measure. For example, there are 32.5 million left-handed people in the United States—almost equaling the entire population of Canada. Yet few products are targeted toward this left-handed segment. The major problem may be that the segment is hard to identify and measure. There are no data on the demographics of lefties, and the U.S. Census Bureau does not keep track of left-handedness in its surveys. Private data companies keep reams of statistics on other demographic segments but not on left-handers.
- *Accessible:* The market segments can be effectively reached and served. Suppose a fragrance company finds that heavy users of its brand are single men and women who stay out late and socialize a lot. Unless this group lives or shops at certain places and is exposed to certain media, its members will be difficult to reach.
- *Substantial:* The market segments are large or profitable enough to serve. A segment should be the largest possible homogenous group worth pursuing with a tailored marketing program. It would not pay, for example, for an automobile manufacturer to develop cars especially for people whose height is greater than seven feet.
- *Differentiable:* The segments are conceptually distinguishable and respond differently to different marketing mix elements and programs. If married and unmarried women respond similarly to a sale on perfume, they do not constitute separate segments.
- *Actionable:* Effective programs can be designed for attracting and serving the segments. For example, although one small airline identified seven market segments, its staff was too small to develop separate marketing programs for each segment.

Linking the Concepts

Slow down a bit and smell the roses. How do the companies you do business with employ the segmentation concepts you're reading about here?

- Can you identify specific companies, other than the examples already discussed, that practice the different types of segmentation just discussed?
- Using the segmentation bases you've just read about, segment the U.S. footwear market. Describe each of the major segments and subsegments. Keep these segments in mind as you read the next section on target market.

Market Targeting

Market segmentation reveals the firm's market segment opportunities. The firm now must evaluate the various segments and decide how many and which segments it can serve best. We now look at how companies evaluate and select target segments.

Evaluating Market Segments

In evaluating different market segments, a firm must look at three factors: segment size and growth, segment structural attractiveness, and company objectives and resources. The company must first collect and analyze data on current segment sales, growth rates, and expected profitability for various segments. It will be interested in segments that have the right size and growth characteristics. But "right size and growth" is a relative matter. The largest, fastest-growing segments are not always the most attractive ones for every company. Smaller companies may lack the skills and resources needed to serve the larger segments. Or they may find these segments too competitive. Such companies may target segments that are smaller and less attractive, in an absolute sense, but that are potentially more profitable for them.

The company also needs to examine major structural factors that affect long-run segment attractiveness.[16] For example, a segment is less attractive if it already contains many strong and aggressive *competitors*. The existence of many actual or potential *substitute products* may limit prices and the profits that can be earned in a segment. The relative *power of buyers* also affects segment attractiveness. Buyers with strong bargaining power relative to sellers will try to force prices down, demand more services, and set competitors against one another—all at the expense of seller profitability. Finally, a segment may be less attractive if it contains *powerful suppliers* who can control prices or reduce the quality or quantity of ordered goods and services.

Even if a segment has the right size and growth and is structurally attractive, the company must consider its own objectives and resources. Some attractive segments can be dismissed quickly because they do not mesh with the company's long-run objectives. Or the company may lack the skills and resources needed to succeed in an attractive segment. The company should enter only segments in which it can create superior customer value and gain advantages over competitors.

Selecting Target Market Segments

After evaluating different segments, the company must now decide which and how many segments it will target. A **target market** consists of a set of buyers who share common needs or characteristics that the company decides to serve. Market targeting can be carried out at several different levels. Figure 6.2 shows that companies can target very broadly (undifferentiated marketing), very narrowly (micromarketing), or somewhere in between (differentiated or concentrated marketing).

Undifferentiated Marketing   Using an **undifferentiated marketing** (or **mass-marketing**) strategy, a firm might decide to ignore market segment differences and target the whole market with one offer. This mass-marketing strategy focuses on what is *common* in the needs of consumers rather than on what is *different*. The company designs a product and a marketing program that will appeal to the largest number of buyers.

As noted earlier in the chapter, most modern marketers have strong doubts about this strategy. Difficulties arise in developing a product or brand that will satisfy all consumers. Moreover, mass marketers often have trouble competing with more-focused firms that do a better job of satisfying the needs of specific segments and niches.

Differentiated Marketing   Using a **differentiated marketing** (or **segmented marketing**) strategy, a firm decides to target several market segments and designs separate offers for each. General Motors tries to produce a car for every "purse, purpose, and personality." Procter & Gamble markets six different laundry detergent brands, which compete with each other on supermarket shelves. And Estée Lauder offers more than two dozen lines of quality skin care, makeup, fragrance, and hair care products aimed at carefully defined segments.

The original Estée Lauder brand, with its gold and blue packaging, appeals to older, 50+ baby boomers. Clinique is perfect for busy middle-aged moms and for younger women

Target market
A set of buyers sharing common needs or characteristics that the company decides to serve.

Undifferentiated (mass) marketing
A market-coverage strategy in which a firm decides to ignore market segment differences and go after the whole market with one offer.

Differentiated (segmented) marketing
A market-coverage strategy in which a firm decides to target several market segments and designs separate offers for each.

FIGURE 6.2   Marketing Targeting Strategies

| Undifferentiated (mass) marketing | Differentiated (segmented) marketing | Concentrated (niche) marketing | Micromarketing (local or individual marketing) |

Targeting broadly   **Targeting narrowly**

■ Differentiated marketing: Estée Lauder offers hundreds of different products aimed at carefully defined segments, from its original Estée Lauder brand appealing to age 50 baby boomers to Aveda, with earthy origins that appeal to younger new age types.

attracted to its classic free gift offers. For young, fashion-forward consumers, there's M.A.C., which provides makeup for clients such as the Dixie Chicks and Mariah Carey. And for the New Age type, there's upscale Aveda, makeup and lifestyle products based on "the art and science of pure flower and plant essences that fulfill the brand's mission of environmental responsibility."[17]

By offering product and marketing variations to segments, companies hope for higher sales and a stronger position within each market segment. Developing a stronger position within several segments creates more total sales than undifferentiated marketing across all segments. Estée Lauder's combined brands give it a much greater market share than any single brand could. The Estée Lauder and Clinique brands alone reap a combined 40 percent share of the prestige cosmetics market. Similarly, Procter & Gamble's multiple detergent brands capture four times the market share of nearest rival Unilever (see Marketing at Work 6.1).

But differentiated marketing also increases the costs of doing business. A firm usually finds it more expensive to develop and produce, say, 10 units of 10 different products than 100 units of one product. Developing separate marketing plans for the separate segments requires extra marketing research, forecasting, sales analysis, promotion planning, and channel management. And trying to reach different market segments with different advertising campaigns increases promotion costs. Thus, the company must weigh increased sales against increased costs when deciding on a differentiated marketing strategy.

Concentrated (niche) marketing
A market-coverage strategy in which a firm goes after a large share of one or a few segments or niches.

Concentrated Marketing Using a **concentrated marketing** (or **niche marketing**) strategy, instead of going after a small share of a large market, the firm goes after a large share of one or a few smaller segments or niches. For example, Whole Foods Market has only about 186 stores and $5.6 billion in sales, compared with goliaths such as Kroger (more than 2,500 stores and sales of $60 billion) and Wal-Mart (6,700 stores and sales of $315 billion).[18] Yet the smaller, upscale retailer is growing faster and more profitably than either of its giant rivals. Whole Foods thrives by catering to affluent customers that the Wal-Marts of the world can't serve well, offering them "organic, natural, and gourmet foods, all swaddled in Earth Day politics." In fact, a typical Whole Foods customer is more likely to boycott the local Wal-Mart than to shop at it.

Through concentrated marketing, the firm achieves a strong market position because of its greater knowledge of consumer needs in the niches it serves and the special reputation it acquires. It can market more *effectively* by fine-tuning its products, prices, and programs to the needs of carefully defined segments. It can also market more *efficiently*, targeting its products or services, channels, and communications programs toward only consumers that it can serve best and most profitably.

Whereas segments are fairly large and normally attract several competitors, niches are smaller and may attract only one or a few competitors. Niching lets smaller companies focus their limited resources on serving niches that may be unimportant to or overlooked by larger competitors. Many companies start as nichers to get a foothold against larger,

6.1 MARKETING AT WORK

P&G: Competing with Itself—and Winning

Procter & Gamble is one of the world's premier consumer-goods companies. Some 99 percent of all U.S. households use at least one of P&G's more than 300 brands, and the typical household regularly buys and uses from one to two *dozen* P&G brands. P&G brands touch the lives of people around the world three billion times a day.

P&G sells six brands of laundry detergent in the United States (Tide, Cheer, Gain, Era, Dreft, and Ivory Snow). It also sells six brands of bath soap (Ivory, Safeguard, Camay, Olay, Zest, and Old Spice); five brands of shampoo (Pantene, Head & Shoulders, Aussie, Herbal Essences, and Infusium 23); four brands of dishwashing detergent (Dawn, Ivory, Joy, and Cascade); three brands each of tissues and towels (Charmin, Bounty, and Puffs) and skin care products (Olay, Gillette Complete Skincare, and Noxzema); and two brands each of deodorant (Secret and Old Spice), fabric softener (Downy and Bounce), cosmetics (Cover Girl and Max Factor), and disposable diapers (Pampers and Luvs).

Moreover, P&G has many additional brands in each category for different international markets. For example, it sells 16 different laundry product brands in Latin America and 19 in Europe, the Middle East, and Africa. (See P&G's Web site at www.pg.com for a full glimpse of the company's impressive lineup of familiar brands.)

These P&G brands compete with one another on the same supermarket shelves. But why would P&G introduce several brands in one category instead of concentrating its resources on a single leading brand? The answer lies in the fact that different people want different *mixes of benefits* from the products they buy. Take laundry detergents as an example. People use laundry detergents to get their clothes clean. But they also want other things from their detergents—such as economy, strength or mildness, bleaching power, fabric softening, fresh smell, and lots of suds or only a few. We all want *some* of every one of these benefits from our detergent, but we may have different *priorities* for each benefit. To some people, cleaning and bleaching power are most important; to others, fabric softening matters most; still others want a mild, fresh-scented detergent. Thus, each segment of laundry detergent buyers seeks a special combination of benefits.

P&G has identified at least six important laundry detergent segments, along with numerous subsegments, and has developed a different brand designed to meet the special needs of each. The six brands are positioned for different segments as follows:

- *Tide* provides "fabric cleaning and care at its best." It's the all-purpose family detergent that "gets to the bottom of dirt and stains to help keep your whites white and your colors bright."
- *Cheer* is the "color expert." It helps protect against fading, color transfer, and fabric wear, with or without bleach. *Cheer Free* is "dermatologist tested . . . contains no irritating perfume or dye."
- *Gain*, originally P&G's "enzyme" detergent, was repositioned as the detergent that gives you "great cleaning power and the smell that says clean." It "cleans and freshens like sunshine."

■ Differentiated marketing: Procter & Gamble markets six different laundry detergents, including Tide—each with multiple forms and formulations—that compete with each other on store shelves. Yet together, these multiple brands capture four times the market share of nearest rival Unilever.

- *Era* is "the power tool for stain removal and pretreating them helps combat many stains that families encounter."
- *Ivory Snow* is "ninety-nine and forty-four one-hundredths percent pure." It provides "mild cleansing benefits for a gentle, pure, and simple clean."
- *Dreft* is specially formulated "to help clean tough baby and toddler stains." It "rinses out thoroughly, leaving clothes soft next to a baby's delicate skin."

Within each segment, P&G has identified even *narrower* niches. For example, you can buy regular Tide (in powder or liquid form) or any of more than 40 different formulations:

- *Tide Powder* helps keep everyday laundry clean and new. It comes in original and special scents: *Tide Mountain Spring* ("the scent of crisp mountain air and fresh wildflowers"); *Tide Clean Breeze* ("the fresh scent of laundry line-dried in a clean breeze"); *Tide Tropical Clean* ("a fresh tropical scent that soothes, relaxes, and refreshes"); and *Tide Free* ("has no scent at all—leaves out the dyes or perfumes").
- *Tide Liquid* combines all the great stain-fighting qualities you've come to expect in Tide powder with the pretreating ease of a liquid detergent. Available in original and Mountain Spring, Clean Breeze, Tropical Clean, and Free scents.

(continues)

- *Tide with Bleach* helps to "clean even the dirtiest laundry without the damaging effects of chlorine bleach." Keeps "your family's whites white and colors bright." Available in Clean Breeze or Mountain Spring scents.
- *Tide Liquid with Bleach Alternative* is the "smart alternative to chlorine bleach." It uses active enzymes in pretreating and washing to break down and remove the toughest stains while whitening whites.
- *Tide with a Touch of Downy* provides "outstanding Tide clean with a touch of Downy softness and freshness." Available in April Fresh, Clean Breeze, and Soft Ocean Mist scents.
- *Tide Coldwater* is specially formulated to help reduce your energy bills by delivering outstanding cleaning, even on the toughest stains, in cold water. Available in both liquid and powder formulas and in two new cool scents—Fresh Scent and Mountain Spring.
- *Tide HE* is specially formulated to unlock the cleaning potential of high-efficiency washers and provides excellent cleaning with the right level of sudsing. Available in Original, Free, and Clean Breeze scents.

- *2X Ultra Tide* is double-concentrated to provide the same cleaning power as regular Tide. One small capful gets your whole wash clean. P&G now offers 2X Ultra versions of all of its major liquid Tide subbrands.

By segmenting the market and having several detergent brands, P&G has an attractive offering for consumers in all important preference groups. As a result, P&G is really cleaning up in the $4.9 billion U.S. laundry detergent market. Tide, by itself, captures a whopping 40 percent of the detergent market. All P&G brands combined take an impressive 60 percent market share—more than four times that of nearest rival Unilever and much more than any single brand could obtain by itself.

Sources: See "Tide Announces Launch of New Liquid Laundry Detergents," *M2PressWIRE*, March 14, 2007; Doris de Guzman, "Colgate Unloads Laundry Brands," *CMR*, July 18–24, 2005, p. 36; and information accessed at www.pg.com and www.tide.com, December 2007.

more-resourceful competitors and then grow into broader competitors. For example, Southwest Airlines began by serving intrastate, no-frills commuters in Texas but is now one of the nation's largest airlines. And Enterprise Rent-A-Car began by building a network of neighborhood offices rather than competing with Hertz and Avis in airport locations. Enterprise is now the nation's largest car rental company.

In contrast, as markets change, some megamarketers develop niche markets to create sales growth. For example, in recent years, Pepsi has introduced several niche products, such as Sierra Mist, Pepsi Twist, Mountain Dew Code Red, and Mountain Dew LiveWire. Initially, these brands, combined, accounted for barely 5 percent of Pepsi's overall soft-drink sales. However, Sierra Mist quickly blossomed and now is the number-two lemon-lime soft drink behind Sprite, and Code Red and LiveWire have revitalized the Mountain Dew brand. Says Pepsi-Cola North America's chief marketing officer, "The era of the mass brand has been over for a long time."[19]

Today, the low cost of setting up shop on the Internet makes it even more profitable to serve seemingly minuscule niches. Small businesses, in particular, are realizing riches from serving small niches on the Web. Consider Zappos:

Zappos sells shoes online—*only* shoes and *only* online. What gives this online nicher an edge? First, Zappos differentiates itself by its selection: Click to the Zappos site and you can pick through some 3.2 million items representing 950 brands—more inventory than any brick-and-mortar shoe peddler could dream of offering. Zappos also gives you convenience: The warehouse is open 24/7, so you can order as late as 11:00 p.m. and still get next-day delivery. Most important, Zappos has a near-fanatical devotion to pleasing its customers. "We offer the absolute best selection of shoes available anywhere," boasts the company, "but much more important to us is offering the absolute best service." Shipping and return shipping are free, and you just can't beat the company's heartfelt returns policy: "If the shoe fits, wear it. If not, ship it back at our expense." All this adds up to a host of satisfied customers. "With Zappos, the shoe store comes to you," says Pamela Leo, a customer in Montclair, New Jersey. "I can try the shoes on in the comfort of my own home. I

■ Concentrated marketing: Web niching is paying off handsomely for shoe seller Zappos and its CEO/Founder Tony Hsieh.

can tell if the shoes I want will really work with a particular suit. It's fabulous." And if the shoes aren't just right, she can click on a Zappos-supplied link to print out a prepaid return shipping label. Web niching is paying off handsomely for Zappos. Although it captures only a small portion of the total $40 billion U.S. shoe market, Zappos is now the Web's number-one shoe seller. Thanks to happy customers like Pamela, sales have soared from "almost nothing" in 1999 to an estimated $800 million this year.[20]

Concentrated marketing can be highly profitable. At the same time, it involves higher-than-normal risks. Companies that rely on one or a few segments for all of their business will suffer greatly if the segment turns sour. Or larger competitors may decide to enter the same segment with greater resources. For these reasons, many companies prefer to diversify in several market segments.

Micromarketing   Differentiated and concentrated marketers tailor their offers and marketing programs to meet the needs of various market segments and niches. At the same time, however, they do not customize their offers to each individual customer. **Micromarketing** is the practice of tailoring products and marketing programs to suit the tastes of specific individuals and locations. Rather than seeing a customer in every individual, micromarketers see the individual in every customer. Micromarketing includes *local marketing* and *individual marketing*.

Local Marketing   **Local marketing** involves tailoring brands and promotions to the needs and wants of local customer groups—cities, neighborhoods, and even specific stores. For example, Kroger designates its supermarkets as "upscale," "mainstream," or "value" based on customer purchase behavior and adjusts its merchandise to match store customer profiles. And Wal-Mart customizes its merchandise store by store to meet the needs of local shoppers.

> Wal-Mart's real-estate teams deeply research the local customer base when scouting for locations. Designers then create a new store's format accordingly—stores near office parks, for example, contain prominent islands featuring ready-made meals for busy workers. Then, using a wealth of customer data on daily sales in every store, Wal-Mart tailors individual store merchandise with similar precision. For example, Wal-Mart stocks about 60 types of canned chili but carries only three nationwide. The rest are allocated according to local tastes. Similarly, Wal-Mart uses more than 200 finely tuned planograms (shelf plans) to match soup assortments to each store's demand patterns. The giant retailer even localizes product packaging to match local preferences. For example, Wal-Mart found that although ant and roach killer sells well in the southern United States, consumers in the northern states are turned off by the word "roach." After labeling the pesticide as "ant killer" in northern states, the company has seen sales increase dramatically.[21]

Local marketing has some drawbacks. It can drive up manufacturing and marketing costs by reducing economies of scale. It can also create logistics problems as companies try to meet the varied requirements of different regional and local markets. Further, a brand's overall image might be diluted if the product and message vary too much in different localities.

Still, as companies face increasingly fragmented markets, and as new supporting technologies develop, the advantages of local marketing often outweigh the drawbacks. Local marketing helps a company to market more effectively in the face of pronounced regional and local differences in demographics and lifestyles. It also meets the needs of the company's first-line customers—retailers—who prefer more fine-tuned product assortments for their neighborhoods.

Individual Marketing   In the extreme, micromarketing becomes **individual marketing**— tailoring products and marketing programs to the needs and preferences of individual customers. Individual marketing has also been labeled *one-to-one marketing, mass customization,* and *markets-of-one marketing.*

The widespread use of mass marketing has obscured the fact that for centuries consumers were served as individuals: The tailor custom-made the suit, the cobbler designed

Micromarketing
The practice of tailoring products and marketing programs to the needs and wants of specific individuals and local customer groups—includes *local marketing* and *individual marketing.*

Local marketing
Tailoring brands and promotions to the needs and wants of local customer groups—cities, neighborhoods, and even specific stores.

Individual marketing
Tailoring products and marketing programs to the needs and preferences of individual customers—also labeled "markets-of-one marketing," "customized marketing," and "one-to-one marketing."

shoes for the individual, the cabinetmaker made furniture to order. Today, however, new technologies are permitting many companies to return to customized marketing. More powerful computers, detailed databases, robotic production and flexible manufacturing, and interactive communication media such as e-mail and the Internet—all have combined to foster "mass customization." *Mass customization* is the process through which firms interact one-to-one with masses of customers to design products and services tailor-made to individual needs.

Dell creates custom-configured computers. Hockey-stick maker Branches Hockey lets customers choose from more than two dozen options—including stick length, blade patterns, and blade curve—and turns out a customized stick in five days. And visitors to Nike's NikeID Web site can personalize their sneakers by choosing from hundreds of colors and putting an embroidered word or phrase on the tongue.

Companies selling all kinds of products—from computers, candy, clothing, and golf clubs to fire trucks—are customizing their offerings to the needs of individual buyers. Consider this example:

> LEGO recently launched LEGO Factory, a Web site (LEGOFactory.com) where LEGO fans can "design their own ultimate LEGO model, show it off, and bring it to life." Using LEGO's free, downloadable Digital Designer software, customers can create any structure they can imagine. Then, if they decide to actually build their creation, the software, which keeps track of which pieces are required, sends the order to LEGO. There, employees put all the pieces into a box, along with instructions, and ship it off. Customers can even design their own boxes. The software also lets proud users share their creations with others in the LEGO community, one of the traditional building blocks of the company's customer loyalty. The LEGO Factory Gallery features winning designs and lets users browse and order the inspired designs of others.[22]

■ Individual marketing: MINI used personalized billboard messages to greet MINI drivers in selected major cities. The messages were triggered by personalized key fobs given to MINI owners.

Marketers are also finding new ways to personalize promotional messages. For example, plasma screens placed in shopping malls around the country can now analyze shoppers' faces and place ads based on an individual shopper's gender, age, or ethnicity. Last year, MINI USA even began using personalized billboard messages to greet MINI drivers in four major cities. The messages were triggered by personalized key fobs given to MINI owners. As the MINI owner passed by, the fob contacted the billboard database, which then transmitted a message such as "Motor on Jim!" or "Great day to be a lawyer in New York, Jim!"[23]

Business-to-business marketers are also finding new ways to customize their offerings. For example, John Deere manufactures seeding equipment that can be configured in more than two million versions to individual customer specifications. The seeders are produced one at a time, in any sequence, on a single production line. Mass customization provides a way to stand out against competitors.

Unlike mass production, which eliminates the need for human interaction, one-to-one marketing has made relationships with customers more important than ever. Just as mass production was the marketing principle of the past century, interactive marketing is becoming a marketing principle for the 21st century. The world appears to be coming full circle—from the good old days when customers were treated as individuals, to mass marketing when nobody knew your name, and back again.

The move toward individual marketing mirrors the trend in consumer *self-marketing*. Increasingly, individual customers are taking more responsibility for shaping both products they buy and the buying experience. Consider two business buyers with two different purchasing styles. The first sees several salespeople, each trying to persuade him to buy his or her product. The second sees no salespeople but rather logs on to the Web. She searches for information on available products; interacts online with various suppliers, users, and product analysts; and then decides which offer is best. The second purchasing agent has taken more responsibility for the buying process, and the marketer has had less influence over the buying decision.

As the trend toward more interactive dialogue and less marketing monologue continues, marketers will need to influence the buying process in new ways. They will need to involve customers more in all phases of the product development and buying processes, increasing opportunities for buyers to practice self-marketing.

Choosing a Targeting Strategy   Companies need to consider many factors when choosing a market-targeting strategy. Which strategy is best depends on *company resources*. When the firm's resources are limited, concentrated marketing makes the most sense. The best strategy also depends on the degree of *product variability*. Undifferentiated marketing is more suited for uniform products such as grapefruit or steel. Products that can vary in design, such as cameras and automobiles, are more suited to differentiation or concentration. The *product's life-cycle stage* also must be considered. When a firm introduces a new product, it may be practical to launch only one version, and undifferentiated marketing or concentrated marketing may make the most sense. In the mature stage of the product life cycle, however, differentiated marketing begins to make more sense.

Another factor is *market variability*. If most buyers have the same tastes, buy the same amounts, and react the same way to marketing efforts, undifferentiated marketing is appropriate. Finally, *competitors' marketing strategies* are important. When competitors use differentiated or concentrated marketing, undifferentiated marketing can be suicidal. Conversely, when competitors use undifferentiated marketing, a firm can gain an advantage by using differentiated or concentrated marketing.

Socially Responsible Target Marketing

Smart targeting helps companies to be more efficient and effective by focusing on the segments that they can satisfy best and most profitably. Targeting also benefits consumers— companies reach specific groups of consumers with offers carefully tailored to their needs. However, target marketing sometimes generates controversy and concern. The biggest issues usually involve the targeting of vulnerable or disadvantaged consumers with controversial or potentially harmful products.

For example, over the years, marketers in a wide range of industries—from cereal and toys to fast food and fashion—have been heavily criticized for their marketing efforts directed toward children. Critics worry that premium offers and high-powered advertising appeals presented through the mouths of lovable animated characters will overwhelm children's defenses.

Other problems arise when the marketing of adult products spills over into the kid segment—intentionally or unintentionally. For example, Victoria's Secret targets its Pink line of young, hip, and sexy clothing to young women 18 to 30 years old. However, critics charge that Pink is now all the rage among girls as young as 11. Responding to Victoria's Secret designs and marketing messages, tweens are flocking into stores and buying Pink, with or without their mothers. More broadly, critics worry that marketers of everything from lingerie and cosmetics to Barbie dolls are directly or indirectly targeting young girls with provocative products, promoting a premature focus on sex and appearance.

> Ten-year-old girls can slide their low-cut jeans over "eye-candy" panties. French maid costumes, garter belt included, are available in preteen sizes. Barbie now comes in a "bling-bling" style, replete with halter top and go-go boots. And it's not unusual for girls under 12 to sing, "Don't cha wish your girlfriend was hot like me?" American girls, say experts, are increasingly being fed a cultural catnip of products and images that promote looking and acting sexy. "The message we're telling our girls is a simple one," laments one reporter about the Victoria's Secret Pink line. "You'll have

a great life if people find you sexually attractive. Grown women struggle enough with this ridiculous standard. Do we really need to start worrying about it at 11?"[24]

The Federal Trade Commission (FTC) and citizen action groups have accused tobacco and beer companies of targeting underage smokers and drinkers. For instance, a recent Adbowl poll found that, in the most recent Super Bowl, Bud Light and Budweiser ads ranked first through fourth in popularity among viewers under age 17.[25] Some critics have even called for a complete ban on advertising to children. To encourage responsible advertising, the Children's Advertising Review Unit, the advertising industry's self-regulatory agency, has published extensive children's advertising guidelines that recognize the special needs of child audiences.

Cigarette, beer, and fast-food marketers have also generated much controversy in recent years by their attempts to target inner-city minority consumers. For example, McDonald's and other chains have drawn criticism for pitching their high-fat, salt-laden fare to low-income, urban residents who are much more likely than are suburbanites to be heavy consumers. Similarly, R.J. Reynolds took heavy flak in the early 1990s when it announced plans to market Uptown, a menthol cigarette targeted toward low-income blacks. It quickly dropped the brand in the face of a loud public outcry and heavy pressure from black leaders.

The meteoric growth of the Internet and other carefully targeted direct media has raised fresh concerns about potential targeting abuses. The Internet allows increasing refinement of audiences and, in turn, more precise targeting. This might help makers of questionable products or deceptive advertisers to more readily victimize the most vulnerable audiences. Unscrupulous marketers can now send tailor-made deceptive messages directly to the computers of millions of unsuspecting consumers. For example, the FBI's Internet Crime Complaint Center Web site alone received more than 207,000 complaints last year.[26]

Not all attempts to target children, minorities, or other special segments draw such criticism. In fact, most provide benefits to targeted consumers. For example, Colgate makes a large selection of toothbrushes and toothpaste flavors and packages for children—from Colgate Barbie, Blues Clues, and SpongeBob SquarePants Sparkling Bubble Fruit toothpastes to Colgate LEGO BIONICLE and Bratz character toothbrushes. Such products help make tooth brushing more fun and get children to brush longer and more often.

American Girl appropriately targets minority consumers with African American, Mexican, and American Indian versions of its highly acclaimed dolls and books. And Nacara Cosmetics markets a multicultural cosmetics and skin care line for all women of color. The line is specially formulated to complement the skin tones of African American, Asian, Latina, and multicultural women.

Thus, in target marketing, the issue is not really *who* is targeted but rather *how* and for *what*. Controversies arise when marketers attempt to profit at the expense of targeted segments—when they unfairly target vulnerable segments or target them with questionable products or tactics. Socially responsible marketing calls for segmentation and targeting that serve not just the interests of the company but also the interests of those targeted.

■ Most target marketing benefits both the marketer and the consumer. Nacara Cosmetiques markets cosmetics for "ethnic women who have a thirst for the exotic."

Linking the Concepts

Time to coast for a bit and take stock.

■ At the last speed bump, you segmented the U.S. footwear market. Refer to Figure 6.2 and select two companies that serve this market. Describe their segmentation and targeting strategies. Can you come up with a company that targets many different segments versus another that focuses on only one or a few segments?

■ How does each company you chose differentiate its market offering and image? Has each done a good job of establishing this differentiation in the minds of targeted consumers? The final section in this chapter deals with such positioning issues.

Differentiation and Positioning

Beyond deciding which segments of the market it will target, the company must decide on a *value proposition*—on how it will create differentiated value for targeted segments and what positions it wants to occupy in those segments. A **product's position** is the way the product is *defined by consumers* on important attributes—the place the product occupies in consumers' minds relative to competing products. "Products are created in the factory, but brands are created in the mind," says a positioning expert.[27]

Product position

The way the product is defined by consumers on important attributes—the place the product occupies in consumers' minds relative to competing products.

Tide is positioned as a powerful, all-purpose family detergent; Ivory Snow is positioned as the gentle detergent for fine washables and baby clothes. At Subway restaurants, you "Eat Fresh"; at Olive Garden, "When You're Here, You're Family"; and at Applebee's, you're "Eatin' Good in the Neighborhood." In the automobile market, the Nissan Versa and Honda Fit are positioned on economy, Mercedes and Cadillac on luxury, and Porsche and BMW on performance. Volvo positions powerfully on safety. And Toyota positions its fuel-efficient, hybrid Prius as a high-tech solution to the energy shortage. "How far will you go to save the planet?" it asks.

Consumers are overloaded with information about products and services. They cannot reevaluate products every time they make a buying decision. To simplify the buying process, consumers organize products, services, and companies into categories and "position" them in their minds. A product's position is the complex set of perceptions, impressions, and feelings that consumers have for the product compared with competing products.

Consumers position products with or without the help of marketers. But marketers do not want to leave their products' positions to chance. They must *plan* positions that will give their products the greatest advantage in selected target markets, and they must design marketing mixes to create these planned positions.

Positioning Maps

In planning their differentiation and positioning strategies, marketers often prepare *perceptual positioning maps,* which show consumer perceptions of their brands versus competing products on important buying dimensions. Figure 6.3 shows a positioning map for the U.S. large luxury sport utility vehicle market.[28] The position of each circle on the map indicates the brand's perceived positioning on two dimensions—price and orientation (luxury versus performance). The size of each circle indicates the brand's relative market share.

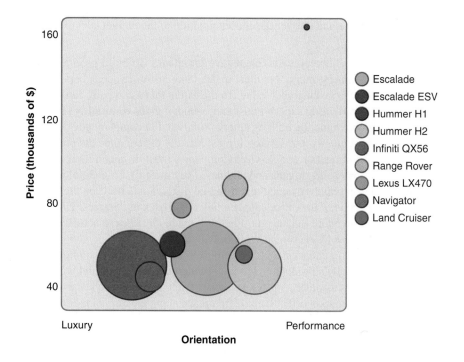

FIGURE 6.3

Positioning Map: Large Luxury SUVs

Source: Based on data provided by WardsAuto.com and Edumunds.com, 2007.

■ Toyota's Land Cruiser retains some of its adventure and performance positioning but with luxury added.

Thus, customers view the original Hummer H1 (the little dot in the upper right corner) as a very high-performance SUV with a price tag to match. The market-leading Cadillac Escalade is positioned as a moderately priced large luxury SUV with a balance of luxury and performance. The Escalade is positioned on urban luxury, and in its case, "performance" probably means power and safety performance. You'll find no mention of off-road adventuring in an Escalade ad. By contrast, Range Rover and Land Cruiser are positioned on luxury with nuances of off-road performance.

For example, the Toyota Land Cruiser began in 1951 as a four-wheel drive, Jeep-like vehicle designed to conquer the world's most grueling terrains and climates. In recent years, Land Cruiser has retained this adventure and performance positioning but with luxury added. Land Cruiser ads show the vehicle in adventurous settings, suggesting that it still has more trails to forge—"from the Dead Sea to the Himalayas," says the company's Web site. "Its husky VVT iV8 will remind you of why Land Cruiser is a legend throughout the world." However, the company adds, "its available Bluetooth hands-free technology, DVD entertainment, and a sumptuous interior have softened its edges."

Choosing a Differentiation and Positioning Strategy

Some firms find it easy to choose a differentiation and positioning strategy. For example, a firm well known for quality in certain segments will go for this position in a new segment if there are enough buyers seeking quality. But in many cases, two or more firms will go after the same position. Then, each will need to find other ways to set itself apart. Each firm must differentiate its offer by building a unique bundle of benefits that appeals to a substantial group within the segment.

The differentiation and positioning task consists of three steps: identifying a set of differentiating competitive advantages upon which to build a position, choosing the right competitive advantages, and selecting an overall positioning strategy. The company must then effectively communicate and deliver the chosen position to the market.

Identifying Possible Value Differences and Competitive Advantages   To build profitable relationships with target customers, marketers must understand customer needs better than competitors do and deliver more customer value. To the extent that a company can differentiate and position itself as providing superior customer value, it gains **competitive advantage**.

Competitive advantage
An advantage over competitors gained by offering greater customer value, either through lower prices or by providing more benefits that justify higher prices.

But solid positions cannot be built on empty promises. If a company positions its product as *offering* the best quality and service, it must actually differentiate the product so that it *delivers* the promised quality and service. Companies must do much more than simply shout out their positions in ad slogans and taglines. They must first *live* the slogan. For example, when Staples' research revealed that it should differentiate itself on the basis of "an easier shopping experience," the office supply retailer held back its "Staples: That was easy" marketing campaign for more than a year. First, it remade its stores to actually deliver the promised positioning (see Marketing at Work 6.2).

To find points of differentiation, marketers must think through the customer's entire experience with the company's product or service. An alert company can find ways to differentiate itself at every customer contact point. In what specific ways can a company differentiate itself or its market offer? It can differentiate along the lines of *product, services, channels, people,* or *image.*

6.2 MARKETING AT WORK

Staples: Positioning Made

These days, Staples really is riding the easy button. But only five years ago, things weren't so easy for the office-supply superstore—or for its customers. The ratio of customer complaints to compliments was running an abysmal eight to one at Staples stores. The company's slogan—"Yeah, we've got that"—had become laughable. Customers griped that items were often out of stock and said the sales staff was unhelpful to boot.

After weeks of focus groups and interviews, Shira Goodman, Staples' executive VP for marketing, had a revelation. "Customers wanted an easier shopping experience," she says. That simple revelation has resulted in one of the most successful marketing campaigns in recent history, built around the now-familiar "Staples: That was easy" tagline. But Staples' positioning turnaround took a lot more than simply bombarding customers with a new slogan. Before it could promise customers a simplified shopping experience, Staples had to actually deliver one. First, it had to *live* the slogan.

When it launched in 1986, Staples all but invented the office-supply superstore. Targeting small- and medium-size businesses, it aimed to sell everything for the office under one roof. But by the mid-1990s, the marketplace was crowded with retailers such as Office Depot, not to mention Target, Wal-Mart, and a slew of other online and off-line sellers. Partly as a result of that competition, Staples' same-store sales fell for the first time in 2001.

Customer research conducted by Goodman and her team revealed that although shoppers expected Staples and its competitors to have everything in stock, they placed little importance on price. Instead, customers overwhelmingly requested a simple, straightforward shopping experience. "They wanted knowledgeable and helpful associates and hassle-free shopping," Goodman says. The "Staples: That was easy" tagline was the simple—yet inspired—outgrowth of that realization.

The slogan, however, was kept under wraps until the company could give its stores a major makeover. Staples removed from its inventory some 800 superfluous items, such as Britney Spears backpacks, that had little use in the corporate world. Office chairs, which had been displayed in the rafters, were moved to the floor so customers could try them out. Staples also added larger signs and retrained sales associates to walk shoppers to the correct aisle. Because customers revealed that the availability of ink was one of their biggest concerns, the company introduced an in-stock guarantee on printer cartridges. Staples even simplified customer communications—a four-paragraph letter sent to prospective customers was cut to two sentences.

Only when all of the customer-experience pieces were in place did Staples begin communicating its new positioning to customers. It took about a year to get the stores up to snuff, Goodman says, but "once we felt that the experience was significantly easier, we changed the tagline."

For starters, the company hired a new ad agency, McCann-Erickson Worldwide, which had also created MasterCard's nine-year-old "Priceless" campaign. A group of McCann copywriters and art directors held a marathon brainstorming session to find ways to illustrate the concept of "easy." As the creative session dragged on, the group's creative director mentioned how nice it would be if she could just push a button to come up with a great ad, so they could go to lunch. The Easy Button was born. "It took an amorphous concept and made it tangible," Goodman says.

The Easy Button soon birthed a string of humorous and popular television commercials, which premiered in January 2005 and also aired during the Super Bowl a month later. In one spot, called "The

Now there's an easy button for your business.

It's called Staples.

Wouldn't it be nice if daily tasks around the office got a little easier? When you shop Staples, it will be as easy as – well – pressing a button. Visit us at **staples.com/easy** to find out what our Easy Button℠ can do for you today.

EASY BUTTON is a service mark of Staples the Office Superstore, LLC.

STAPLES

that was easy:

■ The "Staples: That was easy" marketing campaign has played a major role in repositioning Staples. But marketing promises count for little if not backed by the reality of the customer experience.

Wall," an emperor uses the button to erect a giant barrier as marauders approach; another shows an office worker causing printer cartridges to rain down from above. Online, Staples created a downloadable Easy Button toolbar, which took shoppers directly from their desktops to Staples.com, and billboards reminded commuters that an Easy Button would be helpful in snarled traffic.

As a result of the advertising onslaught, customers began asking about buying real Easy Buttons, so Staples again took the cue. It began selling $5 three-inch red plastic buttons that when pushed say "That was easy." Staples promised to donate $1 million in button profits to charity each year. Within nine months, the company had sold its millionth button. By selling the Easy Button as a sort of modern-day stress ball, Staples has turned its customers into advertisers. Homegrown movies starring the button have appeared on YouTube, and a blogger at Sexy Red-Headed Nuns hacked the button to create a garage door opener; the post was picked up by Digg.com and other sites. "The Easy Button is bigger than its category," says a McCann executive creative director.

(continues)

In all, the repositioning campaign has met with striking success. The five-year rebranding odyssey has helped make Staples the runaway leader in office retail. In addition to the viral success of the buttons, Staples says customer recall of its advertising has doubled to about 70 percent, compared with the industry average of 43 percent. According to Goodman, Staples now receives twice as many compliments as complaints at its stores.

No doubt about it, the "Staples: That was easy" marketing campaign has played a major role in repositioning Staples. Beyond pulling customers to the company's stores and Web site, the Easy Button seems to have insinuated itself into popular culture. But marketing promises count for little if not backed by the reality of the customer experience. Marketing VP Goodman attributes Staples' recent success more to the easy-does-it push within stores than to the "That was easy" catchphrase and campaign. "What has happened at the store has done more to drive the Staples brand than all the marketing in the world," she says.

Source: Adapted from portions of Michael Myser, "Marketing Made Easy," *Business 2.0*, June 2006, pp. 43–44. Also see Pallave Gogoi, "Staples Makes Selling Look Easy," *BusinessWeek Online*, December 7, 2006, accessed at www.BusinessWeek.com; and "Staples," *Hoover's*, accessed at www.hoovers.com, November 2007.

Through *product differentiation,* brands can be differentiated on features, performance, or style and design. Thus, Bose positions its speakers on their striking design and sound characteristics. And Panasonic positions its Toughbook PCs, designed to stand up to rugged use on the road or in the field, as "durable, reliable, wireless—protect your work no matter where you work." The Toughbook Web site offers "Tough Stories," complete with pictures of battered and abused Toughbooks still functioning well.

■ Product differentiation: Panasonic supports its Toughbook's rugged positioning with "real toughbook stories" featuring the PC still functioning well in difficult situations.

Beyond differentiating its physical product, a firm can also differentiate the services that accompany the product. Some companies gain *services differentiation* through speedy, convenient, or careful delivery. For example, Commerce Bank has positioned itself as "the most convenient bank in America"—it remains open seven days a week, including evenings, and you can get a debit card while you wait. Others differentiate their service based on high-quality customer care. Lexus makes fine cars but is perhaps even better known for the quality service that creates outstanding ownership experiences for Lexus owners.

Firms that practice *channel differentiation* gain competitive advantage through the way they design their channel's coverage, expertise, and performance. Amazon.com and GEICO set themselves apart with their smooth-functioning direct channels. Companies can also gain a strong competitive advantage through *people differentiation*—hiring and training better people than their competitors do. Disney people are known to be friendly and upbeat. And Singapore Airlines enjoys an excellent reputation, largely because of the grace of its flight attendants. People differentiation requires that a company select its customer-contact people carefully and train them well. For example, Disney trains its theme park people thoroughly to ensure that they are competent, courteous, and friendly—from the hotel check-in agents, to the monorail drivers, to the ride attendants, to the people who sweep Main Street USA. Each employee is carefully trained to understand customers and to "make people happy."

Even when competing offers look the same, buyers may perceive a difference based on company or brand *image differentiation*. A company or brand image should convey the product's distinctive benefits and positioning. Developing a strong and distinctive image calls for creativity and hard work. A company cannot develop an image in the public's mind overnight using only a few advertisements. If Ritz-Carlton means quality, this image must be supported by everything the company says and does.

Symbols—such as the McDonald's golden arches, the red Travelers umbrella, the Nike swoosh, or Google's colorful logo—can provide strong company or brand recognition and image differentiation. The company might build a brand around a famous person, as Nike did with its Air Jordan basketball shoes and Tiger Woods golfing products. Some companies even become associated with colors, such as IBM (blue), UPS (brown), or Coco-Cola (red). The chosen symbols, characters, and other image elements must be communicated through advertising that conveys the company's or brand's personality.

Choosing the Right Competitive Advantages Suppose a company is fortunate enough to discover several potential differentiations that provide competitive advantages. It now must choose the ones on which it will build its positioning strategy. It must decide *how many* differences to promote and *which ones.*

How Many Differences to Promote Many marketers think that companies should aggressively promote only one benefit to the target market. Ad man Rosser Reeves, for example, said a company should develop a *unique selling proposition* (USP) for each brand and stick to it. Each brand should pick an attribute and tout itself as "number one" on that attribute. Buyers tend to remember number one better, especially in this overcommunicated society. Thus, Wal-Mart promotes its always low prices and Burger King promotes personal choice—"have it your way."

Other marketers think that companies should position themselves on more than one differentiator. This may be necessary if two or more firms are claiming to be best on the same attribute. Today, in a time when the mass market is fragmenting into many small segments, companies are trying to broaden their positioning strategies to appeal to more segments. For example, Unilever introduced the first three-in-one bar soap—Lever 2000—offering cleansing, deodorizing, *and* moisturizing benefits. Clearly, many buyers want all three benefits. The challenge was to convince them that one brand can deliver all three. Judging from the outstanding success of the Lever 2000 brand, Unilever easily met the challenge. However, as companies increase the number of claims for their brands, they risk disbelief and a loss of clear positioning.

Which Differences to Promote Not all brand differences are meaningful or worthwhile; not every difference makes a good differentiator. Each difference has the potential to create company costs as well as customer benefits. A difference is worth establishing to the extent that it satisfies the following criteria:

- *Important:* The difference delivers a highly valued benefit to target buyers.
- *Distinctive:* Competitors do not offer the difference, or the company can offer it in a more distinctive way.
- *Superior:* The difference is superior to other ways that customers might obtain the same benefit.
- *Communicable:* The difference is communicable and visible to buyers.
- *Preemptive:* Competitors cannot easily copy the difference.
- *Affordable:* Buyers can afford to pay for the difference.
- *Profitable:* The company can introduce the difference profitably.

Many companies have introduced differentiations that failed one or more of these tests. When the Westin Stamford Hotel in Singapore once advertised that it is the world's tallest hotel, it was a distinction that was not important to most tourists—in fact, it turned many off. Polaroid's Polarvision, which produced instantly developed home movies, bombed too. Although Polarvision

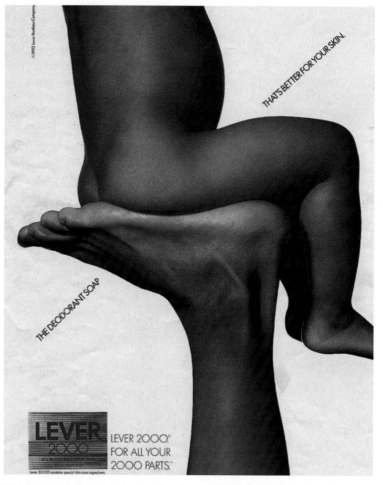

■ Unilever positioned its best-selling Lever 2000 soap on three benefits in one: cleansing, deodorizing, and moisturizing benefits. It's good "for all your 2000 parts."

was distinctive and even preemptive, it was inferior to another way of capturing motion, namely, camcorders. Thus, choosing competitive advantages upon which to position a product or service can be difficult, yet such choices may be crucial to success.

Value proposition

The full positioning of a brand—the full mix of benefits upon which it is positioned.

Selecting an Overall Positioning Strategy The full positioning of a brand is called the brand's **value proposition**—the full mix of benefits upon which the brand is differentiated and positioned. It is the answer to the customer's question "Why should I buy your brand?" Volvo's value proposition hinges on safety but also includes reliability, roominess, and styling, all for a price that is higher than average but seems fair for this mix of benefits.

Figure 6.4 shows possible value propositions upon which a company might position its products. In the figure, the five green cells represent winning value propositions—differentiation and positioning that gives the company competitive advantage. The red cells, however, represent losing value propositions. The center yellow cell represents at best a marginal proposition. In the following sections, we discuss the five winning value propositions upon which companies can position their products: more for more, more for the same, the same for less, less for much less, and more for less.

More for More   "More-for-more" positioning involves providing the most upscale product or service and charging a higher price to cover the higher costs. Ritz-Carlton Hotels, Mont Blanc writing instruments, Mercedes automobiles, Viking appliances—each claims superior quality, craftsmanship, durability, performance, or style and charges a price to match. Not only is the market offering high in quality, it also gives prestige to the buyer. It symbolizes status and a loftier lifestyle. Often, the price difference exceeds the actual increment in quality.

Sellers offering "only the best" can be found in every product and service category, from hotels, restaurants, food, and fashion to cars and household appliances. Consumers are sometimes surprised, even delighted, when a new competitor enters a category with an unusually high-priced brand. Starbucks coffee entered as a very expensive brand in a largely commodity category. When Apple premiered its iPhone, it offered higher-quality features than a traditional cell phone with a hefty price tag to match.

In general, companies should be on the lookout for opportunities to introduce a "more-for-more" brand in any underdeveloped product or service category. Yet "more-for-more" brands can be vulnerable. They often invite imitators who claim the same quality but at a lower price. Luxury goods that sell well during good times may be at risk during economic downturns when buyers become more cautious in their spending.

More for the Same   Companies can attack a competitor's more-for-more positioning by introducing a brand offering comparable quality but at a lower price. For example, Toyota introduced its Lexus line with a "more-for-the-same" value proposition versus Mercedes and BMW. Its first ad headline read: "Perhaps the first time in history that trading a $72,000

FIGURE 6.4
Possible Value Propositions

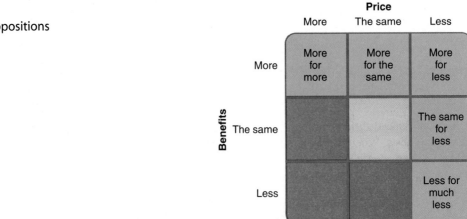

car for a $36,000 car could be considered trading up." It communicated the high quality of its new Lexus through rave reviews in car magazines and through a widely distributed videotape showing side-by-side comparisons of Lexus and Mercedes automobiles. It published surveys showing that Lexus dealers were providing customers with better sales and service experiences than were Mercedes dealerships. Many Mercedes owners switched to Lexus, and the Lexus repurchase rate has been 60 percent, twice the industry average.

The Same for Less   Offering "the same for less" can be a powerful value proposition—everyone likes a good deal. For example, Dell offers equivalent-quality computers at a lower "price for performance." Discount stores such as Wal-Mart and "category killers" such as Best Buy, Circuit City, and Sportmart also use this positioning. They don't claim to offer different or better products. Instead, they offer many of the same brands as department stores and specialty stores but at deep discounts based on superior purchasing power and lower-cost operations. Other companies develop imitative but lower-priced brands in an effort to lure customers away from the market leader. For example, AMD makes less-expensive versions of Intel's market-leading microprocessor chips.

Less for Much Less   A market almost always exists for products that offer less and therefore cost less. Few people need, want, or can afford "the very best" in everything they buy. In many cases, consumers will gladly settle for less than optimal performance or give up some of the bells and whistles in exchange for a lower price. For example, many travelers seeking lodgings prefer not to pay for what they consider unnecessary extras, such as a pool, attached restaurant, or mints on the pillow. Hotel chains such as Ramada Limited suspend some of these amenities and charge less accordingly.

"Less-for-much-less" positioning involves meeting consumers' lower performance or quality requirements at a much lower price. For example, Family Dollar and Dollar General stores offer more affordable goods at very low prices. Sam's Club and Costco warehouse stores offer less merchandise selection and consistency and much lower levels of service; as a result, they charge rock-bottom prices. Southwest Airlines, the nation's most consistently profitable air carrier, also practices less-for-much-less positioning.

From the start, Southwest has positioned itself firmly as *the* no-frills, low-price airline. Southwest's passengers have learned to fly without the amenities. For example, the airline provides no meals—just pretzels. It offers no first-class section, only three-across seating in all of its planes. And there's no such thing as a reserved seat on a Southwest flight. Why, then, do so many passengers love Southwest? Perhaps most importantly, Southwest excels at the basics of getting passengers where they want to go on time, and with their luggage. Beyond the basics, however, Southwest offers shockingly low prices. In fact, prices are so low that when Southwest enters a market, it actually increases total air traffic by attracting customers who might otherwise travel by car or bus. No frills and low prices, however, don't mean drudgery. Southwest's cheerful employees go out of their way to amuse, surprise, or somehow entertain passengers. One analyst sums up Southwest's less-for-much-less positioning this way: "It is not luxurious, but it's cheap and it's fun."

■ Less for much less positioning: Southwest has positioned itself firmly as the no-frills, low-price airline. But no frills doesn't mean drudgery—Southwest's cheerful employees go out of their way to amuse, surprise, or somehow entertain passengers.

More for Less   Of course, the winning value proposition would be to offer "more for less." Many companies claim to do this. And, in the short run, some companies can actually achieve such lofty positions. For example, when it first opened for business, Home Depot had arguably the best product selection, the best service, *and* the lowest prices compared to local hardware stores and other home improvement chains.

Yet in the long run, companies will find it very difficult to sustain such best-of-both positioning. Offering more usually costs more, making it difficult to deliver on the "for-less" promise. Companies that try to deliver both may lose out to more focused competitors. For example, facing determined competition from Lowe's stores, Home Depot must now decide whether it wants to compete primarily on superior service or on lower prices.

All said, each brand must adopt a positioning strategy designed to serve the needs and wants of its target markets. "More for more" will draw one target market, "less for much less" will draw another, and so on. Thus, in any market, there is usually room for many different companies, each successfully occupying different positions. The important thing is that each company must develop its own winning positioning strategy, one that makes it special to its target consumers.

Positioning statement

A statement that summarizes company or brand positioning—it takes this form: *To (target segment and need) our (brand) is (concept) that (point-of-difference).*

Developing a Positioning Statement Company and brand positioning should be summed up in a **positioning statement**. The statement should follow the form: *To (target segment and need) our (brand) is (concept) that (point of difference).*[29] For example: "To *busy, mobile professionals who need to always be in the loop, BlackBerry is a wireless connectivity solution that gives you an easier, more reliable way to stay connected to data, people, and resources while on the go.*"

Note that the positioning first states the product's membership in a category (wireless connectivity solution) and then shows its point of difference from other members of the category (easier, more reliable connections to data, people, and resources). Placing a brand in a specific category suggests similarities that it might share with other products in the category. But the case for the brand's superiority is made on its points of difference.

Sometimes marketers put a brand in a surprisingly different category before indicating the points of difference. DiGiorno is a frozen pizza whose crust rises when the pizza is heated. But instead of putting it in the frozen pizza category, the marketers positioned it in the delivered pizza category. DiGiorno ads show delicious pizzas that look like anything but a frozen pizza, proclaiming "No calling. No tipping. No kidding. It's not delivery, its DiGiorno!" Another ad claims that DiGiorno "Makes mouths water. And delivery guys weep." Such positioning helps highlight DiGiorno's fresh quality and superior taste over the normal frozen pizza.

Communicating and Delivering the Chosen Position

Once it has chosen a position, the company must take strong steps to deliver and communicate the desired position to target consumers. All the company's marketing mix efforts must support the positioning strategy.

Positioning the company calls for concrete action, not just talk. If the company decides to build a position on better quality and service, it must first *deliver* that position. Designing the marketing mix—product, price, place, and promotion—involves working out the tactical details of the positioning strategy. Thus, a firm that seizes on a more-for-more position knows that it must produce high-quality products, charge a high price, distribute through high-quality dealers, and advertise in high-quality media. It must hire and train more service people, find retailers who have a good reputation for service, and develop sales and advertising messages that broadcast its superior service. This is the only way to build a consistent and believable more-for-more position.

No Calling.

No Tipping.

No Kidding.

It's not delivery. It's DiGiorno!

DIGIORNO

■ Points of difference: Sometimes marketers put a brand in a surprisingly different category. Kraft positions its DiGiorno pizza in the delivered pizza category. "No calling. No tipping. No kidding. It's not delivery, its DiGiorno!"

Companies often find it easier to come up with a good positioning strategy than to implement it. Establishing a position or changing one usually takes a long time. In contrast, positions that have taken years to build can quickly be lost. Once a company has built the desired position, it must take care to maintain the position through consistent performance and communication. It must closely monitor and adapt the position over time to match changes in consumer needs and competitors' strategies. However, the company should avoid abrupt changes that might confuse consumers. Instead, a product's position should evolve gradually as it adapts to the ever-changing marketing environment.

REST STOP ⬀ REVIEWING THE CONCEPTS

In this chapter, you've learned about the major elements of a customer-driven marketing strategy: segmentation, targeting, differentiation, and positioning. Marketers know that they cannot appeal to all buyers in their markets, or at least not to all buyers in the same way. Buyers are too numerous, too widely scattered, and too varied in their needs and buying practices. Therefore, most companies today practice *target marketing*—identifying market segments, selecting one or more of them, and developing products and marketing mixes tailored to each.

1. Define the major steps in designing a customer-driven marketing strategy: market segmentation, targeting, differentiation, and positioning.

Customer-driven marketing strategy begins with selecting which customers to serve and deciding on a value proposition that best serves the targeted customers. It consists of four steps. *Market segmentation* is the act of dividing a market into distinct groups of buyers with different needs, characteristics, or behaviors who might require separate products or marketing mixes. Once the groups have been identified, *market targeting* evaluates each market segment's attractiveness and selects one or more segments to serve. Market targeting consists of designing strategies to build the *right relationships* with the *right customers*. *Differentiation* involves actually differentiating the market offering to create superior customer value. *Positioning* consists of positioning the market offering in the minds of target customers.

2. List and discuss the major bases for segmenting consumer and business markets.

There is no single way to segment a market. Therefore, the marketer tries different variables to see which give the best segmentation opportunities. For consumer marketing, the major segmentation variables are geographic, demographic, psychographic, and behavioral. In *geographic segmentation,* the market is divided into different geographical units such as nations, regions, states, counties, cities, or neighborhoods. In *demographic segmentation,* the market is divided into groups based on demographic variables, including age, gender, family size, family life cycle, income, occupation, education, religion, race, generation, and nationality. In *psychographic segmentation,* the market is divided into different groups based on social class, lifestyle, or personality characteristics. In *behavioral segmentation,* the market is divided into groups based on consumers' knowledge, attitudes, uses, or responses to a product.

Business marketers use many of the same variables to segment their markets. But business markets also can be segmented by business consumer *demographics* (industry, company size), *operating characteristics, purchasing approaches, situational factors,* and *personal characteristics.* The effectiveness of segmentation analysis depends on finding segments that are *measurable, accessible, substantial, differentiable,* and *actionable.*

3. Explain how companies identify attractive market segments and choose a market-targeting strategy.

To target the best market segments, the company first evaluates each segment's size and growth characteristics, structural attractiveness, and compatibility with company objectives and resources. It then chooses one of four market-targeting strategies—ranging from very broad to very narrow targeting. The seller can ignore segment differences and target broadly using *undifferentiated (or mass) marketing.* This involves mass producing, mass distributing, and mass promoting about the same product in about the same way to all consumers. Or the seller can adopt *differentiated marketing*—developing different market offers for several segments. *Concentrated marketing* (or *niche marketing*) involves focusing on only one or a few market segments. Finally, *micromarketing* is the practice of tailoring products and marketing programs to suit the tastes of specific individuals and locations. Micromarketing includes *local marketing* and *individual marketing.* Which targeting strategy is best depends on company resources, product variability, product life-cycle stage, market variability, and competitive marketing strategies.

4. Discuss how companies differentiate and position their products for maximum competitive advantage.

Once a company has decided which segments to enter, it must decide on its *differentiation and positioning strategy.* The differentiation and positioning task consists of three steps: identifying a set of possible differentiations that create competitive advantage, choosing advantages upon which to build a position, and selecting an overall positioning strategy. The brand's full positioning is called its *value proposition*—the full mix of benefits upon which the brand is positioned. In general, companies can choose from one of five winning value propositions upon which to position their products: more for more, more for the same, the same for less, less for much less, or more for less.

Company and brand positioning are summarized in positioning statements that state the target segment and need, positioning concept, and specific points of difference. The company must then effectively communicate and deliver the chosen position to the market.

Navigating the Key Terms

Age and life-cycle segmentation (169)
Behavioral segmentation (170)
Benefit segmentation (171)
Competitive advantage (186)
Concentrated (niche) marketing (178)
Demographic segmentation (169)
Differentiated (segmented) marketing (177)
Differentiation (167)
Gender segmentation (170)

Geographic segmentation (168)
Income segmentation (170)
Individual marketing (181)
Intermarket segmentation (175)
Local marketing (181)
Market segmentation (167)
Market targeting (targeting) (167)
Micromarketing (181)
Occasion segmentation (171)

Positioning (167)
Positioning statement (192)
Product position (185)
Psychographic segmentation (171)
Target market (177)
Undifferentiated (mass) marketing (177)
Value proposition (190)

Travel Log

Discussing the Issues

1. List and briefly describe the four major steps in designing customer-driven marketing strategy. (AACSB: Communication)

2. Name and describe the four major variables that might be used in segmenting consumer markets. For each, give an example of a brand using that segmenting variable. (AACSB: Communication; Reflective Thinking)

3. Explain how segmenting business markets is similar to, yet different from, segmenting consumer markets. (AACSB: Communication; Reflective Thinking)

4. After evaluating different segments, marketers must decide which segment(s) to target. Name and describe the options available and discuss the pros and cons of each. (AACSB: Communication)

5. In the context of marketing, what is a product's "position"? How do marketers know what it is? (AACSB: Communication)

6. Name and define the five winning value propositions described in the chapter. Which value proposition describes Starbuck's Coffee? Explain your answer. (AACSB: Communication; Reflective Thinking)

Application Questions

1. The chapter described psychographics as one major variable used by marketers when segmenting consumer markets. SRI

Consulting has developed a typology of consumers based on values and lifestyles. Go to SRI Consulting's Web site (www.sric-bi.com), click on the VALS survey on the right side of the Web site, and complete the VALS survey. How accurately do your primary and secondary VALS types describe you? How can marketers use this information? Write a brief report of your findings. (AACSB: Communication; Use of IT; Reflective Thinking)

2. Suppose you are a brand manager for Van's footwear. You have identified two market segments: young men/boys who are into "pop" culture and skateboarding, and older men wanting shoes that do not need to be tied. You are now deciding which target marketing strategy to pursue. What criteria should you consider to ensure that the identified segments are effective? (AACSB: Communication; Reflective Thinking)

3. In a small group, develop the positioning strategies for an energy drink targeted to three separate target markets segmented by one or more of the four consumer segmenting variables described in the chapter. Describe each market segment and what your brand will offer that target market. For each target market, choose a differentiation and positioning strategy by identifying possible value differences and competitive advantages for your brand, choose the best competitive advantages, select an overall positioning strategy for each target market, and develop a positioning statement for each brand targeted to a specific market. (AACSB: Communication; Reflective Thinking)

Under the Hood: Focus on Technology

Today's micromarketing technology enables marketers to mass customize products ranging from clothing, skin care products, and vitamin supplements to furniture, automobiles, and even postage stamps. And through behavioral targeting technologies, marketing communications also can be customized based on Web surfing behavior and television viewership, often without consumers being aware that their behavior is tracked. Explore micromarketing at the following sites and report on what you find.

1. Consumers can design their own shoes at Nike's Web site. Visit this site at http://NikeID.com and design your own shoe. Print out your shoe design and bring it to class. Do you think the price is appropriate for the value you received

from being able to customize your shoe? Find two other Web sites that allow buyers to customize products and write a brief report on what you learned. (AACSB: Communication; Use of IT)

2. Tacoda Inc. is a behavior ad network that allows marketers to deliver Internet ads to individuals based on their Internet behavior. Visit www.tacoda.com to learn more about this company. Explore this Web site to learn how marketers are able to send Internet ads to targeted consumers and write a brief report explaining behavioral targeting and how marketers are using it. (AACSB: Communication; Use of IT)

Focus on Ethics

As more companies go global, segmentation is becoming more common. However, manufactured goods marketed in one country sometimes end up in another country for which that product was not intended. Or products sometimes end up in intended markets, but through unauthorized channels. This is called gray marketing or parallel importing. It involves genuinely branded products—not counterfeit or "knock-off" products. One factor that encourages such activities is that a given product may be priced differently for different international markets, depending on the economic conditions of those markets. Gray marketers purchase these products at the lower price, import them into another country, and sell them for more than they paid but lower than the price authorized distributors charge in that country.

1. Research gray marketing. Write a report explaining (1) how it occurs, (2) the impact it has on manufacturers and distributors, (3) any positive outcomes of this practice, and (4) what manufacturers can do about it. (AACSB: Communication; Reflective Thinking)

2. As a consumer, do you see any benefits of gray markets? Is it ethical for consumers to purchase products through gray markets? (AACSB: Communication; Reflective Thinking; Ethical Reasoning)

Video Case

Procter & Gamble

Procter & Gamble has one of the world's largest and strongest brand portfolios, including such familiar brands as Pampers, Tide, Ariel, Always, Pantene, Bounty, Folgers, Pringles, Charmin, Downy, Iams, Crest, Secret, and Olay. In fact, in the United States, P&G offers five shampoo brands, six detergent brands, and six brands of soap. In each of these categories, P&G's products compete against each other, in addition to products offered by other companies, for share of the customer's wallet.

How can a company with more than 300 brands sold in more than 140 countries maximize profits without cannibalizing its own sales? It all starts with a solid understanding of consumers and how a brand fits into consumers' lives. Each P&G brand is carefully positioned to target a very specific segment of the market. The result? P&G had more than $68 billion in sales last year.

After viewing the video featuring Procter & Gamble, answer the following questions about segmentation, targeting, and positioning.

1. Visit the Procter & Gamble Web site, choose a specific product category, and review the brands in that category. How does P&G use positioning to differentiate the brands in the product category you selected?

2. What bases of segmentation does P&G use to differentiate the products in the category you selected?

3. How does P&G use its variety of brands to build the right relationships with the right customers?

7

Products, Services, and Brands: Building Customer Value

ROAD MAP Previewing the Concepts

Now that you've had a good look at customer-driven marketing strategy, we'll take a deeper look at the marketing mix—the tactical tools that marketers use to implement their strategies and to deliver superior customer value. In this and the next chapter, we'll study how companies develop and manage products and brands. Then, in the chapters that follow, we'll look at pricing, distribution, and marketing communication tools. The product is usually the first and most basic marketing consideration. We'll start with a seemingly simple question: What *is* a product? As it turns out, however, the answer is not so simple.

Before starting into the chapter, let's look at an interesting branding story. Brands may be the most important tools for creating customer value and profitable customer relationships. Marketing is all about building brands that connect deeply with customers. So, when you think of top brands, which ones pop up first? Here's a tale about one strong brand you may not have considered.

When you think of today's "hottest brands," what names come to mind? Coca-Cola? Nike? Google? Target? Maybe Starbucks? But scan the list of hottest brands prepared each year by respected brand consultancy Landor Associates, and you'll find an unlikely regular entry—Las Vegas. That's right, Las Vegas. Most people wouldn't even think of Vegas as a "product," let alone as a brand. But there it is, number two on the list of the nation's hottest brands behind only Google.

Many old-timers still think of Las Vegas as "Sin City"—an anything-goes gambling town built on smoke-filled casinos, bawdy all-girl revues, all-you-can-eat buffets, Elvis impersonators, and no-wait weddings on the Vegas Strip. But that's the old Las Vegas. The new Vegas has reinvented itself as a luxury destination. Casinos and gaming now account for less than half the city's revenues. Instead, the new Las Vegas brims with classy resort hotel/casinos, expansive shopping malls filled with luxury goods, first-run entertainment, and restaurants bearing the names of world-renown chefs.

However, to the nearly 40 million visitors who flock to Las Vegas each year, the town is much more than just an assortment of facilities and amenities. To visitors, Vegas is an emotional connection, a total brand experience. What *is* the "Las Vegas experience"? To answer that question, the city conducted extensive consumer research. "We talked to old customers and new customers to determine the essence of the brand of Las Vegas," says Rossi Ralenkotter, CEO of the Las Vegas Convention and Visitors Authority (LVCVA).

The research showed that when people come to Las Vegas, they're a little naughtier—a little less inhibited. They stay out longer, eat more, do some gambling, and spend more on shopping and dining. "We found that [the Las Vegas experience] centered on adult freedom," says Ralenkotter. "People could stay up all night and do things they wouldn't normally do in their own towns."

Based on these consumer insights, the LVCVA coined a now-familiar catchphrase—"Only Vegas: What happens here, stays here." The phrase captures the essence of the Las Vegas experience—that it's okay to be a little naughty in Vegas. Now the centerpiece of what has become one of the most successful tourism campaigns in history, that simple phrase has helped transform Las Vegas' brand image from one of a down-and-dirty "Sin City" to an enticing and luxurious "Only Vegas."

In 2003 the LVCVA launched an innovative $75 million "What happens here, stays here" ad campaign. Early ads were based on 2,500 real stories culled from visitors through the market research. True to the brand's positioning, the award-winning campaign showed the naughty nature of people once they arrive in Las Vegas.

In one ad, a woman spontaneously marries a visibly younger man in a Las Vegas wedding chapel. Then, ignoring his ardent pleas, she kisses him goodbye and pulls herself away, insisting that she has to get back to her business convention. In another ad, a suave young man tests different identities on the various women he meets during a night on the town. "I'm a hand model," he declares—or a lifeguard, or a big-game hunter, or a brain doctor. In still another ad, a young woman lounges by the pool with friends at a Vegas hotel, preoccupied with her cell phone. "Okay, what's with the phone?" asks one of the friends. "You had that out all last night." To the friend's chagrin, the woman announces: "Oh, it's not just a phone. It takes photos with this little camera, and it also records little video clips." When she dives into the pool, the phone is shown sinking slowly behind her. At the end, each ad reminds us that, "What happens here, stays here."

The LVCVA is still investing heavily in the bold and provocative campaign. More recent ads show people returning to their normal lives after visiting Las Vegas. When asked by friends what they did in Vegas, they quickly cover their tracks. In one of these newer ads, a guy runs into a woman friend at the supermarket, who asks him where he's been. "Oh, you know, I've been around. . . . I was in Vegas," he says. "Oh!" she responds, "What did you do there?" He hesitates, then fumbles to avoid the sordid truth. "I ate," he replies lamely. "Went to restaurants. Bradley Ogden. Delmonico. I'm a . . . I'm a bit of a 'foodie'." With eyebrows raised, the skeptical woman checks out his shopping cart, which overflows with cupcakes, cheese puffs, popsicles, and soda pop. His deft parting line: "Well, off on a caviar hunt!" The ad signs off with the line: "Our world-class dining can be your alibi." Other ads in the series conclude, "Our fabulous Broadway shows can be your alibi" or "Our fabulous shopping can be your alibi." These new ads extend the "naughty things you'd do only in Vegas" theme, skillfully tying in signature Las Vegas activities such as shopping, seeing shows, and eating at some of the world's best restaurants.

Since the LVCVA campaign began, the "What happens here, stays here" slogan has become a part of the national vernacular, strongly positioning Las Vegas in the minds of potential visitors and setting it apart from the rapidly-growing list of competing destinations. "It's all about branding," says CEO Ralenkotter. "The slogan captures the city's experiences rather than amenities, the image that Las Vegas represents freedom."

Thus, thanks to smart marketing and brand building, Las Vegas really does belong among the ranks of the world's hottest brands. Vegas tourism is booming. By 2011, an estimated 45 million tourists will overindulge in the naughtiness that Vegas affords, secure in the promise that "What happens here, stays here."[1]

A s the Las Vegas example shows, in their quest to create customer relationships, marketers must build and manage products and brands that connect with customers. This chapter begins with a deceptively simple question: *What is a product?* After addressing this question, we look at ways to classify products in consumer and business markets. Then we discuss the important decisions that marketers make regarding individual products, product lines, and product mixes. Next, we look into the critically important issue of how marketers build and manage brands. Finally, we examine the characteristics and marketing requirements of a special form of product—services.

What Is a Product?

Product
Anything that can be offered to a market for attention, acquisition, use, or consumption that might satisfy a want or need.

We define a **product** as anything that can be offered to a market for attention, acquisition, use, or consumption that might satisfy a want or need. Products include more than just tangible objects, such as cars, computers, or cell phones. Broadly defined, "products" also include services, events, persons, places, organizations, ideas, or mixes of these. Throughout this text, we use the term *product* broadly to include any or all of these entities. Thus, an Apple iPod, a Toyota Camry, and a Caffé Mocha at Starbucks are products. But so are a trip to Las Vegas, Fidelity online investment services, and advice from your family doctor.

Because of their importance in the world economy, we give special attention to services. **Services** are a form of product that consists of activities, benefits, or satisfactions offered for sale that are essentially intangible and do not result in the ownership of anything. Examples are banking, hotel, airline, retail, wireless communication, and home-repair services. We will look at services more closely later in this chapter.

Service
Any activity or benefit that one party can offer to another that is essentially intangible and does not result in the ownership of anything.

Products, Services, and Experiences

Product is a key element in the overall *market offering.* Marketing-mix planning begins with building an offering that brings value to target customers. This offering becomes the basis upon which the company builds profitable customer relationships.

A company's market offering often includes both tangible goods and services. At one extreme, the offer may consist of a *pure tangible good,* such as soap, toothpaste, or salt—no services accompany the product. At the other extreme are *pure services,* for which the offer consists primarily of a service. Examples include a doctor's exam or financial services. Between these two extremes, however, many goods-and-services combinations are possible.

Today, as products and services become more commoditized, many companies are moving to a new level in creating value for their customers. To differentiate their offers, beyond simply making products and delivering services, they are creating and managing customer *experiences* with their brands or company.

Experiences have always been an important part of marketing for some companies. Disney has long manufactured dreams and memories through its movies and theme parks. And Nike has long declared, "It's not so much the shoes but where they take you." Today, however, all kinds of firms are recasting their traditional goods and services to create experiences. For example, American Girl Inc. does more than just make and sell high-end dolls. It takes additional steps to create special experiences between the dolls and the girls who adore them.[2]

To put more smiles on the faces of the girls who adore their American Girl dolls, the company has opened American Girl Places in Chicago, New York, Atlanta, and Los Angeles. Some 3 million people made pilgrimages to an American Girl Place last year—most travel three to six hours to get there. The average visit: a startling four hours. Inside a Place are a series of wonderfully engaging experiences for girls, mothers, and grandmothers (not to mention the occasional steamrolled dad). There's a theater with a live play centered on the doll collection, a café for a grown-up dining experience, a salon to style a doll's hair, and a doll hospital to fix one up as good as new. Before, during, and after all these experiences, shopping does go on—and the purchases become memorabilia for the experiences visitors have. Moreover, these same visitors buy more from the catalog, frequent the Web site to purchase items more often, and tell their friends about their American Girl Place experience. Much more than a store that sells dolls, says the company, "it's the place where imaginations soar—from boutiques to special events, from the café to the theater and beyond."

■ Marketing experiences: American Girl, Inc., does more than just make and sell high-end dolls. It takes additional steps to create special experiences between the dolls and the girls who adore them.

Companies that market experiences realize that customers are really buying much more than just products and services. They are buying what those offers will *do* for them.

FIGURE 7.1

Three Levels of Product

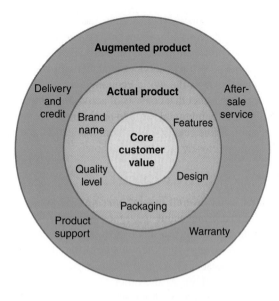

Levels of Product and Services

Product planners need to think about products and services on three levels (see Figure 7.1). Each level adds more customer value. The most basic level is the *core customer value,* which addresses the question *What is the buyer really buying?* When designing products, marketers must first define the core, problem-solving benefits or services that consumers seek. A woman buying lipstick buys more than lip color. Charles Revson of Revlon saw this early: "In the factory, we make cosmetics; in the store, we sell hope." And people who buy a BlackBerry smartphone are buying more than a wireless mobile phone, e-mail device, or personal organizer. They are buying freedom and on-the-go connectivity to people and resources.

At the second level, product planners must turn the core benefit into an *actual product.* They need to develop product and service features, design, a quality level, a brand name, and packaging. For example, the BlackBerry is an actual product. Its name, parts, styling, features, packaging, and other attributes have all been combined carefully to deliver the core customer value of staying connected.

Finally, product planners must build an *augmented product* around the core benefit and actual product by offering additional consumer services and benefits. The BlackBerry solution offers more than just a communications device. It provides consumers with a complete solution to mobile connectivity problems. Thus, when consumers buy a BlackBerry, the company and its dealers also might give buyers a warranty on parts and workmanship, instructions on how to use the device, quick repair services when needed, and a toll-free telephone number and Web site to use if they have problems or questions.

■ Core, actual, and augmented product: People who buy a BlackBerry are buying more than a wireless mobile phone, e-mail device, or organizer. They are buying freedom and on-the-go connectivity to people and resources.

Consumers see products as complex bundles of benefits that satisfy their needs. When developing products, marketers first must identify the *core customer value* that consumers seek from the product. They must then design the *actual* product and find ways to *augment* it in order to create this customer value and the most satisfying customer experience.

Product and Service Classifications

Products and services fall into two broad classes based on the types of consumers that use them—*consumer products* and *industrial products.* Broadly defined, products also include other marketable entities such as experiences, organizations, persons, places, and ideas.

Consumer Products **Consumer products** are products and services bought by final consumers for personal consumption. Marketers usually classify these products and services further based on how consumers go about buying them. Consumer products include *convenience products, shopping products, specialty products,* and *unsought products.* These products differ in the ways consumers buy them and therefore in how they are marketed (see Table 7.1).

Convenience products are consumer products and services that customers usually buy frequently, immediately, and with a minimum of comparison and buying effort. Examples include laundry detergent, candy, magazines, and fast food. Convenience products are usually low priced, and marketers place them in many locations to make them readily available when customers need them.

Shopping products are less frequently purchased consumer products and services that customers compare carefully on suitability, quality, price, and style. When buying shopping products and services, consumers spend much time and effort in gathering information and making comparisons. Examples include furniture, clothing, used cars, major appliances, and hotel and airline services. Shopping products marketers usually distribute their products through fewer outlets but provide deeper sales support to help customers in their comparison efforts.

Specialty products are consumer products and services with unique characteristics or brand identification for which a significant group of buyers is willing to make a special purchase effort. Examples include specific brands of cars, high-priced photographic equipment, designer clothes, and the services of medical or legal specialists. A Lamborghini automobile, for example, is a specialty product because buyers are usually willing to travel great distances to buy one. Buyers normally do not compare specialty products. They invest only the time needed to reach dealers carrying the wanted products.

Unsought products are consumer products that the consumer either does not know about or knows about but does not normally think of buying. Most major new innovations are unsought until the consumer becomes aware of them through advertising. Classic examples of known but unsought products and services are life insurance, preplanned funeral services, and blood donations to the Red Cross. By their very nature, unsought products require a lot of advertising, personal selling, and other marketing efforts.

Industrial Products **Industrial products** are those purchased for further processing or for use in conducting a business. Thus, the distinction between a consumer product and an industrial product is based on the *purpose* for which the product is bought. If a consumer buys a lawn mower for use around home, the lawn mower is a consumer product. If the same consumer buys the same lawn mower for use in a landscaping business, the lawn mower is an industrial product.

Consumer product
Product bought by final consumer for personal consumption.

Convenience product
Consumer product that customers usually buy frequently, immediately, and with a minimum of comparison and buying effort.

Shopping product
Consumer good that the customers, in the process of selection and purchase, characteristically compare on such bases as suitability, quality, price, and style.

Specialty product
Consumer product with unique characteristics or brand identification for which a significant group of buyers is willing to make a special purchase effort.

Unsought product
Consumer product that the consumer either does not know about or knows about but does not normally think of buying.

Industrial product
Product bought by individuals and organizations for further processing or for use in conducting a business.

TABLE 7.1   Marketing Considerations for Consumer Products

Marketing Considerations	Type of Consumer Product			
	Convenience	**Shopping**	**Specialty**	**Unsought**
Customer buying behavior	Frequent purchase, little planning, little comparison or shopping effort, low customer involvement	Less frequent purchase, much planning and shopping effort, comparison of brands on price, quality, style	Strong brand preference and loyalty, special purchase effort, little comparison of brands, low price sensitivity	Little product awareness, knowledge (or, if aware, little or even negative interest)
Price	Low price	Higher price	High price	Varies
Distribution	Widespread distribution, convenient locations	Selective distribution in fewer outlets	Exclusive distribution in only one or a few outlets per market area	Varies
Promotion	Mass promotion by the producer	Advertising and personal selling by both producer and resellers	More carefully targeted promotion by both producer and resellers	Aggressive advertising and personal selling by producer and resellers
Examples	Toothpaste, magazines, laundry detergent	Major appliances, televisions, furniture, clothing	Luxury goods, such as Rolex watches or fine crystal	Life insurance, Red Cross blood donations

The three groups of industrial products and services include materials and parts, capital items, and supplies and services. *Materials and parts* include raw materials and manufactured materials and parts. Raw materials consist of farm products (wheat, cotton, livestock, fruits, vegetables) and natural products (fish, lumber, crude petroleum, iron ore). Manufactured materials and parts consist of component materials (iron, yarn, cement, wires) and component parts (small motors, tires, castings). Most manufactured materials and parts are sold directly to industrial users. Price and service are the major marketing factors; branding and advertising tend to be less important.

Capital items are industrial products that aid in the buyer's production or operations, including installations and accessory equipment. Installations consist of major purchases such as buildings (factories, offices) and fixed equipment (generators, drill presses, large computer systems, elevators). Accessory equipment includes portable factory equipment and tools (hand tools, lift trucks) and office equipment (computers, fax machines, desks). They have a shorter life than installations and simply aid in the production process.

The final group of industrial products is *supplies and services.* Supplies include operating supplies (lubricants, coal, paper, pencils) and repair and maintenance items (paint, nails, brooms). Supplies are the convenience products of the industrial field because they are usually purchased with a minimum of effort or comparison. Business services include maintenance and repair services (window cleaning, computer repair) and business advisory services (legal, management consulting, advertising). Such services are usually supplied under contract.

Organizations, Persons, Places, and Ideas In addition to tangible products and services, marketers have broadened the concept of a product to include other market offerings—organizations, persons, places, and ideas.

Organizations often carry out activities to "sell" the organization itself. *Organization marketing* consists of activities undertaken to create, maintain, or change the attitudes and behavior of target consumers toward an organization. Both profit and not-for-profit organizations practice organization marketing. Business firms sponsor public relations or *corporate image advertising* campaigns to market themselves and polish their images. For example, chemical giant BASF markets itself to the general public as a company whose "invisible contributions" result in "visible success." Its ads show how BASF works behind the scenes with its industrial customers to bring the world visible success in everything from water treatment and agricultural productivity to outdoor clothing, sun protection, and sports and leisure equipment. Similarly, not-for-profit organizations, such as churches, colleges, charities, museums, and performing arts groups, market their organizations in order to raise funds and attract members or patrons.

■ Organizational marketing: Chemical giant BASF markets itself as a company whose "invisible contributions" result in "visible success"—here textile coatings for outdoor clothing that will withstand the toughest conditions.

People can also be thought of as products. *Person marketing* consists of activities undertaken to create, maintain, or change attitudes or behavior toward particular people. People ranging from presidents, entertainers, and sports figures to professionals such as doctors, lawyers, and architects use person marketing to build their reputations. And businesses, charities, and other organizations use well-known personalities to help sell their products or causes. For example, more than a dozen big-name companies—including Nike, Buick, Accenture, EA Sports, American Express, Gillette, and Apple—combine to pay more than $87 million a year to link themselves with golf superstar Tiger Woods.[3]

The skillful use of marketing can turn a person's name into a powerhouse brand. Carefully managed and well-known names such as Michael Jordan, Oprah Winfrey, Martha Stewart, and businessman Donald Trump now adorn everything from sports apparel, housewares, and magazines to book clubs and casinos. Trump, who describes himself as "the hottest brand on the planet," has skillfully made his life a nonstop media event. Says a friend, "He's a skillful marketer, and what he markets is his name."[4]

Such well-known, well-marketed names hold substantial branding power. Consider Rachael Ray:

> Not unlike Oprah or Martha Stewart, Rachael Ray has become a one-woman marketing phenomenon: In less than a decade, she's zipped from nobody to pop-culture icon. Beginning with her 30-Minute Meals cookbooks, followed later by a Food Network TV show, Ray won her way into the hearts of America by demystifying cooking and dishing out a ton of energy. Thanks to her perky personality, which has a dollop of upstate New York twang and a sprinkling of catch phrases such as "yum-o" and "sammies," Rachael Ray has moved far beyond quick meals. Bearing her name are more than a dozen best-selling cookbooks, a monthly lifestyle magazine, two Food Network shows, a syndicated daytime talk show, and assorted licensing deals that have stamped her name on kitchen essentials from knives to her own "E.V.O.O." (extra virgin olive oil for those not familiar with Rayisms). There are even Ray-branded musical CDs and cellular ring tones. Ultimately, Ray's brand power derives from all that she has come to represent. Her brands "begin with food and move briskly on to the emotional, social, and cultural benefits that food gives us." Ray's persona—and hence her brand—is a "celebration of why food matters."[5]

Place marketing involves activities undertaken to create, maintain, or change attitudes or behavior toward particular places. Cities, states, regions, and even entire nations compete to attract tourists, new residents, conventions, and company offices and factories. Texas advertises "It's like a whole other country" and California urges you to "Find yourself here." The Chinese National Tourist Office (CNTO) invites travelers from around the world to "Discover China now!" The CNTO has 15 overseas tourist offices, including two in the United States. Tourism in China has been booming as more and more travelers discover the treasures of China's ancient civilization alongside the towering skylines of modern cities such as Shanghai and Beijing (site of the 2008 Summer Olympics). At its Web site, the CNTO offers information about the country and its attractions, travel tips, lists of tour operators, and much more information that makes it easier to say yes to China travel.[6]

Ideas can also be marketed. In one sense, all marketing is the marketing of an idea, whether it is the general idea of brushing your teeth or the specific idea that Crest toothpastes "create smiles every day." Here, however, we narrow our focus to the marketing of *social ideas*. This area has been called **social marketing**, defined by the Social Marketing Institute as the use of commercial marketing concepts and tools in programs designed to influence individuals' behavior to improve their well-being and that of society.[7]

Social marketing
The use of commercial marketing concepts and tools in programs designed to influence individuals' behavior to improve their well-being and that of society.

Social marketing programs include public health campaigns to reduce smoking, alcoholism, drug abuse, and obesity. Other social marketing efforts include environmental campaigns to promote wilderness protection, clean air, and conservation. Still others address issues such as family planning, human rights, and racial equality. The Ad Council of America has developed dozens of social advertising campaigns, involving issues ranging from preventive health, education, and personal safety to environmental preservation.

But social marketing involves much more than just advertising—the Social Marketing Institute (SMI) encourages the use of a broad range of marketing tools. "Social marketing goes well beyond the promotional '*P*' of the marketing mix to include every other element to achieve its social change objectives," says the SMI's executive director.[8]

Product and Service Decisions

Marketers make product and service decisions at three levels: individual product decisions, product line decisions, and product mix decisions. We discuss each in turn.

Individual Product and Service Decisions

Figure 7.2 shows the important decisions in the development and marketing of individual products and services. We will focus on decisions about *product attributes, branding, packaging, labeling,* and *product support services.*

Product and Service Attributes Developing a product or service involves defining the benefits that it will offer. These benefits are communicated and delivered by product attributes such as *quality, features,* and *style and design.*

Product quality

The characteristics of a product or service that bear on its ability to satisfy stated or implied customer needs.

Product Quality **Product quality** is one of the marketer's major positioning tools. Quality has a direct impact on product or service performance; thus, it is closely linked to customer value and satisfaction. In the narrowest sense, quality can be defined as "freedom from defects." But most customer-centered companies go beyond this narrow definition. Instead, they define quality in terms of creating customer value and satisfaction. The American Society for Quality defines quality as the characteristics of a product or service that bear on its ability to satisfy stated or implied customer needs. Similarly, Siemens defines quality this way: "Quality is when our customers come back and our products don't."[9]

Total quality management (TQM) is an approach in which all the company's people are involved in constantly improving the quality of products, services, and business processes. For most top companies, customer-driven quality has become a way of doing business. Today, companies are taking a "return on quality" approach, viewing quality as an investment and holding quality efforts accountable for bottom-line results.

Product quality has two dimensions—level and consistency. In developing a product, the marketer must first choose a *quality level* that will support the product's positioning. Here, product quality means *performance quality*—the ability of a product to perform its functions. For example, a Rolls-Royce provides higher performance quality than a Chevrolet: It has a smoother ride, provides more "creature comforts," and lasts longer. Companies rarely try to offer the highest possible performance quality level—few customers want or can afford the high levels of quality offered in products such as a Rolls-Royce automobile, a Viking range, or a Rolex watch. Instead, companies choose a quality level that matches target market needs and the quality levels of competing products.

Beyond quality level, high quality also can mean high levels of quality consistency. Here, product quality means *conformance quality*—freedom from defects and *consistency* in delivering a targeted level of performance. All companies should strive for high levels of conformance quality. In this sense, a Chevrolet can have just as much quality as a Rolls-Royce. Although a Chevy doesn't perform at the same level as a Rolls-Royce, it can as consistently deliver the quality that customers pay for and expect.

Product Features A product can be offered with varying features. A stripped-down model, one without any extras, is the starting point. The company can create higher-level models by adding more features. Features are a competitive tool for differentiating the

FIGURE 7.2 Individual Product Decisions

company's product from competitors' products. Being the first producer to introduce a valued new feature is one of the most effective ways to compete.

How can a company identify new features and decide which ones to add to its product? The company should periodically survey buyers who have used the product and ask these questions: How do you like the product? Which specific features of the product do you like most? Which features could we add to improve the product? The answers provide the company with a rich list of feature ideas. The company can then assess each feature's *value* to customers versus its *cost* to the company. Features that customers value highly in relation to costs should be added.

Product Style and Design   Another way to add customer value is through distinctive *product style and design*. Design is a larger concept than style. *Style* simply describes the appearance of a product. Styles can be eye-catching or yawn producing. A sensational style may grab attention and produce pleasing aesthetics, but it does not necessarily make the product *perform* better. Unlike style, *design* is more than skin deep—it goes to the very heart of a product. Good design contributes to a product's usefulness as well as to its looks.

Design begins with a deep understanding of customer needs. More than simply creating product or service attributes, it involves shaping the customer's product-use experience. Consider OXO's outstanding design philosophy and process:[10]

OXO's uniquely designed kitchen and gardening gadgets look pretty cool. But to OXO, good design means a lot more than good looks. It means that OXO tools work—*really* work—for anyone and everyone. For OXO, design means a salad spinner that can be used with one hand; tools with pressure-absorbing, nonslip handles that make them more efficient; or a watering can with a spout that rotates back toward the body, allowing for easier filling and storing. Ever since it came out with its supereffective Good Grips vegetable peeler in 1990, OXO has been known for its clever designs that make everyday living easier.

Much of OXO's design inspiration comes directly from users. "We . . . do a lot of talking to consumers and chefs . . . we do a lot of surveys, we talk to people we know . . . all over the country," says an OXO executive. OXO use-tests its product ideas exhaustively—in the OXO kitchen, in employees' homes, at a cooking school, or by just corralling casual shoppers outside its location near Manhattan's Chelsea Market. For example, after watching people struggle with the traditional Pyrex measuring cup, OXO discovered a critical flaw: You can't tell how full it is without lifting it up to eye level. The resulting OXO measuring cups have markings down the *inside* that can be read from above, big enough to read without glasses.

Interestingly, although OXO offers more than 500 really well-designed products, it doesn't actually do its own designs. Instead, OXOnians focus on the desired end-user experience, and then work with design firms to translate their pie-cutter-in-the-sky notions into eminently usable gadgets.

■ Product design: OXO focuses on the desired end-user experience and then translates its pie-cutter-in-the-sky notions into eminently usable gadgets.

Thus, product designers should think less about product attributes and technical specifications and more about how customers will use and benefit from the product.

Brand
A name, term, sign, symbol, or design or a combination of these that identifies the products or services of one seller or group of sellers and differentiates them from those of competitors.

Branding Perhaps the most distinctive skill of professional marketers is their ability to build and manage brands. A **brand** is a name, term, sign, symbol, or design, or a combination of these, that identifies the maker or seller of a product or service. Consumers view a brand as an important part of a product and branding can add value to a product. For example, most consumers would perceive a bottle of White Linen perfume as a high-quality, expensive product. But the same perfume in an unmarked bottle would likely be viewed as lower in quality, even if the fragrance was identical.

Branding has become so strong that today hardly anything goes unbranded. Salt is packaged in branded containers, common nuts and bolts are packaged with a distributor's label, and automobile parts—spark plugs, tires, filters—bear brand names that differ from those of the automakers. Even fruits, vegetables, dairy products, and poultry are branded—Sunkist oranges, Dole Classic Iceberg Salads, Horizon Organic milk, and Perdue chickens.

Branding helps buyers in many ways. Brand names help consumers identify products that might benefit them. Brands also say something about product quality and consistency—buyers who always buy the same brand know that they will get the same features, benefits, and quality each time they buy. Branding also gives the seller several advantages. The brand name becomes the basis on which a whole story can be built about a product's special qualities. The seller's brand name and trademark provide legal protection for unique product features that otherwise might be copied by competitors. And branding helps the seller to segment markets. For example, Toyota Motor Corporation can offer the major Lexus, Toyota, and Scion brands, each with numerous sub-brands—such as Camry, Prius, Matrix, Yaris, Tundra, Land Cruiser, and others—not just one general product for all consumers.

Building and managing brands are perhaps the marketer's most important tasks. We will discuss branding strategy in more detail later in the chapter.

Packaging
The activities of designing and producing the container or wrapper for a product.

Packaging **Packaging** involves designing and producing the container or wrapper for a product. Traditionally, the primary function of the package was to hold and protect the product. In recent times, however, numerous factors have made packaging an important marketing tool as well. Increased competition and clutter on retail store shelves means that packages must now perform many sales tasks—from attracting attention, to describing the product, to making the sale.

Companies are realizing the power of good packaging to create immediate consumer recognition of a brand. For example, an average supermarket stocks 15,000 items; the average Wal-Mart supercenter carries 142,000 items. The typical shopper passes by some 300 items per minute, and more than 70 percent of all purchase decisions are made in stores. In this highly competitive environment, the package may be the seller's last and best chance to influence buyers. Thus, for many companies, the package itself has become an important promotional medium.[11]

Poorly designed packages can cause headaches for consumers and lost sales for the company. *Consumer Reports* even has an award for the most difficult to open packages, fittingly named the "Oyster Awards" (as in trying to pry open a tight-jawed oyster). One recent winner was packaging for the Bratz Sisterz dolls, which contained some 50 packaging restraints, from rubber bands to molded plastic covers. It took one text subject, a seven-year-old girl, eight minutes to free the dolls. Says one reporter, after wrestling with the packaging, the child was "noticeably agitated and breathing heavily," and the dolls "looked as if they'd just returned from a rough night on the town."[12]

By contrast, innovative packaging can give a company an advantage over competitors and boost sales. Sometimes even seemingly small packaging improvements can make a big difference. For example, Heinz revolutionized the 170-year-old condiments industry by inverting the good old ketchup bottle, letting customers quickly squeeze out even the last bit of ketchup. In the year following the new bottle's debut, Heinz ketchup sales grew at three times the industry rate. It started a packaging trend that quickly spread to other categories. "Companies make a lot of money by making things less annoying," says a packaging expert.[13]

In recent years, product safety has also become a major packaging concern. We have all learned to deal with hard-to-open "childproof" packaging. And after the rash of product tampering scares during the 1980s, most drug producers and food makers now put their products in tamper-resistant packages. In making packaging decisions, the company also must heed growing environmental concerns. Fortunately, many companies have gone "green" by reducing their packaging and using environmentally responsible packaging materials.

Labeling Labels range from simple tags attached to products to complex graphics that are part of the package. They perform several functions. At the very least, the label *identifies* the product or brand, such as the name Sunkist stamped on oranges. The label might also *describe* several things about the product—who made it, where it was made, when it was made, its contents, how it is to be used, and how to use it safely. Finally, the label might help to *promote* the brand, support its positioning, and connect with customers. For many companies, labels have become an important element in broader marketing campaigns.

For example, Pepsi recently recrafted the graphics on its soft drink cans as part of a broader effort to give the brand more meaning and social relevance to its youth audience.[14]

In its quest for a refreshing, more relevant new look, Pepsi created no less than 35 new domestic and international can designs. The first wave of eight new U.S. designs—featuring such exotic names as "Emoticons" and "Groovy"—was timed to coincide with the start of Pepsi's broader "More Happy" ad campaign. Additional new cans were then rolled out about every three weeks throughout 2007. Beyond eye-catching artwork, each Pepsi design carried a unique Web address that linked customers to a microsite created specifically for that design. The first microsites, aptly named "This Is the Beginning," allowed users from around the world to gather in real time to collectively design the next *Pepsi* billboard in Times Square. Additional experiences, such as the music-oriented "Move the Crowd," went live every few weeks in tandem with the can releases, all of which were cataloged at the "*Pepsi* Gallery" Web site. "What we did with the [can designs] and sites is create custom experiences that users discover on their own," said a Pepsi marketing executive. "Every time a consumer buys a Pepsi, they're getting a new experience."

GROOVY

■ Labeling: Pepsi recently recrafted its soft drink cans as part of a broader effort to give the brand more meaning and social relevance to its youth audience.

Along with the positives, labeling also raises concerns. There has been a long history of legal concerns about packaging and labels. The Federal Trade Commission Act of 1914 held that false, misleading, or deceptive labels or packages constitute unfair competition. Labels can mislead customers, fail to describe important ingredients, or fail to include needed safety warnings. As a result, several federal and state laws regulate labeling. The most prominent is the Fair Packaging and Labeling Act of 1966, which set mandatory labeling requirements, encouraged voluntary industry packaging standards, and allowed federal agencies to set packaging regulations in specific industries.

Labeling has been affected in recent times by *unit pricing* (stating the price per unit of standard measure), *open dating* (stating the expected shelf life of the product), and *nutritional labeling* (stating the nutritional values in the product). The Nutritional Labeling and Educational Act of 1990 requires sellers to provide detailed nutritional information on food products, and recent sweeping actions by the Food and Drug Administration regulate the use of health-related terms such as *low fat, light,* and *high fiber.* Sellers must ensure that their labels contain all the required information.

Product Support Services Customer service is another element of product strategy. A company's offer usually includes some support services, which can be a minor or a major part of the total offering. Later in the chapter, we will discuss services as products in themselves. Here, we discuss services that augment actual products.

The first step is to survey customers periodically to assess the value of current services and to obtain ideas for new ones. For example, Cadillac holds regular focus group interviews with owners and carefully watches complaints that come into its dealerships. From this careful monitoring, Cadillac has learned that buyers are very upset by repairs that are not done correctly the first time. GM research indicates that customers who experience good service are five times more likely to repurchase the same brand than those who have had a bad service experience.

Once the company has assessed the quality of various support services to customers, it can take steps to fix problems and add new services that will both delight customers and yield profits to the company. For instance, Cadillac tracks repair data to find out if certain dealerships or even individual technicians are frequently making the same repair mistakes. Then, to promote good first-time repairs, it informs dealers and rewards those that have high customer-service ratings. And to keep customers happier after the sale, Cadillac also offers as a standard feature an early-warning system for mechanical problems, built into the onboard OnStar system.[15]

Many companies are now using a sophisticated mix of phone, e-mail, fax, Internet, and interactive voice and data technologies to provide support services that were not possible before. Consider the following example:

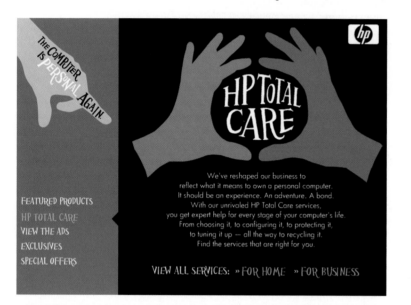

Some online merchants are watching where you surf, then opening a chat window on your screen to ask—just as they would in the store—if you have questions about the goods they see you eyeing. For example, Hewlett-Packard sends pop-up chat boxes to visitors who are shopping on HP.com's pages for digital-photography products. If a shopper loiters a few minutes over some gear, up pops a photo of an attractive woman with the words, "Hello, need information? An HP live chat representative is standing by to assist you." Click on "Go" and type a question, and a live sales agent responds immediately. Since launching its pop-up chat feature, HP has seen a 65 percent surge in online questions. More broadly, HP offers a complete set of sales and after-sale services. It promises "HP Total Care—expert help for every stage of your computer's life. From choosing it, to configuring it, to protecting it, to tuning it up—all the way to recycling it."[16]

■ Product support services: HP promises "HP Total Care—expert help for every stage of your computer's life. From choosing it, to configuring it, to protecting it, to tuning it up—all the way to recycling it."

Product Line Decisions

Product line

A group of products that are closely related because they function in a similar manner, are sold to the same customer groups, are marketed through the same types of outlets, or fall within given price ranges.

Beyond decisions about individual products and services, product strategy also calls for building a product line. A **product line** is a group of products that are closely related because they function in a similar manner, are sold to the same customer groups, are marketed through the same types of outlets, or fall within given price ranges. For example, Nike produces several lines of athletic shoes and apparel and Charles Schwab produces several lines of financial services.

The major product line decision involves *product line length*—the number of items in the product line. The line is too short if the manager can increase profits by adding items; the line is too long if the manager can increase profits by dropping items. Managers need to analyze their product lines periodically to assess each product item's sales and profits and to understand how each item contributes to the line's overall performance.

Product line length is influenced by company objectives and resources. For example, one objective might be to allow for up-selling. Thus BMW wants to move customers up from its 3-series models to 5- and 7-series models. Another objective might be to allow cross-selling: Hewlett-Packard sells printers as well as cartridges. Still another objective might be to protect against economic swings: Gap runs several clothing-store chains (Gap, Old Navy, and Banana Republic) covering different price points.

A company can expand its product line in two ways: by *line filling* or by *line stretching*. *Product line filling* involves adding more items within the present range of the line. There are several reasons for product line filling: reaching for extra profits, satisfying dealers, using excess capacity, being the leading full-line company, and plugging holes to keep out competitors. However, line filling is overdone if it results in cannibalization and customer confusion. The company should ensure that new items are noticeably different from existing ones.

Product line stretching occurs when a company lengthens its product line beyond its current range. The company can stretch its line downward, upward, or both ways. Companies located at the upper end of the market can stretch their lines *downward*. A company may stretch downward to plug a market hole that otherwise would attract a new competitor or to respond to a competitor's attack on the upper end. Or it may add low-end products because it finds faster growth taking place in the low-end segments. Honda stretched downward for all of these reasons by adding its thrifty little Honda Fit to its line. The Fit, economical to drive and priced in the $12,000 to $13,000 range, met increasing consumer demands for more frugal cars and preempted competitors in the new-generation minicar segment.

Companies can also stretch their product lines *upward*. Sometimes, companies stretch upward in order to add prestige to their current products. Or they may be attracted by a faster growth rate or higher margins at the higher end. For example, some years ago, each of the leading Japanese auto companies introduced an upmarket automobile: Honda launched Acura; Toyota launched Lexus; and Nissan launched Infinity. They used entirely new names rather than their own names.

Companies in the middle range of the market may decide to stretch their lines in *both directions*. Marriott did this with its hotel product line. Along with regular Marriott hotels, it added eight new branded hotel lines to serve both the upper and lower ends of the market. For example, Renaissance Hotels & Resorts aims to attract and please top executives; Fairfield Inn by Marriott, vacationers and business travelers on a tight travel budget; and Courtyard by Marriott, salespeople and other "road warriors."[17] The major risk with this strategy is that some travelers will trade down after finding that the lower-price hotels in the Marriott chain give them pretty much everything they want. However, Marriott would rather capture its customers who move downward than lose them to competitors.

Product Mix Decisions

An organization with several product lines has a product mix. A **product mix** (or **product portfolio**) consists of all the product lines and items that a particular seller offers for sale. Some companies manage very complex product portfolios. For example, Sony's diverse portfolio consists of four major product businesses: Sony Electronics, Sony Computer Entertainment (games), Sony Pictures Entertainment (movies, TV shows, music, DVDs), and Sony Financial Services (life insurance, banking, and other offerings).

Each major Sony business consists of several product lines. For example, Sony Electronics includes cameras and camcorders, computers, TV and home entertainment

Product mix (or **product portfolio**) The set of all product lines and items that a particular seller offers for sale.

■ Product line stretching: Marriott offers a full line of hotel brands targeting different segments.

products, mobile electronics, and others. In turn, each of these lines contains many individual items. Sony's TV and home entertainment line includes TVs, DVD players, home audio components, digital home products, and more. Altogether, Sony's product mix includes a diverse collection of hundreds and hundreds of products.

A company's product mix has four important dimensions: width, length, depth, and consistency. Product mix *width* refers to the number of different product lines the company carries. Sony markets a wide range of consumer and industrial products around the world, from TVs and PlayStation consoles to semiconductors. Product mix *length* refers to the total number of items the company carries within its product lines. Sony typically carries many products within each line. The camera and camcorder line, for instance, includes digital cameras, camcorders, photo printers, memory media, and tons of accessories.

Product mix *depth* refers to the number of versions offered of each product in the line. Sony has a very deep product mix. For example, it makes and markets about any kind of TV you'd ever want to buy—tube, flat panel, rear projection, front projection, HD, or low resolution—each in almost any imaginable size. Finally, the *consistency* of the product mix refers to how closely related the various product lines are in end use, production requirements, distribution channels, or some other way. Within each major business, Sony's product lines are fairly consistent in that they perform similar functions for buyers and go through the same distribution channels. Companywide, however, Sony markets a very diverse mix of products. Managing such a broad and diverse product portfolio requires much skill.

These product mix dimensions provide the handles for defining the company's product strategy. The company can increase its business in four ways. It can add new product lines, widening its product mix. In this way, its new lines build on the company's reputation in its other lines. The company can lengthen its existing product lines to become a more full-line company. Or it can add more versions of each product and thus deepen its product mix. Finally, the company can pursue more product line consistency—or less—depending on whether it wants to have a strong reputation in a single field or in several fields.

Linking the Concepts

Slow down for a minute. To get a better sense of how large and complex a company's product offering can become, investigate Procter & Gamble's product mix.

- Using P&G's Web site (www.pg.com), its annual report, or other sources, develop a list of all the company's product lines and individual products. What surprises you about this list of products?
- Is P&G's product mix consistent? What overall strategy or logic appears to have guided the development of this product mix?

Branding Strategy: Building Strong Brands

Some analysts see brands as *the* major enduring asset of a company, outlasting the company's specific products and facilities. A former CEO of McDonald's once declared, "If every asset we own, every building, and every piece of equipment were destroyed in a terrible natural disaster, we would be able to borrow all the money to replace it very quickly because of the value of our brand. . . . The brand is more valuable than the totality of all these assets."[18]

Thus, brands are powerful assets that must be carefully developed and managed. In this section, we examine the key strategies for building and managing brands.

Brand Equity

Brands are more than just names and symbols. They are a key element in the company's relationships with consumers. Brands represent consumers' perceptions and feelings about a product and its performance—everything that the product or service *means* to consumers. In the final analysis, brands exist in the heads of consumers. As one well-respected marketer once said, "Products are created in the factory, but brands are created in the mind."[19]

A powerful brand has high *brand equity*. **Brand equity** is the positive differential effect that knowing the brand name has on customer response to the product or service. It's a measure of the brand's ability to capture consumer preference and loyalty. Brands vary in the amount of power and value they hold in the marketplace. Some brands—such as Coca-Cola, Nike, Disney, GE, McDonald's, Harley-Davidson, and others—become larger-than-life icons that maintain their power in the market for years, even generations. Other brands create fresh consumer excitement and loyalty, brands such as Google, YouTube, Apple, eBay, and Wikipedia. These brands win in the marketplace not simply because they deliver unique benefits or reliable service. Rather, they succeed because they forge deep connections with customers.

Ad agency Young & Rubicam's Brand Asset Valuator measures brand strength along four consumer perception dimensions: *differentiation* (what makes the brand stand out), *relevance* (how consumers feel it meets their needs), *knowledge* (how much consumers know about the brand), and *esteem* (how highly consumers regard and respect the brand). Brands with strong brand equity rate high on all of these dimensions. A brand must be distinct, or consumers will have no reason to choose it over other brands. But the fact that a brand is highly differentiated doesn't necessarily mean that consumers will buy it. The brand must stand out in ways that are relevant to consumers' needs. But even a differentiated, relevant brand is far from a shoe-in. Before consumers will respond to the brand, they must first know about and understand it. And that familiarity must lead to a strong, positive consumer-brand connection (see Marketing at Work 7.1).[20]

Consumers sometimes bond *very* closely with specific brands. Consider the feelings of one Michigan couple about Black & Decker's DeWalt power tool brand:[21]

> **Brand equity**
> The positive differential effect that knowing the brand name has on customer response to the product or service.

Rick and Rose Whitaker weren't comfortable with the idea of a white-gown-and-tux wedding. They kept coming back to the fact that Rick, a carpenter, had a passion for power tools. Specifically, DeWalt power tools. So at the July nuptials, 50-plus guests gathered in Rick's backyard wearing DeWalt's trademark yellow-and-black T-shirts. The Michigan couple—both are now 44—dressed in shirts emblazoned with an image of DeWalt-sponsored NASCAR driver Matt Kenseth. They made their way to a wooden chapel that they had built with their DeWalt gear. There they exchanged power tools, cutting the cake with a power saw.

A brand with high brand equity is a very valuable asset. *Brand valuation* is the process of estimating the total financial value of a brand. Measuring such value is difficult. However, according to one estimate, the brand value of Coca-Cola is $67 billion, Microsoft is $57 billion, and IBM is $56 billion. Other brands rating among the world's most valuable include GE, Nokia, Toyota, McDonald's, Disney, and Mercedes-Benz. Smaller brands with the fastest-growing value include Google, Starbucks, and eBay.[22]

High brand equity provides a company with many competitive advantages. A powerful brand enjoys a high level of consumer brand awareness and loyalty. Because consumers expect stores to carry the brand, the company has more leverage in bargaining with resellers. Because the brand name carries high credibility, the company can more easily launch line and brand extensions. A powerful brand offers the company some defense against fierce price competition.

■ Consumers sometimes bond very closely with specific brands. Jokes the bride: "He loves DeWalt nearly as much as he loves me."

7.1 MARKETING AT WORK

Breakaway Brands: Connecting with Customers

Man, it's been a tough week. My house burned down and my dog ran off. But I've got some good news: I just saved a bunch of money on my car insurance. (Pause for laughter.) If you got that joke, then you're one of the millions of people who have enjoyed—or at least remembered—one-liners from ads run by the auto insurer GEICO. Sure, GEICO hopes you'll recall its value proposition (that 15 minutes could save you 15 percent or more on car insurance). But its clever ads—from a talking gecko to offended cavemen to Little Richard acting out a customer testimonial—also use humor to reinforce its image as a friendly ally of drivers and insurance shoppers everywhere. And that is brand magic.

Ideas about achieving brand strength, that elusive blend of awareness and trust, have changed in the past decade. "It's no longer, 'What can we blast out there about ourselves?'" says one branding expert. "Brand theory now asks, 'How can we connect with the community in a really meaningful way?'" It's a big question. Armed with information about price and quality, today's consumer is a tough challenge. But, says the expert, "if you're willing to talk directly and deeply to your audience, you can become a strong brand without a lot of fanfare."

Each year, brand consultancy Landor Associates, an arm of ad agency Young & Rubicam, conducts a "Breakaway Brands" survey in which it identifies the ten brands with the greatest percentage gains in brand health and business value as a result of superb brand strategy and execution over a three-year period. The survey taps Young & Rubicam's Brand Asset Valuator, a database of responses from 9,000 consumers evaluating 2,500 brands measured across 56 metrics. Landor looks at brand factors such as differentiation, relevance, esteem, and knowledge. At the same time, another consultancy, BrandEconomics, assesses the financial performance of the brand ("Economic Value Added"). Combined, the Brand Asset Valuator and Economic Value Added models provide a brand valuation based on both consumer and financial measures.

The 2006 Breakaway Brands list includes a strange agglomeration, from hot technology brands such as iPod and eBay to seemingly stodgy old consumer goods such as French's and Robitussin to reenergized icons such as Converse.

Top Ten Breakaway Brands

1. iPod	6. Kohl's
2. Viking	7. French's
3. Converse	8. GEICO
4. Robitussin	9. Dove
5. Best Buy	10. eBay

Missing are some brand titans such as Coca-Cola (big but not growing very fast) and fresh-faced young brands such as MySpace (the consumer panel consists of adults 18 and older, so the youth-centric sensation doesn't show up yet). But Landor found that each brand that did make the list embraced one or more of three themes. "Today it's all about *trust, community,* and creating a *dialogue* with your customer that shares real knowledge," says Landor's chief marketing officer. That is, all of the brands really connect with customers.

Consider Robitussin, once a mom's trusted potion of choice for sick kids everywhere. Its growth stems from a fairly dramatic package redesign last year that added a symptom checklist on each box to signal which formula was right for which cold-related maladies. "It's very different from how medicine has been traditionally sold, using doctor portrayals on television," says the Landor marketer. "They spoke directly to the consumer."

Among brands that foster community, the iPod is an obvious winner by virtue of its ability to create an online music ecosystem virtually overnight. "But one of the little-mentioned elements of the iPod's success has been the experience provided for the customer at the Apple stores," says another marketer. Set free from packaging and locked cases, iPod stuff is always available for experimentation and play.

Other brands are more surprising. Viking, the manufacturer of upscale kitchen appliances, has transformed itself into a lifestyle brand by opening 14 cooking schools. Most of the 67,000 students who sign up each year are Gen Xers, younger than Viking's typical moneyed cus-

Above all, however, a powerful brand forms the basis for building strong and profitable customer relationships. The fundamental asset underlying brand equity is *customer equity*—the value of the customer relationships that the brand creates. A powerful brand is important, but what it really represents is a profitable set of loyal customers. The proper focus of marketing is building customer equity, with brand management serving as a major marketing tool. Companies need to think of themselves not as portfolios of products, but as portfolios of customers."[23]

Building Strong Brands

Branding poses challenging decisions to the marketer. Figure 7.3 shows that the major brand strategy decisions involve brand positioning, brand name selection, brand sponsorship, and brand development.

Brand Positioning Marketers need to position their brands clearly in target customers' minds. They can position brands at any of three levels.[24] At the lowest level, they can position the brand on *product attributes*. Thus, The Body Shop marketers can talk about their products' natural, environmentally friendly ingredients, unique scents, and special textures.

tomer. It's a chance to play with the product, yes, but the classes also reinforce the simple pleasures of sharing meals with loved ones.

Perhaps no brand on the list makes deeper consumer connections than Converse, purchased out of bankruptcy in 2001 by sports apparel powerhouse Nike. Whereas parent Nike is strongest on the basketball court, Converse connects best off the court. It has rebuilt its iconic Chuck Taylor All Star canvas shoe into a fashion-oriented but still authentic alternative to today's glitzy performance brands. Converse customers are just plain crazy about their Chucks. The brand's "Get Chucked" ad campaign—with its gritty, irreverent black and white photos and tag lines such as "no soul to sell"—makes a special connection with young consumers eager to show their disregard for mainstream trends and high-priced performance shoes.

Hardcore Converse buffs can spend hours at the ChucksConnection.com Web site, exploring the classic American brand in depth as seen in films, photographs, and television shows or as described in reviews, articles, and stories about why people like wearing Chucks. They can even share photos of themselves in their Chucks, submit short videos defining what Converse means to them, or design their own pairs of personalized shoes. The Converse brand is now on fire. Although still tiny by Nike standards, its market share has tripled over the past five years. When asked about the brand's success, Converse's chief marketer explains, "We don't own Converse anymore. The brand and its meaning are now owned by the consumer."

GEICO ad fans may have noticed a less-revolutionary change in the popular gecko. The mildly skittish, British-accented voice was replaced with that of a real, grittier-sounding Londoner. His face now looks more human too. "We wanted him to seem cooler, like a guy you'd want to grab a pint with," laughs a creative director at the ad agency that created the GEICO campaign. That's what it's all about—brands connecting with customers.

■ Breakaway brands connect meaningfully with customers. Viking's cooking schools create a sense of community around the simple pleasures of sharing meals with loved ones.

Sources: Adapted from Ellen McGirt, "Breakaway Brands," *Fortune,* September 18, 2006, p. 27; with information from "Fortune Magazine Publishes Landor Associates' Second Breakaway Brands Study," September 12, 2006, accessed at www.landor.com; Stephanie Kang, "Nike Takes Chuck Taylors from Antifashion to Fashionista, *Wall Street Journal,* June 23, 2006, p. B.1; and http://chucksconnection.com/, accessed September 2007.

However, attributes are the least desirable level for brand positioning. Competitors can easily copy attributes. More important, customers are not interested in attributes as such; they are interested in what the attributes will do for them.

A brand can be better positioned by associating its name with a desirable *benefit*. Thus, The Body Shop can go beyond product ingredients and talk about the resulting beauty benefits, such as clearer skin from its Tea Tree Oil Facial Wash and sun-kissed cheeks from its Bronzing Powder. Some successful brands positioned on benefits are Volvo (safety), FedEx (guaranteed on-time delivery), Nike (performance), and Lexus (quality).

FIGURE 7.3 Major Brand Strategy Decisions

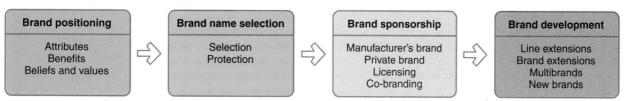

Brand positioning	Brand name selection	Brand sponsorship	Brand development
Attributes Benefits Beliefs and values	Selection Protection	Manufacturer's brand Private brand Licensing Co-branding	Line extensions Brand extensions Multibrands New brands

GODIVA.COM
© 2007 Godiva Brands, Inc. All Rights Reserved. Godiva is a trademark owned by Godiva Brands, Inc.

Flaunt your Passion

■ Brand positioning: The strongest brands go beyond attribute or benefit positioning. Godiva engages customers on a deeper level, touching universal emotions.

The strongest brands go beyond attribute or benefit positioning. They are positioned on strong *beliefs and values*. These brands pack an emotional wallop. Thus, The Body Shop can talk not just about environmentally friendly ingredients and skin-care benefits, but about how purchasing these products empowers its socially conscious customer to "make up your mind, not just your face."[25] Successful brands engage customers on a deep, emotional level. Brands such as Godiva, Starbucks, Apple, and Victoria's Secret rely less on a product's tangible attributes and more on creating surprise, passion, and excitement surrounding a brand.

When positioning a brand, the marketer should establish a mission for the brand and a vision of what the brand must be and do. A brand is the company's promise to deliver a specific set of features, benefits, services, and experiences consistently to the buyers. The brand promise must be simple and honest. Motel 6, for example, offers clean rooms, low prices, and good service but does not promise expensive furniture or large bathrooms. In contrast, Ritz-Carlton offers luxurious rooms and a truly memorable experience but does not promise low prices.

Brand Name Selection A good name can add greatly to a product's success. However, finding the best brand name is a difficult task. It begins with a careful review of the product and its benefits, the target market, and proposed marketing strategies. After that, naming a brand becomes part science, part art, and a measure of instinct.

Desirable qualities for a brand name include the following: (1) It should suggest something about the product's benefits and qualities. Examples: Beautyrest, Die Hard, Curves (women's fitness centers). (2) It should be easy to pronounce, recognize, and remember: Tide, Silk, Palm, JetBlue. (3) The brand name should be distinctive: Lexus, Zappos. (4) It should be extendable: Amazon.com began as an online bookseller but chose a name that would allow expansion into other categories. (5) The name should translate easily into foreign languages. Before changing its name to Exxon, Standard Oil of New Jersey rejected the name Enco, which it learned meant a stalled engine when pronounced in Japanese. (6) It should be capable of registration and legal protection. A brand name cannot be registered if it infringes on existing brand names.

Choosing a new brand name is hard work. After a decade of choosing quirky names (Yahoo!, Google) or trademark-proof made-up names (Novartis, Aventis, Lycos), today's style is to build brands around names that have real meaning. For example, names like Silk (soy milk), Method (home products), Smartwater (beverages), and Blackboard (school software) are simple and make intuitive sense. But with trademark applications soaring, *available* new names can be hard to find. Try it yourself. Pick a product and see if you can come up with a better name for it. How about Moonshot? Tickle? Vanilla? Treehugger? Simplicity? Google them and you'll find that they're already taken.

Once chosen, the brand name must be protected. Many firms try to build a brand name that will eventually become identified with the product category. Brand names such as Kleenex, Levi's, Jell-O, BAND-AID, Scotch Tape, Formica, and Ziploc have succeeded in this way. However, their very success may threaten the company's rights to the name. Many originally protected brand names—such as cellophane, aspirin, nylon, kerosene, linoleum, yo-yo, trampoline, escalator, thermos, and shredded wheat—are now generic names that any seller can use. To protect their brands, marketers present them carefully using the word "brand" and the registered trademark symbol, as in "BAND-AID® Brand Adhesive Bandages."

Brand Sponsorship A manufacturer has four sponsorship options. The product may be launched as a *manufacturer's brand* (or national brand), as when Sony and Kellogg sell their output under their own manufacturer's brand names. Or the manufacturer may sell to resellers who give it a *private brand* (also called a *store brand* or *distributor brand*). Although most manufacturers create their own brand names, others market *licensed brands*. Finally, two companies can join forces and *co-brand* a product.

National Brands Versus Store Brands   National brands (or manufacturers' brands) have long dominated the retail scene. In recent times, however, an increasing number of retailers and wholesalers have created their own **store brands** (or **private brands**). Store brand sales are soaring. In fact, they are growing much faster than national brands. In all, private brands now capture more than 20 percent of all North American consumer packaged-goods sales and will capture an estimated 27 percent by 2010. Private-label apparel, such as Gap, The Limited, Arizona Jeans (JC Penney), and Liz Lange (Target), captures a 45 percent share of all U.S. apparel sales.[26]

Once known as "generic" or "no-name" brands, today's store brands are a far cry from the early no-frills generics. Store brands now offer much greater selection and higher quality. Rather than simply creating low-end generic brands that offer a low-price alternative to national brands, retailers are now moving toward higher-end private brands that boost both the store's revenues and its image. As store brand selection and quality have improved, so have consumer confidence and acceptance. Some 41 percent of U.S. consumers now identify themselves as frequent buyers of store brands, up from just 12 percent in the early 1990s. And 82 percent of consumers now believe that store brands generally match the quality of national brands.[27]

It seems that almost every retailer now carries its own store brands. Wal-Mart's private brands account for a whopping 40 percent of its sales, brands such as Sam's Choice beverages and food products, Equate pharmacy and health and beauty products, and White Cloud brand toilet tissue, diapers, detergent, and fabric softener. Grocery giant Kroger markets some 8,000 items under a variety of private brands, such as Private Selection, Kroger Brand, F.M.V. (For Maximum Value), Naturally Preferred, and Everyday Living. At the other end of the spectrum, upscale retailer Saks Fifth Avenue carries its own clothing line, which features $98 men's ties, $200 halter-tops, and $250 cotton dress shirts.

Costco, the world's largest warehouse club, offers a staggering array of goods and services under its Kirkland Signature brand. Costco customers can buy anything from Kirkland Signature rotisserie chickens to a $3,439-per-person Kirkland Signature Tahitian cruise package. Such private brand offerings are giving national brands a real run for their money:

> Melanie Turner has forgotten her shopping list, but the 42-year-old pension consultant doesn't seem to mind. Entering her local Costco store, Turner knows right where she's going. In the dish detergent section, her hand goes past Procter & Gamble's Cascade to grab two 96-ounce bottles of Kirkland Signature, the in-store brand that Costco has plastered on everything from cashews to crosstrainer sneakers. Trolling for some fresh fish for dinner, she hauls in a 2 1/2-pound package of tilapia—it, too, emblazoned with the bold red, white, and black Kirkland logo. Then it's off to the paper aisle, where she picks up mammoth packs of Kirkland dinner napkins, Kirkland toilet paper, and . . . wait, where are the Kirkland paper towels? Her eyes scan the store's maze of hulking pallets—no sign of them—before coming to rest on a 12-pack of P&G's Bounty. A moment of decision. "I'll wait on this," she says finally.
>
> And there, in microcosm, is why Melanie Turner scares the pants off Procter & Gamble, Unilever, Kraft, and just about every consumer-goods company out there. Her shopping cart is headed for the checkout aisle, and there's hardly a national brand in it.

Store brand (or private brand)
A brand created and owned by a reseller of a product or service.

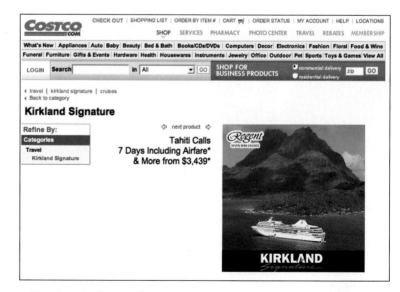

■ Store brands: Costco offers a staggering array of goods and services under its Kirkland Signature brand—anything from Kirkland Signature rotisserie chickens to a $3,439-per-person Kirkland Signature Tahitian cruise package.

. . . A subtle tectonic shift has been reshaping the world of brands. Retailers—once the lowly peddlers of brands that were made and marketed by big, important manufacturers—are now behaving like full-fledged marketers.[28]

In the so-called *battle of the brands* between national and private brands, retailers have many advantages. They control what products they stock, where they go on the shelf, what prices they charge, and which ones they will feature in local circulars. Retailers often price their store brands lower than comparable national brands, thereby appealing to the budget-conscious shopper in all of us. Although store brands can be hard to establish and costly to stock and promote, they also yield higher profit margins for the reseller. And they give resellers exclusive products that cannot be bought from competitors, resulting in greater store traffic and loyalty. Fast-growing retailer Trader Joe's, which carries 80 percent store brands, began creating its own brands so that "we could put our destiny in our own hands," says the company's president.[29]

To compete with store brands, leading brand marketers must invest in R&D to bring out new brands, new features, and continuous quality improvements. They must design strong advertising programs to maintain high awareness and preference. And they must find ways to "partner" with major distributors in a search for distribution economies and improved joint performance.

■ Licensing: Nickelodeon has developed a stable full of hugely popular characters—such as Dora the Explorer, the Rugrats clan, and SpongeBob SquarePants—which generate more than $5.3 billion in annual retail sales.

Licensing   Most manufacturers take years and spend millions to create their own brand names. However, some companies license names or symbols previously created by other manufacturers, names of well-known celebrities, or characters from popular movies and books. For a fee, any of these can provide an instant and proven brand name.

Apparel and accessories sellers pay large royalties to adorn their products—from blouses to ties, and linens to luggage—with the names or initials of well-known fashion innovators such as Calvin Klein, Tommy Hilfiger, Gucci, or Armani. Sellers of children's products attach an almost endless list of character names to clothing, toys, school supplies, linens, dolls, lunch boxes, cereals, and other items. Licensed character names range from classics such as *Sesame Street,* Disney, Peanuts, Winnie the Pooh, the Muppets, Scooby Doo, and Dr. Seuss characters to the more recent Dora the Explorer, Powerpuff Girls, Rugrats, Blue's Clues, and Harry Potter characters. And currently a number of top-selling retail toys are products based on television shows and movies, such as the *Spiderman Deluxe Spinning Web Blaster* and the *Talking Friendship Adventures Dora.*

Name and character licensing has grown rapidly in recent years. Annual retail sales of licensed products in the United States and Canada have grown from only $4 billion in 1977 to $55 billion in 1987 and more than $175 billion today. Licensing can be a highly profitable business for many companies. For example, Nickelodeon has developed a stable full of hugely popular characters—such as Dora the Explorer, Go, Diego, Go!, and SpongeBob SquarePants. Dora alone has generated more than $5.3 billion in retail sales in under five years. "When it comes to licensing its brands for consumer products, Nickelodeon has proved that it has the Midas touch," states a brand licensing expert.[30]

Co-branding

The practice of using the established brand names of two different companies on the same product.

Co-branding   Although companies have been **co-branding** products for many years, there has been a recent resurgence in co-branding. Co-branding occurs when two established brand names of different companies are used on the same product. For example, financial services firms often partner with other companies to create co-branded credit cards, as when Chase and United Airlines joined forces to create the Chase United Travel Card. Similarly, Costco teamed with mattress maker Stearns & Foster to market a line of Kirkland Signature by Stearns & Foster mattress sets. And Italian designer Dolce & Gabbana partnered with Motorola to produce the luxurious $400 gold Dolce & Gabbana Motorola MOTORAZR V3i DC cell phone. In most co-branding situations, one company licenses another company's well-known brand to use in combination with its own.

Co-branding offers many advantages. Because each brand dominates in a different category, the combined brands create broader consumer appeal and greater brand equity. Co-branding also allows a company to expand its existing brand into a category it might otherwise have difficulty entering alone. For example, Nike and Apple co-branded the Nike + iPod Sport Kit, which lets runners link their Nike shoes with their iPod Nanos to track and enhance running performance in real time. "Thanks to a unique partnership between NIKE and Apple, your iPod Nano becomes your coach. Your personal trainer. Your favorite workout companion." The Nike + iPod arrangement gives Apple a presence in the sports and fitness market. At the same time, it helps Nike to bring new value to its customers.[31]

Co-branding also has limitations. Such relationships usually involve complex legal contracts and licenses. Co-branding partners must carefully coordinate their advertising, sales promotion, and other marketing efforts. Finally, when co-branding, each partner must trust the other will take good care of its brand. For example, consider the marriage between Kmart and the Martha Stewart Everyday housewares brand. When Kmart declared bankruptcy, it cast a shadow on Martha Stewart. In turn, when Martha Stewart was convicted and jailed for illegal financial dealings, it created negative associations for Kmart. Kmart was further embarrassed when Martha Stewart Living Omnimedia recently struck major licensing agreements with Macy's and Lowe's, announcing that it would separate from Kmart when the current contract ends in 2009. Thus, as one manager puts it, "Giving away your brand is a lot like giving away your child—you want to make sure everything is perfect."[32]

Brand Development   A company has four choices when it comes to developing brands (see Figure 7.4). It can introduce *line extensions, brand extensions, multibrands,* or *new brands.*

Line Extensions   **Line extensions** occur when a company extends existing brand names to new forms, colors, sizes, ingredients, or flavors of an existing product category. Thus, Morton Salt has expanded its line to include regular iodized salt plus Morton Course Kosher Salt, Morton Sea Salt, Morton Lite Salt (low in sodium), Morton Popcorn Salt, Morton Salt Substitute, and several others. The vast majority of all new-product activity consists of line extensions.

A company might introduce line extensions as a low-cost, low-risk way to introduce new products. Or it might want to meet consumer desires for variety, to use excess capacity, or simply to command more shelf space from resellers. However, line extensions involve some risks. An overextended brand name might lose its specific meaning. Or heavily extended brands can cause consumer confusion or even frustration. For example, you can pick from a dizzying collection of more than 16 varieties of Coca-Cola, ranging from the original Coca-Cola Classic to Coke Zero to Caffeine-Free Diet Coke and Diet Coke Black Cherry Vanilla. It's unlikely that many customers will fully appreciate the differences, and such heavily extended brands can cause consumer confusion or even frustration.

Another risk is that sales of an extension may come at the expense of other items in the line. For example, the original Doritos Tortilla Chips have now morphed into a full line

Line extension

Extending an existing brand name to new forms, colors, sizes, ingredients, or flavors of an existing product category.

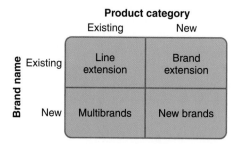

FIGURE 7.4

Brand Development Strategies

■ Line extensions: An overextended brand name might cause consumer confusion or frustration. The original Doritos Tortilla Chips have now morphed into a full line of 20 different types and flavors of chips, making the original Doritos seem like just another flavor.

Brand extension
Extending an existing brand name to new product categories.

of 20 different types and flavors of chips, including such high-decibel flavors as Blazin' Buffalo Ranch, Black Pepper Jack, and Fiery Habanero. Although the line seems to be doing well, the original Doritos chips seem like just another flavor. A line extension works best when it takes sales away from competing brands, not when it "cannibalizes" the company's other items.

Brand Extensions A **brand extension** extends a current brand name to new or modified products in a new category. For example, Kimberly-Clark extended its market-leading Huggies brand from disposable diapers to a full line of toiletries for tots, from shampoos, lotions, and diaper-rash ointments to baby wash, disposable washcloth, and disposable changing pads. Victorinox extended its venerable Swiss Army brand from multitool knives to products ranging from cutlery and ballpoint pens to watches, luggage, and apparel. And P&G has leveraged the strength of its Mr. Clean household cleaner brand to launch several new lines: cleaning pads (Magic Eraser), bathroom cleaning tools (Magic Reach), and home auto cleaning kits (Mr. Clean AutoDry). It's even testing Mr. Clean-branded car washes.

A brand extension gives a new product instant recognition and faster acceptance. It also saves the high advertising costs usually required to build a new brand name. At the same time, a brand extension strategy involves some risk. Brand extensions such as Bic pantyhose, Heinz pet food, LifeSavers gum, and Clorox laundry detergent met early deaths. The extension may confuse the image of the main brand. And if a brand extension fails, it may harm consumer attitudes toward the other products carrying the same brand name.

Further, a brand name may not be appropriate to a particular new product, even if it is well made and satisfying—would you consider flying on Hooters Air or buying an Evian water-filled padded bra (both failed)? Companies that are tempted to transfer a brand name must research how well the brand's associations fit the new product.[33]

Multibrands Companies often introduce additional brands in the same category. Thus, Procter & Gamble markets many different brands in each of its product categories. *Multibranding* offers a way to establish different features and appeal to different buying motives. It also allows a company to lock up more reseller shelf space.

A major drawback of multibranding is that each brand might obtain only a small market share, and none may be very profitable. The company may end up spreading its resources over many brands instead of building a few brands to a highly profitable level. These companies should reduce the number of brands they sell in a given category and set up tighter screening procedures for new brands.

New Brands A company might believe that the power of its existing brand name is waning and a new brand name is needed. Or it may create a new brand name when it enters a new product category for which none of the company's current brand names are appropriate. For example, Toyota created the separate Scion brand, targeted toward Millennial consumers.

As with multibranding, offering too many new brands can result in a company spreading its resources too thin. And in some industries, such as consumer packaged goods, consumers and retailers have become concerned that there are already too many brands, with too few differences between them. Thus, Procter & Gamble, Frito-Lay, and other large consumer-product marketers are now pursuing *megabrand* strategies—weeding out weaker brands and focusing their marketing dollars only on brands that can achieve the number-one or number-two market share positions in their categories. "We . . . sort through our smaller brands," says P&G's CEO, and "divest the ones that don't have a strategic role or cannot deliver."[34]

Managing Brands

Companies must manage their brands carefully. First, the brand's positioning must be continuously communicated to consumers. Major brand marketers often spend huge amounts on advertising to create brand awareness and to build preference and loyalty. For example, Verizon spends more than $1.7 billion annually to promote its brand. McDonald's spends more than $742 million.[35]

Such advertising campaigns can help to create name recognition, brand knowledge, and maybe even some brand preference. However, the fact is that brands are not maintained by advertising but by the *brand experience*. Today, customers come to know a brand through a wide range of contacts and touch points. These include advertising, but also personal experience with the brand, word of mouth, company Web pages, and many others. The company must put as much care into managing these touch points as it does into producing its ads. "A brand is a living entity," says a former Disney executive, "and it is enriched or undermined cumulatively over time, the product of a thousand small gestures."[36]

The brand's positioning will not take hold fully unless everyone in the company lives the brand. Therefore the company needs to train its people to be customer centered. Even better, the company should carry on internal brand building to help employees understand and be enthusiastic about the brand promise. Many companies go even further by training and encouraging their distributors and dealers to serve their customers well.

Finally, companies need to periodically audit their brands' strengths and weaknesses.[37] They should ask: Does our brand excel at delivering benefits that consumers truly value? Is the brand properly positioned? Do all of our consumer touch points support the brand's positioning? Do the brand's managers understand what the brand means to consumers? Does the brand receive proper, sustained support? The brand audit may turn up brands that need more support, brands that need to be dropped, or brands that must be rebranded or repositioned because of changing customer preferences or new competitors.

Services Marketing

Services have grown dramatically in recent years. Services now account for close to 79 percent of U.S. gross domestic product. And the service industry is growing. By 2014, it is estimated that nearly four out of five jobs in the United States will be in service industries. Services are growing even faster in the world economy, making up 64 percent of gross world product.[38]

Service industries vary greatly. *Governments* offer services through courts, employment services, hospitals, military services, police and fire departments, postal service, and schools. *Private not-for-profit organizations* offer services through museums, charities, churches, colleges, foundations, and hospitals. A large number of *business organizations* offer services—airlines, banks, hotels, insurance companies, consulting firms, medical and legal practices, entertainment companies, real-estate firms, retailers, and others.

Nature and Characteristics of a Service

A company must consider four special service characteristics when designing marketing programs: *intangibility, inseparability, variability,* and *perishability* (see Figure 7.5).

Service intangibility means that services cannot be seen, tasted, felt, heard, or smelled before they are bought. For example, people undergoing cosmetic surgery cannot see the result before the purchase. Airline passengers have nothing but a ticket and the promise that they and their luggage will arrive safely at the intended destination, hopefully at the same time. To reduce uncertainty, buyers look for "signals" of service quality. They draw conclusions about quality from the place, people, price, equipment, and communications that they can see.

Service intangibility
A major characteristic of services—they cannot be seen, tasted, felt, heard, or smelled before they are bought.

FIGURE 7.5

Four Service Characteristics

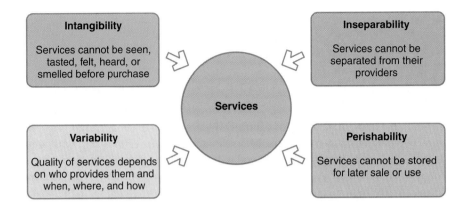

Therefore, the service provider's task is to make the service tangible in one or more ways and to send the right signals about quality. One analyst calls this *evidence management,* in which the service organization presents its customers with organized, honest evidence of its capabilities. The Mayo Clinic practices good evidence management:[39]

> When it comes to hospitals, it's very hard for the average patient to judge the quality of the "product." You can't try it on, you can't return it if you don't like it, and you need an advanced degree to understand it. And so, when we're considering a medical facility, most of us unconsciously turn detective, looking for evidence of competence, caring, and integrity. The Mayo Clinic doesn't leave that evidence to chance. By carefully managing a set of visual and experiential clues, Mayo offers patients and their families concrete evidence of its strengths and values. For example, staff people at the clinic are trained to act in a way that clearly signals its patient-first focus. "My doctor calls me at home to check on how I am doing," marvels one patient. "She wants to work with what is best for my schedule." Mayo's physical facilities also send the right signals. They've been carefully designed to relieve stress, offer a place of refuge, create positive distractions, convey caring and respect, signal competence, accommodate families, and make it easy to find your way around. The result? Exceptionally positive word of mouth and abiding customer loyalty, which have allowed Mayo Clinic to build what is arguably the most powerful brand in health care—with very little advertising.

Service inseparability

A major characteristic of services—they are produced and consumed at the same time and cannot be separated from their providers.

Physical goods are produced, then stored, later sold, and still later consumed. In contrast, services are first sold, then produced and consumed at the same time. **Service inseparability** means that services cannot be separated from their providers, whether the providers are people or machines. If a service employee provides the service, then the employee becomes a part of the service. Because the customer is also present as the service is produced, *provider-customer interaction* is a special feature of services marketing. Both the provider and the customer affect the service outcome.

Service variability

A major characteristic of services—their quality may vary greatly, depending on who provides them and when, where, and how.

Service variability means that the quality of services depends on who provides them as well as when, where, and how they are provided. For example, some hotels—say, Marriott—have reputations for providing better service than others. Still, within a given Marriott hotel, one registration-counter employee may be cheerful and efficient, whereas another standing just a few feet away may be unpleasant and slow. Even the quality of a single Marriott employee's service varies according to his or her energy and frame of mind at the time of each customer encounter.

Service perishability

A major characteristic of services—they cannot be stored for later sale or use.

Service perishability means that services cannot be stored for later sale or use. Some doctors charge patients for missed appointments because the service value existed only at that point and disappeared when the patient did not show up. The perishability of services is not a problem when demand is steady. However, when demand fluctuates, service firms often have difficult problems. For example, because of rush-hour demand, public transportation companies must own much more equipment than they would if demand were even throughout the day. Thus, service firms often design strategies for producing a better match between demand and supply. Hotels and resorts charge lower prices in the off-season to attract more guests. And restaurants hire part-time employees to serve during peak periods.

Marketing Strategies for Service Firms

Just like manufacturing businesses, good service firms use marketing to position themselves strongly in chosen target markets. Target promises "Expect more, pay less." Ritz-Carlton Hotels positions itself as offering a memorable experience that "enlivens the senses, instills well-being, and fulfills even the unexpressed wishes and needs of our guests." At the Mayo Clinic, "the needs of the patient come first." These and other service firms establish their positions through traditional marketing mix activities. However, because services differ from tangible products, they often require additional marketing approaches.

The Service-Profit Chain In a service business, the customer and front-line service employee *interact* to create the service. Effective interaction, in turn, depends on the skills of front-line service employees and on the support processes backing these employees. Thus, successful service companies focus their attention on *both* their customers and their employees. They understand the **service-profit chain**, which links service firm profits with employee and customer satisfaction. This chain consists of five links:[40]

Service-profit chain
The chain that links service firm profits with employee and customer satisfaction.

- *Internal service quality:* superior employee selection and training, a quality work environment, and strong support for those dealing with customers, which results in . . .
- *Satisfied and productive service employees:* more satisfied, loyal, and hardworking employees, which results in . . .
- *Greater service value:* more effective and efficient customer value creation and service delivery, which results in . . .
- *Satisfied and loyal customers:* satisfied customers who remain loyal, repeat purchase, and refer other customers, which results in . . .
- *Healthy service profits and growth:* superior service firm performance.

Therefore, reaching service profits and growth goals begins with taking care of those who take care of customers. In fact, legendary founder and former CEO of Southwest Airlines, Herb Kelleher, always put employees first, not customers. His reasons? "If they're happy, satisfied, dedicated, and energetic, they'll take good care of customers," he says. "When the customers are happy, they come back, and that makes shareholders happy."[41] Consider Wegmans, a 71-store grocery chain in the mid-Atlantic states.

Wegmans customers have a zeal for the store that borders on obsession. Says one regular, "Going there isn't just shopping, it's an event." A recent national survey of food retailer customer satisfaction put Wegmans at the top. Each year, Wegmans receives thousands of letters from around the country from customers wanting a Wegmans in their town or neighborhood. The secret? Wegmans knows that happy, satisfied employees produce happy, satisfied customers. So Wegmans takes care of its employees. It pays higher salaries, shells out money for employee college scholarships, covers 100 percent of health insurance premiums for employees making less than $55,000 a year, and invests heavily in employee training. In fact, for the past several years, Wegmans has regularly placed among the top three on *Fortune* magazine's best-companies-to-work-for list. "The biggest reason Wegmans is a shopping experience like no other is that it is an employer like no other," says a Wegmans watcher.[42]

■ The service-profit chain: Happy employees make for happy customers. "The biggest reason Wegmans is a shopping experience like no other is that it is an employer like no other."

FIGURE 7.6

Three Types of Service Marketing

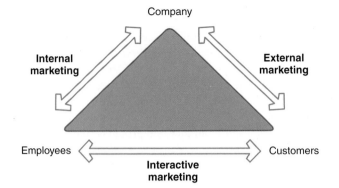

Internal marketing

Orienting and motivating customer-contact employees and the supporting service people to work as a team to provide customer satisfaction.

Interactive marketing

Training service employees in the fine art of interacting with customers to satisfy their needs.

Thus, service marketing requires more than just traditional external marketing using the Four Ps. Figure 7.6 shows that service marketing also requires *internal marketing* and *interactive marketing*. **Internal marketing** means that the service firm must orient and motivate its customer-contact employees and supporting service people to work as a *team* to provide customer satisfaction. Marketers must get everyone in the organization to be customer centered. In fact, internal marketing must *precede* external marketing.

For example, Ritz-Carlton hotels—legendary for its service quality—orients its employees carefully, instills in them a sense of pride, and motivates them by recognizing and rewarding outstanding service deeds. New employees quickly learn that the care and comfort of the luxury hotel chain's guests is their highest mission. The Ritz-Carlton Credo states, "We are ladies and gentlemen serving ladies and gentlemen." Employees are carefully trained to understand that it's their job to deliver the "Ritz-Carlton experience," defined in the Credo as one that "enlivens the senses, instills well-being, and fulfills even the unexpressed wishes and needs of our guests." Then, Ritz-Carlton recognizes and rewards employees who perform outstanding feats of customer service, with everything from plaques, bonuses, and recognition dinners to on-the-spot coupons redeemable for items in the hotel gift shop or free weekend stays at the hotel. As a result, Ritz-Carlton employees know what good service is and are highly motivated to give it.

Interactive marketing means that service quality depends heavily on the quality of the buyer-seller interaction during the service encounter. In product marketing, product quality often depends little on how the product is obtained. But in services marketing, service quality depends on both the service deliverer and the quality of the delivery. Service marketers, therefore, must master interactive marketing skills. Thus, Ritz-Carlton selects only people with an innate "passion to serve" and instructs them carefully in the fine art of interacting with customers to satisfy their every need. In fact, the average Ritz-Carlton employee receives 232 hours of training per year, four times the training at competing hotels.[43]

In today's marketplace, companies must know how to deliver interactions that are not only "high touch" but also "high tech." For example, customers can log onto the Charles Schwab Web site and access account information, investment research, real-time quotes, after-hours trading, and the Schwab learning center. They can also participate in live online events and chat online with customer-service representatives. Customers seeking more-personal interactions can contact service reps by phone or visit a local Schwab branch office to "talk with Chuck." Thus, Schwab has mastered interactive marketing at all three levels—calls, clicks, *and* personal visits.

Today, as competition and costs increase, and as productivity and quality decrease, more service marketing sophistication is needed. Service companies face three major marketing tasks: They want to increase their *service differentiation, service quality,* and *service productivity.*

Managing Service Differentiation In these days of intense price competition, service marketers often complain about the difficulty of differentiating their services from those of competitors. To the extent that customers view the services of different providers as similar, they care less about the provider than the price.

The solution to price competition is to develop a differentiated offer, delivery, and image. The *offer* can include innovative features that set one company's offer apart from competitors' offers. Some hotels offer car-rental, banking, and business-center services in their lobbies and free high-speed Internet connections in their rooms. Airlines differentiate their offers through frequent-flyer award programs and special services. For example, British Airways offers spa services at its Arrivals Lounge at Heathrow airport and softer in-flight beds, plumper pillows, and cozier blankets. Says one ad: "Our simple goal is to deliver the best service you could ask for, without you having to ask."

Service companies can differentiate their service *delivery* by having more able and reliable customer-contact people, by developing a superior physical environment in which the service product is delivered, or by designing a superior delivery process. For example, many grocery chains now offer online shopping and home delivery as a better way to shop than having to drive, park, wait in line, and tote groceries home.

Finally, service companies also can work on differentiating their *images* through symbols and branding. The Harris Bank adopted the lion as its symbol on its stationery, in its advertising, and even as stuffed animals offered to new depositors. The well-known Harris lion confers an image of strength on the bank. Other well-known service symbols include Merrill Lynch's bull, MGM's lion, McDonald's golden arches, Allstate's "good hands," and the Travelers red umbrella.

Managing Service Quality A service firm can differentiate itself by delivering consistently higher quality than its competitors do. Like manufacturers before them, most service industries have now joined the customer-driven quality movement. And like product marketers, service providers need to identify what target customers expect concerning service quality.

Softer flat beds for a deeper sleep.

The best service anticipates your needs. To give you the best possible sleep, we used the latest in cushioning technology to create an even more comfortable flat bed. And to add to your comfort, we include plumper pillows and cozier blankets. Our goal is simple: to deliver the best service you could ask for, without you having to ask. So whether you're enjoying a gourmet meal, or an Arrivals Lounge that feels more like a spa, we think you'll find our business class like no other.

Visit ba.com/clubworld

Business class is different on **BRITISH AIRWAYS**

■ Service differentiation: At British Airways, says this ad, "Our goal is simple: to deliver the best service you can ask for, without you having to ask."

Unfortunately, service quality is harder to define and judge than product quality. For instance, it is harder to agree on the quality of a haircut than on the quality of a hair dryer. Customer retention is perhaps the best measure of quality—a service firm's ability to hang onto its customers depends on how consistently it delivers value to them.

Top service companies set high service-quality standards. They watch service performance closely, both their own and that of competitors. They do not settle for merely good service; they aim for 100 percent defect-free service. A 98 percent performance standard may sound good, but using this standard, UPS would lose or misdirect 312,000 packages each day and U.S. pharmacists would misfill close to 1.4 million prescriptions each week.[44]

Unlike product manufacturers who can adjust their machinery and inputs until everything is perfect, service quality will always vary, depending on the interactions between employees and customers. As hard as they try, even the best companies will have an occasional late delivery, burned steak, or grumpy employee. However, good *service recovery* can turn angry customers into loyal ones. In fact, good recovery can win more customer purchasing and loyalty than if things had gone well in the first place. Therefore, companies should take steps not only to provide good service every time but also to recover from service mistakes when they do occur (see Marketing at Work 7.2).

The first step is to *empower* front-line service employees—to give them the authority, responsibility, and incentives they need to recognize, care about, and tend to customer needs. For example, Nordstrom, the department store chain long known for extraordinary service, gives its employees the autonomy they need to create outstanding customer-service experiences. Here's an example:[45]

In Portland, Oregon, a man walked into Nordstrom asking for an Armani tuxedo to wear to his daughter's wedding. The sales representative took his measurements but

7.2 MARKETING AT WORK

Service Recovery: Doing Things Right When Service Goes Wrong

Southwest Airlines and JetBlue Airlines are both great service companies. For more than three decades, Southwest has set the airline industry standard for efficient service, low fares, and fun flying. And since first taking off in 2000, JetBlue has amassed a soaring list of service honors, including Readers' Choice Awards from discerning *Conde Nast Traveler* magazine for five years running and high rankings in every measured category in the airline satisfaction ratings by J.D. Power & Associates. As a result, Southwest and JetBlue have been the only consistently profitable air carriers in the otherwise troubled U.S. airline industry.

But all service companies, even the great ones, make mistakes once in a while. Perhaps the truest test of good customer service is how well companies do when things go *wrong*. Consider the following tales in which Southwest and JetBlue committed similar service blunders—but with dramatically different outcomes.

SOUTHWEST

Bob Emig was flying home from St. Louis on Southwest Airlines this past December when an all-too-familiar travel nightmare began to unfold. After his airplane backed away from the gate, he and his fellow passengers were told that the plane would need to be de-iced. When the aircraft was ready to fly two and a half hours later, the pilot had reached the hour limit set by the Federal Aviation Administration, and a new pilot was required. By that time, the plane had to be de-iced again. Five hours after the scheduled departure time, Emig's flight was finally ready for takeoff.

A customer-service disaster, right? Not to hear Emig tell it. The pilot walked the aisles, answering questions and offering constant updates. Flight attendants, who Emig says "really seemed like they cared," kept up with the news on connecting flights. And within a couple of days of arriving home, Emig, who travels frequently, received a letter from Southwest that included two free round-trip ticket vouchers. "I could not believe they acknowledged the situation and apologized," says Emig. "Then they gave me a gift, for all intents and purposes, to make up for the time spent sitting on the runway."

Emig's "gift" from Southwest was not the result of an unusually kind customer-service agent who took pity on his plight. Nor was it a scramble to make amends after a disastrous operational fiasco. Rather, it was standard service-recovery procedure for Southwest Airlines. Almost six

■ Service recovery: Following its Valentine's Day customer-service meltdown, JetBlue announced a host of actions to repair its bond with customers. "We've learned from this," said JetBlue Chairman David Needleman, shown here. "That's why it's never going to happen again."

said she'd need time to work on his request. She called later to say that the tuxedo would be ready the next day. As it turned out, Nordstrom did not carry Armani tuxedos at the time. The sales representative had found the tux through a distributor in New York, then had it rushed to Portland and altered to fit the customer in time for the wedding. At Nordstrom, such employee empowerment is built into the process. "It is not a thing of the day," says a Nordstrom store manager, "it is part of our culture."

Managing Service Productivity With their costs rising rapidly, service firms are under great pressure to increase service productivity. They can do so in several ways. They can train current employees better or hire new ones who will work harder or more skillfully. Or they can increase the quantity of their service by giving up some quality. The provider can "in-years ago, Southwest created a new high-level group that oversees all proactive communications with customers. Southwest carefully coordinates information that's sent to all frontline reps in the event of major flight disruptions. It also sends out letters, and in many cases flight vouchers, to customers caught up in flight delays or cancellations, customer bumping incidents, baggage problems, or other travel messes—even those beyond Southwest's control. "It's not something we have to do," says a Southwest executive. "It's just something we feel our customers deserve." Thanks to such caring service recovery, Southwest doesn't just appease wronged customers like Bob Emig, it turns them into even more loyal customers.

JETBLUE

On February 14, 2007—Valentine's Day—a devastating ice storm struck JetBlue's main hub at New York's John F. Kennedy International Airport. The resulting disastrous mix of closed runways, aircraft congestion, and frozen equipment kept many JetBlue customers stranded for hours in grounded planes. So far, this sounds a lot like the Southwest Airlines example just discussed. But rather than recovering with Southwest-like efficiency and caring customer communications, JetBlue experienced a startling, near-total customer-service collapse.

A series of bad decisions resulted in chaos on the tarmac. In a fruitless attempt to eventually get planes off the ground, JetBlue waited too long to cancel flights and to bus enplaned passengers back to the terminal. Many passengers were trapped in planes for as long as 11 hours, as the tires of their planes literally froze to the runway. All the while, increasingly furious customers—both on the stranded planes and in the terminal—were kept pretty much in the dark about what was going to happen and why.

Even after passengers were returned to the terminal, the nightmare continued. Unlike Southwest, the relatively new and rapidly growing JetBlue simply hadn't built the customer-service and operational infrastructure needed to deal with such a crisis. JetBlue flight crews and terminal agents were befuddled and disorganized in helping passengers.

Over the next six days, JetBlue experienced major disruptions throughout its entire system, cancelling more than 1,000 flights and leaving customers fuming over rough handling and lost vacations. During that critical week, JetBlue struggled just to get operations back to normal. The airline did little by way of responding to customers' seething emotions. Whereas Southwest's smooth service recovery created even stronger customer relationships, JetBlue's meltdown created a serious crisis of customer trust.

How much damage will the Valentine's Day service disaster do to JetBlue's hard-earned customer-service reputation? "Will customers forgive JetBlue?" asks an industry analyst. "That depends on how it weathers future storms," he answers. It seems unlikely that this single incident will undo years of good customer relationships. Says the analyst, "JetBlue has this going for it: seven years of goodwill. Its customers largely accept that it cares, because it has demonstrated that it does, flight after flight." In fact, in mid-2007, for the third year running, JetBlue was awarded highest honors in customer satisfaction among low-cost airlines by J.D. Power and Associates. The key is to make certain that there are no future service breakdowns.

JetBlue is now in longer-term service recovery mode. In the weeks following the six-day disaster, JetBlue's Chairman seemed to pop up everywhere—the *New York Times*, the *Late Show* with David Letterman, NPR, even YouTube—accepting responsibility, apologizing repeatedly, and promising refunds and credits to wronged customers. He quickly announced a new Customer Bill of Rights, a unique document that outlines policies for notifying customers about delays and cancellations, sets a limit before ground-delayed passengers must be deplaned, and provides for generous customer compensation for all types of service missteps.

But even more important than apologies, refunds, and guarantees, JetBlue has made sweeping systems changes that will prevent future customer-service debacles. "We should have acted quicker. We should have had contingency plans that were better [tested] to be able to [unload] customers," said the Chairman. "We've learned from this," he declared. "That's why it's never going to happen again."

Thus, even good service companies screw up from time to time. Good service recovery, however, can turn such screw-ups into opportunities to actually strengthen bonds with customers. But companies must think ahead and plan for good service recovery. In these two examples, Southwest was well prepared, JetBlue wasn't. Because JetBlue really cares about its customers, it may well emerge from the Valentine's Day meltdown stronger than ever—but only if it's better prepared to make the right moves when things go wrong.

Sources: Portions adapted from Jena McGregor, "Customer Service Champs," *BusinessWeek*, March 5, 2007, pp. 52–64. Quotes and other information from Justin Bachman, "JetBlue's Fiasco Could Improve Flying," *BusinessWeek*, February 21, 2007, p. 10; Chuck Salter, "Lessons from the Tarmac," *Fast Company*, May 2007, pp. 31–32; Mel Duvall and Doug Bartholomew, "What Really Happened at JetBlue?" *Baseline*, April 2007, pp. 53–59; and "J.D. Power and Associates Reports: JetBlue and Continental Continue to Rank Highest in Airline Customer Satisfaction," June 19, 2007, accessed at www.jdpower.com/corporate/news/releases/pdf/2007097.pdf.

dustrialize the service" by adding equipment and standardizing production, as in McDonald's assembly-line approach to fast-food retailing. Finally, the service provider can harness the power of technology. Although we often think of technology's power to save time and costs in manufacturing companies, it also has great—and often untapped—potential to make service workers more productive.

However, companies must avoid pushing productivity so hard that doing so reduces quality. Attempts to industrialize a service or to cut costs can make a service company more efficient in the short run. But they can also reduce its longer-run ability to innovate, maintain service quality, or respond to consumer needs and desires. Many airlines are learning this lesson the hard way as they attempt to streamline and economize in the face of rising costs.

Over the past year, Northwest Airlines has stopped offering free magazines, pillows, movies, and even minibags of pretzels on its domestic flights. Passengers can still get an in-flight snack of raisins and nuts, but it costs $1. The airline is also charging a $15 fee for a roomier seat on the aisle or in an exit row. Combine that with higher fares and a sharply curtailed schedule, and it's little wonder that flyers rate Northwest dead last among the nation's major airlines. "If at all possible, I don't fly Northwest," says one veteran traveler. "I have found a lack of interest in the customer." A services marketing expert agrees: "The upshot is that some companies, in their passion to drive down costs, have mangled their relationships with customers."[46]

Thus, in attempting to improve service productivity, companies must be mindful of how they create and deliver customer value. In short, they should be careful not to take the "service" out of service.

REST STOP ⏵ REVIEWING THE CONCEPTS

A product is more than a simple set of tangible features. Each product or service offered to customers can be viewed on three levels. The *core customer value* consists of the core problem-solving benefits that consumers seek when they buy a product. The *actual product* exists around the core and includes the quality level, features, design, brand name, and packaging. The *augmented product* is the actual product plus the various services and benefits offered with it, such as warranty, free delivery, installation, and maintenance.

1. Define *product* and the major classifications of products and services.

Broadly defined, a *product* is anything that can be offered to a market for attention, acquisition, use, or consumption that might satisfy a want or need. Products include physical objects but also services, events, persons, places, organizations, ideas, or mixes of these entities. *Services* are products that consist of activities, benefits, or satisfactions offered for sale that are essentially intangible, such as banking, hotel, tax preparation, and home-repair services.

Products and services fall into two broad classes based on the types of consumers that use them. *Consumer products*—those bought by final consumers—are usually classified according to consumer shopping habits (convenience products, shopping products, specialty products, and unsought products). *Industrial products*—purchased for further processing or for use in conducting a business—include materials and parts, capital items, and supplies and services. Other marketable entities—such as organizations, persons, places, and ideas—can also be thought of as products.

2. Describe the decisions companies make regarding their individual products and services, product lines, and product mixes.

Individual product decisions involve product attributes, branding, packaging, labeling, and product support services. *Product attribute* decisions involve product quality, features, and style and design. *Branding* decisions include selecting a brand name and developing a brand strategy. *Packaging* provides many key benefits, such as protection, economy, convenience, and promotion. Package decisions often include designing *labels,* which identify, describe, and possibly promote the product. Companies also develop *product support services* that enhance customer service and satisfaction and safeguard against competitors.

Most companies produce a product line rather than a single product. A *product line* is a group of products that are related in function, customer-purchase needs, or distribution channels. *Line stretching* involves extending a line downward, upward, or in both directions to occupy a gap that might otherwise be filled by a competitor. In contrast, *line filling* involves adding items within the present range of the line. All product lines and items offered to customers by a particular seller make up the *product mix.* The mix can be described by four dimensions: width, length, depth, and consistency. These dimensions are the tools for developing the company's product strategy.

3. Discuss branding strategy—the decisions companies make in building and managing their brands.

Some analysts see brands as *the* major enduring asset of a company. Brands are more than just names and symbols—they embody everything that the product or service *means* to consumers. *Brand equity* is the positive differential effect that knowing the brand name has on customer response to the product or service. A brand with strong brand equity is a very valuable asset.

In building brands, companies need to make decisions about brand positioning, brand name selection, brand sponsorship, and brand development. The most powerful *brand positioning* builds around strong consumer beliefs and values. *Brand name selection* involves finding the best brand name based on a careful review of product benefits, the target market, and proposed marketing strategies. A manufacturer has four *brand sponsorship* options: it can launch a *manufacturer's brand* (or national brand), sell to resellers who use a *private brand,* market *licensed brands,* or join forces with another company to *co-brand* a product. A company also has four choices when it comes to developing brands. It can introduce *line extensions, brand extensions, multibrands,* or *new brands.*

Companies must build and manage their brands carefully. The brand's positioning must be continuously communicated to consumers. Advertising can help. However, brands are not maintained by advertising but by the *brand experience.* Customers come to know a brand through a wide range of contacts and interactions. The company must put as much care into managing these touch points as it does into producing its ads. Thus, managing a company's brand assets can no longer be left only to brand managers. Some companies are now setting up brand asset management teams to manage their major brands. Finally, companies must periodically audit their brands' strengths and weaknesses. In some cases, brands may need to be repositioned because of changing customer preferences or new competitors.

4. Identify the four characteristics that affect the marketing of a service and the additional marketing considerations that services require.

Services are characterized by four key characteristics: they are *intangible, inseparable, variable,* and *perishable.* Each characteristic poses problems and marketing requirements. Marketers work to find ways to make the service more tangible, to increase the productivity of providers who are inseparable from their products, to standardize the quality in the face of variability, and to improve demand movements and supply capacities in the face of service perishability.

Good service companies focus attention on *both* customers and employees. They understand the *service-profit chain,* which links service firm profits with employee and customer satisfaction. Services marketing strategy calls not only for external marketing but also for *internal marketing* to motivate employees and *interactive marketing* to create service delivery skills among service providers. To succeed, service marketers must create *competitive differentiation,* offer high *service quality,* and find ways to increase *service productivity.*

Navigating the Key Terms

Brand (206)
Brand equity (211)
Brand extension (218)
Co-branding (216)
Consumer product (201)
Convenience product (201)
Industrial product (201)
Interactive marketing (222)
Internal marketing (222)

Line extension (217)
Packaging (206)
Product (198)
Product line (208)
Product mix (or product portfolio) (209)
Product quality (204)
Service (199)
Service inseparability (220)
Service intangibility (219)

Service perishability (220)
Service-profit chain (221)
Service variability (220)
Shopping product (201)
Social marketing (203)
Specialty product (201)
Store brand (or private brand) (215)
Unsought product (201)

Travel Log

Discussing the Issues

1. What is a product and how can product planners build customer value? (AACSB: Communication)

2. Name and describe the four types of consumer products. Provide an example of each. (AACSB: Communication; Reflective Thinking)

3. Discuss the individual product and service decisions facing marketers. (AACSB: Communication)

4. Define brand equity. What competitive advantages does high brand equity provide a company? (AACSB: Communication)

5. Compare and contrast the four choices a company has regarding developing brands. Provide an example of each. (AACSB: Communication)

6. Name and describe the four special characteristics of services. How do the services offered by a hair salon differ from those offered by an auto-parts store regarding these

characteristics? (AACSB: Communication; Reflective Thinking)

Application Questions

1. Visit the Kraft Foods Web site (www.kraft.com/brands/index.html) and examine its list of different brands. Name and define the four dimensions of a company's product mix and describe Kraft's product mix on these dimensions. (AACSB: Communication; Reflective Thinking; Use of IT)

2. In a small group, develop a brand name for a line of clothing targeted to college students. Your brand is positioned as affordable yet stylish for the student on the go. Use the desirable qualities for a brand name described in the chapter when selecting your brand name. (AACSB: Communication; Reflective Thinking)

3. Find five examples of service-provider attempts to reduce service intangibility. (AACSB: Communication; Reflective Thinking)

Under the Hood: Focus on Technology

After years of rumors and anticipation, Apple launched the iPhone in June 2007. It's more than just a phone—it's also a music player, a video player, a camera, and an Internet device with Web surfing and e-mail capabilities. Like its predecessor, the iPod, the design is sleek. The touch screen and keyboard enable a world of information at the user's fingertips. This product doesn't come without high costs, however. When it was launched, the 4GB version retailed for $499 and the 8GB version for $599. And because AT&T was the sole service provider, purchasers had to sign up for a two-year service contract with AT&T. Moreover, some businesses were concerned because the iPhone was not compatible with current wireless e-mail systems used by companies. At the time of the launch, most companies were using BlackBerry software and there was fear that iPhone users would circumvent security systems and jeopardize company networks.

1. Visit Apple's Web site to learn more about the iPhone (www.apple.com). Discuss the three levels of this product. (AACSB: Communication; Reflective Thinking; Use of IT)

2. Chapter 5 described the product characteristics influencing the rate of new product adoption. Review these factors and discuss how each factor will influence the rate of adoption of the iPhone. (AACSB: Communication; Reflective Thinking)

Focus on Ethics

Arm & Hammer Baking Soda has been around for more than 150 years. Sodium bicarbonate is a baking ingredient, but this brand has found hundreds of other uses around the house. Use it to eliminate odors in your refrigerator, to brush your teeth, to sooth a stomach ache, to clean battery acid corrosion off your car, or to freshen up your carpet, laundry, or cat's litter box. Arm & Hammer now offers separate products that meet several of these needs, such as laundry detergent, carpet freshener, toothpaste, and kitty litter deodorizer. Whereas a box of Arm & Hammer Baking Soda costs about 50¢, the other products cost $2.00 to $4.00, raising issues about the ethics of Arm & Hammer pricing.

1. Visit Arm & Hammer's Web site (www.armhammer.com) to learn more about this product. Identify four ways this brand can be used other than for baking. For each use, identify a product Arm & Hammer has developed for that use. What brand development strategy is Arm & Hammer using? (AACSB: Communication; Reflective Thinking; Use of IT)

2. Visit a store where the Arm & Hammer products you identified in question 1 can be purchased and find the price of each product. Compare the price per ounce for each of these products to the price per ounce for Arm & Hammer Baking Soda. Is it ethical for Arm & Hammer to sell different products at considerably higher costs to consumers that meet basically the same needs as the other uses identified for the baking soda product? Develop an argument justifying the higher cost for these products. (AACSB: Communication; Ethical Reasoning)

Video Case

Swiss Army

It seems appropriate that Swiss Army Brands, maker of multi-function knives, has become a multiproduct brand. The original company dates back to the late 1800s as a small, family-owned cutlery company. After WWII, the fascination that American GIs had with the multifunction pocket knives of their Swiss ally soldiers led to tremendous growth and expansion. Initially, this meant many different variations of the standard Swiss Army Knife that included such applications as fishing, golf, and an accessory for women's purses.

The popularity of the Swiss Army Knife has enabled the company to expand into all manner of consumer goods including watches, luggage, apparel, and other lines. These brand extensions have been based on consumer research to ensure that each fits within the concept that consumers hold for the brand. The success that Swiss Army Brands has achieved through expansion has even allowed it to open its own retail stores.

After viewing the video featuring Swiss Army Brands, answer the following questions about product and branding strategies.

1. What additional products and lines might Swiss Army Brands consider?

2. How do brand extensions affect a company such as Swiss Army Brands, in both positive and negative ways?

3. Why did Swiss Army Brands open retail stores? How do these stores help the company build its brand?

1. explain how companies find and develop new-product ideas
2. list and define the steps in the new-product development process and the major considerations in managing this process
3. describe the stages of the product life cycle
4. describe how marketing strategies change during the product's life cycle
5. discuss two additional product and services issues: socially responsible product decisions and international product and services marketing

CHAPTER 8

New-Product Development and Product Life-Cycle Strategies

Previewing the Concepts

In the previous chapter, you learned how marketers manage and develop products and brands. In this chapter, we'll look into two additional product topics: developing new products and managing products through their life cycles. New products are the lifeblood of an organization. However, new-product development is risky, and many new products fail. So, the first part of this chapter lays out a process for finding and growing successful new products. Once introduced, marketers want their products to enjoy long and happy lives. In the second part of the chapter, you'll see that every product passes through several life-cycle stages and that each stage poses new challenges requiring different marketing strategies and tactics. Finally, we'll wrap up our product discussion by looking at two additional considerations, social responsibility in product decisions and international product and services marketing.

For openers, consider Apple. An early new-product innovator, Apple got off to a fast and impressive start. But only a decade later, as its creative fires cooled, Apple found itself on the brink of extinction. That set the stage for one of the most remarkable turnarounds in corporate history. Read on to see how Apple's cofounder, Steve Jobs (shown in the picture), used lots of innovation and creative new products to first start the company and then to remake it again 20 years later.

From the very start, the tale of Apple is a tale of dazzling creativity and customer-driven innovation. Under the leadership of its cofounder and creative genius, Steve Jobs, Apple's very first personal computers, introduced in the late 1970s, stood apart because of their user-friendly look and feel. The company's Macintosh computer, unveiled in 1984, and its LazerWriter printers blazed new trails in desktop computing and publishing, making Apple an early industry leader in both innovation and market share.

But then things took an ugly turn for Apple. In 1985, after tumultuous struggles with the new president he'd hired only a year earlier, Steve Jobs left Apple. With Jobs gone, Apple's creative fires cooled. By the late 1980s, the company's fortunes dwindled as a new wave of PC machines, sporting Intel chips and Microsoft software, swept the market. By the mid- to late-1990s, Apple's sales had plunged to $5 billion, 50 percent off previous highs. And its once-commanding share of the personal-computer market had dropped to a tiny 2 percent. Even the most ardent Apple fans—the "macolytes"—wavered, and the company's days seemed numbered.

Yet Apple has engineered a remarkable turnaround. Last years' sales soared to a record $19 billion, more than triple sales just three years earlier. Profits rose a stunning 47-fold in that same three-year period. "To say Apple is hot just doesn't do the company justice," said one analyst. "Apple is smoking, searing, blisteringly hot, not to mention hip, with a side order of funky. . . . Gadget geeks around the world have crowned Apple the keeper of all things cool."

What caused this breathtaking turnaround? Apple rediscovered the magic that had made the company so successful in the first place: customer-driven creativity and new-product innovation. The remarkable makeover began with the return of Steve Jobs in 1997. Since leaving Apple, Jobs had started a new computer company, NeXT. He'd then bought out Pixar Animation Studios, turning it into an entertainment-industry powerhouse. Jobs returned to Apple determined to breathe new creative life and customer focus into the company he'd co-founded 20 years earlier.

Jobs' first task was to revitalize Apple's computer business. For starters, in 1998, Apple launched the iMac personal computer, which featured a sleek, egg-shaped monitor and hard drive, all in one unit, in a futuristic translucent turquoise casing. With its one-button Internet access, this machine was designed specifically for cruising the Internet (hence the "i" in "iMac"). The dramatic iMac won raves for design and lured buyers in droves. Within a year, it had sold more than a million units.

Jobs next unleashed Mac OS X, a ground-breaking new Apple operating system that one observer called "the equivalent of a cross between a Porsche and an Abram's tank." OS X served as the launching pad for a new generation of Apple computers and software products. Consider iLife, a bundle of lifestyle applications that comes with every new Mac. It includes applications such as iMovie (for video editing), iDVD (for recording movies, digital-photo slide shows, and music onto TV-playable DVDs), iPhoto (for managing and touching up digital pictures), GarageBand (for making and mixing your own music), iWeb (for creating Web sites and blogs and getting them online), and iWork (for making presentations and newsletters).

The iMac and Mac OS X put Apple back on the map in personal computing. But Jobs knew that Apple, still a nicher claiming just a 6 percent share of the U.S. market, would never catch up in computers with dominant competitors such as Dell and HP. Real growth and stardom would require even more creative thinking. And it just doesn't get much more creative than iPod and iTunes, innovations that would utterly change the way people acquire and listen to music.

A music buff himself, Jobs noticed that kids by the millions were using computers and CD writers to download digital songs from then-illegal online services such as Napster, and then burning their own music CDs. He moved quickly to make CD burners standard equipment on all Macs. Then, to help users download music and manage their music databases, Apple's programmers created state-of-the-art jukebox software called iTunes.

Even before iTunes hit the streets, according to Apple watcher Brent Schendler, Jobs "recognized that although storing and playing music on your computer was pretty cool, wouldn't it be even cooler if there was a portable, Walkman-type player that could hold all your digital music so that you could listen to it anywhere?" Less than nine months later, Apple introduced the sleek and sexy iPod, a tiny computer with an amazing capacity to store digital music and an easy-to-use interface for managing and playing it. In another 18 months, the Apple iTunes Music Store opened on the Web, enabling consumers to legally download CDs and individual songs.

The results, of course, have been astonishing. The iPod now ranks as one of the greatest consumer electronics hits of all time. By March of 2007, Apple had sold more than 88 million iPods, and more than two billion songs, 50 million TV shows, and 1.3 million movies had been downloaded from the iTunes Store. "We had hoped to sell a million songs in the first six months, but we did that in the first six days," notes an Apple spokesman. The iPod captures more than 70 percent of the music player market; Apple's Music Store grabs nearly 90 percent of the song download business.

Apple's success is attracting a horde of large, resourceful competitors. To stay ahead, the company must keep its eye on the consumer and continue to innovate. So, Apple isn't standing still. It recently introduced a line of new, easy-to-use wireless gadgets that link home and business computers, stereos, and other devices. Its .Mac (pronounced dot-Mac) online subscription service has signed up more than 600,000 members. Apple has also opened more than 174 chic and gleaming Apple Stores, now the world's fastest-growing retail chain. And observers see a host of new products just on or just over the horizon: an iHome (a magical device that powers all your digital home entertainment devices) and an iPod on Wheels (a digital hub that integrates your iPod with your car's entertainment system).

For the third straight year, Apple was named the world's most innovative company in Boston Consulting Group's "Most Innovative Company" survey of 2,500 senior executives worldwide. Apple received an amazing 25 percent of the votes, twice the number of runner-up 3M and three times that of third-place Microsoft.

Thus, almost overnight, it seems, Steve Jobs has transformed Apple from a failing niche computer maker to a major force in consumer electronics, digital music and video, and who knows what else in the future. And he's done it through innovation—by helping those around him to "Think Different" (Apple's motto) in their quest to bring value to customers. *Time* magazine sums it up this way:

[Steve Jobs]'s recipe for success? He's a marketing and creative genius with a rare ability to get inside the imaginations of consumers and understand what will captivate them. He is obsessed with the Apple user's experience. . . . For every product his companies have released, it's clear that someone actually asked, How can we "think different" about this? . . . Whether it's the original Macintosh, the iMac, the iPod, the flat-panel monitor, even the Apple op-

erating system, most of the company's products over the past three decades have had designs that are three steps ahead of the competition. . . . Jobs has a drive and vision that renews itself, again and again. It leaves you waiting for his next move.[1]

As the Apple story suggests, companies that excel at developing and managing new products reap big rewards. Every product seems to go through a life cycle—it is born, goes through several phases, and eventually dies as newer products come along that create greater value for customers. This product life cycle presents two major challenges: First, because all products eventually decline, a firm must be good at developing new products to replace aging ones (the challenge of *new-product development*). Second, the firm must be good at adapting its marketing strategies in the face of changing tastes, technologies, and competition as products pass through life-cycle stages (the challenge of *product life-cycle strategies*). We first look at the problem of finding and developing new products and then at the problem of managing them successfully over their life cycles.

New-Product Development Strategy

A firm can obtain new products in two ways. One is through *acquisition*—by buying a whole company, a patent, or a license to produce someone else's product. The other is through the firm's own **new-product development** efforts. By *new products* we mean original products, product improvements, product modifications, and new brands that the firm develops through its own research-and-development efforts. In this chapter, we concentrate on new-product development.

New products are important—to both customers and the marketers who serve them. "Both consumers and companies love new products," declares a new-product consultant, "consumers because they solve problems and bring variety to their lives, and companies because they are a key source of growth."[2]

Yet, innovation can be very expensive and very risky. For example, Texas Instruments lost $660 million before withdrawing from the home computer business. Webvan burned through a staggering $1.2 billion trying to create a new online grocery business before shuttering its cyberdoors for a lack of customers. And despite a huge investment and fevered speculation that it could be even bigger than the Internet, Segway sold an underwhelming 23,500 of its human transporters in the more than five years following its launch, a tiny fraction of projected sales. Segway has yet to do more than gain small footholds in niche markets, such as urban touring and police departments.[3]

New products face tough odds. Other costly product failures from sophisticated companies include New Coke (Coca-Cola Company), Eagle Snacks (Anheuser-Busch), Zap Mail electronic mail (FedEx), Premier "smokeless" cigarettes (R.J. Reynolds), Arch Deluxe sandwiches (McDonald's), and Breakfast Mates cereal-and-milk combos (Kellogg). Studies indicate that up to 90 percent of all new consumer products fail. For example, of the 30,000 new food, beverage, and beauty products launched each year, an estimated 70 to 90 percent fail within just 12 months.[4]

Why do so many new products fail? There are several reasons. Although an idea may be good, the company may overestimate market size. The actual product may be poorly designed. Or it might be incorrectly positioned, launched at the wrong time, priced too high, or poorly advertised. A high-level executive might push a favorite idea despite poor marketing research findings. Sometimes the costs of product development are higher than expected, and sometimes competitors fight back harder than expected. However, the reasons behind some new-product failures seem pretty obvious. Try the following on for size:[5]

New-product development
The development of original products, product improvements, product modifications, and new brands through the firm's own product development efforts.

■ Visiting the NewProductWorks Showcase and Learning Center is like finding yourself in some nightmare version of a supermarket. Each product failure represents squandered dollars and hopes.

Strolling the aisles at NewProductWorks Showcase and Learning Center collection is like finding yourself in some nightmare version of a supermarket. Many of the 86,553 products on display were abject flops. Behind each of them are squandered dollars and hopes and the classic question, "What were they thinking?" Some products failed because they simply failed to bring value to customers—for example, Look of Buttermilk shampoo, Cucumber antiperspirant spray, or Premier smokeless cigarettes. *Smokeless* cigarettes? What were they thinking? Other companies failed because they attached trusted brand names to something totally out of character. Can you imagine swallowing Ben-Gay aspirin? Or how about Gerber Singles food for adults (perhaps the tasty pureed sweet-and-sour pork or chicken Madeira)? Other misbegotten attempts to stretch a good name include Cracker Jack cereal, Exxon fruit punch, Smucker's premium ketchup, Fruit of the Loom laundry detergent, and Harley-Davidson cake-decorating kits. Really, what were they thinking?

The New-Product Development Process

So companies face a problem—they must develop new products, but the odds weigh heavily against success. In all, to create successful new products, a company must understand its consumers, markets, and competitors and develop products that deliver superior value to customers. It must carry out strong new-product planning and set up a systematic, customer-driven *new-product development process* for finding and growing new products. Figure 8.1 shows the eight major steps in this process.

Idea Generation

Idea generation
The systematic search for new-product ideas.

New-product development starts with **idea generation**—the systematic search for new-product ideas. A company typically generates hundreds of ideas, even thousands, in order to find a few good ones. For example, IBM recently held an "Innovation Jam"—a kind of online suggestion box—in which it invited IBM and customer employees worldwide to submit ideas for new products and services. The mammoth brainstorming session generated some 37,000 ideas from 104 countries. Since the jam fest, however, IBM has whittled down this surge of ideas to only 10 products, businesses, and services that it plans to develop.[6]

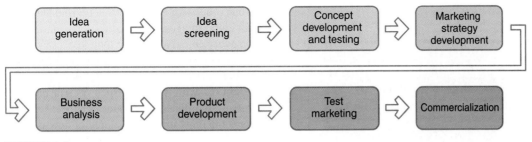

FIGURE 8.1

Major Stages in New-Product Development

Major sources of new-product ideas include internal sources and external sources such as customers, competitors, distributors and suppliers, and others.

Internal Idea Sources Using *internal sources,* the company can find new ideas through formal research and development. Or it can pick the brains of employees—from executives to scientists, engineers, and manufacturing staff to salespeople—as IBM did with its Innovation Jam. Everyone in the company can contribute good new-product ideas. "Most companies operate under the assumption that big ideas come from a few big brains: the inspired founder, the eccentric inventor, the visionary boss," says one analyst. But in today's fast-moving and competitive environment, "it's time to invent a less top-down approach to innovation, to make it everybody's business to come up with great ideas."[7]

Some companies have developed successful "intrapreneurial" programs that encourage employees to think up and develop new-product ideas. For example, Samsung built a special Value Innovation Program (VIP) Center in Suwon, South Korea, to encourage and support internal new-product innovation. The VIP Center is the ultimate round-the-clock idea factory in which company researchers, engineers, and designers commingle to come up with new-product ideas and processes. The center features workrooms, dorm rooms, training rooms, a kitchen, and a basement filled with games, a gym, and sauna. Recent ideas sprouting from the VIP Center include a 102-inch plasma HDTV and a process to reduce material costs on a multifunction printer by 30 percent. The center has helped Samsung, once known as the maker of cheap knock-off products, become one of the world's most innovative and profitable consumer electronics companies.[8]

■ Internal new-product idea sources: Samsung built a special Value Innovation Program Center in which company researchers, engineers, and designers commingle to come up with creative new-product ideas.

External Idea Sources Companies can also obtain good new-product ideas from any of a number of external sources. For example, *distributors and suppliers* can contribute ideas. Distributors are close to the market and can pass along information about consumer problems and new-product possibilities. Suppliers can tell the company about new concepts, techniques, and materials that can be used to develop new products. *Competitors* are another important source. Companies watch competitors' ads to get clues about their new products. They buy competing new products, take them apart to see how they work, analyze their sales, and decide whether they should bring out a new product of their own. Other idea sources include trade magazines, shows, and seminars; government agencies; advertising agencies; marketing research firms; university and commercial laboratories; and inventors.

Some companies seek the help of outside new-product consultancies and design firms, such as ZIBA, Frog Design, or IDEO, for new-product ideas and designs. For example, when Procter & Gamble needed innovative ideas for reinventing its Pringles snack chip line, it turned to IDEO. After interviewing kids and moms about snacking, lunching, and eating habits, IDEO landed on the idea that the uniform chips could have entertainment

■ External idea sources: P&G worked with design firm IDEO to come up with its highly successful Pringles Prints, printable chips with individual images, trivia questions, and jokes printed on every chip.

value. It came up with Pringles Prints, printable chips with individual images, trivia questions, and jokes printed on every chip. Now, more than just a snack, the highly successful Pringles Prints create an interactive customer experience. P&G has even developed co-branding efforts with partners such as Hasbro and Trivial Pursuit to broaden the product's appeal.[9]

Perhaps the most important source of new-product ideas is *customers* themselves. The company can analyze customer questions and complaints to find new products that better solve consumer problems. For example, Staples developed its Easy Rebate program in response to concerns expressed by small-business customers that lost rebates were one of their biggest frustrations.[10]

Company engineers or salespeople can meet with and work alongside customers to get suggestions and ideas. LEGO did just that when it invited 250 LEGO train-set enthusiasts to visit its New York office to assess new designs. "We pooh-poohed them all," says one LEGO fan, an Intel engineer from Portland. But the group gave LEGO lots of new ideas, and the company put them to good use. The result was the "Santa Fe Super Chief" set. Thanks to "word-of-mouse" endorsements from the 250 enthusiasts, LEGO sold out the first 10,000 units in less than two weeks with no additional marketing.[11]

Other companies actively solicit ideas from customers and turn customers into cocreators. For example, Dell set up a Web site forum called IdeaStorm that asks consumers for insights on how to improve its product offering. Users post suggestions, the community votes, and the most popular ideas rise to the top. Only two months after launch, the site had received some 3,850 ideas and 236,000 votes. Michael Dell sees such customer-driven innovation as a key to reenergizing Dell. "We need to think differently about the market and engage our customers in almost everything we do," says Dell.

Finally, customers often create new products and uses on their own, and companies can benefit by putting them on the market. For example, for years customers were spreading the word that Avon Skin-So-Soft bath oil and moisturizer was also a terrific bug repellent. Whereas some consumers were content simply to bathe in water scented with the fragrant oil, others carried it in their backpacks to mosquito-infested campsites or kept a bottle on the decks of their beach houses. Avon turned the idea into a complete line of Skin-So-Soft Bug Guard products, including Bug Guard Mosquito Repellant Moisturizing Towelettes and Bug Guard Plus, a combination moisturizer, insect repellent, and sunscreen.[12]

Although customer input on new products yields many benefits, companies must be careful not to rely *too* heavily on what customers say. For some products, especially highly technical ones, customers may not know what they need. "Merely giving people what they want isn't always enough," says one innovation management consultant. "People want to be surprised; they want something that's better than they imagined, something that stretches them in what they like."[13]

Idea Screening

Idea screening

Screening new-product ideas in order to spot good ideas and drop poor ones as soon as possible.

The purpose of idea generation is to create a large number of ideas. The purpose of the succeeding stages is to *reduce* that number. The first idea-reducing stage is **idea screening**, which helps spot good ideas and drop poor ones as soon as possible. Product development costs rise greatly in later stages, so the company wants to go ahead only with the product ideas that will turn into profitable products.

Many companies require their executives to write up new-product ideas in a standard format that can be reviewed by a new-product committee. The write-up describes the product or service, the proposed customer value proposition, the target market, and the competition. It makes some rough estimates of market size, product price, development time and costs, manufacturing costs, and rate of return. The committee then evaluates the idea against a set of general criteria.

For example, at Kao Corporation, the large Japanese consumer-products company, the new-product committee asks questions such as these: Is the product truly useful to consumers and society? Is it good for our particular company? Does it mesh well with the company's objectives and strategies? Do we have the people, skills, and resources to make it succeed? Does it deliver more value to customers than do competing products? Is it easy to advertise and distribute? Many companies have well-designed systems for rating and screening new-product ideas.

Concept Development and Testing

An attractive idea must be developed into a **product concept**. It is important to distinguish between a product idea, a product concept, and a product image. A *product idea* is an idea for a possible product that the company can see itself offering to the market. A *product concept* is a detailed version of the idea stated in meaningful consumer terms. A *product image* is the way consumers perceive an actual or potential product.

Product concept

A detailed version of the new-product idea stated in meaningful consumer terms.

Concept Development Suppose that a car manufacturer has developed a practical battery-powered all-electric car. Its initial prototype is a sleek, sporty convertible that sells for about $100,000.[14] However, later this decade, it plans to introduce more-affordable, mass-market models that will compete with today's hybrid-powered cars. This 100 percent electric car will accelerate from 0 to 60 in four seconds, travel more than 250 miles on a single charge, recharge from a normal 120-volt electrical outlet, and cost about one cent per mile to power.

Looking ahead, the marketer's task is to develop this new product into alternative product concepts, find out how attractive each concept is to customers, and choose the best one. It might create the following product concepts for the electric car:

Concept 1: An affordably priced midsize car designed as a second family car to be used around town for running errands and visiting friends

Concept 2: A midpriced sporty compact appealing to young singles and couples

Concept 3: A "green" car appealing to environmentally conscious people who want practical, low-polluting transportation

Concept 4: A high-end midsize utility vehicle appealing to those who love the space SUVs provide but lament the poor gas mileage

Concept Testing **Concept testing** calls for testing new-product concepts with groups of target consumers. The concepts may be presented to consumers symbolically or physically. Here, in words, is concept 3:

An efficient, fun-to-drive, battery-powered compact car that seats four. This 100 percent electric wonder provides practical and reliable transportation with no pollution. It goes more than 250 miles on a single charge and costs pennies per mile to operate. It's a sensible, responsible alternative to today's pollution-producing gas-guzzlers. It's priced, fully equipped, at $25,000.

Concept testing

Testing new-product concepts with a group of target consumers to find out if the concepts have strong consumer appeal.

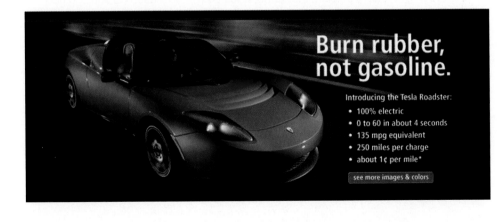

■ Concept testing: The initial Tesla electric car goes from 0-60 mph in 4 seconds, travels 250 miles on a single charge, and costs about a penny a mile to power.

Many firms routinely test new-product concepts with consumers before attempting to turn them into actual new products. For some concept tests, a word or picture description might be sufficient. However, a more concrete and physical presentation of the concept will increase the reliability of the concept test. After being exposed to the concept, consumers then may be asked to react to it by answering questions such as those in Table 8.1.

The answers to such questions will help the company decide which concept has the strongest appeal. For example, the last question asks about the consumer's intention to buy. Suppose 10 percent of consumers say they "definitely" would buy, and another 5 percent say "probably." The company could project these figures to the full population in this target group to estimate sales volume. Even then, the estimate is uncertain because people do not always carry out their stated intentions.

Marketing Strategy Development

Marketing strategy development
Designing an initial marketing strategy for a new product based on the product concept.

Suppose the car maker finds that concept 3 for the fuel-cell-powered electric car tests best. The next step is **marketing strategy development**, designing an initial marketing strategy for introducing this car to the market.

The *marketing strategy statement* consists of three parts. The first part describes the target market; the planned value proposition; and the sales, market share, and profit goals for the first few years. Thus:

The target market is younger, well-educated, moderate- to high-income individuals, couples, or small families seeking practical, environmentally responsible transportation. The car will be positioned as more fun to drive and less polluting than today's internal combustion engine or hybrid cars. The company will aim to sell 100,000 cars in the first year, at a loss of not more than $15 million. In the second year, the company will aim for sales of 120,000 cars and a profit of $25 million.

The second part of the marketing strategy statement outlines the product's planned price, distribution, and marketing budget for the first year:

The battery-powered electric car will be offered in three colors—red, white, and blue—and will have a full set of accessories as standard features. It will sell at a retail price of $25,000—with 15 percent off the list price to dealers. Dealers who sell more than 10 cars per month will get an additional discount of 5 percent on each car sold that month. A marketing budget of $50 million will be split 50-50 between a national media campaign and local event marketing. Advertising and a Web site will emphasize the car's fun spirit and low emissions. During the first year, $100,000 will be spent on marketing research to find out who is buying the car and their satisfaction levels.

The third part of the marketing strategy statement describes the planned long-run sales, profit goals, and marketing mix strategy:

We intend to capture a 3 percent long-run share of the total auto market and realize an after-tax return on investment of 15 percent. To achieve this, product quality will start high and be improved over time. Price will be raised in the second and third years if competition permits. The total marketing budget will be raised each year by about 10 percent. Marketing research will be reduced to $60,000 per year after the first year.

TABLE 8.1 Questions for Battery-Powered Electric Car Concept Test

1. Do you understand the concept of a battery-powered electric car?
2. Do you believe the claims about the car's performance?
3. What are the major benefits of the battery-powered electric car compared with a conventional car?
4. What are its advantages compared with a gas-electric hybrid car?
5. What improvements in the car's features would you suggest?
6. For what uses would you prefer a battery-powered electric car to a conventional car?
7. What would be a reasonable price to charge for the car?
8. Who would be involved in your decision to buy such a car? Who would drive it?
9. Would you buy such a car (definitely, probably, probably not, definitely not)?

Business Analysis

Once management has decided on its product concept and marketing strategy, it can evaluate the business attractiveness of the proposal. **Business analysis** involves a review of the sales, costs, and profit projections for a new product to find out whether they satisfy the company's objectives. If they do, the product can move to the product development stage.

To estimate sales, the company might look at the sales history of similar products and conduct market surveys. It can then estimate minimum and maximum sales to assess the range of risk. After preparing the sales forecast, management can estimate the expected costs and profits for the product, including marketing, R&D, operations, accounting, and finance costs. The company then uses the sales and costs figures to analyze the new product's financial attractiveness.

> **Business analysis**
> A review of the sales, costs, and profit projections for a new product to find out whether these factors satisfy the company's objectives.

Product Development

So far, for many new-product concepts, the product may have existed only as a word description, a drawing, or perhaps a crude mock-up. If the product concept passes the business test, it moves into **product development**. Here, R&D or engineering develops the product concept into a physical product. The product development step, however, now calls for a large jump in investment. It will show whether the product idea can be turned into a workable product.

The R&D department will develop and test one or more physical versions of the product concept. R&D hopes to design a prototype that will satisfy and excite consumers and that can be produced quickly and at budgeted costs. Developing a successful prototype can take days, weeks, months, or even years depending on the product and prototype methods.

Often, products undergo rigorous tests to make sure that they perform safely and effectively, or that consumers will find value in them. Companies can do their own product testing or outsource testing to other firms that specialize in testing. Here are some examples of such product tests:[15]

> **Product development**
> Developing the product concept into a physical product in order to ensure that the product idea can be turned into a workable market offering.

> Thunk. Thunk. Thunk. Behind a locked door in the basement of Louis Vuitton's elegant Paris headquarters, a mechanical arm hoists a brown-and-tan handbag a half-meter off the floor—then drops it. The bag, loaded with an 8-pound weight, will be lifted and dropped, over and over again, for four days. This is Vuitton's test laboratory, a high-tech torture chamber for its fabled luxury goods. Another piece of lab equipment bombards handbags with ultraviolet rays to test resistance to fading. Still another tests zippers by tugging them open and shutting them 5,000 times. There's even a mechanized mannequin hand, with a Vuitton charm bracelet around its wrist, being shaken vigorously to make sure none of the charms fall off.
>
> At Gillette, almost everyone gets involved in new-product testing. Every working day at Gillette, 200 volunteers from various departments come to work unshaven, troop to the second floor of the company's gritty South Boston plant, and enter small booths with a sink and mirror. There they take instructions from technicians on the other side of a small window as to which razor, shaving cream, or aftershave to use. The volunteers evaluate razors for sharpness of blade, smoothness of glide, and ease of handling. In a nearby shower room, women perform the same ritual on their legs, underarms, and what the company delicately refers to as the "bikini area." "We bleed so you'll get a good shave at home," says one Gillette employee.

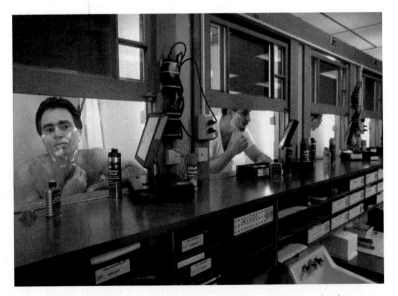

■ Product testing: Gillette uses employee-volunteers to test new shaving products—"We bleed so you'll get a good shave at home," says a Gillette employee.

A new product must have the required functional features and also convey the intended psychological characteristics. The battery-powered electric car, for example, should strike consumers as being well built, comfortable, and safe. Management must learn what makes consumers decide that a car is well built. To some consumers, this means that the car has "solid-sounding" doors. To others, it means that the car is able to withstand heavy impact in crash tests. Consumer tests are conducted in which consumers test-drive the car and rate its attributes.

Test Marketing

Test marketing

The stage of new-product development in which the product and marketing program are tested in realistic market settings.

If the product passes concept and product tests, the next step is **test marketing**, the stage at which the product and marketing program are introduced into realistic market settings. Test marketing gives the marketer experience with marketing the product before going to the great expense of full introduction. It lets the company test the product and its entire marketing program—targeting and positioning strategy, advertising, distribution, pricing, branding and packaging, and budget levels.

The amount of test marketing needed varies with each new product. Test marketing costs can be high, and it takes time that may allow competitors to gain advantages. When the costs of developing and introducing the product are low, or when management is already confident about the new product, the company may do little or no test marketing. In fact, test marketing by consumer-goods firms has been declining in recent years. Companies often do not test-market simple line extensions or copies of successful competitor products.

However, when introducing a new product requires a big investment, or when management is not sure of the product or marketing program, a company may do a lot of test marketing. For instance, McDonald's tested its Redbox subsidiary's automated DVD rental kiosks in its own restaurants and in supermarkets for more than two years in six major U.S. markets. Using the kiosks, consumers can rent DVDs for $1 a day using their credit cards. Based on the success of these test markets—in Denver tests alone, the Redbox kiosks quickly commanded more than a 10 percent share of all DVD rentals—McDonald's is rolling out kiosks in all of its restaurants and in a slew of supermarkets across the country.[16]

Although test-marketing costs can be high, they are often small when compared with the costs of making a major mistake. Still, test marketing doesn't guarantee success. For example, Procter & Gamble tested its Fit produce rinse product heavily for five years and Olay cosmetics for three years. Although market tests suggested the products would be successful, P&G pulled the plug on both shortly after their introductions.[17]

Many marketers are now using new technologies to reduce the costs of test marketing and to speed up the process. For example, Frito-Lay worked with research firm Decision Insight to create an online virtual convenience store in which to test new products and marketing ideas.[18]

■ New test marketing technologies: Frito-Lay worked with research firm Decision Insight to create an online virtual convenience store in which to test new products and marketing ideas.

Decision Insight's SimuShop online shopping environment lets Frito-Lay's marketers test shopper reactions to different extensions, shelf placements, pricing, and packaging of its Lay's, Doritos, Cheetos, and Fritos brands in a variety of store setups without investing huge amounts of time and money on actual in-store research in different locations. Recruited shoppers visit the online store, browse realistic virtual shelves featuring Frito-Lay's and competing products, click on individual products to view them in more detail, and select products to put in their carts. When the shopping is done, selected customers are questioned in one-on-one, on-screen interviews about why they chose the products they did. Watching the entire decision process unfold gives Frito-Lay marketers reams of information about what would happen in the real world. With 200-some bags of Frito-Lay products sitting on a typical store shelf, the company doesn't have the luxury of test marketing in actual market settings. "For us, that can only really be done virtually," says a Frito-Lay marketer. The SimuShop tests produce a 90 percent or better correlation to real shopper behavior when compared with later real-world data.

Commercialization

Test marketing gives management the information needed to make a final decision about whether to launch the new product. If the company goes ahead with **commercialization**— introducing the new product into the market—it will face high costs. The company may need to build or rent a manufacturing facility. And, in the case of a major new consumer packaged good, it may spend hundreds of millions of dollars for advertising, sales promotion, and other marketing efforts in the first year. For example, when Unilever introduced its Sunsilk hair care line, it spent $200 million in the United States alone, including $30 million for nontraditional media such as MySpace ads and profiles, mall displays that used audio to catch passersby, 3-D ads in tavern bathrooms, and cinema ads.[19]

The company launching a new product must first decide on introduction *timing*. If the car maker's new battery-powered electric car will eat into the sales of the company's other cars, its introduction may be delayed. If the car can be improved further, or if the economy is down, the company may wait until the following year to launch it. However, if competitors are ready to introduce their own battery-powered models, the company may push to introduce its car sooner.

Next, the company must decide *where* to launch the new product—in a single location, a region, the national market, or the international market. Few companies have the confidence, capital, and capacity to launch new products into full national or international distribution. They will develop a planned *market rollout* over time. In particular, small companies may enter attractive cities or regions one at a time. Larger companies, however, may quickly introduce new models into several regions or into the full national market. For example, Procter & Gamble launched the Gillette Fusion six-blade razor with a full national $300 million blitz. The launch began with 2006 Super Bowl ads costing more than $6 million. Within the first week of launch, P&G had blanketed U.S. stores with some 180,000 Fusion displays. After three months, Fusion brand awareness exceeded 60 percent, and the new brand contributed to a 44 percent rise in overall U.S. sales of nondisposable razors.[20]

Companies with international distribution systems may introduce new products through swift global rollouts. Microsoft recently did this with its Windows Vista operating system. Microsoft used a mammoth $500 million promotional blitz to launch Vista simultaneously in more than 30 markets worldwide. The campaign targeted 6.6 billion global impressions in just its

Commercialization
Introducing a new product into the market.

■ Commercialization: Microsoft launched its new Windows Vista operating system in a swift global rollout. Its mammoth $500 million "Wow!" promotional blitz hit more than 30 markets worldwide simultaneously, creating some 6.6 billion global impressions in just its first two months.

first two months. "There won't be a PC sold anywhere in the world that doesn't have Vista within the next six months," said an industry analyst at the start of the campaign.[21]

Managing New-Product Development

The new-product development process shown in Figure 8.1 highlights the important activities needed to find, develop, and introduce new products. However, new-product development involves more than just going through a set of steps. Companies must take a holistic approach to managing this process. Successful new-product development requires a customer-centered, team-based, and systematic effort.

Customer-Centered New-Product Development

Customer-centered new-product development
New-product development that focuses on finding new ways to solve customer problems and create more customer-satisfying experiences.

Above all else, new-product development must be customer centered. When looking for and developing new products, companies often rely too heavily on technical research in their R&D labs. But like everything else in marketing, successful new-product development begins with a thorough understanding of what consumers need and value. **Customer-centered new-product development** focuses on finding new ways to solve customer problems and create more customer-satisfying experiences.

One recent study found that the most successful new products are ones that are differentiated, solve major customer problems, and offer a compelling customer value proposition.[22] Thus, for products ranging from bathroom cleaners to jet engines, today's innovative companies are getting out of the research lab and mingling with customers in the search for new customer value. Consider these examples:[23]

> People at all levels of Procter & Gamble, from brand managers to the CEO, look for fresh ideas by tagging along with and talking to customers as they shop for and use the company's products. When one P&G team tackled the problem of "reinventing bathroom cleaning," it started by "listening with its eyes." The group spent many hours watching consumers clean their bathrooms. They focused on "extreme users," ranging from a professional house cleaner who scrubbed grout with his fingernail to four single guys whose idea of cleaning the bathroom was pushing a filthy towel around the floor with a big stick. If they could make both users happy, they figured they had a home run. One big idea—a cleaning tool on a removable stick that could both reach shower walls and get into crannies—got the green light quickly. Consumers loved the prototype, patched together with repurposed plastic, foam, and duct tape. Some refused to return it. The idea became P&G's highly successful Mr. Clean Magic Reach bathroom cleaning tool.
>
> General Electric wants to infuse customer-centered new-product development thinking into all of its diverse divisions. So executives from the GE Money division—which offers credit cards, loans, and other consumer finance solutions—recently took a tour of San Francisco. During the tour, they watched how people use money—where they get it, how they spend it, even how they carry it. Similarly, to unleash creativity in 15 top executives from GE's jet-engine business, the company took them out to talk with airplane pilots and mechanics. "We even went to meet Larry Flynt's private jet team," says a manager who arranged the trip. "It's a way to . . . increase their empathy and strengthen their ability to make innovation decisions."

Thus, customer-centered new-product development begins and ends with solving customer problems. As one expert asks: "What is innovation after all, if not products and services that offer fresh thinking in a way that meets the needs of customers?"[24] Says another expert, "Getting consumer insights at the beginning of the process, using those insights consistently and respectfully throughout the process, and communicating them in a compelling form when you go to market is critical to a product's success in the market these days."[25]

Team-Based New-Product Development

Good new-product development also requires a total-company, cross-functional effort. Some companies organize their new-product development process into the orderly sequence of steps shown in Figure 8.1, starting with idea generation and ending with commercialization. Under this *sequential product development* approach, one company department works individually to complete its stage of the process before passing the new product along to the next department and stage. This orderly, step-by-step process can help bring control to complex and risky projects. But it also can be dangerously slow. In fast-changing, highly competitive markets, such slow-but-sure product development can result in product failures, lost sales and profits, and crumbling market positions.

In order to get their new products to market more quickly, many companies use a **team-based new-product development** approach. Under this approach, company departments work closely together in cross-functional teams, overlapping the steps in the product development process to save time and increase effectiveness. Instead of passing the new product from department to department, the company assembles a team of people from various departments that stays with the new product from start to finish. Such teams usually include people from the marketing, finance, design, manufacturing, and legal departments, and even supplier and customer companies. In the sequential process, a bottleneck at one phase can seriously slow the entire project. In the team-based approach, if one area hits snags, it works to resolve them while the team moves on.

The team-based approach does have some limitations. For example, it sometimes creates more organizational tension and confusion than the more orderly sequential approach. However, in rapidly changing industries facing increasingly shorter product life cycles, the rewards of fast and flexible product development far exceed the risks. Companies that combine a customer-centered approach with team-based new-product development gain a big competitive edge by getting the right new products to market faster (see Marketing at Work 8.1).

> **Team-based new-product development**
> An approach to developing new products in which various company departments work closely together, overlapping the steps in the product development process to save time and increase effectiveness.

Systematic New-Product Development

Finally, the new-product development process should be holistic and systematic rather than compartmentalized and haphazard. Otherwise, few new ideas will surface, and many good ideas will sputter and die. To avoid these problems, a company can install an *innovation management system* to collect, review, evaluate, and manage new-product ideas.

The company can appoint a respected senior person to be the company's innovation manager. It can set up Web-based idea management software and encourage all company stakeholders—employees, suppliers, distributors, dealers—to become involved in finding and developing new products. It can assign a cross-functional innovation management committee to evaluate proposed new-product ideas and help bring good ideas to market. It can create recognition programs to reward those who contribute the best ideas.[26]

The innovation management system approach yields two favorable outcomes. First, it helps create an innovation-oriented company culture. It shows that top management supports, encourages, and rewards innovation. Second, it will yield a larger number of new-product ideas, among which will be found some especially good ones. The good new ideas will be more systematically developed, producing more new-product successes. No longer will good ideas wither for the lack of a sounding board or a senior product advocate.

Thus, new-product success requires more than simply thinking up a few good ideas, turning them into products, and finding customers for them. It requires a holistic approach for finding new ways to create valued customer experiences, from generating and screening new-product ideas to creating and rolling out want-satisfying products to customers.

More than this, successful new-product development requires a whole-company commitment. At companies known for their new-product prowess—such as Apple, Google, 3M, Procter & Gamble, and General Electric—the entire culture encourages, supports, and rewards innovation. Consider GE, which has topped *Fortune's* list of most admired companies 7 of the past 10 years, largely because of its innovative culture. GE's companywide emphasis on innovation is summed up in its well-known advertising tagline: "Imagination at Work."[27]

8.1 MARKETING AT WORK

Electrolux: Cleaning Up with Customer-Centered, Team-Based New-Product Development

You will never meet Catherine, Anna, Maria, or Monica. But the future success of Swedish home appliances maker Electrolux depends on what these four women think. Catherine, for instance, a type A career woman who is a perfectionist at home, loves the idea of simply sliding her laundry basket into a washing machine, instead of having to lift the clothes from the basket and into the washer. That product idea has been moved onto the fast track for consideration.

So, just who are Catherine and the other women? Well, they don't actually exist. They are composites based on in-depth interviews with some 160,000 consumers from around the globe. To divine the needs of these mythical customers, 53 Electrolux employees—in teams that included designers, engineers, and marketers hailing from various divisions—gathered in Stockholm last November for a weeklong brainstorming session. The Catherine team began by ripping photographs out of a pile of magazines and sticking them onto poster boards. Next to a picture of a woman wearing a sharply tailored suit, they scribbled some of Catherine's attributes: driven, busy, and a bit overwhelmed. In similar fashion, other teams addressed the needs of super-efficient Monica, Anna (who just wants to finish her chores as quickly as possible), and Maria, a homebody who dotes on her family.

With the help of these characters, Electrolux product developers are searching for the insights they'll need to dream up the next batch of hot products. It's a new way of doing things for Electrolux, but then again, a lot is new at the company. When Chief Executive Hans Straberg took the helm in 2002, Electrolux—which sells products under the Electrolux, Eureka, and Frigidaire brands—was the world's number-two home appliances maker behind Whirlpool. The company faced spiraling costs while its middle-market products were gradually losing out to cheaper goods from Asia and Eastern Europe. Competition in the United States, where Electrolux gets 40 percent of its sales, was ferocious. The company's stock was treading water.

Straberg had to do something radical, especially in the area of new-product innovation. So he began breaking down barriers between departments and forcing his designers, engineers, and marketers to work together to come up with new products. He also introduced an intense focus on the customer. He set out to become "the leader in our industry in terms of systematic development of new products based on consumer insight."

At the Stockholm brainstorming session, for example, group leader Kim Scott urges everyone "to think of yourselves as Catherine." The room buzzes with discussion. Ideas are refined, sketches drawn up. The group settles on three concepts: Breeze, a clothes steamer that also removes stains; an Ironing Center, similar to a pants press but for shirts; and Ease, the washing machine that holds a laundry basket inside its drum.

Half the group races off to the machine shop to turn out a prototype for Breeze, while the rest stay upstairs to bang out a marketing plan. Over the next hour, designer Lennart Johansson carves and sandpapers a block of peach-colored polyurethane until a contraption that resembles a cross between an electric screwdriver and a handheld vacuum begins to emerge. The designers in the group want the Breeze to be smaller, but engineer Giuseppe Frucco points out that would leave too little space for a charging station for the 1,500-watt unit.

For company veterans such as Frucco, who works at Electrolux's fabric care research and development center in Porcia, Italy, this dynamic groupthink is a refreshing change: "We never used to create new products together," he says. "The designers would come up with something and then tell us to build it." The new way saves time and money by avoiding the technical glitches that crop up as a new design moves from the drafting table to the factory floor. The ultimate goal is to come up with new products that consumers will gladly pay a premium for: gadgets with drop-dead good looks and clever features that ordinary people can understand without having to pore through a thick users' manual. "Consumers are prepared to pay for good design and good performance," says CEO Straberg.

Few companies have pulled off the range of hot new offerings that Electrolux has. One clear hit is a cordless stick and hand vacuum, called Pronto in the United States. Available in an array of metallic hues with a rounded, ergonomic design, this is the Cinderella of vacuums. Too attractive to be locked up in the broom closet, it calls out to be displayed in your kitchen. In Europe, it now commands 50 percent of the market for stick vacs, a coup for a product with fewer than two years on the market. The Pronto is cleaning up in the United States, too. Stacy Silk, a buyer at retail chain Best Buy, says it is one of her hottest sellers, even though it retails for around $100, double the price of comparable models. "The biggest thing is the aesthetics," Silk says. "That gets people to walk over and look."

Electrolux is crafting such new products even while moving away from many traditional customer research tools. The company relies less

At GE, innovation is a key to future growth. But GE's vision of an imagination-driven company can't be realized unless everyone in the company is looking for innovation. So three years ago, GE launched a companywide movement called "Imagination Breakthroughs" that challenged every GE business unit to identify at least five breakthrough big ideas that were capable of generating $50 million to $100 million of new revenue within three to seven years. Under the program, the chief marketing officers in each GE business have become innovation project leaders, responsible for finding new ideas, filtering them, and matching them to customer needs. Marketing executives throughout the company now receive regular creativity training. For example, each year, 60 of GE's most senior marketers experience a three and one-half week "odyssey of creativity." (Remember those customer-interaction field trips by GE executives described in a previous example?) GE's broad-based support for innovation is producing results. Imagination Breakthroughs has already yielded more than 100 projects that

■ Customer-centered new-product development: Electrolux's new-product team starts by watching and talking with consumers to understand their problems. Here, they build a bulletin board packed with pictures and post-its detailing consumers struggling with household cleaning chores and possible product solutions. The team then moves to the lab to create products that solve customer problems. "We were thinking of you when we developed this product," says Electrolux.

heavily on focus groups and now prefers to interview people in their homes where they can be videotaped pushing a vacuum or shoving laundry into the washer. "Consumers think they know what they want, but they often have trouble articulating it," says Electrolux's senior vice president for global design."But when we watch them, we can ask, 'Why do you do that?' We can change the product and solve their problems."

This customer-centered, team-based new-product development approach is producing results. Under the new approach, new-product launches have almost doubled in quantity, and the proportion of new-product launches that result in outsized unit sales is now running at 50 percent of all introductions, up from around 25 percent previously. As a result, Electrolux's sales, profits, and share price are all up sharply.

It all boils down to understanding consumers and giving them what they need and want. According to a recent Electrolux annual report:

"Thinking of you" sums up our product offering. That is how we create value for our customers—and thereby for our shareholders. All

product development and marketing starts with understanding consumer needs, expectations, dreams, and motivation. That's why we contact tens of thousands of consumers throughout the world every year. . . . The first steps in product development are to ask questions, observe, discuss, and analyze. So we can actually say, "We were thinking of you when we developed this product."

Thanks to such thinking, Electrolux has now grown to become the world's biggest household appliances company. Catherine and the other women would be pleased.

Source: Portions adapted from Ariene Sains and Stanley Reed, "Electrolux Cleans Up," *BusinessWeek,* February 27, 2006, pp. 42–43; with quotes and extracts adapted from "Products Developed on the Basis of Consumer Insight," *Acceleration . . . Electrolux Annual Report,* April 7, 2006, p. 7, accessed at www.electrolux.com/node60.aspx. Additional information from Caroline Perry, "Electrolux Doubles Spend with New Strategy," *Marketing Week,* February 16, 2006, pp. 7–9; and Ariane Sains, "Electrolux Redesigns Itself," *BusinessWeek,* November 27, 2006, pp. 13–15.

are on track to meet their $50 million targets. Says GE CEO Jeffrey Immelt, "for GE, imagination is more than a slogan or a tagline. It is a reason for being."

Linking the Concepts

Take a break. Think about new products and how companies find and develop them.

■ Suppose that you're on a panel to nominate the "best new products of the year." What products would you nominate and why? See what you can learn about the new-product development process for one of these products.

■ Applying the new-product development process you've just studied, develop an idea for an innovative new snack-food product and sketch out a brief plan for bringing it to market. Loosen up and have some fun with this.

Product Life-Cycle Strategies

Product life cycle
The course of a product's sales and profits over its lifetime.

After launching the new product, management wants the product to enjoy a long and happy life. Although it does not expect the product to sell forever, the company wants to earn a decent profit to cover all the effort and risk that went into launching it. Management is aware that each product will have a life cycle, although its exact shape and length is not known in advance.

Figure 8.2 shows a typical **product life cycle (PLC)**, the course that a product's sales and profits take over its lifetime. The product life cycle has five distinct stages:

1. *Product development* begins when the company finds and develops a new-product idea. During product development, sales are zero and the company's investment costs mount.
2. *Introduction* is a period of slow sales growth as the product is introduced in the market. Profits are nonexistent in this stage because of the heavy expenses of product introduction.
3. *Growth* is a period of rapid market acceptance and increasing profits.
4. *Maturity* is a period of slowdown in sales growth because the product has achieved acceptance by most potential buyers. Profits level off or decline because of increased marketing outlays to defend the product against competition.
5. *Decline* is the period when sales fall off and profits drop.

Not all products follow this product life cycle. Some products are introduced and die quickly; others stay in the mature stage for a long, long time. Some enter the decline stage and are then cycled back into the growth stage through strong promotion or repositioning. It seems that a well-managed brand could live forever. Such venerable brands as Coca-Cola, Gillette, Budweiser, American Express, Wells-Fargo, Kikkoman, and TABASCO®, for instance, are still going strong after more than 100 years.

The PLC concept can describe a *product class* (gasoline-powered automobiles), a *product form* (SUVs), or a *brand* (the Ford Escape). The PLC concept applies differently in each case. Product classes have the longest life cycles—the sales of many product classes stay in the mature stage for a long time. Product forms, in contrast, tend to have the standard PLC shape. Product forms such as "dial telephones" and "cassette tapes" passed through a regular history of introduction, rapid growth, maturity, and decline.

■ Product life cycle: Some products die quickly; others stay in the mature stage for a long, long time. TABASCO® Sauce is "over 130 years old and yet still able to totally whup your butt!"

A specific brand's life cycle can change quickly because of changing competitive attacks and responses. For example, although laundry soaps (product class) and powdered de-

FIGURE 8.2

Sales and Profits Over the Product's Life from Inception to Decline

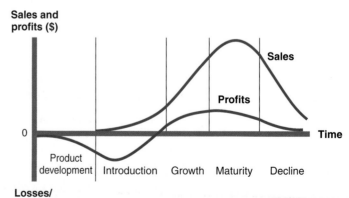

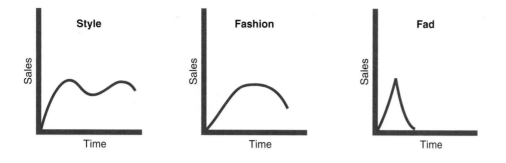

FIGURE 8.3
Styles, Fashions, and Fads

tergents (product form) have enjoyed fairly long life cycles, the life cycles of specific brands have tended to be much shorter. Today's leading brands of powdered laundry soap are Tide and Cheer; the leading brands 75 years ago were Fels-Naptha, Octagon, and Kirkman.

The PLC concept also can be applied to what are known as styles, fashions, and fads. Their special life cycles are shown in Figure 8.3. A **style** is a basic and distinctive mode of expression. For example, styles appear in homes (colonial, ranch, transitional), clothing (formal, casual), and art (realist, surrealist, abstract). Once a style is invented, it may last for generations, passing in and out of vogue. A style has a cycle showing several periods of renewed interest. A **fashion** is a currently accepted or popular style in a given field. For example, the more formal "business attire" look of corporate dress of the 1980s and 1990s gave way to the "business casual" look of today. Fashions tend to grow slowly, remain popular for a while, and then decline slowly.

Fads are temporary periods of unusually high sales driven by consumer enthusiasm and immediate product or brand popularity.[28] A fad may be part of an otherwise normal lifecycle, as in the case of recent surges in the sales of poker chips and accessories and scrapbooking supplies. Or the fad may comprise a brand's or product's entire lifecycle. "Pet rocks" are a classic example. Upon hearing his friends complain about how expensive it was to care for their dogs, advertising copywriter Gary Dahl joked about his pet rock. He soon wrote a spoof of a dog-training manual for it, titled "The Care and Training of Your Pet Rock." Soon Dahl was selling some 1.5 million ordinary beach pebbles at $4 a pop. Yet the fad, which broke one October, had sunk like a stone by the next February. Dahl's advice to those who want to succeed with a fad: "Enjoy it while it lasts." Other examples of such fads include the Rubik's Cube and low-carb diets.[29]

The PLC concept can be applied by marketers as a useful framework for describing how products and markets work. And when used carefully, the PLC concept can help in developing good marketing strategies for different stages of the product life cycle. But using the PLC concept for forecasting product performance or for developing marketing strategies presents some practical problems. For example, managers may have trouble identifying which stage of the PLC the product is in or pinpointing when the product moves into the next stage. They may also find it hard to determine the factors that affect the product's movement through the stages.

In practice, it is difficult to forecast the sales level at each PLC stage, the length of each stage, and the shape of the PLC curve. Using the PLC concept to develop marketing strategy also can be difficult because strategy is both a cause and a result of the product's life cycle. The product's current PLC position suggests the best marketing strategies, and the resulting marketing strategies affect product performance in later life-cycle stages.

Style
A basic and distinctive mode of expression.

Fashion
A currently accepted or popular style in a given field.

Fad
A temporary period of unusually high sales driven by consumer enthusiasm and immediate product or brand popularity.

■ Fads: Pet rocks, introduced one October, had sunk like a stone by the next February.

Moreover, marketers should not blindly push products through the traditional stages of the product life cycle. "As marketers instinctively embrace the old life-cycle paradigm, they needlessly consign their products to following the curve into maturity and decline," notes one marketing professor. Instead, marketers often defy the "rules" of the life cycle and position their products in unexpected ways. By doing this, "companies can rescue products foundering in the maturity phase of their life cycles and return them to the growth phase. And they can catapult new products forward into the growth phase, leapfrogging obstacles that could slow consumers' acceptance."[30]

We looked at the product development stage of the product life cycle in the first part of the chapter. We now look at strategies for each of the other life-cycle stages.

Introduction Stage

Introduction stage
The product life-cycle stage in which the new product is first distributed and made available for purchase.

The **introduction stage** starts when the new product is first launched. Introduction takes time, and sales growth is apt to be slow. Well-known products such as instant coffee and frozen foods lingered for many years before they entered a stage of rapid growth.

In this stage, as compared to other stages, profits are negative or low because of the low sales and high distribution and promotion expenses. Much money is needed to attract distributors and build their inventories. Promotion spending is relatively high to inform consumers of the new product and get them to try it. Because the market is not generally ready for product refinements at this stage, the company and its few competitors produce basic versions of the product. These firms focus their selling on those buyers who are the most ready to buy.

A company, especially the *market pioneer,* must choose a launch strategy that is consistent with the intended product positioning. It should realize that the initial strategy is just the first step in a grander marketing plan for the product's entire life cycle. If the pioneer chooses its launch strategy to make a "killing," it may be sacrificing long-run revenue for the sake of short-run gain. As the pioneer moves through later stages of the life cycle, it must continuously formulate new pricing, promotion, and other marketing strategies. It has the best chance of building and retaining market leadership if it plays its cards correctly from the start.

Growth Stage

Growth stage
The product life-cycle stage in which a product's sales start climbing quickly.

If the new product satisfies the market, it will enter a **growth stage**, in which sales will start climbing quickly. The early adopters will continue to buy, and later buyers will start following their lead, especially if they hear favorable word of mouth. Attracted by the opportunities for profit, new competitors will enter the market. They will introduce new product features, and the market will expand. The increase in competitors leads to an increase in the number of distribution outlets, and sales jump just to build reseller inventories. Prices remain where they are or fall only slightly. Companies keep their promotion spending at the same or a slightly higher level. Educating the market remains a goal, but now the company must also meet the competition.

Profits increase during the growth stage, as promotion costs are spread over a large volume and as unit manufacturing costs fall. The firm uses several strategies to sustain rapid market growth as long as possible. It improves product quality and adds new product features and models. It enters new market segments and new distribution channels. It shifts some advertising from building product awareness to building product conviction and purchase, and it lowers prices at the right time to attract more buyers.

In the growth stage, the firm faces a trade-off between high market share and high current profit. By spending a lot of money on product improvement, promotion, and distribution, the company can capture a dominant position. In doing so, however, it gives up maximum current profit, which it hopes to make up in the next stage.

Maturity Stage

Maturity stage
The product life-cycle stage in which sales growth slows or levels off.

At some point, a product's sales growth will slow down, and the product will enter a **maturity stage**. This maturity stage normally lasts longer than the previous stages, and it poses strong challenges to marketing management. Most products are in the maturity stage of the life cycle, and therefore most of marketing management deals with the mature product.

The slowdown in sales growth results in many producers with many products to sell. In turn, this overcapacity leads to greater competition. Competitors begin marking down prices, increasing their advertising and sales promotions, and upping their product development budgets to find better versions of the product. These steps lead to a drop in profit. Some of the weaker competitors start dropping out, and the industry eventually contains only well-established competitors.

Although many products in the mature stage appear to remain unchanged for long periods, most successful ones are actually evolving to meet changing consumer needs. Product managers should do more than simply ride along with or defend their mature products—a good offense is the best defense. They should consider modifying the market, product, and marketing mix.

In *modifying the market,* the company tries to increase the consumption of the current product. It may look for new users and new market segments, as when John Deere targeted the retiring baby-boomer market with the Gator, a vehicle traditionally used on a farm. For this new market, Deere has repositioned the Gator, promising that it can "take you from a do-it-yourselfer to a do-it-a-lot-easier." As one ad for the Gator XUV puts it, "When your plans include landscaping, gardening, or transporting people and materials on your property, the XUV provides a smooth, comfortable ride with heavy-duty performance."

The manager may also look for ways to increase usage among present customers. For example, Glad Products Company helps customers to find new uses for its Press'n Seal wrap, the plastic wrap that creates a Tupperware-like seal. As more and more customers contacted the company about alternative uses for the product, Glad set up a special "1000s of Uses. What's Yours?" Web site (www.1000uses.com) at which customers could swap usage tips. "We found out our heavy users use it for a lot more than just covering food," says a Glad brand manager. "And they all became heavy users when they had an 'aha' moment with Press'n Seal." Suggested uses for Press'n Seal range from protecting a computer keyboard from dirt and spills and keeping garden seeds fresh to use by soccer moms sitting on damp benches while watching their tykes play. "We just roll out the Glad Press'n Seal over the long benches," says the mom who shared the tip, "and everyone's bottom stays nice and dry."[31]

The company might also try *modifying the product*—changing characteristics such as quality, features, style, or packaging to attract new users and to inspire more usage. It can improve the product's styling and attractiveness. It might improve the product's quality and performance—its durability, reliability, speed, taste. Thus, makers of consumer food and household products introduce new flavors, colors, scents, ingredients, or packages to enhance performance and revitalize consumer buying. For example, P&G regularly adds new versions and features to its Tide line, such as Tide with a Touch of Downey, 2X concentrated liquids, Tide Simple Pleasures scents, and the Tide to Go instant stain removal pen.

■ Modifying the market: To better capture the maturing baby-boomer market, John Deere promises that it can take you from a do-it-yourselfer to a do-it-a-lot-easier.

Finally, the company can try *modifying the marketing mix*—improving sales by changing one or more of the marketing mix elements. The company can offer new or improved services to buyers. It can cut prices to attract new users and competitors' customers. It can launch a better advertising campaign or use aggressive sales promotions—trade deals, cents-off, premiums, and contests. In addition to pricing and promotion, the company can also move into new marketing channels to help serve new users.

Linking the Concepts

Pause for a moment and think about some products that have been around for a long time.

- Ask a grandparent or someone else who shaved back then to compare a 1950s or 1960s Gillette razor to the most current model. Is Gillette's latest razor really a new product or just a "retread" of the previous version? What do you conclude about product life cycles?
- Crayola Crayons have been a household staple for more than 100 years. But the brand remains vital. Sixty-five percent of all American children aged two to eight pick up a crayon at least once a day and color for an average of 28 minutes. Nearly 80 percent of the time, they pick up a Crayola crayon. How has the Binney & Smith division of Hallmark protected the Crayola brand from old age and decline (check out www.crayola.com and www.binney-smith.com)?

Decline Stage

Decline stage
The product life-cycle stage in which a product's sales decline.

The sales of most product forms and brands eventually dip. The decline may be slow, as in the case of oatmeal cereal, or rapid, as in the cases of cassette and VHS tapes. Sales may plunge to zero, or they may drop to a low level where they continue for many years. This is the **decline stage**.

Sales decline for many reasons, including technological advances, shifts in consumer tastes, and increased competition. As sales and profits decline, some firms withdraw from the market. Those remaining may prune their product offerings. They may drop smaller market segments and marginal trade channels, or they may cut the promotion budget and reduce their prices further.

Carrying a weak product can be very costly to a firm, and not just in profit terms. There are many hidden costs. A weak product may take up too much of management's time. It often requires frequent price and inventory adjustments. It requires advertising and sales-force attention that might be better used to make "healthy" products more profitable. A product's failing reputation can cause customer concerns about the company and its other products. The biggest cost may well lie in the future. Keeping weak products delays the search for replacements, creates a lopsided product mix, hurts current profits, and weakens the company's foothold on the future.

For these reasons, companies need to pay more attention to their aging products. The firm's first task is to identify those products in the decline stage by regularly reviewing sales, market shares, costs, and profit trends. Then, management must decide whether to maintain, harvest, or drop each of these declining products.

Management may decide to *maintain* its brand without change in the hope that competitors will leave the industry. For example, Procter & Gamble made good profits by remaining in the declining liquid soap business as others withdrew. Or management may decide to reposition or reinvigorate the brand in hopes of moving it back into the growth stage of the product life cycle. P&G has done this with several brands, including Mr. Clean and Old Spice.

Management may decide to *harvest* the product, which means reducing various costs (plant and equipment, maintenance, R&D, advertising, sales force) and hoping that sales hold up. If successful, harvesting will increase the company's profits in the short run. Or management may decide to *drop* the product from the line. It can sell it to another firm or simply liquidate it at salvage value. In recent years, Procter & Gamble has sold off a number of lesser or declining brands such as Crisco oil, Comet cleanser, Duncan Hines cake mixes, and Jif peanut butter. If the company plans to find a buyer, it will not want to run down the product through harvesting.

Table 8.2 summarizes the key characteristics of each stage of the product life cycle. The table also lists the marketing objectives and strategies for each stage.[32]

TABLE 8.2 Summary of Product Life-Cycle Characteristics, Objectives, and Strategies

Characteristics	Introduction	Growth	Maturity	Decline
Sales	Low sales	Rapidly rising sales	Peak sales	Declining sales
Costs	High cost per customer	Average cost per customer	Low cost per customer	Low cost per customer
Profits	Negative	Rising profits	High profits	Declining profits
Customers	Innovators	Early adopters	Middle majority	Laggards
Competitors	Few	Growing number	Stable number beginning to decline	Declining number
Marketing Objectives				
	Create product awareness and trial	Maximize market share	Maximize profit while defending market share	Reduce expenditure and milk the brand
Strategies				
Product	Offer a basic product	Offer product extensions, service, warranty	Diversify brand and models	Phase out weak items
Price	Use cost-plus	Price to penetrate market	Price to match or beat competitors	Cut price
Distribution	Build selective distribution	Build intensive distribution	Build more intensive distribution	Go selective: phase out unprofitable outlets
Advertising	Build product awareness among early adopters and dealers	Build awareness and interest in the mass market	Stress brand differences and benefits	Reduce to level needed to retain hard-core loyals
Sales Promotion	Use heavy sales promotion to entice trial	Reduce to take advantage of heavy consumer demand	Increase to encourage brand switching	Reduce to minimal level

Source: Philip Kotler and Kevin Lane Keller, *Marketing Management,* 12th ed. (Upper Saddle River, N.J.: Prentice Hall, 2006), p. 332.

Additional Product and Service Considerations

Here, we'll wrap up our discussion of products and services with two additional considerations: social responsibility in product decisions and issues of international product and service marketing.

Product Decisions and Social Responsibility

Product decisions have attracted much public attention. Marketers should carefully consider public policy issues and regulations regarding acquiring or dropping products, patent protection, product quality and safety, and product warranties.

Regarding new products, the government may prevent companies from adding products through acquisitions if the effect threatens to lessen competition. Companies dropping products must be aware that they have legal obligations, written or implied, to their suppliers, dealers, and customers who have a stake in the dropped product. Companies must also obey U.S. patent laws when developing new products. A company cannot make its product illegally similar to another company's established product.

Manufacturers must comply with specific laws regarding product quality and safety. The Federal Food, Drug, and Cosmetic Act protects consumers from unsafe and adulterated food, drugs, and cosmetics. Various acts provide for the inspection of sanitary conditions in the meat- and poultry-processing industries. Safety legislation has been passed to regulate fabrics, chemical substances, automobiles, toys, and drugs and poisons. The Consumer Product Safety Act of 1972 established a Consumer Product Safety Commission, which has the authority to ban or seize potentially harmful products and set severe penalties for violation of the law.

If consumers have been injured by a product that has a defective design, they can sue manufacturers or dealers. Product liability suits are now occurring in federal courts at the rate of almost 24,000 per year. Although manufacturers are found at fault in only 6 percent of all product liability cases, when they are found guilty, the median jury award is $1.5 million and individual awards can run into the tens or even hundreds of millions of dollars. For example, a jury recently ordered Merck to pay $253 million to the widow of a man who died from a heart attack after using the painkiller Vioxx for his arthritis. Although the judge later reduced the award to a "mere" $26.1 million, this was only the first of more than 4,000 Vioxx product liability suits.[33]

This phenomenon has resulted in huge increases in product liability insurance premiums, causing big problems in some industries. Some companies pass these higher rates along to consumers by raising prices. Others are forced to discontinue high-risk product lines. Some companies are now appointing "product stewards," whose job is to protect consumers from harm and the company from liability by proactively ferreting out potential product problems.

Many manufacturers offer written product warranties to convince customers of their products' quality. To protect consumers, Congress passed the Magnuson-Moss Warranty Act in 1975. The act requires that full warranties meet certain minimum standards, including repair "within a reasonable time and without charge" or a replacement or full refund if the product does not work "after a reasonable number of attempts" at repair. Otherwise, the company must make it clear that it is offering only a limited warranty. The law has led several manufacturers to switch from full to limited warranties and others to drop warranties altogether.

International Product and Service Marketing

International product and service marketers face special challenges. First, they must figure out what products and services to introduce and in which countries. Then, they must decide how much to standardize or adapt their products and services for world markets.

On the one hand, companies would like to standardize their offerings. Standardization helps a company to develop a consistent worldwide image. It also lowers the product design, manufacturing, and marketing costs of offering a large variety of products. On the other hand, markets and consumers around the world differ widely. Companies must usually respond to these differences by adapting their product offerings. For example, Cadbury sells kiwi-filled Cadbury Kiwi Royale in New Zealand. Frito-Lay sells Nori Seaweed Lay's potato chips for Thailand and A la Turca corn chips with poppy seeds and a dried tomato flavor for Turkey.[34] And P&G adapts the flavors of its Crest toothpaste to satisfy the palettes of local consumers.

> In America, P&G sells Crest toothpaste in flavors designed for Western palettes—everything from its regular soft mint flavor to vanilla mint, citrus clean mint, lemon ice, and cinnamon. But it has to rethink these flavors for the Chinese market, even *within* the Chinese market. China's rural populations like simplistic natural tastes, such as fruit or herbs. Drawing upon cultural beliefs about good health, P&G devised an herbal formulation. The company also created a salt version, as the Chinese consider salt a teeth-whitening agent. More affluent city dwellers, however, have palettes similar to those of U.S. consumers, preferring more complex flavors like mint. For them, P&G made a tea-flavored Crest, based on the Chinese belief that tea treats halitosis.

Packaging also presents new challenges for international marketers. Packaging issues can be subtle. For example, names, labels, and colors may not translate easily from one country to another. A firm using yellow flowers in its logo might fare well in the United States but meet with disaster in Mexico, where a yellow flower symbolizes death or disrespect. Similarly, although Nature's Gift might be an appealing name for gourmet mushrooms in America, it would be deadly in Germany, where *gift* means poison. Packaging may also need to be tailored to meet the physical characteristics of consumers in various parts of the world. For instance, soft drinks are sold in smaller cans in Japan to fit the smaller Japanese hand better. Thus, although product and package standardization can produce benefits, companies must usually adapt their offerings to the unique needs of specific international markets.

Service marketers also face special challenges when going global. Some service industries have a long history of international operations. For example, the commercial banking industry was one of the first to grow internationally. Banks had to provide global services in order to meet the foreign exchange and credit needs of their home country clients wanting to sell overseas. In recent years, many banks have become truly global. Germany's Deutsche Bank, for example, serves more than 13 million customers through 1,717 branches in 73 countries.

For its clients around the world who wish to grow globally, Deutsche Bank can raise money not only in Frankfurt but also in Zurich, London, Paris, Tokyo, and Moscow.[35]

Professional and business services industries such as accounting, management consulting, and advertising have also globalized. The international growth of these firms followed the globalization of the client companies they serve. For example, as more clients employ worldwide marketing and advertising strategies, advertising agencies have responded by globalizing their own operations. McCann Worldgroup, a large U.S.-based advertising and marketing services agency, operates in more than 130 countries. It serves international clients such as Coca-Cola, General Motors, ExxonMobile, Microsoft, MasterCard, Johnson & Johnson, and Unilever in markets ranging from the United States and Canada to Korea and Kazakhstan. Moreover, McCann Worldgroup is one company in the Interpublic Group of Companies, an immense, worldwide network of advertising and marketing services companies.[36]

■ International services marketing: Retailers are now going global. French-owned Carrefour now operates 12,000 stores in more than 30 countries.

Retailers are among the latest service businesses to go global. As their home markets become saturated, American retailers such as Wal-Mart, Office Depot, and Saks Fifth Avenue are expanding into faster-growing markets abroad. For example, since 1995, Wal-Mart has entered 15 countries; its international division's sales grew more than 11 percent last year, skyrocketing to more than $62.7 billion. Foreign retailers are making similar moves. Asian shoppers can now buy American products in French-owned Carrefour stores. Carrefour, the world's second-largest retailer behind Wal-Mart, now operates in more than 12,000 stores in more than 30 countries. It is the leading retailer in Europe, Brazil, and Argentina and the largest foreign retailer in China.[37]

The trend toward growth of global service companies will continue, especially in banking, airlines, telecommunications, and professional services. Today service firms are no longer simply following their manufacturing customers. Instead, they are taking the lead in international expansion.

REST STOP ⟩ REVIEWING THE CONCEPTS

A company's current products face limited life spans and must be replaced by newer products. But new products can fail—the risks of innovation are as great as the rewards. The key to successful innovation lies in a total-company effort, strong planning, and a systematic *new-product development* process.

1. Explain how companies find and develop new-product ideas.

Companies find and develop new-product ideas from a variety of sources. Many new-product ideas stem from *internal sources.* Companies conduct formal research and development, pick the brains of their employees, and brainstorm at executive meetings. Other ideas come from *external sources.* By conducting surveys and focus groups and analyzing *customer* questions and complaints, companies can generate new-product ideas that will meet specific consumer needs. Companies track *competitors'* offerings and inspect new products, dismantling them, analyzing their performance, and deciding whether to introduce a similar or improved product. *Distributors and suppliers* are close to the market and can pass along information about consumer problems and new-product possibilities.

2. List and define the steps in the new-product development process and the major considerations in managing this process.

The new-product development process consists of eight sequential stages. The process starts with *idea generation.* Next comes *idea screening,* which reduces the number of ideas based on the company's own criteria. Ideas that pass the screening stage continue through *product concept development,* in which a detailed version of the new-product idea is stated in meaningful consumer terms. In the next stage, *concept testing,* new-product concepts are tested with a group of target consumers to determine whether the concepts have strong consumer appeal. Strong concepts proceed to *marketing strategy development,* in which an initial marketing strategy for the new product is developed from the product concept. In the *business analysis* stage, a review of the sales, costs, and profit projections for a new product is conducted to determine whether the new product is likely to satisfy the company's objectives. With positive results here, the ideas become more concrete through *product development* and *test marketing* and finally are launched during *commercialization.*

New-product development involves more than just going through a set of steps. Companies must take a systematic, holistic approach to managing this process. Successful new-product development requires a customer-centered, team-based, systematic effort.

3. Describe the stages of the product life cycle.

Each product has a *life cycle* marked by a changing set of problems and opportunities. The sales of the typical product follow an S-shaped curve made up of five stages. The cycle begins with the *product development stage* when the company finds and develops a new-product idea. The *introduction stage* is marked by slow growth and low profits as the product is distributed to the market. If successful, the product enters a *growth stage,* which offers rapid sales growth and increasing profits. Next comes a *maturity stage* when sales growth slows down and profits stabilize. Finally, the product enters a *decline stage* in which sales and profits dwindle. The company's task during this stage is to recognize the decline and to decide whether it should maintain, harvest, or drop the product.

4. Describe how marketing strategies change during the product's life cycle.

In the *introduction stage,* the company must choose a launch strategy consistent with its intended product positioning. Much money is needed to attract distributors and build their inventories and to inform consumers of the new product and achieve trial. In the *growth stage,* companies continue to educate potential consumers and distributors. In addition, the company works to stay ahead of the competition and sustain rapid market growth by improving product quality, adding new product features and models, entering new market segments and distribution channels, shifting advertising from building product awareness to building product conviction and purchase, and lowering prices at the right time to attract new buyers.

In the *maturity stage,* companies continue to invest in maturing products and consider modifying the market, the product, and the marketing mix. When *modifying the market,* the company attempts to increase the consumption of the current product. When *modifying the product,* the company changes some of the product's characteristics—such as quality, features, or style—to attract new users or inspire more usage. When *modifying the marketing mix,* the company works to improve sales by changing one or more of the marketing-mix elements. Once the company recognizes that a product has entered the *decline stage,* management must decide whether to *maintain* the brand without change, hoping that competitors will drop out of the market; *harvest* the product, reducing costs and trying to maintain sales; or *drop* the product, selling it to another firm or liquidating it at salvage value.

5. Discuss two additional product and services issues: socially responsible product decisions and international product and services marketing.

Marketers must consider two additional product issues. The first is *social responsibility.* This includes public policy issues and regulations involving acquiring or dropping products, patent protection, product quality and safety, and product warranties. The second involves the special challenges facing *international product and service marketers.* International marketers must decide how much to standardize or adapt their offerings for world markets.

Navigating the Key Terms

Business analysis (239)
Commercialization (241)
Concept testing (237)
Customer-centered new product
   development (242)
Decline stage (250)
Fad (247)

Fashion (247)
Growth stage (248)
Idea generation (234)
Idea screening (236)
Introduction stage (248)
Marketing-strategy development (238)
Maturity stage (248)

New-product development (233)
Product concept (237)
Product development (239)
Product life cycle (PLC) (246)
Style (247)
Team-based new-product development (243)
Test marketing (240)

Travel Log

Discussing the Issues

1. Think of a product that failed. Discuss the reasons why new products fail and indicate which reasons you think caused the failure of the product you chose. (AACSB: Communication; Reflective Thinking)

2. Name and describe the major steps in the new-product development process. (AACSB: Communication)

3. Successful new-product development requires a customer-centered, team-based, and systematic effort. Explain what this means. (AACSB: Communication)

4. Briefly describe the five stages of the product life cycle. Identify a product class, form, or brand that is in each stage. (AACSB: Communication; Reflective Thinking)

5. Explain the difference between maintaining, harvesting, and dropping a brand in the decline stage. (AACSB: Communication)

6. Discuss the special challenges facing international product and services marketers. (AACSB: Communication)

Application Questions

1. Visit the Product Development and Management Association's Web site (www.pdma.org) to learn about this organization. Click on "OCI Award" on the left side of the page. Briefly describe the criteria used when granting this award and write a brief report about a company receiving this award. (AACSB: Communication; Use of IT)

2. If your campus is like most college campuses, you probably experience parking frustrations. Wouldn't you like to know where parking spots are available so you don't have to drive around looking for a spot? In a small group, brainstorm ideas for a new product or service that satisfies this need. (AACSB: Communication; Reflective Thinking)

3. Select the product concept from the previous question that you believe is the most viable. Develop a marketing strategy statement and describe how you would conduct a business analysis for the new product based on that concept. (AACSB: Communication; Analytic Skills; Reflective Thinking)

Under the Hood: Focus on Technology

Could you and a fellow student develop a business that would employ more that 10,000 people and be valued at over $120 billion in just over a decade? That's exactly what two Stanford University graduate students, Larry Page and Sergey Brin, did. They founded Google, the world's largest Internet search engine. Google is used in more than 100 countries and generates revenues from its online search services and highly targeted advertising. At Google's headquarters in Mountain View, California, known as "Googleplex," employees ("Googlers") are encouraged to be innovative. As a result, in addition to its original search engine capabilities, Google has launched a host of new products.

1. Identify five products Google has introduced in addition to its search engine service. Are they successful? How many of

these were you aware of before this exercise? Visit Google Labs (labs.google.com) to learn about new products that are still in the testing stage—"a few of our favorite ideas that still aren't quite ready for primetime." Briefly discuss what you found. (AACSB: Communication; Use of IT)

2. Read the article about Google's new-product development process at www.businessweek.com/technology/content/jun2006/tc20060629_411177.htm. What is Google's philosophy regarding new products? Do you think it is appropriate? (AACSB: Communication; Reflective Thinking; Use of IT)

Focus on Ethics

"Green marketing" has been around for a long time and has experienced renewed growth in the past decade. In response, several companies are developing eco-friendly products and touting their environmental conscientiousness. Greenpeace, an environmental activist group, is pushing legislation that would ban the production of incandescent light bulbs. Greenpeace called Philips Electronics a "climate criminal" because it produces these types of light bulbs. However, not all of the new products developed in response to consumers' desires for more environmentally friendly products live up to their promises.

1. Find examples of new products developed in response to growing environmental concern. Have marketers been successful with these new products? (AACSB: Communication; Reflective Thinking)

2. Not all "green" products live up to their claims. Is it ethical for marketers to continue to offer these products? (AACSB: Communication; Ethical Reasoning)

Video Case

ZIBA

How do companies go about designing good new products? Often, they employ specialist firms to help them or even do it for them. That's where design firms such as ZIBA come in. ZIBA is one of a new breed of consultancies whose sole purpose is to help corporations better understand customer needs and to turn that understanding into groundbreaking new products.

ZIBA's novel process for developing successful new products begins with the customer. The firm's novel approach to market research utilizes the likes of social anthropologists and cultural ethnographers to get to the heart of what makes consumers tick. ZIBA researchers often actually follow customers around, observing them in their natural environments and sharing their experiences.

ZIBA's unique approach has earned it contracts with major corporations ranging from P&G and KitchenAid to

Logitech, Microsoft, and Intel, as well as a variety of small start-up companies.

After viewing the video featuring ZIBA, answer the following questions about new-product development.

1. Describe ZIBA's product design process. Is this process consistent with the one detailed in the chapter?

2. Discuss the various ways that ZIBA's process focuses on customer relationships in its design process.

3. Discuss the relevancy of the product life cycle to ZIBA's design efforts. Do ZIBA's activities focus on any particular phase of the life cycle?

Pricing: Understanding and Capturing Customer Value

Previewing the Concepts

We continue your marketing journey with a look at a second major marketing mix tool—pricing. Firms successful at creating customer value with the other marketing mix activities must capture this value in the prices they earn. According to one pricing expert, pricing involves "harvesting your profit potential."[1] If effective product development, promotion, and distribution sow the seeds of business success, effective pricing is the harvest. Yet, despite its importance, many firms do not handle pricing well. In this chapter, we begin with the question: What is a price? Next, we look at customer-value perceptions, costs, and other factors that marketers must consider when setting prices. Finally, we examine pricing strategies for new-product pricing, product mix pricing, price adjustments, and dealing with price changes.

Most U.S. airlines are facing tough times these days. One of the biggest issues is figuring out how to price their services in the face of fierce competition, high fuel costs, and already-disgruntled passengers. But Ryanair—Europe's original, largest, and most profitable low-fares airline—appears to have found a radical new pricing solution: Fly *free*! But surely this strategy is doomed to failure. How can Ryanair make money on free tickets?

The major airlines are facing very difficult pricing strategy decisions in these tough air-travel times. Pricing strategies vary widely. Some airlines offer no-frills flights and charge rock-bottom prices (Southwest, JetBlue, Frontier, Skybus). Others offer luxury and charge higher prices to match (Virgin, Silverjet, Eos, Singapore Airlines). But most airlines haven't yet figured it out, leaving air-travel passengers generally grumpy when it comes to the topic of airline ticket prices. For example, when Northwest Airlines recently charged full fares but still cut basic perks (such as free magazines, pillows, and pretzels) and tacked on irksome new charges for things competitors provide for free (such as in-flight snacks and aisle seats), it dropped to dead last in the industry's customer satisfaction ratings.

But now, one airline appears to have found a radical new pricing solution, one that customers are sure to love: Make flying *free*! According to a *Business 2.0* magazine analyst:

> That's right, Michael O'Leary, chief executive of Ireland's Ryanair, Europe's most profitable airline, wants to make air travel free. Not free as in free from regulation, but free as in zero cost. By the end of the decade, he promises, "more than half of our passengers will fly free." The remarkable thing is, few analysts think his prediction is far-fetched: Ryanair already offers free fares to a quarter of its customers.

Even without free flights, Ryanair has become one of Europe's most popular carriers. Last year it flew 42.5 million passengers to more than 100 European destinations. The airline's sales of more than $2.2 billion were up 28 percent over the previous year, and profits have increased at double-digit rates for the past three years. And although its average fare is just $53 compared with U.S. low-cost leader Southwest's $92, Ryanair's net margins are 18 percent, more than double Southwest's 7 percent. Says one airline industry analyst, "Ryanair has the strongest financials in the European airline industry."

What's the secret? Ryanair's frugal cost structure makes even cost-conscious Southwest look like a reckless spender. In addition, the Irish airline charges for virtually everything except tickets, from baggage check-in to seat-back advertising space. "[Ryanair] thinks like a retailer and charges for absolutely every little thing, except the seat itself," says another analyst. "Imagine the seat as akin to a cell phone: It comes free, or nearly free, but its owner winds up spending on all sorts of services."

Ryanair's low-cost strategy is modeled after Southwest's. In 1991, when Ryanair was just another struggling European carrier, CEO O'Leary went to Dallas to meet with Southwest executives and see what he could learn. The result was a wholesale revamping of the Irish carrier's business model. Following Southwest's lead, to economize, Ryanair began employing only a single type of aircraft—the good old Boeing 737. Also like Southwest, it began focusing on smaller, secondary airports and offering unassigned passenger seating.

But Ryanair has since taken Southwest's low-cost pricing model even further. When it comes to keeping costs down, O'Leary is an absolute fanatic. "We want to be known as the Wal-Mart of flying," he says. Like the giant retailer, Ryanair is constantly on the lookout for new ways to cut costs—for example, by removing seat-back pockets to reduce weight and cleaning expense. Passengers reap the benefits of such savings in the form of lower fares. Ryanair also sells more than 98 percent of its tickets online, cutting down on administration costs and travel agent commissions. Flight crews even buy their own uniforms and headquarters staff supply their own pens.

The penny-pinching airline also charges passengers, for virtually every optional amenity they consume. Notes the *Business 2.0* analyst. "There are no free peanuts or beverages on Ryanair flights; 27 million passengers bought in-flight refreshments on the airline last year, generating sales of $61 million, or an average of $2.25 per person. Last March, Ryanair eliminated its free checked-bag allowance and began charging $3.50 per piece—a 'revenue-neutral' fee that was offset by cutting ticket prices by an average of $3.50. Ryanair expects the move to save $36 million a year by reducing fuel and handling costs." The airline is just as aggressive in its efforts to develop new sources of revenue.

Ryanair has turned its planes into giant billboards, displaying ads for such companies as Vodafone Group, Jaguar, and Hertz. Soon, ads will also stare each passenger in the eye when their seat back trays are up. Once in the air, flight attendants hawk everything from scratch-card games to perfume and digital cameras to their captive audience. Upon arrival at some out-of-the-way airport, Ryanair will sell you a bus or train ticket into town. Ryanair uses its Web site, with 15 million unique visitors each month, to boost related revenues. The company gets commissions from sales of Hertz rental cars, hotel rooms, ski packages, and travel insurance. Last year, such ancillary revenues rose 36 percent, to $332 million. "Every chance they get, Ryanair tries to squeeze just that little bit of extra margin out of its passengers," says an industry consultant.

About Ryanair's outrageously low prices, customers aren't complaining, especially because the additional purchases are discretionary. Moreover, many are entertaining or make life a little easier.

For passengers seeking extra distractions, Ryanair even intends to offer in-flight gambling in the near future, with the airline earning a tiny cut off of each wager. O'Leary thinks gambling could double Ryanair's profits over the next decade, but he's not stopping there. He also envisions a day when the airline can charge passengers for the ability to use their cell phones at 35,000 feet. And he's expressed interest in partnering with operators of airport parking lots and concession stands to capture a bigger slice of the cash that passengers spend on the ground getting to and from his planes.

The *Business 2.0* analyst concludes: "Add it all up—relentless cost cutting on the operations side, combined with innovative efforts to extract more revenue from each traveler—and O'Leary's plan to give away half of Ryanair's seats by 2010 starts to look quite sane. Sure, taking to the skies on Ryanair may feel more like riding in a subway car than an airplane, but you can't beat the prices. And financially strapped U.S. carriers should take note: Flying people from here to there for free could truly be liberating. For Ryanair, not even the sky's the limit.[2]

As the Ryanair story suggests, companies today face a fierce and fast-changing pricing environment. Value-seeking customers have put increased pricing pressure on many companies. "Thank the Wal-Mart phenomenon," says one analyst. "These days, we're all cheapskates in search of a spend-less strategy."[3] In response, it seems that almost every company is looking for ways to slash prices.

In some cases, such as Ryanair or Wal-Mart, low-price strategies work well. Yet, cutting prices is often not the best answer. Reducing prices unnecessarily can lead to lost profits and damaging price wars. It can signal to customers that the price is more important than the customer value a brand delivers. Instead, companies should sell value, not price. They should persuade customers that paying a higher price for the company's brand is justified by the greater value they gain. The challenge is to find the price that will let the company make a fair profit by getting paid for the customer value it creates. "Give people something of value," says Ronald Shaich, CEO of Panera Bread Company, "and they'll happily pay for it."[4]

What Is a Price?

In the narrowest sense, **price** is the amount of money charged for a product or service. More broadly, price is the sum of all the values that customers give up in order to gain the benefits of having or using a product or service. Historically, price has been the major factor affecting buyer choice. In recent decades, nonprice factors have gained increasing importance. However, price still remains one of the most important elements determining a firm's market share and profitability.

■ Pricing: The challenge is to harvest the customer value the company creates. Says Panera's CEO, pictured here, "Give people something of value, and they'll happily pay for it."

Price
The amount of money charged for a product or service, or the sum of all the values that customers give up in order to gain the benefits of having or using a product or service.

Price is the only element in the marketing mix that produces revenue; all other elements represent costs. Price is also one of the most flexible marketing mix elements. Unlike product features and channel commitments, prices can be changed quickly. At the same time, pricing is the number-one problem facing many marketing executives, and many companies do not handle pricing well. One frequent problem is that companies are too quick to reduce prices in order to get a sale rather than convincing buyers that their product's greater value is worth a higher price. Other common mistakes include pricing that is too cost oriented rather than customer-value oriented, and pricing that does not take the rest of the marketing mix into account.

Some managers view pricing as a big headache, preferring instead to focus on the other marketing mix elements. However, smart managers treat pricing as a key strategic tool for creating and capturing customer value. Prices have a direct impact on a firm's bottom line. According to one expert, "a 1 percent price improvement generates a 12.5 percent profit improvement for most organizations."[5] More importantly, as a part of a company's overall value proposition, price plays a key role in creating customer value and building customer relationships. "Instead of running away from pricing," says the expert, "savvy marketers are embracing it."

Factors to Consider When Setting Prices

The price the company charges will fall somewhere between one that is too high to produce any demand and one that is too low to produce a profit. Figure 9.1 summarizes the major considerations in setting price. Customer perceptions of the product's value set the ceiling for prices. If customers perceive that the price is greater than the product's value, they will

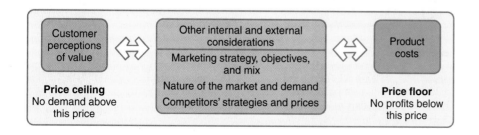

Customer perceptions of value

⟺

Other internal and external considerations

Marketing strategy, objectives, and mix

Nature of the market and demand

Competitors' strategies and prices

⟺

Product costs

Price ceiling
No demand above this price

Price floor
No profits below this price

FIGURE 9.1
Considerations in Setting Price

not buy the product. Product costs set the floor for prices. If the company prices the product below its costs, company profits will suffer. In setting its price between these two extremes, the company must consider a number of other internal and external factors, including its overall marketing strategy and mix, the nature of the market and demand, and competitors' strategies and prices.

Value-Based Pricing

In the end, the customer will decide whether a product's price is right. Pricing decisions, like other marketing mix decisions, must start with customer value. When customers buy a product, they exchange something of value (the price) in order to get something of value (the benefits of having or using the product). Effective, customer-oriented pricing involves understanding how much value consumers place on the benefits they receive from the product and setting a price that captures this value.

Value-based pricing

Setting price based on buyers' perceptions of value rather than on the seller's cost.

Good pricing begins with a complete understanding of the value that a product or service creates for customers. **Value-based pricing** uses buyers' perceptions of value, not the seller's cost, as the key to pricing. Value-based pricing means that the marketer cannot design a product and marketing program and then set the price. Price is considered along with the other marketing mix variables *before* the marketing program is set.

Figure 9.2 compares value-based pricing with cost-based pricing. Cost-based pricing is product driven. The company designs what it considers to be a good product, adds up the costs of making the product, and sets a price that covers costs plus a target profit. Marketing must then convince buyers that the product's value at that price justifies its purchase. If the price turns out to be too high, the company must settle for lower markups or lower sales, both resulting in disappointing profits.

Value-based pricing reverses this process. The company first assesses customer needs and value perceptions. It then sets its target price based on customer perceptions of value. The targeted value and price then drive decisions about what costs can be incurred and the resulting product design. As a result, pricing begins with analyzing consumer needs and value perceptions, and price is set to match consumers' perceived value.

It's important to remember that "good value" is not the same as "low price." For example, prices for a Hermes Birkin Bag start at about $7,000 and can top $25,000—a less-expensive handbag might carry as much, but some consumers place great value on the intangibles they receive from a one-of-a kind handmade bag that has a year-long waiting list. Similarly, some car buyers consider the luxurious Bentley Continental GT automobile a real value, even at an eye-popping price of $150,000:

> Stay with me here, because I'm about to [tell you why] a certain automobile costing $150,000 is not actually expensive, but is in fact a tremendous value. Every Bentley GT is built by hand, an Old World bit of automaking requiring 160 hours per vehicle. Craftsmen spend 18 hours simply stitching the perfectly joined leather of the GT's steering wheel, almost as long as it takes to assemble an entire VW Golf. The results are impressive: Dash and doors are mirrored with walnut veneer, floor pedals are carved from aluminum, window and seat toggles are

FIGURE 9.2　Value-Based Pricing Versus Cost-Based Pricing

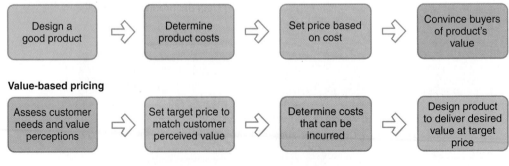

Cost-based pricing

Design a good product ⇒ Determine product costs ⇒ Set price based on cost ⇒ Convince buyers of product's value

Value-based pricing

Assess customer needs and value perceptions ⇒ Set target price to match customer perceived value ⇒ Determine costs that can be incurred ⇒ Design product to deliver desired value at target price

cut from actual metal rather than plastic, and every air vent is perfectly chromed. . . . The sum of all this is a fitted cabin that approximates that of a $300,000 vehicle, matched to an engine the equal of a $200,000 automobile, within a car that has brilliantly incorporated . . . technological sophistication. As I said, the GT is a bargain. [Just ask anyone on the lengthy waiting list.] The waiting time to bring home your very own GT is currently half a year.[6]

A company using value-based pricing must find out what value buyers assign to different competitive offers. However, companies often find it hard to measure the value customers will attach to its product. For example, calculating the cost of ingredients in a meal at a fancy restaurant is relatively easy. But assigning a value to other satisfactions such as taste, environment, relaxation, conversation, and status is very hard. And these values will vary both for different consumers and different situations.

Still, consumers will use these perceived values to evaluate a product's price, so the company must work to measure them. Sometimes, companies ask consumers how much they would pay for a basic product and for each benefit added to the offer. Or a company might conduct experiments to test the perceived value of different product offers. According to an old Russian proverb, there are two fools in every market—one who asks too much and one who asks too little. If the seller charges more than the buyers' perceived value, the company's sales will suffer. If the seller charges less, its products sell very well. But they produce less revenue than they would if they were priced at the level of perceived value.

We now examine two types of value-based pricing: *good-value pricing* and *value-added pricing*.

■ Value-based pricing: "Good value" is not the same as "low price." Some car buyers consider the luxurious Bentley Continental GT automobile a real value, even at an eye-popping price of $150,000.

Good-Value Pricing   During the past decade, marketers have noted a fundamental shift in consumer attitudes toward price and quality. Many companies have changed their pricing approaches to bring them into line with changing economic conditions and consumer price perceptions. More and more, marketers have adopted **good-value pricing** strategies—offering just the right combination of quality and good service at a fair price.

In many cases, this has involved introducing less-expensive versions of established, brand name products. Fast-food restaurants such as Taco Bell and McDonald's offer "value menus." Armani offers the less-expensive, more-casual Armani Exchange fashion line. Volkswagen recently reintroduced the Rabbit, an economical car with a base price under $15,000, to help "get VW on the shopping list of more buyers."[7] In other cases, good-value pricing has involved redesigning existing brands to offer more quality for a given price or the same quality for less.

An important type of good-value pricing at the retail level is *everyday low pricing (EDLP)*. EDLP involves charging a constant, everyday low price with few or no temporary price discounts. In contrast, *high-low pricing* involves charging higher prices on an everyday basis but running frequent promotions to lower prices temporarily on selected items. In recent years, high-low pricing has given way to EDLP in retail settings ranging from Saturn car dealerships to Costco warehouse clubs to furniture stores such as Room & Board. The king of EDLP is Wal-Mart, which practically defined the concept. Except for a few sale items every month, Wal-Mart promises everyday low prices on everything it sells.

Good-value pricing
Offering just the right combination of quality and good service at a fair price.

Value-Added Pricing In many marketing situations, the challenge is to build the company's *pricing power*—its power to escape price competition and to justify higher prices and margins without losing market share. To retain pricing power, a firm must retain or build the value of its market offering. This is especially true for suppliers of commodity products, which are characterized by little differentiation and intense price competition. If companies "rely on price to capture and retain business, they reduce whatever they're selling to a commodity," says an analyst. "Once that happens, there is no customer loyalty."[8]

Value-added pricing

Attaching value-added features and services to differentiate a market offering and support higher prices, rather than cutting prices to match competitors.

To increase their pricing power, many companies adopt **value-added pricing** strategies. Rather than cutting prices to match competitors, they attach value-added features and services to differentiate their offers and thus support higher prices. Consider this example:

The monsoon season in Mumbai, India, is three months of near-nonstop rain. For 147 years, most Mumbaikars protected themselves with a Stag umbrella from venerable Ebrahim Currim & Sons. Like Ford's Model T, the basic Stag was sturdy, affordable, and of any color, as long as it was black. By the end of the 20th century, however, the Stag was threatened by cheaper imports from China. Stag responded by dropping prices and scrimping on quality. It was a bad move: For the first time since the 1940s, the brand began losing money.

Finally, however, the company came to its senses. It abandoned the price war and vowed to improve quality. Surprisingly, even at higher prices, sales of the improved Stag umbrellas actually increased. Then the company started innovating. Noting the new fashion consciousness of Indian men, it launched designer umbrellas in funky designs and cool colors. Teenagers and young adults lapped them up. Stag then launched umbrellas with a built-in high-power flashlight for those who walk unlit roads at night, and models with prerecorded tunes for music lovers. For women who walk secluded streets after dark, there's Stag's Bodyguard model, armed with glare lights, emergency blinkers, and an alarm. Customers willingly pay up to a 100 percent premium for the new products. Under the new value-added strategy, the Stag brand has now returned to profitability. Come the monsoon in June, the grand old black Stags still reappear on the streets of Mumbai—but now priced 15 percent higher than the imports.[9]

■ Value-added pricing: Rather than dropping prices for its venerable Stag umbrella brand to match cheaper imports, Currims successfully launched umbrellas with funky designs, cool colors, and value-added features and sold them at even higher prices.

"Even in today's economic environment, it's not about price," says a pricing expert. "It's about keeping customers loyal by providing [features and] service they can't find anywhere else."[10]

Company and Product Costs

Whereas customer-value perceptions set the price ceiling, costs set the floor for the price that the company can charge. **Cost-based pricing** involved setting prices based on the costs for producing, distributing, and selling the product plus a fair rate of return for its effort and risk. A company's costs may be an important element in its pricing strategy. Many companies, such as Southwest Airlines, Wal-Mart, and Dell, work to become the "low-cost producers" in their industries. Companies with lower costs can set lower prices that result in greater sales and profits.

Cost-based pricing

Setting prices based on the costs for producing, distributing, and selling the product plus a fair rate of return for its effort and risk.

Fixed costs

Costs that do not vary with production or sales level.

Variable costs

Costs that vary directly with the level of production.

Types of Costs A company's costs take two forms, fixed and variable. **Fixed costs** (also known as overhead) are costs that do not vary with production or sales level. For example, a company must pay each month's bills for rent, heat, interest, and executive salaries, whatever the company's output. **Variable costs** vary directly with the level of production. Each

PC produced by Hewlett-Packard involves a cost of computer chips, wires, plastic, packaging, and other inputs. These costs tend to be the same for each unit produced. They are called variable because their total varies with the number of units produced. **Total costs** are the sum of the fixed and variable costs for any given level of production. Management wants to charge a price that will at least cover the total production costs at a given level of production.

The company must watch its costs carefully. If it costs the company more than competitors to produce and sell its product, the company will need to charge a higher price or make less profit, putting it at a competitive disadvantage.

Cost-Based Pricing The simplest pricing method is **cost-plus pricing**—adding a standard markup to the cost of the product. For example, an appliance retailer might pay a manufacturer $20 for a toaster and mark it up to sell at $30, a 50 percent markup on cost. The retailer's gross margin is $10. If the store's operating costs amount to $8 per toaster sold, the retailer's profit margin will be $2.

The manufacturer that made the toaster probably used cost-plus pricing. If the manufacturer's standard cost of producing the toaster was $16, it might have added a 25 percent markup, setting the price to the retailers at $20. Similarly, construction companies submit job bids by estimating the total project cost and adding a standard markup for profit. Lawyers, accountants, architects, and other professionals typically price by adding a standard markup to their costs. Some sellers tell their customers they will charge cost plus a specified markup; for example, aerospace companies price this way to the government.

Does using standard markups to set prices make sense? Generally, no. Any pricing method that ignores demand and competitor prices is not likely to lead to the best price. Still, markup pricing remains popular for many reasons. First, sellers are more certain about costs than about demand. By tying the price to cost, sellers simplify pricing—they do not need to make frequent adjustments as demand changes. Second, when all firms in the industry use this pricing method, prices tend to be similar and price competition is thus minimized. Third, many people feel that cost-plus pricing is fairer to both buyers and sellers. Sellers earn a fair return on their investment but do not take advantage of buyers when buyers' demand becomes great.

Another cost-oriented pricing approach is **break-even pricing**, or a variation called **target profit pricing**. The firm tries to determine the price at which it will break even or make the target profit it is seeking. Target pricing uses the concept of a *break-even chart,* which shows the total cost and total revenue expected at different sales volume levels. Figure 9.3 shows a break-even chart for the toaster manufacturer discussed here. Fixed costs are $6 million regardless of sales volume, and variable costs are $5 per unit. Variable costs are added to fixed costs to form total costs, which rise with volume. The slope of the total revenue curve reflects the price. Here, the price is $15 (for example, the company's revenue is $12 million on 800,000 units, or $15 per unit).

Total costs
The sum of the fixed and variable costs for any given level of production.

Cost-plus pricing
Adding a standard markup to the cost of the product.

Break-even pricing (target profit pricing)
Setting price to break even on the costs of making and marketing a product; or setting price to make a target profit.

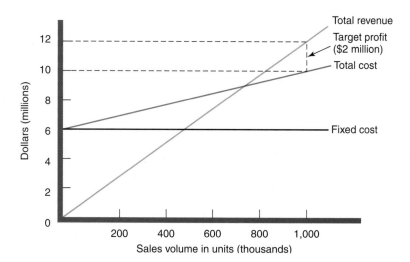

FIGURE 9.3

Break-Even Chart for Determining Price

At the $15 price, the company must sell at least 600,000 units to *break even* [break-even volume = fixed costs ÷ (price – variable costs) = $6,000,000 ÷ ($15 − $5) = 600,000]. That is, at this level, total revenues will equal total costs of $9 million. If the company wants a target profit of $2 million, it must sell at least 800,000 units to obtain the $12 million of total revenue needed to cover the costs of $10 million plus the $2 million of target profits. In contrast, if the company charges a higher price, say $20, it will not need to sell as many units to break even or to achieve its target profit. In fact, the higher the price, the lower the company's break-even point will be.

The major problem with this analysis, however, is that it fails to consider customer value and the relationship between price and demand. As the *price* increases, *demand* decreases, and the market may not buy even the lower volume needed to break even at the higher price. For example, suppose the company calculates that given its current fixed and variable costs, it must charge a price of $30 for the product in order to earn its desired target profit. But marketing research shows that few consumers will pay more than $25. In this case, the company must trim its costs in order to lower the break-even point so that it can charge the lower price consumers expect.

Thus, although break-even analysis and target profit pricing can help the company to determine minimum prices needed to cover expected costs and profits, they do not take the price-demand relationship into account. When using this method, the company must also consider the impact of price on sales volume needed to realize target profits and the likelihood that the needed volume will be achieved at each possible price.

Other Internal and External Considerations Affecting Price Decisions

Customer perceptions of value set the upper limit for prices and costs set the lower limit. However, in setting prices within these limits, the company must consider a number of other internal and external factors. Internal factors affecting pricing include the company's overall marketing strategy, objectives, and marketing mix, as well as other organizational considerations. External factors include the nature of the market and demand, competitors' strategies and prices, and other environmental factors.

Overall Marketing Strategy, Objectives, and Mix Price is only one element of the company's broader marketing strategy. Thus, before setting price, the company must decide on its overall marketing strategy for the product or service. If the company has selected its target market and positioning carefully, then its marketing mix strategy, including price, will be fairly straightforward. For example, when Toyota developed its Lexus brand to compete with European luxury-performance cars in the higher-income segment, this required charging a high price. In contrast, when it introduced its Yaris model—"the car that you can afford to drive is finally the car you actually want to drive"—this positioning required charging a low price. Thus, pricing strategy is largely determined by decisions on market positioning.

General pricing objectives might include survival, current profit maximization, market share leadership, or customer retention and relationship building. At a more specific level, a company can set prices to attract new customers or to profitably retain existing ones. It can set prices low to prevent competition from entering the market or set prices at competitors' levels to stabilize the market. It can price to keep the loyalty and support of resellers or to avoid government intervention. Prices can be reduced temporarily to create excitement for a brand. Or one product may be priced to help the sales of other products in the company's line. Thus, pricing may play an important role in helping to accomplish the company's objectives at many levels.

Price is only one of the marketing mix tools that a company uses to achieve its marketing objectives. Price decisions must be coordinated with product design, distribution, and promotion decisions to form a consistent and effective integrated marketing program. Decisions made for other marketing mix variables may affect pricing decisions. For example, a decision to position the product on high-performance quality will mean that the seller must charge a higher price to cover higher costs. And producers whose resellers are expected to support and promote their products may need to build larger reseller margins into their prices.

Companies often position their products on price and then tailor other marketing mix decisions to the prices they want to charge. Here, price is a crucial product-positioning factor that defines the product's market, competition, and design. Many firms support such price-positioning strategies with a technique called **target costing**, a potent strategic weapon. Target costing reverses the usual process of first designing a new product, determining its cost, and then asking, "Can we sell it for that?" Instead, it starts with an ideal selling price based on customer-value considerations and then targets costs that will ensure that the price is met. For example, when Toyota set out to design the Yaris, it began with the "car you can afford to drive" positioning and price point firmly in mind. It then designed a car with costs that allowed it to give target consumers "a car you actually want to drive" at that targeted price.

Other companies deemphasize price and use other marketing mix tools to create *nonprice* positions. Often, the best strategy is not to charge the lowest price but rather to differentiate the marketing offer to make it worth a higher price. For example, Viking builds more value into its kitchen appliance products and charges a higher price than many competitors. Customers recognize Viking's higher quality and are willing to pay more to get it.

Some marketers even position their products on *high* prices, featuring high prices as part of their product's allure (see Marketing at Work 9.1). For example, Grand Marnier offers a $225 bottle of Cuvée du Cent Cinquantenaire that's marketed with the tagline "Hard to find, impossible to pronounce, and prohibitively expensive." Porsche proudly advertises its curvaceous Cayman as "Starting at $49,400," actually a reasonable price given the brand's high-end prestige, quality, and innovation in performance and design.

Thus, marketers must consider the total marketing strategy and mix when setting prices. If the product is positioned on nonprice factors, then decisions about quality, promotion, and distribution will strongly affect price. If price is a crucial positioning factor, then price will strongly affect decisions made about the other marketing mix elements. But even when featuring price, marketers need to remember that customers rarely buy on price alone. Instead, they seek products that give them the best value in terms of benefits received for the prices paid.

A devil on both shoulders.

With blissfully dark intentions, the new Cayman just begs to be driven. Beneath sculpted curves sits a 2.7-liter, 245-hp mid-mount engine yearning to run. Its rigid body ready to respond instantly to your will. Never has bad felt so good. Porsche. There is no substitute.

The new Cayman. Starting at $49,400.

■ Positioning on high price: Porsche proudly advertises its curvaceous Cayman as "Starting at $49,400," actually a reasonable price given the brand's high-end prestige, quality, and innovation in performance and design.

Target costing
Pricing that starts with an ideal selling price, then targets costs that will ensure that the price is met.

Organizational Considerations   Management must decide who within the organization should set prices. Companies handle pricing in a variety of ways. In small companies, prices are often set by top management rather than by the marketing or sales departments. In large companies, pricing is typically handled by divisional or product line managers. In industrial markets, salespeople may be allowed to negotiate with customers within certain price ranges. Even so, top management sets the pricing objectives and policies, and it often approves the prices proposed by lower-level management or salespeople.

In industries in which pricing is a key factor (airlines, aerospace, steel, railroads, oil companies), companies often have pricing departments to set the best prices or to help others in setting them. These departments report to the marketing department or top management. Others who have an influence on pricing include sales managers, production managers, finance managers, and accountants.

The Market and Demand   As noted earlier, good pricing starts with an understanding how customers' perceptions of value affect the prices they are willing to pay. Both consumer and industrial buyers balance the price of a product or service against the benefits of owning it. Thus, before setting prices, the marketer must understand the relationship between price

9.1 MARKETING AT WORK
Pricing High and Proud of It

Whereas some companies work to achieve irresistibly low prices that will pull in the masses, others take just the opposite tack. They proudly pronounce *higher* prices on brands that appeal to a more select few. The higher prices actually add value, helping to position the brand—and the owner—as something special. Consider the following examples.

FERRARI

Ferraris are anything but cheap. Prices run from a mere $190,000 for the sleek Ferrari F430 to $280,000 for the 599 GTB. These prices don't include the lengthy list of expensive options or the typical markups over list price by dealers. And these are just the street models. For the real Ferrari fanatic, there's the ultralimited-edition FXX that can be driven only on race tracks. It goes out the door for around $2 million, give or take a few tens of thousands.

How can any car be worth such high-octane prices? Part of it's the deeply rooted Ferrari racing heritage, which has established the brand as one of the world's fastest cars. "Racing is in our DNA," says a Ferrari spokesperson. Ferraris also feature some of the most beautiful automotive designs on the planet. These cars are thoroughbreds through and through. But there are plenty of other fast and stylish cars—Corvettes, Vipers, Porsches, Maseratis, Lotuses, and even some Mercedes and BMWs. These cars play in the same performance neighborhood as Ferraris but can be had for a lot less money.

One pillar of Ferrari's special positioning is its exclusivity. People want what they can't get and it's not easy to get a Ferrari. Ferrari made just 5,700 cars worldwide last year (Porsche made about 100,000). Each new Ferrari rolls off the assembly line presold, and the average buyer waits one year to take delivery. Buyers can wait as long as three years depending on the model, options, and location. "It's [part of] the value of the brand," says an investment banker who owns a Ferrari. "It's the cachet of being not easy to obtain."

But what really sets Ferrari apart from less-spendy rivals is what owners sum up as "the Ferrari experience." When you own a Ferrari,

■ Ferraris are anything but cheap. But owners like this one will tell you that when it comes to a Ferrari, price is nothing. The Ferrari experience is everything.

you become a part of something bigger, something special. Ferrari spends millions of dollars annually on managing relationships with its small, elite core of customers. "We have 20,000 owners in the United States and we need to know them by name," says Marco Mattiacci, VP-marketing in North America. The company knows that its millionaire, even billionaire, customers "are looking for more unique things with more adrenaline than a golf game on Sunday." So Ferrari sponsors several owners-only events that fuel owners' driving passions while at the same time making them feel very special.

For example, the automaker sponsors the Ferrari Challenge, a series of six owners-only U.S. races, with the finals held in Italy. And for $5,925, owners can enter the Ferrari Challenge Rally, three-day touring trips on scenic

and demand for the company's product. In this section, we take a deeper look at the price-demand relationship and how it varies for different types of markets. We then discuss methods for analyzing the price-demand relationship.

Pricing in Different Types of Markets   The seller's pricing freedom varies with different types of markets. Economists recognize four types of markets, each presenting a different pricing challenge.

Under *pure competition,* the market consists of many buyers and sellers trading in a uniform commodity such as wheat, copper, or financial securities. No single buyer or seller has much effect on the going market price. A seller cannot charge more than the going price, because buyers can obtain as much as they need at the going price. Nor would sellers charge less than the market price, because they can sell all they want at this price. If price and profits rise, new sellers can easily enter the market. In a purely competitive market, marketing research, product development, pricing, advertising, and sales promotion play little or no role. Thus, sellers in these markets do not spend much time on marketing strategy.

back roads with stays at fine hotels. But the ultimate for owners and their spouses is the Ferrari Driving Experience. For an undisclosed amount, participants are coddled for two-and-a-half days at a five-star hotel. Ferrari loans each participant a sleek and powerful F430. Professional drivers school owners on the technical details of the car and how to get the best performance out of it. Then, Ferrari lets the owners loose on a Formula One race track to apply what they learned in the classroom.

Add it all up and it's not so surprising that Ferrari commands such high prices. Most owners will tell you that when it comes to a Ferrari, price is nothing. The Ferrari experience is everything.

STELLA ARTOIS

Positioning an exclusive, high-performance car on high price is one thing, but can such a strategy work for a more ordinary product—say, beer? Indeed it can. Consider Stella Artois. As a premium lager, Stella Artois has long been positioned as a high-end brew, with a price to match. In its advertising and other promotions, Stella doesn't hide its higher price, it flaunts it. For more than two decades, Stella advertising has carried the tagline, "reassuringly expensive." Years of artful, critically acclaimed television ads featuring this tagline have become a Stella trademark, establishing the brand as something beyond the ordinary.

Stella Artois has even run an award-winning negative-savings coupon campaign featuring a series of authentic-looking Stella Artois coupons. Rather than offering discounts to coupon clippers, the coupons boast deals such as "$1.25 extra," "20% more," and "$4.00, regularly $2.75." The headline in each coupon affirms that Stella is "reassuringly expensive."

To further support the Stella Artois drinking experience, the brewer also promotes its well-known Nine-Step Pouring Ritual in ads and live pub appearances. Under the tutelage of a Stella Artois brewmaster, bar patrons learn important pouring steps, such as "The Purification" (cleansing and rinsing the trademark Stella Artois chalice), "The Liquid Alchemy" (the chalice glass is held at a 45-degree angle during filling), "The Beheading" (while the head is flowing over the edge of the glass, it is gently cut with a knife at a 45-degree angle), and "The Judgment" (the foam is checked to insure two-finger thickness).

You can practice this ritual yourself in a classy, European-style virtual bar—Le Cercle Bar et Brasserie—located at the Stella Artois Web site (www.stella-artois.com). There, you become the star in an interactive drama that begins when you order a Stella and ends when you've completed the nine-step ritual and proven yourself worthy of drinking such a perfect beer. "When you've spent over 600 years crafting the perfect beer," says the company, "you become very fastidious about the way it's served."

Premium pricing has worked well for Stella Artois. Over the years, the company has managed to convince a host of loyal beer drinkers around the globe that its high prices are a good thing, not a bad thing. Although not well-known in the United States, Stella Artois is the number-one selling brand in most of the 80 countries in which it's distributed. The brand has been the number-one seller in the U.K. for years. U.S. sales have grown more than 60 percent over the past five years. Based on this success, Anheuser-Busch recently acquired U.S. distribution rights for the Stella Artois brand, and other U.S. rivals are adopting Stella-like strategies for their premium brands.

What is it that makes Stella Artois worth the premium price to so many beer drinkers? Like Ferrari buyers (okay, maybe with a little less conviction), Stella Artois loyalists will tell you this: It's not the price, it's the Stella experience. Or, maybe the higher price helps to create that experience.

Sources: Harry Hodge, "Stella Artois' 9-Step Ritual," *24 Hours,* April 18, 2007, p. 12; Mike Beirne, "Rivals Crib from Stella's Stellar Marketing Plan," *Brandweek,* January 2, 2007, accessed at www.brandweek.com; Christina Binkley, "Just off the Boat from Italy, the $265K Ferrari," *Wall Street Journal,* October 27, 2006, p. W1; Michael Taylor, "'Red Mist—The Ferrari Mystique," *San Francisco Chronicle,* June 25, 2006, p. J1; Jean Halliday, "For $2M, They Throw in the Sheets," *Advertising Age,* February 6, 2006, p. 14; Gabriel Kahn, "How to Slow Down a Ferrari: Buy It," *Wall Street Journal,* May 8, 2007; and information from www.stella-artois.com, accessed July 2007.

Under *monopolistic competition,* the market consists of many buyers and sellers who trade over a range of prices rather than a single market price. A range of prices occurs because sellers can differentiate their offers to buyers. Either the physical product can be varied in quality, features, or style, or the accompanying services can be varied. Buyers see differences in sellers' products and will pay different prices for them. Sellers try to develop differentiated offers for different customer segments and, in addition to price, freely use branding, advertising, and personal selling to set their offers apart. Thus, Moen differentiates its faucets and other fixtures through strong branding and advertising, reducing the impact of price. Because there are many competitors in such markets, each firm is less affected by competitors' pricing strategies than in oligopolistic markets.

Under *oligopolistic competition,* the market consists of a few sellers who are highly sensitive to each other's pricing and marketing strategies. The product can be uniform (steel, aluminum) or nonuniform (cars, computers). There are few sellers because it is difficult for new sellers to enter the market. Each seller is alert to competitors' strategies and moves. If a steel company slashes its price by 10 percent, buyers will quickly switch to this supplier. The other steelmakers must respond by lowering their prices or increasing their services.

■ Monopolistic competition: Moen sets its products apart through strong branding and advertising, reducing the impact of price.

Demand curve

A curve that shows the number of units the market will buy in a given time period, at different prices that might be charged.

In a *pure monopoly,* the market consists of one seller. The seller may be a government monopoly (the U.S. Postal Service), a private regulated monopoly (a power company), or a private nonregulated monopoly (DuPont when it introduced nylon). Pricing is handled differently in each case. In a regulated monopoly, the government permits the company to set rates that will yield a "fair return." Nonregulated monopolies are free to price at what the market will bear. However, they do not always charge the full price for a number of reasons: a desire not to attract competition, a desire to penetrate the market faster with a low price, or a fear of government regulation.

Analyzing the Price-Demand Relationship Each price the company might charge will lead to a different level of demand. The relationship between the price charged and the resulting demand level is shown in the **demand curve** in Figure 9.4. The demand curve shows the number of units the market will buy in a given time period at different prices that might be charged. In the normal case, demand and price are inversely related; that is, the higher the price, the lower the demand. Thus, the company would sell less if it raised its price from P_1 to P_2. In short, consumers with limited budgets probably will buy less of something if its price is too high.

In the case of prestige goods, the demand curve sometimes slopes upward. Consumers think that higher prices mean more quality. For example, Gibson Guitar Corporation once toyed with the idea of lowering its prices to compete more effectively with Japanese rivals such as Yamaha and Ibanez. To its surprise, Gibson found that its instruments didn't sell as well at lower prices. "We had an inverse [price-demand relationship]," noted Gibson's chief executive. "The more we charged, the more product we sold." At a time when other guitar manufacturers have chosen to build their instruments more quickly, cheaply, and in greater numbers, Gibson still promises guitars that "are made one-at-a-time, by hand. No shortcuts. No substitutions." It turns out that low prices simply aren't consistent with "Gibson's century-old tradition of creating investment-quality instruments that represent the highest standards of imaginative design and masterful craftsmanship."[11] Still, if the company charges too high a price, the level of demand will be lower.

Most companies try to measure their demand curves by estimating demand at different prices. The type of market makes a difference. In a monopoly, the demand curve shows the total market demand resulting from different prices. If the company faces competition, its demand at different prices will depend on whether competitors' prices stay constant or change with the company's own prices.

FIGURE 9.4
Demand Curve

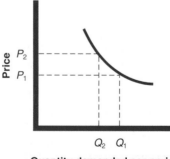

Quantity demanded per period

Price Elasticity of Demand Marketers also need to know **price elasticity**—how responsive demand will be to a change in price. If demand hardly changes with a small change in price, we say demand is *inelastic*. If demand changes greatly, we say the demand is *elastic*.

If demand is elastic rather than inelastic, sellers will consider lowering their prices. A lower price will produce more total revenue. This practice makes sense as long as the extra costs of producing and selling more do not exceed the extra revenue. At the same time, most firms want to avoid pricing that turns their products into commodities. In recent years, forces such as deregulation and the instant price comparisons afforded by the Internet and other technologies have increased consumer price sensitivity, turning products ranging from telephones and computers to new automobiles into commodities in some consumers' eyes.

Marketers need to work harder than ever to differentiate their offerings when a dozen competitors are selling virtually the same product at a comparable or lower price. More than ever, companies need to understand the price sensitivity of their customers and prospects and the trade-offs people are willing to make between price and product characteristics. In the words of marketing consultant Kevin Clancy, those who target only the price sensitive are "leaving money on the table."

Competitors' Strategies and Prices In setting its prices, the company must also consider competitors' costs, prices, and market offerings. Consumers will base their judgments of a product's value on the prices that competitors charge for similar products. A consumer who is thinking about buying a Canon digital camera will evaluate Canon's customer value and price against the value and prices of comparable products made by Kodak, Nikon, Sony, and others.

In addition, the company's pricing strategy may affect the nature of the competition it faces. If Canon follows a high-price, high-margin strategy, it may attract competition. A low-price, low-margin strategy, however, may stop competitors or drive them out of the market. Canon needs to benchmark its costs and value against competitors' costs and value. It can then use these benchmarks as a starting point for its own pricing.

In assessing competitors' pricing strategies, the company should ask several questions. First, how does the company's market offering compare with competitors' offerings in terms of customer value? If consumers perceive that the company's product or service provides greater value, the company can charge a higher price. If consumers perceive less value relative to competing products, the company must either charge a lower price or change customer perceptions to justify a higher price.

Next, how strong are current competitors and what are their current pricing strategies? If the company faces a host of smaller competitors charging high prices relative to the value they deliver, it might charge lower prices to drive weaker competitors out of the market. If the market is dominated by larger, low-price competitors, the company may decide to target unserved market niches with value-added products at higher prices. For example, your local independent bookstore isn't likely to win a price war against Amazon.com or Barnes & Noble. It would be wiser to add special customer services and personal touches that justify higher prices and margins.

Finally, the company should ask, How does the competitive landscape influence customer price sensitivity?[12] For example, customers will be more price sensitive if they see few differences between competing products. They will buy whichever product costs the least. The more information customers have about competing products and prices before buying, the more price sensitive they will be. Easy product comparisons help customers to assess the

Is there a guitar worth half a million dollars in your attic?

In 1963, a Chicago man purchased this beautiful 1958 Gibson Explorer for his son. He paid $247.50. For many years the son preserved the guitar before deciding, for curiosity's sake, to seek out its value. Let's just say he was in for a nice surprise.

In October of 2006, he sold his Gibson Explorer at a Skinner auction in Boston, Massachusetts for a jaw-dropping $611,000.

That's a pretty hefty return on investment. Why so much? Gibson only made 100 of the original '50s Explorers. With their angular, asymmetric design, the eye-popping mahogany electrics were considered ahead of their time, as were many of Gibson's original iconic designs.

What no one knew in 1958 was that those first weird and wonderful Gibson Explorers would become coveted powerhouses of screaming rock and roll. In turn the Explorers grew to be serious collectors' items. Some, like the Explorer on the left, have appreciated by more than half a million dollars in just under 50 years. They aren't alone at the top. Many other vintage Gibson models are experiencing similar surges in value.

These days, collectors are finding that their investments in fine vintage Gibsons—electrics and acoustics, both—are paying off in spades. That's because Gibsons just get better with age.

Today, more collectors are trading both vintage Gibsons and Gibson Custom Shop limited-edition models. Not only are these guitars proving to appreciate rapidly and dramatically, but they're functional works of American art that collectors cherish.

Do you have a guitar worth half a million dollars in your attic? Wouldn't you like to? Go to Gibson.com and find your nearest dealer.

Gibson
PURE

Talk to us at www.gibson.com or 1-800-4GIBSON, (24/7)

© 2007 Gibson Guitar Corp.

This 1958 Gibson Explorer with original Bigsby vibrato and Custom Made plate cover sold for $611,000 at a Skinner auction in Boston, Massachusetts in October 2006.

■ The demand curve sometimes slopes upward: Gibson was surprised to learn that its high-quality instruments didn't sell as well at lower prices. In fact, as this ad suggests, "paying more for a Gibson might even be a good investment."

Price elasticity
A measure of the sensitivity of demand to changes in price.

value of different options and to decide what prices they are willing to pay. Finally, customers will be more price sensitive if they can switch easily from one product alternative to another.

What principle should guide decisions about what price to charge relative to those of competitors? The answer is simple in concept but often difficult in practice: No matter what price you charge—high, low, or in between—be certain to give customers superior value for that price.

Other External Factors When setting prices, the company also must consider a number of other factors in its external environment. *Economic conditions* can have a strong impact on the firm's pricing strategies. Economic factors such as boom or recession, inflation, and interest rates affect pricing decisions because they affect both consumer perceptions of the product's price and value and the costs of producing a product.

The company must also consider what impact its prices will have on other parties in its environment. How will *resellers* react to various prices? The company should set prices that give resellers a fair profit, encourage their support, and help them to sell the product effectively. The *government* is another important external influence on pricing decisions. Finally, *social concerns* may need to be taken into account. In setting prices, a company's short-term sales, market share, and profit goals may need to be tempered by broader societal considerations. We will examine public policy issues in pricing later in the chapter.

Linking the Concepts

The concept of customer value is critical to good pricing and to successful marketing in general. Slow down for a minute and be certain that you appreciate what value really means.

- In an earlier example, one car critic called the Bentley Continental GT a great value at $150,000—"a six-figure steal" in his words. Does this fit with your idea of value?
- Pick two competing brands from a familiar product category (watches, perfume, consumer electronics, restaurants)—one low priced and the other high priced. Which, if either, offers the greatest value?
- Does "value" mean the same thing as "low price"? How do these concepts differ?

We've now seen that pricing decisions are subject to a complex array of customer, company, competitive, and environmental forces. To make things even more complex, a company sets not a single price but rather a *pricing structure* that covers different items in its line. This pricing structure changes over time as products move through their life cycles. The company adjusts prices to reflect changes in demand and costs and to account for variations in buyers and situations. As the competitive environment changes, the company considers when to initiate price changes and when to respond to them.

We now examine the major dynamic pricing strategies available to marketers. In turn, we look at *new-product pricing strategies* for products in the introductory stage of the product life cycle, *product mix pricing strategies* for related products in the product mix, *price-adjustment strategies* that account for customer differences and changing situations, and strategies for initiating and responding to *price changes*.

New-Product Pricing Strategies

Pricing strategies usually change as the product passes through its life cycle. The introductory stage is especially challenging. Companies bringing out a new product face the challenge of setting prices for the first time. They can choose between two broad strategies: *market-skimming pricing* and *market-penetration pricing*.

Market-skimming pricing (price skimming)

Setting a high price for a new product to skim maximum revenues layer by layer from the segments willing to pay the high price; the company makes fewer but more profitable sales.

Market-Skimming Pricing

Many companies that invent new products set high initial prices to "skim" revenues layer by layer from the market. Sony frequently uses this strategy, called **market-skimming pricing** (or **price skimming**). When Sony introduced the world's first high-definition television (HDTV) to the Japanese market in 1990, the high-tech sets cost $43,000. These televisions were purchased only by customers who could afford to pay a high price for the new technology. Sony rapidly reduced the price over the next several years to attract new buyers. By 1993, a 28-inch HDTV cost a Japanese buyer just over $6,000. In 2001, a Japanese consumer could buy a 40-inch HDTV for about $2,000, a price that many more customers could afford. An entry-level HDTV set now sells for less than $500 in the United States, and prices continue to fall. In this way, Sony skimmed the maximum amount of revenue from the various segments of the market.[13]

Market skimming makes sense only under certain conditions. First, the product's quality and image must support its higher price and enough buyers must want the product at that price. Second, the costs of producing a smaller volume cannot be so high that they cancel the advantage of charging more. Finally, competitors should not be able to enter the market easily and undercut the high price.

Market-Penetration Pricing

Rather than setting a high initial price to skim off small but profitable market segments, some companies use **market-penetration pricing**. They set a low initial price in order to *penetrate* the market quickly and deeply—to attract a large number of buyers quickly and win a large market share. The high sales volume results in falling costs, allowing the company to cut its price even further. For example, Wal-Mart and other discount retailers use penetration pricing. And Dell used penetration pricing to enter the personal computer market, selling high-quality computer products through lower-cost direct channels. Its sales soared when HP, Apple, and other competitors selling through retail stores could not match its prices.

■ Market-skimming pricing: Sony priced its early HDTVs high, then reduced prices gradually over the years to attract new buyers.

Several conditions must be met for this low-price strategy to work. First, the market must be highly price sensitive so that a low price produces more market growth. Second, production and distribution costs must fall as sales volume increases. Finally, the low price must help keep out the competition, and the penetration pricer must maintain its low-price position—otherwise, the price advantage may be only temporary. For example, Wal-Mart has faced challenges from other low-cost retailers, such as Costco and Kohl's. However, through its dedication to low operating and purchasing costs, Wal-Mart has retained its price advantage and established itself as the world's number-one retailer.

Market-penetration pricing
Setting a low price for a new product in order to attract a large number of buyers and a large market share.

Product Mix Pricing Strategies

The strategy for setting a product's price often must be changed when the product is part of a product mix. In this case, the firm looks for a set of prices that maximizes the profits on the total product mix. Pricing is difficult because the various products have related demand and costs and face different degrees of competition. We now take a closer look at the five product mix pricing situations summarized in Table 9.1: *product line pricing, optional-product pricing, captive-product pricing, by-product pricing,* and *product bundle pricing.*

Product Line Pricing

Companies usually develop product lines rather than single products. For example, Samsonite offers some 20 different collections of bags of all shapes and sizes at prices that

TABLE 9.1 **Product Mix Pricing Strategies**	Strategy	Description
	Product line pricing	Setting prices across an entire product line
	Optional-product pricing	Pricing optional or accessory products sold with the main product
	Captive-product pricing	Pricing products that must be used with the main product
	By-product pricing	Pricing low-value by-products to get rid of them
	Product bundle pricing	Pricing bundles of products sold together

Product line pricing
Setting the price steps between products in a product line based on cost differences and customer perceptions of the value.

range from under $50 for a Sammie's child's backpack to more than $1,250 for a bag from its Black Label Vintage Collection.[14] In **product line pricing**, management must decide on the price steps to set between the various products in a line.

The price steps should take into account cost differences between the products in the line. More importantly, they should account for differences in customer perceptions of the value of different features. For example, Quicken offers an entire line of financial management software, including Basic, Deluxe, Premier, and Home & Business versions priced at $29.99, $59.99, $79.99, and $89.99. Although it costs Quicken no more to produce the CD containing the Premier version than the CD containing the Basic version, many buyers happily pay more to obtain additional Premier features, such as financial-planning and investment-monitoring tools. Quicken's task is to establish perceived value differences that support the price differences.

■ Product line pricing: Quicken offers an entire line of financial management software, including Basic, Deluxe, Premier, and Home & Business versions priced at $29.99, $59.99, $79.99, and $89.99. Quicken's task is to establish perceived value differences that support the price differences.

Optional-product pricing
The pricing of optional or accessory products along with a main product.

Captive-product pricing
Setting a price for products that must be used along with a main product.

Optional-Product Pricing

Many companies use **optional-product pricing**—offering to sell optional or accessory products along with their main product. For example, a car buyer may choose to order an in-car entertainment system and Bluetooth wireless communication. Refrigerators come with optional ice makers. And when you order a new PC, you can select from a bewildering array of processors, hard drives, docking systems, software options, and carrying cases.

Pricing these options is a sticky problem. Automobile companies must decide which items to include in the base price and which to offer as options. Until recent years, General Motors' normal pricing strategy was to advertise a stripped-down model at a base price to pull people into showrooms and then to devote most of the showroom space to showing option-loaded cars at higher prices. The economy model was stripped of so many comforts and conveniences that most buyers rejected it. Then, GM and other U.S. automakers followed the examples of the Japanese and German companies and included in the sticker price many useful items previously sold only as options. Thus, most advertised prices today represent well-equipped cars.

Captive-Product Pricing

Companies that make products that must be used along with a main product are using **captive-product pricing**. Examples of captive products are razor blade cartridges, video games, and printer cartridges. Producers of the main products (razors, video game consoles, and printers) often price them low and set high markups on the supplies. Thus, Gillette sells low-priced razors but makes money on the replacement cartridges. HP makes very low margins on its printers but very high margins on printer cartridges and other supplies.

Companies using captive-product pricing must be careful— consumers trapped into buying expensive supplies may come to resent the brand that ensnared them. Kodak hopes to reverse the process with its new EasyShare inkjet printers:

> Until recently, printers have been sold at a loss, with profits being made up by the later sales of high-margin ink cartridges. Kodak plans to turn that model upside-down by selling premium-priced printers with no discounts, then selling much cheaper ink cartridges. The printers will be priced from $149 to $299. The company will then sell ink cartridges at $9.99 for black and $14.99 for color. "Our strategy . . . is to crystallize for consumers that they're not only buying a printer today but also buying into three to four years of ink purchases," says a Kodak marketing executive. The strategy is risky—Kodak will need to educate consumers on the benefits of paying more up front in order to reduce long-run printing costs. Initial ads will be built around the idea and visual image "think," with the first two letters in black and the last three in white, creating a "think ink" message. Also, Kodak initially sold the printers only in Best Buy stores to take advantage of the retailer's on-the-floor sales staff and ability to educate buyers.[15]

In the case of services, this captive-product pricing is called *two-part pricing.* The price of the service is broken into a *fixed fee* plus a *variable usage rate.* Thus, at Six Flags and other amusement parks, you pay a daily ticket or season pass charge plus additional fees for food and other in-park features. Theaters charge admission and then generate additional revenues from concessions. And cell phone companies charge a flat rate for a basic calling plan, then charge for minutes over what the plan allows. The service firm must decide how much to charge for the basic service and how much for the variable usage. The fixed amount should be low enough to induce usage of the service; profit can be made on the variable fees.

■ Captive-product pricing: Kodak plans to reverse standard industry pricing strategy by selling premium-price printers without discounts, then selling much cheaper ink cartridges. "You only buy the printer once."

By-Product Pricing

Producing products and services often generates by-products. If the by-products have no value and if getting rid of them is costly, this will affect the pricing of the main product. Using **by-product pricing**, the company seeks a market for these by-products to help offset the costs of disposing of them and to help make the price of the main product more competitive. The by-products themselves can even turn out to be profitable. For example, papermaker MeadWestvaco has turned what was once considered chemical waste into profit-making products.

> MeadWestvaco created a separate company, Asphalt Innovations, which creates useful chemicals entirely from the by-products of MeadWestvaco's wood-processing activities. In fact, Asphalt Innovations has grown to become the world's biggest supplier of specialty chemicals for the paving industry. Using the salvaged chemicals, paving companies can pave roads at a lower temperature, create longer-lasting roads, and more easily recycle road materials when roads need to be replaced. What's more, salvaging the by-product chemicals eliminates the costs and environmental hazards once associated with disposing of them.[16]

By-product pricing
Setting a price for by-products in order to make the main product's price more competitive.

Product Bundle Pricing

Product bundle pricing
Combining several products and offering the bundle at a reduced price.

Using **product bundle pricing**, sellers often combine several of their products and offer the bundle at a reduced price. For example, fast-food restaurants bundle a burger, fries, and a soft drink at a "meal" price. Resorts sell specially priced vacation packages that include airfare, accommodations, meals, and entertainment. And Comcast, Time Warner, and other cable companies bundle cable service, phone service, and high-speed Internet connections at a low combined price. Price bundling can promote the sales of products consumers might not otherwise buy, but the combined price must be low enough to get them to buy the bundle.[17]

Price-Adjustment Strategies

Companies usually adjust their basic prices to account for various customer differences and changing situations. Here we examine the seven price adjustment strategies summarized in Table 9.2: *discount and allowance pricing, segmented pricing, psychological pricing, promotional pricing, geographical pricing, dynamic pricing,* and *international pricing.*

Discount and Allowance Pricing

Most companies adjust their basic price to reward customers for certain responses, such as early payment of bills, volume purchases, and off-season buying. These price adjustments—called *discounts* and *allowances*—can take many forms.

Discount
A straight reduction in price on purchases under stated conditions or during a stated period of time.

The many forms of **discounts** include a *cash discount,* a price reduction to buyers who pay their bills promptly. A typical example is "2/10, net 30," which means that although payment is due within 30 days, the buyer can deduct 2 percent if the bill is paid within 10 days. A *quantity discount* is a price reduction to buyers who buy large volumes. Such discounts provide an incentive to the customer to buy more from one given seller, rather than from many different sources.

A *functional discount* (also called a *trade discount*) is offered by the seller to trade-channel members who perform certain functions, such as selling, storing, and record keeping. A *seasonal discount* is a price reduction to buyers who buy merchandise or services out of season. For example, lawn and garden equipment manufacturers offer seasonal discounts to retailers during the fall and winter months to encourage early ordering in anticipation of the heavy spring and summer selling seasons. Seasonal discounts allow the seller to keep production steady during an entire year.

Allowance
Promotional money paid by manufacturers to retailers in return for an agreement to feature the manufacturer's products in some way.

Allowances are another type of reduction from the list price. For example, *trade-in allowances* are price reductions given for turning in an old item when buying a new one. Trade-in allowances are most common in the automobile industry but are also given for other durable goods. *Promotional allowances* are payments or price reductions to reward dealers for participating in advertising and sales support programs.

TABLE 9.2 Price Adjustment Strategies	Strategy	Description
	Discount and allowance pricing	Reducing prices to reward customer responses such as paying early or promoting the product
	Segmented pricing	Adjusting prices to allow for differences in customers, products, or locations
	Psychological pricing	Adjusting prices for psychological effect
	Promotional pricing	Temporarily reducing prices to increase short-run sales
	Geographical pricing	Adjusting prices to account for the geographic location of customers
	Dynamic pricing	Adjusting prices continually to meet the characteristics and needs of individual customers and situations
	International pricing	Adjusting prices for international markets

Segmented Pricing

Companies will often adjust their basic prices to allow for differences in customers, products, and locations. In **segmented pricing**, the company sells a product or service at two or more prices, even though the difference in prices is not based on differences in costs.

Segmented pricing
Selling a product or service at two or more prices, where the difference in prices is not based on differences in costs.

Segmented pricing takes several forms. Under *customer-segment* pricing, different customers pay different prices for the same product or service. Museums, for example, may charge a lower admission for students and senior citizens. Under *product-form pricing,* different versions of the product are priced differently but not according to differences in their costs. For instance, a 1-liter bottle (about 34 ounces) of Evian mineral water may cost $1.59 at your local supermarket. But a 5-ounce aerosol can of Evian Brumisateur Mineral Water Spray sells for a suggested retail price of $11.39 at beauty boutiques and spas. The water is all from the same source in the French Alps and the aerosol packaging costs little more than the plastic bottles. Yet you pay about 5 cents an ounce for one form and $2.28 an ounce for the other.

Using *location pricing,* a company charges different prices for different locations, even though the cost of offering each location is the same. For instance, theaters vary their seat prices because of audience preferences for certain locations, and state universities charge higher tuition for out-of-state students. Finally, using *time pricing,* a firm varies its price by the season, the month, the day, and even the hour. Some public utilities vary their prices to commercial users by time of day and weekend versus weekday. Resorts give weekend and seasonal discounts.

Segmented pricing goes by many names. Robert Cross, a longtime consultant to the airlines, calls it *revenue management.* According to Cross, the practice ensures that "companies will sell the right product to the right consumer at the right time for the right price." Airlines, hotels, and restaurants call it *yield management* and practice it religiously. The airlines, for example, routinely set prices hour-by-hour—even minute-by-minute—depending on seat availability, demand, and competitor price changes.

Continental Airlines launches more than 3,200 flights every day. Each flight has between 10 and 20 prices. Continental starts booking flights 330 days in advance, and every flying day is different from every other flying day. As a result, at any given moment, Continental may have nearly 7 million prices in the market. It's a daunting marketing task—all of those prices need to be managed, all of the time. For Continental, setting prices is a complex process of balancing demand and customer satisfaction against company profitability.[18]

■ Product-form pricing: Evian water in a 1 liter bottle might cost you 5 cents an ounce at your local supermarket, whereas the same water might run $2.28 an ounce when sold in 5-ounce aerosol cans as Evian Brumisateur Mineral Water Spray moisturizer.

The airlines know full well that we are puzzled by the frantic pricing and repricing that they do—puzzled, that is, when we aren't infuriated. "I do not set the prices," says Jim Compton, senior vice president of pricing and revenue management at Continental Airlines. "The market sets prices." That's point one. Point two: "I have a really perishable product. It's gone when the door of the plane closes. An empty seat is lost revenue." The most valuable airline seat is the one that somebody must have an hour before takeoff and is willing to pay almost any price for. An airline seat gets more profitable with time—right up to the moment it goes from being worth $1,000 one-way to being worth $0.

Here's how Compton and his colleagues think about this: You want to sell every seat on the plane, except that you also want to have a handful left at the very end, for your most profitable (not to mention most grateful) customers. The airlines could easily sell out every seat, every flight, every day. They'd price 'em pretty low, book 'em up, and wait for takeoff. But that would mean there'd never be any seats available two or three weeks before a flight took off. How exasperated would customers be to call and find no seats three days out? When you understand that dilemma, all of a sudden, airline prices don't seem so exploitive. Although all of the seats on that New York–Miami flight are going to the same place, they aren't the same product. You pay less when you commit to a ticket four weeks in advance; Continental assumes a risk for holding a seat until the end—and wants to be paid a lot to balance the times when saving that last seat for you means that the seat flies empty.

For segmented pricing to be an effective strategy, certain conditions must exist. The market must be segmentable, and the segments must show different degrees of demand. The costs of segmenting and watching the market cannot exceed the extra revenue obtained from the price difference. Of course, the segmented pricing must also be legal. Most importantly, segmented prices should reflect real differences in customers' perceived value. Otherwise, in the long run, the practice will lead to customer resentment and ill will.

Psychological Pricing

Price says something about the product. For example, many consumers use price to judge quality. A $100 bottle of perfume may contain only $3 worth of scent, but some people are willing to pay the $100 because this price indicates something special.

Psychological pricing
A pricing approach that considers the psychology of prices and not simply the economics; the price is used to say something about the product.

In using **psychological pricing**, sellers consider the psychology of prices and not simply the economics. For example, consumers usually perceive higher-priced products as having higher quality. When they can judge the quality of a product by examining it or by calling on past experience with it, they use price less to judge quality. But when they cannot judge quality because they lack the information or skill, price becomes an important quality signal:

Some years ago, Heublein produced Smirnoff, then America's leading vodka brand. Smirnoff was attacked by another brand, Wolfschmidt, which claimed to have the same quality as Smirnoff but was priced at one dollar less per bottle. To hold on to market share, Heublein considered either lowering Smirnoff's price by one dollar or holding Smirnoff's price but increasing advertising and promotion expenditures. Either strategy would lead to lower profits and it seemed that Heublein faced a no-win situation. At this point, however, Heublein's marketers thought of a third strategy. They *raised* the price of Smirnoff by one dollar! Heublein then introduced a new brand, Relska, to compete with Wolfschmidt. Moreover, it introduced yet another brand, Popov, priced even *lower* than Wolfschmidt. This clever strategy positioned Smirnoff as the elite brand and Wolfschmidt as an ordinary brand, producing a large increase in Heublein's overall profits. The irony is that Heublein's three brands were pretty much the same in taste and manufacturing costs. Heublein knew that a product's price signals its quality. Using price as a signal, Heublein sold roughly the same product at three different quality positions.

Reference prices
Prices that buyers carry in their minds and refer to when they look at a given product.

Another aspect of psychological pricing is **reference prices**—prices that buyers carry in their minds and refer to when looking at a given product. The reference price might be formed by noting current prices, remembering past prices, or assessing the buying situation. Sellers can influence or use these consumers' reference prices when setting price. For example, a company could display its product next to more expensive ones in order to imply that it belongs in the same class. Department stores often sell women's clothing in separate departments differentiated by price: Clothing found in the more expensive department is assumed to be of better quality.

For most purchases, consumers don't have all the skill or information they need to figure out whether they are paying a good price. They don't have the time, ability, or inclination to research different brands or stores, compare prices, and get the best deals. Instead, they may rely on certain cues that signal whether a price is

■ Psychological pricing: What do the prices marked on this tag suggest about the product and buying solution.

high or low. For example, the fact that a product is sold in a prestigious department store might signal that it's worth a higher price.

Interestingly, such pricing cues are often provided by sellers. A retailer might show a high manufacturer's suggested price next to the marked price, indicating that the product was originally priced much higher. Or the retailer might sell a selection of familiar products for which consumers have accurate price knowledge at very low prices, suggesting that the store's prices on other, less familiar products are low as well. The use of such pricing cues has become a common marketing practice.

Even small differences in price can signal product differences. Consider a stereo receiver priced at $300 compared to one priced at $299.99. The actual price difference is only 1 cent, but the psychological difference can be much greater. For example, some consumers will see the $299.99 as a price in the $200 range rather than the $300 range. The $299.99 will more likely be seen as a bargain price, whereas the $300 price suggests more quality. Some psychologists argue that each digit has symbolic and visual qualities that should be considered in pricing. Thus, 8 is round and even and creates a soothing effect, whereas 7 is angular and creates a jarring effect.[19]

Promotional Pricing

With **promotional pricing**, companies will temporarily price their products below list price and sometimes even below cost to create buying excitement and urgency. Promotional pricing takes several forms. Supermarkets and department stores will price a few products as *loss leaders* to attract customers to the store in the hope that they will buy other items at normal markups. For example, supermarkets often sell disposable diapers at less than cost in order to attract family buyers who make larger average purchases per trip. Sellers will also use *special-event pricing* in certain seasons to draw more customers. Thus, linens are promotionally priced every January to attract weary Christmas shoppers back into stores.

Manufacturers sometimes offer *cash rebates* to consumers who buy the product from dealers within a specified time; the manufacturer sends the rebate directly to the customer. Rebates have been popular with automakers and producers of durable goods and small appliances, but they are also used with consumer packaged goods. Some manufacturers offer *low-interest financing, longer warranties,* or *free maintenance* to reduce the consumer's "price." This practice has become another favorite of the auto industry. Or, the seller may simply offer *discounts* from normal prices to increase sales and reduce inventories.

Promotional pricing, however, can have adverse effects. Used too frequently and copied by competitors, price promotions can create "deal-prone" customers who wait until brands go on sale before buying them. Or, constantly reduced prices can erode a brand's value in the eyes of customers. Marketers sometimes become addicted to promotional pricing, using price promotions as a quick fix instead of sweating through the difficult process of developing effective longer-term strategies for building their brands. The use of promotional pricing can also lead to industry price wars. Such price wars usually play into the hands of only one or a few competitors—those with the most efficient operations. For example, in the face of intense competition with Intel, computer chip maker Advanced Micro Devices (AMD) began to aggressively reduce its prices. Intel retaliated with even lower prices. In the resulting price war, AMD has seen its margins and profits skid against those of its larger rival.[20]

The point is that promotional pricing can be an effective means of generating sales for some companies in certain circumstances. But it can be damaging for other companies or if taken as a steady diet.

Promotional pricing
Temporarily pricing products below the list price, and sometimes even below cost, to increase short-run sales.

■ Promotional pricing: Companies offer promotional prices to create buying excitement and urgency.

Linking the Concepts

Here's a good place to take a brief break. Think about some of the companies and industries you deal with that are "addicted" to promotional pricing.

■ Many industries have created "deal-prone" consumers through the heavy use of promotional pricing—fast food, automobiles, cell phones, airlines, tires, furniture, and others. Pick a company in one of these industries and suggest ways that it might deal with this problem.

■ How does the concept of value relate to promotional pricing? Does promotional pricing add to or detract from customer value?

Geographical Pricing

Geographical pricing
Setting price based on the buyer's geographic location.

A company also must decide how to price its products for customers located in different parts of the country or world. Should the company risk losing the business of more-distant customers by charging them higher prices to cover the higher shipping costs? Or should the company charge all customers the same prices regardless of location? We will look at five **geographical pricing** strategies for the following hypothetical situation:

> The Peerless Paper Company is located in Atlanta, Georgia, and sells paper products to customers all over the United States. The cost of freight is high and affects the companies from whom customers buy their paper. Peerless wants to establish a geographical pricing policy. It is trying to determine how to price a $100 order to three specific customers: Customer A (Atlanta), Customer B (Bloomington, Indiana), and Customer C (Compton, California).

One option is for Peerless to ask each customer to pay the shipping cost from the Atlanta factory to the customer's location. All three customers would pay the same factory price of $100, with Customer A paying, say, $100 for shipping; Customer B, $150; and Customer C, $250. Called *FOB-origin pricing*, this practice means that the goods are placed *free on board* (hence, *FOB*) a carrier. At that point the title and responsibility pass to the customer, who pays the freight from the factory to the destination. Because each customer picks up its own cost, supporters of FOB pricing feel that this is the fairest way to assess freight charges. The disadvantage, however, is that Peerless will be a high-cost firm to distant customers.

Uniform-delivered pricing is the opposite of FOB pricing. Here, the company charges the same price plus freight to all customers, regardless of their location. The freight charge is set at the average freight cost. Suppose this is $150. Uniform-delivered pricing therefore results in a higher charge to the Atlanta customer (who pays $150 freight instead of $100) and a lower charge to the Compton customer (who pays $150 instead of $250). Although the Atlanta customer would prefer to buy paper from another local paper company that uses FOB-origin pricing, Peerless has a better chance of winning over the California customer. Other advantages of uniform-delivered pricing are that it is fairly easy to administer and it lets the firm advertise its price nationally.

Zone pricing falls between FOB-origin pricing and uniform-delivered pricing. The company sets up two or more zones. All customers within a given zone pay a single total price; the more distant the zone, the higher the price. For example, Peerless might set up an East Zone and charge $100 freight to all customers in this zone, a Midwest Zone in which it charges $150, and a West Zone in which it charges $250. In this way, the customers within a given price zone receive no price advantage from the company. For example, customers in Atlanta and Boston pay the same total price to Peerless. The complaint, however, is that the Atlanta customer is paying part of the Boston customer's freight cost.

Using *basing-point pricing*, the seller selects a given city as a "basing point" and charges all customers the freight cost from that city to the customer location, regardless of the city from which the goods are actually shipped. For example, Peerless might set Chicago as the basing point and charge all customers $100 plus the freight from Chicago to their locations. This means that an Atlanta customer pays the freight cost from Chicago to Atlanta, even though the goods may be shipped from Atlanta. If all sellers used the same basing-point city, delivered prices would be the same for all customers and price competition would be eliminated. Industries such as sugar, cement, steel, and automobiles used basing-point pricing for years, but this method has become less popular today. Some companies set up multiple basing points to create more flexibility: They quote freight charges from the basing-point city nearest to the customer.

Finally, the seller who is anxious to do business with a certain customer or geographical area might use *freight-absorption pricing*. Using this strategy, the seller absorbs all or part of the actual freight charges in order to get the desired business. The seller might reason that if it can get more business, its average costs will fall and more than compensate for its extra freight cost. Freight-absorption pricing is used for market penetration and to hold on to increasingly competitive markets.

Dynamic Pricing

Throughout most of history, prices were set by negotiation between buyers and sellers. *Fixed price* policies—setting one price for all buyers—is a relatively modern idea that arose with the development of large-scale retailing at the end of the nineteenth century. Today, most prices are set this way. However, some companies are now reversing the fixed pricing trend. They are using **dynamic pricing**—adjusting prices continually to meet the characteristics and needs of individual customers and situations.

Dynamic pricing
Adjusting prices continually to meet the characteristics and needs of individual customers and situations.

For example, think about how the Internet has affected pricing. From the mostly fixed pricing practices of the past century, the Web seems now to be taking us back—into a new age of fluid pricing. The flexibility of the Internet allows Web sellers to instantly and constantly adjust prices on a wide range of goods based on demand dynamics. In many cases, this involves regular changes in the prices that Web sellers set for their goods. In others, such as eBay or Priceline, consumers negotiate the final prices they pay.

Dynamic pricing offers many advantages for marketers. For example, Internet sellers such as Amazon.com can mine their databases to gauge a specific shopper's desires, measure his or her means, instantaneously tailor products to fit that shopper's behavior, and price products accordingly. Catalog retailers such as L. L. Bean or Spiegel can change prices on the fly according to changes in demand or costs, changing prices for specific items on a day-by-day or even hour-by-hour basis.

Many direct marketers monitor inventories, costs, and demand at any given moment and adjust prices instantly. For example, Dell uses dynamic pricing to achieve real-time balancing of supply and demand for computer components. Author Thomas Friedman describes Dell's dynamic pricing system this way:[21]

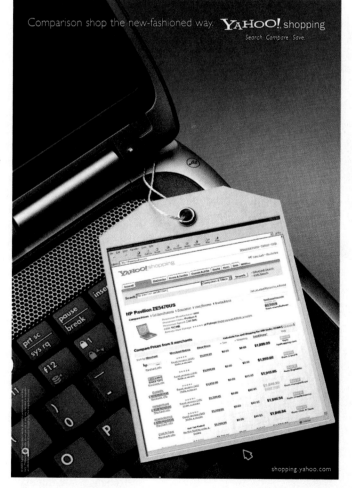

■ Buyers benefit from the Web and dynamic pricing. Sites like Yahoo! Shopping give instant product and price comparisons from thousands of vendors, arming customers with price information they need to get the lowest prices.

> [Dell's] supply chain symphony—from my order over the phone to production to delivery to my house—is one of the wonders of the flat world. . . . Demand shaping goes on constantly. . . . It works like this: At 10 a.m. Austin time, Dell discovers that so many customers have ordered notebooks with 40-gigabyte hard drives since the morning that its supply chain will run short in two hours. That signal is automatically relayed to Dell's marketing department and to Dell.com and to all the Dell phone operators taking orders. If you happen to call to place your Dell order at 10:30 a.m., the Dell representative will say to you, "Tom, it's your lucky day! For the next hour we are offering 60-gigabyte hard drives with the notebook you want—for only $10 more than the 40-gig drive. And if you act now, Dell will throw in a carrying case along with your purchase, because we so value you as a customer." In an hour or two, using such promotions, Dell can reshape the demand for any part of any

notebook or desktop to correspond with the projected supply in its global supply chain. Today memory might be on sale, tomorrow it might be CD-ROMS.

Buyers also benefit from the Web and dynamic pricing. A wealth of *shopping bots*—such as Yahoo! Shopping, Bizrate.com, NexTag.com, epinions.com, PriceGrabber.com, mysimon.com, and PriceScan.com—offer instant product and price comparisons from thousands of vendors. Epinions.com, for instance, lets shoppers browse by category or search for specific products and brands. It then searches the Web and reports back links to sellers offering the best prices along with customer reviews. In addition to simply finding the best product and the vendor with the best price for that product, customers armed with price information can often negotiate lower prices.

Buyers can also negotiate prices at online auction sites and exchanges. Suddenly the centuries-old art of haggling is back in vogue. Want to sell that antique pickle jar that's been collecting dust for generations? Post it on eBay, the world's biggest online flea market. Want to name your own price for a hotel room or rental car? Visit Priceline.com or another reverse auction site. Want to bid on a ticket to a Coldplay show? Check out Ticketmaster.com, which now offers an online auction service for concert tickets.

Dynamic pricing can also be controversial. Most customers would find it galling to learn that the person in the next seat on that flight from Gainesville to Galveston paid 10 percent less just because he or she happened to call at the right time or buy through the right sales channel. Amazon.com learned this some years ago when it experimented with lowering prices to new customers in order to woo their business. When regular customers learned through Internet chatter that they were paying generally higher prices than first-timers, they protested loudly. An embarrassed Amazon.com halted the experiments.

Dynamic pricing makes sense in many contexts—it adjusts prices according to market forces, and it often works to the benefit of the customer. But marketers need to be careful not to use dynamic pricing to take advantage of certain customer groups, damaging important customer relationships.[22]

International Pricing

Companies that market their products internationally must decide what prices to charge in the different countries in which they operate. In some cases, a company can set a uniform worldwide price. For example, Boeing sells its jetliners at about the same price everywhere, whether in the United States, Europe, or a third-world country. However, most companies adjust their prices to reflect local market conditions and cost considerations.

The price that a company should charge in a specific country depends on many factors, including economic conditions, competitive situations, laws and regulations, and development of the wholesaling and retailing system. Consumer perceptions and preferences also may vary from country to country, calling for different prices. Or the company may have different marketing objectives in various world markets, which require changes in pricing strategy. For example, Samsung might introduce a new product into mature markets in highly developed countries with the goal of quickly gaining mass-market share—this would call for a penetration-pricing strategy. In contrast, it might enter a less-developed market by targeting smaller, less price-sensitive segments; in this case, market-skimming pricing makes sense.

Costs play an important role in setting international prices. Travelers abroad are often surprised to find that goods that are relatively inexpensive at home may carry outrageously higher price tags in other countries. A pair of Levi's selling for $30 in the United States might go for $63 in Tokyo and $88 in Paris. A McDonald's Big Mac selling for a modest $2.90 here might cost $6.00 in Reykjavik, Iceland, and an Oral-B toothbrush selling for $2.49 at home may cost $10 in China. Conversely, a Gucci handbag going for only $140 in Milan, Italy, might fetch $240 in the United States. In some cases, such *price escalation* may result from differences in selling strategies or market conditions. In most instances, however, it is simply a result of the higher costs of selling in another country—the additional costs of product modifications, shipping and insurance, import tariffs and taxes, exchange-rate fluctuations, and physical distribution.

Price has become a key element in the international marketing strategies of companies attempting to enter emerging markets, such as China, India, and Brazil. Consider Dell's current China strategy:

It seems that every personal computer maker now wants a piece of China, where PC sales grew at a dazzling 21 percent rate last year, compared with just a 2.6 percent U.S. growth rate. By 2013, China will overtake the United States as the world's largest PC market. To gain a stronger foothold in China, Dell is pursuing a penetration pricing strategy. It recently launched a new, low-priced computer designed especially for the still-developing, less-affluent Chinese market. The $340 Dell EC280 uses only about a quarter of the power of a conventional desktop and has been simplified for first-time computer buyers. "We said to ourselves: 'Let's design something that doesn't have things that people don't use,' " says a Dell international marketing executive. "Those things cost money and add [unneeded] complexity." Smart pricing has helped Dell to increase its share of the Chinese market by almost 30 percent in just the past four years. The PC maker is now adapting the low-cost China PC to Brazil, India, and other emerging markets.[23]

■ International pricing: Smart pricing plays a key role in Dell's marketing in China and other emerging markets.

Thus, international pricing presents some special problems and complexities. We discuss international pricing issues in more detail in Chapter 15.

Price Changes

After developing their pricing structures and strategies, companies often face situations in which they must initiate price changes or respond to price changes by competitors.

Initiating Price Changes

In some cases, the company may find it desirable to initiate either a price cut or a price increase. In both cases, it must anticipate possible buyer and competitor reactions.

Initiating Price Cuts Several situations may lead a firm to consider cutting its price. One such circumstance is excess capacity. Another is falling demand in the face of strong price competition. In such cases, the firm may aggressively cut prices to boost sales and share. But as the airline, fast-food, automobile, and other industries have learned in recent years, cutting prices in an industry loaded with excess capacity may lead to price wars as competitors try to hold on to market share.

A company may also cut prices in a drive to dominate the market through lower costs. Either the company starts with lower costs than its competitors, or it cuts prices in the hope of gaining market share that will further cut costs through larger volume. Bausch & Lomb used an aggressive low-cost, low-price strategy to become an early leader in the competitive soft contact lens market. Costco used this strategy to become the world's largest warehouse retailer.

Initiating Price Increases A successful price increase can greatly improve profits. For example, if the company's profit margin is 3 percent of sales, a 1 percent price increase will boost profits by 33 percent if sales volume is unaffected. A major factor in price increases is cost inflation. Rising costs squeeze profit margins and lead companies to pass cost increases along to customers. Another factor leading to price increases is overdemand: When a company cannot supply all that its customers need, it may raise its prices, ration products to customers, or both. Consider the worldwide oil and gas industry.

When raising prices, the company must avoid being perceived as a price gouger. Customers have long memories, and they will eventually turn away from companies or even whole industries that they perceive as charging excessive prices. There are some techniques for avoiding this problem. One is to maintain a sense of fairness surrounding any price increase. Price increases should be supported by company communications telling customers why prices are being raised. Making low-visibility price moves first is also a good technique: Some examples include dropping discounts, increasing minimum order sizes, and curtailing production of low-margin products. The company sales force should help business customers find ways to economize.

Wherever possible, the company should consider ways to meet higher costs or demand without raising prices. For example, it can consider more cost-effective ways to produce or distribute its products. It can shrink the product or substitute less-expensive ingredients instead of raising the price, as candy bar manufacturers often do. Or it can "unbundle" its market offering, removing features, packaging, or services and separately pricing elements that were formerly part of the offer. IBM, for example, now offers training and consulting as separately priced services.

Buyer Reactions to Price Changes Customers do not always interpret price changes in a straightforward way. They may view a price *cut* in several ways. For example, the Manolo brand name has become synonymous with expensive shoes. But what would you think if designer Manolo Blahnik were to suddenly cut his shoe prices from $400 to $65? You might think that you are getting a better deal on a good pair of designer shoes. More likely, however, you'd think that quality had been reduced or that Manolo had licensed his name to a mass-market shoemaker.

Similarly, a price *increase*, which would normally lower sales, may have some positive meanings for buyers. What would you think if Manolo Blahnik *raised* the price of his latest shoe? On the one hand, you might think that the item is even more exclusive or better made. On the other hand, you might think that Manolo Blahnik is simply being greedy by charging what the traffic will bear.

Competitor Reactions to Price Changes A firm considering a price change must worry about the reactions of its competitors as well as those of its customers. Competitors are most likely to react when the number of firms involved is small, when the product is uniform, and when the buyers are well informed about products and prices.

How can the firm anticipate the likely reactions of its competitors? The problem is complex because, like the customer, the competitor can interpret a company price cut in many ways. It might think the company is trying to grab a larger market share, or that it's doing poorly and trying to boost its sales. Or it might think that the company wants the whole industry to cut prices to increase total demand.

The company must guess each competitor's likely reaction. If all competitors behave alike, this amounts to analyzing only a typical competitor. In contrast, if the competitors do not behave alike—perhaps because of differences in size, market shares, or policies—then separate analyses are necessary. However, if some competitors will match the price change, there is good reason to expect that the rest will also match it.

Responding to Price Changes

Here we reverse the question and ask how a firm should respond to a price change by a competitor. The firm needs to consider several issues: Why did the competitor change the price? Is the price change temporary or permanent? What will happen to the company's market share and profits if it does not respond? Are other competitors going to respond? Besides these issues, the company must also consider its own situation and strategy and possible customer reactions to price changes.

Figure 9.5 shows the ways a company might assess and respond to a competitor's price cut. Suppose the company learns that a competitor has cut its price and decides that this price cut is likely to harm company sales and profits. It might simply decide to hold its current price and profit margin. The company might believe that it will not lose too much market share, or that it would lose too much profit if it reduced its own price. Or it might decide that it should wait and respond when it has more information on the effects of the competitor's price change. However, waiting too long to act might let the competitor get stronger and more confident as its sales increase.

If the company decides that effective action can and should be taken, it might make any of four responses. First, it could *reduce its price* to match the competitor's price. It may

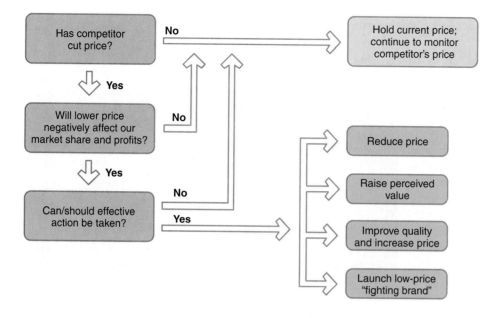

FIGURE 9.5

Assessing and Responding to Competitor Price Changes

decide that the market is price sensitive and that it would lose too much market share to the lower-priced competitor. Cutting the price will reduce the company's profits in the short run. Some companies might also reduce their product quality, services, and marketing communications to retain profit margins, but this will ultimately hurt long-run market share. The company should try to maintain its quality as it cuts prices.

Alternatively, the company might maintain its price but *raise the perceived value* of its offer. It could improve its communications, stressing the relative value of its product over that of the lower-price competitor. The firm may find it cheaper to maintain price and spend money to improve its perceived value than to cut price and operate at a lower margin. Or, the company might *improve quality and increase price,* moving its brand into a higher price-value position. The higher quality creates greater customer value, which justifies the higher price. In turn, the higher price preserves the company's higher margins.

Finally, the company might *launch a low-price "fighting brand"*—adding a lower-price item to the line or creating a separate lower-price brand. This is necessary if the particular market segment being lost is price sensitive and will not respond to arguments of higher quality. Thus, to counter store brands and other low-price entrants, Procter & Gamble turned a number of its brands into fighting brands. Luvs disposable diapers give parents "premium leakage protection for less than pricier brands." And P&G offers popular budget-priced Basic versions of several of its major brands. For example, Charmin Basic is "the quality toilet tissue at a price you'll love." And Bounty Basic is "Practical. Not Pricey." It offers "great strength at a great price—the paper towel that can take care of business without costing a bundle." In all, the Bounty brand claims an astounding 42.5 percent share of the paper towel market, and Bounty Basic has accounted for much of the brand's recent growth.[24]

■ Fighting brands: P&G offers popular budget-priced Basic versions of several of its major brands. For example, Bounty Basic is "Practical. Not Pricey."

Public Policy and Pricing

Price competition is a core element of our free-market economy. In setting prices, companies usually are not free to charge whatever prices they wish. Many federal, state, and even local laws govern the rules of fair play in pricing. In addition, companies must consider

9.2 MARKETING AT WORK

GlaxoSmithKline: Pricing for More than Sales and Profits

The U.S. pharmaceutical industry has historically been one of the nation's most profitable industries. Annual drug industry revenues have grown 33 percent in just the past five years, a growth rate that few industries can match. As the world's second-largest pharmaceuticals company, GlaxoSmithKline (GSK) has played a large role in the industry's success. It produces a medicine cabinet full of well-known prescription drugs that combat infections, depression, skin conditions, asthma, heart and circulatory disease, and cancer. It also makes dozens of familiar over-the-counter remedies, from Contac, Nicorette, and Sensodyne to Tagamet and Tums.

GlaxoSmithKline is doing very well in a high-performing industry. Its sales last year grew by 9 percent; earnings per share grew 17 percent. GSK captures a 7.9 percent share of the U.S. pharmaceuticals market, second only to Pfizer. Around the world, more than 1,100 prescriptions are written for GSK products every minute. And with more drugs in its research and development pipeline than most of its competitors, it appears that GSK's future will be just as bright.

In most situations, we applaud companies for strong profit performance. However, when it comes to pharmaceuticals firms, critics claim that healthy profits may not be so healthy for consumers. Learning that GlaxoSmithKline is reaping big profits leaves a bad taste in the mouths of many consumers—it's like learning that the oil companies are profiting as gas prices soar. Although most consumers appreciate the steady stream of beneficial drugs produced by the U.S. pharmaceutical companies, they sense that the industry's huge success may be coming at their own expense—literally.

Americans spend more than $260 billion a year on prescription medications, nearly half of worldwide spending, and this spending is expected to exceed $450 billion by 2015. Prescription prices have risen rapidly over the years and health care costs continue to jump. A recent AARP report stated that prescription drug prices soared at nearly twice the general inflation rate last year. According to another

■ Most consumers appreciate the steady stream of beneficial drugs produced by pharmaceutical companies like GlaxoSmithKline. However, with the prices of many of the most important drugs skyrocketing, others protest that the industry's huge success may be coming at their own expense—literally.

study, prices for the 10 most prescribed brand-name drugs skyrocketed nearly 7 percent in just the first five months of 2007. High drug prices have sent many consumers, especially seniors with limited budgets and fixed incomes, to Mexico or Canada in search of cheaper alternatives. Says one senior after a visit to Mexico, "If we couldn't get cheap meds, I wouldn't live."

The critics claim that competitive forces don't operate well in the pharmaceutical market, allowing GSK and other companies to charge excessive prices. Unlike purchases of other consumer products, drug purchases cannot be postponed. And consumers don't usually shop for the best deal on medicines—they simply take what the doctor or-

---

broader societal pricing concerns (see Marketing at Work 9.2). The most important pieces of legislation affecting pricing are the Sherman, Clayton, and Robinson-Patman acts, initially adopted to curb the formation of monopolies and to regulate business practices that might unfairly restrain trade. Because these federal statutes can be applied only to interstate commerce, some states have adopted similar provisions for companies that operate locally.

Figure 9.6 shows the major public policy issues in pricing. These include potentially damaging pricing practices within a given level of the channel (price-fixing and predatory pricing) and across levels of the channel (retail price maintenance, discriminatory pricing, and deceptive pricing).[25]

Pricing Within Channel Levels

Federal legislation on *price-fixing* states that sellers must set prices without talking to competitors. Otherwise, price collusion is suspected. Price-fixing is illegal per se—that is, the government does not accept any excuses for price-fixing. Companies found guilty of such practices can receive heavy fines.

Recently, governments at the state and national levels have been aggressively enforcing price-fixing regulations in industries ranging from gasoline, insurance, and concrete to credit cards, CDs, and computer chips. For example, Samsung and two other computer memory-chip makers agreed to pay $160 million to settle a suit alleging a four-year pricing-fixing conders. Because physicians who write the prescriptions don't pay for the medicines they recommend, they have little incentive to be price conscious. Finally, because of patents and FDA approvals, few competing brands exist to force lower prices, and existing brands don't go on sale. The critics claim that these market factors leave pharmaceutical companies free to practice monopoly pricing resulting in unfair practices and price gouging. To add insult to injury, the critics say, drug companies pour $4.5 billion a year into direct-to-consumer advertising and another $16 billion into sampling. These marketing efforts dictate higher prices at the same time that they build demand for more expensive remedies.

As a pharmaceuticals industry leader, GlaxoSmithKline has borne its share of the criticism. For example, as the largest producer of AIDS-fighting antiretroviral drugs, GSK has been accused of pricing its drugs out of the reach of the poor people who need them the most. And the company recently settled claims by the U.S. Department of Justice and 40 states alleging that it had inflated the wholesale prices of drugs used by cancer patients and others. Thus, the severest critics say, GSK may be profiting unfairly—or even at the expense of human life.

But there's another side to the drug-pricing issue. Industry proponents point out that, over the years, GSK has developed a steady stream of medicines that transform people's lives. Developing such new drugs is a risky and expensive endeavor, involving legions of scientists, expensive technology, and years of effort with no certainty of success. The pharmaceuticals industry invests nearly $50 billion a year in R&D—GSK alone invested $6.9 billion last year. GSK now has 158 prescription drugs and vaccines under development. On average, each new drug takes 15 years to develop at a cost of close to $800 million. Then, 70 percent of new drugs never generate enough revenue to recover the cost of development. Although the prices of prescription drugs seem high, they're needed to fund the development of important future drugs.

A recent GlaxoSmithKline ad notes that it took 15 years to complete all the tests and to find the exact right compound for a new heart medicine, at a cost of more than the price of a space shuttle mission. Profits from the heart drug will help to fund critical research on diseases such as multiple sclerosis and Alzheimer's. The ad concludes: "Inventing new medicines isn't easy, but it's worth it.…Today's medicines finance tomorrow's miracles."

And so the controversy continues. As drug prices climb, GSK and the industry are facing pressures from the federal government, insurance companies, managed-care providers, and advocacy groups to exercise restraint in setting prices. Rather than waiting for tougher legislation on prices—or simply because it's the right thing to do—GSK has undertaken several initiatives to make drugs available to those who need but can't afford them. For some years now, it has priced its HIV/AIDS and malaria medicines at cost to customers and not-for-profit organizations in developing countries. In the United States and other developed countries, GSK sponsors patient assistance programs and discount cards that provide prescription medicines to low-income, uninsured patients free or at minimal cost. And GSK regularly donates free medicines in response to disaster relief efforts around the globe.

The pharmaceuticals pricing controversy will no doubt continue. For GlaxoSmithKline, it's more than a matter of sales and profits. In setting prices, short-term financial goals must be tempered by broader societal considerations. GSK's heartfelt mission is "to improve the quality of human life by enabling people to do more, feel better, and live longer." Accomplishing this mission won't come cheap. Most consumers understand that one way or another they'll have to pay the price. All they really ask is that they be treated fairly in the process.

Sources: Jonathan Weisman, "Costs Grow for Common Medicare Drugs," *Washington Post,* May 13, 2007, p. A10; Jim Edwards, "Drug Ad Spend up 9% in '06," *Adweek,* December 26, 2006, accessed at www.adweek.com; "Pharmaceuticals in the United States: Industry Profile," *Datamonitor,* December 2006, pp. 3, 9, and 12; Joel Millman, "Not Your Generic Smugglers—American Seniors Flock to Border Town for Cheap Prescriptions," *Wall Street Journal,* March 20, 2003, p. D3; "GSK to Settle Pricing Claims," *News & Observer,* August 11, 2006, p. 2D; Kerry Capell, "Getting AIDS Drugs to More Sick People," *BusinessWeek,* January 29, 2007, p. 60; Miranda Hitti, "AARP: Prescription Drug Prices Up," *WebMD Medical News,* March 6, 2007; and information from www.gsk.com, accessed December 2007.

spiracy to artificially constrict the supply of D-Ram (dynamic random access memory) chips to computer makers such as Dell and Apple. This control of the supply helped keep prices artificially high, producing higher profits for the conspiring companies. Since that settlement,

FIGURE 9.6   Public Policy Issues in Pricing

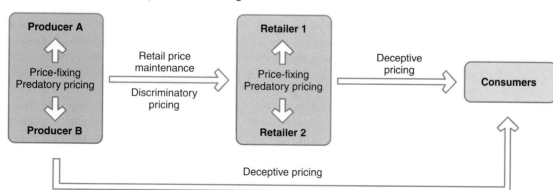

Source: Adapted with permission from Dhruv Grewel and Larry D. Compeau, "Pricing and Public Policy: A Research Agenda and Overview of Special Issue," *Journal of Public Policy and Marketing,* Spring 1999, pp. 3–10, Figure 1.

U.S. state and federal governments and the European Union have filed additional price-fixing lawsuits against various computer memory-chip makers.[26]

Sellers are also prohibited from using *predatory pricing*—selling below cost with the intention of punishing a competitor or gaining higher long-run profits by putting competitors out of business. This protects small sellers from larger ones who might sell items below cost temporarily or in a specific locale to drive them out of business. The biggest problem is determining just what constitutes predatory pricing behavior. Selling below cost to unload excess inventory is not considered predatory; selling below cost to drive out competitors is. Thus, the same action may or may not be predatory depending on intent, and intent can be very difficult to determine or prove.

In recent years, several large and powerful companies have been accused of predatory pricing. For example, Wal-Mart has been sued by dozens of small competitors charging that it lowered prices in their specific geographic areas or on specific products—such as gasoline and generic drugs—to drive them out of business. In fact, the State of New York passed a bill requiring companies to price gas at or above 98 percent of cost to "address the more extreme cases of predatory pricing by big-box stores" such as Wal-Mart. Yet, in North Dakota, the same gas pricing proposal was rejected because state representatives did not view the practice as predatory pricing. And in Colorado, a bill was passed that allowed below-cost fuel.[27]

Pricing Across Channel Levels

The Robinson-Patman Act seeks to prevent unfair *price discrimination* by ensuring that sellers offer the same price terms to customers at a given level of trade. For example, every retailer is entitled to the same price terms from a given manufacturer, whether the retailer is Sears or your local bicycle shop. However, price discrimination is allowed if the seller can prove that its costs are different when selling to different retailers—for example, that it costs less per unit to sell a large volume of bicycles to Sears than to sell a few bicycles to the local dealer.

The seller can also discriminate in its pricing if the seller manufactures different qualities of the same product for different retailers. The seller must prove that these differences are proportional. Price differentials may also be used to "match competition" in "good faith," provided the price discrimination is temporary, localized, and defensive rather than offensive.

Laws also prohibit *retail (or resale) price maintenance*—a manufacturer cannot require dealers to charge a specified retail price for its product. Although the seller can propose a manufacturer's *suggested* retail price to dealers, it cannot refuse to sell to a dealer who takes independent pricing action, nor can it punish the dealer by shipping late or denying advertising allowances. For example, the Florida attorney general's office investigated Nike for allegedly fixing the retail price of its shoes and clothing. It was concerned that Nike might be withholding items from retailers who were not selling its most expensive shoes at prices the company considered suitable.

Deceptive pricing occurs when a seller states prices or price savings that mislead consumers or are not actually available to consumers. This might involve bogus reference or comparison prices, as when a retailer sets artificially high "regular" prices then announces "sale" prices close to its previous everyday prices. For example, Overstock.com recently came under scrutiny for inaccurately listing manufacturer's suggested retail prices, often quoting them higher than the actual price. Such comparison pricing is widespread.

Comparison pricing claims are legal if they are truthful. However, the FTC's *Guides Against Deceptive Pricing* warns sellers not to advertise a price reduction unless it is a saving from the usual retail price, not to advertise "factory" or "wholesale" prices unless such prices are what they are claimed to be, and not to advertise comparable value prices on imperfect goods.[28]

Other deceptive pricing issues include *scanner fraud* and price confusion. The widespread use of scanner-based computer checkouts has led to increasing complaints of retailers overcharging their customers. Most of these overcharges result from poor management—from a failure to enter current or sale prices into the system. Other cases, however, involve intentional overcharges. *Price confusion* results when firms employ pricing methods that make it difficult for consumers to understand just what price they are really paying. For example, consumers are sometimes misled regarding the real price of a home mortgage or car leasing agreement. In other cases, important pricing details may be buried in the "fine print."

Many federal and state statutes regulate against deceptive pricing practices. For example, the Automobile Information Disclosure Act requires automakers to attach a statement to new-car windows stating the manufacturer's suggested retail price, the prices of optional equipment, and the dealer's transportation charges. However, reputable sellers go beyond what is required by law. Treating customers fairly and making certain that they fully understand prices and pricing terms is an important part of building strong and lasting customer relationships.

REST STOP ⤴ REVIEWING THE CONCEPTS

Before you put pricing in the rearview mirror, let's review the important concepts. *Price* can be defined as the sum of all the values that customers give up in order to gain the benefits of having or using a product or service. Pricing decisions are subject to an incredibly complex array of company, environmental, and competitive forces.

1. Discuss the importance of understanding customer-value perceptions and company costs when setting prices.

Good pricing begins with a complete understanding of the value that a product or service creates for customers and setting a price that captures that value. The price the company charges will fall somewhere between one that is too high to produce any demand and one that is too low to produce a profit.

Customer perceptions of the product's value set the ceiling for prices. If customers perceive that the price is greater than the product's value, they will not buy the product. At the other extreme, company and product costs set the floor for prices. If the company prices the product below its costs, its profits will suffer.

Costs are an important consideration in setting prices. However, cost-based pricing is product driven. The company designs what it considers to be a good product and sets a price that covers costs plus a target profit. If the price turns out to be too high, the company must settle for lower markups or lower sales, both resulting in disappointing profits. Value-based pricing reverses this process. The company assesses customer needs and value perceptions and then sets target prices to match targeted value. The targeted value and price then drive decisions about product design and what costs can be incurred. As a result, price is set to match customers' perceived value.

2. Identify and define the other important internal and external factors affecting a firm's pricing decisions.

Other *internal* factors that influence pricing decisions include the company's overall marketing strategy, objectives, mix, and organization for pricing. Price is only one element of the company's broader marketing strategy. If the company has selected its target market and positioning carefully, then its marketing mix strategy, including price, will be fairly straightforward. Some companies position their products on price—high or low—and then tailor other marketing mix decisions to the prices they want to charge. Other companies deemphasize price and use other marketing mix tools to create *nonprice* positions. Common pricing objectives might include survival, current profit maximization, market share leadership, or customer reten-

tion and relationship building. Price decisions must be coordinated with product design, distribution, and promotion decisions to form a consistent and effective marketing program. Finally, in order to coordinate pricing goals and decisions, management must decide who within the organization is responsible for setting price.

Other *external* pricing considerations include the nature of the market and demand, competitors' strategies and prices, and environmental factors such as the economy, reseller needs, and government actions. The seller's pricing freedom varies with different types of markets. Ultimately, the customer decides whether the company has set the right price. The customer weighs the price against the perceived values of using the product—if the price exceeds the sum of the values, consumers will not buy. So the company must understand concepts such as demand curves (the price-demand relationship) and price elasticity (consumer sensitivity to prices). Consumers also compare a product's price to the prices of competitors' products. A company therefore must learn the customer value and prices of competitors' offers.

3. Describe the major strategies for pricing imitative and new products.

Pricing is a dynamic process. Companies design a *pricing structure* that covers all their products. They change this structure over time and adjust it to account for different customers and situations. Pricing strategies usually change as a product passes through its life cycle. In pricing innovative new products, it can follow a *skimming policy* by initially setting high prices to "skim" the maximum amount of revenue from various segments of the market. Or it can use *penetration pricing* by setting a low initial price to penetrate the market deeply and win a large market share.

4. Explain how companies find a set of prices that maximizes the profits from the total product mix.

When the product is part of a product mix, the firm searches for a set of prices that will maximize the profits from the total mix. In *product line pricing*, the company decides on price steps for the entire set of products it offers. In addition, the company must set prices for *optional products* (optional or accessory products included with the main product), *captive products* (products that are required for use of the main product), *by-products* (waste or residual products produced when making the main product), and *product bundles* (combinations of products at a reduced price).

5. Discuss how companies adjust their prices to take into account different types of customers and situations.

Companies apply a variety of *price-adjustment strategies* to account for differences in consumer segments and situations. One is *discount and allowance pricing,* whereby the company establishes cash, quantity, functional, or seasonal discounts, or varying types of allowances. A second strategy is *segmented pricing,* whereby the company sells a product at two or more prices to accommodate different customers, product forms, locations, or times. Sometimes companies consider more than economics in their pricing decisions, using *psychological pricing* to better communicate a product's intended position. In *promotional pricing,* a company offers discounts or temporarily sells a product below list price as a special event, sometimes even selling below cost as a loss leader. Another approach is *geographical pricing,* whereby the company decides how to price to near and distant customers. *Dynamic pricing* involves adjusting prices continually to meet the characteristics and needs of individual customers and situations. Finally, *international pricing* means that the company adjusts its price to meet conditions and expectations in different world markets.

6. Discuss the key issues related to initiating and responding to price changes.

When a firm considers initiating a *price change,* it must consider customers' and competitors' reactions. There are different implications to *initiating price cuts* and *initiating price increases.* Buyer reactions to price changes are influenced by the meaning customers see in the price change. Competitors' reactions flow from a set reaction policy or a fresh analysis of each situation.

There are also many factors to consider in responding to a competitor's price changes. The company that faces a price change initiated by a competitor must try to understand the competitor's intent as well as the likely duration and impact of the change. If a swift reaction is desirable, the firm should preplan its reactions to different possible price actions by competitors. When facing a competitor's price change, the company might sit tight, reduce its own price, raise perceived value, improve quality and raise price, or launch a fighting brand.

Companies are not usually free to charge whatever prices they wish. Many federal, state, and even local laws govern the rules of fair play in pricing. The major public policy issues in pricing include potentially damaging pricing practices within a given level of the channel (price-fixing and predatory pricing) and across levels of the channel (retail price maintenance, discriminatory pricing, and deceptive pricing).

Navigating the Key Terms

Allowance (274)
Break-even pricing (target profit pricing) (263)
By-product pricing (273)
Captive-product pricing (272)
Cost-based pricing (262)
Cost-plus pricing (263)
Demand curve (268)
Discount (274)
Dynamic pricing (279)

Fixed costs (262)
Geographical pricing (278)
Good-value pricing (261)
Market-penetration pricing (271)
Market-skimming pricing (270)
Optional-product pricing (272)
Price (259)
Price elasticity (269)
Product bundle pricing (274)
Product line pricing (272)

Promotional pricing (277)
Psychological pricing (276)
Reference prices (276)
Segmented pricing (275)
Target costing (265)
Total costs (263)
Value-added pricing (262)
Value-based pricing (260)
Variable costs (262)

Travel Log

Discussing the Issues

1. What is price? List five other words that mean the same thing as price (for example, tuition). (AACSB: Communication; Reflective Thinking)

2. Explain the differences between value-based pricing and cost-based pricing and describe the methods of implementing each. (AACSB: Communication)

3. Why would a marketer of high-tech innovative products choose market-skimming pricing rather than market-penetration pricing when launching a new product? (AACSB: Communication)

4. Name and briefly describe the five product mix pricing decisions. (AACSB: Communication)

5. Psychological pricing is a price-adjustment strategy often used by retailers. Explain this pricing strategy. How do reference prices affect psychological pricing decisions? (AACSB: Communication; Reflective Thinking)

6. Under what conditions will a marketer consider a price increase, and what factors must be considered before raising price? (AACSB: Communication)

Application Questions

1. Visit *U.S. News & World Report* at www.usnews.com/usnews/edu/college/rankings/bvrankindex_brief.php for a list of schools that offer the best value. Click on the "Best Colleges Home" tab and then on the "About the Rankings" tab. Under "Methodology," click on "Best Values Methodology" to learn how value is defined. Is this a valid definition of value? (AACSB: Communication; Use of IT; Reflective Thinking)

2. In a small group, brainstorm ideas about a service targeted toward college students (such as laundry pickup and delivery). Have each member of your group talk to five other students about their perceptions of value regarding this service, what they desire in this type of service, and the

price they would be willing to pay for it. Write a brief report on what your group learned and discuss the basis on which price is determined. (AACSB: Communication; Reflective Thinking)

3. You are an owner of a small independent chain of coffee houses competing head-to-head with Starbuck's. The retail price your customers pay for coffee is exactly the same as at Starbuck's. The wholesale price you pay for roasted coffee beans has increased by 25 percent. You know that you cannot absorb this increase and that you must pass it on to your customers. However, you are concerned about the consequences of an open price increase. Discuss three alternative price-increase strategies that address these concerns. (AACSB: Communication; Reflective Thinking)

Under the Hood: Focus on Technology

Consumers have always been price conscious, and price-comparison shopping is now easier than ever. Comparing prices used to require that shoppers visit stores or call to get price information. But now, with the click of a mouse, buyers can compare the prices of several retailers instantaneously. At one time, some experts even predicted that Internet "shopping bots" would make price comparisons so simple that prices would be driven down as retailers were forced to match each others' prices to stay in business.

1. Identify three price-comparison shopping Web sites and shop for an MP3 player of your choice. Compare the price ranges given at these three Web sites. Has price compression occurred as predicted? (AACSB: Communication; Use of IT)

2. Although price is important, other factors influence consumers' purchase decisions. What information, in addition to price, is available from the price-comparison shopping Web sites you accessed? (AACSB: Communication; Use of IT)

Focus on Ethics

Marketers often use pricing to influence consumer behavior. For example, movie theaters smooth out demand by charging less for an afternoon matinee to draw more patrons at this slower time. Similarly, airlines charge lower prices for flyers staying over a Saturday night, causing many buyers to stay an extra night rather than flying home before the weekend. Such pricing shifts demand from one time period to another. A relatively new form of this pricing strategy is called *congestion pricing*. Used in London since 2003, such pricing encourages commuters to use public transportation to relieve congestion—to shift modes of transportation rather than times. However, rather than rewarding individuals for performing the desired behavior, it punishes them for undesirable behavior. Londoners must pay £8 per day to travel across 8.5 square miles of central London. Singapore and Stockholm are using a tolling scheme as well. In the United States, if lawmakers approve Mayor Bloomberg's plan, New York City's proposed congestion pricing plan will receive more than $350 million in federal funding. Although several U.S. cities are congested, New York City is ideal for congestion pricing. Manhattan, the most congested area of New York City, is surrounded by water, making it relatively easy to charge drivers both coming and going.

1. Research congestion pricing and discuss three pros and three cons of this pricing strategy. (AACSB: Communication; Reflective Thinking)

2. Some critics argue that this type of pricing potentially harms small businesses that operate within congested areas (florists, for example) or employees who must travel to such areas for their jobs. Is it ethical for governments to charge drivers in this way? Suggest some compromise solutions. (AACSB: Communication; Ethical Reasoning)

Video Case

GE

When you think of General Electric (GE), you might think first of products such as appliances and light bulbs. But GE is much, much more. The giant $168 billion company also markets financial services, medical imaging equipment, and owns NBC—all under its tagline "imagination at work."

Despite all of its growth and success, several years ago, GE found its appliance business in decline. Prices were dropping and GE's brands stood largely undifferentiated from others on the market. In response, GE applied its considerable marketing muscle to revamp, rebrand, and reprice its entire appliances line. In addition to its core mass-market GE appliance brand, the company added the GE Monogram and GE Profile lines. By doing so, the average retail price paid for GE appliance products has increased more than 15 percent. At the same time, GE's appliances business has delivered five years of double-digit earnings growth.

After viewing the video featuring GE, answer the following questions about pricing strategies.

1. Does GE use a cost-based or value-based pricing approach? Support your response.

2. Which of the product mix pricing strategies discussed in the book most closely describes GE's approach?

3. How did the new positioning statements for the Monogram and Profile lines affect pricing decisions relative to the standard GE line?

CHAPTER 10

Marketing Channels: Delivering Customer Value

ROAD MAP Previewing the Concepts

We now arrive at the third marketing mix tool—distribution. Firms rarely work alone in creating value for customers and building profitable customer relationships. Instead, most are only a single link in a larger supply chain and marketing channel. As such, an individual firm's success depends not only on how well *it* performs but also on how well its *entire marketing channel* competes with competitors' channels. To be good at customer relationship management, a company must also be good at partner relationship management. The first part of this chapter explores the nature of marketing channels and the marketer's channel design and management decisions. We then examine physical distribution—or logistics—an area that is growing dramatically in importance and sophistication. In the next chapter, we'll look more closely at two major channel intermediaries—retailers and wholesalers.

We'll start with a look at Caterpillar. You might think that Caterpillar's success rests on the quality of the heavy construction and mining equipment that it produces. But Caterpillar sees things differently. The company's dominance, it claims, results from its unparalleled distribution and customer-support system—from the strong and caring partnerships that it has built with independent Caterpillar dealers. Read on and see why.

For more than eight decades, Caterpillar has dominated the world's markets for heavy construction, mining, and logging equipment. Its familiar yellow tractors, crawlers, loaders, bulldozers, and trucks are a common sight at any construction area. Caterpillar sells more than 300 products in nearly 200 countries, with sales of more than $41 billion annually. Over the past five years, sales have more than doubled and profits have shot up more than fourfold. The big Cat captures some 37 percent of the worldwide construction and farm equipment business, almost double that of number-two John Deere and three times that of construction equipment rival Komatsu. The waiting line for some of Caterpillar's biggest equipment is years long.

Many factors contribute to Caterpillar's enduring success—high-quality products, flexible and efficient manufacturing, and a steady stream of innovative new products. Yet these are not the most important reasons for Caterpillar's dominance. Instead, Caterpillar credits its focus on customers and its corps of 182 outstanding independent dealers worldwide, who do a superb job of taking care of every customer need. According to former Caterpillar CEO Donald Fites:

After the product leaves our door, the dealers take over. They are the ones on the front line. They're the ones who live with the product for its lifetime. They're the ones customers see. . . . They're out there making sure that when a machine is delivered, it's in the condition it's supposed to be in. They're out there training a customer's operators. They service a product frequently throughout its life, carefully monitoring a machine's health and scheduling repairs to prevent costly downtime. The customer . . . knows that there is a [$41-billion-plus] company called Caterpillar. But the dealers create the image of a company that doesn't stand just *behind* its products but *with* its products, anywhere in the world. Our dealers are the reason that our motto—Buy the Iron, Get the Company—is not an empty slogan.

"Buy the Iron, Get the Company"—that's a powerful value proposition. It means that when you buy Cat equipment, you become a member of the Caterpillar family. Caterpillar and its dealers work in close harmony to find better ways to bring value to customers. Dealers play a vital role in almost every aspect of Caterpillar's operations, from product design and delivery, to product service and support, to market intelligence and customer feedback.

In the heavy-equipment industry, in which equipment downtime can mean big losses, Caterpillar's exceptional service gives it a huge advantage in winning and keeping customers. Consider Freeport-McMoRan, a Cat customer that operates one of the world's largest copper and gold mines, 24 hours a day, 365 days a year. High in the mountains of Indonesia, the mine is accessible only by aerial cableway or helicopter. Freeport-McMoRan relies on more than 500 pieces of Caterpillar mining and construction equipment—worth several hundred million dollars—including loaders, tractors, and mammoth 240-ton, 2,000-plus-horsepower trucks. Many of these machines cost well over $1 million apiece. When equipment breaks down, Freeport-McMoRan loses money fast. Freeport-McMoRan gladly pays a premium price for machines and service it can count on. It knows that it can count on Caterpillar and its outstanding distribution network for superb support.

The close working relationship between Caterpillar and its dealers comes down to more than just formal contracts and business agreements. The powerful partnership rests on a handful of basic principles and practices:

• *Dealer profitability:* Caterpillar's rule: "Share the gain as well as the pain." When times are good, Caterpillar shares the bounty with its dealers rather than trying to grab all the riches for itself. When times are bad, Caterpillar protects its dealers. In the mid-1980s, facing a depressed global construction-equipment market and cutthroat competition, Caterpillar sheltered its dealers by absorbing much of the economic damage. It lost almost $1 billion dollars in just three years but didn't lose a single dealer. In contrast, competitors' dealers struggled and many failed. As a result, Caterpillar emerged with its distribution system intact and its competitive position stronger than ever.

• *Extraordinary dealer support:* Nowhere is this support more apparent than in the company's parts delivery system, the fastest and most reliable in the industry. Caterpillar maintains 36 distribution centers and 1,500 service facilities around the world, which stock 320,000 different parts and ship 84,000 items per day, every day of the year. In turn, dealers have made huge investments in inventory, warehouses, fleets of trucks, service bays, diagnostic and service equipment, and information technology. Together, Caterpillar and its dealers guarantee parts delivery within 48 hours anywhere in the world. The company ships 80 percent of parts orders immediately and 99 percent on the same day the order is received. In contrast, it's not unusual for competitors' customers to wait four or five days for a part.

• *Communications:* Caterpillar communicates with its dealers—fully, frequently, and honestly. According to Fites, "There are no secrets between us and our dealers. We have the financial statements and key operating data of every dealer in the world. . . . In addition, virtually all Caterpillar and dealer employees have real-time access to continually updated databases of service information, sales trends and forecasts, customer satisfaction surveys, and other critical data."

• *Dealer performance:* Caterpillar does all it can to ensure that its dealerships are run well. It closely monitors each dealership's sales, market position, service capability, financial situation, and other performance measures. It genuinely wants each dealer to succeed, and when it sees a problem, it jumps in to help. As a result, Caterpillar dealerships, many of which are family businesses, tend to be stable and profitable.

• *Personal relationships:* In addition to more formal business ties, Cat forms close personal ties with its dealers in a kind of family relationship. One Caterpillar executive relates the following example: "When I see Chappy Chapman, a retired executive vice-president . . . out on the golf course, he always asks about particular dealers or about their children, who may be running the business now. And every time I see those dealers, they inquire, 'How's Chappy?' That's the sort of relationship we have. . . . I consider the majority of dealers personal friends."

Thus, Caterpillar's superb distribution system serves as a major source of competitive advantage. The system is built on a firm base of mutual trust and shared dreams. Caterpillar and its dealers feel a deep pride in what they are accomplishing together. As Fites puts it, "There's a camaraderie among our dealers around the world that really makes it more than just a financial arrangement. They feel that what they're doing is good for the world because they are part of an organization that makes, sells, and tends to the machines that make the world work."[1]

Most firms cannot bring value to customers by themselves. Instead, they must work closely with other firms in a larger value delivery network.

Supply Chains and the Value Delivery Network

Producing a product or service and making it available to buyers requires building relationships not just with customers, but also with key suppliers and resellers in the company's *supply chain*. This supply chain consists of "upstream" and "downstream" partners. Upstream from the company is the set of firms that supply the raw materials, components, parts, information, finances, and expertise needed to create a product or service. Marketers, however, have traditionally focused on the "downstream" side of the supply chain—on the *marketing channels* (or *distribution channels*) that look forward toward the customer. Downstream marketing channel partners, such as wholesalers and retailers, form a vital connection between the firm and its customers.

Both upstream and downstream partners may also be part of other firms' supply chains. But it is the unique design of each company's supply chain that enables it to deliver superior value to customers. An individual firm's success depends not only on how well *it* performs, but also on how well its entire supply chain and marketing channel competes with competitors' channels.

The term *supply chain* may be too limited—it takes a *make-and-sell* view of the business. It suggests that raw materials, productive inputs, and factory capacity should serve as the starting point for market planning. A better term would be *demand chain* because it suggests a *sense-and-respond* view of the market. Under this view, planning starts with the needs of target customers, to which the company responds by organizing a chain of resources and activities with the goal of creating customer value.

Even a demand chain view of a business may be too limited, because it takes a step-by-step, linear view of purchase-production-consumption activities. With the advent of the Internet and other technologies, however, companies are forming more numerous and complex relationships with other firms. For example, Ford manages numerous supply chains. It also sponsors or transacts on many B2B Web sites and online purchasing exchanges as needs arise. Like Ford, most large companies today are engaged in building and managing a continuously evolving *value delivery network*.

As defined in Chapter 2, a **value delivery network** is made up of the company, suppliers, distributors, and ultimately customers who "partner" with each other to improve the performance of the entire system. For example, Nike subsidiary Converse does more than just make and market sneakers. It manages an entire network of materials and equipment suppliers, company shoe designers and manufacturing people, and thousands of online and off-line resellers who must work effectively together to bring superior value to Converse customers. It even involves customers themselves in the value creation process by inviting them to design their own Chucks online or to submit their own "Made by You" Converse video shorts to conversegallery.com.

This chapter focuses on marketing channels—on the downstream side of the value delivery network. However, it is important to remember that this is only part of the full value network. In creating customer value, companies need upstream supplier partners just as they need downstream channel partners. Increasingly, marketers are participating in and influencing their company's upstream activities as well as its downstream activities. More than marketing channel managers, they are becoming full value network managers.

The chapter examines four major questions concerning marketing channels: What is the nature of marketing channels and why are they important? How do channel firms interact and organize to do the work of the channel? What problems do companies face in designing and managing their channels? What role do physical distribution and supply chain management play in attracting and satisfying customers? In Chapter 11, we will look at marketing channel issues from the viewpoint of retailers and wholesalers.

Value delivery network
The network made up of the company, suppliers, distributors, and ultimately customers who "partner" with each other to improve the performance of the entire system in delivering customer value.

The Nature and Importance of Marketing Channels

Marketing channel (distribution channel)
A set of interdependent organizations that help make a product or service available for use or consumption by the consumer or business user.

Few producers sell their goods directly to the final users. Instead, most use intermediaries to bring their products to market. They try to forge a **marketing channel** (or **distribution channel**)—a set of interdependent organizations that help make a product or service available for use or consumption by the consumer or business user.

A company's channel decisions directly affect every other marketing decision. Pricing depends on whether the company works with national discount chains, uses high-quality specialty stores, or sells directly to consumers via the Web. The firm's sales force and communications decisions depend on how much persuasion, training, motivation, and support its channel partners need. Whether a company develops or acquires certain new products may depend on how well those products fit the capabilities of its channel members.

Companies often pay too little attention to their distribution channels, sometimes with damaging results. In contrast, many companies have used imaginative distribution systems to *gain* a competitive advantage. FedEx's creative and imposing distribution system made it a leader in express delivery. Dell revolutionized its industry by selling personal computers directly to consumers rather than through retail stores. Amazon.com pioneered the sales of books and a wide range of other goods via the Internet. And Calyx & Corolla led the way in selling fresh flowers and plants direct to consumers by phone and from its Web site, cutting a week or more off the time it takes flowers to reach consumers through conventional retail channels.

Distribution channel decisions often involve long-term commitments to other firms. For example, companies such as Ford, Hewlett-Packard, or McDonald's can easily change their advertising, pricing, or promotion programs. They can scrap old products and introduce new ones as market tastes demand. But when they set up distribution channels through contracts with franchisees, independent dealers, or large retailers, they cannot readily replace these channels with company-owned stores or Web sites if conditions change. Therefore, management must design its channels carefully, with an eye on tomorrow's likely selling environment as well as today's.

■ Innovative marketing channels: Calyx & Corolla sells fresh flowers and plants direct to consumers by phone and from its Web site, cutting a week or more off the time it takes flowers to reach consumers through conventional retail channels.

How Channel Members Add Value

Why do producers give some of the selling job to channel partners? After all, doing so means giving up some control over how and to whom they sell their products. Producers use intermediaries because they create greater efficiency in making goods available to target markets. Through their contacts, experience, specialization, and scale of operation, intermediaries usually offer the firm more than it can achieve on its own.

Figure 10.1 shows how using intermediaries can provide economies. Figure 10.1A shows three manufacturers, each using direct marketing to reach three customers. This system requires nine different contacts. Figure 10.1B shows the three manufacturers working through one distributor, which contacts the three customers. This system requires only six contacts. In this way, intermediaries reduce the amount of work that must be done by both producers and consumers.

From the economic system's point of view, the role of marketing intermediaries is to transform the assortments of products made by producers into the assortments wanted by

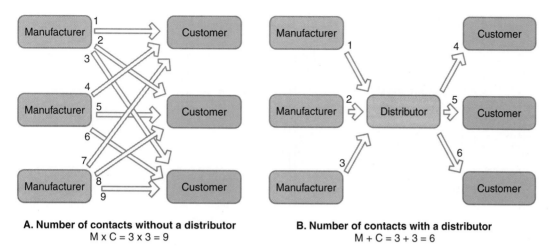

A. Number of contacts without a distributor
M x C = 3 x 3 = 9

B. Number of contacts with a distributor
M + C = 3 + 3 = 6

FIGURE 10.1   How a Distributor Reduces the Number of Channel Transactions

consumers. Producers make narrow assortments of products in large quantities, but consumers want broad assortments of products in small quantities. Marketing channel members buy large quantities from many producers and break them down into the smaller quantities and broader assortments wanted by consumers.

For example, Unilever makes millions of bars of Lever 2000 hand soap each day, but you want to buy only a few bars at a time. So big food, drug, and discount retailers, such as Kroger, Walgreens, and Wal-Mart, buy Lever 2000 by the truckload and stock it on their store's shelves. In turn, you can buy a single bar of Lever 2000, along with a shopping cart full of small quantities of toothpaste, shampoo, and other related products as you need them. Thus, intermediaries play an important role in matching supply and demand.

In making products and services available to consumers, channel members add value by bridging the major time, place, and possession gaps that separate goods and services from those who would use them. Members of the marketing channel perform many key functions. Some help to complete transactions:

• *Information:* Gathering and distributing marketing research and intelligence information about actors and forces in the marketing environment needed for planning and aiding exchange
• *Promotion:* Developing and spreading persuasive communications about an offer
• *Contact:* Finding and communicating with prospective buyers
• *Matching:* Shaping and fitting the offer to the buyer's needs, including activities such as manufacturing, grading, assembling, and packaging
• *Negotiation:* Reaching an agreement on price and other terms of the offer so that ownership or possession can be transferred

Others help to fulfill the completed transactions:

• *Physical distribution:* Transporting and storing goods
• *Financing:* Acquiring and using funds to cover the costs of the channel work
• *Risk taking:* Assuming the risks of carrying out the channel work

The question is not *whether* these functions need to be performed—they must be—but rather *who* will perform them. To the extent that the manufacturer performs these functions, its costs go up and its prices must be higher. When some of these functions are shifted to intermediaries, the producer's costs and prices may be lower, but the intermediaries must charge more to cover the costs of their work. In dividing the work of the channel, the various functions should be assigned to the channel members who can add the most value for the cost.

Number of Channel Levels

Companies can design their distribution channels to make products and services available to customers in different ways. Each layer of marketing intermediaries that performs some

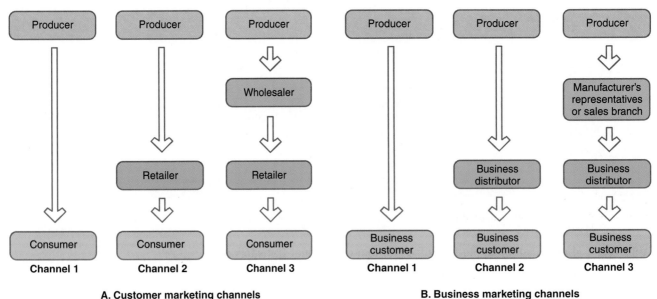

A. Customer marketing channels   B. Business marketing channels

FIGURE 10.2   Consumer and Business Marketing Channels

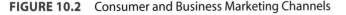

Channel level

A layer of intermediaries that performs some work in bringing the product and its ownership closer to the final buyer.

Direct marketing channel

A marketing channel that has no intermediary levels.

Indirect marketing channel

A channel containing one or more intermediary levels.

work in bringing the product and its ownership closer to the final buyer is a **channel level**. Because the producer and the final consumer both perform some work, they are part of every channel.

The *number of intermediary levels* indicates the *length* of a channel. Figure 10.2A shows several consumer distribution channels of different lengths. Channel 1, called a **direct marketing channel**, has no intermediary levels; the company sells directly to consumers. For example, Mary Kay and Amway sell their products door-to-door, through home and office sales parties, and on the Web; GEICO sells direct via the telephone and the Internet. The remaining channels in Figure 10.2A are **indirect marketing channels**, containing one or more intermediaries.

Figure 10.2B shows some common business distribution channels. The business marketer can use its own sales force to sell directly to business customers. Or it can sell to various types of intermediaries, who in turn sell to these customers. Consumer and business marketing channels with even more levels can sometimes be found, but less often. From the producer's point of view, a greater number of levels means less control and greater channel complexity. Moreover, all of the institutions in the channel are connected by several types of *flows*. These include the *physical flow* of products, the *flow of ownership,* the *payment flow,* the *information flow,* and the *promotion flow.* These flows can make even channels with only one or a few levels very complex.

Channel Behavior and Organization

Distribution channels are more than simple collections of firms tied together by various flows. They are complex behavioral systems in which people and companies interact to accomplish individual, company, and channel goals. Some channel systems consist only of informal interactions among loosely organized firms. Others consist of formal interactions guided by strong organizational structures. Moreover, channel systems do not stand still—new types of intermediaries emerge and whole new channel systems evolve. Here we look at channel behavior and at how members organize to do the work of the channel.

Channel Behavior

A marketing channel consists of firms that have partnered for their common good. Each channel member depends on the others. For example, a Ford dealer depends on Ford to design cars that meet consumer needs. In turn, Ford depends on the dealer to attract consumers, persuade them to buy Ford cars, and service cars after the sale. Each Ford dealer also depends on other dealers to provide good sales and service that will uphold the brand's reputation. In fact, the success of individual Ford dealers depends on how well the entire Ford marketing channel competes with the channels of other auto manufacturers.

Each channel member plays a specialized role in the channel. For example, Samsung's role is to produce consumer electronics products that consumers will like and to create demand through national advertising. Best Buy's role is to display these Samsung products in convenient locations, to answer buyers' questions, and to complete sales. The channel will be most effective when each member assumes the tasks it can do best.

Ideally, because the success of individual channel members depends on overall channel success, all channel firms should work together smoothly. They should understand and accept their roles, coordinate their activities, and cooperate to attain overall channel goals. However, individual channel members rarely take such a broad view. Cooperating to achieve overall channel goals sometimes means giving up individual company goals. Although channel members depend on one another, they often act alone in their own short-run best interests. They often disagree on who should do what and for what rewards. Such disagreements over goals, roles, and rewards generate **channel conflict**.

Horizontal conflict occurs among firms at the same level of the channel. For instance, some Ford dealers in Chicago might complain the other dealers in the city steal sales from them by pricing too low or by advertising outside their assigned territories. Or Holiday Inn franchisees might complain about other Holiday Inn operators overcharging guests or giving poor service, hurting the overall Holiday Inn image.

Vertical conflict, conflicts between different levels of the same channel, is even more common. For example, Goodyear created hard feelings and conflict with its premier independent-dealer channel when it began selling through mass-merchant retailers (see Marketing at Work 10.1). Similarly, Revlon came into serious conflict with its department store channels when it cozied up to mass merchants:[2]

> A few years back, Revlon made a big commitment to mass-market retailers such as Wal-Mart, Target, and CVS, all but snubbing better department stores in the process. That strategy worked well initially. However, the mass merchants are sophisticated and demanding, and they quickly abandon brands that aren't working. That happened recently with Revlon's important new Vital Radiance cosmetics line, which targeted aging boomers. When Revlon failed to deliver on the promised marketing support for Vital Radiance—it spent only $700,000 during the three-month launch versus P&G's $9 million during the same period for its Cover Girl Advanced Radiance cosmetics—the mass-merchant channels backed away from the brand. For example, only 647 of CVS's 5,300 stores carried the new line. Meanwhile, the department stores, which Revlon had chosen to ignore with Vital Radiance, were lukewarm in their reaction to Revlon's attempted launch of a new prestige fragrance, Flair. Federated Department Stores, which operates Macy's and Bloomingdale's, refused to carry Revlon's new fragrance altogether. Says one retailing expert, "The prestige channel [didn't] trust Revlon not to run back to the discount channel if sales for Flair [didn't] fly." In the end, Revlon withdrew Vital Radiance, and Flair never made it to market. Thanks to bungled marketing channel relationships, Revlon lost more than $100 million in one year.

Some conflict in the channel takes the form of healthy competition. Such competition can be good for the channel—without it, the channel could become passive and noninnovative. But severe or prolonged conflict, as in the case of Goodyear and Revlon, can disrupt channel effectiveness and cause lasting harm to channel relationships. Companies should manage channel conflict to keep it from getting out of hand.

Vertical Marketing Systems

For the channel as a whole to perform well, each channel member's role must be specified and channel conflict must be managed. The channel will perform better if it includes a firm, agency, or mechanism that provides leadership and has the power to assign roles and manage conflict.

Channel conflict
Disagreement among marketing channel members on goals and roles—who should do what and for what rewards.

10.1 MARKETING AT WORK

Goodyear Rolls, but No Longer over Its Dealers

For more than 60 years, Goodyear sold replacement tires exclusively through its premier network of 6,900 independent Goodyear dealers. Both Goodyear and its dealers profited from this partnership. Goodyear received the undivided attention and loyalty of its single-brand dealers, and the dealers gained the exclusive right to sell the highly respected Goodyear tire line. In mid-1992, however, Goodyear shattered tradition and jolted its dealers by agreeing to sell its tires through Sears auto centers. Similar pacts soon followed with Wal-Mart and Sam's Club, placing dealers in direct competition with the nation's most potent retailers.

To add insult to injury, beyond selling its branded tires through large retailers, Goodyear began selling private-branded tires though Wal-Mart and other discounters. It even opened its own no-frills, quick-serve Just Tires discount stores designed to fend off low-priced competitors. All of these moves created fierce new competition for Goodyear's independent dealers.

Goodyear claimed that the channel changes were essential. Tires had become more of an impulse item, and value-minded tire buyers were increasingly buying from cheaper, multibrand discount outlets and department stores. The market share of these outlets had grown 30 percent in the previous five years, whereas that of tire dealers had fallen 4 percent. Marketing research showed that one out of four Wal-Mart customers was a potential Goodyear buyer and that these buyers came from a segment not likely to be reached by independent Goodyear dealers. By selling exclusively through its dealer network, Goodyear claimed, it simply wasn't putting its tires where many consumers were going to buy them.

■ Channel conflict: Following more than a decade of damaging conflict with its prized independent dealer network, Goodyear has actively set about repairing fractured dealer relations. The result: a remarkable turnaround that has Goodyear now rolling, rolling, rolling.

Conventional distribution channel
A channel consisting of one or more independent producers, wholesalers, and retailers, each a separate business seeking to maximize its own profits even at the expense of profits for the system as a whole.

Vertical marketing system (VMS)
A distribution channel structure in which producers, wholesalers, and retailers act as a unified system. One channel member owns the others, has contracts with them, or has so much power that they all cooperate.

Corporate VMS
A vertical marketing system that combines successive stages of production and distribution under single ownership—channel leadership is established through common ownership.

Historically, *conventional distribution channels* have lacked such leadership and power, often resulting in damaging conflict and poor performance. One of the biggest channel developments over the years has been the emergence of *vertical marketing systems* that provide channel leadership. Figure 10.3 contrasts the two types of channel arrangements.

A **conventional distribution channel** consists of one or more independent producers, wholesalers, and retailers. Each is a separate business seeking to maximize its own profits, perhaps even at the expense of the system as a whole. No channel member has much control over the other members, and no formal means exists for assigning roles and resolving channel conflict.

In contrast, a **vertical marketing system (VMS)** consists of producers, wholesalers, and retailers acting as a unified system. One channel member owns the others, has contracts with them, or wields so much power that they must all cooperate. The VMS can be dominated by the producer, wholesaler, or retailer.

We look now at three major types of VMSs: *corporate, contractual,* and *administered.* Each uses a different means for setting up leadership and power in the channel.

Corporate VMS A **corporate VMS** integrates successive stages of production and distribution under single ownership. Coordination and conflict management are attained through regular organizational channels. For example, grocery giant Kroger owns and operates 42 factories that crank out more than 8,000 private label items found on its store shelves.

The shifts in consumer buying were also causing problems for dealers. Unfortunately, however, as Goodyear expanded into the needed new channels, it took few steps to protect its prized dealer network. Although it offered an ample variety of premium lines, Goodyear provided its dealers with none of the lower-priced lines that many consumers were demanding. Dealers complained not just about competition from megaretailers but also about shoddy treatment and unfair pricing from Goodyear. For example, to sell more tires, Goodyear offered volume discounts to its biggest retailers and wholesalers. "The result was pricing insanity," notes one observer. "Some smaller dealers were paying more for tires than what Sears charged at retail."

Not surprisingly, Goodyear's aggressive moves into new channels set off a surge of dysfunctional channel conflict, and dealer relations deteriorated rapidly. Some of Goodyear's best dealers defected to competitors. Other angry dealers struck back by taking on competing brands and by aggressively promoting cheaper, private-label tires that offered higher margins to dealers and more appeal to value-conscious consumers. U.S. dealers in California even took Goodyear to court in a class action suit, causing Goodyear to somewhat restrict the tire lines sold through its channels there. Says one former dealer, "After someone punches you in the face a few times, you say, 'Enough is enough.'"

Such dealer actions weakened the Goodyear name and the premium price that it could command. Goodyear's replacement tire sales—which make up 71 percent of the company's revenues—went flat, dropping the company into a decade-long profit funk. By 2002, Goodyear was fighting off rumors of bankruptcy.

In 2003, however, Goodyear regained its senses and refocused its strategy. After years of chasing volume by selling low-margin tires to midmarket buyers, the company began focusing on higher-performance, higher-margin tire lines. More importantly, Goodyear actively set about repairing fractured dealer relations. It began supporting dealers with more fair and consistent pricing, on-time order fulfillment, strong marketing support, and hot new products sold exclusively through the dealer network.

The new strategic direction had an immediate and impressive impact. In the two years following the redirection, Goodyear's sales exploded 30 percent, profits went from searing red to healthy black, and the company's stock price rocketed from a low of $3.35 in 2003 to $24.89 at the end of last year. Goodyear is now rolling, rolling, rolling. And despite the fact that Goodyear now obtains 25 percent of its sales through mass merchandisers, dealer relations have turned around dramatically. At a recent meeting with dealers in Nashville, Tennessee, Goodyear chief executive Robert Keegan received a "roaring standing ovation" from dealers.

Even with its recent successes, however, the company still faces many bumps in the road ahead. Completely patching Goodyear's dealer relations, damaged over many years, will take time. "We still have a long way to go on this," admits Goodyear's VP for replacement tire sales. "We lost sight of the fact that it's in our interest that our dealers succeed." An industry analyst agrees: "Goodyear . . . must stay proactive about keeping dealers satisfied. It's an everyday effort involving all of the company's interactions with dealers."

Sources: Quotes and other information from "No Time to Rest for Goodyear," *Tire Business,* February 13, 2006, p. 8; Kevin Kelleher, "Giving Dealers a Raw Deal," *Business 2.0,* December 2004, pp. 82–84; Jonathan Fahey, "Rolling, Rolling, Rolling," *Forbes,* November 28, 2005, pp. 54–56; "Goodyear Tire Sales," *Associated Press,* December 19, 2006, p. 1; Jack Mckinnon, "Goodyear Tire & Rubber Company," *Knight Ridder Tribune Business News,* April 8, 2007, p. 1; and Goodyear annual reports and other information accessed at www.goodyear.com, December 2007.

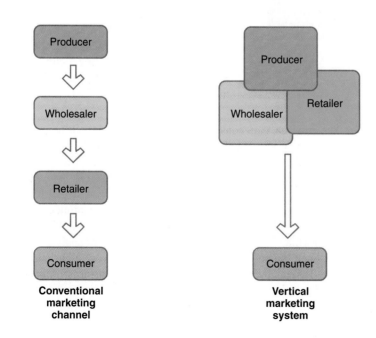

FIGURE 10.3

Comparison of Conventional Distribution Channel with Vertical Marketing System

Similarly, to help supply products for its 1,760 grocery stores, Safeway owns and operates nine milk plants, eight bakery plants, four ice cream plants, four soft drink bottling plants, and four fruit and vegetable processing plants. And little-known Italian eyewear maker Luxottica produces many famous eyewear brands—including its own Ray-Ban brand and licensed brands such as Polo Ralph Lauren, Dolce & Gabbana, Prada, Versace, and Bvlgari. It then sells these brands through two of the world's largest optical chains, LensCrafters and Sunglass Hut, which it also owns.[3]

Controlling the entire distribution chain has turned Spanish clothing chain Zara into the world's fastest-growing fashion retailer.

The secret to Zara's success is its control over almost every aspect of the supply chain, from design and production to its own worldwide distribution network. Zara makes 40 percent of its own fabrics and produces more than half of its own clothes, rather than relying on a hodgepodge of slow-moving suppliers. New designs feed into Zara manufacturing centers, which ship finished products directly to 1,021 Zara stores in 64 countries, saving time, eliminating the need for warehouses, and keeping inventories low. Effective vertical integration makes Zara faster, more flexible, and more efficient than international competitors such as Gap, Benetton, and H&M. And Zara's low costs let it offer midmarket chic at down-market prices.

Last summer, Zara managed to latch onto one of the season's hottest trends in just four weeks (versus an industry average of nine months). The process started when trend-spotters spread the word back to headquarters: White eyelet—cotton with tiny holes in it—was set to become white-hot. A quick telephone survey of Zara store managers confirmed that the fabric could be a winner, so in-house designers got down to work. They zapped patterns electronically to Zara's factory across the street, and the fabric was cut. Local subcontractors stitched white-eyelet V-neck belted dresses—think Jackie Kennedy, circa 1960—and finished them in less than a week. The $129 dresses were inspected, tagged, and transported through a tunnel under the street to a distribution center. From there, they were quickly dispatched to Zara stores from New York to Tokyo—where they were flying off the racks just two days later. In all, the company's stylish but affordable offerings have attracted a cult following. Zara store sales grew 19 percent last year to more than $7 billion.[4]

■ Corporate VMS: Effective vertical integration makes Zara faster, more flexible, and more efficient than competitors. It can take a new line from design to production to worldwide distribution in its own stores in less than a month (versus an industry average of nine months).

Contractual VMS
A vertical marketing system in which independent firms at different levels of production and distribution join together through contracts to obtain more economies or sales impact than they could achieve alone.

Franchise organization
A contractual vertical marketing system in which a channel member, called a franchiser, links several stages in the production-distribution process.

Contractual VMS A **contractual VMS** consists of independent firms at different levels of production and distribution who join together through contracts to obtain more economies or sales impact than each could achieve alone. Channel members coordinate their activities and manage conflict through contractual agreements.

The **franchise organization** is the most common type of contractual relationship—a channel member called a *franchisor* links several stages in the production-distribution process. In the United States alone, some 1,500 franchise businesses and 750,000 franchise outlets account for more than $1.5 trillion in annual sales. Industry analysts estimate that a new franchise outlet opens somewhere in the United States every eight minutes and that about one out of every 12 retail business outlets is a franchised business.[5] Almost every kind of business has been franchised—from motels and fast-food restaurants to dental centers and dating services, from wedding consultants and maid services to fitness centers and funeral homes.

There are three types of franchises. The first type is the *manufacturer-sponsored retailer franchise system*—for example, Ford and its network of independent franchised dealers. The second type is the *manufacturer-sponsored wholesaler franchise system*—Coca-Cola licenses bottlers (wholesalers) in various markets who buy Coca-Cola syrup concentrate and then bottle and sell the finished product to retailers in local markets. The third type is the *service-firm-sponsored retailer franchise system*—examples are found in the auto-rental business (Hertz, Avis), the fast-food service business (McDonald's, Burger King), and the motel business (Holiday Inn, Ramada Inn).

The fact that most consumers cannot tell the difference between contractual and corporate VMSs shows how successfully the contractual organizations compete with corporate chains. Chapter 11 presents a fuller discussion of the various contractual VMSs.

Administered VMS In an **administered VMS**, leadership is assumed not through common ownership or contractual ties but through the size and power of one or a few dominant channel members. Manufacturers of a top brand can obtain strong trade cooperation and support from resellers. For example, General Electric, Procter & Gamble and Kraft can command unusual cooperation from resellers regarding displays, shelf space, promotions, and price policies. Large retailers such as Wal-Mart, Home Depot, and Barnes & Noble can exert strong influence on the manufacturers that supply the products they sell.

Administered VMS
A vertical marketing system that coordinates successive stages of production and distribution, not through common ownership or contractual ties, but through the size and power of one of the parties.

Horizontal Marketing Systems

Another channel development is the **horizontal marketing system**, in which two or more companies at one level join together to follow a new marketing opportunity. By working together, companies can combine their financial, production, or marketing resources to accomplish more than any one company could alone.

Horizontal marketing system
A channel arrangement in which two or more companies at one level join together to follow a new marketing opportunity.

Companies might join forces with competitors or noncompetitors. They might work with each other on a temporary or permanent basis, or they may create a separate company. For example, McDonald's now places "express" versions of its restaurants in Wal-Mart stores. McDonald's benefits from Wal-Mart's heavy store traffic, and Wal-Mart keeps hungry shoppers from needing to go elsewhere to eat.

Such channel arrangements also work well globally. For example, McDonald's recently joined forces with Sinopec, China's largest gasoline retailer, to place drive-through restaurants at Sinopec's more than 31,000 gas stations. The move greatly speeds McDonald's expansion into China while at the same time pulling hungry motorists into Sinopec gas stations.[6] As another example, Coca-Cola and Nestlé formed a joint distribution venture, Beverage Partners Worldwide, to market ready-to-drink coffees, teas, and flavored milks in more than 40 countries worldwide. Coke provides worldwide experience in marketing and distributing beverages, and Nestlé contributes two established brand names—Nescafé and Nestea.[7]

■ Horizontal marketing systems: McDonald's recently joined forces with Sinopec, China's largest gasoline retailer, to place restaurants at its more than 30,000 gas stations. Here, the presidents of the two companies shake hands while announcing the partnership.

Multichannel Distribution Systems

In the past, many companies used a single channel to sell to a single market or market segment. Today, with the proliferation of customer segments and channel possibilities, more and more companies have adopted **multichannel distribution systems**—often called *hybrid*

Multichannel distribution system
A distribution system in which a single firm sets up two or more marketing channels to reach one or more customer segments.

FIGURE 10.4

Multichannel Distribution System

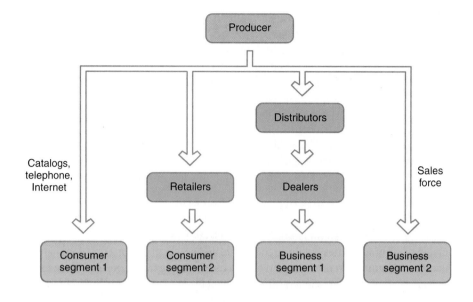

marketing channels. Such multichannel marketing occurs when a single firm sets up two or more marketing channels to reach one or more customer segments. The use of multichannel systems has increased greatly in recent years.

Figure 10.4 shows a multichannel marketing system. In the figure, the producer sells directly to consumer segment 1 using direct-mail catalogs, telemarketing, and the Internet and reaches consumer segment 2 through retailers. It sells indirectly to business segment 1 through distributors and dealers and to business segment 2 through its own sales force.

These days, almost every large company and many small ones distribute through multiple channels. For example, John Deere sells its familiar green and yellow lawn and garden tractors, mowers, and outdoor power products to consumers and commercial users through several channels, including John Deere retailers, Lowe's home improvement stores, and online. It sells and services its tractors, combines, planters, and other agricultural equipment through its premium John Deere dealer network. And it sells large construction and forestry equipment through selected large, full-service dealers and their sales forces.

Apparel and accessories marketer Coldwater Creek started as an out-of-home mail-order business in Sand Point, Idaho. The founder began by selling 18 items and shipping orders by peddling them to the local post office in his backpack. As the company grew, it added new marketing channels to reach new consumers. It now sells through four different catalogs, a direct-response Web site (www.coldwatercreek.com), and more than 250 Coldwater Creek retail outlets, all serviced by a state-of-the-art distribution and customer-service center in West Virginia.[8]

Multichannel distribution systems offer many advantages to companies facing large and complex markets. With each new channel, the company expands its sales and market coverage and gains opportunities to tailor its products and services to the specific needs of diverse customer segments. But such multichannel systems are harder to control, and they generate conflict as more channels compete for customers and sales. For example, when John Deere began selling selected consumer products through Lowe's home improvement stores, many of its dealers felt betrayed and complained loudly. To avoid such conflicts in its Internet marketing channels, the company routes all of its Web site sales to John Deere dealers.

Changing Channel Organization

Changes in technology and the explosive growth of direct and online marketing are having a profound impact on the nature and design of marketing channels. One major trend is toward **disintermediation**—a big term with a clear message and important consequences. Disintermediation occurs when product or service producers cut out intermediaries and go directly to final buyers, or when radically new types of channel intermediaries displace traditional ones.

Thus, in many industries, traditional intermediaries are dropping by the wayside. For example, companies such as Dell and Southwest Airlines sell directly to final buyers, cutting retailers and sales agents from their marketing channels altogether. In other cases, new forms of resellers are displacing traditional intermediaries. For example, online marketing is growing rapidly, taking business from traditional brick-and-mortar retailers. Consumers can buy electronics from sonystyle.com; clothes and accessories from bluefly.com; and books, videos, toys, jewelry, sports, consumer electronics, home and garden items, and almost anything else from Amazon.com; all without ever stepping into a traditional retail store. Online music download services such as iTunes and

■ Disintermediation: Online music download services are threatening to make traditional CD sellers obsolete. For example, once dominant Tower Records recently closed its doors for good.

Musicmatch are threatening the very existence of traditional music-store retailers. In fact, once-dominant music retailer Tower Records recently declared bankruptcy and closed its doors for good.

Disintermediation presents both opportunities and problems for producers and resellers. Channel innovators who find new ways to add value in the channel can sweep aside traditional resellers and reap the rewards. In turn, traditional intermediaries must continue to innovate in order to avoid being swept aside. For example, when Netflix pioneered online video rentals, it sent traditional brick-and-mortar video-rental stores such as Blockbuster reeling. To meet the threat, Blockbuster developed its own online DVD-rental service. Now, both Netflix and Blockbuster face disintermediation threats from an even hotter channel—digital video distribution (see Marketing at Work 10.2)

Similarly, to remain competitive, product and service producers must develop new channel opportunities, such as Internet and other direct channels. However, developing these new channels often brings them into direct competition with their established channels, resulting in conflict.

To ease this problem, companies often look for ways to make going direct a plus for the entire channel. For example, Black & Decker knows that many customers would prefer to buy its power tools and outdoor power equipment online. But selling directly through its Web site would create conflicts with important and powerful retail partners, such as Home Depot, Lowe's, Target, Wal-Mart, and Amazon.com. So, although Black & Decker's Web site provides detailed information about the company's products, you can't buy a Black & Decker cordless drill, laser level, leaf blower, or anything else there. Instead, the Black & Decker site refers you to resellers' Web sites and stores. Thus, Black & Decker's direct marketing helps both the company and its channel partners.

Disintermediation
The cutting out of marketing channel intermediaries by product or service producers, or the displacement of traditional resellers by radical new types of intermediaries.

Linking the Concepts

> Stop here for a moment and apply the distribution channel concepts we've discussed so far.

- Compare the Caterpillar and Goodyear channels. Draw a diagram that shows the types of intermediaries in each channel. What kind of channel system does each company use?
- What are the roles and responsibilities of the members in each channel? How well do these channel members work together toward overall channel success?

10.2 MARKETING AT WORK

Netflix: Disintermediator or Disintermediated?

Baseball great Yogi Berra, known more for his mangled phrasing than for his baseball prowess, once said, "The future ain't what it used to be." For Netflix, the world's largest online movie-rental service, no matter how you say it, figuring out the future is challenging and a bit scary. Netflix faces dramatic changes in how movies and other entertainment content will be distributed. The question: Will Netflix be among the disintermediat*ors* or among the disintermediat*ed*?

Less than a decade ago, if you wanted to watch a movie in the comfort of your own home, your only choice was to roust yourself out of that easy chair and trot down to the local Blockbuster or another neighborhood movie-rental store. In fact, that's how most people still do it. Blockbuster has grown to become the world's largest store-rental chain, with more than 8,000 outlets worldwide and more than $5 billion in annual sales.

But now, thanks to Netflix, that distribution model is changing quickly. In the late 1990s, Netflix pioneered a new way to rent movies—via the Web and direct mail. With Netflix, you pay a monthly subscription fee and create a movie wish list online. Netflix mails you a set number of DVDs from your list at a given time, which you can keep for as long as you like. As you return the DVDs in prepaid return envelopes, Netflix automatically sends you new ones from your list.

Netflix offers lots of advantages over the traditional Blockbuster brick-and-mortar system. With store video rentals, you must make a special trip whenever you want a movie, and if you don't plan ahead, you'll probably find the latest hot releases out of stock. As for finding copies of oldies but goodies, or an old documentary or independent film, forget it—stores can hold only a limited selection of DVDs. Finally, many consumers are frustrated by short due dates and those dreaded late return fees. In contrast, Netflix isn't bound by store-space limitations. It offers a huge selection of more than 80,000 titles and 42 million DVDs total. The Netflix system eliminates store trips—you always have a stack of DVDs on hand. And there are no per-movie charges, no due dates, and no late fees.

Since first opening its virtual doors, Netflix has continued to add innovative features. Its "dynamic queue" lets customers select as many movie titles as they wish and rank them by preference. Netflix has also developed an online recommendation system, called Cinematch, to help customers find movies they'll love based on their own past ratings, member and critic reviews, and top-rented lists.

■ Netflix faces dramatic changes in how movies and other entertainment content will be distributed. Instead of simply watching the developments, Netflix intends to lead them.

Channel Design Decisions

We now look at several channel decisions manufacturers face. In designing marketing channels, manufacturers struggle between what is ideal and what is practical. A new firm with limited capital usually starts by selling in a limited market area. Deciding on the best channels might not be a problem: The problem might simply be how to convince one or a few good intermediaries to handle the line.

If successful, the new firm can branch out to new markets through the existing intermediaries. In smaller markets, the firm might sell directly to retailers; in larger markets, it might sell through distributors. In one part of the country, it might grant exclusive franchises; in another, it might sell through all available outlets. Then, it might add a Web store that sells directly to hard-to-reach customers. In this way, channel systems often evolve to meet market opportunities and conditions.

As a result, more and more customers are signing up with Netflix. Membership has grown to nearly 7 million subscribers, and in just the past three years, sales and profits have more than tripled. Meanwhile, Netflix's success has sent Blockbuster and other video-rental stores reeling. As Netflix sales and profits have soared, Blockbuster's sales have flagged and losses have mounted. Although the traditional brick-and-mortar video-rental market is still alive and kicking, it's stagnating as the red-hot online channel gains momentum.

To meet the disintermediation threat, Blockbuster finally introduced its own online video-rental service. In fact, Blockbuster Total Access takes the new distribution model one step further. Total Access customers can order videos online and then return or exchange them either through the mail or at their local Blockbuster store. Whereas its store sales are sagging, Blockbuster's online business, now 2.2 million subscribers strong, is zooming.

And so the video-rental channels battle continues. Blockbuster claims the advantages of a click-and-mortar model that offers both online and store services. In contrast, Netflix sees physical stores as an unnecessary and costly limitation. Says Netflix founder and CEO Reed Hastings, "For people who'd love never to go into a Blockbuster store ever again, we offer better selection, better tools for choosing movies, and more consistent overnight delivery." Either way, there's no going back to the past—the two competitors are rapidly disintermediating store-only video-rental outfits.

But just as the present isn't what it used to be, neither is the future. At the same time that Netflix is displacing traditional store channels, it faces its own disintermediation threat from a potentially even hotter channel—digital video distribution in the form of digital downloads and video on demand (VOD). Digital distribution is a fact of life in the music industry, where music download services are fast making traditional CD retailers obsolete. Most experts agree that it's only a matter of time until digital video distribution displaces DVD video sales and rentals.

In fact, it's already begun. These days, you can download all kinds of video entertainment—from movies and TV shows to ads and amateur videos—to your computer, iPod, or even your cell phone. Satellite and cable TV companies are promising VOD services that will let you view movies and other video entertainment on television whenever and wherever you wish. And video-rental download services such as CinemaNow and Movielink are already offering a growing list of downloadable titles via the Web.

Digital video downloads and video on demand create obvious cost, distribution, and customer convenience advantages over physically producing and distributing DVDs. For sure, the digital video distribution industry still faces problems. Downloading videos can take a lot of time and yields less-than-DVD quality. Perhaps the biggest barrier so far—Hollywood has been cautious about granting video distribution rights, severely limiting the number of available titles. In time, however, all these limitations will likely dissipate. When that happens, it could be lights out for the DVD sales and rental industry.

Netflix CEO Hastings understands the future challenges. "We're sure that we're going to be buying cars in 25 years, whereas renting DVDs through the mail in 25 years—for sure that's not going to exist," he says. The solution? Keep innovating. Instead of simply watching digital video distribution developments, Netflix intends to lead them. Netflix has already added a "Watch Now" tab on its Web site that allows subscribers to instantly stream near-DVD quality video for a limited but growing list of movie titles. "Our intention," says Hasting, and "is to get Watch Now service to every Internet-connected screen, from cell phones to laptops to Wi-Fi-enabled plasma screens." In this way, Netflix plans to disintermediate its own distribution model before others can do it.

To Hastings, the key to the future is all in how Netflix defines itself. With the right definition, the future remains challenging but perhaps not so menacing. "If [you] think of Netflix as a DVD rental business, [you're] right to be scared," he says. But "if [you] think of Netflix as an online movie service with multiple different delivery models, then [you're] a lot less scared. We're only now starting to deliver [on] that second vision." When asked what Netflix will be like in five years, Hasting responds, "We hope to be much larger, have more subscribers, and be successfully expanding into online video."

Sources: Quotes and other information from Matthew Boyle, "Reed Hastings," *Fortune,* May 28, 2007, p. 30; "Nick Wingfield, "Netflix vs. Naysayers," *Wall Street Journal,* March 27, 2007, p. B1; Yuval Rosenberg, "What's Next for Netflix?" *Fortune,* November 29, 2006, p. 172; "Netflix Ranks No. 18 on Fortune's 100 Fastest-Growing Companies List," *Fortune,* September 20, 2006; Paul R. La Monica, "DVD or Download?" *CNNMoney.com,* June 26, 2006; and information from www.netflix.com, www.blockbuster.com, and www.movielink.com, accessed December 2007.

For maximum effectiveness, however, channel analysis and decision making should be more purposeful. **Marketing channel design** calls for analyzing consumer needs, setting channel objectives, identifying major channel alternatives, and evaluating them.

Analyzing Consumer Needs

As noted previously, marketing channels are part of the overall *customer-value delivery network.* Each channel member and level adds value for the customer. Thus, designing the marketing channel starts with finding out what target consumers want from the channel. Do consumers want to buy from nearby locations or are they willing to travel to more distant centralized locations? Would they rather buy in person, by phone, through the mail, or online? Do they value breadth of assortment or do they prefer specialization? Do consumers want many add-on services (delivery, credit, repairs, installation), or will they obtain these elsewhere? The faster the delivery, the greater the assortment provided, and the more add-on services supplied, the greater the channel's service level.

Marketing channel design
Designing effective marketing channels by analyzing consumer needs, setting channel objectives, identifying major channel alternatives, and evaluating them.

Providing the fastest delivery, greatest assortment, and most services may not be possible or practical. The company and its channel members may not have the resources or skills needed to provide all the desired services. Also, providing higher levels of service results in higher costs for the channel and higher prices for consumers. The company must balance consumer needs not only against the feasibility and costs of meeting these needs but also against customer price preferences. The success of discount retailing shows that consumers will often accept lower service levels in exchange for lower prices.

Setting Channel Objectives

Companies should state their marketing channel objectives in terms of targeted levels of customer service. Usually, a company can identify several segments wanting different levels of service. The company should decide which segments to serve and the best channels to use in each case. In each segment, the company wants to minimize the total channel cost of meeting customer-service requirements.

The company's channel objectives are also influenced by the nature of the company, its products, its marketing intermediaries, its competitors, and the environment. For example, the company's size and financial situation determine which marketing functions it can handle itself and which it must give to intermediaries. Companies selling perishable products may require more direct marketing to avoid delays and too much handling.

In some cases, a company may want to compete in or near the same outlets that carry competitors' products. In other cases, producers may avoid the channels used by competitors. Mary Kay Cosmetics, for example, sells direct to consumers through its corps of more than one million independent beauty consultants in 34 markets worldwide rather than going head-to-head with other cosmetics makers for scarce positions in retail stores. Amazon.com has become the Wal-Mart of the Internet by selling exclusively via the Internet rather than through stores. And GEICO markets auto and homeowner's insurance directly to consumers via the telephone and Web rather than through agents.

Finally, environmental factors such as economic conditions and legal constraints may affect channel objectives and design. For example, in a depressed economy, producers want to distribute their goods in the most economical way, using shorter channels and dropping unneeded services that add to the final price of the goods.

Identifying Major Alternatives

When the company has defined its channel objectives, it should next identify its major channel alternatives in terms of *types* of intermediaries, the *number* of intermediaries, and the *responsibilities* of each channel member.

Types of Intermediaries A firm should identify the types of channel members available to carry out its channel work. For example, suppose a manufacturer of test equipment has developed an audio device that detects poor mechanical connections in machines with moving parts. Company executives think this product would have a market in all industries in which electric, combustion, or steam engines are made or used. The company's current sales force is small, and the problem is how best to reach these different industries. The following channel alternatives might emerge:

Company sales force: Expand the company's direct sales force. Assign outside salespeople to territories and have them contact all prospects in the area, or develop separate company sales forces for different industries. Or, add an inside telesales operation in which telephone salespeople handle small or midsize companies.

Manufacturer's agents: Hire manufacturer's agents—independent firms whose sales forces handle related products from many companies—in different regions or industries to sell the new test equipment.

Industrial distributors: Find distributors in the different regions or industries who will buy and carry the new line. Give them exclusive distribution, good margins, product training, and promotional support.

Number of Marketing Intermediaries Companies must also determine the number of channel members to use at each level. Three strategies are available: intensive distribution, exclusive distribution, and selective distribution. Producers of convenience products and common raw materials typically seek **intensive distribution**—a strategy in which they stock their products in as many outlets as possible. These products must be available where and when consumers want them. For example, toothpaste, candy, and other similar items are sold in millions of outlets to provide maximum brand exposure and consumer convenience. Kraft, Coca-Cola, Kimberly-Clark, and other consumer-goods companies distribute their products in this way.

By contrast, some producers purposely limit the number of intermediaries handling their products. The extreme form of this practice is **exclusive distribution**, in which the producer gives only a limited number of dealers the exclusive right to distribute its products in their territories. Exclusive distribution is often found in the distribution of luxury automobiles and prestige women's clothing. For example, Bentley dealers are few and far between—even large cities may have only one dealer. By granting exclusive distribution, Bentley gains stronger distributor selling support and more control over dealer prices, promotion, credit, and services. Exclusive distribution also enhances the car's image and allows for higher markups.

■ Exclusive distribution: Luxury carmakers such as Bentley sell exclusively through a limited number of retailers. Such limited distribution enhances the car's image and generates stronger retailer support.

Between intensive and exclusive distribution lies **selective distribution**—the use of more than one, but fewer than all, of the intermediaries who are willing to carry a company's products. Most television, furniture, and home appliance brands are distributed in this manner. For example, Whirlpool and General Electric sell their major appliances through dealer networks and selected large retailers. By using selective distribution, they can develop good working relationships with selected channel members and expect a better-than-average selling effort. Selective distribution gives producers good market coverage with more control and less cost than does intensive distribution.

Responsibilities of Channel Members The producer and intermediaries need to agree on the terms and responsibilities of each channel member. They should agree on price policies, conditions of sale, territorial rights, and specific services to be performed by each party. The producer should establish a list price and a fair set of discounts for intermediaries. It must define each channel member's territory, and it should be careful about where it places new resellers.

Mutual services and duties need to be spelled out carefully, especially in franchise and exclusive distribution channels. For example, McDonald's provides franchisees with promotional support, a record-keeping system, training at Hamburger University, and general management assistance. In turn, franchisees must meet company standards for physical facilities and food quality, cooperate with new promotion programs, provide requested information, and buy specified food products.

Evaluating the Major Alternatives

Suppose a company has identified several channel alternatives and wants to select the one that will best satisfy its long-run objectives. Each alternative should be evaluated against economic, control, and adaptive criteria.

Using *economic criteria,* a company compares the likely sales, costs, and profitability of different channel alternatives. What will be the investment required by each channel alternative, and what returns will result? The company must also consider *control issues.* Using intermediaries usually means giving them some control over the marketing of the product, and some intermediaries take more control than others. Other things being equal, the company prefers to keep as much control as possible. Finally, the company must apply *adaptive criteria.* Channels often involve long-term commitments, yet the company wants to keep the channel flexible so that it can adapt to environmental changes. Thus, to be

Intensive distribution
Stocking the product in as many outlets as possible.

Exclusive distribution
Giving a limited number of dealers the exclusive right to distribute the company's products in their territories.

Selective distribution
The use of more than one, but fewer than all, of the intermediaries who are willing to carry the company's products.

considered, a channel involving long-term commitments should be greatly superior on economic and control grounds.

Designing International Distribution Channels

International marketers face many additional complexities in designing their channels. Each country has its own unique distribution system that has evolved over time and changes very slowly. These channel systems can vary widely from country to country. Thus, global marketers must usually adapt their channel strategies to the existing structures within each country.

In some markets, the distribution system is complex and hard to penetrate, consisting of many layers and large numbers of intermediaries. At the other extreme, distribution systems in developing countries may be scattered, inefficient, or altogether lacking. For example, China and India are huge markets, each with populations well over one billion people. However, because of inadequate distribution systems, most companies can profitably access only a small portion of the population located in each country's most affluent cities. "China is a very decentralized market," notes a China trade expert. "[It's] made up of two dozen distinct markets sprawling across 2,000 cities. Each has its own culture. . . . It's like operating in an asteroid belt." China's distribution system is so fragmented that logistics costs amount to 15 percent of the nation's GDP, far higher than in most other countries. After 10 years of effort, even Wal-Mart executives admit that they have been unable to assemble an efficient supply chain in China.[9]

Sometimes customs or government regulation can greatly restrict how a company distributes products in global markets. For example, it wasn't an inefficient distribution structure that caused problems for Avon in China—it was restrictive government regulations. Fearing the growth of multilevel marketing schemes, the Chinese government banned door-to-door selling altogether in 1998, forcing Avon to abandon its traditional direct marketing approach and sell through retail shops. The Chinese government recently gave Avon and other direct sellers permission to sell door-to-door again, but that permission is tangled in a web of restrictions. Fortunately for Avon, its earlier focus on store sales is helping it weather the restrictions better than most other direct sellers.[10]

International marketers face a wide range of channel alternatives. Designing efficient and effective channel systems between and within various country markets poses a difficult challenge. We discuss international distribution decisions further in Chapter 15.

■ International channel complexities: When the Chinese government banned door-to-door selling, Avon had to abandon its traditional direct marketing approach and sell through retail shops.

Channel Management Decisions

Marketing channel management
Selecting, managing, and motivating individual channel members and evaluating their performance over time.

Once the company has reviewed its channel alternatives and decided on the best channel design, it must implement and manage the chosen channel. **Marketing channel management** calls for selecting, managing, and motivating individual channel members and evaluating their performance over time.

Selecting Channel Members

Producers vary in their ability to attract qualified marketing intermediaries. Some producers have no trouble signing up channel members. For example, when Toyota first introduced its Lexus line in the United States, it had no trouble attracting new dealers. In fact, it had to turn down many would-be resellers.

At the other extreme are producers who have to work hard to line up enough qualified intermediaries. When Polaroid started, for example, it could not get photography stores to carry its new cameras, and it had to go to mass-merchandising outlets. Similarly, when the U.S. Time Company first tried to sell its inexpensive Timex watches through regular jewelry stores, most jewelry stores refused to carry them. The company then managed to get its watches into mass-merchandise outlets. This turned out to be a wise decision because of the rapid growth of mass merchandising.

When selecting intermediaries, the company should determine what characteristics distinguish the better ones. It will want to evaluate each channel member's years in business, other lines carried, growth and profit record, cooperativeness, and reputation. If the intermediaries are sales agents, the company will want to evaluate the number and character of other lines carried and the size and quality of the sales force. If the intermediary is a retail store that wants exclusive or selective distribution, the company will want to evaluate the store's customers, location, and future growth potential.

Managing and Motivating Channel Members

Once selected, channel members must be continuously managed and motivated to do their best. The company must sell not only *through* the intermediaries but *to* and *with* them. Most companies see their intermediaries as first-line customers and partners. They practice strong *partner relationship management (PRM)* to forge long-term partnerships with channel members. This creates a marketing system that meets the needs of both the company *and* its marketing partners.

In managing its channels, a company must convince distributors that they can succeed better by working together as a part of a cohesive value delivery system. Thus, Procter & Gamble works closely with Wal-Mart to create superior value for final consumers. The two jointly plan merchandising goals and strategies, inventory levels, and advertising and promotion programs. Similarly, Samsung's Information Technology Division works closely with value-added resellers through the industry-leading Samsung Power Partner Program (P3).

The Samsung P3 program creates close partnerships with important value-added resellers (VARs)—channel firms that assemble IT solutions for their own customers using products from Samsung and other manufacturers. Through the Power Partner Program, Samsung provides extensive presale, selling, and postsale tools and support to some 17,255 registered North America VAR partners at one of three levels—silver, gold, or platinum. For example, platinum-level partners—those selling $500,000 or more of Samsung IT products per year—receive access to a searchable online product and pricing database and downloadable marketing materials. They can tap into partner-only Samsung training programs, special seminars, and conferences. A dedicated Samsung P3 team helps partners to find good sales prospects and initiate sales. Then, a dedicated Samsung field sales rep works with each partner to close deals, and inside sales reps provide the partner with information and technical support. Platinum partners even participate in Samsung's Reseller Council. Finally, the P3 program rewards high-performing reseller-partners with rebates, discount promotions, bonuses, and sales awards. In all, the Power Partner Program turns important resellers

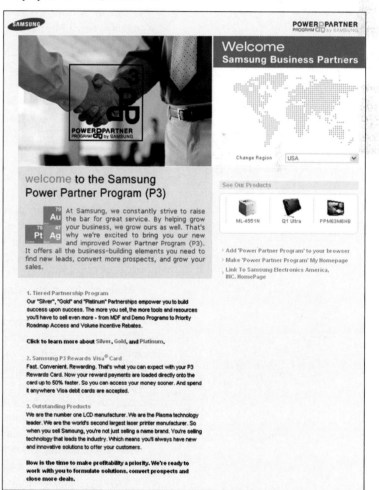

■ Partnering with marketing channel members: The Samsung Power Partner Program turns important resellers into strong, motivated marketing partners by helping them to be more effective and profitable at selling Samsung.

into strong, motivated marketing partners by helping them to be more effective and profitable at selling Samsung.[11]

Many companies are now installing integrated high-tech partner relationship management systems to coordinate their whole-channel marketing efforts. Just as they use customer relationship management (CRM) software systems to help manage relationships with important customers, companies can now use PRM and supply chain management (SCM) software to help recruit, train, organize, manage, motivate, and evaluate relationships with channel partners.

Evaluating Channel Members

The producer must regularly check channel member performance against standards such as sales quotas, average inventory levels, customer delivery time, treatment of damaged and lost goods, cooperation in company promotion and training programs, and services to the customer. The company should recognize and reward intermediaries who are performing well and adding good value for consumers. Those who are performing poorly should be assisted or, as a last resort, replaced. A company may periodically "requalify" its intermediaries and prune the weaker ones.

Finally, manufacturers need to be sensitive to their dealers. Those who treat their dealers poorly risk not only losing dealer support but also causing some legal problems. The next section describes various rights and duties pertaining to manufacturers and their channel members.

Linking the Concepts

Time for another break. This time, compare the Caterpillar and Samsung value-added retailer channel systems.

- Diagram the Caterpillar and Samsung IT Division channel systems. How do they compare in terms of channel levels, types of intermediaries, channel member roles and responsibilities, and other characteristics. How well is each system designed?
- Assess how well Caterpillar and Samsung have managed and supported their channels. With what results?

Public Policy and Distribution Decisions

For the most part, companies are legally free to develop whatever channel arrangements suit them. In fact, the laws affecting channels seek to prevent the exclusionary tactics of some companies that might keep another company from using a desired channel. Most channel law deals with the mutual rights and duties of the channel members once they have formed a relationship.

Many producers and wholesalers like to develop exclusive channels for their products. When the seller allows only certain outlets to carry its products, this strategy is called *exclusive distribution*. When the seller requires that these dealers not handle competitors' products, its strategy is called *exclusive dealing*. Both parties can benefit from exclusive arrangements: The seller obtains more loyal and dependable outlets, and the dealers obtain a steady source of supply and stronger seller support. But exclusive arrangements also exclude other producers from selling to these dealers. This situation brings exclusive dealing contracts under the scope of the Clayton Act of 1914. They are legal as long as they do not substantially lessen competition or tend to create a monopoly and as long as both parties enter into the agreement voluntarily.

Exclusive dealing often includes *exclusive territorial agreements*. The producer may agree not to sell to other dealers in a given area, or the buyer may agree to sell only in its own territory. The first practice is normal under franchise systems as a way to increase dealer enthusiasm and commitment. It is also perfectly legal—a seller has no legal obligation to sell through more outlets than it wishes. The second practice, whereby the producer tries to keep a dealer from selling outside its territory, has become a major legal issue.

Producers of a strong brand sometimes sell it to dealers only if the dealers will take some or all of the rest of the line. This is called full-line forcing. Such *tying agreements* are not necessarily illegal, but they do violate the Clayton Act if they tend to lessen competition substantially. The practice may prevent consumers from freely choosing among competing suppliers of these other brands.

Finally, producers are free to select their dealers, but their right to terminate dealers is somewhat restricted. In general, sellers can drop dealers "for cause." However, they cannot drop dealers if, for example, the dealers refuse to cooperate in a doubtful legal arrangement, such as exclusive dealing or tying agreements.[12]

Marketing Logistics and Supply Chain Management

In today's global marketplace, selling a product is sometimes easier than getting it to customers. Companies must decide on the best way to store, handle, and move their products and services so that they are available to customers in the right assortments, at the right time, and in the right place. Physical distribution and logistics effectiveness have a major impact on both customer satisfaction and company costs. Here we consider the nature and importance of logistics management in the supply chain, goals of the logistics system, major logistics functions, and the need for integrated supply chain management.

Nature and Importance of Marketing Logistics

To some managers, marketing logistics means only trucks and warehouses. But modern logistics is much more than this. **Marketing logistics**—also called **physical distribution**—involves planning, implementing, and controlling the physical flow of goods, services, and related information from points of origin to points of consumption to meet customer requirements at a profit. In short, it involves getting the right product to the right customer in the right place at the right time.

In the past, physical distribution planners typically started with products at the plant and then tried to find low-cost solutions to get them to customers. However, today's marketers prefer customer-centered logistics thinking, which starts with the marketplace and works backward to the factory, or even to sources of supply. Marketing logistics involves not only *outbound distribution* (moving products from the factory to resellers and ultimately to customers) but also *inbound distribution* (moving products and materials from suppliers to the factory) and *reverse distribution* (moving broken, unwanted, or excess products returned by consumers or resellers). That is, it involves entire **supply chain management**—managing upstream and downstream value-added flows of materials, final goods, and related information among suppliers, the company, resellers, and final consumers, as shown in Figure 10.5.

The logistics manager's task is to coordinate activities of suppliers, purchasing agents, marketers, channel members, and customers. These activities include forecasting, information systems, purchasing, production planning, order processing, inventory, warehousing, and transportation planning.

Marketing logistics (physical distribution)
Planning, implementing, and controlling the physical flow of materials, final goods, and related information from points of origin to points of consumption to meet customer requirements at a profit.

Supply chain management
Managing upstream and downstream value-added flows of materials, final goods, and related information among suppliers, the company, resellers, and final consumers.

FIGURE 10.5   Supply Chain Management

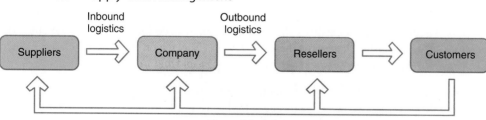

■ The importance of logistics: At any given time, Ford has more than 500 million tons of finished vehicles, production parts, and aftermarket parts in transit, running up an annual logistics bill of around $4 billion.

Companies today are placing greater emphasis on logistics for several reasons. First, companies can gain a powerful competitive advantage by using improved logistics to give customers better service or lower prices. Second, improved logistics can yield tremendous cost savings to both the company and its customers. As much as 20 percent of an average product's price is accounted for by shipping and transport alone. This far exceeds the cost of advertising and many other marketing costs. American companies spend almost $1.2 trillion each year—about 9.6 percent of gross domestic product—to wrap, bundle, load, unload, sort, reload, and transport goods. That's more than the national GDPs of all but 12 countries worldwide. What's more, these costs have risen more than 50 percent over the past decade. By itself, Ford has more than 500 million tons of finished vehicles, production parts, and aftermarket parts in transit at any given time, running up an annual logistics bill of around $4 billion.[13] Shaving off even a small fraction of these costs can mean substantial savings.

Third, the explosion in product variety has created a need for improved logistics management. For example, in 1911 the typical A&P grocery store carried only 270 items. The store manager could keep track of this inventory on about 10 pages of notebook paper stuffed in a shirt pocket. Today, the average A&P carries a bewildering stock of more than 25,000 items. A Wal-Mart Supercenter store carries more than 100,000 products, 30,000 of which are grocery products.[14] Ordering, shipping, stocking, and controlling such a variety of products presents a sizable logistics challenge.

Finally, improvements in information technology have created opportunities for major gains in distribution efficiency. Today's companies are using sophisticated supply chain management software, Web-based logistics systems, point-of-sale scanners, uniform product codes, satellite tracking, and electronic transfer of order and payment data. Such technology lets them quickly and efficiently manage the flow of goods, information, and finances through the supply chain.

Goals of the Logistics System

Some companies state their logistics objective as providing maximum customer service at the least cost. Unfortunately, no logistics system can *both* maximize customer service *and* minimize distribution costs. Maximum customer service implies rapid delivery, large inventories, flexible assortments, liberal return policies, and other services—all of which raise distribution costs. In contrast, minimum distribution costs imply slower delivery, smaller inventories, and larger shipping lots—which represent a lower level of overall customer service.

The goal of marketing logistics should be to provide a *targeted* level of customer service at the least cost. A company must first research the importance of various distribution services to customers and then set desired service levels for each segment. The objective is to maximize *profits,* not sales. Therefore, the company must weigh the benefits of providing higher levels of service against the costs. Some companies offer less service than their competitors and charge a lower price. Other companies offer more service and charge higher prices to cover higher costs.

Major Logistics Functions

Given a set of logistics objectives, the company is ready to design a logistics system that will minimize the cost of attaining these objectives. The major logistics functions include *warehousing, inventory management, transportation,* and *logistics information management.*

Warehousing Production and consumption cycles rarely match. So most companies must store their goods while they wait to be sold. For example, Snapper, Toro, and other lawn mower manufacturers run their factories all year long and store up products for the heavy spring and summer buying seasons. The storage function overcomes differences in needed quantities and timing, ensuring that products are available when customers are ready to buy them.

A company must decide on *how many* and *what types* of warehouses it needs and *where* they will be located. The company might use either *storage warehouses* or *distribution centers*. Storage warehouses store goods for moderate to long periods. **Distribution centers** are designed to move goods rather than just store them. They are large and highly automated warehouses designed to receive goods from various plants and suppliers, take orders, fill them efficiently, and deliver goods to customers as quickly as possible.

Like almost everything else these days, warehousing has seen dramatic changes in technology in recent years. Older, multistoried warehouses with outdated materials-handling methods are steadily being replaced by newer, single-storied *automated warehouses* with advanced, computer-controlled materials-handling systems requiring few employees. Computers and scanners read orders and direct lift trucks, electric hoists, or robots to gather goods, move them to loading docks, and issue invoices.

For example, Wal-Mart operates a network of 129 huge U.S. distribution centers and another 57 around the globe. A single center, which might serve the daily needs of 120 Wal-Mart stores, typically contains some 1 million square feet of space (about 20 football fields) under a single roof. At a typical center, laser scanners route as many as 190,000 cases of goods per day along 11 miles of conveyer belts, and the center's 1,000 workers load or unload some 500 trucks daily. Wal-Mart's Monroe, Georgia, distribution center contains a 127,000-square-foot freezer (that's about 1/2 football fields) that can hold 10,000 pallets—room enough for 58 million Popsicles.[15]

Inventory Management Inventory management also affects customer satisfaction. Here, managers must maintain the delicate balance between carrying too little inventory and carrying too much. With too little stock, the firm risks not having products when customers want to buy. To remedy this, the firm may need costly emergency shipments or production. Carrying too much inventory results in higher-than-necessary inventory-carrying costs and stock obsolescence. Thus, in managing inventory, firms must balance the costs of carrying larger inventories against resulting sales and profits.

Many companies have greatly reduced their inventories and related costs through *just-in-time* logistics systems. With such systems, producers and retailers carry only small inventories of parts or merchandise, often only enough for a few days of operations. For example, Dell, a master just-in-time producer, carries as little as three days of inventory, whereas competitors and their retail channels might carry 40 days or even 60.[16] New stock arrives exactly when needed, rather than being stored in inventory until being used. Just-in-time systems require accurate forecasting along with fast, frequent, and flexible delivery so that new supplies will be available when needed. However, these systems result in substantial savings in inventory-carrying and handling costs.

Marketers are always looking for new ways to make inventory management more efficient. In the not-too-distant future, handling inventory might even become fully automated. For example, in Chapter 3, we discussed RFID or "smart tag" technology, by which small transmitter chips are embedded in or placed on products and packaging on everything from flowers and razors to tires. "Smart" products could make the entire supply chain—which accounts for nearly 75 percent of a product's cost—intelligent and automated.

Companies using RFID would know, at any time, exactly where a product is located physically within the supply chain. "Smart shelves" would not only tell them when it's time to reorder, but would also place the order automatically with their suppliers. Such exciting new information technology applications will revolutionize distribution as we know it. Many large and resourceful marketing companies, such as Wal-Mart, Procter & Gamble, Kraft, IBM, Hewlett-Packard, and Best Buy, are

Distribution center
A large, highly automated warehouse designed to receive goods from various plants and suppliers, take orders, fill them efficiently, and deliver goods to customers as quickly as possible.

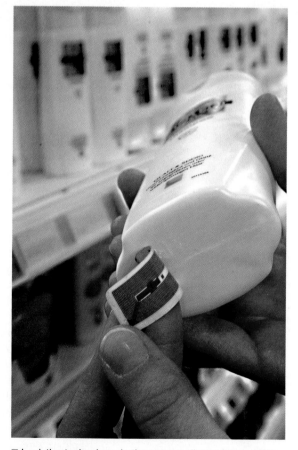

■ Logistics technology: In the not-too-distant future, RFID or "smart tag" technology could make the entire supply chain—which accounts for nearly 75 percent of a product's cost—intelligent and automated.

Everything we know about you goes into everything we do for you.

In business, you deserve people devoted to your success. People who are proactive about customer care. Not reactive. People like the Roadway Customer Care Team. We focus on your specific needs. We're intensely committed to you and the success of your business. Plus, with the entire Roadway team in your corner, you get transportation solutions that are simple, smart, and effective. And that makes everything better for you. **Visit roadway.com or call 888-550-9800.**

Roadway.
your way.

FLEXIBLE TRANSPORTATION SERVICES WORLDWIDE · DEDICATED SUPPORT TEAM · SMART, CUSTOMIZED SOLUTIONS

■ Roadway and other transportation firms have added many services in recent years. Roadway Customer Care Teams focus on specific customer's needs: "With the entire Roadway team in your corner, you get transportation solutions that are simple, smart, and effective."

investing heavily to make the full use of RFID technology a reality.[17]

Transportation   The choice of transportation carriers affects the pricing of products, delivery performance, and condition of the goods when they arrive—all of which will affect customer satisfaction. In shipping goods to its warehouses, dealers, and customers, the company can choose among five main transportation modes: truck, rail, water, pipeline, and air, along with an alternative mode for digital products—the Internet.

Trucks have increased their share of transportation steadily and now account for nearly 35 percent of total cargo ton-miles (more than 60 percent of actual tonnage).[18] Each year in the United States, trucks travel more than 216 billion miles—a distance that has more than doubled over the past 20 years—carrying 11 billion tons of freight worth over $9 trillion. Trucks are highly flexible in their routing and time schedules, and they can usually offer faster service than railroads. They are efficient for short hauls of high-value merchandise. Trucking firms have added many services in recent years. For example, Roadway now offers everything from satellite tracking to logistics planning software and "border ambassadors" who expedite cross-border shipping operations. The Roadway Customer Care Teams focus on specific customer's needs: "With the entire Roadway team in your corner, you get transportation solutions that are simple, smart, and effective. And that makes everything better for you."

Railroads account for 31 percent of total cargo ton-miles moved. They are one of the most cost-effective modes for shipping large amounts of bulk products—coal, sand, minerals, and farm and forest products—over long distances. In recent years, railroads have increased their customer services by designing new equipment to handle special categories of goods, providing flatcars for carrying truck trailers by rail (piggyback), and providing in-transit services such as the diversion of shipped goods to other destinations en route and the processing of goods en route.

Water carriers, which account for about 11 percent of cargo ton-miles, transport large amounts of goods by ships and barges on U.S. coastal and inland waterways. Although the cost of water transportation is very low for shipping bulky, low-value, nonperishable products such as sand, coal, grain, oil, and metallic ores, water transportation is the slowest mode and may be affected by the weather.

Pipelines, which also account for about 16 percent of cargo ton-miles, are a specialized means of shipping petroleum, natural gas, and chemicals from sources to markets. Most pipelines are used by their owners to ship their own products.

Although *air* carriers transport less than 5 percent of the nation's goods, they are an important transportation mode. Airfreight rates are much higher than rail or truck rates, but airfreight is ideal when speed is needed or distant markets must be reached. Among the most frequently airfreighted products are perishables (fresh fish, cut flowers) and high-value, low-bulk items (technical instruments, jewelry). Companies find that airfreight also reduces inventory levels, packaging costs, and the number of warehouses needed.

The *Internet* carries digital products from producer to customer via satellite, cable, or phone wire. Software firms, the media, music companies, and education all make use of the Internet to transport digital products. Although these firms primarily use traditional transportation to distribute DVDs, CDs, newspapers, and more, the Internet holds the potential for lower product distribution costs. Whereas planes, trucks, and trains move freight and packages, digital technology moves information bits.

Shippers also use **intermodal transportation**—combining two or more modes of transportation. *Piggyback* describes the use of rail and trucks; *fishyback,* water and trucks; *trainship,* water and rail; and *airtruck,* air and trucks. Combining modes provides advantages that no single mode can deliver. Each combination offers advantages to the shipper. For example, not only is piggyback cheaper than trucking alone but it also provides flexibility and convenience.

In choosing a transportation mode for a product, shippers must balance many considerations: speed, dependability, availability, cost, and others. Thus, if a shipper needs speed, air and truck are the prime choices. If the goal is low cost, then water or pipeline might be best.

Intermodal transportation
Combining two or more modes of transportation.

Logistics Information Management Companies manage their supply chains through information. Channel partners often link up to share information and to make better joint logistics decisions. From a logistics perspective, information flows such as customer transactions, billing, shipment and inventory levels, and even customer data are closely linked to channel performance. The company wants to design a simple, accessible, fast, and accurate process for capturing, processing, and sharing channel information.

Information can be shared and managed in many ways, but most sharing takes place through traditional or Internet-based *electronic data interchange (EDI),* the computerized exchange of data between organizations. Wal-Mart, for example, maintains EDI links with almost all of its 91,000 suppliers. And where it once took eight weeks, using EDI, Krispy Kreme can now turn around 1,000 supplier invoices and process the checks in only a single week.[19]

In some cases, suppliers might actually be asked to generate orders and arrange deliveries for their customers. Many large retailers—such as Wal-Mart and Home Depot—work closely with major suppliers such as Procter & Gamble or Black & Decker to set up *vendor-managed inventory* (VMI) systems or *continuous inventory replenishment* systems. Using VMI, the customer shares real-time data on sales and current inventory levels with the supplier. The supplier then takes full responsibility for managing inventories and deliveries. Some retailers even go so far as to shift inventory and delivery costs to the supplier. Such systems require close cooperation between the buyer and seller.

Integrated Logistics Management

Today, more and more companies are adopting the concept of **integrated logistics management**. This concept recognizes that providing better customer service and trimming distribution costs require *teamwork,* both inside the company and among all the marketing channel organizations. Inside, the company's various departments must work closely together to maximize the company's own logistics performance. Outside, the company must integrate its logistics system with those of its suppliers and customers to maximize the performance of the entire distribution system.

Integrated logistics management
The logistics concept that emphasizes teamwork, both inside the company and among all the marketing channel organizations, to maximize the performance of the entire distribution system.

Cross-Functional Teamwork Inside the Company Most companies assign responsibility for various logistics activities to many different departments—marketing, sales, finance, operations, purchasing. Too often, each function tries to optimize its own logistics performance without regard for the activities of the other functions. However, transportation, inventory, warehousing, and order-processing activities interact, often in an inverse way. Lower inventory levels reduce inventory-carrying costs. But they may also reduce customer service and increase costs from stockouts, back orders, special production runs, and costly fast-freight shipments. Because distribution activities involve strong trade-offs, decisions by different functions must be coordinated to achieve better overall logistics performance.

The goal of integrated supply chain management is to harmonize all of the company's logistics decisions. Close working relationships among departments can be achieved in several ways. Some companies have created permanent logistics committees, made up of managers responsible for different physical distribution activities. Companies can also create supply chain manager positions that link the logistics activities of functional areas. For example, Procter & Gamble has created supply managers, who manage all of the supply chain activities for each of its product categories. Many companies have a vice president of logistics with cross-functional authority.

Finally, companies can employ sophisticated, systemwide supply chain management software, now available from a wide range of software enterprises large and small, from SAP and Oracle to Infor and Logility. The worldwide market for supply chain management software topped an estimated $6 billion last year.[20] The important thing is that the company must coordinate its logistics and marketing activities to create high market satisfaction at a reasonable cost.

Building Logistics Partnerships Companies must do more than improve their own logistics. They must also work with other channel partners to improve whole-channel distribution. The members of a marketing channel are linked closely in creating customer value and building customer relationships. One company's distribution system is another company's supply system. The success of each channel member depends on the performance of the entire supply chain. For example, IKEA can create its stylish but affordable furniture and deliver the "IKEA lifestyle" only if its entire supply chain—consisting of thousands of merchandise designers and suppliers, transport companies, warehouses, and service providers—operates at maximum efficiency and customer-focused effectiveness.

Smart companies coordinate their logistics strategies and forge strong partnerships with suppliers and customers to improve customer service and reduce channel costs. Many companies have created *cross-functional, cross-company teams.* For example, Procter & Gamble has a team of more than 200 people working in Bentonville, Arkansas, home of Wal-Mart.[21] The P&Gers work jointly with their counterparts at Wal-Mart to find ways to squeeze costs out of their distribution system. Working together benefits not only P&G and Wal-Mart but also their shared final consumers.

Other companies partner through *shared projects.* For example, many large retailers conduct joint in-store programs with suppliers. Home Depot allows key suppliers to use its stores as a testing ground for new merchandising programs. The suppliers spend time at Home Depot stores watching how their product sells and how customers relate to it. They then create programs specially tailored to Home Depot and its customers. Clearly, both the supplier and the customer benefit from such partnerships. The point is that all supply chain members must work together in the cause of bringing value to final consumers.

Third-Party Logistics Most big companies love to make and sell their products. But many loathe the associated logistics "grunt work." They detest the bundling, loading, unloading, sorting, storing, reloading, transporting, customs clearing, and tracking required to supply their factories and to get products out to customers. They hate it so much that a growing number of firms now outsource some or all of their logistics to **third-party logistics (3PL) providers**.

Third-party logistics (3PL) provider
An independent logistics provider that performs any or all of the functions required to get its client's product to market.

These "3PLs"—companies such as UPS Supply Chain Solutions, Penske Logistics, BAX Global, DHL Logistics, Ryder System, FedEx Logistics, or Roadway Logistics Services—help clients to tighten up sluggish, overstuffed supply chains, slash inventories, and get products to customers more quickly and reliably. For example, UPS's Supply Chain Solutions unit provides clients with a wide range of logistics services, from inventory control, warehousing, and transportation management to customer service and fulfillment. According to a recent survey of chief logistics executives at Fortune 500 companies, 82 percent of these companies use third-party logistics (also called *3PL, outsourced logistics,* or *contract logistics*) services. In just the past ten years, the revenues for 3PL companies in the United States has tripled in size to more than $110 billion.[22]

Companies use third-party logistics providers for several reasons. First, because getting the product to market is their main focus, these providers can often do it more efficiently and at lower cost. Outsourcing typically results in 15 percent to 30 percent cost savings. Second, outsourcing logistics frees a company to focus more intensely on its core business. Finally, integrated logistics companies understand increasingly complex logistics environments.

Third-party logistics partners can be especially helpful to companies attempting to expand their global market coverage. For example, companies distributing their products across

Europe face a bewildering array of environmental restrictions that affect logistics, including packaging standards, truck size and weight limits, and noise and emissions pollution controls. By outsourcing its logistics, a company can gain a complete pan-European distribution system without incurring the costs, delays, and risks associated with setting up its own system.

REST STOP ➦ REVIEWING THE CONCEPTS

Marketing channel decisions are among the most important decisions that management faces. A company's channel decisions directly affect every other marketing decision. Management must make channel decisions carefully, incorporating today's needs with tomorrow's likely selling environment. Some companies pay too little attention to their distribution channels, but others have used imaginative distribution systems to gain competitive advantage.

1. Explain why companies use marketing channels and discuss the functions these channels perform.

Most producers use intermediaries to bring their products to market. They try to forge a *marketing channel* (or *distribution channel*)—a set of interdependent organizations involved in the process of making a product or service available for use or consumption by the consumer or business user. Through their contacts, experience, specialization, and scale of operation, intermediaries usually offer the firm more than it can achieve on its own.

Marketing channels perform many key functions. Some help *complete* transactions by gathering and distributing *information* needed for planning and aiding exchange; by developing and spreading persuasive *communications* about an offer; by performing *contact* work—finding and communicating with prospective buyers; by *matching*—shaping and fitting the offer to the buyer's needs; and by entering into *negotiation* to reach an agreement on price and other terms of the offer so that ownership can be transferred. Other functions help to *fulfill* the completed transactions by offering *physical distribution*—transporting and storing goods; *financing*—acquiring and using funds to cover the costs of the channel work; and *risk taking*—assuming the risks of carrying out the channel work.

2. Discuss how channel members interact and how they organize to perform the work of the channel.

The channel will be most effective when each member is assigned the tasks it can do best. Ideally, because the success of individual channel members depends on overall channel success, all channel firms should work together smoothly. They should understand and accept their roles, coordinate their goals and activities, and cooperate to attain overall channel goals. By cooperating, they can more effectively sense, serve, and satisfy the target market.

In a large company, the formal organization structure assigns roles and provides needed leadership. But in a distribution channel made up of independent firms, leadership and power are not formally set. Traditionally, distribution channels have lacked the leadership needed to assign roles and manage conflict. In recent years, however, new types of channel organizations have appeared that provide stronger leadership and improved performance.

3. Identify the major channel alternatives open to a company.

Each firm identifies alternative ways to reach its market. Available means vary from direct selling to using one, two, three, or more intermediary *channel levels*. Marketing channels face continuous and sometimes dramatic change. Three of the most important trends are the growth of *vertical, horizontal,* and *multichannel marketing systems*. These trends affect channel cooperation, conflict, and competition.

Channel design begins with assessing customer channel service needs and company channel objectives and constraints. The company then identifies the major channel alternatives in terms of the *types* of intermediaries, the *number* of intermediaries, and the *channel responsibilities* of each. Each channel alternative must be evaluated according to economic, control, and adaptive criteria. *Channel management* calls for selecting qualified intermediaries and motivating them. Individual channel members must be evaluated regularly.

4. Explain how companies select, motivate, and evaluate channel members.

Producers vary in their ability to attract qualified marketing intermediaries. Some producers have no trouble signing up channel members. Others must work hard to line up enough qualified intermediaries. When selecting intermediaries, the company should evaluate each channel member's qualifications and select those who best fit its channel objectives.

Once selected, channel members must be continuously motivated to do their best. The company must sell not only *through* the intermediaries but *with* them. It should work to forge strong partnerships with channel members to create a marketing system that meets the needs of both the manufacturer *and* the partners. The company must also regularly check channel member performance against established performance standards, rewarding intermediaries who are performing well and assisting or replacing weaker ones.

5. Discuss the nature and importance of marketing logistics and integrated supply chain management.

Just as firms are giving the marketing concept increased recognition, more business firms are paying attention to *marketing logistics* (or *physical distribution*). Logistics is an area of potentially high cost savings and improved customer satisfaction. Marketing logistics addresses not only *outbound distribution* but also *inbound distribution* and *reverse distribution.* That is, it involves entire *supply chain management*—managing value-added flows between suppliers, the company, resellers, and final users. No logistics system can both maximize customer service and minimize distribution costs. Instead, the goal of logistics management is to provide a *targeted* level of service at the least cost. The major logistics functions include *warehousing, inventory management, transportation,* and *logistics information management.*

The *integrated supply chain management concept* recognizes that improved logistics requires teamwork in the form of close working relationships across functional areas inside the company and across various organizations in the supply chain. Companies can achieve logistics harmony among functions by creating cross-functional logistics teams, integrative supply manager positions, and senior-level logistics executives with cross-functional authority. Channel partnerships can take the form of cross-company teams, shared projects, and information-sharing systems. Today, some companies are outsourcing their logistics functions to third-party logistics (3PL) providers to save costs, increase efficiency, and gain faster and more effective access to global markets.

Navigating the Key Terms

Administered VMS (301)
Channel conflict (297)
Channel level (296)
Contractual VMS (300)
Conventional distribution channel (298)
Corporate VMS (298)
Direct marketing channel (296)
Disintermediation (303)
Distribution center (313)
Exclusive distribution (307)

Franchise organization (300)
Horizontal marketing system (301)
Indirect marketing channel (296)
Integrated logistics management (315)
Intensive distribution (307)
Intermodal transportation (315)
Marketing channel (distribution channel) (294)
Marketing channel design (305)
Marketing channel management (308)

Marketing logistics (physical distribution) (311)
Multichannel distribution system (301)
Selective distribution (307)
Supply chain management (311)
Third-party logistics (3PL) provider (316)
Value delivery network (293)
Vertical marketing system (VMS) (298)

Travel Log

Discussing the Issues

1. Explain how channel members add value for manufacturers and consumers. (AACSB: Communication)

2. Discuss the differences between a conventional distribution channel, a corporate VMS, a contractual VMS, and an administered VMS. Give one example of each. (AACSB: Communication; Reflective Thinking)

3. Define *disintermediation.* List three industries for which changes in channel systems have resulted in disintermediation. (AACSB: Communication; Reflective Thinking)

4. Compare and contrast intensive, selective, and exclusive distribution. Give an example of a product or brand that is distributed at each level. (AACSB: Communication; Reflective Thinking)

5. Suppose a company has identified several channel alternatives and wants to select the one that will best satisfy its long-run objectives. Discuss the criteria that should be evaluated in making this decision. (AACSB: Communication)

6. List and briefly describe the major logistics functions. Provide an example of a decision a logistics manager would make for each major function. (AACSB: Communication; Reflective Thinking)

Application Questions

1. Category management is used by channel members to better meet the needs of consumers. Visit www.acnielsen.com/pubs/2004_q3_ci_consumer.shtml to learn about category management, and write a brief report on how marketers and distributors implement it as well as a company such as ACNielsen's role. (AACSB: Communication; Use of IT; Reflective Thinking)

2. In a small group, interview three franchise owners in your community. Ask them why they chose to become a franchisee and the benefits associated with it. Write a brief report describing what you learned about franchising. (AACSB: Communication; Reflective Thinking)

3. Direct selling is a legitimate means for selling products to consumers. However, some people equate direct selling with pyramid selling schemes, which are illegal. Go to www.dsa.org to learn more about direct selling. Explain what it is, the impact it has on distribution, and how it differs from pyramid selling schemes. (AACSB: Communication; Use of IT; Reflective Thinking)

Under the Hood: Focus on Technology

RFID, radio frequency identification, is one of the most exciting recent technical innovations relating to logistics operations. Applications involve placing small tags containing tiny electronic RFID chips on containers, pallets, cartons, or even individual products. The tags transmit a radio signal to readers, which translate and store the product identification data. In the past, RFID tags have been prohibitively expensive. However, thanks to improved semiconductor technology, chips can now be produced at reasonable prices. Improvements in software, telecommunications, and data sharing have all worked to move RFID to center stage for logistics managers. In fact, Wal-Mart, a pioneer in RFID application, has issued mandates to its suppliers, forcing them to begin using RFID tags on pallet shipments. As additional retailers adopt this technology and spread it through their value networks, analysts expect that RFID will become the standard for product identification.

1. What impact will RFID applications have on each of the major logistical functions? (AACSB: Communication; Reflective Thinking)

2. With advancing technology and decreasing costs, it may soon be feasible for potentially every product you purchase to contain an RFID tag. One company has even developed washable RFID tags that can be sewn into clothing. Tags can also be embedded in banknotes. With this technology, there is the potential to know how consumers use products, from purchase all the way to disposal. Discuss the benefits and risks of placing these tags on individual products. (AACSB: Communication; Reflective Thinking)

Focus on Ethics

Firearms-related violence is a major societal issue in the United States. More than 300,000 violent crimes involving firearms are committed each year, killing nearly 30,000 people and injuring another 80,000, costing more than $100 billion for medical, security, and legal services. Although gun sales are legal, most crimes are committed using weapons obtained through diverted sales. The distribution channel for this product is multitiered, with manufacturers selling to wholesale distributors that sell to dealers who sell to the public. Several federal, state, and local laws regulate the sale of firearms. The federal enforcement agency is the Bureau of Alcohol, Tobacco, Firearms, and Explosives (known as the ATF or BATF). Firearms are sold to the public by BATF-licensed dealers, known as federal firearms licensees (FFLs). The FFLs must follow laws and safeguards, selling firearms only to individuals who are considered legal purchasers (for example, over 18 years of age, not a convicted criminal, not mentally defective). However, the major channels for firearms diversion include gun shows, straw man purchases (that is, a legal purchaser buys a gun on behalf of someone who cannot legally buy one), theft, nonstore FFLs (also known as "basement bandits" or "car trunk dealers"), unlicensed sellers, and corrupt FFLs. Gun control advocates, public safety groups, and several municipal governments have launched lawsuits against manufacturers, distributors, and dealers, claiming that industry members are not doing enough to stop diverted sales.

1. One solution to firearms diversion is to completely ban the production and sale of firearms in the United States. What are your thoughts about this solution? Is it right to ban the production and sale of firearms? (AACSB: Communication; Ethical Reasoning)

2. For a discussion on the issue of firearms marketing, see Kevin D. Bradford, Gregory T. Gundlach, and William L. Wilkie, "Countermarketing in the Courts: The Case of Marketing Channels and Firearms Diversion," *Journal of Public Policy & Marketing,* Fall 2005, pp. 284–98. Suggest ways to minimize firearms diversion. (AACSB: Communication; Reflective Thinking)

Video Case

Progressive

From its humble beginnings in 1937, Progressive has grown into the third-largest auto insurance group in the country. Progressive attained its status by not only focusing on growth but by focusing on innovation. Progressive was the first company to offer drive-in claims service, installment payment of premiums, and 24/7 customer service.

But perhaps some of Progressive's most innovative moves have involved its channels of distribution. Whereas most insurance companies distribute their products to consumers via intermediary agents or direct-to-consumer methods, Progressive was one of the first companies to recognize the value in doing both.

In 1995, Progressive moved into the future by becoming the first major insurer in the world to launch a Web site. In 1997, customers could buy auto insurance policies online in real time. Today, customers can do everything from managing their own account information to reporting claims directly through Progressive's Web site.

After viewing the video featuring Progressive, answer the following questions about marketing channels.

1. Apply the concept of the supply chain to Progressive.

2. Using the model of consumer and business channels found in the chapter, sketch out as many channels for Progressive as you can. How does each of these channels meet distinct customer needs?

3. Discuss the various ways that Progressive has had an impact on the insurance industry.

After studying this chapter, you should be able to

1. explain the roles of retailers and wholesalers in the distribution channel

2. describe the major types of retailers and give examples of each

3. describe the major types of wholesalers and give examples of each

4. explain the marketing decisions facing retailers and wholesalers

CHAPTER 11

Retailing and Wholesaling

Previewing the Concepts

In the previous chapter, you learned the basics of delivering customer value through good distribution channel design and management. Now, we'll look more deeply into the two major intermediary channel functions, retailing and wholesaling. You already know something about retailing—you're served every day by retailers of all shapes and sizes. However, you probably know much less about the hoard of wholesalers that work behind the scenes. In this chapter, we'll examine the characteristics of different kinds of retailers and wholesalers, the marketing decisions they make, and trends for the future.

When it comes to retailers, everyone always talks about Wal-Mart, the $351 billion behemoth whose always low prices strategy has made it not only the nation's largest retailer but also the world's largest company. But we'll start the chapter with a story about the nation's *third*-largest retailer, Costco. Surprisingly, although it captures only about one-sixth the sales of Wal-Mart, in warehouse retailing, Costco is trouncing Wal-Mart at its own low-price game.

Giant Wal-Mart is used to beating up on competitors. It outsells Toys "R" Us in the toy market, gives Blockbuster headaches in DVD sales, and puts a big dent in Best Buy's consumer electronics business. With 23 percent of the grocery market, it sells far more groceries than the number-two grocery retailer, Kroger. Almost every retailer, no matter what the category, has its hands full devising strategies by which it can compete with Wal-Mart and survive.

But this isn't a story about Wal-Mart. It's about Costco, the red-hot warehouse retailer that competes head-on with Wal-Mart's Sam's Club. Sam's Club is huge. With more than 550 stores and $40 billion in revenues, if Sam's Club were a separate company, it would be the seventh-largest U.S. retailer. But when it comes to warehouse retailing, it's Costco that's the bully, not the other way around.

With about the same number of members but 50 fewer stores, Costco outsells Sam's Club by 50 percent. Its $60 billion in sales makes Costco the nation's third-largest retailer, behind only Wal-Mart and Home Depot and one step ahead of Target. And unlike Wal-Mart and Sam's Club, Costco is growing at a torrid pace. In just the past four years, Costco's sales have surged 55 percent; profits are up 57 percent. Costco's same-store sales are growing at more than twice the rate of Wal-Mart's. How is Costco beating Sam's Club at its own low-price game? The two retailers are very similar in many ways. But inside the store, Costco adds a certain merchandising magic that Sam's Club just can't match.

Let's start with the similarities. Both Costco and Sam's Club are warehouse retailers. They offer a limited selection of nationally branded and private-label products in a wide range of categories at very low prices to shoppers who pay an annual membership fee. Both retailers stock about 4,000 items, often only jumbo sizes (a typical supermarket stocks 40,000 items; a Wal-Mart supercenter about

150,000). And to keep costs and prices low, both operate out of big, drafty, bare-bones stores and use their substantial buying power to wring low prices from suppliers.

Price is an important part of the equation, and Costco seems addicted to selling every item at the lowest possible price, regardless of competitors' prices. It refuses to mark up any item more than 14 percent above costs. According to Costco founder and CEO Jim Sinegal (shown in the picture), "Many retailers look at an item and say, 'I'm selling this for ten bucks. How can I sell it for 11?' We look at it and say, 'How can we get it to nine bucks?' And then, 'How can we get it to eight?' It is contrary to the thinking of [most retailers]. But once you start doing that, it's like heroin." Costco's operating profit margins average just 2.8 percent; Sam's Club's margins are only 3.5 percent.

Thus, both Costco and Sam's Club excel at low-cost operations and low prices. What is it, then, that sets Costco apart? It has to do with Costco's differentiated value proposition—with the products it carries and sense of urgency that it builds into the Costco shopper's store experience. Alongside the gallon jars of peanut butter and 2,250-count packs of Q-Tips that make other warehouse clubs popular, Costco offers an ever-changing assortment of high-quality products—even luxuries—all at tantalizingly low margins. As one industry analyst puts it, "While Wal-Mart stands for low prices, Costco is a retail treasure hunt, where one's shopping cart could contain a $50,000 diamond ring resting on top of a vat of mayonnaise."

Costco brings flair to an otherwise dreary setting. It has managed to make discount shopping fashionable, even for affluent Americans. It's the place where high-end products meet deep-discount prices. Last year, Costco sold 63 million hot dog and soda combinations (still only $1.50). At the same time, it sold more than 96,000 carats of diamonds at up to $100,000 per item. It's the nation's biggest baster of poultry (77,000 rotisserie chickens a day) but also the country's biggest seller of fine wines (including the likes of a Chateau Cheval Blanc Premier Grand Cru Classe at $1,750 a bottle). It once even offered a Pablo Picasso drawing at Costco.com for only $129,999.99!

Mixed in with its regular stock of staples, Costco features a glittering, constantly-shifting array of one-time specials such as discounted Prada bags, Callaway golf clubs, or Kenneth Cole bags—deals you just won't find at Sam's Club. The changing assortment and great prices keep people coming back, wallets in hand. Says CEO Sinegal, "a customer knows they'd better buy because it will not be there next time, like Waterford crystal. We try to get that sense of urgency in our customers."

There was a time when only the great unwashed masses shopped at off-price retailers. But Costco has changed all that. Even people who don't have to pinch pennies shop there. Not by accident, Costco's stores tend to be located in more affluent locations than Sam's Clubs. One-third of Costco's members have household incomes over $75,000; one-fourth over $100,000.

[Costco] attracts a breed of urban sophisticates attuned to what one retail consultant calls the "new luxury." These shoppers shun Seiko watches for TAG Heuer; Jack Nicklaus golf clubs for Callaway; Maxwell House coffee (it goes without saying) for Starbucks. They "trade up," eagerly spending more for items that make their hearts pound and for which they don't have to pay full price. Then they "trade down" to private labels for things like paper towels, detergent, and vitamins. Catering to this fast-growing segment, Costco has exploded. "It's the ultimate concept in trading up and trading down," says the consultant. "It's a brilliant innovation for the new luxury."

Costco's flair even extends to its store brand—Kirkland Signature. Whereas the Sam's Club Member's Mark store brand covers a limited assortment of generic-priced food, household, and apparel lines, Costco puts the Kirkland Signature brand on a wider range of goods—330 items accounting for 15 percent of its sales. Customers seek out Kirkland Signature products not just for price but also for quality. Costco customers can buy anything from a $20 bottle of Kirkland Signature Tierra de Chile Chilean red wine to a $1,299 Kirkland Signature stainless steel outdoor grill to a $6,330-per-person, 10-day package vacation to South Africa promising "luxury" accommodations.

So, in its own warehouse retailing back yard, it's Costco, not Wal-Mart, that's beating up on competitors. In fact, a mighty but frustrated Wal-Mart is even considering selling off its perennial runner-up Sam's Club division. Costco is more than a big box store that "stacks 'em high sells 'em cheap"—more than just a place to load up on large sizes of consumer staples. Each Costco store is a theater of retail that creates buying urgency and excitement for customers. In many ways, retailing boils down to the unglamorous art of getting the right product in the right place at the right time at the right price. But there's a lot more than that to Costco's value proposition. Says Sinegal: "Do that without being boring. That's the trick."[1]

The Costco story sets the stage for examining the fast-changing world of today's resellers. This chapter looks at *retailing* and *wholesaling*. In the first section, we look at the nature and importance of retailing, major types of store and nonstore retailers, the decisions retailers make, and the future of retailing. In the second section, we discuss these same topics as they relate to wholesalers.

Retailing

What is retailing? We all know that Costco, Home Depot, Macy's, and Target are retailers, but so are Avon representatives, Amazon.com, the local Hampton Inn, and a doctor seeing patients. **Retailing** includes all the activities involved in selling products or services directly to final consumers for their personal, nonbusiness use. Many institutions—manufacturers, wholesalers, and retailers—do retailing. But most retailing is done by **retailers**: businesses whose sales come *primarily* from retailing.

Retailing plays a very important role in most marketing channels. Each year, retailers account for more than $4.3 trillion of sales to final consumers. They connect brands to consumers in what marketing agency OgilvyAction calls "the last mile"—the final stop in the consumer's path to purchase. "Nearly 70 percent of purchase decisions are made near or in the store," explains OgilvyAction's CEO. Thus, retailers "reach consumers at key moments of truth, ultimately [influencing] their actions at the point of purchase."[2]

Although most retailing is done in retail stores, in recent years *nonstore retailing* has been growing much faster than has store retailing. Nonstore retailing includes selling to final consumers through direct mail, catalogs, telephone, the Internet, TV home-shopping shows, home and office parties, door-to-door contact, kiosks and vending machines, and other direct-selling approaches. We discuss such direct-marketing approaches in detail in Chapter 14. In this chapter, we focus on store retailing.

Types of Retailers

Retail stores come in all shapes and sizes—from your local hair-styling salon or family-owned restaurant to national specialty chain retailers such as REI or Williams-Sonoma to megadiscounters such as Costco or Wal-Mart. The most important types of retail stores are described in Table 11.1 and discussed in the following sections. They can be classified in terms of several characteristics, including the *amount of service* they offer, the breadth and depth of their *product lines,* the *relative prices* they charge, and how they are *organized.*

Amount of Service Different types of customers and products require different amounts of service. To meet these varying service needs, retailers may offer one of three service levels—self service, limited service, and full service.

Self-service retailers serve customers who are willing to perform their own "locate-compare-select" process to save time or money. Self-service is the basis of all discount operations and is typically used by retailers selling convenience goods (such as supermarkets) and nationally branded, fast-moving shopping goods (such as Wal-Mart or Kohl's). *Limited-service retailers,* such as Sears or JC Penney, provide more sales assistance because they carry more shopping goods about which customers need information. Their increased operating costs result in higher prices.

In *full-service retailers,* such as high-end specialty stores (for example, Tiffany or Hermes) and first-class department stores (such as Nordstrom or Neiman Marcus), salespeople assist customers in every phase of the shopping process. Full-service stores usually carry more specialty goods for which customers need or want assistance or advice. They provide more services resulting in much higher operating costs, which are passed along to customers as higher prices.

Product Line Retailers also can be classified by the length and breadth of their product assortments. Some retailers, such as **specialty stores**, carry narrow product lines with deep assortments within those lines. Today, specialty stores are flourishing. The increasing use of market segmentation, market targeting, and product specialization has resulted in a greater need for stores that focus on specific products and segments.

In contrast, **department stores** carry a wide variety of product lines. In recent years, department stores have been squeezed between more focused and flexible specialty stores on the one hand, and more efficient, lower-priced discounters on the other. In response, many have added promotional pricing to meet the discount threat. Others have stepped up the use of store brands and single-brand "designer shops" to compete with specialty stores.

Retailing
All activities involved in selling goods or services directly to final consumers for their personal, nonbusiness use.

Retailer
A business whose sales come *primarily* from retailing.

Specialty store
A retail store that carries a narrow product line with a deep assortment within that line.

Department store
A retail organization that carries a wide variety of product lines—each line is operated as a separate department managed by specialist buyers or merchandisers.

TABLE 11.1 Major Store Retailer Types

Type	Description	Examples
Specialty stores	Carry a narrow product line with a deep assortment, such as apparel stores, sporting-goods stores, furniture stores, florists, and bookstores. A clothing store would be a *single-line* store, a men's clothing store would be a *limited-line* store, and a men's custom-shirt store would be a *superspecialty* store.	REI, Tiffany, Radio Shack, Williams-Sonoma
Department stores	Carry several product lines—typically clothing, home furnishings, and household goods—with each line operated as a separate department managed by specialist buyers or merchandisers.	Macy's, Sears, Neiman Marcus
Supermarkets	A relatively large, low-cost, low-margin, high-volume, self-service operation designed to serve the consumer's total needs for grocery and household products.	Kroger, Safeway, Supervalu, Publix
Convenience stores	Relatively small stores located near residential areas, open long hours seven days a week, and carrying a limited line of high-turnover convenience products at slightly higher prices.	7-Eleven, Stop-N-Go, Circle K
Discount stores	Carry standard merchandise sold at lower prices with lower margins and higher volumes.	Wal-Mart, Target, Kohl's
Off-price retailers	Sell merchandise bought at less-than-regular wholesale prices and sold at less than retail, often leftover goods, overruns, and irregulars obtained at reduced prices from manufacturers or other retailers. These include *factory outlets* owned and operated by manufacturers; *independent off-price retailers* owned and run by entrepreneurs or by divisions of larger retail corporations; and *warehouse* (or *wholesale*) *clubs* selling a limited selection of brand-name groceries, appliances, clothing, and other goods at deep discounts to consumers who pay membership fees.	Mikasa (factory outlet); TJ Maxx (independent off-price retailer); Costco, Sam's, BJ's Wholesale Club (warehouse clubs)
Superstores	Very large stores traditionally aimed at meeting consumers' total needs for routinely purchased food and nonfood items. Includes *supercenters,* combined supermarket and discount stores, and *category killers,* which carry a deep assortment in a particular category and have a knowledgeable staff.	Wal-Mart Supercenters, SuperTarget, Super Kmart Center, Meijer (discount stores); Best Buy, PetSmart, Staples, Barnes & Noble (category killers)

Still others are trying catalog, telephone, and Web selling. Service remains the key differentiating factor. Retailers such as Nordstrom, Saks, Neiman Marcus, and other high-end department stores are doing well by emphasizing exclusive merchandise and high-quality service.

Supermarket

A large, low-cost, low-margin, high-volume, self-service store that carries a wide variety of grocery and household products.

Supermarkets are the most frequently shopped type of retail store. Today, however, they are facing slow sales growth because of slower population growth and an increase in competition from discount supercenters on the one hand and upscale specialty food stores on the other. Supermarkets also have been hit hard by the rapid growth of out-of-home eating. In fact, supermarkets' share of the groceries and consumables market plunged from 73 percent in 1998 to 51 percent in 2005.[3] Thus, many traditional supermarkets are facing hard times.

In the battle for "share of stomachs," some supermarkets are cutting costs, establishing more-efficient operations, lowering prices, and attempting to compete more effectively with food discounters. However, they are finding it difficult to profitably match the low prices of superlow-cost operators such as Wal-Mart, now the nation's largest grocery retailer. In contrast, many other large supermarkets are moving upscale, providing improved store environments and higher-quality food offerings, such as from-scratch bakeries, gourmet deli counters, natural foods, and fresh seafood departments. For example, consider Safeway's recent "lifestyle store" strategy:[4]

To raise itself above the cutthroat low-price food frenzy, during the past four years, Safeway has built more than 50 new "lifestyle" stores and remodeled nearly half of its existing stores under the lifestyle store concept. The lifestyle stores feature upscale touches, such as soft lighting and hardwood floors, along with higher-quality fare, including gourmet and organic foods and premium

■ Facing increased competition, many supermarkets are moving upscale. For example, Safeway is converting to "lifestyle" stores—supported by a big-budget "Ingredients for Life" marketing campaign.

brands. The restyled stores are supported by a $100 million "Ingredients for Life" marketing campaign, which assures customers that Safeway's food offerings are designed for the way people live today. The strategy has resulted in increased customer loyalty and a 55 percent growth in earnings last year. Safeway plans to remodel all of its stores under the lifestyle concept by 2009.

Convenience stores are small stores that carry a limited line of high-turnover convenience goods. After several years of stagnant sales, convenience stores are now experiencing healthy growth. Last year, U.S. convenience stores posted sales of $579 billion, a 15 percent increase over the previous year. More than 70 percent of convenience store revenues come from sales of gasoline; a majority of in-store sales are from tobacco products (39 percent) and beer and other beverages (26 percent).[5]

Convenience store

A small store, located near a residential area, that is open long hours seven days a week and carries a limited line of high-turnover convenience goods.

In recent years, convenience store chains have tried to expand beyond their primary market of young, blue-collar men, redesigning their stores to attract female shoppers. They are shedding the image of a "truck stop" where men go to buy beer, cigarettes, or shriveled hotdogs on a roller grill and are instead offering fresh prepared foods and cleaner, safer, more-upscale environments. Consider this example:[6]

There's something familiar about the place, with its muted orange-and-green color scheme. The aisles are wider, though, and the displays tonier. Chilling in the fridge is the house Chardonnay, not far from a glass case packed with baguettes and cream cheese croissants that come piping-hot out of the on-site oven. An aisle away is the snazzy cappuccino machine, which offers up bananas foster and pumpkin spice java. There's sushi and, of course, bouquets of fresh-cut flowers. They're right next to the Slurpee machine. Yes, this decidedly upscale little shoppe is a 7-Eleven—or it will be, once the company's team of ace technologists, trendspotters, and product developers wrap up one of the most ambitious makeovers in business history.

The convenience king, most commonly known for lowbrow if popular features such as the Big Gulp and around-the-clock access to Twinkies, is moving up the food chain in search of flusher customers and fatter margins.

■ Convenience store makeover: 7-Eleven is shedding its "truck stop" image and transforming its stores to offer more upscale assortments and environments.

After all, the majority of convenience store sales come from gasoline and cigarettes—two increasingly stagnant categories. So 7-Eleven is banking on a new, inventive inventory mix that competes more with Starbucks than with Shell. The transformation seems to be working. After declaring bankruptcy in 1990, the company's fortunes turned around in the past couple years—sales are up and profits have jumped.

Superstores are much larger than regular supermarkets and offer a large assortment of routinely purchased food products, nonfood items, and services. Wal-Mart, Target, Meijer, and other discount retailers offer *supercenters* (called *hypermarkets* in some countries), very large combination food and discount stores. Whereas a traditional grocery store brings in about $100,000 a week in sales, a supercenter brings in $600,000 a week. Wal-Mart, which opened its first supercenter in 1988, now has over 2,200 supercenters worldwide and is opening new ones at a rate of 170 per year.[7]

Recent years have also seen the explosive growth of superstores that are actually giant specialty stores, the so-called **category killers**. They feature stores the size of airplane hangars that carry a very deep assortment of a particular line with a knowledgeable staff. Category killers are prevalent in a wide range of categories, including books, baby gear, toys, electronics, home-improvement products, linens and towels, party goods, sporting goods, and even pet supplies.

Finally, for many retailers, the product line is actually a service. **Service retailers** include hotels and motels, banks, airlines, colleges, hospitals, movie theaters, tennis clubs, bowling alleys, restaurants, repair services, hair salons, and dry cleaners. Service retailers in the United States are growing faster than product retailers.

Relative Prices Retailers can also be classified according to the prices they charge (see Table 11.1). Most retailers charge regular prices and offer normal-quality goods and customer service. Others offer higher-quality goods and service at higher prices. The retailers that feature low prices are discount stores and "off-price" retailers.

Discount Stores A **discount store** sells standard merchandise at lower prices by accepting lower margins and selling higher volume. The early discount stores cut expenses by offering few services and operating in warehouse-like facilities in low-rent, heavily traveled districts. Today's discounters have improved their store environments and increased their services, while at the same time keeping prices low through lean, efficient operations. Leading discounters now dominate the retail scene, and world-leading retailer Wal-Mart—what one financial guru calls "the retailing machine of all time"—dominates the discounters (see Marketing at Work 11.1).[8]

Off-Price Retailers As the major discount stores traded up, a new wave of **off-price retailers** moved in to fill the ultralow-price, high-volume gap. Ordinary discounters buy at regular wholesale prices and accept lower margins to keep prices down. In contrast, off-price retailers buy at less-than-regular wholesale prices and charge consumers less than retail. Off-price retailers can be found in all areas, from food, clothing, and electronics to no-frills banking and discount brokerages.

The three main types of off-price retailers are *independents, factory outlets,* and *warehouse clubs*. **Independent off-price retailers** either are independently owned and run or are divisions of larger retail corporations. Although many off-price operations are run by smaller independents, most large off-price retailer operations are owned by bigger retail chains. Examples include store retailers such as TJ Maxx and Marshall's, owned by TJX Companies, and Web sellers such as Overstock.com.

Factory outlets—manufacturer-owned and operated stores by firms such as Liz Claiborne, Carters, Levi Strauss, and others—sometimes group together in *factory outlet malls* and *value-retail centers*, where dozens of outlet stores offer prices as low as 50 percent below retail on a wide range of mostly surplus, discounted, or irregular goods. Whereas outlet malls consist primarily of manufacturers' outlets, value-retail centers combine manufacturers' outlets with off-price retail stores and department store clearance outlets, such as Nordstrom Rack, Neiman Marcus Last Call Clearance Centers, and

---

Superstore
A store much larger than a regular supermarket that offers a large assortment of routinely purchased food products, nonfood items, and services.

Category killer
Giant specialty store that carries a very deep assortment of a particular line and is staffed by knowledgeable employees.

Service retailer
A retailer whose product line is actually a service, including hotels, airlines, banks, colleges, and many others.

Discount store
A retail operation that sells standard merchandise at lower prices by accepting lower margins and selling at higher volume.

Off-price retailer
Retailer that buys at less-than-regular wholesale prices and sells at less than retail. Examples are factory outlets, independents, and warehouse clubs.

Independent off-price retailer
Off-price retailer that is either independently owned and run or is a division of a larger retail corporation.

Factory outlet
Off-price retailing operation that is owned and operated by a manufacturer and that normally carries the manufacturer's surplus, discontinued, or irregular goods.

11.1 MARKETING AT WORK
Wal-Mart: Almost Unimaginably Big

Wal-Mart is almost unimaginably big. It's the world's largest retailer, and it's playing tag-team with ExxonMobil for the title of world's largest *company*. It rang up an incredible $351 billion in sales last year—that's 1.6 times the sales of competitors Costco, Target, Sears, Kmart, JC Penney, and Kohl's *combined*.

Wal-Mart is the number-one seller in several categories of consumer products, including groceries, toys, CDs, and pet care products. It sells more clothes than the Gap and Limited combined and almost twice as many groceries as Kroger, the leading grocery-only food retailer. Incredibly, Wal-Mart sells 30 percent of the disposable diapers purchased in the United States each year, 30 percent of the hair care products, 30 percent of all health and beauty products, 26 percent of the toothpaste, and 20 percent of the pet food. On average, some 130 million people visit Wal-Mart stores each week.

It's also hard to fathom Wal-Mart's impact on the U.S. economy. It's the nation's largest employer—one out of every 230 men, women, and children in the United States is a Wal-Mart associate. Its sales of $1.52 billion on one day in 2003 exceeded the GDPs of 26 countries. According to one study, Wal-Mart was responsible for some 25 percent of the nation's astonishing productivity gains during the 1990s. Another study found that—through its own low prices and through its impact on competitors' prices—Wal-Mart saved the American public $263 billion in 2004 alone—or $2,329 per household.

■ Wal-Mart, the world's largest retailer, is passionately dedicated to its long-time low-price value proposition and what its low prices mean to customers ("Save money. Live better.").

What's behind this spectacular success? First and foremost, Wal-Mart is passionately dedicated to its long-time low-price value proposition and what it means to customers ("Save money. Live better."). Its mission is to "lower the world's cost of living." To accomplish this mission, Wal-Mart offers a broad selection of carefully selected goods at unbeatable prices. No other retailer has come nearly so close to mastering the concepts of everyday low prices and one-stop shopping. As one analyst puts it, "The company gospel . . . is relatively simple: Be an agent for customers—find out what they want, and sell it to them for the lowest possible price." Says Wal-Mart's president and chief executive, "We're obsessed with delivering value to customers."

How does Wal-Mart make money with such low prices? Wal-Mart is a lean, mean, distribution machine—it has the lowest cost structure in the industry. Low costs let the giant retailer charge lower prices but still reap higher profits. For example, grocery prices drop an average of 10 to 15 percent in markets Wal-Mart has entered, and Wal-Mart's food prices average 20 percent less than its grocery store rivals. Lower prices attract more shoppers, producing more sales, making the company more efficient, and enabling it to lower prices even more.

Wal-Mart's low costs result in part from superior management and more sophisticated technology. Its Bentonville, Arkansas, headquarters contains a computer communications system that the U.S. Defense Department would envy, giving managers around the country instant access to sales and operating information. And its huge, fully automated distribution centers employ the latest technology to supply stores efficiently.

Wal-Mart also keeps costs down through good old "tough buying." The company is known for the calculated way it wrings low prices from suppliers. "Don't expect a greeter and don't expect friendly," says one supplier's sales executive after a visit to Wal-Mart's buying offices. "Once you are ushered into one of the spartan little buyers' rooms, ex-

pect a steely eye across the table and be prepared to cut your price. They are very, very focused people, and they use their buying power more forcefully than anyone else in America."

Some critics argue that Wal-Mart squeezes its suppliers too hard, driving some out of business. Wal-Mart proponents counter, however, that it is simply acting in its customers' interests by forcing suppliers to be more efficient. "Wal-Mart is tough, but totally honest and straightforward in its dealings with vendors," says an industry consultant. "Wal-Mart has forced manufacturers to get their acts together."

Despite its incredible success over the past four decades, some analysts are noting chinks in the once seemingly invincible Wal-Mart's armor. True, Wal-Mart's sales are huge, and through new-store and international expansion, Wal-Mart has kept its sales growing at a respectable 9 to 10 percent annually. However, Wal-Mart seems now to be facing a midlife crisis. Profit growth has slowed and Wal-Mart's stock is down 17 percent from five years ago.

Having grown so big, the maturing giant is having difficulty maintaining the speedy growth rates of its youth. "The glory days [of exploding sales and profits] are over," says an analyst. In terms of same-store sales, for example, smaller, spryer competitors such as Costco, Target, Kroger, and Walgreen's are growing two to five times faster than Wal-Mart. To reignite growth, the megaretailer is pushing into new, faster-growing product and service lines, including organic foods, in-store health clinics, and consumer financial services.

Wal-Mart is also grappling with its aging image. To many mid-to-high income consumers, Wal-Mart seems downright dowdy compared with the younger, hipper Target. "Many of its upscale customers . . . come into the store for vegetables, cereal, detergent, and the like—but turn up their noses at higher-margin items like apparel and electronics,"

(continues)

says an analyst. So, in an attempt to capture a larger share of wallet from higher-income consumers, Wal-Mart has recently been giving itself a modest image facelift. It's sprucing up its stores and adding new, higher-quality merchandise. For example, many urban Wal-Marts now carry a slew of higher-end consumer electronics products, from Sony plasma televisions to Toshiba laptops to Apple iPods. And the retailer is now dressing up its apparel racks with more stylish fashion lines under brand names such as Metro 7 and George by designer Mark Eisen. In some ways, Wal-Mart is looking decidedly more like Target. Maybe that's because Wal-Mart's chief marketing officer and the architect of the image makeover, John Fleming, is a 20-year Target marketing veteran.

But don't expect Wal-Mart to try to out-Target Target. Even with its slightly more upscale image, in no way will Wal-Mart ever give up its core low-price value proposition. After all, Wal-Mart is and always will be a discount store. "I don't think Wal-Mart's … ever going to be edgy," says Fleming. "I don't think that fits our brand. Our brand is about saving people money so that they can live better."

Sources: Quotes and other information from Anthony Bianco, "Wal-Mart's Midlife Crisis," *BusinessWeek,* April 30, 2007, p. 46; Michael Barbaro and Stuart Elliot, "Clinging to Its Roots, Wal-Mart Steps Back from an Edgy, New Image," *International Herald Tribune,* December 10, 2006, accessed at www.iht.com/articles/2006/12/10/business/walmart. php; Pallavi Gogoi, "Wal-Mart Gets the Fashion Bug," *BusinessWeek Online,* October 7, 2006, accessed at www.businessweek.com; Elizabeth Woyke, "Buffett, the Wal-Mart Shopper," *BusinessWeek,* May 14, 2007, pp. 66–67; "The Fortune 500," *Fortune,* April 30, 2007, pp. F1–F3; David Kiley, "Wal-Mart Is Out to Change It's Story with New Ads," *BusinessWeek,* September 13, 2007, accessed at www.businessweek.com; and www.walmartstores.com, accessed September 2007.

Off 5th (Saks Fifth Avenue outlets). Factory outlet malls have become one of the hottest growth areas in retailing.

The malls now are moving upscale—and even dropping "factory" from their descriptions—narrowing the gap between factory outlet and more traditional forms of retailers. As the gap narrows, the discounts offered by outlets are getting smaller. However, a growing number of outlet malls now feature brands such as Coach, Polo Ralph Lauren, Dolce & Gabbana, Giorgio Armani, Gucci, and Versace, causing department stores to protest to the manufacturers of these brands. Given their higher costs, the department stores must charge more than the off-price outlets. Manufacturers counter that they send last year's merchandise and seconds to the factory outlet malls, not the new merchandise that they supply to the department stores. Still, the department stores are concerned about the growing number of shoppers willing to make weekend trips to stock up on branded merchandise at substantial savings.

Warehouse clubs (or *wholesale clubs* or *membership warehouses*), such as Costco, Sam's Club, and BJ's, operate in huge, drafty, warehouselike facilities and offer few frills. Customers themselves must wrestle furniture, heavy appliances, and other large items to the checkout line. Such clubs make no home deliveries and often accept no credit cards. However, they do offer ultralow prices and surprise deals on selected branded merchandise.

Although they account for only about 8 percent of total U.S. retail sales, warehouse clubs have grown rapidly in recent years. As we learned in the opening Costco story, these retailers appeal not just to low-income consumers seeking bargains on bare-bones products. They appeal to all kinds of customers shopping for a wide range of goods, from necessities to extravagances.

Organizational Approach Although many retail stores are independently owned, others band together under some form of corporate or contractual organization. The major types of retail organizations—*corporate chains, voluntary chains* and *retailer cooperatives, franchise organizations,* and *merchandising conglomerates*—are described in Table 11.2.

Chain stores are two or more outlets that are commonly owned and controlled. They have many advantages over independents. Their size allows them to buy in large quantities at lower prices and gain promotional economies. They can hire specialists to deal with areas such as pricing, promotion, merchandising, inventory control, and sales forecasting.

The great success of corporate chains caused many independents to band together in one of two forms of contractual associations. One is the *voluntary chain*—a wholesaler-sponsored group of independent retailers that engages in group buying and common merchandising—which we discussed in Chapter 10. Examples include Independent Grocers Alliance (IGA), Western Auto, and Do-It Best hardware. The other type of contractual association is the *retailer cooperative*—a group of independent retailers that band together to set up a jointly owned, central wholesale operation and conduct joint merchandising and promotion efforts. Examples are Associated Grocers and Ace Hardware. These organizations give independents the buying and promotion economies they need to meet the prices of corporate chains.

Warehouse club
Off-price retailer that sells a limited selection of brand name grocery items, appliances, clothing, and a hodgepodge of other goods at deep discounts to members who pay annual membership fees.

Chain stores
Two or more outlets that are commonly owned and controlled.

TABLE 11.2 Major Types of Retail Organizations

Type	Description	Examples
Corporate chain store	Two or more outlets that are commonly owned and controlled. Corporate chains appear in all types of retailing, but they are strongest in department stores, food stores, drug stores, shoe stores, and women's clothing stores.	Sears, Kroger (grocery stores), CVS (drug stores), Williams-Sonoma (cookware and housewares)
Voluntary chain	Wholesaler-sponsored group of independent retailers engaged in group buying and merchandising.	Independent Grocers Alliance (IGA), Do-It Best Hardware, Western Auto, True Value
Retailer cooperative	Group of independent retailers who set up a central buying organization and conduct joint promotion efforts.	Associated Grocers (groceries), Ace (hardware)
Franchise organization	Contractual association between a franchiser (a manufacturer, wholesaler, or service organization) and franchisees (independent businesspeople who buy the right to own and operate one or more units in the franchise system). Franchise organizations are normally based on some unique product or service, on a method of doing business, or on a trade name, goodwill, or patent that the franchiser has developed.	McDonald's, Subway, Pizza Hut, Jiffy Lube, Meineke Mufflers, 7-Eleven
Merchandising conglomerate	A free-form corporation that combines several diversified retailing lines and forms under central ownership, along with some integration of their distribution and management functions.	Limited Brands

Another form of contractual retail organization is a **franchise**. The main difference between franchise organizations and other contractual systems (voluntary chains and retail cooperatives) is that franchise systems are normally based on some unique product or service; on a method of doing business; or on the trade name, goodwill, or patent that the franchiser has developed. Franchising has been prominent in fast food and restaurants, motels, health and fitness centers, auto sales and service, and real estate. But franchising covers a lot more than just burger joints and fitness centers. Franchises have sprung up to meet about any need. For example, franchiser Mad Science Group franchisees put on science programs for schools, scout troops, and birthday parties. And Mr. Handyman provides repair services for homeowners, while Merry Maids tidies up their houses.

Once considered upstarts among independent businesses, franchises now command 40 percent of all retail sales in the United States. These days, it's nearly impossible to stroll down a city block or drive on a city street without seeing a McDonald's, Subway, Jiffy Lube, or Holiday Inn. One of the best-known and most successful franchisers, McDonald's, now has nearly 32,000 stores in 119 countries. It serves nearly 52 million customers a day and racks up over $41 billion in annual systemwide sales. More than 59 percent of McDonald's restaurants worldwide are owned and operated by franchisees. Gaining fast is Subway Sandwiches and Salads, one of the fastest-growing franchises, with more than 27,000 shops in 85 countries, including almost 21,000 in the United States.[9]

Finally, *merchandising conglomerates* are corporations that combine several different retailing forms under central ownership. An example is Limited Brands, which operates

Franchise
A contractual association between a manufacturer, wholesaler, or service organization (a franchiser) and independent businesspeople (franchisees) who buy the right to own and operate one or more units in the franchise system.

■ Franchising: These days, it's nearly impossible to stroll down a city block or drive on a suburban street without seeing a McDonald's, Jiffy Lube, Subway, or Holiday Inn.

The Limited (fashion-forward women's clothing), Express (trendy private-label women's and men's apparel), Victoria's Secret (glamorous lingerie and beauty products), Bath & Body Works (natural but luxurious beauty and body care products), and The White Barn Candle Company (home fragrance and décor items). Such diversified retailing, similar to a multibranding strategy, provides superior management systems and economies that benefit all the separate retail operations.

Retailer Marketing Decisions

Retailers are always searching for new marketing strategies to attract and hold customers. In the past, retailers attracted customers with unique product assortments and more or better services. Today, retail assortments and services are looking more and more alike. Many national-brand manufacturers, in their drive for volume, have placed their brands almost everywhere. You can find most consumer brands not only in department stores but also in mass-merchandise discount stores, off-price discount stores, and on the Web. Thus, it's now more difficult for any one retailer to offer exclusive merchandise.

Service differentiation among retailers has also eroded. Many department stores have trimmed their services, whereas discounters have increased theirs. Customers have become smarter and more price sensitive. They see no reason to pay more for identical brands, especially when service differences are shrinking. For all these reasons, many retailers today are rethinking their marketing strategies.

As shown in Figure 11.1, retailers face major marketing decisions about *segmentation and targeting, store differentiation and positioning,* and the *retail marketing mix.*

Segmentation, Targeting, Differentiation, and Positioning Decision Retailers must first segment and define their target markets and then decide how they will differentiate and position themselves in these markets. Should the store focus on upscale, midscale, or downscale shoppers? Do target shoppers want variety, depth of assortment, convenience, or low prices? Until they define and profile their markets, retailers cannot make consistent decisions about product assortment, services, pricing, advertising, store décor, or any of the other decisions that must support their positions.

Too many retailers fail to define their target markets and positions clearly. They try to have "something for everyone" and end up satisfying no market well. In contrast, successful retailers define their target markets well and position themselves strongly. For example, Wal-Mart positions itself strongly on low prices. In a recent survey testing consumers on their recall of the slogans for American brands, 67 percent of consumers associated Wal-Mart with its "Always low prices. *Always*" promise. Sprite, in second place, scored just 35 percent recognition.[10] Wal-Mart recently extended this positioning to include what those always low prices mean to its consumers. It now promises that customers will "Save money. Live better."

FIGURE 11.1
Retailer Marketing Strategy

If Wal-Mart owns the low-price position, how can other discounters hope to compete? Again, the answer is good targeting and positioning. For example, rather than facing Wal-Mart head-on, Target—or Tar-*zhay* as many fans call it—thrives by aiming at a seemingly oxymoronic "upscale discount" niche. It has become the nation's number-two discount chain by offering discount prices but rising above the discount fray with upmarket style and design and higher-grade service. Target's "expect more, pay less" positioning sets it apart and helps insulate it from Wal-Mart.

Similarly, Whole Foods Market has only 216 stores and less than $6 billion in sales versus Wal-Mart's more than 6,500 stores worldwide and sales of $351 billion. How does this small grocery chain compete with giant Wal-Mart? It doesn't—at least not directly. Whole Foods Market thrives carefully positioning itself *away* from Wal-Mart. It targets a select group of upscale customers and offers them "organic, natural, and gourmet foods, all swaddled in Earth Day politics." In fact, a devoted Whole Foods customer is more likely to boycott the local Wal-Mart than to shop at it. One analyst sums up the Whole Foods shopping experience this way:[11]

Counters groan with creamy hunks of artisanal cheese. Medjool dates beckon amid rows of exotic fruit. Savory breads rest near fruit-drenched pastries, and prepared dishes like sesame-encrusted tuna rival what's sold in fine restaurants. In keeping with the company's positioning, most of the store's goods carry labels proclaiming "organic," "100% natural," and "contains no additives." Staff people smile, happy to suggest wines that go with a particular cheese, or pause to debate the virtues of peanut butter maltballs. And it's all done against a backdrop of eye-pleasing earth-toned hues and soft lighting. This is grocery shopping? Well, not as most people know it. Whole Foods Market has cultivated its mystique with shoppers . . . by being anything but a regular supermarket chain. Whole Foods is, well, special.

■ By positioning itself strongly *away* from Wal-Mart and other discounters, Whole Foods Market has made itself one of the nation's fastest-growing and most profitable food retailers.

Whole Foods can't match Wal-Mart's massive economies of scale, incredible volume purchasing power, ultraefficient logistics, wide selection, and hard-to-beat prices. But then again, it doesn't even try. By positioning itself strongly away from Wal-Mart and other discounters, Whole Foods Market has made itself one of the nation's fastest-growing and most profitable food retailers.

Product Assortment and Services Decision Retailers must decide on three major product variables: *product assortment, services mix,* and *store atmosphere.*

The retailer's *product assortment* should differentiate the retailer while matching target shoppers' expectations. One strategy is to offer merchandise that no other competitor carries, such as store brands or national brands on which it holds exclusives. For example, Saks gets exclusive rights to carry a well-known designer's labels. It also offers its own private-label lines—the Saks Fifth Avenue Signature, Classic, and Sport collections. At JC Penney, private-label brands account for 40 percent of sales.[12]

Another strategy is to feature blockbuster merchandising events—Bloomingdale's is known for running spectacular shows featuring goods from a certain country, such as India or China. Or the retailer can offer surprise merchandise, as when Costco offers surprise assortments of seconds, overstocks, and closeouts. Finally, the retailer can differentiate itself by offering a highly targeted product assortment—Lane Bryant carries plus-size clothing; Brookstone offers an unusual assortment of gadgets in what amounts to an adult toy store.

■ Store atmosphere: Apple's retail stores are very seductive places. Here, people wait in line to enter the new Apple store on Fifth Avenue in New York City. "It has become something of a second home to me," says one shopper, "or, as I jokingly call it, 'my temple.'"

The *services mix* can also help set one retailer apart from another. For example, some retailers invite customers to ask questions or consult service representatives in person or via phone or keyboard. Home Depot offers a diverse mix of services to do-it-yourselfers, from "how-to" classes to a proprietary credit card. Nordstrom promises to "take care of the customer, no matter what it takes."

The *store's atmosphere* is another important element in the reseller's product arsenal. The retailer wants to create a unique store experience, one that suits the target market and moves customers to buy. For example, Apple's retail stores are very seductive places. They're what one analyst calls "a Space-Age vision of a Kubrickian future—full of gleaming white and dull silver hardware."[13] The store design is clean, simple, and just oozing with style—much like an Apple iPod or iPhone. The stores invite shoppers to stay a while, use the equipment, and soak up all of the exciting new technology. One shopper sums up the Apple store atmosphere and experience this way:

It has become something of a second home to me—or, as I jokingly call it, "my temple." I've been known to spend hours at a time there. It seems a trifling thing that I can walk up to any terminal in the place during a . . . shopping break, log in to my e-mail account, and attend to my electronic correspondence. I am also able to freely Web-surf, instant-message, or do a bit of e-shopping (heck, even buy a new Mac or iPod on the online Apple Store). No one rushes or hassles me. It seems like a family room (albeit a gigantic one), with its comfortable theater seating in the back, its library-style shelves lined neatly with Mac software, books, and magazines, its rows of flat-panel screens flashing Pixar trailers, its speaker-connected iPods cranking out catchy tunes, its low-to-the-ground kids' table and ball-shaped chairs for iMac gaming, and its Genius Bar, to which visitors could cozy up for guidance or troubleshooting with an Apple supergeek. That's why I sometimes don't want to leave. In fact, I wrote part of this essay on a MacBook laptop while reclining in one of those airport-style chairs. It's a testament to Apple retail savvy that I felt totally at ease while typing away.[14]

It's no wonder that Apple stores "are going gangbusters," says the analyst. The stores are attracting, on average, 13,800 visitors per week per store. The Fifth Avenue store averages an incredible $4,032 sales per square foot a year. By comparison, Saks, whose flagship store is down the street, generates $362 per square foot; Best Buy stores turn $930—tops for electronics retailers.[15]

Other retailers practice "experiential retailing." Outdoor-goods retailer Cabela's stores are as much natural history museums for outdoor enthusiasts as they are retail outlets. Along with its huge assortment of quality hunting, fishing, and outdoor gear, Cabela's features a two-story mountain replica, complete with waterfalls, cascading streams, and lifelike, museum-quality taxidermy animals in action poses. At an REI store, consumers can try out climbing equipment on a huge wall in the store, or they can test Gore-tex raincoats by going under a simulated rain shower. Similarly, Maytag has set up "try-before-you-buy" stores in which it displays products in realistic home kitchen and laundry room settings, beckoning customers to try out products before making a choice. They can do a load of laundry, bake a sheet of cookies, or listen to a dishwasher to see whether it really is quiet.[16]

Today's successful retailers carefully orchestrate virtually every aspect of the consumer store experience, down to the music, lighting, and even the smells (see Marketing at Work 11.2). All of this confirms that retail stores are much more than simply assortments of goods. They are environments to be experienced by the people who shop in them. Store atmospheres offer a powerful tool by which retailers can differentiate their stores from those of competitors.

Price Decision   A retailer's price policy must fit its target market and positioning, product and service assortment, and competition. All retailers would like to charge high markups and achieve high volume, but the two seldom go together. Most retailers seek *either* high markups on lower volume (most specialty stores) *or* low markups on higher volume (mass merchandisers and discount stores).

Thus, Bijan's boutique, with locations in New York City and on Rodeo Drive in Beverly Hills, sells "the most expensive menswear in the world." Its million-dollar wardrobes include $50 socks, $375 silk ties and $19,000 ostrich-skin vests. Its "by appointment only" policy is designed to make its wealthy, high-profile clients comfortable with these prices. Says Mr. Bijan, "If a man is going to spend $400,000 on his visit, don't you think it's only fair that he have my full attention?"[17] Bijan's sells a low volume but makes hefty profits on each sale. At the other extreme, TJ Maxx sells brand-name clothing at discount prices, settling for a lower margin on each sale but selling at a much higher volume.

■ Bijan's boutique on Rodeo Drive in Beverly Hills sells $375 silk ties and $19,000 ostrich-skin vests. Its "by appointment only" policy makes wealthy, high-profile clients comfortable with these prices.

Retailers must also decide on the extent to which they will use sales and other price promotions. Some retailers use no price promotions at all, competing instead on product and service quality rather than on price. For example, it's difficult to imagine Bijan's holding a two-for-the-price-of-one sale. Other retailers practice *"high-low" pricing*—charging higher prices on an everyday basis, coupled with frequent sales and other price promotions to increase store traffic, clear out unsold merchandise, create a low-price image, or attract customers who will buy other goods at full prices. Still others—such as Wal-Mart, Costco, Home Depot, and other mass retailers—practice *everyday low pricing (EDLP)*, charging constant, everyday low prices with few sales or discounts. Which strategy is best depends on the retailer's marketing strategy and the pricing approaches of competitors.

Promotion Decision   Retailers use any or all of the promotion tools—advertising, personal selling, sales promotion, public relations, and direct marketing—to reach consumers. They advertise in newspapers, magazines, radio, television, and on the Internet. Advertising may be supported by newspaper inserts, catalogs, and direct mail. Personal selling requires careful training of salespeople in how to greet customers, meet their needs, and handle their complaints. Sales promotions may include in-store demonstrations, displays, contests, and visiting celebrities. Public relations activities, such as press conferences and speeches, store openings, special events, newsletters, magazines, and public service activities, are always available to retailers. Most retailers have also set up Web sites, offering customers information and other features and often selling merchandise directly.

Place Decision   Retailers often point to three critical factors in retailing success: *location, location,* and *location*! It's very important that retailers select locations that are accessible to the target market in areas that are consistent with the retailer's positioning. For example, Apple locates its stores in high-end malls and trendy shopping districts—such as the "Miracle Mile" on Chicago's Michigan Avenue or Fifth Avenue in Manhattan—not low-rent strip malls on the edge of town. Small retailers may have to settle for whatever locations they can find or afford. Large retailers, however, usually employ specialists who select locations using advanced methods.

Most stores today cluster together to increase their customer pulling power and to give consumers the convenience of one-stop shopping. *Central business districts* were the main form of retail cluster until the 1950s. Every large city and town had a central business district with department stores, specialty stores, banks, and movie theaters. When people began to move to the suburbs, however, these central business districts, with their traffic, parking, and crime problems, began to lose business. Downtown merchants opened branches in suburban shopping centers, and the decline of the central business districts con-

11.2 MARKETING AT WORK
Orchestrating the Retail Experience

The next time that you step into a retail store—whether it sells consumer electronics, hardware, or high fashion—stop and carefully consider your surroundings. Think about the store's layout and displays. Listen to the background sounds. Smell the smells. Chances are everything in the store, from the layout and lighting to the music and even the smells, has been carefully orchestrated to help shape your shopping experience—and to open your wallet. In most cases, you're probably being affected in ways so subtle that you don't even realize what's happening to you.

It all starts at the store entrance. According to one reporter, "what's in the entrance is the spring on the trap"—it pulls you in and puts you in the mood to buy. "The entrance is important because it hints at what's inside that you must have."

At a JC Penney, a "decompression area" at the front of the store lets shoppers get acclimated and calm down from the noise in the mall or on the street. Dressed mannequins offer a taste of the season's hot trends and set up a line of sight to the shopping ahead. "We're trying to give [shoppers] ideas right as [they're] walking into the store," says JC Penney's VP of store design. In other department stores, the key departments that draw women—the high-volume, high-profit goods—are right up front: handbags, cosmetics, jewelry, and sometimes intimate apparel.

At a new Home Depot in the Atlanta suburb of Buckhead, the entranceway lures shoppers in with an open floor plan so they get a better "vista" of the store. Floor-to-ceiling racks of goods, long the signature of the warehouse store, are now further back. Lower-down displays of expensive goods—riding lawn mowers, upscale porch furniture, and a home design center for redecorating kitchen, bath, and flooring—are clustered so they're visible from the front door. All are ways to engage you in the store and draw you in.

Once inside a store, "how you as a shopper move in and around a store is not, really, up to you," continues the reporter.

In a department store, you're funneled from the entrance past the store's most expensive goods through a maze of aisles and into departments that are set up as stores-within-a-store. Then you find yourself on "the racetrack," an oval aisle that carries you around the entire building to get a look at everything. Mini-displays called "trend stations" are parked in the middle of aisles to stop shoppers' progress and entice them to look and buy.

Meanwhile, everything in a well-designed store is carefully constructed to create just the right moods and actions. At a Sony Style store, for instance, it's all designed to encourage touch, from the silk wallpaper to the smooth maple wood cabinets, to the etched-glass countertops. Products are displayed like museum pieces and set up for you to touch and try. Once you touch something, Sony figures, you'll buy it. Sony Style even has mini-living rooms set up to showcase what its 40-inch flat-panel TV would look like over a fireplace. "We've had customers bring in their architect and say, 'Re-create this in my house. I want the whole setup,'" says a Sony retail executive.

A store's lighting can affect anything from your moods to the pace at which you move and shop. Bright lighting can create excitement, whereas softer lighting can create a mellow mood. Many retailers adjust lighting to regulate shoppers' "blink rates"—the slower you blink, they reason, the more likely you are to browse, pause, and eventually buy.

Sound is another important element of the retail experience. "Music has been used by retailers for decades as a way to identify their stores and affect a shopper's mood, to make you feel happy, nostalgic, or relaxed so that you linger," notes the reporter. "Think of '50s cocktail bar music in a Pottery Barn. But retailers are becoming more sophisticated in how they use music. "They now hire "audio architects" to develop music and sounds that fit their unique positioning. "What does your business sound like?" asks background music provider Muzak. "A bikini and coconut oil or an oil change and a new set of tires? Musak

---

Shopping center
A group of retail businesses planned, developed, owned, and managed as a unit.

tinued. In recent years, many cities have joined with merchants to try to revive downtown shopping areas by building malls and providing underground parking.

A **shopping center** is a group of retail businesses planned, developed, owned, and managed as a unit. A *regional shopping center,* or *regional shopping mall,* the largest and most dramatic shopping center, contains from 40 to over 200 stores, including two or more full-line department stores. It is like a covered mini-downtown and attracts customers from a wide area. A *community shopping center* contains between 15 and 40 retail stores. It normally contains a branch of a department store or variety store, a supermarket, specialty stores, professional offices, and sometimes a bank. Most shopping centers are *neighborhood shopping centers* or *strip malls* that generally contain between 5 and 15 stores. They are close and convenient for consumers. They usually contain a supermarket, perhaps a discount store, and several service stores—dry cleaner, self-service laundry, drugstore, video-rental outlet, barber or beauty shop, hardware store, or other stores.[18]

Combined, the nation's nearly 48,500 shopping centers now account for about 75 percent of U.S. retail activity (not counting cars and gasoline). The average American makes three trips to the mall a month, shopping for an average of 81.5 minutes per trip and spending about $90. However, many experts suggest that America is now "over-malled." During the 1990s, mall shopping space grew at about twice the rate of population growth. As a result, almost 20 percent of America's traditional shopping centers are either dead or dying.[19]

can create the ultimate music experience designed specifically for your business."

Perhaps the hottest store environment frontier these days is scent—that's right, the way the store smells:

Anyone who's walked into a mall has been enticed by the smell of cinnamon buns or chocolate chip cookies. Now, most large retailers are developing "signature scents" that you smell only in their stores. Luxury shirtmaker Thomas Pink pipes the smell of clean, pressed shirts into its stores—its signature "line-dried linen" scent. The essence of lavender wafts out of L'Occitane skin care stores. Bloomingdale's uses different essences in different departments: baby powder in the baby store; suntan lotion in the bathing suit area; lilacs in lingerie; cinnamon and pine scent during the holiday season. Last year, it pumped a sugar-cookie scent into its Christmas shop.

At a Sony Style store, the subtle fragrance of vanilla and mandarin orange—designed exclusively for Sony—wafts down on shoppers, relaxing them and helping them believe that this is a very nice place to be. Sony decided to create its own store scent as one way to make the consumer electronics it sells less intimidating, particularly to women. At Sony's Madison Avenue store in New York, the scent is even pumped onto the street. "From research, we found that scent is closest to the brain and will evoke the most emotion, even faster than the eye," says the Sony retail executive. "Our scent helps us create an environment like no other." A scents expert agrees: "Scent is so closely aligned with your emotions, it's so primitive."

Thus, in their quest to orchestrate the optimal shopper experience, today's successful retailers leave no store environment stone unturned. The next time you visit a store, stop, look, and listen. See if you can spot the subtle and not-so-subtle things that retailers do to affect what you feel, think, and buy in their stores. "Most people know they are being influenced subliminally when they shop," says a retail consumer behavior expert. "They just may not realize how much."

■ Next time you shop, stop, look, and listen. Successful retailers like Sony Style orchestrate every aspect of the shopper store experience, down to the music, lighting, and even the smells (a subtle fragrance of vanilla and mandarin orange).

Sources: Extracts, quotes, and other information from or adapted from Mindy Fetterman and Jayne O'Donnall, "Just Browsing at the Mall? That's What You Think," *USA Today,* September 1, 2006, accessed at www.usatoday.com; and Ylan Q. Mui, "Dollars and Scents," *Washington Post,* December 19, 2006.

Thus, despite the recent development of many new "megamalls," the current trend is toward the so-called *power centers,* huge unenclosed shopping centers consisting of a long strip of retail stores, including large, freestanding anchors such as Wal-Mart, Home Depot, Costco, Best Buy, Michaels, OfficeMax, and CompUSA. Each store has its own entrance with parking directly in front for shoppers who wish to visit only one store. Power centers have increased rapidly during the past few years to challenge traditional indoor malls.

In contrast, *lifestyle centers* are smaller malls with upscale stores, convenient locations, and nonretail activities such as dining and a movie theater. They are usually located near affluent residential neighborhoods and cater to the retail needs of consumers in their areas. "Think of lifestyle centers as part Main Street and part Fifth Avenue," comments an industry observer. In fact, the original power center and lifestyle center concepts are now morphing into hybrid lifestyle-power centers. "The idea is to combine the hominess and community of

■ Shopping centers: The current trend is toward large "power centers" on the one hand and smaller "lifestyle centers" on the other—or a hybrid version of the two called a power-lifestyle center. In all, today's centers are more about creating places to be rather than just places to buy.

an old-time village square with the cachet of fashionable urban stores; the smell and feel of a neighborhood park with the brute convenience of a strip center." In all, today's centers are more about "creating places to be rather than just places to buy."[20]

The Future of Retailing

Retailers operate in a harsh and fast-changing environment, which offers threats as well as opportunities. For example, the industry suffers from chronic overcapacity, resulting in fierce competition for customer dollars. Consumer demographics, lifestyles, and shopping patterns are changing rapidly, as are retailing technologies. To be successful, then, retailers will need to choose target segments carefully and position themselves strongly. They will need to take the following retailing developments into account as they plan and execute their competitive strategies.

New Retail Forms and Shortening Retail Life Cycles   New retail forms continue to emerge to meet new situations and consumer needs, but the life cycle of new retail forms is getting shorter. Department stores took about 100 years to reach the mature stage of the life cycle; more recent forms, such as warehouse stores, reached maturity in about 10 years. In such an environment, seemingly solid retail positions can crumble quickly. Of the top 10 discount retailers in 1962 (the year that Wal-Mart and Kmart began), not one still exists today.

Consider the Price Club, the original warehouse store chain. When Sol Price pioneered his first warehouse store outside San Diego in 1976, he launched a retailing revolution. Selling everything from tires and office supplies to five-pound tubs of peanut butter at super low prices, his store chain was generating $2.6 billion a year in sales within 10 years. But as the industry quickly matured, Price ran headlong into wholesale clubs run by such retail giants as Wal-Mart and Kmart. (In his autobiography, Sam Walton confesses: "I guess I've stolen—I actually prefer the word 'borrowed'—as many ideas from Sol Price as from anybody else in the business.") Only 17 years later, in a stunning reversal of fortune, a faltering Price sold out to competitor Costco. Price's rapid rise and fall shows that even the most successful retailers can't sit back with a winning formula. To remain successful, they must keep adapting.[21]

Many retailing innovations are partially explained by the **wheel-of-retailing concept**.[22] According to this concept, many new types of retailing forms begin as low-margin, low-price, low-status operations. They challenge established retailers that have become "fat" by letting their costs and margins increase. The new retailers' success leads them to upgrade their facilities and offer more services. In turn, their costs increase, forcing them to increase their prices. Eventually, the new retailers become like the conventional retailers they replaced. The cycle begins again when still newer types of retailers evolve with lower costs and prices. The wheel-of-retailing concept seems to explain the initial success and later troubles of department stores, supermarkets, and discount stores and the recent success of off-price retailers.

Growth of Nonstore Retailing   Most of us still make most of our purchases the old-fashioned way: We go to the store, find what we want, wait patiently in line to plunk down our cash or credit card, and bring home the goods. However, consumers now have a broad array of alternatives, including mail-order, television, phone, and online shopping. Americans are increasingly avoiding the hassles and crowds at malls by doing more of their shopping by phone or computer. As we'll discuss in Chapter 13, direct and online marketing are now the fastest-growing forms of marketing.

Only a few years ago, prospects for online retailing were soaring. As more and more consumers flocked to the Web, some experts even saw a day when consumers would bypass stodgy "old economy" store retailers and do almost all of their shopping via the Internet. However, the dot-com meltdown of 2000 dashed these overblown expectations. Many once-brash Web sellers crashed and burned, and expectations reversed almost overnight. The experts began to predict that online retailing was destined to be little more than a tag-on to in-store retailing.

However, today's online retailing is alive, well, and growing. With easier-to-use and more-enticing Web sites, improved online service, and the increasing sophistication of search technologies, online business is booming. In fact, although it currently accounts for only 6 percent

Wheel-of-retailing concept
A concept that states that new types of retailers usually begin as low-margin, low-price, low-status operations but later evolve into higher-priced, higher-service operations, eventually becoming like the conventional retailers they replaced.

of total U.S. retail sales, online buying is growing at a much brisker pace than retail buying as a whole. Last year's U.S. online retail sales reached $259 billion, an 18 percent leap over the previous year.[23] Retailer online sites also influence a large amount of in-store buying.

All types of retailers now employ direct and online channels. The online sales of large brick-and-mortar retailers, such as Sears, Staples, Wal-Mart, and Best Buy are increasing rapidly. Several large online-only retailers—Amazon.com, online auction site eBay, online travel companies such as Travelocity and Expedia, and others—are now making it big on the Web. At the other extreme, hordes of niche marketers are using the Web to reach new markets and expand their sales. Today's more-sophisticated search engines (Google, Yahoo!) and comparison-shopping sites (Shopping.com, Buy.com, Shopzilla, and others) put almost any online retailer within a mouse click or two's reach of millions of customers.

Still, much of the anticipated growth in online sales will go to multichannel retailers—the click-and-brick marketers who can successfully merge the virtual and physical worlds. In a recent ranking of the top 500 online retail sites, 55 percent were multichannel retailers.[24] Consider office-supply retailer Staples. Based on two years of research, Staples recently redesigned its Web site to extend its "Staples—That was easy" marketing promise to online shoppers. The retailer's online sales are now growing at an even faster clip than its store sales. Sales through Staples.com jumped 28 percent last year, now accounting for more than one-quarter of Staples's revenues. But Staples online operations aren't robbing from store sales. Instead, the in-store and online channels complement one another. For example, customers can buy conveniently online and then return unwanted or defective merchandise to their local Staples store. And in-store Staples.com kiosks ensure that customers never leave the store without finding what they need. As a result, for example, the average yearly spending of small-business customers jumps more than fourfold when they combine shopping online with shopping in the store.[25]

■ Online retailing: Today's online retailing is alive, well, and growing, especially for click-and-brick retailers like Staples. Its Web site, staples.com, now accounts for almost more than one-quarter of sales. "That was easy!"

Retail Convergence   Today's retailers are increasingly selling the same products at the same prices to the same consumers in competition with a wider variety of other retailers. For example, you can buy books at outlets ranging from independent local bookstores to warehouse clubs such as Costco, superstores such as Barnes & Noble or Borders, or Web sites such as Amazon.com. When it comes to brand-name appliances, department stores, discount stores, home improvement stores, off-price retailers, electronics superstores, and a slew of Web sites all compete for the same customers. So if you can't find the microwave oven you want at Sears, just step across the street and find one for a better price at Lowe's or Best Buy—or just order one online from Amazon.com.

This merging of consumers, products, prices, and retailers is called *retail convergence.* Such convergence means greater competition for retailers and greater difficulty in differentiating offerings. The competition between chain superstores and smaller, independently owned stores has become particularly heated. Because of their bulk-buying power and high sales volume, chains can buy at lower costs and thrive on smaller margins. The arrival of a superstore can quickly force nearby independents out of business. For example, the decision by electronics superstore Best Buy to sell CDs as loss leaders at rock-bottom prices pushed a number of specialty record-store chains into bankruptcy. And with its everyday low prices, Wal-Mart has been accused of destroying independents in countless small towns around the country who sell the same merchandise.

Yet the news is not all bad for smaller companies. Many small, independent retailers are thriving. They are finding that sheer size and marketing muscle are often no match for the personal touch small stores can provide or the specialty merchandise niches that small stores fill for a devoted customer base.

The Rise of Megaretailers The rise of huge mass merchandisers and specialty superstores, the formation of vertical marketing systems, and a rash of retail mergers and acquisitions have created a core of superpower megaretailers. Through their superior information systems and buying power, these giant retailers can offer better merchandise selections, good service, and strong price savings to consumers. As a result, they grow even larger by squeezing out their smaller, weaker competitors.

The megaretailers are also shifting the balance of power between retailers and producers. A relative handful of retailers now control access to enormous numbers of consumers, giving them the upper hand in their dealings with manufacturers. For example, in the United States, Wal-Mart's sales are more than five times those of Procter & Gamble, and Wal-Mart generates almost 20 percent of P&G's revenues. Wal-Mart can, and often does, use this power to wring concessions from P&G and other suppliers.[26]

Growing Importance of Retail Technology Retail technologies have become critically important as competitive tools. Progressive retailers are using advanced information technology and software systems to produce better forecasts, control inventory costs, interact electronically with suppliers, send information between stores, and even sell to customers within stores. They have adopted sophisticated systems for checkout scanning, RFID inventory tracking, merchandise handling, information sharing, and interacting with customers.

Perhaps the most startling advances in retailing technology concern the ways in which today's retailers are connecting with customers. Many retailers now routinely use technologies such as touch-screen kiosks, customer-loyalty cards, electronic shelf labels and signs, handheld shopping assistants, smart cards, and self-scanning checkout systems. For example, in its new Bloom stores, Southeastern grocery chain Food Lion is using technology to make shopping easier for its customers:

Ever stood in the wine aisle at the grocery store and felt intimidated? You think that bottle of Shiraz looks pretty good but you're not sure what it goes with. It's the sort of problem the creators of Food Lion's new concept store—Bloom— thought about, and one they will use technology to solve. Positioned as "a different kind of grocery store," Bloom relies on technology to enhance the shopping experience and to help customers find products, get information, and check out with greater ease. A computerized kiosk in the wine section lets you scan a bottle and get serving suggestions. The kiosk, and a second one in the meat section, lets you print recipes off the screen. Eight stations with touch screens and scanners around the store let you check an item's price or locate it on the map. To make it easier to keep track of purchases and check out, you can pick up a personal handheld scanner as you walk in the door, then scan and bag items as you shop. Checkout then is just a simple matter of paying as you leave. The personal scanners also give you a running total of the items you've selected as you shop, helping you stay within your budget and avoid surprises at the checkout. And if you drop off a prescription, the pharmacy can send a message to your scanner when your order is ready.[27]

■ Retail technology: In its new pilot store—Bloom—Southeastern grocery chain Food Lion is using technology to make shopping easier for its customers.

Global Expansion of Major Retailers Retailers with unique formats and strong brand positioning are increasingly moving into other countries. Many are expanding internationally to escape mature and saturated home markets. Over the years, some giant U.S. retailers, such as McDonald's, have become globally prominent as a result of their marketing prowess. Others, such as Wal-Mart, are rapidly establishing a global presence. Wal-Mart, which now operates more than 2,700 stores in 14 countries abroad, sees exciting global potential. Its international division alone last year racked up sales of more than $77 billion, an increase of almost 15 percent over the previous year and 30 percent more than rival Target's *total* sales of $59.4 billion.[28]

However, most U.S retailers are still significantly behind Europe and Asia when it comes to global expansion. Eleven of the world's top 20 retailers are U.S. companies; only two of these retailers have set up stores outside of North America (Wal-Mart and Costco). Of the 9 non-U.S. retailers in the world's top 20, eight have stores in at least ten countries. Among foreign retailers that have gone global are France's Carrefour, Germany's Metro and Aldi chains, the Netherlands' Royal Ahold, Britain's Tesco, Japan's Yaohan supermarkets, and Sweden's IKEA home furnishings stores.[29]

French discount retailer Carrefour, the world's second-largest retailer after Wal-Mart, has embarked on an aggressive mission to extend its role as a leading international retailer:

> The Carrefour Group has an interest in more than 7,300 stores in 30 countries in Europe, Asia, and the Americas, including 963 hypermarkets (supercenters). It leads Europe in supermarkets and the world in hypermarkets. Carrefour is outpacing Wal-Mart in several emerging markets, including South America, China, and the Pacific Rim. It's the leading retailer in Brazil and Argentina, where it operates 830 stores, compared to Wal-Mart's 300 units in those two countries. Carrefour is the largest foreign retailer in China, where it operates more than 345 stores versus Wal-Mart's 73. In short, although Wal-Mart has more than three times Carrefour's overall sales, Carrefour is forging ahead of Wal-Mart in most markets outside North America. The only question: Can the French retailer hold its lead? Although no one retailer can safely claim to be in the same league with Wal-Mart as an overall retail presence, Carrefour stands a better chance than most to hold its own in global retailing.[30]

Retail Stores as "Communities" or "Hangouts"   With the rise in the number of people living alone, working at home, or living in isolated and sprawling suburbs, there has been a resurgence of establishments that, regardless of the product or service they offer, also provide a place for people to get together. These places include coffee shops and cafés, shopping malls, bookstores, children's play spaces, superstores, and urban green markets. For example, today's bookstores have become part bookstore, part library, part living room, and part coffee house. On an early evening at your local Barnes & Noble, you'll likely find back-pack-toting high school students doing homework with friends in the coffee bar. Nearby, retirees sit in cushy chairs thumbing through travel or gardening books while parents read aloud to their children. Barnes & Noble sells more than just books, it sells comfort, relaxation, and community.

Retailers don't create communities only in their brick-and-mortar stores. Many also build virtual communities on the Internet. For example, Nike creates community in its giant, interactive Niketown retail stores but also creates online gathering places:

■ Retail "communities": Today's bookstores have become part bookstore, part library, part living room, and part coffee house.

> In just over a decade, Nike's global soccer presence has grown dramatically—from roughly $40 million of sales in 1994 to almost $1.5 billion today. So, when Nike discovered that rival Adidas had gotten the exclusive deal to broadcast ads in the United States during the 2006 World Cup, it had to be innovative. In partnership with Google, Nike created Joga.com, a social networking site for soccer fans. Launched quietly in February of 2006, the site became an instant hit—a bustling online soccer community. More than 1 million members from 140 countries signed up by mid-July. On Joga.com, fans can blog, create communities around favorite teams or players, organize pickup games, download videos, and rant about the encroaching commercialism of the game. Some of the most downloaded videos are clips containing Nike products. According to one marketing analyst, "By enrolling consumers in shaping the [content], Nike is . . . nurturing deeper bonds of loyalty and advocacy." Nike's

CEO agrees: "When someone joins a Nike community or invites Nike into their community, a strong relationship is created."[31]

Wholesaling

Wholesaling
All activities involved in selling goods and services to those buying for resale or business use.

Wholesaler
A firm engaged *primarily* in wholesaling activities.

Wholesaling includes all activities involved in selling goods and services to those buying for resale or business use. We call **wholesalers** those firms engaged *primarily* in wholesaling activities.

Wholesalers buy mostly from producers and sell mostly to retailers, industrial consumers, and other wholesalers. As a result, many of the nation's largest and most important wholesalers are largely unknown to final consumers. For example, you may never have heard of Grainger, even though it's very well known and much valued by its more than 1.7 million business and institutional customers across North America.

Grainger may be the biggest market leader you've never heard of. It's a $5.9 billion business that offers more than 800,000 maintenance, repair, and operating (MRO) products to more than 1.8 million customers. Through its branch network, service centers, sales reps, catalog, and Web site, Grainger links customers with the supplies they need to keep their facilities running smoothly—everything from light bulbs, cleaners, and display cases to nuts and bolts, motors, valves, power tools, and test equipment. Grainger's 600 North American branches, 15 strategically located distribution centers, more than 17,000 employees, and innovative Web site handle more than 100,000 transactions a day. Its customers include organizations ranging from factories, garages, and grocers to schools and military bases. Most American businesses are located within 20 minutes of a Grainger branch. Customers include notables such as Abbott Laboratories, General Motors, Campbell Soup, American Airlines, Chrysler, and the U.S. Postal Service. Grainger operates on a simple value proposition: to make it easier and less costly for customers to find and buy MRO supplies. It starts by acting as a one-stop shop for products to maintain facilities. On a broader level, it builds lasting relationships with customers by helping them find *solutions* to their overall MRO problems. Acting as consultants, Grainger sales reps help buyers with everything from improving their supply chain management to reducing inventories and streamlining warehousing operations. So, how come you've never heard of Grainger? Maybe it's because the company operates in the not-so-glamorous world of MRO supplies, which are important to every business but not so important to consumers. More likely, it's because Grainger is a wholesaler. And like most wholesalers, it operates behind the scenes, selling only to other businesses.[32]

■ Wholesaling: Many of the nation's largest and most important wholesalers—like Grainger—are largely unknown to final consumers. But they are very well known and much valued by the business customers they serve.

Why are wholesalers important to sellers? For example, why would a producer use wholesalers rather than selling directly to retailers or consumers? Simply put, wholesalers add value by performing one or more of the following channel functions:

• *Selling and promoting:* Wholesalers' sales forces help manufacturers reach many small customers at a low cost. The wholesaler has more contacts and is often more trusted by the buyer than the distant manufacturer.

- *Buying and assortment building:* Wholesalers can select items and build assortments needed by their customers, thereby saving the consumers much work.
- *Bulk breaking:* Wholesalers save their customers money by buying in carload lots and breaking bulk (breaking large lots into small quantities).
- *Warehousing:* Wholesalers hold inventories, thereby reducing the inventory costs and risks of suppliers and customers.
- *Transportation:* Wholesalers can provide quicker delivery to buyers because they are closer than the producers.
- *Financing:* Wholesalers finance their customers by giving credit, and they finance their suppliers by ordering early and paying bills on time.
- *Risk bearing:* Wholesalers absorb risk by taking title and bearing the cost of theft, damage, spoilage, and obsolescence.
- *Market information:* Wholesalers give information to suppliers and customers about competitors, new products, and price developments.
- *Management services and advice:* Wholesalers often help retailers train their salesclerks, improve store layouts and displays, and set up accounting and inventory control systems.

Types of Wholesalers

Wholesalers fall into three major groups (see Table 11.3): *merchant wholesalers, agents and brokers,* and *manufacturers' sales branches and offices.* **Merchant wholesalers** are the largest single group of wholesalers, accounting for roughly 50 percent of all wholesaling. Merchant wholesalers include two broad types: full-service wholesalers and limited-service wholesalers. *Full-service wholesalers* provide a full set of services, whereas the various *limited-service wholesalers* offer fewer services to their suppliers and customers. The several different types of limited-service wholesalers perform varied specialized functions in the distribution channel.

Brokers and *agents* differ from merchant wholesalers in two ways: They do not take title to goods, and they perform only a few functions. Like merchant wholesalers, they generally specialize by product line or customer type. A **broker** brings buyers and sellers together and assists in negotiation. **Agents** represent buyers or sellers on a more permanent basis. *Manufacturers' agents* (also called manufacturers' representatives) are the most common type of agent wholesaler. The third major type of wholesaling is that done in **manufacturers' sales branches and offices** by sellers or buyers themselves rather than through independent wholesalers.

Wholesaler Marketing Decisions

Wholesalers now face growing competitive pressures, more-demanding customers, new technologies, and more direct-buying programs on the part of large industrial, institutional, and retail buyers. As a result, they have taken a fresh look at their marketing strategies. As with retailers, their marketing decisions include choices of segmentation and targeting, differentiation and positioning, and the marketing mix—product and service assortments, price, promotion, and distribution (see Figure 11.2).

Segmentation, Targeting, Differentiation; and Positioning Decision Like retailers, wholesalers must segment and define their target markets and differentiate and position themselves effectively—they cannot serve everyone. They can choose a target group by size of customer (only large retailers), type of customer (convenience stores only), need for service (customers who need credit), or other factors. Within the target group, they can identify the more profitable customers, design stronger offers, and build better relationships with them. They can propose automatic reordering systems, set up management-training and advising systems, or even sponsor a voluntary chain. They can discourage less-profitable customers by requiring larger orders or adding service charges to smaller ones.

Marketing-Mix Decision Like retailers, wholesalers must decide on product and service assortments, prices, promotion, and place. Wholesalers add customer value though the *products and services* they offer. They are often under great pressure to carry a full line and to stock enough for immediate delivery. But this practice can damage profits. Wholesalers

---

Merchant wholesaler
Independently owned business that takes title to the merchandise it handles.

Broker
A wholesaler who does not take title to goods and whose function is to bring buyers and sellers together and assist in negotiation.

Agent
A wholesaler who represents buyers or sellers on a relatively permanent basis, performs only a few functions, and does not take title to goods.

Manufacturers' sales branches and offices
Wholesaling by sellers or buyers themselves rather than through independent wholesalers.

TABLE 11.3 Major Types of Wholesalers

Type	Description
Merchant wholesalers	Independently owned businesses that take title to the merchandise they handle. In different trades they are called *jobbers, distributors,* or *mill supply houses.* They include *full-service wholesalers* and *limited-service wholesalers.*
Full-service wholesalers	Provide a full line of services: carrying stock, maintaining a sales force, offering credit, making deliveries, and providing management assistance. There are two types:
Wholesale merchants	Sell primarily to retailers and provide a full range of services. *General merchandise wholesalers* carry several merchandise lines, whereas *general line wholesalers* carry one or two lines in great depth. *Specialty wholesalers* specialize in carrying only part of a line. Examples: health food wholesalers, seafood wholesalers.
Industrial distributors	Sell to manufacturers rather than to retailers. Provide several services, such as carrying stock, offering credit, and providing delivery. May carry a broad range of merchandise, a general line, or a specialty line.
Limited-service wholesalers	Offer fewer services than full-service wholesalers. Limited-service wholesalers are of several types:
Cash-and-carry wholesalers	Carry a limited line of fast-moving goods and sell to small retailers for cash. Normally do not deliver. Example: A small fish store retailer may drive to a cash-and-carry fish wholesaler, buy fish for cash, and bring the merchandise back to the store.
Truck wholesalers (or truck jobbers)	Perform primarily a selling and delivery function. Carry limited line of semiperishable merchandise (such as milk, bread, snack foods), which they sell for cash as they make their rounds to supermarkets, small groceries, hospitals, restaurants, factory cafeterias, and hotels.
Drop shippers	Do not carry inventory or handle the product. On receiving an order, they select a manufacturer, who ships the merchandise directly to the customer. The drop shipper assumes title and risk from the time the order is accepted to its delivery to the customer. They operate in bulk industries, such as coal, lumber, and heavy equipment.
Rack jobbers	Serve grocery and drug retailers, mostly in nonfood items. They send delivery trucks to stores, where the delivery people set up toys, paperbacks, hardware items, health and beauty aids, or other items. They price the goods, keep them fresh, set up point-of-purchase displays, and keep inventory records. Rack jobbers retain title to the goods and bill the retailers only for the goods sold to consumers.
Producers' cooperatives	Are owned by farmer members and assemble farm produce to sell in local markets. The co-op's profits are distributed to members at the end of the year. They often attempt to improve product quality and promote a co-op brand name, such as Sun Maid raisins, Sunkist oranges, or Diamond walnuts.
Mail-order wholesalers	Send catalogs to retail, industrial, and institutional customers featuring jewelry, cosmetics, specialty foods, and other small items. Maintain no outside sales force. Main customers are businesses in small outlying areas. Orders are filled and sent by mail, truck, or other transportation.
Brokers and agents	Do not take title to goods. Main function is to facilitate buying and selling, for which they earn a commission on the selling price. Generally specialize by product line or customer type.
Brokers	Chief function is bringing buyers and sellers together and assisting in negotiation. They are paid by the party who hired them and do not carry inventory, get involved in financing, or assume risk. Examples: food brokers, real estate brokers, insurance brokers, and security brokers.
Agents	Represent either buyers or sellers on a more permanent basis than brokers do. There are several types:
Manufacturers' agents	Represent two or more manufacturers of complementary lines. A formal written agreement with each manufacturer covers pricing, territories, order handling, delivery service and warranties, and commission rates. Often used in such lines as apparel, furniture, and electrical goods. Most manufacturers' agents are small businesses with only a few skilled salespeople as employees. They are hired by small manufacturers who cannot afford their own field sales forces and by large manufacturers who use agents to open new territories or to cover territories that cannot support full-time salespeople.
Selling agents	Have contractual authority to sell a manufacturer's entire output. The manufacturer either is not interested in the selling function or feels unqualified. The selling agent serves as a sales department and has significant influence over prices, terms, and conditions of sale. Found in product areas such as textiles, industrial machinery and equipment, coal and coke, chemicals, and metals.
Purchasing agents	Generally have a long-term relationship with buyers and make purchases for them, often receiving, inspecting, warehousing, and shipping the merchandise to the buyers. They provide helpful market information to clients and help them obtain the best goods and prices available.
Commission merchants	Take physical possession of products and negotiate sales. Normally, they are not employed on a long-term basis. Used most often in agricultural marketing by farmers who do not want to sell their own output and do not belong to producers' cooperatives. The commission merchant takes a truckload of commodities to a central market, sells it for the best price, deducts a commission and expenses, and remits the balance to the producers.
Manufacturers' and retailers' branches and offices	Wholesaling operations conducted by sellers or buyers themselves rather than through independent wholesalers. Separate branches and offices can be dedicated to either sales or purchasing.
Sales branches and offices	Set up by manufacturers to improve inventory control, selling, and promotion. *Sales branches* carry inventory and are found in industries such as lumber and automotive equipment and parts. *Sales offices* do not carry inventory and are most prominent in dry-goods and notions industries.
Purchasing officers	Perform a role similar to that of brokers or agents but are part of the buyer's organization. Many retailers set up purchasing offices in major market centers such as New York and Chicago.

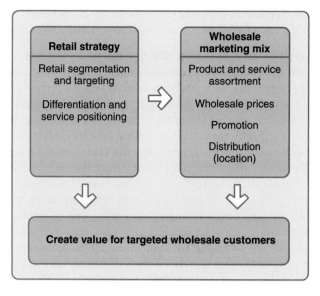

FIGURE 11.2
Wholesaler marketing strategy

today are cutting down on the number of lines they carry, choosing to carry only the more-profitable ones. They are also rethinking which services count most in building strong customer relationships and which should be dropped or paid for by the customer. The key is to find the mix of services most valued by their target customers.

Price is also an important wholesaler decision. Wholesalers usually mark up the cost of goods by a standard percentage—say, 20 percent. Expenses may run 17 percent of the gross margin, leaving a profit margin of 3 percent. In grocery wholesaling, the average profit margin is often less than 2 percent. Wholesalers are trying new pricing approaches. They may cut their margin on some lines in order to win important new customers. They may ask suppliers for special price breaks when they can turn them into an increase in the supplier's sales.

Although *promotion* can be critical to wholesaler success, most wholesalers are not promotion minded. Their use of trade advertising, sales promotion, personal selling, and public relations is largely scattered and unplanned. Many are behind the times in personal selling—they still see selling as a single salesperson talking to a single customer instead of as a team effort to sell, build, and service major accounts. Wholesalers also need to adopt some of the nonpersonal promotion techniques used by retailers. They need to develop an overall promotion strategy and to make greater use of supplier promotion materials and programs.

Finally, *distribution* (location) is important—wholesalers must choose their locations, facilities, and Web locations carefully. There was a time when wholesalers could locate in low-rent, low-tax areas and invest little money in their buildings, equipment, and systems. Today, however, as technology zooms forward, such behavior results in outdated materials-handling, order-processing, and delivery systems.

Instead, today's large and progressive wholesalers have reacted to rising costs by investing in automated warehouses and information technology systems. Orders are fed from the retailer's information system directly into the wholesaler's, and the items are picked up by mechanical devices and automatically taken to a shipping platform where they are assembled. Most large wholesalers are using technology to carry out accounting, billing, inventory control, and forecasting. Modern wholesalers are adapting their services to the needs of target customers and finding cost-reducing methods of doing business.

Trends in Wholesaling

Today's wholesalers face considerable challenges. The industry remains vulnerable to one of the most enduring trends of the last decade—fierce resistance to price increases and the winnowing out of suppliers who are not adding value based on cost and quality. Progressive wholesalers constantly watch for better ways to meet the changing needs of their suppliers and target customers. They recognize that, in the long run, their only reason for existence comes from adding value by increasing the efficiency and effectiveness of the entire marketing channel. For example, Grainger succeeds by making life easier and more efficient for the commercial and institutional buyers and sellers it serves:

> Beyond making it easier for customers to find the products they need, Grainger also helps them streamline their acquisition processes. For most companies, acquiring MRO supplies is a very costly process. In fact, 40 percent of the cost of MRO supplies stems from the purchase process, including finding a supplier, negotiating the best deal, placing the order, receiving the order, and paying the invoice. Grainger constantly seeks ways to reduce the costs associated with MRO supplies acquisition, both internally and externally. One company found that working with Grainger cut MRO requisition time by more than 60 percent; lead times went from days to hours. Its supply chain dropped from 12,000 suppliers to 560—significantly reducing expenses. Similarly, a large timber and paper-products company has come to appreciate Grainger's selection and streamlined ordering process. It orders two-thirds of its supplies from Grainger's Web site at an annual acquisition cost of only $300,000. By comparison, for the remainder of its needs, this company deals with more than 1,300 small distributors at an acquisition cost of $2.4 million each year—eight times the cost of dealing with Grainger for half of the volume. The company is now looking for ways to buy all of its MRO supplies from Grainger. As one Grainger branch manager puts it, "If we don't save [customers] time and money every time they come [to us], they won't come back."[33]

McKesson, the nation's leading wholesaler of pharmaceuticals, health and beauty care, home health care, and medical supply and equipment products, provides another example of progressive, value-adding wholesaling. To survive, McKesson must remain more cost effective than manufacturers' sales branches. Thus, the company has built efficient automated warehouses, established direct computer links with drug manufacturers, and set up extensive online supply management and accounts receivable systems for customers. It offers retail pharmacists a wide range of online resources, including supply management assistance, catalog searches, real-time order tracking, and an account management system. It has also created solutions such as automated pharmaceutical-dispensing machines that assist pharmacists by reducing costs and improving accuracy. Retailers can even use the McKesson system to maintain medical profiles on their customers.

McKesson's medical-surgical supply and equipment customers receive a rich assortment of online solutions and supply management tools, including an online order management system and real-time information on products and pricing, inventory availability, and order status. According to McKesson, it adds value in the channel by providing "supply, information, and health care management products and services designed to reduce costs and improve quality across health care."[34]

The distinction between large retailers and large wholesalers continues to blur. Many retailers now operate formats such as wholesale clubs and supercenters that perform many wholesale functions. In return, many large wholesalers are setting up their own retailing operations. For example, until recently, SuperValu was classified as a food wholesaler, with a majority of its business derived from supplying grocery products to independent grocery retailers. However, over the past decade, SuperValu has started or acquired several retail food chains of its own—including Albertsons, Jewel-Osco, Save-A-Lot, Cub Foods, and others—to become the nation's third-largest food retailer. Thus, even though it remains the country's largest food wholesaler, SuperValu is now classified as a retailer because 75 percent of its $37 billion in sales come from retailing.[35]

Wholesalers will continue to increase the services they provide to retailers—retail pricing, cooperative advertising, marketing and management information reports, accounting services, online transactions, and others. Rising costs on the one hand, and the demand for increased services on the other, will put the squeeze on wholesaler profits. Wholesalers who do not find efficient ways to deliver value to their customers will soon drop by the wayside. However, the increased use of computerized, automated, and Web-based systems will help wholesalers to contain the costs of ordering, shipping, and inventory holding, boosting their productivity.

Finally, facing slow growth in their domestic markets and such developments as the North American Free Trade Agreement, many large wholesalers are now going global. For example, in 1991, McKesson bought out its Canadian partner, Provigo. The company now receives about 3 percent of its total revenues from Canada. Its Information Solutions group operates widely throughout North America, the United Kingdom, and other European countries.

REST STOP ⟶ REVIEWING THE CONCEPTS

In this chapter, we first looked at the nature and importance of retailing, major types of retailers, the decisions retailers make, and the future of retailing. We then examined these same topics for wholesalers.

1. Explain the roles of retailers and wholesalers in the distribution channel.

Retailing and wholesaling consist of many organizations bringing goods and services from the point of production to the point of use. *Retailing* includes all activities involved in selling goods or services directly to final consumers for their personal, non-business use. *Wholesaling* includes all the activities involved in selling goods or services to those who are buying for the purpose of resale or for business use. Wholesalers perform many functions, including selling and promoting, buying and assortment building, bulk breaking, warehousing, transporting, financing, risk bearing, supplying market information, and providing management services and advice.

2. Describe the major types of retailers and give examples of each.

Retail stores come in all shapes and sizes, and new retail types keep emerging. Store retailers can be classified by the *amount of service* they provide (self-service, limited service, or full service), *product line sold* (specialty stores, department stores, supermarkets, convenience stores, superstores, and service businesses), and *relative prices* (discount stores and off-price retailers). Today, many retailers are banding together in corporate and contractual *retail organizations* (corporate chains, vol-untary chains and retailer cooperatives, franchise organizations, and merchandising conglomerates).

3. Describe the major types of wholesalers and give examples of each.

Wholesalers fall into three groups. First, *merchant wholesalers* take possession of the goods. They include *full-service wholesalers* (wholesale merchants, industrial distributors) and *limited-service wholesalers* (cash-and-carry wholesalers, truck wholesalers, drop shippers, rack jobbers, producers' cooperatives, and mail-order wholesalers). Second, *brokers* and *agents* do not take possession of the goods but are paid a commission for aiding buying and selling. Finally, *manufacturers' sales branches and offices* are wholesaling operations conducted by nonwholesalers to bypass the wholesalers.

4. Explain the marketing decisions facing retailers and wholesalers.

Each retailer must make decisions about its target markets and positioning, product assortment and services, price, promotion, and place. Retailers need to choose target markets carefully and position themselves strongly. Today, wholesaling is holding its own in the economy. Progressive wholesalers are adapting their services to the needs of target customers and are seeking cost-reducing methods of doing business. Faced with slow growth in their domestic markets and developments such as the North American Free Trade Agreement, many large wholesalers are also now going global.

Navigating the Key Terms _____

Agent (341)
Broker (341)
Category killer (326)
Chain stores (328)
Convenience store (325)
Department store (323)
Discount store (326)
Factory outlet (326)
Franchise (329)

Independent off-price retailer (326)
Manufacturers' sales branches and offices (341)
Merchant wholesaler (341)
Off-price retailer (326)
Retailer (323)
Retailing (323)
Service retailer (326)
Shopping center (335)

Specialty store (323)
Supermarket (324)
Superstore (326)
Warehouse club (328)
Wheel-of-retailing concept (336)
Wholesaler (340)
Wholesaling (340)

Travel Log

Discussing the Issues

1. Define *retailing* and *wholesaling* and discuss how each adds value to the marketing system. (AACSB: Communication; Reflective Thinking)

2. Distinguish between specialty stores, department stores, supermarkets, convenience stores, superstores, and category killers. Give one example of each. (AASCB: Communication; Reflective Thinking)

3. Discuss the different organizational approaches for retailers and provide an example of each. (AACSB: Communication; Reflective Thinking)

4. What is the wheel-of-retailing concept? Does it apply to online retailing? (AACSB: Communication; Reflective Thinking)

5. List and briefly discuss the trends impacting the future of retailing. (AACSB: Communication)

6. Name and describe the different types of wholesalers. (AACSB: Communication)

Application Questions

1. Store brands (or private labels) have existed for years but have only recently seen increasing popularity in the United States. These are brands that can only be purchased at a specific store, such as Wal-Mart's Great Value or Equate brands. Store brands now account for 15 percent of all retail sales (19 percent of food sales) and are priced about 30 percent below national brands. Visit a grocery store, a drug store, a discount store, and a department store and identify the private-label store brands for each. Compare store-brand prices with national-brand prices and write a brief report of what you found. (AACSB: Communication; Reflective Thinking)

2. Deciding on a target market and positioning for a retail store are very important marketing decisions. In a small group, visit a local mall and evaluate five stores. What is the target market for each store? How is each store positioned? Do the retail atmospherics of each store enhance this positioning effectively to attract and satisfy the target market? (AACSB: Communication; Reflective Thinking)

3. The Mall of America, located in Bloomington, Minnesota, is the largest mall in the world. Visit www.mallofamerica.com to learn more about this shopping center. Write a brief report describing the center and classify what type of shopping center it is. (AACSB: Communication; Reflective Thinking)

Under the Hood: Focus on Technology

Gift card giving has grown dramatically over the past few years, but some consumers feel such cards constitute a thoughtless or impersonal gift. Not anymore! Macy's is testing customized gift card kiosks in some of its stores. The kiosks allow customers to customize gift cards with their photo, message, and color. Each kiosk is equipped with a digital camera for those wanting an impromptu photo, but customers also can upload pictures from a disc or from their own digital camera. Cardways is the company providing this technology, and at its Web site consumers can now customize gift cards for other retailers (such as Circuit City, Linens 'N Things, Lowe's, and Travelocity).

1. This is an example of which retailer marketing decision? Explain your answer. (AACSB: Communication; Reflective Thinking)

2. Go to www.cardways.com and create your own gift card. Was it easy to use? How much does it cost to customize a card and do you think the benefit you receive is worth the cost? (AACSB: Communication; Reflective)

Focus on Ethics

You would think that city officials would want to encourage retail growth, but that isn't always the case. For example, the Chicago City Council passed an ordinance that has been labeled "living wage legislation." It required retailers with more than $1 billion in profits and more than 90,000 square feet of floor space to pay a "living wage" to employees, defined as $10 per hour in pay plus an additional $3 per hour in benefits. As a result, large retailers such as Wal-Mart, Target, and Lowe's threatened to curtail their expansion plans in that city. The mayor of Chicago vetoed the law. But this type of legislation is in effect in other cities, such as Santa Fe, New Mexico, and San Francisco, California. Other cities are considering different kinds of restrictive legislation. For example, Fresno, California, banned altogether stores larger than 100,000 square feet that devote at least 5 percent of that space to groceries (such as Wal-Mart Superstores). And Austin, Texas, requires retail developments greater than 100,000 square feet to obtain conditional use permits and notifies local residents of the development.

1. Why would city officials enact these types of ordinances? (AACSB: Communication; Reflective Thinking)

2. Is it right to single out a few retailers and limit their growth this way? (AACSB: Communication; Ethical Reasoning)

Video Case

Wellbeing

In 2003, Dan Wales and Matt Lennox opened their first Wellbeing restaurant. Their goal was to offer consumers a healthy alternative to typical fast-food options. Working with fresh ingredients, bright and open stores, and a well-crafted, healthy menu, the new chain offered something new. "There are few truly healthy fast-food chains," says Wales. "People have been desperate for healthy options." So it came as no surprise that customers responded with enthusiasm to Wellbeing's new choices as they gobbled up sandwiches, salads, soups, juices, smoothies, and fruit salads. In only a few years, the chain has expanded to 18 stores and expects to nearly double that number in the next two years.

After viewing the video featuring Wellbeing, answer the following questions about retailing and wholesaling.

1. Categorize Wellbeing according to the four characteristics of retailers discussed in the chapter.

2. How is Wellbeing positioned in the marketplace? Which consumers does the chain target? Are its product assortment, pricing, promotion, and place decisions consistent with this targeting and positioning?

3. Which trend affecting the future of retailing do you think will most impact Wellbeing in the coming years?

After studying this chapter, you should be able to

1. discuss the process and advantages of integrated marketing communications in communicating customer value

2. define the five promotion tools and discuss the factors that must be considered in shaping the overall promotion mix

3. describe and discuss the major decisions involved in developing an advertising program

4. explain how companies use public relations to communicate with their publics

12

Communicating Customer Value: Advertising and Public Relations

ROAD MAP Previewing the Concepts

We'll forge ahead now into the last of the marketing mix tools—promotion. Companies must do more than just create customer value. They must also use promotion to clearly and persuasively communicate that value. You'll find that promotion is not a single tool but rather a mix of several tools. Ideally, under the concept of *integrated marketing communications*, the company will carefully coordinate these promotion elements to deliver a clear, consistent, and compelling message about the organization and its products. We'll begin by introducing you to the various promotion mix tools. Next, we'll examine the rapidly changing communications environment and the need for integrated marketing communications. Finally, we'll look more closely at two of the promotion tools—advertising and public relations. In the next chapter, we'll visit two other promotion mix tools—sales promotion and personal selling. In Chapter 14, we'll explore direct and online marketing.

Let's start by looking at an outstanding advertising campaign. Until about ten years ago, GEICO was a little-known nicher in the auto insurance industry. But now, thanks in large part to an industry-changing advertising campaign featuring a likable spokes-lizard, an indignant clan of cavemen, and an enduring tagline, GEICO has grown to become a major industry player. Here's the story.

Founded in 1936, GEICO initially targeted a select customer group of government employees and noncommissioned military officers with exceptional driving records. Unlike its much larger competitors, GEICO has no agents. Instead, the auto insurer markets directly to customers. Founder Leo Goodwin believed that by marketing directly, he could lower costs and pass on the savings in the form of lower premiums. For nearly 60 years, little GEICO relied almost entirely on direct-mail advertising and the telephone to market its services to its select clientele.

In 1994, however, when the company decided to expand its customer base, it knew that it must also expand its marketing. So it hired The Martin Agency, an advertising firm located in Richmond, Virginia. GEICO's advertising adventure began modestly. In 1995, the company spent a paltry $10 million to launch its first national TV, radio, and print ads to support its direct-mail marketing. Then, in 1996, billionaire investor Warren Buffet bought the company and told the marketing group to "speed things up." Did it ever. Over the next 10 years, GEICO's ad spending jumped 50-fold, to more than $500 million.

By now, you probably know a lot about GEICO and its smooth-talking gecko. But at the start, The Martin Agency faced a tough task—introducing a little-known company with a funny name to a national audience. Like all good advertising, the GEICO campaign began with a simple but enduring theme, one that highlights the convenience and savings advantages of GEICO's direct-to-customers system. Every single one of the more than 150 commercials produced in the campaign so far drives home the now-familiar tagline: "15 minutes could save you 15 percent or more on car insurance."

But what really set GEICO's advertising apart was the inspired way the company chose to bring its value proposition to life. At the time, competitors were using serious and sentimental pitches—"You're in good hands with Allstate" or "Like a good neighbor, State Farm is there." To help make its advertising stand out, GEICO decided to deliver its punch line with humor. The creative approach worked and sales began to climb.

As the brand grew, it became apparent that customers had difficulty pronouncing the GEICO name (which stands for Government Employees Insurance Company). Too often, GEICO became "gecko." Enter the charismatic green lizard. In 1999, GEICO ran a 15-second spot in which the now-famous, British-accented gecko calls a press conference and pleads: "I am a gecko, not to be confused with a GEICO, which could save you hundreds on car insurance. So stop calling me." The ad was supposed to be a "throwaway." "It was an odd spot that didn't fit," says Ted Ward, GEICO vice president of marketing, "but we thought it was funny." Consumers agreed. They quickly flooded the company with calls and letters begging to see more of the gecko. The rest, as they say, is history.

Not only has the gecko helped people to pronounce and remember GEICO's name, it's become a pop culture icon. The unlikely lizard has become so well known that it was recently voted one of America's top two favorite icons by attendees of Advertising Week in New York, one of the ad industry's largest and most important gatherings.

Although the gecko ads remain a fixture, one lizard could take the company only so far. Over the past eight years, to keep its advertising fresh and entertaining, GEICO has added several new minicampaigns. Each new campaign has emphasized a different dimension of the brand's positioning. The first new campaign was "Good News," which addressed the difficulties of getting drivers to switch insurance companies. The humorous spots appeared to be about other products or TV programming, say a soap opera or a home improvement program, until one of the characters unexpectedly announced, "I have good news. I just saved a bunch of money on my car insurance by switching to GEICO."

Then came the cavemen. GEICO told The Martin Agency, "Make people understand that GEICO.com is simple." The agency responded with the "Caveman" minicampaign, de-signed to bring younger buyers to the GEICO Web site by showing them how easy it is to purchase insurance online. In the campaign, notes one observer, "a clutch of metrosexual cavemen, having somehow eluded extinction while developing a taste for racquet sports, plasma TVs, and 'duck with mango salsa,' is insulted by the company's advertising slogan, 'It's so easy to use GEICO.com, even a caveman could do it'."

The indignant cavemen have taken on a cult status all their own. They've starred in a host of ads and have their own GEICO created Web site (www.cavemanscrib.com) where you can visit one of the urbane hominids at home with his "iPod docking stations, glossy fashion mags, and hors d'oeuvres on toothpicks." ABC even featured the cavemen on their own sitcom in its fall 2007 lineup.

To open yet another front in its quest to expand customer relationships, GEICO launched its Testimonials campaign, in which real customers recount how GEICO helped them out in tough situations. But the testimonials have been GEICO-ized. Each ad worries that the real customers "aren't paid celebrities, so GEICO paid a real celebrity to help them tell their stories." The result is a set of hilarious commercials in which celebrities such as Little Richard, Peter Graves, Charro, and Burt Bacharach deliver their own unique simultaneous translations of the otherwise plain testimonials (remember Little Richard's "mashed potatoes, gravy, and cranberry sauce—wooooooo!?).

Although different, all of the minicampaigns have a distinctly GEICO flavor. And each closes strongly with the crucial "15 minutes could save you 15 percent" tagline. Also, as we've come to expect, "the ads are fun," says a branding expert. "What makes GEICO so good is that the ads entertain, deliver a message, *and* satisfy a need."

Just how good *is* GEICO's advertising? It helped earn The Martin Agency *Advertising Age's* 2006 "Top Agency A-List" designation last year. And the Caveman and Testimonials ad series were named by *Adweek* as two of the last year's top three ad campaigns. More important, 91 percent of shoppers today say that they've seen or heard at least one GEICO message, and GEICO leads the insurance industry in new customer acquisition. In each of the past five years, GEICO has experienced double-digit market share gains. Rising from relative obscurity only a dozen years ago, the upstart direct marketer now serves more than eight million customers, making it the fourth-largest insurance company, behind State Farm and Allstate, and Progressive, primarily a direct marketer.

Not only have the gecko and cavemen helped GEICO grow, they've changed the face of the auto insurance industry. Many analysts credit GEICO with changing the way insurance companies market their products in this traditionally boring category. "GEICO is spicing it up, and other companies are having to respond," says a communications consultant. "GEICO is exponentially ahead of its competitors in this category." Says another industry observer, "When your advertising has become part of the [contemporary culture], you have hit a home run."[1]

Building good customer relationships calls for more that just developing a good product, pricing it attractively, and making it available to target customers. Companies must also *communicate* their value propositions to customers, and what they communicate should not be left to chance. All of their communications must be planned and blended into carefully integrated marketing communications programs. Just as good communication is important in building and maintaining any kind of relationship, it is a crucial element in a company's efforts to build profitable customer relationships.

The Promotion Mix

A company's total **promotion mix**—also called its **marketing communications mix**—consists of the specific blend of advertising, public relations, personal selling, sales promotion, and direct-marketing tools that the company uses to persuasively communicate customer value and build customer relationships. Definitions of the five major promotion tools follow:[2]

Advertising: Any paid form of nonpersonal presentation and promotion of ideas, goods, or services by an identified sponsor

Sales promotion: Short-term incentives to encourage the purchase or sale of a product or service

Personal selling: Personal presentation by the firm's sales force for the purpose of making sales and building customer relationships

Public relations: Building good relations with the company's various publics by obtaining favorable publicity, building up a good corporate image, and handling or heading off unfavorable rumors, stories, and events

Direct marketing: Direct connections with carefully targeted individual consumers to both obtain an immediate response and cultivate lasting customer relationships—the use of direct mail, the telephone, direct-response television, e-mail, the Internet, and other tools to communicate directly with specific consumers

Each category involves specific promotional tools used to communicate with consumers. For example, advertising includes broadcast, print, Internet, outdoor, and other forms. Sales promotion includes discounts, coupons, displays, and demonstrations. Personal selling includes sales presentations, trade shows, and incentive programs. Public relations includes press releases, sponsorships, special events, and Web pages. And direct marketing includes catalogs, telephone marketing, kiosks, the Internet, and more.

At the same time, marketing communication goes beyond these specific promotion tools. The product's design, its price, the shape and color of its package, and the stores that sell it—*all* communicate something to buyers. Thus, although the promotion mix is the company's primary communication activity, the entire marketing mix—promotion *and* product, price, and place—must be coordinated for greatest communication impact.

Promotion mix (marketing communications mix)
The specific blend of advertising, public relations, personal selling, sales promotion, and direct-marketing tools that the company uses to persuasively communicate customer value and build customer relationships.

Advertising
Any paid form of nonpersonal presentation and promotion of ideas, goods, or services by an identified sponsor.

Sales promotion
Short-term incentives to encourage the purchase or sale of a product or service.

Personal selling
Personal presentation by the firm's sales force for the purpose of making sales and building customer relationships.

Public relations
Building good relations with the company's various publics by obtaining favorable publicity, building up a good "corporate image," and handling or heading off unfavorable rumors, stories, and events.

Direct marketing
Direct connections with carefully targeted individual consumers to both obtain an immediate response and cultivate lasting customer relationships.

Integrated Marketing Communications

In past decades, marketers perfected the art of mass marketing—selling highly standardized products to masses of customers. In the process, they developed effective mass-media communications techniques to support these strategies. Large companies now routinely invest millions or even billions of dollars in television, magazine, or other mass-media advertising, reaching tens of millions of customers with a single ad. Today, however, marketing managers face some new marketing communications realities. Perhaps no other area of marketing is changing so profoundly as marketing communications, creating both exciting and scary times for marketing communicators.

The New Marketing Communications Landscape

Several major factors are changing the face of today's marketing communications. First, consumers are changing. In this digital, wireless age, they are better informed and more communications empowered. Rather than relying on marketer-supplied information, they can use the Internet and other technologies to seek out information on their own. More than that, they can more easily connect with other consumers to exchange brand-related information or even to create their own marketing messages.

■ The new marketing communications landscape: The digital age has spawned a host of new information and communication tools—from cellphones and iPods to the Internet and satellite and cable television systems.

Second, marketing strategies are changing. As mass markets have fragmented, marketers are shifting away from mass marketing. More and more, they are developing focused marketing programs designed to build closer relationships with customers in more narrowly defined micromarkets. Vast improvements in information technology are speeding the movement toward segmented marketing. Today's marketers can amass detailed customer information, keep closer track of customer needs, and tailor their offerings to narrowly target groups.

Finally, sweeping changes in communications technology are causing remarkable changes in the ways in which companies and customers communicate with each other. The digital age has spawned a host of new information and communication tools—from cell phones, and iPods to the Internet and satellite and cable television systems. The new communications technologies give companies exciting new media for interacting with targeted consumers. At the same time, they give consumers more control over the nature and timing of messages they choose to send and receive.

The Shifting Marketing Communications Model

The shift toward segmented marketing and the explosive developments in information and communications technology have had a dramatic impact on marketing communications. Just as mass marketing once gave rise to a new generation of mass-media communications, the shift toward targeted marketing and the changing communications environment are giving birth to a new marketing communications model.

Although television, magazines, and other mass media remain very important, their dominance is declining. Advertisers are now adding a broad selection of more-specialized and highly targeted media to reach smaller customer segments with more-personalized messages. The new media range from specialty magazines, cable television channels, and video on demand (VOD) to Internet catalogs, e-mail, podcasts, and product placements in television programs and video games. In all, companies are doing less *broadcasting* and more *narrowcasting*.

Some advertising industry experts even predict a doom-and-gloom "chaos scenario," in which the old mass-media communications model will collapse entirely. They believe that marketers will increasingly abandon traditional mass media in favor of "the glitzy promise of new digital technologies—from Web sites and e-mail to cell phone content and video on demand. . . . Fragmentation, the bane of network TV and mass marketers everywhere, will become the Holy Grail, the opportunity to reach—and have a conversation with—small clusters of consumers who are consuming not what is force-fed them, but exactly what they want."[3]

Just think about what's happening to television viewing these days. "Adjust your set," says one reporter, "television is changing as quickly as the channels. It's on cell phones. It's on digital music players. It's on almost anything with a screen. Shows can be seen at their regular times or when you want [with or without the commercials]. Some 'TV' programs aren't even on cable or network or satellite; they're being created just for Internet viewing."[4]

Consumers, especially younger ones, appear to be turning away from the major television networks in favor of cable TV or altogether different media. According to a recent study:

> Only one in four 12- to 34-year-olds can name all four major broadcast networks: ABC, NBC, CBS, and Fox. Teens may not be able to name the big four, but they know MTV, Cartoon Network, and Comedy Central. The most popular activity? That would be surfing the Internet, which 84 percent said they did during their idle periods. Hanging out with friends came in second at 76 percent, watching movies third at 71 percent, and TV viewing fourth at 69 percent.[5]

As a result, marketers are losing confidence in television advertising. As mass media costs rise, audiences shrink, ad clutter increases, and viewers use video on demand and TiVo-like systems to skip past disruptive television commercials, many skeptics even predict the demise of the old mass-media mainstay—the 30-second television commercial. "Consider something barely imaginable," says a major "chaos scenario" proponent, a "media world substantially devoid of brand advertising as we have long known it. It's a world in which consumer engagement occurs without consumer interruption . . . in which marketing—and even branding—are conducted without much reliance on the 30-second spot. . . . Because nobody is much interested in seeing [it], and because soon [it] will be largely unnecessary."[6]

Thus, many large advertisers are shifting their advertising budgets away from network television in favor of more targeted, cost-effective, interactive, and engaging media. "The ad industry's plotline used to be a lot simpler: Audiences are splintering off in dozens of new directions, watching TV shows on iPods, watching movies on videogame players, and listening to radio on the Internet," observes one analyst. So marketers must "start planning how to reach consumers in new and unexpected ways." Says the CEO and creative director of one large ad agency, "There's no medium we don't perform in."[7]

Rather than a "chaos scenario," however, other industry insiders see a more gradual shift to the new marketing communications model. They note that broadcast television and other mass media still capture a lion's share of the promotion budgets of most major marketing firms, a fact that isn't likely to change quickly. Although some may question the future of the 30-second spot, it's still very much in use today. TV ad spending actually rose last year by more than 7 percent (although online advertising grew 25 percent). Moreover, television offers many promotional opportunities beyond the 30-second commercial. One advertising expert advises: "Because TV is at the forefront of many technological advances [such as DVRs and video on demand], its audience will continue to increase. So if you think that TV is an aging dinosaur, or you're a national advertiser who is thinking of moving ad dollars away from TV, maybe you should think again."[8]

Thus, it seems likely that the new marketing communications model will consist of a gradually shifting mix of both traditional mass media and a wide array of exciting new, more-targeted, more-personalized media. "We need to reinvent the way we market to consumers," says A.G. Lafley, chief executive of Procter & Gamble. "Mass marketing still has an important role, [but] we need new models to initially coexist with mass marketing, and eventually to succeed it."[9]

The Need for *Integrated* Marketing Communications

The shift toward a richer mix of media and communication approaches poses a problem for marketers. Consumers today are bombarded by commercial messages from a broad range of sources. But consumers don't distinguish between message sources the way marketers do. In the consumer's mind, messages from different media and promotional approaches all become part of a single message about the company. Conflicting messages from these different sources can result in confused company images, brand positions, and customer relationships.

All too often, companies fail to integrate their various communications channels. The result is a hodgepodge of communications to consumers. Mass-media advertisements say one thing, while a price promotion sends a different signal, and a product label creates still another message. Company sales literature says something altogether different, and the company's Web site seems out of sync with everything else.

The problem is that these communications often come from different parts of the company. Advertising messages are planned and implemented by the advertising department or

FIGURE 12.1
Integrated Marketing
Communications

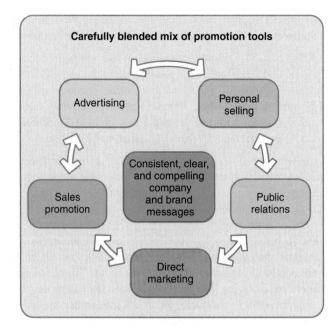

Integrated marketing communications (IMC)
Carefully integrating and coordinating the company's many communications channels to deliver a clear, consistent, and compelling message about the organization and its products.

an advertising agency. Personal selling communications are developed by sales management. Other company specialists are responsible for public relations, sales promotion events, Internet marketing, and other forms of marketing communications. However, whereas these companies have separated their communications tools, customers won't. Mixed communications from these sources will result in blurred consumer brand perceptions.

Today, more companies are adopting the concept of **integrated marketing communications (IMC)**. Under this concept, as illustrated in Figure 12.1, the company carefully integrates its many communications channels to deliver a clear, consistent, and compelling message about the organization and its brands.

IMC calls for recognizing all contact points where the customer may encounter the company and its brands. Each *brand contact* will deliver a message, whether good, bad, or indifferent. Says one advertising executive, "the world has evolved to a place where brands that need to speak to their audience have to understand that everything they do is media."[10] The company wants to deliver a consistent and positive message with each contact. IMC leads to a total marketing communication strategy aimed at building strong customer relationships by showing how the company and its products can help customers solve their problems.

IMC ties together all of the company's messages and images. The company's television and print advertisements have the same message, look, and feel as its e-mail and personal selling communications. And its public relations materials project the same image as its Web site. Often, different media play unique roles in attracting, informing, and persuading consumers, and these roles must be carefully coordinated under the overall marketing communications plan. For example, Nikon used a carefully coordinated mix of media in a recent campaign designed to demonstrate that even ordinary people can take amazing digital pictures with its Nikon D40 camera. To prove the point, Nikon gave 200 of the cameras to people in Georgetown, South Carolina, and then featured the people and their photos in TV and print ads. The ads delivered the brand message and referred consumers to a specially constructed supporting Web site (www.stunningnikon.com/picture-town), where they could explore the stories and people behind the pictures, learn more about the Nikon D40 camera, and find out where to buy one. The ads, Web site, supporting PR, and even the event itself were carefully integrated to deliver a unified message.

In the past, no one person or department was responsible for thinking through the communication roles of the various promotion tools and coordinating the promotion mix. To help implement integrated marketing communications, some companies appoint a marketing communications director who has overall responsibility for the company's communications efforts. This helps to produce better communications consistency and greater sales impact. It places the responsibility in someone's hands—where none existed before—to unify the company's image as it is shaped by thousands of company activities.

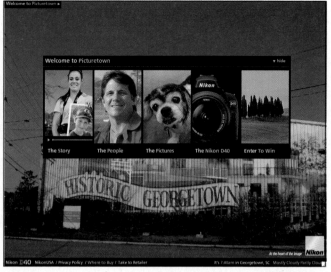

■ Integrated marketing communications: In Nikon's Picturetown campaign, TV and print ads deliver the brand message and refer consumers to a carefully integrated supporting Web site, where they can explore the stories and people behind the pictures, learn more about the Nikon D40 camera, and find out where to buy one.

Shaping the Overall Promotion Mix

The concept of integrated marketing communications suggests that the company must blend the promotion tools carefully into a coordinated *promotion mix*. But how does the company determine what mix of promotion tools it will use? Companies within the same industry differ greatly in the design of their promotion mixes. For example, Mary Kay spends most of its promotion funds on personal selling and direct marketing, whereas competitor Covergirl spends heavily on consumer advertising. HP relies on advertising and promotion through retailers, whereas Dell uses more direct marketing. We now look at factors that influence the marketer's choice of promotion tools.

The Nature of Each Promotion Tool

Each promotion tool has unique characteristics and costs. Marketers must understand these characteristics in shaping the promotion mix.

Advertising Advertising can reach masses of geographically dispersed buyers at a low cost per exposure, and it enables the seller to repeat a message many times. For example, television advertising can reach huge audiences. An estimated 93 million Americans tuned in to at least part of the most recent Super Bowl, about 39.9 million people watched at least part of the last Academy Awards broadcast, and 37.3 million fans tuned in to watch the debut episode of the fifth season of *American Idol*. For companies that want to reach a mass audience, TV is the place to be.[11]

Beyond its reach, large-scale advertising says something positive about the seller's size, popularity, and success. Because of advertising's public nature, consumers tend to view advertised products as more legitimate. Advertising is also very expressive—it allows the company to dramatize its products through the artful use of visuals, print, sound, and color. On the one hand, advertising can be used to build up a long-term image for a product (such as Coca-Cola ads). On the other hand, advertising can trigger quick sales (as when Kohl's advertises weekend specials).

Advertising also has some shortcomings. Although it reaches many people quickly, advertising is impersonal and cannot be as directly persuasive as can company salespeople. For the most part, advertising can carry on only a one-way communication with the audience, and the audience does not feel that it needs to pay attention or respond. In addition,

■ With personal selling, the customer feels a greater need to listen and respond, even if the response is a polite "No thank you."

advertising can be very costly. Although some advertising forms, such as newspaper and radio advertising, can be done on smaller budgets, other forms, such as network TV advertising, require very large budgets.

Personal Selling Personal selling is the most effective tool at certain stages of the buying process, particularly in building up buyers' preferences, convictions, and actions. It involves personal interaction between two or more people, so each person can observe the other's needs and characteristics and make quick adjustments. Personal selling also allows all kinds of customer relationships to spring up, ranging from matter-of-fact selling relationships to personal friendships. An effective salesperson keeps the customer's interests at heart in order to build a long-term relationship by solving customer problems. Finally, with personal selling, the buyer usually feels a greater need to listen and respond, even if the response is a polite "No thank you."

These unique qualities come at a cost, however. A sales force requires a longer-term commitment than does advertising—advertising can be turned on and off, but sales force size is harder to change. Personal selling is also the company's most expensive promotion tool, costing companies $329 on average per sales call. In some industries, the average cost of a sales call reaches $452.[12] U.S. firms spend up to three times as much on personal selling as they do on advertising.

Sales Promotion Sales promotion includes a wide assortment of tools—coupons, contests, cents-off deals, premiums, and others—all of which have many unique qualities. They attract consumer attention, offer strong incentives to purchase, and can be used to dramatize product offers and to boost sagging sales. Sales promotions invite and reward quick response—whereas advertising says, "Buy our product," sales promotion says, "Buy it now." Sales promotion effects are often short-lived, however, and often are not as effective as advertising or personal selling in building long-run brand preference and customer relationships.

Public Relations Public relations is very believable—news stories, features, sponsorships, and events seem more real and believable to readers than ads do. Public relations can also reach many prospects who avoid salespeople and advertisements—the message gets to the buyers as "news" rather than as a sales-directed communication. And, as with advertising, public relations can dramatize a company or product. Marketers tend to underuse public relations or to use it as an afterthought. Yet a well-thought-out public relations campaign used with other promotion mix elements can be very effective and economical.

Direct Marketing Although there are many forms of direct marketing—direct mail and catalogs, telephone marketing, online marketing, and others—they all share four distinctive characteristics. Direct marketing is *nonpublic:* The message is normally directed to a specific person. Direct marketing is *immediate* and *customized:* Messages can be prepared very quickly and can be tailored to appeal to specific consumers. Finally, direct marketing is *interactive:* It allows a dialogue between the marketing team and the consumer, and messages can be altered depending on the consumer's response. Thus, direct marketing is well suited to highly targeted marketing efforts and to building one-to-one customer relationships.

Promotion Mix Strategies

Marketers can choose from two basic promotion mix strategies—*push* promotion or *pull* promotion. Figure 12.2 contrasts the two strategies. The relative emphasis on the specific promotion tools differs for push and pull strategies. A **push strategy** involves "pushing" the product through marketing channels to final consumers. The producer directs its marketing activities (primarily personal selling and trade promotion) toward channel members to induce them to carry the product and to promote it to final consumers.

Using a **pull strategy**, the producer directs its marketing activities (primarily advertising and consumer promotion) toward final consumers to induce them to buy the product. If

Push strategy

A promotion strategy that calls for using the sales force and trade promotion to push the product through channels. The producer promotes the product to channel members to induce them to carry the product and to promote it to final consumers.

Pull strategy

A promotion strategy that calls for spending a lot on advertising and consumer promotion to induce final consumers to buy the product. If the pull strategy is effective, consumers will then demand the product from channel members, who will in turn demand it from producers.

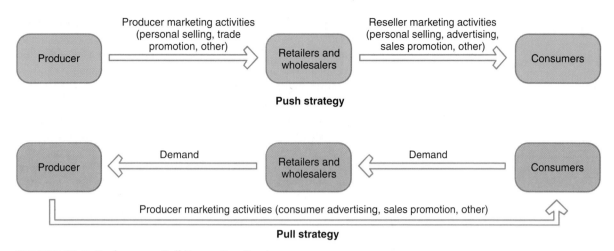

FIGURE 12.2 Push versus Pull Promotion Strategy

the pull strategy is effective, consumers will then demand the product from channel members, who will in turn demand it from producers. Thus, under a pull strategy, consumer demand "pulls" the product through the channels.

Some industrial-goods companies use only push strategies; some direct-marketing companies use only pull. However, most large companies use some combination of both. For example, Kraft uses mass-media advertising and consumer promotions to pull its products and a large sales force and trade promotions to push its products through the channels. In recent years, consumer-goods companies have been decreasing the pull portions of their mixes in favor of more push. This has caused concern that they may be driving short-run sales at the expense of long-term brand equity.

Companies consider many factors when designing their promotion mix strategies, including *type of product/market* and the *product life-cycle stage*. For example, the importance of different promotion tools varies between consumer and business markets. Business-to-consumer (B2C) companies usually "pull" more, putting more of their funds into advertising, followed by sales promotion, personal selling, and then public relations. In contrast, business-to-business (B2B) marketers tend to "push" more, putting more of their funds into personal selling, followed by sales promotion, advertising, and public relations. In general, personal selling is used more heavily with expensive and risky goods and in markets with fewer and larger sellers.

Now that we've examined the concept of integrated marketing communications and the factors that firms consider when shaping their promotion mixes, let's look more closely at the specific marketing communications tools.

Linking the Concepts

Pull over here for a few minutes. Flip back through and link the parts of the chapter you've read so far.

- How do the *integrated marketing communications (IMC)* and *promotion mix* concepts relate to one another?
- How has the changing communications environment affected the ways in which companies communicate with you about their products and services? If you were in the market for a new car, where might you hear about various available models? Where would you *search* for information?

Advertising

Advertising can be traced back to the very beginnings of recorded history. Archaeologists working in the countries around the Mediterranean Sea have dug up signs announcing various events and offers. The Romans painted walls to announce gladiator fights, and the

Phoenicians painted pictures promoting their wares on large rocks along parade routes. During the Golden Age in Greece, town criers announced the sale of cattle, crafted items, and even cosmetics. An early "singing commercial" went as follows: "For eyes that are shining, for cheeks like the dawn / For beauty that lasts after girlhood is gone / For prices in reason, the woman who knows / Will buy her cosmetics from Aesclyptos."

Modern advertising, however, is a far cry from these early efforts. U.S. advertisers now run up an estimated annual advertising bill of more than $285 billion; worldwide ad spending exceeds an estimated $604 billion. Procter & Gamble, the world's largest advertiser, last year spent $4.9 billion on U.S. advertising and $8.2 billion worldwide.[13]

Although advertising is used mostly by business firms, a wide range of not-for-profit organizations, professionals, and social agencies also use advertising to promote their causes to various target publics. In fact, the 29th-largest advertising spender is a not-for-profit organization—the U.S. government. Advertising is a good way to inform and persuade, whether the purpose is to sell Coca-Cola worldwide or to get consumers in a developing nation to use birth control.

Marketing management must make four important decisions when developing an advertising program (see Figure 12.3): *setting advertising objectives, setting the advertising budget, developing advertising strategy (message decisions and media decisions), and evaluating advertising campaigns.*

Setting Advertising Objectives

The first step is to set *advertising objectives*. These objectives should be based on past decisions about the target market, positioning, and the marketing mix, which define the job that advertising must do in the total marketing program. The overall advertising objective is to help build customer relationships by communicating customer value. Here, we discuss specific advertising objectives.

Advertising objective
A specific communication *task* to be accomplished with a specific *target* audience during a specific period of *time*.

An **advertising objective** is a specific communication *task* to be accomplished with a specific *target* audience during a specific period of *time*. Advertising objectives can be classified by primary purpose—whether the aim is to *inform, persuade,* or *remind.* Table 12.1 lists examples of each of these specific objectives.

Informative advertising is used heavily when introducing a new product category. In this case, the objective is to build primary demand. Thus, early producers of DVD players first had to inform consumers of the image quality and convenience benefits of the new product. *Persuasive advertising* becomes more important as competition increases. Here, the company's objective is to build selective demand. For example, once DVD players became established, Sony began trying to persuade consumers that *its* brand offered the best quality for their money.

Some persuasive advertising has become *comparative advertising,* in which a company directly or indirectly compares its brand with one or more other brands. Comparative advertising has been used for products ranging from soft drinks, beer, and pain relievers to com-

FIGURE 12.3 Major Advertising Decisions

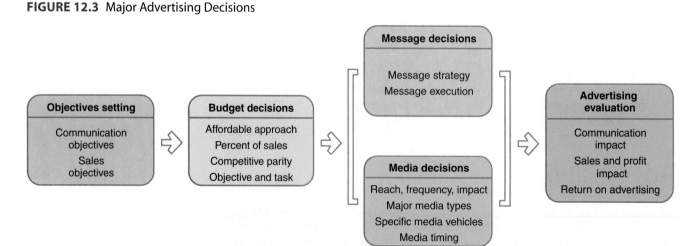

TABLE 12.1 Possible Advertising Objectives

Informative Advertising

Communicating customer value	Suggesting new uses for a product
Building a brand and company image	Informing the market of a price change
Telling the market about a new product	Describing available services and support
Explaining how the product works	Correcting false impressions

Persuasive Advertising

Building brand preference	Persuading customers to purchase now
Encouraging switching to your brand	Persuading customers to receive a sales call
Changing customer's perception of product value	Convincing customers to tell others about the brand

Reminder Advertising

Maintaining customer relationships	Reminding consumers where to buy the product
Reminding consumers that the product may be needed in the near future	Keeping the brand in customer's mind during off-seasons

puters, batteries, car rentals, and credit cards. For example, in its classic comparative campaign, Avis positioned itself against market-leading Hertz by claiming, "We try harder." And Apple's familiar "I'm a PC; I'm a MAC" ads take jabs at rival Windows-based computers.

You see examples of comparative advertising in almost every product category. For example, P&G recently ran ads comparing its Vicks NyQuil to Tylenol Cold multisymptom formula, asking "What good is 4-hour relief if you're trying to sleep for 8?" And Pizza Hut has reignited its long-running rivalry with Papa John's and Domino's with a comparative ad in which delivery drivers from the three chains gather around a table to dig into a Pizza Hut pizza. "Now this is real pizza," one driver tells the others. "Sure tastes better than Domino's," adds another. "And Papa John's," says a third. The announcer confirms that "Americans preferred Pizza Hut's pan pizza almost two to one in a national taste test."[14] Advertisers should use comparative advertising with caution. All too often, such ads invite competitor responses, resulting in an advertising war that neither competitor can win.

Reminder advertising is important for mature products—it helps to maintain customer relationships and keep consumers thinking about the product. Expensive Coca-Cola television ads primarily build and maintain the Coca-Cola brand relationship rather than informing or persuading customers to buy in the short run.

■ Comparative advertising: Recent Pizza Hut ads compare its pizzas directly with those of top competitors. "Sure tastes better than Domino's . . . and Papa John's."

Advertising's goal is to help move consumers through the buying process. Some advertising is designed to move people to immediate action. For example, a direct-response television ad by Sharper Image for its Bionic Breeze air purifier urges consumers to pick up the phone and order right away, and a Sears newspaper ad for a weekend sale encourages store visits. However, many of the other ads focus on building or strengthening long-term customer relationships. For example, a Nike television ad in which well-known athletes "just do it" never directly asks for a sale. Instead, the goal is to somehow change the way the customers think or feel about the brand.

Setting the Advertising Budget

After determining its advertising objectives, the company next sets its **advertising budget** for each product. No matter what method is used, setting the advertising budget is no easy task. Here, we look at four common methods used to set the total budget for advertising:

Advertising budget
The dollars and other resources allocated to a product or company advertising program.

the *affordable method,* the *percentage-of-sales method,* the *competitive-parity method,* and the *objective-and-task method.*[15]

Affordable method

Setting the promotion budget at the level management thinks the company can afford.

Affordable Method Some companies use the **affordable method**: They set the promotion budget at the level they think the company can afford. Small businesses often use this method, reasoning that the company cannot spend more on advertising than it has. They start with total revenues, deduct operating expenses and capital outlays, and then devote some portion of the remaining funds to advertising.

Unfortunately, this method of setting budgets completely ignores the effects of promotion on sales. It tends to place promotion last among spending priorities, even in situations in which advertising is critical to the firm's success. It leads to an uncertain annual promotion budget, which makes long-range market planning difficult. Although the affordable method can result in overspending on advertising, it more often results in underspending.

Percentage-of-sales method

Setting the promotion budget at a certain percentage of current or forecasted sales or as a percentage of the unit sales price.

Percentage-of-Sales Method Other companies use the **percentage-of-sales method**, setting their promotion budget at a certain percentage of current or forecasted sales. Or they budget a percentage of the unit sales price. The percentage-of-sales method has advantages. It is simple to use and helps management think about the relationships between promotion spending, selling price, and profit per unit.

Despite these claimed advantages, however, the percentage-of-sales method has little to justify it. It wrongly views sales as the *cause* of promotion rather than as the *result.* Although studies have found a positive correlation between promotional spending and brand strength, this relationship often turns out to be effect and cause, not cause and effect. Stronger brands with higher sales can afford the biggest ad budgets.

Thus, the percentage-of-sales budget is based on availability of funds rather than on opportunities. It may prevent the increased spending sometimes needed to turn around falling sales. Because the budget varies with year-to-year sales, long-range planning is difficult. Finally, the method does not provide any basis for choosing a *specific* percentage, except what has been done in the past or what competitors are doing.

Competitive-parity method

Setting the promotion budget to match competitors' outlays.

Competitive-Parity Method Still other companies use the **competitive-parity method**, setting their promotion budgets to match competitors' outlays. They monitor competitors' advertising or get industry promotion spending estimates from publications or trade associations, and then set their budgets based on the industry average.

Two arguments support this method. First, competitors' budgets represent the collective wisdom of the industry. Second, spending what competitors spend helps prevent promotion wars. Unfortunately, neither argument is valid. There are no grounds for believing that the competition has a better idea of what a company should be spending on promotion than does the company itself. Companies differ greatly, and each has its own special promotion needs. Finally, there is no evidence that budgets based on competitive parity prevent promotion wars.

Objective-and-task method

Developing the promotion budget by (1) defining specific objectives; (2) determining the tasks that must be performed to achieve these objectives; and (3) estimating the costs of performing these tasks. The sum of these costs is the proposed promotion budget.

Objective-and-Task Method The most logical budget-setting method is the **objective-and-task method**, whereby the company sets its promotion budget based on what it wants to accomplish with promotion. This budgeting method entails (1) defining specific promotion objectives, (2) determining the tasks needed to achieve these objectives, and (3) estimating the costs of performing these tasks. The sum of these costs is the proposed promotion budget.

The advantage of the objective-and-task method is that it forces management to spell out its assumptions about the relationship between dollars spent and promotion results. But it is also the most difficult method to use. Often, it is hard to figure out which specific tasks will achieve stated objectives. For example, suppose Sony wants 95 percent awareness for its latest camcorder model during the six-month introductory period. What specific advertising messages and media schedules should Sony use to attain this objective? How much would these messages and media schedules cost? Sony management must consider such questions, even though they are hard to answer.

Developing Advertising Strategy

Advertising strategy consists of two major elements: creating advertising *messages* and selecting advertising *media*. In the past, companies often viewed media planning as secondary to the message-creation process. The creative department first created good advertisements, and then the media department selected and purchased the best media for carrying these advertisements to desired target audiences. This often caused friction between creatives and media planners.

Today, however, soaring media costs, more-focused target marketing strategies, and the growing array of new media have promoted the importance of the media-planning function. The decision about which medium to use for an ad campaign—Web site, video on demand, cell phone, magazines, broadcast or cable television, or e-mail—is now sometimes more critical than the creative elements of the campaign. As a result, more and more, advertisers are orchestrating a closer harmony between their messages and the media that deliver them.[16]

In fact, in a really good ad campaign, you often have to ask, "Is that a media idea or a creative idea?". For example, BMW created a huge buzz for its quirky, anything-but-ordinary little British-made MINI car with an anything-but-ordinary *Let's Motor* campaign.

> The *Let's Motor* campaign employed a rich mix of unconventional media, carefully integrated to create personality for the car and a tremendous buzz of excitement among consumers. To create buzz, the company put MINIs in all kinds of imaginative places. It mounted them atop Ford Excursion SUVs and drove them around 22 major cities, highlighting the car's sensible size. It set up "MINI Ride" displays outside department stores, featuring an actual MINI that looked like a children's ride. "Rides $16,850. Quarters only," the sign said. Displays in airport terminals featured oversize newspaper vending machines and pay phones next to billboards showing the undersized MINI and proclaiming, "Makes everything else seem a little too big." The car was also promoted on the Internet, in ads painted on city buildings, and on baseball-type cards handed out at auto shows. In addition, BMW created MINI games, MINI booklets, MINI suitcases, and MINI placements in movies. It worked closely with selected magazines to create memorable print ads. For example, ads in *Wired* magazine contained a cardboard fold-out of a MINI, suggesting that readers assemble it and drive it around their desks making 'putt-putt' noises. The *Let's Motor* campaign has been a smashing success, creating an almost cultlike following for the personable little car. Were these clever

Advertising strategy
The strategy by which the company accomplishes its advertising objectives. It consists of two major elements: creating advertising messages and selecting advertising media.

■ Close media-creative partnerships: The MINI Let's Motor campaign used a rich mix of conventional and unconventional media, carefully integrated to create personality for the car and a tremendous buzz of excitement among consumers. Were these clever media ideas or clever creative ideas?

media ideas or clever creative ideas? They were both, the product of a tight media-creative partnership.

■ Advertising clutter: Today's brands are caught up in an explosion of costly clutter. Just to gain and hold attention, advertising messages must be more imaginative and entertaining—and more rewarding to consumers.

Creating the Advertising Message No matter how big the budget, advertising can succeed only if advertisements gain attention and communicate well. Good advertising messages are especially important in today's costly and cluttered advertising environment. In 1950, the average U.S. household received just three network television channels and a handful of major national magazines. Today, there seven networks and 263 subscription channels, and consumers have more than 22,000 magazines from which to choose.[17] Add the countless radio stations and a continuous barrage of catalogs, direct mail, Internet, e-mail, and online ads, and out-of-home media, and consumers are being bombarded with ads at home, at work, and at all points in between. As a result, consumers are exposed to as many as 3,000 to 5,000 commercial messages every day.[18]

Breaking Through the Clutter If all this advertising clutter bothers some consumers, it also causes huge headaches for advertisers. Take the situation facing network television advertisers. They pay an average of $381,000 to make a single 30-second commercial. Then, each time they show it, they regularly pay $250,000 or more for 30 seconds of advertising time during a popular prime-time program. They pay even more if it's an especially popular program such as *Grey's Anatomy* ($344,000), *Desperate Housewives* ($394,000), *American Idol* ($594,000 for an average spot; more than $1.3 million for the season finale), or a megaevent such as the Super Bowl ($2.6 million per 30 seconds!).[19]

Then, their ads are sandwiched in with a clutter of other commercials, announcements, and network promotions, totaling more than nearly 20 minutes of nonprogram material per prime-time hour with commercial breaks coming every six minutes on average. Such clutter in television and other ad media has created an increasingly hostile advertising environment. According to one recent study, 63 percent of Americans believe there are too many ads.[20]

Until recently, television viewers were pretty much a captive audience for advertisers. But today's digital wizardry has given consumers a rich new set of information and entertainment choices. With the growth in cable and satellite TV, the Internet, video on demand (VOD), and DVD rentals, today's viewers have many more options. Digital technology has also armed consumers with an arsenal of weapons for choosing what they watch or don't watch. Increasingly, consumers are choosing *not* to watch ads. They "zap" commercials by fast-forwarding through recorded programs. With the remote control, they mute the sound during a commercial or "zip" around the channels to see what else is on. A recent study found that 40 percent of all television viewers now switch channels when the commercial break starts.[21]

Adding to the problem is the rapid growth of DVR (digital video recorder) systems. Almost 20 percent of American homes now have DVR technology, and an estimated 39 percent will have it by 2011. Although DVRs increase total TV watching, research suggests DVR owners skip 60 percent of commercials in the recorded programs they view. One ad agency executive calls DVR systems "electronic weedwhackers." "In time, the number of people using them to obliterate commercials will totally erode faith in the 30-second commercial," he declares. Similarly, the number of VOD viewers is expected to quadruple during the next five years. These viewers will be able to watch programming on their own time terms, with or without commercials.[22]

Thus, advertisers can no longer force-feed the same old cookie-cutter ad messages to captive consumers through traditional media. Just to gain and hold attention, today's advertising messages must be better planned, more imaginative, more entertaining, and more rewarding to consumers. "Interruption or disruption as the fundamental premise of marketing" no longer works, says one advertising executive. Instead, "you have to create content that is interesting, useful, or entertaining enough to invite [consumers]." According to another, advertisers must now "draw people in. Tell a story. Encourage them to engage in it, and reward them when they do. If you do it right, they'll want to see your ads again and again."[23]

In fact, many marketers are now subscribing to a new merging of advertising and entertainment, dubbed "**Madison & Vine**." You've probably heard of Madison Avenue. It's the New York City street that houses the headquarters of many of the nation's largest advertising agencies. You may also have heard of Hollywood & Vine, the intersection of Hollywood Avenue and Vine Street in Hollywood, California, long the symbolic heart of the U.S. entertainment industry. Now, Madison Avenue and Hollywood & Vine are coming together to form a new intersection—*Madison & Vine*—that represents the merging of advertising and entertainment in an effort to break through the clutter and create new avenues for reaching consumers with more engaging messages (see Marketing at Work 12.1).

Message Strategy   The first step in creating effective advertising messages is to plan a *message strategy*—to decide what general message will be communicated to consumers. The purpose of advertising is to get consumers to think about or react to the product or company in a certain way. People will react only if they believe that they will benefit from doing so. Thus, developing an effective message strategy begins with identifying customer *benefits* that can be used as advertising appeals. Ideally, advertising message strategy will follow directly from the company's broader positioning and customer value strategies.

Message strategy statements tend to be plain, straightforward outlines of benefits and positioning points that the advertiser wants to stress. The advertiser must next develop a compelling **creative concept**—or *"big idea"*—that will bring the message strategy to life in a distinctive and memorable way. At this stage, simple message ideas become great ad campaigns. Usually, a copywriter and art director will team up to generate many creative concepts, hoping that one of these concepts will turn out to be the big idea. The creative concept may emerge as a visualization, a phrase, or a combination of the two.

The creative concept will guide the choice of specific appeals to be used in an advertising campaign. *Advertising appeals* should have three characteristics: First, they should be *meaningful,* pointing out benefits that make the product more desirable or interesting to consumers. Second, appeals must be *believable*—consumers must believe that the product or service will deliver the promised benefits.

However, the most meaningful and believable benefits may not be the best ones to feature. Appeals should also be *distinctive*—they should tell how the product is better than the competing brands. For example, the most meaningful benefit of owning a wristwatch is that it keeps accurate time, yet few watch ads feature this benefit. Instead, based on the distinctive benefits they offer, watch advertisers might select any of a number of advertising themes. For years, Timex has been the affordable watch that "Takes a lickin' and keeps on tickin'." In contrast, Fossil has featured style and fashion, whereas Rolex stresses luxury and status.

Message Execution   The advertiser now must turn the big idea into an actual ad execution that will capture the target market's attention and interest. The creative team must find the best approach, style, tone, words, and format for executing the message. Any message can be presented in different **execution styles**, such as the following:

- *Slice of life:* This style shows one or more "typical" people using the product in a normal setting. For example, a Silk soymilk "Rise and Shine" ad shows a young professional starting the day with a healthier breakfast and high hopes.
- *Lifestyle:* This style shows how a product fits in with a particular lifestyle. For example, an ad for Liquidlogic Kayaks shows kayakers challenging some serious white water and states, "2/3 of the earth is covered in playground—live wet."
- *Fantasy:* This style creates a fantasy around the product or its use. For instance, many ads are built around dream themes. One commercial for the Adidas1 shoes features a guy

Madison & Vine
A term that has come to represent the merging of advertising and entertainment in an effort to break through the clutter and create new avenues for reaching consumers with more engaging messages.

Creative concept
The compelling "big idea" that will bring the advertising message strategy to life in a distinctive and memorable way.

Execution style
The approach, style, tone, words, and format used for executing an advertising message.

12.1 MARKETING AT WORK

Madison & Vine: The New Intersection of Advertising and Entertainment

Welcome to the ever-busier intersection of Madison & Vine, where the advertising industry meets the entertainment industry. In today's cluttered advertising environment, Madison Avenue knows that it must find new ways to engage ad-weary consumers with more-compelling messages. The answer? Entertainment! And who knows more about entertainment than the folks at Hollywood & Vine? The term "Madison & Vine" has come to represent the merging of advertising and entertainment. It takes one of two primary forms: *advertainment* or *branded entertainment*.

The aim of *advertainment* is to make ads themselves so entertaining, or so useful, that people *want* to watch them. It's advertising by invitation rather than by intrusion. There's no chance that you'd watch ads on purpose, you say? Think again. For example, the Super Bowl has become an annual advertainment showcase. Tens of millions of people tune in to the Super Bowl each year, as much to watch the entertaining ads as to see the game.

And rather than bemoaning TiVo and other DVR systems, many advertisers are now using them as a new medium for showing useful or entertaining ads that consumers actually volunteer to watch. For example, GE offered a set of TiVo showcase ads, called "One Second Theater," which embedded additional entertaining material in popular GE television commercials such as "Rail" and "Singin' in the Rain" (remember the dancing elephant?). DVR users could pause the ads and see the new content in its full glory. "One Second Theater" was an unqualified success. According to GE's global director for advertising and branding, "The average time spent in a TiVo showcase by a consumer is about 83 percent of the commercial's duration. That means on average people are watching four-fifths of an ad. By comparison, the average spent on 'One Second Theater' was 352 percent of the commercial time."

Interestingly, studies show that DVR users don't necessarily skip all the ads. One study found that people who own DVRs still watch, on average, two-thirds of the ads. According to another study, 55 percent of DVR users take their finger off the fast-forward button to watch a commercial that is entertaining or relevant, sometimes even watching it more than once. "If advertising is really entertaining, you don't zap it," notes an industry observer. "You might even go out of your way to see it."

Beyond making their regular ads more entertaining, advertisers are also creating new advertising forms that look less like ads and more like short films or shows. For example, as part of a $100 million campaign to introduce its Sunsilk line of hair care products in the United States, Unilever is producing a series of two-minute short programs that resemble sitcom episodes more than ads.

The series, titled "Lovebites: Sunsilk Presents Max and Katie," is running on the TBS cable network. The miniepisodes present a humorous look at the romantic and domestic exploits of Max and

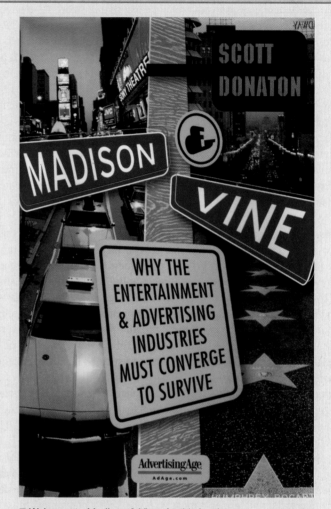

■ Welcome to Madison & Vine. As this book cover suggests, in today's cluttered advertising environment, Madison Avenue must find new ways to engage ad-weary consumers with more compelling messages. The answer? Entertainment!

Katie, a spirited and witty couple who are going through all of life's firsts. Katie—not coincidentally—is a 20-something woman right out of the Sunsilk target audience. In all, Unilever will produce 85 miniepisodes of "Max and Katie," with 65 intended for TBS and the rest to be available online, on cell phones, through e-mail, and at displays in stores. The woman at whom Sunsilk will be aimed "has grown up being marketed to her whole life," says a

dreaming he can outrun everything wearing his Adidas. It closes with the statement "Impossible is nothing."

- *Mood or image:* This style builds a mood or image around the product or service, such as beauty, love, or serenity. Few claims are made about the product except through suggestion. For example, ads for Singapore Airlines feature soft lighting and refined flight attendants pampering relaxed and happy customers.

- *Musical:* This style shows people or cartoon characters singing about the product. For example, one of the most famous ads in history was a Coca-Cola ad built around the song

Unilever marketing manager. "She's open to advertising, if it's entertaining to her."

Branded entertainment (or *brand integrations*) involves making the brand an inseparable part of some other form of entertainment. The most common form of branded entertainment is product placements—imbedding brands as props within other programming. In all, advertisers paid an estimated $3.4 billion on product placements last year, up 37 percent from the previous year. The nature of the placement can vary widely. It might be a brief glimpse of a Starbucks coffee cup sitting on a table on HBO's *Entourage,* or the judges on *American Idol* drinking out of Coca-Cola cups. Or it might involve scripting products into the theme of the program. For example, the boss of *The Office* frequents Chili's restaurant and orders his "awesome blossom, extra awesome"—in one episode, he even broke into the restaurant's catchy "baby back ribs" jingle while entertaining a client there. In another, he sings the praises of Sandals resort in Jamaica—literally. "I've got two tickets to paradise. Pack your bags, we'll leave day after tomorrow," he croons.

Costs of product placements vary widely. "A car manufacturer might be willing to pay $100,000 to $150,000 to show the mirror turns upside down," says one expert. "Going in and completely crafting a whole segment from scratch where the brand is a key player could be a million bucks." For example, blue-chip companies such as Procter & Gamble, General Motors, Staples, Unilever, and Burger King paid $1 to $4 million per episode to integrate their brands into the reality show, *The Apprentice.*

Perhaps no company has gotten more mileage out of such brand integrations than GM's Pontiac division. It all started with an extraordinary giveaway on a popular talk show:

When *The Oprah Winfrey Show* opened its 19th season with a "Wildest Dreams" theme, Oprah electrified the studio audience by giving every one of the 276 people in attendance a new, fully loaded Pontiac G6 sedan worth $28,400. The Oprah giveaway set a new benchmark in the field of branded entertainment. It cost Pontiac about $8 million but generated an estimated $20 million in unpaid media coverage and favorable PR.

Pontiac followed quickly with another stunningly successful placement, this time on *The Apprentice.* Generally viewed as the most successful *Apprentice* brand integration ever, Pontiac used the show to announce a national early-order program for its then-new Solstice two-seat roadster. In a show that included photo shoots of the sleek new car and discussions of Solstice benefits, *Apprentice* teams pulled all-nighters to create Solstice promotion brochures. The result: Pontiac's Web site traffic skyrocketed 1,400 percent the night the episode aired, and some

41,000 people registered online for a chance to place an early order. Expecting to sell 1,000 cars within 10 days, Pontiac blew by that goal in just 41 minutes after the cars went on sale the next day. In all, Pontiac chalked up 7,116 orders during the promotion, more Solstices than it planned to build for the entire year.

Originally created with TV in mind, branded entertainment has spread quickly into other sectors of the entertainment industry. It's widely used in movies—think about Ray Ban sunglasses in *Men in Black,* or the Land Rover LR3 in *Mission: Impossible III.* If you look carefully, you'll also see subtle and not-so-subtle product placements in online video games, magazines, Internet sites, and about anything else—from comic books to Broadway musicals. For example, the script for *Sweet Charity* was revised to fit Jose Cuervo's Gran Centenario tequila into a scene.

So, Madison & Vine is *the* new meeting place for the advertising and entertainment industries. When done right, advertainment and branded entertainment can pay big dividends. However, experts caution that Madison & Vine can also be a dangerous crossing. They worry that making ads too entertaining might detract from the seller's brand message—consumers will remember the clever ad but forget the brand or advertiser. And they note that the intersection is getting pretty congested. With all these new ad formats and product placements, Madison & Vine threatens to create even more of the very clutter that it's designed to break through.

They also worry about potential customer resentment and backlash. Some TV shows outright bristle with product placements. A heavily branded show like *American Idol* contains, on average, more than 66 product placement shots per hour. Last year, in total, prime-time TV bombarded viewers with nearly 80,000 "brand shout-outs." At what point will consumers decide that the intersection of Madison & Vine is just too congested and take yet a different route?

Sources: Quotes and information from Michael Applebaum, "Early Bird Apprentice Draws Solstice Buyers," *Brandweek,* March 13, 2006, pp. R4–R5; Gail Schiller, "Win, Draw for Burnett Branding," *The Hollywood Reporter,* June 1, 2005, accessed at www.hollywoodreporter.com; "Study Spots Ad-Skipping Trends," August 19, 2005, accessed at www.hollywoodreporter.com; Lynn Smith, "Television: When the Plot Pushes Product," *Los Angeles Times,* February 12, 2006, p. E5; Stuart Elliot, "A Sponsor and Its Show, Intertwined," *New York Times,* April 17, 2006, p. C8; Phil Rosenthal, "*Office* Makes Pitch to Viewers: Watch and Buy," *Chicago Tribune,* December 10, 2007; "PQ Media Market Analysis Finds Global Product Placement Grew 37% in 2006," March 14, 2007, accessed at www.pqmedia.com; "U.S. Advertising Spending Rose 4.6% in 2006 Nielsen Monitor-Plus Reports," March 19, 2007, accessed at www.nielsenmedia.com; and Louise Story, "Viewers Fast-Forwarding Pat Ads? Not Always," *New York Times,* February 16, 2007, p. 1.

"I'd Like to Teach the World to Sing." Similarly, Oscar Mayer has long run ads showing children singing its now-classic "I wish I were an Oscar Mayer wiener . . ." jingle. And is there anyone who doesn't know the Chili's advertising song, "I love my baby-back, baby-back, baby-back, . . . baby-back ribs"?

- *Personality symbol:* This style creates a character that represents the product. The character might be *animated* (Mr. Clean, Tony the Tiger, the GEICO gecko) or *real* (the Marlboro man, Ol' Lonely the Maytag repairman, or the AFLAC duck).
- *Technical expertise:* This style shows the company's expertise in making the product. Thus, Maxwell House shows one of its buyers carefully selecting coffee beans, and Jim

Koch of the Boston Beer Company tells about his many years of experience in brewing Samuel Adams beer.

- *Scientific evidence:* This style presents survey or scientific evidence that the brand is better or better liked than one or more other brands. For years, Crest toothpaste has used scientific evidence to convince buyers that Crest is better than other brands at fighting cavities.
- *Testimonial evidence or endorsement:* This style features a highly believable or likable source endorsing the product. It could be ordinary people saying how much they like a given product—as in the Sincerely, JetBlue ads. Or it might be a celebrity presenting the product. For example, Gatorade ran an ad showing how Gatorade helped triathlete Chris Legh win an Ironman triathlon victory following a near-fatal collapse a few years earlier due to dehydration.

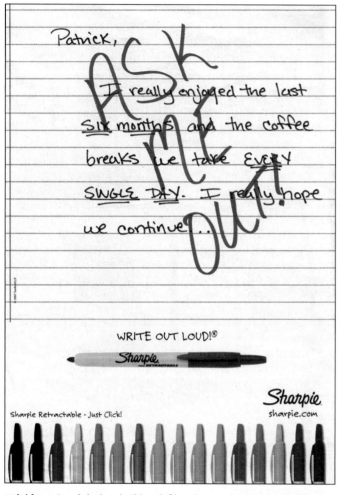

■ Ad format and design: In this ad, Sharpie uses humor along with an attention-getting layout to highlight the benefits of its colorful markers.

The advertiser also must choose a *tone* for the ad. Procter & Gamble always uses a positive tone: Its ads say something very positive about its products. P&G usually avoids humor that might take attention away from the message. In contrast, many advertisers now use edgy humor to break through the commercial clutter. For example, nine of *USA Today*'s ten most popular Super Bowl ads last year employed humor. Six of those nine were Bud Light or Budweiser ads.

The advertiser must use memorable and attention-getting *words* in the ad. For example, rather than claiming simply that "a BMW is a well-engineered automobile," BMW uses more creative and higher-impact phrasing: "The ultimate driving machine." Instead of stating that "K9 Advantix is a topical serum that keeps ticks, fleas, and mosquitoes off your dog," Bayer states it more colorfully—with K9 Advantix, "There ain't no bugs on me!" The World Wildlife Fund doesn't say, "We need your money to help save nature." Instead, it says, "We share the sky. We share the future. Together, we can be a force of nature."

Finally, *format* elements make a difference in an ad's impact as well as in its cost. A small change in ad design can make a big difference in its effect. In a print ad, the *illustration* is the first thing the reader notices—it must be strong enough to draw attention. Next, the *headline* must effectively entice the right people to read the copy. Finally, the *copy*—the main block of text in the ad—must be simple but strong and convincing. Moreover, these three elements must effectively work *together* to persuasively present customer value.

Consumer-Generated Messages Taking advantage of today's interactive technologies, many companies are now tapping consumers for message ideas or actual ads. They are searching existing video sites, setting up their own sites, and sponsoring ad-creation contests and other promotions.

Sometimes, marketers capitalize on consumer videos that are already posted on sites hosted by YouTube, MySpace, Google, and Yahoo!. For example, one of the most viewed amateur videos on the Web last year showed Diet Coke mixed with Mentos candies to produce shooting fountains of soda. The video produced a windfall of free buzz for Coca-Cola. To gain even more mileage, Coca-Cola hired the amateur videographers—a professional juggler and a lawyer—to create another video and to star in a 30-second Coke ad.[24]

Other marketers hold contests or develop brand Web sites of their own that invite consumers to submit ad message ideas and videos. For example, MasterCard sponsored a campaign last spring to create a new consumer-developed MasterCard "Priceless" television ad. Consumers visited the MasterCard lifestyle site (www.priceless.com—"Your Daily Guide to Life's Adventures") and filled in the blanks on preset video images to create their own ads. MasterCard received 100,000 submissions and later aired the ad with the winning text on regular television.

Similarly, Frito-Lay's Doritos brand held a "Crash the Super Bowl Challenge" contest that invited consumers to create their own video ads about the tasty triangular corn chips. Doritos received 1,080 user-generated videos and posted the top five on the contest Web site, where consumers could view the ads and vote for a winner. The five finalists received a $10,000 prize and Frito-Lay showed two winning ads during the Super Bowl. The campaign was a smashing success. A user-generated Doritos ad placed fifth in *USA Today* Ad Meter's most popular Super Bowl ad ratings, and Doritos received a heap of pre- and post-Super Bowl buzz surrounding the contest and the finalist ads.[25]

Not all consumer-generated advertising efforts are so successful. In fact, it can be downright dangerous to give consumers too much creative freedom and control. For example, when Chevrolet ran a promotion for its Tahoe SUV allowing consumers to write their own text for video clips of the vehicle, it got some unexpected negative results. Many of the user-created ads contained critical gibes about the big SUV's poor gas mileage, high operating costs, and harmful environmental impact. Thus, marketers should be cautious when inviting consumer creative inputs. MasterCard, for example, monitors all entries to Priceless.com and posts only suitable ones. "They don't go up live, like on YouTube," says a MasterCard marketer.[26]

If used carefully, however, consumer-generated advertising efforts can produce big benefits. First, for relatively little expense, companies can collect new creative ideas, as well as fresh perspectives on the brand and what it actually means to consumers. "Companies have [their own] vision of what they want their brand to be," says the founder of adcandy.com, a Web site that solicits consumer ideas for product and company taglines. "But if everyone is saying your brand is something else, it may be a battle. Powerful things come from the street, from the people who use the product."[27]

Second, consumer-generated message campaigns can boost consumer involvement and get consumers talking and thinking about a brand and its value to them. Not only do marketers get "a peek into the public's consciousness and what they are thinking . . . [but] by participating and interacting, [consumers] develop a vested interest in your brand," says the adcandy.com founder. Adds a Doritos' marketer, "The return on investment is engagement with the brand."[28]

■ Consumer-generated messages: The Dorito's "Crash the Super Bowl Challenge" contest invited consumers to create their own video ads. Frito-Lay showed winning ads during the Super Bowl.

Selecting Advertising Media   The major steps in **advertising media** selection are (1) deciding on *reach, frequency,* and *impact;* (2) choosing among major *media types;* (3) selecting specific *media vehicles;* and (4) deciding on *media timing.*

Advertising media
The vehicles through which advertising messages are delivered to their intended audiences.

Deciding on Reach, Frequency, and Impact   To select media, the advertiser must decide on the reach and frequency needed to achieve advertising objectives. *Reach* is a measure of the *percentage* of people in the target market who are exposed to the ad campaign during a given period of time. For example, the advertiser might try to reach 70 percent of the target market during the first three months of the campaign. *Frequency* is a measure of how many *times* the average person in the target market is exposed to the message. For example, the advertiser might want an average exposure frequency of three.

But advertisers want to do more than just reach a given number of consumers a specific number of times. The advertiser also must decide on the desired *media impact*—the *qualitative value* of a message exposure through a given medium. For example, the same message in one magazine (say, *Newsweek*) may be more believable than in another (say, the *National Enquirer*). For products that need to be demonstrated, messages on television may have more impact than messages on radio because television uses sight *and* sound. Products for which consumers provide input on design or features might be better promoted at a Web site than in a direct mailing.

More generally, the advertiser wants to choose media that will *engage* consumers rather than simply reach them. For example, for television advertising, "how relevant a program is for its audience and where the ads are inserted are likely to be much more important than whether the program was a Nielsen winner" numbers-wise, says one expert. "This is about 'lean to' TV rather than 'lean back'." Although Nielsen is beginning to measure levels of television *media engagement*, such measures are hard to come by for most media. "All the measurements we have now are media metrics: ratings, readership, listenership, click-through rates," says an executive of the Advertising Research Foundation, but engagement "happens inside the consumer, not inside the medium. What we need is a way to determine how the targeted prospect connected with, got engaged with, the brand idea. With engagement, you're on your way to a relationship. . . ."[29]

Choosing Among Major Media Types The media planner must know the reach, frequency, and impact of each of the major media types. As summarized in Table 12.2, the major media types are television, newspapers, direct mail, magazines, radio, outdoor, and the Internet. Advertisers can also choose from a wide array of new digital media, such as cell phones and other digital devices, that reach consumers directly. Each medium has advantages and limitations. Media planners consider many factors when making their media choices. They want to choose media that will effectively and efficiently present the advertising message to target customers. Thus, they must consider each medium's impact, message effectiveness, and cost.

The mix of media must be reexamined regularly. For a long time, television and magazines dominated in the media mixes of national advertisers, with other media often neglected. However, as discussed previously, the media mix appears to be shifting. As mass-media costs rise, audiences shrink, and exciting new digital media emerge, many advertisers are finding new ways to reach consumers. They are supplementing the traditional

TABLE 12.2 Profiles of Major Media Types	Medium	Advantages	Limitations
	Television	Good mass-marketing coverage; low cost per exposure; combines sight, sound, and motion; appealing to the senses	High absolute costs; high clutter; fleeting exposure; less audience selectivity
	Newspapers	Flexibility; timeliness; good local market coverage; broad acceptability; high believability	Short life; poor reproduction quality; small pass-along audience
	Direct mail	High audience selectivity; flexibility; no ad competition within the same medium; allows personalization	Relatively high cost per exposure; "junk mail" image
	Magazines	High geographic and demographic selectivity; credibility and prestige; high-quality reproduction; long life and good pass-along readership	Long ad purchase lead time; high cost; no guarantee of position
	Radio	Good local acceptance; high geographic and demographic selectivity; low cost	Audio only, fleeting exposure; low attention ("the half-heard" medium); fragmented audiences
	Outdoor	Flexibility; high repeat exposure; low cost; low message competition; good positional selectivity	Little audience selectivity; creative limitations
	Internet	High selectivity; low cost; immediacy; interactive capabilities	Relatively low impact; audience controls exposure

mass media with more-specialized and highly targeted media that cost less, target more effectively, and engage consumers more fully.

For example, cable television and satellite television systems are booming. Such systems allow narrow programming formats such as all sports, all news, nutrition, arts, home improvement and gardening, cooking, travel, history, finance, and others that target select groups. Time Warner, Comcast, and other cable operators are even testing systems that will let them target specific types of ads to specific neighborhoods or to specific types of customers. For example, ads for a Spanish-language newspaper would run only in Hispanic neighborhoods, or only pet owners would see ads from pet food companies.

Advertisers can take advantage of such "narrowcasting" to "rifle in" on special market segments rather than use the "shotgun" approach offered by network broadcasting. Cable and satellite television media seem to make good sense. But, increasingly, ads are popping up in far-less-likely places. In their efforts to find less-costly and more-highly targeted ways to reach consumers, advertisers have discovered a dazzling collection of "alternative media." These days, no matter where you go or what you do, you will probably run into some new form of advertising.[30]

Tiny billboards attached to shopping carts, ads on shopping bags, and advertising decals on supermarket floors urge you to buy Jell-O Pudding Pops or Pampers, while ads roll by on the store's checkout conveyor touting your local Volvo dealer. Even the supermarket eggs are stamped with the names of CBS television shows. Step outside and there goes a city trash truck sporting an ad for Glad trash bags. You escape to the ballpark, only to find billboard-size video screens running Budweiser ads while a blimp with an electronic message board circles lazily overhead. How about a quiet trip in the country? Sorry—you find an enterprising farmer using his milk cows as four-legged billboards mounted with ads for Ben & Jerry's ice cream.

These days, you're likely to find ads—well, anywhere. Boats cruise along public beaches flashing advertising messages for Sundown Sunscreen as sunbathers spread their towels over ads for Snapple pressed into the sand. Taxi cabs sport electronic messaging signs tied to GPS location sensors that can pitch local stores and restaurants wherever they roam. Ad space is being sold on DVD cases, parking-lot tickets, subway turnstiles, golf scorecards, delivery trucks, pizza boxes, gas pumps, ATMs, municipal garbage cans, police cars, doctors' examining tables, and church bulletins. One agency even leases space on the foreheads of college students for temporary advertising tattoos. And the group meeting at the office water cooler has a new member—a "coolertising" ad sitting on top of the water cooler jug trying to start up a conversation about the latest episode of *American Idol*.

■ Marketers have discovered a dazzling collection of "alternative media."

Such alternative media seem a bit far-fetched, and they sometimes irritate consumers who resent it all as "ad nauseam." But for many marketers, these media can save money and provide a way to hit selected consumers where they live, shop, work, and play. Of course, all this may leave you wondering if there are any commercial-free havens remaining for ad-weary consumers. Public elevators, perhaps, or stalls in a public restroom? Forget it! Each has already been invaded by innovative marketers.

Another important trend affecting media selection is the rapid growth in the number of "media multitaskers," people who absorb more than one medium at a time:[31]

It looks like people who aren't satisfied with "just watching TV" are in good company. According to a recent survey, three-fourths of U.S. TV viewers read the newspaper while they watch TV, and two-thirds of them go online during their

TV time. According to the study, 70 percent of media users say they at one time or another try to absorb two or more forms of media at once. What's more, if today's kids are any indication, media multitasking is on the rise. Americans aged 8 to 18 are managing to cram an average 8.5 hours of media consumption into 6.5 hours. It's not uncommon to find a teenage boy chasing down photos of Keira Knightly on Google, IMing several friends at once, listening to a mix of music on iTunes, and talking on the cell phone to a friend all the while, in the midst of the multimedia chaos, trying to complete an essay he's got open in a Word file a few layers down on his desktop.

Media planners need to take such media interactions into account when selecting the types of media they will use.

Selecting Specific Media Vehicles   The media planner now must choose the best *media vehicles*—specific media within each general media type. For example, television vehicles include *Scrubs* and *ABC World News Tonight*. Magazine vehicles include *Newsweek, Vogue,* and *ESPN The Magazine.*

Media planners must compute the cost per thousand persons reached by a vehicle. For example, if a full-page, four-color advertisement in the U.S. national edition of *Newsweek* costs $231,525 and *Newsweek's* readership is 3.1 million people, the cost of reaching each group of 1,000 persons is about $75. The same advertisement in *BusinessWeek* may cost only $104,300 but reach only 900,000 persons—at a cost per thousand of about $115. The media planner ranks each magazine by cost per thousand and favors those magazines with the lower cost per thousand for reaching target consumers.[32]

The media planner must also consider the costs of producing ads for different media. Whereas newspaper ads may cost very little to produce, flashy television ads can be very costly. For example, a typical television commercial might cost $500,000 to $1 million or more to produce. And a few years ago, a two-minute Chanel No. 5 commercial featuring Nicole Kidman and filmed by the director of *Moulin Rouge,* Baz Luhrmann, cost an almost unimaginable $14 million to create. Interestingly, the consumer-generated Doritos Super Bowl ad mentioned previously cost just $12.79, mostly spent on the bags of Doritos used in the ad.[33] There must be a lesson there somewhere for professional ad makers.

In selecting specific media vehicles, the media planner must balance media costs against several media effectiveness factors. First, the planner should evaluate the media vehicle's *audience quality*. For a Huggies disposable diapers advertisement, for example, *Parenting* magazine would have a high exposure value; *Maxim* would have a low-exposure value. Second, the media planner should consider *audience engagement*. Readers of *Vogue,* for example, typically pay more attention to ads than do *Newsweek* readers. Third, the planner should assess the vehicle's *editorial quality*—*Time* and the *Wall Street Journal* are more believable and prestigious than *Star* or the *National Enquirer*.

Deciding on Media Timing   The advertiser must also decide how to schedule the advertising over the course of a year. Suppose sales of a product peak in December and drop in March. The firm can vary its advertising to follow the seasonal pattern, to oppose the seasonal pattern, or to be the same all year. Most firms do some seasonal advertising. For example, The Picture People, the national chain of portraits studios, advertises more heavily before major holidays such as Christmas, Easter, and Valentine's Day. Some marketers do *only* seasonal advertising: For instance, Hallmark advertises its greeting cards only before major holidays.

Finally, the advertiser must choose the pattern of the ads. *Continuity* means scheduling ads evenly within a given period. *Pulsing* means scheduling ads unevenly over a given time period. Thus, 52 ads could either be scheduled at one per week during the year or pulsed in several bursts. The idea behind pulsing is to advertise heavily for a short period to build awareness that carries over to the next advertising period. Those who favor pulsing feel that it can be used to achieve the same impact as a steady schedule but at a much lower cost. However, some media planners believe that although pulsing achieves minimal awareness, it sacrifices depth of advertising communications.

Evaluating Advertising Effectiveness and Return on Advertising Investment

Advertising accountability and **return on advertising investment** have become hot issues for most companies. Two separate recent studies show that advertising effectiveness has fallen 40 percent over the past decade and that 37.3 percent of advertising budgets are wasted. This leaves top management and many companies asking their marketing managers, "How do we know that we're spending the right amount on advertising?" and "What return are we getting on our advertising investment?" According to a recent survey by the Association of National Advertisers (ANA), measuring advertising's efficiency and effectiveness is the number-one issue in the minds of today's advertisers.[34]

Return on advertising investment
The net return on advertising investment divided by the costs of the advertising investment.

Advertisers should regularly evaluate two types of advertising results: the communication effects and the sales and profit effects. Measuring the *communication effects* of an ad or ad campaign tells whether the ads and media are communicating the ad message well. Individual ads can be tested before or after they are run. Before an ad is placed, the advertiser can show it to consumers, ask how they like it, and measure message recall or attitude changes resulting from it. After an ad is run, the advertiser can measure how the ad affected consumer recall or product awareness, knowledge, and preference. Pre- and postevaluations of communication effects can be made for entire advertising campaigns as well.

Advertisers have gotten pretty good at measuring the communication effects of their ads and ad campaigns. However, *sales and profit* effects of advertising are often much harder to measure. For example, what sales and profits are produced by an ad campaign that increases brand awareness by 20 percent and brand preference by 10 percent? Sales and profits are affected by many factors besides advertising—such as product features, price, and availability.

One way to measure the sales and profit effects of advertising is to compare past sales and profits with past advertising expenditures. Another way is through experiments. For example, to test the effects of different advertising spending levels, Coca-Cola could vary the amount it spends on advertising in different market areas and measure the differences in the resulting sales and profit levels. More complex experiments could be designed to include other variables, such as differences in the ads or media used.

However, because so many factors affect advertising effectiveness, some controllable and others not, measuring the results of advertising spending remains an inexact science. For example, dozens of advertisers spend lavishly on high-profile Super Bowl ads each year. Although they sense that the returns are worth the sizable investment, few could actually measure or prove it (see Marketing at Work 12.2). A recent survey of marketing and advertising agency executives concluded that 76 percent of marketers don't measure return on investment because it's just too difficult to measure.[35] The ANA study cited earlier asked advertising managers if they would be able to "forecast the impact on sales" of a 10 percent cut in advertising spending—63 percent said no.

"Marketers are tracking all kinds of data and they still can't answer basic questions" about advertising accountability, says a marketing analyst, "because they don't have real models and metrics by which to make sense of it."[36] Thus, although the situation is improving as marketers seek more answers, managers often must rely on large doses of judgment along with quantitative analysis when assessing advertising performance.

Other Advertising Considerations

In developing advertising strategies and programs, the company must address two additional questions. First, how will the company organize its advertising function—who will perform which advertising tasks? Second, how will the company adapt its advertising strategies and programs to the complexities of international markets?

Organizing for Advertising Different companies organize in different ways to handle advertising. In small companies, advertising might be handled by someone in the sales department. Large companies set up advertising departments whose job it is to set the advertising budget, work with the ad agency, and handle other advertising not done by the

12.2 MARKETING AT WORK

The Super Bowl: The Mother of All Advertising Events. But Is It Worth It?

The Super Bowl is the mother of all advertising events. Each year, dozens of blue chip advertisers showcase some of their best work to huge audiences around the world. But all this doesn't come cheap. Last year, major advertisers plunked down an average of $2.6 million per 30-second spot, and over the past two decades, they've spent a colossal $1.72 billion on just 11 hours of Super Bowl advertising time. But that's just for the air time. Throw in ad production costs—often $1 million or more per showcase commercial—and running even a single Super Bowl ad becomes a superexpensive proposition. Anheuser-Busch ran *10* spots last year.

So every year, as the Super Bowl season nears, up pops the BIG QUESTION: Is Super Bowl advertising worth all that money? Does it deliver a high advertising ROI? As it turns out, there's no easy answer to the question.

Advertiser and industry expert opinion varies widely. Super Bowl stalwarts such as Anheuser-Busch, FedEx, General Motors, CareerBuilder, Diamond Foods, and the Frito-Lay and Pepsi-Cola divisions of PepsiCo must think it's a good investment—they come back year after year. But what about savvy marketers such as P&G and Unilever, who opted out last year? In a survey of board members of the National Sports Marketing Network, 31 percent said they would recommend Super Bowl ads. But 41 percent said no—Super Bowl ads just aren't worth the money.

The naysayers make some pretty good arguments. Super Bowl advertising is outrageously expensive. Advertisers pay 85 percent more per viewer than they'd pay using prime-time network programming. And that $2.6 million would buy a lot of alternative media—for example, 50 different product placements in movies, TV shows, and video games; or two massive billboards in New York's Times Square that would be seen by a million people each day for a year. Beyond the cost, the competition for attention during the Super Bowl is fierce. Every single ad represents the best efforts of a major marketer trying to design a knock-your-socks-off spectacular that will reap high ratings from both critics and consumers. Many advertisers feel they can get more for their advertising dollar in venues that aren't so crowded with bigger-than-life commercials.

Then there's the question of strategic fit. Whereas the Super Bowl might be a perfect advertising event for big-budget companies selling beer, snacks, soft drinks, or sporting goods, it simply doesn't fit the pocketbooks or creative strategies of many other companies and their brands. One media executive likens a Super Bowl ad to a trophy wife:

■ Super Bowl ROI: The Super Bowl plays to a huge and receptive audience—90 million viewers who put away their DVR remotes and watch it live, glued to their screens, ads and all. But is the advertising worth the huge cost?

"It makes sense if you are an advertiser with a huge budget," he says. "But if you're an advertiser with a modest budget, that would not be the best use of your money."

Advertising agency

A marketing services firm that assists companies in planning, preparing, implementing, and evaluating all or portions of their advertising programs.

agency. Most large companies use outside advertising agencies because they offer several advantages.

How does an **advertising agency** work? Advertising agencies were started in the mid- to late-1800s by salespeople and brokers who worked for the media and received a commission for selling advertising space to companies. As time passed, the salespeople began to help customers prepare their ads. Eventually, they formed agencies and grew closer to the advertisers than to the media.

Today's agencies employ specialists who can often perform advertising tasks better than the company's own staff can. Agencies also bring an outside point of view to solving the company's problems, along with lots of experience from working with different clients and situations. So, today, even companies with strong advertising departments of their own use advertising agencies.

As for creative fit, consider Unilever's Dove. Two years ago, the company ran a sentimental 45-second commercial from the Dove "Campaign for Real Beauty." The ad was highly rated by consumers and it created considerable buzz—some 400 million impressions of the ad before and after its single appearance on the Super Bowl. But much of that buzz came from publicity surrounding the issue of girls' self esteem rather than the product. And research showed that the ad produced low levels of involvement with the brand message. Dove got almost equal exposure numbers and more engagement for a lot less money from an outdoor campaign that it ran that same year, and it got a much larger online response from its viral "Dove Evolution" film, which incurred no media cost at all. "The Super Bowl really isn't the right environment for Dove," says a Unilever executive. Last year, instead, Dove opted to run a consumer-generated ad during the more-female-oriented Academy Awards, an event where beauty brands thrive.

Still, the Super Bowl has a lot to offer the right advertisers. It's the most-watched TV event of the year. It plays to a huge and receptive audience—90 million viewers who put away their DVR remotes and watch it live, glued to their screens, ads and all. In fact, to many viewers, the Super Bowl ads are more important than what happens on the gridiron. Last year, the game itself drew an average 41.6 rating; the ads drew 41.22. "There is no other platform quite like the Super Bowl," says the chief creative officer at Anheuser-Busch. "It's worth it. When you can touch that many households [with that kind of impact] in one sitting, it's actually efficient."

What's more, for most advertisers, the Super Bowl ad itself is only the centerpiece of something much bigger. Long after the game is over, ad critics, media pundits, and consumers are still re-viewing, rehashing, and rating the commercials. It's one of the few sports-related events where "it ain't over when it's over." Thus, measuring the effectiveness of Super Bowl advertising involves a lot more than just measuring eyeballs and reach. "Those 30 seconds of fame are only the tip of the iceberg," says the analyst, "with online views, water-cooler chatter, blog buzz, and *USA Today*'s ratings all below the surface."

"The Super Bowl is the only media property where the advertising is as big a story as the content of the show," says Steven Schreibman, VP of advertising and brand management for Nationwide Financial, "so you want to see how much you can leverage it." Schreibman is still agog over the response to Nationwide's Super Bowl spot last year that featured the hunk Fabio demonstrating that "life comes at you fast." Months afterward, consumers were still visiting Web sites such as ifilm.com to watch the commercial. "We got 1.8 million downloads on [just] that one site," says Schreibman. "Fabio himself keeps me apprised of that."

Advertisers don't usually sit back and just hope that consumers will talk about their ads. They build events that help to boost the buzz. For example, last year, leading up to the Super Bowl, at least three advertisers—GM's Chevrolet Division, the NFL, and Doritos—held contests inviting consumers to create their own Super Bowl ads. As noted previously, Doritos' "Crash the Super Bowl Challenge" contest produced more than 1,000 quality entries, considerable media attention, and a bunch of online consumer interest. The winning ad topped the IAG Top 10 Best-Liked Super Bowl Ads list and came in fourth in the *USA Today* Ad Meter rankings.

The Super Bowl's largest advertiser, Anheuser-Busch, extended the festivities far beyond game day. It followed up with a postgame e-mail campaign to keep the fires burning. It also hosted a designated Web site, bud.tv, where consumers could view all of the company's Super Bowl ads and vote for their favorites via the Web site or text messages.

So—back to the original question. Is the Super Bowl advertising really worth the huge investment? It seems that there's no definitive answer—for some advertisers it's "yes"; for others, "no." The real trick is in trying to measure the returns. As the title of one recent article asserts, "Measuring Bowl Return? Good Luck!" The writer's conclusion: "For all the time, energy, and angst marketers spend crafting the perfect Super Bowl spot, [that's] a relative breeze compared to trying to prove its return on investment."

Sources: Quotes and other information from Claire Atkinson, "Measuring Bowl ROI? Good Luck," *Advertising Age,* January 29, 2007, p. 9; Lacey Rose, "Is a Super Bowl Ad a Super Deal?" *Forbes,* January 30, 2007, accessed at www.forbes.com; Angus Loten, "The Best Ads $2.6 Million Can Buy," *Inc.,* February 2, 2007, accessed at www.inc.com; Jack Neff, "P&G, Unilever Sit Out the Super Bowl," *Advertising Age,* January 29, 2007, pp. 1, 36; "IAG Top 10 Best-Liked Super Bowl Ads," *Advertising Age,* February 8, 2007, accessed at http://adage.com/superbowl07/article?article_id=114692; Stuart Elliott, "30 Seconds of Fame at Super Bowl XLI Will Cost $2.6 Million," *New York Times,* January 5, 2007, p. C3; and Stuart Elliott, "Multiplying the Payoffs from a Super Bowl Spot," *New York Times,* January 26, 2007, p. C2.

Some ad agencies are huge—the largest U.S. agency, BBDO Worldwide, has worldwide annual gross revenue of more than $1.5 billion. In recent years, many agencies have grown by gobbling up other agencies, thus creating huge agency holding companies. The largest of these agency "megagroups," Omnicom Group, includes several large advertising, public relations, and promotion agencies with combined worldwide revenues of almost $11.4 billion.[37] Most large advertising agencies have the staff and resources to handle all phases of an advertising campaign for their clients, from creating a marketing plan to developing ad campaigns and preparing, placing, and evaluating ads.

International Advertising Decisions International advertisers face many complexities not encountered by domestic advertisers. The most basic issue concerns the degree to which global advertising should be adapted to the unique characteristics of various country markets. Some large advertisers have attempted to support their global brands with highly standardized worldwide advertising, with campaigns that work as well in Bangkok as they do in Baltimore. For example, McDonald's now unifies its creative elements and brand presentation under the familiar "I'm lovin' it" theme in all of its 100-plus markets worldwide. Coca-Cola coordinates worldwide advertising for its flagship brand under the theme, "The Coke Side of Life." Ads for Gillette Venus razors are almost identical worldwide, with only minor adjustments to suit the local culture.

In recent years, the increased popularity of online social networks and video sharing has boosted the need for advertising standardization for global brands. Most big marketing and advertising campaigns include a large online presence. Connected consumers can now zip easily across borders via the Internet, making it difficult for advertisers to roll out adapted campaigns in a controlled, orderly fashion. As a result, at the very least, most global consumer brands coordinate their Web sites internationally. For example, check out the McDonald's Web sites from Germany to Jordan to China and you'll find the Golden Arches logo, the "I'm lovin it" logo and jingle, a Big Mac equivalent, and maybe even Ronald McDonald himself.

Standardization produces many benefits—lower advertising costs, greater global advertising coordination, and a more consistent worldwide image. But it also has drawbacks. Most importantly, it ignores the fact that country markets differ greatly in their cultures, demographics, and economic conditions. Thus, most international advertisers "think globally but act locally." They develop global advertising *strategies* that make their worldwide advertising efforts more efficient and consistent. Then they adapt their advertising *programs* to make them more responsive to consumer needs and expectations within local markets. For example, Apple uses "I'm a Mac; I'm a PC" commercials in many countries. In some markets, such as Spain, France, Germany, and Italy, it uses U.S. versions of the ads dubbed in the local language. However, it rescripts and reshoots the ads to fit the Japanese culture.

What's funny in one culture can seem ill-mannered in another. In the American ads, a nerdy PC guy keeps getting trumped by his hip Mac counterpart, who uses pointed banter that demonstrates how Macs are better. But in Japanese culture, where direct-comparison ads have long been frowned upon, it's rude to brag about one's strengths. So Japanese versions of the ads include subtle changes to emphasize that Macs and PCs are not that different. Instead of clothes that cast PC clearly as a nerd and Mac as a hipster, PC wears plain office attire and Mac weekend fashion, highlighting the work/home divide between the devices more than personality differences. In the first ad of the series, Mac even gives PC a nickname: waaku—a playful Japanese version of the word "work." PC's body language is a big source of the humor in Japan: Mac looks embarrassed when the

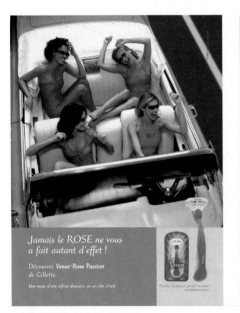

■ Standardized worldwide advertising: Gillette's ads for its Gillette for Women Venus razors are almost identical worldwide, with only minor adjustments to suit the local culture.

PC touches his shoulder or hides behind Mac's legs to avoid viruses. "PC constantly makes friendship-level approaches that Mac rejects in a friendly-irritated way," says a Tokyo brand consultant. "The Western Mac ads would backfire in Japan, because the Mac would appear to lack class." In fact, the jury is still out on whether even the toned-down comparative ads will work there.[38]

Global advertisers face several special problems. For instance, advertising media costs and availability differ vastly from country to country. Countries also differ in the extent to which they regulate advertising practices. Many countries have extensive systems of laws restricting how much a company can spend on advertising, the media used, the nature of advertising claims, and other aspects of the advertising program. Such restrictions often require advertisers to adapt their campaigns from country to country.

For example, alcoholic products cannot be advertised in India or in Muslim countries. In many countries, Sweden and Norway, for example, food ads are banned from kids' TV. To play it safe, McDonald's advertises itself as a family restaurant in Sweden. Comparative ads, although acceptable and even common in the United States and Canada, are less commonly used in the United Kingdom and illegal in India and Brazil. China bans sending e-mail for advertising purposes to people without their permission and all advertising e-mail that is sent must be titled "advertisement."

China also has restrictive censorship rules for TV and radio advertising; for example, the words *the best* are banned, as are ads that "violate social customs" or present women in "improper ways." McDonald's once avoided government sanctions there by publicly apologizing for an ad that crossed cultural norms by showing a customer begging for a discount. Similarly, Coca-Cola's Indian subsidiary was forced to end a promotion that offered prizes, such as a trip to Hollywood, because it violated India's established trade practices by encouraging customers to buy in order to "gamble."[39]

Thus, although advertisers may develop global strategies to guide their overall advertising efforts, specific advertising programs must usually be adapted to meet local cultures and customs, media characteristics, and advertising regulations.

Linking the Concepts

Think about what goes on behind the scenes for the ads we all tend to take for granted.

- Pick a favorite print or television ad. Why do you like it? Do you think that it's effective? Can you think of an ad that people like that may not be effective?
- Dig a little deeper and learn about the campaign *behind* your ad. What are the campaign's objectives? What is its budget? Assess the campaign's message and media strategies. Looking beyond your own feelings about the ad, is the campaign likely to be effective?

Public Relations

Another major mass-promotion tool is public relations—building good relations with the company's various publics by obtaining favorable publicity, building up a good corporate image, and handling or heading off unfavorable rumors, stories, and events. Public relations departments may perform any or all of the following functions:[40]

- *Press relations or press agency:* Creating and placing newsworthy information in the news media to attract attention to a person, product, or service
- *Product publicity:* Publicizing specific products
- *Public affairs:* Building and maintaining national or local community relations
- *Lobbying:* Building and maintaining relations with legislators and government officials to influence legislation and regulation
- *Investor relations:* Maintaining relationships with shareholders and others in the financial community
- *Development:* Public relations with donors or members of nonprofit organizations to gain financial or volunteer support

Public relations is used to promote products, people, places, ideas, activities, organizations, and even nations. Companies use public relations to build good relations with consumers, investors, the media, and their communities. Trade associations have used public relations to rebuild interest in declining commodities such as eggs, apples, milk, and potatoes. The state of New York turned its image around when its "I ♥ New York!" publicity and advertising campaign took root, bringing in millions more tourists. Johnson & Johnson's masterly use of public relations played a major role in saving Tylenol from extinction after its product-tampering scare. Nations have used public relations to attract more tourists, foreign investment, and international support.

The Role and Impact of Public Relations

Public relations can have a strong impact on public awareness at a much lower cost than advertising can. The company does not pay for the space or time in the media. Rather, it pays for a staff to develop and circulate information and to manage events. If the company develops an interesting story or event, it could be picked up by several different media, having the same effect as advertising that would cost millions of dollars. And it would have more credibility than advertising.

Public relations results can sometimes be spectacular. Here's how publisher Scholastic Inc. used public relations to turn a simple new-book introduction into a major international event, all on a very small budget:

Secret codes. A fiercely guarded text. Huddled masses lined up in funny hats at the witching hour. Welcome to one of the biggest literary events in history. As the clock creeps past midnight, kids worldwide rush to buy the next installment of Harry Potter. It's the fastest-shrinking book pile in history. *Harry Potter and the Deathly Hallows,* the seventh and final book in the series, sold an astonishing 8.3 million copies in just the first 24 hours in the United States and Britain alone—some 346,000 per hour. How do you whip up a consumer frenzy with a miserly $1.8 million promotion budget and only a few well-placed ads? The spellbinding plots, written by Scottish welfare-mom-turned-millionaire J. K. Rowling, captivate kids everywhere. But the hidden hand of public relations plays a large role too.

■ Public relations results can sometimes be spectacular. Scholastic sponsored low-cost sleepovers, games, and costume contests to whip up consumer frenzy for the seventh and final installment of its Harry Potter series.

Publisher Scholastic works behind the scenes with retailers to prepare contests, theme parties, and giveaways leading up to each new release. It communicates through amateur fan sites such as The Leaky Cauldron and MuggleNet.com to keep fans informed about print runs and store events. It works with the mainstream media to create a sense of celebration and excitement. NBC's *Today Show* ran an entire week of "Countdown to Harry" events leading up to the publication of the *Deathly Hallows.* Scholastic's Web site reaches out to obsessed fans with essay contests and video clips. Scholastic heightens the tension by keeping each new book's title and book jacket under wraps almost until the last minute, even forcing booksellers to sign secrecy agreements. With all this PR hype, by the time the book hits the shelves, conditions are hot for Harry. And the hype made a lasting impact—the book went on to become the nation's best-selling book of the year.[41]

Despite its potential strengths, public relations is sometimes described as a marketing stepchild because of its often limited and scattered use. The public relations department is usually located at corporate headquarters. Its staff is so busy dealing with various publics—stockholders, employees, legislators, the press—that public relations programs to support product marketing objectives may be ignored. Marketing managers and public relations practitioners do not always speak the same language. Many public relations practitioners see their job as simply communicating. In contrast, marketing managers tend to be much more interested in how advertising and public relations affect brand building, sales and profits, and customer relationships.

This situation is changing, however. Although public relations still captures only a small portion of the overall marketing budgets of most firms, PR is playing an increasingly important brand-building role. Public relations can be a powerful brand-building tool. Two well-known marketing consultants even go so far as to conclude that advertising doesn't build brands, PR does. In their book, *The Fall of Advertising & the Rise of PR*, the consultants proclaim that the dominance of advertising is over, and that public relations is quietly becoming the most powerful marketing communications tool.

> The birth of a brand is usually accomplished with [public relations], not advertising. Our general rule is [PR] first, advertising second. [Public relations] is the nail, advertising the hammer. [PR] creates the credentials that provide the credibility for advertising. . . . Anita Roddick built the Body Shop into a major brand with no advertising at all. Instead, she traveled the world on a relentless quest for publicity. . . . Until recently, Starbucks Coffee didn't spend a hill of beans on advertising either. In 10 years, the company spent less than $10 million on advertising, a trivial amount for a brand that delivers annual sales [in the billions]. Wal-Mart stores became the world's largest retailer . . . with very little advertising. . . . On the Internet, Amazon.com became a powerhouse brand with virtually no advertising.[42]

Although the book created much controversy, and most advertisers wouldn't agree about the "fall of advertising" part of the title, the point is a good one. Advertising and public relations should work hand in hand to build and maintain brands.

Major Public Relations Tools

Public relations uses several tools. One of the major tools is *news.* PR professionals find or create favorable news about the company and its products or people. Sometimes news stories occur naturally, and sometimes the PR person can suggest events or activities that would create news. *Speeches* can also create product and company publicity. Increasingly, company executives must field questions from the media or give talks at trade associations or sales meetings, and these events can either build or hurt the company's image. Another common PR tool is *special events,* ranging from news conferences, press tours, grand openings, and fireworks displays to laser shows, hot air balloon releases, multimedia presentations, or educational programs designed to reach and interest target publics.

Public relations people also prepare *written materials* to reach and influence their target markets. These materials include annual reports, brochures, articles, and company newsletters and magazines. *Audiovisual materials,* such as slide-and-sound programs, DVDs, and online videos are being used increasingly as communication tools. *Corporate identity materials* can also help create a corporate identity that the public immediately recognizes. Logos, stationery, brochures, signs, business forms, business cards, buildings, uniforms, and company cars and trucks—all become marketing tools when they are attractive, distinctive, and memorable. Finally, companies can improve public goodwill by contributing money and time to *public service activities.*

As we discussed in Chapter 5, many marketers are now also designing *buzz marketing* campaigns to generate excitement and favorable word of mouth for their brands. Buzz marketing takes advantage of *social networking* processes by getting consumers themselves to spread information about a product or service to others in their communities. For example, CW Network used buzz marketing to reach often tuned-out and cynical teen girls:

> High schools are always abuzz with talk of one kind or another: sports, music, clothes, and whatever else teens consider indispensable at any given time. But a while back, one piece of chatter weaving its way through select high schools

across America was very specific. It was about the TV series *America's Next Top Model,* then entering its fourth season. While teens did the talking, CW, the network that airs the series, was listening very closely. It had to. CW was essentially sponsoring the whole conversation.

The plan worked like this. With the help of Alloy.com, a shopping and lifestyle site aimed at teen girls, CW created a list of 500 "insiders" who could generate buzz about *Top Model,* which needed a ratings boost. Alloy.com monitored chat within the site and compiled a list of 7,000 girls who, in the course of their banter, had expressed interest in the show. It cut that list to the 500 girls who seemed the best connected—those who had frequently shown up on instant-messaging buddy lists. Alloy.com then provided these gossipy, in-crowd teens with party kits and encouraged them to invite an average of four friends over to their homes for gatherings themed around—you guessed it—*America's Next Top Model.* The girls knew that CW's cash was behind the kits, and "it wasn't a tough sell," say an Alloy.com marketing executive. Tough sell or not, it seems to have worked. "The ratings have been very good," says the executive, "especially among that age group." Whereas most reality shows don't stick around that long, *America's Next Top Model* is now in its eighth season.[43]

■ Company Web sites can be important public relations vehicles. Butterball's site (www.butterball.com), which features cooking and carving tips, once received 550,000 visitors in one day during Thanksgiving week.

A company's Web site is another important public relations vehicle. Consumers and members of other publics often visit Web sites for information or entertainment. Such sites can be extremely popular. For example, Butterball's site (www.butterball.com), which features cooking and carving tips, once received 550,000 visitors in one day during Thanksgiving week. The Web site supplements the Butterball Turkey Talk-Line (1-800-BUTTERBALL)—called by some the "granddaddy of all help lines—staffed by 50 home economists and nutritionists who respond to more than 100,000 questions each November and December. Visitors to the site can even download a series of "Turkey Talk" podcasts containing tips on holiday food preparation.[44]

Web sites can also be ideal for handling crisis situations. For example, when several bottles of Odwalla apple juice sold on the West Coast were found to contain E. coli bacteria, Odwalla initiated a massive product recall. Within only three hours, it set up a Web site laden with information about the crisis and Odwalla's response. Company staffers also combed the Internet looking for newsgroups discussing Odwalla and posted links to the site. In all, in this age where "it's easier to disseminate information through e-mail marketing, blogs, and online chat," notes an analyst, "public relations is becoming a valuable part of doing business in a digital world."[45]

As with the other promotion tools, in considering when and how to use product public relations, management should set PR objectives, choose the PR messages and vehicles, implement the PR plan, and evaluate the results. The firm's public relations should be blended smoothly with other promotion activities within the company's overall integrated marketing communications effort.

REST STOP ⟩⟩ REVIEWING THE CONCEPTS

In this chapter, you've learned how companies use integrated marketing communications (IMC) to communicate customer value. Modern marketing calls for more than just creating customer value by developing a good product, pricing it attractively, and making it available to target customers. Companies also must clearly and persuasively *communicate* that value to current and prospective customers. To do this, they must blend five communication-mix tools, guided by a well-designed and well-implemented integrated marketing communications strategy.

1. Discuss the process and advantages of integrated marketing communications in communicating customer value.

The shift toward segmented marketing and the explosive developments in information and communications technology have had a dramatic impact on marketing communications. The shift toward targeted marketing and the changing communications environment are giving birth to a new marketing communications model. Some advertising industry experts predict a "chaos scenario" in which the old mass-media communications model will collapse entirely. Others, however, predict a gradually shifting mix of both traditional mass media and a wide array of exciting new, more-targeted, more-personalized media.

As marketing communicators adopt a richer mix of media and communication approaches, they risk creating a communications hodgepodge for consumers. To prevent this, more companies are adopting the concept of *integrated marketing communications (IMC)*. Guided by an overall IMC strategy, the company works out the roles that the various promotional tools will play and the extent to which each will be used. It carefully coordinates the promotional activities and the timing of when major campaigns take place. Finally, to help implement its integrated marketing strategy, the company appoints a marketing communications director who has overall responsibility for the company's communications efforts.

2. Define the five promotion tools and discuss factors that must be considered in shaping the overall promotion mix.

A company's total *promotion mix*—also called its *marketing communications mix*—consists of the specific blend of *advertising, personal selling, sales promotion, public relations,* and *direct-marketing* tools that the company uses to persuasively communicate customer value and build customer relationships. Advertising includes any paid form of nonpersonal presentation and promotion of ideas, goods, or services by an identified sponsor. In contrast, public relations focuses on building good relations with the company's various publics by obtaining favorable unpaid publicity. Personal selling is any form of personal presentation by the firm's sales force for the purpose of making sales and building customer relationships. Firms use sales promotion to provide short-term incentives to encourage the purchase or sale of a product or service. Finally, firms seeking immediate response from targeted individual cus-

tomers use direct-marketing tools to communicate with customers. The company wants to create an integrated *promotion mix*. It can pursue a *push* or a *pull* promotional strategy, or a combination of the two. The best specific blend of promotion tools depends on the type of product/market and the product life-cycle stage.

3. Describe and discuss the major decisions involved in developing an advertising program.

Advertising—the use of paid media by a seller to inform, persuade, and remind buyers about its products or organization—is a strong promotion tool that takes many forms and has many uses. *Advertising decision making* involves decisions about the objectives, the budget, the message, the media, and, finally, the evaluation of results. Advertisers should set clear *objectives* as to whether the advertising is supposed to inform, persuade, or remind buyers. The advertising *budget* can be based on what is affordable, on sales, on competitors' spending, or on the objectives and tasks. The *message decision* calls for planning a message strategy and executing it effectively. The *media decision* involves defining reach, frequency, and impact goals; choosing major media types; selecting media vehicles; and deciding on media timing. Message and media decisions must be closely coordinated for maximum campaign effectiveness. Finally, *evaluation* calls for evaluating the communication and sales effects of advertising before, during, and after the advertising is placed and measuring advertising return on investment.

4. Explain how companies use public relations to communicate with their publics.

Public relations involves building good relations with the company's various publics. Its functions include *press agentry, product publicity, public affairs, lobbying, investor relations,* and *development*. Public relations can have a strong impact on public awareness at a much lower cost than advertising can, and public relations results can sometimes be spectacular. Despite its potential strengths, however, public relations sometimes sees only limited and scattered use. Public relations tools include *news, speeches, special events, buzz marketing, written materials, audiovisual materials, corporate identity materials,* and *public service activities*. A company's Web site can be a good public relations vehicle. In considering when and how to use product public relations, management should set PR objectives, choose the PR messages and vehicles, implement the PR plan, and evaluate the results. Public relations should be blended smoothly with other promotion activities within the company's overall integrated marketing communications effort.

Navigating the Key Terms

Advertising (351)
Advertising agency (372)
Advertising budget (359)
Advertising media (367)
Advertising objective (358)

Advertising strategy (361)
Affordable method (360)
Competitive-parity method (360)
Creative concept (363)
Direct marketing (351)

Execution style (363)
Integrated marketing communications (IMC) (354)
Madison & Vine (363)
Objective-and-task method (360)

Percentage-of-sales method (350)
Personal selling (351)
Promotion mix (marketing communica-
tions mix) (351)

Public relations (351)
Pull strategy (356)
Push strategy (356)

Return on advertising investment (371)
Sales promotion (351)

Travel Log

Discussing the Issues

1. List and briefly describe the five major promotion-mix tools. (AASCB: Communication)

2. Discuss the three major factors changing the face of today's marketing communications. (AACSB: Communication)

3. Compare and contrast pull and push promotion strategies. Which promotion tools are most effective in each? (AACSB: Communication)

4. Name and describe the common methods for setting total advertising budgets. (AACSB: Communication)

5. Define the terms *reach, frequency,* and *impact.* (AACSB: Communication)

6. Discuss the tools used by public relations professionals. (AACSB: Communication)

Application Questions

1. Any message can be presented using different message styles. Find two good print advertisements (such as magazine ads) and identify the execution style used. For each advertisement, design an alternative execution style delivering the same message to the target audience but in a different way. (AACSB: Communication; Reflective Thinking)

2. Gather advertising-rate information for a magazine, a newspaper, a local radio station, and a television program (national or local). Which medium has the lowest cost per exposure? Which has the lowest total cost? Which would be most effective for an advertiser like Nike? How about for a local retail store? (AACSB: Communication; Reflective Thinking)

3. In a small group, discuss the major public relations tools and develop three public relations items for the Humane Society in your community. (AACSB: Communication; Reflective Thinking)

Under the Hood: Focus on Technology

Second Life is a virtual world launched in 2003 by Linden Labs in San Francisco, California. It boasts more than nine million inhabitants who connect for fun and to escape. Registered members create online digital alter egos called avatars, and now users can actually speak to each other. The currency is called Linden dollars, with $1 equal to about 270 Linden dollars. Users can purchase land in Second Life to start a business or build a home. The world started with 64 acres but now has more than 65,000 acres as it expanded to meet users' demand. Second Life is not the only virtual world. Approximately $200 million of real money moves through virtual worlds overall. Second Life is more adult oriented but there are other worlds, such as Habbo and Nictropolis, targeted to children. Marketers see opportunities for research and promotion in virtual worlds. Useful insights into consumer preferences and behavior can be gleaned from observing virtual behavior, but some skeptics claim this might not be valid due to consumers not being themselves in these worlds. However, marketers such as IBM, Sony, Adidas, Pontiac, Kraft, and Coca-Cola have a strong presence, much like product placement in other forms of media. Kraft launched 70 new products in a virtual supermarket and found that consumers do go grocery shopping in their fantasy world and that they do read product information.

1. Visit Second Life at www.secondlife.com to learn more about this virtual world. What are some advantages and disadvantages for marketers using a virtual world to promote products? (AACSB: Communication; Use of IT; Reflective Thinking)

2. What other online venues feature brands as part of their content? (AACSB: Communication; Reflective Thinking)

Focus on Ethics

Splenda (sucralose) was introduced to the consumer market in 1999. It is now a common sweetener found in more than 3,500 food products. Splenda's advertising slogan is "made from sugar, so it tastes like sugar." Manufactured and marketed by packaged-goods giant Johnson & Johnson, Splenda now captures a substantial percentage of the artificial sweetener market and is beginning to cut into sugar's market share. But Splenda's campaign has attracted much attention from competitors, social advocacy groups, and nutritional experts. According to these groups, Splenda has clearly violated "truth in advertising" codes with its "made from sugar" slogan. Although currently produced from a sugar molecule, they claim, Splenda is an artificial sweetener that can be produced without sugar. In addition, the chemical name assigned to Splenda—sucralose—is misleading because it closely resembles the chemical name of sugar, sucrose.

The strongest opponent to the Splenda "made from sugar" campaign is The Sugar Association, which has launched a large and expensive campaign of its own to educate the public and to expose Splenda's unethical behavior. The association's Web site (www.truthaboutsplenda.com) urges consumers to take action by contacting friends, sending letters to the FTC and the FDA, and sending letters of complaint directly to Johnson & Johnson.

Another area of the Web site, labeled Fact vs. Fiction, highlights serious consumer misunderstandings that might result from Splenda's advertising. It describes in detail how Splenda is not natural sugar and notes that there exist no conclusive tests regarding long-term safety of consuming Splenda.

1. What is the objective of Splenda's "made from sugar, so it tastes like sugar" message and campaign? Is this slogan effective? (AACSB: Communication; Reflective Thinking)

2. Check the "truth in advertising" guidelines at the FTC Web site (www.ftc.gov/bcp/conline/pubs/buspubs/ad-faqs.htm). Has Splenda followed these guidelines? (AACSB: Communication; Ethical Reasoning)

Video Case

Crispin Porter + Bogusky

Crispin Porter + Bogusky may not be the oldest advertising agency in the world. It may not be the biggest either. But it has been working overtime to prove that it is the most innovative firm at truly integrating marketing promotions. In fact, Crispin relies very little on the king of all advertising channels, broadcast TV. Instead, Crispin has worked miracles for companies such as Virgin Atlantic Airways, BMW's MINI, and Burger King by employing nontraditional campaigns on limited budgets.

Crispin's unique capability to balance strategy with creativity is what produced such groundbreaking campaigns as Burger King's "Subservient Chicken." The interactive Web site that allows visitors to give commands to a person dressed in a large chicken suit drew a record 460 million hits in only 2 years. Although at first skeptical about this type of campaign, the turnaround that Burger King has experienced since signing on with

Crispin has led the fast-food company to rely more and more on Crispin to create new promotions that draw in consumers and sales.

After viewing the video featuring Crispin Porter + Bogusky, answer the following questions about advertising and promotions.

1. Alex Bogusky once said, "Anything and everything is an ad." What does this mean? How is Crispin putting this idea into practice?

2. In what ways has Crispin differentiated itself from other advertising agencies?

3. Give some examples of how Crispin balances strategy with creativity to develop truly integrated marketing communications campaigns.

After studying this chapter, you should be able to

1. discuss the role of a company's salespeople in creating value for customers and building customer relationships

2. identify and explain the six major sales force management steps

3. discuss the personal selling process, distinguishing between transaction-oriented marketing and relationship marketing

4. explain how sales promotion campaigns are developed and implemented

CHAPTER 13

Communicating Customer Value: Personal Selling and Sales Promotion

ROAD MAP Previewing the Concepts

In the previous chapter, you learned about communicating customer value through integrated marketing communications (IMC) and about two elements of the promotion mix—advertising and public relations. In this chapter, we'll look at two more IMC elements—personal selling and sales promotion. Personal selling is the interpersonal arm of marketing communications, in which the sales force interacts with customers and prospects to build relationships and make sales. Sales promotion consists of short-term incentives to encourage purchase or sale of a product or service. As you read on, remember that although this chapter examines personal selling and sales promotion as separate tools, they must be carefully integrated with other elements of the promotion mix.

When someone says "salesperson," what image comes to mind? Perhaps you think about a stereotypical glad-hander who's out to lighten your wallet by selling you something you don't really need. Think again. Today, for most companies, personal selling plays an important role in building profitable customer relationships. Consider CDW Corporation, whose customer-focused sales strategy has helped it grow rapidly while competitors have faltered.

C DW Corporation, a leading provider of multibrand technology products and services, is thriving. In only 23 years since founder Michael Krasny started the business at his kitchen table, CDW has grown to become a high-tech heavyweight in its highly volatile and competitive industry. In just the past four years CDW has increased its sales by 59 percent, to $6.8 billion annually, while profits have grown 52 percent.

How has CDW managed to grow so profitably? The company owes its success to good old-fashioned high-touch personal selling that builds lasting one-to-one customer relationships. The strategy is fueled by a genuine passion for solving customer problems. Under CDW's "Circle of Service" philosophy, "everything revolves around the customer."

CDW sells a complex assortment of more than 100,000 technology products and services—computers, software, accessories, and networking products—including top name brands such as Adobe APC, Apple, Cisco, HP, Lenovo, IBM, Microsoft, Sony, Symantec, Toshiba, and ViewSonic. Many of CDW's competitors chase after a relative handful of very large customers. However, although CDW serves customers of all sizes, one of the company's core customer segments is small and midsize businesses (SMBs). These smaller customers often need lots of advice and support. "Many of our clients don't have IT departments," says one CDW executive, "so they look to us for expertise."

That's where CDW's sales force comes in. The major responsibility for building and managing customer relationships falls to CDW's sales force of over 2,500 account managers. Each customer is assigned an account manager, who helps the customer select the right products and technologies and keep them running smoothly. CDW promises "What You Need. When You Need It. It all starts with your personal account manager."

Account managers orchestrate the efforts of a team of CDW specialist who help customers select the best mix of products, services, and support. But they do more than just sell technology products and services. They work closely with customers to find solutions to their technology problems. "This is a big deal to us," says Jim Grass, CDW's senior director of state and local sales. "We want to go beyond fulfilling the order and become the trusted adviser for them. We [want to] talk . . . about what a customer is trying to accomplish and really add value to the sale, as opposed to just sending out a box."

To become trusted advisors and effective customer-relationship builders, CDW account managers really must know their stuff. And CDW boasts some of the most knowledgeable salespeople in the industry. Before they make a single sales call, new account managers complete a six-week orientation and then a six-month training program. CDW University's College of Sales offers intensive schooling in the science behind the company's products and in the art of consultative selling. But that's just the beginning—the training never ends. Tenured account managers receive ongoing training to enhance their relationship-selling skills. Each year, CDW's sales force completes a whopping 339,000 hours of sales-specific training. John Edwardson, chairman and CEO of CDW and former head of United Airlines, likes to point out that CDW reps get more training than some pilots.

To further support salespeople's customer problem-solving efforts, CDW has also created nine technology teams consisting of about 820 factory-trained specialists and A+ certified technicians on staff. Account managers can draw on these teams to design customer-specific solutions in technology areas such as mobility/wireless, networking, security, and storage.

Customers who want to access CDW's products and expertise without going through their account manager can do so easily at any of several CDW Web sites. Better yet, CDW will create a free personalized CDW@work extranet site that reflects a given customer's pricing, order status, account history, and special considerations. The extranet site serves as a 24-hour extension of the customer's account manager. This resulted in CDW Web sales of more than $1.9 billion last year. But even here, the ever-present account managers are likely to add personal guidance. Account managers receive immediate notification of their customers' online activities. So if a blurry-eyed SMB manager makes a mistake on an emergency order placed in the middle of the night, chances are good that the account manager will find and correct the error first thing in the morning.

Beyond being knowledgeable and ever-present, CDW's account managers are energetic and passionately customer focused. Much of the energy has passed down from CDW founder and former CEO Michael Krasny. Selling has always been a top priority for Krasny, not surprising given that he began the company by selling used personal computers out of his home through classified ads. Krasny's most important legacy is the "Circle of Service" culture that he created—a culture that focuses on taking care of customers, and on the CDW employees who serve them.

So when someone says "salesperson," you may still think of the stereotypical "traveling salesman"—the fast-talking, ever-smiling peddler who travels his territory foisting his wares on reluctant customers. Such stereotypes, however, are out of date. Today, like CDW's account managers, most professional salespeople are well-educated, well-trained men and women who work to build valued customer relationships. They succeed not by taking customers in, but by helping them out—by assessing customer needs and solving customer problems.

CDW's sales force instills loyalty in what are traditionally very price-conscious SMB customers. The company wants to create customer satisfaction at every touch point. Says a former CDW marketing executive, "We're competitively priced, but what's most important is the service and the customers' relationships with their account managers. It's how we actually touch people that creates our most long-lasting [success]."[1]

In this chapter, we examine two more promotion mix tools—*personal selling* and *sales promotion*. Personal selling consists of interpersonal interactions with customers and prospects to make sales and maintain customer relationships. Sales promotion involves using short-term incentives to encourage customer purchasing, reseller support, and sales force efforts.

Personal Selling

Robert Louis Stevenson once noted that "everyone lives by selling something." Companies all around the world use sales forces to sell products and services to business customers and final consumers. But sales forces are also found in many other kinds of organizations. For example, colleges use recruiters to attract new students and churches use membership committees to attract new members. Museums and fine arts organizations use fund-raisers to contact donors and raise money. Even governments use sales forces. The U.S. Postal Service, for instance, uses a sales force to sell Express Mail and other services to corporate customers. In the first part of this chapter, we examine personal selling's role in the organization, sales force management decisions, and the personal selling process.

The Nature of Personal Selling

Personal selling is one of the oldest professions in the world. The people who do the selling go by many names: salespeople, sales representatives, district managers, account executives, sales consultants, sales engineers, agents, and account development reps to name just a few.

People hold many stereotypes of salespeople—including some unfavorable ones. "Salesman" may bring to mind the image of Arthur Miller's pitiable Willy Loman in *Death of a Salesman* or Meredith Willson's cigar-smoking, backslapping, joke-telling Harold Hill in *The Music Man*. These examples depict salespeople as loners, traveling their territories, trying to foist their wares on unsuspecting or unwilling buyers.

However, modern salespeople are a far cry from these unfortunate stereotypes. Today, most salespeople are well-educated, well-trained professionals who add value for customers and maintain long-term customer relationships. They listen to their customers, assess customer needs, and organize the company's efforts to solve customer problems.[2]

> Sales is no longer the avenue of choice for washouts from other fields or for the glad-handers who anticipate doing business over steaks and a three-martini lunch. In today's hypercompetitive markets, "buying is not about transactions any more," says one sales expert. "Salespeople must know their customers' businesses better than they do and align themselves with customers' strategies." That creates an entirely new role for salespeople. These days, "salespeople must have a wheelbarrow full of business savvy, combined with the credibility to sell to [empowered, well-informed buying] executives," says another expert. Today, sales is about building customer relationships through a "focus on differentiation and linking those differences to the customer's realization of value."

Consider Boeing, the aerospace giant competing in the rough-and-tumble worldwide commercial aircraft market. It takes more than fast talk and a warm smile to sell expensive high-tech aircraft. A single big sale can easily run into billions of dollars. Boeing salespeople head up an extensive team of company specialists— sales and service technicians, financial analysts, planners, engineers—all dedicated to finding ways to satisfy airline customer needs. The selling process is nerve-rackingly slow—it can take two or three years from the first sales presentation to the day the sale is announced. After getting the order, salespeople then must stay in almost constant touch to make certain the customer stays satisfied. Success depends on building solid, long-term relationships with customers, based on performance and trust.

The term **salesperson** covers a wide range of positions. At one extreme, a salesperson might be largely an *order taker,* such as the department store salesperson

Personal selling
Personal presentation by the firm's sales force for the purpose of making sales and building customer relationships.

Salesperson
An individual representing a company to customers by performing one or more of the following activities: prospecting, communicating, selling, servicing, information gathering, and relationship building.

■ Professional selling: It takes more than fast talk and a warm smile to sell high-tech aircraft at $100 million or more a copy. Success depends on building solid, long-term relationships with customers.

standing behind the counter. At the other extreme are *order getters,* whose positions demand *creative selling* and *relationship building* for products and services ranging from appliances, industrial equipment, and airplanes to insurance and information technology services. Here, we focus on the more creative types of selling and on the process of building and managing an effective sales force.

The Role of the Sales Force

Personal selling is the interpersonal arm of the promotion mix. Advertising consists largely of nonpersonal communication with target consumer groups. In contrast, personal selling involves interpersonal interactions between salespeople and individual customers—whether face to face, by telephone, through video or Web conferences, or by other means. Personal selling can be more effective than advertising in more complex selling situations. Salespeople can probe customers to learn more about their problems and then adjust the marketing offer and presentation to fit the special needs of each customer.

The role of personal selling varies from company to company. Some firms have no salespeople at all—for example, companies that sell only online or through catalogs, or companies that sell through manufacturer's reps, sales agents, or brokers. In most firms, however, the sales force plays a major role. In companies that sell business products and services, such as IBM or DuPont, the company's salespeople work directly with customers. In consumer product companies such as Procter & Gamble and Nike, the sales force plays an important behind-the-scenes role. It works with wholesalers and retailers to gain their support and to help them be more effective in selling the company's products.

Linking the Company with Its Customers The sales force serves as a critical link between a company and its customers. In many cases, salespeople serve both masters—the seller and the buyer. First, they *represent the company to customers.* They find and develop new customers and communicate information about the company's products and services. They sell products by approaching customers, presenting their products, answering objections, negotiating prices and terms, and closing sales. In addition, salespeople provide customer service and carry out market research and intelligence work.

At the same time, salespeople *represent customers to the company,* acting inside the firm as "champions" of customers' interests and managing the buyer-seller relationship. Salespeople relay customer concerns about company products and actions back inside to those who can handle them. They learn about customer needs and work with other marketing and nonmarketing people in the company to develop greater customer value.

Coordinating Marketing and Sales Ideally, the sales force and the company's other marketing functions should work together closely to jointly create value for both customers and the company. Unfortunately, however, some companies still treat "marketing" and "sales" as separate functions. When this happens, the separated marketing and sales functions often don't get along well. When things go wrong, the marketers (marketing planners, brand managers, and researchers) blame the sales force for its poor execution of an otherwise splendid strategy. The sales team, in turn, blames the marketers for being out of touch with what's really going on with customers. The marketers sometimes feel that salespeople have their "feet stuck in the mud," whereas salespeople feel that the marketers have their "heads stuck in the clouds." In short, neither group fully values the other's contributions. If not repaired, such disconnects between marketing and sales can damage customer relationships and company performance.

A company can take several actions to help bring its marketing and sales functions closer together. At the most basic level, it can *increase communications* between the two groups by arranging joint meetings and by spelling out when and with whom each group should communicate. The company can create *joint assignments.*[3]

> It's important to create opportunities for marketers and salespeople to work together. This will make them more familiar with each other's ways of thinking and acting. It's useful for marketers, particularly brand managers and researchers, to occasionally go along on sales calls. They should also sit in on important account-planning sessions. Salespeople, in turn, should help to develop marketing plans.

They should sit in on product-planning reviews and share their deep knowledge about customers' purchasing habits. They should preview ad and sales-promotion campaigns. Jointly, marketers and salespeople should generate a playbook for expanding business with the top 10 accounts in each market segment. They should also plan events and conferences together.

A company can also create *joint objectives and reward systems* for sales and marketing or appoint *marketing-sales liaisons*—people from marketing who "live with the sales force" and help to coordinate marketing and sales force programs and efforts. Finally, the firm can appoint a *chief revenue officer* (or *chief customer officer*)—a high-level marketing executive who oversees both marketing and sales. Such a person can help infuse marketing and sales with the common goal of creating value for customers in order to capture value in return.

Managing the Sales Force

We define **sales force management** as the analysis, planning, implementation, and control of sales force activities. It includes designing sales force strategy and structure and recruiting, selecting, training, compensating, supervising, and evaluating the firm's salespeople. These major sales force management decisions are shown in Figure 13.1 and are discussed in the following sections.

Sales force management
The analysis, planning, implementation, and control of sales force activities. It includes designing sales force strategy and structure and recruiting, selecting, training, supervising, compensating, and evaluating the firm's salespeople.

Designing Sales Force Strategy and Structure

Marketing managers face several sales force strategy and design questions. How should salespeople and their tasks be structured? How big should the sales force be? Should salespeople sell alone or work in teams with other people in the company? Should they sell in the field or by telephone or on the Web? We address these issues below.

Sales Force Structure   A company can divide sales responsibilities along any of several lines. The decision is simple if the company sells only one product line to one industry with customers in many locations. In that case the company would use a *territorial sales force structure*. However, if the company sells many products to many types of customers, it might need either a *product sales force structure*, a *customer sales force structure*, or a combination of the two.

Territorial Sales Force Structure   In the **territorial sales force structure**, each salesperson is assigned to an exclusive geographic area and sells the company's full line of products or services to all customers in that territory. This organization clearly defines each salesperson's job and fixes accountability. It also increases the salesperson's desire to build local customer relationships that, in turn, improve selling effectiveness. Finally, because each salesperson travels within a limited geographic area, travel expenses are relatively small.

Territorial sales force structure
A sales force organization that assigns each salesperson to an exclusive geographic territory in which that salesperson sells the company's full line.

A territorial sales organization is often supported by many levels of sales management positions. For example, Campbell Soup uses a territorial structure in which each salesperson is responsible for selling all Campbell Soup products. Starting at the bottom of the organization, *sales merchandisers* report to *sales representatives*, who report to *retail supervisors*, who report to *directors of retail sales operations*, who report to 1 of 22 *regional sales managers*. Regional sales managers, in turn, report to 1 of 4 *general sales managers* (West, Central, South, and East), who report to a *vice president* and *general sales manager*.

FIGURE 13.1 Major Steps in Sales Force Management

| Designing sales force strategy and structure | ⇨ | Recruiting and selecting salespeople | ⇨ | Training salespeople | ⇨ | Compensating salespeople | ⇨ | Supervising salespeople | ⇨ | Evaluating salespeople |

Product Sales Force Structure   Salespeople must know their products—especially when the products are numerous and complex. This need, together with the growth of product management, has led many companies to adopt a **product sales force structure**, in which the sales force sells along product lines. For example, Kodak uses a different sales force for its consumer products than for its industrial products. The consumer-products sales force deals with the retailers and dealers who sell its cameras, printers, and other consumer products to retail customers. The industrial-products sales force works with industrial and institutional customers, focusing on the company's more complex imaging products that require technical understanding.

Product sales force structure
A sales force organization under which salespeople specialize in selling only a portion of the company's products or lines.

The product structure can lead to problems, however, if a single large customer buys many different company products. For example, Cardinal Health, the large health care products and services company, has several product divisions, each with a separate sales force. Using a product sales force structure might mean that several Cardinal salespeople end up calling on the same hospital on the same day. This means that they travel over the same routes and wait to see the same customer's purchasing agents. These extra costs must be compared with the benefits of better product knowledge and attention to individual products.

Customer Sales Force Structure   More and more companies are now using a **customer sales force structure**, in which they organize the sales force along customer or industry lines. Separate sales forces may be set up for different industries, for serving current customers versus finding new ones, and for major accounts versus regular accounts. Many companies even have special sales forces set up to handle the needs of individual large customers. For example, Black & Decker has a Home Depot sales organization and a Lowe's sales organization.

Customer sales force structure
A sales force organization under which salespeople specialize in selling only to certain customers or industries.

Organizing the sales force around customers can help a company build closer relationships with important customers. Consider Lear Corporation, one of the largest automotive suppliers in the world.

Each year, Lear Corporation produces almost $18 billion worth of automotive interiors—seat systems, instrument panels, door panels, floor and acoustic systems, overhead systems, and electrical distribution systems. Its customers include all of the world's leading automotive companies, from Ford, General Motors, Chrysler, Toyota, and Volvo to BMW, Ferrari, Rolls-Royce, and more than a dozen others. Perhaps more than any other part of the organization, it's Lear's outstanding 145-person sales force that brings to life the company's credo, "Consumer driven. Customer focused." Lear salespeople work hard at relationship building and doing what's best for the customer. "Our salespeople don't really close deals," notes a senior marketing executive. "They consult and work with customers to learn exactly what's needed and when."

Lear organizes its sales force around major customers. More than that, the company itself is broken up into separate divisions dedicated to specific customers. For example, there's a Ford division, a General Motors division, and a Fiat division. This organization lets Lear's sales teams to get very close to their customers. In fact, Lear often locates its sales offices in customers' facilities. For instance, the team that handles GM's light truck division works at GM's truck operation campus. "We can't just be there to give quotes and ask for orders," says the marketing executive. "We need to be involved with customers every step of the way—from vehicle concept through launch."[4]

■ Automotive supplier Lear Corporation organizes its sales force around major customers. In fact, it often locates its sales offices in customers' facilities. "We need to be involved with customers every step of the way—from vehicle concept through launch."

Complex Sales Force Structures   When a company sells a wide variety of products to many types of customers over a broad geographic area, it often combines several types of sales force structures. Salespeople can be specialized by customer and territory, by product and territory, by product and customer, or by territory, product, and customer. No single structure is best for all companies and situations. Each company should select a sales force structure that best serves the needs of its customers and fits its overall marketing strategy.

A good sales structure can mean the difference between success and failure. Companies should periodically review their sales force organizations to be certain that they serve the needs of the company and its customers. Over time, sales force structures can grow complex, inefficient, and unresponsive to customers' needs. This happened recently to technology giant Hewlett-Packard. To correct the problem, the company's new CEO took dramatic steps to restructure HP's corporate sales force (see Marketing at Work 13.1).[7]

Sales Force Size   Once the company has set its structure, it is ready to consider *sales force size*. Sales forces may range in size from only a few salespeople to tens of thousands. Some sales forces are huge—for example, American Express employs 23,500 U.S. salespeople, PepsiCo 36,000, and The Hartford Financial Services Group 100,000.[5] Salespeople constitute one of the company's most productive—and most expensive—assets. Therefore, increasing their number will increase both sales and costs.

Many companies use some form of *workload approach* to set sales force size. Using this approach, a company first groups accounts into different classes according to size, account status, or other factors related to the amount of effort required to maintain them. It then determines the number of salespeople needed to call on each class of accounts the desired number of times.

The company might think as follows: Suppose we have 1,000 type A accounts and 2,000 type B accounts. Type A accounts require 36 calls a year and type B accounts require 12 calls a year. In this case, the sales force's *workload*—the number of calls it must make per year—is 60,000 calls [(1,000 × 36) + (2,000 × 12) = 36,000 + 24,000 = 60,000]. Suppose our average salesperson can make 1,000 calls a year. Thus, we need 60 salespeople (60,000 ÷ 1,000).[6]

Other Sales Force Strategy and Structure Issues   Sales management must also decide who will be involved in the selling effort and how various sales and sales support people will work together.

Outside and Inside Sales Forces   The company may have an **outside sales force** (or **field sales force**), an **inside sales force**, or both. Outside salespeople travel to call on customers in the field. Inside salespeople conduct business from their offices via telephone, the Internet, or visits from buyers.

Some inside salespeople provide support for the outside sales force, freeing them to spend more time selling to major accounts and finding new prospects. For example, *technical sales-support people* provide technical information and answers to customers' questions. *Sales assistants* provide administrative backup for outside salespeople. They call ahead and confirm appointments, follow up on deliveries, and answer customers' questions when outside salespeople cannot be reached. Using such combinations of inside and outside salespeople can help to serve important customers better. As one sales manager notes, "You have the support and easy access to the inside rep and the face-to-face relationship building of the outside rep."[7]

Other inside salespeople do more than just provide support. *Telemarketers* and *Web sellers* use the phone and Internet to find new leads and qualify prospects or to sell and service accounts directly. Telemarketing and Web selling can be very effective, less costly ways to sell to smaller, harder-to-reach customers. Depending on the complexity of the product and customer, for example, a telemarketer can make from 20 to 33 decision-maker contacts a day, compared to the average of 4 that an outside salesperson can make. And whereas an average business-to-business field sales call costs $329 or more, a routine industrial telemarketing call costs only about $5 and a complex call about $20.[8]

Although the federal government's Do Not Call Registry put a dent in telephone sales to consumers, telemarketing remains a vital tool for many business-to-business marketers.[9]

Outside sales force (or **field sales force**)
Outside salespeople who travel to call on customers in the field.

Inside sales force
Inside salespeople who conduct business from their offices via telephone, the Internet, or visits from prospective buyers.

13.1 MARKETING AT WORK

Hewlett-Packard Overhauls Its Vast Corporate Sales Force

Imagine this scenario: You need a new digital camera. You're not sure which one to buy or even what features you need. So you visit your nearest electronics superstore to talk with a salesperson. You walk through the camera section but can't find anyone to help you. When you finally find a salesperson, he yawns and tells you that he's responsible for selling all the products in the store, so he doesn't really know all that much about cameras—maybe you should talk to someone else. You finally find a camera-savvy salesperson. However, after answering a few questions, she disappears to handle some other task, handing you off to someone new. And the new salesperson seems to contradict what the first salesperson said, even quoting different prices on a couple of models you like.

As incredible as it seems, at least until recently, this is the kind of situation that many large business buyers faced when they attempted to buy from technology giant Hewlett-Packard. Before Mark Hurd took over as HP's new CEO in spring 2005, the company's revenues and profits had flattened and its stock price had plummeted. To find out why, Hurd first talked directly with 400 corporate customers. Mostly what he heard was gripes about HP's corporate sales force.

Customers complained that they had to deal with too many salespeople, and that HP's confusing management layers made it hard to figure out whom to call. They had trouble tracking down HP sales representatives. And once found, the reps often came across as apathetic, leaving the customer to take the initiative. HP reps were responsible for a broad range of complex products, so they sometimes lacked the needed depth of knowledge on any subset of them. Customers grumbled that they received varying price quotes from different sales reps, and that it often took weeks for reps to respond to seemingly simple requests. In all, HP's corporate customers were frustrated, not a happy circumstance for a company that gets more than 70 percent of its revenues from businesses.

But customers weren't the only ones frustrated by HP's unwieldy and unresponsive sales force structure. HP was organized into three main product divisions: the Personal Systems Group (PSG), the

■ HP overhauled its vast sales force, reducing salesperson frustration and helping them to create better value for customers.

Technology Solutions Group (TSG), and the Image and Printing Group (IPG). However, these divisions had little control over the sales process. Instead, HP's corporate sales force was housed in a fourth division, the Customer Sales Group (CSG). All salespeople reported directly to the CSG and were responsible for selling products from all three product divisions. To make matters worse, the CSG was bloated and underperforming. According to one reporter, "of the 17,000 people working in HP's corporate sales, only around 10,000 directly sold to customers. The rest were support staff or in management."

HP division executives were frustrated by the CSG structure. They complained that they had little or no direct control over the salespeople who sold their products. And multiple layers of management slowed sales force decision making and customer responsiveness. Finally, salespeople themselves were frustrated by the structure. They weren't being given the time and support they needed to serve their customers well. Burdened with administrative tasks and bureaucratic

For some smaller companies, telephone and Web selling may be the primary sales approaches. However, larger companies also use these tactics, either to sell directly to small and midsize customers or to help out with larger ones. For example, Avaya, a $5 billion global telecommunications firm, recently formed a telemarketing sales force to service its smaller, more routine, less complex accounts. Not only did the telesales force do a better job of selling to these smaller accounts, it freed Avaya's outside salespeople to focus their attention on the company's highest-value customers and prospects. As a result, the company has experienced 40 percent higher sales in areas where the telesales model is being used.[10]

For many types of products and selling situations, phone or Web selling can be as effective as a personal sales call. Notes a DuPont telemarketer: "I'm more effective on the phone. [When you're in the field], if some guy's not in his office, you lose an hour. On the phone, you lose 15 seconds. . . . Through my phone calls, I'm in the field as much as the rep is." There are other advantages. "Customers can't throw things at you," quips the rep, "and you don't have to outrun dogs."[11]

What's more, although they may seem impersonal, the phone and Internet can be surprisingly personal when it comes to building customer relationships. Remember CDW from our chapter-opening story?

red tape, they were spending less than a third of their time with customers. And they had to work through multiple layers of bureaucracy to get price quotes and sample products for customers. "The customer focus was lacking," says an HP sales vice president. "Trying to navigate inside HP was difficult. It was unacceptable."

As CEO Mark Hurd peeled back the layers, it became apparent that HP's organizational problems went deeper than the sales force. The entire company had become so centralized, with so many layers of management, that it was unresponsive and out of touch with customers. Thus began what one observer called "one of Hurd's biggest management challenges: overhauling HP's vast corporate sales force."

For starters, Hurd eliminated the CSG division, instead assigning salespeople directly to the three product divisions. He also did away with three layers of management and cut hundreds of unproductive sales workers. This move gave divisional marketing and sales executives direct control over a leaner, more efficient sales process, resulting in speedier sales decisions and quicker market response.

Hurd also took steps to reduce salesperson and customer frustrations. Eliminating the CSG meant that each salesperson was responsible for selling a smaller number of products and was able to develop expertise in a specific product area. Hurd urged sales managers to cut back on salesperson administrative requirements and to improve sales support so that salespeople could spend more quality time with customers. As a result, salespeople now spend more than 40 percent of their time with customers, up from just 30 percent last year. And HP salespeople are noticing big changes in the sales support they receive:

Salesman Richard Ditucci began noticing some of the changes late last year. At the time, Ditucci was trying to sell computer servers to Staples. As part of the process, Staples had asked him to provide a sample server for the company to evaluate. In the past, such requests typically took two to three weeks to fulfill because of HP's bureaucracy. This time, Ditucci got the server he needed within three days. The quick turnaround helped him win the contract, valued at several million dollars.

To ensure that important customers are carefully tended, HP assigned each salesperson three or fewer accounts. The top 2,000 accounts were assigned just one salesperson each—"so they'll always know whom to contact." Customers are noticing differences in the attention that they get from HP salespeople:

James Farris, a senior technology executive at Staples, says HP has freed up his salesman to drop by Staples at least twice a month instead of about once a month before. The extra face time enabled the HP salesman to create more valuable interactions, such as arranging a workshop recently for Staples to explain HP's technology to the retailer's executives. As a result, Farris says he is planning to send more business HP's way. Similarly, Keith Morrow, chief information officer of convenience-store chain 7-Eleven, says his HP sales representative is now "here all the time," and has been more knowledgeable in pitching products tailored to his business. As a result, last October, 7-Eleven began deploying in its U.S. stores 10,000 HP pen pads—a mobile device that helps 7-Eleven workers on the sales floor.

So, HP's sales force restructuring appears to be paying off. Since Mr. Hurd's arrival, HP has become a much leaner and more efficient sales organization. HP's earnings have improved 56 percent and profit margins are up 65 percent. More importantly, salespeople are happier and more productive, resulting in happier customers, suggesting that more good news is yet to come for the company. CEO Hurd knows that there's still much more work to be done. But step by step, through restructuring, HP is fixing its sales force to create better value for its business customers. Now, if your local electronics superstore would only do the same for you....

Sources: Quotes and adapted examples from Pui-Wing Tam, "System Reboot: Hurd's Big Challenge at HP: Overhauling Corporate Sales," *Wall Street Journal*, April 3, 2006. Other information from Steven Burke and Craig Zarley, "Tables Have Turned; HP Gaining Ground on Dell," *Computer Reseller News*, May 22, 2006, p. 15; "HP Restructures, Putting More Assignments in Play," *Adweek*, March 27, 2006, accessed at www.adweek.com; Craig Zarley and Robert Faletra, "Team Building," *Computer Reseller News*, April 24, 2006, p. 10; Christopher Hosford, "Rebooting Hewlett-Packard," *Sales & Marketing Management*, July–August 2006, pp. 32–35; Thomas M. Anderson, "Hewlett-Packard: More to Come?" *Kiplinger*, May 25, 2007, accessed at www.kiplinger.com; and www.hp.com, accessed December 2007.

If you're one of CDW Account Manager Ron Kelly's regular customers, you probably know that he's 35 and has a wife named Michelle, a 9-year-old son named Andrew, and a German shepherd named Bones. You know that he majored in journalism and poly sci at SIU (that's Southern Illinois University) and was supposed to attend Northwestern's law school, but instead came to work at CDW. You know that he bleeds red and black for the Chicago Blackhawks. You also know that he knows as much, if not more, about you. Kelly, an affable account manager, is a master at relationship-based selling, CDW's specialty. Customers love it. "He's my sales rep, but he's also my friend," says Todd Greenwald, director of operations for Heartland Computers, which sells barcode scanners. "Most of the time we don't even talk about price. I trust Ron."

What's particularly impressive is that, for the most part, the interaction occurs over the phone and Internet. Despite the lack of face time, CDW account managers forge close ties. One customer invited his CDW contact to his wedding. Kelly and Greenwald share Blackhawks season tickets. It's not uncommon to find customers and reps whose partnership has outlasted job changes, budget cuts, and marriages. Of course, the relationships aren't based solely on being likable.

■ Inside sales force: Although they may seem impersonal, the phone and Internet can be surprisingly personal when it comes to building customer relationships. "He's my business partner," says one CDW customer about her account manager, who manages account relationships almost entirely by phone.

Team selling
Using teams of people from sales, marketing, engineering, finance, technical support, and even upper management to service large, complex accounts.

They're grounded in helping customers succeed. Account managers think like the customer and try to anticipate problems. For instance, before storms rocked Florida one summer, some account managers called or e-mailed clients there with battery and backup-storage solutions. "Instead of just sending a purchase order, we want to ask, 'Why are you buying [that product]?'" says a CDW executive. "That's how you identify customers' needs." In this way, to their customers, CDW account managers are much more than just peddlers. When asked if she thinks of her CDW rep as a salesperson anymore, one customer replied, "Never. He's my business partner." And it all happens over the phone or the Web—both supposedly "arms-length" media.[12]

Team Selling   As products become more complex, and as customers grow larger and more demanding, a single salesperson simply can't handle all of a large customer's needs. Instead, most companies now use **team selling** to service large, complex accounts. Sales teams can unearth problems, solutions, and sales opportunities that no individual salesperson could. Such teams might include experts from any area or level of the selling firm—sales, marketing, technical and support services, R&D, engineering, operations, finance, and others. In team selling situations, the salesperson shifts from "soloist" to "orchestrator."

In many cases, the move to team selling mirrors similar changes in customers' buying organizations. "Today, we're calling on teams of buying people, and that requires more firepower on our side," says one sales vice president. "One salesperson just can't do it all—can't be an expert in everything we're bringing to the customer. We have strategic account teams, led by customer business managers, who basically are our quarterbacks."[13]

Some companies, such as IBM, Xerox, and Procter & Gamble, have used teams for a long time. P&G sales reps are organized into "customer business development (CBD) teams." Each CBD team is assigned to a major P&G customer, such as Wal-Mart, Safeway, or CVS Pharmacy. Teams consist of a customer business development manager, several account executives (each responsible for a specific category of P&G products), and specialists in marketing strategy, operations, information systems, logistics, and finance. This organization places the focus on serving the complete needs of each important customer. It lets P&G "grow business by working as a 'strategic partner' with our accounts, not just as a supplier. Our goal: to grow their business, which also results in growing ours."[14]

Team selling does have some pitfalls. For example, salespeople are by nature competitive and have often been trained and rewarded for outstanding individual performance. Salespeople who are used to having customers all to themselves may have trouble learning to work with and trust others on a team. In addition, selling teams can confuse or overwhelm customers who are used to working with only one salesperson. Finally, difficulties in evaluating individual contributions to the team selling effort can create some sticky compensation issues.

Recruiting and Selecting Salespeople

At the heart of any successful sales force operation is the recruitment and selection of good salespeople. The performance difference between an average salesperson and a top salesperson can be substantial. In a typical sales force, the top 30 percent of the salespeople might bring in 60 percent of the sales. Thus, careful salesperson selection can greatly increase overall sales force performance. Beyond the differences in sales performance, poor selection results in costly turnover. When a salesperson quits, the costs of finding and training a new salesperson—plus the costs of lost sales—can be very high. Also, a sales force with many new people is less productive, and turnover disrupts important customer relationships.

What sets great salespeople apart from all the rest? In an effort to profile top sales performers, Gallup Management Consulting Group, a division of the well-known Gallup polling organization, has interviewed hundreds of thousands of salespeople. Its research suggests that the best salespeople possess four key talents: intrinsic motivation, disciplined work style, the ability to close a sale, and perhaps most important, the ability to build relationships with customers.[15]

Super salespeople are motivated from within—they have an unrelenting drive to excel. Some salespeople are driven by money, a desire for recognition, or the satisfaction of competing and winning. Others are driven by the desire to provide service and to build relationships. The best salespeople possess some of each of these motivations. They also have a disciplined work style. They lay out detailed, organized plans and then follow through in a timely way.

But motivation and discipline mean little unless they result in closing more sales and building better customer relationships. Super salespeople build the skills and knowledge they need to get the job done. Perhaps most important, top salespeople are excellent customer problem solvers and relationship builders. They understand their customers' needs. Talk to sales executives and they'll describe top performers in these terms: Empathetic. Patient. Caring. Responsive. Good listeners. Top performers can put themselves on the buyer's side of the desk and see the world through their customers' eyes. They don't want just to be liked, they want to add value for their customers.

When recruiting, companies should analyze the sales job itself and the characteristics of its most successful salespeople to identify the traits needed by a successful salesperson in their industry. Then, it must recruit the right salespeople. The human resources department looks for applicants by getting names from current salespeople,

■ Great salespeople: The best salespeople, such as Jennifer Hansen of 3M, possess intrinsic motivation, a disciplined work style, the ability to close a sale, and perhaps most important, the ability to build relationships with customers.

using employment agencies, placing classified ads, searching the Web, and working through college placement services. Another source is to attract top salespeople from other companies. Proven salespeople need less training and can be immediately productive.

Recruiting will attract many applicants from whom the company must select the best. The selection procedure can vary from a single informal interview to lengthy testing and interviewing. Many companies give formal tests to sales applicants. Tests typically measure sales aptitude, analytical and organizational skills, personality traits, and other characteristics. But test scores provide only one piece of information in a set that includes personal characteristics, references, past employment history, and interviewer reactions.

Training Salespeople

New salespeople may spend anywhere from a few weeks or months to a year or more in training. Then, most companies provide continuing sales training via seminars, sales meetings, and Web e-learning throughout the salesperson's career. In all, U.S. companies spend more than $7 billion annually on training salespeople. Although training can be expensive, it can also yield dramatic returns. For example, one recent study showed that sales training conducted by a major telecommunications firm paid for itself in 16 days and resulted in a six-month return on investment of 812 percent.[16]

Training programs have several goals. First, salespeople need to know about customers and how to build relationships with them. So the training program must teach them about different types of customers and their needs, buying motives, and buying habits. And it must teach them how to sell effectively and train them in the basics of the selling process. Salespeople also need to know and identify with the company, its products, and its competitors. So an effective training program teaches them about the company's objectives, organization, and chief products and markets, and about the strategies of major competitors.

Today, many companies are adding e-learning to their sales training programs. Most e-learning is Web-based but many companies now offer on-demand training for PDAs, cell phones, and even video iPods. Online and other e-learning approaches cut training costs and make training more efficient. One recent study estimates that companies spend 40 cents

■ Training salespeople: International Rectifier created the online IR University to help keep its hundreds of global sales reps, internal sales staffers, and others trained on the constant stream of new products it introduces.

of every sales training dollar on travel and lodging. Such costs can be greatly reduced through Web-based training. As a result, last year, companies did 33 percent of their corporate training online, up from 24 percent two years earlier.[17]

Online training may range from simple text-based product information to Internet-based sales exercises that build sales skills to sophisticated simulations that re-create the dynamics of real-life sales calls. International Rectifier, a global manufacturer of power management semiconductors, has learned that using the Internet to train salespeople offers many advantages.

> To stay competitive in its complex, fast-changing industry, International Rectifier must continually retrain its sales and support people. For example, IR introduces an average of three or more major new products each month. For each new product, the company must coordinate and train hundreds of sales reps, internal sales staffers, field engineers, key executives, and independent inside sales reps across a variety of time zones in 17 locations around the world.
>
> The answer: International Rectifier's online IR University, which provides timely training in advance of new product launches, along with ongoing training on other company and industry developments. The e-learning center provides enhanced presentations, complete with creative animation and streamlined text, to share knowledge accurately but in a way that excites and captures attention. The center also allows for "real-time" visual and audio communications with the presenter via live chat and conference calls. Beyond learning about new products, salespeople can refresh their memories and sharpen their knowledge on almost any topic before meeting with customers. And evaluation diagnostics help sales managers to identify the skill and knowledge levels of each individual salesperson for ongoing support and training.
>
> The sales force is thrilled about being able to "attend" training sessions at times convenient for them, without leaving their home offices. And online training results in significant cost savings. Approximately 500 IR sales and support people have completed more than 5,500 online courses during the past nine months. The cost? Just an estimated $12 per trainee per course. Compared to the costs associated with onsite training, the online learning system has saved the company approximately $250,000 during the past year. In all, online training has reduced IR's training costs by 75 percent.[18]

Compensating Salespeople

To attract good salespeople, a company must have an appealing compensation plan. Compensation is made up of several elements—a fixed amount, a variable amount, expenses, and fringe benefits. The fixed amount, usually a salary, gives the salesperson some stable income. The variable amount, which might be commissions or bonuses based on sales performance, rewards the salesperson for greater effort and success.

Management must decide what *mix* of these compensation elements makes the most sense for each sales job. Different combinations of fixed and variable compensation give rise to four basic types of compensation plans—straight salary, straight commission, salary plus bonus, and salary plus commission. A recent study of sales force compensation showed that the average salesperson's pay consists of about 67 percent salary and 33 percent incentive pay.[19]

The sales force compensation plan can both motivate salespeople and direct their activities. Compensation should direct salespeople toward activities that are consistent with overall sales force and marketing objectives. For example, if the strategy is to acquire new business, grow rapidly, and gain market share, the compensation plan might include a larger commission component, coupled with a new-account bonus to encourage high sales performance and new-account development. In contrast, if the goal is to maximize current account profitability, the compensation plan might contain a larger base-salary component with additional incentives for current account sales or customer satisfaction.

In fact, more and more companies are moving away from high commission plans that may drive salespeople to make short-term grabs for business. They worry that a salesperson who is pushing too hard to close a deal may ruin the customer relationship. Instead, companies are designing compensation plans that reward salespeople for building customer relationships and growing the long-run value of each customer.

Supervising and Motivating Salespeople

New salespeople need more than a territory, compensation, and training—they need supervision and motivation. The goal of *supervision* is to help salespeople "work smart" by doing the right things in the right ways. The goal of *motivation* is to encourage salespeople to "work hard" and energetically toward sales force goals. If salespeople work smart and work hard, they will realize their full potential, to their own and the company's benefit.

Companies vary in how closely they supervise their salespeople. Many help their salespeople to identify target customers and set call norms. Some may also specify how much time the sales force should spend prospecting for new accounts and set other time management priorities. One tool is the weekly, monthly, or annual *call plan* that shows which customers and prospects to call on and which activities to carry out. Another tool is *time-and-duty analysis*. In addition to time spent selling, the salesperson spends time traveling, waiting, taking breaks, and doing administrative chores.

Figure 13.2 shows how salespeople spend their time. On average, active selling time accounts for only 10 percent of total working time! If selling time could be raised from 10 percent to 30 percent, this would triple the time spent selling.[20] Companies always are looking for ways to save time—simplifying administrative duties, developing better sales-call and routing plans, supplying more and better customer information, and using phones, e-mail, or video conferencing instead of traveling. Consider the changes GE made to increase its sales force's face-to-face selling time.[21]

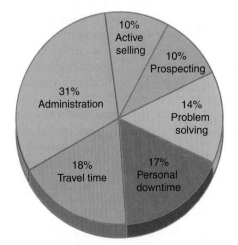

FIGURE 13.2 How Salespeople Spend Their Time

Source: Proudfoot Consulting. Data used with permission.

When Jeff Immelt became General Electric's new chairman, he was dismayed to find that members of the sales team were spending far more time on deskbound administrative chores than in face-to-face meetings with customers and prospects. "He said we needed to turn that around," recalls Venki Rao, an IT leader in global sales and marketing at GE Power Systems, a division focused on energy systems and products. "[We need] to spend four days a week in front of the customer and one day for all the admin stuff." GE Power's salespeople spent much of their time at their desks because they had to go to many sources for the information needed to sell multimillion-dollar turbines, turbine parts, and services to energy companies worldwide. To fix the problem, GE created a new sales portal, a kind of "one-stop shop" for just about everything they need. The sales portal connects the vast array of existing GE databases, providing everything from sales tracking and customer data to parts pricing and information on planned outages. GE also added external data, such as news feeds. "Before, you were randomly searching for things," says Bill Snook, a GE sales manager. Now, he says, "I have the sales portal as my home page, and I use it as the gateway to all the applications that I have." The sales portal has freed Snook and 2,500 other users around the globe from once time-consuming administrative tasks, greatly increasing their face time with customers.

■ Sales force automation: Many sales forces have gone high tech, equipping salespeople with everything from smart phone, wireless Web connections, and videoconferencing to customer-contact and relationship management software that helps them to be more effective and efficient.

Many firms have adopted *sales force automation systems*—computerized, digitized sales force operations that let salespeople work more effectively anytime, anywhere. Companies now routinely equip their salespeople with new-age technologies such as laptops, smart phones, wireless Web connections, Webcams for videoconferencing, and customer-contact and relationship management software. Armed with these technologies, salespeople can more effectively and efficiently profile customers and prospects, analyze and forecast sales, schedule sales calls, make presentations, prepare sales and expense reports, and manage account relationships. The result is better time management, improved customer service, lower sales costs, and higher sales performance.[22]

Perhaps the fastest-growing technology tool is the Internet. The Internet offers explosive potential for conducting sales operations and for interacting with and serving customers. More and more companies are now using the Internet to support their personal selling efforts—not just for selling but for everything from training salespeople to conducting sales meetings and servicing accounts (see Marketing at Work 13.2).

Beyond directing salespeople, sales managers must also motivate them. Some salespeople will do their best without any special urging from management. To them, selling may be the most fascinating job in the world. But selling can also be frustrating. Salespeople often work alone and they must sometimes travel away from home. They may face aggressive competing salespeople and difficult customers. Therefore, salespeople often need special encouragement to do their best.

Management can boost sales force morale and performance through its organizational climate, sales quotas, and positive incentives. *Organizational climate* describes the feeling that salespeople have about their opportunities, value, and rewards for a good performance. Some companies treat salespeople as if they are not very important, and performance suffers accordingly. Other companies treat their salespeople as valued contributors and allow virtually unlimited opportunity for income and promotion. Not surprisingly, these companies enjoy higher sales force performance and less turnover.

13.2 MARKETING AT WORK

Point, Click, and Sell: Welcome to the Web-Based Sales Force

There are few rules at Fisher Scientific International's sales training sessions. The chemical company's salespeople are allowed to show up for new workshops in their pajamas. And no one flinches if they stroll in at midnight for their first class, take a dozen breaks to call clients, or invite the family cat to sleep in their laps while they take an exam. Sound unorthodox? It would be if Fisher's salespeople were trained in a regular classroom. But for the past few years, the company has been using the Internet to teach the majority of its salespeople in the privacy of their homes, cars, hotel rooms, or wherever else they bring their laptops.

To get updates on Fisher's pricing or refresh themselves on one of the company's highly technical products, all salespeople have to do is log on to the Web site and select from the lengthy index. Any time of the day or night, they can get information on a new product, take an exam, or post messages for product experts—all without ever entering a corporate classroom. Welcome to the world of the Web-based sales force.

Sales organizations around the world are now saving money and time by using a host of Web approaches to train reps, hold sales meetings, and even conduct live sales presentations. Fisher Scientific's reps can dial up the Web site at their leisure, and whereas newer reps might spend hours online going through each session in order, more seasoned sellers might just log on for a quick refresher on a specific product before a sales call. "It allows them to manage their time better, because they're only getting training when they need it, in the doses they need it in," says John Pavlik, director of the company's training department. If salespeople are spending less time on training, Pavlik says, they're able to spend more time on what they do best: selling.

Training is only one of the ways sales organizations are using the Internet. Many companies are using the Web to make sales presentations and service accounts. For example, computer and communications equipment maker NEC Corporation has adopted Web-based selling as an essential marketing tool.

After launching a new server line, NEC began looking for ways to cut down on difficult and costly sales force travel. According to Dick Csaplar, marketing manager for the server line, NEC's old sales approach—traveling to customer sites to pitch NEC products—had become unworkable. Instead, NEC adopted a new Web-based sales approach. Although the initial goal was to cut costs and keep people off airplanes, Web selling has now grown into an intrinsic part of NEC's sales efforts. Web selling certainly does reduce travel time and costs. Whereas the average daily cost of salesperson travel is $663, an hour-long Web conference costs just $60. But more importantly, Web selling lets sales reps meet with more prospective customers than ever before, creating a more efficient and effective sales organization. Csaplar estimates that he's doing 10 customer Web conferences a week, during which he and his sales team show prospects product features and benefits. Customers love it because they get a clear understanding of NEC's technology without having to host the NEC team on-site. And Csaplar was pleased to find that Web-based selling is an effective way to interact with customers and to build

■ Online selling support: Sales organizations around the world are now using a host of new Web approaches to train reps, hold sales meetings, and even conduct live sales presentations.

customer relationships. "By the time we're done with the Webcast, the customer understands the technology, the pricing, and the competition, and we understand the customer's business and needs," he says. Without Webcasts, "we'd be lost on how to communicate with the customer without spending a lot of money," says Csaplar. "I don't see us ever going back to the heavy travel thing."

The Web can be a good channel tool for selling to hard-to-reach customers. For example, the big U.S. pharmaceutical companies currently employ some 87,000 sales reps (often called "detailers") to reach roughly 600,000 practicing physicians. However, these reps are finding it harder than ever to get through to the busy doctors. "Doctors need immense amounts of medical information, but their patient loads limit their ability to see pharmaceutical reps or attend outside conferences," says an industry researcher. The answer: Increasingly, it's the Web. The pharmaceutical companies now regularly use product Web sites, e-mail marketing, and video conferencing to help reps deliver useful information to physicians on their home or office PCs. One study found that last year more than 200,000 physicians participated in "e-detailing"—the process of receiving drug marketing information via the Web—a 400 percent jump in only three years. Using direct-to-doctor Web conferences, companies can make live, interactive medical presentations to any physician with a PC and Web access, saving both the customer's and the rep's time.

The Internet can also be a handy way to hold sales strategy meetings. Consider Cisco Systems, which provides networking solutions for the Internet. Sales meetings used to take an enormous bite out of Cisco's travel budget. Now the company saves about $1 million per month by conducting many of those sessions on the Web. Whenever Cisco introduces a new product, it holds a Web meeting to update salespeople, in groups of 100 or more, on the product's marketing and sales strategy.

(*continues*)

Usually led by the product manager or a vice president of sales, the meetings typically begin with a 10-minute slide presentation that spells out the planned strategy. Then, salespeople spend the next 50 or so minutes asking questions via teleconference. The meeting's leader can direct attendees' browsers to competitors' Web sites or ask them to vote on certain issues by using the software's instant polling feature. "Our salespeople are actually meeting more online than they ever were face to face," says Mike Mitchell, Cisco's distance learning manager, adding that some salespeople who used to meet with other reps and managers only a few times a quarter are meeting online nearly every day. "That's very empowering for the sales force, because they're able to make suggestions at every step of the way about where we're going with our sales and marketing strategies."

Thus, Web-based technologies can produce big organizational benefits for sales forces. They help conserve salespeople's valuable time, save travel dollars, and give salespeople a new vehicle for selling and servicing accounts. But the technologies also have some drawbacks. For starters, they're not cheap. And such systems can intimidate low-tech salespeople or clients. "As simple as it is, if your salespeople or clients aren't comfortable using the Web, you're wasting your money," says one marketing communications manager." What's more, Web tools are susceptible to server crashes and other network difficulties, not a happy event when you're in the midst of an important sales meeting or presentation. Finally, there are some things you just can't do or teach via the Web, things that require personal interactions.

For these reasons, some high-tech experts recommend that sales executives use Web technologies to supplement training, sales meetings, and preliminary client sales presentations, but resort to old-fashioned, face-to-face meetings when the time draws near to close the deal. "When push comes to shove, if you've got an account worth closing, you're still going to get on that plane and see the client in person," says sales consultant Sloane. "Your client is going to want to look you in the eye before buying anything from you, and that's still one thing you just can't do online."

Sources: Portions adapted from Rich Thomaselli, "Pharma Replacing Reps," *Advertising Age,* January 2005, p. 50; Tom Kontzer, "Web Conferencing Embraced," *InformationWeek,* May 26, 2003, pp. 68–70; and Melinda Ligos, "Point, Click, and Sell," *Sales & Marketing Management,* May 1999, pp. 51–55. Also see, Daniel Tynan, "Next Best Thing to Being There," *Sales & Marketing Management,* April 2004, p. 22; Judith Lamont, "Collaboration: Web Conferencing Spans the Distance," *KM World,* June 2005, pp. 16–18; Rebecca Aronauer, "Looking Good," *Sales & Marketing Management,* April 2006, pp. 41–44; and Mary M. Long, Thomas Tellefsen, and J. David Lichtenthal, "Internet Integration into the Industrial Selling Process: A Step-By-Step Approach," *Industrial Marketing Management,* July 2007, pp. 676–89.

Sales quota

A standard that states the amount a salesperson should sell and how sales should be divided among the company's products.

Many companies motivate their salespeople by setting **sales quotas**—standards stating the amount they should sell and how sales should be divided among the company's products. Compensation is often related to how well salespeople meet their quotas. Companies also use various *positive incentives* to increase sales force effort. *Sales meetings* provide social occasions, breaks from routine, chances to meet and talk with "company brass," and opportunities to air feelings and to identify with a larger group. Companies also sponsor *sales contests* to spur the sales force to make a selling effort above what would normally be expected. Other incentives include honors, merchandise and cash awards, trips, and profit-sharing plans.

Evaluating Salespeople and Sales Force Performance

We have thus far described how management communicates what salespeople should be doing and how it motivates them to do it. This process requires good feedback. And good feedback means getting regular information about salespeople to evaluate their performance.

Management gets information about its salespeople in several ways. The most important source is *sales reports,* including weekly or monthly work plans and longer-term territory marketing plans. Salespeople also write up their completed activities on *call reports* and turn in *expense reports* for which they are partly or wholly repaid. The company can also monitor the sales and profit performance data in the salesperson's territory. Additional information comes from personal observation, customer surveys, and talks with other salespeople.

Using various sales force reports and other information, sales management evaluates members of the sales force. It evaluates salespeople on their ability to "plan their work and work their plan." Formal evaluation forces management to develop and communicate clear standards for judging performance. It also provides salespeople with constructive feedback and motivates them to perform well.

On a broader level, management should evaluate the performance of the sales force as a whole. Is the sales force accomplishing its customer relationship, sales, and profit objectives? Is it working well with other areas of the marketing and company organization? Are sales force costs in line with outcomes? As with other marketing activities, the company wants to measure its *return on sales investment.*

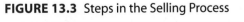

Linking the Concepts

Take a break and reexamine your thoughts about salespeople and sales management.

- Again, when someone says "salesperson," what image comes to mind? Have your perceptions of salespeople changed after what you've read in the chapter so far? How? Be specific.
- Apply each of the steps in sales force management shown in Figure 13.1 to the chapter-opening CDW example.
- Find and talk with someone employed in professional sales. Ask about and report on how this salesperson's company designs its sales force and recruits, selects, trains, compensates, supervises, and evaluates its salespeople. Would you like to work as a salesperson for this company?

The Personal Selling Process

We now turn from designing and managing a sales force to the actual personal selling process. The **selling process** consists of several steps that the salesperson must master. These steps focus on the goal of getting new customers and obtaining orders from them. However, most salespeople spend much of their time maintaining existing accounts and building long-term customer *relationships*. We discuss the relationship aspect of the personal selling process in a later section.

Selling process
The steps that the salesperson follows when selling, which include prospecting and qualifying, preapproach, approach, presentation and demonstration, handling objections, closing, and follow-up.

Steps in the Selling Process

As shown in Figure 13.3, the selling process consists of seven steps: prospecting and qualifying, preapproach, approach, presentation and demonstration, handling objections, closing, and follow-up.

Prospecting and Qualifying The first step in the selling process is **prospecting**—identifying qualified potential customers. Approaching the right potential customers is crucial to selling success. As one sales expert puts it: "If the sales force starts chasing anyone who is breathing and seems to have a budget, you risk accumulating a roster of expensive-to-serve, hard-to-satisfy customers who never respond to whatever value proposition you have." He continues, "The solution to this isn't rocket science. [You must] train salespeople to actively scout the right prospects." Another expert concludes: "Increasing your prospecting effectiveness is the fastest single way to boost your sales."[23]

Prospecting
The step in the selling process in which the salesperson or company identifies qualified potential customers.

FIGURE 13.3 Steps in the Selling Process

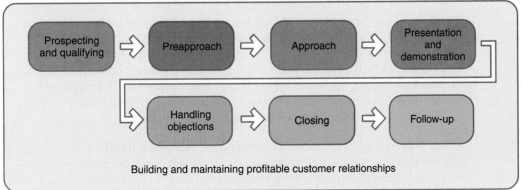

The salesperson must often approach many prospects to get just a few sales. Although the company supplies some leads, salespeople need skill in finding their own. The best source is referrals. Salespeople can ask current customers for referrals and cultivate other referral sources, such as suppliers, dealers, noncompeting salespeople, and bankers. They can also search for prospects in directories or on the Web and track down leads using the telephone and direct mail. Or they can drop in unannounced on various offices (a practice known as "cold calling").

Salespeople also need to know how to *qualify* leads—that is, how to identify the good ones and screen out the poor ones. Prospects can be qualified by looking at their financial ability, volume of business, special needs, location, and possibilities for growth.

Preapproach Before calling on a prospect, the salesperson should learn as much as possible about the organization (what it needs, who is involved in the buying) and its buyers (their characteristics and buying styles). This step is known as the **preapproach**. The salesperson can consult standard industry and online sources, acquaintances, and others to learn about the company.

The salesperson should set *call objectives*, which may be to qualify the prospect, to gather information, or to make an immediate sale. Another task is to decide on the best approach, which might be a personal visit, a phone call, or a letter or e-mail. The best timing should be considered carefully because many prospects are busiest at certain times. Finally, the salesperson should give thought to an overall sales strategy for the account.

Approach During the **approach** step, the salesperson should know how to meet and greet the buyer and get the relationship off to a good start. This step involves the salesperson's appearance, opening lines, and the follow-up remarks. The opening lines should be positive to build goodwill from the beginning of the relationship. This opening might be followed by some key questions to learn more about the customer's needs or by showing a display or sample to attract the buyer's attention and curiosity. As in all stages of the selling process, listening to the customer is crucial.

Presentation and Demonstration During the **presentation** step of the selling process, the salesperson tells the "value story" to the buyer, showing how the company's offer solves the customer's problems. The *customer-solution approach* fits better with today's relationship marketing focus than does a hard-sell or glad-handing approach. Buyers today want answers, not smiles; results, not razzle-dazzle. Moreover, they don't want just products—they want to know how those products will add value to their businesses. They want salespeople who listen to their concerns, understand their needs, and respond with the right products and services.

But before salespeople can *present* customer solutions, they must *develop* solutions to present. Many companies now train their salespeople to go beyond "product thinking." Weyerhaeuser, the $21 billion U.S. forest products company, reorganized its entire sales force around customer-solutions selling:

> Weyerhaeuser, long a product-driven company, undertook an extreme makeover, creating a customer-solutions-focused sales organization called iLevel. Rather than selling wood products piecemeal, Weyerhaeuser wants to be considered the one-stop location for all of the innovation and products required to construct residential home frames—joists, beams, floors, and all. The new iLevel organization assigns a single salesperson to each major builder or dealer. The sales rep leads a coordinated sales team that serves all of the customer's needs. To implement iLevel, Weyerhaeuser retrained its 250 salespeople to present customers with solutions, not products. "It is a consultative selling approach," says a Weyerhaeuser executive. Never again will a salespeople merely sell orders of lumber. "What we want [our sales reps] to do is help our customers find solutions that make them [and us] money."[24]

The solutions approach calls for good listening and problem-solving skills. A recent study revealed that 74 percent of 200 purchasers surveyed at companies nationwide said they would be much more likely to buy from a salesperson if the seller would simply listen to them. Unfortunately, some salespeople believe that talking is more important in sales. "Salespeople

---

Preapproach

The step in the selling process in which the salesperson learns as much as possible about a prospective customer before making a sales call.

Approach

The step in the selling process in which the salesperson meets the customer for the first time.

Presentation

The step in the selling process in which the salesperson tells the "value story" to the buyer, showing how the company's offer solves the customer's problems.

love the chase," says one experienced salesperson. "We get so excited that we often don't spend as much time as we should asking questions and really listening to the answers." Adds another, "When they don't hear what their prospects are saying, they may talk about the wrong products, features, or benefits."[25]

The qualities that buyers *dislike most* in salespeople include being pushy, late, deceitful, and unprepared or disorganized. The qualities they *value most* include good listening, empathy, honesty, dependability, thoroughness, and follow-through. Great salespeople know how to sell, but more importantly they know how to listen and to build strong customer relationships. Says one professional, "Salespeople must have the right answers, certainly, but they also have to learn how to ask those questions and listen."[26]

Finally, salespeople must also plan their presentation methods. Today, advanced presentation technologies allow for full multimedia presentations to only one or a few people. CDs and DVDs, online presentation technologies, and handheld and laptop computers with presentation software have replaced the flip chart. Here's an example:[27]

■ Weyerhaeuser created a customer-solutions-focused sales organization called iLevel. It promises customers "a coordinated sales team that that gives you access to all the products, logistics, tech services, and software you need [to] quickly resolve issues."

> Tina Cox, a technical trainer for Analytical Graphics, a company that produces integrated land, sea, and air analysis software, uses InterWrite software and its integrated wireless tablet-and-pen capabilities to teach new and potential customers how to use the company's products. Just like TV football commentator John Madden, she writes on her prepared screens during the presentation. She draws on freeze-frame images, just as Madden often does when he directs viewers to the significant elements of the previous football play with his trademark squiggly lines. Cox uses her tablet and pen to show her clients the key elements of the slides. If customers ever lose a thread of her sales presentation, they can easily check the information she circled and almost immediately get back on track. Cox believes the technology greatly enhances her presentations, both Web-based and in person, and customers agree.

Handling Objections Customers almost always have objections during the presentation or when asked to place an order. The problem can be either logical or psychological, and objections are often unspoken. In **handling objections**, the salesperson should use a positive approach, seek out hidden objections, ask the buyer to clarify any objections, take objections as opportunities to provide more information, and turn the objections into reasons for buying. Every salesperson needs training in the skills of handling objections.

Handling objections
The step in the selling process in which the salesperson seeks out, clarifies, and overcomes customer objections to buying.

Closing After handling the prospect's objections, the salesperson now tries to close the sale. Some salespeople do not get around to **closing** or do not handle it well. They may lack confidence, feel guilty about asking for the order, or fail to recognize the right moment to close the sale. Salespeople should know how to recognize closing signals from the buyer, including physical actions, comments, and questions. For example, the customer might sit forward and nod approvingly or ask about prices and credit terms.

Salespeople can use one of several closing techniques. They can ask for the order, review points of agreement, offer to help write up the order, ask whether the buyer wants this model or that one, or note that the buyer will lose out if the order is not placed now. The salesperson may offer the buyer special reasons to close, such as a lower price or an extra quantity at no charge.

Closing
The step in the selling process in which the salesperson asks the customer for an order.

Follow-Up The last step in the selling process—**follow-up**—is necessary if the salesperson wants to ensure customer satisfaction and repeat business. Right after closing, the salesperson should complete any details on delivery time, purchase terms, and other matters. The

Follow-up
The last step in the selling process in which the salesperson follows up after the sale to ensure customer satisfaction and repeat business.

salesperson then should schedule a follow-up call when the initial order is received, to make sure there is proper installation, instruction, and servicing. This visit would reveal any problems, assure the buyer of the salesperson's interest, and reduce any buyer concerns that might have arisen since the sale.

Personal Selling and Managing Customer Relationships

The steps in the selling process as just described are *transaction oriented*—their aim is to help salespeople close a specific sale with a customer. But in most cases, the company is not simply seeking a sale: It has targeted a major customer that it would like to win and keep. The company would like to show that it has the capabilities to serve the customer over the long haul in a mutually profitable *relationship*. The sales force usually plays an important role in building and managing profitable customer relationships. Thus, as shown in Figure 13.3, the selling process must be understood in the context of building and maintaining profitable customer relationships.

Today's large customers favor suppliers who can sell and deliver a coordinated set of products and services to many locations, and who can work closely with customer teams to improve products and processes. For these customers, the first sale is only the beginning of the relationship. Unfortunately, some companies ignore these relationship realities. They sell their products through separate sales forces, each working independently to close sales. Their technical people may not be willing to lend time to educate a customer. Their engineering, design, and manufacturing people may have the attitude that "it's our job to make good products and the salesperson's to sell them to customers." Their salespeople focus on pushing products toward customers rather than listening to customers and providing solutions.

Other companies, however, recognize that winning and keeping accounts requires more than making good products and directing the sales force to close lots of sales. It requires listening to customers, understanding their needs, and carefully coordinating the whole company's efforts to create customer value and to build lasting relationships.

Sales Promotion

Sales promotion

Short-term incentives to encourage the purchase or sale of a product or service.

Personal selling and advertising often work closely with another promotion tool, sales promotion. **Sales promotion** consists of short-term incentives to encourage purchase or sales of a product or service. Whereas advertising offers reasons to buy a product or service, sales promotion offers reasons to buy *now*.

Examples of sales promotions are found everywhere. A freestanding insert in the Sunday newspaper contains a coupon offering $1 off Folgers coffee. An e-mail from EddieBauer.com offers free shipping on your next purchase over $100. The end-of-the-aisle display in the local supermarket tempts impulse buyers with a wall of Coke cases. An executive buys a new Sony laptop and gets a free carrying case, or a family buys a new Ford Explorer and receives a factory rebate of $1,000. A hardware store chain receives a 10 percent discount on selected Black & Decker portable power tools if it agrees to advertise them in local newspapers. Sales promotion includes a wide variety of promotion tools designed to stimulate earlier or stronger market response.

Rapid Growth of Sales Promotion

Sales promotion tools are used by most organizations, including manufacturers, distributors, retailers, and not-for-profit institutions. They are targeted toward final buyers (*consumer promotions*), retailers and wholesalers (*trade promotions*), business customers (*business promotions*), and members of the sales force (*sales force promotions*). Today, in the average consumer packaged-goods company, sales promotion accounts for 74 percent of all marketing expenditures.[28]

Several factors have contributed to the rapid growth of sales promotion, particularly in consumer markets. First, inside the company, product managers face greater pressures to increase their current sales, and promotion is viewed as an effective short-run sales tool.

Second, externally, the company faces more competition and competing brands are less differentiated. Increasingly, competitors are using sales promotion to help differentiate their offers. Third, advertising efficiency has declined because of rising costs, media clutter, and legal restraints. Finally, consumers have become more deal oriented, and ever-larger retailers are demanding more deals from manufacturers.

The growing use of sales promotion has resulted in *promotion clutter,* similar to advertising clutter. Consumers are increasingly tuning out promotions, weakening their ability to trigger immediate purchase. Manufacturers are now searching for ways to rise above the clutter, such as offering larger coupon values or creating more dramatic point-of-purchase displays.

In developing a sales promotion program, a company must first set sales promotion objectives and then select the best tools for accomplishing these objectives.

Sales Promotion Objectives

Sales promotion objectives vary widely. Sellers may use *consumer promotions* to urge short-term customer buying or to enhance customer brand involvement. Objectives for *trade promotions* include getting retailers to carry new items and more inventory, buy ahead, or promote the company's products and give them more shelf space. For the *sales force,* objectives include getting more sales force support for current or new products or getting salespeople to sign up new accounts.

Sales promotions are usually used together with advertising, personal selling, direct marketing, or other promotion mix tools. Consumer promotions must usually be advertised and can add excitement and pulling power to ads. Trade and sales force promotions support the firm's personal selling process.

In general, rather than creating only short-term sales or temporary brand switching, sales promotions should help to reinforce the product's position and build long-term *customer relationships.* If properly designed, every sales promotion tool has the potential to build both short-term excitement and long-term consumer relationships. Increasingly, marketers are avoiding "quick fix," price-only promotions in favor of promotions designed to build brand equity.

Examples include all of the "frequency marketing programs" and loyalty clubs that have mushroomed in recent years. Most hotels, supermarkets, and airlines offer frequent-guest/buyer/flyer programs giving rewards to regular customers. All kinds of companies offer rewards programs, even the *Washington Post:*[29]

Washington Post readers can now opt to join the newspaper's new PostPoints rewards program, designed to boost reader involvement and advertiser support. Home-delivery and online customers earn PostPoints by reading and interacting with Post columns and features, supplying information about themselves and their interests, or even by helping the community through activities such as giving blood or participating in charity fund-raising events. They can also earn points by shopping at partnering retail stores—called PostPoints Spots. These retail partners are limited to *Washington Post* advertisers. Once earned, PostPoints can be redeemed for everything from gift cards, merchandise, and event tickets to major appliances and dream trips. Other benefits of membership include invitations to exclusive Post-Points partner events and meet and greets with *Washington Post* writers. In all, the PostPoints loyalty program strengthens the three-way relationship between the newspaper, its customers, and its advertisers. "The innovation is in . . . how this approach relates to [both] customers and advertisers," says a marketing executive at CVS/pharmacy, a PostPoints partner with over 300 stores in the D.C. area. "It's a new dialogue based on community ties and trust."

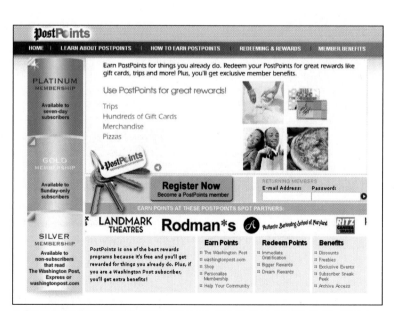

■ Customer-relationship building programs: The Washington Post's PostPoints rewards program strengthens the three-way relationship between the newspaper, its customers, and its advertisers.

Major Sales Promotion Tools

Many tools can be used to accomplish sales promotion objectives. Descriptions of the main consumer, trade, and business promotion tools follow.

Consumer promotions

Sales promotion tools used to boost short-term customer buying and involvement or to enhance long-term customer relationships.

Consumer Promotions The **consumer promotions** include a wide range of tools—from samples, coupons, refunds, premiums, and point-of-purchase displays to contests, sweepstakes, and event sponsorships.

Samples are offers of a trial amount of a product. Sampling is the most effective—but most expensive—way to introduce a new product or to create new excitement for an existing one. Some samples are free; for others, the company charges a small amount to offset its cost. The sample might be delivered door-to-door, sent by mail, handed out in a store, attached to another product, or featured in an ad. Sometimes, samples are combined into sample packs, which can then be used to promote other products and services. Sampling can be a powerful promotional tool.

Coupons are certificates that give buyers a saving when they purchase specified products. Most consumers love coupons. U.S. package-goods companies distributed more than 280 billion coupons last year with an average face value of over $1.25. Consumers redeemed more than 2.6 billion of them for a total savings of about $3.25 billion.[30] Coupons can promote early trial of a new brand or stimulate sales of a mature brand. However, as a result of coupon clutter, redemption rates have been declining in recent years. Thus, most major consumer-goods companies are issuing fewer coupons and targeting them more carefully.

Marketers are also cultivating new outlets for distributing coupons, such as supermarket shelf dispensers, electronic point-of-sale coupon printers, e-mail and online media, or even mobile text-messaging systems. Mobile couponing is very popular in Europe, India, and Japan, and it's now gaining popularity in the United States. For example, consider Cellfire, a mobile couponing company in California:[31]

Cellfire (cellfire.com) distributes digital coupons to the cell phones of consumers nationwide who sign up for its free service. Cellfire's growing list of clients includes Domino's Pizza, TGI Friday, Hollywood Video, 1-800-flowers.com, and Hardee's restaurants. Cellfire sends an ever-changing assortment of digital coupons to users' cell phones. To use the coupons, users simply call up the stored coupon list, navigate to the coupon they want, press the "Use Now" button, and show the digital coupon to the store cashier. Domino's even permits consumers holding the mobile coupons to simply click on a link to have their cell phones dial the nearest Domino's store to place an order.

Coupons distributed through Cellfire offer distinct advantages to both consumers and marketers. Consumers don't have to find and clip paper coupons or print out Web coupons and bring them along when they shop. They always have their cell phone coupons with them. For marketers, mobile coupons allow more careful targeting and eliminate the costs of printing and distributing paper coupons. "We don't pay for distribution of digital coupons," says one client. "We pay on redemptions." And the redemption rates can be dazzling. According to Cellfire's chief executive, Brent Dusing, "We're seeing redemption rates as high as 10 to 15 percent, while the industry average paper response is . . . less than 1 percent."

■ New forms of coupons: Cellfire distributes digital coupons to the cells phones of consumers who sign up for its free service.

Cash refunds (or *rebates*) are like coupons except that the price reduction occurs after the purchase rather than at the retail outlet. The consumer sends a "proof of purchase" to the manufacturer, who then refunds part of the purchase price by mail. For example, Toro ran a clever preseason promotion on some of its snowblower models, offering a rebate if the snowfall in the buyer's market area turned out to be below average. Competitors were not able to match this offer on such short notice, and the promotion was very successful.

Price packs (also called *cents-off deals*) offer consumers savings off the regular price of a product. The producer marks the reduced prices directly on the label or package. Price packs can be single packages sold at a reduced price (such as two for the price of one), or two related products banded together (such as a toothbrush and toothpaste). Price packs are very effective—even more so than coupons—in stimulating short-term sales.

Premiums are goods offered either free or at low cost as an incentive to buy a product, ranging from toys included with kids' products to phone cards and DVDs. A premium may come inside the package (in-pack), outside the package (on-pack), or through the mail. Kellogg often incorporates premiums with its cereals and related products. For instance, it recently offered a free *Pirates of the Caribbean* Skull Projection Alarm Clock to young customers who mailed five Pirate Tokens from specially marked Kellogg's packages.

Advertising specialties, also called *promotional products,* are useful articles imprinted with an advertiser's name, logo, or message that are given as gifts to consumers. Typical items include T-shirts and other apparel, pens, coffee mugs, calendars, key rings, mouse pads, matches, tote bags, coolers, golf balls, and caps. U.S. marketers spent almost $19 billion on advertising specialties last year. Such items can be very effective. The "best of them stick around for months, subtly burning a brand name into a user's brain," notes a promotional products expert. In a recent study, 71 percent of all consumers surveyed had received at least one promotional product in the past 12 months. Seventy-six percent of those were able to recall the advertiser's name on the promotional product they received, compared to only 53.5 percent who could recall the name of an advertiser in a print publication they had read in the past week.[32]

Point-of-purchase (POP) promotions include displays and demonstrations that take place at the point of sale. Think of your last visit to the local Safeway, Costco, CVS, or Bed Bath & Beyond. Chances are good that you were tripping over aisle displays, promotional signs, "shelf talkers," or demonstrators offering free tastes of featured food products. Unfortunately, many retailers do not like to handle the hundreds of displays, signs, and posters they receive from manufacturers each year. Manufacturers have responded by offering better POP materials, offering to set them up, and tying them in with television, print, or online messages.

Contests, sweepstakes, and games give consumers the chance to win something, such as cash, trips, or goods, by luck or through extra effort. A *contest* calls for consumers to submit an entry—a jingle, guess, suggestion—to be judged by a panel that will select the best entries. A *sweepstakes* calls for consumers to submit their names for a drawing. A *game* presents consumers with something—bingo numbers, missing letters—every time they buy, which may or may not help them win a prize. Such promotions can create considerable brand attention and consumer involvement.[33]

Doritos recently ran a "Get It. Taste It. Name It" sweepstakes asking consumers to taste its newest flavor, initially labeled X-13D, and then suggest a name and write an ad for it. Those who submitted a name or ad were entered into the sweeps to become one of 100 Doritos Flavor Masters. Winners were selected through a random drawing. As Flavor Masters, the 100 grand-prize winners will get the chance to take part in Doritos research and development, giving feedback on future flavor ideas. Each also got a year's supply of Doritos, 52 coupons good for one bag per week. The X-13D chips, packaged in a black bag with a label that looks like it's lifted from a science lab, built a lot of buzz. The promotion pulled in more than 100,000 entries within only a month of launch. And the promotion sparked considerable online chatter as bloggers wrote about stumbling upon the distinctive bag in convenience stores and tackled the question of what the flavor really was.

■ Event marketing: P&G recently sponsored a holiday event promotion for its Charmin brand in New York's Times Square, where it can be very difficult to find a public restroom. P&G set up 20 sparkling clean Charmin-themed mini-bathrooms, each with its own sink and a bountiful supply of Charmin.

Event marketing
Creating a brand-marketing event or serving as a sole or participating sponsor of events created by others.

Trade promotions
Sales promotion tools used to persuade resellers to carry a brand, give it shelf space, promote it in advertising, and push it to consumers.

Business promotions
Sales promotion tools used to generate business leads, stimulate purchases, reward customers, and motivate salespeople.

Finally, marketers can promote their brands through **event marketing** (or *event sponsorships*). They can create their own brand-marketing events or serve as sole or participating sponsors of events created by others. The events might include anything from mobile brand tours to festivals, reunions, marathons, concerts, or other sponsored gatherings. Event marketing is huge, and it may be the fastest-growing area of promotion. If you include only consumer events in which the sponsoring brand owns the event or receives top billing, event-marketing spending reached $32.2 billion last year, up 15 percent from a year earlier. If you include brand sponsorships in which another entity owns the event, spending rises to more than $50 billion.[34]

Most companies sponsor brand events. Harley-Davidson holds "HOG Rallies" and Harley biker reunions that draw hundreds of thousands of bikers each year. Nextel is paying $700 million over 10 years to sponsor the NASCAR Nextel Cup Series. Coca Cola, Anheuser-Busch, Nickelodeon, and others jointly sponsor Carnival Miami's culminating event, Calle Ocho, said to be the largest annual celebration of Hispanic culture in the United States. And Procter & Gamble creates numerous events for its major brands. For example, P&G recently sponsored a holiday event promotion for its Charmin brand in New York's Times Square, where it can be very difficult to find a public restroom. P&G set up 20 sparkling clean Charmin-themed mini-bathrooms, each with its own sink and a bountiful supply of Charmin. The event turned out to be the ultimate in experiential marketing—"more than 5,600 people showed up within the first 24 hours of the potty palace premier," notes one observer, and the event touched people in places advertising wouldn't dare to go.[35]

Trade Promotions Manufacturers direct more sales promotion dollars toward retailers and wholesalers (81 percent) than to final consumers (19 percent).[36] **Trade promotions** can persuade resellers to carry a brand, give it shelf space, promote it in advertising, and push it to consumers. Shelf space is so scarce these days that manufacturers often offer price-offs, allowances, buy-back guarantees, or free goods to retailers and wholesalers to get products on the shelf and, once there, to keep them on it.

Manufacturers use several trade promotion tools. Many of the tools used for consumer promotions—contests, premiums, displays—can also be used as trade promotions. Or the manufacturer may offer a straight *discount* off the list price on each case purchased during a stated period of time (also called a *price-off, off-invoice,* or *off-list*). Manufacturers also may offer an *allowance* (usually so much off per case) in return for the retailer's agreement to feature the manufacturer's products in some way. An advertising allowance compensates retailers for advertising the product. A display allowance compensates them for using special displays.

Manufacturers may offer *free goods,* which are extra cases of merchandise, to resellers who buy a certain quantity or who feature a certain flavor or size. They may offer *push money*—cash or gifts to dealers or their sales forces to "push" the manufacturer's goods. Manufacturers may give retailers free *specialty advertising items* that carry the company's name, such as pens, pencils, calendars, paperweights, matchbooks, memo pads, and yardsticks.

Business Promotions Companies spend billions of dollars each year on promotion to industrial customers. **Business promotions** are used to generate business leads, stimulate purchases, reward customers, and motivate salespeople. Business promotions include many of the same tools used for consumer or trade promotions. Here, we focus on two additional major business promotion tools—conventions and trade shows, and sales contests.

Many companies and trade associations organize *conventions and trade shows* to promote their products. Firms selling to the industry show their products at the trade show. Vendors receive many benefits, such as opportunities to find new sales leads, contact customers, introduce new products, meet new customers, sell more to present customers, and educate customers with publications and audiovisual materials. Trade shows also help companies reach many prospects not reached through their sales forces.

Some trade shows are huge. For example, at this year's International Consumer Electronics Show, 2,700 exhibitors attracted more than 140,000 professional visitors. Even more impressive, at the BAUMA mining and construction equipment trade show in Munich, Germany, some 3,000 exhibitors

■ Some trade shows are huge. At this year's International Consumer Electronics Show, 2,500 exhibitors attracted more than 150,000 professional visitors.

from more than 100 countries presented their latest product innovations to more than 500,000 attendees from 190 countries.[37]

A *sales contest* is a contest for salespeople or dealers to motivate them to increase their sales performance over a given period. Sales contests motivate and recognize good company performers, who may receive trips, cash prizes, or other gifts. Some companies award points for performance, which the receiver can turn in for any of a variety of prizes. Sales contests work best when they are tied to measurable and achievable sales objectives (such as finding new accounts, reviving old accounts, or increasing account profitability).

Developing the Sales Promotion Program

Beyond selecting the types of promotions to use, marketers must make several other decisions in designing the full sales promotion program. First, they must decide on the *size of the incentive*. A certain minimum incentive is necessary if the promotion is to succeed; a larger incentive will produce more sales response. The marketer also must set *conditions for participation*. Incentives might be offered to everyone or only to select groups.

Marketers must decide how to *promote and distribute the promotion* program itself. A $2-off coupon could be given out in a package, at the store, via the Internet, or in an advertisement. Each distribution method involves a different level of reach and cost. Increasingly, marketers are blending several media into a total campaign concept. The *length of the promotion* is also important. If the sales promotion period is too short, many prospects (who may not be buying during that time) will miss it. If the promotion runs too long, the deal will lose some of its "act now" force.

Evaluation is also very important. Many companies fail to evaluate their sales promotion programs, and others evaluate them only superficially. Yet marketers should work to measure the returns on their sales promotion investments, just as they should seek to assess the returns on other marketing activities. The most common evaluation method is to compare sales before, during, and after a promotion. Marketers should ask, Did the promotion attract new customers or more purchasing from current customers? Can we hold onto these new customers and purchases? Will the long-run customer relationship and sales gains from the promotion justify its costs?

Clearly, sales promotion plays an important role in the total promotion mix. To use it well, the marketer must define the sales promotion objectives, select the best tools, design the sales promotion program, implement the program, and evaluate the results. Moreover, sales promotion must be coordinated carefully with other promotion mix elements within the overall integrated marketing communications program.

REST STOP ⬁ REVIEWING THE CONCEPTS

This chapter is the second of three chapters covering the final marketing mix element—promotion. The previous chapter dealt with overall integrated marketing communications and with advertising and public relations. This one investigates personal selling and sales promotion. Personal selling is the interpersonal arm of the communications mix. Sales promotion consists of short-term incentives to encourage the purchase or sale of a product or service.

1. Discuss the role of a company's salespeople in creating value for customers and building customer relationships.

Most companies use salespeople and many companies assign them an important role in the marketing mix. For companies selling business products, the firm's salespeople work directly with customers. Often, the sales force is the customer's only direct contact with the company and therefore may be viewed by customers as representing the company itself. In contrast, for consumer-product companies that sell through intermediaries, consumers usually do not meet salespeople or even know about them. The sales force works behind the scenes, dealing with wholesalers and retailers to obtain their support and helping them become effective in selling the firm's products.

As an element of the promotion mix, the sales force is very effective in achieving certain marketing objectives and carrying out such activities as prospecting, communicating, selling and servicing, and information gathering. But with companies becoming more market oriented, a customer-focused sales force also works to produce both *customer satisfaction* and *company profit*. The sales force plays a key role in developing and managing profitable *customer relationships*.

2. Identify and explain the six major sales force management steps.

High sales force costs necessitate an effective sales management process consisting of six steps: designing sales force strategy and structure, recruiting and selecting, training, compensating, supervising, and evaluating salespeople and sales force performance.

In designing a sales force, sales management must address strategy issues such as what type of sales force structure will work best (territorial, product, customer, or complex structure); how large the sales force should be; who will be involved in the selling effort; and how its various salespeople and sales-support people will work together (inside or outside sales forces and team selling).

To hold down the high costs of hiring the wrong people, salespeople must be recruited and selected carefully. In recruiting salespeople, a company may look to job duties and the characteristics of its most successful salespeople to suggest the traits it wants in its salespeople. It must then look for applicants through recommendations of current salespeople, employment agencies, classified ads, the Internet, and contacting college students. In the selection process, the procedure can vary from a single informal interview to lengthy testing and interviewing. After the selection process is complete, training programs familiarize new salespeople not only with the art of selling but also with the company's history, its products and policies, and the characteristics of its market and competitors.

The sales force compensation system helps to reward, motivate, and direct salespeople. In compensating salespeople, companies try to have an appealing plan, usually close to the going rate for the type of sales job and needed skills. In addition to compensation, all salespeople need supervision, and many need continuous encouragement because they must make many decisions and face many frustrations. Periodically, the company must evaluate their performance to help them do a better job. In evaluating salespeople, the company relies on getting regular information gathered through sales reports, personal observations, customers' letters and complaints, customer surveys, and conversations with other salespeople.

3. Discuss the personal selling process, distinguishing between transaction-oriented marketing and relationship marketing.

The art of selling involves a seven-step *selling process*: *prospecting and qualifying, preapproach, approach, presentation and demonstration, handling objections, closing,* and *follow-up.* These steps help marketers close a specific sale and as such are *transaction oriented.* However, a seller's dealings with customers should be guided by the larger concept of *relationship marketing.* The company's sales force should help to orchestrate a whole-company effort to develop profitable long-term relationships with key customers based on superior customer value and satisfaction.

4. Explain how sales promotion campaigns are developed and implemented.

Sales promotion campaigns call for setting sales promotions objectives (in general, sales promotions should be *consumer relationship building*); selecting tools; developing and implementing the sales promotion program by using *consumer promotion tools* (from coupons, refunds, premiums, and point-of-purchase promotions to contests, sweepstakes, and events), *trade promotion tools* (discounts, allowances, free goods, push money), and *business promotion tools* (conventions, trade shows, sales contests), as well as deciding on such things as the size of the incentive, the conditions for participation, how to promote and distribute the promotion package, and the length of the promotion. After this process is completed, the company evaluates its sales promotion results.

Navigating the Key Terms

Approach (400)
Business promotions (406)
Closing (401)
Consumer promotions (404)
Customer sales force structure (388)
Event marketing (405)
Follow-up (401)
Handling objections (401)

Inside sales force (389)
Outside sales force (or field sales force) (389)
Personal selling (385)
Preapproach (400)
Presentation (400)
Product sales force structure (388)
Prospecting (399)
Sales force management (387)

Sales promotion (402)
Sales quota (398)
Salesperson (385)
Selling process (399)
Team selling (392)
Territorial sales force structure (387)
Trade promotions (406)

Travel Log

Discussing the Issues

1. According to the chapter, salespeople serve "two masters." What does this mean? Is it a good or bad thing? (AASCB: Communication)

2. Explain how a company can enable marketing and sales to work better together. (AACSB: Communication)

3. List and briefly describe the three sales-force structures outlined in the chapter. What sales-force structure does CDW employ? (AACSB: Communication)

4. Define *sales promotion* and discuss the factors contributing to its rapid growth. (AACSB: Communication)

5. Name and describe the types of trade sales promotions. (AACSB: Communication)

6. Explain the decisions involved in designing a sales promotion program. (AACSB: Communication)

Application Questions

1. Explain how a company uses the workload method to determine sales-force size. If a company has 4,300 customer accounts, each requiring four calls per year, and if an average salesperson makes 1,000 calls per year, how many salespeople will be needed? (AACSB: Communication; Reflective Thinking)

2. Name and describe the steps in the selling process. In a small group, develop a plan for the selling process that an office equipment firm could use to sell to small businesses in your community. (AACSB: Communication; Reflective Thinking)

3. Name and briefly describe the types of consumer promotions. Find examples of four of them and present them to your class. (AACSB: Communication; Reflective Thinking)

Under the Hood: Focus on Technology

Sales-force automation (or SFA) allows salespeople to spend less time in their office and more time with customers. Web-based sales automation systems provide information at the touch of a button to salespeople out in the field. Such systems became more feasible with the advent of laptop computers. Now, wireless technology allows even more information to be accessed using small mobile devices such as smart phones, pocket PCs, and PDAs. Although not as available as computer-based systems, mobile data applications are expected to grow fastest and to generate more than $100 billion in revenue worldwide by 2012. Intuit Inc. offers mobile solutions through its Eclipse Mobile interface. Whereas most SFA platforms require salespeople to use laptop computers, the new generation of platforms allows the same or more applications to use handheld devices. One leader in sales-force automation is Salesforce.com, but there are many other companies in this field.

1. Visit www.salesforce.com to view a demonstration of how this service is used to automate the selling function. You will need to sign in to view the demonstration. Write a brief report on what you learned and discuss how the use of this type of technology helps a salesperson deliver greater customer value. (AACSB: Communication; Use of IT; Reflective Thinking)

2. Discuss drawbacks of using sales-force automation in general and mobile SFA solutions in particular. (AACSB: Communication; Reflective Thinking)

Focus on Ethics

Slotting fees, a type of allowance trade promotion, consist of a one-time fee paid by food manufacturers to retailers for allotting shelf space to a new product. The manufacturer buys the product's way into the marketing channel. An FTC survey shows that the average slotting fee per chain for a new product is about $10,000, and producers report total slotting fees in the $1,000,000 to $2,000,000 range. The many critics of this system claim that grocery retailers have too much power in this situation. They also assert that the slotting fee system is unfair to small manufacturers who cannot afford such large fees. Slotting fees have been called everything from a bribe to a retailer's addiction, a questionable source of income that many retailers now rely on to survive. Retailers claim that the fees are needed to offset the costs associated with new products. To stock a new product, they must shift other products on the shelf, move products in the warehouse, and update computer systems. In addition, retailers say they run the risk of costs associated with the potential failure of the product. In response to the cries of small manufacturers that these fees create unfair competition, retailers sometimes waive slotting fees for smaller companies.

1. Assess slotting fees from the viewpoints of both retailers and manufacturers. How does this type of allowance differ from the others described in the chapter? Is it fair for retailers to demand slotting fees from manufacturers? (AACSB: Communication; Ethical Reasoning)

2. Go to www.ftc.gov/opa/2003/11/slottingallowance.htm to read about the FTC report on slotting fees. What did you learn from this report? (AACSB: Communication; Reflective Thinking)

Video Case

Nudie

All across the globe, consumers are seeking all-natural, wholesome foods. Even Wal-Mart, a low-price leader, carries organic and all-natural foods. Nudie, a quirky little company in Australia, makes its own contribution to the fast-growing natural foods market—all-natural fruit juices, fruit crushes, and smoothies that provide a day's fruit in every bottle. Amidst a sea of all-natural products, how did Nudie reach customers and encourage them to try its new products? Through a carefully designed program of personal selling and sales promotion.

Nudie uses well-crafted point-of-purchase displays and a devoted, motivated sales force to work with resellers to reach consumers. As a result, Nudie is the fastest-growing juice maker in Australia, attracting an ever-increasing number of highly devoted customers who love Nudie's products. Says one Nudie customer, "Love and happiness are overrated. But Nudies make living worthwhile!"

After viewing the video featuring Nudie, answer the following questions about personal selling and sales promotion.

1. How does Nudie's process for selecting sales representatives compare to the process described in the text?

2. What sales promotion tools does Nudie employ to reach consumers and encourage sales?

3. Select a sales promotion tool not listed in your previous response. How could Nudie use that tool to further promote its products?

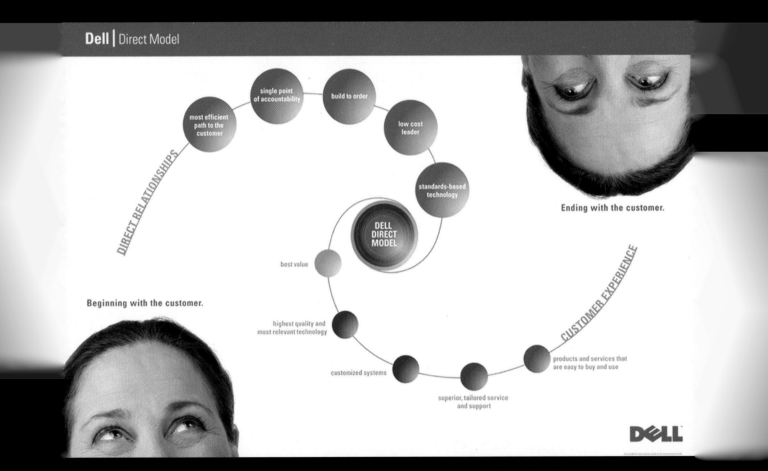

Dell | Direct Model

After studying this chapter, you should be able to

1. define direct marketing and discuss its benefits to customers and companies

2. identify and discuss the major forms of direct marketing

3. explain how companies have responded to the Internet and other powerful new technologies with online marketing strategies

4. discuss how companies go about conducting online marketing to profitably deliver more value to customers

5. overview the public policy and ethical issues presented by direct marketing

CHAPTER 14

Direct and Online Marketing: Building Direct Customer Relationships

ROAD MAP Previewing the Concepts

In the previous two chapters, you learned about communicating customer value through integrated marketing communication (IMC) and about four specific elements of the marketing communications mix—advertising, publicity, personal selling, and sales promotion. In this chapter, we'll look at the final IMC element, direct marketing, and at its fastest-growing form, online marketing. Actually, direct marketing can be viewed as more than just a communications tool. In many ways it constitutes an overall marketing approach—a blend of communication and distribution channels all rolled into one. As you read on, remember that although this chapter examines direct marketing as a separate tool, it must be carefully integrated with other elements of the promotion mix.

As a tune-up, let's look at the world's largest direct marketing company—Dell. Dell owes its incredible success in the fiercely competitive computer industry to a revolutionary business approach—the Dell Direct Model. Says one analyst, "There's no better way to make, sell, and deliver PCs than the way Dell does it, and nobody executes [the direct] model better than Dell." However, in the past few years, Dell's once-rocketing revenues have slowed and profits have fallen off, raising an imposing strategic question: Is the heralded Dell Way running out of gas?

When 19-year-old Michael Dell began selling personal computers out of his college dorm room in 1984, competitors and industry insiders scoffed at the concept of direct computer marketing. Yet young Michael quickly proved the skeptics wrong. In little more than two decades, he has turned his dorm-room mail-order business into the $57 billion Dell computer empire.

In the United States, Dell is now number one in desktop PC sales, number one in laptops, number one in servers, and number three in printers. It captures a 33.5 percent share of the U.S. PC market, compared with number-two HP's 19.4 percent and number-three Gateway's 6.1 percent. Between 1995 and 2005, Dell was the darling of the stock market, producing an average annual return to investors of 39 percent, best among all Fortune 100 companies.

Dell owes its stunning success to its revolutionary business model—the *direct model*. Dell sells the lion's share of its product via the telephone and Internet. Over the years, Dell's direct marketing approach has delivered greater customer value through an unbeatable combination of product customization, low prices, fast delivery, and award-winning customer service. A customer can call 1-800-Buy-Dell or log on to www.dell.com on Monday morning; order a fully customized, state-of-the-art PC to suit his or her special needs; and have the machine delivered to his or her doorstep or desktop before the end of the week—all at prices traditionally well below competitors' prices for a comparably performing PC.

Michael Dell's initial idea was to serve individual buyers by letting them customize machines with the special features they wanted at low prices. However, this one-to-one approach appeals even more strongly to corporate buyers, because Dell can so easily preconfigure each computer to precise requirements. Dell routinely preloads machines with a company's own software and even undertakes tedious tasks such as pasting inventory tags onto each machine so that computers can be delivered directly to a given employee's desk. As a result, more than 85 percent of Dell's sales come from businesses, governments, and educational institutions.

The direct model results in more efficient selling and lower costs, which translate into lower prices for customers. "Nobody, but nobody, makes [and markets] computer hardware more efficiently than Dell," says one analyst. "No unnecessary costs: This is an all-but-sacred mandate of the famous Dell direct business model." Because Dell builds machines to order, it carries barely any inventory—less than three days' worth by some accounts. Dealing one-to-one with customers helps the company react immediately to shifts in demand, so Dell doesn't get stuck with PCs no one wants. Finally, by selling directly, Dell has no dealers or retailers to pay.

Selling direct has given Dell a tremendous competitive advantage. However, after decades of rocketing revenues and profits, the much-heralded Dell growth engine has stalled in the past few years. Last year, sales grew only 2.1 percent and profits fell off 27 percent. To make matters worse, a revitalized HP overtook Dell last year as the global leader in PC sales, and HP continues to eat into Dell's U.S. market share lead. The direct marketing pioneer now faces a key strategic quandary: Is current sluggish growth the result of temporary market conditions and flawed tactical decisions, or does it signal cracks in Dell's vaunted direct marketing model itself?

For sure, Dell has made some tactical errors in implementing the direct marketing model. It appears to have relied *too* heavily on low costs and prices, at the expense of investments in customer service and product innovation. For example, as part of its continual cost-cutting focus, Dell shifted much of its customer service and technical support to temporary employees and to low-cost call centers in places such as India and the Philippines. As a result, customer satisfaction and "likely-to-

repurchase" scores plummeted. Admits Michael Dell, "I think we overemphasized the price element and did not emphasize relationship and customization and experience."

Dell has also been criticized for investing too little in product innovation and design. Its obsession with low costs resulted in a narrow product and operations focus—assembling, selling, and delivering basic machines wrapped in generic grey boxes and counting on low prices to attract customers and sales. This focus on machines has created an "imagination gap" between Dell and more innovative competitors such as Apple. Its lack of design imagination has put Dell at a disadvantage, especially in consumer markets.

Dell is moving to fix these focus, customer-service, and product problems but the imposing strategic question remains: Is the highly regarded Dell Way running out of gas? Can Dell's direct-only model still deliver sales and profit growth for Dell in the fast-changing and highly competitive PC market? The answer depends on whom you ask. Most analysts agree that Dell's direct model still works well for selling complex PC systems to corporate buyers, the bread and butter of Dell's current business. But it may not work as well in consumer markets, Dell's biggest source of potential future growth.

Much of the recent growth in PC demand has come from consumers buying laptops at electronics retailers such as Best Buy and Circuit City. However, boxed in by its direct sales strategy and its focus on corporate customers, Dell has largely missed out on the boom. Further, Dell appears to be stumbling in its attempts to sell an expanding assortment of high-tech consumer electronics products to final buyers. Some analysts suggest that Dell's vaunted direct model may not work well for selling LCD TVs, handhelds, MP3 players, digital cameras, and other personal digital devices—products that consumers want to see and experience first-hand before buying and for which customization is not important.

What's more, in both Dell's business and consumer markets, the direct model doesn't deliver the powerful price punch that it once did. Over the years, Dell's substantial cost advantages forced competitors either to follow or fall away. As a result—under what has come to be known as the "Dell Effect"—competitors such as HP and Lenovo are now both stunningly cost efficient, eroding Dell's price superiority.

Thus, looking ahead, Dell is carefully analyzing its direct-only marketing strategy. In fact, it's already making adjustments by adding some surprising new indirect channels. For example, Dell now sells inexpensive PCs through Wal-Mart and is rumored to be talking with Best Buy, Circuit City, and CompUSA. It has also begun opening its own chain of Dell-branded retail stores, replacing the 100 or so smaller Dell kiosks scattered in malls around the country. These are "the first steps in an evolving global retail strategy," says Michael Dell. "Customers are telling us they want more and new ways to purchase our products. We're committed to finding new ways to reach more customers."

Does this mean that Dell will abandon its previously sacred direct model? Michael Dell says no. "Our direct model still works very well," he asserts. "We wouldn't trade ours for anyone else's!" And although Dell isn't the high-flying growth company it once was, it remains a fearsome competitor. "I do think that Dell's core strengths historically will be its core strengths in the future," says Dell. Still, he leaves the door ajar for future strategic shifts. "The Direct Model has been a revolution," he says, "but it's not a religion."[1]

Many of the marketing and promotion tools that we've examined in previous chapters were developed in the context of *mass marketing:* targeting broad markets with standardized messages and offers distributed through intermediaries. Today, however, with the trend toward more narrowly targeted marketing, many companies are adopting *direct marketing,* either as a primary marketing approach, as in Dell's case, or as a supplement to other approaches. In this section, we explore the exploding world of direct marketing.

Direct marketing consists of direct connections with carefully targeted individual consumers to both obtain an immediate response and cultivate lasting customer relationships. Direct marketers communicate directly with customers, often on a one-to-one, interactive basis. Using detailed databases, they tailor their marketing offers and communications to the needs of narrowly defined segments or even individual buyers.

Beyond brand and relationship building, direct marketers usually seek a direct, immediate, and measurable consumer response. For example, as we learned in the chapter-opening story, Dell interacts directly with customers, by telephone or through its Web site, to design built-to-order systems that meet customers' individual needs. Buyers order directly from Dell, and Dell quickly and efficiently delivers the new computers to their homes or offices.

Direct marketing
Direct connections with carefully targeted individual consumers to both obtain an immediate response and cultivate lasting customer relationships.

The New Direct Marketing Model

Early direct marketers—catalog companies, direct mailers, and telemarketers—gathered customer names and sold goods mainly by mail and telephone. Today, however, fired by rapid advances in database technologies and new marketing media—especially the Internet—direct marketing has undergone a dramatic transformation.

In previous chapters, we've discussed direct marketing as direct distribution—as marketing channels that contain no intermediaries. We also include direct marketing as one element of the promotion mix—as an approach for communicating directly with consumers. In actuality, direct marketing is both these things and more.

Most companies still use direct marketing as a supplementary channel or medium. Thus, Lexus markets mostly through mass-media advertising and its high-quality dealer network but also supplements these channels with direct marketing. Its direct marketing includes promotional DVDs and other materials mailed directly to prospective buyers and a Web page (www.lexus.com) that provides consumers with information about various models, competitive comparisons, financing, and dealer locations. Similarly, most department stores sell the majority of their merchandise off their store shelves but also sell through direct mail and online catalogs.

However, for many companies today, direct marketing is more than just a supplementary channel or advertising medium. For these companies, direct marketing—especially in its most recent transformation, online marketing—constitutes a complete model for doing business. Rather than using direct marketing and the Internet only as supplemental approaches, firms employing this new *direct model* use it as the *only* approach. Companies such as Dell, Amazon.com, eBay, and GEICO have built their entire approach to the marketplace around direct marketing. The direct model is rapidly changing the way companies think about building relationships with customers.

"You could save hundreds by switching to GEICO."

I'm here to save you money.

Get a free rate quote today.
GEICO
geico.com

Online, over the phone, or at your local office.

WITH GEICO, IT'S EASY TO SAVE.
I'm here to save you money. Well...not really here next to your computer, where you can go to **geico.com** to get a free rate quote...but you know what I mean.

People say to me, I don't have time to shop for car insurance. And I say to them, have you ever made $500 in 15 minutes? Go to **geico.com**. Answer some quick questions and you get an accurate rate quote. You can then buy online, over the phone, or at a local office. Do what makes you feel comfortable, and you could save $500.

VALUE. IT'S SAVINGS AND SERVICE.
People know they could save hundreds. But what about GEICO's service? I tell people, GEICO isn't just about saving hundreds. There's also the 24/7 service with real live people. They're on the phones at all hours answering your questions. And you can also get the help you need at **geico.com**.

CLAIMS MADE EASY.
A friend gets into a small accident. Everyone is OK. When he gets home he goes to geico.com, reports the claim and schedules an appointment. Later he goes back to the website, prints out his estimate and views photos of the damage. He then goes to a GEICO-approved shop and his claim repairs are guaranteed for as long as he owns his car. Now that's what I call service.

DEPENDABILITY. IT'S THE GEICO WAY.
I get asked, how dependable is GEICO? They've been consistently protecting drivers and delivering great value for more than 70 years. That sounds dependable to me.

PROTECT LOTS OF THINGS WITH GEICO.
Sure, GEICO does cars. Everyone knows that. But, you could also save big when GEICO insures your motorcycle or ATV. Homeowner's and renter's insurance? GEICO can help you with those, and boats and PWCs, too.

LOOK, IT ALL MAKES A LOT OF SENSE.
It's easy to switch, so contact GEICO. You'll get the value and service all my mates love.

15 minutes could save you 15%.

GEICO
geico.com
1-800-947-AUTO

Obtenga una cotización gratis en español en miGEICO.com.

You could save online, over the phone, or at your local office.

Average savings based on GEICO New Policyholder Survey Data through August 2007. Some discounts, coverages, payment plans, and features are not available in all states or in all GEICO companies. Government Employees Insurance Co. • GEICO General Insurance Co. • GEICO Indemnity Co. • GEICO Casualty Co. These companies are subsidiaries of Berkshire Hathaway Inc. GEICO auto insurance is not available in MA. Homeowner's, motorcycle and ATV insurance are currently not available in some states. Homeowner's, renter's, boat, and PWC coverages are written through non-affiliated insurance companies and are secured through Insurance Counselors Inc., the GEICO Property Agency. The GEICO gecko image © GEICO 1999 – 2007. GEICO: Washington, DC 20076. © 2006-2007 GEICO

■ The new direct marketing model: Companies such as GEICO have built their entire approach to the marketplace around direct marketing: just visit geico.com or call 1-800-947-auto.

Growth and Benefits of Direct Marketing

Direct marketing has become the fastest-growing form of marketing. According to the Direct Marketing Association, U.S. companies spent $166.5 billion on direct marketing last year. These expenditures generated an estimated $1.94 trillion in direct marketing sales, or about 10 percent of total sales in the U.S. economy. And direct marketing-driven sales are growing rapidly. The DMA estimates that direct marketing sales will grow 6.3 percent annually through 2011, compared with a projected 4.8 percent annual growth for total U.S. sales.[2]

Direct marketing continues to become more Web oriented, and Internet marketing is claiming a fast-growing share of direct marketing spending and sales. The Internet now accounts for only about 18 percent of direct marketing-driven sales. However, the DMA predicts that over the next five years Internet marketing expenditures will grow at a blistering 17 percent a year, more than three times faster than expenditures in other direct marketing media. Internet-driven sales will grow by almost 16 percent.

Whether employed as a complete business model or as a supplement to a broader integrated marketing mix, direct marketing brings many benefits to both buyers and sellers.

Benefits to Buyers

For buyers, direct marketing is convenient, easy, and private. Direct marketers never close their doors, and customers don't have to battle traffic, find parking spaces, and trek through stores to find products. From the comfort of their homes or offices, they can browse catalogs or company Web sites at any time of the day or night. Business buyers can learn about products and services without tying up time with salespeople.

Direct marketing gives buyers ready access to a wealth of products. For example, unrestrained by physical boundaries, direct marketers can offer an almost unlimited selection to consumers almost anywhere in the world. For example, by making computers to order and selling directly, Dell can offer buyers thousands of self-designed PC configurations, many times the number offered by competitors who sell preconfigured PCs through retail stores. And just compare the huge selections offered by many Web merchants to the more meager assortments of their brick-and-mortar counterparts. For instance, log on to Bulbs.com, "the Web's number-one light bulb superstore," and you'll have instant access to every imaginable kind of light bulb or lamp—incandescent bulbs, fluorescent bulbs, projection bulbs, surgical bulbs, automotive bulbs—you name it. No physical store could offer handy access to such a vast selection.

Direct marketing channels also give buyers access to a wealth of comparative information about companies, products, and competitors. Good catalogs or Web sites often provide more information in more useful forms than even the most helpful retail salesperson can. For example, the Amazon.com site offers more information than most of us can digest, ranging from top-10 product lists, extensive product descriptions, and expert and user product reviews to recommendations based on customers' previous purchases. And Sears catalogs offer a treasure trove of information about the store's merchandise and services. In fact, you probably wouldn't think it strange to see a Sears salesperson referring to a catalog in the store for more detailed information while trying to advise a customer on a specific product or offer.

Finally, direct marketing is interactive and immediate—buyers can interact with sellers by phone or on the seller's Web site to create exactly the configuration of information, products, or services they desire, and then order them on the spot. Moreover, direct marketing gives consumers a greater measure of control. Consumers decide which catalogs they will browse and which Web sites they will visit.

Benefits to Sellers

For sellers, direct marketing is a powerful tool for building customer relationships. Using database marketing, today's marketers can target small groups or individual consumers and promote their offers through personalized communications. Because of the one-to-one nature of direct marketing, companies can interact with customers by phone or online, learn more about their needs, and tailor products and services to specific customer tastes. In turn, customers can ask questions and volunteer feedback.

Direct marketing also offers sellers a low-cost, efficient, speedy alternative for reaching their markets. Direct marketing has grown rapidly in business-to-business marketing, partly in response to the ever-increasing costs of marketing through the sales force. When personal sales calls cost an average of more than $320 per contact, they should be made only when necessary and to high-potential customers and prospects. Lower-cost-per-contact media—such as telemarketing, direct mail, and company Web sites—often prove more cost effective. Similarly, online direct marketing results in lower costs, improved efficiencies, and speedier handling of channel and logistics functions, such as order processing, inventory handling, and delivery. Direct marketers such as Amazon.com, Dell, or Netflix also avoid the expense of maintaining a store and the related costs of rent, insurance, and utilities, passing the savings along to customers.

Direct marketing can also offer greater flexibility. It allows marketers to make ongoing adjustments to its prices and programs, or to make immediate and timely announcements and offers. For example, Southwest Airlines' Ding! application takes advantage of the flexibility and immediacy of the Web to share low-fare offers directly with customers:[3]

> When Jim Jacobs hears a "ding" coming from his desktop computer, he thinks about discount air fares like the $122 ticket he recently bought for a flight from Tampa to Baltimore on Southwest Airlines. Several times a day, Southwest sends Jacobs and millions of other computer users discounts through an application called Ding! "If I move quickly," says Jacobs, "I can usually save a lot of money."

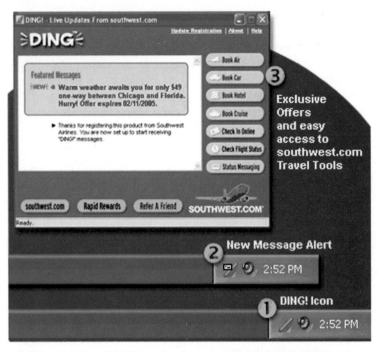

■ Southwest Airlines "DING!" application takes advantage of flexibility and immediacy of the Web to share low-fare offers directly with customers.

The fare to Baltimore underbid the airline's own Web site by $36, he says. Ding! lets Southwest bypass the reservations system and pass bargain fares directly to interested customers. Eventually, Ding! may even allow Southwest to customize fare offers based on each customer's unique characteristics and travel preferences. For now, Ding! provides something any marketer craves: a one-to-one communication link between customer and brand. But its branding power reaches further. Ding! has turned air travel inside-out by transforming what has historically been a planned, premeditated purchase into an impulse buy. Southwest's noisy little icon now boasts more than 2 million subscribers who've booked over $130 million in fares by using it. Forty-five percent of its Ding! users come back to book again, compared to the industry average of just 27 percent.

Finally, direct marketing gives sellers access to buyers that they could not reach through other channels. Smaller firms can mail catalogs to customers outside their local markets and post 1-800 telephone numbers to handle orders and inquiries. Internet marketing is a truly global medium that allows buyers and sellers to click from one country to another in seconds. A Web surfer from Paris or Istanbul can access an online L.L.Bean catalog as easily as someone living in Freeport, Maine, the direct retailer's hometown. Even small marketers find that they have ready access to global markets.

Customer Databases and Direct Marketing

Customer database

An organized collection of comprehensive data about individual customers or prospects, including geographic, demographic, psychographic, and behavioral data.

Effective direct marketing begins with a good customer database. A **customer database** is an organized collection of comprehensive data about individual customers or prospects, including geographic, demographic, psychographic, and behavioral data. A good customer database can be a potent relationship-building tool. The database gives companies "a snapshot of how customers look and behave." Says one expert, "A company is no better than what it knows [about its customers]."[4]

In consumer marketing, the customer database might contain a customer's demographics (age, income, family members, birthdays), psychographics (activities, interests, and opinions), and buying behavior (buying preferences and the recency, frequency, and monetary value—RFM—of past purchases). In business-to-business marketing, the customer profile might contain the products and services the customer has bought; past volumes and prices; key contacts (and their ages, birthdays, hobbies, and favorite foods); competing suppliers; status of current contracts; estimated customer spending for the next few years; and assessments of competitive strengths and weaknesses in selling and servicing the account.

Some of these databases are huge. For example, casino operator Harrah's Entertainment has built a customer database containing 30 terabytes worth of customer information, roughly three times the number of printed characters in the Library of Congress. Internet portal Yahoo! records every click made by every visitor, adding some 400 billion bytes of data per day to its database—the equivalent of 800,000 books. And Wal-Mart captures data on every item, for every customer, for every store, every day. Its database contains more than 570 terabytes of data—that's 570 trillion bytes, far greater than the storage horsepower of 100,000 personal computers.[5]

Companies use their databases in many ways. They use databases to locate good potential customers and to generate sales leads. They can mine their databases to learn about customers in detail, and then fine-tune their market offerings and communications to the special preferences and behaviors of target segments or individuals. In all, a company's database can be an important tool for building stronger long-term customer relationships. For example, financial services provider USAA uses its database to find ways to serve the long-term needs of customers, regardless of immediate sales impact, creating an incredibly loyal customer base:

> USAA provides financial services to U.S. military personnel and their families, largely through direct marketing via the telephone and Internet. It maintains a customer database built from customer purchasing histories and from information collected directly from customers. To keep the database fresh, the organization regularly surveys its more than 5.9 million customers worldwide to learn such things as whether they have children (and if so, how old they are), if they have moved recently, and when they plan to retire. USAA uses the database to tailor direct marketing offers to the specific needs of individual customers. For example, for customers looking toward retirement, it sends information on estate planning. If the family has college-age children, USAA sends those children information on how to manage their credit cards. If the family has younger children, it sends booklets on things such as financing a child's education. One delighted reporter, a USAA customer, recounts how USAA even helped him teach his 16-year-old daughter to drive. Just before her birthday, but before she received her driver's license, USAA mailed a "package of materials, backed by research, to help me teach my daughter how to drive, help her practice, and help us find ways to agree on what constitutes safe driving later on, when she gets her license." What's more, marvels the reporter, "USAA didn't try to sell me a thing. My take-away: that USAA is investing in me for the long term, that it defines profitability not just by what it sells today." Through such skillful use of its database, USAA serves each customer uniquely, resulting in high levels of customer loyalty and sales growth. The average customer household owns almost five USAA products, and the $12 billion company retains 97 percent of its customers.[6]

Like many other marketing tools, database marketing requires a special investment. Companies must invest in computer hardware, database software, analytical programs, communication links, and skilled personnel. The database system must be user-friendly and available to various marketing groups, including those in product and brand management, new-product development, advertising and promotion, direct mail, telemarketing, Web marketing, field sales, order fulfillment, and customer service. However, a well-managed database should lead to sales and customer-relationship gains that will more than cover its costs.

Forms of Direct Marketing

The major forms of direct marketing—as shown in Figure 14.1—include personal selling, direct-mail marketing, catalog marketing, telephone marketing, direct-response television marketing, kiosk marketing, new digital direct marketing technologies, and online marketing. We examined personal selling in depth in Chapter 13. Here, we examine the other direct marketing forms.

Direct-Mail Marketing

Direct-mail marketing involves sending an offer, announcement, reminder, or other item to a person at a particular address. Using highly selective mailing lists, direct marketers send out millions of mail pieces each year—letters, catalogs, ads, brochures, samples, CDs and DVDs, and other "salespeople with wings." Direct mail is by far the largest direct marketing medium. The DMA reports that direct mail (including both catalog and noncatalog mail) drives more than a third of all U.S. direct marketing sales.[7]

Direct-mail marketing
Direct marketing by sending an offer, announcement, reminder, or other item to a person at a particular address.

FIGURE 14.1

Forms of Direct Marketing

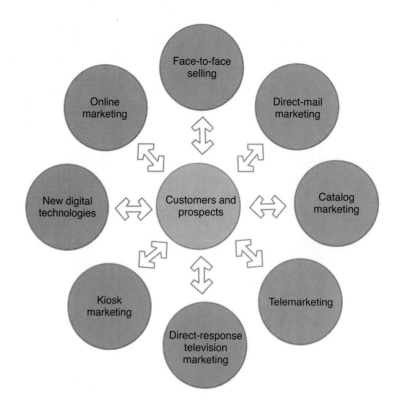

Direct mail is well suited to direct, one-to-one communication. It permits high target-market selectivity, can be personalized, is flexible, and allows easy measurement of results. Although direct mail costs more than mass media such as television or magazines per thousand people reached, the people it reaches are much better prospects. Direct mail has proved successful in promoting all kinds of products, from books, music, DVDs, and magazine subscriptions to insurance, gift items, clothing, gourmet foods, and industrial products. Charities also use direct mail heavily to raise billions of dollars each year.

The direct-mail industry constantly seeks new methods and approaches. For example, CDs and DVDs are now among the fastest-growing direct-mail media. One study showed that including a CD or DVD in a marketing offer generates responses between 50 to 1,000 percent greater than traditional direct mail.[8] New forms of delivery have also become popular, such as *fax mail, voice mail,* and *e-mail*. Fax mail and voice mail are subject to the same do-not-call restrictions as telemarketing, so their use has been limited in recent years. However, e-mail is booming as a direct marketing tool. Today's e-mail messages have moved far beyond the drab text-only messages of old. The new breed of e-mail ad uses animation, interactive links, streaming video, and personalized audio messages to reach out and grab attention.

E-mail and other new forms deliver direct mail at incredible speeds compared to the post office's "snail mail" pace. Yet, much like mail delivered through traditional channels, they may be resented as "junk mail" or SPAM if sent to people who have no interest in them. For this reason, smart marketers are targeting their direct mail carefully so as not to waste their money and recipients' time. They are designing permission-based programs, sending e-mail ads only to those who want to receive them. We will discuss e-mail marketing in more detail later in the chapter.

Catalog Marketing

Catalog marketing

Direct marketing through print, video, or digital catalogs that are mailed to select customers, made available in stores, or presented online.

Advances in technology, along with the move toward personalized, one-to-one marketing have resulted in exciting changes in **catalog marketing**. *Catalog Age* magazine used to define a *catalog* as "a printed, bound piece of at least eight pages, selling multiple products, and offering a direct ordering mechanism." Today, only a few years later, this definition is sadly out of date.

With the stampede to the Internet, more and more catalogs are going digital. A variety of Web-only catalogers have emerged, and most print catalogers have added Web-based catalogs to their marketing mixes. For example, click on the Shop by Catalog link at www.llbean.com and you can flip through the latest L.L.Bean catalog page by page online. One study found that consumers now make 36 percent of their catalog purchases online. Web-based catalogs eliminate production, printing, and mailing costs. And whereas print-catalog space is limited, online catalogs can offer an almost unlimited amount of merchandise. Finally, online catalogs allow real-time merchandising—products and features can be added or removed as needed and prices can be adjusted instantly to match demand.

However, despite the advantages of Web-based catalogs, as your overstuffed mailbox may suggest, printed catalogs are still thriving. Why aren't companies ditching their old-fashioned paper catalogs in this new digital era? It turns out that printed catalogs are still one of the best ways to convince consumers to use the online versions. And printed catalogs can create emotional connections with customers that Web-based sales spaces simply can't (see Marketing at Work 14.1).[9]

In all, catalog marketing—printed and online—has grown explosively during the past 25 years. Annual catalog sales amounted to about $144 billion last year and are expected to grow to top $185 billion by 2011.[10] Some large general-merchandise retailers—such as JC Penney and Spiegel—sell a full line of merchandise through catalogs. In recent years, these giants have been challenged by thousands of specialty catalogs that serve highly specialized market niches. According to one study, there are 8,000 to 10,000 unique catalog titles in the United States.[11]

Consumers can buy just about anything from a catalog. Sharper Image catalogs hawk everything from $300 robot vacuum cleaners to $4,500 see-through kayaks. Each year Lillian Vernon sends out 17 editions of its 3 catalogs with total circulation of 80 million copies to its 20-million-person database, selling more than 700 products in each catalog, ranging from shoes to decorative lawn birds and monogrammed oven mitts.[12] Specialty department stores, such as Neiman Marcus, Bloomingdale's, and Saks Fifth Avenue, use catalogs to cultivate upper-middle-class markets for high-priced, often exotic, merchandise. Want to buy a rocket trip into outer space? It's featured in the latest Neiman Marcus catalog for only $1.7 million.

Telephone marketing
Using the telephone to sell directly to customers.

Telephone Marketing

Telephone marketing involves using the telephone to sell directly to consumers and business customers. Telephone marketing now accounts for 22 percent of all direct marketing-driven sales. We're all familiar with telephone marketing directed toward consumers, but business-to-business marketers also use telephone marketing extensively, accounting for more than 55 percent of all telephone marketing sales.[13]

Marketers use *outbound* telephone marketing to sell directly to consumers and businesses. They use *inbound* toll-free 800 numbers to receive orders from television and print ads, direct mail, or catalogs. The use of 800 numbers has taken off in recent years as more and more companies have begun using them, and as current users have added new features such as toll-free fax numbers. To accommodate this rapid growth, new toll-free area codes, such as 888, 877, and 866, have been added.

Properly designed and targeted telemarketing provides many benefits, including purchasing convenience and increased product and service information. However, the explosion in unsolicited outbound telephone marketing over the years annoyed many consumers, who objected to the almost daily "junk phone calls" that pull them away from the dinner table or fill the answering machine.

■ Marketers use inbound toll-free 800 numbers to receive orders from television and print ads, direct mail, or catalogs. Here, the Carolina Cookie Company urges, "Don't wait another day. Call now to place an order or request a catalog."

14.1 MARKETING AT WORK
Catalogs, Catalogs—*Everywhere!*

For outdoor furniture and garden accessories seller Smith & Hawken, the future lies in cyberspace. Sales of flower pots and gardening gadgets on the company's Web site are blossoming, accounting for 20 percent of its total sales. Meanwhile, catalog sales are wilting, declining to 15 percent of total sales last year, from 19 percent the year before. So why not just ditch the paper catalog? Not a chance, says Felix Carbullido, senior vice-president for marketing. Rather than becoming obsolete in the online age, he says, the old-fashioned catalog is the most effective way to make an emotional appeal to the consumer. And ultimately, he argues, the catalog is the best method to convince customers to go online.

Thanks to e-commerce, as well as rising printing and mailing costs, catalogs were supposed to be dead by now. But a quick visit to the mailbox will confirm that predictions of their death have been vastly exaggerated. In fact, catalogs are more popular than ever—and thriving because of the limitations of shopping by pointing and clicking. Unlike the bulky books of yore, such as the venerable Sears catalog, which at times ran to 1,000 pages, the new breed of catalog is a glossy, magazine-like statement meant to convey to consumers the look and feel of a brand. That's a task the typical home PC just isn't up to, no matter how good the resolution of the monitor. The prototypical new catalogs don't attempt to list everything in the product line. Rather, they simply show a carefully selected and dramatically photographed selection. "We're promoting an entire lifestyle in the garden or patio, not just items," says Carbullido.

Sure, consumers may complain about the stacks of catalogs stuffing their mailboxes. But they're using them anyway, and their actions are speaking louder than their words to retailers. That's why companies are sending out more and more catalogs—the number mailed grew by 5.5 percent last year to 19.2 billion. A big mass-mailer like Victoria's Secret ships 400 million of them annually, or 1.33 for every American citizen. What can Victoria's Secret possibly get out of those 400 million catalogs? Plenty. Last year its catalog and online orders accounted for nearly 28 percent of its overall revenues. And catalog sales grew by 10 percent, more than double the 4 percent increase in store sales.

Even companies that started life on the Web appreciate the allure of a well-designed catalog. Zappos.com, the online shoe giant, now includes its Zappos Life catalog with orders. And tiny candy company JohnandKiras.com started a catalog in October after operating for more than four years only on the Web. The e-commerce site itself is an efficient way to place an order, says co-owner John Doyle but "it's not a good way to attract attention, especially with new customers." Marketing through electronic mail, although cheap, often gets caught in spam filters, he says.

Thus, net shopping isn't rendering print catalogs obsolete, it's just changing their mission. In their new roles as brand-building devices, catalogs are meant only to give consumers ideas instead of listing every product. So they can be smaller and punchier. And in their roles as lures to draw consumers to the Web, paper catalogs are sprinkled throughout with online come-ons. In the current L.L. Bean outdoor gear catalog, page 3, a prominent spot in any catalog, features a blurb about a sales rep's climb up Mt. Everest. "Read about his trip and see his remarkable photographs" at the Bean Web site, it says. Indeed, almost every spread in the

In 2003, U.S. lawmakers responded with a National Do-Not-Call Registry, managed by the Federal Trade Commission. The legislation bans most telemarketing calls to registered phone numbers (although people can still receive calls from nonprofit groups, politicians, and companies with which they have recently done business). Delighted consumers have responded enthusiastically. To date, they have registered more than 132 million phone numbers at www.donotcall.com or by calling 888-382-1222. Businesses that break do-not-call laws can be fined up to $11,000 per violation. As a result, reports an FTC spokesperson, the program "has been exceptionally successful."[14]

Do-not-call legislation has hurt the telemarketing industry, but not all that much. Two major forms of telemarketing—inbound consumer telemarketing and outbound business-to-business telemarketing—remain strong and growing. Telemarketing also remains a major fundraising tool for nonprofits groups. However, many telemarketers are shifting to alternative methods for capturing new customers and sales, from direct mail, direct-response TV, and live-chat Web technology to sweepstakes that prompt customers to call in.

For example, ServiceMaster's TruGreen lawn-care service used to generate about 90 percent of its sales through telemarketing. It now uses more direct mail, as well as having employees go door-to-door in neighborhoods where it already has customers. The new approach appears to be working even better than the old cold-calling one. The company's

Williams-Sonoma catalog tells readers to go online for information ranging from sample Thanksgiving menus to recipes for Brussels sprouts.

Even as they try to drive people to the Web, companies are also working harder to tap into a desire of consumers to have something to touch and hold. "Catalogs are a tangible connection in an intangible, online, all-in-the-ether world," says a retail strategist. For instance, the cover of L.L. Bean's clothing catalog this season features an actual fabric swatch for its Fitness Fleece Pullovers. "Feel the softness and the quality," the cover copy says. Try doing that online.

To fire shoppers' imagination, high-end retailers from Saks Fifth Avenue to Neiman Marcus are upping the number of over-the-top fantasy gifts they're offering, such as Neiman's $1.7 million rocket trip into space. Lavish descriptions of these offerings are more than sales tools. They also make good reading material. "People like to receive a beautifully produced catalog. It's entertaining," says a catalog consultant.

Beyond entertainment, a well-designed catalog can be an effective relationship builder. A recent study conducted by Frank About Women, a marketing-to-women communications company, found that a majority of women who receive catalogs are actively engaged with them.

Eighty-nine percent of the participants revealed that they do more than just browse through the catalogs they receive in the mail. They circle or "tab" the items that they want, fold over the corners of pages, and tear pages out. Some 69 percent save their catalogs to look through again. More than just a buying tool, many women view catalogs as a source of entertainment and inspiration. Women claim to love perusing catalogs almost like reading a woman's magazine, looking for ideas for everything from decorating, to fashion, to that extraspecial gift. More than one-third of women surveyed greet their catalogs with enthusiasm, stating they are the first things they look at when they get their mail. Seventy-five percent of women find catalog browsing really enjoyable, fun, and relaxing, with 74 percent agreeing that they get excited when a new catalog arrives.

To enhance such consumer connections, Smith & Hawken recently completed a top-to-bottom revamping of its catalog design approach. Previously, the typical layout in a Smith & Hawken catalog had as many as six items, each shown in photos of roughly equal size. Lighting was stark. Copy focused heavily on the attributes of the products themselves. In the spread showing the Hadley Peak line of wooden furniture, for instance, the main 5-inch-by-7-inch photo of the furniture was on one page and surrounded by six photos of other products. The lighting in the main photo casts hard shadows of chair legs onto a brick patio. Folded napkins and glasses on the table are unused. The spread, says company creative director Sam Osher, "was item specific. The imagery was based just on the product."

Fast-forward a year to the new design. Using a practice known as "heroing," or blowing up an item so it overshadows everything else in the layout, Smith & Hawken now promotes the same Hadley Peak furniture using a 6-inch-by-11-inch photo spread over the layout. It's surrounded by only three other items in far smaller photos, making the furniture the clear focal point. The table is set with actual food and glasses of beer, one half-consumed to show that "there's life in there. Someone was using this napkin," says Osher.

Patio furniture that tugs at the heartstrings? That's exactly the point. "We're showcasing an environment to be aspirational, inspirational," Osher says. "We want to build a scene that makes you say: 'I want to be there.'"

Sources: Adapted from portions of Louise Lee, "Catalogs, Catalogs, Everywhere," *BusinessWeek,* December 4, 2006, pp. 32–34; with additional information from Janie Curtis, "Catalogs as Portals: Why You Should Keep On Mailing," *Multichannel Merchant,* November 30, 2005, accessed at http://multichannelmerchant.com/news/catalogs_portal_1130/index.html.

sales have grown under the new methods, and less than 50 percent of sales come from telemarketing. "We were nervous, but were thrilled with what we've accomplished," says ServiceMaster's chief executive.[15]

In fact, do-not-call appears to be helping most direct marketers more than it's hurting them. Many of these marketers are shifting their call-center activity from making cold calls on often resentful customers to managing existing customer relationships. They are developing "opt-in" calling systems, in which they provide useful information and offers to customers who have invited the company to contact them by phone or e-mail. These "sales tactics have [produced] results as good—or even better—than telemarketing," declares one analyst. "The opt-in model is proving [more] valuable for marketers [than] the old invasive one."[16]

Direct-Response Television Marketing

Direct-response television marketing takes one of two major forms. The first is *direct-response television advertising* (DRTV). Direct marketers air television spots, often 60 or 120 seconds long, which persuasively describe a product and give customers a toll-free number or Web site for ordering. Television viewers also often encounter full 30-minute or longer advertising programs, or *infomercials,* for a single product.

Direct-response television marketing
Direct marketing via television, including *direct-response television advertising* (or *infomercials*) and *home shopping channels.*

Some successful direct-response ads run for years and become classics. For example, Dial Media's ads for Ginsu knives ran for seven years and sold almost three million sets of knives worth more than $40 million in sales; its Armourcote cookware ads generated more than twice that much. Bowflex has grossed more than $1.3 billion in infomercial sales. And over the past 50 years, infomercial czar Ron Popeil's company, Ronco, has sold billions of dollars worth of TV-marketed gadgets, including the original Veg-O-Matic, the Giant Food Dehydrator and Beef Jerky Machine, and the Showtime Rotisserie & BBQ.[17]

For years, infomercials have been associated with somewhat questionable pitches for juicers and other kitchen gadgets, get-rich-quick schemes, and nifty ways to stay in shape without working very hard at it. In recent years, however, a number of large companies—from Procter & Gamble, Dell, Sears, Disney, Bose, and Revlon to Apple, Land Rover, Anheuser-Busch, and even AARP and the U.S. Navy—have begun using infomercials to sell their wares, refer customers to retailers, send out product information, recruit members, or attract buyers to their Web sites. For example, P&G has used DRTV to market more than a dozen brands, including Dryel, Mr. Clean, CoverGirl, Iams pet food, and Old Spice. An estimated 20 percent of all new infomercials now come to you courtesy of Fortune 1000 companies.[18]

Direct-response TV commercials are usually cheaper to make and the media purchase is less costly. Moreover, unlike most media campaigns, direct-response ads always include a 1-800 number or Web address, making it easier for marketers to track the impact of their pitches. For these reasons, DRTV is growing more quickly than traditional broadcast and cable advertising. Some DRTV experts even predict that in 5 or 10 years, as marketers seek greater returns on their advertising investments, all television advertising will be some form of direct-response advertising. "In a business environment where marketers are obsessed with return on investment," notes one such expert, "direct response is tailor-made—[marketers can] track phone calls and Web-site hits generated by the ads. [They can] use DRTV to build brand awareness while simultaneously generating leads and sales."[19]

Home shopping channels, another form of direct-response television marketing, are television programs or entire channels dedicated to selling goods and services. Some home shopping channels, such as the Quality Value Channel (QVC), Home Shopping Network (HSN), and ShopNBC, broadcast 24 hours a day. Program hosts chat with viewers by phone and offer products ranging from jewelry, lamps, collectible dolls, and clothing to power tools and consumer electronics. Viewers call a toll-free number or go online to order goods. With widespread distribution on cable and satellite television, the top three shopping networks combined now reach 248 million homes worldwide.

Despite their lowbrow images, home shopping channels have evolved into highly sophisticated, very successful marketing operations. Consider QVC:

■ Despite its low-brow image, QVC is a highly sophisticated marketing operation. The network once sold $65 million worth of Dell computers in 24 hours. When Michael Dell later appeared on the network, QVC did $48,000 in sales every minute he chatted on the air.

Wired magazine once described QVC as a place appealing to "trailer-park housewives frantically phoning for another ceramic clown." But look past QVC's reputation and you'll find one of the world's most successful and innovative retailers. Last year, the company rang up $7 billion in sales and $760 million in operating profit, making it nearly as big and roughly twice as profitable as Amazon.com. Although QVC sells no advertising, it's the third-largest U.S. broadcaster in terms of revenue (behind NBC and ABC), and its sales and profits are larger than those of all other TV-based retailers combined. Remarkably, thanks to shrewd coordination with TV programming that drives buyers online, the company's Web site, QVC.com, is now the nation's sixth-largest general merchandise Internet retailer. Moreover, QVC isn't just a place where little-known marketers hawk trinkets and trash at bare-bones prices. Prominent manufacturers such as Estée Lauder, Nextel, and Tourneau now sell through QVC. The network's $80 million single-day sales record happened on December 2, 2001, when Dell sold $65 million worth of PCs in 24 hours. (One month later, Michael Dell went on QVC, doing $48,000 in sales every minute he chatted on air.) Even high-fashion designers such as John Bartlett and Marc Bauer now sell lines on QVC.

QVC has honed the art and science of TV retailing. Its producers react in real time, adjusting offers, camera angles, lighting, and dialogue to maximize sales and profits. QVC has become the gold standard of "retailtainment"—the blending of retailing and entertainment. QVC folks call it the "backyard fence" sell—the feeling that the merchants are neighbors visiting from next door. But according to QVC's president for U.S. commerce, "we aren't really in the business of selling." Instead, QVC uses products to build relationships with customers.[20]

Kiosk Marketing

As consumers become more and more comfortable with computer and digital technologies, many companies are placing information and ordering machines—called *kiosks* (in contrast to vending machines, which dispense actual products)—in stores, airports, and other locations. Kiosks are popping up everywhere these days, from self-service hotel and airline check-in devices to in-store ordering kiosks that let you order merchandise not carried in the store.

In-store Kodak, Fuji, and HP kiosks let customers transfer pictures from memory sticks, mobile phones, and other digital storage devices, edit them, and make high-quality color prints. Kiosks in Hilton hotel lobbies let guests view their reservations, get room keys, view prearrival messages, check in and out, and even change seat assignments and print boarding passes for flights on any of 18 airlines. Outdoor equipment retailer REI has at least four Web-enabled kiosks in each of its 63 stores that provide customers with product information and let them place orders online. Kiosks in Target stores link to articles from *Consumer Reports* magazine, and Mazda dealers let customers use kiosks to research car and truck values through Kelly Blue Book.[21]

Business marketers also use kiosks. For example, Dow Plastics places kiosks at trade shows to collect sales leads and to provide information on its 700 products. The kiosk system reads customer data from encoded registration badges and produces technical data sheets that can be printed at the kiosk or faxed or mailed to the customer. The system has resulted in a 400 percent increase in qualified sales leads.[22]

New Digital Direct Marketing Technologies

Today, thanks to a wealth of new digital technologies, direct marketers can reach and interact with consumers just about anywhere, at anytime, about almost anything. Here, we look into several exciting new digital direct marketing technologies: mobile phone marketing, podcasts and vodcasts, and interactive TV (ITV).

Mobile Phone Marketing With more than 230 million Americans now subscribing to wireless services, many marketers view mobile phones as the next big direct marketing medium. A growing number of consumers—especially younger ones—are using their cell phones as a "third screen" for text messaging, surfing the wireless Web, watching downloaded videos and shows, and checking e-mail. According to one expert, "the cell phone, which makes on-the-go conversing so convenient, is morphing into a content device, a kind of digital Swiss Army knife with the capability of filling its owner's every spare minute with games, music, live and on-demand TV, Web browsing, and, oh yes, advertising."[23] A recent survey found that 89 percent of major brands will be marketed via mobile phones by 2008. More than half of those brands will likely spend up to 25 percent of their marketing budgets on mobile marketing.[24]

Mobile phones and wireless devices have quietly become the newest, hottest frontier for big brands, especially those itching to reach the coveted 18- to 34-year-old

■ Mobile marketing: Mobile phones and wireless devices have quietly become the newest, hottest frontier for big brand messages.

set. TV networks are prodding viewers to send text messages to vote for their favorite reality TV character. Wireless Web sites are lacing sports scores and news digests with banner ads for Lexus, Burger King, and Sheraton. A few companies are even customizing 10-second video ads for short, TV-style episodes that are edging their way onto mobile phones. For advertisers, the young audience is just one selling point. Wireless gad-gets are always-on, ever-present accessories. The fact that a phone is tethered to an individual means that ads can be targeted. And users can respond instantly to time-sensitive offers. The mobile phone is very personal and it's always with you.

Marketers of all kinds—from Pepsi and Nike to P&G, Burger King, Toyota, and McDonald's—are now integrating mobile phones into their direct marketing. Cell phone promotions include everything from ring-tone giveaways, mobile games, and ad-supported content to text-in contests and sweepstakes. For example, McDonald's recently put a promotion code on 20 million Big Mac packages in a joint sweepstakes contest with the House of Blues, urging participants to enter to win prizes and to text in from concerts. Some 40 percent of contest entries came via text messaging, resulting in a 3 percent sales gain for McDonald's. More importantly, 24 percent of those entering via cell phones opted in to receive future promotions and messages.[25]

As with other forms of direct marketing, however, companies must use mobile marketing responsibly or risk angering already ad-weary consumers. Most people are initially skeptical about receiving cell phone ad messages. But they often change their minds if the ads deliver value in the form of lower cell phone bills, useful information, entertaining content, or discounted prices and coupons for their favorite products and services. A recent study found that 42 percent of cell phone users are open to mobile advertising if it's relevant.[26] When used properly, mobile marketing can greatly enrich the buyer's experience. For example, Broadway Marketplace, an upscale Cambridge, Massachusetts, grocery store, successfully replaced its card-based loyalty program with one based on mobile phones:

> The new mobile marketing approach lets Broadway Marketplace deliver promotions directly to each shopper's cell phone based on the shopper's purchase history. Customers sign up for the loyalty program and mobile alerts while they're in the store. Then, a few days before a special sale, discount, or in-store event, the grocer sends an e-mail to enrolled customers, followed by a text-message alert the day of the event. The mobile marketing campaign has been successful from day one. Eighty-two percent of the store's shoppers have enlisted in the program and 64 percent use it actively. Broadway Marketplace's sales, which had been flat for the previous few years, grew 10 percent in the first year of the mobile marketing campaign. For more than a decade, Broadway promoted itself with local cable-TV spots, direct-mail campaigns, in-store fliers, and community outreach. These methods alone, however, failed to bring many customers into the store for scheduled food and cooking demonstrations. "We couldn't get the word out," says owner Charlie Bougas. But "now we can," thanks to mobile marketing.

Podcasts and Vodcasts Podcasting and vodcasting are the latest on-the-go, on-demand technologies. The name *podcast* derives from Apple's now-everywhere iPod. With podcasting, consumers can download audio files (podcasts) or video files (vodcasts) via the Internet to an iPod or other handheld device and then listen to or view them whenever and wherever they wish. They can search for podcast topics through sites such as iTunes or through podcast networks such as PodTrac, Podbridge, or PodShow. These days, you can download podcasts or vodcasts on an exploding array of topics, everything from your favorite National Public Radio show, a recent sit-com episode, or current sports features to the latest music video or Go-Daddy commercial.

One recent study predicts that the U.S. podcast audience will reach 50 million by 2010, up from 5 million in 2005. More than 20 percent of today's podcast listeners make more than $100,000 a year.[27] As a result, this new medium is drawing much attention from marketers. Many are now integrating podcasts and vodcasts into their direct marketing programs in the form of ad-supported podcasts, downloadable ads and informational features, and other promotions.

For example, Volvo sponsors podcasts on Autoblog, and Absolut vodka buys ads on PodShow programs. Hot Topic sponsors its own new music podcast featuring underground bands, and Nestlé Purina publishes podcasts on animal training and behavioral issues. The Walt Disney World Resort offers weekly podcasts on a mix of topics, including behind-the-scenes tours, interviews, upcoming events, and news about new attractions.[28]

Ford recently produced a year-long series of monthly vodcasts as part of its introductory campaign for the Edge crossover vehicle. Called "The Edge Music Videocast," it offered free downloadable videos featuring A-list artists such as Cat Power, Wolfmother, Snow Patrol, Bloc Party, and Air. Ford placed short 15-second ads at the beginning of the videos and between songs but was careful not to make the videos too "corporate," a turn-off to its 30-something urban consumer target market. Narrated clips about the bands were woven between the ads and video. "The content [even has] a hint of NPR-esque, 'programming presented by . . .' flavor rather that the overt, muscular creative that has marked most auto campaigns," says an industry analyst. With the vodcasts, notes the analyst, Ford hopes to reach consumers at one of their most personal and closest touch points—their iPods.[29]

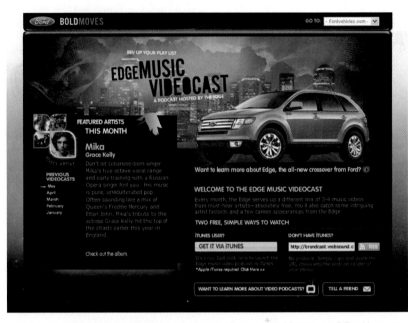

■ Vodcasts: With its year-long series of monthly "Edge Music Videocasts," Ford hopes to reach consumers at one of their most personal and closest touch points—their iPods.

Interactive TV (ITV)   Interactive TV (ITV) lets viewers interact with television programming and advertising using their remote controls. In the past, ITV has been slow to catch on. However, satellite broadcasting systems such as DirecTV, Echostar, and Time Warner are now offering ITV capabilities, and the technology appears poised to take off as a direct marketing medium.

Interactive TV gives marketers an opportunity to reach targeted audiences in an interactive, more involving way. For example, BMW recently ran interactive ads on Echostar that allowed viewers to request catalogs and several screens worth of other information using their remotes. Procter & Gamble ran interactive ads for its Tide to Go brand. The 30-second TV spots contained remote control links giving interested consumers instant access to more information about the product, as well as coupons and the opportunity to enter a sweepstakes to win a trip to an amusement park. Similarly, Disney is combining interactive TV with video-on-demand travel programs:[30]

Couch potatoes rejoice: Now there are even fewer reasons to put down the remote control. Disney is launching an interactive, travel-focused, video-on-demand series, called Travel on Demand. Four shows—available to 9 million Time Warner Cable and Cablevision digital customers—take cable television subscribers behind the scenes at Disney theme parks. The first Travel on Demand episode, "Making the Magic," is an "American Idol"–like reality series that follows an entertainer in his quest to become an elite performer at Walt Disney World Resort. "Disney Fact or Fiction" examines urban legends about Disney parks. On "Dream Makers," unsuspecting guests can win various Disney experiences; and "Disney

Travel Insiders" offers travel tips. Now, here's the interactive part: If viewers like what they see, they can simply push a button on their remote and receive a call from a Disney reservation agent within just 15 minutes.

Mobile phone marketing, podcasts and vodcasts, and interactive TV offer exciting direct marketing opportunities. But marketers must be careful to use these new direct marketing approaches wisely. As with other direct marketing forms, marketers who use them risk backlash from consumers who may resent such marketing as an invasion of their privacy. Marketers must target their direct marketing offers carefully, bringing real value to customers rather than making unwanted intrusions into their lives.

Linking the Concepts

Hold up a moment and think about the impact of direct marketing on your life.

- When was last time that you *bought* something via direct marketing? What did you buy and why did you buy it direct? When was the last time that you *rejected* a direct marketing offer? Why did you reject it? Based on these experiences, what advice would you give to direct marketers?
- For the next week, keep track of all the direct marketing offers that come your way via direct mail and catalogs, telephone, direct-response television, and the Internet. Then analyze the offers by type, source, and what you liked or disliked about each offer and the way it was delivered. Which offer best hit its target (you)? Which missed by the widest margin?

Online Marketing

Online marketing
Company efforts to market products and services and build customer relationships over the Internet.

As noted earlier, **online marketing** is the fastest-growing form of direct marketing. Recent technological advances have created a digital age. Widespread use of the Internet is having a dramatic impact on both buyers and the marketers who serve them. In this section, we examine how marketing strategy and practice are changing to take advantage of today's Internet technologies.

Marketing and the Internet

Internet
A vast public web of computer networks that connects users of all types all around the world to each other and to an amazingly large "information repository."

Much of the world's business today is carried out over digital networks that connect people and companies. The **Internet**, a vast public web of computer networks, connects users of all types all around the world to each other and to an amazingly large information repository. The Web has fundamentally changed customers' notions of convenience, speed, price, product information, and service. As a result, it has given marketers a whole new way to create value for customers and build relationships with them.

Internet usage and impact continues to grow steadily. Last year, Internet household penetration in the United States reached 69 percent, with more than 209 million people now using the Internet at home or at work. The average U.S. Internet user spends some 33 hours a month surfing the Web at home, plus another 80 hours a month at work. Worldwide, almost 500 million people now have Internet access.[31] Moreover, in a recent survey, 33 percent of American consumers chose the Internet as the second-most-essential medium in their lives (close behind TV at 36 percent). However, the Internet came in first as the "most cool and exciting medium."[32]

Click-only companies
The so-called dot-coms, which operate only online without any brick-and-mortar market presence.

All kinds of companies now market online. **Click-only companies** operate only on the Internet. They include a wide array of firms, from *e-tailers* such as Amazon.com and Expedia that sell products and services directly to final buyers via the Net to *search engines and portals* (such as Yahoo!, Google, and MSN), *transaction sites* (eBay), and *content sites* (New York Times on the Web, ESPN.com, and Encyclopedia Britannica Online). After a frenzied and rocky start in the 1990s, many click-only dot-coms are now prospering in today's marketspace.

As the Internet grew, the success of the dot-coms caused existing *brick-and-mortar* manufacturers and retailers to reexamine how they served their markets. Now, almost all of these traditional companies have set up their own online sales and communications channels, becoming **click-and-mortar companies**. It's hard to find a company today that doesn't have a substantial Web presence.

In fact, many click-and-mortar companies are now having more online success than their click-only competitors. In a recent ranking of the top 10 online retail sites, only two were click-only retailers. All of the others were multichannel retailers.[33] For example, Office Depot's more than 1,000 office-supply superstores rack up annual sales of $15 billion in more than 42 countries. But you might be surprised to learn that Office Depot's fastest recent growth has come not from its traditional "brick-and-mortar" channels, but from the Internet.

Office Depot's online sales have soared in recent years, now accounting for 29 percent of total sales. Selling on the Web lets Office Depot build deeper, more personalized relationships with customers large and small. For example, a large customer such as GE or P&G can create lists of approved office products at discount prices and then let company departments or even individuals do their own online purchasing. This reduces ordering costs, cuts through the red tape, and speeds up the ordering process for customers. At the same time, it encourages companies to use Office Depot as a sole source for office supplies. Even the smallest companies find 24-hour-a-day online ordering easier and more efficient. Importantly, Office Depot's Web operations don't steal from store sales. Instead, the OfficeDepot.com site actually builds store traffic by helping customers find a local store and check stock. In return, the local store promotes the Web site through in-store kiosks. If customers don't find what they need on the shelves, they can quickly order it via the Web from the kiosk. Thus, Office Depot now offers a full range of contact points and delivery modes—online, by phone or fax, and in the store. No click-only or brick-only seller can match the call, click, or visit convenience and support afforded by Office Depot's click-and-mortar model.[34]

 Click-and-mortar companies
Traditional brick-and-mortar companies that have added online marketing to their operations.

■ Click-and-mortar marketing: No click-only or brick-only seller can match the call, click, or visit convenience and support afforded by Office Depot's "4 easy ways to shop."

Online Marketing Domains

The four major online marketing domains are shown in Figure 14.2. They include B2C (business to consumer), B2B (business to business), C2C (consumer to consumer), and C2B (consumer to business).

Business to Consumer (B2C) The popular press has paid the most attention to **business-to-consumer (B2C) online marketing**—selling goods and services online to final consumers. Today's consumers can buy almost anything online—from clothing, kitchen gadgets, and airline tickets to computers and cars. Online consumer buying continues to grow at a healthy rate. Some 65 percent of American online users now use the Internet to shop. In 2007, U.S. consumers generated an estimated $259 billion in online retail sales, up 18 percent from the previous year.[35]

Perhaps more importantly, the Internet now influences 27 percent of total retail sales—sales transacted online plus those carried out off-line but encouraged by online research. By 2010, the Internet will influence a staggering 50 percent of total retail sales.[36] Thus, smart

Business-to-consumer (B2C) online marketing
Selling goods and services online to final consumers.

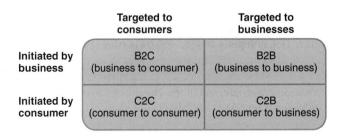

	Targeted to consumers	Targeted to businesses
Initiated by business	B2C (business to consumer)	B2B (business to business)
Initiated by consumer	C2C (consumer to consumer)	C2B (consumer to business)

FIGURE 14.2

Online Domains

marketers are employing integrated multichannel strategies that use the Web to drive sales to other marketing channels.

As more and more people find their way onto the Web, the population of online consumers is becoming more mainstream and diverse. The Web now offers marketers a palette of different kinds of consumers seeking different kinds of online experiences. However, Internet consumers still differ from traditional off-line consumers in their approaches to buying and in their responses to marketing. In the Internet exchange process, customers initiate and control the contact. Traditional marketing targets a somewhat passive audience. In contrast, online marketing targets people who actively select which Web sites they will visit and what marketing information they will receive about which products and under what conditions. Thus, the new world of online marketing requires new marketing approaches.

People now go online to order a wide range of goods—clothing from Gap or L.L.Bean, books or electronics from Amazon.com, furniture from Ethan Allen, major appliances from Sears, flowers from Calyx & Corolla, or even home mortgages from Quicken Loans.[37]

At Quicken Loans (www.quickenloans.com), prospective clients receive a high-tech, high-touch, one-stop mortgage shopping experience. At the site, clients can research a wide variety of home-financing and refinancing options, apply for a mortgage, and receive quick loan approval—all without leaving the comfort and security of their homes. The site provides useful interactive tools that help clients decide how much house they can afford, whether to rent or buy, whether to refinance a current mortgage, the economics of fixing up their current homes rather than moving, and much more. Clients can receive advice by phone or by chatting online with one of 5,000 mortgage experts and sign up for later e-mail rate updates. Quicken Loans is the nation's largest online lender, and expects to close more than $20 billion in home loans in 2007.

■ B2C Web sites: People now go online to order a wide range of goods and services, even home mortgages.

Business-to-business (B2B) online marketing
Using B2B Web sites, e-mail, online product catalogs, online trading networks, and other online resources to reach new business customers, serve current customers more effectively, and obtain buying efficiencies and better prices.

Business to Business (B2B)   Although the popular press has given the most attention to B2C Web sites, **business-to-business (B2B) online marketing** is also flourishing. B2B marketers use B2B Web sites, e-mail, online product catalogs, online trading networks, and other online resources to reach new business customers, serve current customers more effectively, and obtain buying efficiencies and better prices.

Most major business-to-business marketers now offer product information, customer purchasing, and customer-support services online. For example, corporate buyers can visit Sun Microsystems' Web site (www.sun.com), select detailed descriptions of Sun's products and solutions, request sales and service information, and interact with staff members. Some major companies conduct almost all of their business on the Web. Networking equipment and software maker Cisco Systems takes more than 80 percent of its orders over the Internet.

Beyond simply selling their products and services online, companies can use the Internet to build stronger relationships with important business customers. For example, Dell has set up customized Web sites for more than 113,000 business and institutional customers worldwide. These individualized Premier Dell.com sites help business customers to more efficiently manage all phases of their Dell computer buying and ownership. Each customer's Premier Dell.com Web site can include a customized online computer store, purchasing and asset management reports and tools, system-specific technical information, links to useful information throughout Dell's extensive Web site, and more. The site makes all the information a customer needs in order to do business with Dell available in one place, 24 hours a day, 7 days a week.[38]

Consumer to Consumer (C2C) Much **consumer-to-consumer (C2C) online marketing** and communication occurs on the Web between interested parties over a wide range of products and subjects. In some cases, the Internet provides an excellent means by which consumers can buy or exchange goods or information directly with one another. For example, eBay, Amazon.com Auctions, Overstock.com, and other auction sites offer popular marketspaces for displaying and selling almost anything, from art and antiques, coins and stamps, and jewelry to computers and consumer electronics.

EBay's C2C online trading community of more than 220 million registered users worldwide (greater than the combined populations of France, Germany, and Britain!) transacted some $52 billion in trades last year. On any given day, the company's Web site lists more than 16 million items up for auction in more than 50,000 categories. Such C2C sites give people access to much larger audiences than the local flea market or newspaper classifieds (which, by the way, have also gone online at sites such as Craigslist.com and eBay's Kijiji). Interestingly, based on its huge success in the C2C market, eBay has now attracted more than 300,000 B2C sellers, ranging from small businesses peddling their regular wares to large businesses liquidating excess inventory at auction.[39]

In other cases, C2C involves interchanges of information through Internet forums that appeal to specific special-interest groups. Such activities may be organized for commercial or noncommercial purposes. An example is Web logs, or *blogs,* online journals where people post their thoughts, usually on a narrowly defined topic. Blogs can be about anything, from politics or baseball to haiku, car repair, or the latest television series. There are currently about 15 million active blogs read by 57 million people. Such numbers give blogs—especially those with large and devoted followings—substantial influence.[40]

Many marketers are now tapping into blogs as a medium for reaching carefully targeted consumers. One way is to advertise on an existing blog or to influence content there. For example, before General Electric announced a major energy-efficient technology initiative last year, GE executives met with major environmental bloggers to build support. And in an effort to improve its often-battered image, Wal-Mart now works directly with bloggers, feeding them nuggets of positive news, suggesting topics for posting, and even inviting them to visit company headquarters. "Bloggers who agreed to receive the e-mail messages said they were eager to hear Wal-Mart's side of the story, which they . . . felt had been drowned out by critics," says an analyst. The bloggers also "were tantalized by the promise of exclusive news that might attract more visitors to their Web sites."[41]

Other companies set up their own blogs. For example, GM maintains a blog called FastLane that helps it connect with its core consumers in a virtual grassroots kind of way. The log is penned by GM executives, including vice chairman Bob Lutz, who some claim is the big reason for its popularity. The company says it wants all kinds of feedback—so the blog includes both positive and negative comments from readers. Says Lutz, "I'd say the biggest surprise is the passion in which people respond and comment on the blogs. You're getting the real deal there. There is so much passion that even the negative comments are palatable, and indeed, often helpful." FastLane gets up to 10,000 visitors a day, and GM estimates that last year the blog delivered $410,470 worth of customer insight at a cost of only $255,675—a 67 percent return on investment. More important, the blog helps GM build or rebuild relationships with customers. "If there is a gap between GM's excellence and people's perception of it, we believe blogs are a great opportunity to change those perceptions," says GM's digital marketing chief.[42]

Consumer-to-consumer (C2C) online marketing
Online exchanges of goods and information between final consumers.

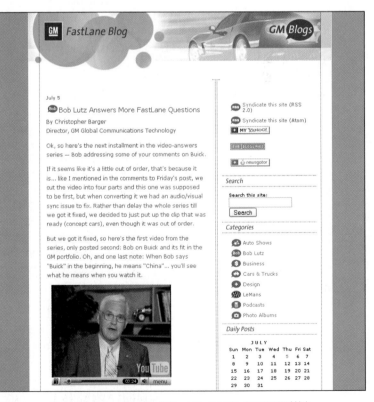

■ Many marketers are now tapping into consumer-to-consumer Web communications by setting up their own blogs. GM's FastLane blog—penned primarily by vice chairman Bob Lutz—helps GM connect with its core consumers in a virtual grassroots kind of way.

As a marketing tool, blogs offer some advantages. They can offer a fresh, original, personal, and cheap way to reach today's fragmented audiences. However, the blogosphere is cluttered and difficult to control. "Blogs may help companies bond with consumers in exciting new ways, but they won't help them control the relationship," says a blog expert. Such Web journals remain largely a C2C medium. "That isn't to suggest companies can't influence the relationship or leverage blogs to engage in a meaningful relationship," says the expert, "but the consumer will remain in control."[43]

Whether or not they actively participate in the blogosphere, companies should show up, monitor, and listen to them. For example, Starbucks draws the line at active participation in blogs but follows the consumer dialogue on the 30 or more online sites devoted to the brand. It then uses the customer insights it gains from blogs to adjust its marketing programs. For instance, it recently altered the remaining installments of a four-part podcast based on the negative blog feedback it gleaned on the first one.[44]

In all, C2C means that online buyers don't just consume product information—increasingly, they create it. As a result, "word of Web" is joining "word of mouth" as an important buying influence.

Consumer-to-business (C2B) online marketing

Online exchanges in which consumers search out sellers, learn about their offers, and initiate purchases, sometimes even driving transaction terms.

Consumer to Business (C2B)   The final online marketing domain is **consumer-to-business (C2B) online marketing**. Thanks to the Internet, today's consumers are finding it easier to communicate with companies. Most companies now invite prospects and customers to send in suggestions and questions via company Web sites. Beyond this, rather than waiting for an invitation, consumers can search out sellers on the Web, learn about their offers, initiate purchases, and give feedback. Using the Web, consumers can even drive transactions with businesses, rather than the other way around. For example, using Priceline.com, would-be buyers can bid for airline tickets, hotel rooms, rental cars, cruises, and vacation packages, leaving the sellers to decide whether to accept their offers.

Consumers can also use Web sites such as PlanetFeedback.com to ask questions, offer suggestions, lodge complaints, or deliver compliments to companies. The site's aim is to help consumers "express their voice" and help companies "prime their ears." The site provides letter templates for consumers to use based on their moods and reasons for contacting the company. The site then forwards the letters to the customer-service manager at each company and helps to obtain a response. "About 80 percent of the companies respond to complaints, some within an hour," says a PlanetFeedback spokesperson.[45]

Linking the Concepts

Pause here and cool your engine for a bit. Think about the relative advantages and disadvantages of *click-only*, *brick-and-mortar only*, and *click-and-mortar* retailers.

- Visit the Amazon.com Web site. Search for a specific book or DVD—perhaps one that's not too well known—and go through the buying process.
- Now visit www.bn.com and shop for the same book or video. Then visit a Barnes & Noble store and shop for the item there.
- What advantages does Amazon.com have over Barnes & Noble? What disadvantages? How does your local independent book store, with its store-only operations, fare against these two competitors?

Setting Up an Online Marketing Presence

Clearly, all companies need to consider moving online. Companies can conduct online marketing in any of the four ways shown in Figure 14.3: creating a Web site, placing ads and promotions online, setting up or participating in online social networks, or using e-mail.

Creating a Web Site   For most companies, the first step in conducting online marketing is to create a Web site. However, beyond simply creating a Web site, marketers must design an attractive site and find ways to get consumers to visit the site, stay around, and come back often.

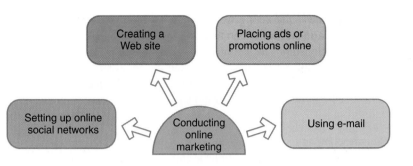

FIGURE 14.3
Setting Up for Online Marketing

Types of Web Sites   Web sites vary greatly in purpose and content. The most basic type is a **corporate (or brand) Web site**. These sites are designed to build customer goodwill, collect customer feedback, and supplement other sales channels, rather than to sell the company's products directly. They typically offer a rich variety of information and other features in an effort to answer customer questions, build closer customer relationships, and generate excitement about the company or brand.

For example, you can't buy anything at P&G's Tide to Go brand site, but you can learn how to use the handy stain remover stick (including a video demo), watch recent ads, and share "Tide to Go saves the day!" stories with others. And Unilever's campaignforrealbeauty.com site doesn't sell soaps and lotions. But it does provide a place for people interested in the cause of women and girl's self-esteem to share their thoughts, view ads and viral videos such as the "Dove Evolution," and download self-esteem assessment tools and workbooks. They can even register for a free training guide to become a Dove Real Beauty Workshop for Girls facilitator. Such Web sites, once brushed aside as digital "brochureware," are now attracting consumers in numbers that vie with flashier consumer sites and even traditional mass media.[46]

Believe it or not, those boring corporate Web sites are pulling in more eyeballs—and more influencers—than flashy prime time TV shows, print magazines, and general-interest sites. Package-goods marketers such as P&G and Unilever don't sell many products directly online. Their low-cost, low-involvement brands tend not to generate much search. Yet P&G and Unilever Web sites now reach nearly 6 million and 3 million unique visitors, respectively, in the United States each month, easily swamping the audiences of many magazines and cable and syndicated TV shows where the companies advertise. But more important than the volume may be who the visitors are. Corporate and brand Web site visitors are much more likely to influence others and to recommend brands to them. Of all options for influencing the online influencers, brand Web sites rank highest both in consumer acceptance and marketer control.

Other companies create a **marketing Web site**. These sites engage consumers in an interaction that will move them closer to a direct purchase or other marketing outcome. For example, visitors to SonyStyle.com can search through dozens of categories of Sony products, learn more about specific items, and read expert product reviews. They can check out the latest hot deals, place orders online, and pay by credit card, all with a few mouse clicks.

Corporate (or brand) Web site
A Web site designed to build customer goodwill, collect customer feedback, and supplement other sales channels, rather than to sell the company's products directly.

■ Corporate Web site: You can't buy anything at P&G's Tide to Go brand site, but you can learn how to use the handy stain remover stick, watch recent ads, and share "Tide to Go saves the day!" stories with others.

Marketing Web site
A Web site that engages consumers in interactions that will move them closer to a direct purchase or other marketing outcome.

MINI USA operates a marketing Web site at www.miniusa.com. Once a potential customer clicks in, the carmaker wastes no time trying to turn the inquiry into a sale, and then into a long-term relationship. The site offers a garage full of useful information and interactive selling features, including detailed and fun descriptions of current MINI models, tools for designing your very own MINI, information on dealer locations and services, and even tools for tracking your new MINI from factory to delivery.

Before Angela DiFabio bought her MINI Cooper last September, she spent untold hours on the company's Web site, playing with dozens of possibilities before coming up with the perfect combination: a chili-pepper-red exterior, white racing stripes on the hood, and a "custom rally badge bar" on the grill. When DiFabio placed her order with her dealer, the same build-your-own tool—and all the price and product details it provided—left her feeling like she was getting a fair deal. "He even used the site to order my car," she says. While she waited for her MINI to arrive, DiFabio logged on to MINI's Web site every day, this time using its "Where's My Baby?" tracking tool to follow her car, like an expensive FedEx package, from the factory in Britain to its delivery. The Web site does more than just provide information or sell products or services. It makes an impact on the customer experience: It's fun, it's individual, it makes users feel like part of the clan.[47]

Designing Effective Web Sites   Creating a Web site is one thing; getting people to *visit* the site is another. To attract visitors, companies aggressively promote their Web sites in offline print and broadcast advertising and through ads and links on other sites. But today's Web users are quick to abandon any Web site that doesn't measure up. The key is to create enough value and excitement to get consumers who come to the site to stick around and come back again. This means that companies must constantly update their sites to keep them current, fresh, and useful.

For some types of products, attracting visitors is easy. Consumers buying new cars, computers, or financial services will be open to information and marketing initiatives from sellers. Marketers of lower-involvement products, however, may face a difficult challenge in attracting Web site visitors. If you're in the market for a computer and you see a banner ad that says, "The top 10 PCs under $800," you'll likely click on the banner. But what kind of ad would get you to visit a site like dentalfloss.com?

A key challenge is designing a Web site that is attractive on first view and interesting enough to encourage repeat visits. Many marketers create colorful, graphically sophisticated Web sites that combine text, sound, and animation to capture and hold attention (for examples, see www.looneytunes.com or www.nike.com). To attract new visitors and to encourage revisits, suggests one expert, online marketers should pay close attention to the seven *C*s of effective Web site design:[48]

- *Context:* the site's layout and design
- *Content:* the text, pictures, sound, and video that the Web site contains
- *Community:* the ways that the site enables user-to-user communication
- *Customization:* the site's ability to tailor itself to different users or to allow users to personalize the site
- *Communication:* the ways the site enables site-to-user, user-to-site, or two-way communication
- *Connection:* the degree that the site is linked to other sites
- *Commerce:* the site's capabilities to enable commercial transactions

And to keep customers coming back to the site, companies need to embrace yet another "C"—constant change.

At the very least, a Web site should be easy to use, professional looking, and physically attractive. Ultimately, however, Web sites must also be *useful*. When it comes to Web surfing and shopping, most people prefer substance over style and function over flash. Thus, effective Web sites contain deep and useful information, interactive tools that help buyers find and evaluate products of interest, links to other related sites, changing promotional offers, and entertaining features that lend relevant excitement.

Placing Ads and Promotions Online   As consumers spend more and more time on the Internet, many companies are shifting more of their marketing dollars to **online advertising** to build their brands or to attract visitors to their Web sites. Online advertising is becoming a major medium. Last year, U.S. companies spent nearly $17 billion on online advertising, up an incredible 35 percent over the previous year, and more than they spend on outdoor and radio advertising combined. Online ad spending will jump to more than $42 billion by 2011, rivaling or surpassing the amounts spent on magazines, newspapers, and even television.[49] Here, we discuss forms of online advertising and promotion and their future.

Online advertising

Advertising that appears while consumers are surfing the Web, including display ads, search-related ads, online classifieds, and other forms.

Forms of Online Advertising   The major forms of online advertising include display ads, search-related ads, and online classifieds. Online display ads might appear anywhere on an Internet user's screen. The most common form is *banners,* banner-shaped ads found at the top, bottom, left, right, or center of a Web page. For instance, a Web surfer looking up airline schedules or fares might encounter a flashing banner that screams, "Rent a car from Alamo and get up to two days free!" Clicking on the ad takes consumers to the Alamo Web site, where they can redeem the promotion.

Interstitials are online display ads that appear between screen changes on a Web site, especially while a new screen is loading. For example, visit www.marketwatch.com and you'll probably see a 10-second ad for Visa, Verizon, Dell, or another sponsor before the homepage loads. *Pop-up*s are online ads that appear suddenly in a new window in front of the window being viewed. Such ads can multiply out of control, creating a major annoyance. As a result, Internet services and Web browser providers have developed applications that let users block most pop-ups. But not to worry. Many advertisers have now developed pop-*under*s, new windows that evade pop-up blockers by appearing behind the page you're viewing.

With the increase in broadband Internet access in American homes, many companies are developing exciting new *rich media* display ads, which incorporate animation, video, sound, and interactivity. Rich media ads attract and hold consumer attention better than traditional banner ads. They employ techniques such as float, fly, and snapback—animations that jump out and sail over the Web page before retreating to their original space. But many rich media ads do more than create a little bit of jumping animation. For example, to attract would-be commodity traders to its Web site, the Chicago Board of Trade runs a small rich media banner ad that explodes into a small site when the user's mouse rolls over it. The mouse-over site features free streaming quotes, sample research, and a virtual trading account, all of which would never fit into a traditional static ad.[50]

Another hot growth area for online advertising is *search-related ads* (or *contextual advertising*), in which text-based ads and links appear alongside search engine results on sites such as Google and Yahoo!. For example, search Google for "HDTV." At the top and side of the resulting search list, you'll see inconspicuous ads for 10 or more advertisers, ranging from Circuit City, Best Buy, and Amazon.com to Dish Network, Nextag.com, and TigerDirect.com. Nearly all of Google's $10.6 billion in revenues come from ad sales. An advertiser buys search terms from the search site and pays only if consumers click through to its site. Search-related ads account for some 42 percent of all online advertising expenditures, more than any other category of online advertising.[51]

Search ads can be an effective way to link consumers to other forms of online promotion. For example, Honda uses keyword searches to lure Web surfers to sites promoting its Element and CR-V models:[52]

> The current Element campaign features the vehicle "talking" to sundry animals—a penguin, a turtle, a lobster, a goat, a rat, and others—in cartoony spots. Honda bought those keyword terms and uses search ads as invitations to "see the penguin in its Element." That link leads consumers to elementandfriends.com, which features Element ads plus an underground world to drive around in. Honda also bought variants of "funny video" and "funny commercials," search terms that have demographic profiles compatible with likely Element buyers. In many cases, the search terms cost just 10 cents or 15 cents per click and drew about 40 percent of the Element's Web site traffic. "It seemed a little quirky, but the more you thought about it, the more it seemed

■ Search ads: Honda uses key word search ads to lure Web surfers to sites like this one promoting its Honda Element models. Within only a month, the search ads drew more than 500,000 people to the site.

Viral marketing
The Internet version of word-of-mouth marketing—Web sites, videos, e-mail messages, or other marketing events that are so infectious that customers will want to pass them along to friends.

to resonate well with the campaign," says Honda's senior manager of marketing. Based on that success, Honda also bought thousands of keywords as part of a new "Crave" campaign for its CR-V, words such as "chocolate," "banana splits," and "celebrity gossip"—all designed to bring searchers to a community Web site Honda created for users to collect and share craves. Within only a month, the search ads drew more than 500,000 people to the site.

Other Forms of Online Promotion Other forms of on-line promotions include content sponsorships, alliances and affiliate programs, and viral advertising.

Using *content sponsorships,* companies gain name exposure on the Internet by sponsoring special content on various Web sites, such as news or financial information or special-interest topics. For example, Scotts, the lawn-and-garden products company, sponsors the Local Forecast section on WeatherChannel.com; and David Sunflower Seeds sponsors the ESPN Fantasy Baseball site at ESPN.com. Sponsorships are best placed in carefully targeted sites where they can offer relevant information or service to the audience. Internet companies can also develop *alliances and affiliate programs,* in which they work with other companies, online and off-line, to "promote each other." For example, through its Amazon Associates Program, Amazon.com has more than 900,000 affiliates who post Amazon.com banners on their Web sites.

Finally, online marketers use **viral marketing**, the Internet version of word-of-mouth marketing. Viral marketing involves creating a Web site, video, e-mail message, or other marketing event that is so infectious that customers will want to pass it along to their friends. One observer describes viral marketing as "addictive, self-propagating advertisement that lives on Web sites, blogs, cell phones, message boards, and even in real-world stunts."[53] Because customers pass the message or promotion along to others, viral marketing can be very inexpensive. And when the information comes from a friend, the recipient is much more likely to open and read it.

Although marketers usually have little control over where their viral messages end up, a well-concocted viral campaign can gain vast exposure. For example, Smirnoff produced a music video called "Tea Partay," featuring "three well-scrubbed, upper-class New Englanders spitting rhymes Beastie Boy-style about the joys of eating finger sandwiches, playing croquet, and drinking Smirnoff Raw Tea, a flavored malt beverage." Smirnoff posted the video only on its own site but it soon found its way to YouTube, where it was viewed 1.3 million times, inspiring several much-watched knockoffs. Those numbers are dwarfed by OfficeMax's holiday ElfYourself Web site, which at its peak had 11 people per second "elfing" themselves, just like Santa's own. The wacky site drew 36 million visits in about five weeks and boosted OfficeMax's holiday online traffic by 20 percent, all with no promotion.[54]

Perhaps the pioneer and real granddaddy of all viral efforts is Burger King's now-classic Subservient Chicken viral campaign:

> The Web site, www.subservientchicken.com, features a dingy living room, where the subservient chicken—someone in a giant chicken suit and a garter belt—hangs out in front of his Web cam and awaits your bidding. Type in commands, and the chicken does exactly what you ask. It will flap its wings, roll over, or jump up and down. It will also moon the viewer, dance the Electric Slide, or die. (Suggestions for lewd acts are met with a "naughty naughty" shake of the wing.) In other words, you can have your way with the chicken. Get it? Have it your way! The site promotes Burger King's TenderCrisp chicken and ties it into Burger King's successful "Have It Your Way" marketing campaign.

"As viral marketing goes, subservientchicken.com is a colossal success," says an advertising expert. "There is great overlap between Web regulars and

Burger King's core audience." If nothing more, the site gets consumers to interact with the brand. And it gets them buzzing about Burger King's edgy positioning. Burger King has never advertised the site. When it was first created, the developer at Crispin Porter + Bogusky (CP+B), the ad agency that created the site, e-mailed the URL to several other CP+B people, asking them to send the link out to friends to test. From that single e-mail, without a peep of promotion, the Subservient Chicken site ended the day with 1 million total hits, and it received 46 million hits in only the first week. Still running, the site has now drawn more than 460 million visits since April 2004. Says one Burger King ad director, the award-winning site helped "sell a lot, a lot, a lot of chicken sandwiches."[55]

Creating or Participating in Online Social Networks As we discussed in Chapter 5, the popularity of the Internet has resulted in a rash of **online social networks** or *Web communities.* Countless independent and commercial Web sites have arisen that give consumers online places to congregate, socialize, and exchange views and information. These days, it seems, almost everyone is buddying up on MySpace or Facebook, tuning into the day's hottest videos at YouTube, or even living a surprisingly real fantasy life as an avatar on Second Life. And, of course, wherever consumers congregate, marketers will surely follow. More and more marketers are now starting to ride the huge social networking wave.

Marketers can engage in online communities in two ways: They can participate in existing Web communities or they can set up their own. Joining existing networks seems easiest. Thus, many major brands—from Burger King, Honda, and Motorola to Estée Lauder and Victoria's Secret have set up MySpace pages and profiles. The Burger King, for instance, has amassed more than 120,000 MySpace "friends," fellow users who have chosen to associate themselves with his profile. Similarly, the Apple Students group on Facebook, which offers information and deals on Apple products, has more than 471,000 members. And companies by the dozens are now hanging up virtual shingles in Second Life—from Nike and Coca-Cola to Dell, Toyota, IBM, 1-800-Flowers, and H&R Block.

But participating successfully in existing online social networks presents challenges. First, online social networks are new and results are hard to measure. Most companies are still experimenting with how to use them effectively. Second, such Web communities are largely user controlled. The company's goal is to make the brand a part of consumers' conversations and their lives. However, marketers can't simply muscle their way into consumers' online interactions—they need to earn the right to be there. "You're talking about conversations between groups of friends," says one analyst. "And in those conversations a brand has no right to be there, unless the conversation is already about that brand." Says another expert, "Being force-fed irrelevant content, or feeling tricked into taking in a brand, is a major turn-off." Rather than intruding, marketers must learn to become a valued part of the online experience.

When it comes to online networks, it's not enough just to be there. For example, when Toyota's Scion first opened a Second Life showroom last year, it quickly became a top destination. But only a few months later, Second Life residents had largely deserted the showroom. Toyota's mistake? It failed to understand that driving adds little value in a virtual world where Second Life avatars can walk underwater, fly, and "beam" themselves around.

Instead, as in any other marketing endeavor, companies participating in Web communities must learn how to add value for consumers in order to capture value in return. For example, compare Pontiac's Second Life experience to Toyota's:[56]

Pontiac's marketing director sums up his brand's unreal-world problem neatly: "In this environment, you've eliminated all physical needs. . . . Why do I need a car when I can fly?" Still, Pontiac has a Second Life presence. Its Motorati Island is dedicated to car enthusiasts and the car culture. Besides the Pontiac store and racetrack, the auto company gives away land to other car-culture-type participants. At Second Life, Pontiac creates an involving community within a community. "Welcome to Motorati Island, powered by Pontiac," screams the flashing banner. "Explore 112 acres of Uncharted Adventures" and "Live the Impossible." "Thrill to the Action at Pontiac Raceway Park"; "Conquer the Karts"; and "Free Your Inner Monster." "Gear Up at the Pontiac Garage" and "Swoon to the Heart-Pounding

■ Viral marketing: Burger King's now classic and colossally successful Subservient Chicken site has gotten consumers interacting with the brand and buzzing about its edgy positioning.

Online social networks
Online social communities—blogs, social networking Web sites, or even virtual worlds—where people socialize or exchange information and opinions.

■ More that just being there, Pontiac's Motorati Island creates involvement and a community within a community, earning it the highest "Dwell" quotient in Second Life.

Spam
Unsolicited, unwanted commercial e-mail messages.

Rhythms of our Nightlife." Such community involvement has netted Pontiac the highest "Dwell" quotient in Second Life, a statistic that measures the number of visitors to its brand-based locale and the amount of time the visitors spend there over time.

To avoid the mysteries and challenges of building a presence on existing online social networks, many companies are now launching their own targeted Web communities. For example, Coca-Cola has developed a Sprite cell phone network—available to Web-ready phones—where members can set up profiles, post pictures, and meet new friends. On Nike's Nike Plus Web site, some 200,000 runners upload, track, and compare their performances. More than half visit the site at least four times a week, and Nike plans eventually to have 15 percent or more of the world's 100 million runners actively participating in the Nike Plus online community.

Procter & Gamble also sponsors several community sites, including Capessa, which features content created by female consumers on a wide range of relevant topics. Such sites provide a place where like-minded consumers can share ideas and solutions with each other and where P&G can interact with consumers and learn how to serve them better (See Marketing at Work 14.2).

Using E-Mail   E-mail is an important and growing online marketing tool. A recent study of ad, brand, and marketing managers found that nearly half of all the companies surveyed use e-mail marketing to reach customers. U.S. companies currently spend about $1.5 billion a year on e-mail marketing, up from just $164 million in 1999. And this spending will grow by an estimated 20 percent annually through 2011.[57]

But there's a dark side to the growing use of e-mail marketing. The explosion of **spam**—unsolicited, unwanted commercial e-mail messages that clog up our e-mailboxes—has produced consumer irritation and frustration. According to one research company, spam now accounts for 88 percent of all e-mail sent. A recent study found that the average consumer received 3,253 spam messages last year.[58] E-mail marketers walk a fine line between adding value for consumers and being intrusive.

To address these concerns, most legitimate marketers now practice *permission-based e-mail marketing,* sending e-mail pitches only to customers who "opt in." Financial services firms such as Charles Schwab use configurable e-mail systems that let customers choose what they want to get. Others, such as Yahoo! or Amazon.com, include long lists of opt-in boxes for different categories of marketing material. Amazon.com targets opt-in customers with a limited number of helpful "we thought you'd like to know" messages based on their expressed preferences and previous purchases. Few customers object and many actually welcome such promotional messages.

When used properly, e-mail can be the ultimate direct marketing medium. Blue-chip marketers such as Amazon.com, Dell, L.L.Bean, Office Depot, Schwab, and others use it regularly, and with great success. E-mail lets these marketers send highly targeted, tightly personalized, relationship-building messages to consumers who actually *want* to receive them. Consider Scotts:

> Scotts, the plant, lawn, and garden products company, designs its e-mail marketing around the customer preferences, season of the year, and the region of the recipient. When individuals sign up for the e-mail program, Scotts asks them a series of questions about where they live and their particular plant and garden interests. It then uses this information to create content and offers that resonate

14.2 MARKETING AT WORK

P&G: Learning About the Hot New World of Online Social Networks

Procter & Gamble is learning fast about the hot new world of online social networking. Like many other major marketing companies these days, P&G is experimenting with all kinds of online community media for its many megabrands. For instance, its Crest brand has a MySpace page featuring a fictional character called "Miss Irresistible," a self-proclaimed "irresistible babe" with a fondness for champagne and strawberries who urges friends to take her Irresistibility iQ quiz and to use her MySpace page to send "a naughty (or nice!)" e-Card. The brand also sponsors the Crest Whitestrips "Smile State" Facebook group that recently sponsored a contest at 20 different colleges and universities. The four schools that had the most students join earned a free on-campus concert for their group by an up-and-coming music artist.

P&G also is no stranger to YouTube and other viral and video community venues: It recently held contests to obtain user-generated video-recorded jingles for its Pringles chips and a Mr. Clean commercial for posting on YouTube. And its Herbal Essences brand launched a "DumpCupid" YouTube campaign last Valentine's Day featuring amateuresque videos of a careless, arrow-slinging cupid. YouTube display ads supporting the campaign reached some 90 million YouTube viewers globally during one week and the DumpCupid.com site became P&G's most-visited brand site.

P&G has also given many of its brand sites more of a community focus. For example, check out Pampers.com, where young parents can learn about child development, receive parenting advice from experts, swap stories with other parents at the site's "community" page, and even set up a personalized Web site experiences catered to their baby's age. Similarly, at the Tide to Go site, consumers can share "True Stories. Real People" tales about how Tide to Go saves the day. And P&G's broader HomeMadeSimple.com site is a community kind of place to go when you need "simple solutions for easy living—ideas to simplify, organize, beautify, and inspire life." However, the site also features P&G brand promotions, free offers, a newsletter, and article archives.

But most of these previous efforts consist more of one-to-one interactions and talking *at* consumers rather than being a part of social networking interactions *among* consumers. So, P&G has recently taken more ambitious social networking steps—creating its own online communities. Here are two examples:

The People's Choice Community. Initially tied to the P&G-produced *People's Choice Awards* television event, P&G is now expanding the site to a year-around forum by which people can share their views on music, movies, actors, TV, and more. People can now use the People's Choice Community site (www.pcavote.com) for everything from voting on the casting of realty TV shows to suggesting the mix of songs for an entertainer's next CD or choosing a model for a major advertising campaign. "How would you like to direct the future of entertainment?" the site asks. "Welcome to the People's Choice Community, where the fans take charge of Hollywood." "We found that the excitement generated by energized consumers going online to vote on the awards was being lost after the show," says P&G spokesperson Robyn Schroeder. "This will let them vote and air their views year-round on what impacts entertainment."

The celebrity- and fan-driven site features Queen Latifah as a host and has "a very jazzy, energized look and feel to it." Consistent

■ Creating online social networks: P&G's new online community sites are less about selling products and more about becoming a part of consumers' interactions to learn they care about.

with its entertainment focus, the People's Choice Community site also includes some P&G marketing, with regular banner ads for P&G and non-P&G products. However, the site's goal isn't so much to deliver marketing messages as to interact with consumers and learn what's important to them.

Capessa. Produced by P&G in partnership with Yahoo!, Capessa is located in the health section of Yahoo! (http://health.yahoo.com/capessa). A true online community, it provides a place where female consumers can discuss a wide range of topics—from women's health, work, pregnancy, and parenting to weight loss, beauty, and relationships—and submit personal stories related to those issues. P&G contacts women with especially compelling submissions and conducts professionally videotaped interviews to help the women share their stories with others at the Capessa site.

Capessa is more subtle and less commercial than the People's Choice Community. Although ads or links to experts might occasionally appear through advertising already running on Yahoo!, P&G won't run any ads on Capessa. The only mention of P&G is a line at the bottom of Web pages that identifies P&G as the site's producer. And although Yahoo! promotes Capessa as a big feature of its health section, given the serious nature of the

(continues)

topics discussed, it doesn't want to overcommercialize the site. "With Capessa, they are providing women with a place where they can learn from and talk with each other, rather than listening to specific views by P&G or some expert," says a marketing consultant. According to Jim Stengel, P&G's global marketing officer, the site should be "engaging not disruptive. If we cross that line, we kill the experience."

P&G is still testing and experimenting with the explosive new online social networking phenomenon, trying to figure out how to harness its enormous potential. In fact, by the time you read this, either or both of the People's Choice Community and Capessa sites might well have evolved or faded. "Success is no slam dunk," notes one analyst. Giant Wal-Mart learned this when it turned out the lights on its teen-targeted social networking site, "The Hub," last year after it failed to connect with consumers.

But such Web communities will no doubt play a big role in P&G's future. Unlike the marketer's brand sites and many of its previous brand-focused social networking efforts, the new online communities are less about building brands and selling products and more about becoming

a part of consumers' interactions to learn how to serve them better. According to the analyst, "Both new sites will act as continuing focus-group-type environments where P&G—by monitoring [and participating in] consumer discussions on the sites—can learn more about its target audience's likes and dislikes and what consumers in different stages of life care about."

Says P&G's Schroder: "By understanding these consumers and giving them a place to express themselves, we feel that ultimately we'll be able to develop products that meet their needs." Marketing chief Stengel strongly agrees: "It's going to be one giant living dynamic learning experience about consumers."

Sources: Quotes and other information from Lisa Cornwell, "P&G Launches Two Social Networking Sites," *Marketing News,* February 1, 2007, p. 21; Suzanne Vranica, "P&G Boosts Social Networking Efforts," *Wall Street Journal,* January 8, 2007, p. B4; Jack Neff, "Unilever, P&G Battle Hits YouTube," *Advertising Age,* February 12, 2007, p. 4; Yuval Rosenburg, "Building a New Nest," *Fast Company,* April 2007, p. 48; Dan Sewell, "P&G Tech Marketing Typical," *The Cincinnati Enquirer,* July 9, 2007, accessed at http://news.enquirer.com; and www.pcavote.com and http://health.yahoo.com/capessa, accessed November 2007.

with each recipient. For example, a city dweller, who may not even have a lawn, gets advice and tips on the care and feeding of houseplants and terrace shrubs, whereas a homeowner in the southwest receives information on maintaining a lawn or garden in a hot and arid climate. To deliver this level of customization, Scotts has developed an e-mail template that allows it to incorporate appropriate, personal content into an otherwise mass e-mailing. Far from thinking of the Scotts' online missives as irritating spam, recipients grow to rely on them as a valuable problem-solving tool.[59]

Given its targeting effectiveness and low costs, e-mail can be an outstanding marketing investment. According to a recent study, return on e-mail marketing investment is $52 for every dollar spent, compared with direct mail at $15 per dollar spent.[60]

The Promise and Challenges of Online Marketing

Online marketing continues to offer both great promise and many challenges for the future. Its most ardent apostles still envision a time when the Internet and online marketing will replace magazines, newspapers, and even stores as sources for information and buying. Most marketers, however, hold a more realistic view. To be sure, online marketing will become a successful business model for some companies, Internet firms such as Amazon.com, eBay, and Google, and direct marketing companies such as Dell. However, for most companies, online marketing will remain just one important approach to the marketplace that works alongside other approaches in a fully integrated marketing mix.

Despite the many challenges, companies large and small are quickly integrating online marketing into their marketing strategies and mixes. As it continues to grow, online marketing will prove to be a powerful direct marketing tool for improving sales, communicating company and product information, delivering products and services, and building customer relationships more efficiently and effectively.

Public Policy Issues in Direct Marketing

Direct marketers and their customers usually enjoy mutually rewarding relationships. Occasionally, however, a darker side emerges. The aggressive and sometimes shady tactics of a few direct marketers can bother or harm consumers, giving the entire industry a black eye. Abuses range from simple excesses that irritate consumers to instances of unfair practices or even outright deception and fraud. The direct marketing industry has also faced growing invasion-of-privacy concerns, and online marketers must deal with Internet security issues.

Irritation, Unfairness, Deception, and Fraud

Direct marketing excesses sometimes annoy or offend consumers. Most of us dislike direct-response TV commercials that are too loud, too long, and too insistent. Our mailboxes fill up with unwanted junk mail, our e-mailboxes bulge with unwanted spam, and our computer screens flash with unwanted banner or pop-under ads.

Beyond irritating consumers, some direct marketers have been accused of taking unfair advantage of impulsive or less sophisticated buyers. TV shopping channels and program-long "infomercials" targeting television-addicted shoppers seem to be the worst culprits. They feature smooth-talking hosts, elaborately staged demonstrations, claims of drastic price reductions, "while they last" time limitations, and unequaled ease of purchase to inflame buyers who have low sales resistance.

Worse yet, so-called heat merchants design mailers and write copy intended to mislead buyers. Even well-known direct mailers have been accused of deceiving consumers. A few years back, sweepstakes promoter Publishers Clearing House paid $52 million to settle accusations that its high-pressure mailings confused or misled consumers, especially the elderly, into believing that they had won prizes or would win if they bought the company's magazines. Even the venerable Reader's Digest has had to pay restitution to consumers for alleged deceptive marketing in its sweepstakes contests.[61]

Fraudulent schemes, such as investment scams or phony collections for charity, have also multiplied in recent years. *Internet fraud,* including identity theft and financial scams, has become a serious problem. Last year alone, the Federal Internet Crime Complaint Center (IC3) received more than 79,000 complaints related to Internet fraud involving monetary loss, with a total dollar loss of $198 million.[62]

One common form of Internet fraud is *phishing,* a type of identity theft that uses deceptive e-mails and fraudulent Web sites to fool users into divulging their personal data. According to one survey, half of all Internet users have received a phishing e-mail. Although many consumers are now aware of such schemes, phishing can be extremely costly to those caught in the net. It also damages the brand identities of legitimate online marketers who have worked to build user confidence in Web and e-mail transactions.[63]

Many consumers also worry about *online security.* They fear that unscrupulous snoopers will eavesdrop on their online transactions, picking up personal information or intercepting credit and debit card numbers. In a recent survey, 68 percent of participants said they were concerned that their credit or debit card information will be stolen if they use their cards for online purchases. More than one-third also see the Internet as the medium most likely to result in identity theft.[64] Internet shoppers are also concerned about contracting annoying or harmful viruses, spyware, and other "malware":

Spyware programs track where you go on the Internet and clutter your screen with annoying pop-up advertisements for everything from pornography to wireless phone plans. Spyware can get stuck in your computer's hard drive as you shop, chat, or download a song. It might arrive attached to that clever

■ Internet fraud has multiplied in recent years. The FBI's Internet Crime Complaint Center provides consumers with a convenient way to alert authorities to suspected violations.

video you just nabbed at no charge. Web security company McAfee estimates that nearly three-quarters of all sites listed in response to Internet searches for popular phrases like "free screen savers" or "digital music" attempt to install some form of advertising software in visitors' computers. Once lodged there, spyware can sap a PC's processing power, slow its functioning, and even cause it to crash.[65]

Another Internet marketing concern is that of *access by vulnerable or unauthorized groups*. For example, marketers of adult-oriented materials have found it difficult to restrict access by minors. In a more specific example, a while back, sellers using eBay found themselves the victims of a 14-year-old boy who'd bid on and purchased more than $3 million worth of high-priced antiques and rare artworks on the site. EBay has a strict policy against bidding by anyone under age 18 but works largely on the honor system. Unfortunately, this honor system did little to prevent the resourceful teenager from taking a cyberspace joyride.[66]

Invasion of Privacy

Invasion of privacy is perhaps the toughest public policy issue now confronting the direct marketing industry. Consumers often benefit from database marketing—they receive more offers that are closely matched to their interests. However, many critics worry that marketers may know *too* much about consumers' lives and that they may use this knowledge to take unfair advantage of consumers. At some point, they claim, the extensive use of databases intrudes on consumer privacy.

These days, it seems that almost every time consumers enter a sweepstakes, apply for a credit card, visit a Web site, or order products by mail, telephone, or the Internet, their names enter some company's already bulging database. Using sophisticated computer technologies, direct marketers can use these databases to "microtarget" their selling efforts. *Online privacy* causes special concerns. Most online marketers have become skilled at collecting and analyzing detailed consumer information.

Some consumers and policy makers worry that the ready availability of information may leave consumers open to abuse if companies make unauthorized use of the information in marketing their products or exchanging databases with other companies. For example, they ask, should phone companies be allowed to sell marketers the names of customers who frequently call the 800 numbers of catalog companies? Should credit card companies be allowed to make data on their millions of cardholders worldwide available to merchants who accept their cards? Is it right for credit bureaus to compile and sell lists of people who have recently applied for credit cards—people who are considered prime direct marketing targets because of their spending behavior? Or is it right for states to sell the names and addresses of driver's license holders, along with height, weight, and gender information, allowing apparel retailers to target tall or overweight people with special clothing offers?

In their drives to build databases, companies sometimes get carried away. For example, Microsoft caused substantial privacy concerns when one version of its Windows software used a "Registration Wizard" that snooped into users computers. When users went online to register, without their knowledge, Microsoft "read" the configurations of their PCs to learn about the major software products they were running. Users protested loudly and Microsoft abandoned the practice.

A Need for Action

All of this calls for strong actions by marketers to prevent privacy abuses before legislators step in to do it for them. For example, to curb direct marketing excesses, various government agencies are investigating not just do-not-call lists but also "do-not-mail" lists and "Can Spam" legislation. And in response to online privacy and security concerns, the federal government has considered numerous legislative actions to regulate how Web operators obtain and use consumer information. State governments are also stepping in. In 2003, California enacted the California Online Privacy Protection Act (OPPA), under which any online business that collects personally identifiable information from California residents must take steps such as posting its privacy policy and notifying consumers about what data will be gathered and how it will be used.[67]

Of special concern are the privacy rights of children. In 1998, the Federal Trade Commission surveyed 212 Web sites directed toward children. It found that 89 percent of the sites collected personal information from children. However, 46 percent of them did not include any disclosure of their collection and use of such information. As a result, Congress passed the Children's Online Privacy Protection Act (COPPA), which requires Web site operators targeting children to post privacy policies on their sites. They must also notify parents about the information they're gathering and obtain parental consent before collecting personal information from children under age 13. Under this act, Interstate Bakeries was recently required to rework its Planet Twinkie Web site after the Children's Advertising Review Unit found that the site allowed children under 13 to submit their full name and phone number without parental consent.[68]

Many companies have responded to consumer privacy and security concerns with actions of their own. Still others are taking an industrywide approach. For example, TRUSTe, a nonprofit self-regulatory organization, works with many large corporate sponsors, including Microsoft, AT&T, and Intuit, to audit companies' privacy and security measures and help consumers navigate the Web safely. According to the company's Web site, "TRUSTe believes that an environment of mutual trust and openness will help make and keep the Internet a free, comfortable, and richly diverse community for everyone." To reassure consumers, the company lends its "trustmark" stamp of approval to Web sites that meet its privacy and security standards.[69]

The direct marketing industry as a whole is also addressing public policy issues. For example, in an effort to build consumer confidence in shopping direct, the Direct Marketing Association (DMA)—the largest association for businesses practicing direct, database, and interactive marketing, with more than 4,800 member companies—launched a "Privacy Promise to American Consumers." The Privacy Promise requires that all DMA members adhere to a carefully developed set of consumer privacy rules. Members must agree to notify customers when any personal information is rented, sold, or exchanged with others. They must also honor consumer requests to "opt out" of receiving further solicitations or having their contact information transferred to other marketers. Finally, they must abide by the DMA's Preference Service by removing the names of consumers who wish not to receive mail, telephone, or e-mail offers.[70]

Direct marketers know that, left untended, such direct marketing abuses will lead to increasingly negative consumer attitudes, lower response rates, and calls for more restrictive state and federal legislation. Most direct marketers want the same things that consumers want: honest and well-designed marketing offers targeted only toward consumers who will appreciate and respond to them. Direct marketing is just too expensive to waste on consumers who don't want it.

REST STOP ⤵ REVIEWING THE CONCEPTS

Let's revisit this chapter's key concepts. This chapter is the last of three chapters covering the final marketing mix element—promotion. The previous chapters dealt with advertising, publicity, personal selling, and sales promotion. This one investigates direct and online marketing.

1. Define direct marketing and discuss its benefits to customers and companies.

Direct marketing consists of direct connections with carefully targeted individual consumers to both obtain an immediate response and cultivate lasting customer relationships. Using detailed databases, direct marketers tailor their offers and communications to the needs of narrowly defined segments or even individual buyers.

For buyers, direct marketing is convenient, easy to use, and private. It gives buyers ready access to a wealth of products and information, at home and around the globe. Direct marketing is also immediate and interactive, allowing buyers to create exactly the configuration of information, products, or services they desire, then order them on the spot. For sellers, direct marketing is a powerful tool for building customer relationships. Using database marketing, today's marketers can target small groups or individual consumers, tailor offers to individual needs, and promote these offers through personalized communications. It also offers them a low-cost, efficient alternative for reaching their markets. As a result of these advantages to both buyers and sellers, direct marketing has become the fastest-growing form of marketing.

2. Identify and discuss the major forms of direct marketing.

The main forms of direct marketing include personal selling, direct-mail marketing, catalog marketing, telephone marketing, direct-response television marketing, kiosk marketing, and online marketing. We discussed personal selling in the previous chapter.

Direct-mail marketing, the largest form of direct marketing, consists of the company sending an offer, announcement, reminder, or other item to a person at a specific address. Recently, new forms of "mail delivery" have become popular, such as e-mail marketing. Some marketers rely on catalog marketing— selling through catalogs mailed to a select list of customers, made available in stores, or accessed on the Web. Telephone marketing consists of using the telephone to sell directly to consumers. Direct-response television marketing has two forms: direct-response advertising (or infomercials) and home shopping channels. Kiosks are information and ordering machines that direct marketers place in stores, airports, and other locations. In recent years, a number of new digital direct marketing technologies have emerged, including mobile marketing, podcasts and vodcasts, and interactive TV. Online marketing involves online channels that digitally link sellers with consumers.

3. Explain how companies have responded to the Internet and other powerful new technologies with online marketing strategies.

Online marketing is the fastest-growing form of direct marketing. The Internet enables consumers and companies to access and share huge amounts of information with just a few mouse clicks. In turn, the Internet has given marketers a whole new way to create value for customers and build customer relationships. It's hard to find a company today that doesn't have a substantial Web marketing presence.

Online consumer buying continues to grow at a healthy rate. Most American online users now use the Internet to shop. Perhaps more importantly, the Internet influences off-line shopping. Thus, smart marketers are employing integrated multichannel strategies that use the Web to drive sales to other marketing channels.

4. Discuss how companies go about conducting online marketing to profitably deliver more value to customers.

Companies of all types are now engaged in online marketing. The Internet gave birth to the *click-only* dot-coms, which oper-

ate only online. In addition, many traditional brick-and-mortar companies have now added online marketing operations, transforming themselves into *click-and-mortar* competitors. Many click-and-mortar companies are now having more online success than their click-only competitors.

Companies can conduct online marketing in any of the four ways: creating a Web site, placing ads and promotions online, setting up or participating in Web communities and online social networks, or using e-mail. The first step typically is to set up a Web site. Beyond simply setting up a site, however, companies must make their sites engaging, easy to use, and useful in order to attract visitors, hold them, and bring them back again.

Online marketers can use various forms of online advertising and promotion to build their Internet brands or to attract visitors to their Web sites. Forms of online promotion include online display advertising, search-related advertising, content sponsorships, alliances and affiliate programs, and viral marketing, the Internet version of word-of-mouth marketing. Online marketers can also participate in online social networks and other Web communities, which take advantage of the C2C properties of the Web. Finally, e-mail marketing has become a fast-growing tool for both B2C and B2B marketers. Whatever direct marketing tools they use, marketers must work hard to integrate them into a cohesive marketing effort.

5. Overview the public policy and ethical issues presented by direct marketing.

Direct marketers and their customers usually enjoy mutually rewarding relationships. Sometimes, however, direct marketing presents a darker side. The aggressive and sometimes shady tactics of a few direct marketers can bother or harm consumers, giving the entire industry a black eye. Abuses range from simple excesses that irritate consumers to instances of unfair practices or even outright deception and fraud. The direct marketing industry has also faced growing concerns about invasion-of-privacy and Internet security issues. Such concerns call for strong action by marketers and public policy makers to curb direct marketing abuses. In the end, most direct marketers want the same things that consumers want: honest and well-designed marketing offers targeted only toward consumers who will appreciate and respond to them.

Navigating the Key Terms

Business-to-business (B2B) online marketing (430)

Business-to-consumer (B2C) online marketing (429)

Catalog marketing (420)

Click-and-mortar companies (429)

Click-only companies (428)

Consumer-to-business (C2B) online marketing (432)

Consumer-to-consumer (C2C) online marketing (431)

Corporate (or brand) Web site (433)

Customer database (418)

Direct-mail marketing (419)

Direct marketing (415)

Direct-response television marketing (423)

Internet (428)

Marketing Web site (433)

Online advertising (435)

Online marketing (428)

Online social networks (437)

Spam (438)

Telephone marketing (421)

Viral marketing (436)

Travel Log

Discussing the Issues

1. Discuss the benefits of direct marketing to both buyers and sellers. (AASCB: Communication)

2. Describe the qualities and features of an effective customer database. (AACSB: Communication)

3. Name and describe the forms of direct-response television marketing and give an example of each. (AACSB: Communication)

4. Describe the four major e-marketing domains and provide an example of each. (AACSB: Communication)

5. Compare and contrast the different forms of online advertising. What factors should a company consider in deciding among these different forms? (AACSB: Communication)

6. Discuss the public policy issues in direct marketing. What are direct marketers doing to address these issues? (AACSB: Communication; Reflective Thinking)

Application Questions

1. In a small group, select a Web site of your choice and evaluate it according to the "7 Cs" of effective Web site design. Present this to the rest of the class. (AACSB: Communication; Use of IT; Reflective Thinking)

2. Visit www.donotcall.gov and click on "more information" to learn more about the National Do Not Call registry. Write a brief report regarding who can register a number, who must comply with the registry, and consequences for noncompliance. (AACSB: Communication; Use of IT; Reflective Thinking)

3. Online marketing to children is of great concern to parents, consumer groups, businesses, and the government. Research the Children's Online Privacy Protection Act (COPPA) and the Children's Advertising Review Unit (CARU) of the National Advertising Division. Discuss a recent case the CARU handled with respect to the COPPA. (AACSB: Communication; Reflective Thinking)

Under the Hood: Focus on Technology

The future of Internet advertising is widgets. Widgets, also known as "gadgets," are tiny computer programs that allow anyone to incorporate professional-looking content into Web pages, such as news feeds, clocks, weather information, and so on. Widgets usually contain a brand name or promotional message. They can be simple or complex, such as those incorporating chat boxes, polls, video, and games. Whereas banner advertising is not very effective and video ads are annoying because they take over the screen, marketers see widgets as a promising route to reach consumers by integrating advertising onto the Web page. Moreover, widgets are a way to get on individuals' personal Web sites and may be the only way to get inside some Web spaces, such as MySpace pages. As with banner ads, marketers can measure widget click-through rates to assess the effectiveness of an ad. Yahoo! offers widgets, Google offers gadgets, and others, such as Microsoft and ThinkGeek, offer free programs for users to download. The only price to users is the promotional content that comes along with it.

1. Search "widgets" and "gadgets" on the Internet to learn more about this Web advertising tool. Search Web sites to see if you can find examples of this type of advertising. Write a brief report of what you learned. (AACSB: Communication; Use of IT; Reflective Thinking)

2. Discuss the different forms of online advertising. Do you think this type of Internet advertising is more effective than the others? Explain why or why not. (AACSB: Communication; Reflective Thinking)

Focus on Ethics

"Junk mail!" We all know what it is, but have you considered the environmental impact of all that unsolicited mail? The Department of the Environment estimates that Americans spend more than $320 million per year to dispose of junk mail. Approximately 42 billion pieces of unsolicited mail are delivered annually, representing 41 pounds of junk mail per adult each year. More than 100 million trees are cut down and 28 billion gallons of water are used each year to feed our junk mail addiction. Statistics such as these have lead some consumers and communities to fight back. For example, the San Francisco and Santa Barbara areas of California started a "Stop Junk Mail" campaign and provide useful tips for consumers at www.stopjunkmail.org. The United States is not the only concerned country. British environment minister David Miliband has declared a "war on junk mail" and has threatened legislation forcing direct marketers to go to an opt-in model of mailing. Charities responded that this was simply "hair-brained lunacy." The direct-mail industry in the United Kingdom is already reeling from a government mandate that 30 percent of delivered direct mail in 2006 be recycled, amounting to proving that more than 600,000 pieces had been recycled by direct marketers by the end of that year.

1. Should the government enact laws to legislate the amount of mail a marketer can send? Is there any benefit to direct mailers of reducing unsolicited mailings? (AACSB: Communication; Ethical Reasoning)

2. Explain the opt-in model. Suggest other ways for direct mailers and consumers to reduce unsolicited mail. Identify organizations that help consumers in this task. (AACSB: Communication; Reflective Thinking)

Video Case

Google

It boggles the mind to realize that only 14 years ago, Google didn't even exist as a concept. Yet the advent of the World Wide Web set the foundation for what would become Google's mission: to organize the world's information and make it universally accessible and useful. Google was not the first Web search engine. But soon after founders Larry Page and Sergey Brin introduced their service based on a unique search technology, Google became *the* go-to way to search for information on the Internet. Google now has dozens of free services, including foreign language translation, stock quotes, maps, phone book listings, images, videos, and news headlines.

But perhaps Google's most revolutionary impact on the dot-com environment is the manner in which it has turned Internet advertising upside down. Today, services such as AdWords (keyword search advertising) and AdSense (a method that generates only the most relevant ads for client Web sites) are breaking new ground because they result in ads that actually help consumers.

After viewing the Google video, answer the following online marketing questions.

1. Brainstorm the many benefits that Google provides for consumers.

2. Brainstorm the many benefits that Google provides for online marketers.

3. Visit www.google.com. Based on what you find there, discuss Google's presence in each of the four major e-marketing domains.

1. discuss how the international trade system and the economic, political-legal, and cultural environments affect a company's international marketing decisions

2. describe three key approaches to entering international markets

3. explain how companies adapt their marketing mixes for international markets

4. identify the three major forms of international marketing organization

The Global Marketplace

ROAD MAP Previewing the Concepts

You've now learned the fundamentals of how companies develop competitive marketing strategies to create customer value and to build lasting customer relationships. In this chapter, we extend these fundamentals to global marketing. We've visited global topics in each previous chapter—it's difficult to find an area of marketing that doesn't contain at least some international issues. Here, however, we'll focus on special considerations that companies face when they market their brands globally. Advances in communication, transportation, and other technologies have made the world a much smaller place. Today, almost every firm, large or small, faces international marketing issues. In this chapter, we will examine six major decisions marketers make in going global.

Before moving into the chapter, let's look first at one of today's hottest global brands—the National Basketball Association. Yes, the NBA! Just like most other large businesses, the once quintessentially American NBA is now seeking growth opportunities beyond its own national boarders. And when it comes to global marketing, the NBA is jamming down one slam dunk after another. Read on and see how.

W hat could be more American than basketball? The sport was invented in the United States, and each year tens of millions of excited fans crowd their local gyms or huddle around their television sets to cheer on their favorite rec league, high school, college, or pro teams. But basketball is rapidly becoming a worldwide craze. Although soccer remains the number-one sport in most of the world, basketball—that's right, basketball—is a solid number two.

Lots of companies are going global these days, but few organizations are doing it better than the National Basketball Association (NBA). During the past two decades, under the leadership of Commissioner David Stern, the NBA has become a truly global marketing enterprise. Nowhere was this more apparent than in last year's NBA finals, which were televised to more than 215 countries in 41 languages, from Armenian, Belorussian, Lithuanian, and Norwegian to Arabic, Cantonese, and Macedonian. In fact, more than 10 percent of the league's $3 billion in revenues come from foreign TV contacts, merchandising, and licensing. More than half the hits on NBA.com, which now features nine country sites in seven languages, originate outside the United States. And 25 percent of all NBA-licensed basketballs, jerseys, backboards, and other merchandise is sold internationally.

The NBA has become a powerful worldwide brand. A *Fortune* article summarizes:

Deployed by global sponsors such as Coca-Cola, Reebok, and McDonald's, well-paid [NBA superstars] hawk soda, sneakers, burgers, and basketball to legions of mostly young fans [worldwide]. That they are recognized from Santiago to Seoul says a lot about the soaring worldwide appeal of hoops—and about the marketing juggernaut known as the NBA. After watching their favorite stars swoop in and slam-dunk on their local TV stations, fans of the league now cheer the *mate* in Latin America, the *trofsla* in Iceland, and the *smash* in France.

Like many other businesses, the NBA's primary motive for going global is growth. The league now sells out most of its games, and domestic licensing revenues have flattened in recent years. "Globalization is a huge opportunity for us," says Commissioner Stern, who recently called basketball a "universal language about to bloom on a global basis." Stern sees huge worldwide potential for the NBA. "If you watch over the years what percentage of profit Coca-Cola makes from overseas, or how Wal-Mart and others are expanding in Europe and China, you'll understand," he says.

Most experts expect slam dunk after slam dunk for the NBA as it extends its international reach. Adding to the league's global appeal is the growing presence of foreign-born players. Some 82 players (more than 20 percent of all NBA pros) hail from outside the United States, and almost every NBA team boasts at least one non-U.S. star. To name just a few, the list includes Yao Ming from China, Dirk Nowitzki from Germany, Tony Kukoc from Croatia, Pau Gasol from Spain, Manu Ginobili from Argentina, and Peja Stojakovic from Serbia. Such players attract large followings in their home countries. German tennis star Boris Becker credits Dirk Nowitzki for the increase in NBA ratings in his homeland. "Thanks to Dirk, basketball has become very, very popular" in Germany.

And many American basketball superstars have developed their own hoards of fanatical fans abroad. For example, according to one report, "Two years ago in Beijing, police were forced to cancel Michael Jordan's first public appearance in the city on his Asian tour after fans trampled flower beds, blocked sidewalks, damaged a car, and ripped down several billboards while angling so they could get a good view of the retired NBA legend. When police pulled the plug on the event at Dongdan Sports Center before Jordan even arrived, the fans became angry, many shouting Jordan's name in unison. Some had [waited] outside the stadium for hours, waving Jordan posters."

Stern is not content to just sit back and let international things happen. He's investing heavily to build the NBA's popularity and business abroad. The NBA now has nine offices in major world cities, including Paris, Tokyo, and Hong Kong. Its international staff numbers more than 100 people, nearly double the number who ran the entire league just two decades ago.

The NBA even has an Hispanic marketing office in Miami, where eight people focus on Latin America and the Hispanic media in other parts of the world.

For Heidi Ueberroth, head of the NBA's international business operations, the U.S. summer off-season is the start of the international marketing season. During last year's summer off-season, the league sponsored 132 international events, with 198 players representing all 30 NBA teams appearing in 87 cities on five continents. It also started what might be its most ambitious global expansion effort ever—called NBA Europe Live. This program took off-season training for four teams—the Suns, Clippers, Sixers, and Spurs—to European cities. Each team was chosen because it has major foreign-born players with international appeal.

NBA Europe Live does much more than simply showcase team training. Each team competes in exhibition games against host teams from Euroleague basketball. According to Stern, "At the culmination of the exhibition games, there will be a four-team tournament featuring the champion of the Euroleague and the runner-up of Euroleague basketball going against two NBA teams." Given that the bulk of the NBA's international fan base is in Europe, NBA Europe Live makes good business sense. Some even see NBA Europe Live as a significant step toward landing an NBA team overseas. "I think somewhere down the road, a European Division or European Conference is certainly a possibility," says an analyst.

If things look good for the NBA in Europe, the league is positively drooling over its prospects in China, with its more than 1.3 billion people and 300 million basketball fans. According to Ueberroth, basketball in China "is the number-one sport for youth 30 and under." It helps that in recent years China's three biggest stars, Yao Ming, Wang ZhiZhi, and Mengke Bateer, left the Chinese Basketball Association to take a shot at NBA careers. The NBA is reaping the benefits. NBA.com's Mandarin language Web site accounts for over 22 percent of all the league's Internet traffic, and 20,000 Chinese retail outlets now sell NBA merchandise. Chinese state-run CCTV airs four NBA games a week, and another 50 stations across the country telecast the games. The league even deploys its Jam Van, complete with hoops and interactive NBA video games, to tour China's provinces.

Despite the dazzling prospects, many challenges remain. "Winning the loyalty of [more than a] billion Chinese won't be a *kou qui*—a slam dunk," suggests one international sports analyst, "but Stern is, well, bullish. . . . Can Ping-Pong survive an NBA invasion? Stay tuned [and see how the ball bounces]."[1]

In the past, U.S. companies paid little attention to international trade. If they could pick up some extra sales through exporting, that was fine. But the big market was at home, and it teemed with opportunities. The home market was also much safer. Managers did not need to learn other languages, deal with strange and changing currencies, face political and legal uncertainties, or adapt their products to different customer needs and expectations. Today, however, the situation is much different. Organizations of all kinds, from Coca-Cola, IBM, and Yahoo! to MTV and even the NBA, have gone global.

Global Marketing Today

The world is shrinking rapidly with the advent of faster communication, transportation, and financial flows. Products developed in one country—Gucci purses, Sony electronics, McDonald's hamburgers, Japanese sushi, German BMWs—have found enthusiastic acceptance in other countries. We would not be surprised to hear about a German businessman wearing an Italian suit meeting an English friend at a Japanese restaurant who later returns home to drink Russian vodka and watch *American Idol* on TV.

International trade is booming. Since 1990, the number of multinational corporations in the world has grown from 30,000 to more than 60,000. Some of these multinationals are true giants. In fact, of the largest 150 "economies" in the world, only 74 are countries. The remaining 76 are multinational corporations. Wal-Mart, the world's largest company, has annual revenues greater than the gross domestic product of all but the world's 23 largest-GDP countries.[2]

Since 2003, total world trade has been growing at 6 to 11 percent annually, whereas global gross domestic product has grown at only 2.5 to 5 percent annually. World trade of products and services was valued at over $14.4 trillion last year, which accounted for about 30 percent of gross domestic product worldwide. This trade growth is most visible in developing countries, such as China, which saw their share in world exports rise sharply to 27 percent last year.[3]

Many U.S. companies have long been successful at international marketing: Coca-Cola, General Electric, IBM, Colgate, Caterpillar, Ford, Boeing, McDonald's, and dozens of other American firms have made the world their market. And in the United States, names such as Sony, Toyota, BP, IKEA, Nestlé, Nokia, and Prudential have become household words. Other products and services that appear to be American are in fact produced or owned by foreign companies: Bantam books, Baskin-Robbins ice cream, GE and RCA televisions, Carnation milk, Pillsbury food products, Universal Studios, and Motel 6, to name just a few. Michelin, the oh-so-French tire manufacturer, now does 35 percent of its business in North America; Johnson & Johnson, the maker of quintessentially all-American products such as Band-Aids and Johnson's Baby Shampoo, does 45 percent of its business abroad.[4]

But while global trade is growing, global competition is intensifying. Foreign firms are expanding aggressively into new international markets, and home markets are no longer as rich in opportunity. Few industries are now safe from foreign competition. If companies delay taking steps toward internationalizing, they risk being shut out of growing markets in Western and Eastern Europe, China and the Pacific Rim, Russia, and elsewhere. Firms that stay at home to play it safe not only might lose their chances to enter other markets but also risk losing their home markets. Domestic companies that never thought about foreign competitors suddenly find these competitors in their own backyards.

Ironically, although the need for companies to go abroad is greater today than in the past, so are the risks. Companies that go global may face highly unstable governments and currencies, restrictive government policies and regulations, and high trade barriers. Corruption is also an increasing problem—officials in several countries often award business not to the best bidder but to the highest briber.

A **global firm** is one that, by operating in more than one country, gains marketing, production, R&D, and financial advantages that are not available to purely domestic competitors. The global company sees the world as one market. It minimizes the importance of national boundaries and develops "transnational" brands. It raises capital, obtains materials

■ Many American companies have made the world their market, and in the United States foreign company names have become so familiar that sometimes products that appear to be American are in fact produced or owned by foreign companies.

Global firm
A firm that, by operating in more than one country, gains R&D, production, marketing, and financial advantages in its costs and reputation that are not available to purely domestic competitors.

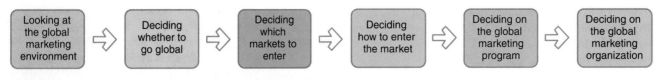

FIGURE 15.1 Major International Marketing Decisions

and components, and manufactures and markets its goods wherever it can do the best job. For example, Otis Elevator, the world's largest elevator maker, achieves four-fifths of its sales from outside the United States. It gets its elevators' door systems from France, small geared parts from Spain, electronics from Germany, and special motor drives from Japan. It uses the United States only for systems integration. "Borders are so 20th century," says one global marketing expert. "Transnationals take 'stateless' to the next level."[5]

This does not mean that small- and medium-size firms must operate in a dozen countries to succeed. These firms can practice global niching. But the world is becoming smaller, and every company operating in a global industry—whether large or small—must assess and establish its place in world markets.

The rapid move toward globalization means that all companies will need to answer some basic questions: What market position should we try to establish in our country, in our economic region, and globally? Who will our global competitors be and what are their strategies and resources? Where should we produce or source our products? What strategic alliances should we form with other firms around the world?

As shown in Figure 15.1, a company faces six major decisions in international marketing. We will discuss each decision in detail in this chapter.

Looking at the Global Marketing Environment

Before deciding whether to operate internationally, a company must understand the international marketing environment. That environment has changed a great deal in the past two decades, creating both new opportunities and new problems.

The International Trade System

U.S. companies looking abroad must start by understanding the international *trade system.* When selling to another country, a firm may face restrictions on trade between nations. Foreign governments may charge *tariffs,* taxes on certain imported products designed to raise revenue or to protect domestic firms. For example, China slaps a 25 percent tariff on U.S. and other imported autos. Or they may set *quotas,* limits on the amount of foreign imports that they will accept in certain product categories. The purpose of a quota is to conserve on foreign exchange and to protect local industry and employment. American firms may also face *exchange controls,* which limit the amount of foreign exchange and the exchange rate against other currencies.

The company also may face *nontariff trade barriers,* such as biases against U.S. company bids, restrictive product standards, or excessive regulations. For example, U.S. foreign policy makers have criticized China for protectionist regulations and other actions that restrict access to several Chinese markets, including banking services.

■ Trade barriers: U.S. and other Western banks have been effectively fenced out of China's huge retail banking market by protectionist regulations.

For years U.S. financial houses have dreamed of the day when they'll be allowed to offer banking services to individual Chinese savers. But critics complain that, despite China's promises to the World Trade Organization, Western banks are effectively fenced out by investment caps and regulations that make going solo frightfully expensive. In theory, foreign banks can open branches from Hainan to Harbin. But in reality, they can open only one branch a year, and each branch must have operating capital of $50 million, a burden local banks don't face. Committing $500 million to open 10 branches in a decade doesn't make a lot of sense, so foreign banks instead have bought stakes in local banks. But Beijing limits total foreign ownership in any Chinese bank to just 25 percent, leaving the foreign investors little say in strategy. Last year, for instance, Bank of America spent $3 billion for 9 percent of China Construction Bank Corp. But the Americans have only one seat on the board and had to abandon their own mainland retail effort as part of the deal. Beijing denies any effort to block access to its market. True, foreigners control just 2 percent of assets in the banking system, notes a Chinese trade expert. "The problem is, the U.S. banking sector is not patient."[6]

At the same time, certain forces *help* trade between nations. Examples include the General Agreement on Tariffs and Trade (GATT) and various regional free trade agreements.

The World Trade Organization and GATT The General Agreement on Tariffs and Trade (GATT) is a 60-year-old treaty designed to promote world trade by reducing tariffs and other international trade barriers. Since the treaty's inception in 1947, member nations (currently numbering 150) have met in eight rounds of GATT negotiations to reassess trade barriers and set new rules for international trade. The first seven rounds of negotiations reduced the average worldwide tariffs on manufactured goods from 45 percent to just 5 percent.[7]

The most recently completed GATT negotiations, dubbed the Uruguay Round, dragged on for seven long years before concluding in 1994. The benefits of the Uruguay Round will be felt for many years as the accord promotes long-term global trade growth. It reduced the world's remaining merchandise tariffs by 30 percent. The agreement also extended GATT to cover trade in agriculture and a wide range of services, and it toughened international protection of copyrights, patents, trademarks, and other intellectual property. Although the financial impact of such an agreement is difficult to measure, research suggests that cutting agriculture, manufacturing, and services trade barriers by one-third would boost the world economy by $613 billion, the equivalent of adding another Argentina to the world economy.[8]

Beyond reducing trade barriers and setting global standards for trade, the Uruguay Round set up the World Trade Organization (WTO) to enforce GATT rules. In general, the WTO acts as an umbrella organization, overseeing GATT, mediating global disputes, and imposing trade sanctions. The previous GATT organization never possessed such authorities. A new round of GATT negotiations, the Doha round, began in Doha, Qatar, in late 2001 and was set to conclude in 2005, but the discussions continue.[9]

Regional Free Trade Zones Certain countries have formed *free trade zones* or **economic communities**. These are groups of nations organized to work toward common goals in the regulation of international trade. One such community is the *European Union (EU)*. Formed in

■ The WTO and GATT: The General Agreement on Tariffs and Trade (GATT) promotes world trade by reducing tariffs in other international trade barriers. The WTO oversees GATT, imposes trade sanctions, and mediates global disputes.

■ Economic communities: The European Union represents one of the world's largest single markets. Its current member countries contain more than half a billion consumers and account for 20 percent of the world's exports.

Economic community

A group of nations organized to work toward common goals in the regulation of international trade.

1957, the European Union set out to create a single European market by reducing barriers to the free flow of products, services, finances, and labor among member countries and by developing policies on trade with nonmember nations. Today, the European Union represents one of the world's largest single markets. Currently, it has 27 member countries containing close to half a billion consumers and accounts for more than 20 percent of the world's exports.[10]

European unification offers tremendous trade opportunities for U.S. and other non-European firms. However, it also poses threats. As a result of increased unification, European companies have grown bigger and more competitive. Perhaps an even greater concern, however, is that lower barriers *inside* Europe will create only thicker *outside* walls. Some observers envision a "Fortress Europe" that heaps favors on firms from EU countries but hinders outsiders by imposing obstacles.

Progress toward European unification has been slow—many doubt that complete unification will ever be achieved. In recent years, 13 member nations have taken a significant step toward unification by adopting the euro as a common currency. Many other countries are expected to follow within the next few years. Widespread adoption of the euro will decrease much of the currency risk associated with doing business in Europe, making member countries with previously weak currencies more attractive markets.[11]

However, even with the adoption of the euro, it is unlikely that the EU will ever go against 2,000 years of tradition and become the "United States of Europe." A community with two dozen different languages and cultures will always have difficulty coming together and acting as a single entity. For example, efforts to forge a single European constitution appear to have failed following French and Dutch "no" votes in mid-2005. And economic disputes between member nations have stalled long-term budget negotiations. Still, although only partly successful so far, unification has made Europe a global force with which to reckon, with a combined annual GDP more than $13.6 trillion.[12]

In 1994, the *North American Free Trade Agreement (NAFTA)* established a free trade zone among the United States, Mexico, and Canada. The agreement created a single market of 443 million people who produce and consume over $15.4 trillion worth of goods and services annually. As it is implemented over a 15-year period, NAFTA will eliminate all trade barriers and investment restrictions among the three countries. Thus far, the agreement has allowed trade between the countries to flourish. In the dozen years following its establishment, trade among the NAFTA nations has risen 173 percent. U.S. merchandise exports to NAFTA partners grew 133 percent, compared with exports to the rest of the world at 77 percent. Canada and Mexico are now the nation's first- and second-largest trading partners.[13]

Following the apparent success of NAFTA, in 2005 the Central American Free Trade Agreement (CAFTA) established a free trade zone between the United States and Costa Rica, the Dominican Republic, El Salvador, Guatemala, Honduras, and Nicaragua. And talks have been underway since 1994 to investigate establishing a Free Trade Area of the Americas (FTAA). This mammoth free trade zone would include 34 countries stretching from the Bering Strait to Cape Horn, with a population of 800 million and a combined gross domestic product of about $17 trillion.[14]

Other free trade areas have formed in Latin America and South America. For example, Mercosur links eleven Latin America and South America countries, and the Andean Community (CAN, for its Spanish initials) links four more. In late 2004, Mercosur and CAN agreed to unite, creating the Union of South American Nations (Unasur), which will be modeled after the European Union. Complete integration between the two trade blocs is expected by the end of 2007, and all tariffs between the nations are to be eliminated by 2019. With a population of more than 379 million, a combined economy of more than $3.5 trillion a year, and exports worth $181 billion, Unasur will make up the largest trading bloc after NAFTA and the European Union.[15]

Each nation has unique features that must be understood. A nation's readiness for different products and services and its attractiveness as a market to foreign firms depend on its economic, political-legal, and cultural environments.

Economic Environment

The international marketer must study each country's economy. Two economic factors reflect the country's attractiveness as a market: the country's industrial structure and its income distribution.

The country's *industrial structure* shapes its product and service needs, income levels, and employment levels. The four types of industrial structures are as follows:

- *Subsistence economies:* In a subsistence economy, the vast majority of people engage in simple agriculture. They consume most of their output and barter the rest for simple goods and services. They offer few market opportunities.
- *Raw material exporting economies:* These economies are rich in one or more natural resources but poor in other ways. Much of their revenue comes from exporting these resources. Examples are Chile (tin and copper), Democratic Republic of Congo (copper, cobalt, and coffee), and Saudi Arabia (oil). These countries are good markets for large equipment, tools and supplies, and trucks. If there are many foreign residents and a wealthy upper class, they are also a market for luxury goods.
- *Industrializing economies:* In an industrializing economy, manufacturing accounts for 10 to 20 percent of the country's economy. Examples include Egypt, India, and Brazil. As manufacturing increases, the country needs more imports of raw textile materials, steel, and heavy machinery, and fewer imports of finished textiles, paper products, and automobiles. Industrialization typically creates a new rich class and a small but growing middle class, both demanding new types of imported goods.
- *Industrial economies:* Industrial economies are major exporters of manufactured goods, services, and investment funds. They trade goods among themselves and also export them to other types of economies for raw materials and semifinished goods. The varied manufacturing activities of these industrial nations and their large middle class make them rich markets for all sorts of goods.

The second economic factor is the country's *income distribution*. Industrialized nations may have low-, medium-, and high-income households. In contrast, countries with subsistence economies may consist mostly of households with very low family incomes. Still other countries may have households with only either very low or very high incomes. However, even poor or developing economies may be attractive markets for all kinds of goods, including luxuries. For example, many luxury-brand marketers are rushing to take advantage of China's rapidly developing consumer markets:[16]

> More than half of China's 1.3 billion consumers can barely afford rice, let alone luxuries. According to The World Bank, more than 400 million Chinese live on less than $2 a day. Yet posh brands—from Gucci and Cartier to Lexus and Bentley— are descending on China in force. How can purveyors of $2,000 handbags, $20,000 watches, and $1 million limousines thrive in a developing economy? Easy, says a Cartier executive. "Remember, even medium-sized cities in China . . . have populations larger than Switzerland's. So it doesn't matter if the percentage of people in those cities who can afford our products is very small." Thus, even though China has only 0.2 millionaires per 1,000 residents (compared with 8.4 per 1,000 in the United States), it trails only the United States, Germany, and the United Kingdom in the total number of millionaires. In 2004, China's luxury-goods consumption accounted for 11 percent of the world's total, slightly under half of that of America's and Japan's. By 2014, however, the figure is expected to jump to 23 percent,

■ Economic environment: Many luxury brand marketers are rushing to take advantage of China's rapidly developing consumer markets.

making China the world's largest consumer of luxury goods. Dazzled by the pace at which China's booming economy is minting million-aires and swelling the ranks of the middle class, luxury brands are rushing to stake out shop space and tout their wares. "The Chinese are a natural audience for luxury goods," notes one analyst. After decades of socialism and poverty, China's elite are suddenly "keen to show off their newfound wealth."

Thus, country and regional economic environments will affect an international marketer's decisions about which global markets to enter and how.

Political-Legal Environment

Nations differ greatly in their political-legal environments. In considering whether to do business in a given country, a company should consider factors such as the country's attitudes toward international buying, government bureaucracy, political stability, and monetary regulations.

Some nations are very receptive to foreign firms; others are less accommodating. For example, India has tended to bother foreign businesses with import quotas, currency restrictions, and other limitations that make operating there a challenge. In contrast, neighboring Asian countries such as Singapore and Thailand court foreign investors and shower them with incentives and favorable operating conditions. Political stability is another issue. For example, India's government is notoriously unstable—the country has elected 10 new governments in the past 20 years—increasing the risk of doing business there. Although most international marketers still find India's huge market attractive, the unstable political situation will affect how they handle business and financial matters.[17]

Companies must also consider a country's monetary regulations. Sellers want to take their profits in a currency of value to them. Ideally, the buyer can pay in the seller's currency or in other world currencies. Short of this, sellers might accept a blocked currency—one whose removal from the country is restricted by the buyer's government—if they can buy other goods in that country that they need themselves or can sell elsewhere for a needed currency. Besides currency limits, a changing exchange rate also creates high risks for the seller.

Most international trade involves cash transactions. Yet many nations have too little hard currency to pay for their purchases from other countries. They may want to pay with other items instead of cash, which has led to a growing practice called **countertrade**. Countertrade takes several forms: *Barter* involves the direct exchange of goods or services, as when Azerbaijan imported wheat from Romania in exchange for crude oil, and Vietnam exchanged rice for Philippine fertilizer and coconuts. Another form is *compensation* (or *buyback*), whereby the seller sells a plant, equipment, or technology to another country and agrees to take payment in the resulting products. Thus, Japan's Fukusuke Corporation sold knitting machines and raw textile materials to Shanghai clothing manufacturer Chinatex in exchange for finished textiles produced on the machines. The most common form of countertrade is *counterpurchase,* in which the seller receives full payment in cash but agrees to spend some of the money in the other country. For example, Boeing sells aircraft to India and agrees to buy Indian coffee, rice, castor oil, and other goods and sell them elsewhere.[18]

Countertrade deals can be very complex. For example, a few years back, DaimlerChrysler agreed to sell 30 trucks to Romania in exchange for 150 Romanian jeeps, which it then sold to Ecuador for bananas, which were in turn sold to a German supermarket chain for German currency. Through this roundabout process, DaimlerChrysler finally obtained payment in German money.

Countertrade
International trade involving the direct or indirect exchange of goods for other goods instead of cash.

Cultural Environment

Each country has its own folkways, norms, and taboos. When designing global marketing strategies, companies must understand how culture affects consumer reactions in each of its world markets. In turn, they must also understand how their strategies affect local cultures.

The Impact of Culture on Marketing Strategy The seller must understand the ways that consumers in different countries think about and use certain products before planning a marketing program. There are often surprises. For example, the average French man uses almost twice as many cosmetics and grooming aids as his wife. The Germans and the French eat more packaged, branded spaghetti than do Italians. Some 49 percent of Chinese eat on the way to work. Most American women let down their hair and take off makeup at bedtime, whereas 15 percent of Chinese women style their hair at bedtime and 11 percent put *on* makeup.[19]

Companies that ignore cultural norms and differences can make some very expensive and embarrassing mistakes. Here are examples:

Nike inadvertently offended Chinese officials when it ran an advertisement featuring LeBron James crushing a number of culturally revered Chinese figures in a kung-fu-themed TV spot. The Chinese government found that the ad violated regulations to uphold national dignity and respect of the "motherland's culture" and yanked the multi-million-dollar campaign. With egg on its face, Nike released a formal apology. Distiller Brown-Forman made a similar mistake when it created a window display in an Athens, Greece, bar showing Hindu Goddess Durga sitting on a tiger holding bottles of its Southern Comfort brand in all eight of her hands. Infuriated Hindus worldwide sent mail and e-mail messages decrying the defamation of their goddess—consuming alcohol is a sin to Hindus. An embarrassed Brown-Forman quickly removed the display, stating "we didn't realize it was the image of a Hindu goddess. It was human error and a violation of our marketing code" (which prohibits the use of religious images in the promotion of the company's alcoholic beverages).[20]

■ Overlooking cultural differences can result in embarrassing mistakes. China imposed a nationwide ban on this "blasphemous" kung fu-themed TV spot featuring LeBron James crushing a number of culturally revered Chinese figures.

Business norms and behavior also vary from country to country. For example, American executives like to get right down to business and engage in fast and tough face-to-face bargaining. However, Japanese and other Asian businesspeople often find this behavior offensive. They prefer to start with polite conversation, and they rarely say no in face-to-face conversations. As another example, South Americans like to sit or stand very close to each other when they talk business—in fact, almost nose-to-nose. The American business executive tends to keep backing away as the South American moves closer. Both may end up being offended. American business executives need to be briefed on these kinds of factors before conducting business in another country.[21]

By the same token, companies that understand cultural nuances can use them to advantage when positioning products and preparing campaigns internationally. Consider the following example:

Johnson & Johnson's Clean & Clear, the United Kingdom's number-one medicated skin care brand, faced a tough challenge when it learned that its core U.K. teen girl audience was finding the brand less "relevant." The brand's "cheesy" U.S.-style TV advertising simply wasn't cutting it with U.K. teen consumers. Research revealed that busy U.K. teens increasingly use media that make them feel part of a group and, more importantly, they use digital media to express themselves and their personalities. MSN Instant Messenger (IM) is considered the absolute must-have application for U.K. teens. So to better connect with U.K. girls, J&J created Clean & Clear Personalized Winks. Users could select one of the 10 Winks (such as "Angel," "You Rock," and "Whatever"), upload a photo of their choice, and send their own personalized, animated Wink to a friend during an IM chat. The campaign also included exclusive online ads on MSN and a special Web site (www.getyourfaceout-there.co.uk). In the end, the U.K. Personalized Winks proved phenomenally successful, with more than 4 million downloads during the first four weeks alone.[22]

Thus, understanding cultural traditions, preferences, and behaviors can help companies not only to avoid embarrassing mistakes but also to take advantage of cross-cultural opportunities.

The Impact of Marketing Strategy on Cultures

Whereas marketers worry about the impact of culture on their global marketing strategies, others may worry about the impact of marketing strategies on global cultures. For example, social critics contend that large American multinationals such as McDonald's, Coca-Cola, Starbucks, Nike, Microsoft, Disney, and MTV aren't just "globalizing" their brands, they are "Americanizing" the world's cultures.

Down in the mall, between the fast-food joint and the bagel shop, a group of young people huddle in a flurry of baggy combat pants, skateboards, and slang. They size up a woman teetering past wearing DKNY, carrying *Time* magazine in one hand and a latte in the other. She brushes past a guy in a Yankees baseball cap who is talking on his Motorola cell phone about the Martin Scorsese film he saw last night.

It's a standard American scene—only this isn't America, it's Britain. U.S. culture is so pervasive, the scene could be played out in any one of dozens of cities. Budapest or Berlin, if not Bogota or Bordeaux. Even Manila or Moscow. As the unrivaled global superpower, America exports its culture on an unprecedented scale. . . . Sometimes, U.S. ideals get transmitted—such as individual rights, freedom of speech, and respect for women—and local cultures are enriched. At other times, materialism or worse becomes the message and local traditions get crushed.[23]

"Today, globalization often wears Mickey Mouse ears, eats big Macs, drinks Coke or Pepsi, and does its computing [with Microsoft] Windows [software]," says Thomas Friedman, in his book *The Lexus and the Olive Tree*.[24] Critics worry that, under such "McDomination," countries around the globe are losing their individual cultural identities. Teens in India watch MTV and ask their parents for more westernized clothes and other symbols of American pop culture and values. Grandmothers in small European villas no longer spend each morning visiting local meat, bread, and produce markets to gather the ingredients for dinner. Instead, they now shop at Wal-Mart Supercenters. Women in Saudi Arabia see American films and question their societal roles. In China, most people never drank coffee before Starbucks entered the market. Now Chinese consumers rush to Starbucks stores "because it's a symbol of a new kind of lifestyle." Similarly, in China, where McDonald's operates 80 restaurants in Beijing alone, nearly half of all children identify the chain as a domestic brand.

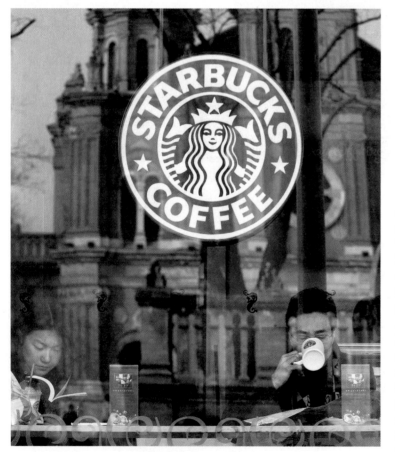

■ Americanization: Social critics contend that large American multinationals aren't just "globalizing" their brands, they are "Americanizing" the world's cultures. In China, most people never drank coffee before Starbucks entered the market.

Such concerns have sometimes led to a backlash against American globalization. Well-known U.S. brands have become the targets of boycotts and protests in some international markets. As symbols of American capitalism, companies such as Coca-Cola, McDonald's, Nike, and KFC have been singled out by antiglobalization protestors in hot spots all around the world, especially when anti-American sentiment peaks.

Despite such problems, defenders of globalization argue that concerns of "Americanization" and the potential damage to American brands are overblown. U.S. brands are doing very well internationally. In the most recent *BusinessWeek*/Interbrand survey of global brands, 11 of the top 15 brands were American-owned. And based on a recent study of 3,300 consumers in 41 countries, researchers concluded that consumers did not appear to translate anti-American sentiment into antibrand sentiment:[25]

> We found that it simply didn't matter to consumers whether the global brands they bought were American. To be sure, many people *said* they cared. A French panelist called American brands "imperialistic threats that undermine French culture." A German told us that Americans "want to impose their way on everybody." But the [talk] belied the reality. When we measured the extent to which consumers' purchase decisions were influenced by products' American roots, we discovered that the impact was negligible.

More fundamentally, most studies reveal that the cultural exchange goes both ways—America gets as well as gives cultural influence:[26]

> Hollywood dominates the global movie market—capturing 90 percent of audiences in some European markets. However, British TV is giving as much as it gets in serving up competition to U.S. shows, spawning such hits as "Who Wants to Be a Millionaire" and "American Idol." And although West Indian sports fans are now watching more basketball than cricket, and some Chinese young people are daubing the names of NBA superstars on their jerseys, the increasing popularity of American soccer has deep international roots. Even American childhood has increasingly been influenced by Asian and European cultural imports. Most kids know all about the Power Rangers, Tamagotchi and Pokemon, Sega and Nintendo. And J. K. Rowling's so-very-British Harry Potter books are shaping the thinking of a generation of American youngsters, not to mention the millions of American oldsters who've fallen under their spell as well. For the moment, English remains cyberspace's dominant language, and having Web access often means that third-world youth have greater exposure to American popular culture. Yet these same technologies enable Balkan students studying in the United States to hear Webcast news and music from Serbia or Bosnia. Thanks to broadband communication, foreign media producers will distribute films and television programs directly to American consumers without having to pass by U.S. gatekeepers.

American companies have also learned that to succeed abroad they must adapt to local cultural values and traditions rather than trying to force their own. Disneyland Paris flopped at first because it failed to take local cultural values and behaviors into account. According to a Euro Disney executive, "When we first launched, there was the belief that it was enough to be Disney. Now we realize that our guests need to be welcomed on the basis of their own culture and travel habits."[27] That realization has made Disneyland Paris the number-one tourist attraction in Europe—with twice as many visitors each year as the Eiffel Tower. The newest attraction there is The Walt Disney Studios Park, a movie-themed park that blends Disney entertainment and attractions with the history and culture of European film. A show celebrating the history of animation features Disney characters speaking six different languages. Rides are narrated by foreign-born stars speaking in their native tongues.

Thus, globalization is a two-way street. If globalization has Mickey Mouse ears, it is also wearing a French beret, talking on a Nokia cell phone, buying furniture at IKEA, driving a Toyota Camry, and watching a Sony big-screen plasma TV.

Deciding Whether to Go Global

Not all companies need to venture into international markets to survive. For example, most local businesses need to market well only in the local marketplace. Operating domestically is easier and safer. Managers don't need to learn another country's language and laws. They don't need to deal with unstable currencies, face political and legal uncertainties, or redesign their products to suit different customer expectations. However, companies that operate in global industries, where their strategic positions in specific markets are affected strongly by their overall global positions, must compete on a regional or worldwide basis to succeed.

Any of several factors might draw a company into the international arena. Global competitors might attack the company's home market by offering better products or lower prices. The company might want to counterattack these competitors in their home markets to tie up their resources. Or the company's home market might be stagnant or shrinking, and foreign markets may present higher sales and profit opportunities. Or the company's customers might be expanding abroad and require international servicing.

Before going abroad, the company must weigh several risks and answer many questions about its ability to operate globally. Can the company learn to understand the preferences and buyer behavior of consumers in other countries? Can it offer competitively attractive products? Will it be able to adapt to other countries' business cultures and deal effectively with foreign nationals? Do the company's managers have the necessary international experience? Has management considered the impact of regulations and the political environments of other countries?

Because of the difficulties of entering international markets, most companies do not act until some situation or event thrusts them into the global arena. Someone—a domestic exporter, a foreign importer, a foreign government—may ask the company to sell abroad. Or the company may be saddled with overcapacity and need to find additional markets for its goods.

Deciding Which Markets to Enter

Before going abroad, the company should try to define its international *marketing objectives and policies*. It should decide what *volume* of foreign sales it wants. Most companies start small when they go abroad. Some plan to stay small, seeing international sales as a small part of their business. Other companies have bigger plans, seeing international business as equal to or even more important than their domestic business.

■ P&G's decision to enter the Chinese toothpaste market with Crest is a no-brainer: China is the world's largest toothpaste market. But P&G must still question whether market size alone is reason enough for investing heavily in China.

The company also needs to choose in *how many* countries it wants to market. Companies must be careful not to spread themselves too thin or to expand beyond their capabilities by operating in too many countries too soon. Next, the company needs to decide on the *types* of countries to enter. A country's attractiveness depends on the product, geographical factors, income and population, political climate, and other factors. The seller may prefer certain country groups or parts of the world. In recent years, many major new markets have emerged, offering both substantial opportunities and daunting challenges.

After listing possible international markets, the company must carefully evaluate each one. It must consider many factors. For example, P&G's decision to enter the Chinese toothpaste market with its Crest is a no-brainer: China's huge population makes it the world's largest toothpaste market. And given that only 20 percent of China's rural dwellers now brush daily, this already huge market can grow even larger. Yet P&G

Demographic characteristics	Sociocultural factors
Education	Consumer lifestyles, beliefs, and values
Population size and growth	Business norms and approaches
Population age composition	Cultural and social norms
	Languages

Geographic characteristics	Political and legal factors
Climate	National priorities
Country size	Political stability
Population density—urban, rural	Government attitudes toward global trade
Transportation structure and market accessibility	Government bureaucracy
	Monetary and trade regulations

Economic factors	
GDP size and growth	
Income distribution	
Industrial infrastructure	
Natural resources	
Financial and human resources	

TABLE 15.1 Indicators of Market Potential

must still question whether market size *alone* is reason enough for investing heavily in China.

P&G should ask some important questions: Can Crest compete effectively with dozens of local competitors, Colgate, and a state-owned brand managed by Unilever? Will the Chinese government remain stable and supportive? Does China provide for the needed production and distribution technologies? Can the company master China's vastly different cultural and buying differences? Crest's current success in China suggests that it could answer yes to all of these questions. "Just 10 years ago, Procter & Gamble's Crest brand was unknown to China's population, most of whom seldom—if ever—brushed their teeth." Says one analyst. "Now P&G . . . sells more tubes of toothpaste there than it does in America, where Crest has been on store shelves for 52 years." Crest now leads all competitors in China with a 25 percent market share.[28]

Possible global markets should be ranked on several factors, including market size, market growth, cost of doing business, competitive advantage, and risk level. The goal is to determine the potential of each market, using indicators such as those shown in Table 15.1. Then the marketer must decide which markets offer the greatest long-run return on investment.

Deciding How to Enter the Market

Once a company has decided to sell in a foreign country, it must determine the best mode of entry. Its choices are *exporting, joint venturing,* and *direct investment*. Figure 15.2 shows three market entry strategies, along with the options each one offers. As the figure shows, each succeeding strategy involves more commitment and risk, but also more control and potential profits.

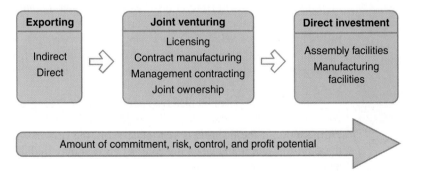

FIGURE 15.2
Market Entry Strategies

Exporting

Exporting
Entering a foreign market by selling goods produced in the company's home country, often with little modification.

The simplest way to enter a foreign market is through **exporting**. The company may passively export its surpluses from time to time, or it may make an active commitment to expand exports to a particular market. In either case, the company produces all its goods in its home country. It may or may not modify them for the export market. Exporting involves the least change in the company's product lines, organization, investments, or mission.

Companies typically start with *indirect exporting,* working through independent international marketing intermediaries. Indirect exporting involves less investment because the firm does not require an overseas marketing organization or network. It also involves less risk. International marketing intermediaries bring know-how and services to the relationship, so the seller normally makes fewer mistakes.

Sellers may eventually move into *direct exporting,* whereby they handle their own exports. The investment and risk are somewhat greater in this strategy, but so is the potential return. A company can conduct direct exporting in several ways: It can set up a domestic export department that carries out export activities. It can set up an overseas sales branch that handles sales, distribution, and perhaps promotion. The sales branch gives the seller more presence and program control in the foreign market and often serves as a display center and customer-service center. The company can also send home-based salespeople abroad at certain times in order to find business. Finally, the company can do its exporting either through foreign-based distributors who buy and own the goods or through foreign-based agents who sell the goods on behalf of the company.

Joint Venturing

Joint venturing
Entering foreign markets by joining with foreign companies to produce or market a product or service.

Licensing
A method of entering a foreign market in which the company enters into an agreement with a licensee in the foreign market, offering the right to use a manufacturing process, trademark, patent, trade secret, or other item of value for a fee or royalty.

A second method of entering a foreign market is **joint venturing**—joining with foreign companies to produce or market products or services. Joint venturing differs from exporting in that the company joins with a host country partner to sell or market abroad. It differs from direct investment in that an association is formed with someone in the foreign country. There are four types of joint ventures: licensing, contract manufacturing, management contracting, and joint ownership.

Licensing **Licensing** is a simple way for a manufacturer to enter international marketing. The company enters into an agreement with a licensee in the foreign market. For a fee or royalty, the licensee buys the right to use the company's manufacturing process, trademark, patent, trade secret, or other item of value. The company thus gains entry into the market at little risk; the licensee gains production expertise or a well-known product or name without having to start from scratch.

Coca-Cola markets internationally by licensing bottlers around the world and supplying them with the syrup needed to produce the product. In Japan, Budweiser beer flows from Kirin breweries and Marlboro cigarettes roll off production lines at Japan Tobacco Inc. Tokyo Disneyland Resort is owned and operated by Oriental Land Company under license from The Walt Disney Company.

Saks recently announced that it will enter the Chinese market through licensing. By licensing its name, Saks will become the first foreign luxury department store in this fast-growing market, but without having to operate the store itself. "Clearly, this minimizes the risk for the company," says Saks' CEO. Licensing also allows Saks to take advantage of global opportunities without diverting its focus from U.S. operations. "Our focus is 99 percent on the U.S. market," says the CEO.[29]

Licensing has potential disadvantages, however. The firm has less control over the licensee than it would over its own operations. Furthermore, if the licensee is very successful, the firm has given up these profits, and if and when the contract ends, it may find it has created a competitor.

■ Licensing: Tokyo Disneyland Resort is owned and operated by the Oriental Land Co. Ltd. (a Japanese development company), under license from The Walt Disney Company.

Contract Manufacturing Another option is **contract manufacturing**—the company contracts with manufacturers in the foreign market to produce its product or provide its service. Sears used this method in opening up department stores in Mexico and Spain, where it found qualified local manufacturers to produce many of the products it sells. The drawbacks of contract manufacturing are decreased control over the manufacturing process and loss of potential profits on manufacturing. The benefits are the chance to start faster, with less risk, and the later opportunity either to form a partnership with or to buy out the local manufacturer.

Management Contracting Under **management contracting**, the domestic firm supplies management know-how to a foreign company that supplies the capital. The domestic firm exports management services rather than products. Hilton uses this arrangement in managing hotels around the world.

Management contracting is a low-risk method of getting into a foreign market, and it yields income from the beginning. The arrangement is even more attractive if the contracting firm has an option to buy some share in the managed company later on. The arrangement is not sensible, however, if the company can put its scarce management talent to better uses or if it can make greater profits by undertaking the whole venture. Management contracting also prevents the company from setting up its own operations for a period of time.

Joint Ownership **Joint ownership** ventures consist of one company joining forces with foreign investors to create a local business in which they share joint ownership and control. A company may buy an interest in a local firm, or the two parties may form a new business venture. Joint ownership may be needed for economic or political reasons. The firm may lack the financial, physical, or managerial resources to undertake the venture alone. Or a foreign government may require joint ownership as a condition for entry.

KFC entered Japan through a joint ownership venture with Japanese conglomerate Mitsubishi. KFC sought a good way to enter the large but difficult Japanese fast-food market. In turn, Mitsubishi, one of Japan's largest poultry producers, understood the Japanese culture and had money to invest. Together, they helped KFC succeed in the semiclosed Japanese market. Surprisingly, with Mitsubishi's guidance, KFC developed decidedly un-Japanese positioning for its Japanese restaurants:

When KFC first entered Japan, the Japanese were uncomfortable with the idea of fast food and franchising. They saw fast food as artificial and unhealthy. To build trust, KFC Japan created ads depicting the most authentic version of Colonel Sanders' beginnings possible. The ads featured the quintessential Southern mother and highlighted the KFC philosophy—the Southern hospitality, old American tradition, and authentic home cooking. With "My Old Kentucky Home" by Stephen Foster playing in the background, the commercial showed Colonel Sanders' mother making and feeding her grandchildren KFC chicken made with 11 secret spices. It conjured up scenes of good home cookin' from the American South, positioning KFC as wholesome, aristocratic food. The campaign was hugely successful—in the end, the Japanese people could not get enough of this special American chicken. Most Japanese grew to know "My Old Kentucky Home" by heart. There are now 1,150 KFC locations in the country.[30]

■ Joint ownership: East joins West—KFC entered Japan through a joint ownership venture with Japanese conglomerate Mitsubishi.

Joint ownership has certain drawbacks. The partners may disagree over investment, marketing, or other policies. Whereas many U.S. firms like to reinvest earnings for growth, local firms often prefer to take out these earnings; and whereas U.S. firms emphasize the role of marketing, local investors may rely on selling.

Contract manufacturing
A joint venture in which a company contracts with manufacturers in a foreign market to produce the product or provide its service.

Management contracting
A joint venture in which the domestic firm supplies the management know-how to a foreign company that supplies the capital; the domestic firm exports management services rather than products.

Joint ownership
A joint venture in which a company joins investors in a foreign market to create a local business in which the company shares joint ownership and control.

Direct investment
Entering a foreign market by developing foreign-based assembly or manufacturing facilities.

Direct Investment

The biggest involvement in a foreign market comes through **direct investment**—the development of foreign-based assembly or manufacturing facilities. If a company has gained experience in exporting and if the foreign market is large enough, foreign production facilities offer many advantages. The firm may have lower costs in the form of cheaper labor or raw materials, foreign government investment incentives, and freight savings. The firm may improve its image in the host country because it creates jobs. Generally, a firm develops a deeper relationship with government, customers, local suppliers, and distributors, allowing it to adapt its products to the local market better. Finally, the firm keeps full control over the investment and therefore can develop manufacturing and marketing policies that serve its long-term international objectives.

The main disadvantage of direct investment is that the firm faces many risks, such as restricted or devalued currencies, falling markets, or government changes. In some cases, a firm has no choice but to accept these risks if it wants to operate in the host country.

Linking the Concepts

Slow down here and think again about McDonald's global marketing issues.

- To what extent can McDonald's standardize for the Chinese market? What marketing strategy and program elements can be similar to those used in the United States and other parts of the Western world? Which ones must be adapted? Be specific.
- To what extent can McDonald's standardize its products and programs for the Canadian market? What elements can be standardized and which must be adapted?
- To what extent are McDonald's "globalization" efforts contributing to "Americanization" of countries and cultures around the world? What are the positives and negatives of such cultural developments?

Deciding on the Global Marketing Program

Standardized global marketing
An international marketing strategy for using basically the same marketing strategy and mix in all the company's international markets.

Adapted global marketing
An international marketing strategy for adjusting the marketing strategy and mix elements to each international target market, bearing more costs but hoping for a larger market share and return.

Companies that operate in one or more foreign markets must decide how much, if at all, to adapt their marketing strategies and programs to local conditions. At one extreme are global companies that use **standardized global marketing**, using largely the same marketing strategy approaches and marketing mix worldwide. At the other extreme is an **adapted global marketing**. In this case, the producer adjusts the marketing strategy and mix elements to each target market, bearing more costs but hoping for a larger market share and return.

The question of whether to adapt or standardize the marketing strategy and program has been much debated in recent years. On the one hand, some global marketers believe that technology is making the world a smaller place and that consumer needs around the world are becoming more similar. This paves the way for "global brands" and standardized global marketing. Global branding and standardization, in turn, result in greater brand power and reduced costs from economies of scale.

On the other hand, the marketing concept holds that marketing programs will be more effective if tailored to the unique needs of each targeted customer group. If this concept applies within a country, it should apply even more in international markets. Despite global convergence, consumers in different countries still have widely varied cultural backgrounds. They still differ significantly in their needs and wants, spending power, product preferences, and shopping patterns. Because these differences are hard to change, most marketers adapt their products, prices, channels, and promotions to fit consumer desires in each country.

However, global standardization is not an all-or-nothing proposition. It's a matter of degree. Most international marketers suggest that companies should "think globally but act locally"—that they should seek a balance between standardization and adaptation. The corporate level gives global strategic direction; regional or local units focus on individual consumer differences across global markets. Simon Clift, head of marketing for global consumer-goods giant Unilever, puts it this way: "We're trying to strike a balance between being mindlessly global and hopelessly local."[31]

McDonald's operates this way. It uses the same basic fast-food look, layout, and operating model in its restaurants around the world but adapts its menu to local tastes. In Japan, it offers up Ebi Filet-O-Shrimp burgers and fancy Salad Macs salad plates. In Korea it sells the Bulgogi Burger, a grilled pork patty on a bun with a garlicky soy sauce. In India, where cows are considered sacred, McDonald's serves McChicken, Filet-O-Fish, McVeggie (a vegetable burger), Pizza McPuffs, McAloo Tikki (a spiced-potato burger), and the Maharaja Mac—two all-chicken patties, special sauce, lettuce, cheese, pickles, onions on a sesame-seed bun.

Similarly, South Korean electronics and appliance powerhouse LG Electronics makes and markets its brands globally but carefully localizes its products to the needs of specific country markets. By acting locally, it succeeds globally (see Marketing at Work 15.1).

Product

Five strategies allow for adapting product and marketing communication strategies to a global market (see Figure 15.3).[32] We first discuss the three product strategies and then turn to the two communication strategies.

Straight product extension means marketing a product in a foreign market without any change. Top management tells its marketing people, "Take the product as is and find customers for it." The first step, however, should be to find out whether foreign consumers use that product and what form they prefer.

Straight product extension
Marketing a product in a foreign market without any change.

Straight extension has been successful in some cases and disastrous in others. Kellogg cereals, Gillette razors, Heineken beer, and Black & Decker tools are all sold successfully in about the same form around the world. But General Foods introduced its standard powdered Jell-O in the British market only to find that British consumers prefer a solid wafer or cake form. Likewise, Philips began to make a profit in Japan only after it reduced the size of its coffeemakers to fit into smaller Japanese kitchens and its shavers to fit smaller Japanese hands. Straight extension is tempting because it involves no additional product development costs, manufacturing changes, or new promotion. But it can be costly in the long run if products fail to satisfy foreign consumers.

Product adaptation involves changing the product to meet local conditions or wants. For example, Finnish cell phone maker Nokia customizes its cell phones for every major market. Developers build in rudimentary voice recognition for Asia where keyboards are a problem and raise the ring volume so phones can be heard on crowded Asian streets. Nokia is also making a major push to create full-featured but rugged and low-cost phones that meet the needs of less-affluent consumers in large developing countries such as India, China, and Kenya.[33]

Product adaptation
Adapting a product to meet local conditions or wants in foreign markets.

Looking for ways to make cell phones practical for people living in developing countries, Nokia has trekked to far corners of the globe, from the narrow alleys of Mumbai to the vast slums of Nairobi. The result is a slew of new features especially designed for places with harsh weather and harsher living conditions. One example: The company created dustproof keypads—crucial in dry, hot countries with many unpaved roads, as Nokia executives learned from visits to customers' homes in India. Low price is also important. On a recent visit to slums outside Nairobi, members of the emerging markets team discovered that many people form buying clubs, pooling their money to buy handsets one at a time until every

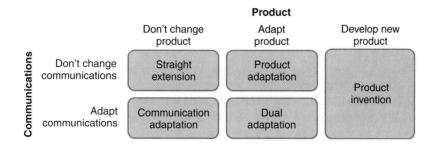

FIGURE 15.3

Five Global Product and Communications Strategies

15.1 MARKETING AT WORK

LG Electronics: Thinking Locally, Succeeding Globally

If you've got kimchi in your fridge, it's hard to keep it a secret. Made from fermented cabbage seasoned with garlic and chili, kimchi is served with most meals in Korea. But when it's stored inside a normal refrigerator, its pungent odor taints nearby foods. That's why, two decades ago, South Korean appliance manufacturer LG Electronics introduced the kimchi refrigerator, a product specifically designed to address the odor problem. Featuring a dedicated compartment that isolates smelly kimchi from other foods, the fridge gradually became a must-have in Korean homes, inspiring rivals such as Samsung to offer similar models. Kimchi refrigerators have become a fixture in 65 percent of Korean homes, and after facing down the competition, LG is the country's top-selling manufacturer.

The kimchi fridge has become a model for the approach that LG uses to expand into new global markets—a passionate focus on in-depth localization. LG insists on understanding and catering to the unique characteristics of local markets through in-country research, manufacturing, and marketing. Localization has been a key element of LG's successful global expansion. "Gone are the days where you could just roll out one product for the global market," explains LG's Middle East marketing director. "We speak to consumers individually."

LG certainly has been successful globally. The $38 billion electronics powerhouse claims that it's the world's top producer of air conditioners and one of the top three global players in washing machines, microwaves, and refrigerators. LG aims to make customers

■ By thinking locally, LG Electronics is succeeding globally. It makes a kimchi fridge for the Korean market, a shish kebab microwave for the Iranians, karaoke phones for the Russians, and gold-plated 71-inch flat-screen televisions for Middle Easterners with a taste for gilded opulence.

happy worldwide by creating products that change their lives, no matter where they live.

Nowhere is the success of LG's localization approach more evident than in India, where the company is now the clear leader in virtually every appliance and electronics category—from microwaves to televisions—despite having entered the market in 1997, two years after Samsung. With a population of more than 1 billion that spans

---

member has one. Now Nokia is looking for ways to encourage this form of self-financing. Communal finance is a far cry from manufacturing mobile phones, but Nokia knows it has to try all sorts of product and service ideas if it wants to capture its share of the industry's next 1 billion customers.

Product invention consists of creating something new for a specific country market. This strategy can take two forms. It might mean maintaining or reintroducing earlier product forms that happen to be well adapted to the needs of a given country. Or a company might create a new product to meet a need in a given country. For example, Sony added the "U" model to its VAIO personal computer line to meet the unique needs of Japanese consumers. It found that Japanese commuters had difficulty using standard laptops on crowded rush-hour trains—standing commuters have no laps. So it created the U as a "standing computer." The U is lightweight and small: only seven inches wide with a five-inch diagonal screen. And it includes a touch screen and small keyboard that can be used while standing or on the move. Although the model is popular in Japan, response to similar Sony ultraportable models in the United States has been lukewarm. Far more Americans touch-type than do Japanese (a few Japanese characters convey a lot) and touch typists are likely to resist on-screen keyboards.[34]

Product invention
Creating new products or services for foreign markets.

Promotion

Companies can either adopt the same communication strategy they used in the home market or change it for each local market. Consider advertising messages. Some global companies use a standardized advertising theme around the world. Of course, even in highly standardized communications campaigns, some adjustments might be required for language and cultural differences. For example, although McDonald's uses it's standardized "I'm lovin' it" theme

several religions and languages, India functions like dozens of smaller regional markets. LG initially differentiated itself by introducing a line of health-oriented products, such as televisions that reduced eyestrain. By 1999, however, it had set up local research and design facilities, manufacturing plants, and a network of service centers.

To meet the needs of Indian consumers, LG rolled out refrigerators with larger vegetable- and water-storage compartments, surge-resistant power supplies, and brightly colored finishes that reflect local preferences (red in the south, green in Kashmir). Some of LG's Indian microwaves have dark-colored interiors to hide masala stains. In 1999, LG introduced a television for cricket fans that came with a built-in cricket video game. After research showed that many Indians use their TVs to listen to music as well, the company offered its Ballad television with extraloud sound. Over time, these efforts have paid off. LG says it dominates in India, with sales that are projected to reach $1.8 billion this year. In some categories, such as washing machines, LG's market share is more than twice that of its nearest competitor.

Localization helps LG gain traction in emerging markets, where consumers have few preexisting brand loyalties. In Iran, LG offers a microwave oven with a preset button for reheating shish kebabs—a favorite dish. LG now claims to command roughly 40 percent of the Iranian microwave market. Meanwhile, LG's Primian refrigerator includes a special compartment for storing dates, a Middle Eastern staple fruit that spoils easily.

Although not always huge sellers, LG's localized products clearly generate buzz. The company recently made headlines throughout the Middle East by unveiling a gold-plated 71-inch flat-screen television that sells for $80,000—a tribute to the region's famous affinity for gilded opulence. In Russia, LG's research revealed that many people entertain at home during the country's long winters, prompting the company to develop a karaoke phone that can be programmed with the top 100 Russian songs, whose lyrics scroll across the screen when they're played. Introduced in late 2004, the phone has been a hit, selling more than 220,000 handsets, LG says.

All this experience will be put to the test as LG moves to make its presence felt in China, the world's biggest consumer market, where major international brands must compete against domestic rivals such as Haier. Just as it did in India, LG is establishing extensive in-country facilities in China—from research to manufacturing to product marketing. LG opened research and development operations in Beijing in 2002 and has since ramped up its staff to more than 1,500. The company also reached out to local consumers by creating an "LG village," a high-profile initiative that transformed a decrepit agricultural community into a showcase for LG technologies. The efforts seem to be paying off: With help from such simple touches as making the exteriors of products red—a lucky color in China—LG raked in sales of $8 billion on the mainland last year.

Thus, from Korean kimchi to Indian cricket mania to Russian karaoke, LG's unrelenting commitment to localization is winning the company waves of new customers around the globe. By thinking locally, LG is succeeding globally.

Sources: Adapted from Elizabeth Esfahani, "Thinking Locally, Succeeding Globally," *Business 2.0,* December 2005, pp. 96–98; with information from Evan Ramstas, "LG Electronics' Net Surges 91 Percent as Cell Phone Margins Improve," *Wall Street Journal,* January 25, 2006, p. B2; and www.lge.com, accessed January 2008.

worldwide, it varies its interpretations of the theme in different countries. In China, for instance, it presents the Quarter Pounder as a lot more than just a big U.S.-style burger.[35]

> Many Chinese hold the traditional view that eating beef boosts energy and heightens sex appeal. The word "beef" in Chinese has connotations of manliness, strength, and skill. That's the message McDonald's is sending Chinese consumers as it tries to seduce them into eating more hamburgers. One racy Quarter Pounder poster hanging in restaurants features a close-up of a women's lips. "Flirt with your senses," the sign says. The burger chain's Quarter Pounder TV commercials are even steamier. In one, a man and a woman eat the burgers, and close-up shots of the woman's neck and mouth are interspersed with images of fireworks and spraying water. As the actors suck their fingers, the voice-over says: "You can feel it. Thicker. You can taste it. Juicier." A series of light-hearted print ads in trendy magazines lay out scenarios in which beef saves the day. In one, a young man frets that five women he has met online want to go out on dates with him the next day. The ad offers some solutions: Hire four friends. Split up the meetings. Or "have enough beef tonight" to "be able to handle five princesses tomorrow."

Colors also are changed sometimes to avoid taboos in other countries. Purple is associated with death in most of Latin America, white is a mourning color in Japan, and green is associated with jungle sickness in Malaysia. Even names must sometimes be adjusted. The global name for Microsoft's new operating system, Vista, turns out to be a disparaging term for a frumpy old woman in Latvia. And in the Americas, Mitsubishi changed the Japanese name of its Pajero SUV to Montero—it seems that *pajero* in Spanish is a slang term for sexual self-gratification. (See Marketing at Work 15.2 for more on language blunders in international marketing.)

Communication adaptation
A global communication strategy of fully adapting advertising messages to local markets.

Other companies follow a strategy of **communication adaptation**, fully adapting their advertising messages to local markets. Kellogg ads in the United States promote the taste and nutrition of Kellogg's cereals versus competitors' brands. In France, where consumers drink little milk and eat little for breakfast, Kellogg's ads must convince consumers that cereals are a tasty and healthful breakfast. In India, where many consumers eat heavy, fried breakfasts, Kellogg's advertising convinces buyers to switch to a lighter, more nutritious breakfast diet.

Similarly, Coca-Cola sells its low-calorie beverage as Diet Coke in North America, the United Kingdom, and the Middle and Far East but as Light elsewhere. According to Diet Coke's global brand manager, in Spanish-speaking countries Coke Light ads "position the soft drink as an object of desire, rather than as a way to feel good about yourself, as Diet Coke is positioned in the United States." This "desire positioning" plays off research showing that "Coca-Cola Light is seen in other parts of the world as a vibrant brand that exudes a sexy confidence."[36]

Media also need to be adapted internationally because media availability varies from country to country. TV advertising time is very limited in Europe, for instance, ranging from four hours a day in France to none in Scandinavian countries. Advertisers must buy time months in advance, and they have little control over airtimes. Magazines also vary in effectiveness. For example, magazines are a major medium in Italy but a minor one in Austria. Newspapers are national in the United Kingdom but are only local in Spain.[37]

Price

Companies also face many considerations in setting their international prices. For example, how might Black & Decker price its power tools globally? It could set a uniform price all around the world, but this amount would be too high a price in poor countries and not high enough in rich ones. It could charge what consumers in each country would bear, but this strategy ignores differences in the actual costs from country to country. Finally, the company could use a standard markup of its costs everywhere, but this approach might price Black & Decker out of the market in some countries where costs are high.

Regardless of how companies go about pricing their products, their foreign prices probably will be higher than their domestic prices for comparable products. A Gucci handbag may sell for $60 in Italy and $240 in the United States. Why? Gucci faces a *price escalation* problem. It must add the cost of transportation, tariffs, importer margin, wholesaler margin, and retailer margin to its factory price. Depending on these added costs, the product may need to sell for two to five times as much in another country to make the same profit.

To overcome this problem when selling to less affluent consumers in developing countries, many companies make simpler or smaller versions of their products that can be sold at lower prices. For example, in China and other emerging markets, Dell sells its simplified Dell EC280 model for $340 dollars, and P&G sells everything from shampoo to toothpaste in less costly formulations and smaller packages at more affordable prices.

Another problem involves setting a price for goods that a company ships to its foreign subsidiaries. If the company charges a foreign subsidiary too much, it may end up paying higher tariff duties even while paying lower income taxes in that country. If the company charges its subsidiary too little, it can be charged with *dumping*. Dumping occurs when a company either charges less than its costs or less than it charges in its home market. For example, the U.S. Southern Shrimp Alliance, which represents thousands of small shrimp operations in the southeastern United States, recently complained that six countries (China, Thailand, Vietnam, Ecuador, India, and Brazil) have been dumping excess supplies of farmed shrimp on the U.S. market. The U.S. International Trade Commission agreed and the Commerce Department imposed duties as high as 112.81 percent on shrimp imports from the offending countries.[38] Various governments are always watching for dumping abuses, and they often force companies to set the price charged by other competitors for the same or similar products.

Recent economic and technological forces have had an impact on global pricing. For example, in the European Union, the transition to the euro is reducing the amount of price differentiation. As consumers recognize price differentiation by country, companies are being forced to harmonize prices throughout the countries that have adopted the single currency. Companies and marketers that offer the most unique or necessary products or services will be least affected by such "price transparency."[39]

15.2 MARKETING AT WORK
Watch Your Language!

Many global companies have had difficulty crossing the language barrier, with results ranging from mild embarrassment to outright failure. Seemingly innocuous brand names and advertising phrases can take on unintended or hidden meanings when translated into other languages. Careless translations can make a marketer look downright foolish to foreign consumers.

The classic language blunders involve standardized brand names that do not translate well. When Coca-Cola first marketed Coke in China in the 1920s, it developed a group of Chinese characters that, when pronounced, sounded like the product name. Unfortunately, the characters actually translated as "bite the wax tadpole." Now, the characters on Chinese Coke bottles translate as "happiness in the mouth."

Several modern-day marketers have had similar problems when their brand names crashed into the language barrier. Chevy's Nova translated into Spanish as *no va*—"it doesn't go." GM changed the name to Caribe (Spanish for Caribbean) and sales increased. Microsoft's new operating system, Vista, turns out to be a disparaging term for a frumpy old woman in Latvia. Rolls-Royce avoided the name Silver Mist in German markets, where *mist* means "manure." Sunbeam, however, entered the German market with its Mist Stick hair-curling iron. As should have been expected, the Germans had little use for a "manure wand." IKEA marketed a children's workbench named FARTFULL (the word means "speedy" in Swedish)—it soon discontinued the product.

Interbrand of London, the firm that created household names such as Prozac and Acura, recently developed a brand-name "hall of shame" list, which contained these and other foreign brand names you're never likely to see inside the local Safeway: Krapp toilet paper (Denmark), Crapsy Fruit cereal (France), Poo curry powder (Argentina), and Pschitt lemonade (France).

Travelers often encounter well-intentioned advice from service firms that takes on meanings very different from those intended. The menu in one Swiss restaurant proudly stated, "Our wines leave you nothing to hope for." Signs in a Japanese hotel pronounced, "You are invited to take advantage of the chambermaid." At a laundry in Rome, it was, "Ladies, leave your clothes here and spend the afternoon having a good time."

Advertising themes often lose—or gain—something in the translation. The Coors beer slogan "get loose with Coors" in Spanish came out as "get the runs with Coors." Coca-Cola's "Coke adds life" theme in Japanese translated into "Coke brings your ancestors back from the dead." The milk industry learned too late that its American advertising question "Got Milk?" translated in Mexico as a more provocative "Are you lactating?" In Chinese, the KFC slogan "finger-lickin' good" came

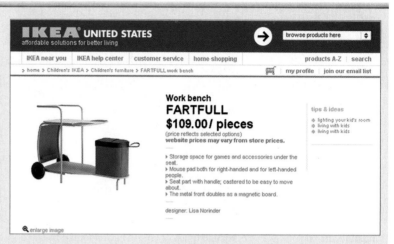

■ Global language barriers: Some standardized brand names do not translate well globally.

out as "eat your fingers off." And Motorola's Hellomoto ring tone sounds like "Hello, Fatty" in India. Even when the language is the same, word usage may differ from country to country. Thus, the British ad line for Electrolux vacuum cleaners—"Nothing sucks like an Electrolux"—would capture few customers in the United States.

Thus, crossing the language barrier involves much more than simple translating names and slogans into other languages. You can't uproot a concept and just translate it and put it into another market," says one translation consultant. "It's not really about translating word for word, but actually adapting a certain meaning." Beyond just word meanings and nuances, international marketers must also consider things such as phonetic appeal and even associations with historical figures, legends, and other factors. The consultant points to the Chinese adaptation of the name for eBay's online free classified ads service—Kijiji (which means "village" in Swahili)—as a localization success story. "In Chinese, the three characters used to phonetically represent the Kijiji name map almost exactly to the English pronunciation," she says. "Plus, they have the meaning of people pulling together to share things, which is totally descriptive of the business and brand."

Sources: Quotes from Randall Frost, "Lost in Translation," *Brandchannel.com,* November 13, 2006. For the above and other examples, see David A. Ricks, "Perspectives: Translation Blunders in International Business," *Journal of Language for International Business* 7, no. 2, 1996, pp. 50–55; Thomas T. Sermon, "Cutting Corners in Language Risky Business," *Marketing News,* April 23, 2001, p. 9; Martin Croft, "Mind Your Language," *Marketing,* June 19, 2003, pp. 35–39; Mark Lasswell, "Lost in Translation," *Business 2.0,* August 2004, pp. 68–70; "Lost in Translation," *Hispanic,* May 2005, p. 12; and Ross Thomson, "Lost in Translation," *Medical Marketing and Media,* March 2005, p. 82.

For Marie-Claude Lang, a 72-year-old retired Belgian postal worker, the euro is the best thing since bottled water—or French country sausage. Always on the prowl for bargains, Ms. Lang is now stalking the wide aisles of an Auchan hypermarket in Roncq, France, a 15-minute drive from her Wervick home. . . . Ms. Lang has been coming to France every other week for years to stock up on bottled water, milk, and yogurt. But the launch of the euro . . . has opened her eyes to many more products that she now sees cost less across the border. Today she sees that "saucisse de campagne" is cheaper "by about five euro cents," a savings she didn't notice when she had to calculate the

■ International pricing: Twelve European Union countries have adopted the euro as a common currency creating "pricing transparency" and forcing companies to harmonize their prices throughout Europe.

Whole-channel view
Designing international channels that take into account the entire global supply chain and marketing channel, forging and effective global value delivery network.

difference between Belgian and French francs. At Europe's borders, the euro is turning into the coupon clipper's delight. Sure, price-conscious Europeans have long crossed into foreign territory to find everything from cheaper television sets to bargain bottles of Coca-Cola. But the new transparency is making comparisons a whole lot easier.

The Internet is also making global price differences more obvious. When firms sell their wares over the Internet, customers can see how much products sell for in different countries. They can even order a given product directly from the company location or dealer offering the lowest price. This is forcing companies toward more standardized international pricing.

Distribution Channels

The international company must take a **whole-channel view** of the problem of distributing products to final consumers. Figure 15.4 shows the two major links between the seller and the final buyer. The first link, *channels between nations,* moves company products from points of production to the borders of countries within which they are sold. The second link, *channels within nations,* moves the products from their market entry points to the final consumers. The whole-channel view takes into account the entire global supply chain and marketing channel. It recognizes that to compete well internationally, the company must effectively design and manage an entire *global value delivery network.*

Channels of distribution within countries vary greatly from nation to nation. There are the large differences in the numbers and types of intermediaries serving each country market, and in the transportation infrastructure serving these intermediaries. For example, whereas large-scale retail chains dominate the U.S. scene, much retailing in other countries is done by many small, independent retailers. In India, millions of retailers operate tiny shops or sell in open markets. Thus, in its efforts to sell rugged, affordable phones to Indian consumers, Nokia has had to forge its own distribution structure.[40]

In India, Nokia estimates there are 90,000 points-of-sale for its phones, ranging from modern stores to makeshift kiosks. That makes it difficult to control how products are displayed and pitched to consumers. "You have to understand where people live, what the shopping patterns are," says a Nokia executive. "You have to work with local means to reach people—even bicycles or rickshaws." To reach rural India, Nokia has outfitted its own fleet of distinctive blue Nokia-branded vans that prowl the rutted country roads. Staffers park these advertisements-on-wheels in villages, often on market or festival days. There, with crowds clustering around, Nokia reps explain the basics of how the phones work and how to buy them. Nokia has extended the concept to minivans, which can reach even more remote places.

Similarly, when Coke first entered China, customers bicycled up to bottling plants to get their soft drinks. Many shopkeepers still don't have enough electricity to run soft-drink coolers. Now, Coca-Cola has set up direct distribution channels, investing heavily in refrigerators and trucks and upgrading wiring so that more retailers can install coolers. The company has also built an army of more than 10,000 sales representatives who make regular visits on re-

FIGURE 15.4
Whole-channel Concept for International Marketing

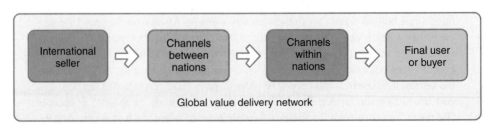

International seller → Channels between nations → Channels within nations → Final user or buyer

Global value delivery network

sellers, often on foot or bicycle, to check on stocks and record sales. Still, to reach the most isolated spots in the country, Coca-Cola relies on some pretty unlikely business partners—teams of delivery donkeys. "Massive advertising budgets can drum up demand," says one observer, "but if the distribution network doesn't exist properly or doesn't work, the potential of China's vast market cannot be realized."[41]

Deciding on the Global Marketing Organization

■ Distribution channels vary greatly from nation to nation. In its efforts to sell rugged, affordable phones to Indian consumers, Nokia forged its own distribution structure, including a fleet of distinctive blue Nokia-branded vans that prowl rutted country roads to visit remote villages.

Companies manage their international marketing activities in at least three different ways: Most companies first organize an export department, then create an international division, and finally become a global organization.

A firm normally gets into international marketing by simply shipping out its goods. If its international sales expand, the company organizes an *export department* with a sales manager and a few assistants. As sales increase, the export department can expand to include various marketing services so that it can actively go after business. If the firm moves into joint ventures or direct investment, the export department will no longer be adequate.

Many companies get involved in several international markets and ventures. A company may export to one country, license to another, have a joint ownership venture in a third, and own a subsidiary in a fourth. Sooner or later it will create *international divisions* or subsidiaries to handle all its international activity.

International divisions are organized in a variety of ways. An international division's corporate staff consists of marketing, manufacturing, research, finance, planning, and personnel specialists. It plans for and provides services to various operating units, which can be organized in one of three ways. They can be *geographical organizations,* with country managers who are responsible for salespeople, sales branches, distributors, and licensees in their respective countries. Or the operating units can be *world product groups,* each responsible for worldwide sales of different product groups. Finally, operating units can be *international subsidiaries,* each responsible for its own sales and profits.

Many firms have passed beyond the international division stage and become truly *global organizations.* They stop thinking of themselves as national marketers who sell abroad and start thinking of themselves as global marketers. The top corporate management and staff plan worldwide manufacturing facilities, marketing policies, financial flows, and logistical systems. The global operating units report directly to the chief executive or executive committee of the organization, not to the head of an international division. Executives are trained in worldwide operations, not just domestic *or* international. The company recruits management from many countries, buys components and supplies where they cost the least, and invests where the expected returns are greatest.

Today, major companies must become more global if they hope to compete. As foreign companies successfully invade their domestic markets, companies must move more aggressively into foreign markets. They must change from companies that treat their international operations as secondary to companies that view the entire world as a single borderless market.

REST STOP ⏩ REVIEWING THE CONCEPTS

Companies today can no longer afford to pay attention only to their domestic market, regardless of its size. Many industries are global industries, and firms that operate globally achieve lower costs and higher brand awareness. At the same time, global marketing is risky because of variable exchange rates, unstable governments, protectionist tariffs and trade barriers, and several other factors. Given the potential gains and risks of international marketing, companies need a systematic way to make their global marketing decisions.

1. Discuss how the international trade system and the economic, political-legal, and cultural environments affect a company's international marketing decisions.

A company must understand the *global marketing environment,* especially the international trade system. It must assess each foreign market's *economic, political-legal,* and *cultural* characteristics. The company must then decide whether it wants to go abroad and consider the potential risks and benefits. It must decide on the volume of international sales it wants, how many countries it wants to market in, and which specific markets it wants to enter. This decision calls for weighing the probable rate of return on investment against the level of risk.

2. Describe three key approaches to entering international markets.

The company must decide how to enter each chosen market—whether through *exporting, joint venturing,* or *direct investment.* Many companies start as exporters, move to joint ventures, and finally make a direct investment in foreign markets. In *exporting,* the company enters a foreign market by sending and selling products through international marketing intermediaries (indirect exporting) or the company's own department, branch, or sales representative or agents (direct exporting). When es-

tablishing a *joint venture,* a company enters foreign markets by joining with foreign companies to produce or market a product or service. In *licensing,* the company enters a foreign market by contracting with a licensee in the foreign market, offering the right to use a manufacturing process, trademark, patent, trade secret, or other item of value for a fee or royalty.

3. Explain how companies adapt their marketing mixes for international markets.

Companies must also decide how much their products, promotion, price, and channels should be adapted for each foreign market. At one extreme, global companies use *standardized global marketing* worldwide. Others use an *adapted global marketing,* in which they adjust the marketing strategy and mix to each target market, bearing more costs but hoping for a larger market share and return. However, global standardization is not an all-or-nothing proposition. It's a matter of degree. Most international marketers suggest that companies should "think globally but act locally"—that they should seek a balance between standardization and adaptation.

4. Identify the three major forms of international marketing organization.

The company must develop an effective organization for international marketing. Most firms start with an *export department* and graduate to an *international division.* A few become *global organizations,* with worldwide marketing planned and managed by the top officers of the company. Global organizations view the entire world as a single, borderless market.

Navigating the Key Terms

Adapted global marketing (464)
Communication adaptation (468)
Contract manufacturing (463)
Countertrade (456)
Direct investment (464)
Economic community (453)

Exporting (462)
Global firm (451)
Joint ownership (463)
Joint venturing (462)
Licensing (462)
Management contracting (463)

Product adaptation (465)
Product invention (466)
Standardized global marketing (464)
Straight product extension (465)
Whole-channel view (470)

Travel Log

Discussing the Issues

1. Explain what is meant by the term *global firm.* (AASCB: Communication)

2. Name and describe the various restrictions on international trade. (AACSB: Communication)

3. Discuss the factors that a business must consider when deciding whether to go global and factors considered in deciding which market to enter. (AACSB: Communication)

4. Compare and contrast the three ways to enter foreign markets. Which is the best? (AACSB: Communication; Reflective Thinking)

5. Define standardized global marketing and adapted global marketing and discuss the implications of each. (AACSB: Communication)

6. Explain the differences in organizing the international marketing function as an export department, an international division, or a global organization. What drives the evolution from one organizational form to another? (AACSB: Communication; Reflective Thinking)

Application Questions

1. Convert $1.00 U.S. to euros and to the currencies of five other countries. One Web site that converts currencies is www.xe.com/ucc/. Is the dollar stronger or weaker than each other currency? Is a strong dollar good or bad for United States businesses doing business in other countries? (AACSB: Communication; Use of IT; Reflective Thinking)

2. The political-legal environment in countries such as Russia and Venezuela has had a significant impact on foreign oil

companies. Research these countries and write a brief report on the impact of the political-legal environment on foreign oil companies. (AACSB: Communication; Use of IT; Reflective Thinking)

3. Form teams of four students and discuss how the following products might adapt their marketing mixes when entering the Chinese market: Oreo cookies, Herbal Essences Conditioner, Ben and Jerry's ice cream, and Hummer H3 SUVs. (AACSB: Communication; Reflective Thinking)

Under the Hood: Focus on Technology

GMI (Global Market Insight) is a leader in global market research. It offers an online global panel of more than 5 million members in 200 countries. Panelists speak more than 37 different languages and are available in the Americas, Europe, Asia Pacific, and the Middle East. In addition to consumer markets, GMI provides access to hard-to-reach business consumers, including B2B specialty medical markets of physicians, nurses, and patients with a variety of chronic illnesses. GMI differentiates itself from competitors with claims that it has the highest standards of panel integrity.

1. What questions might a U.S. manufacturer of blood diagnostic equipment ask the members of the GMI medical panel when considering entry into a new country? (AACSB: Communication; Reflective Thinking)

2. Sign up to be a GMI survey respondent at www.globaltestmarket.com. After going through the registration process, do you think that GMI has a rigid standard for its survey respondents? (AACSB: Communication; Reflective Thinking)

Focus on Ethics

Global companies face many challenges when expanding abroad. Cultural differences in particular are difficult. In several emerging markets, such as parts of Asia, Africa, the Middle East, the former Soviet Union, Eastern Europe, and South America, bribery is considered "standard operating procedure." The World Bank estimates bribery in international trade to be about $1 trillion annually.

The Foreign Corrupt Practices Act (FCPA) has existed in the United States since 1977, but the Securities and Exchange Commission and the U.S. Department of Justice have only recently stepped up enforcement. This law prohibits U.S. companies from giving corrupt payments to foreign officials to obtain favor in business transactions. To get around this law, many companies have used third parties to do their dirty deeds. However, many companies are now confessing their misdeeds rather than remaining silent and hoping to avoid detection. This is because of provisions of the 2002 Sarbanes-Oxley law regarding accounting reporting practices. Under this law, American senior executives can go to prison for violations.

For a long time, the United States was one of few leaders in battling corruption in foreign trade, but now many more countries are joining the fight. In China, bribery is punishable by death, which makes the multimillion dollar penalties levied from FCPA violations seem light. Aside from financial penalties (the largest being over $40 million so far), guilty companies may also be prohibited from doing business with the U.S. government or may be denied export licenses.

1. Is it right for U.S. companies to be penalized for going along with cultural norms in other countries? Is it right for the United States and other countries to demand that businesses in other countries follow our laws? (AACSB: Communication; Ethical Reasoning)

2. What are the consequences for U.S. companies of not doing what foreign businesses and governments expect or what competitors foreign markets do? (AACSB: Communication; Reflective Thinking)

Video Case

Nivea

In 1911, German company Nivea introduced the revolutionary Nivea Crème in a simple blue tin. Today, that Crème is the centerpiece of a wide range of personal care products. The product line includes everything from soap, shampoo, and shaving products to baby care products, deodorant, and sunscreen. From small beginnings, the company's products are sold today in more than 150 countries worldwide.

But despite this global presence, most Nivea consumers believe that the products they buy are produced and marketed locally. Why? Although Nivea looks for commonalities between consumers around the globe, the company's marketers also recognize the differences between consumers in different markets. So Nivea adapts its marketing mix to reach local consumers while keeping its message consistent everywhere its products are sold. This globally consistent, locally customized marketing strategy has sold more than 11 billion tins of the traditional Nivea Crème.

After viewing the video featuring Nivea, answer the following questions about the company and the global marketplace.

1. Which of the five strategies for adapting products and promotion for the global market does Nivea employ? How does it do so?

2. Visit Nivea's Web site, www.nivea.com, and tour the sites for several different countries. How does Nivea market its products differently in different countries? How does the company maintain the consistency of its brand across countries?

WE STARTED OUT AS BOOTMAKERS, but we're about much more. Like you, we care about the strength of our neighborhoods, the well-being of our environment, and the quality of life in our communities. We believe in making a difference and invite you to join us.

Timberland
Make it better.™

INFORM   INSPIRE   ENGAGE

After studying this chapter, you should be able to

1. identify the major social criticisms of marketing
2. define *consumerism* and *environmentalism* and explain

how they affect marketing strategies
3. describe the principles of socially responsible marketing

4. explain the role of ethics in marketing

CHAPTER 16

Marketing Ethics and Social Responsibility

ROAD MAP Previewing the Concepts

In this final chapter, we'll focus on marketing as a social institution. First, we'll look at some common criticisms of marketing as it impacts individual consumers, other businesses, and society as a whole. Then, we'll examine consumerism, environmentalism, and other citizen and public actions to keep marketing in check. Finally, we'll see how companies themselves can benefit from proactively pursuing socially responsible and ethical practices that bring value not just to individual customers but to society as a whole. You'll see that social responsibility and ethical actions are more than just the right thing to do; they're also good for business.

First, let's visit the concept of social responsibility in business. Perhaps no one gets more fired up about corporate social responsibility than Jeffery Swartz, CEO of footwear and apparel maker Timberland. He's on a passionate mission to use the resources of his company to combat the world's social ills. But he knows that to do this, his company must also be profitable. Swartz believes firmly that companies actually can do both—that it can do well by doing good. Here's the story.

Timberland CEO Jeffrey Swartz recently strode purposefully into a New York office packed with McDonald's executives. Dressed in a blazer, jeans, and Timberland boots, he was there to convince the fast-food giant that it should choose his $1.6 billion shoe and clothing company to provide its new uniforms. The executives waited expectantly for him to unzip a bag and reveal the sleek new prototype.

"We didn't bring any designs," Swartz said flatly. Eyebrows arched. Instead, he launched into an impassioned speech that had virtually nothing to do with clothes or shoes. What Timberland really had to offer McDonald's, Swartz said, was the benefit to the company—and the world at large—of helping it build a unified, motivated, purposeful workforce. "Other people can do uniforms," Swartz said, his Yankee accent asserting itself. "This is about partnership. We can create a partnership together that will be about value and values."

As unorthodox as it sounds, Swartz wasn't pitching Timberland's creativity or craftsmanship. Rather, he was pitching its culture, and the ways that culture could rub off on McDonald's. Growing more and more animated, Swartz talked about how Timberland's employees get 40 hours paid leave every year to pursue volunteer projects. He discussed Serv-a-palooza, Timberland's daylong burst of do-goodism that this year will host 170 service projects in 25 countries, covering 53,000 volunteer hours of work. And he talked about City Year, the nonprofit that Timberland has supported for more than a decade, which brings young people into public service for a year. As for McDonald's, it was part of practically every community in the country, Swartz explained, but was it helping every community?

The room was silent. Swartz couldn't tell whether they thought he was a touchy-feely freak or whether what he said had struck a deep chord (McDonald's wouldn't make a final decision for many months). Yet Swartz was elated all the same. "I told my team to find me 10 more places where I can have this conversation," he said. "No one believes in this more than we do, and that is our competitive advantage."

The "this" that gets Swartz, a third-generation CEO whose grandfather founded the company in 1952, so fired up is expressed in Timberland's slogan: "Boots, Brand, Belief." What Swartz is really trying to do—no kidding—is to use the resources, energy, and profits of a publicly traded footwear and apparel company to combat social ills, help the environment, and improve conditions for laborers around the globe. And rather than using his company as a charity, he's using the hard financial metrics of profit, return on investment, and, oh yes, shareholder return, to try to prove that companies actually can do well by doing good.

So far, Swartz has done a more-than-respectable job of proving the point. Over the past seven years, the company, which sells outdoor-themed clothes, shoes, and accessories, has shown good sales and earnings performance. At the same time, it is viewed as a trailblazer by companies many times larger when it comes to corporate social responsibility. But Swartz's big ambitions also draw doubters who question whether Timberland's drive for sustainability is itself sustainable in a profit-driven world—whether the amoral world of capitalism and the spiritual world of service can be merged.

Those who think Timberland must choose between profits and passion have not spent much time with Swartz, an earnest, funny, hyperkinetic 45-year-old who can barely sit still, so anxious is he to discuss the beautiful—and profitable—nexus between, in his words, "commerce and justice." Although Swartz knows the business inside and out, it's hard to get him to talk about it. Asked if he cares about shoes, he looks shocked. "Am I proud of the boots and shoes we make? Desperately." But making good gear, he says, doesn't matter enough. "I can't care enough about shoes or clothes to do what I do unless there is a different kind of purpose to it."

Swartz's quest has created a cohesive culture at Timberland. In the most recent employee survey, 75 percent of employees said they would choose Timberland again if they were looking for work, and 79 percent said Timberland's reputation had played a big role in their decision to come to the company. "I love my job," says Michael Moody, a staff attorney. "The core values are humanity, humility, integrity, and excellence, and I see those values used as a touchstone in all conversations."

Betsy Blaisdell, manager for environmental stewardship, laughs when she thinks how horrified she originally was at the thought of working for a big, bad corporation. With Swartz's support, however, she has helped push through such initiatives as a $3,000 cash incentive for employees to purchase hybrid cars (six have taken advantage so far) and the company's $3.5 million solar array at its Ontario, California, distribution center. The array will provide 60 percent of the center's energy and eliminate the creation of 480,000 pounds of carbon emissions. Although it may take as many as 20 years to show a return, that's just fine with Swartz.

For Timberland, service is not something you do once a year. Although volunteer projects are always under way, many of them have been organized under the rubric of Serv-a-palooza, held in late September. Last year's projects included a massive effort to clean up and reclaim public spaces around Lawrence, Massachusetts, and a plan to improve a center for handicapped kids in Ho Chi Minh City, Vietnam. Timberland supports these efforts for their own sake, but the potential corporate benefits do not go unnoticed. As his pitch to McDonald's shows, Swartz also sees service as a powerful differentiator for Timberland with its current and potential customers.

Although Timberland's message seems to be getting through to its business customers, it's not at all clear that consumers have any clue what the brand stands for beyond cool stuff. Nor is it clear that they care. "The vast majority of footwear is purchased by teenagers," says an industry analyst, "and some don't believe in advertising at all, so it's tough to reach them." But Swartz insists that it's simply a matter of time until consumers refuse to patronize companies that don't tell them what they're doing for the community. "I believe that there's a storm coming against the complacent who say good enough is good enough," he says.

To inspire consumers to ask questions and make more informed purchase decisions, every Timberland shoebox carries a label, modeled after the nutrition labels on food products, outlining the ecological footprint created by the manufacture and distribution of the footwear inside. And Timberland is now introducing a Green Index hang tag, which provides product-specific ratings on environmental factors such as climate impact, chemical usage, and the amount of sustainable or organic materials used.

Probably Swartz's biggest challenge is getting Wall Street to buy into the doing-good side of the story. Sure, the brand's a success, says the analyst. "But investors would rather see Timberland doing things like increasing dividends or share buybacks. Nobody's investing in Timberland just because Jeff's a nice guy. They expect results."

Although compelling, the lofty notion of serving a doubled bottom line of values and profits will present significant challenges for Timberland. Can one man and his band of devotees really change the role of the corporation? To Swartz, it's only a matter of time. After all, he's trying to save the world. The funny thing is that he's trying to do it by running a large, profitable, publicly traded shoe company. Some call him the messiah for a new age of social awareness. Others think he could be headed for a fall. But all agree he's challenging the system.[1]

Responsible marketers discover what consumers want and respond with market offerings that create value for buyers in order to capture value in return. The *marketing concept* is a philosophy of customer value and mutual gain. Its practice leads the economy by an invisible hand to satisfy the many and changing needs of millions of consumers.

Not all marketers follow the marketing concept, however. In fact, some companies use questionable marketing practices, and some marketing actions that seem innocent in themselves strongly affect the larger society. Consider the sale of cigarettes. On the face of it, companies should be free to sell cigarettes and smokers should be free to buy them. But this private transaction involves larger questions of public policy. For example, the smokers are harming their health and may be shortening their own lives. Smoking places a financial burden on the smoker's family and on society at large. Other people around smokers may suffer discomfort and harm from secondhand smoke. Finally, marketing cigarettes to adults might also influence young people to begin smoking. Thus, the marketing of tobacco products has sparked substantial debate and negotiation in recent years.

This chapter examines the social effects of private marketing practices. We examine several questions: What are the most frequent social criticisms of marketing? What steps have private citizens taken to curb marketing ills? What steps have legislators and government agencies taken to curb marketing ills? What steps have enlightened companies taken to carry out socially responsible and ethical marketing that creates value for both individual customers and society as a whole?

Social Criticisms of Marketing

Marketing receives much criticism. Some of this criticism is justified; much is not. Social critics claim that certain marketing practices hurt individual consumers, society as a whole, and other business firms.

Marketing's Impact on Individual Consumers

Consumers have many concerns about how well the American marketing system serves their interests. Surveys usually show that consumers hold mixed or even slightly unfavorable attitudes toward marketing practices. Consumer advocates, government agencies, and other critics have accused marketing of harming consumers through high prices, deceptive practices, high-pressure selling, shoddy or unsafe products, planned obsolescence, and poor service to disadvantaged consumers.

High Prices Many critics charge that the American marketing system causes prices to be higher than they would be under more "sensible" systems. They point to three factors—*high costs of distribution, high advertising and promotion costs,* and *excessive markups.*

High Costs of Distribution   A long-standing charge is that greedy channel intermediaries mark up prices beyond the value of their services. Critics charge that there are too many intermediaries, that intermediaries are inefficient, or that they provide unnecessary or duplicate services. As a result, distribution costs too much, and consumers pay for these excessive costs in the form of higher prices.

How do resellers answer these charges? They argue that intermediaries do work that would otherwise have to be done by manufacturers or consumers. Markups reflect services that consumers themselves want—more convenience, larger stores and assortments, more service, longer store hours, return privileges, and others. In fact, they argue, retail competition is so intense that margins are actually quite low. For example, after taxes, supermarket chains are typically left with barely 1 percent profit on their sales. If some resellers try to charge too much relative to the value they add, other resellers will step in with lower prices. Low-price stores such as Wal-Mart, Costco, and other discounters pressure their competitors to operate efficiently and keep their prices down.

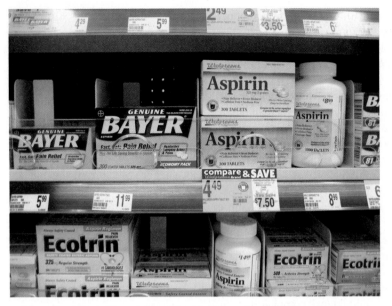

■ A heavily promoted brand of aspirin sells for much more than a virtually identical non-branded or store-branded product. Critics charge that promotion adds only psychological value to the product rather than functional value.

High Advertising and Promotion Costs Modern marketing is also accused of pushing up prices to finance heavy advertising and sales promotion. For example, a few dozen tablets of a heavily promoted brand of pain reliever sell for the same price as 100 tablets of less-promoted brands. Differentiated products—cosmetics, detergents, toiletries—include promotion and packaging costs that can amount to 40 percent or more of the manufacturer's price to the retailer. Critics charge that much of the packaging and promotion adds only psychological value to the product rather than functional value.

Marketers respond that advertising does add to product costs. But it also adds value by informing potential buyers of the availability and merits of a brand. Brand name products may cost more but branding gives buyers assurances of consistent quality. Moreover, consumers can usually buy functional versions of products at lower prices. However, they *want* and are willing to pay more for products that also provide psychological benefits—that make them feel wealthy, attractive, or special. Also, heavy advertising and promotion may be necessary for a firm to match competitors' efforts—the business would lose "share of mind" if it did not match competitive spending. At the same time, companies are cost conscious about promotion and try to spend their money wisely.

Excessive Markups Critics also charge that some companies mark up goods excessively. They point to the drug industry, where a pill costing five cents to make may cost the consumer $2 to buy. They point to the pricing tactics of funeral homes that prey on the confused emotions of bereaved relatives and to the high charges for auto repair and other services.

Marketers respond that most businesses try to deal fairly with consumers because they want to build customer relationships and repeat business. Most consumer abuses are unintentional. When shady marketers do take advantage of consumers, they should be reported to Better Business Bureaus and to state and federal agencies. Marketers also respond that consumers often don't understand the reasons for high markups. For example, pharmaceutical markups must cover the costs of purchasing, promoting, and distributing existing medicines plus the high research and development costs of formulating and testing new medicines. As pharmaceuticals company GlaxoSmithKline states in its ads, "Today's medicines finance tomorrow's miracles."

Deceptive Practices Marketers are sometimes accused of deceptive practices that lead consumers to believe they will get more value than they actually do. Deceptive practices fall into three groups: pricing, promotion, and packaging. *Deceptive pricing* includes practices such as falsely advertising "factory" or "wholesale" prices or a large price reduction from a phony high retail list price. *Deceptive promotion* includes practices such as misrepresenting the product's features or performance or luring the customers to the store for a bargain that is out of stock. *Deceptive packaging* includes exaggerating package contents through subtle design, using misleading labeling, or describing size in misleading terms.

To be sure, questionable marketing practices do occur. Consider the advertising of airline ticket prices:[2]

When is $49 not $49? When it's the advertised price for an airline ticket. In newspaper ads and radio commercials, we are lured with the promise of $49 round-trip tickets to Bermuda. But by the time you add in all the extras, that bargain ticket will cost nearly $200. What ever happened to truth in advertising? Technically, the advertising is legal. But the average airline consumer needs a magnifying glass to get an idea of the actual ticket cost. For the Bermuda ticket, radio commercials warn that the discount price comes with conditions and fees, but you must read the fine print across the bottom of a newspaper ad to discover the true cost. "Prepaid government taxes and fees of up to $86.00, September 11 Security Fees of up to $10.00, and Passenger Facility Charges up to $18.00 per person . . . are not included in listed prices," we're told. "Listed prices include fuel-related and all other increases as of 7/1, but may increase additionally due to unanticipated expenses beyond our control." Add them up, and that ticket costs $163, not counting whatever fuel surcharge may have been imposed over the past nine months. Not quite the $49 in the big print at the top of the ad.

Deceptive practices have led to legislation and other consumer protection actions. For example, in 1938, Congress reacted to such blatant deceptions as Fleischmann's Yeast's claim to straighten crooked teeth by enacting the Wheeler-Lea Act giving the Federal Trade Commission (FTC) power to regulate "unfair or deceptive acts or practices." The FTC has published several guidelines listing deceptive practices. Despite new regulations, some critics argue that deceptive claims are still the norm.

The toughest problem is defining what is "deceptive." For instance, an advertiser's claim that its powerful laundry detergent "makes your washing machine 10 feet tall," showing a surprised homemaker watching her appliance burst through her laundry room ceiling, isn't intended to be taken literally. Instead, the advertiser might claim, it is "puffery"— innocent exaggeration for effect. One noted marketing thinker, Theodore Levitt, once claimed that advertising puffery and alluring imagery are bound to occur—and that they may even be desirable: "There is hardly a company that would not go down in ruin if it refused to provide fluff, because nobody will buy pure functionality. . . . Worse, it denies . . . people's honest needs and values. Without distortion, embellishment, and elaboration, life would be drab, dull, anguished, and at its existential worst."[3]

However, others claim that puffery and alluring imagery can harm consumers in subtle ways. Think about the popular and long-running MasterCard Priceless commercials that paint pictures of consumers fulfilling their priceless dreams despite the costs. Similarly, Visa invites consumers to "Enjoy life's opportunities." Both suggest that your credit card can make it happen. But critics charge that such imagery by credit card companies encourages a spend-now-pay-later attitude that causes many consumers to *over*use their cards. The critics point to statistics showing that sixty percent of Americans are carrying a balance on their credit cards and that one in every four American families is maxed out on at least one credit card. One in every seven Americans today is dealing with a debt collector because they can't make their payments.[4]

Marketers argue that most companies avoid deceptive practices because such practices harm their business in the long run. Profitable customer relationships are built upon a foundation of value and trust. If consumers do not get what they expect, they will switch to more reliable products. In addition, consumers usually protect themselves from deception. Most consumers recognize a marketer's selling intent and are careful when they buy, sometimes to the point of not believing completely true product claims.

■ Deceptive practices: Technically legal, ads like this one lure readers with promises of low, low prices. But you need a magnifying glass to figure out the actual ticket cost.

High-Pressure Selling Salespeople are sometimes accused of high-pressure selling that persuades people to buy goods they had no thought of buying. It is often said that insurance, real estate, and used cars are *sold,* not *bought.* Salespeople are trained to deliver smooth, canned talks to entice purchase. They sell hard because sales contests promise big prizes to those who sell the most.

But in most cases, marketers have little to gain from high-pressure selling. Such tactics may work in one-time selling situations for short-term gain. However, most selling involves building long-term relationships with valued customers. High-pressure or deceptive selling can do serious damage to such relationships. For example, imagine a Procter & Gamble account manager trying to pressure a Wal-Mart buyer, or an IBM salesperson trying to browbeat a General Electric information technology manager. It simply wouldn't work.

Shoddy, Harmful, or Unsafe Products   Another criticism concerns poor product quality or function. One complaint is that, too often, products are not made well and services are not performed well. A second complaint is that many products deliver little benefit, or that they might even be harmful. For example, many critics have pointed out the dangers of today's fat-laden fast food. In fact, McDonald's recently faced a class-action lawsuit charging that its fare has contributed to the nationwide obesity epidemic:

> [Four years ago,] the parody newspaper *Onion* ran a joke article under the headline "Hershey's Ordered to Pay Obese Americans $135 Billion." The hypothesized class-action lawsuit said that Hershey "knowingly and willfully" marketed to children "rich, fatty candy bars containing chocolate and other ingredients of negligible nutritional value," while "spiking" them with "peanuts, crisped rice, and caramel to increase consumer appeal." Some joke. [In 2002,] New York City attorney Sam Hirsch filed a strikingly similar suit—against McDonald's—on behalf of a class of obese and overweight children. He alleged that the fast-food chain "negligently, recklessly, carelessly, and/or intentionally" markets to children food products that are "high in fat, salt, sugar, and cholesterol" while failing to warn of those ingredients' links to "obesity, diabetes, coronary heart disease, high blood pressure, strokes, elevated cholesterol intake, related cancers," and other conditions. Industry defenders decried the suit as frivolous. It is ridiculous, they claimed, to blame the fast-food industry for consumers' "own nutritional ignorance, lack of willpower, genetic predispositions, failure to exercise, or whatever else may play a role in [their] obesity." A federal judge agreed and dismissed the suit, explaining that "it is not the place of the law to protect them from their own excess." And to prevent similar lawsuits, in 2005 the United States House of Representatives passed The Personal Responsibility in Food Consumption Act, dubbed the "Cheeseburger Bill," which bans obesity-related lawsuits in state and federal courts.[5]

Who's to blame for the nation's obesity problem? And what should responsible food companies do about it? As with most social responsibility issues, there are no easy answers. McDonald's has worked to improve its fare and make its menu and its customers healthier. However, other fast feeders seem to be going the other way. Hardee's, for example, serves up a 1,410-calorie Monster Thickburger, and Burger King promotes its Enormous Omelet breakfast sandwich, packing an unapologetic 47 grams of fat. Are these companies being socially irresponsible? Or are they simply serving customers choices they want? (See Marketing at Work 16.1.)

A third complaint concerns product safety. Product safety has been a problem for several reasons, including company indifference, increased product complexity, and poor quality control. For years, Consumers Union—the nonprofit testing and information organization that publishes the *Consumer Reports* magazine and Web site—has reported various hazards in tested products: electrical dangers in appliances, carbon monoxide poisoning from room heaters, injury risks from lawn mowers, and faulty automobile design, among many others. The organization's testing and other activities have helped consumers make better buying decisions and encouraged businesses to eliminate product flaws.

However, most manufacturers *want* to produce quality goods. The way a company deals with product quality and safety problems can damage or help its reputation. Companies selling poor-quality or unsafe products risk damaging conflicts with consumer groups and regulators. Unsafe products can result in product liability suits and large awards for damages. More fundamentally, consumers who are unhappy with a firm's products may avoid future purchases and talk other consumers into doing the same. Thus, quality missteps can have severe consequences. Today's marketers know that good quality results in customer value and satisfaction, which in turn creates profitable customer relationships.

Planned Obsolescence   Critics also have charged that some companies practice planned obsolescence, causing their products to become obsolete before they actually should need replacement. Some producers are accused of using materials and components that will break, wear, rust, or rot sooner than they should. One writer put it this way: "The marvels of modern technology include the development of a soda can which, when discarded, will last forever—and a . . . car, which, when properly cared for, will rust out in two or three years."[6]

16.1 MARKETING AT WORK
The National Obesity Debate: Who's to Blame?

As you've no doubt heard, the United States is facing an obesity epidemic. Everyone seems to agree on the problem—as a nation, we're packing on the pounds. But still unresolved is another weighty issue: Who's to blame? Is it the fault of self-indulgent consumers who just can't say no to sticky buns, fat burgers, and other tempting treats? Or is it the fault of greedy food marketers who are cashing in on vulnerable consumers, turning us into a nation of overeaters?

The problem is a big one. Studies show that some 66 percent of American adults and 17 percent of children and teens are overweight or obese. According to a Rand Corporation study, the number of people in the United States who are 100 pounds or more overweight quintupled between 2000 and 2005, from one adult in 200 to one in 40. This weight increase comes despite repeated medical studies showing that excess weight brings increased risks for heart disease, diabetes, and other maladies, even cancer.

So, here's that weighty question again. If we know that we're overweight and that it's bad for us, why do we keep putting on the pounds? Who's to blame? The answer, of course, depends on whom you ask. However, these days, lots of people are blaming food marketers. In the national obesity debate, food marketers have become a favorite target of almost everyone, from politicians, public policy makers, and the press to overweight consumers themselves. And some food marketers are looking pretty much guilty as charged.

Take Hardee's, for example. At a time when other fast-food chains such as McDonald's, Wendy's, and Subway were getting "leaner," Hardee's introduced the decadent Thickburger, featuring a third of a pound of Angus beef. It followed up with the *Monster* Thickburger: two-thirds of a pound of Angus beef, four strips of bacon, and three slices of American cheese, all nestled in a buttered sesame-seed bun slathered with mayonnaise! The Monster Thickburger weighs in at a whopping 1,410 calories and 107 grams of fat, far greater than the government's recommended fat intake for an entire day.

Surely, you say, Hardee's made a colossal blunder here. Not so! At least, not from a profit viewpoint. Sales at Hardee's 1,990 outlets have climbed 20 percent since it introduced the Thickburger line, resulting in fatter profits. It seems that some consumers, especially in Hardee's target market of young men aged 18 to 34, just love fat burgers. A reporter asked a 27-year-old construction worker who was downing a Monster Thickburger if he'd thought about its effect on his health. "I've never even thought about it," he replied, "and to be honest, I don't really care. It just tastes good."

Hardee's certainly isn't hiding the nutritional facts. Here's how it describes Thickburgers on its Web site:

There's only one thing that can slay the hunger of a young guy on the move: the Thickburger line at Hardee's. With nine cravable varieties, including the classic Original Thickburger and the monument to decadence, the Monster Thickburger, quick service goes premium with 100% Angus beef and all the fixings.... If you want to indulge in a big, delicious, juicy burger, look no further than Hardee's.

Hardee's even offers a Nutrition Calculator on it's Web site showing the calories, fat, and other content of all its menu items.

So, should Hardee's hang its head in shame? Is it being socially irresponsible by aggressively promoting overindulgence to ill-informed or

■ The obesity debate: Is Hardee's being socially irresponsible or simply practicing good marketing by giving customers a big juicy burger that clearly pings their taste buds? Judging by the nutrition calculator at its Web site, the company certainly isn't hiding the nutritional facts.

unwary consumers? Or is it simply practicing good marketing, creating more value for its customers by offering a big, juicy burger that clearly pings their taste buds and letting them make their own choices? Critics claim the former; industry defenders claim the latter.

Hardee's clearly targets adult men with its products and marketing. However, the question of blame gets even murkier when it comes to child obesity. The debate rages over the marketing of everything from fast food and soft drinks in our nation's school cafeterias to cereal, cookies, and other "not-so-good-for-you" products targeted toward kids and teens, who are seen as especially vulnerable to seductive or misleading marketing pitches. Once again, many public and private advocacy groups point the finger at food marketers. U.S. companies spend $15 billion a year marketing and advertising to children under 12, and a recent Federal Trade Commission study found that half of all ads for junk food, sugary cereals, and soft drinks are on children's programs. The FTC and critics have called on food marketers to voluntarily adopt more responsible children's marketing practices.

The food industry itself seems split on the issue. However, under increasing pressure from politicians and the press, most major children's food marketers are responding with voluntary restrictions. For example, early on, Kraft Foods announced that it would no longer advertise products such as Oreos, Chips Ahoy!, and most of its Oscar Mayer Lunchables meals on programs targeted to children aged 6 to 11—programs such as *SpongeBob SquarePants* and *All Grown Up*. Similarly, Kellogg voluntarily stopped child-directed advertising for products that don't meet specific guidelines for calories, sugar, fat, and sodium. The voluntary ban applies to about half the products that Kellogg markets to children, including Froot Loops, Apple Jacks, and Pop Tarts.

Other marketers have undertaken efforts to educate children about healthy eating and lifestyles. For example, a group of 11 major companies who account for more than two-thirds of food and beverage ads that children see—including titans such as Coca-Cola, Hershey, McDonald's, Kellogg, and General Mills—have pledged to devote at least half of their

(continues)

advertising directed to children "toward furthering the goal of promoting healthy dietary choices and healthy lifestyles." Still, many critics claim that such actions constitute too little too late. In the extreme, they call for a complete ban on marketing to children by food and beverage makers.

So, back to that big question: Who's to blame for our nation's obesity epidemic? Is it the marketers who promote unhealthy but irresistible fare to vulnerable consumers? Or is it the fault of consumers themselves for failing to take personal responsibility for their own health and well-being? It's a weighty decision for many food marketers. And, as is the case with most social responsibility issues, finding the an-

swer to that question is even harder than trying to take off some of those extra pounds.

Sources: See, Rand Health, "Obesity and Disability: The Shape of Things to Come," accessed at www.rand.org/pubs/research_briefs/2007/RAND_RB9043-1.pdf, October 2007; Ira Teinowitz, "Kellogg Move Bodes Ill for Ads to Kids," *Advertising Age,* June 18, 2007, pp. 1, 33; Andrew Martin, "Kellogg to Curb Marketing of Foods to Children," *New York Times,* June 14, 2007, accessed at www.nytimes.com; Jonathan Birchallin, "Foodmakers Tighten Code to Avoid Ads Ban," *Financial Times,* July 18, 2007, p. 4; Tara Parker-Pope, "Watching Food Ads on TV May Program Kids to Overeat," *Wall Street Journal,* July 10, 2007, p. D1; and information from www.hardees.com/menu/, accessed December 2007.

Others are charged with continually changing consumer concepts of acceptable styles to encourage more and earlier buying. An obvious example is constantly changing clothing fashions. Still others are accused of introducing planned streams of new products that make older models obsolete. Critics claim that this occurs in the consumer electronics and computer industries. For example, consider this writer's tale about an aging cell phone:

Today, most people, myself included, are all agog at the wondrous outpouring of new technology, from cell phones to iPods, iPhones, laptops, BlackBerries, and on and on. Even though I am a techno-incompetent and like to think I shun these new devices, I actually have a drawer filled with the detritus of yesterday's hottest product, now reduced to the status of fossils. I have video cameras that use tapes no longer available, laptops with programs incompatible with anything on today's market, portable CD players I no longer use, and more. But what really upsets me is how quickly some still-useful gadgets become obsolete, at least in the eyes of their makers.

I recently embarked on an epic search for a cord to plug into my wife's cell phone to recharge it. We were traveling and the poor phone kept bleating that it was running low and the battery needed recharging. So, we began a search—from big-box technology superstores to smaller suppliers and the cell phone companies themselves—all to no avail. Finally, a salesperson told my wife, "That's an old model, so we don't stock the charger any longer." "But I only bought it last year," she sputtered. "Yeah, like I said, that's an old model," he replied without a hint of irony or sympathy. So, in the world of insanely rapid obsolescence, each successive model is incompatible with the previous one it replaces. The proliferation and sheer waste of this type of practice is mind-boggling.[7]

■ Planned obsolescence: Almost everyone, it seems, has a drawer filled with the detritus of yesterday's hottest product, now reduced to the status of fossils.

Marketers respond that consumers *like* style changes; they get tired of the old goods and want a new look in fashion. Or they *want* the latest high-tech innovations, even if older models still work. No one has to buy the new product, and if too few people like it, it will simply fail. Finally, most companies do not design their products to break down earlier, because they do not want to lose customers to other brands. Instead, they seek constant improvement to ensure that products will consistently meet or exceed customer expectations. Much of the so-called planned obsolescence is the working of the competitive and technological forces in a free society—forces that lead to ever-improving goods and services.

Poor Service to Disadvantaged Consumers Finally, the American marketing system has been accused of serving disadvantaged consumers poorly. For example, critics claim that the urban poor often must shop in smaller stores that carry inferior goods and charge higher prices. The presence of large national chain stores in low-income neighborhoods would help to keep prices down. However, the critics accuse major chain retailers of "redlining," drawing a red line around disadvantaged neighborhoods and avoiding placing stores there.[8]

Similar redlining charges have been leveled at the insurance, consumer lending, banking, and health care industries. Home and auto insurers have been accused of assigning higher premiums to people with poor credit ratings. The insurers claim that individuals with bad credit tend to make more insurance claims, and that this justifies charging them higher premiums. However, critics and consumer advocates have accused the insurers of a new form of redlining. Says one writer, "This is a new excuse for denying coverage to the poor, elderly, and minorities."[9]

More recently, consumer advocates have charged that income tax preparers such as H&R Block and Jackson Hewitt are taking advantage of the working poor by offering them "rapid refunds" after preparing their taxes. Customers receive these rapid refunds when their taxes are prepared, rather than waiting two weeks to a month for the IRS to send the refund. The big problem is that the refunds are not free. In fact, they're "refund anticipation loans" (RALs) with fees starting around $130, which represents an APR (annual percentage rate) of 245 percent of the average working poor person's refund. In one year alone, more than 10.6 million low-income families requested rapid refunds, and tax preparers made more than $1.4 billion in profits on them. Consumer advocates are pressuring state legislatures to pass laws requiring loan materials to be written in a language that the average consumer can understand. And the state of California recently filed a lawsuit against H&R Block for deceptive practices associated with RALs.[10]

■ Public policymakers have charged that income tax preparers such as H&R Block and Jackson Hewitt are taking advantage of vulnerable consumers by offering them "rapid refunds" after preparing their taxes. The big problem is that the refunds are not free.

Clearly, better marketing systems must be built to service disadvantaged consumers. In fact, many marketers profitably target such consumers with legitimate goods and services that create real value. In cases where marketers do not step in to fill the void, the government likely will. For example, the FTC has taken action against sellers who advertise false values, wrongfully deny services, or charge disadvantaged customers too much.

Linking the Concepts

Hit the brakes for a moment and cool down. Few marketers *want* to abuse or anger consumers—it's simply not good business. Instead, as you know well by now, most marketers work to build long-term, profitable customer relationships based on real value and caring. Still, some marketing abuses do occur.

■ Think back over the past three months or so and list any instances in which you've suffered a marketing abuse such as those just discussed. Analyze your list: What kinds of companies were involved? Were the abuses intentional? What did the situations have in common?

■ Pick one of the instances you listed and describe it in detail. How might you go about righting this wrong? Write out an action plan and then do something to remedy the abuse. If we all took such actions when wronged, there would be far fewer wrongs to right!

Marketing's Impact on Society as a Whole

The American marketing system has been accused of adding to several "evils" in American society at large. Advertising has been a special target—so much so that the American Association of Advertising Agencies once launched a campaign to defend advertising against what it felt to be common but untrue criticisms.

False Wants and Too Much Materialism Critics have charged that the marketing system urges too much interest in material possessions. People are judged by what they *own* rather than by who they *are*. This drive for wealth and possessions hit new highs in the 1980s and 1990s, when phrases such as "greed is good" and "shop till you drop" seemed to characterize the times.

In the current decade, many social scientists have noted a reaction against the opulence and waste of the previous decades and a return to more basic values and social commitment. However, our infatuation with material things continues.

> If you made a graph of American life since the end of World War II, every line concerning money and the things that money can buy would soar upward, a statistical monument to materialism. Inflation-adjusted income per American has almost tripled. The size of the typical new house has more than doubled. A two-car garage was once a goal; now we're nearly a three-car nation. Designer everything, personal electronics, and other items that didn't even exist a half-century ago now affordable. Although our time spent shopping has dropped in recent years to just three hours a week, American households currently spend on average $1.22 for every $1 earned. Some consumers will let nothing stand between them and their acquisitions. Recently, in a Florida Wal-Mart, post-Thanksgiving shoppers rushing to buy DVD players (on sale for $29) knocked down a woman, trampled her, and left her unconscious.[11]

The critics do not view this interest in material things as a natural state of mind but rather as a matter of false wants created by marketing. Businesses hire Madison Avenue to stimulate people's desires for goods, and Madison Avenue uses the mass media to create materialistic models of the good life. People work harder to earn the necessary money. Their purchases increase the output of American industry, and industry in turn uses Madison Avenue to stimulate more desire for the industrial output.

Thus, marketing is seen as creating false wants that benefit industry more than they benefit consumers. Some critics even take their concerns to the streets.

> For almost a decade Bill Talen, also known as Reverend Billy, has taken to the streets, exhorting people to resist temptation—the temptation to shop. With the zeal of a street-corner preacher and the schmaltz of a street-corner Santa, Reverend Billy will tell anyone willing to listen that people are walking willingly into the hellfires of consumption. Reverend Billy, leader of the Church of Stop Shopping believes that shoppers have almost no resistance to the media messages that encourage them, around the clock, to want things and buy them. He sees a population lost in consumption, the meaning of individual existence vanished in a fog of wanting, buying, and owning too many things, ultimately leading to a "Shopocalypse." Sporting a televangelist's pompadour, a priest's collar, and a white megaphone, Reverend Billy is often accompanied by his gospel choir when he strides into stores he considers objectionable or shows up at protests like the annual post-Thanksgiving Buy Nothing Parade in front of Macy's in Manhattan. When the choir, which is made up of volunteers, erupts in song, it is hard to ignore: "Stop shopping! Stop shopping! We will never shop again!"[12]

■ Materialism: With the zeal of a street-corner preacher and the schmaltz of a street-corner Santa, Reverend Billy—founder of the Church of Stop Shopping—will tell anyone who will listen that people are walking willingly into the hellfires of consumption.

These criticisms overstate the power of business to create needs, however. People have strong defenses against advertising and other marketing tools. Marketers are most effective when they appeal to existing wants rather than when they attempt to create new ones. Furthermore, people seek information when making important purchases and often do not rely on single sources. Even minor purchases that may be affected by advertising messages lead to repeat purchases only if the product delivers the promised customer value. Finally, the high failure rate of new products shows that companies are not able to control demand.

On a deeper level, our wants and values are influenced not only by marketers but also by family, peer groups, religion, cultural background, and education. If Americans are highly materialistic, these values arose out of basic socialization processes that go much deeper than business and mass media could produce alone.

Too Few Social Goods Business has been accused of overselling private goods at the expense of public goods. As private goods increase, they require more public services that are usually not forthcoming. For example, an increase in automobile ownership (private good) requires more highways, traffic control, parking spaces, and police services (public goods). The overselling of private goods results in "social costs." For cars, some of the social costs include traffic congestion, gasoline shortages, and air pollution. For example, in 85 of the most congested U.S. urban areas, drivers sat through 3.7 billion hours of traffic delays in one year. In the process, they wasted 2.3 billion gallons of fuel and emitted millions of tons of greenhouse gases.[13]

A way must be found to restore a balance between private and public goods. One option is to make producers bear the full social costs of their operations. The government could require automobile manufacturers to build cars with more efficient engines and better pollution-control systems. Automakers would then raise their prices to cover extra costs. If buyers found the price of some cars too high, however, the producers of these cars would disappear. Demand would then move to those producers that could support the sum of the private and social costs.

A second option is to make consumers pay the social costs. For example, many cities around the world are starting to charge "congestion tolls" in an effort to reduce traffic congestion. To unclog its streets, the city of London now levies a congestion charge of $16.50 per day per car to drive in an eight-square-mile area downtown. The charge has not only reduced traffic congestion by 30 percent and increased mass transit use by 16 percent, it also raises money to shore up London's public transportation system.

Based on London's success, cities such as San Diego and Denver have turned some of their HOV (high-occupancy vehicle) lanes into HOT (high-occupancy toll) lanes for drivers carrying too few passengers. Regular drivers can use the HOV lanes, but they must pay tolls ranging from $0.50 off-peak to $8.50 during rush hour. The U.S. government has recently proposed a bill that would create rush-hour fees in congested urban areas across the country. If the costs of driving rise high enough, the government hopes, consumers will travel at nonpeak times or find alternative transportation modes, ultimately helping to curb America's oil addiction.[14]

■ Balancing private and public goods: In response to lane-clogging traffic congestion like that above, London now levies a congestion charge. The charge has reduced congestion by 30 percent and raised money to shore up the city's public transportation system.

Cultural Pollution Critics charge the marketing system with creating *cultural pollution*. Our senses are being constantly assaulted by marketing and advertising. Commercials interrupt serious programs; pages of ads obscure magazines; billboards mar beautiful scenery; spam fills our e-mailboxes. These interruptions continually pollute people's minds with messages of materialism, sex, power, or status. A recent study found that 63 percent of Americans feel constantly bombarded with too many marketing messages, and some critics call for sweeping changes.[15]

Marketers answer the charges of "commercial noise" with these arguments: First, they hope that their ads reach primarily the target audience. But because of mass-communication channels, some ads are bound to reach people who have no interest in the product and are therefore bored or annoyed. People who buy magazines addressed to their interests—such as *Vogue* or *Fortune*—rarely complain about the ads because the magazines advertise products of interest.

Second, ads make much of television and radio free to users and keep down the costs of magazines and newspapers. Many people think commercials are a small price to pay for these benefits. Finally, today's consumers have alternatives. For example, they can zip or zap TV commercials on recorded programs or avoid them altogether on many paid cable or satellite channels. Thus, to hold consumer attention, advertisers are making their ads more entertaining and informative.

Marketing's Impact on Other Businesses

Critics also charge that a company's marketing practices can harm other companies and reduce competition. Three problems are involved: acquisitions of competitors, marketing practices that create barriers to entry, and unfair competitive marketing practices.

Critics claim that firms are harmed and competition reduced when companies expand by acquiring competitors rather than by developing their own new products. The large number of acquisitions and the rapid pace of industry consolidation over the past several decades have caused concern that vigorous young competitors will be absorbed and that competition will be reduced. In virtually every major industry—retailing, entertainment, financial services, utilities, transportation, automobiles, telecommunications, health care—the number of major competitors is shrinking.

Acquisition is a complex subject. Acquisitions can sometimes be good for society. The acquiring company may gain economies of scale that lead to lower costs and lower prices. A well-managed company may take over a poorly managed company and improve its efficiency. An industry that was not very competitive might become more competitive after the acquisition. But acquisitions can also be harmful and, therefore, are closely regulated by the government.

Critics have also charged that marketing practices bar new companies from entering an industry. Large marketing companies can use patents and heavy promotion spending or tie up suppliers or dealers to keep out or drive out competitors. Those concerned with antitrust regulation recognize that some barriers are the natural result of the economic advantages of doing business on a large scale. Other barriers could be challenged by existing and new laws. For example, some critics have proposed a progressive tax on advertising spending to reduce the role of selling costs as a major barrier to entry.

Finally, some firms have in fact used unfair competitive marketing practices with the intention of hurting or destroying other firms. They may set their prices below costs, threaten to cut off business with suppliers, or discourage the buying of a competitor's products. Various laws work to prevent such predatory competition. It is difficult, however, to prove that the intent or action was really predatory.

In recent years, Wal-Mart has been accused of using predatory pricing in selected market areas to drive smaller, mom-and-pop retailers out of business. Wal-Mart has become a lightning rod for protests by citizens in dozens of towns who worry that the megaretailer's unfair practices will choke out local businesses. However, whereas critics charge that Wal-Mart's actions

■ Predatory business practices: Wal-Mart has become a lightning rod for protests by citizens who worry that the megaretailer's unfair practices will choke out local businesses. Wal-Mart defenders claim that it's healthy competition of a more efficient company against less efficient ones.

are predatory, others assert that its actions are just the healthy competition of a more efficient company against less efficient ones.

For instance, when Wal-Mart recently began a program to sell generic drugs at $4 a prescription, local pharmacists complained of predatory pricing. They charged that at those low prices, Wal-Mart must be selling under cost to drive them out of business. But Wal-Mart claimed that, given its substantial buying power and efficient operations, it could make a profit at those prices. The $4 pricing program was not aimed at putting competitors out of business. Rather, it was simply a good competitive move that served customers better and brought more of them in the door.[16]

Citizen and Public Actions to Regulate Marketing

Because some people view business as the cause of many economic and social ills, grassroots movements have arisen from time to time to keep business in line. The two major movements have been *consumerism* and *environmentalism*.

Consumerism

American business firms have been the target of organized consumer movements on three occasions. The first consumer movement took place in the early 1900s. It was fueled by rising prices, Upton Sinclair's writings on conditions in the meat industry, and scandals in the drug industry. The second consumer movement, in the mid-1930s, was sparked by an upturn in consumer prices during the Great Depression and another drug scandal.

The third movement began in the 1960s. Consumers had become better educated, products had become more complex and potentially hazardous, and people were unhappy with American institutions. Ralph Nader appeared on the scene to force many issues, and other well-known writers accused big business of wasteful and unethical practices. President John F. Kennedy declared that consumers had the right to safety and to be informed, to choose, and to be heard. Congress investigated certain industries and proposed consumer-protection legislation. Since then, many consumer groups have been organized and several consumer laws have been passed. The consumer movement has spread internationally and has become very strong in Europe.

But what is the consumer movement? **Consumerism** is an organized movement of citizens and government agencies to improve the rights and power of buyers in relation to sellers. Traditional *sellers' rights* include:

Consumerism
An organized movement of citizens and government agencies to improve the rights and power of buyers in relation to sellers.

- The right to introduce any product in any size and style, provided it is not hazardous to personal health or safety; or, if it is, to include proper warnings and controls
- The right to charge any price for the product, provided no discrimination exists among similar kinds of buyers
- The right to spend any amount to promote the product, provided it is not defined as unfair competition
- The right to use any product message, provided it is not misleading or dishonest in content or execution
- The right to use any buying incentive programs, provided they are not unfair or misleading

Traditional *buyers' rights* include:

- The right not to buy a product that is offered for sale
- The right to expect the product to be safe
- The right to expect the product to perform as claimed

Comparing these rights, many believe that the balance of power lies on the seller's side. True, the buyer can refuse to buy. But critics feel that the buyer has too little information, education, and protection to make wise decisions when facing sophisticated sellers. Consumer advocates call for the following additional consumer rights:

- The right to be well informed about important aspects of the product
- The right to be protected against questionable products and marketing practices

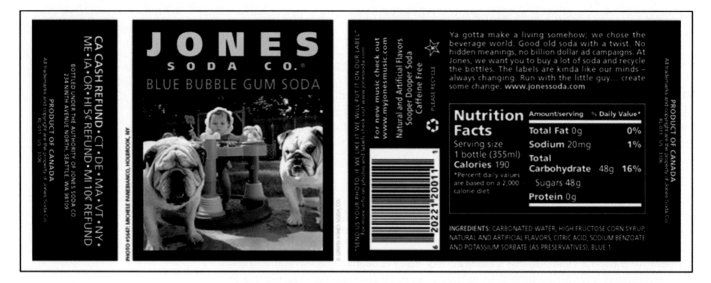

■ Consumer desire for more information led to packing labels with useful facts, from ingredients and nutrition facts to recycling and country of origin information. Jones Soda even puts customer-submitted photos on its labels.

• The right to influence products and marketing practices in ways that will improve the "quality of life"

Each proposed right has led to more specific proposals by consumerists. The right to be informed includes the right to know the true interest on a loan (truth in lending), the true cost per unit of a brand (unit pricing), the ingredients in a product (ingredient labeling), the nutritional value of foods (nutritional labeling), product freshness (open dating), and the true benefits of a product (truth in advertising). Proposals related to consumer protection include strengthening consumer rights in cases of business fraud, requiring greater product safety, ensuring information privacy, and giving more power to government agencies. Proposals relating to quality of life include controlling the ingredients that go into certain products and packaging, reducing the level of advertising "noise," and putting consumer representatives on company boards to protect consumer interests.

Consumers have not only the *right* but also the *responsibility* to protect themselves instead of leaving this function to someone else. Consumers who believe they got a bad deal have several remedies available, including contacting the company or the media; contacting federal, state, or local agencies; and going to small-claims courts.

Environmentalism

Environmentalism

An organized movement of concerned citizens and government agencies to protect and improve people's living environment.

Whereas consumerists consider whether the marketing system is efficiently serving consumer wants, environmentalists are concerned with marketing's effects on the environment and with the environmental costs of serving consumer needs and wants. **Environmentalism** is an organized movement of concerned citizens, businesses, and government agencies to protect and improve people's living environment.

Environmentalists are not against marketing and consumption; they simply want people and organizations to operate with more care for the environment. The marketing system's goal, they assert, should not be to maximize consumption, consumer choice, or consumer satisfaction, but rather to maximize life quality. And "life quality" means not only the quantity and quality of consumer goods and services, but also the quality of the environment. Environmentalists want environmental costs included in both producer and consumer decision making.

The first wave of modern environmentalism in the United States was driven by environmental groups and concerned consumers in the 1960s and 1970s. They were concerned with damage to the ecosystem caused by strip-mining, forest depletion, acid rain, loss of the atmosphere's ozone layer, toxic wastes, and litter. They also were concerned with the loss of recreational areas and with the increase in health problems caused by bad air, polluted water, and chemically treated food.

	Today: Greening	Tomorrow: Beyond Greening
Internal	**Pollution prevention** Eliminating or reducing waste before it is created	**New clean technology** Developing new sets of environmental skills and capabilities
External	**Product stewardship** Minimizing environmental impact throughout the entire product lifecycle	**Sustainability vision** Creating a strategic framework for future sustainability

FIGURE 16.1

The Environmental Sustainability Portfolio

Source: Stuart L. Hart, "Innovation, Creative Destruction, and Sustainability," *Research Technology Management*, September–October 2005, pp. 21–27.

The second environmentalism wave was driven by government, which passed laws and regulations during the 1970s and 1980s governing industrial practices impacting the environment. This wave hit some industries hard. Steel companies and utilities had to invest billions of dollars in pollution control equipment and costlier fuels. The auto industry had to introduce expensive emission controls in cars. The packaging industry had to find ways to reduce litter. These industries and others have often resented and resisted environmental regulations, especially when they have been imposed too rapidly to allow companies to make proper adjustments. Many of these companies claim they have had to absorb large costs that have made them less competitive.

The first two environmentalism waves have now merged into a third and stronger wave in which companies are accepting more responsibility for doing no harm to the environment. They are shifting from protest to prevention, and from regulation to responsibility. More and more companies are adopting policies of **environmental sustainability**. Simply put, environmental sustainability is about generating profits while helping to save the planet. Sustainability is a crucial but difficult societal goal.

Some companies have responded to consumer environmental concerns by doing only what is required to avert new regulations or to keep environmentalists quiet. Enlightened companies, however, are taking action not because someone is forcing them to, or to reap short-run profits, but because it is the right thing to do—for both the company and for the planet's environmental future.

Figure 16.1 shows a grid that companies can use to gauge their progress toward environmental sustainability. In includes both internal and external "greening" activities that will pay off for the firm and environment in the short run and "beyond greening" activities that will pay off in the longer term. At the most basic level, a company can practice *pollution prevention*. This involves more than pollution control—cleaning up waste after it has been created. Pollution prevention means eliminating or minimizing waste before it is created. Companies emphasizing prevention have responded with internal "green marketing" programs—designing and developing ecologically safer products, recyclable and biodegradable packaging, better pollution controls, and more energy-efficient operations.

For example, Sony has reduced the amount of heavy metals—such as lead, mercury, and cadmium—in its electronic products. Nike produces PVC-free shoes, recycles old sneakers, and educates young people about conservation, reuse, and recycling. And UPS is now developing a "green fleet" of alternative-fuel vehicles to replace its old fleet of boxy brown, smoke-belching diesel delivery trucks. It recently deployed 50 new next-generation hybrid electric delivery vehicles to join the roughly 20,000 low-emission and alternative-fuel trucks already in use. The hybrid vehicles produce 45 percent better fuel economy and a dramatic decrease in vehicle emissions.[17]

At the next level, companies can practice *product stewardship*—minimizing not just pollution from production and product design but all environmental impacts throughout the full product life cycle, and all the while reducing costs. Many companies are adopting *design for environment (DFE)* and *cradle-to-cradle* practices. This involves thinking ahead to design products that are easier to recover, reuse, or recycle and developing programs to reclaim products at the end of their lives. DFE not only helps to sustain the environment, it can be highly profitable for the company.

An example is Xerox Corporation's Equipment Remanufacture and Parts Reuse Program, which converts end-of-life office equipment into new products and parts. Equipment returned to Xerox can be remanufactured reusing 70 to 90 percent by weight of old machine components, while still meeting performance standards for equipment made

Environmental sustainability
A management approach that involves developing strategies that both sustain the environment and produce profits for the company.

with all new parts. The program creates benefits for both the environment and for the company. So far, it has diverted nearly two billion pounds of waste from landfills. And it reduces the amount of raw material and energy needed to produce new parts. Energy savings from parts reuse total an estimated 320,000 megawatt hours annually—enough energy to light more than 250,000 U.S. homes for the year.[18]

Today's "greening" activities focus on improving what companies already do to protect the environment. The "beyond greening" activities identified in Figure 16.1 look to the future. First, internally, companies can plan for *new clean technology*. Many organizations that have made good sustainability headway are still limited by existing technologies. To create fully sustainable strategies, they will need to develop innovative new technologies. Wal-Mart is doing this. It recently opened two experimental superstores designed to test dozens of environmentally friendly and energy-efficient technologies:[19]

■ Wal-Mart has opened two experimental superstores designed to test dozens of environmentally friendly and energy-efficient technologies. The façade of this store features rows and rows of windows to let in as much natural light as possible, and it's "urban forest" landscaping uses native, well-adapted plants, cutting down on watering, mowing, and the amount of fertilizer and other chemicals needed.

A 143-foot-tall wind turbine stands outside a Wal-Mart Supercenter in Aurora, Colorado. Incongruous as it might seem, it is clearly a sign that something about this particular store is different. On the outside, the store's facade features row upon row of windows to allow in as much natural light as possible. The landscaping uses native, drought-tolerant plants well adapted to the hot, dry Colorado summers, cutting down on watering, mowing, and the amount of fertilizer and other chemicals needed. Inside the store, an efficient high-output linear fluorescent lighting system saves enough electricity annually from this store alone to supply the needs of 52 single-family homes. The store's heating system burns recovered cooking oil from the deli's fryers. The oil is collected, mixed with waste engine oil from the store's Tire and Lube Express, and burned in the waste-oil boiler. All organic waste, including produce, meats, and paper, is placed in an organic waste compactor, which is then hauled off to a company that turns it into mulch for the garden.

These and dozens more technological touches make the supercenter a laboratory for efficient and Earth-friendly retail operations. In the long run, Wal-Mart's environmental goals are to use 100 percent renewable energy, to create zero waste, and to sell products that sustain its resources and environment. Moreover, Wal-Mart is eagerly spreading the word by encouraging visitors—even from competing companies. "We had Target in here not too long ago, and other retail chains and independents have also taken a tour of the store," notes the store manager. "This is not something we're keeping to ourselves. We want everyone to know about it."

Finally, companies can develop a *sustainability vision,* which serves as a guide to the future. It shows how the company's products and services, processes, and policies must evolve and what new technologies must be developed to get there. This vision of sustainability provides a framework for pollution control, product stewardship, and new environmental technology for the company and others to follow.

Most companies today focus on the upper-left quadrant of the grid in Figure 16.1, investing most heavily in pollution prevention. Some forward-looking companies practice product stewardship and are developing new environmental technologies. Few companies have well-defined sustainability visions. However, emphasizing only one or a few quadrants in the environmental sustainability grid can be shortsighted. Investing only in the left half of the grid puts a company in a good position today but leaves it vulnerable in the future. In contrast, a heavy emphasis on the right half suggests that a company has good environmental vision but lacks the skills needed to implement it. Thus, companies should work at developing all four dimensions of environmental sustainability.

Alcoa, the world's leading producer of aluminum is doing just that. For three years running, it has been named one of the most sustainable corporations in the annual *Global 100 Most Sustainable Corporations in the World* ranking:

> Alcoa has distinguished itself as a leader through its sophisticated approach to identifying and managing the material sustainability risks that it faces as a company. From pollution prevention via greenhouse gas emissions reduction programs to engaging stakeholders over new environmental technology, such as controversial hydropower projects, Alcoa has the sustainability strategies in place needed to meld its profitability objectives with society's larger environmental protection goals. . . . Importantly, Alcoa's approach to sustainability is firmly rooted in the idea that sustainability programs can indeed add financial value. Perhaps the best evidence is the company's efforts to promote the use of aluminum in transportation, where aluminum—with its excellent strength-to-weight ratio—is making inroads as a material of choice that allows automakers to build low-weight, fuel-efficient vehicles that produce fewer tailpipe emissions. This kind of forward-thinking strategy of supplying the market with the products that will help solve pressing global environmental problems shows a company that sees the future, has plotted a course, and is aligning its business accordingly. Says CEO Alain Belda, "Our values require us to think and act not only on the present challenges, but also with the legacy in mind that we leave for those who will come after us . . . as well as the commitments made by those that came before us."[20]

Environmentalism creates some special challenges for global marketers. As international trade barriers come down and global markets expand, environmental issues are having an ever-greater impact on international trade. Countries in North America, Western Europe, and other developed regions are developing strict environmental standards. In the United States, for example, more than two dozen major pieces of environmental legislation have been enacted since 1970, and recent events suggest that more regulation is on the way. A side accord to the North American Free Trade Agreement (NAFTA) set up the Commission for Environmental Cooperation resolving environmental matters. The European Union has passed "end-of-life" regulations affecting automobiles and consumer electronics products. And the EU's Eco-Management and Audit Scheme provides guidelines for environmental self-regulation.[21]

However, environmental policies still vary widely from country to country. Countries such as Denmark, Germany, Japan, and the United States have fully developed environmental policies and high public expectations. But major countries such as China, India, Brazil, and Russia are in only the early stages of developing such policies. Moreover, environmental factors that motivate consumers in one country may have no impact on consumers in another. For example, PVC soft-drink bottles cannot be used in Switzerland or Germany. However, they are preferred in France, which has an extensive recycling process for them. Thus, international companies have found it difficult to develop standard environmental practices that work around the world. Instead, they are creating general policies and then translating these policies into tailored programs that meet local regulations and expectations.

Public Actions to Regulate Marketing

Citizen concerns about marketing practices will usually lead to public attention and legislative proposals. New bills will be debated—many will be defeated, others will be modified, and a few will become workable laws.

Many of the laws that affect marketing are listed in Chapter 3. The task is to translate these laws into the language that marketing executives understand as they make decisions about competitive relations, products, price, promotion, and channels of distribution. Figure 16.2 illustrates the major legal issues facing marketing management.

FIGURE 16.2

Major Marketing Decision Areas
That May Be Called Into Question
Under the Law

Selling decisions
Bribing?
Stealing trade secrets?
Disparaging customers?
Misrepresenting?
Disclosure of customer
rights?
Unfair discrimination?

Product decisions
Product additions and
deletions?
Patent protection?
Product quality and
safety?
Product warranty?

Advertising decisions
False advertising?
Deceptive advertising?
Bait-and-switch advertising?
Promotional allowances and
services?

Packaging decisions
Fair packaging and
labeling?
Excessive cost?
Scarce resources?
Pollution?

Channel decisions
Exclusive dealing?
Exclusive territorial
distributorship?
Tying agreements?
Dealer's rights?

Price decisions
Price fixing?
Predatory pricing?
Price discrimination?
Minimum pricing?
Price increases?
Deceptive pricing?

Competitive relations decisions
Anticompetitive acquisition?
Barriers to entry?
Predatory competition?

Business Actions Toward Socially Responsible Marketing

At first, many companies opposed consumerism and environmentalism. They thought the criticisms were either unfair or unimportant. But by now, most companies have grown to embrace the new consumer rights, at least in principle. They might oppose certain pieces of legislation as inappropriate ways to solve specific consumer problems, but they recognize the consumer's right to information and protection. Many of these companies have responded positively to consumerism and environmentalism as a way to create greater customer value and to strengthen customer relationships.

Enlightened Marketing

Enlightened marketing
A marketing philosophy holding that a company's marketing should support the best long-run performance of the marketing system.

The philosophy of **enlightened marketing** holds that a company's marketing should support the best long-run performance of the marketing system. Enlightened marketing consists of five principles: *consumer-oriented marketing, customer-value marketing, innovative marketing, sense-of-mission marketing,* and *societal marketing.*

Consumer-oriented marketing
The philosophy of enlightened marketing that holds that the company should view and organize its marketing activities from the consumer's point of view.

Consumer-Oriented Marketing **Consumer-oriented marketing** means that the company should view and organize its marketing activities from the consumer's point of view. It should work hard to sense, serve, and satisfy the needs of a defined group of customers. All of the good marketing companies that we've discussed in this text have had this in common: an all-consuming passion for delivering superior value to carefully chosen customers. Only by seeing the world through its customers' eyes can the company build lasting and profitable customer relationships.

Customer-value marketing
A principle of enlightened marketing that holds that a company should put most of its resources into customer value-building marketing investments.

Customer-Value Marketing According to the principle of **customer-value marketing**, the company should put most of its resources into customer-value-building marketing investments. Many things marketers do—one-shot sales promotions, cosmetic packaging changes, direct-response advertising—may raise sales in the short run but add less *value* than would actual improvements in the product's quality, features, or convenience. Enlightened marketing calls for building long-run consumer loyalty and relationships by continually improving the value consumers receive from the firm's market offering. By creating value *for* consumers, the company can capture value *from* consumers in return.

Innovative Marketing The principle of **innovative marketing** requires that the company continuously seek real product and marketing improvements. The company that overlooks new and better ways to do things will eventually lose customers to another company that has found a better way. An excellent example of an innovative marketer is Samsung Electronics:

> A dozen years ago, Samsung was a copycat consumer electronics brand you bought off a shipping pallet at Costco if you couldn't afford a Sony. But today, the brand holds a high-end, cutting-edge aura. In 1996, Samsung Electronics made an inspired decision. It turned its back on cheap knock-offs and set out to overtake rival Sony. The company hired a crop of fresh, young designers, who unleashed a torrent of new products—not humdrum, me-too products, but sleek, bold, and beautiful products targeted to high-end users. Samsung called them "lifestyle works of art"—from brightly colored cell phones and elegantly thin DVD players to flat-panel TV monitors that hung on walls like paintings. Every new product had to pass the "Wow!" test: If it didn't get a "Wow!" reaction during market testing, it went straight back to the design studio.
>
> Samsung also changed its distribution to match its new caché. It initially abandoned low-end distributors such as Wal-Mart and Kmart, instead building strong relationships with specialty retailers such as Best Buy and Circuit City. Interbrand calculates Samsung's brand value at more than $16 billion, highest in the consumer electronics business and 38 percent higher than Sony's. Samsung is the world leader in CDMA cell phones and is battling for the number-two spot in total handsets sold. It's also number-one worldwide in color TVs, flash memory, and LCD panels. "Samsung's performance continues to astound brand watchers," says one analyst. The company has become a model for others that "want to shift from being a cheap supplier to a global brand." Says a Samsung designer, "We're not el cheapo anymore."[22]

Sense-of-Mission Marketing **Sense-of-mission marketing** means that the company should define its mission in broad *social* terms rather than narrow *product* terms. When a company defines a social mission, employees feel better about their work and have a clearer sense of direction. Brands linked with broader missions can serve the best long-run interests of both the brand and consumers. For example, Dove wants to do more than just sell its beauty care products. It's on a mission to discover "real beauty" and to help women be happy just the way they are (see Marketing at Work 16.2).

Some companies define their overall corporate missions in broad societal terms. For example, defined in narrow product terms, the mission of Unilever's Ben & Jerry's unit might be "to sell ice cream." However, Ben & Jerry's states its mission more broadly, as one of "linked prosperity," including product, economic, and social missions. From its beginnings, Ben & Jerry's championed a host of social and environmental causes, and it donated a whopping 7.5 percent of pretax profits to support worthy causes. By the mid-1990s, Ben & Jerry's had become the nation's number-two superpremium ice cream brand.

However, having a "double bottom line" of values and profits is no easy proposition. Throughout the 1990s, as competitors not shackled by "principles before profits" missions invaded its markets, Ben & Jerry's growth and profits flattened. In 2000, after several years of less-than-stellar financial returns, Ben & Jerry's was acquired by giant food producer Unilever. Looking back, the company appears to have focused too much on social issues at the expense of sound business management. Cohen once commented, "There came a time when I had to admit 'I'm a businessman.' And I had a hard time mouthing those words."[23]

Such experiences taught the socially responsible business movement some hard lessons. The result is a new generation of activist entrepreneurs—not social activists with big

Innovative marketing
A principle of enlightened marketing that requires that a company seek real product and marketing improvements.

Sense-of-mission marketing
A principle of enlightened marketing that holds that a company should define its mission in broad social terms rather than narrow product terms.

16.2 REAL MARKETING

Dove on a Mission: "Normal Is the New Beautiful"

How do you define beauty? Flip open the latest copy of *Vogue* or *Cosmopolitan* and check out the ads for cosmetics and beauty care products. Look at the models in those ads—the classic beauties with incredibly lean, sexy figures and flawless features. Does anyone *you* know look like the women in those ads? Probably not. They're one-of-a-kind supermodels, chosen to portray ideal beauty. The ads are meant to be aspirational. But real women, who compare themselves to these idealized images day in and day out, too often come away feeling diminished by thoughts that they could never really look like that.

Unilever's Dove brand is on a mission to change all of this. Its Dove Campaign for Real Beauty hopes to do much more than just sell Dove beauty creams and lotions. It aims to change the traditional definition of beauty—to "offer in its place a broader, healthier, more democratic view of beauty." It tells women to be happy just the way they are. "In Dove ads," says one advertising expert, "normal is the new beautiful."

It all started with a Unilever study that examined the impact on women of a society that narrowly defines beauty by the images seen in entertainment, in advertising, and on fashion runways. The startling result: Only 2 percent of 3,300 women and girls surveyed in 10 countries around the world considered themselves beautiful. Unilever's research revealed that among women ages 15 to 64 worldwide, 90 percent want to change at least one aspect of their physical appearance; 67 percent withdraw from life-engaging activities because they are uncomfortable with their looks. Unilever's conclusion: It's time to redefine beauty. "We believe that beauty comes in different shapes, sizes, and ages," says Dove marketing director Philippe Harousseau. "Our mission is to make more women feel beautiful every day by broadening the definition of beauty."

Unilever launched the Dove Campaign for Real Beauty globally in 2004, with ads that featured candid and confident images of real women of all types (not actresses or models) and headlines that prompted consumers to ponder their perceptions of beauty. Among others, it featured full-bodied women ("Oversized or Outstanding?"), older women ("Gray or Gorgeous?" "Wrinkled or Wonderful?"), and a heavily freckled woman ("Flawed or Flawless?"). In 2005, the campaign's popularity skyrocketed as Dove introduced six new "real beauties" of various ethnicities and proportions, in sizes ranging from 6 to 14. These women appeared in magazines and on billboards wearing nothing but their underwear and big smiles, with headlines proclaiming, "Let's face it, firming the thighs of a size 2 supermodel is no challenge," or "New Dove Firming: As Tested on Real Curves."

In 2006, Dove took the campaign to a new level, with a groundbreaking spot in the mother of all ad showcases, the Super Bowl. This ad didn't feature curvy, confident women. Instead, it presented young girls battling self-esteem issues—not models but real girls picked from schools, sports leagues, and Girl Scout troops. In the ad, one dark-haired girl "wishes she were a blond." Another "thinks she's ugly." A pretty young redhead "hates her freckles." The ad also promoted the Dove Self-Esteem Fund, which supports, among other causes, the Girl Scouts' Uniquely Me program. It urged viewers to "get involved" at the campaignforrealbeauty.com Web site. "We want to raise awareness of self-esteem being a real issue [for a young girl]," says Harousseau. "Every single one of us can get engaged and can change the way we interact with her to increase self-esteem."

■ Unilever's Dove brand is on a mission. The Dove Campaign for Real Beauty aims to change the traditional definition of beauty.

The latest real beauty entry is the campaign's award-winning, made-for-the-Web "Dove Evolution" video, which has garnered even more impressions than the Super Bowl ad. "Evolution" shows an ordinary young woman being transformed into a beautiful poster model with a lot of help from a make-up artist and photo-editing software. The ad's endline: "It's no wonder our perception of beauty is distorted."

As the campaign has taken off, so have sales of Dove products. And calls to Unilever's consumer call center have surged, as has traffic to the campaignforrealbeauty.com Web site. Women, girls, and even men praise Dove for addressing a too-long-ignored social issue. Debora Boyda, managing partner at Ogilvy & Mather, the ad agency that created the campaign, received a phone call from an emotional father. His teenage daughter had just recovered from a four-year battle with anorexia. The father thanked her and stressed how important he thought the ad was. "That to me was the high point of what the ad achieved," says Boyda.

In addition to the positive reactions, however, the Dove Campaign for Real Beauty has also received criticism. Critics point out that the "real women" in Dove's ads are still head-turners, with smooth skin, straight teeth, and not an ounce of cellulite. Although these unretouched beauties are more realistic than supermodels, they still represent a lofty standard of beauty. Fans of the campaign counter that, compared with typical ad-industry portrayals, the Dove women represent an image of beauty that is healthy, constructive, and much closer to reality. For example, after seeing a Dove billboard in Chicago, one young woman gushed, "Most girls don't have that (supermodel) type of body and they know they won't get to that. But seeing this [Dove ad] they say, 'I can do that.'"

Other critics claim that the campaign is hypocritical, celebrating less-than-perfect bodies while at the same time selling products designed to restore them, such as firming lotions. "Any change in the culture of advertising that allows for a broader definition of beauty and encourages women to be more accepting and comfortable with their natural appearance is a step in the right direction," says noted psychologist and author Mary Pipher. "But embedded within this is a contradiction. They are still saying you have to use this product to be beautiful." Still, she concedes, "It's better than what we've had in the past."

Yvonne, a woman featured in one of the Dove ads, takes issue with the criticism. "That's like saying, why be into fashion? Women are women. We love to be the best we can be. It's not contradictory; it's just taking care of yourself." Ad executive Boyda also defends Unilever's intentions: "We are telling [women] we want them to take care of themselves, take care of their beauty," she says. "That's very different from sending them the message to look like something they're not."

Still others criticize Unilever for capitalizing on women's low self-esteem just to make a buck. But the company responds that it has created a lot more than just a series of ads. It's promoting a philosophy, one supported by a substantial advertising budget, the Dove Self-Esteem Fund, and a Web site full of resources designed to build the self-esteem of women and young girls.

To be sure, Dove does have financial objectives for its brand—most consumers understand and except that fact. And if women are not buying Dove's message about the nature of real beauty, then they aren't buying its products either. But the people behind the Dove brand and the Campaign for Real Beauty have noble motives beyond sales and profits. According to Fernando Acosta, Dove vice president of brand development, Dove's bold and compelling mission to redefine beauty and reassure women ranks well above issues of dollars and cents. "You should see the faces of the people working on this brand now," he says. "There is a real love for the brand."

Sources: See, Laurel Wentz, "'Evolution' Win Marks Dawn of New Cannes Era," *Advertising Age,* June 25, 2007, p. 1; Don Babwin, "Dove Ads with 'Real' Women Get Attention," *Associated Press Financial Wire,* July 29, 2005; Theresa Howard, "Ad Campaign Tells Women to Celebrate How They Are," *USA Today,* August 7, 2005, accessed at www.usatoday.com; Pallavi Gogoi, "From Reality TV to Reality Ads," *BusinessWeek Online,* August 17, 2005, accessed at www.businessweek.com; Patricia Odell, "Real Girls," *Promo,* March 1, 2006, p. 24; "Beyond Stereotypes: Rebuilding the Foundation of Beauty Beliefs," February 2006, accessed at www. campaignforrealbeauty.com; "Cause: Conscience Marketing. You Stand for Something. Shouldn't Your Brand?" *Strategy,* June 2007, p. 22; and information found at www.campaignforrealbeauty.com, accessed December 2007.

hearts who hate capitalism, but well-trained business managers and company builders with a passion for a cause. For example, consider Honest Tea:

> Honest Tea has a social mission. "We strive to live up to our name in the way we conduct our business," states the company's "Philoso-tea." "We do this in every way we can—whether we are working with growers and suppliers, answering our customers' questions, or trying to leave a lighter environmental footprint." It all starts with a socially responsible product, an "Honest Tea"—tasty, barely sweetened, and made from all-natural ingredients, many purchased from poorer communities seeking to become more self-sufficient. But unlike old revolutionaries like Ben and Jerry, Honest Tea's founders are businesspeople—and proud of it—who appreciate solid business training. Cofounder Seth Goldman won a business-plan competition as a student at the Yale School of Management and later started the company with one of his professors.

> Honest Tea's managers know that good deeds alone don't work. They are just as dedicated to building a viable, profitable business as to shaping a mission. For Honest Tea, social responsibility is not about marketing and hype. It goes about its good deeds quietly. A few years ago, Honest Tea became the first (and only) company to sell a Fair Trade bottled tea—every time the company purchases the tea for its Peach Oo-la-long tea, a donation is made to the workers who pick the tea leaves. The workers invest the money in their community for a variety of uses, including a computer lab for children in the village and a fund for families. Royalties from sales of Honest Tea's First Nation Peppermint tea go to I'tchik Herbal Tea, a small woman-owned company on the Crow Reservation in Montana, as well as a Native American organization called Pretty Shield Foundation, which includes foster care among its activities. However, "when we first brought out our peppermint tea, our label didn't mention that we were sharing the revenues with the Crow Nation," says Goldman. "We didn't want people to think that was a gimmick."[24]

■ Societal marketing: Today's new activist entrepreneurs are not social activists with big hearts who hate capitalism, but well-trained business managers and company builders with a passion for a cause. TeaEO Seth Goldman takes a break with workers in a fair trade tea garden in India.

FIGURE 16.3

Societal Classification of Products

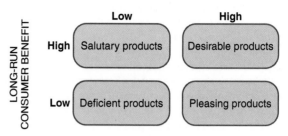

IMMEDIATE SATISFACTION

	Low	High
High	Salutary products	Desirable products
Low	Deficient products	Pleasing products

LONG-RUN CONSUMER BENEFIT

Societal marketing

A principle of enlightened marketing that holds that a company should make marketing decisions by considering consumers' wants, the company's requirements, consumers' long-run interests, and society's long-run interests.

Deficient products

Products that have neither immediate appeal nor long-run benefits.

Pleasing products

Products that give high immediate satisfaction but may hurt consumers in the long run.

Societal Marketing Following the principle of **societal marketing**, an enlightened company makes marketing decisions by considering consumers' wants and interests, the company's requirements, and society's long-run interests. The company is aware that neglecting consumer and societal long-run interests is a disservice to consumers and society. Alert companies view societal problems as opportunities.

A societally oriented marketer wants to design products that are not only pleasing but also beneficial. The difference is shown in Figure 16.3. Products can be classified according to their degree of immediate consumer satisfaction and long-run consumer benefit. **Deficient products**, such as bad-tasting and ineffective medicine, have neither immediate appeal nor long-run benefits. **Pleasing products** give high immediate satisfaction but may hurt consumers in the long run. Examples include cigarettes and junk food. **Salutary products** have low appeal but may benefit consumers in the long run; for instance, bicycle helmets or some insurance products. **Desirable products** give both high immediate satisfaction and high long-run benefits, such as a tasty *and* nutritious breakfast food.

Examples of desirable products abound. GE's Energy Smart compact fluorescent lightbulb provides good lighting at the same time that it gives long life and energy savings. Toyota's hybrid Prius gives both a quiet ride and fuel efficiency. Maytag's front-loading Neptune washer provides superior cleaning along with water savings and energy efficiency. And Haworth's Zody office chair is not only attractive and functional but also environmentally responsible:

> Let's talk about your butt—specifically, what it's sitting on. Chances are, your chair is an unholy medley of polyvinyl chloride and hazardous chemicals that drift into your lungs each time you shift your weight. It was likely produced in a fossil-fuel-swilling factory that in turn spews toxic pollution and effluents. And it's ultimately destined for a landfill or incinerator, where it will emit carcinogenic dioxins and endocrine-disrupting phthalates, the kind of hormone-mimicking nasties that give male fish female genitalia and small children cancer (or is it the other way around?). Now, envision what you might be sitting on in 2016. Actually, never mind: Office-furniture outfit Haworth already built it. It's called the Zody, and it's made without PVC, CFCs, chrome, or any other toxic fixin's. Ninety-eight percent of it can be recycled; some 50 percent of it already has been. The energy used in the manufacturing process is completely offset by wind-power credits, and when the chair is ready to retire, the company will take it off your hands and reuse its components. And the award-winning Zody's not just good for the environment, it's also good for your body. It was the first chair to be endorsed by the American Physical Therapy Association.[25]

Companies should try to turn all of their products into desirable products. The challenge posed by pleasing products is that they sell very well but may end up hurting the consumer. The product opportunity, therefore, is to add long-run benefits without reducing the product's

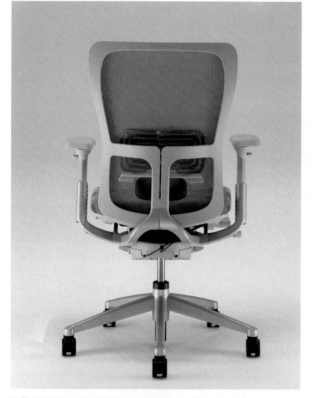

■ Desirable products: Haworth's Zody office chair is not only attractive and functional but also environmentally responsible.

pleasing qualities. The challenge posed by salutary products is to add some pleasing qualities so that they will become more desirable in consumers' minds.

Marketing Ethics

Conscientious marketers face many moral dilemmas. The best thing to do is often unclear. Because not all managers have fine moral sensitivity, companies need to develop *corporate marketing ethics policies*—broad guidelines that everyone in the organization must follow. These policies should cover distributor relations, advertising standards, customer service, pricing, product development, and general ethical standards.

The finest guidelines cannot resolve all the difficult ethical situations the marketer faces. Table 16.1 lists some difficult ethical situations marketers could face during their careers. If marketers choose immediate sales-producing actions in all these cases, their marketing behavior might well be described as immoral or even amoral. If they refuse to go along with *any* of the actions, they might be ineffective as marketing managers and unhappy because of the constant moral tension. Managers need a set of principles that will help them figure out the moral importance of each situation and decide how far they can go in good conscience.

But *what* principle should guide companies and marketing managers on issues of ethics and social responsibility? One philosophy is that such issues are decided by the free market and legal system. Under this principle, companies and their managers are not responsible for making moral judgments. Companies can in good conscience do whatever the market and legal systems allow.

A second philosophy puts responsibility not on the system but in the hands of individual companies and managers. This more enlightened philosophy suggests that a company should have a "social conscience." Companies and managers should apply high standards of ethics and morality when making corporate decisions, regardless of "what the

Salutary products
Products that have low appeal but may benefit consumers in the long run.

Desirable products
Products that give both high immediate satisfaction and high long-run benefits.

---

1. You work for a cigarette company. Public policy debates over the past many years leave no doubt in your mind that cigarette smoking and cancer are closely linked. Although your company currently runs an "if you don't smoke, don't start" promotion campaign, you believe that other company promotions might encourage young (although legal age) nonsmokers to pick up the habit. What would you do?

2. Your R&D department has changed one of your products slightly. It is not really "new and improved," but you know that putting this statement on the package and in advertising will increase sales. What would you do?

3. You have been asked to add a stripped-down model to your line that could be advertised to pull customers into the store. The product won't be very good, but salespeople will be able to switch buyers up to higher-priced units. You are asked to give the green light for the stripped-down version. What would you do?

4. You are thinking of hiring a product manager who has just left a competitor's company. She would be more than happy to tell you all the competitor's plans for the coming year. What would you do?

5. One of your top dealers in an important territory recently has had family troubles, and his sales have slipped. It looks like it will take him a while to straighten out his family trouble. Meanwhile you are losing many sales. Legally, on performance grounds, you can terminate the dealer's franchise and replace him. What would you do?

6. You have a chance to win a big account that will mean a lot to you and your company. The purchasing agent hints that a "gift" would influence the decision. Your assistant recommends sending a big-screen HDTV television to the buyer's home. What would you do?

7. You have heard that a competitor has a new product feature that will make a big difference in sales. The competitor will demonstrate the feature in a private dealer meeting at the annual trade show. You can easily send a snooper to this meeting to learn about the new feature. What would you do?

8. You have to choose between three ad campaigns outlined by your agency. The first (a) is a soft-sell, honest, straight-information campaign. The second (b) uses sex-loaded emotional appeals and exaggerates the product's benefits. The third (c) involves a noisy, somewhat irritating commercial that is sure to gain audience attention. Pretests show that the campaigns are effective in the following order: c, b, and a. What would you do?

9. You are interviewing a capable female applicant for a job as salesperson. She is better qualified than the men you just interviewed. Nevertheless, you know that in your industry some important customers prefer dealing with men, and you will lose some sales if you hire her. What would you do?

TABLE 16.1 Some Morally Difficult Situations in Marketing

system allows." History provides an endless list of examples of company actions that were legal but highly irresponsible.

Each company and marketing manager must work out a philosophy of socially responsible and ethical behavior. Under the societal marketing concept, each manager must look beyond what is legal and allowed and develop standards based on personal integrity, corporate conscience, and long-run consumer welfare. A clear and responsible philosophy will help the company deal with knotty issues such as the one faced by 3M:

> In late 1997, a powerful new research technique for scanning blood kept turning up the same odd result: Tiny amounts of a chemical 3M had made for nearly 40 years were showing up in blood drawn from people living all across the country. If the results held up, it meant that virtually all Americans may be carrying some minuscule amount of the chemical, called perfluorooctane sulfonate (PFOS), in their systems. Even though at the time they had yet to come up with a definitive answer as to what harm the chemical might cause, the company reached a drastic decision. In mid-2000, although under no mandate to act, 3M voluntarily phased out products containing PFOS and related chemicals, including its popular Scotchgard fabric protector. This was no easy decision. Since there was as yet no replacement chemical, it meant a potential loss of $500 million in annual sales. 3M's voluntary actions drew praise from regulators. "3M deserves great credit for identifying the problem and coming forward," says an Environmental Protection Agency administrator. "It took guts," comments another government scientist. "The fact is that most companies . . . go into anger, denial, and the rest of that stuff. [We're used to seeing] decades-long arguments about whether a chemical is really toxic." For 3M, however, it wasn't all that difficult a decision—it was simply the right thing to do. The company has since introduced reformulated Scotchgard products that it claims work even better than the original formula—and sell just as well.[26]

As with environmentalism, the issue of ethics presents special challenges for international marketers. Business standards and practices vary a great deal from one country to the next. For example, whereas bribes and kickbacks are illegal for U.S. firms, they are standard business practice in many South American countries. One recent study found that companies from some nations were much more likely to use bribes when seeking contracts in emerging-market nations. The most flagrant bribe-paying firms were from India, Russia, and China. Other countries where corruption is common include Iraq, Myanmar, and Haiti. The least corrupt were companies from Iceland, Finland, New Zealand, and Denmark.[27]

The question arises as to whether a company must lower its ethical standards to compete effectively in countries with lower standards. The answer: No. Companies should make a commitment to a common set of shared standards worldwide. For example, John Hancock Mutual Life Insurance Company operates successfully in Southeast Asia, an area that by Western standards has widespread questionable business and government practices. Despite warnings from locals that Hancock would need to bend its rules to succeed, the company set out strict guidelines. "We told our people that we had the same ethical standards, same procedures, and same policies in these countries that we have in the United States, and we do," says Hancock Chairman Stephen Brown. "We just felt that things like payoffs were wrong—and if we had to do business that way, we'd rather not do business." Hancock employees feel good about the consistent levels of ethics. "There may be countries where you have to do that kind of thing," says Brown. "We haven't found that country yet, and if we do, we won't do business there."[28]

Many industrial and professional associations have suggested codes of ethics, and many companies are now adopting their own codes. For example, the American Marketing Association, an international association of marketing managers and scholars, developed the code of ethics shown in Table 16.2. Companies are also developing programs to teach managers about important ethics issues and help them find the proper responses. They hold ethics workshops and seminars and set up ethics committees. Furthermore, most major U.S. companies have appointed high-level ethics officers to champion ethics issues and to help resolve ethics problems and concerns facing employees.

TABLE 16.2 American Marketing Association Code of Ethics

Ethical Norms and Values for Marketers

Preamble

The American Marketing Association commits itself to promoting the highest standard of professional ethical norms and values for its members. Norms are established standards of conduct that are expected and maintained by society and/or professional organizations. Values represent the collective conception of what people find desirable, important, and morally proper. Values serve as the criteria for evaluating the actions of others. Marketing practitioners must recognize that they not only serve their enterprises but also act as stewards of society in creating, facilitating, and executing the efficient and effective transactions that are part of the greater economy. In this role, marketers should embrace the highest ethical norms of practicing professionals and the ethical values implied by their responsibility toward stakeholders (e.g., customers, employees, investors, channel members, regulators, and the host community).

General Norms

1. Marketers must do no harm. This means doing work for which they are appropriately trained or experienced so that they can actively add value to their organizations and customers. It also means adhering to all applicable laws and regulations and embodying high ethical standards in the choices they make.

2. Marketers must foster trust in the marketing system. This means that products are appropriate for their intended and promoted uses. It requires that marketing communications about goods and services are not intentionally deceptive or misleading. It suggests building relationships that provide for the equitable adjustment and/or redress of customer grievances. It implies striving for good faith and fair dealing so as to contribute toward the efficacy of the exchange process.

3. Marketers must embrace, communicate, and practice the fundamental ethical values that will improve consumer confidence in the integrity of the marketing exchange system. These basic values are intentionally aspirational and include honesty, responsibility, fairness, respect, openness, and citizenship.

Ethical Values

Honesty —to be truthful and forthright in our dealings with customers and stakeholders.
- We will tell the truth in all situations and at all times.
- We will offer products of value that do what we claim in our communications.
- We will stand behind our products if they fail to deliver their claimed benefits.
- We will honor our explicit and implicit commitments and promises.

Responsibility —to accept the consequences of our marketing decisions and strategies.
- We will make strenuous efforts to serve the needs of our customers.
- We will avoid using coercion with all stakeholders.
- We will acknowledge the social obligations to stakeholders that come with increased marketing and economic power.
- We will recognize our special commitments to economically vulnerable segments of the market such as children, the elderly, and others who may be substantially disadvantaged.

Fairness —to try to balance justly the needs of the buyer with the interests of the seller.
- We will represent our products in a clear way in selling, advertising, and other forms of communication; this includes the avoidance of false, misleading, and deceptive promotion.
- We will reject manipulations and sales tactics that harm customer trust.
- We will not engage in price fixing, predatory pricing, price gouging, or "bait-and-switch" tactics.
- We will not knowingly participate in material conflicts of interest.

Respect —to acknowledge the basic human dignity of all stakeholders.
- We will value individual differences even as we avoid stereotyping customers or depicting demographic groups (e.g., gender, race, sexual orientation) in a negative or dehumanizing way in our promotions.
- We will listen to the needs of our customers and make all reasonable efforts to monitor and improve their satisfaction on an ongoing basis.
- We will make a special effort to understand suppliers, intermediaries, and distributors from other cultures.
- We will appropriately acknowledge the contributions of others, such as consultants, employees, and coworkers, to our marketing endeavors.

Openness —to create transparency in our marketing operations.
- We will strive to communicate clearly with all our constituencies.
- We will accept constructive criticism from our customers and other stakeholders.
- We will explain significant product or service risks, component substitutions, or other foreseeable eventualities that could affect customers or their perception of the purchase decision.
- We will fully disclose list prices and terms of financing as well as available price deals and adjustments.

Citizenship —to fulfill the economic, legal, philanthropic, and societal responsibilities that serve stakeholders in a strategic manner.
- We will strive to protect the natural environment in the execution of marketing campaigns.
- We will give back to the community through volunteerism and charitable donations.
- We will work to contribute to the overall betterment of marketing and its reputation.
- We will encourage supply chain members to ensure that trade is fair for all participants, including producers in developing countries.

Implementation

Finally, we recognize that every industry sector and marketing subdiscipline (e.g., marketing research, e-commerce, direct selling, direct marketing, advertising) has its own specific ethical issues that require policies and commentary. An array of such codes can be accessed through links on the AMA Web site. We encourage all such groups to develop and/or refine their industry and discipline-specific codes of ethics to supplement these general norms and values.

Source: Reprinted with permission of the American Marketing Association.

PricewaterhouseCoopers (PwC) is a good example. In 2002, PwC established a global ethics office and comprehensive ethics program, headed by a high-level global ethics officer. The ethics program begins with a code of conduct, called "The Way We Do Business." PwC employees learn about the code of conduct and about how to handle thorny ethics issues in comprehensive ethics training programs, which start when the employee joins the company and continue through the employee's career. The program also includes an ethics help line and regular communications at all levels. "It is obviously not enough to distribute a document," says PwC's CEO, Samuel DiPiazza. "Ethics is in everything we say and do."[29]

Still, written codes and ethics programs do not ensure ethical behavior. Ethics and social responsibility require a total corporate commitment. They must be a component of the overall corporate culture. According to PwC's DiPiazza, "I see ethics as a mission-critical issue . . . deeply imbedded in who we are and what we do. It's just as important as our product development cycle or our distribution system. . . . It's about creating a culture based on integrity and respect, not a culture based on dealing with the crisis of the day. . . . We ask ourselves every day, 'Are we doing the right things?'"[30]

REST STOP ⚡ REVIEWING THE CONCEPTS

Well—here you are at the end of your introductory marketing travels! In this chapter, we've closed with many important concepts involving marketing's sweeping impact on individual consumers, other businesses, and society as a whole. You learned that responsible marketers discover what consumers want and respond with the right market offerings, priced to give good value to buyers and profit to the producer. A marketing system should deliver customer value and improve the quality of consumers' lives.

1. Identify the major social criticisms of marketing.

Marketing's *impact on individual consumer welfare* has been criticized for its high prices, deceptive practices, high-pressure selling, shoddy or unsafe products, planned obsolescence, and poor service to disadvantaged consumers. Marketing's *impact on society* has been criticized for creating false wants and too much materialism, too few social goods, cultural pollution, and too much political power. Critics have also criticized marketing's *impact on other businesses* for harming competitors and reducing competition through acquisitions, practices that create barriers to entry, and unfair competitive marketing practices. Some of these concerns are justified; some are not.

2. Define *consumerism* and *environmentalism* and explain how they affect marketing strategies.

Concerns about the marketing system have led to *citizen action movements*. *Consumerism* is an organized social movement intended to strengthen the rights and power of consumers relative to sellers. Alert marketers view it as an opportunity to serve consumers better by providing more consumer information, education, and protection. *Environmentalism* is an organized social movement seeking to minimize the harm done to the environment and quality of life by marketing practices. The

first wave of modern environmentalism was driven by environmental groups and concerned consumers, whereas the second wave was driven by government, which passed laws and regulations governing industrial practices impacting the environment. The first two environmentalism waves are now merging into a third and stronger wave in which companies are accepting responsibility for doing no environmental harm. Companies now are adopting policies of *environmental sustainability*—developing strategies that both sustain the environment and produce profits for the company.

3. Describe the principles of socially responsible marketing.

Many companies originally opposed these social movements and laws, but most of them now recognize a need for positive consumer information, education, and protection. Some companies have followed a policy of *enlightened marketing*, which holds that a company's marketing should support the best long-run performance of the marketing system. Enlightened marketing consists of five principles: *consumer-oriented marketing, customer-value marketing, innovative marketing, sense-of-mission marketing,* and *societal marketing*.

4. Explain the role of ethics in marketing.

Increasingly, companies are responding to the need to provide company policies and guidelines to help their managers deal with questions of *marketing ethics*. Of course even the best guidelines cannot resolve all the difficult ethical decisions that individuals and firms must make. But there are some principles that marketers can choose to follow. One principle states that such issues should be decided by the free market and legal system. A second, and more enlightened principle, puts responsibility not on the system but in the hands of individual companies and managers. Each firm and marketing manager must work out a philosophy of socially responsible and ethical behavior. Under the societal marketing concept, managers must look beyond what is legal and allowable and develop standards based on personal integrity, corporate conscience, and long-term consumer welfare.

Because business standards and practices vary from country to country, the issue of ethics poses special challenges for international marketers. The growing consensus among today's marketers is that it is important to make a commitment to a common set of shared standards worldwide.

Navigating the Key Terms

Consumerism (487)
Consumer-oriented marketing (492)
Customer-value marketing (492)
Deficient products (496)
Desirable products (496)

Enlightened marketing (492)
Environmental sustainability (489)
Environmentalism (488)
Innovative marketing (493)
Pleasing products (496)

Salutary products (496)
Sense-of-mission marketing (493)
Societal marketing (496)

Travel Log

Discussing the Issues

1. In what ways do consumers believe that marketers make products more expensive to the end consumer? (AASCB: Communication)

2. Marketing's impact on society as a whole has been criticized. Discuss the issues relevant to this impact. (AACSB: Communication)

3. Discuss the types of harmful impact that marketing practices can have on competition and the associated problems. (AACSB: Communication)

4. Can an organization focus on both consumerism and environmentalism at the same time? Explain. (AACSB: Communication)

5. Define enlightened marketing and explain the five principles associated with it. (AACSB: Communication)

6. Discuss the philosophies that guide marketers facing ethical issues. (AACSB: Communication)

Application Questions

1. Consumers can contact the U.S. Consumer Product Safety Commission (CPSC) if they have a complaint about an unsafe product. Visit www.cpsc.gov to learn about this agency. Discuss a recent recall. (AACSB: Communication; Use of IT; Reflective Thinking)

2. In a small group, discuss the pros and cons of the proposed merger between the two satellite radio companies, XM Radio and Sirius. Is the merger good or bad for competition and society as a whole? (AACSB: Communication; Reflective Thinking)

3. Identify a company you believe is environmentally responsible. Does this influence your opinion of the company? Does it increase the likelihood that you'll buy from the company? Explain. (AACSB: Communication; Reflective Thinking)

Under the Hood: Focus on Technology

We are living in a time when technological advancement causes technological obsolescence. We like technological advances but they create problems. For example, you may be too young to remember 5-inch floppy computer disks or even the smaller 3-inch disks that replaced them. USB drives now replace disks and CDs as a data storage device. Most new computers can no longer access data that were stored on disks, so what will it be like five, ten, or twenty years from now? How many people have video cameras but can no longer purchase the tapes they use to record videos? Or what about a cell phone for which you can no longer purchase a charger?

1. Think of other instances of technological obsolescence and discuss them with others in your class. (AACSB: Communication; Reflective Thinking)

2. Is this obsolescence just a ploy by manufacturers to force consumers to purchase new products or is it based on consumer demand for new products? Explain your position. (AACSB: Communication; Reflective Thinking)

Focus on Ethics

Take a look at any advertisement in a women's fashion magazine and you'll see that thin is in. Fashion designers are criticized for their use of ultra thin models. However, the president of Italy's fashion-group, Marlo Boselli, is spearheading a drive to encourage designers and media to use "fuller-bodied models" and several designers agree. One designer, however, might have gone too far. To bring this issue to light in a more graphic manner, Nolita, an Italian label, pictured an emaciated, naked young woman in an ad with the line, "No. Anorexia." Some critics claim that this advertisement may encourage young women to be unhealthily thin due to all the attention it is getting. Others claim that Nolita is trying to profit from a deadly disease and scream "hypocrisy" because, like all designers in the industry, Nolita uses thin models. The Italian government has taken this issue so seriously that it developed a set of guidelines for fashion houses and magazines for using healthier-looking models. The guidelines include models providing doctors' certificates as to their health, limiting the use of models younger than 16, and banning models with body-mass indexes of 18.5 or less, which is considered to be underweight by the World Health Organization.

1. Do fashion designers and advertisements encourage young women to be unhealthily thin? (AACSB: Communication; Ethical Reasoning)

2. Create a set of guidelines for the fashion and advertising industries that promote more ethical presentations of women. (AACSB: Communication; Reflective Thinking)

Video Case

NFL

Think of the NFL and you might conjure up images of burly football players and adrenaline-filled stadiums. But the League offers fans much more than Sunday afternoons full of football. Players and teams alike consider football and community involvement to be the twin pillars of the NFL. Through more than twenty separate community programs, the NFL focuses considerable human efforts to give back to the community and encourage others to do the same.

One of the NFL's biggest efforts to engage in socially responsible behavior is its partnership with the United Way, which has been ongoing for more than 30 years. This partnership is exhibited through various types of team and player support as well as through public service ads. With help from the NFL, United Way fund-raising has skyrocketed from $800 million in 1974 to nearly $4 billion today. And the NFL benefits by building stronger relationships with fans through its community involvement.

After viewing the video featuring the NFL, answer the following questions about marketing and social responsibility.

1. Why does the NFL partner with United Way? How does that partnership impact your opinion of the League? How does it impact your interest in volunteering?

2. Make a list of social criticisms of the NFL. Then visit www.JoinTheTeam.com and read more about the NFL's outreach programs. Do these efforts alleviate any concerns you have about the League's negative impact on society?

3. By the text's definition, does the NFL practice "enlightened marketing"?

Appendix 1 Company Cases

Company Case 1

Build-A-Bear: Build-A-Memory

In the late 1990s, it was all about the dot-coms. While venture capital poured into the high-tech sector and the stock prices of dot-com start-ups rose rapidly, the performance of traditional companies paled in comparison. This era seemed like a very bad time to start a chain of brick-and-mortar mall stores selling stuffed animals. Indeed, when Maxine Clark founded Build-A-Bear Workshop in 1996, many critics thought that she was making a very poor business decision.

But as the company moves into its second decade, it has more cheerleaders than naysayers. In 2005, one retail consultancy named Build-A-Bear one of the five hottest retailers. The company hit number 25 on *BusinessWeek's* Hot Growth list of fast-expanding small companies. And founder and CEO Maxine Clark won *Fast Company's* Customer-Centered Leader Award. How does a small start-up company achieve such accolades?

THE PRODUCT

On paper, it all looks simple. Maxine Clark opened the first company store in 1996. Since then, the company has opened more than 200 stores and has custom-made more than 30 million teddy bears and other stuffed animals. Annual revenues reached $359 million for 2005 and are growing at a steady and predictable 20 percent annually. After going public in November of 2004, the company's stock price soared 56 percent in just two years. Annual sales per square foot are $600, roughly double the average for U.S. mall stores. In fact, Build-A-Bear Workshops typically earns back almost all of its investment in a new store within the first year, a feat that is unheard of in retail. And on top of all this, the company's Internet sales are exploding.

But what all these numbers don't illustrate is *how* the company is achieving such success. That success comes not from the tangible object that children clutch as they leave a store. It comes from what Build-A-Bear is really selling: the experience of participating in the creation of personalized entertainment.

When children enter a Build-A-Bear store, they step into a cartoon land, a genuine fantasy world organized around a child-friendly assembly line comprised of clearly labeled work stations. The process begins at the "Choose Me" station where customers select an unstuffed animal from a bin. At the "Stuff Me" station, the animal literally comes to life as the child operates a foot pedal that blows in the amount of "fluff" that she or he (25 percent of Build-A-Bear customers are boys) chooses. Other stations include "Hear Me" (where customers decide whether or not to include a "voice box"), "Stitch Me" (where the child stitches the animal shut), "Fluff Me" (where the child can give the animal a blow-dry spa treatment), "Dress Me" (filled with accessories galore), and "Name Me" (where a birth certificate is created with the child-selected name).

Unlike most retail stores, waiting in line behind other customers is not an unpleasant activity. In fact, because the process is much of the fun; waiting actually enhances the experience. By the time children leave the store, they have a product unlike any they've ever bought or received. They have a product that they have created. More than just a stuffed animal that they can have and hold, it's entrenched with the memory created on their visit to the store. And because of the high price-to-delight ratio (bears start as low as $10 and average $25), parents love Build-A-Bear as much as the kids.

WHY THE CONCEPT WORKS

The outside observer might assume that Build-A-Bear is competing with other toy companies or with other makers of stuffed animals, such as the Vermont Teddy Bear Company. Touting its product as the only bear made in America and guaranteed for life, Vermont Teddy Bear hand-makes all of its bears at a central factory in Vermont. Customers choose their bears through a catalog or Web site, receiving their bear in the mail without the experience of having taken part in the creation of the bear. Quality is the key selling point (reinforce by its price of $50–$100).

Although Vermont Teddy Bear has achieved great success since it sold its first bear in 1981, Maxine Clark does not consider it to be a serious Build-A-Bear competitor. "Our concept is based on customization," says Clark. "Most things today are high tech and hard touch. We are soft touch. We don't think of ourselves as a toy store—we think of ourselves as an experience." It is widely recognized in many industries that the personalization feature builds fiercely loyal customers. As evidence, Clark points out that unlike the rest of the toy industry, Build-A-Bear sales do not peak during the holiday season, but are evenly distributed throughout the year.

Although not very common in the toy industry, Maxine Clark asserts that personalization is emerging because it lets customers be creative and express themselves. It provides far more value for the customer than they receive from mass-produced products. "It's empowerment—it lets the customer do something in their control," she adds. Build-A-Bear has capitalized on this concept by not just allowing for customization, but by making it a key driver of customer value. The extensive customer involvement in the personalization process is more of the "product" than the resulting item.

Although Build-A-Bear has performed impressively, some analysts question whether or not it is just another toy industry fad, comparing the brand to Beanie Babies and Cabbage Patch Kids. Although Maxine Clark has considered this, she is confident that the Build-A-Bear product and experience will evolve as quickly as the fickle tastes of children. Although some outfits and accessories might be trendy (the company added Spiderman costumes to the bear-size clothing line at the peak of the movie's popularity), accessories assortment are changed 11 times each year.

KNOWING THE CUSTOMER

Maxine Clark has been viewed as the strategic visionary—and even the genius—who has made the Build-A-Bear concept work. But her success as CEO derives from more than just business skills relating to strategy development and implementation. Clark attributes her success to "never forgetting what it's like to be a customer." Given that Clark has no children of her own, this is an amazing feat indeed. Although understanding customers is certainly not a new concept, Clark has employed both low-tech and high-tech methods for making Build-A-Bear a truly customer-centric organization.

To put herself in the customer's shoes, Clark walks where they walk. Every week, she visits two or three of the more than 200 Build-A-Bear stores. She doesn't do this just to see how the stores are running operationally. She takes the opportunity to interact with her customer base by chatting with preteens and parents. She actually puts herself on the front line, assisting employees in serving customers. She even hands out business cards.

As a result, Clark receives thousands of e-mails each week, and she's added to the buddy lists of preteens all over the world. Clark doesn't take this honor lightly, and she tries to respond to as many of those messages as possible via her BlackBerry. Also, to capitalize on these customer communications, she has created what she calls the "Virtual Cub Advisory Council," a panel of children on her e-mail list. And what does Clark get in return from all this high-tech communication? "Ideas," she says. "I used to feel like I had to come up with all the ideas myself, but it's so much easier relying on my customers for help."

From the location of stores to accessories that could be added to the Build-A-Bear line, Build-A-Bear actually puts customer ideas into practice. As the ideas come in, Clark polls the Cub Council to get real-time feedback from customers throughout the areas where the company does business. Miniscooters, mascot bears at professional sports venues, and sequined purses are all ideas generated by customers that have become very successful additions.

The future holds great potential as more ideas are being considered and implemented. Soon, Build-A-Bear Workshops will house in-store galleries of bear-sized furniture designed by kids for kids. The company will add NASCAR to the sports licensing agreements that it currently has with the NBA, MLB, NHL, and NFL. Clark's research efforts have also lead to a current media campaign focusing on the tween segment by playing up ideas of fashion and imagination.

But growth for Build-A-Bear will come from more than just these improvements to same-store sales. Clark's expansion efforts include building a base of at least 350 stores in the United States, 120 stores in Europe, and franchising an additional 300 stores in other parts of the world. And Clark is taking action on the flood of "build-your-own" concepts that have come across her desk since the first Build-A-Bear Workshop opened. She will give much more attention to a new line of stores called "Friends 2B Made," a concept built around the personalization of dolls rather than stuffed animals. This year also sees the opening of the first Ridemakerz store, a make-and-outfit your own toy car shop that Build-A-Bear is backing with a 25 percent ownership stake.

Although Maxine Clark may communicate with only a fraction of her customers, she sees her efforts as the basis for a personal connection with all customers. "With each child that enters our store, we have an opportunity to build a lasting memory," she says. "Any business can think that way, whether you're selling a screw, a bar of soap, or a bear."

Questions for Discussion

1. Give examples of needs, wants, and demands that Build-A-Bear customers demonstrate, differentiating each of these three concepts. What are the implications of each on Build-A-Bear's actions?

2. In detail, describe all facets of Build-A-Bear's product. What is being exchanged in a Build-A-Bear transaction?

3. Which of the five marketing management concepts best describes Build-A-Bear Workshop?

4. Discuss in detail the value that Build-A-Bear creates for its customers.

5. Is Build-A-Bear likely to be successful in continuing to build customer relationships? Why or why not?

Sources: Joanne Kaufman, "After Build-A-Bear, Build-A-Toy-Car," *New York Times,* May 29, 2007; "Build-A-Bear Brings Out the Bulls," *BusinessWeek,* June 28, 2007, accessed at www.businessweek.com; Aaron Baar, "Build-A-Bear Effort Targets Tweens," *Adweek.com,* May 4, 2007, accessed at www.adweek.com; Parija Bhatnagar, "The Next Hot Retailers?" *CNNMoney.com,* January 9, 2006; Lucas Conley, "Customer-Centered Leader: Maxine Clark," *Fast Company,* October 2005, p. 54; "The Mini-Me School of Marketing," *Brand Strategy,* November 2, 2005, p. 12; Dody Tsiantar, "Not Your Average Bear," *Time,* July 3, 2005, accessed at www.time.com; Roger Crockett, "Build-A-Bear Workshop: Retailing Gets Interactive with Toys Designed by Tots," *BusinessWeek,* June 6, 2005, p. 77.

Company Case 2

Trap-Ease America: The Big Cheese of Mousetraps

CONVENTIONAL WISDOM

One April morning, Martha House, president of Trap-Ease America, entered her office in Costa Mesa, California. She paused for a moment to contemplate the Ralph Waldo Emerson quote that she had framed and hung near her desk:

> "If a man [can] . . . make a better mousetrap than his neighbor . . . the world will make a beaten path to his door."

Perhaps, she mused, Emerson knew something that she didn't. She had the better mousetrap—Trap-Ease—but the world didn't seem all that excited about it.

The National Hardware Show Martha had just returned from the National Hardware Show in Chicago. Standing in the trade show display booth for long hours and answering the same questions hundreds of times had been tiring. Yet, all the hard work had paid off. Each year, National Hardware Show officials held a contest to select the best new product introduced at that year's show. The Trap-Ease had won the contest this year, beating out over 300 new products.

Such notoriety was not new for the Trap-Ease mousetrap, however. People magazine had run a feature article on the trap, and the trap had been the subject of numerous talk shows and articles in various popular press and trade publications.

Despite all of this attention, however, the expected demand for the trap had not materialized. Martha hoped that this award might stimulate increased interest and sales.

BACKGROUND

A group of investors had formed Trap-Ease America in January after it had obtained worldwide rights to market the innovative mousetrap. In return for marketing rights, the group agreed to pay the inventor and patent holder, a retired rancher, a royalty fee for each trap sold. The group then hired Martha to serve as president and to develop and manage the Trap-Ease America organization.

Trap-Ease America contracted with a plastics-manufacturing firm to produce the traps. The trap consisted of a square, plastic tube measuring about 6 inches long and 1-1/2 inches in diameter. The tube bent in the middle at a 30-degree angle, so that when the front part of the tube rested on a flat surface, the other end was elevated. The elevated end held a removable cap into which the user placed bait (cheese, dog food, or some other aromatic tidbit). The front end of the tube had a hinged door. When the trap was "open," this door rested on two narrow "stilts" attached to the two bottom corners of the door. (See Exhibit 1.)

The simple trap worked very efficiently. A mouse, smelling the bait, entered the tube through the open end. As it walked up the angled bottom toward the bait, its weight made the elevated

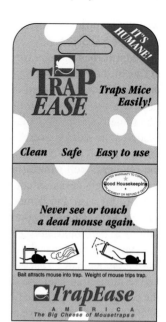

end of the trap drop downward. This action elevated the open end, allowing the hinged door to swing closed, trapping the mouse. Small teeth on the ends of the stilts caught in a groove on the bottom of the trap, locking the door closed. The user could then dispose of the mouse while it was still alive, or the user could leave it alone for a few hours to suffocate in the trap.

Martha believed the trap had many advantages for the consumer when compared with traditional spring-loaded traps or poisons. Consumers could use it safely and easily with no risk of catching their fingers while loading it. It posed no injury or poisoning threat to children or pets. Furthermore, with Trap-Ease, consumers avoided the unpleasant "mess" they often encountered with the violent spring-loaded traps. The Trap-Ease created no "clean-up" problem. Finally, the user could reuse the trap or simply throw it away.

Martha's early research suggested that women were the best target market for the Trap-Ease. Men, it seemed, were more willing to buy and use the traditional, spring-loaded trap. The targeted women, however, did not like the traditional trap. These women often stayed at home and took care of their children. Thus, they wanted a means of dealing with the mouse problem that avoided the unpleasantness and risks that the standard trap created in the home.

To reach this target market, Martha decided to distribute Trap-Ease through national grocery, hardware, and drug chains such as Safeway, Kmart, Hechingers, and CB Drug. She sold the trap directly to these large retailers, avoiding any wholesalers or other middlemen.

The traps sold in packages of two, with a suggested retail price of $2.49. Although this price made the Trap-Ease about five to ten times more expensive than smaller, standard traps, consumers appeared to offer little initial price resistance. The manufacturing cost for the Trap-Ease, including freight and packaging costs, was about 31 cents per unit. The company paid an additional 8.2 cents per unit in royalty fees. Martha priced the traps to retailers at 99 cents per unit (two units to a package) and estimated that, after sales and volume discounts, Trap-Ease would produce net revenue from retailers of 75 cents per unit.

To promote the product, Martha had budgeted approximately $60,000 for the first year. She planned to use $50,000 of this amount for travel costs to visit trade shows and to make sales calls on retailers. She planned to use the remaining $10,000 for advertising. So far, however, because the mousetrap had generated so much publicity, she had not felt that she needed to do much advertising. Still, she had placed advertising in Good Housekeeping (after all, the trap had earned the Good Housekeeping Seal of Approval) and in other "home and shelter" magazines. Martha was the company's only salesperson, but she intended to hire more salespeople soon.

Martha had initially forecasted Trap-Ease's first-year sales at five million units. Through April, however, the company had only sold several hundred thousand units. Martha wondered if most new products got off to such a slow start, or if she was doing something wrong. She had detected some problems, although none seemed overly serious. For one, there had not been enough repeat buying. For another, she had noted that many of the retailers upon whom she called kept their sample mousetraps on their desks as conversation pieces—she wanted the traps to be used and demonstrated. Martha wondered if consumers were also buying the traps as novelties rather than as solutions to their mouse problems.

Martha knew that the investor group believed that Trap-Ease America had a "once-in-a-lifetime chance" with its innovative mousetrap, and she sensed the group's impatience with the company's progress so far. She had budgeted approximately $250,000 in administrative and fixed costs for the first year (not including marketing costs). To keep the investors happy, the company needed to sell enough traps to cover those costs and make a reasonable profit.

BACK TO THE DRAWING BOARD

In these first few months, Martha had learned that marketing a new product was not an easy task. Some customers were very demanding. For example, one national retailer had placed a large order with instructions that Trap-Ease America was to deliver the order to the loading dock at one of the retailer's warehouses between 1:00 and 3:00 p.m. on a specified day. When the truck delivering the order arrived after 3 p.m., the retailer had refused to accept the shipment. The retailer had told Martha it would be a year before she got another chance.

As Martha sat down at her desk, she realized she needed to rethink her marketing strategy. Perhaps she had missed something or made some mistake that was causing sales to be so slow. Glancing at the quotation again, she thought that perhaps she should send the picky retailer and other customers a copy of Emerson's famous quote.

Questions for Discussion

1. Martha and the Trap-Ease America investors believe they face a once-in-a-lifetime opportunity. What information do they need to evaluate this opportunity? How do you think the group would write its mission statement? How would you write it?

2. Has Martha identified the best target market for Trap-Ease? What other market segments might the firm target?

3. How has the company positioned the Trap-Ease for the chosen target market? Could it position the product in other ways?

4. Describe the current marketing mix for Trap-Ease. Do you see any problems with this mix?

5. Who is Trap-Ease America's competition?

6. How would you change Trap-Ease's marketing strategy? What kinds of control procedures would you establish for this strategy?

Company Case 3

Prius: Leading a Wave of Hybrids

Americans love their cars. In a country where SUVs sell briskly and the biggest sport is stockcar racing, you wouldn't expect a small, hybrid, sluggish vehicle to sell well. Despite such expectations, Honda successfully introduced the Insight in 1999 as a 2000 model. Toyota closely followed Honda's lead, bringing the 2001 Prius to market one year later. Introducing a fuel sipper in a market where vehicle size and horsepower have reigned led one Toyota executive to profess, "Frankly, it was one of the biggest crapshoots I've ever been involved in." Considering these issues, it is nothing short of amazing that a mere five years later, the Prius is such a runaway success that Toyota Motor Sales U.S.A. president Jim Press has dubbed it "the hottest car we've ever had."

THE NUTS AND BOLTS OF THE PRIUS

Like other hybrids currently available or in development, the Prius (pronounced PREE-us, not PRY-us) combines a gas engine with an electric motor. Different hybrid vehicles employ this combination of power sources in different ways to boost both fuel efficiency and power. The Prius runs on only the electric motor when starting up and under initial acceleration. At roughly 15 mph, the gas engine kicks in. This means that the auto gets power from only the battery at low speeds, and from both the gas engine and electric motor during heavy acceleration.

Once up to speed, the gas engine sends power directly to the wheels and, through the generator, to the electric motor or battery. When braking, energy from the slowing wheels—energy that is wasted in a conventional car—is sent back through the electric motor to charge the battery. At a stop, the gas engine shuts off, saving fuel. When starting up and operating at low speeds, the auto makes no noise, which seems eerie to some drivers and to pedestrians who don't hear it coming!

The original Prius was a small, cramped compact car with a dull design. It had a total of 114 horsepower—70 from its four-cylinder gas engine and 44 from the electric motor. It went from 0 to 60 in a woeful 14.5 seconds. But it got 42 miles per gallon. Although the second-generation 2004 Prius benefited from a modest power increase, the car was still anything but a muscle car. However, there were countless other improvements. The sleek, Asian-inspired design was much better looking than the first generation Prius and came in seven colors. The interior was roomy and practical, with plenty of rear leg room and gobs of storage space.

The new Prius also provided expensive touches typically found only in luxury vehicles. A single push button brought the car to life. A seven-inch energy monitor touch screen displayed fuel consumption, outside temperature, and battery charge level. It also indicated when the car was running on gas, electricity, regenerated energy, or a combination of these. Multiple screens within the monitor also provided controls for air conditioning, audio, and a satellite navigation system. But perhaps the most important improvement was an increase in fuel efficiency to a claimed 60 miles per gallon in city driving.

A RUNAWAY SUCCESS

Apparently, consumers liked the improvements. In its inaugural year, the Prius saw moderate sales of just over 15,000 units—not bad considering Toyota put minimal promotional effort behind the new vehicle. But sales for the carbon fuel miser have increased exponentially ever since. Toyota expects to sell 175,000 Priuses in the United States alone in 2007, a 70 percent increase over 2006 sales. That makes the Prius Toyota's third-best-selling passenger car following the Camry and Corolla. Perhaps more significantly, Toyota announced that as of May, 2007, it had sold more than 1 million hybrid vehicles worldwide. More than half of those were Priuses.

The rapid increase in demand for the Prius has created a rare automotive phenomenon. During a period when most automotive companies had to offer substantial incentives to move vehicles, many Toyota dealers had no problem getting price premiums of up to $5,000 over sticker price for the Prius. By June 2004, waiting lists for the Prius stretched to six months or more. At one point, spots on dealers' waiting lists were being auctioned on eBay for $500. By 2006, the Prius had become the "hottest" car in the United States, based on industry metrics of time spent on dealer lots, sales incentives, and average sale price relative to sticker price. In fact, demand for new Priuses in 2006 was so strong that Kelley Blue Book puts the price of a used 2005 Prius with 20,000 miles at $25,970, more than $4,500 above the original sticker price.

There are many reasons for the success of the Prius. For starters, Toyota's targeting strategy has been spot-on from the beginning. It focused first on early adopters, techies who were attracted by the car's advanced technology. Such buyers not only bought the car but found ways to modify it by hacking into the Prius's computer system. Soon, owners were sharing their hacking secrets through chat rooms such as Priusenvy.com, boasting such modifications as using the dashboard display screen to play video games, show files from a laptop, watch TV, and look at images taken by a rear-view camera. One savvy owner found a way to plug the Prius into a wall socket and boost fuel efficiency to as much as 100 miles per gallon.

By 2004, Toyota had skimmed off the market of techies and early adopters. It knew that the second-generation Prius needed to appeal to a wider market. Toyota anticipated that environmentally conscious consumers as well as those desiring more fuel efficiency would be drawn to the vehicle. To launch the new Prius, Toyota spent more than $40 million dollars on advertising in consumer-oriented magazines and on TV. With the accuracy of a fortune teller, Toyota hit the nail right on the head. In the summer of 2004, gasoline prices began to rise—going to more than $2 a gallon in some locations. By the summer of 2005, gas prices had skyrocketed to more than $3 a gallon. As a result, buyers moved toward smaller SUVs, compact cars, and hybrids, while sales of full-sized SUVs such as the Ford Expedition, Chevy Tahoe, and Hummer H2 fell significantly.

In addition to Toyota's effective targeting tactics, various external incentives helped to spur Prius sales. For example, some states allow single-occupant hybrids in HOV (high-occupancy vehicle) lanes. Some cities, including Albuquerque, Los Angeles, San Jose, and New Haven, provide free parking for hybrids. But the biggest incentives have been monetary. The federal government gave huge tax breaks amounting to thousands of dollars. Some state governments gave additional tax breaks, in some cases matching the federal tax break. On top of all that, some eco-friendly companies such as Timberland, Google, and Hyperion Solutions also joined in the incentive game, giving employees as much as $5,000 toward the purchase of hybrids.

FUELING THE HYBRID CRAZE

Although Honda's Insight was the first hybrid to market in the United States, its sales were miniscule compared to those of the Prius. Honda dropped the Insight after the 2006 model year. And although Toyota's Japanese rival has had much better success with its Civic hybrid, it sold only over 20,000 units for 2006, less than one-fourth of Prius sales. The overall category of gas-electric vehicles in the United States appears to be hotter than ever, with unit sales expected to hit 345,000 for 2007, an increase of more than 400 percent from 2004. But the Prius alone commands more than 50 percent of the market and is largely responsible for category growth.

It appears that consumers like their green cars very green. Although sales of the ultra-high-mileage Prius and Civic have grown significantly each year since their introductions, less efficient (and more expensive) hybrid models such as the Honda Accord (now discontinued), the Ford Escape, and the Mercury Mariner have not fared nearly as well. Some analysts believe it is because consumers are doing the math and realizing that even with better fuel efficiency, they may not save money with a hybrid. In fact, a widely publicized report by *Consumer Reports* revealed that of six hybrid models studied, the Prius and the Civic were the only two to recover the price premium and save consumers money after five years and 75,000 miles. Even as new government-imposed standards for rating the fuel efficiency of hybrids have reduced the Prius's estimate mileage from 60 miles per gallon in city driving to a more realistic 48, this has not slowed the pace of Prius sales.

However, although car makers are scaling back on some models, almost every automotive nameplate wants a piece of the growing pie. Ford blames the lack of success with the Escape and Mariner on a bungled promotional effort. It has lofty plans to put more money into campaigns for its existing models as well as to introduce new hybrid models, including the Ford Fusion and Mercury Milan.

General Motors also has big plans, beginning with the Saturn Vue Greenline, which will have the advantage of a low $2,000 price tag for the hybrid option. GM plans to extend the Saturn hybrid line to almost every vehicle in the lineup. It also plans to introduce hybrids in other divisions, including full-size trucks and SUVs. And while Subaru, Nissan, Hyundai, and Honda are all promoting upcoming hybrid models, Audi, BMW, and numerous others are busy developing hybrid vehicles of their own.

Even with all the activity from these automotive brands, Toyota is currently the clear leader in hybrid sales and likely will be for some time to come. And with market conditions changing, Toyota is also showing its ability to adapt. In addition to the increased level of competition, the Prius faces more internal competition from new Toyota models such as the Camry. Although Toyota has ramped up Prius production to match consumer demand, government tax incentives have also dropped considerably and will eventually be phased out. Thus, Toyota is now offering modest incentives on the Prius to keep sales growing. Toyota has also introduced a "standard" version of the Prius with less standard equipment and a base price that's $1,375 less than the price of the more upscale Touring model.

All indications show that Toyota plans to maintain its hybrid momentum, doubling its line to 12 models and increasing its worldwide hybrid sales to 1 million vehicles by the early 2010s. At that time, it plans to unleash an entirely new lineup of hybrids based on next-generation lithium-ion batteries, which pack more power than the current nickel-metal-hydride batteries. If the past is any indication, Toyota's future looks very green.

Questions for Discussion

1. What microenvironmental factors affected the introduction and relaunch of the Toyota Prius? How well has Toyota dealt with these factors?

2. Outline the major macroenvironmental factors—demographic, economic, natural, technological, political and cultural—that affected the introduction and relaunch of the Toyota Prius. How well has Toyota dealt with each of these factors?

3. Evaluate Toyota's marketing strategy so far. What has Toyota done well? How might it improve its strategy?

4. GM's marketing director for new ventures, Ken Stewart, says, "If you want to get a lot of hybrids on the road, you put them in vehicles that people are buying now." This seems to summarize the U.S. automakers' approach to hybrids. Would you agree with Mr. Stewart? Why or why not?

Sources: Peter Valdes-Dapena, "Prius Still King as Hybrid Auto Sales Rise," *CNNMoney.com,* August 2, 2007; "Toyota Reportedly Eyes 1M Hybrids a Year," *CNNMoney.com,* June 12, 2007; David Kushner, "How to Hack a Hybrid," *Business 2.0,* July 13, 2006, accessed at www.money.cnn.com; Norihiko Shirouzu, "Toyota Seeks to Improve Prius and Plans to Produce Car in U.S.," *Wall Street Journal,* May 22, 2006; Peter Valdes-Dapena, "Mad Market for Used Fuel Sippers," *CNNMoney.com,* May 18, 2006; David Kiley and David Welch, "Invasion of the Hybrids," *BusinessWeek,* January 10, 2006; "Testing Toyota's Hybrid Car," *GP,* June 7, 2004; Gary S. Vasilash, "Is Toyota Prius the Most Important 2004 Model?" *Motor Trend,* November 11, 2003; John D. Stoll and Gina Chon, "Consumer Drive for Hybrid Autos Is Slowing Down, *Wall Street Journal,* April 7, 2006; "Toyota to Offer Hybrids for All Vehicle Classes by 2012," *Wall Street Journal,* April 1, 2006, accessed at www.wsj.com; Peter Valdes-Dapena, "Toyota Tops Hottest Cars in America," *CNNMoney.com,* March 18, 2006.

Company Case 4

Enterprise Rent-A-Car: Measuring Service Quality

SURVEYING CUSTOMERS

Kevin Kirkman wheeled his shiny blue BMW coupe into his driveway, put the gearshift into park, set the parking brake, and got out to check his mailbox as he did every day when he returned home. As he flipped through the deluge of catalogs and credit card offers, he noticed a letter from Enterprise Rent-A-Car. He wondered why Enterprise would be writing him.

THE WRECK

Then he remembered. Earlier that month, Kevin had been involved in a wreck. As he was driving to work one rainy morning, another car had been unable to stop on the slick pavement and had plowed into his car as he waited at a stoplight. Thankfully, neither he nor the other driver was hurt, but both cars had sustained considerable damage. In fact, he was not able to drive his car.

Kevin had used his cell phone to call the police, and while he was waiting for the officers to come, he had called his auto insurance agent. The agent had assured Kevin that his policy included coverage to pay for a rental car while he was having his car repaired. He told Kevin to have the car towed to a nearby auto repair shop and gave him the telephone number for the Enterprise Rent-A-Car office that served his area. The agent noted that his company recommended using Enterprise for replacement rentals and that Kevin's policy would cover up to $20 per day of the rental fee.

Once Kevin had checked his car in at the body shop and made the necessary arrangements, he telephoned the Enterprise office. Within 10 minutes, an Enterprise employee had driven to the repair shop and picked him up. They drove back to the Enterprise office, where Kevin completed the paperwork and rented a Ford Taurus. He drove the rental car for 12 days before the repair shop completed work on his car.

"Don't know why Enterprise would be writing me," Kevin thought. "The insurance company paid the $20 per day, and I paid the extra because the Taurus cost more than that. Wonder what the problem could be?"

TRACKING SATISFACTION

Kevin tossed the mail on the passenger's seat and drove up the driveway. Once inside his house, he opened the Enterprise letter to find that it was a survey to determine how satisfied he was with his rental. The survey itself was only one page long and consisted of 13 questions (see Exhibit 1).

Enterprise's executives believed that the company had become the largest rent-a-car company in the U.S. (in terms of number of cars, rental locations, and revenue) because of its laserlike focus on customer satisfaction and because of its concentration on serving the home-city replacement market. It aimed to serve customers like Kevin who were involved in wrecks and suddenly found themselves without a car. While the more well known companies like Hertz and Avis battled for business in the cutthroat airport market, Enterprise quietly built its business by cultivating insurance agents and body-shop managers as referral agents so that when one of their clients or customers needed a replacement vehicle, they would recommend Enterprise. Although such replacement rentals accounted for about 80 percent of the company's business, it also served the discretionary market (leisure/vacation rentals), and the business market (renting cars to businesses for their short-term needs). It had also begun to provide on-site and off-site service at some airports.

Throughout its history, Enterprise had followed founder Jack Taylor's advice. Taylor believed that if the company took care of its customers and employees first, profits would follow. So the company was careful to track customer satisfaction.

About one in 20 randomly selected customers received a letter like Kevin's. An independent company mailed the letter and a postage-paid return envelope to the selected customers. Customers who completed the survey used the envelope to return it to the independent company. That company compiled the results and provided them to Enterprise.

CONTINUOUS IMPROVEMENT

Meanwhile, back at Enterprise's St. Louis headquarters, the company's top managers were interested in taking the next steps in their customer satisfaction program. Enterprise had used the percentage of customers who were completely satisfied to develop its Enterprise Service Quality index (ESQi). It used the survey results to calculate an overall average ESQi score for the company and a score for each individual branch. The company's branch managers believed in and supported the process.

However, top management believed that to really "walk the walk" on customer satisfaction, it needed to make the ESQi a key factor in the promotion process. The company wanted to take the ESQi for the branch or branches a manager supervised into consideration when it evaluated that manager for a promotion. Top management believed that such a process would ensure that its managers and all its employees would focus on satisfying Enterprise's customers.

However, the top managers realized they had two problems in taking the next step. First, they wanted a better survey response rate. Although the company got a 25 percent response rate, which was good for this type of survey, it was concerned that it might still be missing important information. Second, it could take up to two months to get results back, and Enterprise believed it needed a process that would get the customer satisfaction information more quickly, at least on a monthly basis, so its branch managers could identify and take action on customer service problems quickly and efficiently.

Enterprise's managers wondered how they could improve the customer-satisfaction-tracking process.

EXHIBIT 1

SERVICE QUALITY SURVEY

Please mark the box that best reflects your response to each question.

	Completely Satisfied	Somewhat Satisfied	Neither Satisfied Nor Dissatisfied	Somewhat Dissatisfied	Completely Dissatisfied
1. Overall, how satisfied were you with your recent car rental from Enterprise on January 1, 2003?	☐	☐	☐	☐	☐

2. What, if anything, could Enterprise have done better? *(Please be specific)* _____

_____

3a. Did you experience any problems during the rental process?	Yes ☐ No ☐	3b.	If you mentioned any problems to Enterprise, did they resolve them to your satisfaction?	Yes ☐ No ☐ Did not mention ☐

	Excellent	Good	Fair	Poor	N/A
4. If you personally called Enterprise to reserve a vehicle, how would you rate the telephone reservation process?	☐	☐	☐	☐	☐

	Both at start and end of rental	Just at start of rental	Just at end of rental	Neither time
5. Did you go to the Enterprise office. . . .	☐	☐	☐	☐

	Both at start and end of rental	Just at start of rental	Just at end of rental	Neither time
6. Did an Enterprise employee give you a ride to help with your transportation needs. . . .	☐	☐	☐	☐

7. After you arrived at the Enterprise office, how long did it take you to:	Less than 5 minutes	5–10 minutes	11–15 minutes	16–20 minutes	21–30 minutes	More than 30 minutes	N/A
• pick up your rental car?	☐	☐	☐	☐	☐	☐	☐
• return your rental car?	☐	☐	☐	☐	☐	☐	☐

8. How would you rate the . . .	Excellent	Good	Fair	Poor	N/A
• timeliness with which you were either picked up at the start of the rental or dropped off afterwards?	☐	☐	☐	☐	☐
• timeliness with which the rental car was either brought to your location and left with you or picked up from your location afterwards?	☐	☐	☐	☐	☐
• Enterprise employee who handled your paperwork . . .					
at the START of the rental?	☐	☐	☐	☐	☐
at the END of the rental?	☐	☐	☐	☐	☐
• mechanical condition of the car?	☐	☐	☐	☐	☐
• cleanliness of the car interior/exterior?	☐	☐	☐	☐	☐

	Yes	No	N/A
9. If you asked for a specific type or size of vehicle, was Enterprise able to meet your needs?	☐	☐	☐

	Car repairs due to accident	All other car repairs/ maintenance	Car was stolen	Business	Leisure/ vacation	Some other reason
10. For what reason did you rent this car?	☐	☐	☐	☐	☐	☐

	Definitely will call	Probably will call	Might or might not call	Probably will not call	Definitely will not call
11. The next time you need to pick up a rental car in the city or area in which you live, how likely are you to call Enterprise?	☐	☐	☐	☐	☐

	Once—this was first time	3–5 2 times	6–10 times	11 or more times	times
12. Approximately how many times in total have you rented from Enterprise (including this rental)?	☐	☐	☐	☐	☐

13. Considering *all rental companies,* approximately how many times *within the past year* have you rented a car in the city or area in which you live (including this rental)?	0 times	1 time	2 times	3–5 times	6–10 times	11 or more times
	☐	☐	☐	☐	☐	☐

Questions for Discussion

1. Analyze Enterprise's Service Quality Survey. What information is it trying to gather? What are its research objectives?

2. What decisions has Enterprise made with regard to primary data collection—research approach, contact methods, sampling plan, and research instruments?

3. In addition to or instead of the mail survey, what other means could Enterprise use to gather customer satisfaction information?

4. What specific recommendations would you make to Enterprise to improve the response rate and the timeliness of feedback from the process?

Source: Officials at Enterprise Rent-A-Car contributed to and supported development of this case.

Company Case 5

Victoria's Secret Pink: Keeping the Brand Hip

When most people think of Victoria's Secret, they think of lingerie. Indeed, the Limited Brands division has done a very good job of developing this association by placing images of supermodels donning its signature bras, panties, and "sleepwear" in everything from standard broadcast and print advertising to the controversial prime-time television fashion shows that the company airs each year. Such promotional tactics have paid off for Victoria's Secret, a subsidiary of Limited Brands, which continues to achieve healthy sales and profit growth.

How does a successful company ensure that its hot sales don't cool off? One approach is to sell more to existing customers. Another is to find new customers. Victoria's Secret is doing plenty of both. One key component in its quest to find new customers is the launch and growth of its subbrand, Pink.

EXPANDING THE TARGET MARKET

Victoria's Secret launched its line of Pink products in 50 test markets in 2003. Based on very positive initial results, the company expanded the subbrand quickly to a national level. With the Pink introduction, Victoria's Secret hoped to add a new segment to its base: young, hip, and fashionable customers. "Young" in this case means 18 to 30 years of age. More specifically, Pink is geared toward college coeds. According to company spokesman Anthony Hebron, "It's what you see around the dorm. It's the fun, playful stuff she needs, but is still fashionable."

The company classifies the Pink product line as "loungewear," a very broad term that includes sweatpants, T-shirts, pajamas, bras and panties, pillows and bedding, and even dog accessories. In keeping with the "young and fun" image, the product line includes bright colors (Pink is not a misnomer) and often incorporates stripes and polka dots. The garments feature comfortable cuts and mostly soft cotton fabrics. To keep things fresh for the younger segment, stores introduce new Pink products every three or four weeks.

According to those at Victoria's Secret, in sharp contrast to the sexy nature of the core brand, Pink is positioned as cute and playful. "It's spirited and collegiate. It's not necessarily sexy—it's not sexy at all—but young, hip, and casual. It's fashion forward and accessible," said Mary Beth Wood, a spokeswoman for Victoria's Secret. The Pink line does include underwear that some might consider to be on par with standard Victoria's Secret items. But management is quick to point out that the designs such as heart-covered thongs are more cute than racy. Displays of Pink merchandise often incorporate stuffed animals and many articles display Pink's trademark mascot, a pink dog.

Originally, Pink was considered to be a store-within-a-store concept. But Pink sales have surpassed expectations. This prompted the opening of three stand-alone Pink stores in 2006. With Pink revenues expected to reach somewhere near $900 million for 2007, the company is giving far more serious consideration to expanding the presence of Pink lifestyle shops in several markets.

A KEY DRIVER OF VICTORIA'S SECRET'S FUTURE GROWTH

Limited Brands has been experiencing good times and executives have been quick to recognize that Victoria's Secret is a huge part of that success. In fact, the Victoria's Secret and Bath & Body Works divisions have accounted for roughly 70 percent of revenue (Victoria's Secret alone was good for more than 50 percent) and almost all the profit in recent years. With sales at the Express and Limited stores declining, Limited Brands recently chose to sell those two units off and focus on its stars.

But Limited Brands CEO Les Wexner is not content to let the chain rest. "The Victoria brand is really the power of the business," he says. "We can double the Victoria's Secret business in the next five years." This would mean increasing the division's sales from $5 billion to $10 billion. The umbrella strategy for achieving this growth is to continually broaden the customer base. This will include a focus on new and emerging lines, such as IPEX and Angels Secret Embrace (bras), Intimissimi (a line of Italian lingerie for women and men appealing to younger customers), and a new line of fitness apparel called VSX. Pink is a key component of this multibrand strategy.

The future of Victoria's Secret will also include a move toward bigger stores. Currently, the typical Victoria's Secret store is approximately 6,000 square feet. More than 80 percent of Victoria's Secret stores will be remodeled over the next five years, nearly doubling its average store size to 11,000 square feet. Larger stores will allow the company to give more space and attention to the store-within-a-store brands, such as Pink.

BROADENING THE CUSTOMER BASE . . . TOO FAR?

Although Victoria's Secret's introduction and expansion of Pink seems well founded, it has raised some eyebrows. As Pink's young and cute line has expanded rapidly, it has become apparent that the brand's appeal goes far beyond that of its intended target market. Some women much older than 30 have shown an interest (41-year-old Courtney Cox Arquette was photographed wearing Pink sweats). But stronger interest is being shown by girls younger than 18. Girls as young as 11 years old are visiting Victoria's Secret stores to buy Pink items, with and without their mothers.

Two such 11-year-olds, Lily Feingold and Brittany Garrison, were interviewed while shopping at a Victoria's Secret store with Lily's mother. As they browsed exclusively through the Pink merchandise, the two confessed that Victoria's Secret was one of their favorite stores. Passing up cotton lounge pants because each already had multiple pairs, both girls bought $68 pairs of sweatpants with the "Pink" label emblazoned on the derriere. The girls denied buying the items because they wanted to seem more grown up, instead saying that they simply liked the clothes.

The executives at Victoria's Secret are quick to say that they are not targeting girls younger than 18. Perhaps that is due to the backlash that retailer Abercrombie & Fitch experienced not long ago for targeting teens and preteens with sexually charged promotional materials and merchandise. But regardless of Victoria's Secret's intentions, Pink is fast becoming popular among teens and "tweens." Most experts agree that by the time children reach 10, they are rejecting childlike images and aspiring to more mature things associated with being a teenager. Called "age compression," it explains the trend toward preteens leaving their childhoods earlier and giving up traditional toys for more mature interests, such as cell phones, consumer electronics, and fashion products.

Tweens are growing in size and purchase power. Whereas the 33 million teens (ages 12 to 19) in the United States spend more than $175 billion annually (more than 60 percent have jobs), the 25 million tweens spend $51 billion annually, a number that continues to increase. But even more telling is the $170 billion per year that is spent by parents and other family members directly for the younger consumers who may not have as much income as their older siblings. Although boys are a part of this group, it is widely recognized that girls account for the majority of dollars spent. With this kind of purchasing power, as they find revenue for their older target markets leveling off, marketers everywhere are focusing on the teen and tween segments.

Although executives at Victoria's Secret deny targeting the youth of America, experts disagree. David Morrison, president of marketing research agency TwentySomething, says he is not surprised that Victoria's Secret denies marketing to teens and preteens. "If Victoria's Secret is blatantly catering to seventh and eighth graders, that might be considered exploitative." Morrison also acknowledges that the age group is drawn to the relative maturity and sophistication of the Pink label.

Natalie Weathers, assistant professor of fashion-industry management at Philadelphia University, says that Victoria's Secret is capitalizing on a trend known as coshopping—mothers and tweens shopping together. "They are advising their daughters about their purchases, and their daughters are advising them," she said. This type of activity may have been strange 20 years ago, but according to Weathers, the preteens of today are more savvy and, therefore, more likely to be shopping partners for moms. "They are not little girls, and they aren't teenagers, but they have a lot of access to sophisticated information about what the media says is beautiful, what is pretty, what is hot and stylish and cool. They are very visually literate."

In general, introducing a brand to younger consumers is considered a sound strategy for growth and for creating long-term relationships. Marketers of everything from packaged foods to shampoo use this strategy. In most cases, it's not considered controversial to engender aspirational motives in young consumers through an entry-level product line. But many critics have questioned the aspirations that Pink engenders in tweens. Specifically, to what does it make them aspire? Based on years of experience working as a creative director for ad agencies in New York, Timothy Matz calls Pink "beginner-level lingerie." Matz does not question the practice of gateway marketing (getting customers to use the brand at an earlier age). But he admits that a "gateway" to a sexy lingerie shop may make parents nervous. "Being a 45-year-old dad, do I want my 10-year-old going to Victoria's Secret?"

Thus far, Victoria's Secret has avoided the negative reactions of the masses who opposed Abercrombie & Fitche's bla-

tant marketing of thong underwear to preteens. Perhaps that's because it adamantly professes its exclusive focus on young adults. But it may also be because Victoria's Secret is not alone in its efforts to capitalize on the second-fastest-growing apparel category (loosely defined as "lingerie") by focusing on the younger target market. An almost exhaustive list of retailers are expanding their lingerie lines. Companies that specifically target the same Pink segment include the Gap, Kohl's, Macy's, and JC Penney. But the biggest competition comes from fellow mall store American Eagle Outfitters, which has rolled out its own new Aerie line of "fun lingerie." The Aerie collection of dorm-wear and intimates includes "bras, undies, camis, hoodies, robes, boxers, sweats and leggings for the AE girl. Designed to be sweetly sexy, comfortable and cozy, aerie offers AE customers a new way to express their personal style everyday, from the dormroom to the coffee shop to the classroom."

But Victoria's Secret was the first-to-market with lingerie for young adults and still has the greatest presence. And whether Pink's appeal to the preadult crowd is intentional or unintentional, many critics question the effort. Big tobacco companies have been under fire for years for using childlike imagery to draw the interest of youth to an adult product. Is Pink the Joe Camel of early adolescent sexuality? Are Pink's extreme low-rise string bikini panties the gateway drug to push-up teddies and Pleasure State Geisha thongs? These are questions that Victoria's Secret may have to address more directly at some point in the near future.

Questions for Discussion

1. Analyze the buyer decision process of a typical Pink customer.

2. Apply the concept of aspirational groups to Victoria's Secret's Pink line. Should marketers have boundaries with regard to this concept?

3. Explain how both positive and negative consumer attitudes toward a brand like Pink develop. How might someone's attitude toward Pink change?

4. What role does Pink appear to be playing in the self-concept of tweens, teens, and young adults?

Sources: Heather Burke, "Victoria's Secret to Expand Its Stores," *International Herald Tribune,* August 13, 2007; Amy Merrick, "Victoria's Secret Chief Expects Athletic Wear to Be Growth Area," *Wall Street Journal,* August 10, 2007, accessed at www.wsj.com; Ann Zimmerman, "Retailers' Panty Raid on Victoria's Secret New Lines Target Hot Fashion Lingerie," *Wall Street Journal,* June 20, 2007; Alycia De Mesa, "Marketing and Tweens," *BusinessWeek,* October 12, 2005, accessed at www.businessweek.com; Fae Goodman, "Lingerie Is Luscious and Lovely—For Grown-Ups," *Chicago Sun Times,* February 19, 2006; Vivian McInerny, "Pink Casual Loungewear Brand Nicely Colors Teen Girls' World," *City? Oregonian,* May 7, 2006; Randy Schmelzer, "Victoria's Secret Has Designs on Putting Everyone in the Pink," *PR Week,* March 13, 2006, p. 3; Jane M. Von Bergen, "Victoria's Secret? Kids," *Philadelphia Inquirer,* December 22, 2005; and www.ae.com, January 2008.

Company Case 6

Saturn: An Image Makeover

Things are changing at Saturn. The General Motors brand had only three iterations of the same compact car for the entire decade of the 1990s. But Saturn has just introduced an all-new lineup of vehicles that includes a mid-sized sport sedan, an eight-passenger crossover vehicle, a two-seat roadster, a new compact, and a hybrid SUV. Having anticipated the brand's renaissance for years, Saturn executives, employees, and customers are beside themselves with joy.

But with all this change, industry observers wonder whether Saturn will be able to maintain the very characteristics that have distinguished the brand since its inception. Given that Saturn established itself based on a very narrow line of compact vehicles, many believe that a move from targeting one segment of customers to targeting multiple segments will be challenging. Will a newly positioned Saturn still meet the needs of one of the most loyal cadres of customers in the automotive world?

A NEW KIND OF CAR COMPANY

In the early '80s, GM recognized its inferiority to the Japanese big three (Honda, Toyota, and Nissan) with respect to compact vehicles. The Japanese carmakers had a lower cost structure yet built better cars. It was during this time that GM gave the green light to Group 99, a secretive task force that resulted in formation of the Saturn Corporation in 1985.

From the beginning, Saturn set out to break through the GM bureaucracy and become "A different kind of car. A different kind of company." As the single-most defining characteristic of the new company, Saturn proclaimed that its sole focus would be people: customers, employees, and communities. Saturn put significant resources into customer research and product development. The first Saturn cars were made "from scratch," without any allegiance to the GM parts bin or suppliers. The goal was to produce not only a high-quality vehicle but one known for safety and innovative features that would "wow" the customer.

Saturn's focus on employees began with an unprecedented contract with United Auto Workers (UAW). The contract was so simple, it fit into a shirt pocket. It established progressive work rules, with special emphasis given to benefits, work teams, and the concept of empowerment. At the retail end, Saturn selected dealers based on carefully crafted criteria. It paid service personnel and sales associates a salary rather than commission. This would help create an environment that would reverse the common customer perception of the dealer as a nemesis.

Finally, in addition to customer and employee relations, Saturn focused on social responsibility. Human resources policies gave equal opportunities to women, ethnic minorities, and people with disabilities. Saturn designed environmentally responsible manufacturing processes, even going beyond legal requirements. The company also gave heavy philanthropic support to various causes. All of these actions earned Saturn a number of awards recognizing its environmentally and socially responsible actions.

When the first Saturn vehicles rolled off the assembly line on July 30, 1990, the company offered a sedan, a coupe, and a wagon in two trim levels each, all based on a single compact vehicle platform. Despite this minimal approach, sales quickly exceeded expectations. By 1992, Saturn had sold 500,000 vehicles. That same year, the company achieved the highest new-car sales per retail outlet, something that had not been done by a domestic car company for 15 years.

Indeed, customers were drawn to all the things that Saturn had hoped they would be. They loved the innovations, such as dent-resistant body panels, the high-tech paint job designed to resist oxidization and chipping longer than any in the industry, and safety features such as traction control, antilock brakes, and unparalleled body reinforcements. They were overwhelmed by the fresh sales approach that included no-haggle pricing, a 30-day return policy, and no hassle from the sales associates. The noncommissioned associates spent as much time with each customer as they wished, even going on extended test drives. Absent were typical high-pressure tactics so commonly used by automotive salespeople.

By 1994, Saturn had developed an unusually loyal customer base. The depth of customer relationships became apparent when 38,000 Saturn loyalists made the trek to company headquarters in Tennessee to celebrate the brand's first five years at the company's Spring Hill Homecoming. It was "just like Woodstock without all the patchouli oil," beamed one proud SL2 owner. The homecoming set the mold for many company-sponsored customer gatherings to follow.

During Saturn's first years of operations, the accolades rolled in. The list included "Best Car" picks from numerous magazines and organizations, along with awards for quality, engineering, safety, and ease of maintenance. But the crowning achievement occurred in 1995, as the 1,000,000th Saturn took to the road. That year, Saturn ranked number one out of all automotive nameplates on the J.D. Power and Associates Sales Satisfaction Index Study, achieving the highest score ever given by the organization. It would be the only company ever to achieve the highest marks in all three categories ranked by the satisfaction index (salesperson performance, delivery activities, and initial product quality). Saturn earned that honor for an astounding four consecutive years, and it was the only nonluxury brand to be at or near the top of J.D. Power's scores for the better part of a decade.

THE HONEYMOON ENDS

Looking back, Saturn unquestionably defied the odds. To launch an all-new automotive company in such a fiercely competitive and barrier-entrenched industry is one thing. To achieve the level of sales, the customer base, and the list of awards that Saturn achieved in such a short period of time is truly remarkable. But despite all of Saturn's initial successes, one thing has always been missing from the GM division. Profit. In the 17 years Saturn has been around, GM has sunk between $5 billion and $6 billion into the brand, without ever seeing a nickel of return on that investment. In fact, in recent years, Saturn has faced losses of up to $1 billion. One of the biggest reasons for this is that Saturn revenues flattened out quickly. Sales peaked in 1994 at 286,000 and settled in at an average of about 250,000 units per year.

The lack of continued growth may have been due partly to the fact that Saturn released no new models in the 1990s. Finally, in the 2000 model year, Saturn introduced its long-awaited mid-sized L-series with an optional V6 engine. But unlike the S-series, the L-series was a generally bland and forgettable car.

In 2002, Saturn broadened the lineup with the Vue, a compact SUV model. In January of 2003, it replaced the S-series with the Ion, a totally new compact that offered more options than before. But although these new vehicles addressed the issue of a lack of model options, they brought with them a new concern. Saturn's history of high quality and its long-cherished J.D. Power ratings began to slide. In the early part of the new millennium, not only was Saturn's J.D. Power initial-quality rating not near the top, it fell to below the industry average.

Even with the new models, Saturn's sales did not improve. In fact, they declined. This was partly due to an industry-wide downturn in sales wrought by a recession. But Jill Lajdziak, Saturn's general manager, has conceded that for too long Saturn sold utilitarian vehicles. In 2005, Saturn sales fell to a low of 213,000 units, only about 1 percent of the overall market. It seems that sales of the L-series and Vue were coming almost entirely from loyal Saturn customers who were trading up to something different, something bigger, and, unfortunately, something not as good.

A NEW KIND OF SATURN

With all that Saturn had done wrong, the fact that dealers still moved 213,000 vehicles in 2005 against competitors with better reputations and better cars testifies to the things it had done right. With its rock-solid dealer network, high purchase-process satisfaction ratings, and loyal customer base, Saturn had valuable assets to build upon. It is these core assets as well as the identified mistakes that lie at the heart of a major Saturn turnaround.

Plowing $3 billion into the Saturn line, GM hopes to perform a makeover by 2008 similar to the one it achieved with Cadillac. With the billions of dollars in annual losses at GM in recent years, the world's biggest carmaker is clearly putting faith in one of its smallest brands to help turn the tide. GM's goal is to raise Saturn's sales to 400,000 units by the end of 2007. If all goes as planned, sales could reach 500,000 not long after that. With higher prices and margins, this would represent an even greater growth in revenues and profits.

In 2006, Jill Lajdziak said, "Saturn's initial image as a smart innovation small-car company was blurred by bumps in quality and slow model turnover. We didn't grow the portfolio fast enough, and this year we're growing it in a huge way." At Vancouver's Pacific International Auto Show in the spring 2007, Lajdziak introduced one shiny new model after another: the 2007 Sky two-seat roadster, the 2007 Outlook crossover wagon, the completely redesigned 2008 Vue, the 2007 mid-sized Aura sedan, and the 2008 Astra hatchbacks. Not a single one of these models was available in January 2006.

"By the end of this year, the oldest product in a Saturn showroom will be the Sky," said Lajdziak. Of GM's investment, she remarked, "We've asked for beautifully designed products with a level of refinement, interiors, vehicle dynamics—we think we have it all. And we've got that married up with what consumers believe is the best industry experience in the marketplace." Commenting on the magnitude of the changes at Saturn, she continued, "Nobody else has ever tried to grow the portfolio and turn it over as fast as we are, maintain industry-best customer satisfaction, and obviously deliver the [profit] results all at the same time."

At the heart of this makeover is something else that is all new to Saturn: taking advantage of the GM family of vehicles and parts bins to achieve efficiencies of scale. In fact, the new Saturn models are largely rebadged Opels, GM's European division. In the future, new-product development will be carried out in a joint venture fashion between the two divisions. For a company that in the past has been known as making the "car for people who hate cars," this is a 180-degree turnaround.

"The biggest advantage to rebranding Opel vehicles as Saturns is that it doesn't mean additional costs to GM," said Guido Vildozo, a senior market analyst and industry forecaster at Global Insight Inc. "And since Opel is a kind of sporty European brand, Saturn will adopt this image too, or at least that is what they hope to happen." Some industry analysts suggest that because Saturn is such a new company, it can reposition itself more easily than other brands.

As far as positioning is concerned, GM makes it clear that with Saturn, it's not trying to make another Chevrolet. Chevrolet will remain the only GM brand positioned as "all things to all people." Along with the other GM brands, Saturn will play a niche roll and target a specific segment of the market. In fact, GM says that it's just trying to help Saturn do more of what it has been doing all along—reach the type of import-buying customer it can't reach with any of its other brands. Indeed, top executives at GM acknowledge that many Saturn owners already believe their car is an Asian brand, not a domestic one. "Saturn has always been the one brand in the GM lineup suitable for attracting import-intenders," commented one GM executive.

Although it may be too early to tell, initial indications are that Saturn's efforts are working. Sales data for early 2007, even before most of the new models rolled out, indicated that revenues were up by as much as 60 percent over the year before. "We're seeing more cross-shopping than ever," said Lajdziak. "Our retailers are seeing people they've never seen before in their showrooms, in terms of demographics and what they are trading in." But more important, Saturn sales appear to be increasing at the expense of Honda, Nissan, and Toyota. And better yet, Saturn is not cannibalizing other GM brands. In fact, not a single GM model ranks among the top 10 vehicles cross-shopped by potential Saturn buyers.

The new Saturn strategy is a big change: new positioning, new vehicles, even a new advertising agency. But despite all this change, Saturn is remaining focused on the core elements that have always made Saturn a different kind of car company: innovation, social responsibility, a focus on employees, and creating and maintaining strong customer relationships. This unique combination of change and consistency may just result in Saturn finally living up to its role as GM's import fighter.

Questions for Discussion

1. Using the full spectrum of segmentation variables, describe how GM has segmented the automobile market.

2. What segment(s) is Saturn now targeting? How is GM now positioning Saturn? How do these strategies differ from those employed with the original Saturn S-series?

3. Describe the role that social responsibility plays in Saturn's targeting strategy.

4. Do you think that GM will accomplish its goals with the "new Saturn"? Why or why not?

5. What segmentation, targeting, and positioning recommendations would you make to GM for future Saturn models?

Sources: Gregory Solman, "Saturn Asks Americans to 'Rethink' Its Brand," *Adweek,* May 21, 2007, accessed at www.adweek.com; Jeremy Cato, "Saturn's Revival Shows What the 'New GM' Can Do," *Globe and Mail,* April 5, 2007; Leslie J. Allen, "Saturn's Rebirth Vexes Chevy Dealers," *Automotive News,* February 20, 2006, p. 1; Sharon Silke Carty, "Saturn Puts Its Models Where Its Mouth Is," *USA Today,* April 21, 2006; Barbara Powell, "GM's Saturn Seeks to Shake Up Humdrum Image," *Ottawa Citizen,* April 12, 2006; David Welch, "Saturn's Second Liftoff?" *BusinessWeek,* April 13, 2006, accessed at www.businessweek.com; and "Our Story," accessed at www.saturn.com, September 2007.

Company Case 7

Converse: We Love You, Chucks!

The first Olympic basketball team wore them; they dominated the basketball courts—amateur and professional—for more than 40 years; Dr. J made them famous; Kurt Cobain died in them. What are they? Converse All Stars—more particularly the famous Chuck Taylor All Stars, known around the world as Chucks.

Compared to today's marvels of performance engineering, Chucks have always been very basic shoes. The first Chucks were introduced in 1923 as high-top canvas lace-ups with rubber-covered toes in black, white, and red with a blue label on the back that read "Made in the U.S.A." More than 80 years and 750 million pairs later, that formula has changed very little. But although they may be basic, they are also downright affordable. At a standard pair of Chuck Taylor high-tops still costs only about $38.

Converse invented basketball shoes, and by the mid-1970s, 70 to 80 percent of basketball players still wore Converse. But by the year 2000, the company's market share had dwindled to only about 1 percent of the total athletic shoe market. In 2001, Converse declared Chapter 11 bankruptcy and was purchased by an investment group. In 2003, Nike bought the wavering company for $305 million. What would a behemoth like Nike want with a bankrupt brand? Before dealing with that question, let's look at Converse's history.

THE LEGEND BEGINS

Converse was founded in 1908 in North Reading, Massachusetts, by Marquis. In 1917, the company introduced a canvas, high-top called the All Star. By 1923, it was renamed the Chuck Taylor, after a semiprofessional basketball player from Akron, Ohio. After his basketball career ended, Charles "Chuck" Taylor became an aggressive member of the Converse sales force. He drove throughout the Midwest, stopping at playgrounds to sell the high-tops to players. Some consider Taylor to be the original Phil Knight, Nike's CEO, who also started out selling his shoes at track meets from the back of his van. Throughout the '30s, '40s, '50s, and '60s, Chucks were *the* shoes to have.

By the early 1980s, with a secure hold on the basketball shoe market (it thought), Converse branched out, introducing both tennis and running shoes. This strategy appeared to be successful, helping to boost revenue in 1983 by 21 percent to $209 million. By 1986, however, Converse's fortunes had taken a turn for the worse, and it was acquired by consumer-products maker and retailer Interco for approximately $132 million. By the late 1980s, Converse had been overtaken by a host of competitors. In 1989, the top four athletic shoe companies were Nike with a 26 percent market share, Reebok with 23 percent, L.A. Gear with 13 percent, and Converse with 5 percent. Strangely, although Nike was grabbing basketball shoe sales at a rapid clip, Converse was still the official shoe of the NBA, which gave it the right to use the NBA logo in its advertising.

By 1993, an ailing Converse had changed its positioning strategy. Instead of focusing on basketball and Chucks, it aimed at capitalizing on an image that was both sexy and streetwise.

Converse launched a provocative, edgy ad campaign where nothing was sacred. And without the aid of advertising, the venerable Chuck Taylor All Star was dissociated from basketball and given new life as a fashion statement. Candy Pratts, fashion director of shoes and accessories at Vogue, used high-top canvas sneakers on models in numerous layouts. The best part, according to Candy, was that this trend didn't come from advertising but from the kids on the street.

But financially, things only continued to get worse for Converse. In 1992, it was forced to abandon the treasured "Made in the U.S.A." label, sending manufacturing to India in order to cut costs. In 1996, Converse restructured, cutting 594 jobs from a little over 2,000 and reorganizing its product line into four categories: basketball, athletic-leisure, cross-training, and children's. (Notice the absence of tennis and running shoes, although Converse had once been big in those areas.) To boost its basketball shoes, Converse put the famous Chuck Taylor signature patch on a new line of performance wear—the All Star 2000 collection.

Encouraged by the successful relaunch of the All Star 2000, the company chose to launch another new line called Dr. J 2000. A remake of a '70s shoe, it was backed by heavy advertising. Dr. J was chosen because kids told Converse researchers that Dr. J was cool enough to have a shoe. The campaign tagline was "Take the Soul to the Hole," and ads consisted of a cartoon Julius Irving performing his famous moves to a Stevie Wonder soundtrack. Unfortunately, the Dr. J 2000 produced disappointing results.

At the turn of the century, nostalgia was in. Jimi Hendrix was on Rolling Stone and the VW Beetle was a hot-selling car. Consumers were looking for "retro," so companies were redesigning classic products. And no athletic shoe was more classic than Chucks. So Converse introduced an updated black shoe, the EZ Chucks. In addition to this bump from the nostalgia trend, classic Chucks enjoyed a counterculture following that dated back to the punk rock movement of the '70s and '80s. Remembered for being worn by icons such as Joey Ramone and Kurt Cobain, Converse appealed to the antiflash group, tired of polyester and synthetic, Michael Jordan-endorsed shoes. In 2000, Converse capitalized on this segment and introduced a line of shoes for skateboarders.

NIKE TO THE RESCUE

Converse was hanging on but only by the skin of its teeth. In 2001, the company had 180 employees and sales of $185 million. But Converse had global brand recognition and strong brand equity in the market. The question was, "Could the company make the products to back up its reputation?" Enter Nike and the buyout. Initially, Nike left Converse management alone to implement its own business strategy. It also allowed Converse products to go without the famous Swoosh, unlike other acquired brands such as Bauer hockey equipment (now Nike Bauer Hockey). But Nike did help Converse with advertising dollars. In 2001, Converse had spent a mere $163,500 on promotions. In 2004, Nike poured more than $4 million into advertising for Converse, quadrupling promotional expenses in 2005 to over $17 million.

After nearly a decade-long absence from TV advertising, Converse produced ads with the tagline "The first school." The focus was on basketball, not famous players. The ads featured a basketball being dribbled and shot, but no player. They were "narrated" by Mos Def. "Before Mr. Taylor taught the world to play. Before fiberglass. Before parquet. Before the word 'doctor' was spelled with a J. And ballrooms were ball courts where renaissance played. Before the hype and before the dunk. After the rhythm, but before the funk. Before the money and before the fame. Before new and old school. Before school had a name. There was only the ball and the soul of the game." The ad ended with shots of the Converse logo or the Chuck Taylor All Star.

So, back to the original question. What does megabrand Nike do with a fading icon like Converse? Converse's new parent gave that question considerable thought. Some observers believed that Converse should become a second-tier brand. Nike could use Converse to sell millions and millions of shoes in Wal-Mart and Target—a sort of "Sam Walton meets Chuck Taylor" scenario. But Nike filled that void in 2004 when it bought Exeter Brands Group, the maker of the lower-price Starter line of apparel and footwear that now sell in Wal-Mart.

Instead, Nike has taken Converse in two different directions. After many years without the endorsement of a professional athlete, Converse is back on pro basketball courts as a performance shoe. The "Wade," named for Miami Heat superstar Dwyane Wade, hit the shelves of athletic footwear chains in 2005. Sales surpassed expectations. So much so, that Wade's original endorsement contract of $500,000 a year was renegotiated to about $10 million a year. The latest Converse basketball shoe, the DWade 2.0, was created down to the laces by Wade. And Converse is expanding the Wade line from basketball shoes to casual and active attire.

A DIFFERENT KIND OF CHUCKS?

But while Converse is currently retesting the waters of the performance shoe market, it is springboarding off the Chucks' trendy roots and doing a cannonball dive into the fashion shoe market. The current line-up of the longest-selling athletic shoe includes the classic high- and low-top canvas Chucks. But pricey variations include gold-metallic Chucks ($72), knee-high shearling-lined Chucks ($175), tattooed Chucks ($52), and customer-designed Chucks ($65 and up); there's even a "limited edition" snakeskin high-top going for $1,800. In all, Converse currently offers more than 1,000 different types of Chucks in outlets ranging from retail chains such as Foot Locker and Journeys to upscale stores such as Saks, Bloomingdales, and Barneys. This may seem like a big order for the tiny 12-person design team at Converse. But Nike has opened the doors to the parent company's creative labs, giving the team access to its designers, engineers, and biomechanics experts.

As if this weren't enough, Converse has enlisted the talent of designer John Varvatos to not only design a line of Chucks but to put the "C. Taylor" label on a full line of men's and women's clothing that includes blazers, merino wool hoodies, military coats, jeans, and T-shirts. Prices range from $55 to $125 for T-shirts and from $295 to $795 for outerwear and jackets.

But this new fashion strategy begs an interesting question. Can the affordable, antiestablishment image of the Chuck Taylor All Star survive what can only be viewed as the antithesis? Some of the Converse old guard are not pleased with Nike's new handiwork. One skate shop manager says the new Chucks don't have the same vibe as the classics. "What's happening is that Converse has now gotten greedy. That's why those are not as cool."

Converse may well lose some of its devoted Chuck Taylor customer base. But given that U.S. sales of Converse footwear hit $400 million in 2005, it may not care. That's still only 1.5 percent of the market, but it's more than double the company's revenue from just four years earlier. And sales are continuing on an upward trend. In fact, Converse and the other Nike subsidiary brands (a portfolio that includes Cole Haan, Hurley, Nike Bauer, and Nike Golf) increased their revenue by 16 percent for fiscal year 2007 to $2.3 billion. Nike CEO Mark Parker has recognized this performance specifically as a key factor in another year of record revenue, earnings, and cash flow.

Converse plans more fashion variations for the Chucks line, asserting that the possibilities are endless. And encouraged by the success of the Wade, Converse is set to launch "All Star Revolution," a shoe with the Chuck Taylor look but performance features and technology. In light of this drastic turnaround at Converse, it appears that Nike may have once again demonstrated its magic touch.

Questions for Discussion

1. What are the core, actual, and augmented product benefits of the Converse Chuck?

2. When Converse outsourced production of its shoes to India, it entered into a licensing arrangement. What are the benefits and risks of that action? Do you think it has helped or hurt the company? The brand?

3. What are the sources of brand equity for both Converse and Chuck Taylor All Stars?

4. Analyze the Nike-era direction of Converse. (a) Assess the benefits and risks of the fashion and performance strategies individually, and of the combined two-tiered approach. (b) What targeting and positioning would you recommend for the Converse brand in the future?

Sources: Nicholas Casey, "Nike's Six Subsidiaries Power 32% Profit Jump," *Wall Street Journal,* June 27, 2007; Roger O. Crockett, "Building a Megabrand Named Dwyane," *BusinessWeek,* February 12, 2007, accessed at www.businessweek.com; Stephanie Kang, "Nike Takes Chuck Taylors from Antifashion to Fashionista," *Wall Street Journal,* June 23, 2006; Michelle Jeffers, "Word on the Street," *Adweek,* May 16, 2005, accessed at www.adweek.com; Donna Goodison, "Converse Is Convert to Designer Clothing," *Boston Herald,* May 16, 2006; "From Court to Street, Converse Kicks It Double Time with Dwyane Wade Signature Product in Two-Pack," *PR Newswire,* February 13, 2006.

Company Case 8

Sony: Betting It All on Blu-Ray

The year was 1976. Sony was entering into a format war with other consumer electronics manufacturers. The victor would capture the prize of owning the consumer home video market. Wait a minute . . . are we talking about 1976 or 2006? Actually, it could be either.

In 1976, Sony introduced the first VCR for home use. Called the Betamax, it was as big as a microwave oven and cost a whopping $1,295 (more than $6,000 in today's dollars). A year later, RCA was the first of many manufacturers to introduce a VCR using a different technology: VHS. In terms of image quality, Beta was considered superior to VHS. Sony also had the advantage of being first to market. But VHS machines were cheaper and allowed longer recording times (initially, 4 hours versus Beta's 2 hours). In addition, there were far more movies available for purchase or rent in VHS than in Beta. Ultimately, consumers decided that those features were more important. VHS quickly surpassed Beta in market share, eventually wiping out Beta entirely. In 1988, after an eight-year battle, Sony surrendered by making the switch from Beta to VHS.

TWO MODERN TECHNOLOGIES: BLU-RAY VERSUS HD DVD

Today, once again, Sony finds itself at the forefront of a format war in the consumer home video market. This time, Sony is going to battle with Blu-ray technology, pitted against the competing HD DVD format. As in 1976, the two technologies are competing for dominance of the home video market, now worth more than $24 billion. Since the first DVD players appeared in 1997, many companies have been working on a format capable of delivering high-definition video to the home market. Of the many technologies under development, Blu-ray and HD DVD have emerged as the frontrunners.

Blu-ray was developed by the Blu-ray Disc Association, a coalition of companies that includes Sony, Hitachi, Pioneer, Philips, Panasonic, Samsung, LG, Sharp, Apple, HP, and a host of other companies. HD DVD was developed by a similar coalition and is being backed commercially by Toshiba, Sanyo, Kenwood, Intel, NEC, and Microsoft, among others. Although each of the technologies was developed by a coalition of companies, Sony and Toshiba appear to be the dominant players in their respective camps. And whereas Sony stood pretty much alone in pitting Beta against VHS, its Blu-ray forum has more corporate firepower in this battle.

In a situation in which the differences between the two technologies seem critical, the formats are surprisingly similar. Both use physical discs that are identical in diameter and thickness to current DVD discs. This allows the developers of the new-generation players to make them backward compatible (able to play previous generation DVDs). Additionally, each technology employs a blue laser of the same wave length, as well as similar video encoding and basic copyright protection features.

WILL THE DIFFERENCES MATTER?

Despite the similarities, the Blu-ray and HD DVD formats have notable differences. Interestingly, some of the key differences likely to affect the success of the two new DVD formats are the same features that differentiated Beta and VHS 30 years ago. Specifically, both sides are vying for image quality, disc capacity, price, and availability of content advantages. At least initially, Blu-ray captures the quality advantage in this race. However, although both Blu-ray and HD DVD produce high-definition video far superior to current DVD images, the quality difference between the two may be indistinguishable by the average human eye.

Blu-ray and HD DVD discs look identical. However, there are fundamental differences in the way the discs are put together. Each technology utilizes multiple layers of data encoding, but Blu-ray uses more layers and can store more data on each layer. Thus, Blu-ray discs can store far more information—up to 200 GB versus HD DVD's 90 GB. For home video, this means that a single Blu-ray disc can hold longer movies. "Capacity is always going to be your number-one concern," says Andy Parsons, spokesman for the Blu-ray Disc Association and senior vice president of advanced product development for Pioneer.

However, whereas capacity was critical in Beta versus VHS, many observers believe that it is less of an issue today. Both Blu-ray and HD DVD discs have more than enough capacity to hold a feature length high-definition film. But Parsons is quick to point out that the consumers really like the bonus features on DVDs, so much so that many titles now come in two-disc sets—one disc for the movie and the other for bonus features. "We . . . have learned . . . not to try to squeeze the most we can out of mid-'90s technology, which is what the HD DVD guys have done." Even so, given the compact size of modern discs, capacity may be less of an issue than it was when video tapes were the size of paperback books. Additionally, it has yet to be determined how many layers could be added to either technology, ultimately affecting data capacity.

Whether or not capacity emerges as an important feature, price could be another story. Toshiba introduced the first HD DVD players in April of 2006 at price points of $499 and $799. Pioneer introduced the first Blu-ray machine in June 2006 with a much higher price tag of $1,800. This price difference parallels that of Beta versus VHS in the 1970s. However, Andy Parsons shares some insights on the implications of Toshiba's introductory strategy:

> As part of a marketing strategy, certain companies such as Toshiba say, "Even though it costs us this much money to make this product, we're going to price it lower, even if it's below our factory cost, because taking that kind of loss up front might help to get the market populated with our product and help accelerate adoption." That kind of thinking is generally not very successful, because it ignores one very important element: You have to build awareness for the new technology before you can assume that price is an important or overriding factor.

This is why we have a natural curve with an early-adopter group of people who are very focused on technology and performance. Right now in this space, the big buzzword is 1080P progressive scan, 24 frames per second, full-resolution HD TV—this is the Holy Grail, because it's the closest you can get to a theater experience in terms of frame rates, and [it's] a hot button for people who are following this story at the consumer level.

Consumers interested in buying technology that gives them the best display or audio quality won't balk at the price. This is why our player is $1,800. We focused on getting 1080P, because that is something we knew would resonate with the initial target market, whereas the $499 strategy is probably going off in the wrong direction, because the folks who are really paying attention to this right now want the highest resolution.

But the pricing issue is likely to play much less of a role as prices drop. In just over one year after the introduction of the first machines, the cheapest players had dropped to under $300 for an HD DVD and about $450 for a Blu-ray. That price differential is getting very close to being a nonfactor.

Whereas capacity and pricing may be fizzling out as factors in this war, the issue of content availability seems to be the issue upon which battle lines are being drawn. Taking another cue from Beta versus VHS, the Blu-ray and HD DVD camps have fought to get the support of major movie studios. The idea is that the format offering more movies will have the advantage. Warner Bros. and DreamWorks are among the studios that release movies in both formats. But Blu-ray has the lead in the number of studios that release movies exclusively. Soldiers on its side include Sony Corp., Walt Disney, and Fox. Adding to its advantage of exclusive content providers, Blu-ray has also managed to nail down exclusive retail contracts. Blockbuster and BJ's Wholesale Club have agreed to stock only Blu-ray discs, and Target has agreed to sell only Blu-ray players.

The HD DVD camp has no such exclusive retailer contracts. And until recently, NBC's Universal was the only major studio providing content exclusively in HD DVD. But in August 2007, Paramount mixed things up dramatically by changing its strategy from one of dual distribution to only releasing movies in the HD DVD format. Some experts say that this move is so substantial that it alone could draw out the format war for at least two more holiday seasons. At the very least, it tempers the advantages of Blu-ray's exclusive contracts.

In the Beta versus VHS competition, image quality, capacity, price, and content availability were the deciding factors. In the current format war, only time will tell if these points of difference will have the same impact. But the HD DVD forum claims that new issues this time around will give its technology the advantage. For starters, manufacturing costs for Blu-ray will be significantly higher. (The Blu-ray camp counters that the cost difference is minimal and will disappear as volumes increase.) HD DVD software will also allow consumers to make copies of their discs to computer hard drives and portable devices. And with its iHD technology, HD DVD discs promise greater inter-activity by allowing for enhanced content and navigation, as well as fancy features such as picture-in-picture capability.

However, an additional issue could tilt the scales in favor of Blu-ray. Toshiba and HD DVD enjoyed a brief first-to-market advantage. To date, more than 400,000 HD DVD players have been sold, whereas the number of Blu-ray players sold is around 300,000. However, Blu-ray has another huge feather in its cap. Sony Playstation 3 video game consoles have the feature of playing Blu-ray movie discs. More than five million PS3 consoles have been distributed worldwide. Whereas Microsoft's Xbox 360 has an optional HD DVD upgrade, fewer than 300,000 customers have opted for the add-on. This may explain why Blu-ray discs outsold HD DVD discs by a ratio of nearly two-to-one for the first half of 2007.

WILL THE POINT BE MOOT?

Drawing comparisons to the Beta/VHS format war assumes that one of the two current competing formats will ultimately win and the other will die out. However, two other possibilities exist. First, both formats could succeed and do well. Most of the difference issues may become nonissues as the Blu-ray and HD DVD technologies evolve. Either of the technologies could adopt features of the other. Additionally, given that both formats use a physical disc that is identical in size and shape, it seems logical that dual-format players could easily emerge as a viable option. LG Electronics already has one such player on the market. Others are sure to follow. Stephen Nickerson, senior vice president at Warner Home Video, believes that both formats could easily succeed. "The [video] games industry since the early '90s has had two or three incompatible formats and it hasn't slowed the adoption of game platforms."

Alternatively, both formats might fail. Ted Schadler, analyst with Forrester Research, believes that most people are missing an important point. "The irony of this format war is that it comes at the tail end of the century-long era of physical media. While a high-definition video format does bring benefits over today's standard-definition discs, in movies as in music, consumers are moving beyond shiny discs." The consumption of all kinds of entertainment products, even television programming, has evolved dramatically since the mid-1990s. Consumers have far more options than they used to, and the dust has yet to settle on which options will dominate for any given type of product.

For home video, more customers are choosing on-demand, nonphysical media, including online video and video-on-demand television. Internet video is also spreading rapidly, with 46 percent of online consumers now watching movies via the Web. Additionally, with the success of the video iPod, major Hollywood studios are now assessing how they can make money by selling movies directly to consumers to be played on portable devices. Even Microsoft's Bill Gates has his doubts about the current DVD format war. "Understand that this is the last physical format there will ever be. Everything's going to be streamed directly or on a hard disk."

That nonphysical media options for viewing home video are rapidly emerging gives credence to those who believe that the HD format war will ultimately end in failure for both HD camps. Walter Mossberg, personal technology columnist for the *Wall Street Journal*, says, "Until the electronics and movie companies support universal high-definition players and/or universal high-definition discs, I don't recommend that most people invest in either technology. [So] why prolong a war that's bad for consumers?"

Although the dual-format alternative may seem like a logical outcome to this saga, Andy Parsons downplays it strongly. "Either a single format wins, or nobody wins." But just as speculation grows, there is still plenty of steam left in the DVD market and in the Blu-ray/HD DVD battle, enough to muster the sale of 3.7 million HD discs in the first half of 2007. Physical discs still hold many advantages over the nonphysical media. And even with the significant threat of VHS, Beta survived for eight years. On top of all that, it should be remembered that no format lasts forever. Only nine years passed between the introductions of the first home DVD and HD DVD players. So although a home video war will continue raging, the bigger questions concern who will be fighting and on what fronts.

Questions for Discussion

1. Classify the high-definition DVD market using the product life-cycle framework. Based on this analysis, what objectives and strategies should Sony and the other competitors pursue? Are any of the competitors deviating from this formula?

2. As sales of the new DVD players increase, what will happen to the characteristics of the home video market and the strategies employed by Sony and other competitors?

3. Analyze the development of Blu-ray and HD DVD according to the stages of the new-product development process.

4. Who are the current combatants in the battle for the home video market? Who will they be in five years?

Sources: Catherine Holahan, "DVD Wars: Not Over Yet," *BusinessWeek,* August 20, 2007, accessed at www.businessweek.com; Sarah McBride, "Paramount Chooses HD DVD over Blu-Ray," *Wall Street Journal,* August 21, 2007; Walter Mossberg, "Don't Get Caught in a Losing Battle over DVD Technology," *Wall Street Journal,* March 8, 2007; Beth Snyder Bulik, "Marketing War Looms for Dueling DVD Formats," *Advertising Age,* April 10, 2006, p. 20; Gary Gentile, "Beta/VHS-Like Battle Shaping Up for New High-Def DVDs," *Associated Press Worldstream,* January 6, 2006; Ann Steffora Mutschler, "The Convergence War," *Electronic Business,* May 1, 2006, p. 44; Sue Zeidler, "Hold On Tight: Going to the Store to Rent a DVD May Soon Be a Thing of the Past," *Calgary Sun,* information on Beta and VHS accessed at www.totalrewind.org.

Company Case 9

Southwest Airlines: Waging War in Philly

BATTLE STATIONS!

In March 2004, US Airways CEO David Siegel addressed his employees via a Webcast. "They're coming for one reason: They're coming to kill us. They beat us on the West Coast, they beat us in Baltimore, but if they beat us in Philadelphia, they are going to kill us." Siegel exhorted his employees on, emphasizing that US Airways had to repel Southwest Airlines when the no-frills carrier began operations at the Philadelphia International Airport in May—or die.

On Sunday, May 9, 2004, at 5:05 A.M. (yes, A.M.), leisure passengers and some thrift-minded business people lined up to secure seats on Southwest's 7 A.M. flight from Philadelphia to Chicago—its inaugural flight from the new market. Other passengers scurried to get in line for a flight to Orlando. And why not? One family of six indicated it bought tickets for $49 each way, or $98 round trip. An equivalent round-trip ticket on US Airways would have cost $200.

Southwest employees, dressed in golf shirts and khaki pants or shorts, had decorated the ticket counters with lavender, red, and gold balloons and hustled to assist the throng of passengers. As the crowd blew noisemakers and hurled confetti, Herb Kelleher, Southwest's quirky CEO, shouted, "I hereby declare Philadelphia free from the tyranny of high fares!" At 6:59 A.M., Southwest flight 741 departed for Chicago.

WAR ON!

Was Southwest's entry into the Philadelphia market worth all this fuss? After all, US Airways was firmly entrenched in Philadelphia, the nation's eighth-largest market, offering more than 375 flights per day and controlling two-thirds of the airport's 120 gates. Further, in 2004, little Southwest served a total of 58 cities and 59 airports in 30 states and was offering only 14 flights a day from Philly out of only two gates. And until its entry into Philadelphia, Southwest had a history of entering smaller, less expensive, more out-of-the-way airports where it didn't pose a direct threat to the major airlines like US Airways. Did Southwest really have a chance?

Southwest was used to that question. In 1971, when Kelleher and a partner concocted a business plan on a cocktail napkin, most people didn't give Southwest much chance. Its strategy completely countered the industry's conventional wisdom. Southwest's planes flew from "point-to-point" rather than using the "hub-and-spoke" pattern that is the backbone of the major airlines. This allowed more flexibility to move planes around based on demand. Southwest served no meals, only snacks. It did not charge passengers a fee to change same-fare tickets. It had no assigned seats. It had no electronic entertainment, relying on comic flight attendants to entertain passengers. The airline did not offer a retirement plan; rather, it offered its employees a profit-sharing plan. Because of all this, Southwest had much lower costs than its competitors and was able to crush the competition with low fares.

For 32 years, Southwest achieved unbelievable success by sticking to this basic no-frills, low-price strategy. Since it began operations in 1972, it was the only airline to post a profit every year. In 2003, just prior to taking the plunge in Philly, the company earned $442 million—more than all the other U.S. airlines *combined*. In the three prior years, Southwest had earned $1.2 billion, while its competitors *lost* a combined $22 billion. In May 2003, for the first time, Southwest boarded more domestic customers than any other airline. From 1972 through 2002, Southwest had the nation's best-performing stock—growing at a compound annual rate of 26 percent over the period. Moreover, whereas competing airlines laid off thousands of workers following the September 11 tragedy, Southwest didn't lay off a single employee. In 2004, its cost per average seat mile (CASM—the cost of flying one seat one mile) was 8.09 cents, as compared with between 9.42 to 11.18 for the big carriers.

THE MAJORS: LOW ON AMMUNITION

In the early 2000s, the major (or legacy) airlines, such as US Airways, Delta, United, American, and Continental, faced three major problems. First, "little" Southwest was no longer little. Second, other airlines, such as JetBlue, AirTran, ATA, and Virgin Atlantic, had adopted Southwest-like strategies. In fact, JetBlue and America West had CASMs of 5.90 and 7.72 cents, respectively. In 1990, discount airlines flew on just 159 of the nation's top 1,000 routes. By 2004, that number had risen to 754. As a result, the majors, who had always believed they could earn a 30 percent price premium, were finding it hard to get a 10 percent premium, if that. Third, and most importantly, the major airlines had high cost structures that were difficult to change. They had more long-service employees who earned higher pay and received expensive pension and health benefits. Many had unions, which worked hard to protect employee pay and benefits.

ATTACK AND COUNTERATTACK

US Airways had experienced Southwest's attacks before. In the late 1980s, Southwest entered the California market, where US Airways had a 58 percent market share on its routes. By the mid-90s, Southwest had forced US Airways to abandon those routes. On the Oakland-to-Burbank route, average one-way fares fell from $104 to just $42 and traffic tripled. In the early '90s, Southwest entered Baltimore Washington International Airport, where US Airways had a significant hub and a 55 percent market share. By 2004, US Airways had only 4.9 percent of BWI traffic, with Southwest ranking number one at 47 percent.

Knowing it was in for a fight in Philly, US Airways reluctantly started to make changes. In preparation for Southwest's arrival, it began to reshape its image as a high-fare, uncooperative carrier. It spread out its scheduling to reduce congestion and the resulting delays and started using two seldom-used runways to reduce bottlenecks. The company also lowered fares to match Southwest's and dropped its requirement for a Saturday-night stayover on discounted flights. US Airways also began some new promotion tactics. It launched local TV spots on popular shows to promote free massages, movie tickets, pizza, and flowers.

On the other side, Southwest knew that Philadelphia posed a big challenge. Philadelphia International was one of the biggest airports it had ever attempted to enter. And with US Airways' strong presence, it was also one of the most heavily guarded. Finally, the airport was known for its delays, congestion, bureaucracy, and baggage snafus, making Southwest's strategy of 20-minute turnarounds very difficult.

Therefore, Southwest unveiled a new promotion plan for Philly. Ditching its tried-and-true cookie-cutter approach, the airline held focus groups with local travelers to get their ideas on how it should promote its service—a first for Southwest. As a result, the airline developed a more intense ad campaign and assigned 50 percent more employees to the airport than it typically had for other launches. Southwest also recruited volunteers to stand on local street corners handing out free inflatable airline hats, luggage tags, and antenna toppers. The airline used billboards, TV, and radio to trumpet the accessibility of its low fares as well as its generous frequent flier program.

Two short years after Southwest began service to Philadelphia, the market took on a dramatically different look. Southwest had boosted daily nonstop flights from 14 to 53. It had added service to 11 new cities and quadrupled its number of gates from two to eight, with its eye on four more. The number of Southwest employees in Philly approached 200, a huge increase over its postlaunch total of less than 30.

But the external impact of Southwest's first two years in Philadelphia was a classic example of what has come to be known as "the Southwest effect"—a phenomenon in which all carriers' fares drop and more people fly. In Philadelphia, the intense competition brought on by Southwest's arrival caused airfares on some routes to drop by as much as 70 percent. In 2005, airline passenger traffic for Philadelphia International was up 15 percent over 2004. The airport attributed much of that increase to Southwest. In all, by the end of 2005, Southwest had captured 10 percent of total passenger traffic. In turn, US Airways' share fell about five percentage points.

Just as US Airways was absorbing Southwest's blows in Philadelphia, the underdog airline struck again. In May of 2005, Southwest started service to Pittsburgh, another major US Airways hub. Shortly thereafter, Southwest announced that it would also soon enter Charlotte, North Carolina, US Airways' last stronghold.

THE END OF AN ERA?

Today, although it appears that Southwest is on cloud nine, many factors are forcing the nation's most profitable air carrier to change its flight plans. First, the best-known discount airline has more competition than ever before. Upstarts such as Frontier, AirTran, and JetBlue are doing very well with Southwest's model. And they are trumping Southwest's low fares by adding amenities such as free TV and XM satellite radio at each seat.

Even the legacy carriers are now in better positions to take on Southwest's lower fares. All of the major airlines have ruthlessly slashed costs, mostly in the areas of wages and pensions. Some, like US Airways, have used bankruptcy to force steep union concessions. In fact, Southwest now has some of the highest paid employees in the industry.

At the same time that competition is becoming leaner and meaner, Southwest's cost structure is actually on the rise. Because Southwest already has such a lean cost structure, it has much less room for improvement. For example, travel agent commissions have been at zero for some time (Southwest doesn't work through agents). Sixty-five percent of Southwest customers already buy their tickets online, minimizing its call center expense. And Southwest is quickly losing another of its traditional cost advantages. For years, through some smartly negotiated fuel-hedging contracts, Southwest has enjoyed fuel prices far below those paid by the rest of the industry. But with those contracts expiring, Southwest paid 47 percent more for jet fuel in 2006 than it did in 2005. For others, the cost increase was much less.

Although Southwest still holds a cost advantage over the major carriers, the gap is narrowing. Southwest's CASM for 2006 was 8.8 cents, up 17 percent from 7.5 cents four years earlier. With the cost structure of the big airlines decreasing, Southwest's cost advantage has narrowed from 42 percent to 31 percent. With the momentum on both sides, this gap could soon be as little as 20 percent.

As these factors have quickly turned the tables on Southwest, some analysts are questioning the company's current strategic direction. "Slowly, Southwest is becoming what its competitors used to be," says industry consultant Steven Casley. Serving congested hub airports, linking with rivals through code-sharing, and hunting the big boys on their own turf are all things that Southwest would previously have never considered.

But Gary Kelly, Southwest's new CEO, defends the company's actions. "Hey, I can admit it, our competitors are getting better," says Kelly. "Sure, we have an enormous cost advantage. Sure, we're the most efficient. The problem is, I just don't see how that can be indefinitely sustained without some sacrifice." Kelly has his eye on change, in the areas of both cost and revenue. Although costs are already low at Southwest, the low-cost carrier is doing all that it can on that front. But the revenue side poses some greater potential.

In 2006, Southwest raised ticket prices, boosting average fares by 11.4 percent over 2005. But fares can only go up so much before customers stop jumping on board. So Kelly is considering many tactics that Southwest long avoided. Some of the possibilities include an assigned seating system and an in-flight entertainment system. By 2009, Southwest will be booking international flights through ATA Airlines. And in another first, Southwest has begun selling tickets through third-party distribution agents Galileo and Sabre Holdings.

When asked if he was worried about Southwest losing its competitive advantage, Mr. Kelly responded confidently:

> We know people shop first for fares, and we've got the fares. [But] ultimately, our industry is a customer-service business, and we have the best people to provide that special customer service . . . that's our core advantage. Since the U.S. Department of Transportation began collecting and publishing operating statistics, we've excelled at on-time performance, baggage handling, fewest complaints, and fewest canceled flights. Besides, we're still the low-cost producer and the low-fare leader in the United States. We have no intention of conceding that position.

By almost any measure, Southwest is still the healthiest airline in the business. However, that might be like saying it's the least sick patient in the hospital. As the industry as a whole has suffered in the post-September 11th world, Southwest's 2005 earnings of $313 million were half of what the company made in 2000. The airline's stock prices continue to hover somewhere between $11 and $14 a share, more than 30 percent below 2001 levels. As the other patients get better, Southwest can only hope that its future initiatives will be the new medicine that it needs.

Questions for Discussion

1. How do Southwest's marketing objectives and its marketing-mix strategy affect its pricing decisions?

2. Discuss factors that have affected the nature of costs in the airline industry since the year 2000. How have these factors affected pricing decisions?

3. How do the nature of the airline market and the demand for airline service affect Southwest's decisions?

4. What general pricing approaches have airlines pursued?

5. Do you think that Southwest will be able to continue to maintain a competitive advantage based on price? What will happen if others carriers match the low-price leader?

Sources: Melanie Trottman, "As Competition Rebounds, Southwest Faces Squeeze," *Wall Street Journal,* June 27, 2007; "Southwest Airlines Adds Sales Outlet," *Wall Street Journal,* May 17, 2007; Chris Walsh, "A Philadelphia Success Story: Southwest's Quick Growth in City Shows Its Potential in Denver," *Rocky Mountain News,* December 30, 2005; Susan Warren, "Keeping Ahead of the Pack," *Wall Street Journal,* December 19, 2005; Barney Gimbel, "Southwest's New Flight Plan," *Fortune,* May 16, 2005, accessed at www.money.cnn.com; "Let the Battle Begin," *Air Transport World,* May 2004, p. 9; Micheline Maynard, "Southwest Comes Calling, and a Race Begins," *New York Times,* May 10, 2004; Melanie Trottman, "Destination: Philadelphia," *Wall Street Journal,* May 4, 2004; Andy Serwer and Kate Bonamici, "Southwest Airlines: The Hottest Thing in the Sky," *Fortune,* March 8, 2004, p. 86.

Company Case 10

Zara: The Technology Giant of the Fashion World

One global retailer is expanding at a dizzying pace. It's on track for what appears to be world domination of its industry. Having built its own state-of-the art distribution network, the company is leaving the competition in the dust in terms of sales and profits, not to mention speed of inventory management and turnover. Wal-Mart you might think? Dell possibly? Although these two retail giants definitely fit the description, we're talking here about Zara, the flagship specialty chain of Spain-based clothing conglomerate Inditex.

This dynamic retailer is known for selling stylish designs that resemble those of big-name fashion houses but at moderate prices. "We sell the latest trends at low prices, but our clients value our design, quality, and constant innovation," a company spokesman said. "That gives us the advantage even in highly competitive, developed markets, including Britain." More interesting is the way that Zara achieves its mission.

FAST FASHION—THE NEWEST WAVE

A handful of European specialty clothing retailers are taking the fashion world by storm with a business model that has come to be known as "fast fashion." In short, these companies can recognize and respond to fashion trends very quickly, create products that mirror the trends, and get those products onto shelves much faster and more frequently than the industry norm. Fast-fashion retailers include Sweden's Hennes & Mauritz (H&M), Britain's Top Shop, Spain's Mango, and the Netherlands' Mexx. Although all of these companies are successfully employing the fast-fashion concept, Zara leads the pack on virtually every level.

For example, "fast" at Zara means that it can take a product from concept through design, manufacturing, and store shelf placement in as little as two weeks, much quicker than any of its fast-fashion competitors. For more mainstream clothing chains, such as the U.S.'s Gap and Abercrombie and Fitch, the process takes months.

This gives Zara the advantage of virtually copying fashions from the pages of *Vogue* and having them on the streets in dozens of countries before the next issue of the magazine even hits the newsstands! When Spain's Crown Prince Felipe and Letizia Ortiz Rocasolano announced their engagement in 2003, the bride-to-be wore a stylish white trouser suit. This raised some eyebrows, given that it violated royal protocol. But European women loved it and within a few weeks, hundreds of them were wearing a nearly identical outfit they had purchased from Zara.

But Zara is more than just fast. It's also prolific. In a typical year, Zara launches about 11,000 new items. Compare that to the 2,000 to 4,000 items introduced by both H&M and Gap. In the fashion world, this difference is huge. Zara stores receive new merchandise two to three times each week, whereas most clothing retailers get large shipments on a seasonal basis, four to six times per year.

By introducing new products with frequency and in higher numbers, Zara produces smaller batches of items. Thus, it assumes less risk if an item doesn't sell well. But smaller batches also means exclusivity, a unique benefit from a mass-market retailer that draws young fashionistas through Zara's doors like a magnet. When items sell out, they are not restocked with another shipment. Instead, the next Zara shipment contains something new, something different. Popular items can appear and disappear within a week. Consumers know that if they like something, they must buy it or miss out. Customers are enticed to check out store stock more often, leading to very high levels of repeat patronage. But it also means that Zara doesn't need to follow the industry pattern of marking products down as the season progresses. Thus, Zara reaps the benefit of prices that average much closer to the list price.

THE VERTICAL SECRET TO ZARA'S SUCCESS

Just how does Zara achieve such mind-blowing responsiveness? The answer lies in its distribution system. In 1975, Amancio Ortega opened the first Zara store in Spain's remote northwest town of La Coruña, home to Zara's headquarters. Having already worked in the textile industry for two decades, his experience led him to design a system in which he could control every aspect of the supply chain, from design and production to distribution and retailing. He knew, for example, that in the textile business, the biggest mark-ups were made by wholesalers and retailers. He was determined to maintain control over these activities.

Ortega's original philosophy forms the heart of Zara's unique, rapid-fire supply chain today. But it's Zara's high-tech information system that has taken vertical integration in the company to an unprecedented level. According to CEO Pablo Isla, "Our information system is absolutely avant-garde. It's what links the shop to our designers and our distribution system."

Zara's vertically integrated system makes the starting point of a product concept hard to nail down. At Zara's headquarters, creative teams of more than 300 professionals carry out the design process. But they act on information fed to them from the stores. This goes far beyond typical point-of-sales data. Store managers act as trend spotters. Every day they report hot fads to headquarters, enabling popular lines to be tweaked and slow movers to be whisked away within hours. If customers are asking for a rounded neck on a vest rather than a V neck, such an item can be in stores in 7 to 10 days. This process would take traditional retailers months.

Managers also consult a personal digital assistant every evening to check what new designs are available and place their orders according to what they think will sell best to their customers. Thus, store managers help shape designs by ensuring that the creative teams have real-time information based on the observed tastes of actual consumers. Mr. Ortega refers to this as the democratization of fashion.

When it comes to sourcing, Zara's supply chain is unique as well. Current conventional wisdom calls for manufacturers in all industries to outsource their goods globally to the cheapest provider. Thus, most of Zara's competitors contract manufacturing out to low-wage countries, notably Asia. But Zara makes 40 percent of its own fabrics and produces more than half of its own clothes, rather than relying on a hodgepodge of slow-moving suppliers. Even things that are farmed out are done locally in order to maximize time efficiency. Nearly all Zara clothes for its stores worldwide are produced in its remote northeast corner of Spain.

As it completes designs, Zara cuts fabric in-house. It then sends the designs to one of several hundred local co-operatives for sewing, minimizing the time for raw material distribution. When items return to Zara's facilities, they are ironed by an assembly line of workers who specialize in a specific task (lapels, shoulders, on so on). Clothing items are wrapped in plastic and transported on conveyor belts to a group of giant warehouses.

Zara's warehouses are a vision of modern automation as swift and efficient as any automotive or consumer electronics plant. Human labor is a rare sight in these cavernous buildings. Customized machines patterned after the equipment used by overnight parcel services process up to 80,000 items an hour. The computerized system sorts, packs, labels, and allocates clothing items to every one of Zara's 1,000-plus stores. For stores within a 24-hour drive, Zara delivers goods by truck, whereas it ships merchandise via cargo jet to stores farther away.

DOMESTIC MANUFACTURING PAYS OFF

The same philosophy that has produced such good results for Zara has led parent company Inditex to diversify. Its other chains now include underwear retailer Oysho, teen-oriented Bershka and Stradivarius, children's Kiddy's Class, menswear Massimo Duti, and casual and sportswear chain Pull & Bear. Recently, Inditex opened its first nonclothing chain, Zara Home. Each chain operates under the same style of vertical integration honed at Zara.

Making speed the main goal of its supply chain has really paid off for Inditex. 2005 sales grew by a whopping 21 percent over the prior year to $8.15 billion (retail revenue growth worldwide averages single-digit increases). That puts Inditex ahead of H&M in the fast-fashion category for the first time. During the same period, profits soared by 26 percent to $973 million. Most of this performance was driven by Zara, now ranked number 73 on Interbrand's list of top 100 most valuable worldwide brands.

Although Inditex has grown rapidly, it only wants more. In 2006, it opened almost 500 new stores worldwide (H&M added only 145) and has plans to do the same in 2007. It is even considering an entry into the fast-growing Indian market. Global retailers are pushing into India in droves in response to India's thirst for premium brands. Zara is very capable of capitalizing on this trend. With more than one ribbon-cutting ceremony per day, Inditex could increase its number of stores from the current 3,300 to as many as 5,000 stores in 70 countries by the end of this decade.

European fast-fashion retailers have thus far expanded very cautiously in the United States (Zara has only 25 stores stateside). But the threat has U.S. clothing retailers rethinking the models they have relied on for years. According to one analyst, the industry may soon experience a reversal from outsourcing to China to "Made in the U.S.A."

> "U.S. retailers are finally looking at lost sales as lost revenue. They know that in order to capture maximum sales, they need to turn their inventory much quicker. The disadvantage of importing from China is that it requires a longer lead time of between three to six months from the time an order is placed to when the inventory is stocked in stores. By then the trends may have changed and you're stuck with all the unsold inventory. If retailers want to refresh their merchandise quicker, they will have to consider sourcing at least some of the merchandise locally."

So being the fastest of the fast-fashion retailers has not only paid off for Zara, its model has reconfigured the fashion landscape everywhere. Zara has blazed a trail for cheaper and cheaper fashion-led mass retailers, has put the squeeze on mid-priced fashion, and has forced luxury brands to scramble to find ways to set themselves apart from Zara's look-a-like designs. Leadership certainly has its perks.

Questions for Discussion

1. As completely as possible, sketch the supply chain for Zara from raw materials to consumer purchase.

2. Discuss the concepts of horizontal and vertical conflict as they relate to Zara.

3. Which type of vertical marketing system does Zara employ? List all the benefits that Zara receives by having adopted this system.

4. Does Zara experience disadvantages from its "fast-fashion" distribution system? Are these disadvantages offset by the advantages?

5. How does Zara add value for the customer through major logistics functions?

Sources: Lisa Berwin, "Zara Weighs a Push into India as Market Hots Up," *Retail Week,* August 3, 2007, accessed at www.retail-week.com; "The Future of Fast Fashion," *Economist,* June 18, 2005, accessed at www.economist.com; Rachel Tiplady, "Zara: Taking the Lead in Fast Fashion," *BusinessWeek,* April 4, 2006, accessed at www.business-week.com; John Tagliabue, "A Rival to Gap that Operates Like Dell," *New York Times,* May 30, 2003; Elizabeth Nash, "Dressed for Success," *Independent,* March 31, 2006; Parija Bhatnagar, "Is 'Made in U.S.A.' Back in Vogue?" *CNNMoney.com,* March 1, 2006; Sarah Mower, "The Zara Phenomenon," *Evening Standard,* January 13, 2006; and www.inditex.com, accessed September 2007.

Company Case 11

Peapod: Thriving in the World of Online Groceries

After years of marketing consumer products for both Procter & Gamble and Kraft Foods, Andrew Parkinson was ready for a change. His brother Thomas, who owned a software company, was also ready for something new. The two decided to partner and enter the online grocery business. Given that the Internet grocery business has produced a high number of casualties, it may seem that venture was a suicide mission. But this case is very different from that of other online grocery companies. Andrew and Thomas Parkinson made their decision to start a company selling groceries online in 1989, years before the Internet and the World Wide Web would become available to the public. Today, not only is their company, Peapod LLC, still in business, it is the leading online grocery retailer.

FROM IDEA TO REALITY

For decades, the retail grocery industry has been characterized by fierce competition, low margins, and powerful chains. Their vision included giving customers the ability to place orders from their homes at any hour of the day, have the orders hand assembled and then have them delivered to customers' homes, even to be placed on the kitchen counter if desired.

Aspiring to succeed in the online grocery business in 1989 was indeed a pioneering venture. At that time, the general public had no concept of online communications. Peapod had to supply customers with a modem and software that would allow their home PCs to dial in and communicate with the company system. Given that most customers had never used a modem, they had to be taught how to do that as well. In the first few years of operations, Peapod focused exclusively on the metro Chicago area. Andrew and Thomas took care of all the aspects of running the business, from selling the service to packing orders and delivering them in their own cars.

From the beginning, Andrew and Thomas settled on a concept that would serve as the foundation for their business model: partnering with existing grocery chains. Rather than trying to tackle the challenges of online order fulfillment along with those of starting a free-standing grocery chain, they chose to serve as the order-and-delivery service for existing chains. Today, as a wholly owned subsidiary of Netherlands-based Royal Ahold, the parent company of Stop & Shop and Giant, Peapod continues to follow its original model.

Peapod has come a long way since its humble beginnings. On February 7, 2007, Andrew and Thomas Parkinson revisited their roots by delivering a grocery order—Peapod's 10 millionth order. "It's staggering to consider how much food Peapod has delivered since its inception," said Thomas. "Peapod's delivery of 25 million bananas could be strung together from San Francisco to Washington, D.C. We have sold enough milk to fill 21 Olympic-sized pools and have sold nearly 2 million pounds of coffee. That's a lot of caffeinated people!"

Peapod assembles orders in one of two 75,000-square-foot warehouses, and in more than a dozen 7,500-square-foot "warerooms" located adjacent to partner stores. Although Peapod is far from providing service on a national level, the company covers 1,500 zip codes containing almost 13,000,000 households. Peapod has grown conservatively, yet it has averaged 25 percent annual revenue increases, a phenomenal feat in an industry characterized by single-digit growth rates.

PROVIDING CUSTOMER VALUE BY OVERCOMING NEGATIVE PERCEPTIONS

Customers most commonly cite convenience as their reason for purchasing groceries online. Many find the benefit of grocery shopping at any hour of the day from the comfort of home or the office very motivating. Yet many potential customers perceive numerous disadvantages that prevent them from ever trying online grocery services. The Parkinson brothers have always focused on providing customer value by addressing the following commonly perceived disadvantages.

Ordering on the Web is too complex and time consuming. Retail experts have widely recognized that the Internet is not well suited to shopping for and purchasing low-dollar, routinely purchased consumables. If it takes customers 30 minutes online to find the type and brand of bread, milk, cheese, and apples they want, they might as well just stop by the store on the way home from work.

The basic Peapod system requires an initial account setup that includes establishing a shopping list of commonly purchased items. Given that most people buy many of the same items regularly, this list becomes the basis for each order. The customer's core list is flexible to additions and deletions. As customers purchase new items, the Peapod system remembers those items and makes them available for future purchases without searching. Being able to quickly find an item through a keyword search can be much easier than trying to locate the same item in the aisles of a grocery store.

Finding new items is enhanced by Express Shop. This feature lets shoppers jot down an entire list and then provides matching products instantly. Any resulting products being compared can be sorted by price, nutritional content (sodium, fat, carbs, etc.), or even best-seller status. In a similar manner, shoppers can also personalize their lists around dietary needs or recipe requirements. To keep searching and browsing simple, Peapod offers a maximum of 8,000 items, as opposed to the 30,000 to 40,000 items available in the typical partner store.

People often do not know what they want until they browse the store. Even as customers go to the store with shopping lists, they often discover things as they walk the aisles. The Peapod Web site approximates in-store shopping by letting the customer browse for products in a traditional grocery store aisle format if they choose. Additionally, a "New Arrivals" icon highlights new products that customers might not think of before shopping. Shoppers can also easily find hundreds of weekly specials by clicking on the "Specials" tab or by looking for red tags in normal browsing.

The quality of the delivered products might not be as good. The vast majority of food purchased in grocery stores is prepackaged. However, a commonly cited reason consumers give for not getting groceries online is that an unknown, unseen person will select their produce, meats, and bakery items. E-marketing analyst David Berkowitz says, "People who go in and feel fruit have no idea what they're doing, but it's still so important for them."

However, Peapod believes that it can do a better job of selecting foods and of transporting those foods in a way that maximizes quality. It trains order assemblers so that they know what to look for in a piece of produce. "I would pick your fruit the way I pick fruit for myself," said one trained shopper. Many customers don't stop to consider that the interior of a car on a hot summer day can wreak havoc on fresh produce, dairy products, and frozen foods. But Peapod equips its facilities and delivery vans with multiple climate-controlled zones, so the rotisserie chicken stays warm, the produce stays cool, and the ice cream stays rock hard.

Online groceries are priced too high. For the most part, Peapod's grocery prices match those found in partner stores. Peapod adds a modest flat fee that covers the cost of delivery: $6.95 for orders greater than $100 and $9.95 for orders between $50 and $100 (orders have a $50 minimum). Moreover, Peapod offers easily located "in-store" specials and drivers accept all manufacturer coupons and credits them to the next order.

Waiting to meet the delivery person is too inconvenient. When considering Peapod's delivery option, many potential customers envision spending hours "waiting for the cable installer." In actuality, customers can choose a two-hour delivery window that is convenient for them. What's more, they place orders seven days a week, as soon as the next day or as far as two weeks ahead. For people living in high-rise apartments, orders can be left with the doorman at any time.

THE COMPETITIVE LANDSCAPE

The first thing that comes to mind when most people think of online groceries is the string of high-profile dot-com failures of the late 1990s. The most notable failure was Webvan in California, a company that burned through $830 million in venture capital and declared bankruptcy in 2001, without ever turning a profit. Experts now agree that Webvan grew too fast and took on too many of the aspects of the business without first establishing a foundation.

Contrary to Webvan, however, other online grocers have been slowly and quietly expanding. Peapod's growth model allowed the company not only to achieve stability before the dot-com blitz of online grocers, but to weather the dot-com meltdown and emerge strong and profitable. The current list of notable online grocers consists almost entirely of existing grocery chain companies that have ventured into the online sector. The list includes Safeway, Albertson's, Pathmark, Shoprite, Waldbaum's, Roche Bros., and Sam's Club. New York-based Freshdirect.com is the only other online grocer without a brick-and-mortar chain to have achieved measurable success.

Each of these companies has rolled out services on a regional basis. The regions generally correspond to where chains have a brick-and-mortar presence. Companies are also wisely expanding in urban areas that are densely populated with potential customers that fit the proper profile: affluent, Internet-savvy, time-pressed consumers. This includes high-income households that are also two-paycheck or single-parent households. As a secondary market, people with physical disabilities are attracted to grocery delivery service.

Because the existing Internet grocers serve only select regional areas, they don't often compete with each other. Peapod's most notable competitors are Safeway in the Washington, D.C./Baltimore area, Roche Bros. in Boston and Cape Cod, and Freshdirect in Westchester County, New York. These companies offer many comparable features. But each company also has points of differentiation. For example, Roche Bros. does not have a minimum order price, offers 20,000 items, and does not allow tipping (Peapod encourages it).

Such differences don't concern Peapod much. In any given market, Peapod faces at most one other formidable competitor. And although some experts question whether or not a single metro area can support two major online grocers, Peapod believes that there is plenty of business to go around. Peapod spokesperson Elana Margolis welcomes competition. "It validates the service. People are recognizing what we've realized all along, that people want options," she says. "It's a big enough market I think it can hold more than one grocery delivery business."

The online grocery industry is indeed growing. According to one analyst, online grocery sales were $2.4 billion in 2004, just 0.4 percent of the total $570 billion grocery market. However, by 2008, overall online grocery sales are expected to hit $6.5 billion. Although that still represents only about 1 percent of the total market, it amounts to an annual growth rate of 42 percent, 10 times that of the overall industry. Safeway estimates that Internet sales could account for up to 5 percent of its total sales within a few years, without significant cannibalization of in-store sales.

If the past is any predictor of success, Peapod has a bright future. However, as overall sales for online grocers continue to grow, Peapod and its competitors will likely face emerging challenges. According to University of Michigan professor Claes Fornell, "more Internet shopping options have given consumers the upper hand in brick-and-mortar retail stores. [Consumers] are more powerful relative to the seller than they ever have been in the past. There is more pressure on the company to try to satisfy the customer." Although Peapod continues to meet the challenges of growing its business today, it will likely have to deal with a rising bar in the future.

Questions for Discussion

1. Visit www.Peapod.com and click on the "Groceries for your home" link. Enter a Chicago-area zip code (say 60602). Compare the Peapod customer experience to a brick-and-mortar grocery shopping experience. What benefits does a customer receive by using Peapod? What are the disadvantages?

2. Using the various characteristics for classifying types of retailers, develop a profile of Peapod.

3. Who does Peapod target? How does it position itself in this market? Does its marketing mix support this targeting and positioning?

4. Apply the wheel-of-retailing concept to the entire grocery industry, defining Peapod's role.

5. What does the future hold for Peapod, in both the short term and the long term?

Sources: "Peapod Is in the "Growth"ery Business," February 7, 2007, accessed at www.peapod.com; Steve Adams, "Fresh Rivalry," *Patriot Ledger,* October 29, 2005; Dina ElBoghdady, "Safeway Rolls Out Online Shopping," *Washington Post,* September 19, 2005; Jen Haberkorn, "Going the Extra Smile," *Washington Times,* November 16, 2005; Bruce Mohl, "Like Peapod, Roche Bros. Now Aims to Deliver," *Boston Globe,* October 23, 2005; Jason Straziuso, "After Flashy Failures, Online Groceries Quietly Grow," *CNNMoney.com,* May 19, 2004; Eileen Gunn, "Picking Up an Online Grocery Order," *Wall Street Journal,* April 6, 2006; "Company Information," accessed at www. peapod.com, December 2007.

Company Case 12

Burger King: Promoting a Food Fight

PASS THE MUSTARD

In early 2004, as Burger King's CEO Brad Blum reviewed the company's 2003 performance, he decided once again that he had to do something to spice up BK's bland performance. Industry leader McDonald's had just reported a 9 percent sales jump in 2003 to a total of $22.1 billion, whereas number-two BK's U.S. sales had *slipped* about 5 percent to $7.9 billion. Further, number-three Wendy's sales had spiked 11 percent to $7.4 billion, putting it in position to overtake BK.

Blum surprised the fast-food industry by abruptly firing the firm's advertising agency, Young & Rubicam (Y&R) and awarding its global creative account to a small, Miami-based, upstart firm Crispin Porter + Bogusky (Crispin). The switch marked the fifth time in four years that BK had moved its account! Ad agency Y&R had gotten the $350 million BK account only 10 months earlier. To help revive BK's sales, it had developed a campaign with the theme "The Fire's Ready," which focused on BK's flame-broiled versus frying cooking method. However, observers found the message to be flat and uninspiring, and the sales decline sealed Y&R's fate.

With the move to Crispin, there was no shortage of speculation that the fickle Burger King would soon move again. Many saw BK as a bad client, impossible to work for. Others noted that the "win" of this account would ruin Crispin's quirky culture.

CHALLENGING CONVENTIONAL WISDOM

In announcing the Crispin selection, Blum indicated he had challenged the firm to develop "groundbreaking, next-level, results-oriented, and innovative advertising that strongly connects with our core customers." BK automatically became the small firm's largest client, but Crispin was not without an impressive track record.

Chuck Porter joined Crispin in 1988. A middle-aged windsurfer, he wanted to be near the water. Alex Bogusky joined the firm later as a 24-year-old art director who raced motorbikes. The Porter-Bogusky combination clicked, and Crispin Porter + Bogusky racked up local awards for its ad campaigns. A Sunglass Hut billboard featured a huge pair of sunglasses with the headline "What to Wear to a Nude Beach." Because its clients often had little money for advertising, Crispin found inexpensive ways to gain attention. For a local homeless shelter, it placed ads on shopping carts, trash dumpsters, and park benches.

In 1997, with Bogusky serving as creative director, Crispin finally got national attention with its unconventional "Truth" campaign aimed at convincing Florida teens to stop smoking. The campaign was so successful that the American Legacy Foundation picked it up and turned it into a national promotion, leading to a big-budget ad at the Super Bowl—the "Shards O'Glass Freeze Pop." Crispin followed with award-winning, low-budget campaigns for BMW's MINI Cooper, IKEA furniture, and Virgin Atlantic Airways, forging Crispin's reputation as an out-of-the-box, results-oriented agency. Along the way, Crispin developed some loose "rules." Among them were:

- Zero in on the product.
- Kick the TV commercial habit.
- Find the sweet spot (the overlap between product characteristics and customer needs).
- Surprise = buzz = exposure.
- Don't be timid.
- Think of advertising as a product rather than a service.

BACK TO THE FUTURE

Within a month of getting BK's account, rather than recommending some outrageous new idea, Crispin recommended going back to the firm's "Have It Your Way" tagline, developed by BK's second advertising agency, BBDO, in 1974. Crispin argued that it could take that old phrase and make it relevant to today's customers.

But although Crispin's initial pitch may have initially seemed "same-old," it was anything but. Uncharacteristically, Crispin kicked off the new campaign with TV commercials. In a series of off-beat ads that were a takeoff on a British comedy series, *The Office,* office workers competed and compared their "made my way" BK burgers, reinforcing the message that each customer could have a custom-made burger—no matter how unusual it might be. Crispin planned an entire package of promotions around the new-old theme, including everything from in-store signage to messages on cups.

Although the "office" ads were unusual and catchy, they were also mainstream media. The TV campaign created an environment for the real Crispin approach to emerge. To promote BK's TenderCrisp chicken, Crispin launched a Web site, www.subservientchicken.com. When people visited the site, they saw what appeared to be a Web camera focused on a somewhat seedy living room. In the room was a man dressed like a chicken (except for one subtle accessory, a lady's garter belt). The site invited the visitor to "Get chicken just the way you like it. Type in your command here." The visitor could type in a command, such as "stand on your head" or "do jumping jacks" and the chicken would respond. If someone typed in a risqué request, the chicken would wave a wing at the camera, as if to say "no-no."

Below the chicken video area were five other icons. "Subservient TV" featured three video clips with various people "having their way" with the chicken. "Photos" presented five "glamour" shots of the chicken. The "Chicken Mask" icon produced a printable chicken mask that one could print, cut out, and wear. The mask's instructions were to "cut along dotted line, put on chicken face, be subservient." A fourth icon, "Tell a friend," pulled up an Outlook Express e-mail document that invited you to send an e-mail to a friend with the text: "Finally, somebody in a chicken costume who will do whatever you want. Check it out. www.subservientchicken.com." The last icon was marked "BK TenderCrisp" and was linked to the Burger King homepage. This was the only indication of BK's sponsorship on the site, reflecting Crispin's desire to avoid seeming too commercial and "uncool." Unless a visitor clicked on that last icon, he or she would have no indication that the site had anything to do with Burger King.

When Crispin launched the site, it told only 20 people—all of whom were friends of people who worked at the agency. Within the first 10 *days*, 20 million people visited the site, with the average visitor spending more than seven minutes. Many visitors apparently selected the "tell a friend" icon, sending e-mails flying like feathers.

SUBSERVIENT CHICKEN—CHAPTER 2

In 2005, as a follow-up to the Subservient Chicken promotion, Crispin created a campaign to launch a new BK product, Chicken Fries. The promotion was based on a heavy metal band called Coq Roq with lead singer, Fowl Mouth. Crispin set up a Web site, www.coqroq.com, in world-class rock band fashion. It showcased the band's songs, including "Bob Your Head," "One-Armed Bandit," and "Nice Box." There was even a video for the "hit song" "Cross the Road," directed by music video biggie Paul Hunter. Fans could purchase T-shirts, CDs, cell phone ring tones, and other fowl merchandise. There was even talk of a tour and a DVD! Was this a real band or just a promotion? Crispin's Coq Roq campaign was so well done, it was difficult to tell. Soon after the Web site launch, Hunter-directed music-video-style ads began airing on MTV and VH-1.

Crispin targeted this campaign squarely at what it perceived to be the main BK target market—young men. Although the campaign was well received by this target segment, many others groups were not so entertained. The campaign ruffled the feathers of real metal band Slipknot. It filed suit, claiming violation of publicity and trademark rights. Other critics saw the campaign for what it was—a crude attempt to generate buzz among teenagers through childish genital humor. In fact, with relations already rocky between Burger King and its franchisees, the campaign only threw more fuel on the fire. The franchisees hated it, as they did the eerie 2004 campaign that featured a bobblehead-looking ceramic King with a gargantuan head. But none of this bothered Burger King's sales. The fast feeder sold more than 100 million orders of Chicken Fries in the first four weeks of the new-product launch.

A VIRAL TURNAROUND

Crispin clearly demonstrated with both the Subservient Chicken and the Cog Roq campaigns that it was a master at viral marketing—using unusual methods to get attention and to generate buzz and word of mouth. Despite the success of these campaigns in producing lots of Web site hits, many analysts wondered if they would lead to increased sales and turn around BK's sliding market share. There was also speculation as to whether or not Crispin could continue to produce ideas that would keep BK strong in the fast-food fights.

But at Burger King's 2006 annual franchisee convention, the feeling in the air was "long live the king." CEO Blum debuted a new Crispin ad entitled, "Manthem." A parody of the Helen Reddy Song, "I Am Woman," the spot was yet another example of BK's strategy to unapologetically embrace the young, male, fast-food "super fan." The lyrics of "Manthem" spurned "chick food" and gleefully exalted the meat, cheese, and more meat and cheese combos that can turn "innies into outies," all the while showing guys burning their briefs and pushing a minivan off a bridge.

After openly revolting at the convention the year before, BK's restaurant operators rose to their feet in a thunderous ovation, demanding an encore. They now embraced the kind of uncomfortably edgy advertising that they had rejected not so long before. Why this sudden change of heart?

Perhaps it was because Burger King was on the verge of a public offering. Or maybe it was because sales and profits go a long way in healing wounds. "I feel much better this year than I have in the last three, four, or five years," said Mahendra Nath, owner operator of 90 stores in the upper Midwest and Florida. "I've been up 7.8 percent in 2004, 4.8 percent for 2005 and up 2.8 percent for this quarter so far. Now I think we are believers and hopefully the trend is going to keep going." Alex Salgueiro, another franchisee who was seeing results similar to Nath's, said, "I think our competitors are scared of the King. . . . They should be. They say, 'What's with the King?' and my answer is 'It's better than clowns.'"

With BK's fortunes apparently changing, franchisees were much less likely to question the irreverent Crispin promotional tactics, whether they liked them or not. And why would they? With the young male demographic providing nearly half of all Burger King visits, Mr. Salguiero said it best: "All opinions boil down to traffic and sales. Once that happens, everybody has to shut up with their opinion. We have a very old-franchisee base at this point and some of us don't understand our customers. We have a lot of gray hair."

Despite the early speculation, Crispin is now into its fourth year as Burger King's promotional agency, with no sign of being shown the door. The creative ads have continued to flow, including the humorous series to promote the Western Whopper. The spots, based on the tagline, "Bring out your inner cowboy," feature people from all walks of life developing huge handlebar mustaches after eating Burger King fare. The ads are accompanied by a link to www.petmoustache.com, where people can register, upload a photo, and design a custom mustache. The mustache then takes on a life of its own. "It sends you e-mails that say, 'Hey, I miss you and why haven't you waxed me?' If you neglect it, it grows willy-nilly and wild," explains Rob Reilly, creative director for Crispin.

Crispin's knack for viral and nontraditional approaches to advertising are also illustrated in a recent effort that places BK characters (the bobble-headed king, the subservient chicken, and a big Whopper Jr. character) in video games that can be played on Microsoft's Xbox 360. The games cost only $3.99 each and are expected to place the brand firmly among the desirable video gamer segment.

All of this just seems to be adding more to Burger King's fire. Revenue for fiscal-year 2007 was up 9 percent to $2.23 billion, topping the company's growth goal of 6 to 7 percent. Burger King is also showing healthy profits, rising stock prices, and strong international growth. As long as Crispin continues to hit home runs with its creative promotions, its franchisees, shareholders, and customers alike will continue to shout, "Long live the King."

Questions for Discussion

1. What are Burger King's communication objectives for its target audience?

2. With its focus on the "super fan," does BK risk alienating other customers? What are the implications of this?

3. Why is viral or buzz marketing effective? Analyze the design of the subservient chicken Web site's message, including content, structure, and format. What can you conclude from this analysis?

4. Do the TV and viral elements of the BK's campaigns work well together? What additional elements and media might Crispin add to the integrated marketing communications campaign?

5. What other recommendations would you make to BK and Crispin to help them improve the integration of Burger King's promotion mix?

Sources: Kevin Kingsbury, "Burger King Swings to Net Profit," *Wall Street Journal,* August 24, 2007, accessed at www.wsj.com; Barbara Lippert, "King of All Media," *Adweek,* November 20, 2006, accessed at www.adweek.com; Kamau High, "BK Intros 'Inner Cowboy,'" *Adweek,* June 05, 2007, accessed at www.adweek.com; Kate Macarthur, "BK Rebels Fall in Love with King," *Advertising Age,* May 1, 2006, p. 1; Elaine Walker, "Franchisees, Burger King Work to Mend Rift," *Miami Herald,* March 27, 2006; Michael Paoletta and Susan Butler, "For BK and Slipknot, a Game of Chicken," *Billboard,* September 3, 2005; Bob Garfield, "Garfield's Ad Review," *Advertising Age,* August 1, 2005, p. 29; Catharine P. Taylor, "Playing Chicken," *Adweek,* April 19, 2004, p. 19; Warren Berger, "Dare-Devils: The Ad World's Most Buzzed-About Agency Is Miami's Crispin Porter & Bogusky," *Business 2.0,* April 2004, p. 110; Kate McArthur, "Burger King's Big Idea: Have It Your Way, Again," *Advertising Age,* February 16, 2004, p. 1.

Company Case 13

Personal Selling at the Lear Corporation

When someone says "salesperson," what image comes to mind? Perhaps it's the stereotypical "traveling salesman"—the fast-talking, ever-smiling peddler who travels his territory foisting his wares on reluctant customers. Such stereotypes, however, are sadly out of date. Today, most professional salespeople are well-educated, well-trained men and women who work to build long-term, value-producing relationships with their customers. They succeed not by taking customers in but by helping them out—by assessing customer needs and solving customer problems.

One company that has been able to employ such a customer-centric sales philosophy is the Lear Corporation. From its humble beginnings in 1917 as a manufacturer of tubular assemblies for the automotive and aircraft industries, Lear has grown into one of the largest and most successful automotive suppliers in the world. In 2007, Lear achieved revenues of $17.8 billion, 130th on the Fortune 500.

For decades, Lear dominated the automotive parts industry as a maker of seat systems. But through 18 major acquisitions since it went public in 1994, Lear has broadened its product line to include all five major vehicle interior systems—instrument panels, cockpits, door and trim, overhead and flooring, and acoustic systems. Lear is also one of the leading global suppliers of automotive electronics and electrical distribution systems.

Lear's customers include most of the world's leading automotive companies, from high-volume producers such as Ford, Chrysler, General Motors, Fiat, and Toyota to boutique brands such as Ferrari and Rolls-Royce. Lear has been able to successfully follow global automotive growth trends by gaining business among European and Asian manufacturers. Currently, Lear products are found in new products produced by more than 300 nameplates around the world. With 104,000 employees, Lear designs, engineers, and manufactures products in more than 275 facilities in 33 countries.

Along with all this growth, Lear has experienced periods of superb financial performance. The company achieved record-breaking sales and earnings growth throughout the 1990s. During that decade, its "average content per car" in North America increased more than fourfold. Not surprisingly, Lear's revenues more than doubled in the latter half of the '90s. Currently, the company owns roughly 30 percent of the North American interior components market.

Lear has achieved its growth and financial success by focusing on the customer. In a description of its business philosophy, Lear states:

> "The success of Lear is a result of our dedication to provide the best possible service to the world's automakers—which includes understanding their customers, the automotive consumer—by delivering increased value through the latest vehicle interior technologies and the continuous improvement of our processes and product quality. All of this is reflected in Lear's exclusive People-Vehicle-Interface Methodology. By utilizing the PVI Method, Lear employs an innovation development discipline that turns market opportunities into the products that consumers want and customers need in their vehicles."

ACHIEVING CUSTOMER ORIENTATION

Lear's customer orientation is evident in all aspects of operations, from design through manufacturing. But perhaps more than any other part of the organization, it's Lear's outstanding sales force that makes the company's credo, "Consumer driven. Customer focused," ring true. Lear's sales force was recently rated by *Sales & Marketing Management* magazine as one of "America's Best Sales Forces." What makes this an outstanding sales force? Lear knows that good selling these days takes much more than just a sales rep covering a territory and convincing customers to buy the product. It takes teamwork, relationship building, and doing what's best for the customer. Lear's sales force excels at these tasks.

Lear's sales depend completely on the success of its customers. If the automakers don't sell cars, Lear doesn't sell interiors. So the Lear sales force strives to create not just sales, but customer success. In fact, Lear salespeople aren't "sales reps," they're "account managers" who function more as consultants than as order getters. "Our salespeople don't really close deals," notes a senior marketing executive. "They consult and work with customers to learn exactly what's needed and when."

Lear's growth and expansion of its product line have been driven by the quest to better meet customers' needs. As Lear has diversified its product line from seats to all parts of a vehicle's interior, it has become a kind of "one-stop shopping" source. As the provision of complete interior solutions benefits customers, it also benefits Lear. "It used to be that we'd build a partnership and then get only a limited amount of revenue from it," the executive says. "Now we can get as much as possible out of our customer relationships."

Lear's heavy customer focus has lead to a structure that is broken up into separate divisions dedicated to specific customers. For example, there's a Ford division and a General Motors division, and each operates as its own profit center. Within each division, high-level "platform teams"—made up of salespeople, engineers, and program managers—work closely with their customer counterparts. These platform teams are closely supported by divisional manufacturing, finance, quality, and advanced technology groups.

The platform team structure has allowed Lear to be very responsive to customer needs. In 1999, leaders at GM wanted to expand their commercial van business. One idea was to create a new model by fitting an existing van shell with deluxe leather seating; flip-down, flat-panel screens; and other high-tech gadgets. "It would have taken two, maybe three years to make a van like this in the GM system," says Larry Szydlowski, GM's program manager for the Express LT. In that time, the demand for such a van might have come and gone. Or a competitor might have been first to market with a product fitting that concept.

But based on efficiencies derived from its platform teams, Lear confidently predicted that it could go from contract to product in just one year. The claim was so outrageous that GM hesitated. So Lear took a risk and invested in a physical prototype on its own. GM was so impressed that it awarded the lucrative contract to Lear. One year later, as promised, the Express LT was in production.

Lear has achieved another sales-team efficiency by limiting its customer base to fewer major customers rather than many small-contract customers. This has allowed sales teams to get very close to their customers. "Our teams don't call on purchasers; they're linked to customer operations at all levels," the marketer notes. "We try to put a system in place that creates continuous contact with customers." In fact, Lear often locates its sales offices in customers' plants. For example, the team that handles GM's light truck division works at GM's truck operation campus. "We can't just be there to give quotes and ask for orders," says the marketing executive. "We need to be involved with customers every step of the way—from vehicle concept through launch."

THE TIDE SHIFTS FOR LEAR

Whereas the 1990s were golden years for Lear, numerous factors combined to create a dismal situation as the new millennium unfolded. Despite the fact that Lear captured 2005 revenues of more than $17 billion, it posted a net loss of $1.3 billion. Almost half of that loss came in the fourth quarter alone. Ironically, many of the factors responsible for Lear's earlier success were leading to this downturn.

For starters, gas prices went up. Although this was nothing that Lear could have prevented, as gas prices have risen, industry-wide vehicle sales have slowed. The biggest casualties were SUVs and light trucks, models that litter the product lines for the Big Three auto makers. Additionally, the downturn in SUV and truck sales came at an inopportune time. The large American car companies were already losing market share to foreign competitors in other categories as well. Whereas Lear's strategy of limiting its customer base allowed it to achieve close customer relationships, tough times for these large customers was wreaking havoc on Lear's sales.

Lear's product diversification strategy, which has been a key to building customer relationships, has also contributed to current losses. In 2005, the company spent a record $586 million on capital investments, in part to become a total supplier for its largest customers. At the same time, however, these large customers abandoned their strategy of sourcing all vehicle-interior components to one supplier.

Although Lear has continued to suffer heavy losses, its strengths may now be shining through. Even as Lear suffered a net loss of more than $700 million in 2006, it fended off a buyout offer and implemented a massive restructuring plan that included selling off the poor performing interior systems business. As a result, its stock price increased by almost 100 percent to a high of more than $40 per share in mid-2007. This demonstrates that Wall Street is confident that Lear's few years of losses are little more than a blip on the radar and that better times are already on the way.

Maintaining profitable relationships with large customers takes much more than a nice smile and a firm handshake. And certainly there's no place for the "smoke and mirrors" or "flim-flam" sometimes mistakenly associated with personal selling. Success in such a selling environment requires careful teamwork among well-trained, dedicated sales professionals who are bent on profitably taking care of their customers. But even as Lear has focused on these principles, it has found that maintaining solid customer relationships can at times be very difficult.

Questions for Discussion

1. Classify Lear's sales-force structure. What role has this structure played in the company's successes and failures?

2. What role does team selling play in Lear's sales-force strategy? Should Lear make any changes to this strategy?

3. What implications does selling its interior systems division have on Lear's sales force and its ability to serve its customers? How can Lear overcome the possible problems associated with this sale?

4. Make other recommendations for how Lear can reverse the difficulties that it now faces? How would you implement each recommendation?

Sources: Brent Snavely, "Despite Loss, Lear Has Wall Street Impressed," *Crain's Detroit Business,* January 29, 2007, p. 4; Phil Nussel and Brent Snavely, "Stock Price Climbs After Lear Shareholders Reject Icahn Bid," *Crain's Detroit Business,* July 23, 2007, p. 26; Andy Cohen, "Top of the Charts: Lear Corporation," *Sales & Marketing Management,* July 1998, p. 40; Fara Warner, "Lear Won't Take a Back Seat," *Fast Company,* June 2001, pp. 178–85; "Lear Corporation," *Sales & Marketing Management,* July 1999, p. 62; Jesse Eisinger, "Lear Case Shows Sometimes Investors Can Detect Crises Before Management," *Wall Street Journal,* March 15, 2006; Terry Kosdrosky, "Lear's Profit Climbs 15%," *Wall Street Journal,* April 26, 2006, accessed at www.wsj.com; "About Lear," accessed at www.lear.com, September 2007.

Company Case 14

StubHub: Ticket Scalping Becomes Respectable

As the Rolling Stones geared up for their "A Bigger Bang" tour, Roger felt like reliving some old memories. Just because he was in his 50s didn't mean he was too old to rock. After all, he was an original Stones fan dating back to the '60s. It had been years since he had gone to a concert for any band. But on the day the Stones tickets went on sale, he grabbed a lawn chair and headed to his local Ticketmaster outlet to "camp out" in line. Roger knew that the terminal, located inside a large chain music store, wouldn't open until 10 A.M. when tickets went on sale. He got to the store at 6 A.M. to find only three people ahead of him. "Fantastic," Roger thought. With so few people in front of him, getting good seats would be a snap. Maybe he would even score something close to the stage.

By the time the three people in front of him had their tickets, it was 10:13. As the clerk typed away on the Ticketmaster computer terminal, Roger couldn't believe what he heard. No tickets were available. The show at the Forum in Los Angeles was sold out. Dejected, Roger turned to leave. As he made his way out the door, another customer said, "You can always try StubHub." As the fellow Stones fan explained what StubHub was, it occurred to Roger that the world had become a very different place with respect to buying concert tickets.

Indeed, in this Internet age, buying tickets for live events has changed dramatically since Roger's concert-going days. Originators such as Ticketmaster now sell tickets online for everything from Broadway shows to sporting events. Increasingly, however, event tickets are resold through Web sites such as eBay, RazorGator, TicketsNow, Craigslist, and StubHub, the fastest-growing company in the business. According to one survey conducted at a U2 concert, 29 percent of the fans said that they had purchased their tickets from a resale Web site, a statistic that reflects ticket buying industry wide. This secondary market for online sports and entertainment tickets has grown to an estimated $3 billion in annual revenues.

And although prices are all over the map, tickets for sold-out shows of hot events routinely sell for double or triple their face value. In some cases, the markup is astronomical. Prices for a seat at Super Bowl XLI in Miami sold for as high as $10,000. Tickets to see Coldplay in San Jose went for as much as $3,000 each. Elton John's 60th birthday bash? Try $5,500. And a pair of Stone's tickets at New York's Madison Square Garden, close enough to see a geriatric Mick Jagger perspire, went up for more than $14,000. Extreme cases? Yes. But not uncommon.

When most people think of buying a ticket from a reseller, they probably envision a seedy scalper standing in the shadows near an event venue. But scalping is moving mainstream. Because the Internet and other technologies have allowed professional ticket agents to purchase event tickets in larger numbers, anyone with a computer and broadband connection can instantly become a scalper. And regular folks, even fans, are routinely doing so. "Because we allowed people to buy four [tickets], if they only need two, they put the other two up for sale," said Dave Holmes, manager for Coldplay. This dynamic, occurring for events across the board, has dramatically increased the number of ticket resellers.

STUBHUB ENTERS THE GAME

With the ticket resale market booming, StubHub started operations in 2000 under the name Liquid Seats. It all started with an idea by two first-year students at the Stanford Graduate School of Business. Eric Baker and Jeff Fluhr had been observing the hysteria on the ticket resale market. In their opinion, the market was highly fragmented and rampant with fraud and distorted pricing. Two buyers sitting side by side at the same event might find they'd paid wildly different prices for essentially the same product. Even with heavy hitter eBay as the biggest ticket reseller at the time, Baker and Fluhr saw an opportunity to create a system that would bring buyers and sellers together in a more efficient manner.

They entered their proposal in a new-business plan competition. Fluhr was utterly convinced the concept would work. So much so, that he withdrew the proposal from the competition and dropped out of school in order to launch the business. At a time when dot-coms were dropping like flies, this might have seemed like a very poor decision. But Fluhr is now CEO of StubHub, the leader and fastest-growing company in a $10-billion-a-year industry.

Home to 230 employees, StubHub utilizes 20,000 square feet of prime office space in San Francisco's pricey financial district, seven satellite offices, and two call centers. Even more telling is the company's financial performance. From 2003–2006, StubHub posted a staggering growth rate of more than 3,200 percent, increasing its volume to 3.3 million tickets. That amounts to roughly $100 million in commissions. Most of that was profit. According to comScore Networks, a firm that tracks Web traffic, StubHub.com is the leading site among more than a dozen competitors in the ticket-resale category.

THE DEVIL IS IN THE DETAILS

Sharing his own experience, a *New York Times* writer provides the following description of how StubHub works:

> "To test the system, I started with the New York Yankees. A series with the Seattle Mariners was coming up, just before the Yankees left town for a long road trip. Good tickets would be scarce. I went to StubHub. Lots of tickets there, many priced stratospherically. I settled on two Main Box seats in Section 313, Row G. They were in the right-field corner, just one section above field level. The price was $35 each, or face price for a season ticket holder. This was a tremendous value for a sold-out game. I registered with StubHub, creating a user name and password, ordered the tickets, then sealed the deal by providing my credit card number. An e-mail message arrived soon after, confirming the order and informing me that StubHub was contacting the seller to arrange for shipment. My card would not be charged until the seller had confirmed to StubHub the time and method of delivery. A second e-mail message arrived a day later giving the delivery details.

The tickets arrived on the Thursday before the game, and the seller was paid by StubHub on confirmation of delivery. On Saturday, under a clear, sunny sky, the Yankees were sending a steady stream of screaming line drives into the right-field corner."

From the beginning, Baker and Fluhr set out to provide better options for both buyers and sellers by making StubHub different. Like eBay, StubHub has no ticket inventory of its own, reducing its risk. It simply provides the venue that gives buyers and sellers the opportunity to come together. But it's the differences, perhaps, that have allowed StubHub to achieve such success in such a short period of time.

One of the first differences noticed by buyers and sellers is StubHub's ticket-listing procedure. Sellers can list tickets by auction or at a fixed price, a price that declines as the event gets closer. Whereas some sites charge fees just to list tickets, StubHub lists them for free. Thus, initially, the seller has no risk whatsoever. StubHub's system is simpler than most, splitting the fee burden between buyer and seller. It charges sellers a 15 percent commission and buyers a 10 percent fee.

StubHub's Web site structure also creates a marketplace that comes closer to pure competition than any other reseller's Web site. All sellers are equal on StubHub, as ticket listings are identical in appearance and seller identity is kept anonymous. StubHub even holds the shipping method constant, via FedEx. This makes the purchase process much more transparent for buyers. They can browse tickets by event, venue, and section. Comparison shopping is very easy as shoppers can simultaneously view different pairs of tickets in the same section, even in the same row.

Although prices still vary, this system makes tickets more of a commodity and allows market forces to narrow the gap considerably from one seller to another. In fact, although tickets often sell for high prices, this reselling model can also have the effect of pushing ticket prices down below face value. Many experts believe that the emergence of Internet resellers such as StubHub is having an equalizing effect, often resulting in fair prices determined by market forces.

Perhaps the biggest and most important difference between StubHub and competitors is the company's 100 percent guarantee. Initially, it might seem more risky buying from a seller whose identity is unknown. But StubHub puts the burden of responsibility on the seller, remaining involved after the purchase where competing sites bow out. Buyers aren't charged until they confirm receipt of the tickets. "If you open the package and it contains two squares of toilet paper instead of the tickets," Baker explains, "then we debit the seller's credit card for the amount of the purchase." StubHub will also revoke site privileges for fraudulent or unreliable sellers. In contrast, the eBay system is largely self-policing and does not monitor the shipment or verification of the purchased items.

WHAT THE FUTURE HOLDS

When StubHub was formed, it targeted professional ticket brokers and ordinary consumers. In examining individuals as sellers, Baker and Fluhr capitalized on the underexploited assets of sports team season ticket holders. "If you have season tickets to the Yankees, that's 81 games," Mr. Baker said. "Unless you're unemployed or especially passionate, there's no way you're going to attend every game." StubHub entered the equation, not only giving ticket holders a way to recoup some of their investment, but allowing them to have complete control over the process rather than selling to a ticket agent.

It quickly became apparent to StubHub's founders that the benefits of season ticket holders selling off unused tickets extended to the sports franchises as well. Being able to sell unwanted tickets encourages season ticket holders to buy again. It also puts customers in seats that would otherwise go empty—customers who buy hot dogs, souvenirs, and programs. Thus, StubHub began entering into signed agreements with professional sports teams. The company has signed agreements with numerous NFL, NBA, and NHL teams to be their official secondary marketplace for season ticket holders.

But most recently, StubHub scored a huge breakthrough deal by becoming the official online ticket reseller for Major League Baseball and its 30 teams. Given that an estimated $10 billion worth of baseball tickets are resold each year, this single move will likely bring tremendous growth to StubHub. "This is the final vindication for the secondary ticketing market," StubHub spokesman Sean Pate said. "That really puts the final stamp of approval on StubHub," he said.

Revenues from sporting events account for more than half of all StubHub sales. So it's not surprising that the company continues to pursue new partnerships with collegiate sports organizations and even media organizations, such as Sporting News and CBS Sportsline. However, it has arranged similar contractual agreements with big-name performers such as Coldplay, Britney Spears, Jewel, Christina Aguilera, Alanis Morissette, and country music's rising star, Bobby Pinson. Arrangements allow StubHub to offer exclusive event packages with a portion of the proceeds supporting charities designated by the performer.

The reselling of event tickets is here to stay. With the rise of safe and legal reseller Web sites and the repeal of long-standing antiscalping laws in many states, scalping continues to gain legitimacy. There are numerous hands in the fast-growing cookie jar that is the secondary ticket market. StubHub founder Eric Baker left the company in 2004 and formed Viagogo, a European ticket reseller site that is entering the U.S. market. Even Ticketmaster—the long-standing dominant force in primary ticket sales—has jumped into the act. Not only has the ticket powerhouse turned to auctioning a certain portion of premium tickets to the highest bidders, but it has its own resale arm, TicketExchange.

But although there is more than one channel to buy or sell, StubHub's future looks bright. The company's model of entering into partnerships with event-producing organizations is establishing it as "the official" ticket reseller. At this point, there is no end in sight to StubHub's growth curve. Who knows, at some point, ticket-seeking consumers may even think of StubHub before thinking of Ticketmaster.

Questions for Discussion

1. Conduct a brief analysis of the marketing environment and the forces shaping the development of StubHub.

2. Discuss StubHub's business model. What general benefits does it afford to buyers and sellers? Which benefits are

most important in terms of creating value for buyers and sellers?

3. Discuss StubHub as a new intermediary. What effects has this new type of intermediary had on the ticket industry?

4. Apply the text's e-marketing domains framework to StubHub's business model. How has each domain played a role in the company's success?

5. What recommendations can you make for improving StubHub's future growth and success?

6. What are the legal or ethical issues, if any, for ticket-reselling Web sites?

Sources: Amy Feldman, "Hot Tickets," *Fast Company,* September 1, 2007, p. 44; Kristina Dell, "Going After Ticketmaster," *Time,* May 24, 2007, accessed at www.time.com; "Ticket Reseller StubHub Hits a Home Run," *Rueters,* August 2, 2007; William Grimes, "That Invisible Hand Guides the Game of Ticket Hunting," *New York Times,* June 18, 2004; Henry Fountain, "The Price of Admission in a Material World," *New York Times,* April 16, 2006; Steve Stecklow, "Can't Get No . . . Tickets?" *Wall Street Journal,* January 7, 2006; Steve Stecklow, "StubHub's Ticket to Ride," *Wall Street Journal,* January 17, 2006; Bob Tedeschi, "New Era of Ticket Resales: Online and Aboveboard," *New York Times,* August 29, 2005; information from "About Us," accessed at www.stubhub.com, December, 2007.

Company Case 15

Wal-Mart Takes on the World

Wal-Mart is the world's largest retailer. It has more than 7,000 stores worldwide, employing nearly 2.0 million people, and has annual sales of more than $350 billion. The next-largest global retailer, Carrefour (a French discount retailer), has sales of $99 billion, and Wal-Mart's nearest U.S. competitor in the general merchandise category, Target, has $59 billion in annual sales. More than 70 percent of Wal-Mart's merchandise comes from China. If Wal-Mart were a country, it would be China's eighth-largest trading partner, ahead of Russia and Great Britain.

Although the bulk of Wal-Mart's sales come from the United States, its international division contributes significantly to the corporate bottom line. Roughly 40 percent of Wal-Mart stores are located in 13 markets outside the United States and account for about 25 percent of sales. In fact, Wal-Mart's international operations generated a larger sales gain in 2006 than its U.S. unit ($17.9 billion versus $16.4 billion). In order to appeal to consumers of differing levels of affluence and sophistication in various countries, you might expect that Wal-Mart would need to change its strategy. But that is not the case. The giant retailer's strategy is the same everywhere in the world—Everyday Low Prices (EDLP) and Everyday Low Costs (EDLC). It carries this strategy out to near perfection through its own version of global sourcing and distribution that has other retailers clamoring to copy.

WAL-MART'S INTERNATIONAL GROWTH

Wal-Mart operates in North and South America, Europe, and Asia. It has used multiple entry strategies in various countries.

North and South America

Canada　Wal-Mart's first international venture was Canada—a market similar to that of the United States. Wal-Mart initially bought 122 Canadian Woolco stores, and today it operates 290 stores in that country.

Mexico　In Mexico, Wal-Mart used an acquisition strategy (buying Suburbia stores that sell clothing to young women, VIPS restaurants, Superama supermarkets, and 62 percent of Cifra, then Mexico's largest retailer). It also established its own Mexican Wal-Mart stores and Sam's Clubs. Mexico has been a big success for Wal-Mart, largely because of Cifra's thorough understanding of the Mexican consumer. Wal-Mart is now the largest retailer in Mexico with more than 900 stores. Outside of the United States, Mexico is Wal-Mart's largest market. Wal-Mart's Mexican operations achieve a 4.5 percent net margin—better than the 3.5 percent overall Wal-Mart margin.

Puerto Rico　This is another big success for Wal-Mart. It established its own stores in Puerto Rico and bought Supermercados Amigo—Puerto-Rico's second-largest grocery retailer.

Brazil and Argentina　Wal-Mart entered these countries in the mid-1990s with disappointing results. Both countries faced miserable economic situations, with inflation spiraling out of control, devaluation of currencies, and defaults on loans, plus a political maelstrom in which Argentina's presidency seemed to be a revolving door. To this day, Wal-Mart has opened only 15 stores in Argentina.

Despite the economic situation and considerable competition, Wal-Mart has fared much better in Brazil. Carrefour entered Brazil in 1975 and was well entrenched as the number-one retailer. Upon Wal-Mart's entry, Carrefour started a price war and located hypermarkets next to Wal-Mart stores. In retaliation, Wal-Mart opened smaller-format stores called "Todo Dia," which sell mostly groceries and a little general merchandise. These smaller stores give Wal-Mart a presence in crowded Brazilian neighborhoods and enable it to sell to lower-income consumers who buy daily.

In early 2004, Wal-Mart bolstered its Brazilian market share from sixth to third by buying the 118-unit Bompreco supermarket chain. In late 2005, it bought an additional 140 hypermarkets, supermarkets, and wholesale outlets from Portuguese conglomerate Sonae. Increased market share will create lower costs and lower prices, making Wal-Mart more competitive with Carrefour and with Companhania Brasiliera de Distribuicao (CBD), the largest grocery retailer in Brazil. Wal-Mart's acquisitions have raised its presence in Brazil to more than 290 stores.

Europe

Germany　In 1998, Wal-Mart bought the 21-unit Wertkauf chain in Germany, and a year later it purchased the 74-unit Interspar hypermarkets. As the third-largest retail market in the world (behind the United States and Japan), Germany initially looked very attractive. But from the start, Germany was a nightmare for Wal-Mart. First, there were real estate issues: strict zoning laws, scarcity of land, and high real estate prices. Then there were well-entrenched unions, which were unlikely to allow their members to gather in the morning to respond to Wal-Mart's "Give me a W . . . Give me an A . . ." rallying cheer.

In addition, Wal-Mart faced much greater competition in Germany—five of the world's top 25 global retailers are German, with two of them in the top 10. Finally, German consumers are among the most demanding in the world. They are extremely quality conscious and are less price conscious. To top all that, Wal-Mart had purchased two chains with declining sales, poor locations, and dirty stores.

Wal-Mart executives admit in hindsight that they moved too fast in Germany and failed to take advantage of the managerial expertise in their acquisitions. In July of 2006, after nine years of trying to make a go of it, Wal-Mart sold its German stores to rival Metro.

United Kingdom　Although Wal-Mart struggled in Germany, it scored a home run when it purchased the U.K.'s ASDA chain. These U.K. outlets are the biggest contributor to the profits of Wal-Mart's International Division. Why? ASDA had for years modeled itself on the Wal-Mart format—right down to the rah-rah philosophy and low prices. It was not a struggling chain, but rather a top-notch retailer that "knows food retailing" and shares that knowledge throughout Wal-Mart's other global operations.

With Wal-Mart's backing, ASDA cut prices (undercutting rivals), added general merchandise, and took advantage of Wal-Mart's logistics prowess. ASDA has been so successful that its sales per square foot go as high as $2,000, four times higher than an average Sam's Club. For the Christmas season in 2003, 9 of the 10 top-selling Wal-Mart stores worldwide were in the United Kingdom. This does not mean a lack of competition—two other U.K. retailers, Tesco and Sainsbury's, also rank among the top 25 global retailers. Wal-Mart's store count in the United Kingdom now stands at more than 330 and growing.

Asia

Japan Wal-Mart entered Japan in 2002 by buying a 38 percent stake in Seiyu Ltd., Japan's fifth-largest supermarket chain. Although Seiyu had 400 stores with good locations, the stores were shabby and the chain faced declining sales. Anxious not to repeat the German mistakes in another land of demanding consumers, Wal-Mart has moved slowly to remodel Seiyu's stores. Unfortunately, this gives Japanese competitors such as Aeon time to get a jump on Wal-Mart.

Wal-Mart faces many of the same problems in Japan as in China and Germany, such as pricey real estate and few available locations. Until recently, Japanese laws protecting small retailers, who make up 58 percent of the Japanese retailing system, restricted store size and opening hours. In addition, in Japan's complicated and sometimes convoluted distribution systems, retailers go through layers of middlemen with long-standing relationships instead of buying directly from suppliers. As a result, goods may pass through three or more hands before reaching a retailer.

Then there are the Japanese consumers, who are among the world's quirkiest and most demanding. They want fresher foods, the most clean and orderly stores, short checkout lines, and an abundance of clerks. And they don't understand the EDLP strategy. Trained by Japanese retailers in the past, consumers still expect discounts offered in newspaper ads, which must be in color. Shoppers also don't understand jargon such as "rollback," so Wal-Mart must translate terms that it considers standard in the rest of the world. Worse, Japanese consumers think very low prices indicate poor quality. Thus, its very-low-price strategy could hurt Wal-Mart's image and sales.

Despite Wal-Mart's elaborate planning and preparation, results in Japan have been disappointing. Seiyu continues to lose money (almost $500 million in 2006) and blames the sluggish economy and unusual weather—not to mention the competition. Wal-Mart has yet to articulate a clear strategy with the struggling chain, but giving up does not appear to be an option. Following Mexico, there are more Wal-Mart stores in Japan than in any other country outside the United States. Wal-Mart has spent more than $1 billion in Japan. Sluggish sales are merely a challenge to be overcome.

China Wal-Mart began operations in China in 1995. For years, growth was slow due to the many challenges of operating in the Chinese market. Like Germany, there is a shortage of land and stores tend to be smaller. Wal-Mart located one of its first store in a subway station, placed to cater to busy commuters.

Competition is also a factor. Carrefour and a handful of Chinese supermarket chains (including China's own Wumart) are expanding much more rapidly.

These problems are magnified by a bigger problem: the government. In an effort to limit competition, the government designated territories within which each retailer must locate, and Wal-Mart was confined mostly to southern China. For some time, this meant no stores in Shanghai, the fastest-growing, most Western, highest-income market in China. However, the government has started relaxing such restrictions.

China's friendlier regulatory environment, timed with the failures and struggles that Wal-Mart has faced in Germany, South Korea, and Japan, has led the Bentonville giant to make bigger moves. In 2006, Wal-Mart acquired Trust-Mart, one of China's biggest retailers. This more than doubled the number of Wal-Mart stores in China (currently at 185). But more importantly, it gave Wal-Mart immediate placement in both Shanghai and Beijing.

Chinese consumers couldn't be happier, having now embraced the world's largest retailer. And many experts say that it is about time that Wal-Mart picked up the pace, given China's blistering economic growth and the world's largest population. "China is the only country in the world that offers Wal-Mart the chance to replicate what they have accomplished in the U.S.," said Bill Dreher, an analyst at Deutsche Bank Securities.

WHAT'S NEXT?

For some time, Wal-Mart's next big move appeared to be Russia. Based on factors such as market saturation, political risk, economic growth, and consumer demographics, Russia constitutes the second most attractive global retail market. Wal-Mart's developer arm, Gazeley, has been involved in speculative ventures in and around Moscow. But in recent times, Wal-Mart has not shown concrete signs of opening stores in this large country.

Whereas Russia is the second most attractive global retail destination, India is number one, and Wal-Mart is taking serious notice. India has nearly 1.1 billion people and is growing fast. In one year, India's population will grow by over 400,000 people, far outpacing China's growth. Analysts predict that India's $350 billion retail market will grow by 13 percent annually. Moreover, India boasts a fast-expanding middle class, one of the fastest-growing economies in the world, and a retail sector that is dominated by small, family-run stores.

In 2007, after years of research on the Indian market, Wal-Mart created a 50-50 joint venture with Bharti Enterprises Ltd. This entry strategy is unique to Wal-Mart in that it does not immediately provide for any retail outlets. Rather, the venture gives Wal-Mart wholesale and supply chain management operations. Bharti Wal-Mart will sell goods to small retailers, manufacturers, and farmers. By the end of 2008, however, the venture plans to open its first retail store, and it will open 15 more such facilities in the years to follow.

Wal-Mart refers to its international strategy as "majoring in the majors." It is focusing efforts on the big markets where it does best or has the potential to gain the biggest impact. For the most part, this strategy centers on developing countries with huge low-income populations. Thus, it is no surprise that Wal-Mart's greatest growth is taking place in Central America, China, Brazil, and now India. Although it has not yet decided how it will enter Russia, that is another market that fits its strategy. When it comes to global marketing, Wal-Mart faces a world of opportunity.

Questions for Discussion

1. In what countries has Wal-Mart done well? Can you identify any common consumer, market, retailer, or entry strategy traits across these countries that might account for Wal-Mart's success?

2. In what countries has Wal-Mart done poorly? Can you identify any common traits across these countries that might account for Wal-Mart's lack of success?

3. In your opinion, will Wal-Mart succeed in Japan? Why or why not?

4. Beyond India, what countries should Wal-Mart consider entering? What factors are important in making this decision? Be prepared to defend the countries that you chose.

Sources: Nitin Luthra and Kris Hudson, "Wal-Mart Makes Move into India," *Wall Street Journal,* August 7, 2007; William Holstein, "Why Wal-Mart Can't Find Happiness in Japan," *Fortune,* July 27, 2007, accessed at www.money.cnn.com; David Ellis, "Wal-Mart Tops Fortune 500 List," *CNNMoney.com,* April 15, 2007; David Barboza and Michael Barbaro, "Wal-Mart Buys Retailer in Bid for China Market," *International Herald Tribune,* October 17, 2006; Kate Norton, "Wal-Mart's German Retreat," *BusinessWeek,* July 28, 2006, accessed at www.businessweek.com; Alan Clendenning, "Wal-Mart Buys Brazil Stores for Expansion," *Associated Press,* December 14, 2005; Clay Chandler, "The Great Wal-Mart of China," *Fortune,* July 25, 2005, accessed at www.money.cnn.com; Laura Heller, "Latin Market Never Looked So Bueno," *DSN Retailing Today,* June 10, 2002, p. 125; www.walmartstores.com, accessed September 2007.

Company Case 16

Vitango: Fighting Malnutrition

Imagine teaching an elementary school class in which students are constantly inattentive and falling asleep—not because they are bored but because they are malnourished. In many countries, this is not an unusual problem. Two billion people around the globe suffer from anemia—an iron deficiency. Iron deficiency leads to reduced resistance to disease, lowers learning ability in children, and contributes to the death of one out of five pregnant mothers. Two hundred million children do not get enough Vitamin A. As a result, 250,000 of them go blind each year and 2.2 million children under five die each year from diarrhea. Many malnourished children suffer from zinc deficiency, which leads to growth failure and infections. Close to two billion people do not get enough iodine, and iodine deficiency is the leading cause of preventable mental retardation in the world. If they only used the ordinary table salt found in homes and restaurants all across the United States, this wouldn't happen.

Although estimates vary widely, it is clear that a substantial portion of the world's population suffers from malnutrition of some kind. Malnutrition exists everywhere, but one estimate places as many as 95 percent of the world's malnourished people in developing countries, where poverty levels are the highest. And although malnutrition is clearly a direct result of poverty, it also perpetuates poverty. Malnourished children are more likely to drop out of school, are less likely to benefit from schooling even if they remain enrolled, and end up having lower incomes as adults. According to Jean-Louis Sarbib, Senior Vice President for Human Development at the World Bank, malnutrition costs developing countries up to 3 percent of their yearly GDP. "Put this in the context that the economies of many developing countries are growing at the rate of 2 to 3 percent annually, and improving nutrition could potentially double these rates," says Sarbib.

What can U.S. businesses do about this deplorable situation? Quite a bit. Companies such as Coca-Cola and Procter & Gamble have invested millions of dollars in research of micronutrients. They are learning how to fortify everyday food and beverages with additional minerals and vitamins to wipe out deficiencies and keep school children around the world alert and mentally prepared for school.

Fortifying foods is not new or unusual in the United States. Iodine has been added to ordinary table salt for decades; milk contains Vitamin D and calcium; and cornflakes list all the micronutrients found in them on the box. A quick check of your pantry reveals that many drinks and other foods have vitamins and minerals added to them. What are new are the efforts of companies to identify deficiencies in specific countries and to develop new technologies for adding micronutrients to foodstuffs in order to eliminate or reduce them. A good example is a Coca-Cola beverage product called Vitango in Botswana.

Coca-Cola spent years developing a powdered beverage that, when mixed with water, looks and tastes like a sweeter version of Hi-C. The beverage is fortified with 12 vitamins and with minerals that are chronically lacking in the diets of people in developing countries. Coca-Cola tested this product in Botswana in

Project Mission. Every day for eight weeks, nurses visited schools where they mixed the beverage and passed out paper cups of the "new Hi-C." At the end of the test period, levels of iron and zinc in the children's blood levels had grown. Some parents noted that their children had become more attentive at school. After the Botswana tests, Coca-Cola also ran tests in Peru to determine how well the nutrients are absorbed into the bloodstream.

Although Vitango may seem like a miracle solution, Coca-Cola has faced challenges in releasing it. One issue is the powdered product form. Given the impurities of much water in Africa, Coca-Cola wants to package it in a ready-to-drink formula, not in the powdered version now available. That would require reformulation that could actually drive down the price.

Procter & Gamble has also developed micronutrient-enriched drinks for distribution in developing countries. In the 1990s, P&G developed its own proprietary iron, Vitamin A, and iodine fortification technology, which it called GrowthPlus. GrowthPlus was the basic ingredient in a product called Nutridelight that P&G launched in the Philippines. Unfortunately it didn't sell well—primarily because it was priced at 50 percent above the market price of other powdered drinks.

More recently, P&G has launched another product in Venezuela, Nutristar, containing eight vitamins and five minerals. Sold at most food stores, it comes in flavors such as mango and passion fruit and promises to produce "taller, stronger, and smarter kids." To date, Nutristar is doing quite well. One reason is that it's available at McDonald's, where it is chosen by consumers with about half of all happy meals sold. P&G is also offering free samples in schools.

The major problem with both Coca-Cola's and P&G's nutritional products is price. These products were expensive to develop because of long lead times, the need to enlist the help of nutritional experts around the world, and the need to develop products that appeal to the local population's tastes. If offered at "reasonable" prices, they would be out of the reach of the world's desperately poor, the group that needs them most. Consider P&G's Nutristar. The poor people in other countries are *not* eating at McDonald's. In countries such as Botswana, they are barely existing on cornmeal and rice. They simply cannot afford to buy fortified sweetened drinks or, for that matter, any sweetened drinks.

How can P&G and Coca-Cola market such products without pricing them too high for the intended market? Learning its lesson in the Philippines, P&G priced Nutristar about 25 percent higher than other powdered drinks and 30 percent below carbonated soft drinks. Even so, that's still too high for the poverty-stricken. Coca-Cola originally planned to sell Vitango for about 20 cents for an 8-ounce liquid serving but realizes that this price is too high. That's part of the reason for continuing developmental work on the product.

One solution to the pricing problem is to work with governments, but many of them are too poor to be able to afford the products. Many also lack the resources to educate their people on the merits of fortified foods. Additionally, some policy makers fail to recognize the connection between malnutrition and the severe problems that it causes.

Enter GAIN—the Global Alliance for Improved Nutrition—an international consortium set up by the Bill and

Melinda Gates Charitable Foundation. GAIN offers assistance to companies in order to profitably market fortified foods in developing countries. One $70 million GAIN program gives money to local governments in order to increase the demand for fortified foods, through means including large-scale public relations campaigns or a government "seal of approval." GAIN also actively lobbies for favorable tariffs and tax rates and for speedier regulatory review of new products in targeted countries. Of course, Coca-Cola and P&G can work with governments on their own, but their actions may be distrusted. After all, these are "for profit" organizations whose motives may be suspect. GAIN has the advantage that it's a not-for-profit organization.

Another GAIN project provides $20 million to fortify salt, flour, and staple foods in developing countries by working directly with a network of more than a dozen manufacturers and retailers, as well as with governments. The idea is to motivate food-producing and distributing companies to make fortified foods available. After the initial funding period, the companies would then continue fortifying these foods without the need for additional aid money. Two such projects include GAIN-funded efforts that assist the government of Zambia in a three-year project to fortify maize meal and a project in China to produce and promote iron-fortified soy sauce.

In all, once fully implemented, GAIN projects will reach almost 700 million people with fortified food. "We are aiming for a realistic target of eliminating vitamin and mineral deficiencies in the next 10 years," said Marc Van Ameringen, executive director of GAIN. "Adding vitamins and minerals to the foods that people eat every day is a proven solution to a genuine health and development problem and it only costs around 25 cents per person per year."

Although GAIN seems like a wonderful resource for helping malnourished peoples, it does have critics. The critics point out that selling or giving away fortified foods does not solve the underlying problem of poverty. Nor does it teach people good nutritional habits. Moreover, in addition to vitamins and minerals, many of the "fortified" foods also contain overly large amounts of fat, sugar, and salt. So, for example, whereas the foods might help reduce iron deficiency, they could also lead to obesity. Some observers claim that it would be better to teach people how to grow fruits and vegetables. The problem is that people will die from malnutrition before poverty is eliminated or trees bear fruit.

Other issues must also be addressed. A fortified beverage such as Vitango will help in dealing with malnutrition but can't eliminate it. People will still need to eat a variety of other foods, which makes education very important. Remember that these products contain no juice. They are intended as supplements, not as substitutes for a proper diet. Lack of understanding about how to use products has landed other companies, such as Nestlé with its infant formula, in trouble when the products were used inappropriately.

Given all these problems, why would Coca-Cola and P&G develop these products in the first place? One answer is future sales and profits. Products such as Nutristar and Vitango could create a basis from which to launch other Coca-Cola or P&G products, such as snack foods or juice drinks. As sales of carbonated beverages around the world have slowed, these fortified drinks pose a growth opportunity for the companies.

Another answer is "goodwill," and not just goodwill for the companies involved. September 11, 2001, taught us in the United States that our country is the focus of both the world's envy and its hatred. Efforts to help share our wealth of technology and research in ways that improve the lot of other peoples may be a major deterrent to future attacks and the growth of terrorism. By helping other nations of the world, U.S. corporations can help create environments where freedom can flourish. One writer insists that when U.S. corporations help people as consumers to buy the goods and services that our companies sell, they also enhance our government's ability to sell our country.

Questions for Discussion

1. Which of the textbook's criticisms of marketing's impact on consumers, if any, are evident in the cases of Vitango and Nutristar?

2. Which of the criticisms of marketing's impact on society are evident in the Vitango and Nutristar cases?

3. Could Vitango and Nutristar be considered enlightened marketing efforts? Why or why not?

4. Are the development and marketing of such products as fortified foods and beverages ethical and socially responsible?

5. How should Coca-Cola proceed with the development and marketing of Vitango?

Sources: Shan Juan, "Iron-Fortified Soy Sauce for Every Kitchen," *Chinadaily.com.cn,* July 14, 2007; "Zambia Gains Support for Decision to Fortify Maize Meal with Vitamins, Minerals," *Times of Zambia,* September 28, 2006, accessed online through LexisNexis; Sanjay Suri, "Development: Nutrient-Packed Food Headed for 200 Million," *Inter Press Service,* April 9, 2006; "World Bank: Malnutrition Causes Heavy Economic Losses," *M2 Presswire,* March 3, 2006; Jill Bruss, "Reaching the World," *Beverage Industry,* December 2001, p. 28; Rance Crain, "U.S. Marketers Must Develop Products to Help Third World," *Advertising Age,* December 3, 2001, p. 20; Betsy McKay, "Drinks for Developing Countries," *Wall Street Journal,* November 27, 2001; George Carpenter, "P&G and Sustainable Development—Finding Opportunity in Responsibility," April 1, 2003, accessed at www.eu.pg.com; "Hunger Kills Six Million Children Annually," *Advertiser,* November 22, 2005, p. 40; Betsy McKay, "Effort to Combat Malnutrition Cites Economic Impact," *Wall Street Journal,* March 3, 2006.

Appendix 2 Marketing Plan

The Marketing Plan: An Introduction

As a marketer, you'll need a good marketing plan to provide direction and focus for your brand, product, or company. With a detailed plan, any business will be better prepared to launch a new product or build sales for existing products. Nonprofit organizations also use marketing plans to guide their fund-raising and outreach efforts. Even government agencies put together marketing plans for initiatives such as building public awareness of proper nutrition and stimulating area tourism.

The Purpose and Content of a Marketing Plan

Unlike a business plan, which offers a broad overview of the entire organization's mission, objectives, strategy, and resource allocation, a marketing plan has a more limited scope. It serves to document how the organization's strategic objectives will be achieved through specific marketing strategies and tactics, with the customer as the starting point. It is also linked to the plans of other departments within the organization. Suppose a marketing plan calls for selling 200,000 units annually. The production department must gear up to make that many units, the finance department must arrange funding to cover the expenses, the human resources department must be ready to hire and train staff, and so on. Without the appropriate level of organizational support and resources, no marketing plan can succeed.

Although the exact length and layout will vary from company to company, a marketing plan usually contains the sections described in Chapter 2. Smaller businesses may create shorter or less formal marketing plans, whereas corporations frequently require highly structured marketing plans. To guide implementation effectively, every part of the plan must be described in considerable detail. Sometimes a company will post its marketing plan on an internal Web site, which allows managers and employees in different locations to consult specific sections and collaborate on additions or changes.

The Role of Research

Marketing plans are not created in a vacuum. To develop successful strategies and action programs, marketers need up-to-date information about the environment, the competition, and the market segments to be served. Often, analysis of internal data is the starting point for assessing the current marketing situation, supplemented by marketing intelligence and research investigating the overall market, the competition, key issues, and threats and opportunities. As the plan is put into effect, marketers use a variety of research techniques to measure progress toward objectives and identify areas for improvement if results fall short of projections.

Finally, marketing research helps marketers learn more about their customers' requirements, expectations, perceptions, and satisfaction levels. This deeper understanding provides a foundation for building competitive advantage through well-informed segmenting, targeting, differentiating, and positioning decisions. Thus, the marketing plan should outline what marketing research will be conducted and how the findings will be applied.

The Role of Relationships

The marketing plan shows how the company will establish and maintain profitable customer relationships. In the process, however, it also shapes a number of internal and external relationships. First, it affects how marketing personnel work with each other and with other departments to deliver value and satisfy customers. Second, it affects how the company works with suppliers, distributors, and strategic alliance partners to achieve the objectives listed in the plan. Third, it influences the company's dealings with other stakeholders, including government regulators, the media, and the community at large. All of these relationships are important to the organization's success, so they should be considered when a marketing plan is being developed.

From Marketing Plan to Marketing Action

Companies generally create yearly marketing plans, although some plans cover a longer period. Marketers start planning well in advance of the implementation date to allow time for marketing research, thorough analysis, management review, and coordination between departments. Then, after each action program begins, marketers monitor ongoing results, compare them with projections, analyze any differences, and take corrective steps as needed. Some marketers also prepare contingency plans for implementation if certain conditions emerge. Because of inevitable and sometimes unpredictable environmental changes, marketers must be ready to update and adapt marketing plans at any time.

For effective implementation and control, the marketing plan should define how progress toward objectives will be measured. Managers typically use budgets, schedules, and performance standards for monitoring and evaluating results. With budgets, they can compare planned expenditures with actual expenditures for a given week, month, or other period. Schedules allow management to see when tasks were supposed to be completed—and when they were actually completed. Performance standards track the outcomes of marketing programs to see whether the company is moving toward its objectives. Some examples of performance standards are: market share, sales volume, product profitability, and customer satisfaction.

Sample Marketing Plan for Sonic

This section takes you inside the sample marketing plan for Sonic, a hypothetical start-up company. The company's first product is the Sonic 1000, a multimedia, cellular/Wi-Fi-enabled personal digital assistant (PDA), also known as a handheld computer. Sonic will be competing with Palm, Hewlett-Packard, Motorola, and other well-established rivals in a crowded, fast-changing marketplace where smart phones and many other electronics devices have PDA functionality. The annotations explain more about what each section of the plan should contain and why.

Executive Summary

Executive summary
This section summarizes the main goals, recommendations, and points as an overview for senior managers who will read and approve the marketing plan. Generally a table of contents follows this section, for management convenience.

Sonic is preparing to launch a new multimedia, dual-mode PDA product, the Sonic 1000, in a mature market. We can compete with both PDAs and smart phones because our product offers a unique combination of advanced features and functionality at a value-added price. We are targeting specific segments in the consumer and business markets, taking advantage of opportunities indicated by higher demand for easy-to-use PDAs with expanded communications, entertainment, and storage functionality.

The primary marketing objective is to achieve first-year U.S. market share of 3 percent with unit sales of 240,000. The primary financial objectives are to achieve first-year sales revenues of $60 million, keep first-year losses to less than $10 million, and break even early in the second year.

Current Marketing Situation

Current marketing situation
In this section, marketing managers discuss the overall market, identify the market segments they will target, and provide information about the company's current situation.

Sonic, founded 18 months ago by two entrepreneurs with experience in the PC market, is about to enter the now-mature PDA market. Multifunction cell phones, e-mail devices, and wireless communication devices are increasingly popular for both personal and professional use. Competition is therefore more intense even as PDA demand flattens, industry consolidation continues, and pricing pressures squeeze profitability. More than 5 million PDAs are sold worldwide every year, with Palm and Hewlett-Packard the market leaders. To gain market share in this dynamic environment, Sonic must carefully target specific segments with features that deliver benefits valued by each customer group.

Market description
Describing the targeted segments in detail provides context for the marketing strategies and detailed action programs discussed later in the plan.

Market Description   Sonic's market consists of consumers and business users who prefer to use a single device for communication, information storage and exchange, and entertainment on the go. Specific segments being targeted during the first year include professionals, cor-

Targeted Segment	Customer Need	Corresponding Feature/Benefit
Professionals (consumer market)	• Stay in touch conveniently and securely while on the go	• Built-in cell phone and push-to-talk to communicate anywhere at any time; wireless e-mail/Web access from anywhere; Linux operating system less vulnerable to hackers
	• Perform many functions hands-free without carrying multiple gadgets	• Voice-activated applications are convenient; GPS function, camera add value
Students (consumer market)	• Perform many functions hands-free without carrying multiple gadgets	• Compatible with numerous applications and peripherals for convenient, cost-effective note taking and functionality
	• Express style and individuality	• Wardrobe of PDA cases in different colors, patterns, and materials
Corporate users (business market)	• Security and adaptability for proprietary tasks	• Customizable to fit corporate tasks and networks; Linux-based operating system less vulnerable to hackers
	• Obtain driving directions to business meetings	• Built-in GPS allows voice-activated access to directions and maps
Entrepreneurs (business market)	• Organize and access contacts, schedule details, business and financial files	• No-hands, wireless access to calendar, address book, information files for checking appointments and data, connecting with contacts
	• Get in touch fast	• Push-to-talk instant calling speeds up communications
Medical users (business market)	• Update, access, and exchange medical records	• No-hands, wireless recording and exchange of information to reduce paperwork and increase productivity
	• Photograph medical situations to maintain a visual record	• Built-in camera allows fast and easy photography, stores images for later retrieval

TABLE A2.1   Segment Needs and Corresponding Features/Benefits of Sonic PDA

porations, students, entrepreneurs, and medical users. Table A2.1 shows how the Sonic 1000 addresses the needs of targeted consumer and business segments.

PDA purchasers can choose between models based on several different operating systems, including systems from Palm, Microsoft, and Symbian, plus Linux variations. Sonic licenses a Linux-based system because it is somewhat less vulnerable to attack by hackers and viruses. Hard drives and flash drives are commonplace in the PDA market, so Sonic is equipping its first product with an ultrafast five-gigabyte drive for information and entertainment storage. Technology costs are decreasing even as capabilities are increasing, which makes value-priced models more appealing to consumers and to business users with older PDAs who want to trade up to new, high-end multifunction units.

Benefits and product features
Table A2.1 clarifies the benefits that product features will deliver to satisfy the needs of customers in each targeted segment.

Product Review   Our first product, the Sonic PDA 1000, offers the following standard features with a Linux OS:

• Voice recognition for hands-free operation
• Built-in dual cell phone/Internet phone functionality and push-to-talk instant calling
• Digital music/video/television recording, wireless downloading, and playback
• Wireless Web and e-mail, text messaging, and instant messaging
• Three-inch color screen for easy viewing
• Organization functions, including calendar, address book, and synchronization
• Global positioning system for directions and maps
• Integrated four-megapixel digital camera
• Ultrafast five-gigabyte drive with expansion potential
• Interchangeable case wardrobe of different colors and patterns

Product review
The product review summarizes the main features for all of the company's products, organized by product line, type of customer, market, or order of product introduction.

First-year sales revenues are projected to be $60 million, based on sales of 240,000 Sonic 1000 units at a wholesale price of $250 each. During the second year, we plan to introduce the Sonic 2000, also with Linux OS, as a higher-end product offering the following standard features:

• Global phone and messaging compatibility
• Translation capabilities to send English text as Spanish text (other languages to be offered as add-on options)
• Integrated eight-megapixel camera with flash

Competitive review
The purpose of a competitive review is to identify key competitors, describe their market positions, and briefly discuss their strategies.

Competitive Review   The emergence of new multifunction smart phones, including the Apple iPhone, has increased competitive pressure. Dell has already left the PDA market; the remaining competitors are continually adding features and sharpening price points. Competition from specialized devices for text and e-mail messaging, such as BlackBerry devices, is a major factor, as well. Key competitors include:

• *Palm.* As the PDA market leader, with a 34 percent share, Palm has excellent distribution in multiple channels and alliances with a number of U.S. and European telecommunications carriers. However, Palm's smart phone share is well below that of Nokia and other handset marketers. Palm products use either the proprietary Palm operating system or Windows.
• *Hewlett-Packard.* HP holds 22 percent of the PDA market and targets business segments with its numerous iPAQ Pocket PC devices. Some of its PDAs can send documents to Bluetooth-equipped printers and prevent data loss if batteries run down. For extra security, one model allows access by fingerprint match as well as by password. HP enjoys widespread distribution and offers a full line of PDAs at various price points.
• *Motorola.* Motorola, a global giant, has sold 100 million of its RAZR clamshell phones in three years. The RAZR2 is even smaller and lighter than earlier models. In addition, the Motorola Q targets professionals and business users with PDA and e-mail functions, a tiny keyboard, Bluetooth connections, multimedia capabilities, and more.
• *Apple.* The iPhone, priced at $500 and up during introduction, is a smart phone with a 3.5-inch color screen designed with entertainment enthusiasts in mind. It's well equipped for music, video, and Web access, plus calendar and contact management functions. Apple forecast first-year iPhone sales of 10 million units, initially partnering only with the AT&T network, and quickly cut the price of its 8GB model to $399.99 to accelerate first-year holiday sales.
• *RIM.* Research in Motion makes the lightweight BlackBerry wireless phone/PDA products that are popular among corporate users. RIM's continuous innovation and solid customer-service support clearly strengthen its competitive standing as it introduces multifunction smart phone and PDA products.
• *Samsung.* Value, style, function: Samsung is a strong competitor, offering a variety of smart phones and Ultra mobile PCs for consumer and business segments. Some of its smart phones are available for specific telecommunications carriers and some are "unlocked," ready for any compatible telecommunications network.

Despite this strong competition, Sonic can carve out a definite image and gain recognition among the targeted segments. Our voice-recognition system for completely hands-off operation is a critical point of differentiation for competitive advantage. Also, offering GPS as a standard feature gives us a competitive edge compared with similarly priced PDAs. Moreover, our product is speedier than most and runs the Linux OS, which is an appealing alternative for customers concerned about security. Table A2.2 shows a sample of competitive products and prices.

Channels and logistics review
In this section, marketers list the most important channels, provide an overview of each channel arrangement, and identify developing issues in channels and logistics.

Channels and Logistics Review   Sonic-branded products will be distributed through a network of retailers in the top 50 U.S. markets. Among the most important channel partners being contacted are:

• *Office supply superstores.* Office Max and Staples will both carry Sonic products in stores, in catalogs, and online.

Competitor	Model	Features	Price
Apple	iPhone	Stylish multimedia smart phone/iPod with 3.5-inch screen, touch-screen dialing, virtual keyboard, cell phone and Wi-Fi access, organizer features, 8-GB memory, camera, Bluetooth, OS X (4.8 ounces)	$399.99
Hewlett-Packard	iPAQ hw6940	PDA and phone functions, wireless radio and Bluetooth connection, GPS, backlit keyboard, multiple cell phone system compatibility, Windows Mobile OS (6.3 ounces)	$599.99
Motorola	RAZR 2	Slimmer, improved version of popular RAZR, with 2-megapixel camera, digital music player, Bluetooth connection, 2-inch high-resolution screen, streaming video/television capability, Linux OS	$299.99
Palm	T|X Handheld	PDA with color screen, Web browser, Wi-Fi and Bluetooth, 128-MB flash memory, digital media player, work with e-mail and Microsoft Office documents, e-book reader, text messaging, Palm OS (5.25 ounces)	$299.99
RIM	BlackBerry Pearl	Smart phone with PDA functions, voice-activated dialing, e-mail and instant messaging, Web browser, built-in camera and keyboard, multimedia player, BlackBerry OS (3.1 ounces)	$499.99
Samsung	u740	Ultra-thin PDA phone with swivel-out keyboard, voice commands, Wi-Fi Web access, Bluetooth connection, camera and camcorder, digital music and video capabilities (3.6 ounces)	$399.99

TABLE A2.2 Sample of Competitive Products and Pricing

- *Computer stores.* Independent computer retailers will carry Sonic products.
- *Electronics specialty stores.* Circuit City and Best Buy will feature Sonic PDAs.
- *Online retailers.* Amazon.com will carry Sonic PDAs and, for a promotional fee, will give Sonic prominent placement on its homepage during the introduction.

Initially, our channel strategy will focus on the United States; according to demand, we plan to expand into Canada and beyond, with appropriate logistical support.

Strengths, Weaknesses, Opportunities, and Threat Analysis

Sonic has several powerful strengths on which to build, but our major weakness is lack of brand awareness and image. The major opportunity is demand for multimedia PDAs that deliver a number of valued benefits, eliminating the need for customers to carry more than one device. We also face the threat of ever-higher competition from consumer electronics manufacturers, as well as downward pricing pressure. Table A2.3 summarizes Sonic's main strengths, weaknesses, opportunities, and threats.

Strengths Sonic can build on three important strengths:

1. *Innovative product.* The Sonic 1000 offers a combination of features that would otherwise require customers to carry multiple devices: speedy, hands-free, dual-mode cell/Wi-Fi telecommunications capabilities, GPS functions, and digital video/music/TV program storage/playback.

2. *Security.* Our PDA uses a Linux-based operating system that is less vulnerable to hackers and other security threats that can result in stolen or corrupted data.

3. *Pricing.* Our product is priced lower than competing multifunction models—none of which offer the same bundle of features—which gives us an edge with price-conscious customers.

Strengths
Strengths are internal capabilities that can help the company reach its objectives.

TABLE A2.3 Sonic's Strengths, Weaknesses, Opportunities, and Threats

Strengths	Weaknesses
• Innovative combination of functions operated hands-free in one portable device	• Lack of brand awareness and image
• Value pricing	• Heavier and thicker than most competing models
• Security due to Linux-based operating system	

Opportunities	Threats
• Increased demand for multimedia models with diverse functions and benefits	• Intense competition
• Lower technology costs	• Downward pricing pressure
	• Compressed product life

Weaknesses

Weaknesses are internal elements that may interfere with the company's ability to achieve its objectives.

Weaknesses By waiting to enter the PDA market until considerable consolidation of competitors has occurred, Sonic has learned from the successes and mistakes of others. Nonetheless, we have two main weaknesses:

1. *Lack of brand awareness.* Sonic has no established brand or image, whereas Palm, Apple, and others have strong brand recognition. We will address this issue with aggressive promotion.

2. *Physical specifications.* The Sonic 1000 is slightly heavier and thicker than most competing models because it incorporates multiple features, offers sizable storage capacity, and is compatible with numerous peripheral devices. To counteract this weakness, we will emphasize our product's benefits and value-added pricing, two compelling competitive strengths.

Opportunities

Opportunities are external elements that the company may be able to exploit to its advantage.

Opportunities Sonic can take advantage of two major market opportunities:

1. *Increasing demand for multimedia models with multiple functions.* The market for multimedia, multifunction devices is growing much faster than the market for single-use devices. Growth will accelerate as dual-mode capabilities become mainstream, giving customers the flexibility to make phone calls over cell or Internet connections. PDAs and smart phones are already commonplace in public, work, and educational settings, which is boosting primary demand. Also, customers who bought entry-level models are replacing older models with more advanced models.

2. *Lower technology costs.* Better technology is now available at a lower cost than ever before. Thus, Sonic can incorporate advanced features at a value-added price that allows for reasonable profits.

Threats

Threats are current or emerging external elements that could potentially challenge the company's performance.

Threats We face three main threats at the introduction of the Sonic 1000:

1. *Increased competition.* More companies are entering the U.S. PDA market with models that offer some but not all of the features and benefits provided by Sonic's PDA. Therefore, Sonic's marketing communications must stress our clear differentiation and value-added pricing.

2. *Downward pressure on pricing.* Increased competition and market-share strategies are pushing PDA prices down. Still, our objective of seeking a 10% profit on second-year sales of the original model is realistic, given the lower margins in the PDA market.

3. *Compressed product life cycle.* PDAs have reached the maturity stage of their life cycle more quickly than earlier technology products. We have contingency plans to keep sales growing by adding new features, targeting additional segments, and adjusting prices as needed.

Objectives and issues

The company's objectives should be defined in specific terms so management can measure progress and plan corrective action if needed to stay on track. This section describes any major issues that might affect the company's marketing strategy and implementation.

Objectives and Issues

We have set aggressive but achievable objectives for the first and second years of market entry.

First-year Objectives During the Sonic 1000's initial year on the market, we are aiming for a 3 percent share of the U.S. PDA market through unit sales volume of 240,000.

Second-year Objectives   Our second-year objectives are to achieve a 6 percent share based on sales of two models and to achieve breakeven early in this period.

Issues   In relation to the product launch, our major issue is the ability to establish a well-regarded brand name linked to a meaningful positioning. We will invest heavily in marketing to create a memorable and distinctive brand image projecting innovation, quality, and value. We also must measure awareness and response so we can adjust our marketing efforts as necessary.

Marketing Strategy

Sonic's marketing strategy is based on a positioning of product differentiation. Our primary consumer target is middle- to upper-income professionals who need one portable device to coordinate their busy schedules, communicate with family and colleagues, get driving directions, and be entertained on the go. Our secondary consumer target is high school, college, and graduate students who want a multimedia, dual-mode device. This segment can be described demographically by age (16–30) and education status.

Our primary business target is mid- to large-sized corporations that want to help their managers and employees stay in touch and input or access critical data when out of the office. This segment consists of companies with more than $25 million in annual sales and more than 100 employees. We are also targeting entrepreneurs and small-business owners as well as medical users who want to update or access patients' medical records and to reduce paperwork.

Positioning   Using product differentiation, we are positioning the Sonic PDA as the most versatile, convenient, value-added model for personal and professional use. Our marketing will focus on the hands-free operation of multiple communication, entertainment, and information capabilities differentiating the Sonic 1000.

Product Strategy   The Sonic 1000, including all the features described in the earlier Product Review section, will be sold with a one-year warranty. We will introduce a more compact, powerful high-end model (the Sonic 2000) during the following year. Building the Sonic brand is an integral part of our product strategy. The brand and logo (Sonic's distinctive yellow thunderbolt) will be displayed on the product and its packaging and reinforced by its prominence in the introductory marketing campaign.

Pricing Strategy   The Sonic 1000 will be introduced at $250 wholesale/$350 estimated retail price per unit. We expect to lower the price of this first model when we expand the product line by launching the Sonic 2000, to be priced at $350 wholesale per unit. These prices reflect a strategy of (1) attracting desirable channel partners and (2) taking share from Palm and other established competitors.

Distribution Strategy   Our channel strategy is to use selective distribution, marketing Sonic PDAs through well-known stores and online retailers. During the first year, we will add channel partners until we have coverage in all major U.S. markets and the product is included in the major electronics catalogs and Web sites. We will also investigate distribution through cell phone outlets maintained by major carriers such as Verizon Wireless. In support of our channel partners, Sonic will provide demonstration products, detailed specification handouts, and full-color photos and displays featuring the product. Finally, we plan to arrange special payment terms for retailers that place volume orders.

Marketing Communications Strategy   By integrating all messages in all media, we will reinforce the brand name and the main points of product differentiation. Research about media consumption patterns will help our advertising agency choose appropriate media and timing to reach prospects before and during product introduction. Thereafter, advertising will appear on a pulsing basis to maintain brand awareness and communicate various differentiation messages. The agency will also coordinate public relations efforts to build the Sonic brand and support the differentiation message. To create buzz, we will host a

Positioning

A positioning built on meaningful differentiation, supported by appropriate strategy and implementation, can help the company build competitive advantage.

Marketing tools

These sections summarize the broad logic that will guide decisions made about the marketing tools to be used during the period covered by the plan.

FIGURE A2.1

Sonic's Marketing Organization

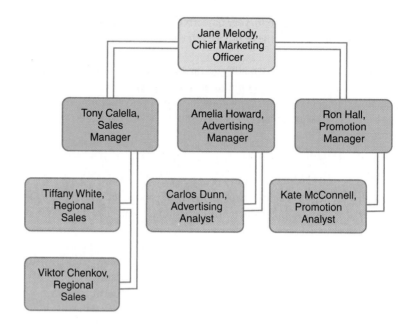

user-generated video contest on our Web site. To attract, retain, and motivate channel partners for a push strategy, we will use trade sales promotions and personal selling. Until the Sonic brand has been established, our communications will encourage purchases through channel partners rather than from our Web site.

Marketing Research   Using research, we are identifying the specific features and benefits that our target market segments value. Feedback from market tests, surveys, and focus groups will help us develop the Sonic 2000. We are also measuring and analyzing customers' attitudes toward competing brands and products. Brand awareness research will help us determine the effectiveness and efficiency of our messages and media. Finally, we will use customer satisfaction studies to gauge market reaction.

Marketing Organization   Sonic's chief marketing officer, Jane Melody, holds overall responsibility for all of the company's marketing activities. Figure A2.1 shows the structure of the eight-person marketing organization. Sonic has hired Worldwide Marketing to handle national sales campaigns, trade and consumer sales promotions, and public relations efforts.

Action Programs

The Sonic 1000 will be introduced in February. Following are summaries of the action programs we will use during the first six months of next year to achieve our stated objectives.

January We will launch a $200,000 trade sales promotion campaign and exhibit at the major industry trade shows to educate dealers and generate channel support for the product launch in February. Also, we will create buzz by providing samples to selected product reviewers, opinion leaders, influential bloggers, and celebrities. Our training staff will work with retail sales personnel at major chains to explain the Sonic 1000's features, benefits, and advantages.

February We will start an integrated print/radio/Internet campaign targeting professionals and consumers. The campaign will show how many functions the Sonic PDA can perform and emphasize the convenience of a single, powerful handheld device. This multimedia campaign will be supported by point-of-sale signage as well as online-only ads and video tours.

March As the multimedia advertising campaign continues, we will add consumer sales promotions such as a contest in which consumers post videos to our Web site, showing how they use the Sonic in creative and unusual ways. We will also distribute new point-of-purchase displays to support our retailers.

Marketing research
This section shows how marketing research will be used to support development, implementation, and evaluation of strategies and action programs.

Marketing organization
The marketing department may be organized by function, as in this sample, by geography, by product, or by customer (or some combination).

Action programs
Action programs should be coordinated with the resources and activities of other departments, including production, finance, and purchasing.

April We will hold a trade sales contest offering prizes for the salesperson and retail organization that sells the most Sonic PDAs during the four-week period.

May We plan to roll out a new national advertising campaign this month. The radio ads will feature celebrity voices telling their Sonic PDAs to perform functions such as initiating a phone call, sending an e-mail, playing a song or video, and so on. The stylized print and online ads will feature avatars of these celebrities holding their Sonic PDAs.

June Our radio campaign will add a new voice-over tagline promoting the Sonic 1000 as a graduation gift. We will also exhibit at the semiannual electronics trade show and provide channel partners with new competitive comparison handouts as a sales aid. In addition, we will tally and analyze the results of customer satisfaction surveys for use in future promotions and to provide feedback for product and marketing activities.

Budgets

Total first-year sales revenue for the Sonic 1000 is projected at $60 million, with an average wholesale price of $250 per unit and variable cost per unit of $150 for unit sales volume of 240,000. We anticipate a first-year loss of up to $10 million on the Sonic 1000 model. Break-even calculations indicate that the Sonic 1000 will become profitable after the sales volume exceeds 267,500, early in the product's second year. Our break-even analysis of Sonic's first PDA product assumes per-unit wholesale revenue of $250 per unit, variable cost of $150 per unit, and estimated first-year fixed costs of $26,750,000. Based on these assumptions, the break-even calculation is:

$$\frac{\$26{,}750{,}000}{\$250/\text{unit} - \$150/\text{unit}} = 267{,}500 \text{ units}$$

Budgets
Managers use budgets to project profitability and plan for each marketing program's expenditures, scheduling, and operations.

Controls

We are planning tight control measures to closely monitor quality and customer-service satisfaction. This will enable us to react very quickly in correcting any problems that may occur. Other early warning signals that will be monitored for signs of deviation from the plan include monthly sales (by segment and channel) and monthly expenses. Given the market's volatility, we are developing contingency plans to address fast-moving environmental changes such as new technology and new competition.

Controls
Controls help management assess results after the plan is implemented, identify any problems or performance variations, and initiate corrective action.

Marketing Plan Tools

Prentice Hall offers two valuable resources to assist you in developing a marketing plan:

• *The Marketing Plan Handbook* by Marian Burk Wood explains the process of creating a marketing plan, complete with detailed checklists and dozens of real-world examples.
• *Marketing Plan Pro* is an award-winning software package that includes sample plans, step-by-step guides, an introductory video, help wizards, and customizable charts for documenting a marketing plan.

Sources: Background information and market data adapted from "Roam If You Want To," *PC World,* September 2007, p. 134; Sascha Segan, "Exclusive: One RAZR2, Four Ways to Cut It," *PC Magazine Online,* August 13, 2007, www.pcmag.com; "Apple Unlikely to Budge Anytime Soon on iPhone Pricing," *InformationWeek,* July 26, 2007; "Smart Phones Get Smarter, Thanks in Part to the iPhone," *InformationWeek,* July 21, 2007; "Nine Alternatives to Apple's iPhone," *InformationWeek,* June 28, 2007; "Hospital Uses PDA App for Patient Transport," *Health Data Management,* June 2007, p. 14; "Smart Phones Force Dell from Handhelds," *MicroScope,* April 23, 2007; "2005 PDA Shipments Set Record," *Business Communications Review,* April 2006, p. 6; "Smartphone Market Grows Fast Despite Challenges," *Appliance,* March 2006, p. 16.

Appendix 3 Marketing by the Numbers

Marketing managers are facing increased accountability for the financial implications of their actions. This appendix provides a basic introduction to measuring marketing financial performance. Such financial analysis guides marketers in making sound marketing decisions and in assessing the outcomes of those decisions.

The appendix is built around a hypothetical manufacturer of high-definition consumer electronics products—HDX-treme. In the past, HDX-treme has concentrated on making high-definition televisions for the consumer market. However, the company is now entering the accessories market. Specifically, HDX-treme is introducing a new product—a high-definition optical disc player (DVD) that uses the Blu-ray format. In this appendix, we will discuss and analyze the various decisions HDX-treme's marketing managers must make before and after the new-product launch.

The appendix is organized into *three sections*. The *first section* introduces pricing, break-even, and margin analysis assessments that will guide the introduction of HDX-treme's new product. The *second section* discusses demand estimates, the marketing budget, and marketing performance measures. It begins with a discussion of estimating market potential and company sales. It then introduces the marketing budget, as illustrated through a *pro forma* profit-and-loss statement followed by the actual profit-and-loss statement. Next, we discuss marketing performance measures, with a focus on helping marketing managers to better defend their decisions from a financial perspective. In the *third section,* we analyze the financial implications of various marketing tactics, such as increasing advertising expenditures, adding sales representatives to increase distribution, lowering price, or extending the product line.

Each of the three sections ends with a set of quantitative exercises that provide you with an opportunity to apply the concepts you learned to situations beyond HDX-treme.

Pricing, Break-Even, and Margin Analysis

Pricing Considerations

Determining price is one of the most important marketing-mix decisions, and marketers have considerable leeway when setting prices. The limiting factors are demand and costs. Demand factors, such as buyer-perceived value, set the price ceiling. The company's costs set the price floor. In between these two factors, marketers must consider competitors' prices and other factors such as reseller requirements, government regulations, and company objectives.

Current competing high-definition DVD products in this relatively new product category were introduced in 2006 and sell at retail prices between $500 and $1,200. HDX-treme plans to introduce its new product at a lower price in order to expand the market and to gain market share rapidly. We first consider HDX-treme's pricing decision from a cost perspective. Then, we consider consumer value, the competitive environment, and reseller requirements.

Determining Costs   Recall from Chapter 10 that there are different types of costs. **Fixed costs** do not vary with production or sales level and include costs such as rent, interest, depreciation, and clerical and management salaries. Regardless of the level of output, the company must pay these costs. Whereas total fixed costs remain constant as output increases, the fixed cost per unit (or average fixed cost) will decrease as output increases because the total fixed costs are spread across more units of output. **Variable costs** vary directly with the level of production and include costs related to the direct production of the product (such as costs of goods sold—COGS) and many of the marketing costs associated with selling it. Although these costs tend to be uniform for each unit produced, they are called variable because their total varies with the number of units produced. **Total costs** are the sum of the fixed and variable costs for any given level of production.

Fixed costs
Costs that do not vary with production or sales level.

Variable costs
Costs that vary directly with the level of production.

Total costs
The sum of the fixed and variable costs for any given level of production.

HDX-treme has invested $10 million in refurbishing an existing facility to manufacture the new DVD product. Once production begins, the company estimates that it will incur fixed costs of $20 million per year. The variable cost to produce each DVD player is estimated to be $250 and is expected to remain at that level for the output capacity of the facility.

Setting Price Based on Costs

HDX-treme starts with the cost-based approach to pricing discussed in Chapter 10. Recall that the simplest method, **cost-plus pricing** (or **markup pricing**), simply adds a standard markup to the cost of the product. To use this method, however, HDX-treme must specify an expected unit sales so that total unit costs can be determined. Unit variable costs will remain constant regardless of the output, but *average unit fixed costs* will decrease as output increases.

To illustrate this method, suppose HDX-treme has fixed costs of $20 million, variable costs of $250 per unit, and expects unit sales of 1 million units. Thus, the cost per DVD player is given by:

$$\text{Unit cost} = \text{variable cost} + \frac{\text{fixed costs}}{\text{unit sales}} = \$250 + \frac{\$20,000,000}{1,000,000} = \$270$$

Note that we do *not* include the initial investment of $10 million in the total fixed cost figure. It is not considered a fixed cost because it is not a *relevant* cost. **Relevant costs** are those that will occur in the future and that will vary across the alternatives being considered. HDX-treme's investment to refurbish the manufacturing facility was a one-time cost that will not reoccur in the future. Such past costs are *sunk costs* and should not be considered in future analyses.

Also notice that if HDX-treme sells its DVD player for $270, the price is equal to the total cost per unit. This is the **break-even price**—the price at which unit revenue (price) equals unit cost and profit is zero.

Suppose HDX-treme does not want to merely break even but rather wants to earn a 25% markup on sales. HDX-treme's markup price is:[1]

$$\text{Markup price} = \frac{\text{unit cost}}{(1 - \text{desired return on sales})} = \frac{\$270}{1 - .25} = \$360$$

This is the price that HDX-treme would sell the DVD player to resellers such as wholesalers or retailers to earn a 25% profit on sales.

Another approach HDX-treme could use is called **return on investment (ROI) pricing** (**or target-return pricing**). In this case, the company *would* consider the initial $10 million investment, but only to determine the dollar profit goal. Suppose the company wants a 30% return on its investment. The price necessary to satisfy this requirement can be determined by:[2]

$$\text{ROI price} = \text{unit cost} + \frac{\text{ROI} \times \text{investment}}{\text{unit sales}} = \$270 + \frac{0.3 \times \$10,000,000}{1,000,000} = \$273$$

That is, if HDX-treme sells its DVD players for $273 each, it will realize a 30% return on its initial investment of $10 million.

In these pricing calculations, unit cost is a function of the expected sales, which were estimated to be 1 million units. But what if actual sales were lower? Then the unit cost would be higher because the fixed costs would be spread over fewer units, and the realized percentage markup on sales or ROI would be lower. Alternatively, if sales are higher than the estimated 1 million units, unit cost would be lower than $270, so a lower price would produce the desired markup on sales or ROI. It's important to note that these cost-based pricing methods are *internally* focused and do not consider demand, competitors' prices, or reseller requirements. Because HDX-treme will be selling these DVD players to consumers through wholesalers and retailers offering competing brands, the company must consider markup pricing from this perspective.

Cost-plus pricing (or **markup pricing**)
A standard markup to the cost of the product.

Relevant costs
Costs that will occur in the future and that will vary across the alternatives being considered.

Break-even price
The price at which total revenue equals total cost and profit is zero.

Return on investment (ROI) pricing (or **target-return pricing**)
A cost-based pricing method that determines price based on a specified rate of return on investment.

Setting Price Based on External Factors

Whereas costs determine the price floor, HDX-treme also must consider external factors when setting price. HDX-treme does not have the final say concerning the final price to consumers—retailers do. So it must start with its suggested retail price and work back. In doing so, HDX-treme must consider the markups required by resellers that sell the product to consumers.

In general, a dollar **markup** is the difference between a company's selling price for a product and its cost to manufacture or purchase it. For a retailer, then, the markup is the difference between the price it charges consumers and the cost the retailer must pay for the product. Thus, for any level of reseller:

$$\text{Dollar markup} = \text{selling price} - \text{cost}$$

Markups are usually expressed as a percentage, and there are two different ways to compute markups—on *cost* or on *selling price*:

$$\text{Markup percentage on cost} = \frac{\text{dollar markup}}{\text{cost}}$$

$$\text{Markup percentage on selling price} = \frac{\text{dollar markup}}{\text{selling price}}$$

To apply reseller margin analysis, HDX-treme must first set the suggested retail price and then work back to the price at which it must sell the DVD player to a wholesaler. Suppose retailers expect a 30% margin and wholesalers want a 20% margin based on their respective selling prices. And suppose that HDX-treme sets a manufacturer's suggested retail price (MSRP) of $599.99 for its high-definition DVD player.

Recall that HDX-treme wants to expand the market by pricing low and generating market share quickly. HDX-treme selected the $599.99 MSRP because it is much lower than most competitors' prices, which can be as high as $1,200. And the company's research shows that it is below the threshold at which more consumers are willing to purchase the product. By using buyers' perceptions of value and not the seller's cost to determine the MSRP, HDX-treme is using **value-based pricing**. For simplicity, we will use an MSRP of $600 in further analyses.

To determine the price HDX-treme will charge wholesalers, we must first subtract the retailer's margin from the retail price to determine the retailer's cost ($600 – ($600 × 0.30) = $420). The retailer's cost is the wholesaler's price, so HDX-treme next subtracts the wholesaler's margin ($420 – ($420 × 0.20) = $336). Thus, the **markup chain** representing the sequence of markups used by firms at each level in a channel for HDX-treme's new product is:

Suggested retail price:	$600
minus retail margin (30%):	– $180
Retailer's cost/wholesaler's price:	$420
minus wholesaler's margin (20%):	– $ 84
Wholesaler's cost/HDX-treme's price:	$336

By deducting the markups for each level in the markup chain, HDX-treme arrives at a price for the DVD player to wholesalers of $336.

Break-Even and Margin Analysis

The previous analyses derived a value-based price of $336 for HDX-treme's DVD player. Although this price is higher than the break-even price of $270 and covers costs, that price assumed a demand of 1 million units. But how many units and what level of dollar sales must HDX-treme achieve to break even at the $336 price? And what level of sales must be

Markup
The difference between a company's selling price for a product and its cost to manufacture or purchase it.

Value-based pricing
Offering just the right combination of quality and good service at a fair price.

Markup chain
The sequence of markups used by firms at each level in a channel.

achieved to realize various profit goals? These questions can be answered through break-even and margin analysis.

Determining Break-Even Unit Volume and Dollar Sales

Break-even analysis

Analysis to determine the unit volume and dollar sales needed to be profitable given a particular price and cost structure.

Based on an understanding of costs, consumer value, the competitive environment, and reseller requirements, HDX-treme has decided to set its price to wholesalers at $336. At that price, what sales level will be needed for HDX-treme to break even or make a profit? **Break-even analysis** determines the unit volume and dollar sales needed to be profitable given a particular price and cost structure. At the break-even point, total revenue equals total costs and profit is zero. Above this point, the company will make a profit; below it, the company will lose money. HDX-treme can calculate break-even volume using the following formula:[3]

$$\text{Break-even volume} = \frac{\text{fixed costs}}{\text{price} - \text{unit variable cost}}$$

Unit contribution

The amount that each unit contributes to covering fixed costs—the difference between price and variable costs.

The denominator (price − unit variable cost) is called **unit contribution** (sometimes called contribution margin). It represents the amount that each unit contributes to covering fixed costs. Break-even volume represents the level of output at which all (variable and fixed) costs are covered. In HDX-treme's case, break-even unit volume is:

$$\text{Break-even volume} = \frac{\text{fixed cost}}{\text{price} - \text{variable cost}} = \frac{\$20,000,000}{\$336 - \$250} = 232,558.1 \text{ units}$$

Thus, at the given cost and pricing structure, HDX-treme will break even at 232,559 units.

To determine the break-even dollar sales, simply multiply unit break-even volume by the selling price:

$$\text{BE sales} = \text{BE}_{\text{vol}} \times \text{price} = 232,559 \times \$336 = \$78,139,824$$

Contribution margin

The unit contribution divided by the selling price.

Another way to calculate dollar break-even sales is to use the percentage contribution margin (hereafter referred to as **contribution margin**), which is the unit contribution divided by the selling price:

$$\text{Contribution margin} = \frac{\text{price} - \text{variable cost}}{\text{price}} = \frac{\$336 - \$250}{\$336} = 0.256 \text{ or } 25.6\%$$

Then,

$$\text{Break-even sales} = \frac{\text{fixed costs}}{\text{contribution margin}} = \frac{\$20,000,000}{0.256} = \$78,125,000$$

Note that the difference between the two break-even sales calculations is due to rounding.

Such break-even analysis helps HDX-treme by showing the unit volume needed to cover costs. If production capacity cannot attain this level of output, then the company should not launch this product. However, the unit break-even volume is well within HDX-treme's capacity. Of course, the bigger question concerns whether HDX-treme can sell this volume at the $336 price. We'll address that issue a little later.

Understanding contribution margin is useful in other types of analyses as well, particularly if unit prices and unit variable costs are unknown or if a company (say, a retailer) sells many products at different prices and knows the percentage of total sales variable costs represent. Whereas unit contribution is the difference between unit price and unit variable costs, total contribution is the difference between total sales and total variable costs. The overall contribution margin can be calculated by:

$$\text{Contribution margin} = \frac{\text{total sales} - \text{total variable costs}}{\text{total sales}}$$

Regardless of the actual level of sales, if the company knows what percentage of sales is represented by variable costs, it can calculate contribution margin. For example, HDX-treme's unit variable cost is $250, or 74% of the selling price ($250 ÷ $336 = 0.74). That means for every $1 of sales revenue for HDX-treme, $0.74 represents variable costs, and the difference ($0.26) represents contribution to fixed costs. But even if the company doesn't know its unit price and unit variable cost, it can calculate the contribution margin from total sales and total variable costs or from knowledge of the total cost structure. It can set total sales equal to 100% regardless of the actual absolute amount and determine the contribution margin:

$$\text{Contribution margin} = \frac{100\% - 74\%}{100\%} = \frac{1 - 0.74}{1} = 1 - 0.74 = 0.26 \text{ or } 26\%$$

Note that this matches the percentage calculated from the unit price and unit variable cost information. This alternative calculation will be very useful later when analyzing various marketing decisions.

Determining "Breakeven" for Profit Goals

Although it is useful to know the break-even point, most companies are more interested in making a profit. Assume HDX-treme would like to realize a $5 million profit in the first year. How many DVD players must it sell at the $336 price to cover fixed costs and produce this profit? To determine this, HDX-treme can simply add the profit figure to fixed costs and again divide by the unit contribution to determine unit sales:[4]

$$\text{Unit volume} = \frac{\text{fixed cost} - \text{profit goal}}{\text{price} - \text{variable cost}} = \frac{\$20,000,000 + \$5,000,000}{\$336 - \$250} = 290,697.7 \text{ units}$$

Thus, to earn a $5 million profit, HDX-treme must sell 290,698 units. Multiply by price to determine dollar sales needed to achieve a $5 million profit:

$$\text{Dollar sales} = 290,698 \text{ units} \times \$336 = \$97,674,528$$

Or use the contribution margin:

$$\text{Sales} = \frac{\text{fixed cost} + \text{profit goal}}{\text{contribution margin}} = \frac{\$20,000,000 + \$5,000,000}{0.256} = \$97,656,250$$

Again, note that the difference between the two break-even sales calculations is due to rounding.

As we saw previously, a profit goal can also be stated as a return on investment goal. For example, recall that HDX-treme wants a 30% return on its $10 million investment. Thus, its absolute profit goal is $3 million ($10,000,000 × 0.30). This profit goal is treated the same way as in the previous example:[5]

$$\text{Unit volume} = \frac{\text{fixed cost} + \text{profit goal}}{\text{price} - \text{variable cost}} = \frac{\$20,000,000 + \$3,000,000}{\$336 - \$250} = 267,442 \text{ units}$$

$$\text{Dollar sales} = 267,442 \text{ units} \times \$336 = \$89,860,512$$

Or

$$\text{Dollar sales} = \frac{\text{fixed cost} + \text{profit goal}}{\text{contribution margin}} = \frac{\$20,000,000 + \$3,000,000}{0.256} = \$89,843,750$$

Finally, HDX-treme can express its profit goal as a percentage of sales, which we also saw in previous pricing analyses. Assume HDX-treme desires a 25% return on sales. To determine the unit and sales volume necessary to achieve this goal, the calculation is a little different from the previous two examples. In this case, we incorporate the profit goal into the unit contribution as an additional variable cost. Look at it this way: If 25% of each sale must go toward profits, that leaves only 75% of the selling price to cover fixed costs. Thus, the equation becomes:[6]

$$\text{Unit volume} = \frac{\text{fixed cost}}{\text{price} - \text{variable cost} - (0.25 \times \text{price})} \text{ or } \frac{\text{fixed cost}}{(0.75 \times \text{price}) - \text{variable cost}}$$

So,

$$\text{Unit volume} = \frac{\$20,000,000}{(0.75 \times \$336) - \$250} = 10,000,000 \text{ units}$$

Dollar sales necessary = 10,000,000 units × $336 = $3,360,000,000

Thus, HDX-treme would need more than $3 billion in sales to realize a 25% return on sales given its current price and cost structure! Could it possibly achieve this level of sales? The major point is this: Although break-even analysis can be useful in determining the level of sales needed to cover costs or to achieve a stated profit goal, it does not tell the company whether it is *possible* to achieve that level of sales at the specified price. To address this issue, HDX-treme needs to estimate demand for this product.

Before moving on, however, let's stop here and practice applying the concepts covered so far. Now that you have seen pricing and break-even concepts in action as they related to HDX-treme's new DVD player, here are several exercises for you to apply what you have learned in other contexts.

Marketing by the Numbers Exercise Set One

Now that you've studied pricing, break-even, and margin analysis as they relate to HDX-treme's new-product launch, use the following exercises to apply these concepts in other contexts.

1.1 Sanborn, a manufacturer of electric roof vents, realizes a cost of $55 for every unit it produces. Its total fixed costs equal $2 million. If the company manufactures 500,000 units, compute the following:
   a.   unit cost
   b.   markup price if the company desires a 10% return on sales
   c.   ROI price if the company desires a 25% return on an investment of $1 million

1.2 An interior decorator purchases items to sell in her store. She purchases a lamp for $125 and sells it for $225. Determine the following:
   a.   dollar markup
   b.   markup percentage on cost
   c.   markup percentage on selling price

1.3 A consumer purchases a toaster from a retailer for $60. The retailer's markup is 20%, and the wholesaler's markup is 15%, both based on selling price. For what price does the manufacturer sell the product to the wholesaler?

1.4 A vacuum manufacturer has a unit cost of $50 and wishes to achieve a margin of 30% based on selling price. If the manufacturer sells directly to a retailer who then adds a set margin of 40% based on selling price, determine the retail price charged to consumers.

1.5 Advanced Electronics manufactures DVDs and sells them directly to retailers who typically sell them for $20. Retailers take a 40% margin based on the retail selling price. Advanced's cost information is as follows:

DVD package and disc	$2.50/DVD
Royalties	$2.25/DVD
Advertising and promotion	$500,000
Overhead	$200,000

Calculate the following:
   a.   contribution per unit and contribution margin
   b.   break-even volume in DVD units and dollars
   c.   volume in DVD units and dollar sales necessary if Advanced's profit goal is 20% profit on sales
   d.   net profit if 5 million DVDs are sold

Demand Estimates, the Marketing Budget, and Marketing Performance Measures

Market Potential and Sales Estimates

HDX-treme has now calculated the sales needed to break even and to attain various profit goals on its DVD player. However, the company needs more information regarding demand in order to assess the feasibility of attaining the needed sales levels. This information is also needed for production and other decisions. For example, production schedules need to be developed and marketing tactics need to be planned.

The **total market demand** for a product or service is the total volume that would be bought by a defined consumer group in a defined geographic area in a defined time period in a defined marketing environment under a defined level and mix of industry marketing effort. Total market demand is not a fixed number but a function of the stated conditions. For example, next year's total market demand for high-definition DVD players will depend on how much Samsung, Sony, Pioneer, Toshiba, and other producers spend on marketing their brands. It also depends on many environmental factors, such as government regulations, economic conditions, and the level of consumer confidence in a given market. The upper limit of market demand is called **market potential**.

One general but practical method that HDX-treme might use for estimating total market demand uses three variables: (1) the number of prospective buyers, (2) the quantity purchased by an average buyer per year, and (3) the price of an average unit. Using these numbers, HDX-treme can estimate total market demand as follows:

$$Q = n \times q \times p$$

where

Q = total market demand
n = number of buyers in the market
q = quantity purchased by an average buyer per year
p = price of an average unit

A variation of this approach is the **chain ratio method**. This method involves multiplying a base number by a chain of adjusting percentages. For example, HDX-treme's high-definition DVD player is designed to play high-definition DVD movies on high-definition televisions. Thus, consumers who do not own a high-definition television will not likely purchase this player. Additionally, not all HDTV households will be willing and able to purchase the new high-definition DVD player. HDX-treme can estimate U.S. demand using a chain of calculations like the following:

Total number of U.S. households
× The percentage of U.S. households owning a high-definition television
× The percentage of these households willing and able to buy a high-definition DVD player

ACNielsen, the television ratings company, estimates that there are more than 110 million TV households in the United States.[7] The Consumer Electronics Association estimates that 38% of TV households will own HDTVs by the end of 2007.[8] However, HDX-treme's research indicates that only 44.5% of HDTV households possess the discretionary income needed and are willing to buy a high-definition DVD player. Then, the total number of households willing and able to purchase this product is:

110 million households × 0.38 × 0.445 = 18.6 million households

Because HDTVs are relatively new and expensive products, most households have only one of these televisions, and it's usually the household's primary television.[9] Thus, consumers who buy a high-definition DVD player will likely buy only one per household.

Total market demand
The total volume that would be bought by a defined consumer group in a defined geographic area in a defined time period in a defined marketing environment under a defined level and mix of industry marketing effort.

Market potential
The upper limit of market demand.

Chain ratio method
Estimating market demand by multiplying a base number by a chain of adjusting percentages.

Assuming the average retail price across all brands is $750 for this product, the estimate of total market demand is as follows:

18.6 million households $\times$ 1 DVD player per household $\times$ $750 = $14 billion

This simple chain of calculations gives HDX-treme only a rough estimate of potential demand. However, more detailed chains involving additional segments and other qualifying factors would yield more accurate and refined estimates. Still, these are only *estimates* of market potential. They rely heavily on assumptions regarding adjusting percentages, average quantity, and average price. Thus, HDX-treme must make certain that its assumptions are reasonable and defendable. As can be seen, the overall market potential in dollar sales can vary widely given the average price used. For this reason, HDX-treme will use unit sales potential to determine its sales estimate for next year. Market potential in terms of units is 18.6 million DVD players (18.6 million households $\times$ 1 DVD player per household).

Assuming that HDX-treme wants to attain 2% market share (comparable to its share of the HDTV market) in the first year after launching this product, then it can forecast unit sales at 18.6 million units $\times$ 0.02 = 372,000 units. At a selling price of $336 per unit, this translates into sales of $124.99 million (372,000 units $\times$ $336 per unit). For simplicity, further analyses will use forecasted sales of $125 million.

This unit volume estimate is well within HDX-treme's production capacity and exceeds not only the break-even estimate (232,559 units) calculated earlier, but also the volume necessary to realize a $5 million profit (290,698 units) or a 30% return on investment (267,442 units). However, this forecast falls well short of the volume necessary to realize a 25% return on sales (10 million units!) and may require that HDX-treme revise expectations.

To assess expected profits, we must now look at the budgeted expenses for launching this product. To do this, we will construct a pro forma profit-and-loss statement.

The Profit-and-Loss Statement and Marketing Budget

All marketing managers must account for the profit impact of their marketing strategies. A major tool for projecting such profit impact is a **pro forma** (or projected) **profit-and-loss statement** (also called an **income statement** or **operating statement**). A pro forma statement shows projected revenues less budgeted expenses and estimates the projected net profit for an organization, product, or brand during a specific planning period, typically a year. It includes direct product production costs, marketing expenses budgeted to attain a given sales forecast, and overhead expenses assigned to the organization or product. A profit-and-loss statement typically consists of several major components (see Table A3.1):

Pro forma (or projected) **profit-and-loss statement** (or **income statement** or **operating statement**) A statement that shows projected revenues less budgeted expenses and estimates the projected net profit for an organization, product, or brand during a specific planning period, typically a year.

- *Net sales*—gross sales revenue minus returns and allowances (for example, trade, cash, quantity, and promotion allowances). HDX-treme's net sales for 2007 are estimated to be $125 million, as determined in the previous analysis.
- *Cost of goods sold* (sometimes called *cost of sales*)—the actual cost of the merchandise sold by a manufacturer or reseller. It includes the cost of inventory, purchases, and other costs associated with making the goods. HDX-treme's cost of goods sold is estimated to be 50% of net sales, or $62.5 million.
- *Gross margin (or gross profit)*—the difference between net sales and cost of goods sold. HDX-treme's gross margin is estimated to be $62.5 million.
- *Operating expenses*—the expenses incurred while doing business. These include all other expenses beyond the cost of goods sold that are necessary to conduct business. Operating expenses can be presented in total or broken down in detail. Here, HDX-treme's estimated operating expenses include *marketing expenses* and *general and administrative expenses*.

    Marketing expenses include sales expenses, promotion expenses, and distribution expenses. The new product will be sold though HDX-treme's sales force, so the company budgets $5 million for sales salaries. However, because sales representatives earn a 10% commission on sales, HDX-treme must also add a variable component to sales expenses of $12.5 million (10% of $125 million net sales), for a total budgeted sales expense of

			% of Sales
Net Sales		$125,000,000	100%
Cost of Goods Sold		62,500,000	50%
Gross Margin		$ 62,500,000	50%
Marketing Expenses			
Sales expenses	$17,500,000		
Promotion expenses	15,000,000		
Freight	12,500,000	45,000,000	36%
General and Administrative Expenses			
Managerial salaries and expenses	$2,000,000		
Indirect overhead	3,000,000	5,000,000	4%
Net Profit Before Income Tax		$12,500,000	10%

TABLE A3.1 Pro Forma Profit-and-Loss Statement for the 12-Month Period Ended December 31, 2007

$17.5 million. HDX-treme sets its advertising and promotion to launch this product at $10 million. However, the company also budgets 4% of sales, or $5 million, for cooperative advertising allowances to retailers who promote HDX-treme's new product in their advertising. Thus, the total budgeted advertising and promotion expenses are $15 million ($10 million for advertising plus $5 million in co-op allowances). Finally, HDX-treme budgets 10% of net sales, or $12.5 million, for freight and delivery charges. In all, total marketing expenses are estimated to be $17.5 million + $15 million + $12.5 million = $45 million.

General and administrative expenses are estimated at $5 million, broken down into $2 million for managerial salaries and expenses for the marketing function and $3 million of indirect overhead allocated to this product by the corporate accountants (such as depreciation, interest, maintenance, and insurance). Total expenses for the year, then, are estimated to be $50 million ($45 million marketing expenses + $5 million in general and administrative expenses).

• *Net profit before taxes*—profit earned after all costs are deducted. HDX-treme's estimated net profit before taxes is $12.5 million.

In all, as Table A3.1 shows, HDX-treme expects to earn a profit on its new DVD player of $12.5 million in 2007. Also note that the percentage of sales that each component of the profit-and-loss statement represents is given in the right-hand column. These percentages are determined by dividing the cost figure by net sales (that is, marketing expenses represent 36% of net sales determined by $45 million ÷ $125 million). As can be seen, HDX-treme projects a net profit return on sales of 10% in the first year after launching this product.

Marketing Performance Measures

Now let's fast-forward a year. HDX-treme's high-definition DVD player has been on the market for one year and management wants to assess its sales and profit performance. One way to assess this performance is to compute performance ratios derived from HDX-treme's **profit-and-loss statement** (or **income statement** or **operating statement**).

Whereas the pro forma profit-and-loss statement shows *projected* financial performance, the statement given in Table A3.2 shows HDX-treme's *actual* financial performance based on actual sales, cost of goods sold, and expenses during the past year. By comparing the profit-and-loss statement from one period to the next, HDX-treme can gauge performance against goals, spot favorable or unfavorable trends, and take appropriate corrective action.

The profit-and-loss statement shows that HDX-treme lost $1 million rather than making the $12.5 million profit projected in the pro forma statement. Why? One obvious reason is that net sales fell $25 million short of estimated sales. Lower sales translated into lower variable costs associated with marketing the product. However, both fixed costs and the cost of goods sold as a percentage of sales exceeded expectations. Hence, the product's

Profit-and-loss statement (or income statement or operating statement)
A statement that shows actual revenues less expenses and net profit for an organization, product, or brand during a specific planning period, typically a year.

		% of Sales
Net Sales	$100,000,000	100%
Cost of Goods Sold	55,000,000	55%
Gross Margin	$ 45,000,000	45%
Marketing Expenses		
Sales expenses	$15,000,000	
Promotion expenses	14,000,000	
Freight	10,000,000	39,000,000	39%
General and Administrative Expenses		
Managerial salaries and expenses	$2,000,000	
Indirect overhead	5,000,000	7,000,000	7%
Net Profit Before Income Tax		($1,000,000)	(–1%)

TABLE A3.2 Profit-and-Loss Statement for the 12-Month Period Ended December 31, 2007

contribution margin was 21% rather than the estimated 26%. That is, variable costs represented 79% of sales (55% for cost of goods sold, 10% for sales commissions, 10% for freight, and 4% for co-op allowances). Recall that contribution margin can be calculated by subtracting that fraction from one $(1 - 0.79 = 0.21)$. Total fixed costs were $22 million, $2 million more than estimated. Thus, the sales that HDX-treme needed to break even given this cost structure can be calculated as:

$$\text{Break-even sales} = \frac{\text{fixed costs}}{\text{contribution margin}} = \frac{\$22,000,000}{0.21} = \$104,761,905$$

If HDX-treme had achieved another $5 million in sales, it would have earned a profit.

Although HDX-treme's sales fell short of the forecasted sales, so did overall industry sales for this product. Overall industry sales were only $2.5 billion. That means that HDX-treme's **market share** was 4% ($100 million ÷ $2.5 billion = 0.04 = 4%), which was higher than forecasted. Thus, HDX-treme attained a higher-than-expected market share but the overall market sales were not as high as estimated.

Market share
Company sales divided by market sales.

Analytic Ratios

The profit-and-loss statement provides the figures needed to compute some crucial **operating ratios**—the ratios of selected operating statement items to net sales. These ratios let marketers compare the firm's performance in one year to that in previous years (or with industry standards and competitors' performance in that year). The most commonly used operating ratios are the *gross margin percentage,* the *net profit percentage,* and the *operating expense percentage.* The *inventory turnover rate* and *return on investment (ROI)* are often used to measure managerial effectiveness and efficiency.

The **gross margin percentage** indicates the percentage of net sales remaining after cost of goods sold that can contribute to operating expenses and net profit before taxes. The higher this ratio, the more a firm has left to cover expenses and generate profit. HDX-treme's gross margin ratio was 45%:

Operating ratios
The ratios of selected operating statement items to net sales.

Gross margin percentage
The percentage of net sales remaining after cost of goods sold—calculated by dividing gross margin by net sales.

$$\text{Gross margin percentage} = \frac{\text{gross margin}}{\text{net sales}} = \frac{\$45,000,000}{\$100,000,000} = 0.45 = 45\%$$

Note that this percentage is lower than estimated, and this ratio is seen easily in the percentage of sales column in Table A2.2. Stating items in the profit-and-loss statement as a percent of sales allows managers to quickly spot abnormal changes in costs over time. If there was previous history for this product and this ratio was declining, management should examine it more closely to determine why it has decreased (that is, because of a decrease in sales volume or price, an increase in costs, or a combination of these). In HDX-treme's case, net sales were $25 million lower than estimated, and cost of goods sold was higher than estimated (55% rather than the estimated 50%).

The **net profit percentage** shows the percentage of each sales dollar going to profit. It is calculated by dividing net profits by net sales:

$$\text{Net profit percentage} = \frac{\text{net profit}}{\text{net sales}} = \frac{-\$1,000,000}{\$100,000,000} = -0.01 = -1.0\%$$

Net profit percentage
The percentage of each sales dollar going to profit—calculated by dividing net profits by net sales.

This ratio is easily seen in the percent of sales column. HDX-treme's DVD player generated negative profits in the first year, not a good situation given that before the product launch net profits before taxes were estimated at more than $12 million. Later in this appendix, we will discuss further analyses the marketing manager should conduct to defend the product.

The **operating expense percentage** indicates the portion of net sales going to operating expenses. Operating expenses include marketing and other expenses not directly related to marketing the product, such as indirect overhead assigned to this product. It is calculated by:

Operating expense percentage
The portion of net sales going to operating expenses—calculated by dividing total expenses by net sales.

$$\text{Operating expense percentage} = \frac{\text{total expenses}}{\text{net sales}} = \frac{\$46,000,000}{\$100,000,000} = 0.46 = 46\%$$

This ratio can also be quickly determined from the percent of sales column in the profit-and-loss statement by adding the percentages for marketing expenses and general and administrative expenses (39% + 7%). Thus, 46 cents of every sales dollar went for operations. Although HDX-treme wants this ratio to be as low as possible, and 46% is not an alarming amount, it is of concern if it is increasing over time or if a loss is realized.

Another useful ratio is the **inventory turnover rate** (also called **stockturn rate** for resellers). The inventory turnover rate is the number of times an inventory turns over or is sold during a specified time period (often one year). This rate tells how quickly a business is moving inventory through the organization. Higher rates indicate that lower investments in inventory are made, thus freeing up funds for other investments. It may be computed on a cost, selling price, or unit basis. The formula based on cost is:

Inventory turnover rate (or stockturn rate)
The number of times an inventory turns over or is sold during a specified time period (often one year)—calculated based on costs, selling price, or units.

$$\text{Inventory turnover rate} = \frac{\text{cost of goods sold}}{\text{average inventory at cost}}$$

Assuming HDX-treme's beginning and ending inventories were $30 million and $20 million, respectively, the inventory turnover rate is:

$$\text{Inventory turnover rate} = \frac{\$55,000,000}{(\$30,000,000 + \$20,000,000)/2} = \frac{\$55,000,000}{\$25,000,000} = 2.2$$

That is, HDX-treme's inventory turned over 2.2 times in 2007. Normally, the higher the turnover rate, the higher the management efficiency and company profitability. However, this rate should be compared to industry averages, competitors' rates, and past performance to determine if HDX-treme is doing well. A competitor with similar sales but a higher inventory turnover rate will have fewer resources tied up in inventory, allowing it to invest in other areas of the business.

Companies frequently use **return on investment (ROI)** to measure managerial effectiveness and efficiency. For HDX-treme, ROI is the ratio of net profits to total investment required to manufacture the new product. This investment includes capital investments in land, buildings, and equipment (here, the initial $10 million to refurbish the manufacturing facility) plus inventory costs (HDX-treme's average inventory totaled $25 million), for a total of $35 million. Thus, HDX-treme's ROI for the DVD player is:

Return on investment (ROI)
A measure of managerial effectiveness and efficiency—net profit before taxes divided by total investment.

$$\text{Return on investment} = \frac{\text{net profit before taxes}}{\text{investment}} = \frac{-\$1,000,000}{\$35,000,000} = -.0286 = -2.86\%$$

ROI is often used to compare alternatives, and a positive ROI is desired. The alternative with the highest ROI is preferred to other alternatives. HDX-treme needs to be concerned with the ROI realized. One obvious way HDX-treme can increase ROI is to increase net profit by reducing expenses. Another way is to reduce its investment, perhaps by investing less in inventory and turning it over more frequently.

Marketing Profitability Metrics

Given the above financial results, you may be thinking that HDX-treme should drop this new product. But what arguments can marketers make for keeping or dropping this product? The obvious arguments for dropping the product are that first-year sales were well below expected levels and the product lost money, resulting in a negative return on investment.

So what would happen if HDX-treme did drop this product? Surprisingly, if the company drops the product, the profits for the total organization will decrease by $4 million! How can that be? Marketing managers need to look closely at the numbers in the profit-and-loss statement to determine the *net marketing contribution* for this product. In HDX-treme's case, the net marketing contribution for the DVD player is $4 million, and if the company drops this product, that contribution will disappear as well. Let's look more closely at this concept to illustrate how marketing managers can better assess and defend their marketing strategies and programs.

Net marketing contribution (NMC)
A measure of marketing profitability that includes only components of profitability controlled by marketing.

Net Marketing Contribution   **Net marketing contribution (NMC)**, along with other marketing metrics derived from it, measures *marketing* profitability. It includes only components of profitability that are controlled by marketing. Whereas the previous calculation of net profit before taxes from the profit-and-loss statement includes operating expenses not under marketing's control, NMC does not. Referring back to HDX-treme's profit-and-loss statement given in Table A2.2, we can calculate net marketing contribution for the DVD player as:

$$\text{NMC} = \text{net sales} - \text{cost of goods sold} - \text{marketing expenses}$$
$$= \$100 \text{ million} - \$55 \text{ million} - \$41 \text{ million} = \$4 \text{ million}$$

The marketing expenses include sales expenses ($15 million), promotion expenses ($14 million), freight expenses ($10 million), and the managerial salaries and expenses of the marketing function ($2 million), which total $41 million.

Thus, the DVD player actually contributed $4 million to HDX-treme's profits. It was the $5 million of indirect overhead allocated to this product that caused the negative profit. Further, the amount allocated was $2 million more than estimated in the pro forma profit-and-loss statement. Indeed, if only the estimated amount had been allocated, the product would have earned a *profit* of $1 million rather than losing $1 million. If HDX-treme drops the DVD player product, the $5 million in fixed overhead expenses will not disappear—it will simply have to be allocated elsewhere. However, the $4 million in net marketing contribution *will* disappear.

Marketing Return on Sales and Investment   To get an even deeper understanding of the profit impact of marketing strategy, we'll now examine two measures of marketing efficiency—*marketing return on sales* (marketing ROS) and *marketing return on investment* (marketing ROI).[10]

Marketing return on sales (or marketing ROS)
The percent of net sales attributable to the net marketing contribution—calculated by dividing net marketing contribution by net sales.

Marketing return on sales (or **marketing ROS**) shows the percent of net sales attributable to the net marketing contribution. For our DVD player, ROS is:

$$\text{Marketing ROS} = \frac{\text{net marketing contribution}}{\text{net sales}} = \frac{\$4,000,000}{\$100,000,000} = 0.04 = 4\%$$

Thus, out of every $100 of sales, the product returns $4 to HDX-treme's bottom line. A high marketing ROS is desirable. But to assess whether this is a good level of performance, HDX-treme must compare this figure to previous marketing ROS levels for the product, the ROSs of other products in the company's portfolio, and the ROSs of competing products.

Marketing return on investment (or marketing ROI)
A measure of the marketing productivity of a marketing investment—calculated by dividing net marketing contribution by marketing expenses.

Marketing return on investment (or **marketing ROI**) measures the marketing productivity of a marketing investment. In HDX-treme's case, the marketing investment is represented by $41 million of the total expenses. Thus, marketing ROI is:

$$\text{Marketing ROI} = \frac{\text{net marketing contribution}}{\text{net sales}} = \frac{\$4,000,000}{\$41,000,000} = 0.0976 = 9.76\%$$

As with marketing ROS, a high value is desirable, but this figure should be compared with previous levels for the given product and with the marketing ROIs of competitors' products. Note from this equation that marketing ROI could be greater than 100%. This can be achieved by attaining a higher net marketing contribution and/or a lower total marketing expense.

In this section, we estimated market potential and sales, developed profit-and-loss statements, and examined financial measures of performance. In the next section, we discuss methods for analyzing the impact of various marketing tactics. However, before moving on to those analyses, here's another set of quantitative exercises to help you apply what you've learned to other situations.

Marketing by the Numbers Exercise Set Two

2.1 Determine the market potential for a product that has 50 million prospective buyers who purchase an average of 3 per year and price averages $25. How many units must a company sell if it desires a 10% share of this market?

2.2 Develop a profit-and-loss statement for the Westgate division of North Industries. This division manufactures light fixtures sold to consumers through home improvement and hardware stores. Cost of goods sold represents 40% of net sales. Marketing expenses include selling expenses, promotion expenses, and freight. Selling expenses include sales salaries totaling $3 million per year and sales commissions (5% of sales). The company spent $3 million on advertising last year, and freight costs were 10% of sales. Other costs include $2 million for managerial salaries and expenses for the marketing function and another $3 million for indirect overhead allocated to the division.
   a.   Develop the profit-and-loss statement if net sales were $20 million last year.
   b.   Develop the profit-and-loss statement if net sales were $40 million last year.
   c.   Calculate Westgate's break-even sales.

2.3 Using the profit-and-loss statement you developed in question 2.2b, and assuming that Westgate's beginning inventory was $11 million, ending inventory was $7 million, and total investment was $20 million including inventory, determine the following:
   a.   gross margin percentage
   b.   net profit percentage
   c.   operating expense percentage
   d.   inventory turnover rate
   e.   return on investment (ROI)
   f.   net marketing contribution
   g.   marketing return on sales (marketing ROS)
   h.   marketing return on investment (marketing ROI)
   i.   Is the Westgate division doing well? Explain your answer.

Financial Analysis of Marketing Tactics

Although the first-year profit performance for HDX-treme's DVD player was less than desired, management feels that this attractive market has excellent growth opportunities. Although the sales of HDX-treme's DVD player were lower than initially projected, they were not unreasonable given the size of the current market. Thus, HDX-treme wants to explore new marketing tactics to help grow the market for this product and increase sales for the company.

For example, the company could increase advertising to promote more awareness of the new DVD player and its category. It could add salespeople to secure greater product distribution. HDX-treme could decrease prices so that more consumers could afford its player. Finally, to expand the market, HDX-treme could introduce a lower-priced model in addition to the higher-priced original offering. Before pursuing any of these tactics, HDX-treme must analyze the financial implications of each.

Increase Advertising Expenditures

Although most consumers understand DVD players, they may not be aware of high-definition DVD players. Thus, HDX-treme is considering boosting its advertising to make more people aware of the benefits of high-definition DVD players in general and of its own brand in particular.

What if HDX-treme's marketers recommend increasing national advertising by 50% to $15 million (assume no change in the variable cooperative component of promotional expenditures)? This represents an increase in fixed costs of $5 million. What increase in sales will be needed to break even on this $5 million increase in fixed costs?

A quick way to answer this question is to divide the increase in fixed cost by the contribution margin, which we found in a previous analysis to be 21%:

$$\text{Increase in sales} = \frac{\text{increase in fixed cost}}{\text{contribution margin}} = \frac{\$5,000,000}{0.21} = \$23,809,524$$

Thus, a 50% increase in advertising expenditures must produce a sales increase of almost $24 million to just break even. That $24 million sales increase translates into an almost 1 percentage point increase in market share (1% of the $2.5 billion overall market equals $25 million). That is, to break even on the increased advertising expenditure, HDX-treme would have to increase its market share from 4% to 4.95% ($123,809,524 ÷ $2.5 billion = 0.0495 or 4.95% market share). All of this assumes that the total market will not grow, which might or might not be a reasonable assumption.

Increase Distribution Coverage

HDX-treme also wants to consider hiring more salespeople in order to call on new retailer accounts and increase distribution through more outlets. Even though HDX-treme sells directly to wholesalers, its sales representatives call on retail accounts to perform other functions in addition to selling, such as training retail salespeople. Currently, HDX-treme employs 60 sales reps who earn an average of $50,000 in salary plus 10% commission on sales. The DVD player is currently sold to consumers through 1,875 retail outlets. Suppose HDX-treme wants to increase that number of outlets to 2,500, an increase of 625 retail outlets. How many additional salespeople will HDX-treme need, and what sales will be necessary to break even on the increased cost?

Workload method
An approach to determining sales force size based on the workload required and the time available for selling.

One method for determining what size sales force HDX-treme will need is the **workload method**. The workload method uses the following formula to determine the salesforce size:

$$NS = \frac{NC \times FC \times LC}{TA}$$

where

NS = number of salespeople
NC = number of customers
FC = average frequency of customer calls per customer
LC = average length of customer call
TA = time an average salesperson has available for selling per year

HDX-treme's sales reps typically call on accounts an average of 20 times per year for about 2 hours per call. Although each sales rep works 2,000 hours per year (50 weeks per year × 40 hours per week), they spent about 15 hours per week on nonselling activities such as administrative duties and travel. Thus, the average annual available selling time per sales rep per year is 1,250 hours (50 weeks × 25 hours per week). We can now calculate how many sales reps HDX-treme will need to cover the anticipated 2,500 retail outlets:

$$NS = \frac{2,500 \times 20 \times 2}{1,250} = 80 \text{ salespeople}$$

Therefore, HDX-treme will need to hire 20 more salespeople. The cost to hire these reps will be $1 million (20 salespeople × $50,000 salary per sales person).

What increase in sales will be required to break even on this increase in fixed costs? The 10% commission is already accounted for in the contribution margin, so the contribution margin remains unchanged at 21%. Thus, the increase in sales needed to cover this increase in fixed costs can be calculated by:

$$\text{Increase in sales} = \frac{\text{increase in fixed cost}}{\text{contribution margin}} = \frac{\$1,000,000}{0.21} = \$4,761,905$$

That is, HDX-treme's sales must increase almost $5 million to break even on this tactic. So, how many new retail outlets will the company need to secure to achieve this sales increase? The average revenue generated per current outlet is $53,333 ($100 million in sales divided by 1,875 outlets). To achieve the nearly $5 million sales increase needed to break even, HDX-treme would need about 90 new outlets ($4,761,905 ÷ $53,333 = 89.3 outlets), or about 4.5 outlets per new rep. Given that current reps cover about 31 outlets apiece (1,875 outlets ÷ 60 reps), this seems very reasonable.

Decrease Price

HDX-treme is also considering lowering its price to increase sales revenue through increased volume. The company's research has shown that demand for most types of consumer electronics products is elastic—that is, the percentage increase in the quantity demanded is greater than the percentage decrease in price. It has also been found that when the price of HDTVs goes down, the quantity of DVD players demanded increases because they are complementary products.

What increase in sales would be necessary to break even on a 10% decrease in price? That is, what increase in sales will be needed to maintain the total contribution that HDX-treme realized at the higher price? The current total contribution can be determined by multiplying the contribution margin by total sales:[11]

Current total contribution = contribution margin × sales = .21 × $100 million = $21 million

Price changes result in changes in unit contribution and contribution margin. Recall that the contribution margin of 21% was based on variable costs representing 79% of sales. Therefore, unit variable costs can be determined by multiplying the original price by this percentage: $336 × 0.79 = $265.44 per unit. If price is decreased by 10%, the new price is $302.40. However, variable costs do not change just because price decreased, so the contribution and contribution margin decrease as follows:

	Old	New (reduced 10%)
Price	$336	$302.40
– Unit variable cost	$265.44	$265.44
= Unit contribution	$70.56	$36.96
Contribution margin	$70.56/$336 = 0.21 or 21%	$36.96/$302.40 = 0.12 or 12%

So a 10% reduction in price results in a decrease in the contribution margin from 21% to 12%.[12] To determine the sales level needed to break even on this price reduction, we calculate the level of sales that must be attained at the new contribution margin to achieve the original total contribution of $21 million:

New contribution margin × new sales level = original total contribution

So,

$$\text{New sales level} = \frac{\text{original contribution}}{\text{new contribution margin}} = \frac{\$21,000,000}{0.12} = \$175,000,000$$

Thus, sales must increase by $75 million ($175 million – $100 million) just to break even on a 10% price reduction. This means that HDX-treme must increase market share to 7% ($175 million ÷ $2.5 billion) to achieve the current level of profits (assuming no increase in the total market sales). The marketing manager must assess whether or not this is a reasonable goal.

Extend the Product Line

As a final option, HDX-treme is considering extending its DVD player product line by offering a lower-priced model. Of course, the new, lower-priced product would steal some sales from the higher-priced model. This is called **cannibalization**—the situation in which one product sold by a company takes a portion of its sales from other company products. If the new product has a lower contribution than the original product, the company's total contribution will decrease on the cannibalized sales. However, if the new product can generate enough new volume, it is worth considering.

Cannibalization
The situation in which one product sold by a company takes a portion of its sales from other company products.

To assess cannibalization, HDX-treme must look at the incremental contribution gained by having both products available. Recall in the previous analysis we determined that unit variable costs were $265.44 and unit contribution was just over $70. Assuming costs remain the same next year, HDX-treme can expect to realize a contribution per unit of approximately $70 for every unit of the original DVD player sold.

Assume that the first model high-definition DVD player offered by HDX-treme is called HD1 and the new, lower-priced model is called HD2. HD2 will retail for $400, and resellers will take the same markup percentages on price as they do with the higher-priced model. Therefore, HD2's price to wholesalers will be $224 as follows:

Retail price:	$400
minus retail margin (30%):	– $120
Retailer's cost/wholesaler's price:	$280
minus wholesaler's margin (20%):	– $ 56
Wholesaler's cost/HDX-treme's price	$224

If HD2's variable costs are estimated to be $174, then its contribution per unit will equal $50 ($224 − $174 = $50). That means for every unit that HD2 cannibalizes from HD1, HDX-treme will *lose* $20 in contribution toward fixed costs and profit (that is, contribution$_{HD2}$ − contribution$_{HD1}$ = $50 − $70 = −$20). You might conclude that HDX-treme should not pursue this tactic because it appears as though the company will be worse off if it introduces the lower-priced model. However, if HD2 captures enough *additional* sales, HDX-treme will be better off even though some HD1 sales are cannibalized. The company must examine what will happen to *total* contribution, which requires estimates of unit volume for both products.

Originally, HDX-treme estimated that next year's sales of HD1 would be 600,000 units. However, with the introduction of HD2, it now estimates that 200,000 of those sales will be cannibalized by the new model. If HDX-treme sells only 200,000 units of the new HD2 model (all cannibalized from HD1), the company would lose $4 million in total contribution (200,000 units × −$20 per cannibalized unit = −$4 million)—not a good outcome. However, HDX-treme estimates that HD2 will generate the 200,000 of cannibalized sales plus an *additional* 500,000 unit sales. Thus, the contribution on these additional HD2 units will be $25 million (i.e., 500,000 units × $50 per unit = $25 million). The net effect is that HDX-treme will gain $21 million in total contribution by introducing HD2.

The following table compares HDX-treme's total contribution with and without the introduction of HD2:

	HD1 only	HD1 and HD2
HD1 contribution	600,000 units × $70	400,000 units × $70
	= $42,000,000	= $28,000,000
HD2 contribution	0	700,000 units × $50
		= $35,000,000
Total contribution	$42,000,000	$63,000,000

The difference in the total contribution is a net gain of $21 million ($63 million − $42 million). Based on this analysis, HDX-treme should introduce the HD2 model because it results in a positive incremental contribution. However, if fixed costs will increase by more than $21 million as a result of adding this model, then the net effect will be negative and HDX-treme should not pursue this tactic.

Now that you have seen these marketing tactic analysis concepts in action as they related to HDX-treme's new DVD player, here are several exercises for you to apply what you have learned in this section in other contexts.

Marketing by the Numbers Exercise Set Three

3.1 Kingsford, Inc. sells small plumbing components to consumers through retail outlets. Total industry sales for Kingsford's relevant market last year were $80 million, with Kingsford's sales representing 10% of that total. Contribution margin is 25%. Kingsford's sales force calls on retail outlets and each sales rep earns $45,000 per year plus 1% commission on all sales. Retailers receive a 40% margin on selling price and generate average revenue of $10,000 per outlet for Kingsford.

  a. The marketing manager has suggested increasing consumer advertising by $300,000. By how much would dollar sales need to increase to break even on this expenditure? What increase in overall market share does this represent?

  b. Another suggestion is to hire three more sales representatives to gain new consumer retail accounts. How many new retail outlets would be necessary to break even on the increased cost of adding three sales reps?

  c. A final suggestion is to make a 20% across-the-board price reduction. By how much would dollar sales need to increase to maintain Kingsford's current contribution? (See endnote 12 to calculate the new contribution margin.)

  d. Which suggestion do you think Kingsford should implement? Explain your recommendation.

3.2 PepsiCo sells its soft drinks in approximately 400,000 retail establishments, such as supermarkets, discount stores, and convenience stores. Sales representatives call on each retail account weekly, which means each account is called on by a sales rep 52 times per year. The average length of a sales call is 75 minutes (or 1.25 hours). An average salesperson works 2,000 hours per year (50 weeks per year × 40 hours per week), but each spends 10 hours a week on nonselling activities, such as administrative tasks and travel. How many sales people does PepsiCo need?

3.3 Hair Zone manufactures a brand of hair-styling gel. It is considering adding a modified version of the product—a foam that provides stronger hold. Hair Zone's variable costs and prices to wholesalers are:

	Current Hair Gel	New Foam Product
Unit selling price	2.00	2.25
Unit variable costs	.85	1.25

Hair Zone expects to sell 1 million units of the new styling foam in the first year after introduction, but it expects that 60% of those sales will come from buyers who normally purchase Hair Zone's styling gel. Hair Zone estimates that it would sell 1.5 million units of the gel if it did not introduce the foam. If the fixed cost of launching the new foam will be $100,000 during the first year, should Hair Zone add the new product to its line? Why or why not?

Appendix 4 Careers in Marketing

Now that you have completed this course in marketing, you have a good idea of what the field entails. You may have decided you want to pursue a marketing career because it offers constant challenge, stimulating problems, the opportunity to work with people, and excellent advancement opportunities. But you still may not know which part of marketing best suits you—marketing is a very broad field offering a wide variety of career options.

This appendix helps you discover what types of marketing jobs best match your special skills and interests, shows you how to conduct the kind of job search that will get you the position you want in the company of your choice, describes marketing career paths open to you, and suggests other information resources.

Marketing Careers Today

The marketing field is booming, with nearly a third of all Americans now employed in marketing-related positions. Marketing salaries may vary by company, position, and region, and salary figures change constantly. In general, entry-level marketing salaries usually are only slightly below those for engineering and chemistry but equal or exceed starting salaries in economics, finance, accounting, general business, and the liberal arts. Moreover, if you succeed in an entry-level marketing position, it's likely that you will be promoted quickly to higher levels of responsibility and salary. In addition, because of the consumer and product knowledge you will gain in these jobs, marketing positions provide excellent training for the highest levels in an organization.

In conducting your job search, consider the following facts and trends that are changing the world of marketing.

Focus on customers: More and more, companies are realizing that they win in the marketplace only by creating superior value for customers. To capture value from customers, they must first find new and better ways to solve customer problems and improve customer brand experiences. This increasing focus on the customer puts marketers at the forefront in many of today's companies. As the primary customer-facing function, marketing's mission is to get all company departments to "think customer."

Technology: Technology is changing the way marketers work. For example, price coding allows instantaneous retail inventorying. Software for marketing training, forecasting, and other functions is changing the ways we market. And the Internet is creating new jobs and new recruiting rules. Consider the explosive growth in new media marketing. Whereas advertising firms have traditionally recruited "generalists" in account management, "generalist" has now taken on a whole new meaning—advertising account executives must now have both broad and specialized knowledge.

Diversity: The number of women and minorities in marketing continues to rise. They also are rising rapidly into marketing management. For example, women now outnumber men by nearly two to one as advertising account executives. As marketing becomes more global, the need for diversity in marketing positions will continue to increase, opening new opportunities.

Global: Companies such as Coca-Cola, McDonald's, IBM, Wal-Mart, and Procter & Gamble have become multinational, with manufacturing and marketing operations in hundreds of countries. Indeed, such companies often make more profit from sales outside the United States than from within. And it's not just the big companies that are involved in international marketing. Organizations of all sizes have moved into the global arena. Many new marketing opportunities and careers will be directly linked to the expanding global marketplace. The globalization of business also means that you will need more cultural, language, and people skills in the marketing world of the 21st century.

Not-for-profit organizations: Increasingly, colleges, arts organizations, libraries, hospitals, and other not-for-profit organizations are recognizing the need for effectively marketing their "products" and services to various publics. This awareness has led to new marketing positions—with these organizations hiring their own marketing directors and marketing vice presidents or using outside marketing specialists.

Looking for a Job in Today's Marketing World

To choose and find the right job, you will need to apply the marketing skills you've learned in this course, especially marketing analysis and planning. Follow these nine steps for marketing yourself: (1) Conduct a self-assessment and seek career counseling; (2) examine job descriptions; (3) explore the job market and assess opportunities; (4) develop search strategies; (5) prepare a résumé; (6) write a cover letter, follow up, and assemble supporting documents; (7) interview for jobs; and (8) follow up.

Conduct a Self-Assessment and Seek Career Counseling

If you're having difficulty deciding what kind of marketing position is the best fit for you, start out by doing some self-testing or get some career counseling. Self-assessments require that you honestly and thoroughly evaluate your interests, strengths, and weaknesses. What do you do well (your best and favorite skills) and not so well? What are your favorite interests? What are your career goals? What makes you stand out from other job seekers?

The answers to such questions may suggest which marketing careers you should seek or avoid. For help in making an effective self-assessment, look at the following books in your local bookstore: Susan Johnston, *The Career Adventure: Your Guide to Personal Assessment, Career Exploration, and Decision Making,* 4th edition (Prentice Hall, 2006) and Richard Bolles, *What Color Is Your Parachute 2008?* (Ten Speed Press, 2007). Many Web sites also offer self-assessment tools, such as the Keirsey Temperament Theory and the Temperament Sorter, a free but broad assessment available at AdvisorTeam.com. For a more specific evaluation, CareerLeader.com offers a complete online business career self-assessment program designed by the Directors of MBA Career Development at Harvard Business School. You can use this for a fee.

For help in finding a career counselor to guide you in making a career assessment, Richard Bolles' *What Color Is Your Parachute 2008?* contains a useful state-by-state sampling. CareerLeader.com also offers personal career counseling. (Some counselors can help you in your actual job search, too.) You can also consult the career counseling, testing, and placement services at your college or university.

Examine Job Descriptions

After you have identified your skills, interests, and desires, you need to see which marketing positions are the best match for them. Two U.S. Labor Department publications (available in your local library or online)—the *Occupation Outlook Handbook* (www.bls.gov/oco) and the *Dictionary of Occupational Titles* (www.occupationalinfo.org)—describe the duties involved in various occupations, the specific training and education needed, the availability of jobs in each field, possibilities for advancement, and probable earnings.

Your initial career shopping list should be broad and flexible. Look for different ways to achieve your objectives. For example, if you want a career in marketing management, consider the public as well as the private sector, and local and regional as well as national and international firms. Be open initially to exploring many options, then focus on specific industries and jobs, listing your basic goals as a way to guide your choices. Your list might include "a job in a start-up company, near a big city on the West Coast, doing new-product planning with a computer software firm."

Explore the Job Market and Assess Opportunities

At this stage, you need to look at the market and see what positions are actually available. You do not have to do this alone. Any of the following may assist you.

Career Development Centers   Your college's career development center is an excellent place to start. Besides checking with your career development center for specific job openings, check the current edition of the National Association of Colleges and Employers *Job Outlook* (www.jobweb.com). It contains a national forecast of hiring intentions of employers as they relate to new college graduates. More and more, college career develop-ment centers are also going online. For example, the Web site of the undergraduate career services of Indiana University's Kelley School of Business has a list of career links (http://ucso.indiana.edu/cgi-bin/students/careerResources/) that can help to focus your job search.

In addition, find out everything you can about the companies that interest you by consulting business magazines, Web sties, annual reports, business reference books, faculty, career counselors, and others. Try to analyze the industry's and the company's future growth and profit potential, advancement opportunities, salary levels, entry positions, travel time, and other factors of significance to you.

Job Fairs   Career development centers often work with corporate recruiters to organize on-campus job fairs. You might also use the Internet to check on upcoming career fairs in your region. For example, visit JobWeb's College Career Fairs page at www.jobweb.com/employ/fairs/public_fairs.asp.

Networking and the Yellow Pages   Networking, or asking for job leads from friends, family, people in your community, and career centers, is one of the best ways to find a marketing job. Studies estimate that 60 to 90 percent of jobs are found through networking. The idea is to spread your net wide, contacting anybody and everybody.

The phone book's yellow pages are another effective way to job search. Check out employers in your field of interest in whatever region you want to work, then call and ask if they are hiring for the position of your choice.

Cooperative Education and Internships   According to a survey by CBcampus.com, CareerBuilder.com's college job search site, employers on average give full-time employment offers to about 61 percent of students who have had internships with their companies. Many company Internet sites have separate internship areas. For example, check out WetFeet (www.wetfeet.internship programs.com), MonsterTRAK.com (www.monstertrak.monster.com), CampusCareerCenter.com (www.campuscareercenter.com/students/intern.asp), InternJobs.com, and InternAbroad.com. If you know of a company for which you wish to work, go to that company's corporate Web site, enter the human resources area, and check for internships. If none are listed, try e-mailing the human resources department, asking if internships are offered.

The Internet   A constantly increasing number of sites on the Internet deal with job hunting. You can also use the Internet to make contacts with people who can help you gain information on companies and research companies that interest you. The Riley Guide offers a great introduction to what jobs are available (www.rileyguide.com). Other helpful sites are DisabilityInfo.gov (www.disabilityinfo.gov) and HireDiversity (www.hire diversity.com), which contain information on opportunities for African Americans, Hispanic Americans, Asian Americans, and Native Americans.

Most companies have their own Web sites on which they post job listings. This may be helpful if you have a specific and fairly limited number of companies that you are keeping your eye on for job opportunities. But if this is not the case, remember that to find out what interesting marketing jobs the companies themselves are posting, you may have to visit hundreds of corporate sites.

Develop Search Strategies

Once you've decided which companies you are interested in, you need to contact them. One of the best ways is through on-campus interviews. But not every company you are interested in will visit your school. In such instances, you can write, e-mail, or phone the company directly or ask marketing professors or school alumni for contacts.

Prepare a Résumé

A résumé is a concise yet comprehensive written summary of your qualifications, including your academic, personal, and professional achievements, that showcases why you are the best candidate for the job. Because an employer will spend an average of 15 to 20 seconds reviewing your résumé, you want to be sure that you prepare a good one.

In preparing your résumé, remember that all information on it must be accurate and complete. Résumés typically begin with the applicant's full name, telephone and fax numbers, and mail and e-mail addresses. A simple and direct statement of career objectives generally appears next, followed by work history and academic data (including awards and internships), and then by personal activities and experiences applicable to the job sought.

The résumé sometimes ends with a list of references the employer may contact (at other times, references may be listed separately). If your work or internship experience is limited, nonexistent, or irrelevant, then it is a good idea to emphasize your academic and nonacademic achievements, showing skills related to those required for excellent job performance.

There are three types of résumés. Reverse *chronological* résumés, which emphasize career growth, are organized in reverse chronological order, starting with your most recent job. They focus on job titles within organizations, describing the responsibilities required for each job. *Functional* résumés focus less on job titles and work history and more on assets and achievements. This format works best if your job history is scanty or discontinuous. *Mixed,* or *combination,* résumés take from each of the other two formats. First, the skills used for a specific job are listed, then the job title is stated. This format works best for applicants whose past jobs are in other fields or seemingly unrelated to the position.

Your local bookstore or library has many books that can assist you in developing your résumé. Popular guides are Brenda Greene, *Get the Interview Every Time: Fortune 500 Hiring Professionals' Tips for Writing Winning Résumés and Cover Letters* (Dearborn Trade, 2004) and Susan Britton Whitcomb, *Résumé Magic: Trade Secrets of a Professional Résumé Writer* (JIST Works, 2006). Computer software programs, such as *RésuméMaker Professional,* provide hundreds of sample résumés and ready-to-use phrases and guide you through the résumé preparation process. America's Career InfoNet (www. acinet.org/acinet/resume/resume_intro.asp) offers a step-by-step résumé tutorial, and Monster (http://content.monster.com/resume/home.aspx) offers résumé advice and writing services.

Finally, you can even create your own personalized online résumé at sites such as optimalresume.com.

Use of the Internet as a tool in the job search process is increasing, so it's a good idea to have your résumé ready for the online environment. You can forward an electronic résumé to networking contacts or recruiting professionals through e-mail. You can also post it in online databases with the hope that employers and recruiters will find it.

Successful electronic résumés require a different strategy than paper résumés. For instance, when companies search résumé banks, they search key words and industry buzz words that describe a skill or core work required for each job, so nouns are much more important than verbs. Two good resources for preparing electronic résumés are Susan Ireland's *Electronic Résumé Guide* (http://susanireland.com/eresumeguide/) and *The Riley Guide* (www.rileyguide.com/eresume.html).

After you have written your electronic résumé, you need to post it. The following sites may be good locations to start: Monster.com (www.monster.com) and Yahoo! hotjobs (www.hotjobs.yahoo.com). However, use caution when posting your résumé on various sites. In this era of identity theft, you need to select sites with care so as to protect your privacy. Limit access to your personal contact information and don't use sites that offer to "blast" your résumé into cyberspace.

Résumé Tips

- Communicate your worth to potential employers in a concrete manner, citing examples whenever possible.
- Be concise and direct.
- Use active verbs to show you are a doer.
- Do not skimp on quality or use gimmicks. Spare no expense in presenting a professional résumé.
- Have someone critique your work. A single typo can eliminate you from being considered.
- Customize your résumé for specific employers. Emphasize your strengths as they pertain to your targeted job.
- Keep your résumé compact, usually one page.
- Format the text to be attractive, professional, and readable. Times New Roman is often the font of choice. Avoid too much "design" or gimmicky flourishes.

Write a Cover Letter, Follow Up, and Assemble Supporting Documents

Cover Letter You should include a cover letter informing the employer that a résumé is enclosed. But a cover letter does more than this. It also serves to summarize in one or two paragraphs the contents of the résumé and explains why you think you are the right person for the position. The goal is to persuade the employer to look at the more detailed résumé. A typical cover letter is organized as follows: (1) the name and position of the person you are contacting; (2) a statement identifying the position you are applying for, how you heard of the vacancy, and the reasons for your interest; (3) a summary of your qualifications for the job; (4) a description of what follow-ups you intend to make, such as phoning in two weeks to see if the résumé has been received; (5) an expression of gratitude for the opportunity of being a candidate for the job. America's Career InfoNet (www.acinet.org/acinet/resume/resume_intro.asp) offers a step-by-step tutorial on how to create a cover letter, and Susan Ireland's Web site contains more than 50 cover letter samples (http://susanireland.com/coverletterindex.htm).

Follow-Up Once you send your cover letter and résumé to perspective employers via the method they prefer—e-mail, their Web site, fax, or regular mail—it's often a good idea to follow up. In today's market, job seekers can't afford to wait for interviews to find them. A quality résumé and an attractive cover letter are crucial, but a proper follow-up may be the key to landing an interview. However, before you engage your potential employer, be sure to research the company. Knowing about the company and understanding its place in the industry will help you shine. When you place a call, send an e-mail, or mail a letter to a company contact, be sure to restate your interest in the position, check on the status of your résumé, and ask the employer about any questions they may have.

Letters of Recommendation Letters of recommendation are written references by professors, former and current employers, and others that testify to your character, skills, and abilities. Some companies may request letters of recommendation to be submitted either with the résumé or at the interview. Even if letters of recommendation aren't requested, it's a good idea to bring them with you to the interview. A good reference letter tells why you would be an excellent candidate for the position. In choosing someone to write a letter of recommendation, be confident that the person will give you a good reference. In addition, do not assume the person knows everything about you or the position you are seeking. Rather, provide the person with your résumé and other relevant data. As a courtesy, allow the reference writer at least a month to complete the letter and enclose a stamped, addressed envelope with your materials.

In the packet containing your résumé, cover letter, and letters of recommendation, you may also want to attach other relevant documents that support your candidacy, such as academic transcripts, graphics, portfolios, and samples of writing.

Interview for Jobs

As the old saying goes, "The résumé gets you the interview; the interview gets you the job." The job interview offers you an opportunity to gather more information about the organization, while at the same time allowing the organization to gather more information about you. You'll want to present your best self. The interview process consists of three parts: before the interview, the interview itself, and after the interview. If you pass through these stages successfully, you will be called back for the follow-up interview.

Before the Interview In preparing for your interview, do the following:

1. Understand that interviewers have diverse styles, including the "chitchat," let's-get-to-know-each-other style; the interrogation style of question after question; and the tough-

probing "why, why, why" style, among others. So be ready for anything.

2. With a friend, practice being interviewed and then ask for a critique. Or, videotape yourself in a practice interview so that you can critique your own performance. Your college placement service may also offer "mock" interviews to help you.

3. Prepare at least five good questions whose answers are not easily found in the company literature, such as "What is the future direction of the firm?" "How does the firm differentiate itself from competitors?" "Do you have a new-media division?"

4. Anticipate possible interview questions, such as "Why do you want to work for this company?" or "Why should we hire you?" Prepare solid answers before the interview. Have a clear idea of why you are interested in joining the company and the industry to which it belongs. (See Susan Ireland's site, http://susanireland.com/interviewwork.html, for additional interview questions.)

5. Avoid back-to-back interviews—they can be exhausting and it is unpredictable how long they will last.

6. Prepare relevant documents that support your candidacy, such as academic transcripts, letters of recommendation, graphics, portfolios, and samples of writing. Bring multiple copies to the interview.

7. Dress conservatively and professionally. Be neat and clean.

8. Arrive 10 minutes early to collect your thoughts and review the major points you intend to cover. Check your name on the interview schedule, noting the name of the interviewer and the room number. Be courteous and polite to office staff.

9. Approach the interview enthusiastically. Let your personality shine through.

During the Interview During the interview, do the following:

1. Shake hands firmly in greeting the interviewer. Introduce yourself, using the same form of address the interviewer uses. Focus on creating a good initial impression.

2. Keep your poise. Relax, smile when appropriate, and be upbeat throughout.

3. Maintain eye contact, good posture, and speak distinctly. Don't clasp your hands or fiddle with jewelry, hair, or clothing. Sit comfortably in your chair. Do not smoke, even if it's permitted.

4. Along with the copies of relevant documents that support your candidacy, carry extra copies of your résumé with you.

5. Have your story down pat. Present your selling points. Answer questions directly. Avoid either one-word or too-wordy answers.

6. Let the interviewer take the initiative but don't be passive. Find an opportunity to direct the conversation to things about yourself that you want the interviewer to hear.

7. To end on a high note, make your most important point or ask your most pertinent question during the last part of the interview.

8. Don't hesitate to "close." You might say, "I'm very interested in the position, and I have enjoyed this interview."

9. Obtain the interviewer's business card or address and phone number so that you can follow up later.

A tip for acing the interview: Before you open your mouth, find out *what it's like* to be a brand manager, sales representative, market researcher, advertising account executive, or other position for which you're interviewing. See if you can find a "mentor"—someone in a position similar to the one you're seeking, perhaps with another company. Talk with this mentor about the ins and outs of the job and industry.

After the Interview After the interview, do the following:

1. After leaving the interview, record the key points that arose. Be sure to note who is to follow up and when a decision can be expected.

2. Analyze the interview objectively, including the questions asked, the answers to them, your overall interview presentation, and the interviewer's responses to specific points.

3. Immediately send a thank-you letter or e-mail, mentioning any additional items and your willingness to supply further information.

4. If you do not hear within the specified time, write, e-mail, or call the interviewer to determine your status.

Follow-Up Interview

If your first interview takes place off-site, such as at your college or at a job fair, and if you are successful with that initial interview, you will be invited to visit the organization. The in-company interview will probably run from several hours to an entire day. The organization will examine your interest, maturity, enthusiasm, assertiveness, logic, and company and functional knowledge. You should ask questions about issues of importance to you. Find out about the working environment, job role, responsibilities, opportunity for advancement, current industrial issues, and the company's personality. The company wants to discover if you are the right person for the job, whereas you want to find out if it is the right job for you. The key is to determine if the right *fit* exists between you and the company.

Marketing Jobs

This section describes some of the key marketing positions.

Advertising

Advertising is one of today's hottest fields in marketing. In fact, *Money* magazine lists a position in advertising as among the 50 best jobs in America.

Job Descriptions Key advertising positions include copywriter, art director, production manager, account executive, and media planner/buyer.

- *Copywriters* write advertising copy and help find the concepts behind the written words and visual images of advertisements.

- *Art directors,* the other part of the creative team, help translate the copywriters' ideas into dramatic visuals called "layouts." Agency artists develop print layouts, package designs, television layouts (called "storyboards"), corporate logotypes, trademarks, and symbols.
- *Production managers* are responsible for physically creating ads, in-house or by contracting through outside production houses.
- *Account development executives* research and understand clients' markets and customers and help develop marketing and advertising strategies to impact them.
- *Account executives* serve as liaisons between clients and agencies. They coordinate the planning, creation, production, and implementation of an advertising campaign for the account.
- *Account planners* serve as the voice of the consumer in the agency. They research consumers to understand their needs and motivations as a basis for developing effective ad campaigns.
- *Media planners (or buyers)* determine the best mix of television, radio, newspaper, magazine, and other media for the advertising campaign.

Skills Needed, Career Paths, and Typical Salaries Work in advertising requires strong people skills in order to interact closely with an often-difficult and demanding client base. In addition, advertising attracts people with high skills in planning, problem solving, creativity, communication, initiative, leadership, and presentation. Advertising involves working under high levels of stress and pressure created by unrelenting deadlines. Advertisers frequently have to work long hours to meet deadlines for a presentation. But work achievements are very apparent, with the results of creative strategies observed by thousands or even millions of people.

Because they are so sought after, positions in advertising sometimes require an MBA. But there are many jobs open for business, graphics arts, and liberal arts undergraduates. Advertising positions often serve as gateways to higher-level management. Moreover, with large advertising agencies opening offices all over the world, there is the possibility of eventually working on global campaigns.

Starting advertising salaries are relatively low compared to some other marketing jobs because of strong competition for entry-level advertising jobs. You may even want to consider working for free to break in. Compensation will increase quickly as you move into account executive or other management positions. For more facts and figures, see the Web pages of *Advertising Age,* a key ad industry publication (www.adage.com, click on the Job Bank button), and the American Association of Advertising Agencies (www.aaaa.org).

Brand and Product Management

Brand and product managers plan, direct, and control business and marketing efforts for their products. They are involved with research and development, packaging, manufacturing, sales and distribution, advertising, promotion, market research, and business analysis and forecasting.

Job Descriptions   A company's brand management team consists of people in several positions.

- *Brand managers* guide the development of marketing strategies for a specific brand.
- *Assistant brand managers* are responsible for certain strategic components of the brand.
- *Product managers* oversee several brands within a product line or product group.
- *Product category managers* direct multiple product lines in the product category.
- *Market analysts* research the market and provide important strategic information to the project managers.
- *Project directors* are responsible for collecting market information on a marketing or product project.
- *Research directors* oversee the planning, gathering, and analyzing of all organizational research.

Skills Needed, Career Paths, and Typical Salaries   Brand and product management requires high problem-solving, analytical, presentation, communication, and leadership skills, as well as the ability to work well in a team. Product management requires long hours and involves the high pressure of running large projects. In consumer-goods companies, the newcomer—who usually needs an MBA—joins a brand team as an assistant and learns the ropes by doing numerical analyses and watching senior brand people. This person eventually heads the team and later moves on to manage a larger brand, then several brands.

Many industrial-goods companies also have product managers. Product management is one of the best training grounds for future corporate officers. Product management also offers good opportunities to move into international marketing. Product managers command relatively high salaries. Because this job category encourages or requires a master's degree, starting pay tends to be higher than in other marketing categories such as advertising or retailing.

Sales and Sales Management

Sales and sales management opportunities exist in a wide range of profit and not-for-profit organizations and in product and service organizations, including financial, insurance, consulting, and government organizations.

Job Descriptions   Key jobs include consumer sales, industrial sales, national account manager, service support, sales trainers, sales management, and tellesellers.

- *Consumer* sales involves selling consumer products and services through retailers.
- *Industrial sales* involves selling products and services to other businesses.
- *National account managers (NAM)* oversee a few very large accounts.
- *Service support* personnel support salespeople during and after the sale of a product.
- *Sales trainers* train new hires and provide refresher training for all sales personnel.

- *Sales management* includes a sequence of positions ranging from district manager to vice president of sales.
- The *teleseller* (not to be confused with the home consumer telemarketer) offers service and support to field salespeople.

Salespeople enjoy active professional lives, working outside the office and interacting with others. They manage their own time and activities. And successful salespeople can be very well paid. Competition for top jobs can be intense. Every sales job is different, but some positions involve extensive travel, long workdays, and working under pressure. You can also expect to be transferred more than once between company headquarters and regional offices. However, most companies are now working to bring good work-life balance to their salespeople and sales managers.

Skills Needed, Career Paths, and Typical Salaries   Selling is a people profession in which you will work with people every day, all day long. Besides people skills, sales professionals need sales and communication skills. Most sales positions also require high problem-solving, analytical, presentation, and leadership ability as well as creativity and initiative. Teamwork skills are increasingly important.

Career paths lead from salesperson to district, regional, and higher levels of sales management and, in many cases, to the top management of the firm. Today, most entry-level sales management positions require a college degree. Increasingly, people seeking selling jobs are acquiring sales experience in an internship capacity or from a part-time job before graduating. Sales positions are great springboards to leadership positions, with more CEOs starting in sales than in any other entry-level position. Possibly this explains why competition for top sales jobs is intense.

Starting base salaries in sales may be moderate, but compensation is often supplemented by significant commission, bonus, or other incentive plans. In addition, many sales jobs include a company car or car allowance. Successful salespeople are among most companies' highest paid employees.

Other Marketing Jobs

Retailing   Retailing provides an early opportunity to assume marketing responsibilities. Key jobs include store manager, regional manager, buyer, department manager, and salesperson. *Store managers* direct the management and operation of an individual store. *Regional managers* manage groups of stores across several states and report performance to headquarters. *Buyers* select and buy the merchandise that the store carries. The *department manager* acts as store manager of a department, such as clothing, but on the department level. The *salesperson* sells merchandise to retail customers. Retailing can involve relocation, but generally there is little travel, unless you are a buyer. Retailing requires high people and sales skills because retailers are constantly in contact with customers. Enthusiasm, willingness, and communication skills are very helpful for retailers, too.

Retailers work long hours, but their daily activities are often more structured than some types of marketing positions.

Starting salaries in retailing tend to be low, but pay increases as you move into management or some retailing specialty job.

Marketing Research   Marketing researchers interact with managers to define problems and identify the information needed to resolve them. They design research projects, prepare questionnaires and samples, analyze data, prepare reports, and present their findings and recommendations to management. They must understand statistics, consumer behavior, psychology, and sociology. A master's degree helps. Career opportunities exist with manufacturers, retailers, some wholesalers, trade and industry associations, marketing research firms, advertising agencies, and governmental and private nonprofit agencies.

New-Product Planning   People interested in new-product planning can find opportunities in many types of organizations. They usually need a good background in marketing, marketing research, and sales forecasting; they need organizational skills to motivate and coordinate others; and they may need a technical background. Usually, these people work first in other marketing positions before joining the new-product department.

Marketing Logistics (Physical Distribution)   Marketing logistics, or physical distribution, is a large and dynamic field, with many career opportunities. Major transportation carriers, manufacturers, wholesalers, and retailers all employ logistics specialists. Increasingly, marketing teams include logistics specialists, and marketing managers' career paths include marketing logistics assignments. Coursework in quantitative methods, finance, accounting, and marketing will provide you with the necessary skills for entering the field.

Public Relations   Most organizations have a public relations staff to anticipate problems with various publics, handle complaints, deal with media, and build the corporate image. People interested in public relations should be able to speak and write clearly and persuasively, and they should have a background in journalism, communications, or the liberal arts. The challenges in this job are highly varied and very people oriented.

Not-for-Profit Services   The key jobs in nonprofits include marketing director, director of development, event coordinator, publication specialist, and intern/volunteer. The *marketing director* is in charge of all marketing activities for the organization. The *director of development* organizes, manages, and directs the fund-raising campaigns that keep a nonprofit in existence. An *event coordinator* directs all aspects of fund-raising events, from initial planning through implementation. The *publication specialist* oversees publications designed to promote awareness of the organization.

Although typically an unpaid position, the *intern/volunteer* performs various marketing functions, and this work can be an important step to gaining a full-time position. The nonprofit sector is typically not for someone who is money driven. Rather, most nonprofits look for people with a strong sense of community spirit and the desire to help others. So starting pay is usually lower than in other marketing fields. However, the bigger the nonprofit, the better your chance of rapidly increasing your income when moving into upper management.

Other Resources

Professional marketing associations and organizations are another source of information about careers. Marketers belong to many such societies. You may want to contact some of the following in your job search:

Advertising Women of New York, 25 West 45th Street, New York, NY 10036. (212) 221-7969 (www.awny.org)

American Advertising Federation, 1101 Vermont Avenue, NW, Suite 500, Washington, DC 20005. (202) 898-0089 (www.aaf.org)

American Marketing Association, 311 South Wacker Drive, Suite 5800, Chicago, IL 60606. (800) AMA-1150 (www.ama.org)

Market Research Association, 2189 Silas Deane Highway, Suite 5, Rocky Hill, CT 06067. (860) 257-4008 (www.mra-net.org)

National Association of Sales Professionals, 11000 North 130th Place, Scottsdale, AZ 85259. (480) 951-4311 (www.nasp.com)

National Management Association, 2210 Arbor Boulevard, Dayton, OH 45439. (937) 294-0421 (www.nma1.org)

National Retail Federation, 325 Seventh Street NW, Suite 1100, Washington, DC 20004. (800) NRF-HOW2 (www.nrf.com)

Product Development and Management Association, 15000 Commerce Parkway, Suite C Mount Laurel, NJ 08054. (800) 232-5241 (www.pdma.org)

Public Relations Society of America, 33 Maiden Lane, Eleventh Floor, New York, NY 10038. (212) 460-1400 (www.prsa.org)

Sales and Marketing Executives International, PO Box 1390, Sumas, WA 98295-1390. (312) 893-0751 (www.smei.org)

The Association of Women in Communications, 3337 Duke Street, Alexandria, VA 22314. (703) 370-7436 (www.womcom.org)

Glossary

Adapted global marketing An international marketing strategy for adjusting the marketing strategy and mix elements to each international target market, bearing more costs but hoping for a larger market share and return.

Administered VMS A vertical marketing system that coordinates successive stages of production and distribution, not through common ownership or contractual ties, but through the size and power of one of the parties.

Adoption process The mental process through which an individual passes from first hearing about an innovation to final adoption.

Advertising Any paid form of nonpersonal presentation and promotion of ideas, goods, or services by an identified sponsor.

Advertising agency A marketing services firm that assists companies in planning, preparing, implementing, and evaluating all or portions of their advertising programs.

Advertising budget The dollars and other resources allocated to a product or company advertising program.

Advertising media The vehicles through which advertising messages are delivered to their intended audiences.

Advertising objective A specific communication task to be accomplished with a specific target audience during a specific period of time.

Advertising strategy The strategy by which the company accomplishes its advertising objectives. It consists of two major elements: creating advertising messages and selecting advertising media.

Affordable method Setting the promotion budget at the level management thinks the company can afford.

Age and life-cycle segmentation Dividing a market into different age and life-cycle groups.

Agent A wholesaler who represents buyers or sellers on a relatively permanent basis, performs only a few functions, and does not take title to goods.

Allowance Promotional money paid by manufacturers to retailers in return for an agreement to feature the manufacturer's products in some way.

Approach The step in the selling process in which the salesperson meets the customer for the first time.

Attitude A person's consistently favorable or unfavorable evaluations, feelings, and tendencies toward an object or idea.

Baby boomers The 78 million people born during the baby boom following World War II and lasting until 1964.

Behavioral segmentation Dividing a market into groups based on consumer knowledge, attitudes, uses, or responses to a product.

Belief A descriptive thought that a person holds about something.

Benefit segmentation Dividing the market into groups according to the different benefits that consumers seek from the product.

Brand A name, term, sign, symbol, or design or a combination of these that identifies the products or services of one seller or group of sellers and differentiates them from those of competitors.

Brand equity The positive differential effect that knowing the brand name has on customer response to the product or service.

Brand extension Extending an existing brand name to new product categories.

Break-even pricing (target profit pricing) Setting price to break even on the costs of making and marketing a product; or setting price to make a target profit.

Broker A wholesaler who does not take title to goods and whose function is to bring buyers and sellers together and assist in negotiation.

Business analysis A review of the sales, costs, and profit projections for a new product to find out whether these factors satisfy the company's objectives.

Business buyer behavior The buying behavior of the organizations that buy goods and services for use in the production of other products and services or for the purpose of reselling or renting them to others at a profit.

Business portfolio The collection of businesses and products that make up the company.

Business promotions Sales promotion tools used to generate business leads, stimulate purchases, reward customers, and motivate salespeople.

Business-to-business (B2B) online marketing Using B2B Web sites, e-mail, online product catalogs, online trading networks, and other online resources to reach new business customers, serve current customers more effectively, and obtain buying efficiencies and better prices.

Business-to-consumer (B2C) online marketing Selling goods and services online to final consumers.

Buying center All the individuals and units that participate in the business buying-decision process.

By-product pricing Setting a price for by-products in order to make the main product's price more competitive.

Captive-product pricing Setting a price for products that must be used along with a main product, such as blades for a razor and film for a camera.

Catalog marketing Direct marketing through print, video, or electronic catalogs that are mailed to a select customers, made available in stores, or presented online.

Category killer Giant specialty store that carries a very deep assortment of a particular line and is staffed by knowledgeable employees.

Causal research Marketing research to test hypotheses about cause-and-effect relationships.

Chain stores Two or more outlets that are commonly owned and controlled.

Channel conflict Disagreement among marketing channel members on goals and roles—who should do what and for what rewards.

Channel level A layer of intermediaries that performs some work in bringing the product and its ownership closer to the final buyer.

Click-and-mortar companies Traditional brick-and-mortar companies that have added online marketing to their operations.

Click-only companies The so-called dot-coms, which operate only online without any brick-and-mortar market presence.

Closing The step in the selling process in which the salesperson asks the customer for an order.

Co-branding The practice of using the established brand names of two different companies on the same product.

Cognitive dissonance Buyer discomfort caused by postpurchase conflict.

Commercialization   Introducing a new product into the market.

Commercial online databases   Computerized collections of information available from online commercial sources or via the Internet.

Communication adaptation   A global communication strategy of fully adapting advertising messages to local markets.

Competitive advantage   An advantage over competitors gained by offering greater customer value, either through lower prices or by providing more benefits that justify higher prices.

Competitive-parity method   Setting the promotion budget to match competitors' outlays.

Concentrated (niche) marketing   A market-coverage strategy in which a firm goes after a large share of one or a few segments or niches.

Concept testing   Testing new-product concepts with a group of target consumers to find out if the concepts have strong consumer appeal.

Consumer buyer behavior   The buying behavior of final consumers—individuals and households who buy goods and services for personal consumption.

Consumer market   All the individuals and households who buy or acquire goods and services for personal consumption.

Consumer product   Product bought by final consumer for personal consumption.

Consumer-generated marketing   Marketing messages, ads, and other brand exchanges created by consumers themselves—both invited and uninvited.

Consumer promotions   Sales promotion tools used to boost short-term customer buying and involvement or to enhance long-term customer relationships.

Consumerism   An organized movement of citizens and government agencies to improve the rights and power of buyers in relation to sellers.

Consumer-oriented marketing   The philosophy of enlightened marketing that holds that the company should view and organize its marketing activities from the consumer's point of view.

Consumer-to-business (C2B) online marketing   Online exchanges in which consumers search out sellers, learn about their offers, and initiate purchases, sometimes even driving transaction terms.

Consumer-to-consumer (C2C) online marketing   Online exchanges of goods and information between final consumers.

Contract manufacturing   A joint venture in which a company contracts with manufacturers in a foreign market to produce the product or provide its service.

Contractual VMS   A vertical marketing system in which independent firms at different levels of production and distribution join together through contracts to obtain more economies or sales impact than they could achieve alone.

Convenience product   Consumer product that customers usually buy frequently, immediately, and with a minimum of comparison and buying effort.

Convenience store   A small store, located near a residential area, that is open long hours seven days a week and carries a limited line of high-turnover convenience goods.

Conventional distribution channel   A channel consisting of one or more independent producers, wholesalers, and retailers, each a separate business seeking to maximize its own profits even at the expense of profits for the system as a whole.

Corporate VMS   A vertical marketing system that combines successive stages of production and distribution under single ownership—channel leadership is established through common ownership.

Corporate (or brand) Web site   A Web site designed to build customer goodwill, collect customer feedback, and supplement other sales channels, rather than to sell the company's products directly.

Cost-based pricing   Setting prices based on the costs for producing, distributing, and selling the product plus a fair rate of return for its effort and risk.

Cost-plus pricing   Adding a standard markup to the cost of the product.

Countertrade   International trade involving the direct or indirect exchange of goods for other goods instead of cash.

Creative concept   The compelling "big idea" that will bring the advertising message strategy to life in a distinctive and memorable way.

Cultural environment   Institutions and other forces that affect society's basic values, perceptions, preferences, and behaviors.

Culture   The set of basic values, perceptions, wants, and behaviors learned by a member of society from family and other important institutions.

Customer database   An organized collection of comprehensive data about individual customers or prospects, including geographic, demographic, psychographic, and behavioral data.

Customer equity   The total combined customer lifetime values of all of the company's customers.

Customer insights   Fresh understandings of customers and the marketplace derived from marketing information that become the basis for creating customer value and relationships.

Customer lifetime value   The value of the entire stream of purchases that the customer would make over a lifetime of patronage.

Customer relationship management (CRM)   Managing detailed information about individual customers and carefully managing customer "touch points" in order to maximize customer loyalty; The overall process of building and maintaining profitable customer relationships by delivering superior customer value and satisfaction.

Customer sales force structure   A sales force organization under which salespeople specialize in selling only to certain customers or industries.

Customer satisfaction   The extent to which a product's perceived performance matches a buyer's expectations.

Customer-centered new-product development   New-product development that focuses on finding new ways to solve customer problems and create more customer-satisfying experiences.

Customer-perceived value   The customer's evaluation of the difference between all the benefits and all the costs of a marketing offer relative to those of competing offers.

Customer-value marketing   A principle of enlightened marketing that holds that a company should put most of its resources into customer value-building marketing investments.

Decline stage   The product life-cycle stage in which a product's sales decline.

Deficient products   Products that have neither immediate appeal nor long-run benefits.

Demand curve   A curve that shows the number of units the market will buy in a given time period, at different prices that might be charged.

Demands   Human wants that are backed by buying power.

Demographic segmentation   Dividing the market into groups based on variables such as age, gender, family size, family life cycle, income, occupation, education, religion, race, generation, and nationality.

Demography   The study of human populations in terms of size, density, location, age, gender, race, occupation, and other statistics.

Department store A retail organization that carries a wide variety of product lines—each line is operated as a separate department managed by specialist buyers or merchandisers.

Derived demand Business demand that ultimately comes from (derives from) the demand for consumer goods.

Descriptive research Marketing research to better describe marketing problems, situations, or markets, such as the market potential for a product or the demographics and attitudes of consumers.

Desirable products Products that give both high immediate satisfaction and high long-run benefits.

Differentiated (segmented) marketing A market-coverage strategy in which a firm decides to target several market segments and designs separate offers for each.

Differentiation Actually differentiating the market offering to create superior customer value.

Direct investment Entering a foreign market by developing foreign-based assembly or manufacturing facilities.

Direct-mail marketing Direct marketing by sending an offer, announcement, reminder, or other item to a person at a particular address.

Direct marketing Direct connections with carefully targeted individual consumers to both obtain an immediate response and cultivate lasting customer relationships.

Direct marketing channel A marketing channel that has no intermediary levels.

Direct-response television marketing Direct marketing via television, including direct-response television advertising (or infomercials) and home shopping channels.

Discount A straight reduction in price on purchases under stated conditions or during a stated period of time.

Discount store A retail operation that sells standard merchandise at lower prices by accepting lower margins and selling at higher volume.

Disintermediation The cutting out of marketing channel intermediaries by product or service producers, or the displacement of traditional resellers by radical new types of intermediaries.

Distribution center A large, highly automated warehouse designed to receive goods from various plants and suppliers, take orders, fill them efficiently, and deliver goods to customers as quickly as possible.

Diversification A strategy for company growth through starting up or acquiring businesses outside the company's current products and markets.

Downsizing Reducing the business portfolio by eliminating products of business units that are not profitable or that no longer fit the company's overall strategy.

Dynamic pricing Adjusting prices continually to meet the characteristics and needs of individual customers and situations.

Economic community A group of nations organized to work toward common goals in the regulation of international trade.

Economic environment Factors that affect consumer buying power and spending patterns.

Engel's laws Differences noted over a century ago by Ernst Engel in how people shift their spending across food, housing, transportation, health care, and other goods and services categories as family income rises.

Enlightened marketing A marketing philosophy holding that a company's marketing should support the best long-run performance of the marketing system.

Environmental sustainability A management approach that involves developing strategies that both sustain the environment and produce profits for the company.

Environmentalism An organized movement of concerned citizens and government agencies to protect and improve people's living environment.

Ethnographic research A form of observational research that involves sending trained observers to watch and interact with consumers in their "natural habitat."

Event marketing Creating a brand-marketing event or serving as a sole or participating sponsor of events created by others.

Exchange The act of obtaining a desired object from someone by offering something in return.

Exclusive distribution Giving a limited number of dealers the exclusive right to distribute the company's products in their territories.

Execution style The approach, style, tone, words, and format used for executing an advertising message.

Experimental research Gathering primary data by selecting matched groups of subjects, giving them different treatments, controlling related factors, and checking for differences in group responses.

Exploratory research Marketing research to gather preliminary information that will help define problems and suggest hypotheses.

Exporting Entering a foreign market by selling goods produced in the company's home country, often with little modification.

Factory outlet Off-price retailing operation that is owned and operated by a manufacturer and that normally carries the manufacturer's surplus, discontinued, or irregular goods.

Fad A temporary period of unusually high sales driven by consumer enthusiasm and immediate product or brand popularity.

Fashion A currently accepted or popular style in a given field.

Fixed costs Costs that do not vary with production or sales level.

Focus group interviewing Personal interviewing that involves inviting six to ten people to gather for a few hours with a trained interviewer to talk about a product, service, or organization. The interviewer "focuses" the group discussion on important issues.

Follow-up The last step in the selling process in which the salesperson follows up after the sale to ensure customer satisfaction and repeat business.

Franchise A contractual association between a manufacturer, wholesaler, or service organization (a franchiser) and independent businesspeople (franchisees) who buy the right to own and operate one or more units in the franchise system.

Franchise organization A contractual vertical marketing system in which a channel member, called a franchiser, links several stages in the production-distribution process.

Gender segmentation Dividing a market into different groups based on gender.

Generation X The 45 million people born between 1965 and 1976 in the "birth dearth" following the baby boom.

Geographic segmentation Dividing a market into different geographical units such as nations, states, regions, counties, cities, or neighborhoods.

Geographical pricing Setting price based on the buyer's geographic location.

Global firm A firm that, by operating in more than one country, gains R&D, production, marketing, and financial advantages in its costs and reputation that are not available to purely domestic competitors.

Good-value pricing Offering just the right combination of quality and good service at a fair price.

Group Two or more people who interact to accomplish individual or mutual goals.

Growth-share matrix A portfolio-planning method that evaluates a company's strategic business units in terms of their market growth rate and relative market share. SBUs are classified as stars, cash cows, question marks, or dogs.

Growth stage The product life-cycle stage in which a product's sales start climbing quickly.

Handling objections The step in the selling process in which the salesperson seeks out, clarifies, and overcomes customer objections to buying.

Horizontal marketing system A channel arrangement in which two or more companies at one level join together to follow a new marketing opportunity.

Idea generation The systematic search for new-product ideas.

Idea screening Screening new-product ideas in order to spot good ideas and drop poor ones as soon as possible.

Income segmentation Dividing a market into different income groups.

Independent off-price retailer Off-price retailer that is either independently owned and run or is a division of a larger retail corporation.

Indirect marketing channel Channel containing one or more intermediary levels.

Individual marketing Tailoring products and marketing programs to the needs and preferences of individual customers—also labeled "markets-of-one marketing," "customized marketing," and "one-to-one marketing."

Industrial product Product bought by individuals and organizations for further processing or for use in conducting a business.

Innovative marketing A principle of enlightened marketing that requires that a company seek real product and marketing improvements.

Inside sales force Inside salespeople who conduct business from their offices via telephone, the Internet, or visits from prospective buyers.

Integrated logistics management The logistics concept that emphasizes teamwork, both inside the company and among all the marketing channel organizations, to maximize the performance of the entire distribution system.

Integrated marketing communications (IMC) Carefully integrating and coordinating the company's many communications channels to deliver a clear, consistent, and compelling message about the organization and its products.

Intensive distribution Stocking the product in as many outlets as possible.

Interactive marketing Training service employees in the fine art of interacting with customers to satisfy their needs.

Intermarket segmentation Forming segments of consumers who have similar needs and buying behavior even though they are located in different countries.

Intermodal transportation Combining two or more modes of transportation.

Internal databases Electronic collections of consumer and market information obtained from data sources within the company network.

Internal marketing Orienting and motivating customer-contact employees and the supporting service people to work as a team to provide customer satisfaction.

Internet A vast public web of computer networks that connects users of all types all around the world to each other and to an amazingly large "information repository."

Introduction stage The product life-cycle stage in which the new product is first distributed and made available for purchase.

Joint ownership A joint venture in which a company joins investors in a foreign market to create a local business in which the company shares joint ownership and control.

Joint venturing Entering foreign markets by joining with foreign companies to produce or market a product or service.

Learning Changes in an individual's behavior arising from experience.

Licensing A method of entering a foreign market in which the company enters into an agreement with a licensee in the foreign market, offering the right to use a manufacturing process, trademark, patent, trade secret, or other item of value for a fee or royalty.

Lifestyle A person's pattern of living as expressed in his or her activities, interests, and opinions.

Line extension Extending an existing brand name to new forms, colors, sizes, ingredients, or flavors of an existing product category.

Local marketing Tailoring brands and promotions to the needs and wants of local customer groups—cities, neighborhoods, and even specific stores.

Macroenvironment The larger societal forces that affect the microenvironment—demographic, economic, natural, technological, political, and cultural forces.

Madison & Vine A term that has come to represent the merging of advertising and entertainment in an effort to break through the clutter and create new avenues for reaching consumers with more engaging messages.

Management contracting A joint venture in which the domestic firm supplies the management know-how to a foreign company that supplies the capital; the domestic firm exports management services rather than products.

Manufacturers' sales branches and offices Wholesaling by sellers or buyers themselves rather than through independent wholesalers.

Market The set of all actual and potential buyers of a product or service.

Market development A strategy for company growth by identifying and developing new market segments for current company products.

Market offering Some combination of products, services, information, or experiences offered to a market to satisfy a need or want.

Market penetration A strategy for company growth by increasing sales of current products to current market segments without changing the product.

Market segment A group of consumers who respond in a similar way to a given set of marketing efforts.

Market segmentation Dividing a market into distinct groups of buyers who have distinct needs, characteristics, or behavior and who might require separate products or marketing programs.

Market targeting The process of evaluating each market segment's attractiveness and selecting one or more segments to enter.

Marketing Marketing is the activity, set of institutions, and processes for creating, communicating, delivering, and exchanging offerings that have value for customers, clients, partners, and society at-large.

Marketing audit A comprehensive, systematic, independent, and periodic examination of a company's environment, objectives, strategies, and activities to determine problem areas and opportunities and to recommend a plan of action to improve the company's marketing performance.

Marketing channel (distribution channel) A set of interdependent organizations that help make a product or service available for use or consumption by the consumer or business user.

Marketing channel design Designing effective marketing channels by analyzing consumer needs, setting channel objectives, identifying major channel alternatives, and evaluating them.

Marketing channel management Selecting, managing, and motivating individual channel members and evaluating their performance over time.

Marketing concept The marketing management philosophy that holds that achieving organizational goals depends on knowing the needs and wants of target markets and delivering the desired satisfactions better than competitors do.

Marketing control The process of measuring and evaluating the results of marketing strategies and plans and taking corrective action to ensure that objectives are achieved.

Marketing environment The actors and forces outside marketing that affect marketing management's ability to build and maintain successful relationships with target customers.

Marketing implementation The process that turns marketing strategies and plans into marketing actions in order to accomplish strategic marketing objectives.

Marketing information system (MIS) People and procedures for assessing information needs, developing the needed information, and helping decision makers to use the information to generate and validate actionable customer and market insights.

Marketing intelligence The systematic collection and analysis of publicly available information about consumers, competitors, and developments in the marketing environment.

Marketing intermediaries Firms that help the company to promote, sell, and distribute its goods to final buyers.

Marketing logistics (physical distribution) Planning, implementing, and controlling the physical flow of materials, final goods, and related information from points of origin to points of consumption to meet customer requirements at a profit.

Marketing management The art and science of choosing target markets and building profitable relationships with them.

Marketing mix The set of controllable tactical marketing tools—product, price, place, and promotion—that the firm blends to produce the response it wants in the target market.

Marketing myopia The mistake of paying more attention to the specific products a company offers than to the benefits and experiences produced by these products.

Marketing research The systematic design, collection, analysis, and reporting of data relevant to a specific marketing situation facing an organization.

Marketing strategy The marketing logic by which the business unit hopes to create customer value and achieve profitable customer relationships.

Marketing strategy development Designing an initial marketing strategy for a new product based on the product concept.

Marketing Web site A Web site that engages consumers in interactions that will move them closer to a direct purchase or other marketing outcome.

Market-penetration pricing Setting a low price for a new product in order to attract a large number of buyers and a large market share.

Market-skimming pricing (price skimming) Setting a high price for a new product to skim maximum revenues layer by layer from the segments willing to pay the high price; the company makes fewer but more profitable sales.

Maturity stage The product life-cycle stage in which sales growth slows or levels off.

Merchant wholesaler Independently owned business that takes title to the merchandise it handles.

Microenvironment The actors close to the company that affect its ability to serve its customers—the company, suppliers, marketing intermediaries, customer markets, competitors, and publics.

Micromarketing The practice of tailoring products and marketing programs to the needs and wants of specific individuals and local customer groups—includes local marketing and individual marketing.

Millennials (or Generation Y) The 83 million children of the baby boomers, born between 1977 and 2000.

Mission statement A statement of the organization's purpose—what it wants to accomplish in the larger environment.

Modified rebuy A business buying situation in which the buyer wants to modify product specifications, prices, terms, or suppliers.

Motive (drive) A need that is sufficiently pressing to direct the person to seek satisfaction of the need.

Multichannel distribution system A distribution system in which a single firm sets up two or more marketing channels to reach one or more customer segments.

Natural environment Natural resources that are needed as inputs by marketers or that are affected by marketing activities.

Needs States of felt deprivation.

New product A good, service, or idea that is perceived by some potential customers as new.

New-product development The development of original products, product improvements, product modifications, and new brands through the firm's own product development efforts.

New task A business buying situation in which the buyer purchases a product or service for the first time.

Objective-and-task method Developing the promotion budget by (1) defining specific objectives; (2) determining the tasks that must be performed to achieve these objectives; and (3) estimating the costs of performing these tasks. The sum of these costs is the proposed promotion budget.

Observational research Gathering primary data by observing relevant people, actions, and situations.

Occasion segmentation Dividing the market into groups according to occasions when buyers get the idea to buy, actually make their purchase, or use the purchased item.

Off-price retailer Retailer that buys at less-than-regular wholesale prices and sells at less than retail. Examples are factory outlets, independents, and warehouse clubs.

Online advertising Advertising that appears while consumers are surfing the Web, including display ads, search-related ads, online classifieds, and other forms.

Online focus groups Gathering a small group of people online with a trained moderator to chat about a product, service, or organization and gain qualitative insights about consumer attitudes and behavior.

Online marketing Company efforts to market products and services and build customer relationships over the Internet.

Online marketing research Collecting primary data online through Internet surveys, online focus groups, Web-based experiments, or tracking consumers online behavior.

Online social networks   Online social communities—blogs, social networking Web sites, or even virtual worlds—where people socialize or exchange information and opinions.

Opinion leader   Person within a reference group who, because of special skills, knowledge, personality, or other characteristics, exerts influence on others.

Optional-product pricing   The pricing of optional or accessory products along with a main product.

Outside sales force   (or **field sales force**) Outside salespeople who travel to call on customers in the field.

Packaging   The activities of designing and producing the container or wrapper for a product.

Partner relationship management   Working closely with partners in other company departments and outside the company to jointly bring greater value to customers.

Percentage-of-sales method   Setting the promotion budget at a certain percentage of current or forecasted sales or as a percentage of the unit sales price.

Perception   The process by which people select, organize, and interpret information to form a meaningful picture of the world.

Personal selling   Personal presentation by the firm's sales force for the purpose of making sales and building customer relationships.

Personality   The unique psychological characteristics that lead to relatively consistent and lasting responses to one's environment.

Pleasing products   Products that give high immediate satisfaction but may hurt consumers in the long run.

Political environment   Laws, government agencies, and pressure groups that influence and limit various organizations and individuals in a given society.

Portfolio analysis   The process by which management evaluates the products and businesses making up the company.

Positioning   Arranging for a market offering to occupy a clear, distinctive, and desirable place relative to competing products in the minds of target consumers.

Positioning statement   A statement that summarizes company or brand positioning—it takes this form: To (target segment and need) our (brand) is (concept) that (point-of-difference).

Preapproach   The step in the selling process in which the salesperson learns as much as possible about a prospective customer before making a sales call.

Presentation   The step in the selling process in which the salesperson tells the "value story" to the buyer, showing how the company's offer solves the customer's problems.

Price   The amount of money charged for a product or service, or the sum of all the values that customers give up in order to gain the benefits of having or using a product or service.

Price elasticity   A measure of the sensitivity of demand to changes in price.

Primary data   Information collected for the specific purpose at hand.

Product   Anything that can be offered to a market for attention, acquisition, use, or consumption that might satisfy a want or need.

Product adaptation   Adapting a product to meet local conditions or wants in foreign markets.

Product bundle pricing   Combining several products and offering the bundle at a reduced price.

Product concept   A detailed version of the new-product idea stated in meaningful consumer terms; The idea that consumers will favor products that offer the most quality, performance, and features and that the organization should therefore devote its energy to making continuous product improvements.

Product development   A strategy for company growth by offering modified or new products to current market segments; Developing the product concept into a physical product in order to ensure that the product idea can be turned into a workable market offering.

Product invention   Creating new products or services for foreign markets.

Product life cycle   The course of a product's sales and profits over its lifetime.

Product line   A group of products that are closely related because they function in a similar manner, are sold to the same customer groups, are marketed through the same types of outlets, or fall within given price ranges.

Product line pricing   Setting the price steps between various products in a product line based on cost differences between the products and customer perceptions of the value of different features.

Product/market expansion grid   A portfolio-planning tool for identifying company growth opportunities through market penetration, market development, product development, or diversification.

Product mix (or product portfolio)   The set of all product lines and items that a particular seller offers for sale.

Product position   The way the product is defined by consumers on important attributes—the place the product occupies in consumers' minds relative to competing products.

Product quality   The characteristics of a product or service that bear on its ability to satisfy stated or implied customer needs.

Product sales force structure   A sales force organization under which salespeople specialize in selling only a portion of the company's products or lines.

Production concept   The idea that consumers will favor products that are available and highly affordable and that the organization should therefore focus on improving production and distribution efficiency.

Promotion mix (marketing communications mix)   The specific blend of advertising, public relations, personal selling, sales promotion, and direct-marketing tools that the company uses to persuasively communicate customer value and build customer relationships.

Promotional pricing   Temporarily pricing products below the list price, and sometimes even below cost, to increase short-run sales.

Prospecting   The step in the selling process in which the salesperson or company identifies qualified potential customers.

Psychographic segmentation   Dividing a market into different groups based on social class, lifestyle, or personality characteristics.

Psychological pricing   A pricing approach that considers the psychology of prices and not simply the economics; the price is used to say something about the product.

Public   Any group that has an actual or potential interest in or impact on an organization's ability to achieve its objectives.

Public relations   Building good relations with the company's various publics by obtaining favorable publicity, building up a good "corporate image," and handling or heading off unfavorable rumors, stories, and events.

Pull strategy   A promotion strategy that calls for spending a lot on advertising and consumer promotion to induce final consumers to buy the product. If the pull strategy is effective, consumers will then demand the product from channel members, who will in turn demand it from producers.

Push strategy   A promotion strategy that calls for using the sales force and trade promotion to push the product through channels. The producer promotes the product to channel members to induce them to carry the product and to promote it to final consumers.

Reference prices   Prices that buyers carry in their minds and refer to when they look at a given product.

Retailer   A business whose sales come primarily from retailing.

Retailing   All activities involved in selling goods or services directly to final consumers for their personal, nonbusiness use.

Return on advertising investment   The net return on advertising investment divided by the costs of the advertising investment.

Return on marketing investment (or marketing ROI)   The net return from a marketing investment divided by the costs of the marketing investment.

Sales promotion   Short-term incentives to encourage the purchase or sale of a product or service.

Sales quota   A standard that states the amount a salesperson should sell and how sales should be divided among the company's products.

Sales-force management   The analysis, planning, implementation, and control of sales force activities. It includes designing sales force strategy and structure and recruiting, selecting, training, supervising, compensating, and evaluating the firm's salespeople.

Salesperson   An individual representing a company to customers by performing one or more of the following activities: prospecting, communicating, selling, servicing, information gathering, and relationship building.

Salutary products   Products that have low appeal but may benefit consumers in the long run.

Sample   A segment of the population selected for marketing research to represent the population as a whole.

Secondary data   Information that already exists somewhere, having been collected for another purpose.

Segmented pricing   Selling a product or service at two or more prices, where the difference in prices is not based on differences in costs.

Selective distribution   The use of more than one, but fewer than all, of the intermediaries who are willing to carry the company's products.

Selling concept   The idea that consumers will not buy enough of the firm's products unless it undertakes a large-scale selling and promotion effort.

Selling process   The steps that the salesperson follows when selling, which include prospecting and qualifying, preapproach, approach, presentation and demonstration, handling objections, closing, and follow-up.

Sense-of-mission marketing   A principle of enlightened marketing that holds that a company should define its mission in broad social terms rather than narrow product terms.

Service   Any activity or benefit that one party can offer to another that is essentially intangible and does not result in the ownership of anything.

Service inseparability   A major characteristic of services—they are produced and consumed at the same time and cannot be separated from their providers.

Service intangibility   A major characteristic of services—they cannot be seen, tasted, felt, heard, or smelled before they are bought.

Service perishability   A major characteristic of services—they cannot be stored for later sale or use.

Service-profit chain   The chain that links service firm profits with employee and customer satisfaction.

Service retailer   A retailer whose product line is actually a service, including hotels, airlines, banks, colleges, and many others.

Service variability   A major characteristic of services—their quality may vary greatly, depending on who provides them and when, where, and how.

Share of customer   The portion of the customer's purchasing that a company gets in its product categories.

Shopping center   A group of retail businesses planned, developed, owned, and managed as a unit.

Shopping product   Consumer good that the customers, in the process of selection and purchase, characteristically compare on such bases as suitability, quality, price, and style.

Social class   Relatively permanent and ordered divisions in a society whose members share similar values, interests, and behaviors.

Social marketing   The use of commercial marketing concepts and tools in programs designed to influence individuals' behavior to improve their well-being and that of society; A principle of enlightened marketing that holds that a company should make marketing decisions by considering consumers' wants, the company's requirements, consumers' long-run interests, and society's long-run interests.

Societal marketing concept   The idea that a company's marketing decisions should consider consumers' wants, the company's requirements, consumers' long-run interests, and society's long-run interests.

Spam   Unsolicited, unwanted commercial e-mail messages.

Specialty product   Consumer product with unique characteristics or brand identification for which a significant group of buyers is willing to make a special purchase effort.

Specialty store   A retail store that carries a narrow product line with a deep assortment within that line.

Standardized global marketing   An international marketing strategy for using basically the same marketing strategy and mix in all the company's international markets.

Store brand (or private brand)   A brand created and owned by a reseller of a product or service.

Straight product extension   Marketing a product in a foreign market without any change.

Straight rebuy   A business buying situation in which the buyer routinely reorders something without any modifications.

Strategic planning   The process of developing and maintaining a strategic fit between the organization's goals and capabilities and its changing marketing opportunities.

Style   A basic and distinctive mode of expression.

Subculture   A group of people with shared value systems based on common life experiences and situations.

Supermarket   A large, low-cost, low-margin, high-volume, self-service store that carries a wide variety of grocery and household products.

Superstore   A store much larger than a regular supermarket that offers a large assortment of routinely purchased food products, nonfood items, and services.

Supply chain management   Managing upstream and downstream value-added flows of materials, final goods, and related information among suppliers, the company, resellers, and final consumers.

Survey research   Gathering primary data by asking people questions about their knowledge, attitudes, preferences, and buying behavior.

SWOT analysis   An overall evaluation of the company's strengths (S), weaknesses (W), opportunities (O), and threats (T).

Systems selling (or solutions selling)   Selling a complete solution to a problem, helping buyers to avoid all the separate decisions involved in a complex buying situation.

Target costing   Pricing that starts with an ideal selling price, then targets costs that will ensure that the price is met.

Target market   A set of buyers sharing common needs or characteristics that the company decides to serve.

Team-based new-product development   An approach to developing new products in which various company departments work closely together, overlapping the steps in the product development process to save time and increase effectiveness.

Team selling   Using teams of people from sales, marketing, engineering, finance, technical support, and even upper management to service large, complex accounts.

Technological environment   Forces that create new technologies, creating new product and market opportunities.

Telephone marketing   Using the telephone to sell directly to customers.

Territorial sales force structure   A sales force organization that assigns each salesperson to an exclusive geographic territory in which that salesperson sells the company's full line.

Test marketing   The stage of new-product development in which the product and marketing program are tested in realistic market settings.

Third-party logistics (3PL) provider   An independent logistics provider that performs any or all of the functions required to get their client's product to market.

Total costs   The sum of the fixed and variable costs for any given level of production.

Trade promotions   Sales promotion tools used to persuade resellers to carry a brand, give it shelf space, promote it in advertising, and push it to consumers.

Undifferentiated (mass) marketing   A market-coverage strategy in which a firm decides to ignore market segment differences and go after the whole market with one offer.

Unsought product   Consumer product that the consumer either does not know about or knows about but does not normally think of buying.

Value analysis   An approach to cost reduction in which components are studied carefully to determine if they can be redesigned, standardized, or made by less costly methods of production.

Value chain   The series of departments that carry out value-creating activities to design, produce, market, deliver, and support a firm's products.

Value delivery network   The network made up of the company, suppliers, distributors, and ultimately customers who "partner" with each other to improve the performance of the entire system in delivering customer value.

Value-added pricing   Attaching value-added features and services to differentiate a market offering and support higher prices, rather than cutting prices to match competitors.

Value-based pricing   Setting price based on buyers' perceptions of value rather than on the seller's cost.

Value proposition   The full positioning of a brand—the full mix of benefits upon which it is positioned.

Variable costs   Costs that vary directly with the level of production.

Vertical marketing system (VMS)   A distribution channel structure in which producers, wholesalers, and retailers act as a unified system. One channel member owns the others, has contracts with them, or has so much power that they all cooperate.

Viral marketing   The Internet version of word-of-mouth marketing—Web sites, videos, e-mail messages, or other marketing events that are so infectious that customers will want to pass them along to friends.

Wants   The form human needs take as shaped by culture and individual personality.

Warehouse club   Off-price retailer that sells a limited selection of brand name grocery items, appliances, clothing, and a hodgepodge of other goods at deep discounts to members who pay annual membership fees.

Wheel-of-retailing concept   A concept that states that new types of retailers usually begin as low-margin, low-price, low-status operations but later evolve into higher-priced, higher-service operations, eventually becoming like the conventional retailers they replaced.

Whole-channel view   Designing international channels that take into account the entire global supply chain and marketing channel, forging and effective global value delivery network.

Wholesaler   A firm engaged primarily in wholesaling activities.

Wholesaling   All activities involved in selling goods and services to those buying for resale or business use.

References

Chapter 1

1. Quotes and other information from Jonah Bloom, "Stengel Exhorts 4As: It's Not About Telling and Selling," *Advertising Age,* March 1, 2007, accessed at http://adage.com/4asmedia07/article?article_id=115259; Robert Berner, "Detergent Can Be So Much More," *BusinessWeek,* May 1, 2006, pp. 66–67; Jack Neff, "New Tide Campaign Goes Beyond Stains," *Advertising Age,* February 13, 2006, p. 16; Dan Sewell, "P&G to Build Relationships," *Akron Beacon Journal,* July 22, 2007, accessed at www.ohio.com/business/8789492.html; "Case Study: Tide Knows Fabrics Best," accessed at www.thearf.org/awards/ogilvy-current-winners.html, September 2007; and "P&G: Our Purpose, Values, and Principles," accessed at www.pg.com/company/who_we_are/ppv.jhtml, November 2007.

2. Statement made in an address to the American Association of Advertising Agencies conference, accessed via Jonah Bloom, "Stengel Exhorts 4As: It's Not About 'Telling and Selling,' " *Advertising Age,* March 1, 2007, at http://adage.com/print?article_id=115259.

3. See "Markets: Since Launch of First Generation of iPod, Apple Inc. Has Sold More Than 88.7 Million Units Worldwide," *Associated Press Financial Wire,* March 14, 2007; "Apple," *BusinessWeek,* March 26, 2007, p. 84; and "Global 500: World's Largest Corporations," *Fortune,* July 23, 2007, p. 133.

4. As quoted in Carolyn P. Neal, "From the Editor," *Marketing Management,* January–February 2006, p. 3.

5. The American Marketing Association offers the following definition: "Marketing is an organizational function and a set of processes for creating, communicating, and delivering value to customers and for managing customer relationships in ways that benefit the organization and its stakeholders." Accessed at www.marketingpower.com/mg-dictionary-view1862.php?, November 2007.

6. Lucas Conley, "Customer-Centered Leader: Winner Maxine Clark," *Fast Company,* October 2005, p. 54; and Walter F. Loeb, "Bringing Concepts to Bear," *Stores,* March 2007, p. 88.

7. See Theodore Levitt's classic article, "Marketing Myopia," *Harvard Business Review,* July–August 1960, pp. 45–56. For more recent discussions, see Yves Doz, Jose Santos, and Peter J. Williamson, "Marketing Myopia Re-Visited: Why Every Company Needs to Learn from the World," *Ivey Business Journal,* January–February 2004, p. 1; Lon Zimmerman, "Product Positioning Maps Secure Future," *Marketing News,* October 15, 2005, p. 47; and "What Business Are You In?" *Harvard Business Review,* October 2006, pp. 127–37.

8. Scott Pelley, "Howard Schultz: The Star of Starbucks," *CBS News,* April 23, 2006, accessed at www.cbsnews.com/stories/2006/04/21/60minutes/main1532246.shtml.

9. Information from "The Computer Is Personal Again," an HP ad appearing in *Business 2.0,* June 2006, p. 33; and www.hp.com/personal, accessed November 2007.

10. See Rand Health, "Obesity and Disability: The Shape of Things to Come," accessed October 2007 at www.rand.org/pubs/research_briefs/2007/RAND_RB9043-1.pdf; "Prince Charles Says Ban McDonald's Food," *Associated Press,* February 28, 2007; and information from www.hardees.com/menu/, accessed October 2007.

11. See Alex Taylor III, "Can J&J Keep the Magic Going?" *Fortune,* May 27, 2002, pp. 117–21; Larry Edwards et al., "75 Years of Ideas," *Advertising Age,* February 14, 2005, p. 14; "America's Most Admired Companies," *Fortune,* accessed at http://money.cnn.com/magazines/fortune/mostadmired/2007/index.html, August 2007; "The Top 10 PR Endeavors," PR News, October 30, 2006, p.1; and www.jnj.com/our_company/our_credo/index.htm, accessed January 2008.

12. Quotes and information from Blanca Torres, "Jeans' Genes Part of Price Tag Formula," *Knight Ridder Tribune Business News,* November 8, 2006, p. 1; Stephanie King, "The Queen of Jeans," *London Independent,* July 17, 2006; "Paige Denim Week," *Toronto Fashion Monitor,* October 30, 2006, accessed at http://toronto.fashion-monitor.com/events.php/56; and www.paigepremiumdenim.com, accessed October 2007.

13. For more on how to measure customer satisfaction, see D. Randall Brandt, "For Good Measure," *Marketing Management,* January–February 2007, pp. 21–25.

14. Example adapted from Denny Hatch and Ernie Schell, "Delight Your Customers," *Target Marketing,* April 2002, pp. 32–39; with additional information from "Lexus Earns Best-Selling Brand Title for Sixth Consecutive Year," January 4, 2006, accessed at www.lexus.com/about/press_releases/index.html; and www.lexus.com/about/corporate/lexus_covenant.html, accessed November 2007.

15. Information accessed at www.incircle.com, July, 2007.

16. Information about the Harley Owners Group accessed at www.hog.com, October 2007. For more on loyalty programs, see Joseph C. Nunes and Xavier Dreze, "Your Loyalty Program Is Betraying You," *Harvard Business Review,* April 2006, pp. 124–31; Deborah L. Vence, "Create Expectations," *Marketing News,* October 6, 2007, p. 25; and "Do Loyalty Programs Retain Profitable Customers?" *Business Wire,* May 23, 2007.

17. Quotes and other information from "Gunning for the Best Buy," *Knight Ridder Tribune Business News,* May 28, 2006, p. 1; Gary McWilliams, "Analyzing Customers, Best Buy Decides Not All Are Welcome," *Wall Street Journal,* November 8, 2004; Shirley A. Lazo, "Let's Go Shopping," *Barron's,* June 26, 2006, p. 28; Matthew Boyle, "Best Buy's Giant Gamble," *Fortune,* April 3, 2006, pp. 69–75; "Best Buy Co. Inc.," *Hoover's Company Records,* July 15, 2007, p. 10209; Devendra Mishra, "Tale of Two Retailers," Dealerscope, March 2007, p. 36; and www.bestbuy.com, accessed November 2007.

18. Andrew Walmsley, "The Year of Consumer Empowerment," *Marketing,* December 20, 2006, p. 9.

19. Walmsley, "The Year of Consumer Empowerment," p. 9.

20. Adapted from information in Jonathan Birchall, "Just Do It, Marketers Say," *Financial Times,* April 30, 2007, accessed at http://i-advertising.com/?p=23.

21. Matthew Creamer, "John Doe Edges Out Jeff Goodby," *Advertising Age,* January 8, 2007, pp. S4–S5.

22. Philip Kotler and Kevin Lane Keller, *Marketing Management,* 12th ed. (Upper Saddle River, NJ: Prentice Hall, 2006), p. 27.

23. For more on the relationship between customers satisfaction, loyalty, and company performance, see Ben McConnell and Jackie Huba, "Learning to Leverage the Lunatic Fringe," *Point,* July–August 2006, pp. 14–15; Fred Reichheld, *The Ultimate Question: Driving Good Profits and True Growth* (Boston: Harvard Business School Press, 2006); Bruce Cooil, Timothy L. Keiningham, Lerzan Aksoy, and Michael Hsu, "A Longitudinal Analysis of Customer Satisfaction and Share of Wallet: Investigating the Moderating Effects of Customer Characteristics," *Journal of Marketing,* January 2007, pp. 67–83; and Murali Chandrahsekaran, Kristin Rotte, Stephen S. Tax, and Rajdeep Grewal, "Satisfaction, Strength, and Customer Loyalty," *Journal of Marketing Research,* February 2007, pp. 153–63.

24. "Stew Leonard's," *Hoover's Company Records,* July 15, 2007, p. 104226; and www.stew-leonards.com/html/about.cfm, accessed October 2007.

25. For interesting discussions on assessing and using customer lifetime value, see Rajkumar Venkatesan and V. Kumar, "A Customer Lifetime Value Framework for Customer Selection and Resource Allocation Strategy," *Journal of Marketing,* October 2004, pp. 106–25; Rajkumar Venkatesan, V. Kumar, and Timothy Bohling, "Selecting Valuable Customers Using a Customer Lifetime Value Framework," Marketing Science Institute, Report No. 05–121, 2005; Lynette Ryals, "Making Customer Relationships Management Work: The Measurement and Profitable Management of Customer Relationships," *Journal of Marketing,* October 2005, pp. 252–61; Sunil Gupta et al., "Modeling Customer Lifetime Value," *Journal of Service Research,* November 2006, pp. 139–46; and "Determining 'CLV' Can Lead to Making Magical Marketing Decisions," *BtoB,* May 7, 2007, p. 18.

26. Don Peppers and Martha Rogers, "Customer Loyalty: A Matter of Trust," *Sales & Marketing Management,* June 2006, p. 22.

27. Don Peppers and Martha Rogers, "Customers Don't Grow on Trees," *Fast Company,* July 2005, p. 26.

28. See Roland T. Rust, Valerie A. Zeithaml, and Katherine A. Lemon, *Driving Customer Equity* (New York: Free Press, 2000); Robert C. Blattberg, Gary Getz, and Jacquelyn S. Thomas, Customer Equity (Boston: Harvard Business School Press, 2001); Rust, Lemon, and Zeithaml, "Return on Marketing: Using Customer Equity to Focus Marketing Strategy," *Journal of Marketing,* January 2004, pp. 109–27; Rust, Zeithaml, and Lemon, "Customer-Centered Brand Management," *Harvard Business Review,* September 2004, p. 110; Don Peppers and Martha Rogers, "Hail to the Customer," *Sales & Marketing Management,* October 2005, pp. 49–51; and Robert P. Leone et al., "Linking Brand Equity to Customer Equity," *Journal of Service Marketing,* November 2006, pp. 125–38.

29. This example is adapted from information in Rust, Lemon, and Zeithaml, "Where Should the Next Marketing Dollar Go?" *Marketing Management,* September–October 2001, pp. 24–28. Also see David Welch and David Kiley, "Can Caddy's Driver Make GM Cool?" *BusinessWeek,* September 20, 2004, pp. 105–6; Jamie LaReau, "Cadillac Wants to Boost Sales, Customer Service," *Automotive News,* February 20, 2006, p. 46; and Jon Kamp, "GM Optimistic About Cadillac," *Dow Jones Newswires,* January 8, 2007.

30. Ravi Dhar and Rashi Glazer, "Hedging Customers," *Harvard Business Review,* May 2003, pp. 86–92. Also see Ian Gordon, "Relationship Marketing: Managing Wasteful or Worthless Customer Relationships," *Ivey Business Journal,* March–April 2006, pp. 1–4.

31. Werner Reinartz and V. Kumar, "The Mismanagement of Customer Loyalty," *Harvard Business Review,* July 2002, pp. 86–94. For more on customer equity management, see Michael D. Johnson and Fred Selnes, "Customer Portfolio Management: Toward a Dynamic Theory of Exchange Relationships," *Journal of Marketing,* April 2004, pp. 1–17; Sunil Gupta and Donald R. Lehman, *Managing Customers as Investments* (Philadelphia: Wharton School Publishing, 2005); Roland T. Rust, Katherine N. Lemon, and Das Narayandas, *Customer Equity Management* (Upper Saddle River, NJ: Prentice Hall, 2005); and Kathy Stevens, "Using Customer Equity Models to Improve Loyalty and Profits," *The Journal of Consumer Marketing* 23, 2006, p. 379.

32. "Population Explosion!" *ClickZ Stats,* April 12, 2006, accessed at www.clickz.com/stats/sectors/geographics/article.php/151151; and www.internetworldstats.com/stats.htm, accessed March 2007.

33. See Allison Enright, "Get Clued In: Mystery of Web 2.0 Resolved," *Marketing News,* January 15, 2007, pp. 20–22.

34. "Jupiter Research Forecasts Online Retail Spending Will Reach $144 Billion in 2010, a CAGR of 12% from 2005," February 6, 2006, accessed at www.jupitermedia.com/corporate/releases/06.02.06-new jupresearch.html.

35. See annual reports and other information found at www.mcdonalds.com, www.viacom.com, and www.nikebiz.com, accessed October 2007.

36. Quotes and information found at www.patagonia.com/web/us/contribution/patagonia.go?assetid=2329, accessed October 2007.

37. Information and quotes from "White Alligator, ZooFest Make Magical Day at SF Zoo," accessed at www.coastnews.com/f001.htm, August 2007; and www.sfzoo.org/kids/about.htm, accessed October 2007.

38. For other examples, and for a good review of nonprofit marketing, see Philip Kotler and Alan R. Andreasen, *Strategic Marketing for Nonprofit Organizations,* 6th ed. (Upper Saddle River, NJ: Prentice Hall, 2003); Philip Kotler and Karen Fox, *Strategic Marketing for Educational Institutions* (Upper Saddle River, NJ: Prentice Hall, 1995); Philip Kotler, John Bowen, and James Makens, *Marketing for Hospitality and Tourism,* 3rd ed. (Upper Saddle River, NJ: Prentice Hall, 2003); and Philip Kotler and Nancy Lee, *Marketing in the Public Sector: A Roadmap for Improved Performance* (Philadelphia, PA: Wharton School Publishing, 2007).

39. "100 Leading National Advertisers," Advertising Age, June 25, 2007, p. S4. For more on social marketing, see Philip Kotler, Ned Roberto, and Nancy R. Lee, *Social Marketing: Improving the Quality of Life,* 2nd ed. (Thousand Oaks, CA: Sage, 2002).

Chapter 2

1. Quotes and other information from Paul Farriss, "NASCAR Rides the Fast Track," *Marketing,* April 11, 2005, pp. 11–12; Mark Woods, "Readers Try to Explain Why Racin' Rocks," *Florida Times Union,* February 16, 2003; Tony Kontzer, "Backseat Drivers—NASCAR Puts You in the Race," *InformationWeek,* March 25, 2002, p. 83; Paul Owens, "Office Depot to Sponsor NASCAR," *Knight Ridder Tribune Business News,* January 28, 2005, p. 1; Jenny Kincaid, "NASCAR Beefs Up Its Brand Loyalty," *Knight Ridder Tribune Business News,* April 1, 2006, p. 1; Robert McGarvery, "UPS Roars into Action," *Sales & Marketing Management,* May 2005, pp. 58–65; Rich Thomaselli, "Hitch a Ride with NASCAR for Under $5M," *Advertising Age,* November 6, 2006, pp. 4, 80; Michael A. Prospero, "NASCAR," *Fast Company,* September 2006, p. 52; Rich Thomaselli, "How NASCAR Plans to Get Back on the Fast Track," *Advertising Age,* February 12, 2007, pp. 3–5; and www.NASCAR.com, accessed November 2007.

2. For more on mission statements, see Frank Buytendijk, "Five Keys to Building a High-Performance Organization," *Business Performance Management,* February 2006, pp. 24–29; Joseph Peyrefitte and Forest R. David, "A Content Analysis of Mission Statements of United States Firms in Four Industries," *International Journal of Management,* June 2006, pp. 296–301; and Jeffrey Abrahams, *101 Mission Statements from Top Companies* (Berkeley, CA: Ten Speed Press, 2007).

3. Nike and eBay mission statements from www.nike.com/nikebiz/nikebiz.jhtml?page=4 and http://pages.ebay.com/aboutebay/thecompany/companyoverview.html, respectively, accessed November 2007.

4. Thomas Walsh, "Mission Statement or Mission: Impossible?" *Central New York Business Journal,* May 26, 2006, pp. 23, 27.

5. See the BASF Innovations Web page, accessed at www.corporate.basf.com/en/innovationen/?id=Z_1-HA6M0bcp4PX, November 2007.

6. See "BASF Expands Innovative Agricultural Products to Asian Growth Markets," February 28, 2007, accessed at www.corporate.basf.com/en/presse/mitteilungen/pm.htm?pmid=2586&id=Z_1-HA6M0bcp4PX.

7. The following discussion is based in part on information found at www.bcg.com/this_is_BCG/mission/growth_share_matrix.html, accessed December 2007.

8. H. Igor Ansoff, "Strategies for Diversification," *Harvard Business Review,* September–October 1957, pp. 113–24. Quotes and information about Starbucks in this discussion are from Bruce Horovitz, "Starbucks Nation," *USA Today,* May 19, 2006, accessed at www.usatoday.com/

money/industries/food/2006-05-18-starbucks-usat_x.htm; Melissa Allison, "Starbucks Sprouted Up Here, There, Everywhere," *Knight Ridder Tribune Business News*, February 1, 2007, p. 1; "Joni Mitchell Set to 'Shine' on Hear Music," *Business Wire*, July 25, 2007, p. 1; Burt Helm, "Saving Starbucks' Soul," *BusinessWeek*, April 9, 2007, pp. 56–61; and the company fact sheet, annual report, and other information accessed at www.starbucks.com, November 2007.

9. Michael E. Porter, *Competitive Advantage: Creating and Sustaining Superior Performance* (New York: Free Press, 1985); and Michel E. Porter, "What Is Strategy?" *Harvard Business Review*, November–December 1996, pp. 61–78. Also see Kim B. Clark et al., *Harvard Business School on Managing the Value Chain* (Boston: Harvard Business School Press, 2000); "Buyer Value and the Value Chain," *Business Owner*, September–October 2003, p. 1; and "The Value Chain," accessed at www.quickmba.com/strategy/value-chain/, November 2007.

10. Phillip Kotler, *Kotler on Marketing* (New York: Free Press, 1999), pp. 20–22; and Marianne Seiler, "Transformation Trek," *Marketing Management*, January–February 2006, pp. 32–39.

11. "McDonald's Fetes 50th Birthday, Opens Anniversary Restaurant," *Knight Ridder Tribune Business News*, April 15, 2005, p. 1; and information from www.mcdonalds.com/corp.html, accessed September 2007.

12. Quotes and other information from Jeffery K. Liker and Thomas Y. Choi, "Building Deep Supplier Relationships," *Harvard Business Review*, December 2004, pp. 104–13; Lindsay Chappell, "Toyota Aims to Satisfy Its Suppliers," *Automotive News*, February 21, 2005, p. 10; and www.toyotasupplier.com, accessed november 2006; Lindsay Chappell, "Toyota: Suppliers Should Squawk," *Automotive News*, August 14, 2006, p. 22; and "Survey Ranks Relations with Parts Suppliers," *Light & Medium Trucks*, July 2007, p. 9.

13. Jack Trout, "Branding Can't Exist Without Positioning," *Advertising Age*, March 14, 2005, p. 28.

14. Ford Motor Company 2006 Annual report, accessed at www.ford.com, and "100 Leading National Advertisers," special issue of *Advertising Age*, June 25, 2007, p. 10.

15. The four Ps classification was first suggested by E. Jerome McCarthy, *Basic Marketing: A Managerial Approach* (Homewood, IL: Irwin, 1960). For the 4Cs, other proposed classifications, and more discussion, see Robert Lauterborn, "New Marketing Litany: 4Ps Passé; C-Words Take Over," *Advertising Age*, October 1, 1990, p. 26; Don E. Schultz, "New Definition of Marketing Reinforces Idea of Integration," *Marketing News*, January 15, 2005, p. 8; and Phillip Kotler, "Alphabet Soup," *Marketing Management*, March–April 2006, p. 51.

16. For more on brand and product management, see Kevin Lane Keller, *Strategic Brand Management*, 3rd ed. (Upper Saddle River, NJ: Prentice Hall, 2008).

17. For details, see Kotler and Keller, *Marketing Management*, pp. 719–25. Also see Neil A. Morgan, Bruce H. Clark, and Rich Gooner, "Marketing Productivity, Marketing Audits, and Systems for Marketing Performance Assessment: Integrating Multiple Perspectives," *Journal of Marketing*, May 2002, pp. 363–75. For a case study on a marketing audit, see Tom McCarthy, "Internal Marketing Audit Pays for Itself," *Lodging Hospitality*, August 2005, p. 22.

18. Adapted from Diane Brady, "Making Marketing Measure Up," *BusinessWeek*, December 13, 2004, pp. 112–13; with information from "Kotler Readies World for One-on-One," *Point*, June 2005, p. 3. Also see Darryl E. Owens, "Champion ROI to Prove Worth," *Marketing News*, March 1, 2007, pp. 13, 22.

19. Mark McMaster, "ROI: More Vital Than Ever," *Sales & Marketing Management*, January 2002, pp. 51–52. Also see Gordon A. Wyner, "Beyond ROI," *Marketing Management*, May–June 2006, pp. 8–9; Pat LaPointe, "Building Blocks," *Marketing Management*, May–June, 2007, pp. 19–26; James Lenskold, "Unlock Profit Potential," *Marketing Management*, May–June, 2007, pp. 26–31; and Steven H. Seggie, Erin Cavusgil, and Steven Phelan, "Measurement of Return on Marketing Investment: A Conceptual Framework and the Future of Marketing Metrics," *Industrial Marketing Management*, August 2007, pp. 834–41.

20. See David Skinner and Doug Brooks, "Move from Metrics Overload to Actionable Insights," *Advertising Age*, May 28, 2007, pp. 14–15.

21. Matthew Creamer, "Shops Push Affinity, Referrals over Sales," *Advertising Age*, June 20, 2005, p. S4.

22. For more discussion, see Michael Karuss, "Marketing Dashboards Drive Better Decisions," *Marketing News*, October 1, 2005, p. 7; Richard Karpinski, "Making the Most of a Marketing Dashboard," *BtoB*, March 13, 2006, p. 18; Bruce H. Clark, Andrew V. Abela, and Tim Ambler, "Behind the Wheel," *Marketing Management*, May–June 2006, pp. 19–23; and Christopher Hosford, "Driving Business with Dashboards," *BtoB*, December 11, 2006, p. 18.

23. For a full discussion of this model and details on customer-centered measures of return on marketing investment, see Roland T. Rust, Katherine N. Lemon, and Valarie A. Zeithaml, "Return on Marketing: Using Customer Equity to Focus Marketing Strategy," *Journal of Marketing*, January 2004, pp. 109–27; Roland T. Rust, Katherine N. Lemon, and Das Narayandas, *Customer Equity Management* (Upper Saddle River, NJ: Prentice Hall, 2005); Allison Enright, "Serve Them Right," *Marketing News*, May 1, 2006, pp. 21–22; and David Tiltman, "Everything You Know Is Wrong," *Marketing*, June 13, 2007, pp. 28–29.

24. Deborah L. Vence, "Return on Investment," *Marketing News*, October 15, 2005, pp. 13–14.

Chapter 3

1. Michael Arndt, "McDonald's 24/7," *BusinessWeek*, February 5, 2007, pp. 64–72; Sherri Day, "After Years at Top, McDonald's Strives to Regain Ground," *New York Times*, March 3, 2003; Pallavi Gogoi, "Mickey D's McMakeover," *BusinessWeek*, May 15, 2006, pp. 42–43; Michael Bush, "McDonald's Taps Moms as Online Correspondents," *PRweek*, June 18, 2007, p. 43; and financial information and other facts accessed at www.mcdonalds.com/corp/invest.html and http://mcdonalds.com/corp/about/factsheets.html, November 2007.

2. Mya Frazier, "Look Who's Putting the Squeeze on Brands," *Advertising Age*, March 27, 2006, pp. 1, 46.

3. Information from Robert J. Benes, Abbie Jarman, and Ashley Williams, "2007 NRA Sets Records," accessed at www.chefmagazine.com/nra.htm, September 2007; and http://www.cokesolutions.com/, accessed November 2007.

4. World POPClock, U.S. Census Bureau, accessed online at www.census.gov, September 2007. This Web site provides continuously updated projections of the U.S. and world populations.

5. See Frederik Balfour, "Educating the 'Little Emperors': There's a Big Market for Products That Help China's Coddled Kids Get Ahead," *BusinessWeek*, November 10, 2003, p. 22; Clay Chandler, "Little Emperors," *Fortune*, October 4, 2004, pp. 138–50; and "Hothousing Little Tykes," *Beijing Review*, May 5, 2005, accessed at www.bjreview.com.cn/En-2005/05-18-e/china-5.htm; and "China's 'Little Emperors,' " *Financial Times*, May 5, 2007, p. 1.

6. Adapted from information in Janet Adamy, "Different Brew: Eyeing a Billion Tea Drinkers, Starbucks Pours It On in China," *Wall Street Journal*, November 29, 2006. Also see, "Where the Money Is," *Financial Times*, May 12, 2007, p. 8.

7. See "China's Golden Oldies," *The Economist*, February 26, 2005, p. 74; "China Economy: How Do You Prepare for the Retirement of 1.3bn People?" *EIU ViewsWire*, March 27, 2006; and Chris Dalby, "How China Respects Its Elders," *Spiked.com*, July 16, 2007.

8. U.S. Census Bureau projections and POPClock Projection, U.S. Census Bureau, accessed at www.census.gov, September 2007.

9. Louise Lee, "Love Those Boomers," *BusinessWeek,* October 24, 2005, pp. 94–102; Tom Ramstack, "The New Gray: Boomers Spark Retirement Revolution," *Washington Times,* December 29, 2005; and "Baby Boomers in the United States Have an Estimated Annual Spending Power of Over $2 Trillion," *Business Wire,* April 27, 2007.

10. Claudia H. Deutsch, "Not Getting Older, Just More Scrutinized," *New York Times,* October 11, 2006, accessed at www.nyt.com.

11. Dee Depass, "Designed with a Wink, Nod at Boomers," *Minneapolis-St. Paul Star Tribune,* April 1, 2006, p. 1.

12. Jack Neff, "Unilever Resuscitates the Demo Left for Dead," *Advertising Age,* May 28, 2007, pp. 1, 26.

13. Stuart Elliott, "Flower Power in Ad Land," *New York Times,* April 11, 2006; and Jack Willoughby, "Good Morning, Ameriprise: A Financial-Services Giant Awakens," *Barron's,* August 21, 2006, pp. 15–16. Also see Laura Petrecca, "More Marketers Target Boomers' Eyes, Wallets," *USA Today,* February 26, 2007.

14. Scott Schroder and Warren Zeller, "Get to Know Gen X and Its Segments," *Multichannel News,* March 21, 2005, p. 55; and Jim Shelton, "When Children of Divorce Grow Up," *Knight Ridder Tribune Business News,* March 4, 2007, p. 1.

15. Quotes from "Mixed Success: One Who Targeted Gen X and Succeeded—Sort Of," *Journal of Financial Planning,* February 2004, p. 15; and Paul Greenberg, "Move Over, Baby Boomers; Gen Xers Want Far More Collaboration with Companies, Both as Consumers and Employees," *CIO,* March 1, 2006, p. 1.

16. Adapted from information found in Mark Ritson, "Have You Got the Gen X Factor?" *Marketing,* April 25, 2007, p. 25; and "75 Wall Street to Be a Hyatt Andaz Property," April 25, 2007, accessed at www.hotelchatter.com/tag/Andaz%20Hotels.

17. Julie Liesse, "Getting to Know the Millennials," *Advertising Age,* July 9, 2007, pp. A1–A6.

18. John Jullens, "Marketers: Meet the Millennial Generation," *Strategy + Business,* Spring 2007, pp. 16–18.

19. Sharon Jayson, "Totally Wireless on Campus," *USA Today,* October 2, 2006, accessed at www.usatoday.com/tech/news/2006-10-02-gennext-tech_x.htm. Also see Barbara Rose, "Generation Y a Learning Experience for Firms," *Chicago Tribune,* March 4, 2007.

20. See Mark Rechtin, "Scion's Dilemma: Be Hip—But Avoid the Mainstream," *Automotive News,* May 22, 2006, pp. 42–45; Julie Bosman, "Hey, Kid, You Want to Buy a Scion?" *New York Times,* June 14, 2006; and Mark Rechtin, "Marketing to Stay Outside the Mainstream," *Automotive News,* May 7, 2007, p. 8.

21. See "America's Families and Living Arrangements: 2006," U.S. Census Bureau, accessed at www.census.gov/population/www/socdemo/hh-fam.html, November 2007.

22. See Paul Nyhan, "Stay-Home Dads Connect with New Full-Time Job: Pay Stinks, but Benefits Are Great," *Seattle Post-Intelligencer,* April 25, 2006; and U.S. Census Bureau, "Facts for Features," April 17, 2007, accessed at www.census.gov/Press-Release/www/2007/cb07ff-08.pdf.

23. "Peapod Is in the 'Growth'ery Business: 10 Millionth Order Delivered, 10 Million Hours Saved," *PR Newswire,* February 7, 2007, p. 1; and information from www.peapod.com/corpinfo/GW_index.jhtml, accessed September 2007.

24. U.S. Census Bureau, "Geographical Mobility/Migration," accessed at www.census.gov/population/www/socdemo/migrate.html, September 2007.

25. See U.S. Census Bureau, accessed at www.census.gov/population/www/estimates/aboutmetro.html, June 2007; and Gordon F. Mulligan

and Alexander C. Vias, "Growth and Change in Micropolitan Areas," *The Annals of Regional Science,* June 2006, p. 203.

26. Kate Lorenz, "What's the Advantage to Telecommuting," accessed at www.cnn.com, April 27, 2007.

27. Mike Bergman, "Earnings Gap Highlighted by Census Bureau Data on Educational Attainment," U.S. Census Bureau, March 15, 2007, accessed at www.census.gov/Press-Release/www/releases/archives/education/009749.html.

28. See U.S. Bureau of Labor Statistics, "Labor Force, Employment, and Earnings," p. 416, accessed at http://landview.census.gov/prod/2001pubs/statab/sec13.pdf, June 2004; and U.S. Department of Labor, *Occupational Outlook Handbook, 2006–07 Edition,* June 29, 2006, accessed at www.bls.gov/emp/home.htm.

29. See Robert Bernstein, "Minority Population Tops 100 Million," May 17, 2007, accessed at www.census.gov; Farai Chidey, "American-Born Hispanic Population Rising," *National Public Radio,* May 16, 2006; U.S. Census Bureau reports accessed at www.census.gov, September 2007; and Ewen MacAskill, "Rapid Growth in Hispanic Population Means U.S. Politics Will Have to Change," *Guardian Weekly,* May 25, 2007, p. 9.

30. Adapted from William F. Gloede, "The Art of Cultural Correctness," *American Demographics,* November 2004, pp. 27–33. See also, Meg Green, "Perfect Prospects," *Best Review,* August 2005, pp. 22–26.

31. Information accessed at www.rivendellmarketing.com/ngng/ngng_profiles_set.html, June 2005; Deborah L. Vence, "Younger GLBT Market Spells Opportunities," *Marketing News,* April 1, 2006, pp. 17, 19; Stuart Elliott, "Hey, Gay Spender, Marketers Spending Time with You," *New York Times,* June 26, 2006; Michael Paoletta, "Gay-Oriented Entertainment Emerges as Powerful Industry," *Billboard,* July 5, 2007, www.billboard.com; and www.planetoutinc.com/sales/market.html, accessed November 2007.

32. For these and other examples, see Edward Iwata, "More Marketing Aimed at Gay Consumers," *USA Today,* November 2, 2006, accessed at www.usatoday.com; and Andrew Hampp, "An Ad in Which Boy Gets Girl . . . or Boy," *Advertising Age,* August 6, 2007, p. 4.

33. Joan Voight, "Accessibility of Disability," *Adweek,* March 27, 2006, p. 20; and Nadine Vogel, "Not Marketing to People with Disabilities? You're Missing Out," *Advertising Age,* July 31, 2006, p. 18. Also see H. H. Friedman, "Frontiers in Multicultural Marketing: The Disabilities Market," *Journal of International Marketing & Marketing Research,* February 2007, pp. 25–39.

34. Quotes from Voight, "Accessibility of Disability," *Adweek,* p. 20. Avis example is adapted from "Avis to Sponsor Achilles Track Club Athletes," *PR Newswire,* March 16, 2006. See also, Joan Leotta, "Avis Really Tries Harder," accessed at www.avis.com, October 2007.

35. Bradley Johnson, "Recession's Long Gone, but America's Average Income Isn't Budging," *Advertising Age,* April 17, 2006, p. 22. See also, Jeremy J. Siegel, "Why the Rich Got Richer," *Kiplinger's Personal Finance,* July 2007, p. 532; and Frederic L. Pryor, "The Anatomy of Increasing Inequity of U.S. Family Incomes," *Journal of Socio-Economics,* August 2007, p. 595.

36. Eric Wilson and Michael Barbaro, "Can You Be Too Fashionable?" *New York Times,* June 17, 2007; and Kelly Nolan, "Mass Movement of High Fashion," *Retailing Today,* January 8, 2007, pp. 4–6.

37. Andrew Zolli, "Business 3.0," *Fast Company,* March 2007, pp. 64–70.

38. Adapted from Lorraine Woellert, "HP Wants Your Old PC Back," *BusinessWeek,* April 10, 2006, pp. 82–83. Also see Beth Snyder Bulik, "Green Past Doesn't Satisfy HP," *Advertising Age,* June 11, 2007, p. S2. For more discussion, see the "Environmentalism" section in Chapter 16.

39. See Renee Boucher, "Wal-Mart Forges Ahead with RFID," *eWeek,* March 6, 2006; Michael Garry, "Wal-Mart Expands RFID Program to Atlanta," *Supermarket News,* June 12, 2006, p. 24; Marc L. Songini,

"Procter & Gamble: Wal-Mart RFID Effort Effective," *Computerworld*, February 26, 2007, p. 14; "RFID Market Nears $7B," *Journal of Commerce Online Edition*, July 9, 2007; Lynn A. Fish and Wayne C. Forrest, "A Worldwide Look at RFID," *Supply Chain Management Review*, April 2007, pp. 48–55; and information accessed online at www. autoidlabs.org, August 2007.

40. See "R&D Funding Forecast: Industry Retakes Leadership Role," *PR Newswire*, January 25, 2007, p. 1.

41. Sarah Pinsky, "KaBoom! and the Home Depot Announce Partnership with Swing-N-Slide," KaBoom! press release, March 9, 2006, accessed at www.kaboom.org; Bowdeya Tweh, "Let's Build a Playground," *Knight Ridder Tribune Business News*, June 15, 2007, p1; and information accessed at www.causemarketingforum.com/page.asp?ID=442, August 2007.

42. Wendy Meillo, "The Greed for Goodwill," *Adweek*, March 13, 2006, p. 14; and "The Growth of Cause Marketing," accessed at www. causemarketingforum.com/page.asp?ID=188, August 2007.

43. Adapted from descriptions found at www.yankelovich.com/products/ lists.aspx, accessed August 2006.

44. Adapted from Ronald Grover, "Trading the Bleachers for the Couch," *BusinessWeek*, August 22, 2005, p. 32. Also see, "Examine the Impact Cocooning Is Having on Consumer Markets," *Business Wire*, February 22, 2007.

45. "Decked Out," *Inside*, Spring 2006, pp. 76–77. See also, "Meet Me at the Oasis: From Saunas to Spas, People Are Turning Their Homes into a Personal Paradise," *Ottawa Citizen*, April 18, 2007.

46. Laura Feldmann, "After 9/11 Highs, America's Back to Good Ol' Patriotism," *Christian Science Monitor*, July 5, 2006, p. 1.

47. L. A. Chung, "New Greetings of Hybrid Fans: Aloha, LOHAS," *Mercury News*, April 29, 2005, accessed at www.mercurynews.com/ mld/mercurynews/news/columnists/la_chung/11520890.htm; Becky Ebenkamp, "Livin' la Vida Lohas," *Brandweek*, May 1, 2006, p. 22; and Heidi Petelinz Benson, "Green Marketing: Why Dow XLA Joined the LOHAS Movement," *Daily News Record*, January 2007.

48. See "Wal-Mart Launches Live Better Index with First Focus on the Environment," April 17, 2007, accessed at www.walmartfacts.com/ articles/4960.aspx; and Steve Bonser, "Retailers Realizing that Environmentally Driven Public Packs a 'Wallet,'" *Knight Ridder Tribune Business News*, April 22, 2007, p. 1.

49. See Doug Desjardins, "Latest Natural-Food Trend Going to the Dogs," *DSN Retailing Today*, March 14, 2005, p. 26; Steven Gray, "Organic Food Goes Mass Market," *Wall Street Journal*, May 4, 2006; Libby Quib, "Appetite for Organic Outstripping Supply," *Durham Herald Sun*, July 7, 2006; and "Organic Food Is Best for Kids, Say Parents," *M2 Presswire*, June 12, 2007.

50. Quotes from Myra Stark, "Celestial Season," *Brandweek*, November 16, 1998, pp. 25–26; and Becky Ebankamp, "The Young and Righteous," *Brandweek*, April 5, 2004, p. 18.

51. See Philip Kotler, *Kotler on Marketing* (New York: Free Press, 1999), p. 3; and Kotler, *Marketing Insights from A to Z* (Hoboken, NJ: John Wiley & Sons, 2003), pp. 23–24.

52. Adapted from Jayne O'Donnell, "Online Rumor Mill Dogs Companies," *USA Today*, October 29, 2005. See also, Betty Lin-Fisher," Question Forwarded E-Mails," *Knight Ridder Tribune*, January 22, 2006, p. 1.

Chapter 4

1. Portions adapted from Bill Breen, "The Mind Reader," *Fast Company*, October 2006, pp. 70–74; with other information from www.ziba.com and www.cleret.com, accessed September 2007.

2. Unless otherwise noted, quotes in this section are from the excellent discussion of customer insights found in Mohanbir Sawhney, "Insights into Customer Insights," accessed at www.mohansawhney.com/ registered/content/TradeArticle/Insights%20into%20Customer%20 Insights.pdf, March 15, 2007. The Apple iPod example is also adapted from this article.

3. See Charles Babcock, "Data, Data, Everywhere," *InformationWeek*, January 9, 2006, pp. 49–53; and Holly Wright, "Data Overload," *Marketing Direct*, June 2006, pp. 43–46.

4. Michael Fassnacht, "Beyond Spreadsheets," *Advertising Age*, February 19, 2007, p. 15.

5. Mohanbir Sawhney, "Insights into Customer Insights," p. 3.

6. See Steve Wills and Sally Webb, "Measuring the Value of Insight—It Can and Must Be Done," *International Journal of Market Research* 49, no. 2, 2007, pp. 155–65.

7. See "Pizza Hut and Its Local Agency Win Direct Marketing Association Award," *Pegasus Newswire*, November 18, 2006, accessed at www. pegasusnews.com; Jennifer Brown, "Pizza Hut Delivers Hot Results Using Data Warehousing," *Computing Canada*, October 17, 2003, p. 24; http://newspapergrl.wordpress.com/2006/03/22/pizza-hut%E2%80% 99s-vip-club/; and www.yum.com/investors/fact/asp, accessed March 2007.

8. See Jean Halliday, "Car Talk: Ford Listens in on Consumers' Online Chatter," *Advertising Age*, February 5, 2007, pp. 3, 34.

9. See Richard L. Wilkins, "Competitive Intelligence: The New Supply Chain Edge," *Supply Chain Management Review*, January–February 2007, pp. 18–27.

10. Tracey Tyler, "WestJet Accuses Rival of Trap in Spy Case," *Toronto Star*, February 14, 2006; and "WestJet to Settle in Air Canada Spy Suit," *Airfinance Journal*, July 2006, p. 38.

11. Fred Vogelstein and Peter Lewis, "Search and Destroy," *Fortune*, May 2, 2005.

12. James Curtis, "Behind Enemy Lines," *Marketing*, May 21, 2001, pp. 28–29. Also see Brian Caufield, "Know Your Enemy," *Business 2.0*, June 2004, p. 89; Michael Fielding, "Damage Control: Firms Must Plan for Counterintelligence," *Marketing News*, September 15, 2004, pp. 19–20; and Bill DeGenaro, "A Case for Business Counterintelligence," *Competitive Intelligence Magazine*, September–October 2005, pp. 5+; and Jim Middlemiss, "Firms Look to Intelligence to Gain a Competitive Edge," *Law Times*, March 5, 2007, accessed at www. lawtimesnews.com.

13. See Shaun Prolux, "Boys Smell . . . Real Good," *Globe and Mail*, September 30, 2006; "What We Buy . . . ," *Time*, October 30, 2006, p. 54; "What's Hot: Axe Extends its Aromatic Reach," *Drug Store News*, December 11, 2006, p. 67; and information from www.unilever.com/ ourbrands/personalcare/Axe.asp, accessed September 2007.

14. See Shaun Prolux, "Boys Smell . . . Real Good," *Globe and Mail*, September 30, 2006; "What We Buy . . . ," *Time*, October 30, 2006, p. 54; "What's Hot: Axe Extends its Aromatic Reach," *Drug Store News*, December 11, 2006, p. 67; and information from www.unilever.com/ ourbrands/personalcare/Axe.asp, accessed September 2007.

15. For more on research firms that supply marketing information, see Jack Honomichl, "Honomichl 50," special section, *Marketing News*, June 15, 2006, pp. H1–H67. Other information from www.infores. com; www.smrb.com; www.acnielsen.com; and www.yankelovich. com/products/monitor.aspx, accessed August 2007.

16. See http://us.infores.com/page/solutions/market_content/infoscan, accessed April 5, 2007.

17. Adapted from an example in David Kiley, "Shoot the Focus Group," *BusinessWeek*, November 14, 2005, pp. 120–21.

18. Adapted from an example in Spencer E. Ante, "The Science of Desire," *BusinessWeek,* June 5, 2006, pp. 99–106.

19. Spencer E. Ante, "The Science of Desire," *BusinessWeek,* June 5, 2006, p. 100. Also see Jane Fulton and Suzanne Gibbs Howard, "Going Deeper, Seeing Further: Enhancing Ethnographic Interpretations to Reveal More Meaningful Opportunities to Design," *Journal of Advertising Research,* September 2006, pp. 246–50.

20. David Kiley, "Shoot the Focus Group," *BusinessWeek,* p. 120. Also see Peter Noel Murray, "Focus Groups Are Valid When Done Right," *Marketing News,* September 1, 2006, pp. 21, 25.

21. Emily Spensieri, "A Slow, Soft Touch," *Marketing,* June 5, 2006, pp. 15–16.

22. The online research stats in this section come from Bradley Johnson, "Forget Phone and Mail: Online's the Best Place to Administer Surveys," *Advertising Age,* July 17, 2006, p. 23; and Gabriel M. Gelb, "Online Options Change Biz a Bit—and a Lot," *Marketing News,* November 1, 2006, pp. 23–24.

23. Gelb, "Online Options Change Biz a Bit—and a Lot," p. 23.

24. Johnson, "Forget Phone and Mail: Online's the Best Place to Administer Surveys," p. 23.

25. Adapted from an example in David Kiley, "Shoot the Focus Group," *BusinessWeek,* November 14, 2005, pp. 120–21.

26. Enid Burns, "U.S. Internet Adoption to Slow," February 24, 2006, accessed at www.clickz.com/showPage.html?page=3587496.

27. For more on Internet privacy, see Larry Dobrow, "Privacy Issues Loom for Marketers," *Advertising Age,* March 13, 2006, p. S6; and Jessica E. Vascellaro "They've Got Your Number (and a Lot More)," *Wall Street Journal,* March 13, 2007.

28. Josh Goldstein, "Branding on the Brain," *News & Observer,* December 6, 2006.

29. This example is adapted from Rebecca Harris, "Brain Waves," *Marketing,* June 5, 2006, pp. 15–17. Also see "Creating Computers That Know How You Feel," accessed at www.almaden.ibm.com/cs/BlueEyes/index.html, July 2007.

30. Barney Beal, "CRM, Customer Services Still Driving Technology Spending," www.searchcrm.com, January 18, 2007.

31. Mike Freeman, "Data Company Helps Wal-Mart, Casinos, Airlines Analyze Customers," *San Diego Union Tribune,* February 24, 2006.

32. Michael Krauss, "At Many Firms, Technology Obscures CRM," *Marketing News,* March 18, 2002, p. 5. Also see William Boulding et al., "A Customer Relationship Management Roadmap: What Is Known, Potential Pitfalls, and Where to Go," *Journal of Marketing,* October 2005, pp. 155–66; Darrell K. Rigby and Dianne Ledingham, "CRM Done Right," *Harvard Business Review,* November 2004, pp. 129; Julia Chang, "Missing the Target with Your Customer Relationship Management Strategy?" *Sales & Marketing Management,* January–February 2007, pp. 24–27; and Gordon A. Wyner, "Relationship Management Revisited," *Marketing Management,* January–February 2007, pp. 10–11.

33. See Robert McLuhan, "How to Reap the Benefits of CRM," *Marketing,* May 24, 2001, p. 35; Stewart Deck, "Data Mining," *Computerworld,* March 29, 1999, p. 76; Jason Compton, "CRM Gets Real," *Customer Relationship Management,* May 2004, pp. 11–12; Ellen Neuborne, "A Second Act of CRM," *Inc.,* March 2005, p. 40; and "Value Added with mySAP CRM: Benchmarking Study," accessed at www.sap.com/solutions/business-suite/crm/pdf/Misc_CRM_Study.pdf, June 2007.

34. See Darell K. Rigby and Vijay Vishwanath, "Localization: The Revolution in Consumer Markets," *Harvard Business Review,* April 2006, pp. 82–92; and information found at www.partnersonline.com, accessed September 2007.

35. Adapted from information in Ann Zimmerman, "Small Business; Do the Research," *Wall Street Journal,* May 9, 2005; with information from www.bibbentuckers.com, accessed July 2007.

36. Zimmerman, "Small Business; Do the Research," *Wall Street Journal.*

37. For some good advice on conducting market research in a small business, see "Marketing Research . . . Basics 101," accessed at www.sba.gov/starting_business/marketing/research.html, August 2007; and "Researching Your Market," U.S. Small Business Administration, accessed at www.sba.gov/library/pubs/mt-8.doc, August 2007.

38. See Jack Honomichl, "Honomichl Global Top 25," a special insert to *Marketing News,* August 15, 2006, pp. H3–H4; and Robert B. Young and Rajshekhar G. Javalgi, "International Marketing Research: A Global Project Management Perspective," *Business Horizons,* March–April 2007, pp. 113–22.

39. See ACNielsen International Research Web site, accessed at www2.acnielsen.com/company/where.php, July 2007.

40. Phone, PC, and other country media stats are from www.nationmaster.com, accessed July 2007.

41. Subhash C. Jain, *International Marketing Management,* 3rd ed. (Boston: PWS-Kent, 1990), p. 338. For more discussion on international marketing research issues and solutions, see Gary Kaplan, "Global Research Needs Local Coordination," *Marketing News,* May 15, 2005, p. 43; C. Samuel Craig and Susan P. Douglas, "International Research Frame Needs Reworking," *Marketing News,* February 15, 2006, pp. 33–34; Michael Fielding, "Shift the Focus: Ethnography Proves Fruitful in Emerging Economies," *Marketing News,* September 1, 2006, pp. 18, 20; and Robert B. Young and Rajshekhar G. Javalgi, "International Marketing Research: A Global Project Management Perspective," *Business Horizons,* March–April 2007, pp. 113–22.

42. Portions of this example are adapted from "Listening to the Internet," *Economist,* March 11, 2006, p. 8. Other information accessed at www.nielsenbuzzmetrics.com, June 2007.

43. Margaret Webb Pressler, "Too Personal to Tell?" *Washington Post,* April 18, 2004; and "E-Mail Privacy Statistics," accessed at www.relemail.com/statistics.html, June 2007.

44. "ICC/ESOMAR International Code of Marketing and Social Research Practice," accessed at www.iccwbo.org/home/menu_advert_marketing.asp, July 2007. Also see "Respondent Bill of Rights," accessed at www.cmor.org/rc/tools.cfm?topic=4, July 2007.

45. Jaikumar Vijayan, "Disclosure Laws Driving Data Privacy Efforts, Says IBM Exec," *Computerworld,* May 8, 2006, p. 26. Also see Thornton A. May, "The What and Why of CPOs," *Computerworld,* November 27, 2006, p. 18.

46. Information accessed at www10.americanexpress.com/sif/cda/page/0,1641,14271,00.asp, July 2007.

47. Cynthia Crossen, "Studies Galore Support Products and Positions, but Are They Reliable?" *Wall Street Journal,* November 14, 1991. Also see Allan J. Kimmel, "Deception in Marketing Research and Practice: An Introduction," *Psychology and Marketing,* July 2001, pp. 657–61; Alvin C. Burns and Ronald F. Bush, *Marketing Research* (Upper Saddle River, NJ: Prentice Hall, 2005), pp. 63–75; and Jack Neff, "Who's No. 1? Depends on Who's Analyzing the Data," *Advertising Age,* June 12, 2006, p. 8.

48. Information accessed at www.casro.org/codeofstandards.cfm#intro, July 2007.

Chapter 5

1. Quotes and other information from Ludmilla Lelis, "Biker Billy: Eat to Ride, Ride to Eat," *Orlando Sentinel,* March 3, 2007; Greg Schneider, "Rebels with Disposable Income: Aging Baby Boomers Line Up to Buy High-End Versions of Youthful Indulgences," *Washington Post,*

April 27, 2003, p. F1; Ian P. Murphy, "Aided by Research, Harley Goes Whole Hog," *Marketing News,* December 2, 1996, pp. 16–17; Ted Bolton, "Tattooed Call Letters: The Ultimate Test of Brand Loyalty," accessed online at www.boltonresearch.com, April 2003; Marc Gerstein, "The Road Ahead for Harley," *Reuters,* April 13, 2006; Joseph Weber, "Harley Just Keeps on Cruisin'," *BusinessWeek,* November 6, 2006, p. 71; and the Harley-Davidson Web site at www.Harley-Davidson.com, accessed November 2007.

2. GDP figures from *The World Fact Book,* March 12, 2007, accessed at www.cia.gov/cia/publications/factbook/. Population figures from the World POPClock, U.S. Census Bureau, www.census.gov, accessed October 2007. This Web site provides continuously updated projections of the U.S. and world populations.

3. Jim Edwards, "Why Buy?" *Brandweek,* October 5, 2005, pp. 21–24.

4. Statistics from Stanley Perman, "How to Tap the Hispanic Market," *BusinessWeek Online,* July 12, 2006, accessed at www.businessweek.com; Scott D. Schroeder, "The U.S. Hispanic Population—One Market or Many?" www.dmnews.com, August 10, 2006; "Beyond Black and White," *Incentive,* January 2007, p. 9; and Deborah L. Vence, "Segmentation: Multicultural—Scratch the Surface," *Marketing News,* February 15, 2007, pp. 17–18.

5. See Deborah L. Vence, "Avoid Shortcuts: Hispanic Marketing Requires Distinct, Inventive Marketing," *Marketing News,* February 2006, pp. 23–24; and Brad Pomerance, "Marketers Use Finesse in Reaching Hispanics," *TelevisionWeek,* November 27, 2006, p. 18.

6. See Elizabeth Aguilera, "Marketing in Espanol," DenverPost.com, December 24, 2007; and Nancy Ayala, "Speaking Same Language: Bilingual Web Sites Target Young Hispanics," *Adweek's Marketing y Medios,* January 15, 2007, accessed at www.marketingymedios.com.

7. "Media Report 2006: Top Advertisers in the Hispanic Market," *Hispanic Business,* December 2006, accessed at www.hispanicbusiness.com/news/newsbyid.asp?id=50532.

8. Example adapted from Elaine Walker, "Home Depot Offers Colors in Spanish," *Miami Herald,* September 15, 2005, p. 1; with information from "The Home Depot Introduces Colores Origenes," Hispanic Association on Corporate Responsibility press release, September 23, 2005, accessed at www.hacr.org/mediacenter/pubID.93/pub_detail.asp; and Laurel Wentz, "Home Depot Paint Line Connects with Hispanics," *Advertising Age,* July 3, 2006, p. 19.

9. See Deborah L. Vence, "Scratch the Surface," *Marketing News,* February 2007, pp. 17–18; "Increasingly Affluent African American Market Set to Reach $981 Billion by 2010," *PR Newswire,* February 22, 2006; and U.S. Census Bureau reports accessed online at www.census.gov, August 2007.

10. Facts from Cliff Peale, "P&G Showed the Way: Company's Ads Targeted to Blacks Paid Off," *Cincinnati Enquirer,* February 25, 2007, accessed at http://news.enquirer.com. Quote from "Queen Latifah Turns Cover-Girl," February 2, 2007, accessed at http://blogs.chron.com/shopgirl/archives/2006/02/queen_latifah_t.html.

11. Cliff Peale, "Procter & Gamble Campaigns for Black Consumers Paying Off," *Cincinnati Inquirer,* March 6, 2007, accessed at www.clarionledger.com.

12. See Randi Schmelzer, "The Asian Answer," *PR Week,* March 13, 2006; "Asian Americans in the U.S.," Packaged Facts, August 1, 2006, accessed at www.marketresearch.com/product/display.asp?productid=1119537&xs=r; and U.S. Census Bureau reports accessed at www.census.gov, July 2007.

13. Jeffrey M. Humphreys, "The Multicultural Economy 2004," *Georgia Business and Economic Conditions,* The Selig Center for Economic Growth, third quarter 2004; Christopher Reynolds, "Far East Moves West," *American Demographics,* October 2004, p. 56; Mike Troy, "Wal-Mart Unveils Asian Ad Campaign," *DSN Retailing Today,* April 11,

2005, pp. 5–6; Randi Schmelzer, "The Asian Answer," *PR Week,* March 13, 2006; and U.S. Internet Industry Association, *Proposed Legislation and Its Impact on Consumer's Use of Broadband and IP Services,* accessed at www.usiia.org, April 11, 2006.

14. Based on conversations with PNC bank, July 26, 2007.

15. Information accessed at www.census.gov, August 2007. Also see Sherry L. Jarrell, "Picture of Retiree Spending Is Changing," *Marketing News,* September 15, 2006, p. 40; and "Mature Market in the U.S.," *M2 Presswire,* March 2, 2007.

16. For a discussion of influencers, see Edward Keller and Jonathan Berry, *The Influentials* (New York: Free Press, 2003); and Ronald E. Goldsmith, "The Influentials," *Journal of Product & Brand Management,* 2005, pp. 371–72. The study results and quotes are from Kenneth Hein, "Report Explores What Influences the Influencers," *Brandweek,* February 5, 2007, p. 13.

17. Adapted from Anya Kamenetz, "The Network Unbound," *Fast Company,* June 2006, pp. 69–73. Also see A. Weinstein, "Ads in Social Nets Booming," *Red Herring,* November 1, 2006, accessed at www.redherring.com; and Brad Stone, "Social Networking's Next Phase," *New York Times,* March 3, 2007, accessed at www.nytimes.com.

18. See Saul Hansell, "For MySpace, Making Friends Was Easy. Big Profit Is Tougher," *New York Times,* April 23, 2006, p. 3; and Anick Jesdanun, "MySpace Tops Yahoo! in November," December 13, 2006, accessed at www.newsfactor.com.

19. Allison Enright, "How the Second Half Lives," *Marketing News,* February 15, 2007, pp. 12–14; and http://secondlife.com, accessed November 2007.

20. Quote and information from "Colored Vision Adidas Unleashes Seven-Film Mobile Media," *Boards,* May 2006, p. 15.

21. See Yuval Rosenberg, "Building a New Nest," *Fast Company,* April 27, 2007, p. 48.

22. Quote from Anya Kamenetz, "The Network Unbound," *Fast Company,* June 2006, p. 73. Also see Julie Bosman, "Chevy Tries a Write-Your-Own-Ad Approach," *New York Times,* April 4, 2006, p. C1.

23. See Pallavi Gogoi, "I Am Woman, Hear Me Shop," *BusinessWeek Online,* February 14, 2005, accessed at www.bwonline.com; "Finance and Economics: A Guide to Womenomics," *Economist,* April 15, 2006, p. 80; and Marti Barletta, "Who's Really Buying That Car? Ask Her," *Brandweek,* September 4, 2006, p. 20.

24. Adapted from Pallavi Gogoi, "Meet Jane Geek," *BusinessWeek,* November 28, 2005, pp. 94–95.

25. Kevin Downey, "What Children Teach Their Parents," *Broadcasting & Cable,* March 13, 2006, p. 26; Debra Kaufman, "Kid's Spending: Big and Getting Bigger," *Television Week,* February 12, 2007, pp. 11–12; Laura A. Flurry, "Children's Influence in Family Decision Making: Examining the Impact of the Changing American Family," *Journal of Business Research,* April 2007, pp. 322–30.

26. Alice Dragoon, "How to Do Customer Segmentation Right," *CIO,* October 1, 2005, p. 1. For another example, see Teri Koenke, "Destroying Demographics: The New Art of Strategic Customer Communications," *U.S. Banker,* October 2006, pp. 22–23.

27. Quotes and examples from www.carhartt.com, accessed November 2006.

28. Portions adapted from Linda Tischler, "How Pottery Barn Wins with Style," *Fast Company,* June 2003, pp. 106–13; and Carole Sloan, "Lifestyle Specialists Enjoy Strong Year," *Furniture Today,* August 28, 2006, p. 28; with information from www.potterybarn.com; www.potterybarnkids.com, and www.pbteen.com, accessed October 2007.

29. Jennifer Aaker, "Dimensions of Measuring Brand Personality," *Journal of Marketing Research,* August 1997, pp. 347–56. Also see Aaker, "The

Malleable Self: The Role of Self-Expression in Persuasion," *Journal of Marketing Research,* May 1999, pp. 45–57; and Audrey Azoulay and Jean-Noel Kapferer, "Do Brand Personality Scales Really Measure Brand Personality?" *Journal of Brand Management,* November 2003, p. 143.

30. Seth Stevenson, "Ad Report Card: Mac Attack," June 19, 2006, accessed at www.slate.com/id/2143810; and "Apple Debuts New 'Get a Mac' Ads," *Apple Matters,* January 17, 2007.

31. See Mark Tadajewski, "Remembering Motivation Research: Toward an Alternative Genealogy of Interpretive Consumer Research," *Marketing Theory,* December 2006, pp. 429–66; and Leon G. Schiffman and Leslie L. Kanuk, *Consumer Behavior,* 9th ed. (Upper Saddle River, NJ: Prentice Hall, 2007), chapter 4.

32. See Abraham H. Maslow, "A Theory of Human Motivation," *Psychological Review* 50, 1943, pp. 370–96. Also see Maslow, *Motivation and Personality,* 3rd ed. (New York: HarperCollins, 1987); and Barbara Marx Hubbard, "Seeking Our Future Potentials," *Futurist,* May 1998, pp. 29–32.

33. Louise Story, "Anywhere the Eye Can See, It's Likely to See an Ad," *New York Times,* January 15, 2007, accessed at www.nytimes.com; and Matthew Creamer, "Caught in the Clutter Crossfire: Your Brand," *Advertising Age,* April 1, 2007, pp. 1, 35.

34. Bob Garfield, "'Subliminal' Seduction and Other Urban Myths," *Advertising Age,* September 18, 2000, pp. 4, 105; and Lewis Smith, "Subliminal Advertising May Work, but Only If You're Paying Attention," *Times,* March 9, 2007. Also see Sheri J. Broyles, "Subliminal Advertising and the Perpetual Popularity of Playing People's Paranoia," *Journal of Consumers Affairs,* Winter 2006, pp. 392–406; and Alastair Goode, "The Implicit and Explicit Role of Ad Memory in Ad Persuasion: Rethinking the Hidden Persuaders," *International Journal of Marketing Research* 49, no. 2, 2007, pp. 95–116.

35. See Jeff Manning and Kevin Lane Keller, "Got Advertising That Works?" *Marketing Management,* January–February 2004, pp. 16–20; Alice Z. Cuneo, "Now Even Cell Phones Have Milk Mustaches," *Advertising Age,* February 26, 2007, p. 8; and information from www.bodybymilk.com, accessed November 2007.

36. Douglas Pruden and Terry G. Vavra, "Controlling the Grapevine," *Marketing Management,* July–August 2004, pp. 25–30. See also John Goodman, "Treat Your Customers as Prime Media Reps," *Brandweek,* September 12, 2005, pp. 16–17.

37. See Leon Festinger, *A Theory of Cognitive Dissonance* (Stanford, CA: Stanford University Press, 1957); Schiffman and Kanuk, *Consumer Behavior,* pp. 219–20; "Cognitive Dissonance and the Stability of Service Quality Perceptions," *Journal of Services Marketing,* 2004, p. 433+; and Cynthia Crossen, "'Cognitive Dissonance' Became a Milestone in the 1950s Psychology," *Wall Street Journal,* December 12, 2006, p. B1.

38. The following discussion draws from the work of Everett M. Rogers. See his *Diffusion of Innovations,* 5th ed. (New York: Free Press, 2003).

39. Patrick J. Robinson, Charles W. Faris, and Yoram Wind, *Industrial Buying Behavior and Creative Marketing* (Boston: Allyn & Bacon, 1967). Also see James C. Anderson and James A. Narus, *Business Market Management,* 2nd ed. (Upper Saddle River, NJ: Prentice Hall, 2004), chapter 3; James C. Anderson, James A. Narus, and Wouter van Rossum, "Customer Value Propositions in Business Markets," *Harvard Business Review,* March 2006, pp. 91–99; and Philip Kotler and Kevin Lane Keller, *Marketing Management,* 12th ed. (Upper Saddle River, NJ: Prentice Hall, 2006), chapter 7.

40. Example adapted from information found in "Nikon Focuses on Supply Chain Innovation—and Makes New Product Distribution a Snap," UPS case study, accessed at www.ups.com/media/en/cs_nikon.pdf, November 2007.

41. Renee Houston Zemanski, "Buyer, Show Yourself," *Selling Power,* November–December 2006, pp. 28–31.

42. For more discussion, see Stefan Wuyts and Inge Geyskens, "The Formation of Buyer-Seller Relationships: Detailed Contract Drafting and Close Partner Selection," *Harvard Business Review,* October 2005, pp. 103–17; and Robert McGarvey, "The Buyer's Emotional Side," *Selling Power,* April 2006, pp. 35–36.

43. Robinson, Faris, and Wind, *Industrial Buying Behavior,* p. 14.

44. For this and other examples, see Kate Maddox, "10 Great Web Sites," *BtoB Online,* September 11, 2006; all accessed at www.btobonline.com. Other information from www.sun.com, accessed November 2007.

45. Karen Prema, "National Aquarium Reels in Savings with Online Buying," accessed at www.purchasing.com, March 2, 2006; Karen Prema, "SRM + E-Auctions: Tools in the Toolbox," *Purchasing,* April 6, 2006, pp. 46–47; and Susan Avery, "At HP, Indirect Procurement Takes More of a Leadership Role," accessed at www.purchasing.com, May 25, 2006.

46. Demir Barlas, "E-Procurement: Steady Value" *Line56.com,* January 4, 2005, accessed at www.line56.com.

47. Michael A. Verespej, "E-Procurement Explosion," *Industry Week,* March 2002, pp. 25–28.

Chapter 6

1. Adapted from portions of Janet Adamy, "Battle Brewing: Dunkin' Donuts Tries to Go Upscale, but Not Too Far," *Wall Street Journal,* April 8, 2006, p. A1; with quotes and other information from Julie Bosman, "This Joe's for You," *New York Times,* June 8, 2006, p. C1; Matthew Boyle, "Dunkin's Coffee Buzz," *Fortune,* September 28, 2006, pp. 51–53; Chris Reidy, "The New Face of Dunkin' Donuts," *Boston Globe,* March 9, 2007; and www.dunkindonuts.com, accessed November 2007.

2. For these and other examples, see Darell K. Rigby and Vijay Vishwanath, "Localization: The Revolution in Consumer Markets," *Harvard Business Review,* April 2006, pp. 82–92.

3. Based on information from Patti Bond, "Home Depot to Test Superstores, Ministores," *Atlanta Journal-Constitution,* March 23, 2007.

4. See Mike Troy, "Taking Back the Neighborhood," *Retailing Today,* February 12, 2007, pp. 6–8.

5. See Reena Jana, "Nintendo's New Brand Game," June 22, 2006, accessed at www.businessweek.com/innovate/content/jun2006/id20060622_124931.htm?chan=search; Catherine Arnst, "Chicken Soup for the Aging Brain," *BusinessWeek,* September 25, 2006, pp. 94–96; and Sara Cardine, "Small Challenges Keep Older Brains Growing," *Stockton Record,* February 20, 2007.

6. Solvej Schou, "Sisters Doing It for Themselves," *Associated Press,* March 12, 2007.

7. Debbie Howell, "Dollar," *DSN Retailing Today,* November 21, 2005, pp. 11–12; Bernadette Casey, "Retailers Better Learn the Real Value of a Dollar," *DSN Retailing Today,* March 13, 2006, p. 6; and David Wellman, "The Buck Spends Here," *Retail Merchandiser,* January 2007, pp. 24–25.

8. Information from www.smartertravel.com, www.rssc.com, and www.royalcaribbean.com, accessed November 2007.

9. See Louise Story, "Finding Love and the Right Linens," *New York Times,* December 13, 2006, accessed at www.nytimes.com.

10. Kate MacArthur, "BK Rebels Fall in Love with King," *Advertising Age,* May 1, 2006, pp. 1, 86; and Kenneth Hein, "BK 'Lifestyle' Goods Aim for Young Males," *Adweek,* June 12, 2006, p. 8.

11. See Jennifer Ordonez, "Fast-Food Lovers, Unite!" *Newsweek,* May 24, 2004, p. 56.

12. Portions adapted from Alan T. Saracevic, "Author Plumbs Bottomless Depth of Mac Worship," December 12, 2004, accessed at www.sfgate.com. Definition from www.urbandictionary.com/define.php?term=Macolyte&r=d, accessed November 2007.

13. See the "PRIZM NE Lifestyle Segmentation System" brochure and other cluster information, accessed at www.claritas.com, November 2007.

14. Information from https://home.americanexpress.com/home/open.shtml, accessed August 2007.

15. Portions of this example adapted from Edward Cone, "Putting Customers to Work," *CIO Insight,* November 8, 2006, accessed at www.cioinsight.com/print_article2/0,1217,a=193622,00.asp. Also see "Coke Sees Growth Abroad," *Associate Press,* February 22, 2007.

16. See Michael Porter, *Competitive Advantage* (New York: Free Press, 1985), pp. 4–8, 234–36. For more recent discussions, see Stanley Slater and Eric Olson, "A Fresh Look at Industry and Market Analysis," *Business Horizons,* January–February 2002, p. 15–22; Kenneth Sawka and Bill Fiora, "The Four Analytical Techniques Every Analyst Must Know: 2. Porter's Five Forces Analysis," *Competitive Intelligence Magazine,* May–June 2003, p. 57; and Philip Kotler and Kevin Lane Keller, *Marketing Management,* 12th ed. (Upper Saddle River, NJ: Prentice Hall, 2006), pp. 342–43.

17. Information accessed at www.elcompanies.com, July 2007.

18. Store information found at www.wholefoodsmarket.com//investor/index.html; www.walmartfacts.com; and www.kroger.com, accessed July 2007.

19. See Gerry Khermouch, "Call It the Pepsi Blue Generation," *Business Week,* February 3, 2003, p. 96; Phyllis Furman, "Mist-Takes Made Again: New Ads for Sierra Mist," *Knight Ridder Tribune Business News,* April 10, 2006, p. 1; and Duane D. Stanford, "Coke, Pepsi Cola Sales Down, Other Sodas Grow," *Cox News Service,* March 8, 2007.

20. Quotes and information from Sidra Durst, "Shoe In," *Business 2.0,* December 2006, p. 54; Kimberly Weisul, "A Shine on Their Shoes," *BusinessWeek,* December 12, 2006, p. 84; and "About Zappos," accessed at www.zappos.com/about.zhtml, April 2007.

21. Adapted from examples in Darell K. Rigby and Vijay Vishwanath, "Localization: The Revolution in Consumer Markets," *Harvard Business Review,* April 2006, pp. 82–92. Also see Jenny McTaggart, "Wal-Mart Unveils New Segmentation Scheme," *Progressive Grocer,* October 1, 2006, pp. 10–11.

22. Example adapted from Michael Prospero, "Lego's New Building Blocks," *Fast Company,* October 2005, p. 35; with information from http://factory.lego.com/, accessed November 2007.

23. See Gigi Stone, "Advertisers Try New Way to Get into Your Head," December 16, 2006, accessed at http://abcnews.go.com/WNY/print?id=2731799; and Steve Miller, "Who Said That?" *Brandweek,* Jaunary 30, 2007, accessed at www.brandweek.com.

24. Adapted from portions of Fae Goodman, "Lingerie Is Luscious and Lovely-for Grown-Ups: But Is the Pink?" *Chicago Sun-Times,* February 19, 2006, p. B02; and Stacy Weiner, "Goodbye to Girlhood," *Washington Post,* February 20, 2007, p. HE01. Also, see Jayne O'Donnell, "As Kids Get Savvy, Marketers Move down the Age Scale," *USA Today,* April 11, 2007, accessed at www.usatoday.com.

25. Andrew Adam Newman, "Youngsters Enjoy Beer Ads, Arousing Industry's Critics," *New York Times,* February 13, 2006, p. C15; and www.adbowl.com, accessed March 2007.

26. See "FBI Internet Crime Complaint Center Releases Stats," *States News Service,* March 16, 2007.

27. Jack Trout, "Branding Can't Exist Without Positioning," *Advertising Age,* March 14, 2005, p. 28.

28. Adapted from a positioning map prepared by students Brian May, Josh Payne, Meredith Schakel, and Bryana Sterns, University of North Carolina, April 2003. SUV sales data furnished by WardsAuto.com, October 2007. Price data from www.edmunds.com, accessed October 2007.

29. See Bobby J. Calder and Steven J. Reagan, "Brand Design," in *Kellogg on Marketing,* ed. Dawn Iacobucci (New York: John Wiley & Sons, 2001) p. 61. The Mountain Dew example is from Alice M. Tybout and Brian Sternthal, "Brand Positioning," in *Kellogg on Marketing,* p. 54. Also see Philip Kotler and Kevin Lane Keller, *Marketing Management* (Upper Saddle River, NJ: Prentice Hall, 2007). pp. 315–16.

Chapter 7

1. Quotes and other information from Damon Hodge, "Tourism Chief Aims to Continue Vegas' Hot Streak," *Travel Weekly,* February 12, 2007, p. 64; Greg Lindsay, "Players Place Bets on Brands," *Advertising Age,* June 5, 2006; Bob Garfield, "This Time, Vegas Tourism Gets the Credit It Deserves," *Advertising Age,* August 21, 2006, p. 25; Theresa Howard, "Vegas Goes for Edgier Ads," *USA Today,* August 3, 2003, accessed at www.usatoday.com; Ned Potter, Transcript for *ABC News Now,* November 10, 2006; Joe Scarborough, Transcript for *Scarborough Country,* October 25, 2006; Arnold M. Knightly, "Las Vegas Convention Authority, Vegas.com Win Adrian Awards," *Las Vegas Review-Journal,* February 2, 2007; and Parija Kavilanz "Hot in '07: Google, Vegas. Not: Paris, Britney," accessed online at *CNNMoney.com,* January 12, 2007.

2. Adapted from an example in B. Joseph Pine II and James H. Gilmore, "Trade in Ads for Experiences," *Advertising Age,* September 27, 2004, p. 36; and Keith H. Hammonds, "American Girl," *Fast Company,* September 2006, p. 54; with information from www.americangirlplace.com, accessed September 2007.

3. See Rich Thomaselli, "Dream Endorser: Tiger Woods as a Giant of Marketing ROI," *Advertising Age,* September 25, 2006, p. 37; and Jenn Abelson, "Gillette Lands a Trio of Star Endorsers," *Boston Globe,* February 5, 2007.

4. See Diane Brady, "It's All Donald, All the Time," *BusinessWeek,* January 22, 2007, p. 51.

5. Based on Sonia Reyes, "Faster Than a Ray of Light," *Brandweek,* October 9, 2006, pp. M28–M31; Grant McCracken, "Rachael Ray: Branding Goddess?" *This Blog Sits at the Intersection of Anthropology and Economics,* October 17, 2006, accessed at www.cultureby.com/trilogy/2006/10/rachael_ray_bra.html; and Alec Foege, "The Rachael Way," *Adweek,* March 5, 2007, pp. SR22–SR24.

6. Information from www.cnto.org/aboutchina.asp, accessed April 2007. Also see www.TravelTex.com, and www.visitcalifornia.com, accessed November 2007.

7. Accessed online at www.social-marketing.org/aboutus.html, November 2007.

8. See Alan R. Andreasen, Rob Gould, and Karen Gutierrez, "Social Marketing Has a New Champion," *Marketing News,* February 7, 2000, p. 38. Also see Philip Kotler, Ned Roberto, and Nancy Lee, *Social Marketing: Improving the Quality of Life,* 2nd ed. (Thousand Oaks, CA: Sage Publications, 2002); and www.social-marketing.org, accessed August 2007.

9. Quotes and definitions from Philip Kotler, *Kotler on Marketing* (New York: Free Press, 1999), p. 17; and www.asq.org, accessed November 2007.

10. Quotes and other information from Regina Schrambling, "Tool Department; The Sharpest Knives in the Drawer," *Los Angeles Times,*

March 8, 2006, p. F1; Arricca Elin SanSone, "OXO: Universal Design Innovator," *Cooking Light,* April 2007, p. 118; and www.oxo.com/OA_HTML/oxo/about_what.htm, accessed September 2007.

11. See Mya Frazier, "How Can Your Package Stand Out?" *Advertising Age,* October 16, 2006, p. 14; "Supermarket Facts," accessed at www.fmi.org/facts_figs/superfact.htm, April 2007; and "Wal-Mart Facts," accessed at www.walmartfacts.com/StateByState/?id=2, April 2007.

12. "The Oyster Awards," *Consumer Reports,* March 2007, p. 12.

13. For this and other examples, see Susanna Hamner, "Packaging That Pays," *Business 2.0,* July 2006, pp. 68–69.

14. Example adapted from "Pepsi's New Set of Cans," *Creativity,* March 2007, p. 76; with quote from Martinne Geller, "PepsiCo Invites Designers to New Pepsi Challenge," *The San Diego Union-Tribute,* April 4, 2007, accessed at www.SignOnSanDiego.com. Also see www.pepsigallery.com.

15. See Jena McGregor, "Customer Service Champs," *BusinessWeek,* March 5, 2007, pp. 52–64; and David Welch, "Looser Rules, Happier Clients," *BusinessWeek,* March 5, 2007, p. 62.

16. Example adapted from Michelle Higgins, "Pop-Up Sales Clerks: Web Sites Try the Hard Sell," *Wall Street Journal,* April 15, 2004, p. D.1.

17. Information accessed online at www.marriott.com, November 2007.

18. See "McAtlas Shrugged," *Foreign Policy,* May–June 2001, pp. 26–37; and Philip Kotler and Kevin Lane Keller, *Marketing Management,* 12th ed. (Upper Saddle River, NJ: Prentice Hall, 2006), pp. 290–91.

19. See Jack Trout, "'Branding' Simplified," *Forbes,* April 19, 2007, accessed at www.forbes.com.

20. For more on Y&R's Brand Asset Evaluator, see W. Ronald Lane, Karen Whitehill King, and J. Thomas Russell, *Kleppner's Advertising Procedure* (Englewood Cliffs, NJ: Prentice Hall, 2005), p. 90; and Ellen McGirt, "Breakaway Brands," *Fortune,* September 18, 2006, pp. 27–30.

21. Al Ehrbar, "Breakaway Brands," *Fortune,* October 31, 2005, pp. 153–70. Also see "DeWalt Named Breakaway Brand," *Snips,* January 2006, p. 66.

22. "The 100 Top Brands," *BusinessWeek,* August 6, 2007, pp. 59–64. For other rankings, see Normandy Madden, "Hold the Phone," *Advertising Age,* April 10, 2006, pp. 4, 64; Tachel Sanderson, "YouTube, Wikipedia Storm into 2006 Top Brand Ranking," January 26, 2007, accessed at www.reuters.com; and "Google Tops List of Most Valuable Brands," April 23, 2007, accessed at CNNMoney.com.

23. See Larry Selden and Yoko S. Selden, "Profitable Customer: Key to Great Brands," *Point,* July–August, 2006, pp. 7–9; and Robert Leone et al., "Linking Brand Equity to Customer Equity," *Journal of Service Research,* November 2006, pp. 125–38.

24. See Scott Davis, *Brand Asset Management,* 2nd ed. (San Francisco: Jossey-Bass, 2002). For more on brand positioning, see Philip Kotler and Kevin Lane Keller, *Marketing Management,* 12th ed. (Upper Saddle River, NJ: Prentice Hall, 2006), chapter 10.

25. See Jacquelyn A. Ottman, Edwin R. Strattford, and Cathy L. Hartman, "Avoiding Green Marketing Myopia," *Environment,* June 2006, pp. 22–37.

26. See Michelle Moran, "Discovering Your Own Private Label," *Gourmet Retailer,* October 1, 2006, accessed at www.gourmetretailer.com; Michael Fielding, "No Longer Plain, Simple," *Marketing News,* May 15, 2006, pp. 11–13; and Nirmalya Kumar and Jan-Benedict E. M. Steenkamp, *Private Label Strategy* (Boston: Harvard Business School Press, 2007), pp. 1–12.

27. See Jana Reena, "The Revenge of the Generic," *BusinessWeekOnline,* December 12, 2006, accessed at www.businessweekonline; and "Private

Label Food and Beverage Sales Set to Soar Past $56 Billion by 2011," *M2PressWIRE,* January 31, 2007.

28. Example adapted from Matthew Boyle, "Brand Killers," *Fortune,* August 11, 2003, pp. 89–100. See also "Battle of the Brands," *Consumer Reports,* August 2005, pp. 12–15; and Marcia Blomberg, "Simply Upscale: Shop & Stop Debuts Private Label Food Items," *Sunday Republican,* January 28, 2007, p. D1.

29. Nirmalya Kumar and Jan-Benedict E. M. Steenkamp, *Private Label Strategy* (Boston: Harvard Business School Press, 2007), p. 5.

30. Jay Sherman, "Nick Puts Muscle Behind EverGirl," *TelevisionWeek,* January 5, 2004, p. 3; "Nickelodeon Unveils Three New Toy Lines Based on Hit Properties," *PR Newswire,* February 10, 2006; "Dora the Explorer Takes the Lead as Sales Growth Elevates Property to Megabrand Status as Number-One Toy License in 2006," *PR Newswire,* February 8, 2007; and Doug DesJardins, "Hit Movies Play into Latest Toy Licenses," *Retailing Today,* February 12, 2007, pp. 36–37.

31. See Michael Beckerman, "Doing the Math," *Marketing,* October 9–16, 2006, p. 32. Quote from www.apple.com/ipod/nike/, accessed April 2007.

32. Gabrielle Solomon, "Co-branding Alliances: Arranged Marriages Made by Marketers," *Fortune,* October 12, 1998, p. 188; "Martha Stewart Upgrading from Kmart to Macy's," *FinancialWire,* April 26, 2006, p. 1; Doug Desjardins, "Lowe's to Carry Martha Stewart Paint," *Retailing Today,* October 9, 2006, p. 68; and Becky Edenkamp, "Behind the 'Just Duet' Music," *Brandweek,* February 26, 2007, p. 18.

33. For more on the use of line and brand extensions and consumer attitudes toward them, see Franziska Volckner and Henrik Sattler, "Drivers of Brand Extension Success," *Journal of Marketing,* April 2006, pp. 18–34; and Chris Pullig, Carolyn J. Simmons, and Richard G. Netemeyer, "Brand Dilution: When Do New Brands Hurt Existing Brands?" *Journal of Marketing,* April 2006, pp. 52–66; and Lucas Conley, "When Brand Extensions Go Bad," *Fast Company,* October 2006, p. 38.

34. Constantine von Hoffman, "P&G's House Cleaning May Sweep Away Classics," *Brandweek,* May 15, 2006, p. 5.

35. "Megabrands," *Advertising Age,* July 17, 2006, p. S1.

36. Stephen Cole, "Value of the Brand," *CA Magazine,* May 2005, pp. 39–40.

37. See Kevin Lane Keller, "The Brand Report Card," *Harvard Business Review,* January 2000, pp. 147–57; Keller, *Strategic Brand Management,* pp. 766–67; David A. Aaker, "Even Brands Need Spring Cleaning," *Brandweek,* March 8, 2004, pp. 36–40; and Jane Simms, "What's Your Brand Worth?" *Marketing,* October 4, 2006, pp. 26–27.

38. See CIA, *The World Factbook,* accessed at www.cia.gov/cia/publications/factbook/index.html, August 2007; and information from the Bureau of Labor Statistics, www.bls.gov, accessed August 2007.

39. Adapted from information in Leonard Berry and Neeli Bendapudi, "Clueing In Customers," *Harvard Business Review,* February 2003, pp. 100–106; with information accessed at www.mayoclinic.org, August 2007. See also Leonard L. Berry and Kent D. Selman, "Building a Strong Services Brand: Lessons from Mayo Clinic," *Business Horizons,* May–June 2007, pp. 199–209.

40. See James L. Heskett, W. Earl Sasser Jr., and Leonard A. Schlesinger, *The Service Profit Chain: How Leading Companies Link Profit and Growth to Loyalty, Satisfaction, and Value* (New York: Free Press, 1997); Heskett, Sasser, and Schlesinger, *The Value Profit Chain: Treat Employees Like Customers and Customers Like Employees* (New York: Free Press, 2003); and "Recovering from Service Failure," *Strategic Direction,* June 2006, pp. 37–40.

41. William C. Johnson and Larry G. Chiagouris, "So Happy Together," *Marketing Management,* March–April 2006, pp. 47–50.

42. Based on Matthew Boyle, "The Wegmans Way," *Fortune,* January 24, 2005, pp. 62–68; with information from Mark Hamstra, "Wegmans, H-E-B Lead in Customer Satisfaction Study," *Supermarket News,* April 17, 2006, p. 22; Robert Levering and Milton Moskowitz, "In Good Company," *Fortune,* January 22, 2007, p. 94; and www.wegmans. com/about/jobs/index.asp, accessed June 2007.

43. See Robert Rappa and Evan Hirsch, "The Luxury Touch," *Strategy+Business,* Spring 2007, pp. 32–37.

44. See "Prescription Drug Trends," Kaiser Family Foundation, June 2006, accessed at www.kff.org/rxdrugs/upload/3057-05.pdf; and "UPS Fact Sheet," accessed at http://pressroom.ups.com/mediakits/factsheet/0,2305,866,00.html, August 2007.

45. Based on information in Rappa and Hirsch, "The Luxury Touch," p. 34.

46. Brian Hindo, "Satisfacton Not Guaranteed," *BusinessWeek,* June 19, 2006, pp. 32–36. Also see Frances X. Frei, "Breaking the Trade-Off Between Efficiency and Service," *Harvard Business Review,* November 2006, pp. 93–99.

Chapter 8

1. Quotes and other information in this Apple story from Terry Semel, "Steve Jobs: Perpetual Innovation Machine," *Time,* April 18, 2005, p. 78; Brent Schlender, "How Big Can Apple Get," *Fortune,* February 21, 2005, pp. 67–76; "Markets: Since Launch of First Generation of iPod, Apple Inc. Has Sold More than 88.7 Million Units Worldwide," *Associated Press Financial Wire,* March 14, 2007; "Apple," *BusinessWeek,* March 26, 2007, p. 84; Karlene Lukovitz, "Marketer of the Year: Apple Computer," *MediaPostPublications,* January 2, 2007, accessed at http://publications.mediapost.com; ; "The World's Most Innovative Companies," *BusinessWeek,* May 14, 2007, p. 55; and Apple annual reports and other information accessed at www.apple.com, September 2007.

2. Robert S. Shulman, "Material Whirl," *Marketing Management,* March–April, 2006, pp. 25–27.

3. Rick Romell, "Moving in the Right Direction: Segways Catch on in Niche Markets," *Milwaukee Journal Sentinel,* June 10, 2006, p. 1D; and Unmesh Kher, "What the Recall Reveals About Segway," *Time,* September 24, 2006, accessed at www.time.com/time/business/article/0,8599,1535267,00.html?cnn=yes.

4. For these and other facts and examples, see Jena McGregor, "How Failure Breeds Success," *BusinessWeek,* July 10, 2006, p. 42; and John T. Gourville, "Eager Sellers & Stony Buyers," *Harvard Business Review,* June 2006, pp. 98–106.

5. Information and examples from Robert M. McMath and Thom Forbes, *What Were They Thinking? Money-Saving, Time-Saving, Face-Saving Marketing Lessons You Can Learn from Products That Flopped* (New York: Times Business, 1999); Beatriz Cholo, "Living with Your 'Ex': A Brand New World," *Brandweek,* December 5, 2005, p. 4; and www.newproductworks.com/npw_difference/product_collection.html, accessed September 2007.

6. "IBM Taps Into Its Workers' Bright Ideas," *Irish Times,* October 27, 2006, p. 12; and Luke Collins, "Embedding Innovation into the Firm," *Research Technology Management,* March–April 2007, pp. 5–6.

7. William C. Taylor, "Here's an Idea: Let Everyone Have Ideas," *New York Times,* March 26, 2006, p. 3.3.

8. Based on material from Peter Lewis, "A Perpetual Crisis Machine," *Fortune,* September 19, 2005, pp. 58–67. Also see "Camp Samsung," *BusinessWeek Online,* July 3, 2006, accessed at www.businessweek.com.

9. Example from http://ideo.com/portfolio/re.asp?x=19008910, accessed July 2007.

10. Paul Gillin, "Get Customers Involved in Innovations," *BtoB,* March 12, 2007, p. 111. See also Patricia B. Seybold, *Outside Innovation: How Your Customers Will Co-Design Your Company's Future* (New York: Collins, 2006); and Patricia B. Seybold's blog: http://outsideinnovation.blogs.com, accessed April 2007.

11. Based on quotes and information from Robert D. Hof, "The Power of Us," *BusinessWeek,* June 20, 2005, pp. 74–82. See also Robert Weisman, "Firms Turn R&D on Its Head, Looking Outside for Ideas," *Boston Globe,* May 14, 2006, p. E1.

12. Information accessed online at www.avon.com, August 2007.

13. Robert Gray, "Not Invented Here," *Marketing,* May 6, 2004, pp. 34–37.

14. Information for this example obtained from www.teslamotors.com, April 2007; and Elizabeth Corcoran, "Can Silicon Valley Reinvent the Car?" *Forbes,* March 19, 2007, accessed at www.forbes.com.

15. Examples adapted from those found in Carol Matlack, "The Vuitton Machine," *BusinessWeek,* March 22, 2004, pp. 98–102; and Brendan Koerner, "For Every Sport, A Super Sock," *New York Times,* March 27, 2005, p. 3.2.

16. Joshua Freed, "Redbox Aims to Up Presence of DVD Kiosks," *Associated Press Online,* April 25, 2006; Trisha Evans, "Would You Like a DVD with Those Fries?" *Knight Ridder Tribune Business News,* February 17, 2007, p. 1; and Melissa S. Monroe, "Do You Want a DVD with That? McDonald's Adds Service to Attract Families," *San Antonio Express-News,* April 4, 2007.

17. Jack Neff, "Is Testing the Answer?" *Advertising Age,* July 9, 2001, p. 13; and Dale Buss, "P&G's Rise," *Potentials,* January 2003, pp. 26–30. For more on test marketing, see Philip Kotler and Kevin Lane Keller, *Marketing Management,* 12th ed. (Upper Saddle River, NJ: Prentice Hall, 2006), pp. 653–55.

18. Example developed from information found in Allison Enright, "Best Practices: Frito-Lay Get Real Results from a Virtual World," *Marketing News,* December 15, 2006, p. 20.

19. See Steve McClellan, "Unilever's Sunsilk Launch Goes Far Beyond the Box," *Adweek,* August 21–28, 2006, p. 9.

20. See William C. Symonds, "Gillette's New Edge," *BusinessWeek,* February 6, 2006, p. 44; and "Sales Are Razor Sharp," *Drug Store News,* April 10, 2006, p. 25.

21. See Beth Snyder Bulik, "$500 Million for Vista? Wow," *Advertising Age,* January 29, 2007, pp. 1, 30.

22. Robert G. Cooper, "Formula for Success," *Marketing Management,* March–April 2006, pp. 19–23.

23. Examples adapted from information in Jennifer Reingold, "The Interpreter," *Fast Company,* June 2005, pp. 59–61; and Jonah Bloom, "Beth Has an Idea," *Point,* September 2005, pp. 9–14. Also see Paul Bennett, "Listening Lessons: Make Consumers Part of the Design Process by Tuning In," *Point,* March 2006, pp. 9–10; and Larry Selden and Ian C. MacMillan, "Manage Customer-Centric Innovation—Systematically," *Harvard Business Review,* April 2006, pp. 108–16.

24. Lawrence A. Crosby and Sheree L. Johnson, "Customer-Centric Innovation," *Marketing Management,* March–April 2006, pp. 12–13.

25. Teressa Iezzi, "Innovate, but Do It for Customers," *Creativity,* September 2006, pp. 8–11.

26. See Philip Kotler, *Kotler on Marketing* (New York: Free Press, 1999), pp. 43–44; Judy Lamont, "Idea Management: Everyone's an Innovator," *KM World,* November–December 2004, pp. 14–16; "Anatomy of an Innovation Management System," *CIO Insight,* June 2005, p. 18; and J. Roland Ortt, "Innovation Management: Different Approaches to Cope with the Same Trends," *Management,* Fall 2006, pp. 296–318.

27. Portions adapted from Jonah Bloom, "Beth Has a Big Idea," *Point,* September 2005, pp. 9–14; with information from www.ge.com/en/product/imagination_break.html and http://cwcdn.geimaginationatwork.com/@v=092520050111@/imaginationatwork/flash.html, accessed September 2007. Also see Anne Fisher, "America's Most Admired Companies," *Fortune,* March 19, 2007, p. 88–94.

28. This definition is based on one found in Bryan Lilly and Tammy R. Nelson, "Fads: Segmenting the Fad-Buyer Market," *Journal of Consumer Marketing* 20, no. 3, Fall 2003, pp. 252–65.

29. See Katya Kazakina and Robert Johnson, "A Fad's Father Seeks a Sequel," *New York Times,* May 30, 2004, p. 3.2; Debbie Howell, "Retailers Piece Together New Crafting Opportunities," *DSN Retailing Today,* January 23, 2006, pp. 11–12; Timothy L. O'Brien, "Is Poker Losing Its First Flush?" *New York Times,* April 16, 2006, sec. 3, pp. 1-8; Tom McGhee, "Spotting Trends, Eschewing Fads," *Denver Post,* May 29, 2006; and www.crazyfads.com, accessed April 2007.

30. Youngme Moon, "Break Free from the Product Life Cycle," *Harvard Business Review,* May 2005, pp. 87–94.

31. See Constantine von Hoffman, "Glad Gives Seal of Approval to Alternate Wrap Uses," *Brandweek,* November 27, 2006, p. 10; and www.1000uses.com, accessed May 2007.

32. For a more comprehensive discussion of marketing strategies over the course of the product life cycle, see Philip Kotler and Kevin Lane Keller, *Marketing Management,* 12th ed. (Upper Saddle River, NJ: Prentice Hall, 2006), pp. 321–35.

33. See "Verdict Warns Drug Makers Not to Suppress Known Risks," *Tampa Tribune,* August 23, 2005, p. 10; "Year-by-Year Analysis Reveals an Overall Compensatory Award of $1,500,000 for Products Liability Cases," *Personal Injury Verdict Reviews,* July 3, 2006; Emily Umbright, "Report Finds Product Liability Cases on the Decline," *St. Louis Daily Record,* July 10, 2006; and "Top 100 Verdicts," accessed at www.verdictsearch.com, April 2007.

34. For these and other examples, see Darell K. Rigby and Vijay Vishwanath, "Localization: The Revolution in Consumer Markets," *Harvard Business Review,* April 2006, pp. 82–92; and Noreen O'Leary, "Bright Lights, Big Challenge," *Adweek,* January 15, 2007, pp. 22-28.

35. Information accessed online at www.deutsche-bank.com, September 2007.

36. Information accessed online at www.interpublic.com and www.mccann.com, September 2007.

37. See "2007 Global Powers of Retailing," *Stores,* January 2007, accessed at www.stores.org; "Wal-Mart International Operations," accessed at www.walmartstores.com, September 2007; and information accessed at www.carrefour.com/english/groupecarrefour/profil.jsp, September 2007.

Chapter 9

1. Thomas T. Nagle and Reed K. Holden, *The Strategy and Tactics of Pricing,* 4th ed. (Upper Saddle River, NJ: Prentice Hall, 2005), chapter 1.

2. Quotes and excerpts from or adapted from Matthew Maier, "A Radical Fix for Airlines: Make Flying Free," *Business 2.0,* April 2006, pp. 32–34; and Kerry Capell, "Wal-Mart with Wings," *BusinessWeek,* November 27, 2006, pp. 44–46. Also see "Ryanair Offers Gambling Web Site," *Associated Press,* November 1, 2006; Will Sullivan, "Flying on the Cheap," *U.S. News & World Report,* March 26, 2007, p. 47; "Ryanair Offers Ad Space in Planes," *Marketing,* February 28, 2007; Mark Tatge, "Nightmare at 30,000 Feet," *Forbes,* June 4, 2007, p. 56; and www.ryanair.com, accessed December 2007.

3. George Mannes, "The Urge to Unbundle," *Fast Company,* February 27, 2005, pp. 23–24.

4. Linda Tischler, "The Price Is Right," *Fast Company,* November 2003, pp. 83–91. See also Wendy Melillo, "The Gold Standard," *Brandweek,* June 5, 2006, pp. 18–20.

5. Paul S. Hunt, "Seizing the Fourth P," *Marketing Management,* May–June 2005, pp. 40–44.

6. John Tayman, "The Six-Figure Steal," *Business 2.0,* June 2005, pp. 148–50; and Annie Groer, "Hermes v. Hermes," June 28, 2006, accessed at www.washingtonpost.com.

7. Diana T. Kuryiko, "VW Goes Downscale, Lowers Prices," *Automotive News,* January 8, 2007, p. 4.

8. William F. Kendy, "The Price Is Too High," *Selling Power,* April 2006, pp. 30–33.

9. Example adapted from Anupam Mukerji, "Monsoon Marketing," *Fast Company,* April 2007, p. 22.

10. Erin Stout, "Keep Them Coming Back for More," *Sales & Marketing Management,* February 2002, pp. 51–52. Also see Gerald E. Smith and Thomas T. Nagle, "A Question of Value," *Marketing Management,* July–August 2005, pp. 39–44; William F. Kendy, "Value as a Sales Tool," *Selling Power,* July–August 2006, pp. 39–41; and Nirmalya Kumar, "Strategies to Fight Low-Cost Rivals," *Harvard Business Review,* December 2006, pp. 104–12.

11. Joshua Rosenbaum, "Guitar Maker Looks for a New Key," *Wall Street Journal,* February 11, 1998; and information accessed online at www.gibson.com, December 2007.

12. See Robert J. Dolan, "Pricing: A Value-Based Approach," *Harvard Business School Publishing,* November 3, 2003.

13. See Philip Kotler and Kevin Lane Keller, *Marketing Management,* 12th ed. (Upper Saddle River, NJ: Prentice Hall, 2006), p. 438; and Kenneth Hein, "Not a Pretty Picture: HDTV Prices Continue to Erode," *Brandweek,* April 16, 2007, pp. 10–11.

14. See Susan Berfield, "Sleek. Stylish. Samsonite?" *BusinessWeek,* February 26, 2007, p. 106.

15. Example adapted from information found in Beth Snyder Bulik, "Kodak Develops New Model: Expensive Printer, Cheap Ink," *Advertising Age,* March 12, 2007, pp. 4, 45.

16. Information accessed at www.meadwestvaco.com, July 2007.

17. See Nagle and Hogan, *The Strategy and Tactics of Pricing,* pp. 244–47; Stefan Stremersch and Gerard J. Tellis, "Strategic Bundling of Products and Prices: A New Synthesis for Marketing," *Journal of Marketing Research,* January 2002, pp. 55–72; Chris Janiszewski and Marcus Cunha Jr., "The Influence of Price Discount Framing on the Evaluation of a Product Bundle," *Journal of Marketing Research,* March 2004, pp. 534–46; "Save a Bundle, Comcast Says," *Tacoma News Tribune,* July 25, 2006; and Rob Doctors et al., "Bundles with Sharp Teeth: Effective Combinations," *Journal of Business Strategy* 27, no. 5, 2006, pp. 10–16.

18. Example adapted from Charles Fishman, "Which Price Is Right?" *Fast Company,* March 2003, pp. 92–96. Additional data from "Continental Airlines Reports April 2007 Operational Performance," Continental Financial and Traffic Releases, accessed at www.continental.com/company/investor/news.asp.

19. For more discussion, see Manoj Thomas and Vicki Morvitz, "Penny Wise and Pound Foolish: The Double-Digit Effect in Price Cognition," *Journal of Consumer Research,* June 2005, pp. 54–64; Heyong Min Kim and Luke Kachersky, "Dimensions of Price Salience: A Conceptual Framework for Perceptions of Multi-Dimensional Prices," *Journal of Product and Brand Management* 15, no. 2, 2006, pp. 139–47; and Alex Mindlin, "For a Memorable Price, Trim Syllables," *New York Times,* August 14, 2006, accessed at www.nytimes.com.

20. Karyn McCormack, "Price War Leaves AMD Reeling," *BusinessWeek Online,* January 25, 2007, p. 4.

21. Thomas L. Friedman, *The World Is Flat: A Brief History of the Twenty-First Century* (New York: Farrar, Straus, and Giroux, 2005), pp. 417–18.

22. For a discussion of consumer perceptions of fairness in dynamic pricing, see Kelly L. Haws and William O. Bearden, "Dynamic Pricing and Consumer Fairness Perceptions," *Journal of Consumer Research,* December 2006, pp. 304–11.

23. Based on information found in Bruce Einhorn, "Grudge Match in China," *BusinessWeek,* April 2, 2007, pp. 42–43.

24. Jack Neff, "Flourishing Viva Paper-Towel Brand Beefs Up Its Marketing," *Advertising Age,* June 5, 2007, accessed at www.adage.com.

25. For discussions of these issues, see Dhruv Grewel and Larry D. Compeau, "Pricing and Public Policy: A Research Agenda and Overview of Special Issue," *Journal of Public Policy and Marketing,* Spring 1999, pp. 3–10; and Michael V. Marn, Eric V. Roegner, and Craig C. Zawada, *The Price Advantage* (Hoboken, NJ: John Wiley & Sons, 2004), appendix 2.

26. "Three Chipmakers Settle Antitrust Lawsuit," *FinancialWire,* May 11, 2006, p. 1; Kevin Allison, "Chipmakers Face Suit over Price-Fixing," *Financial Times,* July 14, 2006, p. 23; and Mark Jacoby, "Politics & Economics: EU Investigators Urge Intel Charge," *Wall Street Journal,* January 17, 2007.

27. "Predatory-Pricing Law Passed by New York Governor," *National Petroleum News,* December 2003, p. 7; Brenden Timpe, "House Rejects Bill to Protect Gas Stations from Wal-Mart-Style Competition," *Knight Ridder Tribune Business News,* March 26, 2005, p. 1; Charles Ashby, "Senate OKs Bill to Allow Below-Cost Fuel," *Knight Ridder Tribune Business News,* March 14, 2007, p. 1; and Martin Sipkoff, "Wal-Mart, Other Discounters Facing Predatory-Pricing Concerns," *Drug Topics,* April 2, 2007, pp. 10–12.

28. "FTC Guides Against Deceptive Pricing," accessed at www.ftc.gov/bcp/guides/decptprc.htm, January 2008.

Chapter 10

1. Quotes and other information from Donald V. Fites, "Make Your Dealers Your Partners," *Harvard Business Review,* March–April 1996, pp. 84–95; Michael Arndt, "Cat Claws Its Way into Services," *BusinessWeek,* December 5, 2005, pp. 56–59; "Global Construction & Farm Machinery: Industry Profile," *Datamonitor,* June 2006, accessed at www.datamonitor.com; Pallavi Gogoi, "What Buffet Might Buy," *BusinessWeek Online,* May 8, 2007, p. 1; and information accessed at www.caterpillar.com, December 2007.

2. Based on information from Stephanie Thompson and Jack Neff, "Retailer Revolt Causes $40M Loss at Revlon," *Advertising Age,* July 17, 2006, pp. 3, 28; and Molly Prior and Matthew W. Evans, "Revlon Posts $5.5M Loss in 4th Quarter," *Women's Wear Daily,* March 14, 2007, p. 2.

3. Matthew Boyle, "Brand Killers," *Fortune,* August 11, 2003, pp. 89–100; and information accessed at www.kroger.com, www.safeway.com, and www.luxottica.com/english/profilo_aziendale/index_keyfacts.html, December 2007.

4. Adapted from information found in Kerry Capell, "Fashion Conquistador," *BusinessWeek,* September 4, 2006, pp. 38–39; Miguel Helft, "Fashion Fast Forward," *Business 2.0,* May 2002, p. 60; Kasra Ferdows, Michael A. Lewis, and Jose A. D. Machuca, "Rapid-Fire Fulfillment," *Harvard Business Review,* November 2004, pp. 104–10; and the Inditext Press Kit, accessed at www.inditex.com/en/press/information/press_kit, December 2007.

5. Franchising facts from www.franchise.org/content.asp?contentid=379 and www.azfranchises.com/franchisefacts.htm, accessed July 2007.

6. See Geoff Dyer, "Hunger for Cars Feeds Drive-Thru Fast-Food Outlets Across China," *Financial Times,* November 18, 2006, p. 8; and http://english.sinopec.com/faq/faq.shtml; accessed December 2007.

7. Information accessed at www.mind-advertising.com/ch/nestea_ch.htm, September 2007.

8. Information from www.coldwatercreek.com, accessed July 2007.

9. Quotes and information from Normandy Madden, "Two Chinas," *Advertising Age,* August 16, 2004, pp. 1, 22; Russell Flannery, "China: The Slow Boat," *Forbes,* April 12, 2004, p. 76; and Jeff Berman, "U.S. Providers Say Logistics in China on the Right Track," *Logistics Management,* March 2007, p. 22.

10. Nanette Byrnes, "Avon Calls. China Opens the Door," *BusinessWeek Online,* February 28, 2006, p. 19; and Mei Fong, "Avon's Calling, but China Opens Door Only a Crack," *Wall Street Journal,* February 26, 2007, p. B1.

11. See Steven Burke, "Samsung Launches Revamped Partner Program," *CRN,* February 12, 2007, accessed at www.crn.com/it-channel/197005419; and "Program Details: Samsung Electronics America, IT Divison," *VAR Business 2007 Partner Programs Guide,* accessed at www.crn.com/var/apps/2007/ppg/ppg_details.jhtml?c=54, July 2007.

12. For a full discussion of laws affecting marketing channels, see Anne Coughlin, Erin Anderson, Louis W. Stern, and Adel El-Ansary, *Marketing Channels,* 7th ed. (Upper Saddle River, NJ: Prentice Hall, 2006), chapter 10.

13. Kathy Doherty, "Logistics Costs Skyrocket," *Food Logistics,* October 10, 2006, p. 4; Neil Shister, "Redesigned Supply Chain Positions Ford for Global Competition," *World Trade,* May 2005, pp. 20–26; "Logistics Costs on the Rise," *Modern Materials Handling,* July 2006, p. 11; and supply chain facts from www.cscmp.org/Website/AboutCSCMP/Media/FastFacts.asp, accessed October 2007.

14. Shlomo Maital, "The Last Frontier of Cost Reduction," *Across the Board,* February 1994, pp. 51–52; "Wal-Mart to Expand Supercenters to California," *BusinessJournal,* May 15, 2002, accessed online at http://sanjose.bizjournals.com; and information accessed online at www.walmartstores.com, August 2007.

15. Gail Braccidiferro, "One Town's Rejection Is Another's 'Let's Do Business'," *New York Times,* June 15, 2003, p. 2; Dan Scheraga, "Wal-Smart," *Chain Store Age,* January 2006 supplement, pp. 16A–21A; and facts from www.walmart.com and www.statemaster.com, accessed October 2007.

16. William Hoffman, "Dell's Direct-to-Logistics Strategy," *Traffic World,* March 5, 2007, p. 1.

17. See "A Worldwide Look at RFID," *Supply Chain Management Review,* April 2007, pp. 48–55; Owen Davis, "Time to Roll with RFID," *Supply & Demand Chain Executive,* February–March 2007, p. 56; and "Wal-Mart Extends Commitment to RFID," *Material Handling Management,* May 2007, p. 8.

18. Transportation percentages and other figures in this section are from Bureau of Transportation Statistics, "Freight in America," January 2006, accessed at www.bts.gov/publications; and Bureau of Transportation Statistics, "Pocket Guide to Transportation 2006," January 2006, accessed at www.bts.gov/publications/pocket_guide_to_transportation/2006/.

19. See Laurie Sullivan, "Hey, Wal-Mart, a New Case of Pampers Is on the Way," *InformationWeek,* January 23, 2006, p. 28; Connie Robbins Gentry, "No More Holes at Krispy Kreme," *Chain Store Age,* July 2006, pp. 64–65; Rebecca Logan, "EDI Still a Fresh, Hot App," *Stores Magazine,* October 2006, pp. 118–20; and "Collaborative Supply Chain

Practices and Evolving Technological Approaches," *Supply Chain Management,* May 2007, pp. 210–20.

20. See Bob Trebilock, "Top 20 Supply Chain Management Software Providers," *Modern Materials Handling,* May 2007, p. 47; and "The 2007 Supply & Demand Chain Executive 100," *Supply & Demand Chain Executive,* May 2007, accessed at www.sdcexec.com/web/online/None/2007-Supply-and-Demand-Chain-Executive-100/6$9086.

21. Michelle Bradford, "Vendor Families Propel Region's Shift to Affluence," *Arkansas Democrat-Gazette,* February 5, 2006; and "It Takes a People Company to Know a People Company," *Retailing Today,* February–March 2007, pp. 23–27.

22. John Paul Quinn, "3PLs Hit Their Stride," *Logistics Management/Supply Chain Management Review,* July 2006, pp. 3T–8T; and "U.S. and Global Third-Party Logistics (3PL) Market Analysis Is Released," *PR Newswire,* April 12, 2007.

Chapter 11

1. Quotes and other information from "Costco vs. Sam's Club," *Consumer Reports,* May 2007, pp. 16–19; Matthew Boyle, "Why Costco Is So Addictive," *Fortune,* October 25, 2006, pp. 126–32; Anthony Bianco, "Wal-Mart's Midlife Crisis," *BusinessWeek,* April 30, 2007, pp. 46–55; John Helyar, "The Only Company Wal-Mart Fears," *Fortune,* November 24, 2003, pp. 158–66; Reena Jana, "The Revenge of the Generic," *BusinessWeek,* December 27, 2006, accessed at www.businessweek.com/innovate/content/dec2006/id20061227_049239.htm; Pat Regnief, "Hunting Big Savings at Costco," *Money,* June 22, 2006; Andrew Bary, "Everybody's Store," *Barron's,* February 12, 2007, pp. 29–32; and www.costco.com, accessed December 2007.

2. Quote from "Ogilvy Gets Activated," *MediaPostPublications,* January 8, 2007, accessed at http://publications.mediapost.com/index.cfm?fuseaction=Articles.showArticle&art_aid=53477. Retail sales statistics from "Annual Revision of Monthly Retail and Food Services: Sales and Inventories—January 1992–2007," U.S. Census Bureau, March 2007, p. 3.

3. "Supermarkets' Shrinking Share in Food Retailing Marketing Sparks Opportunities for Alternative Food Retail Channels," *M2PressWIRE,* March 31, 2006.

4. Blanca Torres, "4th Quarter Profit Soars at Safeway," *Knight Ridder Tribune Business News,* February 23, 2007, p. 1; Justin Hibbard, "Put Your Money Where Your Mouth Is," *BusinessWeek,* September 18, 2007, pp. 61–63; and Blanca Torres, "Safeway Sees Sales, Profits Rise," *Knight Ridder Tribune Business News,* April 17, 2007, p. 1.

5. "Convenience Store Industry Sales Top $569 Billion, NACS Reports," April 11, 2007, accessed online at http://www.nacsonline.com/.

6. Adapted from Elizabeth Esfahani, "7-Eleven Gets Sophisticated," *Business 2.0,* January–February 2005, pp. 93–100. Also see Tatiana Serafin, "Smokes and Sandwiches," *Forbes,* February 13, 2006, p. 120; and "Rivals Want a Big Gulp of 7-Eleven's Business," *Knight Ridder Tribune Business News,* June 12, 2007, p. 1.

7. "SN Top 75 2007," accessed at http://supermarketnews.com/top75/, June 2007; and Gary McWilliams and Kris Hodson, "Wal-Mart Reins In Plan for New U.S. Stores," *Wall Street Journal,* June 2, 2007, p. A3.

8. Elizabeth Woyke, "Buffett, the Wal-Mart Shopper," *BusinessWeek,* May 14, 2007, pp. 66–67.

9. Company information from www.subway.com and www.mcdonalds.com/corp.html, accessed September 2007.

10. "Who Said That?" *Marketing Management,* January–February 2005, p. 4.

11. The Whole Foods example is based on quotes and information from Diane Brady, "Eating Too Fast at Whole Foods," *BusinessWeek,* October 24, 2005, pp. 82–84; Kim Wright Wiley, "Think Organic," *Sales & Marketing Management,* January–February 2007, pp. 54–59; Julie Schlosser, "After a Dip, Whole Foods Looks Tasty," *Fortune,* April 3, 2006, p. 115; "Whole Food Market Inc.," *Hoovers Company Records,* June 1, 2007, p. 10952, p.1; and www.wholefoods.com, accessed December 2007.

12. Laurie Sullivan, "Brand This: Department Stores Capitalize on Their Names," *InformationWeek,* April 18, 2005, p. 61–67; Kelly Nolan, "Claiborne, Miller Add to Exclusives," *Retailing Today,* October 23, 2006, pp. 3–4; and Kelly Nolan, "Staking Success on Brand Push," *Retailing Today,* January 8, 2007, pp. 1–2.

13. Leander Kahney, "The Genius of Apple's Stores," *WiredNews,* May 2, 2006, accessed at www.wired.com/news/columns/0,70787-0.html. See also Ray Allegrezza, "In Search of That Special Feeling," *Furniture Today,* March 26, 2007, p. 4.

14. Adapted from "At Home in the Apple Store: A Welcoming Temple to a Devout Member of the Cult," *Saint Paul Pioneer Press,* June 19, 2006.

15. Jerry Useem, "Simply Irresistible," *Fortune,* March 19, 2007, p. 107.

16. See John Torella, "Brilliant! In-Store Marketing," *Strategy,* April 2006, p. 8.

17. Lauren Monsen, "Iranian-American Menswear Designer Conquers the Luxury Market," *State Department Documents and Publications,* April 18, 2007, p. 1; and information accessed at www.bijan.com/boutique, December 2007.

18. For definitions of these and other types of shopping centers, see "Dictionary of Marketing Terms," American Marketing Association, accessed at www.marketingpower.com/mg-dictionary.php, September 2007.

19. Paul Lukas, "Our Malls, Ourselves," *Fortune,* October 18, 2004, pp. 243–56; Ryan Chittum, "Mall-Building Industry Takes Stock," *Wall Street Journal,* May 17, 2006, p. B7; Kelsey Volkmann, "Business Malls Evolving to Imitate Traditional Downtowns," *Associated Press,* January 31, 2007, p. 1; and the International Council of Shopping Centers, "U.S. Mall Report," April 2007, accessed at www.icsc.org.

20. Dean Starkman, "The Mall, Without the Haul—'Lifestyle Centers' Slip Quietly into Upscale Areas, Mixing Cachet and 'Curb Appeal'," *Wall Street Journal,* July 25, 2001, p. B1; Michael Fickes, "Everything's Coming Up Lifestyle," *Chain Store Age,* March 2007, pp. 130–33; Paul Grimaldi, "Shopping for a New Look: Lifestyle Centers Are Replacing Enclosed Malls," *Providence (RI) Journal,* April 29, 2007, p. F10; and information accessed on the International Council of Shopping Centers Web site, www.icsc.org, December 2007.

21. See Amy Barrett, "A Retailing Pacesetter Pulls Up Lame," *BusinessWeek,* July 12, 1993, pp. 122–23; and John Helyar, "The Only Company Wal-Mart Fears," *Fortune,* November 24, 2003, pp. 158–66; Heather Todd, "Club Stores Pack 'Em In," *Beverage World,* April 15, 2005, pp. 44–45.

22. See Malcolm P. McNair and Eleanor G. May, "The Next Revolution of the Retailing Wheel," *Harvard Business Review,* September–October 1978, pp. 81–91; Stephen Brown, "The Wheel of Retailing: Past and Future," *Journal of Retailing,* Summer 1990, pp. 143–147; Stephen Brown, "Variations on a Marketing Enigma: The Wheel-of-Retailing Theory," *Journal of Marketing Management* 7, no. 2, April 1991, pp. 131–55; Jennifer Negley, "Retrenching, Reinventing, and Remaining Relevant," *Discount Store News,* April 5, 1999, p. 11; and Don E. Schultz, "Another Turn of the Wheel," *Marketing Management,* March–April 2002, pp. 8–9; and Carol Krol, "Staples Preps Easier E-Commerce Site," *BtoB,* March 14, 2005, pp. 3–4.

23. "Online Clothing Sales Surpass Computers, According to Shop.org/ Forrester Research Study," May 14, 2007, accessed at www.shop.org/ press/07/051407.asp.

24. See Sungwook Min and Mary Wolfinbarger, "Market Share, Profit Margin, and Marketing Efficiency of Early Movers, Bricks and Clicks, and Specialists in E-Commerce," *Journal of Business Research,* August 2005, pp. 1030+; and "Facts About America's Top 500 E-Retailers," *Internet Retailer,* accessed online at www.internetretailer.com/top500/ facts.asp, May 2007.

25. Joseph Pereira, "Staples Posts Strong Earnings on High-Margin Internet Sales," *Wall Street Journal,* March 5, 2004; "The BusinessWeek 50: Staples Inc.," *BusinessWeek,* April 3, 2006, p. 97; and information accessed online at www.staples.com, October 2007.

26. See "The Fortune 500," *Fortune,* April 30, 2007, p. F1.

27. Adapted from information found in Christina Rexrode, "Concept Store in Bloom," *Herald-Sun,* June 6, 2004, pp. F1, F3; Victor Reklaitis, "Bloom Is Coming to Food Lion," *Knight Ridder Tribune Business News,* May 30, 2007, p. 1; and www.shopbloom.com, accessed October 2007.

28. "Wal-Mart International Operations," September 2007, accessed online at www.walmartstores.com.

29. See "2007 Global Powers of Retailing," *Stores,* January 2007, accessed at www.nxtbook.com/nxtbooks/nrfe/stores-globalretail07/.

30. See Dexter Roberts, Wendy Zellner, and Carol Matlack, "Let the Retail Wars Begin," *BusinessWeek,* January 17, 2005, pp. 44–45; "Top 250 Global Retailers," *Stores,* January 2007, accessed at www.nxtbook. com/nxtbooks/nrfe/stores-globalretail07/; and information from www. walmartstores.com and www.carrefour.com, accessed October 2007.

31. Adapted from information in "Nike Will Outfit U.S. Men's National Soccer Team in Germany This Summer," *Business Wire,* May 2, 2006; and Stanley Holmes, "Nike: It's Not a Shoe It's a Community," *BusinessWeek,* July 24, 2006, p. 50. Also see Jonathan Birchall, "Cyber Persuaders Gain Ground: Consumer Communities," *Financial Times,* April 23, 2007, p. 2.

32. See the Grainger 2007 Fact Book and other information accessed at www.grainger.com, December 2007.

33. See Dale Buss, "The New Deal," *Sales & Marketing Management,* June 2002, pp. 25–30; and Colleen Gourley, "Redefining Distribution," *Warehousing Management,* October 2000, pp. 28–30; Steve Konicki and Eileen Colkin, "Attitude Adjustment," *InformationWeek,* March 25, 2002, pp. 20–22; and Stewart Scharf, "Grainger: Tooled Up for Growth," *BusinessWeek Online,* April 25, 2006, p. 8. Also see Victoria Fraza Kickham, "Go Global, But Stay Local," *Industrial Distribution,* January 2007, p. 1.

34. "McKesson: Raising Expectations," *Modern Materials Handling,* February 2004, p. 53; and information from "About Us" and "Supply Management Online," accessed online at www.mckesson.com, October 2007.

35. Facts accessed at www.supervalu.com, December 2007.

Chapter 12

1. Quotes and other information from Linda Tischler, "Clan of the Caveman," *Fast Company,* June 2007, pp. 105–8; "A Legend in Its Time," *Best's Review,* January 2006, p. 53; Jim Lovel, "Loving the Lizard," *Adweek,* October 24, 2005, pp. 32–33; Mya Frazier, "Ad Spending Booms in War of Car Insurers," *Advertising Age,* March 13, 2006, p. 4; Suzanne Vranica, "How a Gecko Shook Up Insurance Ads," *Wall Street Journal,* January 2, 2007, p. B1; and Mya Frazier, "Geico's Big Spending Pays Off, Study Says," *Advertising Age,* June 26, 2007, accessed at http://adage.com/print?article_id=118844.

2. The first four of these definitions are adapted from Peter D. Bennett, *The AMA Dictionary of Marketing Terms,* 2nd ed. (New York: McGraw-Hill, 1995). Other definitions can be found at www.marketingpower .com/live/mg-dictionary.php?.

3. Bob Garfield, "The Chaos Scenario," *Advertising Age,* April 4, 2005, pp. 1, 57+; and "Readers Respond to 'Chaos Scenario'," *Advertising Age,* April 18, 2005, pp. 1+.

4. Chase Squires and Dave Gussow, "The Ways in Which We Watch TV Are Changing Right Before Our Eyes," *St. Petersburg Times,* April 27, 2006; and Geoff Colvin, "TV Is Dying? Long Live TV!" *Fortune,* February 5, 2007, p. 43.

5. Abbey Klaassen, "Study: Only One in Four Teens Can Name Broadcast Networks," *Advertising Age,* May 15, 2006.

6. Bob Garfield, "The Chaos Scenario 2.0: The Post-Advertising Age," *Advertising Age,* March 26, 2007, pp. 1, 12–13.

7. Brian Steinberg and Suzanne Vranica, "As 30-Second Spot Fades, What Will Advertisers Do Next?" *Wall Street Journal,* January 3, 2006, p. A15; and Warren Berger, "A Hard Sell," *Business 2.0,* May 2007, pp. 91–96.

8. Mike Shaw, "Direct Your Advertising Dollars Away from TV at Your Own Risk," *Advertising Age,* February 27, 2006, p. 29. TV advertising stats from "Domestic Advertising Spending Totals by Medium," *Advertising Age,* June 25, 2007, p. 8.

9. Jack Neff, "P&G Chief: We Need New Model Now," *Advertising Age,* November 15, 2004, pp. 1, 53.

10. Bob Garfield, "Lee Chow on What's Changed Since '1984'," *Advertising Age,* June 11, 2007, p. 3.

11. See Scott Collins, "'Idol' Viewership Goes Up, Up, Up for Fox," *Los Angeles Times,* January 18, 2007, p. E4; "CBS Gets 93 Million Viewers to Tune In to Super Bowl," *Associated Press Financial Wire,* February 6, 2007; and Scott Collins, "Channel Island: Smaller Films, Low-Key Host Affect Ratings," *Los Angeles Times,* February 27, 2007, p. E1.

12. Roy Chitwood, "Making the Most out of Each Outside Sales Call," February 4, 2005, accessed at http://seattle.bizjournals.com/seattle/ stories/2005/02/07/smallb3.html; and "The Cost of the Average Sales Call Today Is More Than $400," *Business Wire,* February 28, 2006.

13. For information on U.S. and international advertising spending, see "Top 100 Global Marketers," *Advertising Age,* November 20, 2006, p. 4; and "100 Leading National Advertisers," special issue of *Advertising Age,* June 25, 2007, p. S4.

14. For these and other examples, see Kate MacArthur, "Why Big Brands Are Getting Bigger," *Advertising Age,* May 2007, p. 6.

15. For more on setting promotion budgets, see W. Ronald Lane, Karen Whitehill King, and J. Thomas Russell, *Kleppner's Advertising Procedure,* 17th ed. (Upper Saddle River, NJ: Prentice Hall, 2008), chapter 6.

16. For more discussion, see Brian Steinberg and Suzanne Vranica, "Agencies Rethink Wall Between Creative, Media: Fragmentation of Audience Undercuts the Rationale for Separate Buying Units," *Wall Street Journal,* March 1, 2006, p. B3; Suzanne Vranica, "'Aligning' Creative and Media: An Old Idea with a New Twist," *Wall Street Journal,* November 1, 2006; and Mark Dominiak, "Get Creative Teamed Up with Media," *TelevisionWeek,* December 18–25, 2006, p. 10.

17. "Commercial Conundrum," *Marketing Management,* April 2006, p. 6; and "Number of Magazines by Category," accessed at www.magazine. org/editorial/editorial_trends_and_magazine_handbook/1145.cfm, August 2007.

18. Louise Story, "Anywhere the Eye Can See, It's Likely to See an Ad," *New York Times,* January 15, 2007, accessed at www.nytimes.com; and

Matthew Creamer, "Caught in the Clutter Crossfire: Your Brand," *Advertising Age,* April 1, 2007, pp. 1, 35.

19. See Paul R. La Monica, "'Idol' Fatigue? Think Again," *CNNMoney.com,* January 10, 2007; and Andrew Hampp, "'American Idol' vs. the Super Bowl," *Advertising Age,* May 28, 2007, p. 3.

20. Ken Krimstein, "Tips for the Ad World," *Forbes,* October 16, 2006, p. 34; and Bob Garfield, "The Chaos Scenario: The Post-Advertising Age," *Advertising Age,* March 26, 2007, pp. 1, 12–13.

21. John Consoli, "Broadcast, Cable Ad Clutter Continues to Rise," *MediaWeek,* May 4, 2006, accessed at www.mediaweek.com.

22. Ronald Grover, "The Sound of Many Hands Zapping," *BusinessWeek,* May 22, 2006, p. 38; Louise Story, "Viewers Fast-Forwarding Past Ads? Not Always," *New York Times,* February 16, 2007, p. 1; and David Lieberman, "Forecaster Says DRVs Will Help Networks Make Money," *USA Today,* June 20, 2007, accessed at www.usatoday.com.

23. See Theresa Howard, "'Viral' Advertising Spreads Through Marketing Plans," *USA Today,* June 6, 2005, accessed at www.usatoday.com/money/advertising/2005-06-22-viral-usat_x.htm; and Steve McKee, "Advertising: Less Is Much More," *BusinessWeek Online,* May 10, 2006, accessed at www.businessweek.com.

24. For this and other examples, see Wendy Tanaka, "D.I.Y. Ads," *Red Herring,* January 29, 2007, accessed at www.redherring.com/Article.aspx?a=20955&hed=D.I.Y.+Ads.

25. See Brian Steinberg, "Super Bowl Advertisers Hand Amateurs the Ball," *Wall Street Journal,* January 12, 2007, p. B1; and "How All the Ads Ranked in *USA Today*'s Super Bowl Ad Meter," *USA Today,* February 5, 2007, accessed at www.usatoday.com.

26. Tanaka, "D.I.Y. Ads," p. 3.

27. Enright, "Let Them Decide," *Marketing News,* June 1, 2006, pp. 10–11.

28. Tanaka, "D.I.Y. Ads"; Enright, "Let Them Decide."

29. Stuart Elliot, "New Rules of Engagement," *New York Times,* March 21, 2006, p. C7; Abbey Klaassen, "New Wins Early Battle in Viewer-Engagement War," *Advertising Age,* March 20, 2006, p. 1; Mike DiFranza, "Rules of Engagement," *MediaWeek,* January 15, 2007, p. 9; and Andrew Hampp, "Water Cooler," *Advertising Age,* April 16, 2007, p. 32.

30. For these and other examples and quotes, see Chris Walsh, "Ads on Board," *Rocky Mountain News,* February 27, 2007; David H. Freedman, "The Future of Advertising Is Here," *Inc.,* August 2005, pp. 70–78; David Kiley, "Rated M for Mad Ave," *BusinessWeek,* February 26, 2006, pp. 76–77; "Global Trends Watch—Innovative Advertising," *Brand Strategy,* April 10, 2006, p. 14; Cliff Peale, "Advertising Takes Many Forms," *Cincinnati Enquirer,* December 3, 2006, accessed at http://news.enquirer.com; and Louise Story, "Anywhere the Eye Can See, It's Likely to See an Ad," *New York Times,* January 15, 2007, p. A12.

31. Adapted from information found in "Multi-Taskers," *Journal of Marketing Management,* May–June 2004, p. 6; "Kids Today: Media Multitaskers," March 9, 2005, accessed at www.cbsnews.com/stories/2005/03/09/tech/main678999.shtml; Claudia Wallis, "The Multitasking Generation," *Time,* March 27, 2006, accessed at www.time.com; and Curtis L. Taylor, "Teens' Balancing Act: New Study Shows Young People Are Spending More Time Multitasking," *Knight Ridder Tribune BusinessNews,* December 16, 2006, p. 1.

32. *Newsweek* and *BusinessWeek* cost and circulation data accessed online at http://mediakit.businessweek.com and www.newsweekmediakit.com, August 2007.

33. See Frank Ahrens, "$2 Million Airtime, $13 Ad," *Washington Post,* January 31, 2007, p. D1.

34. See Stuart Elliot, "How Effective Is This Ad, in Real Numbers? Beats Me," *New York Times,* July 20, 2005, p. C8; Jack Neff, "Half Your Advertising Isn't Wasted—Just 37.3 Percent," *Advertising Age,* August 7, 2006, pp. 1, 32; and Ben Richards and Faris Yakob, "The New Quid pro Quo," *Adweek,* March 19, 2007, p. 17.

35. Chris Daniels, "ROI or Else," *Marketing,* March 26, 2007, p. 6.

36. Elliot, "How Effective Is This Ad, in Real Numbers? Beats Me," p. C8. Also see, Dan Lippe, "Media Scorecard: How ROI Adds Up," *Advertising Age,* June 20, 2005, p. S6; and Pat LaPointe, "For Better ROI, Think Sailing, Not Driving," *Brandweek,* January 30, 2006, pp. 17–18.

37. Information on advertising agency revenues from "Agency Report 2007," *Advertising Age,* April 25, 2007, accessed at www.adage.com.

38. Adapted from information in Geoffrey A. Fowler, Brian Steinberg, and Aaron O. Patrick, "Mac and PC's Overseas Adventures," *Wall Street Journal,* March 1, 2007, p. B1.

39. See Alexandra Jardine and Laurel Wentz, "It's a Fat World After All," *Advertising Age,* March 7, 2005, p. 3; George E. Belch and Michael A. Belch, *Advertising and Promotion* (New York: McGraw-Hill/Irwin, 2004), pp. 666–68; Jonathan Cheng, "China Demands Concrete Proof of Ads," *Wall Street Journal,* July 8, 2005, p. B1; Cris Prystay, "India's Brewers Cleverly Dodge Alcohol-Ad Ban," *Wall Street Journal,* June 15, 2005, p. B1; Dean Visser, "China Puts New Restrictions on Cell Phone, E-Mail Advertising," *Marketing News,* March 15, 2006, p. 23; and Steve Inskeep, "Ban Thwarts 'Year of the Pig' Ads in China," *National Public Radio,* February 6, 2007.

40. Adapted from Scott Cutlip, Allen Center, and Glen Broom, *Effective Public Relations,* 9th ed. (Upper Saddle River, NJ: Prentice Hall, 2006), chapter 1.

41. Based on and adapted from information found in Diane Brady, "Wizard of Marketing," *BusinessWeek,* July 24, 2000, pp. 84–87; Mira Serrill-Robins, "Harry Potter and the Cyberpirates," *BusinessWeek,* August 1, 2005, p. 9; Keith O'Brien, "Publisher Puts Fans First for New Harry Potter Release," *PRWeek,* July 18, 2005, p. 3; and "Harry Potter Tops U.S. Best-Seller List for 2005," *China Daily,* January 11, 2006, p. 14.

42. Al Ries and Laura Ries, "First Do Some Publicity," *Advertising Age,* February 8, 1999, p. 42. Also see Al Ries and Laura Ries, *The Fall of Advertising and the Rise of PR* (New York: HarperBusiness, 2002). For points and counterpoints and discussions of the role of public relations, see O. Burtch Drake, "'Fall' of Advertising? I Differ," *Advertising Age,* January 13, 2003, p. 23; Robert E. Brown, "Book Review: The Fall of Advertising & the Rise of PR," *Public Relations Review,* March 2003, pp. 91–93; Mark Cheshire, "Roundtable Discussion—Making & Moving the Message," *Daily Record,* January 30, 2004, p. 1; and David Robinson. "Public Relations Comes of Age," *Business Horizons,* May–June 2006, pp. 247+.

43. Adapted from Todd Wasserman, "Word Games," *Brandweek,* April 24, 2006, pp. 24–28.

44. See "Butterball Turkey Talk-Line Fact Sheet," accessed at www.butterball.com, October 2007.

45. Paul Holmes, "Senior Marketers Are Sharply Divided About the Role of PR in the Overall Mix," *Advertising Age,* January 24, 2005, pp. C1–C2.

Chapter 13

1. Quotes and other information from Jeff O'Heir, "Michael Krasny—IT Sales Innovator," *Computer Reseller News,* November 18, 2002; Ed Lawler, "Integrated Campaign Winner: CDW Computer Centers," *BtoB,* December 9, 2002, p. 20; Chuck Salter, "The Soft Sell," *Fast Company,* January 2005, pp. 72–73; "CDW Corporation," *Hoover's Company Records,* June 15, 2007, p. 16199; Paolo Del Nibletto, "CDW Goes to Class," *Computer Dealer News,* May 25, 2007, p. 20; and www.cdw.com, accessed October 2007.

2. Based on information in Jennifer J. Salopek, "Bye, Bye, Used Car Guy," *T+D*, April 2007, pp. 22–25.

3. This extract and strategies that follow are based on Philip Kotler, Neil Rackham, and Suj Krishnaswamy, "Ending the War Between Sales and Marketing," *Harvard Business Review*, July–August 2006, pp. 68–78. Also see, Timothy Smith, Srinath Gopalakrishna, and Rabikar Chatterjee, "A Three-Stage Model of Integrated Marketing Communications at the Marketing-Sales Interface," *Journal of Marketing Research*, November 2006, pp. 564–79.

4. See "Lear Corp. Honored by GM as Supplier of the Year," *St. Charles County Business Record*, May 10, 2006, p. 1; Andy Cohen, "Top of the Charts: Lear Corporation," *Sales & Marketing Management*, July 1998, p. 40; and "Lear Corporation," *Hoover's Company Records*, June 15, 2007, p. 17213.

5. "Selling Power 500," accessed at www.sellingpower.com/sp500/index.asp, October 2007.

6. For more on this and other methods for determining sales force size, see William L. Cron and Thomas E. DeCarlo, *Sales Management*, 9th ed. (New York: John Wiley & Sons, 2006), pp. 84–85.

7. Theodore Kinni, "The Team Solution," *Selling Power*, April 2007, pp. 27–29.

8. Roy Chitwood, "Making the Most out of Each Outside Sales Call," February 4, 2005, accessed at http://seattle.bizjournals.com/seattle/stories/2005/02/07/smallb3.html; and "The Cost of the Average Sales Call Today Is More Than $400," *Business Wire*, February 28, 2006.

9. See Kristine M. Becker, "When the Law Says 'Do Not Call'," *ABA Bank Marketing*, May 2007, pp. 36–41.

10. Carol Krol, "Telemarketing Team Rings Up Sales for Avaya," *BtoB*, October 10, 2005, p. 34. For more on the Avaya's sales strategy, see Julia Chang, "On Top of the World," *Sales & Marketing Management*, January–February 2006, pp. 31–36.

11. See Martin Everett, "It's Jerry Hale on the Line," *Sales & Marketing Management*, December 1993, pp. 75–79. Also see, Irene Cherkassky, "Target Marketing," *BtoB*, October 2006, pp. 22–24.

12. Adapted from Chuck Salter, "The Soft Sell," *Fast Company*, January 2005, pp. 72–73. See also, "Minding Our Business," *Multichannel Merchant*, March 2006, p. 1.

13. William F. Kendy, "No More Lone Rangers," *Selling Power*, April 2004, pp. 70–74. Also see, Michelle Nichols, "Pull Together—Or Fall Apart," *BusinessWeek Online*, December 2, 2005, accessed at www.businessweek.com; and Theodore Kinni, "The Team Solution," *Selling Power*, April 2007, pp. 27–29.

14. "Customer Business Development," accessed at www.pg.com/jobs/jobs_us/work_we_offer/advisor_overview.jhtml?sl=jobs_advisor_business_development, November 2007.

15. For more information and discussion, see Benson Smith, *Discover Your Strengths: How the World's Greatest Salespeople Develop Winning Careers* (New York: Warner Business Books, 2003); Henry Canaday, "Recruiting the Right Stuff," *Selling Power*, April 2004, pp. 94–96; Tom Andel, "How to Cultivate Sales Talent," *Official Board Markets*, April 23, 2005, pp. 14–16; Kevin McDonald, "Therapist, Social Worker, or Consultant?" *CRN*, December 2005–January 2006, p. 24; and Tom Reilly, "Planning for Success," *Industrial Distribution*, May 2007, p. 25.

16. Geoffrey James, "The Return of Sales Training," *Selling Power*, May 2004, pp. 86–91. See also, Rebecca Aronauer, "Tracking Your Investment," *Sales & Marketing Management*, October 2006, p. 13; and Geoffrey James, "Training: A Wise Choice," *Selling Power*, January–February 2007, pp. 88–90.

17. David Chelan, "Revving Up E-Learning to Drive Sales," *EContent*, March 2006, pp. 28–32. Also see, "E-Learning Evolves into Mature Training Tool," *T+D*, April 2006, p. 20; Rebecca Aronauer, "The Classroom vs. E-Learning," *Sales & Marketing Management*, October 2006, p. 21; and Harry Sheff, "Agent Training Beyond the Classroom," *Call Center Magazine*, April 2007, p. 18.

18. From David Chelan, "Revving Up E-Learning to Drive Sales," *EContent*, March 2006, pp. 28–32; and "International Rectifier Drives Sales with Global E-Leaning Initiative," GeoLearning case study, accessed at www.geolearning.com/main/customers/ir.cfm, October 2007.

19. Joseph Kornak, "'07 Compensation Survey: What's It All Worth?" *Sales & Marketing Management*, May 2007, pp. 28–39.

20. See Henry Canady, "How to Increase the Times Reps Spend Selling," *Selling Power*, March 2005, p. 112; George Reinfeld, "8 Tips to Help Control the Hand of Time," *Printing News*, January 9, 2006, p. 10; and David J. Cichelli, "Plugging Sales 'Time Leaks'," *Sales & Marketing Management*, April 2006, p. 23; Rebecca Aronauer, "Time Well Spent," *Sales & Marketing Management*, January–February 2007, p. 7; and Dave Bradford, "Finding More Time for Selling," *Electrical Wholesaling*," April 2007, pp. 66–67.

21. See Gary H. Anthes, "Portal Powers GE Sales," *Computerworld*, June 2, 2003, pp. 31–32. Also see, Betsy Cummings, "Increasing Face Time," *Sales & Marketing Management*, January 2004, p. 12; David J. Cichelli, "Plugging Sales 'Time Leaks'," *Sales & Marketing Management*, April 2006, p. 23; and Tom Reilly, "Planning for Success," *Industrial Distribution*, May 2007, p. 25.

22. For extensive discussions of sales force automation, see the May 2005 issue of *Industrial Marketing Management*, which is devoted to the subject; Gary K. Hunter and William D. Perreault, "Making Sales Technology Effective," *Journal of Marketing*, January 2007, pp. 16–34; and Mary M. Long, Thomas Tellefsen, and J. David Lichtenthal, "Internet Integration into the Industrial Selling Process: A Step-By-Step Approach," *Industrial Marketing Management*, July 2007, pp. 676–89.

23. Quotes from Bob Donath, "Delivering Value Starts with Proper Prospecting," *Marketing News*, November 10, 1997, p. 5; and Bill Brooks, "Power-Packed Prospecting Pointers," *Agency Sales*, March 2004, p. 37. Also see, Gerhard Gschwandtner, "The Basics of Successful Selling," *Selling Power*, 25th anniversary issue, 2007, pp. 22–26.

24. Adapted from Charlotte Huff, "EXTREME Makeover," *Workforce Management*, May 8, 2006, p. 1.

25. Quotes from William Kendy, "Learning to Listen," *Selling Power*, July–August 2006, p. 25; and Gerhard Gschwandtner, "The Basics of Successful Selling," *Selling Power*, 25th anniversary issue, 2007, pp. 22–26.

26. Betsy Cummings, "Listening for Deals," *Sales & Marketing Management*, August 2005, p. 8. Also see, Michele Marchetti, "Listen to Me!" *Sales and Marketing Management*, April 2007, p. 12.

27. Adapted from Rebecca Aronauer, "Looking Good," *Sales and Marketing Management*, April 2006, pp. 41–45.

28. *Shopper-Centric Trade: The Future of Trade Promotion* (Cannondale Associates: Wilton, CT, October 2007), p. 15.

29. Based on information and quotes from Helen Leggatt, "PostPoints Rewards Readers for Reading," *Biz Report: Loyalty Marketing*, April 2, 2007, accessed at www.bizreport.com; and www.washingtonpost.com/postpoints, October 2007.

30. See Donna L. Montaldo, "2006 Coupon Usage Trends," accessed at http://couponing.about.com, May 2007; and Jack Neff, "Package-Goods Players Just Can't Quit Coupons," *Advertising Age*, May 14, 2007, p. 8.

31. Quotes and other information from Alan J. Liddle, "Hardee's Connects with Mobile Device Users, Offer Discounts," *Nation's Restaurant News*, May 14, 2007, p. 16; and www.cellfire.com, accessed August 2007.

32. See "Promotional Products—Impact, Exposure, and Influence" at Promotional Products Association International Web site, www.ppai.org, accessed October 2007; Stacey Burling, "Your Logo Sells Here," *The Philadelphia Enquirer*, May 31, 2006, accessed at www.philly.com/mld/philly/business/14702529.htm; and "The 2006 Estimate of Promotional Products Distributor Sales," accessed at Promotional Products Association International Web site, www.ppai.org, October 2007.

33. Adapted from information found in Betsey Spethmann, "Doritos Experiments with Sampling and Sweeps," *Promo*, June 19, 2007, accessed at http://promomagazine.com/contests/news/doritos_experiments_sampling_sweeps_061907/.

34. Jack Neff, "Specialists Thrive in Fast-Growing Events Segment," *Advertising Age*, March 19, 2007, pp. S2–S4.

35. Martha T. Moore, "Charmin Rolls Out 20 Restrooms in Times Square," *USA Today*, November 11, 2006, accessed at www.usatoday.com/news/nation/2006-11-21-charmin_x.htm.

36. *Shopper-Centric Trade: The Future of Trade Promotion* (Cannondale Associates: Wilton, CT, October 2007), p. 15.

37. See "International CES Defined by New Convergence of Broadband, Content, and Consumer Electronics," Consumer Electronics Association press release, January 11, 2007, accessed at Web site, www.cesweb.org; and "Worldwide Boom in Construction Helps Bauma to a Truly Superlative Performance," closing report 2007, accessed at www.bauma.de, June 2007.

Chapter 14

1. Quotes and other information from Nanette Byrnes et al., "Where Dell Went Wrong," *BusinessWeek*, February 19, 2007, p. 62; Christopher Lawton and Joann S. Lublin, "Dell's Founder Returns as CEO as Rollins Quits," *Wall Street Journal*, February 1, 2007, p. A1; Louise Lee, "It's Dell vs. the Dell Way," *BusinessWeek*, March 6, 2006, pp. 61–62; Kevin Allison, "Dell Broadens Sales Model," FT.com, May 16, 2007, p. 1; Christopher Lawton, "Dell to Rely Less on Direct Sales," *Wall Street Journal*, May 25, 2007, p. A3; "Dell to Sell Computers at Wal-Mart," *Financial Times*, May 25, 2007, p. 24, and www.dell.com/us/en/gen/corporate/access_company_direct_model.htm, accessed November 2007.

2. For these and other direct marketing statistics in this section, see Direct Marketing Association, "The DMA 2007 Statistical Fact Book," June 2007, pp. 223–24; and a wealth of other information accessed at www.the-dma.org, August 2007.

3. Portions adapted from Mike Beirne, *Brandweek*, October 23, 2006, p. 22; and Christopher Elliott, "Your Very Own Personal Air Fare," *New York Times*, August 9, 2005, p. C5.; "Southwest Airlines Announces San Francisco Treat," *PR Newswire*, May 11, 2007; Michael Leis, "What Happens in Vegas Stays on the Desktop," *iMedia Connection*, August 7, 2007, accessed at www.imediaconnection.com/content/16034.asp; and "What Is DING!?" accessed at www.southwest.com/ding/, November 2007.

4. Alicia Orr Suman, "Ideas You Can Take to the Bank! 10 Big Things All Direct Marketers Should Be Doing Now," *Target Marketing*, February 2003, pp. 31–33; Mary Ann Kleinfelter, "Know Your Customer," *Target Marketing*, January 2005, pp. 28–31; and Michele Fitzpatrick, "Socialize the Database Beyond Marketing," at www.dmnews.com, January 29, 2007.

5. Daniel Lyons, "Too Much Information," *Forbes*, December 13, 2004, p. 110; Mike Freeman, "Data Company Helps Wal-Mart, Casinos, Airlines Analyze Data," *Knight Ridder Business Tribune News*, February 24, 2006, p. 1; and John Foley, "Exclusive: Inside HP's Data Warehouse Gamble," *InformationWeek*, January 1–8, 2007, pp. 30–35.

6. Quotes from Scott Horstein, "Use Care with the Database," *Sales & Marketing Management*, May 2006, p. 22. Also see, Geoffrey Brewer, "The Customer Stops Here," *Sales & Marketing Management*, March 1998, pp. 31–36; "The Art of Service," *Fast Company*, October 2005, pp. 47–59; *Hoover's Company Records*, July 1, 2007, p. 40508; Travis E. Poling, "Business Week Says USAA Is Best in Nation When It Comes to Customer Service," *Knight Ridder Tribune Business News*, April 9, 2007, p. 1; and information from www.usaa.com, accessed November 2007.

7. Direct Marketing Association, "The DMA 2007 Statistical Fact Book," June 2007, p. 224.

8. David Ranii, "Compact Discs, DVDs Get More Use as Promotional Tool," *Knight Ridder Tribune Business News*, May 5, 2004, p. 1; and "DVD & CD Serious Cardz Increase Response Rate over 1,000% over Traditional Direct Marketing," *Market Wire*, January 10, 2007, p. 1.

9. See Louise Lee, "Catalogs, Catalogs, Everywhere," *BusinessWeek*, December 4, 2006, p. 32.

10. Direct Marketing Association, "The DMA 2007 Statistical Fact Book," June 2007, p. 224.

11. Karen E. Kleing, "Making It with Mail-Order," *BusinessWeek*, January 23, 2006, accessed at www.businessweek.com.

12. See "About Lillian Vernon," accessed at www.lillianvernon.com, August 2007.

13. Direct Marketing Association, "The DMA 2006 Statistical Fact Book," June 2006, p. 250.

14. Christopher S. Rugaber, "Do Not Call List Expanded 23% to 132M U.S. Phone Numbers in 2006, Federal Agency Says," *Associated Press*, April 5, 2007.

15. Ira Teinowitz, "Do Not Call Does Not Hurt Direct Marketing," *Advertising Age*, April 11, 2005, pp. 3, 95.

16. Teinowitz, "'Do Not Call Does Not Hurt Direct Marketing," p. 3.

17. Ron Donoho, "One-Man Show," *Sales & Marketing Management*, June 2001, pp. 36–42; information accessed at www.ronco.com, March 2004; and Brian Steinberg, "Read This Now!; But Wait! There's More! The Infomercial King Explains," *Wall Street Journal*, March 9, 2005, p. 1.

18. Jack Neff, "What Procter & Gamble Learned from Veg-O-Matic," *Advertising Age*, April 10, 2006, pp. 1, 65; and Jack Neff, "P&G Turns Lights Out on DRTV Players," *Advertising Age*, March 19, 2007, p. 3.

19. Steve McLellan, "For a Whole New DRTV Experience, Call Now," *Adweek*, September 5, 2005, p. 10; Jack Neff, "What Procter & Gamble Learned from Veg-O-Matic," p. 1; and "Analysis: Can DRTV Really Build Brands Better Than Image Ads?" *Precision Marketing*, February 9, 2007, p. 11.

20. Adapted from portions of Elizabeth Esfahani, "A Sales Channel They Can't Resist," *Business 2.0*, September 2005, pp. 91–96. Also see, Stacey Burling, "The Ultimate Sell Job," *Knight Ridder Tribune Business News*, February 18, 2007, p. 1.

21. Diane Anderson, "HP Developing Retail Kiosks to Reach 'iMoms'," *Brandweek*, March 6, 2006, p. 12; Chris Jones, "Kiosks Put Shopper in Touch," *Knight Ridder Tribune Business News*, April 11, 2006, p. 1; David Eisen, "Hilton Debuts Air Checkin Kiosk," *Business Travel News*, May 1, 2006, p. 8; and Linda Formichelli, "Putting Kiosks to Work," *Multichannel Merchant*, May 1, 2007, p. 87.

22. "Interactive: Ad Age Names Finalists," *Advertising Age*, February 27, 1995, pp. 12–14.

23. Alice Z. Cuneo, "Scramble for Content Drives Mobile," *Advertising Age*, October 24, 2005, p. S6; and "CTIA: The Wireless Association," accessed June 2007 at www.ctia.org.

24. "Mobile Marketing," *Marketing News,* April 1, 2006, p. 4. The following example is adapted from Paul Davidson, "Ad Campaigns for Your Tiny Cell Phone Screen Get Bigger," *USA Today,* August 9, 2006, accessed at www.usatoday.com/tech/wireless/2006-08-08-mobile-ads_x.htm.

25. For this and other examples, see Alice Z. Cuneo, "Marketers Get Serious About the Third Screen," *Advertising Age,* July 11, 2005, p. 6; and Louise Story, "Madison Avenue Calling," *New York Times,* January 20, 2007, accessed at www.nytimes.com.

26. Davidson, "Ad Campaigns for Your Tiny Cell Phone Screen Get Bigger," p. 2; Julie Schlosser, "Get Outta My Phone," *Fortune,* February 10, 2007, p. 20; and Emily Burg, "Acceptance of Mobile Ads on the Rise," *MediaPostPublications,* March 16, 2007, accessed at http://publications.mediapost.com.

27. See Abbey Klaassen and Leslie Taylor, "Few Compete to Settle Podcasting's Wild West," *Advertising Age,* April 24, 2006, p. 13; "E-Marketer Sees Big Future for Podcast Ads," *BtoB,* March 13, 2006, p. 6; Jim Pollock, "Suddenly, It's the Podcast Era," *Des Moines Business Record,* April 17, 2006, p. 1; and "Don't Quit Your Day Job Podcasters," *BusinessWeek,* April 9, 2007, p. 72.

28. For these and other examples, see Karyn Strauss and Derek Gale, *Hotels,* March 2006, p. 22; "Disneyland Offers Behind-the-Scenes Podcast," *Wireless News,* February 19, 2006, p. 1; and Kate Calder, "Hot Topic Cranks Its Music Biz," *Kidscreen,* May 2007, p. 22.

29. Steve Miller, "Ford to Use Video, Music to Snare Buyers," *Brandweek,* January 29, 2007, accessed at www.brandweek.com.

30. See Daisy Whitney, "Marketers Quick to Say 'Yes' to Opt-In TV Fare," *Advertising Age,* October 24, 2005, p. S4; "Nickelodeon Runs SeaWord iTV Ads," *New Media Age,* April 27, 2006, p. 3; and Joe Mandese, "P&G Goes Interactive for Tide to Go," *MediaPostPublications,* October 17, 2006, accessed at www.publications.mediapost.com. The Disney example is adapted from Kimi Yoshino, "Disney Aims to Sell Trips via TV Remote," *Los Angeles Times,* May 16, 2007, p. C1.

31. For these and other statistics on Internet usage, see "United States: Average Web Usage," *Nielsen/NetRatings,* June 2007, accessed at www.nielsen-netratings.com.

32. See Les Luchter, "Study: Internet 2nd Most Essential Medium, but #1 in Coolness," June 27, 2007, accessed at www.publications.mediapost.com.

33. See "America's Top Ten Retail Businesses," accessed at www.internetretailer.com/top500/list.asp, August 2007.

34. See Tom Sullivan, "A Lot More than Paper Clips," *Barron's,* April 16, 2007, pp. 23–25; and information from www.officedepot.com, accessed November 2007.

35. See "Consumer Internet Usage," *Advertising Age FactPack,* April 23, 2007, p. 28; and "Online Clothing Sales Surpass Computers, According to Shop.Org/Forrester Research Study," May 14, 2007, accessed at www/shop.org.

36. "JupiterResearch Forecasts Online Retail Spending Will Reach $144 Billion in 2010, a CAGR of 12% from 2005," February 6, 2006, accessed at www.jupitermedia.com/corporate/releases/06.02.06-newjupresearch.html.

37. Information for this example accessed at http://quickenloans.quicken.com, November 2007.

38. Information for this example accessed at www.dell.com/html/us/segments/pub/premier/tutorial/users_guide.html, August 2007.

39. See Kim Wright Wiley, "Meg Whitman: The $40 Billion eBay Sales Story," *Selling Power,* November–December, 2005, pp. 63–70; "eBay Inc.," *Hoover's Company Records,* June 1, 2007, p. 56307; and facts from eBay annual reports and other information accessed at www.ebay.com, September 2007.

40. Beth Snyder Bulik, "Who Blogs?" *Advertising Age,* June 4, 2007, p. 20.

41. Michael Barbaro, "Wal-Mart Enlists Bloggers in Its Public Relations Campaign," *New York Times,* March 7, 2006, p. C1.

42. See David Ward, "GM Blog Keeps Everyone up to Speed," *PRWeek,* April 3, 2006, p. 7; "Corporate Blogging Pays Off," *COMMWEB,* January 26, 2007; and Kate Fitzgerald, "GM, Suzuki Use Medium to Connect with Car Junkies," *Advertising Age,* March 5, 2007, p. S4.

43. Pete Blackshaw, "Irrational Exuberance? I Hope We're Not Guilty," *Barcode Blog,* August 26, 2005, accessed at www.barcodefactory.com/wordpress/?p=72.

44. Laurie Peterson, "When It Comes to Blogs, It Pays to Listen," *MediaPostPublications,* September 29, 2006, accessed at www.publications.com.

45. Michelle Slatalla, "Toll-Free Apology Soothes Savage Beast," *New York Times,* February 12, 2004, p. G4; and information from www.planetfeedback.com/consumer, accessed August 2007.

46. Adapted from Jack Neff, "Media Owners Take Heed: P&G's Staid Old Web Site Has You Licked," *Advertising Age,* December 4, 2007, pp. 1, 38.

47. Adapted from Jena McGregor, "High-Tech Achiever: MINI USA," *Fast Company,* October 2004, p. 86; with information from www.miniusa.com, accessed November 2007.

48. Jeffrey F. Rayport and Bernard J. Jaworski, *e-Commerce* (New York: McGraw-Hill, 2001), p. 116. Also see, Goutam Chakraborty, "What Do Customers Consider Important in B2B Web Sites?" *Journal of Advertising,* March 2003, p. 50; and "Looks Are Everything," *Marketing Management,* March–April 2006, p. 7.

49. Internet Advertising Bureau, "Internet Advertising Revenues Grow 35% in 2006, Hitting a Record Close to $17 Billion," May 23, 2007, accessed at www.iab.net/news/pr_2007_05_23.asp; and Brain Morrissey, "Web Ad Spend Hits Record High," *Adweek,* March 7, 2007, accessed at www.adweek.com.

50. Elliis Booker, "Vivid 'Experiences' as the New Frontier," *BtoB,* March 14, 2005, p. 14; Karen J. Bannan, "Rich Media Rule Book," *BtoB,* March 13, 2006, pp. 27–30; and Lee Gomes, "As Web Ads Grow, Sites Get Trickier About Targeting You," *Wall Street Journal,* May 9, 2007, p. B1.

51. "U.S. Online Ad Spending by Format," *Digital Marketing and Media Fact Pack,* supplement to *Advertising Age,* April 23, 2007, p. 6; and Kaye, "2006 Online Ad Spending Hits Nearly $17 Billion," May 23, 2007, accessed at www.clickz.com.

52. Adapted from Jon Fine, "Rise of the Lowly Search Ad," *BusinessWeek,* April 24, 2006, p. 24; and Brian Morrissey, "Like Honda for Chocolate: Branding via Keywords," *Adweek,* October 23, 2006, p. 14.

53. Danielle Sacks, "Down the Rabbit Hole," *Fast Company,* November 2006, pp. 86–93.

54. See Devin Leonard, "Viral Ads: It's an Epidemic," *Fortune,* October 2, 2006, p. 61; and T. L. Stanley, "Eat That, Subservient Chicken: OfficeMax Site Draws 36M," *Advertising Age,* January 29, 2007, pp. 4, 35.

55. Adapted from information found in Bob Garfield, "War & Peace and Subservient Chicken," April 26, 2004, accessed at www.adage.com; Gregg Cebrzynski, "Burger King Says It's OK to Have Your Way with the Chicken," *Nation's Restaurant News,* May 10, 2004, p. 16; and Bruce Horowitz, "Burger King of Cool," *USA Today,* February 7, 2007, accessed at www.usatoday.com.

56. Example from information in Brooke Capps, "How to Succeed in Second Life," *Advertising Age,* May 28, 2007, p. 6; information from www.motoratilife.com, accessed August 2007.

57. See "U.S. E-Mail Marketing Spending and User Data," *Digital Marketing and Media Fact Pack,* supplement to *Advertising Age,* April 23,

2007, p. 44; and Direct Marketing Association, "The DMA 2007 Statistical Fact Book," June 2007, p. 223.

58. "May Spam and Virus Statistics Released by Softscan," *Telecomworldwire,* June 4, 2007, p. 1.

59. Adapted from Regina Brady, "Profitable E-Mail," *Target Marketing,* April 2007, pp. 21–22.

60. Linda Zebian, "Special Report: Achieving A Bigger Payoff Through Targeted E-Mail Marketing Solutions," *Folio,* March 2007, pp. 42–44.

61. "Sweepstakes Groups Settles with States," *New York Times,* June 27, 2001, p. A14; "PCH Reaches $34 Million Sweepstakes Settlement with 26 States," *Direct Marketing,* September 2001, p. 6; and Steve Higgins, "Reader's Digest Will Pay Up in Connecticut Sweepstakes Settlement," *Knight Ridder Tribune Business News,* March 29, 2005, p. 1.

62. See Internet Crime Complaint Center, "Internet Crime Report 2006," accessed at www.ic3.gov/media/annualreport/2006_IC3Report.pdf; and Ed Finegold, "Internet-Like Services Bring Internet-Like Crime," *Billing World and OSS Today,* May 2007.

63. See Don Oldenburg, "Hook, Line, and Sinker: Personalized Phishing Scams Use Customers' Names to Attract Attention," *Washington Post,* April 2, 2006, p. F05; and "Is Someone 'Phishing' for Your Information?" accessed at www.ftc.gov/bcp/conline/pubs/alerts/phishregsalrt.shtm, June 2007.

64. See "Consumer Security Fears Continue to Rise in Banking Industry," *Business Wire,* December 14, 2006; and Tom Wright, "Online Card Use Stirs Fears Despite Relatively Low Fraud," *Cards and Payments,* April 2007, p. 16.

65. Adapted from Ben Elgin, "The Plot to Hijack Your Computer," *BusinessWeek,* July 17, 2006, p. 40. Also see, Joseph Menn, "Online Tunes Are More Risky Than Web Porn," *Los Angeles Times,* June 4, 2007, p. C3.

66. "14-Year-Old Bids over $3M for Items in eBay Auctions," *USA Today,* April 30, 1999.

67. See Jaikumar Vijayan, "First Online Data Privacy Law Looms in California," *Computerworld,* June 28, 2004, p. 12; "Does Your Privacy Policy Comply with the California Online Privacy Protection Act?" Banking and Financial Services Policy Report, January 2005, p. 7; Damon Darlin, "Don't Call. Don't Write. Let Me Be," *New York Times,* January 20, 2007; and Ira Tenowitz and Ken Wheaton, "Do Not Call," *Advertising Age,* March 12, 2007, pp. 1, 44.

68. See Jennifer DiSabatino, "FTC OKs Self-Regulation to Protect Children's Privacy," *Computerworld,* February 12, 2001, p. 32; Ann Mack, "Marketers Challenged on Youth Safeguards," *Adweek,* June 14, 2004, p. 12; Hiawatha Bray, "Google Faces Order to Give Up Records," *Knight Ridder Tribune Business News,* March 15, 2006, p. 1; and "COPPA Protects Children but Challenges Lie Ahead," *US Fed News,* February 27, 2007.

69. Information on TRUSTe accessed at www.truste.com, November 2007.

70. Information on the DMA Privacy Promise obtained at www.dmaconsumers.org/privacy.html, November 2007.

Chapter 15

1. Quotes and other information from John Dorschner, "World Catches NBA Fever," *Miami Herald,* June 15, 2006, accessed online at www.miamiherald.com; Marc Gunther, "They All Want to Be Like Mike," *Fortune,* July 21, 1997, pp. 51–53; Jon Robinson, "EA Sports Sponsors the NBA's Euroleague Invasion," accessed online at www.sports.ign.com, June 14, 2005; Janny Hu, "Europe Beckons, League Follows," *San Francisco Chronicle,* December 25, 2005, p. C5; Carol Matlack, "*Le Basket* Struggles to Score," *BusinessWeek,* May 22, 2006, p. 45; Russell Adams, "NBA Commissioner Gets Kudos but Has Work to

Do,"*Associated Press,* January 17, 2007; Christopher Bodeen, "Cavaliers, Magic Coming to China," *Associated Press,* March 29, 2007; and Steve Wiseman, "NBA Site Produces International Hits," *Knight Ridder Tribune Business News,* June 3, 2007, p.1.

2. Data from Michael V. Copeland, "The Mighty Micro-Multinational," *Business 2.0,* July 28, 2006, accessed at cnnmoney.com; "Fortune 500," *Fortune,* April 30, 2007, accessed at http://money.cnn.com/magazines/fortune/fortune500/2007/; and "List of Countries by GDP," *Wikipedia,* accessed at http://en.wikipedia.org/wiki/List_of_countries_by_GDP_%28nominal%29, November 2007.

3. World Bank, *Global Economic Prospects, 2007,* June 3, 2005, accessed at www.worldbank.org; CIA, *The World Factbook,* accessed at www.cia.gov, June 2007; and WTO, "Risks Lie Ahead Following Stronger Trade in 2006, WTO Reports," WTO press release, April 12, 2007, accessed at www.wto.org/english/news_e/pres07_e/pr472_e.htm.

4. Information from www.michelin.com/corporate and www.jnj.com, accessed October 2007.

5. Steve Hamm, "Borders Are So 20th Century," *BusinessWeek,* September 22, 2003, pp. 68–73; and "Otis Elevator Company," *Hoover's Company Records,* June 15, 2007, p. 56332.

6. Adapted from information in Brian Bremner and Dexter Robests, "How Beijing Is Keeping Banks at Bay," *BusinessWeek,* October 2, 2006, p. 42.

7. "What Is the WTO?" accessed at www.wto.org/english/thewto_e/whatis_e/whatis_e.htm, September 2007.

8. See *WTO Annual Report 2005,* accessed at www.wto.org, September 2007; and World Trade Organization, "10 Benefits of the WTO Trading System," accessed at www.wto.org/english/thewto_e/whatis_e/whatis_e.htm, September 2007.

9. Peter Coy, "Why Free-Trade Talks Are in Free Fall," *BusinessWeek,* May 22, 2006, p. 44; and "Congress Faces Key Decisions as Efforts to Reach Doha Agreement Intensify," *GAO Reports,* March 5, 2007.

10. "The European Union at a Glance," accessed online at http://europa.eu/abc/index-en.htm, September 2007.

11. "Overviews of European Union Activities: Economic and Monetary Affairs," accessed at http://europa.eu.int/pol/emu/overview_en.htm, September 2007.

12. See "European Union's Heated Budget Negotiations Collapse," *New York Times,* June 18, 2005, p. A3; "Leaders: A Constitutional Conundrum," *Economist,* June 16, 2007, p. 14; CIA, *The World Factbook,* accessed at http://www.cia.gov, June 2007.

13. Statistics and other information from CIA, *The World Factbook,* accessed at www.cia.gov, June 2007; and "Trade Facts: NAFTA—A Strong Record of Success," Office of the United States Trade Representative, March 2006, accessed at www.ustr.gov/assets/Document_Library/Fact_Sheets/2006/asset_upload_file242_9156.pdf.

14. See Angela Greiling Keane, "Counting on CAFTA," *Traffic World,* August 8, 2005, p. 1; "Integrating the Americas: FTAA and Beyond," *Journal of Common Market Studies,* June 2005, p. 430; Diana Kinch, "Latin America: Mercosul Boosted," *Metal Bulletin Monthly,* February 2006, p. 1; "Foreign Trade Statistics," accessed at www.census.gov, June 2007; Kevin Z. Jiang, "Americas: Trading Up?" *Harvard International Review,* Spring 2006, pp. 10–12; and Peter Hadekel, "FTAA Much Tougher Sell These Days," *Montreal Gazette,* June 22, 2007, p. B1.

15. Mary Turck, "South American Community of Nations," Resource Center of the Americas.org, accessed at www.americas.org, August 2006; "Former Ecuador President Borja Accepts S. America Union Presidency," *Xinhua General News Service,* May 9, 2007; and "Union of South American Nations," *Wikipedia,* accessed at http://en.wikipedia.org/wiki/South_American_Community_of_Nations, July 2007.

16. Adapted from information found in Clay Chandler, "China Deluxe," *Fortune,* July 26, 2004, pp. 148–56; and "Brand Strategy in China: Luxury Looks East," *Brand Strategy,* June 12, 2007, p. 56.

17. See Om Malik, "The New Land of Opportunity," *Business 2.0,* July 2004, pp. 72–79; "India Economy: South Asia's Worst Business Environment," *EIU ViewsWire,* January 2006; and Andy Stone, "India's Roads to Riches," *Forbes,* May 21, 2007, pp. 84–86.

18. Ricky Griffin and Michael Pustay, *International Business,* 4th ed. (Upper Saddle River, NJ: Prentice Hall, 2005), pp. 522–23.

19. For other examples, see Emma Hall, "Do You Know Your Rites? BBDO Does," *Advertising Age,* May 21, 2007, p. 22.

20. Jamie Bryan, "The Mintz Dynasty," *Fast Company,* April 2006, pp. 56–61; and Viji Sundaram, "Offensive Durga Display Dropped," *India-West,* February 2006, p. A1.

21. For other examples and discussion, see www.executiveplanet.com, accessed December 2006; *Dun & Bradstreet's Guide to Doing Business Around the World* (Upper Saddle River, NJ: Prentice Hall, 2000); Ellen Neuborne, "Bridging the Culture Gap," *Sales & Marketing Management,* July 2003, p. 22; Richard Pooley, "When Cultures Collide," *Management Services,* Spring 2005, pp. 28–31; and Helen Deresky, *International Management,* 5th ed. (Upper Saddle River, NJ: Prentice Hall, 2006).

22. Danielle Long, "Clean & Clear," *Revolution,* February 1, 2007, p. 69.

23. Adapted from Mark Rice-Oxley, "In 2,000 Years, Will the World Remember Disney or Plato?" *Christian Science Monitor,* January 15, 2004, p. 16.

24. Thomas L. Friedman, *The Lexus and the Olive Tree: Understanding Globalization* (New York: Anchor Books, 2000).

25. Robert Berner and David Kiley, "Global Brands," *BusinessWeek,* August 1, 2005, pp. 86–94; and "The 100 Top Brands 2006," *BusinessWeek,* August 7, 2006, accessed at www.businessweek.com. Also see, Millward Brown, "2007 BRANDZ Top 100 Most Powerful Brands," accessed at www.millwardbrown.com, August 2007.

26. Portions adapted from information found in Mark Rice-Oxley, "In 2,000 Years, Will the World Remember Disney or Plato?" *Christian Science Monitor,* January 15, 2004, p. 16. See also, Liz Robbins, "The NBA and China Hope They've Found the Next Yao," *New York Times,* June 25, 2007, accessed at www.nytimes.com

27. Paulo Prada and Bruce Orwall, "A Certain 'Je Ne Sais Quoi' at Disney's New Park—Movie-Themed Site Near Paris Is Multilingual, Serves Wine—and Better Sausage Variety," *Wall Street Journal,* March 12, 2002, p. B1. Also see "Euro Disney S. C. A.," *Hoover's Company Records,* June 15, 2007, p. 90721.

28. See Noreen O'Leary, "Bright Lights, Big Challenge," *Adweek,* January 15, 2007, pp. 22–28.

29. Vanessa O'Connell and Mei Fong, "Saks to Follow Luxury Brands into China," *Wall Street Journal,* April 18, 2006, p. B1; and "Saks Fifth Avenue Hits Roadblock in China," *Women's Wear Daily,* March 12, 2007, p. 2.

30. See Cynthia Kemper, "KFC Tradition Sold Japan on Chicken," *Denver Post,* June 7, 1998, p. J4; and Yum Brands Inc. restaurant count, accessed at www.yum.com/investors/restcounts.asp, August 2007. See also Susan Hamaker, "A Christmas Tradition?" accessed at www.internet-okinawa.com/articles/kfc/index.htm, June 25, 2007.

31. Quotes from Pankaj Ghemawat, "Regional Strategies for Global Leadership," *Harvard Business Review,* December 2005, pp. 97–108; and Ben Laurance, "Unilever Learns to Join the Dots," *Sunday Times,* March 18, 2007, p. B1. Also see, Pankaj Ghemawat, "Managing Differences," *Harvard Business Review,* March 2007, pp. 59–68.

32. Warren J. Keegan, *Global Marketing Management,* 7th ed. (Upper Saddle River, NJ: Prentice Hall, 2002), pp. 346–51. Also see, Phillip Kotler and Kevin Lane Keller, *Marketing Management,* 12th ed. (Upper Saddle River, NJ: 2006), pp. 677–84.

33. Adapted from Jack Ewing, "First Mover in Mobile; How It's Selling Cell Phones to the Developing World," *BusinessWeek,* May 14, 2007, p. 60.

34. See Douglas McGray, "Translating Sony into English," *Fast Company,* January 2003, p. 38; James Coates, "Chicago Tribune Binary Beat Column," *Chicago Tribune,* January 9, 2005, p. 1; and Daniel Robinson, "Ultra-Mobile Punches Above Its Weight," *IT Week,* May 7, 2007, p. 16.

35. Adapted from Gordon Fairclough and Janet Adamy, "Sex, Skin, Fireworks, Licked Fingers—It's a Quarter Pounder Ad in China," *Wall Street Journal,* September 21, 2006, p. B1.

36. Kate MacArthur, "Coca-Cola Light Employs Local Edge," *Advertising Age,* August 21, 2000, pp. 18–19; and "Case Studies: Coke Light Hottest Guy," *Advantage Marketing,* msn India, accessed at http://advantage.msn.co.in, March 15, 2004.

37. See Alicia Clegg, "One Ad One World?" *Marketing Week,* June 20, 2002, pp. 51–52; Ira Teinowitz, "International Advertising Code Revised," *Advertising Age,* January 23, 2006, p. 3; and George E. Belch and Michael A. Belch, *Advertising and Promotion: An Integrated Marketing Communications Perspective,* 7th ed. (New York: McGraw Hill, 2007), chapter 20.

38. Michael Schroeder, "The Economy: Shrimp Imports to U.S. May Face Antidumping Levy," *Wall Street Journal,* February 18, 2004, p. A.2; Woranuj Maneerungsee, "Shrimpers Suspect Rivals of Foul Play," *Knight Ridder Tribune Business News,* April 28, 2005, p. 1; David Bierderman, "Tough Journey," *Journal of Commerce,* March 13, 2006, p. 1; Clay Chandler, "Vietnam VroooooM," *Fortune,* December 11, 2006, p. 147.

39. Sarah Ellison, "Revealing Price Disparities, the Euro Aids Bargain-Hunters," *Wall Street Journal,* January 30, 2002, p. A15.

40. Adapted from Jack Ewing, "First Mover in Mobile; How It's Selling Cell Phones to the Developing World," *BusinessWeek,* May 14, 2007, p. 60.

41. See Leslie Chang, Chad Terhune, and Betsy McKay, "A Global Journal Report; Rural Thing—Coke's Big Gamble in Asia," *Wall Street Journal,* August 11, 2004, p. A1; and Ann Chen and Vijay Vishwanath, "Expanding in China," *Harvard Business Review,* March 1, 2005.

Chapter 16

1. Adapted from Jennifer Reingold, "Walking the Walk," *Fast Company,* November 2005, pp. 81–85; with additional information from "Timberland Celebrates Earthday 2007 by Hosting More Than 170 Service Projects and 9,000 Volunteers," *Business Wire,* April 19, 2007; and Mya Frazier, "Timberland 'Walks the Walk'," *Advertising Age,* June 11, 2007, p. S8.

2. Adapted from Kevin DeMarrais, "You Can't Believe Airlines' Ticket Ads," *Knight Ridder Tribune Business News,* April 2, 2006, p. 1.

3. Theodore Levitt, "The Morality (?) of Advertising," *Harvard Business Review,* July–August 1970, pp. 84–92. For counterpoints, see Heckman, "Don't Shoot the Messenger," *Marketing News,* May 24, 1999, pp. 1, 9.

4. "Elizabeth Warren on the Credit Card Industry," NRP's *Fresh Air,* March 27, 2007, accessed at www.npr.org/templates/story/story.php?storyId=9156929.

5. Roger Parloff, "Is Fat the Next Tobacco?" *Fortune,* February 3, 2003, pp. 51–54; "'Big Food' Get the Obesity Message," *New York Times,*

July 10, 2003, p. A22; Carl Hulse, "Vote in House Offers Shield in Obesity Suits," *New York Times,* March 11, 2004, p. A1; Amy Garber, "Twice-Tossed McD Obesity Suit Back on Docket," *Nation's Restaurant News,* February 7, 2005, pp. 1+; Marguerite Higgins, "Obesity-Lawsuit Bill Passes in House," *Washington Times,* October 20, 2005, p. C8; Lisa Bertagnoli, "Capitol Concerns," *Restaurants and Institutions,* January 1, 2006, pp. 47–48; and "Message from McDonald's," *Campaign,* April 20, 2007, p. 9.

6. Cliff Edwards, "Where Have All the Edsels Gone?" *Greensboro News & Record,* May 24, 1999, p. B6; Tim Cooper, "Inadequate Life? Evidence of Consumer Attitudes to Product Obsolescence," *Journal of Consumer Policy,* December 2004, pp. 421–48; David Hunter, "Planned Obsolescence Well Entrenched in Society," *Knoxville News-Sentinel,* August 15, 2005, p. B5; Atsuo Utaka, "Planned Obsolescence and Social Welfare," *Journal of Business,* January 2006, pp. 137–47; and Jessiac Harbert and Caleb Heeringga, "Pari Camp Out for Days to Be First to Buy Apple iPhones," *Knight Ridder Tribune Business News,* June 30, 2007, p. 1.

7. Adapted from David Suzuki, "We All Pay for Technology," *Niagara Falls Review,* March 15, 2007, p. A4.

8. For more discussion, see Denver D'Rozario and Jerome D. Williams, "Retail Redlining: Definition, Theory, Typology, and Measurement," *Journal of Macromarketing,* December 2005, pp. 175+.

9. See Brian Grow and Pallavi Gogoi, "A New Way to Squeeze the Weak?" *BusinessWeek,* January 28, 2002, p. 92; Judith Burns, "Study Finds Links in Credit Scores, Insurance Claims," *Wall Street Journal,* February 28, 2005, p. D3; Erik Eckholm, "Black and Hispanic Home Buyers Pay Higher Interest on Mortgages, Study Finds," *New York Times,* June 1, 2006, p. A22; and Frank Phillips, "Battle Brewing on Auto Insurance," *Knight Ridder Tribune Business News,* July 1, 2007, p. 1.

10. "Increasing Incomes and Reducing the Rapid Refund Rip-Off," A report from the ACORN Financial Justice Center, September 2004, pp. 3–4; Tracy Turner, "H&R Block Makes Changes in Rapid-Refund Program," *Knight Ridder Tribune Business News,* January 29, 2005, p. 1; "California Sues H&R Block," *Knight-Ridder Tribune Business News,* February 16, 2006; and Candace Jarrett, "State: Be Aware of Rapid Loan Fees," *Knight Ridder Tribune Business News,* February 10, 2007, p. 1.

11. Information from "Shop 'til They Drop?" *Christian Science Monitor,* December 1, 2003, p. 8; Gregg Easterbrook, "The Real Truth About MONEY," *Time,* January 17, 2005, pp. 32–35; Bradley Johnson, "Day in the Life: How Consumers Divvy Up All the Time They Have," *Advertising Age,* May 2, 2005; Rich Miller, "Too Much Money," *BusinessWeek,* July 11, 2005, pp. 59–66; and "Bankers Encourage 'Consumer Generation' to Save," *Texas Banking,* March 2006, pp. 25–26. For more on materialism as it relates to quality of life, see James A. Roberts and Aimee Clement, "Materialism and Satisfaction with Over-All Quality of Life Domains," *Social Indicators Research,* May 2007, pp. 72–92.

12. Portions adapted from Constance L. Hays, "Preaching to Save Shoppers from 'Evil' of Consumerism," *New York Times,* January 1, 2003, p. C1; and "A Preacher's Plea to Stop the 'Shopocalypse'," *Knight Ridder Tribune Business News,* December 11, 2006. Also see, Jo Littler, "Beyond the Boycott," *Cultural Studies,* March 2005, pp. 227–52; and www.revbilly.com, accessed July 2007.

13. See Larry Copeland, "Traffic Jams Delay Drivers Millions of Hours," *USA Today,* May 10, 2005, accessed at www.usatoday.com.

14. See Dan Sturges, Gregg Moscoe, and Cliff Henke, "Innovations at Work: Transit and the Changing Urban Landscapes," *Mass Transit,* July–August 2006, pp. 34–38; John D. McKinnon, "Politics & Economics: Bush Plays Traffic Cop in Budget Request," *Wall Street Journal,* February 5, 2007, p. A6; and "A Rush-Hour Tax on Urban Drivers," *Christian Science Monitor,* February 7, 2007.

15. See Allison Linn, "Ads Inundate Public Places," *MSNBC.com,* January 22, 2007; and Bob Garfield, "The Chaos Scenario: The Post Advertising Age," *Advertising Age,* March 26, 2007, pp. 1, 12–13.

16. For more discussion, see Martin Sipkoff, "Wal-Mart, Other Discounters Facing Predatory-Pricing Concerns," *Drug Topics,* April 2007, pp. S10–S11.

17. See "UPS 'Green Fleet' Expands with 50 Hybrid Electric Vehicles," UPS press release, May 22, 2007, accessed at www.pressroom.ups.com.

18. Information from "Because We Can't Remanufacture the Earth . . . ," March 2005, accessed at www.xerox.com/downloads/usa/en/e/ehs_remanufacture_2005.pdf; and "Environmental Solutions that Work," April 2007, accessed at www.xerox.com/downloads/usa/en/e/Environmental_Overview.pdf.

19. Adapted from information found in Joseph Tarnowski, "Green Monster," *Progressive Grocer,* April 1, 2006, pp. 20–26. Also see "Wal-Mart Announces Solar Power Pilot Project; Pilot Project Marks Major Step Toward Its Goal of Being Supplied by 100 Percent Renewable Energy," *PR Newswire,* May 7, 2007; Sue Stock, "Wal-Mart Cutting Energy Use," *Raleigh News and Observer,* June 15, 2007, pp. 1D, 3D; and Danielle Sacks, "Working with the Enemy," *Fast Company,* September 2007, pp. 74–81.

20. Adapted from "The Top 3 in 2005," *Global 100,* accessed at www.global100.org, July 2005. See also, "Alcoa Named One of the Most Sustainable Corporations in the World for Third Year in a Row," January 25, 2007, accessed at www.aloca.com; and information from www.global100.org, accessed September 2007. For further information on Alcoa's sustainability program, see Alcoa's Sustainability Report found at www.alcoa.com.

21. See "EMAS: What's New?" accessed at http://europa.eu.int/comm/environment/emas, August 2007; "Special Report: Free Trade on Trial—Ten Years of NAFTA," *Economist,* January 3, 2004, p. 13; Daniel J. Tschopp, "Corporate Social Responsibility: A Comparison Between the United States and Europe," *Corporate Social-Responsibility and Environmental Management,* March 2005, pp. 55–59; "Three Countries Working Together to Protect our Shared Environment," Commission for Environmental Cooperation, accessed at www.cec.org/who_we_are/index.cfm?varlan=english, August 2007.

22. Information and quotes from Andy Milligan, "Samsung Points the Way for Asian Firms in Global Brand Race," *Media,* August 8, 2003, p. 8; Bill Breen, "The Seoul of Design," *Fast Company,* December 2005, pp. 91–98; "The 100 Top Brands," *BusinessWeek,* August 7, 2006, pp. 60–66; and Samsung Annual Reports and other information accessed at www.samsung.com, September 2007.

23. Information from Mike Hoffman, "Ben Cohen: Ben & Jerry's Homemade, Established in 1978," *Inc,* April 30, 2001, p. 68; and the Ben & Jerry's Web site at www.benjerrys.com, accessed September 2007.

24. Quotes and other information from Thea Singer, "Can Business Still Save the World?" *Inc,* April 30, 2001, pp. 58–71; and www.honesttea.com, accessed September 2007. Also see, Sarah Theodore, "More Than Tea, 'Honestly'," *Beverage Industry,* May 2007, pp. 22–25.

25. Adapted from Chip Giller and David Roberts, "Resources: The Revolution Begins," *Fast Company,* March 2006, pp. 73–78. Also see, "American Physical Therapy Association; Physical Therapists Endorse Office Chair," *Healthcare Mergers, Acquisitions & Ventures Week,* February 4, 2006, p. 15; Joseph Ogando, "Green Engineering," *Design News,* January 9, 2006, p. 65; and information accessed online at www.haworth.com, August 2007.

26. Joseph Webber, "3M's Big Cleanup," *BusinessWeek,* June 5, 2000, pp. 96–98. Also see, "What You Should Know about 3M's 'Next Generation' Scotchgard Protector Products," accessed at http://solutions.

3m.com/wps/portal/3M/en_US/Scotchgard/Home/Resources/Environmental/, August 2007.

27. See *Global Corruption Report 2007,* Transparency International, accessed at www.transparency.org/publications/gcr/download_gcr#download.

28. John F. McGee and P. Tanganath Nayak, "Leaders' Perspectives on Business Ethics," *Prizm,* First Quarter 1994, pp. 71–72. Also see, Adrian Henriques, "Good Decision—Bad Business?" *International Journal of Management & Decision Making,* 2005, p. 273; and Marylyn Carrigan, Svetla Marinova, and Isabelle Szmigin, "Ethics and International Marketing: Research Background and Challenges," *International Marketing Review,* 2005, pp. 481–94.

29. See Samuel A. DiPiazza, "Ethics in Action," *Executive Excellence,* January 2002, pp. 15–16; Samuel A. DiPiazza Jr., "It's All Down to Personal Values," accessed online at www.pwcglobal.com, August 2003; and "Code of Conduct: The Way We Do Business," accessed at www.pwcglobal.com/gx/eng/ins-sol/spec-int/ethics/index.html, September 2007. [PricewaterhouseCoopers (www.pwc.com) provides industry-focused assurance, tax, and advisory services to build public trust and enhance value for its clients and their stakeholders. More than 130,000 people in 148 countries across its network share their thinking, experience, and solutions to develop fresh perspectives and practical advice. 'PricewaterhouseCoopers' refers to the network of member firms of PricewaterhouseCoopers International limited, each of which is a separate and independent legal entity.]

30. DiPiazza, "Ethics in Action," p. 15.

Appendix 3

1. This is derived by rearranging the following equation and solving for price: Percentage markup = (price − cost) ÷ price.

2. The equation is derived from the basic profit = total revenue − total cost equation. Profit is set to equal the return on investment times the investment (ROI × I), total revenue equals price times quantity (P × Q), and total costs equals quantity times unit cost (Q × UC): ROI × I = (P × Q) − (Q × UC). Solving for P gives P = ((ROI × I) ÷ Q) + UC.

3. The breakeven volume equation can also be derived from the basic profit = total revenue − total cost equation. At the breakeven point, profit is equal to zero, and it is best to separate fixed and variable costs: 0 = (P × Q) − TFC − (Q = UVC). Solving for Q gives Q = TFC ÷ (P − UVC).

4. As in the previous note, this equation is derived from the basic profit = total revenue − total cost equation. However, unlike the break-even calculation, in which profit was set to equal zero, we set the profit equal to the dollar profit goal: Dollar profit goal = (P × Q) − TFC − (Q × UVC). Solving for Q gives Q = (TFC + dollar profit goal) ÷ (P − UVC).

5. Again, using the basic profit equation, we set profit equal to ROI × I: ROI × I = (P × Q) − TFC − (Q × UVC). Solving for Q gives Q = (TFC + (ROI × I)) ÷ (P − UVC).

6. Again, using the basic profit equation, we set profit equal to 25% of sales, which is 0.25 × P × Q: 0.25 × P × Q = (P × Q) − TFC − (Q × UVC). Solving for Q gives Q = TFC ÷ (P − UVC − (0.25 × P)) or TFC ÷ ((0.75 × P) − UVC).

7. "Nielson Finds More TVs; Hispanics Top 11 Million," *Advertising Age,* August 29, 2005, p. 1.

8. Consumer Electronics Association available at www.ce.org, accessed July 25, 2006.

9. Daisy Whitney, " '06 HDTV Sales to Outpace Analog," *Television Week,* October 31, 2005, 19–24.

10. See Roger J. Best, *Market-Based Management,* 4th ed. (Upper Saddle River, NJ: Prentice Hall, 2005).

11. Total contribution can also be determined from the unit contribution and unit volume: Total contribution = unit contribution × unit sales. Total units sold in 2006 were 297,619 units, which can be determined by dividing total sales by price per unit ($100 million ÷ $336). Total contribution = $70 contribution per unit × 297,619 units = $20,833,330 (difference due to rounding).

12. Recall that the contribution margin of 21% was based on variable costs representing 79% of sales. Therefore, if we do not know price, we can set it equal to $1.00. If price equals $1.00, 79 cents represents variable costs and 21 cents represents unit contribution. If price is decreased by 10%, the new price is $0.90. However, variable costs do not change just because price decreased, so the unit contribution and contribution margin decrease as follows:

	Old	New (reduced 10%)
Price	$1.00	$0.90
− Unit variable cost	$0.79	$0.79
= Unit contribution	$0.21	$0.11
Contribution margin	$0.21/$1.00 = 0.21 or 21%	$0.11/$0.90 = 0.12 or 12%

Credits

Chapter 1

2 Copyright © 2007 The Procter & Gamble Company. All rights reserved. Reprinted with permission. Images used with permission of actors. Talent: Frederika Kesten, Alejandro Quijano, and Emily Sullivan. **7** Photo by Jim White. Courtesy of LaSalle Bank. **10** Copyright © 2007 Ford Motor Company. All rights reserved. Reprinted with permission. Courtesy of RKCR/Y&R. **12** Courtesy of Johnson & Johnson. Reprinted with permission. **15** Courtesy of Bike Friday. **16** © 2007 Toyota Motor Sales. All rights reserved. Used with permission. **17** © 2007 Neiman Marcus. All rights reserved. Reprinted with permission. **18** AP Wide World Photos. **19** © 2007 Toyota Motor Sales. All rights reserved. Used with permission. **20** These materials have been reproduced with the permission of EepyBird.com and Atypical Entertainment. **23** Courtesy of Stew Leonard. **24** Copyright © 2007 GM. All rights reserved. Used with permission. **26** YouTube: Courtesy of YouTube, Inc. Used with permission. Doritoes commercial still is courtesy of Frito-Lay Inc. **28** Courtesy of Corbis/Bettmann. **34** Courtesy of Corbis/Bettmann.

Chapter 2

38 © 2007 EBAY INC. ALL RIGHTS RESERVED. **39** Courtesy of BASF Corporation. All rights reserved. Photographer: Ed James. **41** Courtesy of Corbis/Bettmann. **42** Courtesy of Corbis/Bettmann. **45** AP Wide World Photos. **46** Used with permission of Toyota Motor Manufacturing North America, Inc. All rights reserved. **50** Courtesy of Veterinary Pet Insurance Company. Used with permission. **49** © 2007 Helio LLC. All rights reserved. Used with permission. **55** Courtesy of Corbis. **57** © 2007 Marketing NPV LLC. All rights reserved. Used with permission.

Chapter 3

62 Used with permission from McDonald's Corporation. **67** "Coca-Cola and the Dynamic Ribbon design are registered trademarks of The Coca-Cola Company." **68** Used with permission of Wal-Mart Stores, Inc. All rights reserved. **69** Courtesy of Getty Images. **71** The following marks, New Retirement Mindscape^{SM}, Dream > Plan > Track >®, Dream Book® and Dreams don't retire.^{SM} are registered trademarks and servicemarks exclusively of Ameriprise Financial, Inc. © 2007 Ameriprise Financial, Inc. All rights reserved. Used with permission. **73** Courtesy of Corbis. **75** © 2006 Visa U.S.A. Inc. All rights reserved. Reprinted with permission. **76** Used with permission of Allstate. Photographer: Huey Tran. **77** Courtesy of Avis Rent A Car System. Used with permission. **80** © 2005 General Electric Company. All rights reserved. Used with permission. Courtesy of BBDO, New York. **81** Courtesy of Getty Images. **85** Courtesy of Getty Images. **86** © 2007 MasterCard Inc. All rights reserved. Used with permission. **88** © 2007 Earthbound Farm. All rights reserved. Used with permission. **90** Courtesy of Wal-Mart Stores, Inc. **94** Copyright © 2007 Sirius Satellite Radio, Inc. All rights reserved. Reprinted with permission.

Chapter 4

97 Courtesy of Corbis. **99** Courtesy of Corbis. **101** Courtesy of Getty Images. **105** Courtesy of Simmons Market Research Bureau. **106** Courtesy of Getty Images. **108** Courtesy of Corbis. **110** © 2007 Channel M2, LLC. All rights reserved. Used with permission. **115** © 2007 Salesforce.com, Inc. All rights reserved. Used with permission. **116** Courtesy of Digistock. **119** Copyright © 2005 Bibbentuckers. All rights reserved. Reprinted with permission. **120** © 2005 ACNielsen. All rights reserved. **124** © 1994–2005 American Express Company. All rights reserved. Used with permission.

Chapter 5

122 Courtesy of Getty Images. **128** Courtesy of Corbis/Bettmann. **133** Product photographer: Olof Wahlund. Beauty photographer: Patrick Demarchelier. Copyright © 2007 The Procter & Gamble Company. All rights reserved. Reprinted with permission. **134** Copyright © 2007 The PNC Financial Services Group, Inc. All rights reserved. Reprinted with permission. Ad provided courtesy of AdAsia Communications, Inc. **136** Copyright © 2007 The Procter & Gamble Company. All rights reserved. Reprinted with permission. Photographs © Stockbyte/Getty Images and Kevin Dodge/Corbis. **138** Courtesy of Adidas AG. Reprinted with permission. **139** General Motors Corp. Used with permission, GM Media Archives. **141** Copyright © 2007 Georgia Boot. All rights reserved. Used with permission. Photo © Craig Aurness/Corbis. **142** Courtesy of Getty Images. **144** Courtesy of Corbis. **145** Courtesy of the National Fluid Milk Processor Promotion Board. Reprinted with permission. **146** CLOROX is a registered trademark of The Clorox Company. Used with permission. **148** Copyright © 2007 The Procter & Gamble Company. All rights reserved. Reprinted with permission. **151** © 2007 Intel Corporation. All rights reserved. Photograph: Zach Gold. Used with permission. **152** Courtesy of Bilderberg Archiv der Fotografen. **155** Courtesy of Cardinal Health, Medical Products & Services. **156** © 1998 Volvo Trucks North America, Inc. © RIP-SAW, Inc. **158** Copyright © 2007 Sharp Electronics Company. All rights reserved. Photographer: Carl Zapp. Reprinted with permission. **160** © 2007 Sun Microsystems, Inc. All rights reserved. Used with permission.

Chapter 6

164 Courtesy of Corbis/Bettmann. **169** Courtesy of Getty Images. **170** © 2007 American Express Company. All rights reserved. Used with permission. **171** © 2007 The Coca-Cola Company. All rights reserved. Used with permission. **172** Reprinted courtesy of Doug Hardman, www.hardman.org. **173** © 2005 Claritas Inc. All Rights Reserved. **175** © 2007 The Coca-Cola Company. All rights reserved. Used with permission. **176** Courtesy of Anything Left-Handed. All rights reserved. **178** Photographer: Amanda Kamen. **179** Copyright © 2007 The Procter & Gamble Company. All rights reserved. Reprinted with permission. **180** Courtesy of Tony Hsieh. **182** © 2007 MINI, a division of BMW of North America, LLC. All rights reserved. The MINI and BMW trademark, model names and logo are registered trademarks. Photo courtesy of Newscast and MINI, a Division of BMW of North America, LLC. **184** Used with permission of Nacara Cosmetiques. All rights reserved. Not for reproduction. **186** © 2007 Toyota Motor Sales. All rights reserved. Used with permission. **187** © 2007 Staples Inc. All rights reserved. Used with permission. **188** © 2007 Panasonic Corporation of North America. All rights reserved. Used with permission. **189** Copyright © 2007 Unilever PLC. All rights reserved. Reprinted with permission. **191** Courtesy of AP Wide World Photos. **192** © 2007 Kraft Foods Inc. All rights reserved. Used with permission.

Chapter 7

196 Courtesy of Jupiter Images. **199** Courtesy of AP Images. **200** © 2007 Research In Motion Limited. All rights reserved. Used with permission. **202** Courtesy of BASF Corporation. All rights reserved. **205** © 2007 OXO International Inc. All rights reserved. Used with permission. **207** Courtesy of Pepsi-Cola North America, Inc. All rights reserved. **208** © 2007 Hewlett-Packard Development Company, L.P. Reproduced with permission. **209** Courtesy of Marriott International, Inc. All rights reserved. **213** © 2007 Viking Range Corporation. All rights reserved. Used with permission. **211** Courtesy of Redux Pictures. **214** Copyright © 2007 Godiva Chocolatier Inc. All rights reserved. Reprinted with permission. **215** Copyright © 2007 Costco Wholesale Corporation. All rights reserved. Reprinted with permission. **216** Courtesy of Nickelodeon. **223** Copyright © 2007 British Airways Plc. All rights reserved. Reprinted with permission. **224** Courtesy of Corbis. **224** Photographer: Alyson Aliano.

Chapter 8

230 Courtesy of Corbis. **234** Courtesy of NewProductWorks, a division of the Arbor Strategy Group. Used with permission. **235** Photographer: Ki Ho Park. **236** Copyright © 2007 The Procter & Gamble Company. All rights reserved. Reprinted with permission. **237** © 2007 Tesla Motors. All rights reserved. Used with permission. **239** Courtesy of Corbis/Sygma. **240** Copyright © 2007 Decision Insight. All rights reserved. Reprinted with permission. **241** Copyright © 2007 Microsoft Corporation. All rights reserved. Reprinted with permission. **245** Courtesy of Procter & Gamble. **246** The TABASCO® marks, bottle and label designs are registered trademarks and servicemarks exclusively of McIlhenny Company, Avery Island, LA 70513. www.TABASCO.com **247** Courtesy of Getty Images/Time Life Pictures. **249** © 2007 Deere & Company. All rights reserved. Used with permission. **253** Courtesy of Getty Images.

Chapter 9

256 Copyright © 2007 Ryanair Ltd. All rights reserved. Reprinted with permission. **259** Courtesy of AP Wide World Photos. **261** © 2007 Bentley Motors Inc. All rights reserved. Used with permission. **262** Photographer: Raghu Rai **265** PORSCHE and the PORSCHE CREST are registered trademarks and CAYMAN is a trademark and the distinctive shapes of PORSCHE automobiles are trade dress of Dr. Ing. H.c.F.Porsche AG. Used with permission of Porsche Cars North America, Inc. and Dr. Ing. H.c.F. Porsche AG. Copyrighted by Porsche Cars North America, Inc. **266** Alex Quesada/The New York Times/Redux. **268** © 2004 Moen Incorporated. All rights reserved. **269** © 2007 Gibson Guitar Corp. All rights reserved. Reprinted with permission. **271** Used by permission of Sony Electronics Inc. **272** Screen shot © Intuit Inc. All rights reserved. **273** © 2007 Eastman Kodak Company. All rights reserved. Used with permission. **276** Courtesy of D. Young-Wolf/PhotoEdit, Inc. **277** Courtesy of AP Wide World Photos. **279** Reproduced with permission of Yahoo! Inc. © 2007 by Yahoo! Inc. YAHOO! and the YAHOO! logo are trademarks of Yahoo! Inc. **281** © 2007 Dell Inc. All rights reserved. Used with permission. **283** © 2007 The Procter & Gamble Company. All rights reserved. Used with permission. **284** Courtesy of Getty Images.

Chapter 10

290 Reprinted courtesy of Caterpillar, Inc. **294** Courtesy of Calyx & Corolla. **298** Photographer: Joe and Kathy Heiner. **300** Courtesy of INDITEK. **301** Courtesy of Getty Images. **303** Courtesy of Redux Pictures. **304** © 1997–2007 Netflix, Inc. All rights reserved. Netflix and the Netflix logo are trademarks and/or service marks of Netflix, Inc. Used with permission. **307** Used with permission of Bentley Houston. **308** Courtesy of Corbis/Bettmann. **309** Copyright © 2007 Samsung Electronics America, Inc. All rights reserved. Reprinted with permission. **312** Courtesy of Fine Image Photography. **313** Prentice Hall School Division. **314** © 2007 Roadway Express, Inc. All rights reserved. Used with permission. **320** Photographer: Michael O'Neill. Used with permission.

Chapter 11

325 Courtesy of OrangeTwice. **325** Courtesy of Corbis/Bettmann. **327** Courtesy of Reuters. **329** Courtesy of Getty Images. **331** Courtesy of AP Wide World Photos. **332** Courtesy of Getty Images. **335** Used by permission of Sony Electronics Inc. **333** Courtesy of Getty Images. **335** Courtesy of New Town Associates, LLC. **337** © 2007 Staples Inc. All rights reserved. Used with permission. **338** © 2005 Food Lion, LLC. All rights reserved. **339** Courtesy of Getty Images. **340** Courtesy of W. W. Grainger, Inc. **348** © 2007 GEICO. All rights reserved. Used with permission.

Chapter 12

352 © moodboard/Corbis. **355** Nikon: Photographer: Sam Bayer. © 2007 Nikon Inc. All rights reserved. Used with permission. **356** Courtesy of Corbis/Photography veer Inc. **359** © 2007 Pizza Hut, Inc. All rights reserved. Used with permission. **361** © 2005 BMW of North America, LLC. All rights reserved. **362** Photo-Illustration by John Kucazala. **364** Cover image of Madison & Vine, by Scott Donaton. © 2004 The McGraw-Hill Companies.

Used with permission. **366** © 2007 Sanford, a Newell Rubbermaid Company. All rights reserved. Used with permission. **367** Advertisement provided courtesy of Frito-Lay, Inc. **369** Copyright © 2007 The Procter & Gamble Company. All rights reserved. Reprinted with permission. **372** Courtesy of Jupiter Images. **374** Used with permission of Gillette. All rights reserved. **376** Photographer: F. Carter Smith/Polaris Images. **378** Copyright © 2007 Butterball, LLC. All rights reserved. Reprinted with permission. **383** © 2007 CDW Corporation. All rights reserved. Used with permission.

Chapter 13

385 Courtesy of Boeing Commercial Airplane Group. **388** Courtesy of Lear Corporation. **390** Courtesy of Mark Hurd/Redux. **392** © 2005 CDW Corporation. All rights reserved. Used with permission. **393** Used with permission of Jennifer Hansen. Photographer: Linda Ford. **394** © 2007 International Rectifier. All rights reserved. Used with permission. **396** Courtesy of Jupiter Images. **397** Courtesy of Corbis/Bettmann. **401** Copyright © 2007 Weyerhaeuser Company. All rights reserved. Reprinted with permission. **403** © 2007 The Washington Post. All rights reserved. Used with permission. **404** Copyright © 2007 Cellfire Inc. All Rights Reserved. Used with permission. **406** Courtesy of Getty Images. **406** Courtesy of Reuters. **407** Courtesy of Consumer Electronics Association (CEA). **412** Used with permission of Dell Inc. All rights reserved.

Chapter 14

416 © 2007 GEICO. All rights reserved. Used with permission. **418** Courtesy of Southwest Airlines. Reprinted with permission. **422** Photo-Illustration by John Kucazala. **421** Used with permission of the Carolina Cookie Company. All rights reserved. **424** Courtesy of QVC. **426** Courtesy of the New York Times. **427** Copyright © 2007 Ford Motor Company. All rights reserved. Reprinted with permission. **429** Used with permission of Office Depot. All rights reserved. **430** Courtesy of Quicken Loans. Used with permission. **431** General Motors Corp. Used with permission, GM Media Archives. **433** Copyright © 2007 The Procter & Gamble Company. All rights reserved. Reprinted with permission. **436** Courtesy of American Honda Motor Co. Inc. Used with permission. **437** ™ & © 2005 Burger King Brands, Inc. (USA only). ™ & © 2005 Burger King Corporation (outside USA). All rights reserved. **438** General Motors Corp. Used with permission, GM Media Archives. **439** Reproduced with permission of Yahoo! Inc. © 2007 by Yahoo! Inc. YAHOO! and the YAHOO! logo are trademarks of Yahoo! Inc. **441** Courtesy of the U.S. Government.

Chapter 15

448 Photographer: REUTERS/Claro Cortes Photographer: Liu Gin/Getty. **451** Courtesy of Still Media. **452** Photographer: Zhang Zhe/Chinafotopress. **453** Courtesy of the WTO. **453** Courtesy of Corbis Royalty Free. **454** © European Community, 2007. **457** Courtesy of Getty Images—Agence France Presse. **458** Courtesy of Getty Images. **460** Courtesy of Sinopix. **462** Courtesy of Getty Images. **463** Courtesy of IKJELD.com. **466** Courtesy of LG Electronics, Inc. **469** © Inter IKEA Systems B.V. 1999–2005. All rights reserved. **468** Audiovisual Library of the European Commission. **471** Courtesy of PANOS.co.uk. **474** © 2007 The Timberland Company. Used with permission.

Chapter 16

478 Pearson Education/PH College. **479** Jim Whitmer Photography. **481** Courtesy of Aurora/Getty Images. **482** Courtesy of Corbis. **483** Courtesy of Corbis/Bettmann. **484** Courtesy of Corbis—NY. **485** Courtesy of The Image Works. **486** © Jim West/ZUMA Press. **488** © Jones Soda Seattle. All rights reserved. **490** Courtesy of Wal-Mart. **494** Courtesy of Dove. **495** Courtesy of Honest Tea. Used with permission. **496** Courtesy of Zody.

Indexes